Essentials *of* Investments

Ninth Edition

ZVI BODIE
Boston University

ALEX KANE
University of California, San Diego

ALAN J. MARCUS
Boston College

FI 320
Bentley University

1 2 3 4 5 6 7 8 9 0 QMF QMF 15 14 13

ISBN-13: 978-1-259-17118-5
ISBN-10: 1-259-17118-3

Learning Solutions Consultant: Anthony Mansella
Associate Project Manager: Michele McNulty
Cover Photo Credits:
010BI1.tif – (DAL) © Copyright 1997 IMS Communications Ltd/Capstone Design. All Rights Reserved.
17014.tif – (DAL) Neil Beer/Getty Images
73040.tif – (DAL) Daisuke Morita/Getty Images
A14FK1.tif – (DAL) Idealink Photography/Alamy
C029-09424.tif – (DAL) © imageshop/PunchStock
104205247 – Ralf Siemieniec
200352796-001 – Tom Brakefield

About the Authors

Zvi Bodie

Boston University

Zvi Bodie is Professor of Finance and Economics at Boston University School of Management. He holds a PhD from the Massachusetts Institute of Technology and has served on the finance faculty at Harvard Business School and MIT's Sloan School of Management. Professor Bodie has published widely on pension finance and investment strategy in leading professional journals. His books include *Foundations of Pension Finance, Pensions in the U.S. Economy, Issues in Pension Economics,* and *Financial Aspects of the U.S. Pension System.* Professor Bodie is a member of the Pension Research Council of the Wharton School, University of Pennsylvania. His latest book is *Worry-Free Investing: A Safe Approach to Achieving Your Lifetime Financial Goals.*

Alex Kane

University of California, San Diego

Alex Kane is Professor of Finance and Economics at the Graduate School of International Relations and Pacific Studies at the University of California, San Diego. He holds a PhD from the Stern School of Business of New York University and has been Visiting Professor at the Faculty of Economics, University of Tokyo; Graduate School of Business, Harvard; Kennedy School of Government, Harvard; and Research Associate, National Bureau of Economic Research. An author of many articles in finance and management journals, Professor Kane's research is mainly in corporate finance, portfolio management, and capital markets.

Alan J. Marcus

Boston College

Alan Marcus is the Mario J. Gabelli Professor of Finance in the Carroll School of Management at Boston College. He received his PhD from MIT, has been a Visiting Professor at MIT's Sloan School of Management and Athens Laboratory of Business Administration, and has served as a Research Fellow at the National Bureau of Economic Research, where he participated in both the Pension Economics and the Financial Markets and Monetary Economics Groups. Professor Marcus also spent two years at the Federal Home Loan Mortgage Corporation (Freddie Mac), where he helped to develop mortgage pricing and credit risk models. Professor Marcus has published widely in the fields of capital markets and portfolio theory. He currently serves on the Research Foundation Advisory Board of the CFA Institute.

Brief Contents

Contents

Part ONE

A Note From the Authors . . .

The year 2012 capped three decades of rapid and profound change in the investment industry as well as a financial crisis of historic magnitude. The vast expansion of financial markets over recent decades was due in part to innovations in securitization and credit enhancement that gave birth to new trading strategies. These strategies were in turn made feasible by developments in communication and information technology, as well as by advancements in the theory of investments.

Yet the crisis was rooted in the cracks of these developments. Many of the innovations in security design facilitated high leverage and an exaggerated notion of the efficacy of risk transfer strategies. This engendered complacency about risk that was coupled with relaxation of regulation as well as reduced transparency that masked the precarious condition of many big players in the system.

Of necessity, our text has evolved along with financial markets. We devote increased attention in this edition to recent breathtaking changes in market structure and trading technology. At the same time, however, many basic *principles* of investments remain important. We continue to organize the book around one basic theme—that security markets are nearly efficient, meaning that you should expect to find few obvious bargains in these markets. Given what we know about securities, their prices usually appropriately reflect their risk and return attributes; free lunches are few and far apart in markets as competitive as these. This starting point remains a powerful approach to security valuation. While the degree of market efficiency is and will always be a matter of debate, this first principle of valuation, specifically that in the absence of private information prices are the best guide to value, is still valid. Greater emphasis on risk analysis is the lesson we have weaved into the text.

This text also continues to emphasize *asset allocation* more than most other books. We prefer this emphasis for two important reasons. First, it corresponds to the procedure that most individuals actually follow when building an investment portfolio. Typically, you start with all of your money in a bank account, only then considering how much to invest in something riskier that might offer a higher expected return. The logical step at this point is to consider other risky asset classes, such as stock, bonds, or real estate. This is an asset allocation decision. Second, in most cases the asset allocation choice is far more important than specific security-selection decisions in determining overall investment performance. Asset allocation is the primary determinant of the risk-return profile of the investment portfolio, and so it deserves primary attention in a study of investment policy.

Our book also focuses on investment analysis, which allows us to present the practical applications of investment theory and to convey insights of practical value. In this edition of the text, we have continued to expand a systematic collection of Excel spreadsheets that give you tools to explore concepts more deeply than was previously possible. These spreadsheets are available on the text's website (**www.mhhe.com/bkm**) and provide a taste of the sophisticated analytic tools available to professional investors.

In our efforts to link theory to practice, we also have attempted to make our approach consistent with that of the CFA Institute. The Institute administers an education and certification program to candidates seeking designation as a Chartered Financial Analyst (CFA). The CFA curriculum represents the consensus of a committee of distinguished scholars and practitioners regarding the core of knowledge required by the investment professional. We continue to include questions from previous CFA exams in our end-of-chapter problems and have added to this edition new CFA-style questions derived from the Kaplan-Schweser CFA preparation courses.

This text will introduce you to the major issues of concern to all investors. It can give you the skills to conduct a sophisticated assessment of current issues and debates covered by both the popular media and more specialized finance journals. Whether you plan to become an investment professional or simply a sophisticated individual investor, you will find these skills essential.

Zvi Bodie
Alex Kane
Alan J. Marcus

Organization of the Ninth Edition

Essentials of Investments, Ninth Edition, is intended as a textbook on investment analysis most applicable for a student's first course in investments. The chapters are written in a modular format to give instructors the flexibility to either omit certain chapters or rearrange their order. The highlights in the margins describe updates for this edition.

Pedagogical Features

Learning Objectives

Each chapter begins with a summary of the chapter learning objectives, providing students with an overview of the concepts they should understand after reading the chapter. The end-of-chapter problems and CFA questions are tagged with the corresponding learning objective.

Learning Objectives:

LO1-1 Define an investment.

LO1-2 Distinguish between real assets and financial assets.

LO1-3 Explain the economic functions of financial markets and how various securities are related to the governance of the corporation.

LO1-4 Describe the major steps in the construction of an investment portfolio.

LO1-5 Identify different types of financial markets and the major participants in each of those markets.

Chapter Overview

Each chapter begins with a brief narrative to explain the concepts that will be covered in more depth. Relevant websites related to chapter material can be found on the book's website at **www.mhhe.com/bkm.** These sites make it easy for students to research topics further and retrieve financial data and information.

You learned in Chapter 1 that the process of building an investment portfolio usually begins by deciding how much money to allocate to broad classes of assets, such as safe money market securities or bank accounts, longer-term bonds, stocks, or even asset classes such as real estate or precious metals. This process is called *asset allocation.* Within each class the investor then selects specific assets from a more detailed menu. This is called *security selection.* marketable, liquid, low-risk debt securities. Money market instruments sometimes are called *cash equivalents,* or just *cash* for short. Capital markets, in contrast, include longer-term and riskier securities. Securities in the capital market are much more diverse than those found within the money market. For this reason, we will subdivide the capital market into three segments: longer-term debt markets, equity markets, and derivative markets in which options and futures trade.

Key Terms in the Margin

Key terms are indicated in color and defined in the margin the first time the term is used. A full list of key terms is included in the end-of-chapter materials.

Commercial Paper

commercial paper
Short-term unsecured debt issued by large corporations.

The typical corporation is a net borrower of both long-term funds (for capital investments) and short-term funds (for working capital). Large, well-known companies often issue their own short-term unsecured debt notes directly to the public, rather than borrowing from banks. These notes are called **commercial paper** (CP). Sometimes, CP is backed by a bank line of credit, which gives the borrower access to cash that can be used if needed to pay off the paper at maturity.

CP maturities range up to 270 days; longer maturities require registration with the Securities and Exchange Commission and so are almost never issued. CP most commonly is issued with maturities of less than one or two months in denominations of multiples of $100,000. Therefore, small investors can invest in commercial paper only indirectly, through money market mutual funds.

Numbered Equations

Key equations are called out in the text and identified by equation numbers. These key formulas are listed at the end of each chapter. Equations that are frequently used are also featured on the text's end sheets for convenient reference.

One way of comparing bonds is to determine the interest rate on taxable bonds that would be necessary to provide an after-tax return equal to that of municipals. To derive this value, we set after-tax yields equal and solve for the *equivalent taxable yield* of the tax-exempt bond. This is the rate a taxable bond would need to offer in order to match the after-tax yield on the tax-free municipal.

$$r(1 - t) = r_m \quad \textbf{(2.1)}$$

or

$$r = \frac{r_m}{1 - t} \quad \textbf{(2.2)}$$

Thus, the equivalent taxable yield is simply the tax-free rate divided by $1 - t$. Table 2.2 presents equivalent taxable yields for several municipal yields and tax rates.

On the **MARKET FRONT**

MONEY MARKET FUNDS AND THE FINANCIAL CRISIS OF 2008

Money market funds are mutual funds that invest in the short-term debt instruments that comprise the money market. In 2008, these funds had investments totaling about $3.4 trillion. They are required to hold only short-maturity debt of the highest quality: The average maturity of their holdings must be maintained at less than three months. Their biggest investments tend to be in commercial paper, but they also hold sizable fractions of their portfolios in certificates of deposit, repurchase agreements, and Treasury securities. Because of this very conservative investment profile, money market funds typically experience extremely low price risk. Investors for their part usually acquire check-writing privileges with their funds and often use them as a close substitute for a bank account. This is feasible because the funds almost always maintain share value at $1 and pass along all investment earnings to their investors as interest.

Until 2008, only one fund had "broken the buck," that is, suffered losses large enough to force value per share below $1. But when Lehman Brothers filed for bankruptcy protection on September 15, 2008, several funds that had invested heavily in its commercial paper suffered large losses. The next day, Reserve Primary Fund, the oldest money market fund, broke the buck when its value per share fell to only $.97.

The realization that money market funds were at risk in the credit crisis led to a wave of investor redemptions similar to a run on a bank. Only three days after the Lehman bankruptcy, Putman's Prime Money Market Fund announced that it was liquidating due to heavy redemptions. Fearing further outflows, the U.S. Treasury announced that it would make federal insurance available to money market funds willing to pay an insurance fee. This program would thus be similar to FDIC bank insurance. With the federal insurance in place, the outflows were quelled.

However, the turmoil in Wall Street's money market funds had already spilled over into "Main Street." Fearing further investor redemptions, money market funds had become afraid to commit funds even over short periods, and their demand for commercial paper had effectively dried up. Firms that had been able to borrow at 2% interest rates in previous weeks now had to pay up to 8%, and the commercial paper market was on the edge of freezing up altogether. Firms throughout the economy had come to depend on those markets as a major source of short-term finance to fund expenditures ranging from salaries to inventories. Further breakdown in the money markets would have had an immediate crippling effect on the broad economy. Within days, the Federal government put forth its first plan to spend $700 billion to stabilize the credit markets.

On the Market Front Boxes

Current articles from financial publications such as *The Wall Street Journal* are featured as boxed readings. Each box is referred to within the narrative of the text, and its real-world relevance to the chapter material is clearly defined.

CONCEPT check 2.5

Reconsider companies XYZ and ABC from Concept Check Question 2.4. Calculate the percentage change in the market value-weighted index. Compare that to the rate of return of a portfolio that holds $500 of ABC stock for every $100 of XYZ stock (i.e., an index portfolio).

Concept Checks

These self-test questions in the body of the chapter enable students to determine whether the preceding material has been understood and then reinforce understanding before students read further. Detailed Solutions to the Concept Checks are found at the end of each chapter.

EXAMPLE 2.4

Value-Weighted Indexes

To illustrate how value-weighted indexes are computed, look again at Table 2.3. The final value of all outstanding stock in our two-stock universe is $690 million. The initial value was $600 million. Therefore, if the initial level of a market value–weighted index of stocks ABC and XYZ were set equal to an arbitrarily chosen starting value such as 100, the index value at year-end would be $100 \times (690/600) = 115$. The increase in the index would reflect the 15% return earned on a portfolio consisting of those two stocks held in proportion to outstanding market values.

Unlike the price-weighted index, the value-weighted index gives more weight to ABC. Whereas the price-weighted index fell because it was dominated by higher-price XYZ, the value-weighted index rose because it gave more weight to ABC, the stock with the higher total market value.

Note also from Tables 2.3 and 2.4 that market value–weighted indexes are unaffected by stock splits. The total market value of the outstanding XYZ stock increases from $100 million to $110 million regardless of the stock split, thereby rendering the split irrelevant to the performance of the index.

Numbered Examples

Numbered and titled examples are integrated in each chapter. Using the worked-out solutions to these examples as models, students can learn how to solve specific problems step-by-step as well as gain insight into general principles by seeing how they are applied to answer concrete questions.

Excel Integration

Excel Applications

Since many courses now require students to perform analyses in spreadsheet format, Excel has been integrated throughout the book. It is used in examples as well as in this chapter feature which shows students how to create and manipulate spreadsheets to solve specific problems. This feature starts with an example presented in the chapter, briefly discusses how a spreadsheet can be valuable for investigating the topic, shows a sample spreadsheet, and asks students to apply the data to answer questions. These applications also direct the student to the web to work with an interactive version of the spreadsheet. The student can obtain the actual spreadsheet from the book's website (**www.mhhe.com/bkm**); available spreadsheets are denoted by an icon. As extra guidance, the spreadsheets include a comment feature that documents both inputs and outputs. Solutions for these exercises are located on the password-protected instructor site only, so instructors can assign these exercises either for homework or just for practice.

Excel application spreadsheets are available for the following:

Chapter 3: Buying on Margin; Short Sales
Chapter 7: Estimating the Index Model
Chapter 11: Immunization; Convexity
Chapter 15: Options, Stock, and Lending; Straddles and Spreads
Chapter 17: Parity and Spreads
Chapter 18: Performance Measures; Performance Attribution
Chapter 19: International Portfolios

Spreadsheet exhibit templates are also available for the following:

Chapter 5: Spreadsheet 5.1
Chapter 6: Spreadsheets 6.1–6.6
Chapter 10: Spreadsheets 10.1 & 10.2
Chapter 11: Spreadsheets 11.1 & 11.2
Chapter 13: Spreadsheets 13.1 & 13.2
Chapter 16: Spreadsheet 16.1
Chapter 21: Spreadsheets 21.1–21.10

EXCEL APPLICATIONS Buying on Margin

Please visit us at www.mhhe.com/bkm

The Excel spreadsheet model below makes it easy to analyze the impacts of different margin levels and the volatility of stock prices. It also allows you to compare return on investment for a margin trade with a trade using no borrowed funds.

	A	B	C	D	E	F	G	H
1								
2			**Action or Formula**	**Ending**	**Return on**		**Ending**	**Return with**
3			**for Column B**	**St Price**	**Investment**		**St Price**	**No Margin**
4	Initial Equity Investment	$10,000.00	Enter data		−42.00%			−19.00%
5	Amount Borrowed	$10,000.00	(B4/B10)−B4	$20.00	−122.00%		$20.00	−59.00%
6	Initial Stock Price	$50.00	Enter data	25.00	−102.00%		25.00	−49.00%
7	Shares Purchased	400	(B4/B10)/B6	30.00	−82.00%		30.00	−39.00%
8	Ending Stock Price	$40.00	Enter data	35.00	−62.00%		35.00	−29.00%
9	Cash Dividends During Hold Per.	$0.50	Enter data	40.00	−42.00%		40.00	−19.00%
10	Initial Margin Percentage	50.00%	Enter data	45.00	−22.00%		45.00	−9.00%
11	Maintenance Margin Percentage	30.00%	Enter data	50.00	−2.00%		50.00	1.00%
12				55.00	18.00%		55.00	11.00%
13	Rate on Margin Loan	8.00%	Enter data	60.00	38.00%		60.00	21.00%
14	Holding Period in Months	6	Enter data	65.00	58.00%		65.00	31.00%
15				70.00	78.00%		70.00	41.00%
16	**Return on Investment**			75.00	98.00%		75.00	51.00%
17	Capital Gain on Stock	−$4,000.00	B7*(B8−B6)	80.00	118.00%		80.00	61.00%
18	Dividends	$200.00	B7*B9					
19	Interest on Margin Loan	$400.00	B5*(B14/12)*B13					
20	Net Income	−$4,200.00	B17+B18−B19			**LEGEND:**		
21	Initial Investment	$10,000.00	B4			**Enter data**		
22	Return on Investment	−42.00%	B20/B21			**Value calculated**		

Excel Questions

1. Suppose you buy 100 shares of stock initially selling for $50, borrowing 25% of the necessary funds from your broker; that is, the initial margin on your purchase is 25%. You pay an interest rate of 8% on margin loans.
   a. How much of your own money do you invest? How much do you borrow from your broker?
   b. What will be your rate of return for the following stock prices at the end of a one-year holding period? (i) $40, (ii) $50, (iii) $60.

End-of-Chapter Features

PROBLEM SETS  Select problems are available in McGraw-Hill's *Connect Finance*. Please see the Supplements section of the book's frontmatter for more information.

Basic

1. Define the following types of bonds: *(LO 10-1)*
   a. Catastrophe bond.
   b. Eurobond.

c. What is the Treynor measure for the Miranda Fund and the S&P 500?
d. What is the Jensen measure for the Miranda Fund?

17. Go to **www.mhhe.com/bkm** and link to the material for Chapter 18, where you will find five years of monthly returns for two mutual funds, Vanguard's U.S. Growth Fund and U.S. Value Fund, as well as corresponding returns for the S&P 500 and the Treasury-bill rate. *(LO 18-2)*
   a. Set up a spreadsheet to calculate each fund's excess rate of return over T-bills in each month.
   b. Calculate the standard deviation of each fund over the five-year period.
   c. What was the beta of each fund over the five-year period? (You may wish to review the spreadsheets from Chapters 5 and 6 on the Index model.)
   d. What were the Sharpe, Jensen, and Treynor measures for each fund?

eXcel Please visit us at www.mhhe.com/bkm

Problem Sets

We strongly believe that practice in solving problems is a critical part of learning investments, so we provide a good variety. We have separated questions by level of difficulty: Basic, Intermediate, and Challenge.

Excel Problems

Select end-of-chapter questions require the use of Excel. These problems are denoted with an icon. A template is available at the book's website, **www.mhhe.com/bkm.**

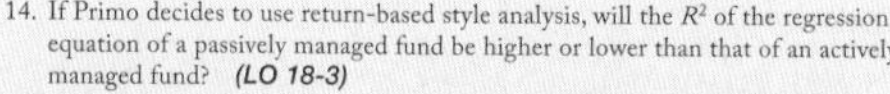

14. If Primo decides to use return-based style analysis, will the R^2 of the regression equation of a passively managed fund be higher or lower than that of an actively managed fund? *(LO 18-3)*
15. Which of the following statements about Primo's global fund is most correct? Primo appears to have a positive currency allocation effect as well as: *(LO 18-4)*
    a. A negative market allocation effect and a positive security allocation effect.
    b. A negative market allocation effect and a negative security allocation effect.
    c. A positive market allocation effect and a negative security allocation effect.
16. Kelli Blakely is a portfolio manager for the Miranda Fund (Miranda), a core large-cap equity fund. The market proxy and benchmark for performance measurement purposes is the S&P 500. Although the Miranda portfolio generally mirrors the asset class and sector weightings of the S&P, Blakely is allowed a significant amount of leeway in man-

Kaplan-Schweser Problems

Each chapter contains select CFA-style questions derived from the Kaplan-Schweser CFA preparation courses. These questions are tagged with an icon for easy reference.

CFA Problems

1. The following multiple-choice problems are based on questions that appeared in past CFA examinations.
   a. A bond with a call feature: *(LO 10-4)*
      (1) Is attractive because the immediate receipt of principal plus premium produces a high return.
      (2) Is more apt to be called when interest rates are high because the interest saving will be greater.
      (3) Will usually have a higher yield to maturity than a similar noncallable bond.
      (4) None of the above.
   b. In which *one* of the following cases is the bond selling at a discount? *(LO 10-2)*
      (1) Coupon rate is greater than current yield, which is greater than yield to maturity.
      (2) Coupon rate, current yield, and yield to maturity are all the same.
      (3) Coupon rate is less than current yield, which is less than yield to maturity.
      (4) Coupon rate is less than current yield, which is greater than yield to maturity.
   c. Consider a five-year bond with a 10% coupon selling at a yield to maturity of 8%. If interest rates remain constant, one year from now the price of this bond will be: *(LO 10-3)*

CFA Problems

We provide several questions from past CFA exams in applicable chapters. These questions represent the kinds of questions that professionals in the field believe are relevant to the practicing money manager. Appendix B, at the back of the book, lists each CFA question and the level and year of the CFA Exam it was included in, for easy reference when studying for the exam.

WEB *master*

1. Go to the website of Standard & Poor's at **www.standardandpoors.com.** Look for *Rating Services (Find a Rating).* Find the ratings on bonds of at least 10 companies. Try to choose a sample with a wide range of ratings. Then go to a website such as **money.msn.com** or **finance.yahoo.com** and obtain, for each firm, as many of the financial ratios tabulated in Table 10.3 as you can find. What is the relationship between bond rating and these ratios? Can you tell from your sample which of these ratios are the more important determinants of bond rating?
2. The FINRA operates the TRACE (Trade Reporting and Compliance Engine) system, which reports over-the-counter secondary market trades of fixed-income securities. Go to the FINRA home page at **www.finra.org** and click on the link for *Industry Professionals.* Search (located at the top right) for the "TRACE Fact Book" and click the first link that appears. Find the detailed data tables and locate the table with information on issues, excluding convertible bonds (typically Table 1). For each of the last three years, calculate

Web Master Exercises

These exercises are a great way to allow students to test their skills on the Internet. Each exercise consists of an activity related to practical problems and real-world scenarios.

Supplements

ONLINE SUPPORT

Online Learning Center

www.mhhe.com/bkm

Find a wealth of information online! At this book's website instructors have access to teaching supports such as electronic files of the ancillary materials. Students have access to study materials created specifically for this text, and much more. All Excel spreadsheets, denoted by an icon in the text, are located at this site. Links to the following support material, as described below, are also included.

FOR THE INSTRUCTOR

Instructor's Manual

Revised by Catherine Teutsch, University of Denver, this instructional tool provides an integrated learning approach revised for this edition. Each chapter includes a Chapter Overview, Learning Objectives, and Presentation of Material that outlines and organizes the material around the PowerPoint Presentation.

Test Bank

Prepared by Maryellen Epplin, University of Central Oklahoma, the Test Bank contains more than 1,200 questions and includes over 300 new questions. Each question is ranked by level of difficulty (easy, medium, hard) and tagged with the learning objective, the topic, AACSB, and Bloom's Taxonomy, which allows greater flexibility in creating a test.

Computerized Test Bank

A comprehensive bank of test questions is provided within a computerized test bank powered by McGraw-Hill's flexible electronic testing program, EZ Test Online (**www.eztestonline.com**). You can select questions from multiple McGraw-Hill test banks or write your own and then either print the test for paper distribution or give it online. This user-friendly program allows you to sort questions by format, edit existing questions or add new ones, and scramble questions for multiple versions of the same test. You can export your tests for use in WebCT, Blackboard, PageOut, and Apple's iQuiz. Sharing tests with colleagues, adjuncts, and TAs is easy! Instant scoring and feedback are provided, and EZ Test's grade book is designed to easily export to your grade book.

PowerPoint Presentation

These presentation slides, developed by Catherine Teutsch, contain figures and tables from the text, key points, and summaries in a visually stimulating collection of slides. These slides follow the order of the chapters, but if you have PowerPoint software, you may customize the program to fit your lecture.

Solutions Manual

Fiona Chou, University of California–San Diego, prepared detailed solutions to the end-of-chapter problems. Students can purchase the Solutions Manual, with instructor approval, using the ISBN-13: 9780077502249; ISBN-10: 0077502248. This supplement can also be packaged with the text. Please contact your McGraw-Hill/Irwin representative for additional information.

FOR THE STUDENT

Related Websites

A list of suggested websites is provided for each chapter. To keep them up to date, the suggested sites as well as their links are now provided online. Each chapter contains specific sites of particular use.

Excel Templates

There are templates for selected spreadsheets featured within the text, as well as the ones featured among the Excel Applications boxes. Select end-of-chapter problems have also been designated as Excel problems, in which there is a template available for students to solve the problem and gain experience using spreadsheets. Each template can also be found at the book's website and is denoted by an icon.

Wall Street Survivor

Students receive free access to this web-based portfolio simulation with a hypothetical $100,000 brokerage account to buy and sell stocks and mutual funds.

Students can use the real data found at this site in conjunction with the chapters on investments. They can also compete against students around the United States. This site is powered by Stock-Trak, the leading provider of investment simulation services to the academic community.

MCGRAW-HILL *CONNECT FINANCE*

Less Managing. More Teaching. Greater Learning.

McGraw-Hill *Connect Finance* is an online assignment and assessment solution that connects students with the tools and resources they'll need to achieve success.

McGraw-Hill *Connect Finance* helps prepare students for their future by enabling faster learning, more efficient studying, and higher retention of knowledge.

McGraw-Hill *Connect Finance* features

Connect Finance offers a number of powerful tools and features to make managing assignments easier, so faculty can spend more time teaching. With *Connect Finance,* students can engage with their coursework anytime and anywhere, making the learning process more accessible and efficient. *Connect Finance* offers you the features described below.

Simple assignment management

With *Connect Finance* creating assignments is easier than ever, so you can spend more time teaching and less time managing. The assignment management function enables you to:

- Create and deliver assignments easily with selectable end-of-chapter questions and test bank items.
- Streamline lesson planning, student progress reporting, and assignment grading to make classroom management more efficient than ever.
- Go paperless with the eBook and online submission and grading of student assignments.

Smart grading

When it comes to studying, time is precious. *Connect Finance* helps students learn more efficiently by providing feedback and practice material when they need it, where they need it. When it comes to teaching, your time also is precious. The grading function enables you to:

- Have assignments scored automatically, giving students immediate feedback on their work and side-by-side comparisons with correct answers.
- Access and review each response; manually change grades or leave comments for students to review.
- Reinforce classroom concepts with practice tests and instant quizzes.

Instructor library

The *Connect Finance* Instructor Library is your repository for additional resources to improve student engagement in and out of class. You can select and use any asset that enhances your lecture.

Student study center

The *Connect Finance* Student Study Center is the place for students to access additional resources. The Student Study Center:

- Offers students quick access to lectures, practice materials, eBooks, and more.
- Provides instant practice material and study questions, easily accessible on the go.
- Gives students access to the Self Quiz and Study described below.

Self Quiz and Study

The Self Quiz and Study (SQS) connects each student to the learning resources needed for success in the course. For each chapter, students:

- Take a practice test to initiate the Self Quiz and Study.
- Immediately upon completing the practice test, see how their performance compares to the learning objectives to be achieved within each section of the chapters.

- Receive a Study Plan that recommends specific readings from the text, supplemental study material, and practice work that will improve their understanding and mastery of each learning objective.

Student progress tracking

Connect Finance keeps instructors informed about how each student, section, and class is performing, allowing for more productive use of lecture and office hours. The progress-tracking function enables you to:

- View scored work immediately and track individual or group performance with assignment and grade reports.
- Access an instant view of student or class performance relative to learning objectives.

Lecture capture through Tegrity Campus

For an additional charge Lecture Capture offers new ways for students to focus on the in-class discussion, knowing they can revisit important topics later. This can be delivered through Connect or separately. See below for more details.

MCGRAW-HILL *CONNECT PLUS FINANCE*

McGraw-Hill reinvents the textbook learning experience for the modern student with *Connect Plus Finance.* A seamless integration of an eBook and *Connect Finance, Connect Plus Finance* provides all of the *Connect Finance* features plus the following:

- An integrated eBook, allowing for anytime, anywhere access to the textbook.
- Dynamic links between the problems or questions you assign to your students and the location in the eBook where that problem or question is covered.
- A powerful search function to pinpoint and connect key concepts in a snap.

In short, *Connect Finance* offers you and your students powerful tools and features that optimize your time and energies, enabling you to focus on course content, teaching, and student learning. *Connect Finance* also offers a wealth of content resources for both instructors and students. This state-of-the-art, thoroughly tested system supports you in preparing students for the world that awaits.

For more information about Connect, go to **www.mcgrawhillconnect.com** or contact your local McGraw-Hill sales representative.

TEGRITY CAMPUS: LECTURES 24/7

Tegrity Campus is a service that makes class time available 24/7 by automatically capturing every lecture in a searchable format for students to review when they study and complete assignments. With a simple one-click start-and-stop process, you capture all computer screens and corresponding audio. Students can replay any part of any class with easy-to-use browser-based viewing on a PC or Mac.

Educators know that the more students can see, hear, and experience class resources, the better they learn. In fact, studies prove it. With Tegrity Campus, students quickly recall key moments by using Tegrity Campus's unique search feature. This search helps students efficiently find what they need, when they need it, across an entire semester of class recordings. Help turn all your students' study time into learning moments immediately supported by your lecture.

To learn more about Tegrity, watch a 2-minute Flash demo at **http://tegritycampus.mhhe.com.**

Assurance of Learning Ready

Many educational institutions today are focused on the notion of *assurance of learning,* an important element of many accreditation standards. *Essentials of Investments,* Ninth Edition, is designed specifically to support your assurance-of-learning initiatives with a simple, yet powerful, solution.

Each chapter in the book begins with a list of numbered learning objectives, which also appear in the end-of-chapter problems. Every Test Bank question for *Essentials of Investments* maps to a specific chapter learning objective in the textbook. Each Test Bank question also identifies the topic area, level of difficulty, Bloom's Taxonomy level, and AACSB skill area. You can use our Test Bank software, *EZ Test* and *EZ Test Online,* or *Connect Finance* to easily search for learning objectives that directly relate to the learning objectives for your course. You can then use the reporting features of *EZ Test* to aggregate student results in similar fashion, making the collection and presentation of assurance-of-learning data simple and easy.

AACSB Statement

McGraw-Hill/Irwin is a proud corporate member of AACSB International. Understanding the importance and value of AACSB accreditation, *Essentials of Investments,* Ninth Edition, recognizes the curricula guidelines detailed in the AACSB standards for business accreditation by connecting selected questions in the Test Bank to the general knowledge and skill guidelines in the AACSB standards.

The statements contained in *Essentials of Investments,* Ninth Edition, are provided only as a guide for the users of this textbook. The AACSB leaves content coverage and assessment within the purview of individual schools, the mission of the school, and the faculty. While *Essentials of Investments,* Ninth Edition, and the teaching package make no claim of any specific AACSB qualification or evaluation, we have labeled selected questions according to the six general knowledge and skills areas.

McGraw-Hill Customer Care Contact Information

At McGraw-Hill, we understand that getting the most from new technology can be challenging. That's why our services don't stop after you purchase our products. You can e-mail our Product Specialists 24 hours a day to get product-training online. Or you can search our knowledge bank of Frequently Asked Questions on our support website. For Customer Support, call **800-331-5094,** e-mail **hmsupport@mcgraw-hill.com,** or visit **www.mhhe.com/support.** One of our Technical Support Analysts will be able to assist you in a timely fashion.

Acknowledgments

We received help from many people as we prepared this book. An insightful group of reviewers commented on this and previous editions of this text. Their comments and suggestions improved the exposition of the material considerably. These reviewers all deserve special thanks for their contributions.

Anna Agapova *Florida Atlantic University, Boca Raton*
Sandro C. Andrade *University of Miami*
Bala Arshanapalli *Indiana University Northwest*
Rasha Ashraf *Georgia State University*
Anand Bhattacharya *Arizona State University, Tempe*
Randall S. Billingsley *Virginia Polytechnic Institute and State University*
Howard Bohnen *St. Cloud State University*
Paul Bolster *Northeastern University*
Lyle Bowlin *University of Northern Iowa*
Brian Boyer *Brigham Young University*
Nicole Boyson *Northeastern University*
Ben Branch *University of Massachussets, Amherst*
Thor W. Bruce *University of Miami*
Timothy Burch *University of Miama, Coral Gables*
Alyce R. Campbell *University of Oregon*
Mark Castelino *Rutgers University*
Greg Chaudoin *Loyola University*
Ji Chen *University of Colorado, Denver*
Joseph Chen *University of California, Davis*
Mustafa Chowdhury *Louisiana State University*
Ron Christner *Loyola University, New Orleans*
Shane Corwin *University of Notre Dame*
Brent Dalrymple *University of Central Florida*
Praveen Das *University of Louisiana, Lafayette*
Diane Del Guercio *University of Oregon*
David C. Distad *University of California at Berkeley*
Gary R. Dokes *University of San Diego*
James Dow *California State University, Northridge*
Robert Dubil *University of Utah, Salt Lake City*
John Earl *University of Richmond*
Jeff Edwards *Portland Community College*
Peter D. Ekman *Kansas State University*
John Elder *Colorado State University*
Richard Elliott *University of Utah, Salt Lake City*
James Falter *Franklin University*
Philip Fanara *Howard University*
Joseph Farinella *University of North Carolina, Wilmington*
Greg Feigel *University of Texas, Arlington*
James F. Feller *Middle Tennessee State University*
James Forjan *York College*
Beverly Frickel *University of Nebraska, Kearney*
Ken Froewiss *New York University*
Phillip Ghazanfari *California State University, Pomona*
Eric Girard *Siena College*
Richard A. Grayson *University of Georgia*
Richard D. Gritta *University of Portland*
Deborah Gunthorpe *University of Tennessee*
Weiyu Guo *University of Nebraska, Omaha*
Pamela Hall *Western Washington University*
Thomas Hamilton *St. Mary's University*
Bing Han *University of Texas, Austin*
Yvette Harman *Miami University of Ohio*
Gay Hatfield *University of Mississippi*
Larry C. Holland *Oklahoma State University*
Harris Hordon *New Jersey City University*
Stephen Huffman *University of Wisconsin, Oshkosh*
Ron E. Hutchins *Eastern Michigan University*
David Ikenberry *University of Illinois, Urbana-Champaign*
A. Can (John) Inci *Florida State University*
Victoria Javine *University of Southern Alabama*
Nancy Jay *Mercer University*
Richard Johnson *Colorado State University*
Douglas Kahl *University of Akron*
Richard J. Kish *Lehigh University*
Tom Krueger *University of Wisconsin, La Crosse*
Donald Kummer *University of Missouri, St. Louis*

Merouane Lakehal-Ayat *St. John Fisher College*
Reinhold P. Lamb *University of North Florida*
Angeline Lavin *University of South Dakota*
Hongbok Lee *Western Illinois University*
Kartono Liano *Mississippi State University*
Jim Locke *Northern Virginia Community College*
John Loughlin *St. Louis University*
David Louton *Bryant College*
David Loy *Illinois State University*
Christian Lundblad *Indiana University*
Robert A. Lutz *University of Utah*
Laurian Casson Lytle *University of Wisconsin, Whitewater*
Leo Mahoney *Bryant College*
Herman Manakyan *Salisbury State University*
Steven V. Mann *University of South Carolina*
Jeffrey A. Manzi *Ohio University*
James Marchand *Westminster College*
Robert J. Martel *Bentley College*
Linda J. Martin *Arizona State University*
Stanley A. Martin *University of Colorado, Boulder*
Thomas Mertens *New York University*
Edward Miller *University of New Orleans*
Michael Milligan *California State University, Fullerton*
Rosemary Minyard *Pfeiffer University*
Walter Morales *Louisiana State University*
Mbodja Mougoue *Wayne State University*
Shabnam Mousavi *Georgia State University*
Majed Muhtaseb *California State Polytechnic University*
Deborah Murphy *University of Tennessee, Knoxville*
Mike Murray *Winona State University*
C. R. Narayanaswamy *Georgia Institute of Technology*
Walt Nelson *Missouri State University*
Karyn Neuhauser *SUNY, Plattsburgh*
Mike Nugent *SUNY Stonybrook*
Raj Padmaraj *Bowling Green University*
Elisabeta Pana *Illinois Wesleyan University*
John C. Park *Frostburg State University*
Percy Poon *University of Nevada, Las Vegas*
Robert B. Porter *University of Florida*
Dev Prasad *University of Massachusetts, Lowell*
Rose Prasad *Central Michigan University*
Elias A. Raad *Ithaca College*
Murli Rajan *University of Scranton*
Kumoli Ramakrishnan *University of South Dakota*
Rathin Rathinasamy *Ball State University*
Craig Rennie *University of Arkansas*
Cecilia Ricci *Montclair University*
Craig Ruff *Georgia State University*
Tom Sanders *University of Miami*
Jeff Sandri *University of Colorado, Boulder*
David Schirm *John Carroll University*
Chi Sheh *University of Houston*
Ravi Shukla *Syracuse University*
Allen B. Snively, Jr. *Indiana University*
Andrew Spieler *Hofstra University*
Kim Staking *Colorado State University*
Edwin Stuart *Southeastern Oklahoma State University*
George S. Swales *Southwest Missouri State University*
Paul Swanson *University of Cincinnati*
Bruce Swensen *Adelphi University*
Glenn Tanner *University of Hawaii*
John L. Teall *Pace University*
Anne Macy Terry *West Texas A&M University*
Donald J. Thompson *Georgia State University*
Steven Thorley *Brigham Young University*
James Tipton *Baylor University*
Steven Todd *DePaul University*
Michael Toyne *Northeastern State University*
William Trainor *Western Kentucky University*
Andrey Ukhov *Indiana University, Bloomington*
Cevdet Uruk *University of Memphis*
Joseph Vu *DePaul University*
Jessica Wachter *New York University*
Joe Walker *University of Alabama at Birmingham*
Richard Warr *North Carolina State University*
William Welch *Florida International University*
Russel Wermers *University of Maryland*
Andrew L. Whitaker *North Central College*
Howard Whitney *Franklin University*
Alayna Williamson *University of Utah, Salt Lake City*
Michael E. Williams *University of Texas at Austin*
Michael Willoughby *University of California, San Diego*
Tony Wingler *University of North Carolina*
Annie Wong *Western Connecticut State University*
David Wright *University of Wisconsin, Parkside*
Richard H. Yanow *North Adams State College*
Tarek Zaher *Indiana State University*
Allan Zebedee *San Diego State University*
Zhong-guo Zhou *California State University, Northridge*
Thomas J. Zwirlein *University of Colorado, Colorado Springs*

For granting us permission to include many of their examination questions in the text, we are grateful to the CFA Institute.

Much credit is also due to the development and production team of McGraw-Hill/Irwin: Michele Janicek, Executive Brand Manager; Noelle Bathurst, Development Editor; Dana Pauley, Senior Project Manager; Melissa Caughlin, Senior Marketing Manager; Jennifer Jelinski, Marketing Specialist; Michael McCormick, Lead Production Supervisor; Laurie Entringer, Designer; and Daryl Horrocks, Lead Media Project Manager.

Finally, once again, our most important debts are to Judy, Hava, and Sheryl for their unflagging support.

Zvi Bodie
Alex Kane
Alan J. Marcus

Elements of Investments

PART 1

Even a cursory glance at *The Wall Street Journal* reveals a bewildering collection of securities, markets, and financial institutions. But although it may appear so, the financial environment is not chaotic: There is rhyme and reason behind the vast array of financial instruments and the markets in which they trade.

These introductory chapters provide a bird's-eye view of the investing environment. We will give you a tour of the major types of markets in which securities trade, the trading process, and the major players in these arenas. You will see that both markets and securities have evolved to meet the changing and complex needs of different participants in the financial system.

Markets innovate and compete with each other for traders' business just as vigorously as competitors in other industries. The competition between NASDAQ, the New York Stock Exchange (NYSE), and several other electronic and non-U.S. exchanges is fierce and public.

Trading practices can mean big money to investors. The explosive growth of online electronic trading has saved them many millions of dollars in trading costs. On the other hand, some worry that lightning-fast electronic trading has put the stability of security markets at risk. All agree, however, that these advances will change the face of the investments industry, and Wall Street firms are scrambling to formulate strategies that respond to these changes.

These chapters will give you a good foundation with which to understand the basic types of securities and financial markets as well as how trading in those markets is conducted.

Chapters in This Part:

Chapter 1

Investments: Background and Issues

Learning Objectives:

- LO1-1 Define an investment.
- LO1-2 Distinguish between real assets and financial assets.
- LO1-3 Explain the economic functions of financial markets and how various securities are related to the governance of the corporation.
- LO1-4 Describe the major steps in the construction of an investment portfolio.
- LO1-5 Identify different types of financial markets and the major participants in each of those markets.
- LO1-6 Explain the causes and consequences of the financial crisis of 2008.

investment

Commitment of current resources in the expectation of deriving greater resources in the future.

An **investment** is the *current* commitment of money or other resources in the expectation of reaping *future* benefits. For example, an individual might purchase shares of stock anticipating that the future proceeds from the shares will justify both the time that her money is tied up as well as the risk of the investment. The time you will spend studying this text (not to mention its cost) also is an investment. You are forgoing either current leisure or the income you could be earning at a job in the expectation that your future career will be sufficiently enhanced to justify this commitment of time and effort. While these two investments differ in many ways, they share one key attribute that is central to all investments: You sacrifice something of value now, expecting to benefit from that sacrifice later.

This text can help you become an informed practitioner of investments. We will focus on investments in securities such as stocks, bonds, or options and futures contracts, but much of what we discuss will be useful in the analysis of any type of investment. The text will provide you with background in the organization of various securities markets, will survey the valuation and risk management principles useful in particular markets, such as those for bonds or stocks, and will introduce you to the principles of portfolio construction.

Broadly speaking, this chapter addresses three topics that will provide a useful perspective for the material that is to come later. First, before delving into the topic of "investments," we consider the role of financial assets in the economy. We discuss the relationship between securities and the "real" assets that actually produce goods and services for consumers, and we consider why financial assets are important to the functioning of a developed economy. Given this background, we then take a first look at the types of decisions that confront investors as they assemble a portfolio of assets. These investment decisions are made in an environment where higher returns usually can be obtained only at the price of greater risk and in which it is rare to find assets that are so mispriced as to be obvious bargains. These themes—the risk-return trade-off and the efficient pricing of financial assets—are central to the investment process, so it is worth pausing for a brief discussion of their implications as we begin the text. These implications will be fleshed out in much greater detail in later chapters.

We provide an overview of the organization of security markets as well as the various players that participate in those markets. Together, these introductions should give you a feel for who the major participants are in the securities markets as well as the setting in which they act. Finally, we discuss the financial crisis that began playing out in 2007 and peaked in 2008. The crisis dramatically illustrated the connections between the financial system and the "real" side of the economy. We look at the origins of the crisis and the lessons that may be drawn about systemic risk. We close the chapter with an overview of the remainder of the text.

Related websites for this chapter are available at www.mhhe.com/bkm.

1.1 REAL ASSETS VERSUS FINANCIAL ASSETS

The material wealth of a society is ultimately determined by the productive capacity of its economy, that is, the goods and services its members can create. This capacity is a function of the **real assets** of the economy: the land, buildings, equipment, and knowledge that can be used to produce goods and services.

real assets

Assets used to produce goods and services.

In contrast to such real assets are **financial assets** such as stocks and bonds. Such securities are no more than sheets of paper or, more likely, computer entries and do not directly contribute to the productive capacity of the economy. Instead, these assets are the means by which individuals in well-developed economies hold their claims on real assets. Financial assets are claims to the income generated by real assets (or claims on income from the government). If we cannot own our own auto plant (a real asset), we can still buy shares in Honda or Toyota (financial assets) and, thereby, share in the income derived from the production of automobiles.

financial assets

Claims on real assets or the income generated by them.

While real assets generate net income to the economy, financial assets simply define the allocation of income or wealth among investors. Individuals can choose between consuming their wealth today or investing for the future. If they choose to invest, they may place their wealth in financial assets by purchasing various securities. When investors buy these securities from companies, the firms use the money so raised to pay for real assets, such as plant, equipment, technology, or inventory. So investors' returns on securities ultimately come from the income produced by the real assets that were financed by the issuance of those securities.

The distinction between real and financial assets is apparent when we compare the balance sheet of U.S. households, shown in Table 1.1, with the composition of national wealth in the United States, shown in Table 1.2. Household wealth includes financial assets such as bank accounts, corporate stock, or bonds. However, these securities, which are financial assets of households, are *liabilities* of the issuers of the securities. For example, a bond that you treat as

TABLE 1.1 Balance sheet of U.S. households, 2011

Assets	$ Billion	% Total	Liabilities and Net Worth	$ Billion	% Total
Real assets					
Real estate	$18,117	25.2%	Mortgages	$10,215	14.2%
Consumer durables	4,665	6.5	Consumer credit	2,404	3.3
Other	303	0.4	Bank and other loans	384	0.5
Total real assets	$23,085	32.1%	Security credit	316	0.4
			Other	556	0.8
			Total liabilities	$13,875	19.3%
Financial assets					
Deposits	$ 8,038	11.2%			
Life insurance reserves	1,298	1.8			
Pension reserves	13,419	18.7			
Corporate equity	8,792	12.2			
Equity in noncorp. business	6,585	9.2			
Mutual fund shares	5,050	7.0			
Debt securities	4,129	5.7			
Other	1,536	2.1			
Total financial assets	48,847	67.9	*Net worth*	58,058	80.7
Total	$71,932	100.0%		$71,932	100.0%

Note: Column sums may differ from total because of rounding error.
Source: *Flow of Funds Accounts of the United States,* Board of Governors of the Federal Reserve System, June 2011.

TABLE 1.2 Domestic net worth

Assets	$ Billion
Commercial real estate	$14,248
Residential real estate	18,117
Equipment & software	4,413
Inventories	1,974
Consumer durables	4,665
Total	$43,417

Note: Column sums may differ from total because of rounding error.
Source: *Flow of Funds Accounts of the United States,* Board of Governors of the Federal Reserve System, June 2011.

an asset because it gives you a claim on interest income and repayment of principal from Toyota is a liability of Toyota, which is obligated to make these payments to you. Your asset is Toyota's liability. Therefore, when we aggregate over all balance sheets, these claims cancel out, leaving only real assets as the net wealth of the economy. National wealth consists of structures, equipment, inventories of goods, and land.[1]

[1]You might wonder why real assets held by households in Table 1.1 amount to $23,085 billion, while total real assets in the domestic economy (Table 1.2) are far larger, at $43,417 billion. One major reason is that real assets held by firms, for example, property, plant, and equipment, are included as *financial* assets of the household sector, specifically through the value of corporate equity and other stock market investments. Another reason is that equity and stock investments in Table 1.1 are measured by market value, whereas plant and equipment in Table 1.2 are valued at replacement cost.

We will focus almost exclusively on financial assets. But you shouldn't lose sight of the fact that the successes or failures of the financial assets we choose to purchase ultimately depend on the performance of the underlying real assets.

CONCEPT check 1.1

Are the following assets real or financial?

a. Patents *b.* Lease obligations *c.* Customer goodwill
d. A college education *e.* A $5 bill

1.2 FINANCIAL ASSETS

It is common to distinguish among three broad types of financial assets: debt, equity, and derivatives. **Fixed-income** or **debt securities** promise either a fixed stream of income or a stream of income that is determined according to a specified formula. For example, a corporate bond typically would promise that the bondholder will receive a fixed amount of interest each year. Other so-called floating-rate bonds promise payments that depend on current interest rates. For example, a bond may pay an interest rate that is fixed at two percentage points above the rate paid on U.S. Treasury bills. Unless the borrower is declared bankrupt, the payments on these securities are either fixed or determined by formula. For this reason, the investment performance of debt securities typically is least closely tied to the financial condition of the issuer.

fixed-income (debt) securities

Pay a specified cash flow over a specific period.

Nevertheless, debt securities come in a tremendous variety of maturities and payment provisions. At one extreme, the *money market* refers to fixed-income securities that are short term, highly marketable, and generally of very low risk. Examples of money market securities are U.S. Treasury bills or bank certificates of deposit (CDs). In contrast, the fixed-income *capital market* includes long-term securities such as Treasury bonds, as well as bonds issued by federal agencies, state and local municipalities, and corporations. These bonds range from very safe in terms of default risk (for example, Treasury securities) to relatively risky (for example, high-yield or "junk" bonds). They also are designed with extremely diverse provisions regarding payments provided to the investor and protection against the bankruptcy of the issuer. We will take a first look at these securities in Chapter 2 and undertake a more detailed analysis of the fixed-income market in Part Three.

Unlike debt securities, common stock, or **equity,** in a firm represents an ownership share in the corporation. Equityholders are not promised any particular payment. They receive any dividends the firm may pay and have prorated ownership in the real assets of the firm. If the firm is successful, the value of equity will increase; if not, it will decrease. The performance of equity investments, therefore, is tied directly to the success of the firm and its real assets. For this reason, equity investments tend to be riskier than investments in debt securities. Equity markets and equity valuation are the topics of Part Four.

equity

An ownership share in a corporation.

Finally, **derivative securities** such as options and futures contracts provide payoffs that are determined by the prices of *other* assets such as bond or stock prices. For example, a call option on a share of Intel stock might turn out to be worthless if Intel's share price remains below a threshold or "exercise" price such as $20 a share, but it can be quite valuable if the stock price rises above that level.[2] Derivative securities are so named because their values derive from the prices of other assets. For example, the value of the call option will depend on the price of Intel stock. Other important derivative securities are futures and swap contracts. We will treat these in Part Five.

derivative securities

Securities providing payoffs that depend on the values of other assets.

Derivatives have become an integral part of the investment environment. One use of derivatives, perhaps the primary use, is to hedge risks or transfer them to other parties. This is

[2]A call option is the right to buy a share of stock at a given exercise price on or before the option's expiration date. If the market price of Intel remains below $20 a share, the right to buy for $20 will turn out to be valueless. If the share price rises above $20 before the option expires, however, the option can be exercised to obtain the share for only $20.

done successfully every day, and the use of these securities for risk management is so commonplace that the multitrillion-dollar market in derivative assets is routinely taken for granted. Derivatives also can be used to take highly speculative positions, however. Every so often, one of these positions blows up, resulting in well-publicized losses of hundreds of millions of dollars. While these losses attract considerable attention, they do not negate the potential use of such securities as risk management tools. Derivatives will continue to play an important role in portfolio construction and the financial system. We will return to this topic later in the text.

Investors and corporations regularly encounter other financial markets as well. Firms engaged in international trade regularly transfer money back and forth between dollars and other currencies. Well more than a trillion dollars of currency is traded each day in the market for foreign exchange, primarily through a network of the largest international banks.

Investors also might invest directly in some real assets. For example, dozens of commodities are traded on exchanges such as the New York Mercantile Exchange or the Chicago Board of Trade. You can buy or sell corn, wheat, natural gas, gold, silver, and so on.

Commodity and derivative markets allow firms to adjust their exposure to various business risks. For example, a construction firm may lock in the price of copper by buying copper futures contracts, thus eliminating the risk of a sudden jump in the price of its raw materials. Wherever there is uncertainty, investors may be interested in trading, either to speculate or to lay off their risks, and a market may arise to meet that demand.

1.3 FINANCIAL MARKETS AND THE ECONOMY

We stated earlier that real assets determine the wealth of an economy, while financial assets merely represent claims on real assets. Nevertheless, financial assets and the markets in which they trade play several crucial roles in developed economies. Financial assets allow us to make the most of the economy's real assets.

The Informational Role of Financial Markets

Stock prices reflect investors' collective assessment of a firm's current performance and future prospects. When the market is more optimistic about the firm, its share price will rise. At that higher price, fewer shares must be issued to raise the funds necessary to finance a prospective project, for example, a research and development effort or an expansion of operations. And when fewer shares are issued, a smaller proportion of profits are absorbed by the new shareholders, leaving more for the existing shareholders and making the potential investment more attractive. The firm therefore is more inclined to pursue the opportunity. In this manner, stock prices play a major role in the allocation of capital in market economies, directing capital to the firms and applications with the greatest perceived potential.

Do capital markets actually channel resources to the most efficient use? At times, they appear to fail miserably. Companies or whole industries can be "hot" for a period of time (think about the dot-com bubble that peaked in 2000), attract a large flow of investor capital, and then fail after only a few years. The process seems highly wasteful.

But we need to be careful about our standard of efficiency. No one knows with certainty which ventures will succeed and which will fail. It is therefore unreasonable to expect that markets will never make mistakes. The stock market encourages allocation of capital to those firms that appear *at the time* to have the best prospects. Many smart, well-trained, and well-paid professionals analyze the prospects of firms whose shares trade on the stock market. Stock prices reflect their collective judgment.

You may well be skeptical about resource allocation through markets. But if you are, then take a moment to think about the alternatives. Would a central planner make fewer mistakes? Would you prefer that Congress make these decisions? To paraphrase Winston Churchill's comment about democracy, markets may be the worst way to allocate capital except for all the others that have been tried.

Consumption Timing

Some individuals in an economy are earning more than they currently wish to spend. Others, for example, retirees, spend more than they currently earn. How can you shift your purchasing power from high-earnings periods to low-earnings periods of life? One way is to "store" your wealth in financial assets. In high-earnings periods, you can invest your savings in financial assets such as stocks and bonds. In low-earnings periods, you can sell these assets to provide funds for your consumption needs. By so doing, you can "shift" your consumption over the course of your lifetime, thereby allocating your consumption to periods that provide the greatest satisfaction. Thus, financial markets allow individuals to separate decisions concerning current consumption from constraints that otherwise would be imposed by current earnings.

Allocation of Risk

Virtually all real assets involve some risk. When Toyota builds its auto plants, for example, it cannot know for sure what cash flows those plants will generate. Financial markets and the diverse financial instruments traded in those markets allow investors with the greatest taste for risk to bear that risk, while other, less risk-tolerant individuals can, to a greater extent, stay on the sidelines. For example, if Toyota raises the funds to build its auto plant by selling both stocks and bonds to the public, the more optimistic or risk-tolerant investors can buy shares of stock in Toyota, while the more conservative ones can buy Toyota bonds. Because the bonds promise to provide a fixed payment, the stockholders bear most of the business risk but reap potentially higher rewards. Thus, capital markets allow the risk that is inherent to all investments to be borne by the investors most willing to bear that risk.

This allocation of risk also benefits the firms that need to raise capital to finance their investments. When investors are able to select security types with the risk-return characteristics that best suit their preferences, each security can be sold for the best possible price. This facilitates the process of building the economy's stock of real assets.

Separation of Ownership and Management

Many businesses are owned and managed by the same individual. This simple organization is well suited to small businesses and, in fact, was the most common form of business organization before the Industrial Revolution. Today, however, with global markets and large-scale production, the size and capital requirements of firms have skyrocketed. For example, in 2010 General Electric listed on its balance sheet about $103 billion of property, plant, and equipment, and total assets in excess of $750 billion. Corporations of such size simply cannot exist as owner-operated firms. GE actually has over 600,000 stockholders with an ownership stake in the firm proportional to their holdings of shares.

Such a large group of individuals obviously cannot actively participate in the day-to-day management of the firm. Instead, they elect a board of directors that in turn hires and supervises the management of the firm. This structure means that the owners and managers of the firm are different parties. This gives the firm a stability that the owner-managed firm cannot achieve. For example, if some stockholders decide they no longer wish to hold shares in the firm, they can sell their shares to other investors, with no impact on the management of the firm. Thus, financial assets and the ability to buy and sell those assets in the financial markets allow for easy separation of ownership and management.

How can all of the disparate owners of the firm, ranging from large pension funds holding hundreds of thousands of shares to small investors who may hold only a single share, agree on the objectives of the firm? Again, the financial markets provide some guidance. All may agree that the firm's management should pursue strategies that enhance the value of their shares. Such policies will make all shareholders wealthier and allow them all to better pursue their personal goals, whatever those goals might be.

Do managers really attempt to maximize firm value? It is easy to see how they might be tempted to engage in activities not in the best interest of shareholders. For example, they might engage in empire building or avoid risky projects to protect their own jobs or overconsume luxuries such as corporate jets, reasoning that the cost of such perquisites is largely borne by the shareholders. These potential conflicts of interest are called **agency problems** because managers, who are hired as agents of the shareholders, may pursue their own interests instead.

agency problems

Conflicts of interest between managers and stockholders.

Several mechanisms have evolved to mitigate potential agency problems. First, compensation plans tie the income of managers to the success of the firm. A major part of the total compensation of top executives is typically in the form of stock options, which means that the managers will not do well unless the stock price increases, benefiting shareholders. (Of course, we've learned more recently that overuse of options can create its own agency problem. Options can create an incentive for managers to manipulate information to prop up a stock price temporarily, giving them a chance to cash out before the price returns to a level reflective of the firm's true prospects. More on this shortly.) Second, while boards of directors have sometimes been portrayed as defenders of top management, they can, and in recent years increasingly have, forced out management teams that are underperforming. Third, outsiders such as security analysts and large institutional investors such as pension funds monitor the firm closely and make the life of poor performers at the least uncomfortable.

Finally, bad performers are subject to the threat of takeover. If the board of directors is lax in monitoring management, unhappy shareholders in principle can elect a different board. They can do this by launching a *proxy contest* in which they seek to obtain enough proxies (i.e., rights to vote the shares of other shareholders) to take control of the firm and vote in another board. However, this threat is usually minimal. Shareholders who attempt such a fight have to use their own funds, while management can defend itself using corporate coffers. Most proxy fights fail. The real takeover threat is from other firms. If one firm observes another underperforming, it can acquire the underperforming business and replace management with its own team. The stock price should rise to reflect the prospects of improved performance, which provides incentive for firms to engage in such takeover activity.

EXAMPLE 1.1

Carl Icahn's Proxy Fight with Yahoo!

In February 2008, Microsoft offered to buy Yahoo! by paying its current shareholders $31 for each of their shares, a considerable premium to its closing price of $19.18 on the day before the offer. Yahoo!'s management rejected that offer and a better one at $33 a share; Yahoo!'s CEO Jerry Yang held out for $37 per share, a price that Yahoo! had not reached in over two years. Billionaire investor Carl Icahn was outraged, arguing that management was protecting its own position at the expense of shareholder value. Icahn notified Yahoo! that he had been asked to "lead a proxy fight to attempt to remove the current board and to establish a new board which would attempt to negotiate a successful merger with Microsoft."[3] To that end, he had purchased approximately 59 million shares of Yahoo! and formed a 10-person slate to stand for election against the current board. Despite this challenge, Yahoo!'s management held firm in its refusal of Microsoft's offer, and with the support of the board, Yang managed to fend off both Microsoft and Icahn. In July, Icahn agreed to end the proxy fight in return for three seats on the board to be held by his allies. But the 11-person board was still dominated by current Yahoo! management. Yahoo!'s share price, which had risen to $29 a share during the Microsoft negotiations, fell back to around $21 a share. Given the difficulty that a well-known billionaire faced in defeating a determined management, it is no wonder that proxy contests are rare. Historically, about three of four proxy fights go down to defeat.

Corporate Governance and Corporate Ethics

We've argued that securities markets can play an important role in facilitating the deployment of capital resources to their most productive uses. But market signals will help to allocate capital efficiently only if investors are acting on accurate information. We say that markets need to be *transparent* for investors to make informed decisions. If firms can mislead the public about their prospects, then much can go wrong.

[3]Open letter from Carl Icahn to Board of Directors of Yahoo!, May 15, 2008, published in press release from ICAHN CAPITAL LP.

Despite the many mechanisms to align incentives of shareholders and managers, the three years between 2000 and 2002 were filled with a seemingly unending series of scandals that collectively signaled a crisis in corporate governance and ethics. For example, the telecom firm WorldCom overstated its profits by at least $3.8 billion by improperly classifying expenses as investments. When the true picture emerged, it resulted in the largest bankruptcy in U.S. history, at least until Lehman Brothers smashed that record in 2008. The next-largest U.S. bankruptcy was Enron, which used its now notorious "special purpose entities" to move debt off its own books and similarly present a misleading picture of its financial status. Unfortunately, these firms had plenty of company. Other firms such as Rite Aid, HealthSouth, Global Crossing, and Qwest Communications also manipulated and misstated their accounts to the tune of billions of dollars. And the scandals were hardly limited to the U.S. Parmalat, the Italian dairy firm, claimed to have a $4.8 billion bank account that turned out not to exist. These episodes suggest that agency and incentive problems are far from solved.

Other scandals of that period included systematically misleading and overly optimistic research reports put out by stock market analysts (their favorable analysis was traded for the promise of future investment banking business, and analysts were commonly compensated not for their accuracy or insight but for their role in garnering investment banking business for their firms) and allocations of initial public offerings to corporate executives as a quid pro quo for personal favors or the promise to direct future business back to the manager of the IPO.

What about the auditors who were supposed to be the watchdogs of the firms? Here too, incentives were skewed. Recent changes in business practice made the consulting businesses of these firms more lucrative than the auditing function. For example, Enron's (now defunct) auditor Arthur Andersen earned more money consulting for Enron than auditing it; given its incentive to protect its consulting profits, it should not be surprising that it, and other auditors, were overly lenient in their auditing work.

In 2002, in response to the spate of ethics scandals, Congress passed the Sarbanes-Oxley Act to tighten the rules of corporate governance. For example, the act requires corporations to have more independent directors, that is, more directors who are not themselves managers (or affiliated with managers). The act also requires each CFO to personally vouch for the corporation's accounting statements, creates a new oversight board to oversee the auditing of public companies, and prohibits auditors from providing various other services to clients.

Wall Street and its regulators have learned (admittedly belatedly) that markets require trust to function. In the wake of the scandals, the value of reputation and straightforward incentive structures has increased. As one Wall Street insider put it, "This is an industry of trust; it's one of its key assets. . . . [Wall Street] is going to have to invest in getting [that trust] back . . . without that trust, there's nothing."[4] Ultimately, a firm's reputation for integrity is key to building long-term relationships with its customers and is therefore one of its most valuable assets. Indeed, the motto of the London Stock Exchange is "My word is my bond." Every so often firms forget this lesson, but in the end, investments in reputation are in fact good business practice.

1.4 THE INVESTMENT PROCESS

An investor's *portfolio* is simply his collection of investment assets. Once the portfolio is established, it is updated or "rebalanced" by selling existing securities and using the proceeds to buy new securities, by investing additional funds to increase the overall size of the portfolio, or by selling securities to decrease the size of the portfolio.

asset allocation

Allocation of an investment portfolio across broad asset classes.

Investment assets can be categorized into broad asset classes, such as stocks, bonds, real estate, commodities, and so on. Investors make two types of decisions in constructing their portfolios. The **asset allocation** decision is the choice among these broad asset classes, while the **security selection** decision is the choice of which particular securities to hold *within* each asset class.

security selection

Choice of specific securities within each asset class.

[4] *BusinessWeek,* "How Corrupt Is Wall Street?" May 13, 2002.

"Top-down" portfolio construction starts with asset allocation. For example, an individual who currently holds all of his money in a bank account would first decide what proportion of the overall portfolio ought to be moved into stocks, bonds, and so on. In this way, the broad features of the portfolio are established. For example, while the average annual return on the common stock of large firms since 1926 has been about 12% per year, the average return on U.S. Treasury bills has been less than 4%. On the other hand, stocks are far riskier, with annual returns (as measured by the Standard & Poor's 500 Index) that have ranged as low as −46% and as high as 55%. In contrast, T-bill returns are effectively risk-free: You know what interest rate you will earn when you buy the bills. Therefore, the decision to allocate your investments to the stock market or to the money market where Treasury bills are traded will have great ramifications for both the risk and the return of your portfolio. A top-down investor first makes this and other crucial asset allocation decisions before turning to the decision of the particular securities to be held in each asset class.

security analysis

Analysis of the value of securities.

Security analysis involves the valuation of particular securities that might be included in the portfolio. For example, an investor might ask whether Merck or Pfizer is more attractively priced. Both bonds and stocks must be evaluated for investment attractiveness, but valuation is far more difficult for stocks because a stock's performance usually is far more sensitive to the condition of the issuing firm.

In contrast to top-down portfolio management is the "bottom-up" strategy. In this process, the portfolio is constructed from the securities that seem attractively priced without as much concern for the resultant asset allocation. Such a technique can result in unintended bets on one or another sector of the economy. For example, it might turn out that the portfolio ends up with a very heavy representation of firms in one industry, from one part of the country, or with exposure to one source of uncertainty. However, a bottom-up strategy does focus the portfolio on the assets that seem to offer the most attractive investment opportunities.

1.5 MARKETS ARE COMPETITIVE

Financial markets are highly competitive. Thousands of well-backed analysts constantly scour securities markets searching for the best buys. This competition means that we should expect to find few, if any, "free lunches," securities that are so underpriced that they represent obvious bargains. There are several implications of this no-free-lunch proposition. Let's examine two.

The Risk-Return Trade-Off

Investors invest for anticipated future returns, but those returns rarely can be predicted precisely. There will almost always be risk associated with investments. Actual or realized returns will almost always deviate from the expected return anticipated at the start of the investment period. For example, in 1931 (the worst calendar year for the market since 1926), the stock market lost 46% of its value. In 1933 (the best year), the stock market gained 55%. You can be sure that investors did not anticipate such extreme performance at the start of either of these years.

Naturally, if all else could be held equal, investors would prefer investments with the highest expected return.[5] However, the no-free-lunch rule tells us that all else cannot be held equal. If you want higher expected returns, you will have to pay a price in terms of accepting higher investment risk. If higher expected return can be achieved without bearing extra risk, there will be a rush to buy the high-return assets, with the result that their prices will be driven up. Individuals considering investing in the asset at the now-higher price will find the investment less attractive: If you buy at a higher price, your expected rate of return (that is, profit per dollar invested) is lower. The asset will be considered attractive and its price will continue to rise until its expected return is no more than commensurate with risk. At this point, investors can anticipate a "fair" return relative

[5] The "expected" return is not the return investors believe they necessarily will earn, or even their most likely return. It is instead the result of averaging across all possible outcomes, recognizing that some outcomes are more likely than others. It is the average rate of return across possible economic scenarios.

to the asset's risk, but no more. Similarly, if returns were independent of risk, there would be a rush to sell high-risk assets. Their prices would fall (and their expected future rates of return rise) until they eventually were attractive enough to be included again in investor portfolios. We conclude that there should be a **risk-return trade-off** in the securities markets, with higher-risk assets priced to offer higher expected returns than lower-risk assets.

risk-return trade-off

Assets with higher expected returns entail greater risk.

Of course, this discussion leaves several important questions unanswered. How should one measure the risk of an asset? What should be the quantitative trade-off between risk (properly measured) and expected return? One would think that risk would have something to do with the volatility of an asset's returns, but this guess turns out to be only partly correct. When we mix assets into diversified portfolios, we need to consider the interplay among assets and the effect of diversification on the risk of the entire portfolio. *Diversification* means that many assets are held in the portfolio so that the exposure to any particular asset is limited. The effect of diversification on portfolio risk, the implications for the proper measurement of risk, and the risk-return relationship are the topics of Part Two. These topics are the subject of what has come to be known as *modern portfolio theory.* The development of this theory brought two of its pioneers, Harry Markowitz and William Sharpe, Nobel Prizes.

Efficient Markets

Another implication of the no-free-lunch proposition is that we should rarely expect to find bargains in the security markets. We will spend all of Chapter 8 examining the theory and evidence concerning the hypothesis that financial markets process all available information about securities quickly and efficiently, that is, that the security price usually reflects all the information available to investors concerning the value of the security. According to this hypothesis, as new information about a security becomes available, the price of the security quickly adjusts so that at any time, the security price equals the market consensus estimate of the value of the security. If this were so, there would be neither underpriced nor overpriced securities.

One interesting implication of this "efficient market hypothesis" concerns the choice between active and passive investment-management strategies. **Passive management** calls for holding highly diversified portfolios without spending effort or other resources attempting to improve investment performance through security analysis. **Active management** is the attempt to improve performance either by identifying mispriced securities or by timing the performance of broad asset classes—for example, increasing one's commitment to stocks when one is bullish on the stock market. If markets are efficient and prices reflect all relevant information, perhaps it is better to follow passive strategies instead of spending resources in a futile attempt to outguess your competitors in the financial markets.

passive management

Buying and holding a diversified portfolio without attempting to identify mispriced securities.

active management

Attempting to identify mispriced securities or to forecast broad market trends.

If the efficient market hypothesis were taken to the extreme, there would be no point in active security analysis; only fools would commit resources to actively analyze securities. Without ongoing security analysis, however, prices eventually would depart from "correct" values, creating new incentives for experts to move in. Therefore, in Chapter 9, we examine challenges to the efficient market hypothesis. Even in environments as competitive as the financial markets, we may observe only *near*-efficiency, and profit opportunities may exist for especially insightful and creative investors. This motivates our discussion of active portfolio management in Part Six. More importantly, our discussions of security analysis and portfolio construction generally must account for the likelihood of nearly efficient markets.

1.6 THE PLAYERS

From a bird's-eye view, there would appear to be three major players in the financial markets:

1. Firms are net demanders of capital. They raise capital now to pay for investments in plant and equipment. The income generated by those real assets provides the returns to investors who purchase the securities issued by the firm.
2. Households typically are suppliers of capital. They purchase the securities issued by firms that need to raise funds.

3. Governments can be borrowers or lenders, depending on the relationship between tax revenue and government expenditures. Since World War II, the U.S. government typically has run budget deficits, meaning that its tax receipts have been less than its expenditures. The government, therefore, has had to borrow funds to cover its budget deficit. Issuance of Treasury bills, notes, and bonds is the major way that the government borrows funds from the public. In contrast, in the latter part of the 1990s, the government enjoyed a budget surplus and was able to retire some outstanding debt.

Corporations and governments do not sell all or even most of their securities directly to individuals. For example, about half of all stock is held by large financial institutions such as pension funds, mutual funds, insurance companies, and banks. These financial institutions stand between the security issuer (the firm) and the ultimate owner of the security (the individual investor). For this reason, they are called *financial intermediaries.* Similarly, corporations do not directly market their securities to the public. Instead, they hire agents, called investment bankers, to represent them to the investing public. Let's examine the roles of these intermediaries.

Financial Intermediaries

Households want desirable investments for their savings, yet the small (financial) size of most households makes direct investment difficult. A small investor seeking to lend money to businesses that need to finance investments doesn't advertise in the local newspaper to find a willing and desirable borrower. Moreover, an individual lender would not be able to diversify across borrowers to reduce risk. Finally, an individual lender is not equipped to assess and monitor the credit risk of borrowers.

financial intermediaries

Institutions that "connect" borrowers and lenders by accepting funds from lenders and loaning funds to borrowers.

For these reasons, **financial intermediaries** have evolved to bring together the suppliers of capital (investors) with the demanders of capital (primarily corporations). These financial intermediaries include banks, investment companies, insurance companies, and credit unions. Financial intermediaries issue their own securities to raise funds to purchase the securities of other corporations.

For example, a bank raises funds by borrowing (taking deposits) and lending that money to other borrowers. The spread between the interest rates paid to depositors and the rates charged to borrowers is the source of the bank's profit. In this way, lenders and borrowers do not need to contact each other directly. Instead, each goes to the bank, which acts as an intermediary between the two. The problem of matching lenders with borrowers is solved when each comes independently to the common intermediary.

Financial intermediaries are distinguished from other businesses in that both their assets and their liabilities are overwhelmingly financial. Table 1.3 presents the aggregated balance sheet of commercial banks, one of the largest sectors of financial intermediaries. Notice that the balance sheet includes only very small amounts of real assets. Compare Table 1.3 to the aggregated balance sheet of the nonfinancial corporate sector in Table 1.4 for which real assets are about half of all assets. The contrast arises because intermediaries simply move funds from one sector to another. In fact, the primary social function of such intermediaries is to channel household savings to the business sector.

Other examples of financial intermediaries are investment companies, insurance companies, and credit unions. All these firms offer similar advantages in their intermediary role. First, by pooling the resources of many small investors, they are able to lend considerable sums to large borrowers. Second, by lending to many borrowers, intermediaries achieve significant diversification, so they can accept loans that individually might be too risky. Third, intermediaries build expertise through the volume of business they do and can use economies of scale and scope to assess and monitor risk.

investment companies

Firms managing funds for investors. An investment company may manage several mutual funds.

Investment companies, which pool and manage the money of many investors, also arise out of economies of scale. Here, the problem is that most household portfolios are not large enough to be spread among a wide variety of securities. It is very expensive in terms of brokerage fees and research costs to purchase one or two shares of many different firms. Mutual

TABLE 1.3 Balance sheet of commercial banks, 2011

Assets	$ Billion	% Total	Liabilities and Net Worth	$ Billion	% Total
Real assets			Liabilities		
Equipment and premises	$ 110.4	0.9%	Deposits	$ 8,674.6	71.4%
Other real estate	46.6	0.4	Debt and other borrowed funds	1,291.8	10.6
Total real assets	$ 157.0	1.3%	Federal funds and repurchase agreements	499.1	4.1
			Other	308.4	2.5
			Total liabilities	$10,773.9	88.6%
Financial assets					
Cash	$ 1,066.3	8.8%			
Investment securities	2,406.1	19.8			
Loans and leases	6,279.1	51.6			
Other financial assets	1,153.9	9.5			
Total financial assets	$10,905.4	89.7%			
Other assets					
Intangible assets	$ 373.9	3.1%			
Other	721.0	5.9			
Total other assets	1,094.9	9.0	*Net worth*	1,383.4	11.4
Total	$12,157.3	100.0%		$12,157.3	100.0%

Note: Column sums may differ from total because of rounding error.
Source: Federal Deposit Insurance Corporation, **www.fdic.gov,** July 2011.

TABLE 1.4 Balance sheet of U.S. nonfinancial corporations, 2011

Assets	$ Billion	% Total	Liabilities and Net Worth	$ Billion	% Total
Real assets			Liabilities		
Equipment and software	$ 4,109	14.6%	Bonds and mortgages	$ 5,321	18.9%
Real estate	7,676	27.2	Bank loans	538	1.9
Inventories	1,876	6.7	Other loans	1,227	4.4
Total real assets	$13,661	48.5%	Trade debt	1,863	6.6
			Other	4,559	16.2
Financial assets			*Total liabilities*	$13,509	47.9%
Deposits and cash	$ 1,009	3.6%			
Marketable securities	899	3.2			
Trade and consumer credit	2,388	8.5			
Other	10,239	36.3			
Total financial assets	14,535	51.5			
Total	$28,196	100.0%	*Net worth*	14,687	52.1
				$28,196	100.0%

Note: Column sums may differ from total because of rounding error.
Source: *Flow of Funds Accounts of the United States,* Board of Governors of the Federal Reserve System, June 2011.

funds have the advantage of large-scale trading and portfolio management, while participating investors are assigned a prorated share of the total funds according to the size of their investment. This system gives small investors advantages they are willing to pay for via a management fee to the mutual fund operator.

On the MARKET FRONT

THE END OF THE STAND-ALONE INVESTMENT BANKING INDUSTRY

Until 1999, the Glass-Steagall Act had prohibited banks from both accepting deposits and underwriting securities. In other words, it forced a separation of the investment and commercial banking industries. But when Glass-Steagall was repealed, many large commercial banks began to transform themselves into "universal banks" that could offer a full range of commercial and investment banking services. In some cases, commercial banks started their own investment banking divisions from scratch, but more commonly they expanded through merger. For example, Chase Manhattan acquired J. P. Morgan to form JPMorgan Chase. Similarly, Citigroup acquired Salomon Smith Barney to offer wealth management, brokerage, investment banking, and asset management services to its clients. Most of Europe had never forced the separation of commercial and investment banking, so their giant banks such as Credit Suisse, Deutsche Bank, HSBC, and UBS had long been universal banks. Until 2008, however, the stand-alone investment banking sector in the U.S. remained large and apparently vibrant, including such storied names as Goldman Sachs, Morgan Stanley, Merrill Lynch, and Lehman Brothers.

But the industry was shaken to its core in 2008, when several investment banks were beset by enormous losses on their holdings of mortgage-backed securities. In March, on the verge of insolvency, Bear Stearns was merged into JPMorgan Chase. On September 14, Merrill Lynch, also suffering steep mortgage-related losses, negotiated an agreement to be acquired by Bank of America. The next day, Lehman Brothers entered into the largest bankruptcy in U.S. history, having failed to find an acquirer who was able and willing to rescue it from its steep losses. The next week, the only two remaining major independent investment banks, Goldman Sachs and Morgan Stanley, decided to convert from investment banks to traditional bank holding companies. In so doing, they became subject to the supervision of national bank regulators such as the Federal Reserve and the far tighter rules for capital adequacy that govern commercial banks.[6] The firms decided that the greater stability they would enjoy as commercial banks, particularly the ability to fund their operations through bank deposits and access to emergency borrowing from the Fed, justified the conversion. These mergers and conversions marked the effective end of the independent investment banking industry—but not of investment banking. Those services now will be supplied by the large universal banks.

Investment companies also can design portfolios specifically for large investors with particular goals. In contrast, mutual funds are sold in the retail market, and their investment philosophies are differentiated mainly by strategies that are likely to attract a large number of clients.

Like mutual funds, *hedge funds* also pool and invest the money of many clients. But they are open only to institutional investors such as pension funds, endowment funds, or wealthy individuals. They are more likely to pursue complex and higher-risk strategies. They typically keep a portion of trading profits as part of their fees, whereas mutual funds charge a fixed percentage of assets under management.

Economies of scale also explain the proliferation of analytic services available to investors. Newsletters, databases, and brokerage house research services all engage in research to be sold to a large client base. This setup arises naturally. Investors clearly want information, but with small portfolios to manage, they do not find it economical to personally gather all of it. Hence, a profit opportunity emerges: A firm can perform this service for many clients and charge for it.

Investment Bankers

investment bankers

Firms specializing in the sale of new securities to the public, typically by underwriting the issue.

Just as economies of scale and specialization create profit opportunities for financial intermediaries, so too do these economies create niches for firms that perform specialized services for businesses. Firms raise much of their capital by selling securities such as stocks and bonds to the public. Because these firms do not do so frequently, however, **investment bankers** that specialize in such activities can offer their services at a cost below that of maintaining an in-house security issuance division.

[6]For example, a typical leverage ratio (total assets divided by bank capital) at commercial banks in 2008 was about 10 to 1. In contrast, leverage at investment banks reached 30 to 1. Such leverage increased profits when times were good but provided an inadequate buffer againts losses and left the banks exposed to failure when their investment portfolios were shaken by large losses.

Investment bankers advise an issuing corporation on the prices it can charge for the securities issued, appropriate interest rates, and so forth. Ultimately, the investment banking firm handles the marketing of the security in the **primary market,** where new issues of securities are offered to the public. In this role, the banks are called *underwriters.* Later, investors can trade previously issued securities among themselves in the so-called **secondary market.**

primary market

A market in which new issues of securities are offered to the public.

secondary market

Previously issued securities are traded among investors.

For most of the last century, investment banks and commercial banks in the U.S. were separated by law. While those regulations were effectively eliminated in 1999, until 2008 the industry known as "Wall Street" still comprised large, independent investment banks such as Goldman Sachs, Merrill Lynch, or Lehman Brothers. But that stand-alone model came to an abrupt end in September 2008, when all the remaining major U.S. investment banks were absorbed into commercial banks, declared bankruptcy, or reorganized as commercial banks. The nearby box presents a brief introduction to these events.

Venture Capital and Private Equity

While large firms can raise funds directly from the stock and bond markets with help from their investment bankers, smaller and younger firms that have not yet issued securities to the public do not have that option. Start-up companies rely instead on bank loans and investors who are willing to invest in them in return for an ownership stake in the firm. The equity investment in these young companies is called **venture capital (VC).** Sources of venture capital are dedicated venture capital funds, wealthy individuals known as *angel investors,* and institutions such as pension funds.

venture capital (VC)

Money invested to finance a new firm.

Most venture capital funds are set up as limited partnerships. A management company starts with its own money and raises additional capital from limited partners such as pension funds. That capital may then be invested in a variety of start-up companies. The management company usually sits on the start-up company's board of directors, helps recruit senior managers, and provides business advice. It charges a fee to the VC fund for overseeing the investments. After some period of time, for example, 10 years, the fund is liquidated and proceeds are distributed to the investors.

Venture capital investors commonly take an active role in the management of a start-up firm. Other active investors may engage in similar hands-on management but focus instead on firms that are in distress or firms that may be bought up, "improved," and sold for a profit. Collectively, these investments in firms that do not trade on public stock exchanges are known as **private equity** investments.

private equity

Investments in companies that are not traded on a stock exchange.

1.7 THE FINANCIAL CRISIS OF 2008

This chapter has laid out the broad outlines of the financial system, as well as some of the links between the financial side of the economy and the "real" side, in which goods and services are produced. The financial crisis of 2008 illustrated in a painful way the intimate ties between these two sectors. We present in this section a capsule summary of the crisis, attempting to draw some lessons about the role of the financial system as well as the causes and consequences of what has become known as *systemic risk.* Some of these issues are complicated; we consider them briefly here but will return to them in greater detail later in the text once we have more context for analysis.

Antecedents of the Crisis

In early 2007, most observers thought it inconceivable that within two years the world financial system would be facing its worse crisis since the Great Depression. At the time, the economy seemed to be marching from strength to strength. The last significant macroeconomic threat had been from the collapse of the high-tech bubble in 2000–2002. But the Federal Reserve responded to an emerging recession by aggressively reducing interest rates.

FIGURE 1.1

Short-term LIBOR and Treasury-bill rates and the TED spread

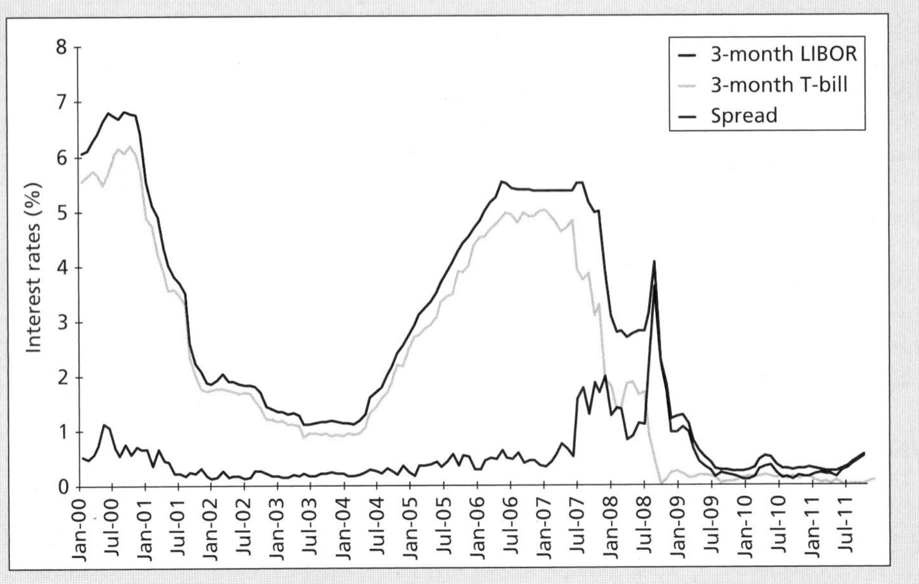

FIGURE 1.2

Cumulative returns on a $1 investment in the S&P 500 Index

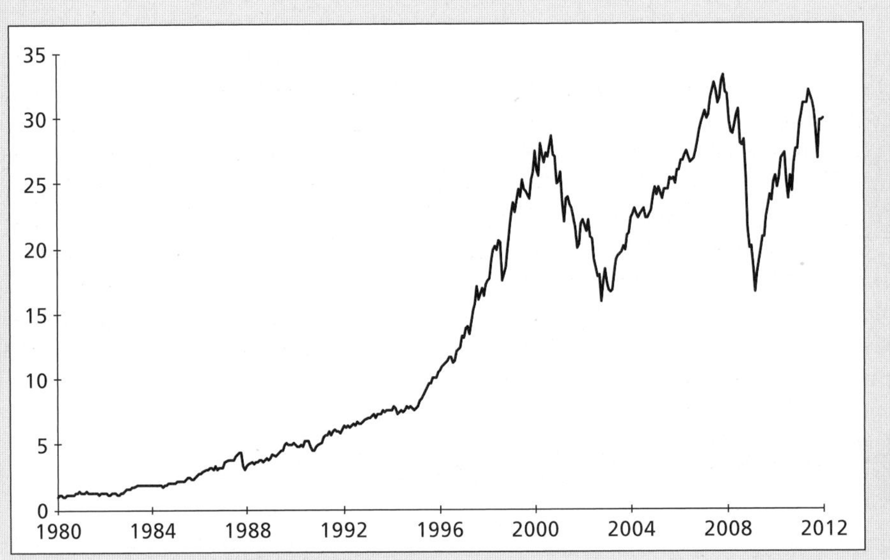

Figure 1.1 shows that Treasury bill rates dropped drastically between 2001 and 2004, and the LIBOR rate, which is the interest rate at which major money-center banks lend to each other, fell in tandem.[7] These actions appeared to have been successful, and the recession was short-lived and mild.

By mid-decade the economy was once again apparently healthy. While the stock market had declined substantially between 2001 and 2002, Figure 1.2 shows that it reversed direction just as dramatically beginning in 2003, fully recovering all of its post-tech-meltdown losses within a few years. Of equal importance, the banking sector seemed healthy. The spread

[7] *LIBOR* stands for "London Interbank Offer Rate." It is a rate charged on dollar-denominated loans in an interbank lending market outside the U.S. (largely centered in London). The rate is typically quoted for three-month loans.

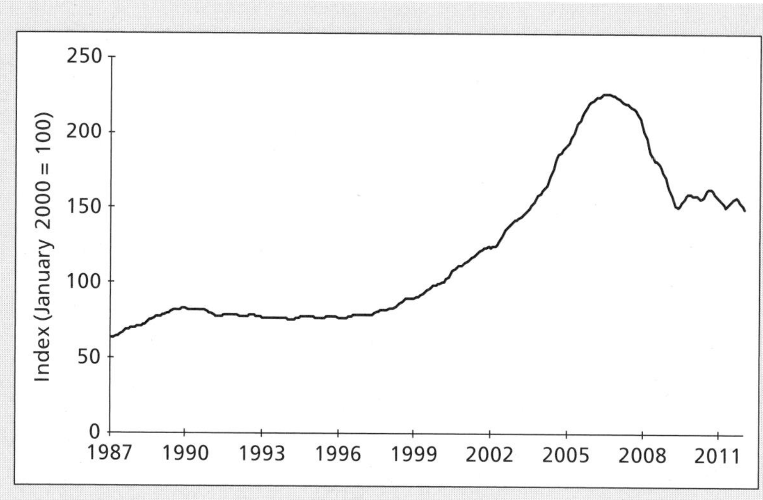

FIGURE 1.3

The Case-Shiller index of U.S. housing prices

between the LIBOR rate (at which banks borrow from each other) and the Treasury-bill rate (at which the U.S. government borrows), a common measure of credit risk in the banking sector (often referred to as the *TED spread*[8]), was only around .25% in early 2007 (see the bottom line in Figure 1.1), suggesting that fears of default or "counterparty" risk in the banking sector were extremely low.

The combination of dramatically reduced interest rates and an apparently stable economy fed a historic boom in the housing market. Figure 1.3 shows that U.S. housing prices began rising noticeably in the late 1990s and accelerated dramatically after 2001 as interest rates plummeted. In the 10 years beginning 1997, average prices in the U.S. approximately tripled.

But confidence in the power of macroeconomic policy to reduce risk, the impressive recovery of the economy from the high-tech implosion, and particularly the housing price boom following the aggressive reduction in interest rates may have sown the seeds for the debacle that played out in 2008. On the one hand, the Fed's policy of reducing interest rates had resulted in low yields on a wide variety of investments, and investors were hungry for higher-yielding alternatives. On the other hand, low volatility and growing complacency about risk encouraged greater tolerance for risk in the search for these higher-yielding investments. Nowhere was this more evident than in the exploding market for securitized mortgages. The U.S. housing and mortgage finance markets were at the center of a gathering storm.

Changes in Housing Finance

Prior to 1970, most mortgage loans would come from a local lender such as a neighborhood savings bank or credit union. A homeowner would borrow funds for a home purchase and repay it over a long period, commonly 30 years. A typical thrift institution would have as its major asset a portfolio of these long-term home loans, while its major liability would be the accounts of its depositors. This landscape began to change in the 1970s when Fannie Mae (FNMA, or Federal National Mortgage Association) and Freddie Mac (FHLMC, or Federal Home Loan Mortgage Corporation) began buying large quantities of mortgage loans from originators and bundling them into pools that could be traded like any other financial asset. These pools, which were essentially claims on the underlying mortgages, were soon dubbed "mortgage-backed securities," and the process

[8] *TED* stands for "Treasury-Eurodollar spread." The Eurodollar rate in this spread is in fact LIBOR.

FIGURE 1.4

Cash flows in a mortgage pass-through security

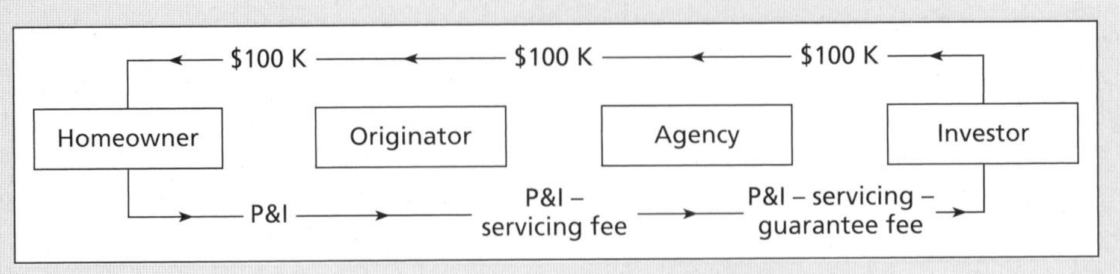

securitization

Pooling loans into standardized securities backed by those loans, which can then be traded like any other security.

was called **securitization.** Fannie and Freddie quickly became the behemoths of the mortgage market, between them buying more than half of all mortgages originated by the private sector.

Figure 1.4 illustrates how cash flows passed from the original borrower to the ultimate investor in a mortgage-backed security. The loan originator, for example, the savings and loan, might make a $100,000 loan to a homeowner. The homeowner would repay principal and interest (P&I) on the loan over 30 years. But then the originator would sell the mortgage to Freddie Mac or Fannie Mae and recover the cost of the loan. The originator could continue to service the loan (e.g., collect monthly payments from the homeowner) for a small servicing fee, but the loan payments net of that fee would be passed along to the agency. In turn, Freddie or Fannie would pool the loans into mortgage-backed securities and sell the securities to investors such as pension funds or mutual funds. The agency (Fannie or Freddie) typically would guarantee the credit or default risk of the loans included in each pool, for which it would retain a guarantee fee before passing along the rest of the cash flow to the ultimate investor. Because the mortgage cash flows were passed along from the homeowner to the lender, to Fannie or Freddie, and finally to the investor, the mortgage-backed securities were also called *pass-throughs.*

Until the last decade, the vast majority of the mortgages that had been securitized into pass-throughs were held or guaranteed by Freddie Mac or Fannie Mae. These were low-risk *conforming* mortgages, meaning that eligible loans for agency securitization couldn't be too big and homeowners had to meet underwriting criteria establishing their ability to repay the loan. For example, the ratio of loan amount to house value could be no more than 80%.

While conforming loans were pooled almost entirely through Freddie Mac and Fannie Mae, once the securitization model took hold, it created an opening for a new product: securitization by private firms of *nonconforming* "subprime" loans with higher default risk. One important difference between the government-agency pass-throughs and these so-called private-label pass-throughs was that the investor in the private-label pool would bear the risk that homeowners might default on their loans. Thus, originating mortgage brokers had little incentive to perform due diligence on the loan *as long as the loans could be sold to an investor.* These investors, of course, had no direct contact with the borrowers and could not perform detailed underwriting concerning loan quality. Instead, they relied on borrowers' credit scores, which steadily came to replace conventional underwriting.

A strong trend toward low-documentation and then no-documentation loans entailing little verification of a borrower's ability to carry a loan soon emerged. Other subprime underwriting standards also quickly deteriorated. For example, allowed leverage on home loans (as measured by the loan-to-value ratio) rose dramatically. By 2006, the majority of subprime borrowers purchased houses by borrowing the *entire* purchase price! When housing prices began falling, these highly leveraged loans were quickly "underwater," meaning that the house was worth less than the loan balance, and many homeowners decided to "walk away" or abandon their homes—and their loans.

Adjustable rate mortgages (ARMs) also grew in popularity, quickly becoming the standard in the subprime market. These loans offered borrowers low initial or "teaser" interest rates, but these rates eventually would reset to current market interest yields, for example, the Treasury-bill rate plus 3%. While many of these borrowers had "maxed out" their borrowing capacity at the teaser rate, as soon as the loan rate was reset, their monthly payments would soar, especially if market interest rates had increased.

Despite these obvious risks, the ongoing increase in housing prices over the last decade seemed to have lulled many investors into complacency, with a widespread belief that continually rising home prices would bail out poorly performing loans. But starting in 2004, the ability of refinancing to save a loan began to diminish. First, higher interest rates put payment pressure on homeowners who had taken out adjustable rate mortgages. Second, as Figure 1.3 shows, housing prices peaked by 2006, so homeowners' ability to refinance a loan using built-up equity in the house declined. Housing default rates began to surge in 2007, as did losses on mortgage-backed securities. The crisis was ready to shift into high gear.

Mortgage Derivatives

One might ask: Who was willing to buy all of these risky subprime mortgages? Securitization, restructuring, and credit enhancement provide a big part of the answer. New risk-shifting tools enabled investment banks to carve out AAA-rated securities from original-issue "junk" loans. Collateralized debt obligations, or CDOs, were among the most important and eventually damaging of these innovations.

CDOs were designed to concentrate the credit (i.e., default) risk of a bundle of loans on one class of investors, leaving the other investors in the pool relatively protected from that risk. The idea was to prioritize claims on loan repayments by dividing the pool into senior versus junior slices called *tranches*. The senior tranches had first claim on repayments from the entire pool. Junior tranches would be paid only after the senior ones had received their cut. For example, if a pool were divided into two tranches, with 70% of the pool allocated to the senior tranche and 30% allocated to the junior one, the senior investors would be repaid in full as long as 70% or more of the loans in the pool performed, i.e., as long as the default rate on the pool remained below 30%. Even with pools comprised of risky subprime loans, default rates above 30% seemed extremely unlikely, and thus senior tranches were commonly granted the highest (i.e., AAA) rating by the major credit rating agencies, Moody's, Standard & Poor's, and Fitch. Large amounts of AAA-rated securities were thus carved out of pools of low-rated mortgages. (We will describe CDOs in more detail in Chapter 10.)

Of course, we know now that these ratings were wrong. The senior-subordinated structure of CDOs provided far less protection to senior tranches than investors anticipated. When housing prices across the entire country began to fall in unison, defaults in all regions increased and the hoped-for benefits from diversifying loans geographically never materialized.

Why had the rating agencies so dramatically underestimated credit risk in these subprime securities? First, default probabilities had been estimated using historical data from an unrepresentative period characterized by a housing boom and an uncommonly prosperous economy. Moreover, the ratings analysts had extrapolated historical default experience to a new sort of borrower pool—one without down payments, with exploding payment loans, and with low- or no-documentation loans (often called *liar loans*). Past default experience was largely irrelevant given these profound changes in the market. Moreover, there was excessive optimism about the power of cross-regional diversification to minimize risk.

Finally, there were apparent agency problems. The ratings agencies were paid to provide ratings by the issuers of the securities—not the purchasers. They faced pressure from the issuers, who could shop around for the most favorable treatment, to provide generous ratings.

CONCEPT check 1.2

When Freddie Mac and Fannie Mae pooled conforming mortgages into securities, they guaranteed the underlying mortgage loans against homeowner defaults. In contrast, there were no guarantees on the mortgages pooled into subprime mortgage–backed securities, so investors would bear credit risk. Were either of these arrangements necessarily a better way to manage and allocate default risk?

Credit Default Swaps

In parallel to the CDO market, the market in *credit default swaps* also exploded in this period. A credit default swap, or CDS, is in essence an insurance contract against the default of one or more borrowers. (We will describe these in more detail in Chapter 10.) The purchaser of the swap pays an annual premium (like an insurance premium) for the protection from credit risk. Credit default swaps became an alternative method of credit enhancement, seemingly allowing investors to buy subprime loans and insure their safety. But, in practice, some swap issuers ramped up their exposure to credit risk to unsupportable levels, without sufficient capital to back those obligations. For example, the large insurance company AIG alone sold more than $400 billion of CDS contracts on subprime mortgages.

The Rise of Systemic Risk

By 2007, the financial system displayed several troubling features. Many large banks and related financial institutions had adopted an apparently profitable financing scheme: borrowing short term at low interest rates to finance holdings in higher-yielding, long-term, illiquid[9] assets and treating the interest rate differential between their assets and liabilities as economic profit. But this business model was precarious: By relying primarily on short-term loans for their funding, these firms needed to constantly refinance their positions (i.e., borrow additional funds as the loans matured), or else face the necessity of quickly selling off their less liquid asset portfolios, which would be difficult in times of financial stress. Moreover, these institutions were highly leveraged and had little capital as a buffer against losses. Large investment banks on Wall Street in particular had sharply increased leverage, which added to an underappreciated vulnerability to refunding requirements—especially if the value of their asset portfolios came into question. Even small portfolio losses could drive their net worth negative, at which point no one would be willing to extend them loans.

Another source of fragility was widespread investor reliance on credit protection through products like CDOs. Many of the assets underlying these pools were illiquid, hard to value, and highly dependent on forecasts of future performance of other loans. In a widespread downturn, with rating downgrades, these assets would prove difficult to sell.

The steady displacement of formal exchange trading by informal "over-the-counter" markets created other problems. In formal exchanges such as futures or options markets, participants must put up collateral called *margin* to guarantee their ability to make good on their obligations. Prices are computed each day, and gains or losses are continually added to or subtracted from each trader's margin account. If a margin account runs low after a series of losses, the investor can be required to either contribute more collateral or close out the position before actual insolvency ensues. Positions, and thus exposures to losses, are transparent to other traders. In contrast, the over-the-counter markets where CDS contracts trade are effectively private contracts between two parties with less public disclosure of positions and less opportunity to recognize either cumulative gains or losses over time or the resultant credit exposure of each trading partner.

systemic risk

Risk of breakdown in the financial system, particularly due to spillover effects from one market into others.

This new financial model was brimming with **systemic risk,** a potential breakdown of the financial system when problems in one market spill over and disrupt others. When lenders such as banks have limited capital, and are afraid of further losses, they may rationally choose to hoard their capital instead of lending it out to customers such as small firms, thereby exacerbating funding problems for their customary borrowers.

The Shoe Drops

By fall of 2007, housing prices were in decline (Figure 1.3), mortgage delinquencies increased, and the stock market entered its own free fall (Figure 1.2). Many investment banks, which had large investments in mortgages, also began to totter.

[9] *Liquidity* refers to the speed and the ease with which investors can realize the cash value of an investment. Illiquid assets, for example, real estate, can be hard to sell quickly, and a quick sale may require a substantial discount from the price at which the asset could be sold in an unrushed situation.

The crisis peaked in September 2008. On September 7, the giant federal mortgage agencies Fannie Mae and Freddie Mac, both of which had taken large positions in subprime mortgage–backed securities, were put into conservatorship. (We will have more to say on their travails in Chapter 2.) The failure of these two mainstays of the U.S. housing and mortgage finance industries threw financial markets into a panic. By the second week of September, it was clear that both Lehman Brothers and Merrill Lynch were on the verge of bankruptcy. On September 14, Merrill Lynch was sold to Bank of America. The next day, Lehman Brothers, which was denied equivalent treatment, filed for bankruptcy protection. Two days later, on September 17, the government reluctantly lent $85 billion to AIG, reasoning that its failure would have been highly destabilizing to the banking industry, which was holding massive amounts of its credit guarantees (i.e., CDS contacts). The next day, the Treasury unveiled its first proposal to spend $700 billion to purchase "toxic" mortgage-backed securities.

A particularly devastating fallout of the Lehman bankruptcy was on the "money market" for short-term lending. Lehman had borrowed considerable funds by issuing very short-term unsecured debt called *commercial paper.* Among the major customers in the commercial paper were money market mutual funds, which invest in short-term, high-quality debt of commercial borrowers. When Lehman faltered, fear spread that these funds were exposed to losses on their large investments in commercial paper, and money market fund customers across the country rushed to withdraw their funds. In turn, the funds rushed out of commercial paper into safer and more liquid Treasury bills, essentially shutting down short-term financing markets.

The freezing up of credit markets was the end of any dwindling possibility that the financial crisis could be contained to Wall Street. Larger companies that had relied on the commercial paper market were now unable to raise short-term funds. Banks similarly found it difficult to raise funds. (Look back to Figure 1.1, where you will see that the TED spread, a measure of bank insolvency fears, skyrocketed in 2008.) With banks unwilling or unable to extend credit to their customers, thousands of small businesses that relied on bank lines of credit also became unable to finance their normal business operations. Capital-starved companies were forced to scale back their own operations precipitously. The unemployment rate rose rapidly, and the economy was in its worst recession in decades. The turmoil in the financial markets had spilled over into the real economy, and Main Street had joined Wall Street in a bout of protracted misery.

The Dodd-Frank Reform Act

The crisis engendered many calls for reform of Wall Street. These eventually led to the passage in 2010 of the Dodd-Frank Wall Street Reform and Consumer Protection Act, which proposes several mechanisms to mitigate systemic risk.

The act calls for stricter rules for bank capital, liquidity, and risk management practices, especially as banks become larger and their potential failure would be more threatening to other institutions. With more capital supporting banks, the potential for one insolvency to trigger another could be contained. In addition, when banks have more capital, they have less incentive to ramp up risk, as potential losses will come at their own expense and not the FDIC's.

Dodd-Frank also mandates increased transparency, especially in derivative markets. For example, one suggestion is to standardize CDS contracts so they can trade in centralized exchanges where prices can be determined in a deep market and gains or losses can be settled on a daily basis. Margin requirements, enforced daily, would prevent CDS participants from taking on greater positions than they can handle, and exchange trading would facilitate analysis of the exposure of firms to losses in these markets.

The act also attempts to limit the risky activities in which banks can engage. The so-called Volcker Rule, named after former chairman of the Federal Reserve Paul Volcker, limits a bank's ability to trade for its own account and to own or invest in a hedge fund or private equity fund.

The law also addresses shortcomings of the regulatory system that became apparent in 2008. The U.S. has several financial regulators with overlapping responsibility, and some institutions were accused of "regulator shopping," seeking to be supervised by the most lenient regulator. Dodd-Frank seeks to unify and clarify lines of regulatory authority and responsibility in one or a smaller number of government agencies.

The act addresses incentive issues. Among these are proposals to force employee compensation to reflect longer-term performance. The act requires public companies to set "clawback provisions" to take back executive compensation if it was based on inaccurate financial statements. The motivation is to discourage excessive risk taking by large financial institutions in which big bets can be wagered with the attitude that a successful outcome will result in a big bonus while a bad outcome will be borne by the company, or worse, the taxpayer.

The incentives of the bond rating agencies are also a sore point. Few are happy with a system that has the ratings agencies paid by the firms they rate. The act creates an Office of Credit Ratings within the Securities and Exchange Commission to oversee the credit rating agencies.

It is still too early to know which, if any, of these reforms will stick. The implementation of Dodd-Frank is still subject to considerable interpretation by regulators, and the act is still under attack by some members of Congress. But the crisis surely has made clear the essential role of the financial system in the functioning of the real economy.

1.8 OUTLINE OF THE TEXT

The text has six parts, which are fairly independent and may be studied in a variety of sequences. Part One is an introduction to financial markets, instruments, and trading of securities. This part also describes the mutual fund industry.

Part Two is a fairly detailed presentation of "modern portfolio theory." This part of the text treats the effect of diversification on portfolio risk, the efficient diversification of investor portfolios, the choice of portfolios that strike an attractive balance between risk and return, and the trade-off between risk and expected return. This part also treats the efficient market hypothesis as well as behavioral critiques of theories based on investor rationality.

Parts Three through Five cover security analysis and valuation. Part Three is devoted to debt markets and Part Four to equity markets. Part Five covers derivative assets, such as options and futures contracts.

Part Six is an introduction to active investment management. It shows how different investors' objectives and constraints can lead to a variety of investment policies. This part discusses the role of active management in nearly efficient markets, considers how one should evaluate the performance of managers who pursue active strategies, and takes a close look at hedge funds. It also shows how the principles of portfolio construction can be extended to the international setting.

www.mhhe.com/bkm

SUMMARY

- Real assets create wealth. Financial assets represent claims to parts or all of that wealth. Financial assets determine how the ownership of real assets is distributed among investors.
- Financial assets can be categorized as fixed-income (debt), equity, or derivative instruments. Top-down portfolio construction techniques start with the asset allocation decision—the allocation of funds across broad asset classes—and then progress to more specific security-selection decisions.
- Competition in financial markets leads to a risk-return trade-off, in which securities that offer higher expected rates of return also impose greater risks on investors. The presence of risk, however, implies that actual returns can differ considerably from expected returns at the beginning of the investment period. Competition among security analysts also results in financial markets that are nearly informationally efficient, meaning that prices reflect all available information concerning the value of the security. Passive investment strategies may make sense in nearly efficient markets.

- Financial intermediaries pool investor funds and invest them. Their services are in demand because small investors cannot efficiently gather information, diversify, and monitor portfolios. The financial intermediary, in contrast, is a large investor that can take advantage of scale economies.
- Investment banking brings efficiency to corporate fund raising. Investment bankers develop expertise in pricing new issues and in marketing them to investors. By the end of 2008, all the major stand-alone U.S. investment banks had been absorbed into commercial banks or had reorganized themselves into bank holding companies. In Europe, where universal banking had never been prohibited, large banks had long maintained both commercial and investment banking divisions.
- The financial crisis of 2008 showed the importance of systemic risk. Systemic risk can be limited by transparency that allows traders and investors to assess the risk of their counterparties, capital requirements to prevent trading participants from being brought down by potential losses, frequent settlement of gains or losses to prevent losses from accumulating beyond an institution's ability to bear them, incentives to discourage excessive risk taking, and accurate and unbiased analysis by those charged with evaluating security risk.

KEY TERMS

active management, 11
agency problems, 8
asset allocation, 9
derivative securities, 5
equity, 5
financial assets, 3
financial intermediaries, 12
fixed-income (debt) securities, 5
investment, 2
investment bankers, 14
investment companies, 12
passive management, 11
primary market, 15
private equity, 15
real assets, 3
risk-return trade-off, 11
secondary market, 15
securitization, 18
security analysis, 10
security selection, 9
systemic risk, 20
venture capital (VC), 15

PROBLEM SETS

Select problems are available in McGraw-Hill's *Connect Finance.* Please see the Supplements section of the book's frontmatter for more information.

Basic

1. What are the differences between equity and fixed-income securities? *(LO 1-5)*
2. What is the difference between a primary asset and a derivative asset? *(LO 1-1)*
3. What is the difference between asset allocation and security selection? *(LO 1-4)*
4. What are agency problems? What are some approaches to solving them? *(LO 1-3)*
5. What are the differences between real and financial assets? *(LO 1-2)*
6. How does investment banking differ from commercial banking? *(LO 1-5)*

Intermediate

7. For each transaction, identify the real and/or financial assets that trade hands. Are any financial assets created or destroyed in the transaction? *(LO 1-2)*
   a. Toyota takes out a bank loan to finance the construction of a new factory.
   b. Toyota pays off its loan.
   c. Toyota uses $10 million of cash on hand to purchase additional inventory of spare auto parts.
8. Suppose that in a wave of pessimism, housing prices fall by 10% across the entire economy. *(LO 1-2)*
   a. Has the stock of real assets of the economy changed?
   b. Are individuals less wealthy?
   c. Can you reconcile your answers to (*a*) and (*b*)?

www.mhhe.com/bkm

9. Lanni Products is a start-up computer software development firm. It currently owns computer equipment worth \$30,000 and has cash on hand of \$20,000 contributed by Lanni's owners. For each of the following transactions, identify the real and/or financial assets that trade hands. Are any financial assets created or destroyed in the transaction? ***(LO 1-2)***
   a. Lanni takes out a bank loan. It receives \$50,000 in cash and signs a note promising to pay back the loan over three years.
   b. Lanni uses the cash from the bank plus \$20,000 of its own funds to finance the development of new financial planning software.
   c. Lanni sells the software product to Microsoft, which will market it to the public under the Microsoft name. Lanni accepts payment in the form of 5,000 shares of Microsoft stock.
   d. Lanni sells the shares of stock for \$25 per share and uses part of the proceeds to pay off the bank loan.
10. Reconsider Lanni Products from the previous problem. ***(LO 1-2)***
    a. Prepare its balance sheet just after it gets the bank loan. What is the ratio of real assets to total assets?
    b. Prepare the balance sheet after Lanni spends the \$70,000 to develop its software product. What is the ratio of real assets to total assets?
    c. Prepare the balance sheet after Lanni accepts the payment of shares from Microsoft. What is the ratio of real assets to total assets?
11. What reforms to the financial system might reduce its exposure to systemic risk? ***(LO 1-6)***
12. Examine the balance sheet of commercial banks in Table 1.3. What is the ratio of real assets to total assets? What is that ratio for nonfinancial firms (Table 1.4)? Why should this difference be expected? ***(LO 1-2)***
13. Why do financial assets show up as a component of household wealth, but not of national wealth? Why do financial assets still matter for the material well-being of an economy? ***(LO 1-2)***
14. Discuss the advantages and disadvantages of the following forms of managerial compensation in terms of mitigating agency problems, that is, potential conflicts of interest between managers and shareholders. ***(LO 1-3)***
    a. A fixed salary.
    b. Stock in the firm that must be held for five years.
    c. A salary linked to the firm's profits.
15. We noted that oversight by large institutional investors or creditors is one mechanism to reduce agency problems. Why don't individual investors in the firm have the same incentive to keep an eye on management? ***(LO 1-3)***
16. Wall Street firms have traditionally compensated their traders with a share of the trading profits that they generated. How might this practice have affected traders' willingness to assume risk? What is the agency problem this practice engendered? ***(LO 1-3)***
17. Why would you expect securitization to take place only in highly developed capital markets? ***(LO 1-6)***
18. What would you expect to be the relationship between securitization and the role of financial intermediaries in the economy? For example, what happens to the role of local banks in providing capital for mortgage loans when national markets in mortgage-backed securities become highly developed? ***(LO 1-6)***
19. Give an example of three financial intermediaries, and explain how they act as a bridge between small investors and large capital markets or corporations. ***(LO 1-5)***
20. Firms raise capital from investors by issuing shares in the primary markets. Does this imply that corporate financial managers can ignore trading of previously issued shares in the secondary market? ***(LO 1-4)***

21. The average rate of return on investments in large stocks has outpaced that on investments in Treasury bills by about 7% since 1926. Why, then, does anyone invest in Treasury bills? ***(LO 1-1)***
22. You see an advertisement for a book that claims to show how you can make $1 million with no risk and with no money down. Will you buy the book? ***(LO 1-1)***

WEB *master*

1. Log on to **finance.yahoo.com** and enter the ticker symbol "RRD" in the *Get Quotes* box to find information about R.R. Donnelley & Sons.
   a. Click on company *Profile.* What is Donnelly's main line of business?
   b. Now go to *Key Statistics.* How many shares of the company's stock are outstanding? What is the total market value of the firm? What were its profits in the most recent fiscal year?
   c. Look up *Major Holders* of the company's stock. What fraction of total shares is held by insiders?
   d. Now go to *Analyst Opinion.* What is the average price target (i.e., the predicted stock price of the Donnelly shares) of the analysts covering this firm? How does that compare to the price at which the stock is currently trading?
   e. Look at the company's *Balance Sheet.* What were its total assets at the end of the most recent fiscal year?
2. Visit the website of the Securities and Exchange Commission, **www.sec.gov.** What is the mission of the SEC? What information and advice does the SEC offer to beginning investors?
3. Now visit the website of the NASD, **www.finra.org.** What is its mission? What information and advice does it offer to beginners?
4. Now visit the website of the IOSCO, **www.iosco.org.** What is its mission? What information and advice does it offer to beginners?

SOLUTIONS TO CONCEPT *checks*

1.1 *a.* Real
b. Financial
c. Real
d. Real
e. Financial

1.2 The central issue is the incentive to monitor the quality of loans both when originated and over time. Freddie and Fannie clearly had incentive to monitor the quality of conforming loans that they had guaranteed, and their ongoing relationships with mortgage originators gave them opportunities to evaluate track records over extended periods of time. In the subprime mortgage market, the ultimate investors in the securities (or the CDOs backed by those securities), who were bearing the credit risk, should not have been willing to invest in loans with a disproportional likelihood of default. If they properly understood their exposure to default risk, then the (correspondingly low) prices they would have been willing to pay for these securities would have imposed discipline on the mortgage originators and servicers. The fact that they were willing to hold such large positions in these risky securities suggests that they did not appreciate the extent of their exposure. Maybe they were led astray by overly optimistic projections for housing prices or by biased assessments from the credit reporting agencies. While in principle either arrangement for default risk could have provided the appropriate discipline on the mortgage originators, in practice the informational advantages of Freddie and Fannie probably made them the better "recipients" of default risk. The lesson is that information and transparency are some of the preconditions for well-functioning markets.

Chapter 2

Asset Classes and Financial Instruments

Learning Objectives:

- LO2-1 Distinguish among the major assets that trade in money markets and in capital markets.
- LO2-2 Describe the construction of stock market indexes.
- LO2-3 Calculate the profit or loss on investments in options and futures contracts.

You learned in Chapter 1 that the process of building an investment portfolio usually begins by deciding how much money to allocate to broad classes of assets, such as safe money market securities or bank accounts, longer-term bonds, stocks, or even asset classes such as real estate or precious metals. This process is called *asset allocation.* Within each class the investor then selects specific assets from a more detailed menu. This is called *security selection.*

Each broad asset class contains many specific security types, and the many variations on a theme can be overwhelming. Our goal in this chapter is to introduce you to the important features of broad classes of securities. Toward this end, we organize our tour of financial instruments according to asset class.

Financial markets are traditionally segmented into money markets and capital markets. Money market instruments include short-term, marketable, liquid, low-risk debt securities. Money market instruments sometimes are called *cash equivalents,* or just *cash* for short. Capital markets, in contrast, include longer-term and riskier securities. Securities in the capital market are much more diverse than those found within the money market. For this reason, we will subdivide the capital market into three segments: longer-term debt markets, equity markets, and derivative markets in which options and futures trade.

We first describe money market instruments. We then move on to debt and equity securities. We explain the structure of various stock market indexes in this chapter because market benchmark portfolios play an important role in portfolio construction and evaluation. Finally, we survey the derivative security markets for options and futures contracts. A selection of the markets, instruments, and indexes covered in this chapter appears in Table 2.1.

Related websites for this chapter are available at www.mhhe.com/bkm.

2.1 THE MONEY MARKET

The **money market** is a subsector of the debt market. It consists of very short-term debt securities that are highly marketable. Many of these securities trade in large denominations and so are out of the reach of individual investors. Money market mutual funds, however, are easily accessible to small investors. These mutual funds pool the resources of many investors and purchase a wide variety of money market securities on their behalf.

money markets

Include short-term, highly liquid, and relatively low-risk debt instruments.

Treasury Bills

U.S. **Treasury bills** (T-bills, or just bills, for short) are the most marketable of all money market instruments. T-bills represent the simplest form of borrowing. The government raises money by selling bills to the public. Investors buy the bills at a discount from the stated maturity value. At the bill's maturity, the holder receives from the government a payment equal to the face value of the bill. The difference between the purchase price and the ultimate maturity value represents the investor's earnings.

Treasury bills

Short-term government securities issued at a discount from face value and returning the face amount at maturity.

T-bills are issued with initial maturities of 4, 13, 26, or 52 weeks. Individuals can purchase T-bills directly from the Treasury or on the secondary market from a government securities dealer. T-bills are highly liquid; that is, they are easily converted to cash and sold at low transaction cost and with little price risk. Unlike most other money market instruments, which sell in minimum denominations of $100,000, T-bills sell in minimum denominations of only $100, although $10,000 denominations are far more common. While the income earned on T-bills is taxable at the federal level, it is exempt from all state and local taxes, another characteristic distinguishing T-bills from other money market instruments.

Figure 2.1 is a partial listing of T-bills from *The Wall Street Journal Online* (look for the *Markets* tab, and then for the *Market Data* tab). Rather than providing prices of each bill, the financial press reports yields based on those prices. You will see yields corresponding to both bid and asked prices. The *asked price* is the price you would have to pay to buy a T-bill from a securities dealer. The *bid price* is the slightly lower price you would receive if you wanted to sell a bill to a dealer. The *bid–asked spread* is the difference in these prices, which is the dealer's source of profit.

The first two yields in Figure 2.1 are reported using the *bank-discount method.* This means that the bill's discount from its maturity, or face, value is "annualized" based on a 360-day year and then reported as a percentage of face value. For example, for the highlighted bill maturing on March 8, 2012, days to maturity are 245 and the yield under the column labeled "ASKED" is given as .07%. This means that a dealer was willing to sell the bill at a discount from face value of .07% × (245/360) = .0476%. So a bill with $10,000 face value could be purchased for $10,000 × (1 − .000476) = $9,995.236. Similarly, on the basis of the bid yield of .085%, a dealer would

TABLE 2.1 Financial markets and indexes

The money market	**The bond market**
Treasury bills	Treasury bonds and notes
Certificates of deposit	Federal agency debt
Commercial paper	Municipal bonds
Bankers' acceptances	Corporate bonds
Eurodollars	Mortgage-backed securities
Repos and reverses	**Equity markets**
Federal funds	Common stocks
Brokers' calls	Preferred stocks
Indexes	**Derivative markets**
Dow Jones averages	Options
Standard & Poor's indexes	Futures and forwards
Bond market indicators	Swaps
International indexes	

FIGURE 2.1

Treasury bill listings

Source: *The Wall Street Journal Online*, July 7, 2011. Reprinted by permission of *The Wall Street Journal*, Copyright © 2011 Dow Jones & Company, Inc. All Rights Reserved Worldwide.

Treasury Bills

MATURITY	DAYS TO MAT	BID	ASKED	CHG	ASK YLD
Sep 01 11	56	0.045	0.015	0.030	0.005
Oct 06 11	91	0.025	0.015	0.005	0.015
Nov 03 11	119	0.040	0.020	0.015	0.020
Jan 05 12	182	0.070	0.060	0.070	0.061
Mar 08 12	245	0.085	0.070	0.005	0.071
Jun 28 12	357	0.185	0.180	0.015	0.183

be willing to purchase the bill for $10,000 × (1 − .00085 × 245/360) = $9,994.215. Notice that prices and yields are inversely related, so the higher bid *yield* reported in Figure 2.1 implies a lower bid *price.*

The bank discount method for computing yields has a long tradition, but it is flawed for at least two reasons. First, it assumes that the year has only 360 days. Second, it computes the yield as a fraction of face value rather than of the price the investor paid to acquire the bill.[1] An investor who buys the bill for the asked price and holds it until maturity will see her investment grow over 245 days by a multiple of $10,000/$9,995.236 = 1.000477, for a gain of .0477%. Annualizing this gain using a 365-day year results in a yield of .0477% × 365/245 = .071%, which is the value reported in the last column, under "asked yield." This last value is called the Treasury bill's *bond-equivalent yield.*

Certificates of Deposit

certificate of deposit

A bank time deposit.

A **certificate of deposit** (CD) is a time deposit with a bank. Time deposits may not be withdrawn on demand. The bank pays interest and principal to the depositor only at the end of the fixed term of the CD. CDs issued in denominations larger than $100,000 are usually negotiable, however; that is, they can be sold to another investor if the owner needs to cash in the certificate before its maturity date. Short-term CDs are highly marketable, although the market significantly thins out for maturities of three months or more. CDs are treated as bank deposits by the Federal Deposit Insurance Corporation, so they are insured for up to $250,000 in the event of a bank insolvency.

Commercial Paper

commercial paper

Short-term unsecured debt issued by large corporations.

The typical corporation is a net borrower of both long-term funds (for capital investments) and short-term funds (for working capital). Large, well-known companies often issue their own short-term unsecured debt notes directly to the public, rather than borrowing from banks. These notes are called **commercial paper** (CP). Sometimes, CP is backed by a bank line of credit, which gives the borrower access to cash that can be used if needed to pay off the paper at maturity.

CP maturities range up to 270 days; longer maturities require registration with the Securities and Exchange Commission and so are almost never issued. CP most commonly is issued with maturities of less than one or two months in denominations of multiples of $100,000. Therefore, small investors can invest in commercial paper only indirectly, through money market mutual funds.

CP is considered to be a fairly safe asset, given that a firm's condition presumably can be monitored and predicted over a term as short as one month. CP trades in secondary markets and so is quite liquid. Most issues are rated by at least one agency such as Standard & Poor's. The yield on CP depends on its time to maturity and credit rating.

While most CP historically was issued by nonfinancial firms, in recent years there was a sharp increase in so-called *asset-backed commercial paper* issued by financial firms such as banks. This short-term CP typically was used to raise funds for the institution to invest in other assets, most notoriously, subprime mortgages. These assets in turn were used as

[1]Both of these "errors" were dictated by computational simplicity in the days before computers. It is easier to compute percentage discounts from a round number such as face value than from purchase price. It is also easier to annualize using a 360-day year, since 360 is an even multiple of so many numbers.

collateral for the CP—hence the label "asset-backed." This practice led to many difficulties starting in the summer of 2007 when those subprime mortgages began defaulting. The banks found themselves unable to issue new CP to refinance their positions as the old paper matured.

Bankers' Acceptances

A **bankers' acceptance** starts as an order to a bank by a bank's customer to pay a sum of money at a future date, typically within six months. At this stage, it is like a postdated check. When the bank endorses the order for payment as "accepted," it assumes responsibility for ultimate payment to the holder of the acceptance. At this point, the acceptance may be traded in secondary markets much like any other claim on the bank. Bankers' acceptances are considered very safe assets, as they allow traders to substitute the bank's credit standing for their own. They are used widely in foreign trade where the creditworthiness of one trader is unknown to the trading partner. Acceptances sell at a discount from the face value of the payment order, just as T-bills sell at a discount from par value.

bankers' acceptance

An order to a bank by a customer to pay a sum of money at a future date.

Eurodollars

Eurodollars are dollar-denominated deposits at foreign banks or foreign branches of American banks. By locating outside the United States, these banks escape regulation by the Federal Reserve Board. Despite the tag "Euro," these accounts need not be in European banks, although that is where the practice of accepting dollar-denominated deposits outside the United States began.

Most Eurodollar deposits are for large sums, and most are time deposits of less than six months' maturity. A variation on the Eurodollar time deposit is the Eurodollar certificate of deposit. A Eurodollar CD resembles a domestic bank CD except it is the liability of a non-U.S. branch of a bank, typically a London branch. The advantage of Eurodollar CDs over Eurodollar time deposits is that the holder can sell the asset to realize its cash value before maturity. Eurodollar CDs are considered less liquid and riskier than domestic CDs, however, and so offer higher yields. Firms also issue Eurodollar bonds, that is, dollar-denominated bonds outside the U.S., although such bonds are not a money market investment by virtue of their long maturities.

Eurodollars

Dollar-denominated deposits at foreign banks or foreign branches of American banks.

Repos and Reverses

Dealers in government securities use **repurchase agreements,** also called repos, or RPs, as a form of short-term, usually overnight, borrowing. The dealer sells securities to an investor on an overnight basis, with an agreement to buy back those securities the next day at a slightly higher price. The increase in the price is the overnight interest. The dealer thus takes out a one-day loan from the investor. The securities serve as collateral for the loan.

A *term repo* is essentially an identical transaction, except the term of the implicit loan can be 30 days or more. Repos are considered very safe in terms of credit risk because the loans are collateralized by the securities. A *reverse repo* is the mirror image of a repo. Here, the dealer finds an investor holding government securities and buys them with an agreement to resell them at a specified higher price on a future date.

repurchase agreements (repos)

Short-term sales of government securities with an agreement to repurchase the securities at a higher price.

Brokers' Calls

Individuals who buy stocks on margin borrow part of the funds to pay for the stocks from their broker. The broker in turn may borrow the funds from a bank, agreeing to repay the bank immediately (on call) if the bank requests it. The rate paid on such loans is usually about one percentage point higher than the rate on short-term T-bills.

Federal Funds

Federal funds

Funds in the accounts of commercial banks at the Federal Reserve Bank.

Just as most of us maintain deposits at banks, banks maintain deposits of their own at the Federal Reserve Bank, or the Fed. Each member bank of the Federal Reserve System is required to maintain a minimum balance in a reserve account with the Fed. The required balance depends on the total deposits of the bank's customers. Funds in the bank's reserve account are called **Federal funds** or *Fed funds.* At any time, some banks have more funds than required at the Fed. Other banks, primarily big New York and other financial center banks, tend to have a shortage of Federal funds. In the Federal funds market, banks with excess funds lend to those with a shortage. These loans, which are usually overnight transactions, are arranged at a rate of interest called the *Federal funds rate.*

Although the Fed funds market arose primarily as a way for banks to transfer balances to meet reserve requirements, today the market has evolved to the point that many large banks use Federal funds in a straightforward way as one component of their total sources of funding. Therefore, the Fed funds rate is simply the rate of interest on very short-term loans among financial institutions. While most investors cannot participate in this market, the Fed funds rate commands great interest as a key barometer of monetary policy.

The LIBOR Market

LIBOR

Lending rate among banks in the London market.

The **London Interbank Offer Rate (LIBOR)** is the rate at which large banks in London are willing to lend money among themselves. This rate has become the premier short-term interest rate quoted in the European money market and serves as a reference rate for a wide range of transactions. A corporation might borrow at a rate equal to LIBOR plus two percentage points, for example. Like the Fed funds rate, LIBOR is a statistic widely followed by investors.

LIBOR interest rates may be tied to currencies other than the U.S. dollar. For example, LIBOR rates are widely quoted for transactions denominated in British pounds, yen, euros, and so on. There is also a similar rate called EURIBOR (European Interbank Offer Rate) at which banks in the euro zone are willing to lend euros among themselves.

Yields on Money Market Instruments

Although most money market securities are of low risk, they are not risk-free. The securities of the money market promise yields greater than those on default-free T-bills, at least in part because of their greater relative risk. Investors who require more liquidity also will accept lower yields on securities, such as T-bills, that can be more quickly and cheaply sold for cash. Figure 2.2 shows that bank CDs, for example, consistently have paid a risk premium over T-bills. Moreover, as Figure 2.2 shows, that premium increases with economic crises such as

FIGURE 2.2

Spread between three-month CD and T-bill rates

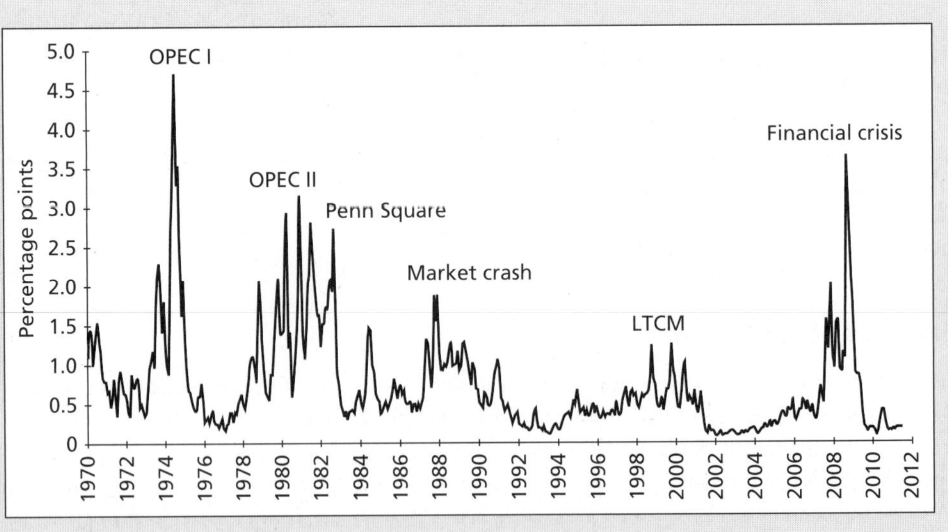

On the MARKET FRONT

MONEY MARKET FUNDS AND THE FINANCIAL CRISIS OF 2008

Money market funds are mutual funds that invest in the short-term debt instruments that comprise the money market. In 2008, these funds had investments totaling about $3.4 trillion. They are required to hold only short-maturity debt of the highest quality: The average maturity of their holdings must be maintained at less than three months. Their biggest investments tend to be in commercial paper, but they also hold sizable fractions of their portfolios in certificates of deposit, repurchase agreements, and Treasury securities. Because of this very conservative investment profile, money market funds typically experience extremely low price risk. Investors for their part usually acquire check-writing privileges with their funds and often use them as a close substitute for a bank account. This is feasible because the funds almost always maintain share value at $1 and pass along all investment earnings to their investors as interest.

Until 2008, only one fund had "broken the buck," that is, suffered losses large enough to force value per share below $1. But when Lehman Brothers filed for bankruptcy protection on September 15, 2008, several funds that had invested heavily in its commercial paper suffered large losses. The next day, Reserve Primary Fund, the oldest money market fund, broke the buck when its value per share fell to only $.97.

The realization that money market funds were at risk in the credit crisis led to a wave of investor redemptions similar to a run on a bank. Only three days after the Lehman bankruptcy, Putman's Prime Money Market Fund announced that it was liquidating due to heavy redemptions. Fearing further outflows, the U.S. Treasury announced that it would make federal insurance available to money market funds willing to pay an insurance fee. This program would thus be similar to FDIC bank insurance. With the federal insurance in place, the outflows were quelled.

However, the turmoil in Wall Street's money market funds had already spilled over into "Main Street." Fearing further investor redemptions, money market funds had become afraid to commit funds even over short periods, and their demand for commercial paper had effectively dried up. Firms that had been able to borrow at 2% interest rates in previous weeks now had to pay up to 8%, and the commercial paper market was on the edge of freezing up altogether. Firms throughout the economy had come to depend on those markets as a major source of short-term finance to fund expenditures ranging from salaries to inventories. Further breakdown in the money markets would have had an immediate crippling effect on the broad economy. Within days, the Federal government put forth its first plan to spend $700 billion to stabilize the credit markets.

the energy price shocks associated with the Organization of Petroleum Exporting Countries (OPEC) disturbances, the failure of Penn Square Bank, the stock market crash in 1987, the collapse of Long Term Capital Management in 1998, and the financial crisis resulting from the breakdown of the subprime mortgage market beginning in 2007. If you look back to Figure 1.1 in Chapter 1, you'll see that the TED spread, the difference between the LIBOR rate and the Treasury-bill rate, also peaked during the financial crisis.

Money market funds are mutual funds that invest in money market instruments and have become major sources of funding to that sector. The nearby box discusses the fallout of the financial crisis of 2008 on those funds.

2.2 THE BOND MARKET

The bond market is composed of longer-term borrowing or debt instruments than those that trade in the money market. This market includes Treasury notes and bonds, corporate bonds, municipal bonds, mortgage securities, and federal agency debt.

These instruments are sometimes said to comprise the *fixed-income capital market,* because most of them promise either a fixed stream of income or stream of income that is determined according to a specified formula. In practice, these formulas can result in a flow of income that is far from fixed. Therefore, the term "fixed income" is probably not fully appropriate. It is simpler and more straightforward to call these securities either debt instruments or bonds.

Treasury Notes and Bonds

The U.S. government borrows funds in large part by selling **Treasury notes** and **bonds.** T-notes are issued with original maturities ranging up to 10 years, while T-bonds are issued with maturities ranging from 10 to 30 years. Both bonds and notes may be issued in increments of $100 but far more commonly trade in denominations of $1,000. Both bonds and notes make semiannual interest payments called *coupon payments,* so named because in

Treasury notes or bonds

Debt obligations of the federal government with original maturities of one year or more.

FIGURE 2.3

Listing of Treasury issues

Source: Compiled from data from *The Wall Street Journal Online,* July 6, 2011. Reprinted by permission of *The Wall Street Journal,* Copyright © 2011 Dow Jones & Company, Inc. All Rights Reserved Worldwide.

MATURITY	COUPON	BID	ASKED	CHG	YLD TO MATURITY
2011 Nov 15	1.750	100.5859	100.6016	−0.008	0.051
2013 Nov 15	4.250	108.4375	108.4844	−0.234	0.613
2015 Nov 15	4.500	112.9375	113.0000	−0.438	1.410
2018 Feb 15	3.500	107.2969	107.3594	−0.547	2.294
2020 Feb 15	8.500	143.6875	143.7344	−0.547	2.756
2025 Aug 15	6.875	134.4844	134.5166	−0.531	3.710
2030 May 15	6.250	129.1406	129.1719	−0.484	4.026
2040 Nov 15	4.250	97.9531	98.0000	−0.313	4.371

precomputer days, investors would literally clip a coupon attached to the bond and present it to receive the interest payment.

Figure 2.3 is an excerpt from a listing of Treasury issues. The highlighted bond matures in November 2015. The coupon income or interest paid by the bond is 4.5% of par value, meaning that for a $1,000 face value bond, $45 in annual interest payments will be made in two semiannual installments of $22.50 each.

The bid price of the highlighted bond is 112.9375. (This is the decimal version of 112 60/64. The minimum *tick size,* or spread between prices in the Treasury-bond market, is 1/64 of a point.) The asked price is 113. Although bonds are typically traded in denominations of $1,000 par value, prices are quoted as a percentage of par. Thus, the asked price of 103 should be interpreted as 103% of par, or $1,030 for the $1,000 par value bond. Similarly, the bond could be sold to a dealer for $1,129.375. The −.4375 change means that the closing price on this day fell by .4375% of par value (equivalently, by 7/16 of a point) from the previous day's close. Finally, the yield to maturity based on the asked price is 1.41%.

The *yield to maturity* reported in the last column is a measure of the annualized rate of return to an investor who buys the bond and holds it until maturity. It accounts for both coupon income as well as the difference between the purchase price of the bond and its final value of $1,000 at maturity. We discuss the yield to maturity in detail in Chapter 10.

CONCEPT check 2.1

What were the bid price, asked price, and yield to maturity of the 3.5% February 2018 Treasury bond displayed in Figure 2.3? What was its asked price the previous day?

Inflation-Protected Treasury Bonds

The best place to start building an investment portfolio is at the least risky end of the spectrum. Around the world, governments of many countries, including the U.S., have issued bonds that are linked to an index of the cost of living in order to provide their citizens with an effective way to hedge inflation risk.

In the United States, inflation-protected Treasury bonds are called *TIPS* (Treasury Inflation Protected Securities). The principal amount on these bonds is adjusted in proportion to increases in the Consumer Price Index. Therefore, they provide a constant stream of income in real (inflation-adjusted) dollars, and the real interest rates you earn on these securities are risk-free if you hold them to maturity. We return to TIPS bonds in more detail in Chapter 10.

Federal Agency Debt

Some government agencies issue their own securities to finance their activities. These agencies usually are formed for public policy reasons to channel credit to a particular sector of the economy that Congress believes is not receiving adequate credit through normal private sources.

The major mortgage-related agencies are the Federal Home Loan Bank (FHLB), the Federal National Mortgage Association (FNMA, or Fannie Mae), the Government National

Mortgage Association (GNMA, or Ginnie Mae), and the Federal Home Loan Mortgage Corporation (FHLMC, or Freddie Mac).

Although the debt of federal agencies was never explicitly insured by the federal government, it had long been assumed that the government would assist an agency nearing default. Those beliefs were validated when Fannie Mae and Freddie Mac actually encountered severe financial distress in September 2008. With both firms on the brink of insolvency, the government stepped in and put them both into conservatorship, assigned the Federal Housing Finance Agency to run the firms, but did in fact agree to make good on the firm's bonds. (Turn back to Chapter 1 for more discussion of the Fannie and Freddie failures.)

International Bonds

Many firms borrow abroad and many investors buy bonds from foreign issuers. In addition to national capital markets, there is a thriving international capital market, largely centered in London.

A *Eurobond* is a bond denominated in a currency other than that of the country in which it is issued. For example, a dollar-denominated bond sold in Britain would be called a *Eurodollar bond.* Similarly, investors might speak of Euroyen bonds, yen-denominated bonds sold outside Japan. Since the European currency is called the *euro,* the term *Eurobond* may be confusing. It is best to think of them simply as international bonds.

In contrast to bonds that are issued in foreign currencies, many firms issue bonds in foreign countries but in the currency of the investor. For example, a Yankee bond is a dollar-denominated bond sold in the U.S. by a non-U.S. issuer. Similarly, Samurai bonds are yen-denominated bonds sold in Japan by non-Japanese issuers.

Municipal Bonds

municipal bonds

Tax-exempt bonds issued by state and local governments.

Municipal bonds ("munis") are issued by state and local governments. They are similar to Treasury and corporate bonds, except their interest income is exempt from federal income taxation. The interest income also is usually exempt from state and local taxation in the issuing state. Capital gains taxes, however, must be paid on munis if the bonds mature or are sold for more than the investor's purchase price.

There are basically two types of municipal bonds. *General obligation bonds* are backed by the "full faith and credit" (i.e., the taxing power) of the issuer, while *revenue bonds* are issued to finance particular projects and are backed either by the revenues from that project or by the municipal agency operating the project. Typical issuers of revenue bonds are airports, hospitals, and turnpike or port authorities. Revenue bonds are riskier in terms of default than general obligation bonds.

An *industrial development bond* is a revenue bond that is issued to finance commercial enterprises, such as the construction of a factory that can be operated by a private firm. In effect, this device gives the firm access to the municipality's ability to borrow at tax-exempt rates, and the federal government limits the amount of these bonds that may be issued.[2] Figure 2.4 plots outstanding amounts of industrial revenue bonds as well as general obligation municipal bonds.

Like Treasury bonds, municipal bonds vary widely in maturity. A good deal of the debt issued is in the form of short-term *tax anticipation notes* that raise funds to pay for expenses before actual collection of taxes. Other municipal debt may be long term and used to fund large capital investments. Maturities range up to 30 years.

The key feature of municipal bonds is their tax-exempt status. Because investors pay neither federal nor state taxes on the interest proceeds, they are willing to accept lower yields on these securities.

An investor choosing between taxable and tax-exempt bonds needs to compare after-tax returns on each bond. An exact comparison requires the computation of after-tax rates of return with explicit recognition of taxes on income and realized capital gains. In practice, there is a simpler rule of thumb. If we let t denote the investor's combined federal plus local

[2]A warning, however. Although interest on industrial development bonds usually is exempt from federal tax, it can be subject to the alternative minimum tax if the bonds are used to finance projects of for-profit companies.

FIGURE 2.4

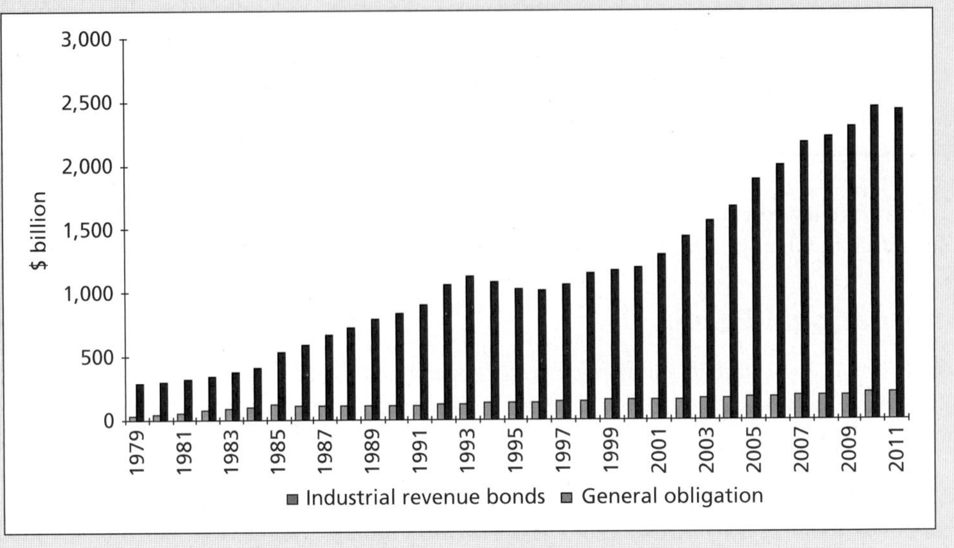

Outstanding tax-exempt debt

Source: *Flow of Funds Accounts of the U.S.*, Board of Governors of the Federal Reserve System, June 2011.

marginal tax rate and r denote the total before-tax rate of return available on taxable bonds, then $r(1 - t)$ is the after-tax rate available on those securities.[3] If this value exceeds the rate on municipal bonds, r_m, the investor does better holding the taxable bonds. Otherwise, the tax-exempt municipals provide higher after-tax returns.

One way of comparing bonds is to determine the interest rate on taxable bonds that would be necessary to provide an after-tax return equal to that of municipals. To derive this value, we set after-tax yields equal and solve for the *equivalent taxable yield* of the tax-exempt bond. This is the rate a taxable bond would need to offer in order to match the after-tax yield on the tax-free municipal.

$$r(1 - t) = r_m \quad \textbf{(2.1)}$$

or

$$r = \frac{r_m}{1 - t} \quad \textbf{(2.2)}$$

Thus, the equivalent taxable yield is simply the tax-free rate divided by $1 - t$. Table 2.2 presents equivalent taxable yields for several municipal yields and tax rates.

TABLE 2.2 Equivalent taxable yields corresponding to various tax-exempt yields

	Tax-Exempt Yield				
Marginal Tax Rate	**1%**	**2%**	**3%**	**4%**	**5%**
20%	1.25%	2.50%	3.75%	5.00%	6.25%
30	1.43	2.86	4.29	5.71	7.14
40	1.67	3.33	5.00	6.67	8.33
50	2.00	4.00	6.00	8.00	10.00

[3]An approximation to the combined federal plus local tax rate is just the sum of the two rates. For example, if your federal tax rate is 28% and your state rate is 5%, your combined tax rate would be approximately 33%. A more precise approach would recognize that state taxes are deductible at the federal level. You owe federal taxes only on income net of state taxes. Therefore, for every dollar of income, your after-tax proceeds would be $(1 - t_{\text{federal}}) \times (1 - t_{\text{state}})$. In our example, your after-tax proceeds on each dollar earned would be $(1 - .28) \times (1 - .05) = .684$, which implies a combined tax rate of $1 - .684 = .316$, or 31.6%.

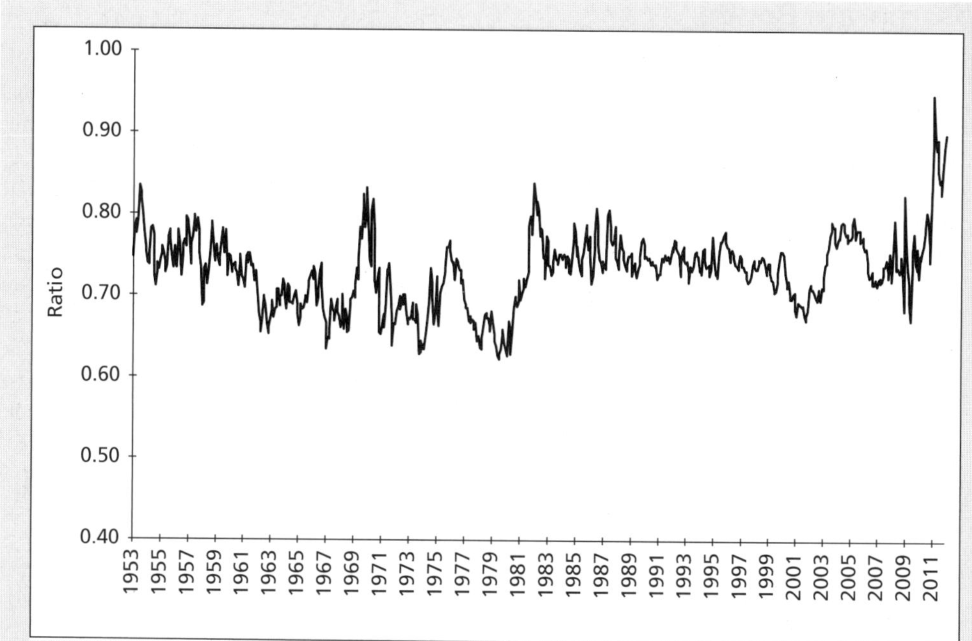

FIGURE 2.5

Ratio of yields on tax-exempt to taxable bonds

Source: **www.federalreserve.gov/releases/h15/data.htm.**

This table frequently appears in the marketing literature for tax-exempt mutual bond funds because it demonstrates to high-tax-bracket investors that municipal bonds offer highly attractive equivalent taxable yields. Each entry is calculated from Equation 2.2. If the equivalent taxable yield exceeds the actual yields offered on taxable bonds, after taxes the investor is better off holding municipal bonds. The equivalent taxable interest rate increases with the investor's tax bracket; the higher the bracket, the more valuable the tax-exempt feature of municipals. Thus, high-bracket individuals tend to hold municipals.

We also can use Equation 2.1 or 2.2 to find the tax bracket at which investors are indifferent between taxable and tax-exempt bonds. The cutoff tax bracket is given by solving Equation 2.1 for the tax bracket at which after-tax yields are equal. Doing so, we find

$$t = 1 - \frac{r_m}{r} \tag{2.3}$$

Thus, the yield ratio r_m/r is a key determinant of the attractiveness of municipal bonds. The higher the yield ratio, the lower the cutoff tax bracket, and the more individuals will prefer to hold municipal debt. Figure 2.5 graphs the yield ratio since 1955.[4]

EXAMPLE 2.1

Taxable versus Tax-Exempt Yields

Figure 2.5 shows that for most of the last 30 years, the ratio of tax-exempt to taxable yields fluctuated around .75. What does this imply about the cutoff tax bracket above which tax-exempt bonds provide higher after-tax yields? Equation 2.3 shows that an investor whose combined tax bracket (federal plus local) exceeds 1 − .75 = .25, or 25%, will derive a greater after-tax yield from municipals. Note, however, that it is difficult to control precisely for differences in the risks of these bonds, so the cutoff tax bracket must be taken as approximate.

CONCEPT check 2.2

Suppose your tax bracket is 28%. Would you prefer to earn a 6% taxable return or a 4% tax-free yield? What is the equivalent taxable yield of the 4% tax-free yield?

[4]Figure 2.5 plots the ratio of 20-year municipal debt yields to the average of the yields on Aaa-rated and Baa-rated corporate debt. The default risk of these corporate and municipal bonds may be comparable but certainly will fluctuate somewhat over time. For example, the sharp run-up in the ratio in 2011 probably reflects increased concern at the time about the precarious financial condition of several states and municipalities.

Corporate Bonds

corporate bonds

Long-term debt issued by private corporations typically paying semiannual coupons and returning the face value of the bond at maturity.

Corporate bonds are the means by which private firms borrow money directly from the public. These bonds are structured much like Treasury issues in that they typically pay semiannual coupons over their lives and return the face value to the bondholder at maturity. Where they differ most importantly from Treasury bonds is in risk.

Default risk is a real consideration in the purchase of corporate bonds. We treat this issue in considerable detail in Chapter 10. For now, we distinguish only among secured bonds, which have specific collateral backing them in the event of firm bankruptcy; unsecured bonds, called *debentures,* which have no collateral; and subordinated debentures, which have a lower priority claim to the firm's assets in the event of bankruptcy.

Corporate bonds sometimes come with options attached. *Callable bonds* give the firm the option to repurchase the bond from the holder at a stipulated call price. *Convertible bonds* give the bondholder the option to convert each bond into a stipulated number of shares of stock. These options are treated in more detail in Part Three.

Mortgages and Mortgage-Backed Securities

Because of the explosion in mortgage-backed securities, almost anyone can invest in a portfolio of mortgage loans, and these securities have become a major component of the fixed-income market.

As described in Chapter 1, a *mortgage-backed security* is either an ownership claim in a pool of mortgages or an obligation that is secured by such a pool. Most pass-throughs traditionally comprised *conforming mortgages,* which meant that the loans had to satisfy certain underwriting guidelines (standards for the creditworthiness of the borrower) before they could be purchased by Fannie Mae or Freddie Mac. In the years leading up to the financial crisis, however, a large amount of *subprime mortgages,* that is, riskier loans made to financially weaker borrowers, were bundled and sold by "private-label" issuers. Figure 2.6 illustrates the explosive growth of these securities, at least through 2007.

FIGURE 2.6

Mortgage-backed securities outstanding

Source: *Flow of Funds Accounts of the U.S.,* Board of Governors of the Federal Reserve System, June 2011.

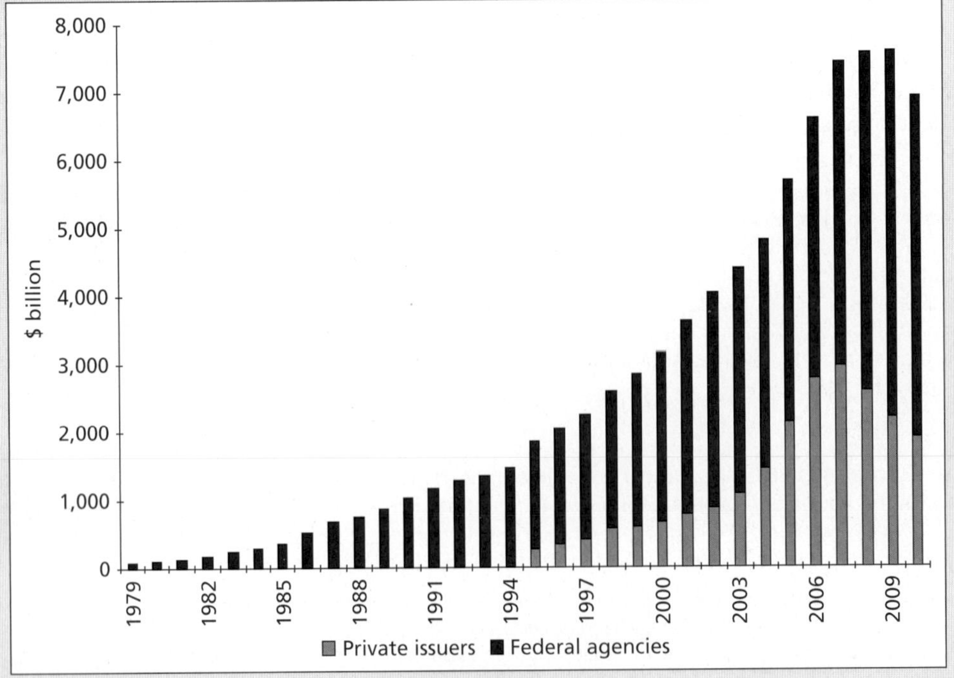

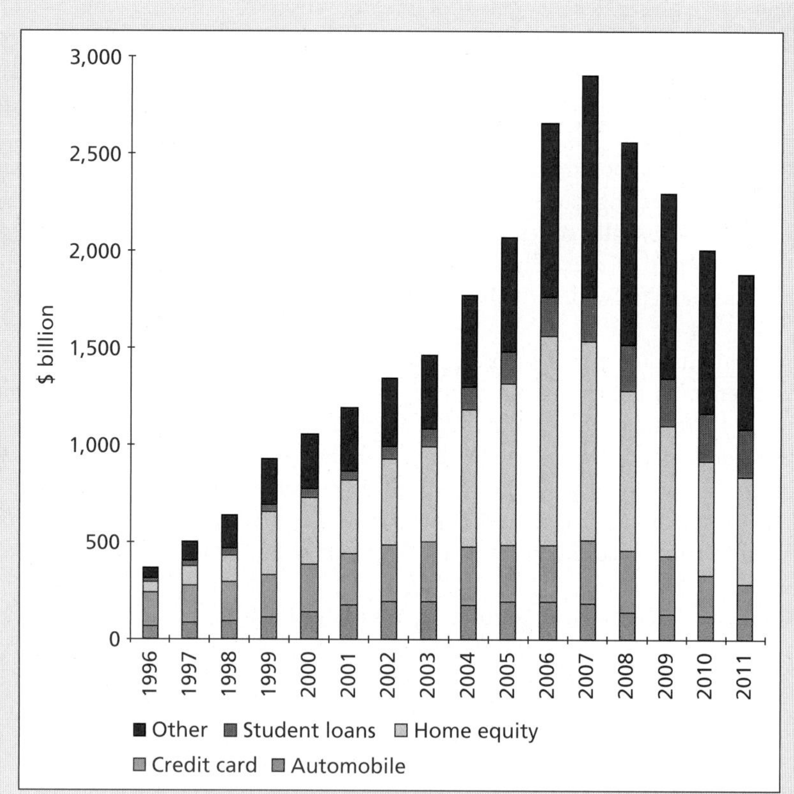

FIGURE 2.7

Asset-backed securities outstanding

Source: Securities Industry & Financial Markets Association, **www.sifma.org.**

In an effort to make housing more affordable to low-income households, the government sponsored enterprises were encouraged to buy subprime mortgage securities. These loans turned out to be disastrous, with trillion-dollar losses spread among banks, hedge funds, and other investors, as well as Freddie and Fannie, which lost billions of dollars on the subprime mortgages they had purchased. You can see from Figure 2.6 that, starting in 2007, the market in private-label mortgage pass-throughs began to shrink rapidly.

Despite these troubles, few believe that securitization itself will cease, although it is certain that practices in this market will be far more conservative than in previous years, particularly with respect to the credit standards that must be met by the ultimate borrower. Indeed, securitization has become an increasingly common staple of many credit markets. For example, it is now common for car loans, student loans, home equity loans, credit card loans, and even debt of private firms to be bundled into pass-through securities that can be traded in the capital market. Figure 2.7 documents the rapid growth of nonmortgage asset-backed securities. The market expanded more than fivefold in the decade ending 2007. After the financial crisis, it contracted considerably as the perceived risks of credit card and home equity loans skyrocketed, but the asset-backed market is still substantial.

2.3 EQUITY SECURITIES

Common Stock as Ownership Shares

Common stocks, also known as equity securities, or equities, represent ownership shares in a corporation. Each share of common stock entitles its owners to one vote on any matters of corporate governance put to a vote at the corporation's annual meeting and to a share in the financial benefits of ownership (e.g., the right to any dividends that the corporation may choose to distribute).[5]

common stocks

Ownership shares in a publicly held corporation. Shareholders have voting rights and may receive dividends.

[5]Sometimes a corporation issues two classes of common stock, one bearing the right to vote, the other not. Because of their restricted rights, the nonvoting stocks sell for a lower price, reflecting the value of control.

A corporation is controlled by a board of directors elected by the shareholders. The board, which meets only a few times each year, selects managers who run the corporation on a day-to-day basis. Managers have the authority to make most business decisions without the board's approval. The board's mandate is to oversee management to ensure that it acts in the best interests of shareholders.

The members of the board are elected at the annual meeting. Shareholders who do not attend the annual meeting can vote by proxy, empowering another party to vote in their name. Management usually solicits the proxies of shareholders and normally gets a vast majority of these proxy votes. Thus, management usually has considerable discretion to run the firm as it sees fit, without daily oversight from the equityholders who actually own the firm.

We noted in Chapter 1 that such separation of ownership and control can give rise to "agency problems," in which managers pursue goals not in the best interests of shareholders. However, there are several mechanisms designed to alleviate these agency problems. Among these are compensation schemes that link the success of the manager to that of the firm; oversight by the board of directors as well as outsiders such as security analysts, creditors, or large institutional investors; the threat of a proxy contest in which unhappy shareholders attempt to replace the current management team; or the threat of a takeover by another firm.

The common stock of most large corporations can be bought or sold freely on one or more of the stock markets. A corporation whose stock is not publicly traded is said to be *closely held*. In most closely held corporations, the owners of the firm also take an active role in its management. Takeovers generally are not an issue.

Characteristics of Common Stock

The two most important characteristics of common stock as an investment are its residual claim and its limited liability features.

Residual claim means stockholders are the last in line of all those who have a claim on the assets and income of the corporation. In a liquidation of the firm's assets, the shareholders have claim to what is left after paying all other claimants, such as the tax authorities, employees, suppliers, bondholders, and other creditors. In a going concern, shareholders have claim to the part of operating income left after interest and income taxes have been paid. Management either can pay this residual as cash dividends to shareholders or reinvest it in the business to increase the value of the shares.

Limited liability means that the most shareholders can lose in event of the failure of the corporation is their original investment. Shareholders are not like owners of unincorporated businesses, whose creditors can lay claim to the personal assets of the owner—such as houses, cars, and furniture. In the event of the firm's bankruptcy, corporate stockholders at worst have worthless stock. They are not personally liable for the firm's obligations: Their liability is limited.

CONCEPT check 2.3

a. If you buy 100 shares of IBM common stock, to what are you entitled?
b. What is the most money you can make over the next year?
c. If you pay $95 per share, what is the most money you could lose over the year?

Stock Market Listings

Figure 2.8 presents key trading data for a small sample of stocks traded on the New York Stock Exchange. The NYSE is one of several markets in which investors may buy or sell shares of stock. We will examine issues of trading in these markets in the next chapter.

To interpret Figure 2.8, consider the listing for General Electric, the last listed stock. The table provides the ticker symbol (GE), the closing price of the stock (19.30), and its change (+0.25) from the previous trading day. Over 44 million shares of GE traded on this day.

NAME	SYMBOL	CLOSE	CHG	VOLUME	52 WK HIGH	52 WK LOW	DIV	P/E	YIELD	YTD% CHG
Gannett	GCI	14.60	0.22	2,485,119	18.93	11.65	0.16	6.55	1.10	−3.25
Gap	GPS	19.28	0.95	13,621,775	23.73	16.62	0.45	10.54	2.33	−12.92
Gardner Denver	GDI	87.15	−0.66	450,263	88.70	44.24	0.20	22.99	0.23	26.63
Gartner	IT	41.40	0.11	230,999	43.39	22.89	....	39.06	....	24.70
GATX	GMT	38.85	0.36	203,912	42.84	25.40	1.16	22.33	2.99	10.12
Gaylord Entertainment	GET	31.90	0.89	806,280	38.22	22.45	....	.... dd	....	−11.24
GenCorp	GY	6.38	0.05	298,903	7.09	4.30	....	24.54	....	23.40
Genco Shipping & Trading	GNK	7.49	0.10	409,701	18.08	6.28	....	2.18	....	−47.99
Generac Holdings	GNRC	19.55	0.04	65,811	21.10	11.70	....	7.29	....	20.90
General Cable	BGC	43.41	0.61	418,968	49.32	21.68	....	20.19	....	23.71
General Dynamics	GD	75.60	0.97	2,236,585	78.27	55.46	1.88	10.92	2.49	6.54
General Electric	GE	19.30	0.25	44,235,766	21.65	13.96	0.60	15.32	3.11	5.52

Note: dd means that P/E cannot be computed because earnings were negative.

FIGURE 2.8

Listing of stocks traded on the New York Stock Exchange

Source: Compiled from data from *The Wall Street Journal Online,* July 8, 2011. Reprinted by permission of *The Wall Street Journal,* Copyright © 2011 Dow Jones & Company, Inc. All Rights Reserved Worldwide.

The table also provides the highest and lowest price at which GE has traded in the last 52 weeks. The 0.60 value in the DIV column means that the last quarterly dividend payment was \$.15 per share, which is consistent with annual dividend payments of $\$.15 \times 4 = \$.60$. This corresponds to a dividend yield (i.e., annual dividend per dollar paid for the stock) of $.60/19.30 = .0311$, or 3.11%.

The dividend yield is only part of the return on a stock investment. It ignores prospective *capital gains* (i.e., price increases) or losses. Shares in low-dividend firms presumably offer greater prospects for capital gains, or investors would not be willing to hold these stocks in their portfolios. If you scan Figure 2.8, you will see that dividend yields vary widely across companies.

The P/E ratio, or price-to-earnings ratio, is the ratio of the current stock price to last year's earnings. The P/E ratio tells us how much stock purchasers must pay per dollar of earnings the firm generates for each share. For GE, the ratio of price to earnings is 15.32. The P/E ratio also varies widely across firms. Where the dividend yield and P/E ratio are not reported in Figure 2.8, the firms have zero dividends, or zero or negative earnings. We shall have much to say about P/E ratios in Part Four. Finally, we see that GE's stock price has increased by 5.52% since the beginning of the year.

Preferred Stock

Preferred stock has features similar to both equity and debt. Like a bond, it promises to pay to its holder a fixed stream of income each year. In this sense, preferred stock is similar to an infinite-maturity bond, that is, a perpetuity. It also resembles a bond in that it does not give the holder voting power regarding the firm's management.

preferred stock

Nonvoting shares in a corporation, usually paying a fixed stream of dividends.

Preferred stock is an equity investment, however. The firm retains discretion to make the dividend payments to the preferred stockholders: It has no contractual obligation to pay those dividends. Instead, preferred dividends are usually *cumulative;* that is, unpaid dividends cumulate and must be paid in full before any dividends may be paid to holders of common stock. In contrast, the firm does have a contractual obligation to make timely interest payments on the debt. Failure to make these payments sets off corporate bankruptcy proceedings.

Preferred stock also differs from bonds in terms of its tax treatment for the firm. Because preferred stock payments are treated as dividends rather than as interest on debt, they are not tax-deductible expenses for the firm. This disadvantage is largely offset by the fact that corporations may exclude 70% of dividends received from domestic corporations in the computation of their taxable income. Preferred stocks, therefore, make desirable fixed-income investments for some corporations.

Even though preferred stock ranks after bonds in terms of the priority of its claim to the assets of the firm in the event of corporate bankruptcy, preferred stock often sells at lower yields than corporate bonds. Presumably this reflects the value of the dividend exclusion, because the higher risk of preferred stock would tend to result in higher yields than those offered by bonds. Individual investors, who cannot use the 70% exclusion, generally will find preferred stock yields unattractive relative to those on other available assets.

Corporations issue preferred stock in variations similar to those of corporate bonds. Preferred stock can be callable by the issuing firm, in which case it is said to be *redeemable.* It also can be convertible into common stock at some specified conversion ratio. A relatively recent innovation is adjustable-rate preferred stock, which, like adjustable-rate bonds, ties the dividend rate to current market interest rates.

Depository Receipts

American Depository Receipts, or ADRs, are certificates traded in U.S. markets that represent ownership in shares of a foreign company. Each ADR may correspond to ownership of a fraction of a foreign share, one share, or several shares of the foreign corporation. ADRs were created to make it easier for foreign firms to satisfy U.S. security registration requirements. They are the most common way for U.S. investors to invest in and trade the shares of foreign corporations.

2.4 STOCK AND BOND MARKET INDEXES

Stock Market Indexes

The daily performance of the Dow Jones Industrial Average is a staple portion of the evening news report. While the Dow is the best-known measure of the performance of the stock market, it is only one of several indicators. Other more broadly based indexes are computed and published daily. In addition, several indexes of bond market performance are widely available.

The ever-increasing role of international trade and investments has made indexes of foreign financial markets part of the general news. Thus, foreign stock exchange indexes such as the Nikkei Average of Tokyo or the *Financial Times* index of London have become household names.

Dow Jones Averages

The Dow Jones Industrial Average (DJIA) of 30 large, "blue-chip" corporations has been computed since 1896. Its long history probably accounts for its preeminence in the public mind. (The average covered only 20 stocks until 1928.)

Originally, the DJIA was calculated as the average price of the stocks included in the index. So, if there were 30 stocks in the index, one would add up the prices of the 30 stocks and divide by 30. The percentage change in the DJIA would then be the percentage change in the average price of the 30 shares.

This procedure means that the percentage change in the DJIA measures the return (excluding any dividends paid) on a portfolio that invests one share in each of the 30 stocks in the index. The value of such a portfolio (holding one share of each stock in the index) is the sum of the 30 prices. Because the percentage change in the *average* of the 30 prices is the same as the percentage change in the *sum* of the 30 prices, the index and the portfolio have the same percentage change each day.

price-weighted average

An average computed by adding the prices of the stocks and dividing by a "divisor."

The Dow measures the return (excluding dividends) on a portfolio that holds one share of each stock. The amount of money invested in each company in that portfolio is therefore proportional to the company's share price, so the Dow is called a **price-weighted average.**

TABLE 2.3 Data to construct stock price indexes

Stock	Initial Price	Final Price	Shares (millions)	Initial Value of Outstanding Stock ($ million)	Final Value of Outstanding Stock ($ million)
ABC	$ 25	$30	20	$500	$600
XYZ	100	90	1	100	90
Total				$600	$690

EXAMPLE 2.2

Price-Weighted Average

Consider the data in Table 2.3 for a hypothetical two-stock version of the Dow Jones Average. Let's compare the changes in the value of the portfolio holding one share of each firm and the price-weighted index. Stock ABC starts at $25 a share and increases to $30. Stock XYZ starts at $100, but falls to $90.

Portfolio: Initial value = $25 + $100 = $125

Final value = $30 + $90 = $120

Percentage change in portfolio value = −5/125 = −.04 = −4%

Index: Initial index value = (25 + 100)/2 = 62.5

Final index value = (30 + 90)/2 = 60

Percentage change in index = −2.5/62.5 = −.04 = −4%

The portfolio and the index have identical 4% declines in value.

Notice that price-weighted averages give higher-priced shares more weight in determining the performance of the index. For example, although ABC increased by 20% while XYZ fell by only 10%, the index dropped in value. This is because the 20% increase in ABC represented a smaller dollar price gain ($5 per share) than the 10% decrease in XYZ ($10 per share). The "Dow portfolio" has four times as much invested in XYZ as in ABC because XYZ's price is four times that of ABC. Therefore, XYZ dominates the average. We conclude that a high-price stock can dominate a price-weighted average.

You might wonder why the DJIA is (in mid-2012) at a level of about 13,000 if it is supposed to be the average price of the 30 stocks in the index. The DJIA no longer equals the average price of the 30 stocks because the averaging procedure is adjusted whenever a stock splits or pays a stock dividend of more than 10% or when one company in the group of 30 industrial firms is replaced by another. When these events occur, the divisor used to compute the "average price" is adjusted so as to leave the index unaffected by the event.

EXAMPLE 2.3

Splits and Price-Weighted Averages

Suppose firm XYZ from Example 2.2 were to split two for one so that its share price fell to $50. We would not want the average to fall, as that would incorrectly indicate a fall in the general level of market prices. Following a split, the divisor must be reduced to a value that leaves the average unaffected. Table 2.4 illustrates this point. The initial share price of XYZ, which was $100 in Table 2.3, falls to $50 if the stock splits at the beginning of the period. Notice that the number of shares outstanding doubles, leaving the market value of the total shares unaffected.

We find the new divisor as follows: The index value before the stock split was 125/2 = 62.5. We must find a new divisor, d, that leaves the index unchanged after XYZ splits and its price falls to $50. Therefore we solve for d in the following equation:

$$\frac{\text{Price of ABC} + \text{Price of XYZ}}{d} = \frac{25 + 50}{d} = 62.5$$

which implies that the divisor must fall from its original value of 2.0 to a new value of 1.20.

(continued)

EXAMPLE 2.3

Splits and Price-Weighted Averages (concluded)

Because the split changes the price of stock XYZ, it also changes the relative weights of the two stocks in the price-weighted average. Therefore, the return of the index is affected by the split.

At period-end, ABC will sell for $30, while XYZ will sell for $45, representing the same negative 10% return it was assumed to earn in Table 2.3. The new value of the price-weighted average is (30 + 45)/1.20 = 62.5. The index is unchanged, so the rate of return is zero, greater than the −4% return that would have resulted in the absence of a split. The relative weight of XYZ, which is the poorer-performing stock, is reduced by a split because its price is lower; so the performance of the average is higher. This example illustrates that the implicit weighting scheme of a price-weighted average is somewhat arbitrary, being determined by the prices rather than by the outstanding market values (price per share times number of shares) of the shares in the average.

TABLE 2.4 Data to construct stock price indexes after stock split

Stock	Initial Price	Final Price	Shares (millions)	Initial Value of Outstanding Stock ($ million)	Final Value of Outstanding Stock ($ million)
ABC	$25	$30	20	$500	$600
XYZ	50	45	2	100	90
Total				$600	$690

In the same way that the divisor is updated for stock splits, if one firm is dropped from the average and another firm with a different price is added, the divisor has to be updated to leave the average unchanged by the substitution. By mid-2012, the divisor for the Dow Jones Industrial Average had fallen to a value of about .132.

Because the Dow Jones averages are based on small numbers of firms, care must be taken to ensure that they are representative of the broad market. As a result, the composition of the average is changed every so often to reflect changes in the economy. Table 2.5 presents the composition of the Dow industrials in 1928 as well as its composition today, in 2012. The table presents striking evidence of the changes in the U.S. economy in the last century. Many of the "bluest of the blue chip" companies in 1928 no longer exist, and the industries that were the backbone of the economy in 1928 have given way to ones that could not have been imagined at the time.

CONCEPT check 2.4

Suppose XYZ's final price in Table 2.3 increases to $110, while ABC falls to $20. Find the percentage change in the price-weighted average of these two stocks. Compare that to the percentage return of a portfolio that holds one share in each company.

Dow Jones & Company also computes a Transportation Average of 20 airline, trucking, and railroad stocks; a Public Utility Average of 15 electric and natural gas utilities; and a Composite Average combining the 65 firms of the three separate averages. Each is a price-weighted average and thus overweights the performance of high-priced stocks.

market value-weighted index

Index return equals the weighted average of the returns of each component security, with weights proportional to outstanding market value.

Standard & Poor's Indexes

The Standard & Poor's Composite 500 (S&P 500) stock index represents an improvement over the Dow Jones averages in two ways. First, it is a more broadly based index of 500 firms. Second, it is a **market value–weighted index.** In the case of the firms XYZ and

TABLE 2.5 Companies included in the Dow Jones Industrial Average: 1928 and 2011

Dow Industrials in 1928	Current Dow Companies	Ticker Symbol	Industry	Year Added to Index
Wright Aeronautical	3M	MMM	Diversified industrials	1976
Allied Chemical	Alcoa	AA	Aluminum	1959
North American	American Express	AXP	Consumer finance	1982
Victor Talking Machine	AT&T	T	Telecommunications	1999
International Nickel	Bank of America	BAC	Banking	2008
International Harvester	Boeing	BA	Aerospace & defense	1987
Westinghouse	Caterpillar	CAT	Construction	1991
Texas Gulf Sulphur	Chevron	CVX	Oil and gas	2008
General Electric	Cisco Systems	CSCO	Computer equipment	2009
American Tobacco	Coca-Cola	KO	Beverages	1987
Texas Corp	DuPont	DD	Chemicals	1935
Standard Oil (NJ)	ExxonMobil	XOM	Oil & gas	1928
Sears Roebuck	General Electric	GE	Diversified industrials	1907
General Motors	Hewlett-Packard	HPQ	Computers	1997
Chrysler	Home Depot	HD	Home improvement retailers	1999
Atlantic Refining	Intel	INTC	Semiconductors	1999
Paramount Publix	IBM	IBM	Computer services	1979
Bethlehem Steel	Johnson & Johnson	JNJ	Pharmaceuticals	1997
General Railway Signal	JPMorgan Chase	JPM	Banking	1991
Mack Trucks	Kraft Foods	KFT	Food processing	2008
Union Carbide	McDonald's	MCD	Restaurants	1985
American Smelting	Merck	MRK	Pharmaceuticals	1979
American Can	Microsoft	MSFT	Software	1999
Postum Inc	Pfizer	PFE	Pharmaceuticals	2004
Nash Motors	Procter & Gamble	PG	Household products	1932
American Sugar	Travelers	TRV	Insurance	2009
Goodrich	United Technologies	UTX	Aerospace	1939
Radio Corp	Verizon	VZ	Telecommunications	2004
Woolworth	Wal-Mart	WMT	Retailers	1997
U.S. Steel	Walt Disney	DIS	Broadcasting & entertainment	1991

ABC in Example 2.2, the S&P 500 would give ABC five times the weight given to XYZ because the market value of its outstanding equity is five times larger, $500 million versus $100 million.

The S&P 500 is computed by calculating the total market value of the 500 firms in the index and the total market value of those firms on the previous day of trading.[6] The percentage increase in the total market value from one day to the next represents the increase in the index. The rate of return of the index equals the rate of return that would be earned by an investor holding a portfolio of all 500 firms in the index in proportion to their market value, except that the index does not reflect cash dividends paid by those firms.

[6]Actually, most indexes today use a modified version of market value weights. Rather than weighting by total market value, they weight by the market value of "free float," that is, by the value of shares that are freely tradable among investors. For example, this procedure does not count shares held by founding families or governments, which are effectively not available for investors to purchase. The distinction is more important in Japan and Europe, where a higher fraction of shares are held in such nontraded portfolios.

EXAMPLE 2.4

Value-Weighted Indexes

To illustrate how value-weighted indexes are computed, look again at Table 2.3. The final value of all outstanding stock in our two-stock universe is $690 million. The initial value was $600 million. Therefore, if the initial level of a market value–weighted index of stocks ABC and XYZ were set equal to an arbitrarily chosen starting value such as 100, the index value at year-end would be 100 × (690/600) = 115. The increase in the index would reflect the 15% return earned on a portfolio consisting of those two stocks held in proportion to outstanding market values.

Unlike the price-weighted index, the value-weighted index gives more weight to ABC. Whereas the price-weighted index fell because it was dominated by higher-price XYZ, the value-weighted index rose because it gave more weight to ABC, the stock with the higher total market value.

Note also from Tables 2.3 and 2.4 that market value–weighted indexes are unaffected by stock splits. The total market value of the outstanding XYZ stock increases from $100 million to $110 million regardless of the stock split, thereby rendering the split irrelevant to the performance of the index.

A nice feature of both market value–weighted and price-weighted indexes is that they reflect the returns to straightforward portfolio strategies. If one were to buy each share in the index in proportion to its outstanding market value, the value-weighted index would perfectly track capital gains on the underlying portfolio. Similarly, a price-weighted index tracks the returns on a portfolio comprised of equal shares of each firm.

Investors today can easily buy market indexes for their portfolios. One way is to purchase shares in mutual funds that hold shares in proportion to their representation in the S&P 500 as well as other stock indexes. These *index funds* yield a return equal to that of the particular index and so provide a low-cost passive investment strategy for equity investors. Another approach is to purchase an *exchange-traded fund,* or ETF, which is a portfolio of shares that can be bought or sold as a unit, just as a single share would be traded. Available ETFs range from portfolios that track extremely broad global market indexes all the way to narrow industry indexes. We discuss both mutual funds and ETFs in detail in Chapter 4.

Standard & Poor's also publishes a 400-stock Industrial Index, a 20-stock Transportation Index, a 40-stock Utility Index, and a 40-stock Financial Index.

CONCEPT check 2.5

Reconsider companies XYZ and ABC from Concept Check Question 2.4. Calculate the percentage change in the market value–weighted index. Compare that to the rate of return of a portfolio that holds $500 of ABC stock for every $100 of XYZ stock (i.e., an index portfolio).

Other U.S. Market Value Indexes

The New York Stock Exchange publishes a market value–weighted composite index of all NYSE-listed stocks, in addition to subindexes for industrial, utility, transportation, and financial stocks. These indexes are even more broadly based than the S&P 500. The National Association of Securities Dealers publishes an index of more than 3,000 firms traded on the NASDAQ market.

The ultimate U.S. equity index so far computed is the Wilshire 5000 Index of the market value of essentially all actively traded stocks in the U.S. Despite its name, the index actually includes more than 5,000 stocks. The performance of many of these indexes appears daily in *The Wall Street Journal.*

Equally Weighted Indexes

Market performance is sometimes measured by an equally weighted average of the returns of each stock in an index. Such an averaging technique, by placing equal weight on each return, corresponds to a portfolio strategy that places equal dollar values in each stock. This is in contrast to both price weighting, which requires equal numbers of shares of each stock, and market value weighting, which requires investments in proportion to outstanding value.

equally weighted index
An index computed from a simple average of returns.

Unlike price- or market value–weighted indexes, **equally weighted indexes** do not correspond to buy-and-hold portfolio strategies. Suppose you start with equal dollar investments in the two stocks of Table 2.3, ABC and XYZ. Because ABC increases in value by 20% over the year, while XYZ decreases by 10%, your portfolio is no longer equally weighted but is now more heavily invested in ABC. To reset the portfolio to equal weights, you would need to rebalance: Sell some ABC stock and/or purchase more XYZ stock. Such rebalancing would be necessary to align the return on your portfolio with that on the equally weighted index.

Foreign and International Stock Market Indexes

Development in financial markets worldwide includes the construction of indexes for these markets. Among these are the Nikkei (Japan), FTSE (U.K., pronounced "footsie"), DAX (Germany), Hang Seng (Hong Kong), and TSX (Toronto). A leader in the construction of international indexes has been MSCI (Morgan Stanley Capital International), which computes over 50 country indexes and several regional indexes. Table 2.6 presents many of the indexes computed by MSCI.

Bond Market Indicators

Just as stock market indexes provide guidance concerning the performance of the overall stock market, several bond market indicators measure the performance of various categories of bonds. The three most well-known groups of indexes are those of Merrill Lynch, Barclays (formerly Lehman Brothers), and Salomon Smith Barney (now part of Citigroup). Table 2.7 lists the components of the bond market in 2011.

TABLE 2.6 MSCI stock indexes

Regional Indexes		Countries	
Developed Markets	**Emerging Markets**	**Developed Markets**	**Emerging Markets**
EAFE (Europe, Australasia, Far East)	Emerging Markets (EM)	Australia	Brazil
EASEA (EAFE excluding Japan)	EM Asia	Austria	Chile
Europe	EM Far East	Belgium	China
EMU	EM Latin America	Canada	Colombia
Far East	EM Eastern Europe	Denmark	Czech Republic
Kokusai (World excluding Japan)	EM Europe	Finland	Egypt
Nordic Countries	EM Europe & Middle East	France	Hungary
North America		Germany	India
Pacific		Greece	Indonesia
World		Hong Kong	Korea
G7 countries		Ireland	Malaysia
World excluding U.S.		Israel	Mexico
		Italy	Peru
		Japan	Philippines
		Netherlands	Poland
		New Zealand	Russia
		Norway	South Africa
		Portugal	Taiwan
		Singapore	Thailand
		Spain	Turkey
		Sweden	
		Switzerland	
		U.K.	
		U.S.	

Source: MSCI, **www.msci.com**. Reprinted by permission.

TABLE 2.7 The U.S. bond market

Sector	Size ($ billion)	% of Market
Treasury	$ 9,434.6	29.5%
Federal agency and gov't sponsored enterprise	6,437.3	20.1
Corporate	4,653.9	14.6
Tax-exempt*	2,636.7	8.3
Mortgage-backed	6,908.0	21.6
Other asset-backed	1,877.9	5.9
Total	$31,948.4	100.0%

*Includes private-purpose tax-exempt debt.

Source: *Flow of Funds Accounts of the United States: Flows and Outstandings,* Board of Governors of the Federal Reserve System, June 2011.

The major problem with these indexes is that true rates of return on many bonds are difficult to compute because bonds trade infrequently, which makes it hard to get reliable, up-to-date prices. In practice, some prices must be estimated from bond-valuation models. These so-called matrix prices may differ from true market values.

2.5 DERIVATIVE MARKETS

derivative asset

A security with a payoff that depends on the prices of other securities.

A significant development in financial markets in recent years has been the growth of futures and options markets. Futures and options provide payoffs that depend on the values of other assets, such as commodity prices, bond and stock prices, or market index values. For this reason, these instruments sometimes are called **derivative assets.** Their values derive from the values of other assets. We discuss derivative assets in detail in Part Five.

Options

call option

The right to buy an asset at a specified price on or before a specified expiration date.

A **call option** gives its holder the right to purchase an asset for a specified price, called the *exercise* or *strike price,* on or before some specified expiration date. An October call option on Apple stock with exercise price $355, for example, entitles its owner to purchase Apple stock for a price of $355 at any time up to and including the option's expiration date in October. Each option contract is for the purchase of 100 shares, with quotations made on a per share basis. The holder of the call need not exercise the option; it will make sense to exercise only if the market value of the asset that may be purchased exceeds the exercise price.

When the market price exceeds the exercise price, the option holder may "call away" the asset for the exercise price and reap a benefit equal to the difference between the stock price and the exercise price. Otherwise, the option will be left unexercised. If not exercised before the expiration date, the option expires and no longer has value. Calls, therefore, provide greater profits when stock prices increase and so represent bullish investment vehicles.

put option

The right to sell an asset at a specified exercise price on or before a specified expiration date.

In contrast, a **put option** gives its holder the right to sell an asset for a specified exercise price on or before a specified expiration date. An October put on Apple with exercise price $355 entitles its owner to sell Apple stock to the put writer at a price of $355 at any time before expiration in October even if the market price of Apple is lower than $355. Whereas profits on call options increase when the asset increases in value, profits on put options increase when the asset value falls. The put is exercised only if its holder can deliver an asset worth less than the exercise price in return for the exercise price.

Figure 2.9 is an excerpt of the options quotations for Apple from the online edition of *The Wall Street Journal.* The price of Apple shares on this date was $357.20. The first two columns give the expiration month and exercise (or strike) price for each option. We have included listings for call and put options with exercise prices ranging from $350 to $360 per share and with expiration dates in July, August, and October 2011 and January 2012.

FIGURE 2.9

Stock options on Apple

Source: From *The Wall Street Journal Online,* July 8, 2011. Reprinted by permission of *The Wall Street Journal,* Copyright © 2011 Dow Jones & Company, Inc. All Rights Reserved Worldwide.

Prices at close July 7, 2011

Apple (AAPL) — Underlying stock price: 357.20

		Call			Put		
Expiration	Strike	Last	Volume	Open Interest	Last	Volume	Open Interest
Jul	350	9.00	32874	46311	1.73	15148	9711
Aug	350	16.50	5883	24232	8.95	4457	6421
Oct	350	24.90	751	8526	16.70	138	1732
Jan	350	33.95	859	30028	25.35	316	8067
Jul	355	5.60	43911	40395	0.90	18762	1061
Aug	355	13.70	4624	8952	11.10	2859	3146
Oct	355	21.98	760	2146	18.85	176	938
Jan	355	31.27	383	2842	27.45	175	1279
Jul	360	3.15	43485	50184	3.50	3811	114
Aug	360	11.15	8692	43183	13.55	1864	1176
Oct	360	19.41	693	4669	21.34	134	868
Jan	360	28.50	1018	14117	29.98	305	1564

The next columns provide the closing prices, trading volume, and open interest (outstanding contracts) of each option. For example, 43,911 contracts traded on the July 2011 expiration call with an exercise price of $355. The last trade was at $5.60, meaning that an option to purchase one share of Apple at an exercise price of $355 sold for $5.60. Each option *contract* (on 100 shares) therefore costs $560.

Notice that the prices of call options decrease as the exercise price increases. For example, the July 2011 expiration call with exercise price $360 costs only $3.15. This makes sense, as the right to purchase a share at a higher exercise price is less valuable. Conversely, put prices increase with the exercise price. The right to sell a share of Apple in July at a price of $355 costs $.90, while the right to sell at $360 costs $3.50.

Option prices also increase with time until expiration. Clearly, one would rather have the right to buy Apple for $355 at any time until October 2011 than at any time until July 2011. Not surprisingly, this shows up in a higher price for the more-distant expiration options. For example, the call with exercise price $355 expiring in October 2011 sells for $21.98, compared to only $5.60 for the July 2011 call.

CONCEPT check 2.6

What would be the profit or loss per share of stock to an investor who bought the July 2011 expiration Apple call option with exercise price $355, if the stock price at the expiration of the option is $365? What about a purchaser of the put option with the same exercise price and expiration?

Futures Contracts

A **futures contract** calls for delivery of an asset (or, in some cases, its cash value) at a specified delivery or maturity date, for an agreed-upon price, called the *futures price,* to be paid at contract maturity. The long position is held by the trader who commits to purchasing the commodity on the delivery date. The trader who takes the short position commits to delivering the commodity at contract maturity.

futures contract

Obliges traders to purchase or sell an asset at an agreed-upon price at a specified future date.

Figure 2.10 illustrates the listing of the corn futures contract on the Chicago Board of Trade for July 8, 2011. Each contract calls for delivery of 5,000 bushels of corn. Each row details prices for contracts expiring on various dates. The first row is for the nearest term or "front" contract, with maturity in July 2011. The most recent price was $6.7225 per bushel.

FIGURE 2.10

Corn futures prices in the Chicago Board of Trade, July 8, 2011

Source: Data from *The Wall Street Journal Online,* July 8, 2011. Reprinted by permission of *The Wall Street Journal,* Copyright © 2011 Dow Jones & Company, Inc. All Rights Reserved Worldwide.

MONTH	LAST	CHG	OPEN	HIGH	LOW	VOLUME	OPEN INT
Jul '11	672'2	22'2	652'4	672'0	652'4	2575	6043
Sep '11	642'2	17'2	626'0	646'4	626'0	51128	380602
Dec '11	637'0	21'4	615'6	638'0	615'6	130702	487465
Mar '12	649'2	20'6	628'6	650'2	628'6	13351	112108
May '12	656'2	19'4	637'4	657'0	637'0	3632	24787
Jul '12	662'4	18'4	644'6	664'0	644'4	5692	70374
Sep '12	644'0	18'0	628'4	643'0	627'4	696	6079
Dec '12	614'0	12'2	600'0	615'0	600'0	3506	71122

(The numbers after each apostrophe denote eighths of a cent.) That price is up $.2225 from yesterday's close. The next columns show the contract's opening price that day as well as the high and low price over each contract's life. Volume is the number of contracts trading that day; open interest is the number of outstanding contracts.

The trader holding the long position profits from price increases. Suppose that at expiration, corn is selling for $6.9225 per bushel. The long position trader who entered the contract at the futures price of $6.7225 on July 8 would pay the previously agreed-upon $6.7225 for each bushel of corn, which at contract maturity would be worth $6.9225.

Because each contract calls for delivery of 5,000 bushels, the profit to the long position, ignoring brokerage fees, would equal 5,000 × ($6.9225 − $6.7225) = $1,000. Conversely, the short position must deliver 5,000 bushels for the previously agreed-upon futures price. The short position's loss equals the long position's profit.

The *right* to purchase an asset at an agreed-upon price versus the *obligation* to purchase it distinguishes a call option from a long position in a futures contract. A futures contract *obliges* the long position to purchase the asset at the futures price; the call option merely *conveys the right* to purchase the asset at the exercise price. The purchase will be made only if it yields a profit.

Clearly, the holder of a call has a better position than the holder of a long position on a futures contract with a futures price equal to the option's exercise price. This advantage, of course, comes only at a price. Call options must be purchased; futures investments are entered into without cost. The purchase price of an option is called the *premium.* It represents the compensation the purchaser of the call must pay for the ability to exercise the option only when it is profitable to do so. Similarly, the difference between a put option and a short futures position is the right, as opposed to the obligation, to sell an asset at an agreed-upon price.

SUMMARY

- Money market securities are very short-term debt obligations. They are usually highly marketable and have relatively low credit risk. Their low maturities and low credit risk ensure minimal capital gains or losses. These securities often trade in large denominations, but they may be purchased indirectly through money market funds.
- Much of U.S. government borrowing is in the form of Treasury bonds and notes. These are coupon-paying bonds usually issued at or near par value. Treasury bonds are similar in design to coupon-paying corporate bonds.
- Municipal bonds are distinguished largely by their tax-exempt status. Interest payments (but not capital gains) on these securities are exempt from income taxes.

www.mhhe.com/bkm

- Mortgage pass-through securities are pools of mortgages sold in one package. Owners of pass-throughs receive all principal and interest payments made by the borrower. The firm that originally issued the mortgage merely services the mortgage, simply "passing through" the payments to the purchasers of the mortgage. Payments of interest and principal on government agency pass-through securities are guaranteed, but payments on private-label mortgage pools are not.
- Common stock is an ownership share in a corporation. Each share entitles its owner to one vote on matters of corporate governance and to a prorated share of the dividends paid to shareholders. Stock, or equity, owners are the residual claimants on the income earned by the firm.
- Preferred stock usually pays a fixed stream of dividends for the life of the firm: It is a perpetuity. A firm's failure to pay the dividend due on preferred stock, however, does not set off corporate bankruptcy. Instead, unpaid dividends simply cumulate. Varieties of preferred stock include convertible and adjustable-rate issues.
- Many stock market indexes measure the performance of the overall market. The Dow Jones averages, the oldest and best-known indicators, are price-weighted indexes. Today, many broad-based, market value–weighted indexes are computed daily. These include the Standard & Poor's Composite 500 stock index, the NYSE index, the NASDAQ index, the Wilshire 5000 Index, and several international indexes, including the Nikkei, FTSE, and DAX.
- A call option is a right to purchase an asset at a stipulated exercise price on or before an expiration date. A put option is the right to sell an asset at some exercise price. Calls increase in value, while puts decrease in value, as the price of the underlying asset increases.
- A futures contract is an obligation to buy or sell an asset at a stipulated futures price on a maturity date. The long position, which commits to purchasing, gains if the asset value increases, while the short position, which commits to delivering the asset, loses.

KEY TERMS

bankers' acceptance, 29
call option, 46
certificate of deposit, 28
commercial paper, 28
common stocks, 37
corporate bonds, 36
derivative asset, 46
equally weighted index, 44
Eurodollars, 29
Federal funds, 30
futures contract, 47
London Interbank Offer Rate (LIBOR), 30
market value–weighted index, 42
money markets, 27
municipal bonds, 33
preferred stock, 39
price-weighted average, 40
put option, 46
repurchase agreements, 29
Treasury bills, 27
Treasury bonds, 31
Treasury notes, 31

KEY FORMULAS

Equivalent taxable yield: $\frac{r_{\text{muni}}}{1 - \text{tax rate}}$ where r_{muni} is the rate on tax-free municipal debt

Cutoff tax rate (for indifference to taxable versus tax-free bonds): $1 - \frac{r_{\text{muni}}}{r_{\text{taxable}}}$

PROBLEM SETS

Select problems are available in McGraw-Hill's *Connect Finance.* Please see the Supplements section of the book's frontmatter for more information.

Basic

1. What are the key differences between common stock, preferred stock, and corporate bonds? ***(LO 2-1)***
2. Why do most professionals consider the Wilshire 5000 a better index of the performance of the broad stock market than the Dow Jones Industrial Average? ***(LO 2-2)***

3. What features of money market securities distinguish them from other fixed-income securities? ***(LO 2-1)***
4. What are the major components of the money market? ***(LO 2-1)***
5. Describe alternative ways that an investor may add positions in international equity to his or her portfolio. ***(LO 2-1)***
6. Why are high-tax-bracket investors more inclined to invest in municipal bonds than are low-bracket investors? ***(LO 2-1)***
7. What is meant by the LIBOR rate? The Federal funds rate? ***(LO 2-1)***
8. How does a municipal revenue bond differ from a general obligation bond? Which would you expect to have a lower yield to maturity? ***(LO 2-1)***
9. Why are corporations more apt to hold preferred stock than are other potential investors? ***(LO 2-1)***
10. What is meant by limited liability? ***(LO 2-1)***

KAPLAN SCHWESER

11. Which of the following **correctly** describes a repurchase agreement? ***(LO 2-1)***
    a. The sale of a security with a commitment to repurchase the same security at a specified future date and a designated price.
    b. The sale of a security with a commitment to repurchase the same security at a future date left unspecified, at a designated price.
    c. The purchase of a security with a commitment to purchase more of the same security at a specified future date.

Intermediate

12. Why are money market securities sometimes referred to as "cash equivalents"? ***(LO 2-1)***
13. A municipal bond carries a coupon rate of 6¾% and is trading at par. What would be the equivalent taxable yield of this bond to a taxpayer in a 35% tax bracket? ***(LO 2-1)***
14. Suppose that short-term municipal bonds currently offer yields of 4%, while comparable taxable bonds pay 5%. Which gives you the higher after-tax yield if your tax bracket is: ***(LO 2-1)***
    a. Zero
    b. 10%
    c. 20%
    d. 30%
15. An investor is in a 30% combined federal plus state tax bracket. If corporate bonds offer 9% yields, what must municipals offer for the investor to prefer them to corporate bonds? ***(LO 2-1)***
16. Find the equivalent taxable yield of the municipal bond in Problem 14 for tax brackets of zero, 10%, 20%, and 30%. ***(LO 2-1)***
17. Turn back to Figure 2.3 and look at the Treasury bond maturing in November 2040. ***(LO 2-1)***
    a. How much would you have to pay to purchase one of these bonds?
    b. What is its coupon rate?
    c. What is the current yield (i.e., coupon income as a fraction of bond price) of the bond?
18. Turn to Figure 2.8 and look at the listing for General Dynamics. ***(LO 2-1)***
    a. What was the firm's closing price *yesterday?*
    b. How many shares could you buy for $5,000?
    c. What would be your annual dividend income from those shares?
    d. What must be General Dynamics' earnings per share?

19. Consider the three stocks in the following table. P_t represents price at time t, and Q_t represents shares outstanding at time t. Stock C splits two-for-one in the last period. ***(LO 2-2)***

	P_0	Q_0	P_1	Q_1	P_2	Q_2
A	90	100	95	100	95	100
B	50	200	45	200	45	200
C	100	200	110	200	55	400

a. Calculate the rate of return on a price-weighted index of the three stocks for the first period ($t = 0$ to $t = 1$).
b. What must happen to the divisor for the price-weighted index in year 2?
c. Calculate the rate of return of the price-weighted index for the second period ($t = 1$ to $t = 2$).

20. Using the data in the previous problem, calculate the first-period rates of return on the following indexes of the three stocks: ***(LO 2-2)***
a. A market value–weighted index
b. An equally weighted index

21. What problems would confront a mutual fund trying to create an index fund tied to an equally weighted index of a broad stock market? ***(LO 2-2)***

22. What would happen to the divisor of the Dow Jones Industrial Average if FedEx, with a current price of around $95 per share, replaced AT&T (with a current value of about $31 per share)? ***(LO 2-2)***

23. A T-bill with face value $10,000 and 87 days to maturity is selling at a bank discount ask yield of 3.4%. What is the price of the bill? What is its bond equivalent yield? ***(LO 2-1)***

24. Which security should sell at a greater price? ***(LO 2-3)***
a. A 10-year Treasury bond with a 9% coupon rate or a 10-year T-bond with a 10% coupon.
b. A three-month expiration call option with an exercise price of $40 or a three-month call on the same stock with an exercise price of $35.
c. A put option on a stock selling at $50 or a put option on another stock selling at $60. (All other relevant features of the stocks and options are assumed to be identical.)

25. Look at the futures listings for corn in Figure 2.10. ***(LO 2-3)***
a. Suppose you buy one contract for December 2011 delivery. If the contract closes in December at a price of $6.43 per bushel, what will be your profit or loss? (Each contract calls for delivery of 5,000 bushels.)
b. How many December 2011 maturity contracts are outstanding?

26. Turn back to Figure 2.9 and look at the Apple options. Suppose you buy an August expiration call option with exercise price $355. ***(LO 2-3)***
a. If the stock price in August is $367, will you exercise your call? What are the profit and rate of return on your position?
b. What if you had bought the August call with exercise price $360?
c. What if you had bought an August put with exercise price $355?

27. What options position is associated with: ***(LO 2-3)***
a. The right to buy an asset at a specified price?
b. The right to sell an asset at a specified price?
c. The obligation to buy an asset at a specified price?
d. The obligation to sell an asset at a specified price?

28. Why do call options with exercise prices higher than the price of the underlying stock sell for positive prices? ***(LO 2-3)***

www.mhhe.com/bkm

29. Both a call and a put currently are traded on stock XYZ; both have strike prices of $50 and maturities of six months. What will be the profit to an investor who buys the call for $4 in the following scenarios for stock prices in six months? (*a*) $40; (*b*) $45; (*c*) $50; (*d*) $55; (*e*) $60. What will be the profit in each scenario to an investor who buys the put for $6? ***(LO 2-3)***
30. What would you expect to happen to the spread between yields on commercial paper and Treasury bills if the economy were to enter a steep recession? ***(LO 2-1)***
31. Examine the stocks listed in Figure 2.8. For how many of these stocks is the 52-week high price at least 50% greater than the 52-week low price? What do you conclude about the volatility of prices on individual stocks? ***(LO 2-1)***
32. Find the after-tax return to a corporation that buys a share of preferred stock at $40, sells it at year-end at $40, and receives a $4 year-end dividend. The firm is in the 30% tax bracket. ***(LO 2-1)***

Challenge

33. Explain the difference between a put option and a short position in a futures contract. ***(LO 2-3)***
34. Explain the difference between a call option and a long position in a futures contract. ***(LO 2-3)***

CFA Problems

1. Preferred stock yields often are lower than yields on bonds of the same quality because of: ***(LO 2-1)***
   a. Marketability
   b. Risk
   c. Taxation
   d. Call protection

WEB *master*

1. Go to **finance.yahoo.com,** and enter the ticker symbol DIS (for Walt Disney Co.) in the *Get Quotes* box. Now click on *SEC Filings* and look for the link to Disney's most recent annual report (its 10-K). Financial tables are available from the *Summary* link, and Disney's full annual report may be obtained from the *EDGAR* link. Locate the company's Consolidated Balance Sheets and answer these questions:
   a. How much preferred stock is Disney authorized to issue? How much has been issued?
   b. How much common stock is Disney authorized to issue? How many shares are currently outstanding?
   c. Search for the term "Financing Activities." What is the total amount of borrowing listed for Disney? How much of this is medium-term notes?
   d. What other types of debt does Disney have outstanding?
2. Not all stock market indexes are created equal. Different methods are used to calculate various indexes, and different indexes will yield different assessments of "market performance." Using one of the following data sources, retrieve the stock price for five different firms on the first and last trading days of the previous month.

   www.nasdaq.com—Get a quote; then select *Charts* and specify one month. When the chart appears, click on a data point to display the underlying data.

   www.bloomberg.com—Get a quote; then plot the chart; next, use the moving line to see the closing price today and one month ago.

   finance.yahoo.com—Get a quote; then click on *Historical Data* and specify a date range.

   a. Compute the monthly return on a price-weighted index of the five stocks.
   b. Compute the monthly return on a value-weighted index of the five stocks.
   c. Compare the two returns and explain their differences. Explain how you would interpret each measure.

SOLUTIONS TO CONCEPT *checks*

2.1 The bid price is 107.297% of par or \$1,072.97, and the ask price is \$1,073.59. This ask price corresponds to a yield of 2.294%. The ask price fell .547 from its level yesterday, so the ask price then must have been 107.906.

2.2 A 6% taxable return is equivalent to an after-tax return of 6(1 − .28) = 4.32%. Therefore, you would be better off in the taxable bond. The equivalent taxable yield of the tax-free bond is 4/(1 − .28) = 5.55%. So a taxable bond would have to pay a 5.55% yield to provide the same after-tax return as a tax-free bond offering a 4% yield.

2.3 *a.* You are entitled to a prorated share of IBM's dividend payments and to vote in any of IBM's stockholder meetings.

b. Your potential gain is unlimited because IBM's stock price has no upper bound.

c. Your outlay was \$95 × 100 = \$9,500. Because of limited liability, this is the most you can lose.

2.4 The price-weighted index increases from 62.50[=(100 + 25)/2] to 65[=(110 + 20)/2], a gain of 4%. An investment of one share in each company requires an outlay of \$125 that would increase in value to \$130, for a return of 4% (=5/125), which equals the return to the price-weighted index.

2.5 The market value–weighted index return is calculated by computing the increase in value of the stock portfolio. The portfolio of the two stocks starts with an initial value of \$100 million + \$500 million = \$600 million and falls in value to \$110 million + \$400 million = \$510 million, a loss of 90/600 = .15, or 15%. The index portfolio return is a weighted average of the returns on each stock with weights of $\frac{1}{6}$ on XYZ and $\frac{5}{6}$ on ABC (weights proportional to relative investments). Because the return on XYZ is 10%, while that on ABC is −20%, the index portfolio return is ($\frac{1}{6}$) 10 + ($\frac{5}{6}$) (−20) = −15%, equal to the return on the market value–weighted index.

2.6 The payoff to the call option is \$365 − \$355 = \$10. The call cost \$9. The profit is \$10 − \$9 = \$1 per share. The put will pay off zero—it expires worthless since the stock price exceeds the exercise price. The loss is the cost of the put, \$1.75.

Chapter 3

Securities Markets

Learning Objectives:

LO3-1 Describe how firms issue securities to the public.

LO3-2 Identify various types of orders investors can submit to their brokers.

LO3-3 Describe trading practices in dealer markets, specialist-directed stock exchanges, and electronic communication networks.

LO3-4 Compare the mechanics and investment implications of buying on margin and short-selling.

This chapter will provide you with a broad introduction to the many venues and procedures available for trading securities in the United States and international markets. We will see that trading mechanisms range from direct negotiation among market participants to fully automated computer crossing of trade orders.

The first time a security trades is when it is issued to the public. Therefore, we begin with a look at how securities are first marketed to the public by investment bankers, the midwives of securities. We turn next to a broad survey of how already-issued securities may be traded among investors, focusing on the differences between dealer markets, electronic markets, and specialist markets. With this background, we then turn to specific trading arenas such as the New York Stock Exchange, NASDAQ, and several all-electronic markets. We compare the mechanics of trade execution and the ongoing quest for cross-market integration of trading.

We then turn to the essentials of some specific types of transactions, such as buying on margin and short-selling stocks. We close the chapter with a look at some important aspects of the regulations governing security trading, including insider trading laws, circuit breakers, and the role of security markets as self-regulating organizations.

Related websites for this chapter are available at www.mhhe.com/bkm.

3.1 HOW FIRMS ISSUE SECURITIES

Firms regularly need to raise new capital to help pay for their many investment projects. Broadly speaking, they can raise funds either by borrowing money or by selling shares in the firm. Investment bankers are generally hired to manage the sale of these securities in what is called a **primary market** for newly issued securities. Once these securities are issued, however, investors might well wish to trade them among themselves. For example, you may decide to raise cash by selling some of your shares in Apple to another investor. This transaction would have no impact on the total outstanding number of Apple shares. Trades in existing securities take place in the **secondary market.**

primary market

Market for new issues of securities.

secondary market

Market for already-existing securities.

Shares of *publicly listed* firms trade continually on well-known markets such as the New York Stock Exchange or the NASDAQ Stock Market. There, any investor can choose to buy shares for his or her portfolio. These companies are also called *publicly traded, publicly owned,* or just *public companies.* Other firms, however, are *private corporations,* whose shares are held by small numbers of managers and investors. While ownership stakes in the firm are still determined in proportion to share ownership, those shares do not trade in public exchanges. Some private firms are relatively young companies that have not yet chosen to make their shares generally available to the public, others may be more established firms that are still largely owned by the company's founders or families, and others may simply have decided that private organization is preferable.

Privately Held Firms

A privately held company is owned by a relatively small number of shareholders. Privately held firms have fewer obligations to release financial statements and other information to the public. This saves money and frees the firm from disclosing information that might be helpful to its competitors. Some firms also believe that eliminating requirements for quarterly earnings announcements gives them more flexibility to pursue long-term goals free of shareholder pressure.

At the moment, however, privately held firms may have only up to 499 shareholders. This limits their ability to raise large amounts of capital from a wide base of investors. Thus, almost all of the largest companies in the U.S. are public corporations.

When private firms wish to raise funds, they sell shares directly to a small number of institutional or wealthy investors in a **private placement.** Rule 144A of the SEC allows them to make these placements without preparing the extensive and costly registration statements required of a public company. While this is attractive, shares in privately held firms do not trade in secondary markets such as a stock exchange, and this greatly reduces their liquidity and presumably reduces the prices that investors will pay for them. *Liquidity* has many specific meanings, but generally speaking, it refers to the ability to trade an asset at a fair price on short notice. Investors demand price concessions to buy illiquid securities.

private placement

Primary offerings in which shares are sold directly to a small group of institutional or wealthy investors.

As firms increasingly chafe against the informational requirements of going public, federal regulators have come under pressure to loosen the constraints entailed by private ownership, and they are currently reconsidering some of the restrictions on private companies. They may raise the number of shareholders that private firms can have before they are required to disclose financial information beyond 499, and they may make it easier to publicize share offerings.

Trading in private corporations also has evolved in recent years. To get around the 499-investor restriction, middlemen have formed partnerships to buy shares in private companies; the partnership counts as only one investor, even though many individuals may participate in it.

Very recently, some firms have set up computer networks to enable holders of private-company stock to trade among themselves. However, unlike the public stock markets regulated by the SEC, these networks require little disclosure of financial information and provide correspondingly little oversight of the operations of the market. For example, in the run-up to its 2012 IPO, Facebook enjoyed huge valuations in these markets, but skeptics worried that investors in these markets could not obtain a clear view of the firm, the interest among other investors in the firm, or the process by which trades in the firm's shares were executed.

Publicly Traded Companies

initial public offering (IPO)

First sale of stock by a formerly private company.

underwriters

Underwriters purchase securities from the issuing company and resell them to the public.

prospectus

A description of the firm and the security it is issuing.

When a private firm decides that it wishes to raise capital from a wide range of investors, it may decide to *go public.* This means that it will sell its securities to the general public and allow those investors to freely trade those shares in established securities markets. The first issue of shares to the general public is called the firm's **initial public offering,** or **IPO.** Later, the firm may go back to the public and issue additional shares. A *seasoned equity offering* is the sale of additional shares in firms that already are publicly traded. For example, a sale by Apple of new shares of stock would be considered a seasoned new issue.

Public offerings of both stocks and bonds typically are marketed by investment bankers who in this role are called **underwriters.** More than one investment banker usually markets the securities. A lead firm forms an underwriting syndicate of other investment bankers to share the responsibility for the stock issue.

Investment bankers advise the firm regarding the terms on which it should attempt to sell the securities. A preliminary registration statement must be filed with the Securities and Exchange Commission (SEC), describing the issue and the prospects of the company. When the statement is in final form, and approved by the SEC, it is called the **prospectus.** At this point, the price at which the securities will be offered to the public is announced.

In a typical underwriting arrangement, the investment bankers purchase the securities from the issuing company and then resell them to the public. The issuing firm sells the securities to the underwriting syndicate for the public offering price less a spread that serves as compensation to the underwriters. This procedure is called a *firm commitment.* In addition to the spread, the investment banker also may receive shares of common stock or other securities of the firm. Figure 3.1 depicts the relationships among the firm issuing the security, the lead underwriter, the underwriting syndicate, and the public.

Shelf Registration

An important innovation in the issuing of securities was introduced in 1982 when the SEC approved Rule 415, which allows firms to register securities and gradually sell them to the public for two years following the initial registration. Because the securities are already registered, they can be sold on short notice, with little additional paperwork. Moreover, they can be sold in small amounts without incurring substantial flotation costs. The securities are "on the shelf," ready to be issued, which has given rise to the term *shelf registration.*

CONCEPT check 3.1

Why does it make sense for shelf registration to be limited in time?

FIGURE 3.1

Relationship among a firm issuing securities, the underwriters, and the public

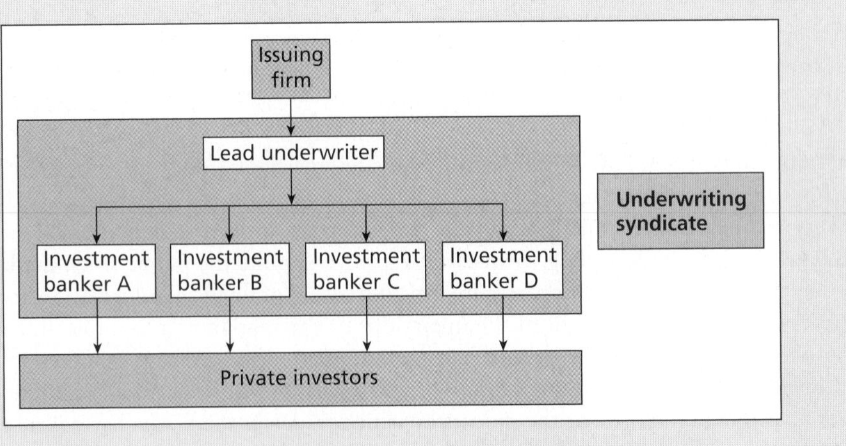

Initial Public Offerings

Investment bankers manage the issuance of new securities to the public. Once the SEC has commented on the registration statement and a preliminary prospectus has been distributed to interested investors, the investment bankers organize *road shows* in which they travel around the country to publicize the imminent offering. These road shows serve two purposes. First, they generate interest among potential investors and provide information about the offering. Second, they provide information to the issuing firm and its underwriters about the price at which they will be able to market the securities. Large investors communicate their interest in purchasing shares of the IPO to the underwriters; these indications of interest are called a *book* and the process of polling potential investors is called *bookbuilding*. These indications of interest provide valuable information to the issuing firm because institutional investors often will have useful insights about both the market demand for the security as well as the prospects of the firm and its competitors. It is common for investment bankers to revise both their initial estimates of the offering price of a security and the number of shares offered based on feedback from the investing community.

Why do investors truthfully reveal their interest in an offering to the investment banker? Might they be better off expressing little interest, in the hope that this will drive down the offering price? Truth is the better policy in this case because truth telling is rewarded. Shares of IPOs are allocated across investors in part based on the strength of each investor's expressed interest in the offering. If a firm wishes to get a large allocation when it is optimistic about the security, it needs to reveal its optimism. In turn, the underwriter needs to offer the security at a bargain price to these investors to induce them to participate in bookbuilding and share their information. Thus, IPOs commonly are underpriced compared to the price at which they could be marketed. Such underpricing is reflected in price jumps that occur on the date when the shares are first traded in public security markets. The November 2011 IPO of Groupon was a typical example of underpricing. The company issued about 35 million shares to the public at a price of $20. The stock price closed that day at $26.11, a bit more than 30% above the offering price.

While the explicit costs of an IPO tend to be around 7% of the funds raised, such underpricing should be viewed as another cost of the issue. For example, if Groupon had sold its shares for the $26.11 that investors obviously were willing to pay for them, its IPO would have raised 30% more money than it actually did. The money "left on the table" in this case far exceeded the explicit cost of the stock issue. This degree of underpricing is perhaps more dramatic than is common, but underpricing seems to be a universal phenomenon. For example, Figure 3.2 presents average first-day returns on IPOs of stocks across the world. The results consistently indicate that IPOs are marketed to investors at attractive prices.

Pricing of IPOs is not trivial and not all IPOs turn out to be underpriced. Some do poorly after issue. Six months after its IPO, Groupon shares were selling for about half the $20 offer price and two weeks after its IPO, Facebook shares were down around 25%. Other IPOs cannot even be fully sold to the market. Underwriters left with unmarketable securities are forced to sell them at a loss on the secondary market. Therefore, the investment banker bears the price risk of an underwritten issue.

Interestingly, despite their dramatic initial investment performance, IPOs have been poor long-term investments. Ritter calculates the returns to a hypothetical investor who bought equal amounts of each U.S. IPO between 1980 and 2009 and held each position for three years. That portfolio would have underperformed the broad U.S. stock market on average by 19.8% for three-year holding periods and underperformed "style-matched" portfolios of firms with comparable size and ratio of book value to market value by 7.3%.[1]

3.2 HOW SECURITIES ARE TRADED

Financial markets develop to meet the needs of particular traders. Consider what would happen if organized markets did not exist. Any household wishing to invest in some type of financial asset would have to find others wishing to sell. Soon, venues where interested traders

[1]Professor Jay Ritter's website contains a wealth of information and data about IPOs: **http://bear.warrington.ufl.edu/ritter/ipodata.htm.**

FIGURE 3.2

Average initial returns for (A) U.S. and European and (B) non-European IPOs

Source: Provided by Professor J. Ritter of the University of Florida, 2008. This is an updated version of the information contained in T. Loughran, J. Ritter, and K. Rydqvist, "Initial Public Offerings: International Insights," *Pacific-Basin Finance Journal* 2 (1994), pp. 165–199. Copyright May 1994. Used with permission from Elsevier.

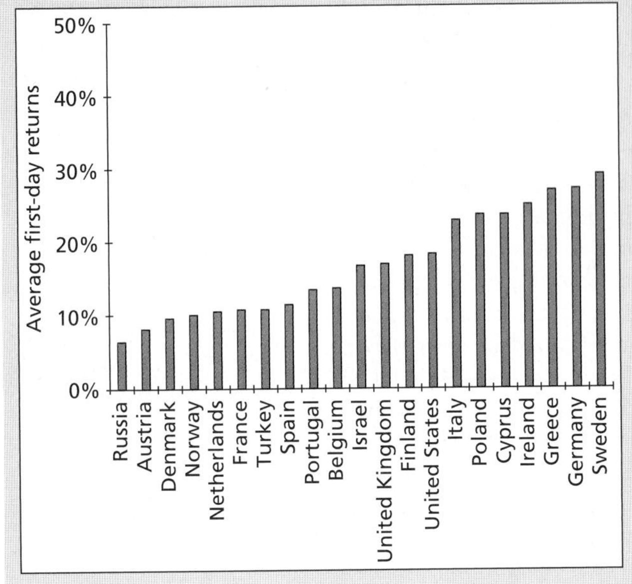

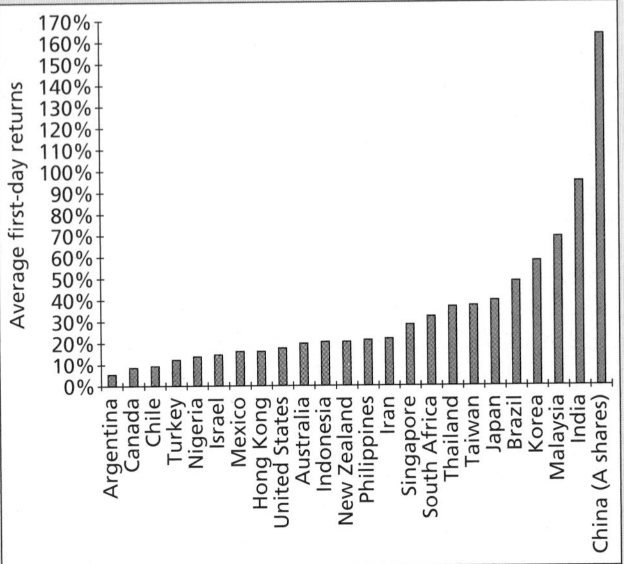

could meet would become popular. Eventually, financial markets would emerge from these meeting places. Thus, a pub in old London called Lloyd's launched the maritime insurance industry. A Manhattan curb on Wall Street became synonymous with the financial world.

Types of Markets

We can differentiate four types of markets: direct search markets, brokered markets, dealer markets, and auction markets.

Direct search markets A *direct search market* is the least organized market. Buyers and sellers must seek each other out directly. An example of a transaction in such a market is the sale of a used refrigerator where the seller advertises for buyers on Craigslist. Such markets are characterized by sporadic participation and low-priced and nonstandard goods. It would not pay for most people or firms to specialize in such markets.

Brokered markets The next level of organization is a *brokered market.* In markets where trading in a good is active, brokers find it profitable to offer search services to buyers and sellers. A good example is the real estate market, where economies of scale in searches for available homes and for prospective buyers make it worthwhile for participants to pay brokers to conduct the searches. Brokers in particular markets develop specialized knowledge on valuing assets traded in that market.

An important brokered investment market is the *primary market,* where new issues of securities are offered to the public. In the primary market, investment bankers who market a firm's securities to the public act as brokers; they seek investors to purchase securities directly from the issuing corporation.

dealer markets

Markets in which traders specializing in particular assets buy and sell for their own accounts.

Dealer markets When trading activity in a particular type of asset increases, **dealer markets** arise. Dealers specialize in various assets, purchase these assets for their own accounts, and later sell them for a profit from their inventory. The spreads between dealers' buy (or "bid") prices and sell (or "ask") prices are a source of profit. Dealer markets save traders on search costs because market participants can easily look up the prices at which they can buy from or sell to dealers. A fair amount of market activity is required before dealing in a market is an attractive source of income. Most bonds trade in over-the-counter dealer markets.

Auction markets The most integrated market is an **auction market,** in which all traders converge at one place (either physically or "electronically") to buy or sell an asset. The New York Stock Exchange (NYSE) is an example of an auction market. An advantage of auction markets over dealer markets is that one need not search across dealers to find the best price for a good. If all participants converge, they can arrive at mutually agreeable prices and save the bid–ask spread.

auction market

A market where all traders meet at one place to buy or sell an asset.

Notice that both over-the-counter dealer markets and stock exchanges are secondary markets. They are organized for investors to trade existing securities among themselves.

CONCEPT check 3.2

Many assets trade in more than one type of market. What types of markets do the following trade in?

a. Used cars
b. Paintings
c. Rare coins

Types of Orders

Before comparing alternative trading practices and competing security markets, it is helpful to begin with an overview of the types of trades an investor might wish to have executed in these markets. Broadly speaking, there are two types of orders: market orders and orders contingent on price.

Market orders Market orders are buy or sell orders that are to be executed immediately at current market prices. For example, our investor might call her broker and ask for the market price of FedEx. The broker might report back that the best **bid price** is $90 and the best **ask price** is $90.05, meaning that the investor would need to pay $90.05 to purchase a share and could receive $90 a share if she wished to sell some of her own holdings of FedEx. The **bid–ask spread** in this case is $.05. So an order to buy 100 shares "at market" would result in purchase at $90.05, and an order to "sell at market" would be executed at $90.

bid price

The price at which a dealer or other trader is willing to purchase a security.

ask price

The price at which a dealer or other trader will sell a security.

bid–ask spread

The difference between the bid and asked prices.

This simple scenario is subject to a few potential complications. First, posted price quotes actually represent commitments to trade up to a specified number of shares. If the market order is for more than this number of shares, the order may be filled at multiple prices. For example, if the asked price is good for orders up to 1,000 shares, and the investor wishes to purchase 1,500 shares, it may be necessary to pay a slightly higher price for the last 500 shares. Figure 3.3 shows the average *depth* of the markets for shares of stock (i.e., the total number of shares offered for trading at the best bid and ask prices). Notice that depth is considerably higher for the large stocks in the S&P 500 than for the smaller stocks that constitute the Russell 2000 index. Depth is considered another component of liquidity. Second, another trader may beat our investor to the quote, meaning that her order would then be executed at a worse price. Finally, the best price quote may change before her order arrives, again causing execution at a different price than the one at the moment of the order.

Price-contingent orders Investors also may place orders specifying prices at which they are willing to buy or sell a security. A **limit buy order** for Intel may instruct the broker to buy some number of shares if and when they may be obtained at or below a stipulated price. Conversely, a **limit sell** instructs the broker to sell if and when the stock price rises *above* a specified limit. A collection of limit orders waiting to be executed is called a *limit order book.*

limit buy (sell) order

An order specifying a price at which an investor is willing to buy or sell a security.

FIGURE 3.3

Average market depth for large (S&P 500) and small (Russell 2000) firms

Source: Adapted from James J. Angel, Lawrence E. Harris, and Chester Spatt, "Equity Trading in the 21st Century," *Quarterly Journal of Finance* 1 (2011), pp. 1–53; Knight Capital Group.

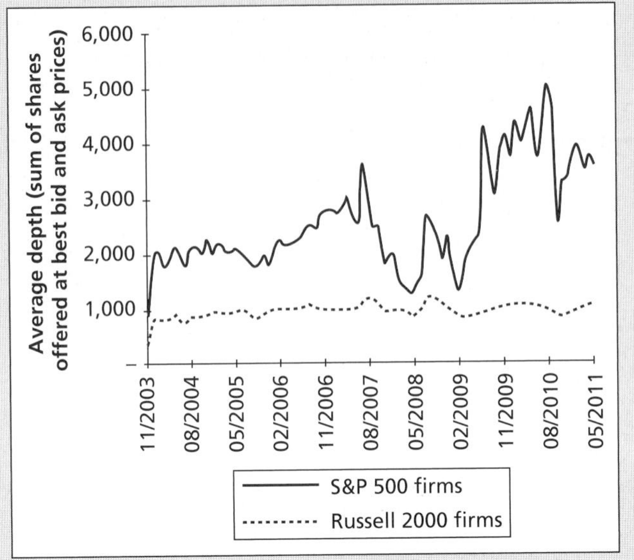

FIGURE 3.4

The limit order book for Intel on the NYSE Arca market, July 22, 2011

Source: NYSE Euronext.

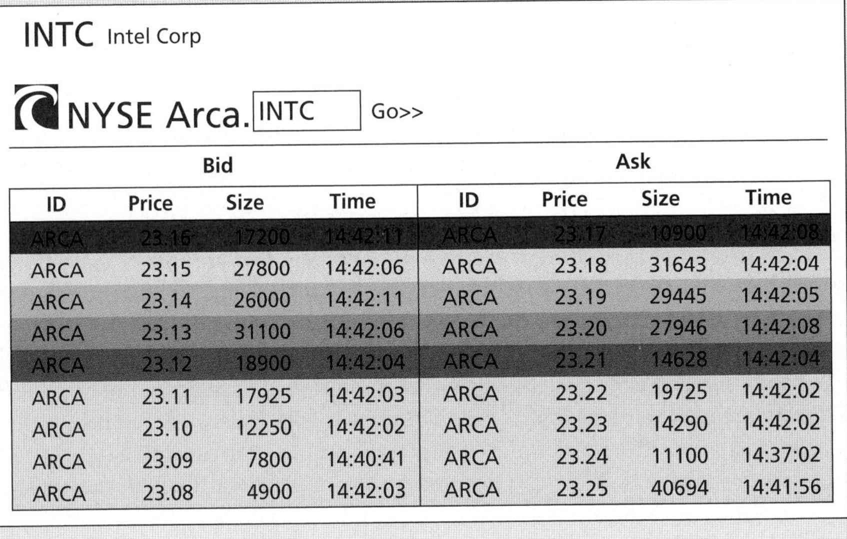

INTC Intel Corp

NYSE Arca. INTC Go>>

Bid				Ask			
ID	Price	Size	Time	ID	Price	Size	Time
ARCA	23.16	17200	14:42:11	ARCA	23.17	10900	14:42:08
ARCA	23.15	27800	14:42:06	ARCA	23.18	31643	14:42:04
ARCA	23.14	26000	14:42:11	ARCA	23.19	29445	14:42:05
ARCA	23.13	31100	14:42:06	ARCA	23.20	27946	14:42:08
ARCA	23.12	18900	14:42:04	ARCA	23.21	14628	14:42:04
ARCA	23.11	17925	14:42:03	ARCA	23.22	19725	14:42:02
ARCA	23.10	12250	14:42:02	ARCA	23.23	14290	14:42:02
ARCA	23.09	7800	14:40:41	ARCA	23.24	11100	14:37:02
ARCA	23.08	4900	14:42:03	ARCA	23.25	40694	14:41:56

Figure 3.4 is a portion of the limit order book for shares in Intel taken from the NYSE Arca exchange (one of several electronic exchanges; more on these shortly). Notice that the best orders are at the top of the list: the offers to buy at the highest price and to sell at the lowest price. The buy and sell orders at the top of the list—$23.16 and $23.17—are called the *inside quotes;* they are the highest buy and lowest sell orders. For Intel, the inside spread at this time was only 1 cent. Note, however, that order sizes at the inside quotes can be fairly small. Therefore, investors interested in larger trades face an *effective* spread greater than the nominal one since they cannot execute their entire trades at the inside price quotes.

stop order

Trade is not to be executed unless stock hits a price limit.

Stop orders are similar to limit orders in that the trade is not to be executed unless the stock hits a price limit. For *stop-loss orders,* the stock is to be *sold* if its price falls *below* a stipulated level. As the name suggests, the order lets the stock be sold to stop further losses from accumulating. Similarly, *stop-buy orders* specify that a stock should be bought when its price rises above a limit. These trades often accompany *short sales* (sales of securities you don't own but have borrowed from your broker) and are used to limit potential losses from the short position. Short sales are discussed in greater detail later in this chapter. Figure 3.5 organizes these types of trades in a convenient matrix.

FIGURE 3.5

Price-contingent orders

Action	Condition: Price falls below the limit	Condition: Price rises above the limit
Buy	Limit buy order	Stop-buy order
Sell	Stop-loss order	Limit sell order

CONCEPT check 3.3

What type of trading order might you give to your broker in each of the following circumstances?

a. You want to buy shares of Intel to diversify your portfolio. You believe the share price is approximately at the "fair" value, and you want the trade done quickly and cheaply.

b. You want to buy shares of Intel but believe that the current stock price is too high given the firm's prospects. If the shares could be obtained at a price 5% lower than the current value, you would like to purchase shares for your portfolio.

c. You plan to purchase a condominium sometime in the next month or so and will sell your shares of Intel to provide the funds for your down payment. While you believe that Intel share price is going to rise over the next few weeks, if you are wrong and the share price drops suddenly, you will not be able to afford the purchase. Therefore, you want to hold on to the shares for as long as possible but still protect yourself against the risk of a big loss.

Trading Mechanisms

An investor who wishes to buy or sell shares will place an order with a brokerage firm. The broker charges a commission for arranging the trade on the client's behalf. Brokers have several avenues by which they can execute that trade, that is, find a buyer or seller and arrange for the shares to be exchanged.

Broadly speaking, there are three trading systems employed in the United States: over-the-counter dealer markets, electronic communication networks, and specialist markets. The best-known markets such as NASDAQ or the New York Stock Exchange actually use a variety of trading procedures, so before delving into these markets, it is useful to understand the basic operation of each type of trading system.

Dealer markets Roughly 35,000 securities trade on the **over-the-counter** or OTC **market.** Thousands of brokers register with the SEC as security dealers. Dealers quote prices at which they are willing to buy or sell securities. A broker then executes a trade by contacting a dealer listing an attractive quote.

over-the-counter (OTC) market

An informal network of brokers and dealers who negotiate sales of securities.

Before 1971, all OTC quotations were recorded manually and published daily on so-called pink sheets. In 1971, the National Association of Securities Dealers introduced its Automatic Quotations System, or NASDAQ, to link brokers and dealers in a computer network where price quotes could be displayed and revised. Dealers could use the network to display the bid price at which they were willing to purchase a security and the ask price at which they were willing to sell. The difference in these prices, the bid–ask spread, was the source of the dealer's profit. Brokers representing clients could examine quotes over the computer network, contact the dealer with the best quote, and execute a trade.

As originally organized, NASDAQ was more of a price quotation system than a trading system. While brokers could survey bid and ask prices across the network of dealers in the search for the best trading opportunity, actual trades required direct negotiation (often over the phone) between the investor's broker and the dealer in the security. However,

NASDAQ Stock Market The computer-linked price quotation and trade execution system.

as we will see, NASDAQ has progressed far beyond a pure price quotation system. While dealers still post bid and ask prices over the network, what is now called the **NASDAQ Stock Market** allows for electronic execution of trades at quoted prices without the need for direct negotiation, and the vast majority of trades are executed electronically.

electronic communication networks (ECNs) Computer networks that allow direct trading without the need for market makers.

Electronic communication networks (ECNs) **Electronic communication networks** allow participants to post market and limit orders over computer networks. The limit order book is available to all participants. An example of such an order book from NYSE Arca, one of the leading ECNs, appears in Figure 3.4. Orders that can be "crossed," that is, matched against another order, are done so automatically without requiring the intervention of a broker. For example, an order to buy a share at a price of $50 or lower will be immediately executed if there is an outstanding asked price of $50. Therefore, ECNs are true trading systems, not merely price quotation systems.

ECNs offer several attractions. Direct crossing of trades without using a broker-dealer system eliminates the bid–ask spread that otherwise would be incurred. Instead, trades are automatically crossed at a modest cost, typically less than a penny per share. ECNs are attractive as well because of the speed with which a trade can be executed. Finally, these systems offer investors considerable anonymity in their trades.

specialist A trader who makes a market in the shares of one or more firms and who maintains a "fair and orderly market" by dealing personally in the market.

Specialist markets Specialist systems have been largely replaced by electronic communication networks, but as recently as a decade ago, they were still a dominant form of market organization for trading in stocks. In these systems, exchanges such as the NYSE assign responsibility for managing the trading in each security to a **specialist.** Brokers wishing to buy or sell shares for their clients direct the trade to the specialist's post on the floor of the exchange. While each security is assigned to only one specialist, each specialist firm makes a market in many securities. The specialist maintains the limit order book of all outstanding unexecuted limit orders. When orders can be executed at market prices, the specialist executes or "crosses" the trade. The highest outstanding bid price and the lowest outstanding ask price "win" the trade.

Specialists are also mandated to maintain a "fair and orderly" market when the book of limit buy and sell orders is so thin that the spread between the highest bid price and lowest ask price becomes too wide. In this case, the specialist firm would be expected to offer to buy and sell shares from its own inventory at a narrower bid–ask spread. In this role, the specialist serves as a dealer in the stock and provides liquidity to other traders. In this context, liquidity providers are those who stand willing to buy securities from or sell securities to other traders.

3.3 THE RISE OF ELECTRONIC TRADING

When first established, NASDAQ was primarily an over-the-counter dealer market and the NYSE was a specialist market. But today both are primarily electronic markets. These changes were driven by an interaction of new technologies and new regulations. New regulations allowed brokers to compete for business, broke the hold that dealers once had on information about best-available bid and ask prices, forced integration of markets, and allowed securities to trade in ever-smaller price increments (called *tick sizes*). Technology made it possible for traders to rapidly compare prices across markets and direct their trades to the markets with the best prices. The resulting competition drove down the cost of trade execution to a tiny fraction of its value just a few decades ago.

In 1975, fixed commissions on the NYSE were eliminated, which freed brokers to compete for business by lowering their fees. In that year also, Congress amended the Securities Exchange Act to create the National Market System to at least partially centralize trading across exchanges and enhance competition among different market makers. The idea was to implement centralized reporting of transactions as well as a centralized price quotation system to give traders a broader view of trading opportunities across markets.

The aftermath of a 1994 scandal at NASDAQ turned out to be a major impetus in the further evolution and integration of markets. NASDAQ dealers were found to be colluding to maintain wide bid–ask spreads. For example, if a stock was listed at $30 bid–$30½ ask, a retail client who wished to buy shares from a dealer would pay \$30½ while a client who wished to sell shares would receive only \$30. The dealer would pocket the ½-point spread as profit. Other traders may have been willing to step in with better prices (e.g., they may have been willing to buy shares for \$30⅛ or sell them for \$30⅜), but those better quotes were not made available to the public, enabling dealers to profit from artificially wide spreads at the public's expense. When these practices came to light, an antitrust lawsuit was brought against NASDAQ.

In response to the scandal, the SEC instituted new order-handling rules. Published dealer quotes now had to reflect limit orders of customers, allowing them to effectively compete with dealers to capture trades. As part of the antitrust settlement, NASDAQ agreed to integrate quotes from ECNs into its public display, enabling the electronic exchanges to also compete for trades. Shortly after this settlement, the SEC adopted Regulation ATS (Alternative Trading Systems), giving ECNs the right to register as stock exchanges. Not surprisingly, they captured an ever-larger market share, and in the wake of this new competition, bid–ask spreads narrowed.

Even more dramatic narrowing of trading costs came in 1997, when the SEC allowed the minimum tick size to fall from one-eighth of a dollar to one-sixteenth. Not long after, in 2001, "decimalization" allowed the tick size to fall to 1 cent. Bid–ask spreads again fell dramatically. Figure 3.6 shows estimates of the "effective spread" (the cost of a transaction) during three distinct time periods defined by the minimum tick size. Notice how dramatically effective spread falls along with the minimum tick size.

Technology was also changing trading practices. The first ECN, Instinet, was established in 1969. By the 1990s, exchanges around the world were rapidly adopting fully electronic trading systems. Europe led the way in this evolution, but eventually American exchanges followed suit. The National Association of Securities Dealers (NASD) spun off the NASDAQ Stock Market as a separate entity in 2000, which quickly evolved into a centralized limit-order matching system—effectively a large ECN. The NYSE acquired the electronic Archipelago Exchange in 2006 and renamed it NYSE Arca.

In 2005, the SEC adopted Regulation NMS (National Market System), which was fully implemented in 2007. The goal was to link exchanges electronically, thereby creating in effect one integrated electronic market. The regulation required exchanges to honor quotes of other

FIGURE 3.6

The effective spread (measured in dollars per share) fell dramatically as the minimum tick size fell. (Value-weighted average of NYSE-listed shares)

Source: Tarun Chordia, Richard Roll, and Avanidhar Subrahmanyam, "Liquidity and Market Efficiency," *Journal of Financial Economics* 87 (2008), pp. 249–268. Copyright © February 2008, with permission from Elsevier.

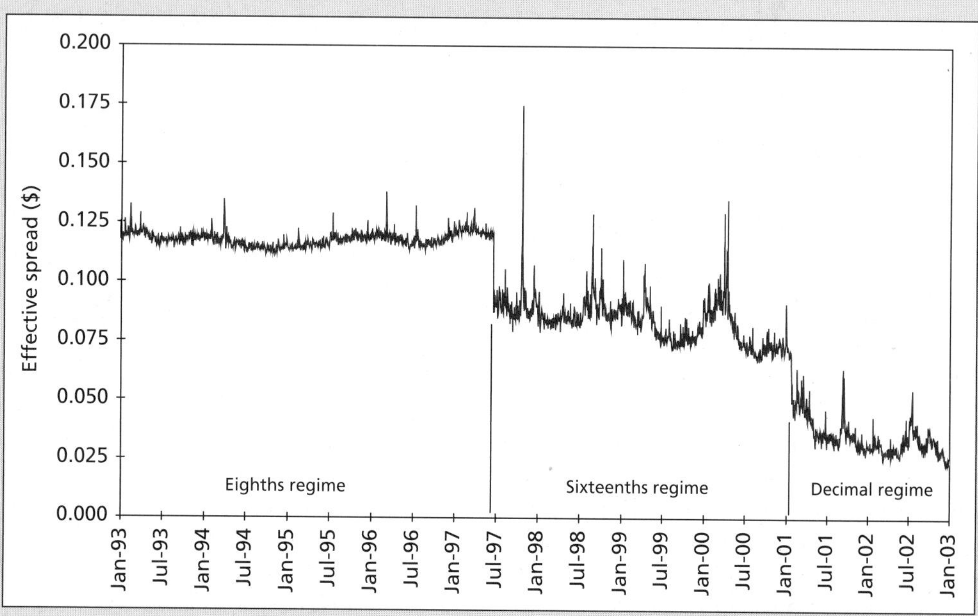

FIGURE 3.7

Market share of trading in NYSE-listed shares

Source: James J. Angel, Lawrence E. Harris, and Chester Spatt, "Equity Trading in the 21st Century," *Quarterly Journal of Finance* 1 (2011), pp. 1–53.

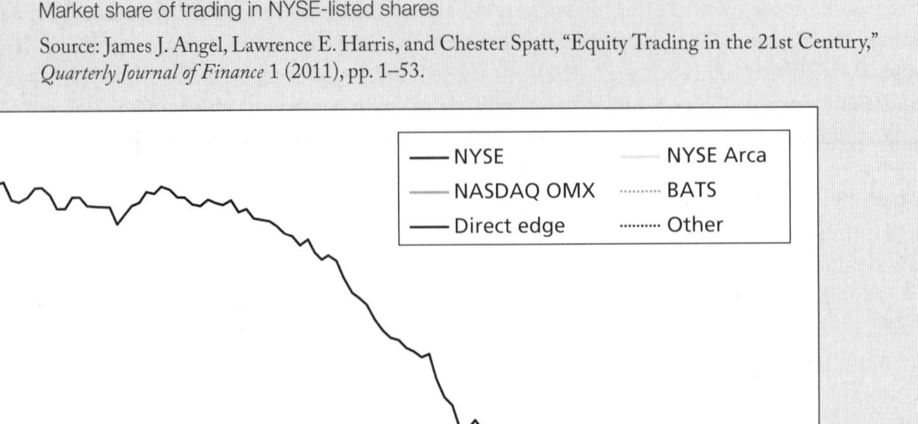

exchanges when they could be executed automatically. An exchange that could not handle a quote electronically would be labeled a "slow market" under Reg NMS and could be ignored by other market participants. The NYSE, which was still devoted to the specialist system, was particularly at risk of being passed over, and in response to this pressure, it moved aggressively toward automated execution of trades. Electronic trading networks and the integration of markets in the wake of Reg NMS made it much easier for exchanges around the world to compete; the NYSE lost its effective monopoly in trading its own listed stocks, and by the end of the decade, its share in the trading of NYSE-listed stocks fell from about 75% to 25%.

While specialists still exist, trading today is overwhelmingly electronic, at least for stocks. Bonds are still traded in more traditional dealer markets. In the U.S., the share of electronic trading in equities rose from about 16% in 2000 to over 80% by the end of the decade. In the rest of the world, the dominance of electronic trading is even greater.

3.4 U.S. MARKETS

The NYSE and the NASDAQ Stock Market remain the two largest U.S. stock markets. But electronic communication networks have steadily increased their market share. Figure 3.7 shows the comparative trading volume of NYSE-listed shares on the NYSE and NASDAQ as well as on the major ECNs, namely, BATS, NYSE Arca, and Direct Edge. The "Other" category, which recently has risen above 30%, includes so-called dark pools, which we will discuss shortly.

NASDAQ

The NASDAQ Stock Market lists around 3,000 firms. It has steadily introduced ever-more sophisticated trading platforms, which today handle the great majority of its trades. The current version, called the NASDAQ Market Center, consolidates NASDAQ's previous electronic markets into one integrated system. NASDAQ merged in 2008 with OMX, a Swedish-Finnish company that controls seven Nordic and Baltic stock exchanges, to form NASDAQ OMX Group. In addition to maintaining the NASDAQ Stock Market, it also maintains several stock markets in Europe as well as an options and futures exchange in the U.S.

NASDAQ has three levels of subscribers. The highest, level 3 subscribers, are registered market makers. These are firms that make a market in securities, maintain inventories of securities, and post bid and ask prices at which they are willing to buy or sell shares. Level 3 subscribers can enter and change bid–ask quotes continually and have the fastest execution of trades. They profit from the spread between bid and ask prices.

Level 2 subscribers receive all bid and ask quotes but cannot enter their own quotes. They can see which market makers are offering the best prices. These subscribers tend to be brokerage firms that execute trades for clients but do not actively deal in stocks for their own account.

Level 1 subscribers receive only inside quotes (i.e., the best bid and ask prices) but do not see how many shares are being offered. These subscribers tend to be investors who are not actively buying or selling but want information on current prices.

The New York Stock Exchange

The NYSE is the largest U.S. **stock exchange.** In 2006, the NYSE merged with the Archipelago Exchange to form a publicly held company called the NYSE Group, and then in 2007, it merged with the European exchange Euronext to form NYSE Euronext. The firm acquired the American Stock Exchange in 2008, which has since been renamed NYSE Amex and focuses on small firms. More than a billion shares trade daily on the NYSE. NYSE Arca is the firm's electronic communications network, and this is where the bulk of exchange-traded funds trade.

stock exchanges

Secondary markets where already-issued securities are bought and sold by members.

The NYSE was long committed to its specialist trading system, which relied heavily on human participation in trade execution. It began its transition to electronic trading for smaller trades in 1976 with the introduction of its DOT (Designated Order Turnaround) and later SuperDOT systems, which could route orders directly to the specialist. In 2000, the exchange launched Direct+, which could automatically cross smaller trades (up to 1,099 shares) without human intervention, and in 2004, it began eliminating the size restrictions on Direct+ trades. The change of emphasis dramatically accelerated in 2006 with the introduction of the NYSE Hybrid Market, which allowed brokers to send orders either for immediate electronic execution or to the specialist, who could seek price improvement from another trader. The Hybrid system allowed the NYSE to qualify as a fast market for the purposes of Regulation NMS but still offer the advantages of human intervention for more complicated trades. In contrast, NYSE's Arca marketplace is fully electronic.

ECNs

Over time, more fully automated markets have gained market share at the expense of less automated ones, in particular, the NYSE. Some of the biggest ECNs today are Direct Edge, BATS, and NYSE Arca. Brokers that have an affiliation with an ECN have computer access and can enter orders in the limit order book. As orders are received, the system determines whether there is a matching order, and if so, the trade is immediately crossed.

Originally, ECNs were open only to other traders using the same system. But following the implementation of Reg NMS, ECNs began listing limit orders on other networks. Traders could use their computer systems to sift through the limit order books of many ECNs and instantaneously route orders to the market with the best prices. Those cross-market links have become the impetus for one of the more popular strategies of so-called high-frequency traders, which seek to profit from even small, transitory discrepancies in prices across markets. Speed is obviously of the essence here, and ECNs compete in terms of the speed they can offer. **Latency** refers to the time it takes to accept, process, and deliver a trading order. BATS, for example, advertises (in 2012) latency times of around 200 microseconds, i.e., .0002 second.

latency

The time it takes to accept, process, and deliver a trading order.

3.5 NEW TRADING STRATEGIES

The marriage of electronic trading mechanisms with computer technology has had far-ranging impacts on trading strategies and tools. *Algorithmic trading* delegates trading decisions to computer programs. *High-frequency trading* is a special class of algorithmic trading in which computer programs initiate orders in tiny fractions of a second, far faster than any human could process the information driving the trade. Much of the market liquidity that once was provided by brokers making a market in a security has been displaced by these high-frequency traders. But when high-frequency traders abandon the market, as in the so-called flash crash of 2010, liquidity can likewise evaporate in a flash. *Dark pools* are trading venues that preserve anonymity but also affect market liquidity. We will address these emerging issues later in this section.

Algorithmic Trading

algorithmic trading

The use of computer programs to make rapid trading decisions.

Algorithmic trading is the use of computer programs to make trading decisions. Well more than half of all equity volume in the U.S. is believed to be initiated by computer algorithms. Many of these trades exploit very small discrepancies in security prices and entail numerous and rapid cross-market price comparisons that are well suited to computer analysis. These strategies would not have been feasible before decimalization of the minimum tick size.

Some algorithmic trades attempt to exploit very short-term trends (as short as a few seconds) as new information about a firm becomes reflected in its stock price. Others use versions of *pairs trading* in which normal price relations between pairs (or larger groups) of stocks seem temporarily disrupted and offer small profit opportunities as they move back into alignment. Still others attempt to exploit discrepancies between stock prices and prices of stock-index futures contracts.

Some algorithmic trading involves activities akin to traditional market making. The traders seek to profit from the bid–ask spread by buying a stock at the bid price and rapidly selling it at the ask price before the price can change. While this mimics the role of a market maker who provides liquidity to other traders in the stock, these algorithmic traders are not registered market makers and so do not have an affirmative obligation to maintain both bid and ask quotes. If they abandon a market during a period of turbulence, the shock to market liquidity can be disruptive. This seems to have been a problem during the flash crash of May 6, 2010, when the stock market encountered extreme volatility, with the Dow Jones average falling by 1,000 points before recovering around 600 points in intraday trading. The nearby box discusses this amazing and troubling episode.

High-Frequency Trading

high-frequency trading

A subset of algorithmic trading that relies on computer programs to make very rapid trading decisions.

It is easy to see that many algorithmic trading strategies require extremely rapid trade initiation and execution. **High-frequency trading** is a subset of algorithmic trading that relies on computer programs to make extremely rapid decisions. High-frequency traders compete for trades that offer very small profits. But if those opportunities are numerous enough, they can accumulate to big money.

We pointed out that one high-frequency strategy entails a sort of market making, attempting to profit from the bid–ask spread. Another relies on cross-market arbitrage, in which even tiny price discrepancies across markets allow the firm to buy a security at one price and simultaneously sell it at a slightly higher price. The competitive advantage in these strategies lies with the firms that are quickest to identify and execute these profit opportunities. There is a tremendous premium on being the first to "hit" a bid or ask price.

Trade execution times for high-frequency traders are now measured in milliseconds, even microseconds. This has induced trading firms to "co-locate" their trading centers next to the computer systems of the electronic exchanges. When execution or latency periods are less than a millisecond, the extra time it takes for a trade order to travel from a remote location to a New York exchange would be enough to make it nearly impossible to win the trade.

To understand why co-location has become a key issue, consider this calculation: Even light can travel only 186 miles in one millisecond, and ECNs today claim latency periods less than one millisecond. So an order originating in Chicago transmitted at the speed of light would take almost five milliseconds to reach New York. That order could not possibly compete with one launched from a co-located facility.

In some ways, co-location is a new version of an old phenomenon. Think about why, even before the advent of the telephone, so many brokerage firms originally located their headquarters in New York: They were "co-locating" with the NYSE so that their brokers could bring

On the MARKET FRONT

THE FLASH CRASH OF MAY 2010

At 2:42 New York time on May 6, 2010, the Dow Jones Industrial Average was already down about 300 points for the day. The market was demonstrating concerns about the European debt crisis, and nerves were on edge. Then, in the next five minutes, the Dow dropped an *additional* 600 points. And only 20 minutes after that, it had recovered most of those 600 points. Besides the staggering intraday volatility of the broad market, trading in individual shares and ETFs was even more disrupted. The iShares Russell 1000 Value Fund temporarily fell from $59 a share to 8 cents. Shares in the large consulting company Accenture, which had just sold for $38, traded at 1 cent only a minute or two later. At the other extreme, share prices of Apple and Hewlett-Packard momentarily increased to over $100,000. These markets were clearly broken.

The causes of the flash crash are still debated. An SEC report issued after the trade points to a $4 billion sale of market index futures contracts by a mutual fund (believed to be Waddell & Reed Financial). As market prices began to tumble, many algorithmic trading programs withdrew from the markets, and those that remained became net sellers, further pushing down equity prices. As more and more of these algorithmic traders shut down, liquidity in these markets evaporated: Buyers for many stocks simply disappeared.

Finally, trading was halted for a short period. When it resumed, buyers decided to take advantage of many severely depressed stock prices, and the market rebounded almost as quickly as it had crashed. Given the intraday turbulence and the clearly distorted prices at which some trades had been executed, the NYSE and NASDAQ decided to cancel all trades that were executed more than 60% away from a "reference price" close to the opening price of the day. Almost 70% of those canceled trades involved ETFs.

The SEC has since approved experimentation with new circuit breakers to halt trading for five minutes in large stocks that rise or fall by more than 10% in a five-minute period. The idea is to prevent trading algorithms from moving share prices quickly before human traders have a chance to determine whether those prices are moving in response to fundamental information.

The flash crash highlighted the fragility of markets in the face of huge variation in trading volume created by algorithmic traders. The potential for these high-frequency traders to withdraw from markets in periods of turbulence remains a concern, and many observers are not convinced that we are protected from future flash crashes.

trades to the exchange quickly and efficiently. Today, trades are transmitted electronically, but competition among traders for fast execution means that the need to be near the market (now embodied in computer servers) remains.

Dark Pools

Many large traders seek anonymity. They fear that if others see them executing a buy or a sell program, their intentions will become public and prices will move against them. Very large trades (called **blocks,** usually defined as a trade of more than 10,000 shares) have traditionally been brought to "block houses," brokerage firms specializing in matching block buyers and sellers. Part of the expertise of block brokers is in identifying traders who might be interested in a large purchase or sale if given an offer. These brokers discreetly arrange large trades out of the public eye, and so avoid moving prices against their clients.

blocks

Large transactions in which at least 10,000 shares of stock are bought or sold.

Block trading today has been displaced to a great extent by **dark pools,** trading systems in which participants can buy or sell large blocks of securities without showing their hand. Not only are buyers and sellers in dark pools hidden from the public, but even trades may not be reported, or if they are reported, they may be lumped with other trades to obscure information about particular participants.

dark pools

Electronic trading networks where participants can anonymously buy or sell large blocks of securities.

Dark pools are somewhat controversial because they contribute to the fragmentation of markets. When many orders are removed from the consolidated limit order book, there are fewer orders left to absorb fluctuations in demand for the security, and the public price may no longer be "fair" in the sense that it reflects all the potentially available information about security demand.

Another approach to dealing with large trades is to split them into many small trades, each of which can be executed on electronic markets, attempting to hide the fact that the total number of shares ultimately to be bought or sold is large. This trend has led to rapid decline in average trade size, which today is less than 300 shares.

Bond Trading

In 2006, the NYSE obtained regulatory approval to expand its bond trading system to include the debt issues of any NYSE-listed firm. In the past, each bond needed to be registered before listing; such a requirement was too onerous to justify listing most bonds. In conjunction with these new listings, the NYSE has expanded its electronic bond-trading platform, which is now called NYSE Bonds, and is the largest centralized bond market of any U.S. exchange.

Nevertheless, the vast majority of bond trading occurs in the OTC market among bond dealers, even for bonds that are actually listed on the NYSE. This market is a network of bond dealers such as Merrill Lynch (now part of Bank of America), Salomon Smith Barney (a division of Citigroup), and Goldman Sachs that is linked by a computer quotation system. However, because these dealers do not carry extensive inventories of the wide range of bonds that have been issued to the public, they cannot necessarily offer to sell bonds from their inventory to clients or even buy bonds for their own inventory. They may instead work to locate an investor who wishes to take the opposite side of a trade. In practice, however, the corporate bond market often is quite "thin," in that there may be few investors interested in trading a bond at any particular time. As a result, the bond market is subject to a type of liquidity risk, for it can be difficult to sell one's holdings quickly if the need arises.

3.6 GLOBALIZATION OF STOCK MARKETS

Figure 3.8 shows that the NYSE Euronext is by far the largest equity market, as measured by the total market value of listed firms. All major stock markets today are effectively electronic.

Securities markets have come under increasing pressure in recent years to make international alliances or mergers. Much of this pressure is due to the impact of electronic trading. To a growing extent, traders view stock markets as networks that link them to other traders, and there are increasingly fewer limits on the securities around the world that they can trade. Against this background, it becomes more important for exchanges to provide the cheapest and most efficient mechanism by which trades can be executed and cleared. This argues for global alliances that can facilitate the nuts and bolts of cross-border trading and can benefit from economies of scale. Exchanges feel that they eventually need to offer 24-hour global markets. Finally, companies want to be able to go beyond national borders when they wish to raise capital.

These pressures have resulted in a broad trend toward market consolidation. In the last decade, most of the mergers were "local," that is, involving exchanges operating in the same continent. In the U.S., the NYSE merged with the Archipelago ECN in 2006, and in 2008 acquired the American Stock Exchange. NASDAQ acquired Instinet (which operated the other major ECN, INET) in 2005 and the Boston Stock Exchange in 2007. In the derivatives market, the Chicago Mercantile Exchange acquired the Chicago Board of Trade in 2007. In Europe, Euronext was formed by the merger of the Paris, Brussels, Lisbon, and Amsterdam exchanges and shortly thereafter purchased LIFFE, the derivatives exchange based in London. The LSE merged in 2007 with Borsa Italiana, which operates the Milan exchange.

There has also been a wave of intercontinental consolidation. The NYSE Group and Euronext merged in 2007. Germany's Deutsche Börse and the NYSE Euronext agreed to merge in late 2011. The merged firm would have been able to support trading in virtually every type of investment. However, in early 2012, the proposed merger ran into trouble when European Union antitrust regulators recommended that the combination be blocked. Still, the attempt at the merger indicates the thrust of market pressures, and other combinations continue to develop. The NYSE and the Tokyo stock exchange have announced their intention to link their networks to give customers of each access to both markets. In 2007, the NASDAQ Stock Market merged with OMX, which operates seven Nordic and Baltic stock exchanges, to form NASDAQ OMX Group. In 2008, Euronext took over International Securities Exchange (ISE), to form a major options exchange.

3.7 TRADING COSTS

Part of the cost of trading a security is obvious and explicit. Your broker must be paid a commission. Individuals may choose from two kinds of brokers: full-service or discount brokers. Full-service brokers who provide a variety of services often are referred to as account executives or financial consultants.

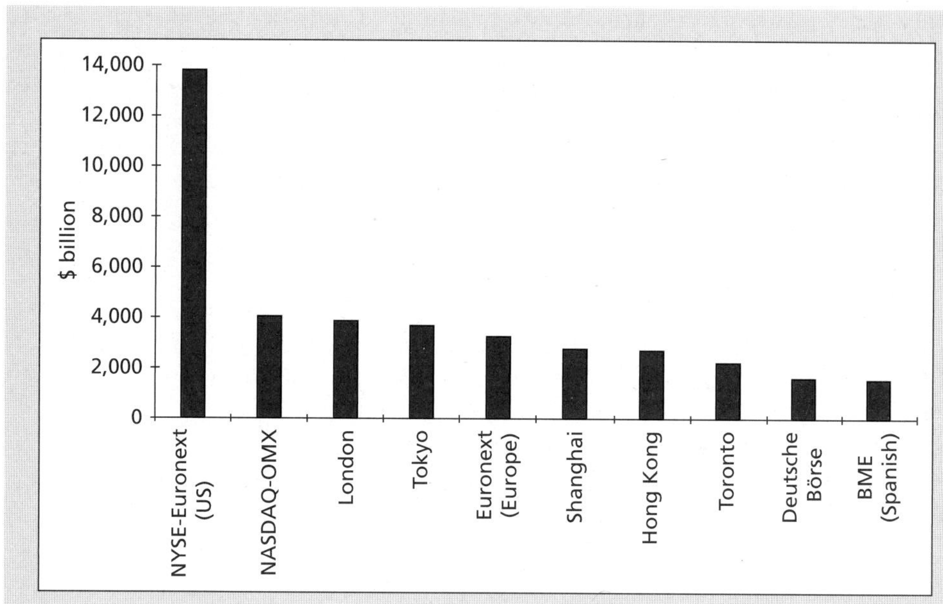

FIGURE 3.8

Market capitalization of major world stock exchanges, 2011

Source: World Federation of Exchanges.

Besides carrying out the basic services of executing orders, holding securities for safekeeping, extending margin loans, and facilitating short sales, brokers routinely provide information and advice relating to investment alternatives.

Full-service brokers usually depend on a research staff that prepares analyses and forecasts of general economic as well as industry and company conditions and often makes specific buy or sell recommendations. Some customers take the ultimate leap of faith and allow a full-service broker to make buy and sell decisions for them by establishing a *discretionary account.* In this account, the broker can buy and sell prespecified securities whenever deemed fit. (The broker cannot withdraw any funds, though.) This action requires an unusual degree of trust on the part of the customer, for an unscrupulous broker can "churn" an account, that is, trade securities excessively with the sole purpose of generating commissions.

Discount brokers, on the other hand, provide "no-frills" services. They buy and sell securities, hold them for safekeeping, offer margin loans, facilitate short sales, and that is all. The only information they provide about the securities they handle is price quotations. Discount brokerage services have become increasingly available in recent years. Many banks, thrift institutions, and mutual fund management companies now offer such services to the investing public as part of a general trend toward the creation of one-stop "financial supermarkets." Stock trading fees have fallen steadily over the last decade, and discount brokerage firms such as Schwab, E*Trade, or Ameritrade now offer commissions below $10.

In addition to the explicit part of trading costs—the broker's commission—there is an implicit part—the dealer's bid–ask spread. Sometimes the broker is a dealer in the security being traded and charges no commission but instead collects the fee entirely in the form of the bid–ask spread. Another implicit cost of trading that some observers would distinguish is the price concession an investor may be forced to make for trading in quantities greater than those associated with the posted bid or asked prices.

3.8 BUYING ON MARGIN

When purchasing securities, investors have easy access to a source of debt financing called *broker's call loans.* The act of taking advantage of broker's call loans is called *buying on margin.*

Purchasing stocks on margin means the investor borrows part of the purchase price of the stock from a broker. The **margin** in the account is the portion of the purchase price contributed by the investor; the remainder is borrowed from the broker. The brokers in turn borrow

margin

Describes securities purchased with money borrowed in part from a broker. The margin is the net worth of the investor's account.

money from banks at the call money rate to finance these purchases; they then charge their clients that rate (defined in Chapter 2), plus a service charge for the loan. All securities purchased on margin must be maintained with the brokerage firm in street name, for the securities are collateral for the loan.

The Board of Governors of the Federal Reserve System limits the extent to which stock purchases can be financed using margin loans. The current initial margin requirement is 50%, meaning that at least 50% of the purchase price must be paid for in cash, with the rest borrowed.

EXAMPLE 3.1

Margin

The percentage margin is defined as the ratio of the net worth, or the "equity value," of the account to the market value of the securities. To demonstrate, suppose an investor initially pays $6,000 toward the purchase of $10,000 worth of stock (100 shares at $100 per share), borrowing the remaining $4,000 from a broker. The initial balance sheet looks like this:

Assets		Liabilities and Owners' Equity	
Value of stock	$10,000	Loan from broker	$4,000
		Equity	$6,000

The initial percentage margin is

$$\text{Margin} = \frac{\text{Equity in account}}{\text{Value of stock}} = \frac{\$6{,}000}{\$10{,}000} = .60, \text{ or } 60\%$$

If the price declines to $70 per share, the account balance becomes:

Assets		Liabilities and Owners' Equity	
Value of stock	$7,000	Loan from broker	$4,000
		Equity	$3,000

The assets in the account fall by the full decrease in the stock value, as does the equity. The percentage margin is now

$$\text{Margin} = \frac{\text{Equity in account}}{\text{Value of stock}} = \frac{\$3{,}000}{\$7{,}000} = .43, \text{ or } 43\%$$

If the stock value in Example 3.1 were to fall below $4,000, owners' equity would become negative, meaning the value of the stock is no longer sufficient collateral to cover the loan from the broker. To guard against this possibility, the broker sets a *maintenance margin.* If the percentage margin falls below the maintenance level, the broker will issue a *margin call,* which requires the investor to add new cash or securities to the margin account. If the investor does not act, the broker may sell securities from the account to pay off enough of the loan to restore the percentage margin to an acceptable level.

EXAMPLE 3.2

Maintenance Margin

Suppose the maintenance margin is 30%. How far could the stock price fall before the investor would get a margin call?

Let P be the price of the stock. The value of the investor's 100 shares is then $100P$, and the equity in the account is $100P - \$4{,}000$. The percentage margin is $(100P - \$4{,}000)/100P$. The price at which the percentage margin equals the maintenance margin of .3 is found by solving the equation

(continued)

EXAMPLE 3.2

Maintenance Margin (concluded)

$$\frac{100P - 4{,}000}{100P} = .3$$

which implies that $P = \$57.14$. If the price of the stock were to fall below \$57.14 per share, the investor would get a margin call.

CONCEPT check 3.4

Suppose the maintenance margin in Example 3.2 is 40%. How far can the stock price fall before the investor gets a margin call?

Why do investors buy securities on margin? They do so when they wish to invest an amount greater than their own money allows. Thus, they can achieve greater upside potential, but they also expose themselves to greater downside risk.

To see how, let's suppose an investor is bullish on IBM stock, which is selling for \$100 per share. An investor with \$10,000 to invest expects IBM to go up in price by 30% during the next year. Ignoring any dividends, the expected rate of return would be 30% if the investor invested \$10,000 to buy 100 shares.

But now assume the investor borrows another \$10,000 from the broker and invests it in IBM, too. The total investment in IBM would be \$20,000 (for 200 shares). Assuming an interest rate on the margin loan of 9% per year, what will the investor's rate of return be now (again ignoring dividends) if IBM stock goes up 30% by year's end?

The 200 shares will be worth \$26,000. Paying off \$10,900 of principal and interest on the margin loan leaves \$15,100 (i.e., \$26,000 − \$10,900). The rate of return in this case will be

$$\frac{\$15{,}100 - \$10{,}000}{\$10{,}000} = 51\%$$

The investor has parlayed a 30% rise in the stock's price into a 51% rate of return on the \$10,000 investment.

Doing so, however, magnifies the downside risk. Suppose that, instead of going up by 30%, the price of IBM stock goes down by 30% to \$70 per share. In that case, the 200 shares will be worth \$14,000, and the investor is left with \$3,100 after paying off the \$10,900 of principal and interest on the loan. The result is a disastrous return of

$$\frac{\$3{,}100 - \$10{,}000}{\$10{,}000} = -69\%$$

Table 3.1 summarizes the possible results of these hypothetical transactions. If there is no change in IBM's stock price, the investor loses 9%, the cost of the loan.

TABLE 3.1 Illustration of buying stock on margin

Change in Stock Price	End-of-Year Value of Shares	Repayment of Principal and Interest*	Investor's Rate of Return
30% increase	\$26,000	\$10,900	51%
No change	20,000	10,900	−9
30% decrease	14,000	10,900	−69

*Assuming the investor buys \$20,000 worth of stock by borrowing \$10,000 at an interest rate of 9% per year.

EXCEL APPLICATIONS

Buying on Margin

Please visit us at www.mhhe.com/bkm

The Excel spreadsheet model below makes it easy to analyze the impacts of different margin levels and the volatility of stock prices. It also allows you to compare return on investment for a margin trade with a trade using no borrowed funds.

	A	B	C	D	E	F	G	H
1								
2			**Action or Formula**	**Ending**	**Return on**		**Ending**	**Return with**
3			**for Column B**	**St Price**	**Investment**		**St Price**	**No Margin**
4	Initial Equity Investment	$10,000.00	Enter data		−42.00%			−19.00%
5	Amount Borrowed	$10,000.00	(B4/B10)−B4	$20.00	−122.00%		$20.00	−59.00%
6	Initial Stock Price	$50.00	Enter data	25.00	−102.00%		25.00	−49.00%
7	Shares Purchased	400	(B4/B10)/B6	30.00	−82.00%		30.00	−39.00%
8	Ending Stock Price	$40.00	Enter data	35.00	−62.00%		35.00	−29.00%
9	Cash Dividends During Hold Per.	$0.50	Enter data	40.00	−42.00%		40.00	−19.00%
10	Initial Margin Percentage	50.00%	Enter data	45.00	−22.00%		45.00	−9.00%
11	Maintenance Margin Percentage	30.00%	Enter data	50.00	−2.00%		50.00	1.00%
12				55.00	18.00%		55.00	11.00%
13	Rate on Margin Loan	8.00%	Enter data	60.00	38.00%		60.00	21.00%
14	Holding Period in Months	6	Enter data	65.00	58.00%		65.00	31.00%
15				70.00	78.00%		70.00	41.00%
16	**Return on Investment**			75.00	98.00%		75.00	51.00%
17	Capital Gain on Stock	−$4,000.00	B7*(B8−B6)	80.00	118.00%		80.00	61.00%
18	Dividends	$200.00	B7*B9					
19	Interest on Margin Loan	$400.00	B5*(B14/12)*B13					
20	Net Income	−$4,200.00	B17+B18−B19			**LEGEND:**		
21	Initial Investment	$10,000.00	B4			**Enter data**		
22	Return on Investment	−42.00%	B20/B21			**Value calculated**		

Excel Questions

1. Suppose you buy 100 shares of stock initially selling for $50, borrowing 25% of the necessary funds from your broker; that is, the initial margin on your purchase is 25%. You pay an interest rate of 8% on margin loans.
   a. How much of your own money do you invest? How much do you borrow from your broker?
   b. What will be your rate of return for the following stock prices at the end of a one-year holding period? (i) $40, (ii) $50, (iii) $60.
2. Repeat Question 1 assuming your initial margin was 50%. How does margin affect the risk and return of your position?

CONCEPT check 3.5

Suppose that in the IBM example above, the investor borrows only $5,000 at the same interest rate of 9% per year. What will the rate of return be if the price of IBM goes up by 30%? If it goes down by 30%? If it remains unchanged?

3.9 SHORT SALES

short sale

The sale of shares not owned by the investor but borrowed through a broker and later purchased to replace the loan.

Normally, an investor would first buy a stock and later sell it. With a short sale, the order is reversed. First, you sell and then you buy the shares. In both cases, you begin and end with no shares.

A **short sale** allows investors to profit from a decline in a security's price. An investor borrows a share of stock from a broker and sells it. Later, the short-seller must purchase a share of the same stock in order to replace the share that was borrowed.[2] This is called *covering the short position.* Table 3.2 compares stock purchases to short sales.

[2]*Naked short-selling* is a variant on conventional short-selling. In a naked short, a trader sells shares that have not yet been borrowed, assuming that the shares can be acquired and delivered whenever the short sale needs to be closed out.

TABLE 3.2 Cash flows from purchasing versus short-selling shares of stock

Purchase of Stock

Time	Action	Cash Flow*
0	Buy share	−Initial price
1	Receive dividend, sell share	Ending price + Dividend

Profit = (Ending price + Dividend) − Initial price

Short Sale of Stock

Time	Action	Cash Flow*
0	Borrow share; sell it	+Initial price
1	Repay dividend and buy share to replace the share originally borrowed	−(Ending price + Dividend)

Profit = Initial price − (Ending price + Dividend)

*Note: A negative cash flow implies a cash *outflow*.

The short-seller anticipates the stock price will fall, so that the share can be purchased later at a lower price than it initially sold for; if so, the short-seller will reap a profit. Short-sellers must not only replace the shares but also pay the lender of the security any dividends paid during the short sale.

In practice, the shares loaned out for a short sale are typically provided by the short-seller's brokerage firm, which holds a wide variety of securities of its other investors in street name (i.e., the broker holds the shares registered in its own name on behalf of the client). The owner of the shares need not know that the shares have been lent to the short-seller. If the owner wishes to sell the shares, the brokerage firm will simply borrow shares from another investor. Therefore, the short sale may have an indefinite term. However, if the brokerage firm cannot locate new shares to replace the ones sold, the short-seller will need to repay the loan immediately by purchasing shares in the market and turning them over to the brokerage house to close out the loan.

Finally, exchange rules require that proceeds from a short sale must be kept on account with the broker. The short-seller cannot invest these funds to generate income, although large or institutional investors typically will receive some income from the proceeds of a short sale being held with the broker. Short-sellers also are required to post margin (cash or collateral) with the broker to cover losses should the stock price rise during the short sale.

EXAMPLE 3.3

Short Sales

To illustrate the mechanics of short-selling, suppose you are bearish (pessimistic) on Dot Bomb stock, and its market price is $100 per share. You tell your broker to sell short 1,000 shares. The broker borrows 1,000 shares either from another customer's account or from another broker.

The $100,000 cash proceeds from the short sale are credited to your account. Suppose the broker has a 50% margin requirement on short sales. This means you must have other cash or securities in your account worth at least $50,000 that can serve as margin on the short sale.

Let's say that you have $50,000 in Treasury bills. Your account with the broker after the short sale will then be:

Assets		Liabilities and Owners' Equity	
Cash	$100,000	Short position in Dot Bomb stock (1,000 shares owed)	$100,000
T-bills	50,000	Equity	50,000

(continued)

EXAMPLE 3.3

Short Sales (concluded)

Your initial percentage margin is the ratio of the equity in the account, \$50,000, to the current value of the shares you have borrowed and eventually must return, \$100,000:

$$\text{Percentage margin} = \frac{\text{Equity}}{\text{Value of stock owed}} = \frac{\$50{,}000}{\$100{,}000} = .50$$

Suppose you are right and Dot Bomb falls to \$70 per share. You can now close out your position at a profit. To cover the short sale, you buy 1,000 shares to replace the ones you borrowed. Because the shares now sell for \$70, the purchase costs only \$70,000.[3] Because your account was credited for \$100,000 when the shares were borrowed and sold, your profit is \$30,000: The profit equals the decline in the share price times the number of shares sold short.

Like investors who purchase stock on margin, a short-seller must be concerned about margin calls. If the stock price rises, the margin in the account will fall; if margin falls to the maintenance level, the short-seller will receive a margin call.

EXAMPLE 3.4

Margin Calls on Short Positions

Suppose the broker has a maintenance margin of 30% on short sales. This means the equity in your account must be at least 30% of the value of your short position at all times. How much can the price of Dot Bomb stock rise before you get a margin call?

Let P be the price of Dot Bomb stock. Then the value of the shares you must pay back is $1{,}000P$, and the equity in your account is $\$150{,}000 - 1{,}000P$. Your short position margin ratio is equity/value of stock $= (150{,}000 - 1{,}000P)/1{,}000P$. The critical value of P is thus

$$\frac{\text{Equity}}{\text{Value of shares owed}} = \frac{150{,}000 - 1{,}000P}{1{,}000P} = .3$$

which implies that $P = \$115.38$ per share. If Dot Bomb stock should *rise* above \$115.38 per share, you will get a margin call, and you will either have to put up additional cash or cover your short position by buying shares to replace the ones borrowed.

CONCEPT check 3.6

a. Construct the balance sheet if Dot Bomb goes up to \$110.

b. If the short position maintenance margin in Example 3.4 is 40%, how far can the stock price rise before the investor gets a margin call?

You can see now why stop-buy orders often accompany short sales. Imagine that you short-sell Dot Bomb when it is selling at \$100 per share. If the share price falls, you will profit from the short sale. On the other hand, if the share price rises, let's say to \$130, you will lose \$30 per share. But suppose that when you initiate the short sale, you also enter a stop-buy order at \$120. The stop-buy will be executed if the share price surpasses \$120, thereby limiting your losses to \$20 per share. (If the stock price drops, the stop-buy will never be executed.) The stop-buy order thus provides protection to the short-seller if the share price moves up.

Short-selling periodically comes under attack, particularly during times of financial stress when share prices fall. The last few years have been no exception to this rule, and the nearby box examines the controversy surrounding short sales in greater detail.

3.10 REGULATION OF SECURITIES MARKETS

Trading in securities markets in the United States is regulated by a myriad of laws. The major governing legislation includes the Securities Act of 1933 and the Securities Exchange Act of 1934. The 1933 act requires full disclosure of relevant information relating to the issue of new

[3]Notice that when buying on margin, you borrow a given amount of dollars from your broker, so the amount of the loan is independent of the share price. In contrast, when short-selling, you borrow a given number of *shares,* which must be returned. Therefore, when the price of the shares changes, the value of the loan also changes.

On the MARKET FRONT

SHORT-SELLING COMES UNDER FIRE—AGAIN

Short-selling has long been viewed with suspicion, if not outright hostility. England banned short sales for a good part of the eighteenth century. Napoleon called short-sellers enemies of the state. In the U.S., short-selling was widely viewed as contributing to the market crash of 1929, and in 2008, short-sellers were blamed for the collapse of the investment banks Bear Stearns and Lehman Brothers. With share prices of other financial firms tumbling in September 2008, the SEC instituted a temporary ban on short-selling for about 800 of those firms. Similarly, the Financial Services Authority, the financial regulator in the U.K., prohibited short sales on about 30 financial companies, and Australia banned shorting altogether.

The motivation for these bans is that short sales put downward pressure on share prices that in some cases may be unwarranted: rumors abound of investors who first put on a short sale and then spread negative rumors about the firm to drive down its price. More often, however, shorting is an innocent bet that a share price is too high and is due to fall. Nevertheless, during the market stresses of late 2008, the widespread feeling was that even if short positions were legitimate, regulators should do what they could to prop up the affected institutions.

Hostility to short-selling may well stem from confusion between bad news and the bearer of that news. Short-selling allows investors whose analysis indicates a firm is overpriced to take action on that belief—and to profit if they are correct. Rather than *causing* the stock price to fall, shorts may simply be *anticipating* a decline in the stock price. Their sales simply force the market to reflect the deteriorating prospects of troubled firms sooner than it might have otherwise. In other words, short-selling is part of the process by which the full range of information and opinion—pessimistic as well as optimistic—is brought to bear on stock prices.

For example, short-sellers took large (negative) positions in firms such as WorldCom, Enron, and Tyco even before these firms were exposed by regulators. In fact, one might argue that these emerging short positions helped regulators identify the previously undetected scandals. And in the end, Lehman and Bear Stearns were brought down by their very real losses on their mortgage-related investments—not by unfounded rumors.

Academic research supports the conjecture that short sales contribute to efficient "price discovery." For example, the greater the demand for shorting a stock, the lower its future returns tend to be; moreover, firms that attack short-sellers with threats of legal action or bad publicity tend to have especially poor future returns.[4] Short-sale bans may in the end be nothing more than an understandable, but nevertheless misguided, impulse to "shoot the messenger."

securities. This is the act that requires registration of new securities and issuance of a prospectus that details the financial prospects of the firm. SEC approval of a prospectus or financial report is not an endorsement of the security as a good investment. The SEC cares only that the relevant facts are disclosed; investors must make their own evaluation of the security's value.

The 1934 act established the Securities and Exchange Commission to administer the provisions of the 1933 act. It also extended the disclosure principle of the 1933 act by requiring periodic disclosure of relevant financial information by firms with already-issued securities on secondary exchanges.

The 1934 act also empowers the SEC to register and regulate securities exchanges, OTC trading, brokers, and dealers. While the SEC is the administrative agency responsible for broad oversight of the securities markets, it shares responsibility with other regulatory agencies. The Commodity Futures Trading Commission (CFTC) regulates trading in futures markets, while the Federal Reserve has broad responsibility for the health of the U.S. financial system. In this role, the Fed sets margin requirements on stocks and stock options and regulates bank lending to securities markets participants.

The Securities Investor Protection Act of 1970 established the Securities Investor Protection Corporation (SIPC) to protect investors from losses if their brokerage firms fail. Just as the Federal Deposit Insurance Corporation provides depositors with federal protection against bank failure, the SIPC ensures that investors will receive securities held for their account in street name by a failed brokerage firm up to a limit of $500,000 per customer. The SIPC is financed by levying an "insurance premium" on its participating, or member, brokerage firms.

In addition to being governed by federal regulations, security trading is subject to state laws, known generally as *blue sky laws* because they are intended to give investors a clearer view of investment prospects. State laws to outlaw fraud in security sales existed before the Securities Act of 1933. Varying state laws were somewhat unified when many states adopted portions of the Uniform Securities Act, which was enacted in 1956.

[4]See, for example, C. Jones and O. A. Lamont, "Short Sale Constraints and Stock Returns," *Journal of Financial Economics,* November 2002, pp. 207–239, or O. A. Lamont, "Go Down Fighting: Short Sellers vs. Firms," *Yale ICF Working Paper No. 04-20,* July 2004.

Short Sale

eXcel

Please visit us at www.mhhe.com/bkm

This Excel spreadsheet model was built using the text example for Dot Bomb. The model allows you to analyze the effects of returns, margin calls, and different levels of initial and maintenance margins. The model also includes a sensitivity analysis for ending stock price and return on investment.

	A	B	C	D	E
1					
2			**Action or Formula**	**Ending**	**Return on**
3			**for Column B**	**St Price**	**Investment**
4	Initial Investment	$50,000.00	Enter data		60.00%
5	Initial Stock Price	$100.00	Enter data	$170.00	−140.00%
6	Number of Shares Sold Short	1,000	(B4/B9)/B5	160.00	−120.00%
7	Ending Stock Price	$70.00	Enter data	150.00	−100.00%
8	Cash Dividends Per Share	$0.00	Enter data	140.00	−80.00%
9	Initial Margin Percentage	50.00%	Enter data	130.00	−60.00%
10	Maintenance Margin Percentage	30.00%	Enter data	120.00	−40.00%
11				110.00	−20.00%
12	**Return on Short Sale**			100.00	0.00%
13	Capital Gain on Stock	$30,000.00	B6*(B5−B7)	90.00	20.00%
14	Dividends Paid	$0.00	B8*B6	80.00	40.00%
15	Net Income	$30,000.00	B13−B14	70.00	60.00%
16	Initial Investment	$50,000.00	B4	60.00	80.00%
17	Return on Investment	60.00%	B15/B16	50.00	100.00%
18				40.00	120.00%
19	**Margin Positions**			30.00	140.00%
20	Margin Based on Ending Price	114.29%	(B4+(B5*B6)−B14−(B6*B7))/(B6*B7)	20.00	160.00%
21				10.00	180.00%
22	Price for Margin Call	$115.38	(B4+(B5*B6)−B14)/(B6*(1+B10))		
23				**LEGEND:**	
24				**Enter data**	
25				**Value calculated**	

Excel Questions

1. Suppose you sell short 100 shares of stock initially selling for $100 a share. Your initial margin requirement is 50% of the value of the stock sold. You receive no interest on the funds placed in your margin account.
   a. How much do you need to contribute to your margin account?
   b. What will be your rate of return for the following stock prices at the end of a one-year holding period (assume the stock pays no dividends)? (i) $90; (ii) $100; (iii) $110.
2. Repeat Question 1 (*b*) but now assume that the stock pays dividends of $2 per share at year-end. What is the relationship between the total rate of return on the stock and the return to your short position?

Self-Regulation

In addition to government regulation, there is considerable self-regulation of the securities market. The most important overseer in this regard is the Financial Industry Regulatory Authority (FINRA), which is the largest nongovernmental regulator of all securities firms in the United States. FINRA was formed in 2007 through the consolidation of the National Association of Securities Dealers (NASD) with the self-regulatory arm of the New York Stock Exchange. It describes its broad mission as the fostering of investor protection and market integrity. It examines securities firms, writes and enforces rules concerning trading practices, and administers a dispute resolution forum for investors and registered firms.

There is also self-regulation among the community of investment professionals. For example, the CFA Institute has developed standards of professional conduct that govern the behavior of members with the Chartered Financial Analysts designation, commonly referred to as CFAs. The nearby box presents a brief outline of those principles.

The Sarbanes-Oxley Act

The scandals of 2000–2002 centered largely on three broad practices: allocations of shares in initial public offerings, tainted securities research and recommendations put out to the public, and, probably most important, misleading financial statements and accounting practices.

On the MARKET FRONT

EXCERPTS FROM CFA INSTITUTE STANDARDS OF PROFESSIONAL CONDUCT

I. Professionalism

- Knowledge of law. Members must understand knowledge of and comply with all applicable laws, rules, and regulations including the Code of Ethics and Standards of Professional Conduct.
- Independence and objectivity. Members shall maintain independence and objectivity in their professional activities.
- Misrepresentation. Members must not knowingly misrepresent investment analysis, recommendations, or other professional activities.

II. Integrity of Capital Markets

- Non-public information. Members must not exploit material non-public information.
- Market manipulation. Members shall not attempt to distort prices or trading volume with the intent to mislead market participants.

III. Duties to Clients

- Loyalty, prudence, and care. Members must place their clients' interests before their own and act with reasonable care on their behalf.
- Fair dealing. Members shall deal fairly and objectively with clients when making investment recommendations or taking actions.
- Suitability. Members shall make a reasonable inquiry into a client's financial situation, investment experience, and investment objectives prior to making appropriate investment recommendations.
- Performance presentation. Members shall attempt to ensure that investment performance is presented fairly, accurately, and completely.
- Confidentiality. Members must keep information about clients confidential unless the client permits disclosure.

IV. Duties to Employers

- Loyalty. Members must act for the benefit of their employer.
- Compensation. Members must not accept compensation from sources that would create a conflict of interest with their employer's interests without written consent from all involved parties.
- Supervisors. Members must make reasonable efforts to detect and prevent violation of applicable laws and regulations by anyone subject to their supervision.

V. Investment Analysis and Recommendations

- Diligence. Members must exercise diligence and have reasonable basis for investment analysis, recommendations, or actions.
- Communication. Members must distinguish fact from opinion in their presentation of analysis and disclose general principles of investment processes used in analysis.

VI. Conflicts of Interest

- Disclosure of conflicts. Members must disclose all matters that reasonably could be expected to impair their objectivity or interfere with their other duties.
- Priority of transactions. Transactions for clients and employers must have priority over transactions for the benefit of a member.

VII. Responsibilities as Member of CFA Institute

- Conduct. Members must not engage in conduct that compromises the reputation or integrity of the CFA Institute or CFA designation.

SOURCE: Excerpts from "Code of Ethics and Standards of Professional Conduct," *Standards of Practice Handbook*, 10th Ed.

The Sarbanes-Oxley Act was passed by Congress in 2002 in response to these problems. Among the key reforms are:

- Creation of the Public Company Accounting Oversight Board to oversee the auditing of public companies.
- Rules requiring independent financial experts to serve on audit committees of a firm's board of directors.
- CEOs and CFOs must now personally certify that their firms' financial reports "fairly represent, in all material respects, the operations and financial condition of the company," and are subject to personal penalties if those reports turn out to be misleading. Following the letter of GAAP rules may still be necessary, but it is no longer sufficient accounting practice.
- Auditors may no longer provide several other services to their clients. This is intended to prevent potential profits on consulting work from influencing the quality of their audit.
- The board of directors must be composed of independent directors and hold regular meetings of directors in which company management is not present (and therefore cannot impede or influence the discussion).

More recently, there has been a fair amount of push-back on Sarbanes-Oxley. Many observers believe that the compliance costs associated with the law are too onerous, especially for smaller firms, and that heavy-handed regulatory oversight is giving foreign locales an undue advantage over the United States when firms decide where to list their securities.

Moreover, the efficacy of single-country regulation is being tested in the face of increasing globalization and the ease with which funds can move across national borders.

One of the most contentious issues in regulation has to do with "rules" versus "principles." Rules-based regulation attempts to lay out specifically what practices are or are not allowed. This has generally been the American approach, particularly at the SEC. In contrast, principles-based regulation relies on a less explicitly defined set of understandings about risk taking, the goals of regulation, and the sorts of financial practices considered allowable. This has been the dominant approach in the U.K. and seems to be the more popular model for regulators throughout the world.

Insider Trading

inside information

Nonpublic knowledge about a corporation possessed by corporate officers, major owners, or other individuals with privileged access to information about the firm.

Regulations also prohibit insider trading. It is illegal for anyone to transact in securities to profit from **inside information,** that is, private information held by officers, directors, or major stockholders that has not yet been divulged to the public. But the definition of insiders can be ambiguous. While it is obvious that the chief financial officer of a firm is an insider, it is less clear whether the firm's biggest supplier can be considered an insider. Yet a supplier may deduce the firm's near-term prospects from significant changes in orders. This gives the supplier a unique form of private information, yet the supplier is not technically an insider. These ambiguities plague security analysts, whose job is to uncover as much information as possible concerning the firm's expected prospects. The distinction between legal private information and illegal inside information can be fuzzy. (We return to this issue in Chapter 12.)

The SEC requires officers, directors, and major stockholders to report all transactions in their firm's stock. A compendium of insider trades is published monthly in the SEC's *Official Summary of Securities Transactions and Holdings.* The idea is to inform the public of any implicit vote of confidence or no confidence made by insiders.

Insiders *do* exploit their knowledge. Three forms of evidence support this conclusion. First, there have been well-publicized convictions of principals in insider trading schemes.

Second, there is considerable evidence of "leakage" of useful information to some traders before any public announcement of that information. For example, share prices of firms announcing dividend increases (which the market interprets as good news concerning the firm's prospects) commonly increase in value a few days *before* the public announcement of the increase. Clearly, some investors are acting on the good news before it is released to the public. Share prices still rise substantially on the day of the public release of good news, however, indicating that insiders, or their associates, have not fully bid up the price of the stock to the level commensurate with the news.

A third form of evidence on insider trading has to do with returns earned on trades by insiders. Researchers have examined the SEC's summary of insider trading to measure the performance of insiders. In one of the best known of these studies, Jaffe (1974) examined the abnormal return of stocks over the months following purchases or sales by insiders. For months in which insider purchasers of a stock exceeded insider sellers of the stock by three or more, the stock had an abnormal return in the following eight months of about 5%. Moreover, when insider sellers exceeded insider buyers, the stock tended to perform poorly.

SUMMARY

- Firms issue securities to raise the capital necessary to finance their investments. Investment bankers market these securities to the public on the primary market. Investment bankers generally act as underwriters who purchase the securities from the firm and resell them to the public at a markup. Before the securities may be sold to the public, the firm must publish an SEC-approved prospectus that provides information on the firm's prospects.
- Already-issued securities are traded on the secondary market, that is, in organized stock markets, or, primarily for bonds, on the over-the-counter market. Brokerage firms holding licenses to trade on an exchange sell their services to individuals, charging commissions for executing trades on their behalf.
- Trading may take place in dealer markets, via electronic communication networks, or in specialist markets. In dealer markets, security dealers post bid and ask prices at which they are willing to trade. Brokers for individuals execute trades at the best available prices. In

www.mhhe.com/bkm

electronic markets, the existing book of limit orders provides the terms at which trades can be executed. Mutually agreeable offers to buy or sell securities are automatically crossed by the computer system operating the market. In specialist markets, the specialist acts to maintain an orderly market with price continuity. Specialists maintain a limit order book but also sell from or buy for their own inventories of stock.

- NASDAQ was traditionally a dealer market in which a network of dealers negotiated directly over sales of securities. The NYSE was traditionally a specialist market. In recent years, however, both exchanges dramatically increased their commitment to electronic and automated trading. Most trades today are electronic.
- Buying on margin means borrowing money from a broker in order to buy more securities than can be purchased with one's own money alone. By buying securities on a margin, an investor magnifies both the upside potential and the downside risk. If the equity in a margin account falls below the required maintenance level, the investor will get a margin call from the broker.
- Short-selling is the practice of selling securities that the seller does not own. The short-seller borrows the securities sold through a broker and may be required to cover the short position at any time on demand. The cash proceeds of a short sale are kept in escrow by the broker, and the broker usually requires that the short-seller deposit additional cash or securities to serve as margin (collateral) for the short sale.
- Securities trading is regulated by the Securities and Exchange Commission, by other government agencies, and through self-regulation of the exchanges. Many of the important regulations have to do with full disclosure of relevant information concerning the securities in question. Insider trading rules also prohibit traders from attempting to profit from inside information.

KEY TERMS

algorithmic trading, 66
ask price, 59
auction market, 59
bid–ask spread, 59
bid price, 59
blocks, 67
dark pools, 67
dealer markets, 58
electronic communication networks (ECNs), 62
high-frequency trading, 66
initial public offering (IPO), 56
inside information, 78
latency, 65
limit buy (sell) order, 59
margin, 69
NASDAQ Stock Market, 62
over-the-counter (OTC) market, 61
primary market, 55
private placement, 55
prospectus, 56
secondary market, 55
short sale, 72
specialist, 62
stock exchanges, 65
stop order, 60
underwriters, 56

PROBLEM SETS

Select problems are available in McGraw-Hill's *Connect Finance.* Please see the Supplements section of the book's frontmatter for more information.

Basic

1. What is the difference between an IPO (initial public offering) and an SEO (seasoned equity offering)? ***(LO 3-1)***
2. What are some different components of the effective costs of buying or selling shares of stock? ***(LO 3-3)***
3. What is the difference between a primary and secondary market? ***(LO 3-3)***
4. How do security dealers earn their profits? ***(LO 3-3)***
5. In what circumstances are private placements more likely to be used than public offerings? ***(LO 3-1)***
6. What are the differences between a stop-loss order, a limit sell order, and a market order? ***(LO 3-3)***
7. Why have average trade sizes declined in recent years? ***(LO 3-3)***
8. What is the role of an underwriter? A prospectus? ***(LO 3-1)***
9. How do margin trades magnify both the upside potential and downside risk of an investment portfolio? ***(LO 3-4)***

10. A market order has: *(LO 3-2)*
    a. Price uncertainty but not execution uncertainty.
    b. Both price uncertainty and execution uncertainty.
    c. Execution uncertainty but not price uncertainty.

11. Where would an illiquid security in a developing country *most likely* trade? *(LO 3-3)*
    a. Broker markets.
    b. Electronic crossing networks.
    c. Electronic limit-order markets.

Intermediate

12. Suppose you short-sell 100 shares of IBM, now selling at $200 per share. *(LO 3-4)*
    a. What is your maximum possible loss?
    b. What happens to the maximum loss if you simultaneously place a stop-buy order at $210?
13. Call one full-service broker and one discount broker and find out the transaction costs of implementing the following strategies: *(LO 3-3)*
    a. Buying 100 shares of IBM now and selling them six months from now.
    b. Investing an equivalent amount in six-month at-the-money call options on IBM stock now and selling them six months from now.
14. DRK, Inc., has just sold 100,000 shares in an initial public offering. The underwriter's explicit fees were $60,000. The offering price for the shares was $40, but immediately upon issue, the share price jumped to $44. *(LO 3-1)*
    a. What is your best guess as to the total cost to DRK of the equity issue?
    b. Is the entire cost of the underwriting a source of profit to the underwriters?
15. Dée Trader opens a brokerage account and purchases 300 shares of Internet Dreams at $40 per share. She borrows $4,000 from her broker to help pay for the purchase. The interest rate on the loan is 8%. *(LO 3-4)*
    a. What is the margin in Dée's account when she first purchases the stock?
    b. If the share price falls to $30 per share by the end of the year, what is the remaining margin in her account? If the maintenance margin requirement is 30%, will she receive a margin call?
    c. What is the rate of return on her investment?
16. Old Economy Traders opened an account to short-sell 1,000 shares of Internet Dreams from the previous question. The initial margin requirement was 50%. (The margin account pays no interest.) A year later, the price of Internet Dreams has risen from $40 to $50, and the stock has paid a dividend of $2 per share. *(LO 3-4)*
    a. What is the remaining margin in the account?
    b. If the maintenance margin requirement is 30%, will Old Economy receive a margin call?
    c. What is the rate of return on the investment?
17. Consider the following limit order book for a share of stock. The last trade in the stock occurred at a price of $50. *(LO 3-3)*

Limit Buy Orders		Limit Sell Orders	
Price	**Shares**	**Price**	**Shares**
$49.75	500	$50.25	100
49.50	800	51.50	100
49.25	500	54.75	300
49.00	200	58.25	100
48.50	600		

    a. If a market buy order for 100 shares comes in, at what price will it be filled?
    b. At what price would the next market buy order be filled?
    c. If you were a security dealer, would you want to increase or decrease your inventory of this stock?

Please visit us at www.mhhe.com/bkm

18. You are bullish on Telecom stock. The current market price is $50 per share, and you have $5,000 of your own to invest. You borrow an additional $5,000 from your broker at an interest rate of 8% per year and invest $10,000 in the stock. *(LO 3-4)*
    a. What will be your rate of return if the price of Telecom stock goes up by 10% during the next year? (Ignore the expected dividend.)
    b. How far does the price of Telecom stock have to fall for you to get a margin call if the maintenance margin is 30%? Assume the price fall happens immediately.

Please visit us at www.mhhe.com/bkm

19. You are bearish on Telecom and decide to sell short 100 shares at the current market price of $50 per share. *(LO 3-4)*
    a. How much in cash or securities must you put into your brokerage account if the broker's initial margin requirement is 50% of the value of the short position?
    b. How high can the price of the stock go before you get a margin call if the maintenance margin is 30% of the value of the short position?
20. Here is some price information on Marriott:

	Bid	Asked
Marriott	19.95	20.05

You have placed a stop-loss order to sell at $20. What are you telling your broker? Given market prices, will your order be executed? *(LO 3-2)*

21. Here is some price information on Fincorp stock. Suppose first that Fincorp trades in a dealer market. *(LO 3-2)*

Bid	Asked
55.25	55.50

    a. Suppose you have submitted an order to your broker to buy at market. At what price will your trade be executed?
    b. Suppose you have submitted an order to sell at market. At what price will your trade be executed?
    c. Suppose you have submitted a limit order to sell at $55.62. What will happen?
    d. Suppose you have submitted a limit order to buy at $55.37. What will happen?
22. Now reconsider the previous problem assuming that Fincorp sells in an exchange market like the NYSE. *(LO 3-2)*
    a. Is there any chance for price improvement in the market orders considered in parts (*a*) and (*b*)?
    b. Is there any chance of an immediate trade at $55.37 for the limit buy order in part (*d*)?
23. You've borrowed $20,000 on margin to buy shares in Disney, which is now selling at $40 per share. Your account starts at the initial margin requirement of 50%. The maintenance margin is 35%. Two days later, the stock price falls to $35 per share. *(LO 3-4)*
    a. Will you receive a margin call?
    b. How low can the price of Disney shares fall before you receive a margin call?
24. On January 1, you sold short one round lot (that is, 100 shares) of Snow's stock at $21 per share. On March 1, a dividend of $3 per share was paid. On April 1, you covered the short sale by buying the stock at a price of $15 per share. You paid 50 cents per share in commissions for each transaction. What is the value of your account on April 1? *(LO 3-4)*

Challenge

Please visit us at www.mhhe.com/bkm

25. Suppose that Intel currently is selling at $40 per share. You buy 500 shares using $15,000 of your own money, borrowing the remainder of the purchase price from your broker. The rate on the margin loan is 8%. *(LO 3-4)*
    a. What is the percentage increase in the net worth of your brokerage account if the price of Intel *immediately* changes to (i) $44; (ii) $40; (iii) $36? What is the relationship between your percentage return and the percentage change in the price of Intel?

b. If the maintenance margin is 25%, how low can Intel's price fall before you get a margin call?

c. How would your answer to (*b*) change if you had financed the initial purchase with only $10,000 of your own money?

d. What is the rate of return on your margined position (assuming again that you invest $15,000 of your own money) if Intel is selling *after one year* at (i) $44; (ii) $40; (iii) $36? What is the relationship between your percentage return and the percentage change in the price of Intel? Assume that Intel pays no dividends.

e. Continue to assume that a year has passed. How low can Intel's price fall before you get a margin call?

Please visit us at www.mhhe.com/bkm

26. Suppose that you sell short 500 shares of Intel, currently selling for $40 per share, and give your broker $15,000 to establish your margin account. ***(LO 3-4)***

a. If you earn no interest on the funds in your margin account, what will be your rate of return after one year if Intel stock is selling at (i) $44; (ii) $40; (iii) $36? Assume that Intel pays no dividends.

b. If the maintenance margin is 25%, how high can Intel's price rise before you get a margin call?

c. Redo parts (*a*) and (*b*), but now assume that Intel also has paid a year-end dividend of $1 per share. The prices in part (*a*) should be interpreted as ex-dividend, that is, prices after the dividend has been paid.

CFA® PROBLEMS

CFA Problems

1. If you place a stop-loss order to sell 100 shares of stock at $55 when the current price is $62, how much will you receive for each share if the price drops to $50? ***(LO 3-2)***
   a. $50
   b. $55
   c. $54.87
   d. Cannot tell from the information given
2. Specialists on the New York Stock Exchange traditionally did all of the following *except:* ***(LO 3-3)***
   a. Act as dealers for their own accounts.
   b. Execute limit orders.
   c. Help provide liquidity to the marketplace.
   d. Act as odd-lot dealers.

WEB *master*

There are several factors that should be considered when you are choosing which brokerage firm(s) to use to execute your trades. There are also a wide range of services that claim to objectively recommend brokerage firms. Many are actually sponsored by the brokerage firms themselves.

Go to the website **www.consumersearch.com/online-brokers/reviews** and read the information provided under "Our Sources." Then follow the link for the Barron's ratings. Here you can read the Barron's annual broker survey and download the "How the Brokers Stack Up" report, which contains a list of fees. Suppose that you have $3,000 to invest and want to put it in a non-IRA account.

1. Are all of the brokerage firms suitable if you want to open a cash account? Are they all suitable if you want a margin account?
2. Choose two of the firms listed. Assume that you want to buy 200 shares of LLY stock using a market order. If the order is filled at $42 per share, how much will the commission be for the two firms if you place an online order?
3. Are there any maintenance fees associated with the account at either brokerage firm?
4. Now assume that you have a margin account and the balance is $3,000. Calculate the interest rate you would pay if you borrowed money to buy stock.

SOLUTIONS TO CONCEPT checks

3.1 Limited-time shelf registration was introduced because of its favorable trade-off of saving issue costs versus providing disclosure. Allowing unlimited shelf registration would circumvent "blue sky" laws that ensure proper disclosure as the financial circumstances of the firm change over time.

3.2 *a.* Used cars trade in dealer markets (used-car lots or auto dealerships) and in direct search markets when individuals advertise in local newspapers or Internet listings.

b. Paintings trade in broker markets when clients commission brokers to buy or sell art for them, in dealer markets at art galleries, and in auction markets.

c. Rare coins trade in dealer markets, for example, in coin shops or shows, but they also trade in auctions and in direct search markets when individuals advertise they want to buy or sell coins.

3.3 *a.* You should give your broker a market order. It will be executed immediately and is the cheapest type of order in terms of brokerage fees.

b. You should give your broker a limit buy order, which will be executed only if the shares can be obtained at a price about 5% below the current price.

c. You should give your broker a stop-loss order, which will be executed if the share price starts falling. The limit or stop price should be close to the current price to avoid the possibility of large losses.

3.4 Solving

$$\frac{100P - \$4{,}000}{100P} = .4$$

yields $P = \$66.67$ per share.

3.5 The investor will purchase 150 shares, with a rate of return as follows:

Year-End Change in Price	Year-End Value of Shares	Repayment of Principal and Interest	Investor's Rate of Return
30%	$19,500	$5,450	40.5%
No change	15,000	5,450	−4.5
−30%	10,500	5,450	−49.5

3.6 *a.* Once Dot Bomb stock goes up to $110, your balance sheet will be:

Assets		Liabilities and Owners' Equity	
Cash	$100,000	Short position in Dot Bomb	$110,000
T-bills	50,000	Equity	40,000

b. Solving

$$\frac{\$150{,}000 - 1{,}000P}{1{,}000P} = .4$$

yields $P = \$107.14$ per share.

Chapter 4

Mutual Funds and Other Investment Companies

Learning Objectives:

- **LO4-1** Cite advantages and disadvantages of investing with an investment company rather than buying securities directly.
- **LO4-2** Contrast open-end mutual funds with closed-end funds, unit investment trusts, hedge funds, and exchange-traded funds.
- **LO4-3** Define *net asset value* and measure the rate of return on a mutual fund.
- **LO4-4** Classify mutual funds according to investment style.
- **LO4-5** Demonstrate the impact of expenses and turnover on mutual fund investment performance.

The previous chapter provided an introduction to the mechanics of trading securities and the structure of the markets in which securities trade. Increasingly, however, individual investors are choosing not to trade securities directly for their own accounts. Instead, they direct their funds to investment companies that purchase securities on their behalf. The most important of these financial intermediaries are mutual funds, which are currently owned by about one-half of U.S. households. Other types of investment companies, such as unit investment trusts and closed-end funds, also merit distinction.

We begin the chapter by describing and comparing the various types of investment companies available to investors—unit investment trusts, closed-end investment companies, and open-end investment companies, more commonly known as mutual funds. We devote most of our attention to mutual funds, examining the functions of such funds, their investment styles and policies, and the costs of investing in these funds.

Next, we take a first look at the investment performance of these funds. We consider the impact of expenses and turnover on net performance and examine the extent to which performance is consistent from one period to the next. In other words, will the mutual funds that were the best past performers be the best *future* performers? Finally, we discuss sources of information on mutual funds and consider in detail the information provided in the most comprehensive guide, Morningstar's *Mutual Fund Sourcebook.*

Related websites for this chapter are available at www.mhhe.com/bkm.

4.1 INVESTMENT COMPANIES

Investment companies are financial intermediaries that collect funds from individual investors and invest those funds in a potentially wide range of securities or other assets. Pooling of assets is the key idea behind investment companies. Each investor has a claim to the portfolio established by the investment company in proportion to the amount invested. These companies thus provide a mechanism for small investors to "team up" to obtain the benefits of large-scale investing.

investment companies

Financial intermediaries that invest the funds of individual investors in securities or other assets.

Investment companies perform several important functions for their investors:

1. *Record keeping and administration.* Investment companies issue periodic status reports, keeping track of capital gains distributions, dividends, investments, and redemptions, and they may reinvest dividend and interest income for shareholders.
2. *Diversification and divisibility.* By pooling their money, investment companies enable investors to hold fractional shares of many different securities. They can act as large investors even if any individual shareholder cannot.
3. *Professional management.* Investment companies can support full-time staffs of security analysts and portfolio managers who attempt to achieve superior investment results for their investors.
4. *Lower transaction costs.* Because they trade large blocks of securities, investment companies can achieve substantial savings on brokerage fees and commissions.

While all investment companies pool the assets of individual investors, they also need to divide claims to those assets among those investors. Investors buy shares in investment companies, and ownership is proportional to the number of shares purchased. The value of each share is called the **net asset value,** or **NAV.** Net asset value equals assets minus liabilities expressed on a per-share basis:

net asset value (NAV)

Assets minus liabilities expressed on a per-share basis.

$$\text{Net asset value} = \frac{\text{Market value of assets minus liabilities}}{\text{Shares outstanding}}$$

Consider a mutual fund that manages a portfolio of securities worth \$120 million. Suppose the fund owes \$4 million to its investment advisers and owes another \$1 million for rent, wages due, and miscellaneous expenses. The fund has 5 million shares. Then

$$\text{Net asset value} = \frac{\$120 \text{ million} - \$5 \text{ million}}{5 \text{ million shares}} = \$23 \text{ per share}$$

CONCEPT check 4.1

Consider these data from the March 2011 balance sheet of the Growth and Income mutual fund sponsored by the Vanguard Group. (All values are in millions.) What was the net asset value of the portfolio?

Assets:	\$3,352.8
Liabilities:	\$ 270.3
Shares:	110.2

4.2 TYPES OF INVESTMENT COMPANIES

In the United States, investment companies are classified by the Investment Company Act of 1940 as either unit investment trusts or managed investment companies. The portfolios of unit investment trusts are essentially fixed and thus are called "unmanaged." In contrast, managed companies are so named because securities in their investment portfolios continually are bought and sold: The portfolios are managed. Managed companies are further classified as either closed-end or open-end. Open-end companies are what we commonly call *mutual funds.*

Unit Investment Trusts

unit investment trusts

Money pooled from many investors that is invested in a portfolio fixed for the life of the fund.

Unit investment trusts are pools of money invested in a portfolio that is fixed for the life of the fund. To form a unit investment trust, a sponsor, typically a brokerage firm, buys a portfolio of securities which are deposited into a trust. It then sells to the public shares, or "units," in the trust, called *redeemable trust certificates.* All income and payments of principal from the portfolio are paid out by the fund's trustees (a bank or trust company) to the shareholders.

There is little active management of a unit investment trust because once established, the portfolio composition is fixed; hence these trusts are referred to as *unmanaged.* Trusts tend to invest in relatively uniform types of assets; for example, one trust may invest in municipal bonds, another in corporate bonds. The uniformity of the portfolio is consistent with the lack of active management. The trusts provide investors a vehicle to purchase a pool of one particular type of asset, which can be included in an overall portfolio as desired. The lack of active management of the portfolio implies that management fees can be lower than those of managed funds.

Sponsors of unit investment trusts earn their profit by selling shares in the trust at a premium to the cost of acquiring the underlying assets. For example, a trust that has purchased $5 million of assets may sell 5,000 shares to the public at a price of $1,030 per share, which (assuming the trust has no liabilities) represents a 3% premium over the net asset value of the securities held by the trust. The 3% premium is the trustee's fee for establishing the trust.

Investors who wish to liquidate their holdings of a unit investment trust may sell the shares back to the trustee for net asset value. The trustees can either sell enough securities from the asset portfolio to obtain the cash necessary to pay the investor, or they may instead sell the shares to a new investor (again at a slight premium to net asset value).

Unit investment trusts have steadily lost market share to mutual funds in recent years. Assets in such trusts declined from $105 billion in 1990 to only $51 billion in 2010.

Managed Investment Companies

There are two types of managed companies: closed-end and open-end. In both cases, the fund's board of directors, which is elected by shareholders, hires a management company to manage the portfolio for an annual fee that typically ranges from .2% to 1.5% of assets. In many cases the management company is the firm that organized the fund. For example, Fidelity Management and Research Corporation sponsors many Fidelity mutual funds and is responsible for managing the portfolios. It assesses a management fee on each Fidelity fund. In other cases, a mutual fund will hire an outside portfolio manager. For example, Vanguard has hired Wellington Management as the investment adviser for its Wellington Fund. Most management companies have contracts to manage several funds.

open-end fund

A fund that issues or redeems its shares at net asset value.

closed-end fund

Shares may not be redeemed, but instead are traded at prices that can differ from net asset value.

Open-end funds stand ready to redeem or issue shares at their net asset value (although both purchases and redemptions may involve sales charges). When investors in open-end funds wish to "cash out" their shares, they sell them back to the fund at NAV. In contrast, **closed-end funds** do not redeem or issue shares. Investors in closed-end funds who wish to cash out must sell their shares to other investors. Shares of closed-end funds are traded on organized exchanges and can be purchased through brokers just like other common stock; their prices therefore can differ from NAV.

FIGURE 4.1

Closed-end mutual funds

Source: Compiled from data obtained from *The Wall Street Journal Online,* July 14, 2011. Reprinted by permission of *The Wall Street Journal,* © 2011 Dow Jones & Company, Inc. All Rights Reserved Worldwide.

CLOSED-END FUNDS

FUND	NAV	MKT PRICE	PREM/DISC	52 WEEK RETURN %
Adams Express Company (ADX)	12.89	11.11	−13.81	26.13
Advent/Clay Enhcd G & I (LCM)	12.16	11.58	−4.77	23.52
BlackRock Equity Div (BDV)	10.65	10.03	−5.82	27.39
BlackRock Str Eq Div Achv (BDT)	11.80	10.68	−9.49	26.17
Cohen & Steers CE Oppty (FOF)	14.64	13.46	−8.06	25.17
Cohen & Steers Dvd Mjrs (DVM)	14.70	13.82	−5.99	49.28
Eaton Vance Tax Div Inc (EVT)	18.75	17.19	−8.32	29.89
Gabelli Div & Inc Tr (GDV)	18.64	16.58	−11.05	43.52
Gabelli Equity Trust (GAB)	6.08	6.10	0.33	48.48
General Amer Investors (GAM)	32.71	28.26	−13.60	30.93
Guggenheim Enh Eq Inc (GPM)	9.58	9.65	0.73	38.93

Figure 4.1 is a listing of closed-end funds from *The Wall Street Journal Online.* The first column gives the fund's name and ticker symbol. The next two columns give the fund's most recent net asset value and closing share price. The premium or discount is the percentage difference between price and NAV: (Price − NAV)/NAV. Notice that there are more funds selling at discounts to NAV (indicated by negative differences) than premiums. Finally, the 52-week return based on the percentage change in share price plus dividend income is presented in the last column.

The common divergence of price from net asset value, often by wide margins, is a puzzle that has yet to be fully explained. To see why this is a puzzle, consider a closed-end fund that is selling at a discount from net asset value. If the fund were to sell all the assets in the portfolio, it would realize proceeds equal to net asset value. The difference between the market price of the fund and the fund's NAV would represent the per-share increase in the wealth of the fund's investors. Despite this apparent profit opportunity, sizable discounts seem to persist for long periods of time.

Moreover, several studies have shown that, on average, fund premiums or discounts tend to dissipate over time, so funds selling at a discount receive a boost to their rate of return as the discount shrinks. Pontiff (1995) estimates that a fund selling at a 20% discount would have an expected 12-month return more than 6% greater than funds selling at net asset value.

Interestingly, while many closed-end funds sell at a discount from net asset value, the prices of these funds when originally issued are often above NAV. This is a further puzzle, as it is hard to explain why investors would purchase these newly issued funds at a premium to NAV when the shares tend to fall to a discount shortly after issue.

In contrast to closed-end funds, the price of open-end funds cannot fall below NAV, because these funds stand ready to redeem shares at NAV. The offering price will exceed NAV, however, if the fund carries a **load.** A load is, in effect, a sales charge. Load funds are sold by securities brokers and directly by mutual fund groups.

load

A sales commission charged on a mutual fund.

Unlike closed-end funds, open-end mutual funds do not trade on organized exchanges. Instead, investors simply buy shares from and liquidate through the investment company at net asset value. Thus, the number of outstanding shares of these funds changes daily. In early 2011, about $240 billion of assets were held in closed-end funds.

Other Investment Organizations

Some intermediaries are not formally organized or regulated as investment companies but nevertheless serve similar functions. Among the more important are commingled funds, real estate investment trusts, and hedge funds.

Commingled funds Commingled funds are partnerships of investors that pool funds. The management firm that organizes the partnership, for example, a bank or insurance company, manages the funds for a fee. Typical partners in a commingled fund might be trust or retirement accounts that have portfolios much larger than those of most individual investors but are still too small to warrant managing on a separate basis.

Commingled funds are similar in form to open-end mutual funds. Instead of shares, though, the fund offers *units,* which are bought and sold at net asset value. A bank or insurance company may offer an array of different commingled funds, for example, a money market fund, a bond fund, and a common stock fund.

Real Estate Investment Trusts (REITs) A REIT is similar to a closed-end fund. REITs invest in real estate or loans secured by real estate. Besides issuing shares, they raise capital by borrowing from banks and issuing bonds or mortgages. Most of them are highly leveraged, with a typical debt ratio of 70%.

There are two principal kinds of REITs. *Equity trusts* invest in real estate directly, whereas *mortgage trusts* invest primarily in mortgage and construction loans. REITs generally are established by banks, insurance companies, or mortgage companies, which then serve as investment managers to earn a fee.

hedge fund

A private investment pool, open to wealthy or institutional investors, that is exempt from SEC regulation and can therefore pursue more speculative policies than mutual funds.

Hedge funds Like mutual funds, **hedge funds** are vehicles that allow private investors to pool assets to be invested by a fund manager. Unlike mutual funds, however, hedge funds are commonly structured as private partnerships and thus are not subject to many SEC regulations. Typically they are open only to wealthy or institutional investors. Many require investors to agree to initial "lock-ups," that is, periods as long as several years in which investments cannot be withdrawn. Lock-ups allow hedge funds to invest in illiquid assets without worrying about meeting demands for redemption of funds. Moreover, since hedge funds are only lightly regulated, their managers can pursue other investment strategies that are not open to mutual fund managers, for example, heavy use of derivatives, short sales, and leverage.

Hedge funds by design are empowered to invest in a wide range of investments, with various funds focusing on derivatives, distressed firms, currency speculation, convertible bonds, emerging markets, merger arbitrage, and so on. Other funds may jump from one asset class to another as perceived investment opportunities shift.

Hedge funds enjoyed great growth in the last several years, with assets under management ballooning from about $50 billion in 1990 to nearly $2 trillion in 2011. Because of their recent prominence, we devote all of Chapter 20 to these funds.

4.3 MUTUAL FUNDS

Mutual fund is the common name for an open-end investment company. This is the dominant investment company in the U.S. today, accounting for about 90% of investment company assets. Assets under management in the U.S. mutual fund industry were nearly $12 trillion in early 2011. Roughly another $11 trillion was invested in mutual funds of non-U.S. sponsors.

Investment Policies

Each mutual fund has a specified investment policy, which is described in the fund's prospectus. For example, money market mutual funds hold the short-term, low-risk instruments of the money market (see Chapter 2 for a review of these securities), while bond funds hold fixed-income securities. Some funds have even more narrowly defined mandates. For example, some bond funds will hold primarily Treasury bonds, others primarily mortgage-backed securities.

Management companies manage a family, or "complex," of mutual funds. They organize an entire collection of funds and then collect a management fee for operating them. By managing a collection of funds under one umbrella, these companies make it easy for investors to allocate assets across market sectors and to switch assets across funds while still benefiting from centralized record keeping. Some of the most well-known management companies are Fidelity, Vanguard, Putnam, and Dreyfus. Each offers an array of open-end mutual funds with different investment policies. In early 2011, there were over 8,000 mutual funds in the United States, which were offered by 669 fund complexes.

Some of the more important fund types, classified by investment policy, are discussed next.

Money market funds These funds invest in money market securities such as commercial paper, repurchase agreements, or certificates of deposit. The average maturity of these assets tends to be a bit more than one month. They usually offer check-writing features, and net asset value is fixed at $1 per share,[1] so that there are no tax implications such as capital gains or losses associated with redemption of shares.

Equity funds Equity funds invest primarily in stock, although they may, at the portfolio manager's discretion, also hold fixed-income or other types of securities. Equity funds commonly will hold about 5% of total assets in money market securities to provide the liquidity necessary to meet potential redemption of shares.

Stock funds are traditionally classified by their emphasis on capital appreciation versus current income. Thus *income funds* tend to hold shares of firms with high dividend yields that provide high current income. *Growth funds* are willing to forgo current income, focusing instead on prospects for capital gains. While the classification of these funds is couched in terms of income versus capital gains, it is worth noting that in practice the more relevant distinction concerns the level of risk these funds assume. Growth stocks—and therefore growth funds—are typically riskier and respond more dramatically to changes in economic conditions than do income funds.

Specialized sector funds Some equity funds, called *sector funds,* concentrate on a particular industry. For example, Fidelity markets dozens of "select funds," each of which invests in a specific industry such as biotechnology, utilities, precious metals, or telecommunications. Other funds specialize in securities of particular countries.

Bond funds As the name suggests, these funds specialize in the fixed-income sector. Within that sector, however, there is considerable room for further specialization. For example, various funds will concentrate on corporate bonds, Treasury bonds, mortgage-backed securities, or municipal (tax-free) bonds. Indeed, some municipal bond funds invest only in bonds of a particular state (or even city!) in order to satisfy the investment desires of residents of that state who wish to avoid local as well as federal taxes on interest income. Many funds also specialize by maturity, ranging from short-term to intermediate to long-term, or by the credit risk of the issuer, ranging from very safe to high-yield or "junk" bonds.

International funds Many funds have international focus. *Global funds* invest in securities worldwide, including the United States. In contrast, *international funds* invest in securities of firms located outside the U.S. *Regional funds* concentrate on a particular part of the world, and *emerging market funds* invest in companies of developing nations.

Balanced funds Some funds are designed to be candidates for an individual's entire investment portfolio. These *balanced funds* hold both equities and fixed-income securities in relatively stable proportions. *Life-cycle funds* are balanced funds in which the asset mix can range from aggressive (primarily marketed to younger investors) to conservative (directed at older investors). Static allocation life-cycle funds maintain a stable mix across stocks and bonds, while *targeted-maturity funds* gradually become more conservative as the investor ages.

[1]The box in Chapter 2 noted that money market funds are able to maintain NAV at $1 because they invest in short-maturity debt of the highest quality with minimal price risk. In rare circumstances, funds have experienced losses sufficient to drive NAV below $1. In September 2008, Reserve Primary Fund, the nation's oldest money market fund, broke the buck when it suffered losses on its holding of Lehman Brothers commercial paper, and its NAV fell to $.97.

funds of funds

Mutual funds that primarily invest in shares of other mutual funds.

Many balanced funds are in fact **funds of funds.** These are mutual funds that primarily invest in shares of other mutual funds. Balanced funds of funds invest in equity and bond funds in proportions suited to their investment goals.

Asset allocation and flexible funds These funds are similar to balanced funds in that they hold both stocks and bonds. However, asset allocation funds may dramatically vary the proportions allocated to each market in accord with the portfolio manager's forecast of the relative performance of each sector. Hence, these funds are engaged in market timing and are not designed to be low-risk investment vehicles.

Index funds An index fund tries to match the performance of a broad market index. The fund buys shares in securities included in a particular index in proportion to the security's representation in that index. For example, the Vanguard 500 Index Fund is a mutual fund that replicates the composition of the Standard & Poor's 500 stock price index. Because the S&P 500 is a value-weighted index, the fund buys shares in each S&P 500 company in proportion to the market value of that company's outstanding equity. Investment in an index fund is a low-cost way for small investors to pursue a passive investment strategy—that is, to invest without engaging in security analysis. Nearly 25% of assets invested in equity funds in 2012 were in index funds.

Of course, index funds can be tied to nonequity indexes as well. For example, Vanguard offers a bond index fund and a real estate index fund.

Table 4.1 breaks down the number of mutual funds by investment orientation. Sometimes the fund name describes its investment policy. For example, Vanguard's GNMA Fund invests in mortgage-backed securities, the Municipal Intermediate Fund invests in intermediate-term municipal bonds, and the High-Yield Corporate Bond Fund invests in large part in

TABLE 4.1 U.S. mutual funds by investment classification

	Assets ($ billion)	Percent of Total Assets	Number of Funds
Equity Funds			
Capital appreciation focus	$ 2,912	24.2%	3,037
World/international	1,660	13.8	968
Total return	1,950	16.2	762
Total equity funds	$ 6,522	54.2%	4,767
Bond Funds			
Corporate	$ 301	2.5%	293
High yield	157	1.3	206
World	84	0.7	122
Government	203	1.7	301
Strategic income	560	4.7	370
Single-state municipal	156	1.3	451
National municipal	218	1.8	224
Total bond funds	$ 1,679	14.0%	1,967
Hybrid (bond/stock) funds	$ 713	5.9%	488
Money market funds			
Taxable	$ 2,642	22.0%	548
Tax-exempt	465	3.9	259
Total money market funds	$ 3,107	25.8%	807
Total	$12,021	100.0%	8,029

Note: Column sums subject to rounding error.

Source: Investment Company Institute, *2011 Mutual Fund Fact Book.* Copyright © 2011 by the Investment Company Institute.

speculative grade, or "junk," bonds with high yields. However, names of common stock funds often reflect little or nothing about their investment policies. Examples are Vanguard's Windsor and Wellington funds.

How Funds Are Sold

Mutual funds are generally marketed to the public either directly by the fund underwriter or indirectly through brokers acting on behalf of the underwriter. Direct-marketed funds are sold through the mail, various offices of the fund, over the phone, and, increasingly, over the Internet. Investors contact the fund directly to purchase shares. For example, if you look at the financial pages of your local newspaper, you will see several advertisements for funds, along with toll-free phone numbers that you can call to receive a fund's prospectus and an application to open an account.

About half of fund sales today are distributed through a sales force. Brokers or financial advisers receive a commission for selling shares to investors. (Ultimately, the commission is paid by the investor. More on this shortly.)

Investors who rely on their broker's advice to select their mutual funds should be aware that brokers may have a conflict of interest with regard to fund selection. This arises from a practice called *revenue sharing,* in which fund companies pay the brokerage firm for preferential treatment when making investment recommendations. The payment sometimes comes in the form of direct payments, computed either as a one-time payment based on sales of the mutual fund or as an ongoing payment based on fund assets held by the brokerage's clients.

Many funds also are sold through "financial supermarkets" that can sell shares in funds of many complexes. These programs allow customers to buy funds from many different fund groups. Instead of charging customers a sales commission, the supermarket splits management fees with the mutual fund company. Another advantage is unified record keeping for all funds purchased from the supermarket, even if the funds are offered by different complexes. On the other hand, many contend that these supermarkets result in higher expense ratios because mutual funds pass along the costs of participating in these programs in the form of higher management fees.

4.4 COSTS OF INVESTING IN MUTUAL FUNDS

Fee Structure

An individual investor choosing a mutual fund should consider not only the fund's stated investment policy and past performance, but also its management fees and other expenses. Comparative data on virtually all important aspects of mutual funds are available in the annual reports prepared by CDA/Wiesenberger or in Morningstar's *Mutual Fund Sourcebook,* which can be found in many academic and public libraries. You should be aware of four general classes of fees.

Operating expenses Operating expenses are the costs incurred by the mutual fund in operating the portfolio, including administrative expenses and advisory fees paid to the investment manager. These expenses, usually expressed as a percentage of total assets under management, may range from 0.2% to 2%. Shareholders do not receive an explicit bill for these operating expenses; however, the expenses periodically are deducted from the assets of the fund. Shareholders pay for these expenses through the reduced value of the portfolio.

The simple average of the expense ratio of equity funds in the U.S. was 1.43% in 2011. But larger funds tend to have lower expense ratios (and investors place more of their assets in lower-cost funds), so the average expense ratio weighted by assets under management is considerably smaller, .79%.

In addition to operating expenses, most funds assess fees to pay for marketing and distribution costs. These charges are used primarily to pay the brokers or financial advisers who sell the funds to the public. Investors can avoid these expenses by buying shares directly from the fund sponsor, but many investors are willing to incur these distribution fees in return for the advice they may receive from their broker.

Front-end load A front-end load is a commission or sales charge paid when you purchase the shares. These charges, which are used primarily to pay the brokers who sell the funds, may not exceed 8.5%, but in practice they are rarely higher than 6%. *Low-load funds* have loads that range up to 3% of invested funds. *No-load funds* have no front-end sales charges. About half of all funds today (measured by assets) are no load. Loads effectively reduce the amount of money invested. For example, each $1,000 paid for a fund with a 6% load results in a sales charge of $60 and fund investment of only $940. You need cumulative returns of 6.4% of your net investment (60/940 = .064) just to break even.

Back-end load A back-end load is a redemption, or "exit," fee incurred when you sell your shares. Typically, funds that impose back-end loads start them at 5% or 6% and reduce them by one percentage point for every year the funds are left invested. Thus, an exit fee that starts at 6% would fall to 4% by the start of your third year. These charges are known more formally as "contingent deferred sales charges."

12b-1 fees

Annual fees charged by a mutual fund to pay for marketing and distribution costs.

12b-1 charges The Securities and Exchange Commission allows the managers of so-called 12b-1 funds to use fund assets to pay for distribution costs such as advertising, promotional literature including annual reports and prospectuses, and, most important, commissions paid to brokers who sell the fund to investors. These **12b-1 fees** are named after the SEC rule that permits use of these plans. Funds may use annual 12b-1 charges instead of, or in addition to, front-end loads to generate the fees with which to pay brokers. As with operating expenses, investors are not explicitly billed for 12b-1 charges. Instead, the fees are deducted from the assets of the fund. Therefore, 12b-1 fees (if any) must be added to operating expenses to obtain the true annual expense ratio of the fund. The SEC now requires that all funds include in the prospectus a consolidated expense table that summarizes all relevant fees. The 12b-1 fees are limited to 1% of a fund's average net assets per year.[2]

Many funds offer "classes" which represent ownership in the same portfolio of securities, but with different combinations of fees. Typical Class A shares have front-end loads and a small 12b-1 fee, often around .25%. Class B shares rely on larger 12b-1 fees, commonly 1%, and often charge a modest back-end load. If an investor holds Class B shares for a long enough duration, typically 6–8 years, the shares often will convert into Class A shares which have lower 12b-1 fees. Class C shares generally rely on 12b-1 fees and back-end loads. These shares usually will not convert to Class A shares.

EXAMPLE 4.1

Fees for Various Classes (Dreyfus Equity Growth Fund)

Here are fees for different classes of the Dreyfus Equity Growth Fund in 2011. Notice the trade-off between the front-end loads and the 12b-1 charges.

	Class A	Class B	Class C
Front-end load	0–5.75%[a]	0	0
Back-end load	0	0–4%[b]	0–1%[b]
12b-1 fees[c]	.25%	1.0	1.0
Expense ratio	1.0%	1.72%	1.05%

Notes:
[a]Depending on size of investment.
[b]Depending on years until holdings are sold.
[c]Including service fee of .25%.

[2]The maximum 12b-1 charge for the sale of the fund is .75%. However, an additional service fee of .25% of the fund's assets also is allowed for personal service and/or maintenance of shareholder accounts.

Each investor must choose the best combination of fees. Obviously, pure no-load no-fee funds distributed directly by the mutual fund group are the cheapest alternative, and these will often make the most sense for knowledgeable investors. But as we noted earlier, many investors are willing to pay for financial advice, and the commissions paid to advisers who sell these funds are the most common form of payment. Alternatively, investors may choose to hire a fee-only financial manager who charges directly for services instead of collecting commissions. These advisers can help investors select portfolios of low- or no-load funds (as well as provide other financial advice). Independent financial planners have become increasingly important distribution channels for funds in recent years.

If you do buy a fund through a broker, the choice between paying a load and paying 12b-1 fees will depend primarily on your expected time horizon. Loads are paid only once for each purchase, whereas 12b-1 fees are paid annually. Thus, if you plan to hold your fund for a long time, a one-time load may be preferable to recurring 12b-1 charges.

Fees and Mutual Fund Returns

The rate of return on an investment in a mutual fund is measured as the increase or decrease in net asset value plus income distributions such as dividends or distributions of capital gains expressed as a fraction of net asset value at the beginning of the investment period. If we denote the net asset value at the start and end of the period as NAV_0 and NAV_1, respectively, then

$$\text{Rate of return} = \frac{\text{NAV}_1 - \text{NAV}_0 + \text{Income and capital gain distributions}}{\text{NAV}_0}$$

For example, if a fund has an initial NAV of $20 at the start of the month, makes income distributions of $.15 and capital gain distributions of $.05, and ends the month with NAV of $20.10, the monthly rate of return is computed as

$$\text{Rate of return} = \frac{\$20.10 - \$20.00 + \$.15 + \$.05}{\$20.00} = .015, \text{ or } 1.5\%$$

Notice that this measure of the rate of return ignores any commissions such as front-end loads paid to purchase the fund.

On the other hand, the rate of return is affected by the fund's expenses and 12b-1 fees. This is because such charges are periodically deducted from the portfolio, which reduces net asset value. Thus the rate of return on the fund equals the gross return on the underlying portfolio minus the total expense ratio.

EXAMPLE 4.2

Expenses and Rates of Return

To see how expenses can affect rate of return, consider a fund with $100 million in assets at the start of the year and with 10 million shares outstanding. The fund invests in a portfolio of stocks that provides no income but increases in value by 10%. The expense ratio, including 12b-1 fees, is 1%. What is the rate of return for an investor in the fund?

The initial NAV equals $100 million/10 million shares = $10 per share. In the absence of expenses, fund assets would grow to $110 million and NAV would grow to $11 per share, for a 10% rate of return. However, the expense ratio of the fund is 1%. Therefore, $1 million will be deducted from the fund to pay these fees, leaving the portfolio worth only $109 million, and NAV equal to $10.90. The rate of return on the fund is only 9%, which equals the gross return on the underlying portfolio minus the total expense ratio.

Fees can have a big effect on performance. Table 4.2 considers an investor who starts with $10,000 and can choose between three funds that all earn an annual 12% return on investment before fees but have different fee structures. The table shows the cumulative amount in each fund after several investment horizons. Fund A has total operating expenses of .5%, no load, and no 12b-1 charges. This might represent a low-cost producer like Vanguard. Fund B has no load but has 1% management expenses and .5% in 12b-1 fees. This level of charges

TABLE 4.2 Impact of costs on investment performance

	Cumulative Proceeds (all dividends reinvested)		
	Fund A	Fund B	Fund C
Initial investment*	$10,000	$10,000	$ 9,200
5 years	17,234	16,474	15,502
10 years	29,699	27,141	26,123
15 years	51,183	44,713	44,018
20 years	88,206	73,662	74,173

Notes: Fund A is no-load with .5% expense ratio, Fund B is no-load with 1.5% total expense ratio, and Fund C has an 8% load on purchases and a 1% expense ratio. Gross return on all funds is 12% per year before expenses.

*After front-end load, if any.

is fairly typical of actively managed equity funds. Finally, Fund C has 1% in management expenses, has no 12b-1 charges, but assesses an 8% front-end load on purchases.

Note the substantial return advantage of low-cost Fund A. Moreover, that differential is greater for longer investment horizons.

CONCEPT check 4.2

The Equity Fund sells Class A shares with a front-end load of 4% and Class B shares with 12b-1 fees of .5% annually as well as back-end load fees that start at 5% and fall by 1% for each full year the investor holds the portfolio (until the fifth year). Assume the rate of return on the fund portfolio net of operating expenses is 10% annually. What will be the value of a $10,000 investment in Class A and Class B shares if the shares are sold after (*a*) 1 year, (*b*) 4 years, (*c*) 10 years? Which fee structure provides higher net proceeds at the end of each investment horizon?

soft dollars

The value of research services that brokerage houses provide "free of charge" in exchange for the investment manager's business.

Although expenses can have a big impact on net investment performance, it is sometimes difficult for the investor in a mutual fund to measure true expenses accurately. This is because of the common practice of paying for some expenses in **soft dollars.** A portfolio manager earns soft-dollar credits with a brokerage firm by directing the fund's trades to that broker. Based on those credits, the broker will pay for some of the mutual fund's expenses, such as databases, computer hardware, or stock-quotation systems. The soft-dollar arrangement means that the stockbroker effectively returns part of the trading commission to the fund. Purchases made with soft dollars are not included in the fund's expenses, so funds with extensive soft-dollar arrangements may report artificially low expense ratios to the public. However, the fund will have paid its brokers needlessly high commissions to obtain its soft-dollar "rebates." The impact of the higher trading commissions shows up in net investment performance rather than the reported expense ratio.

The SEC allows soft-dollar arrangements as long as the proceeds are used for research that may ultimately benefit the mutual fund shareholder. About half of such funds have been used to purchase stock research reports. There have certainly been cases in which soft dollars were used for purposes other than the welfare of shareholders, however, and consumer advocates periodically propose that their use be curtailed.

4.5 TAXATION OF MUTUAL FUND INCOME

Investment returns of mutual funds are granted "pass-through status" under the U.S. tax code, meaning that taxes are paid only by the investor in the mutual fund, not by the fund itself. The income is treated as passed through to the investor as long as the fund meets several requirements, most notably that the fund be sufficiently diversified and that virtually all income is distributed to shareholders.

A fund's short-term capital gains, long-term capital gains, and dividends are passed through to investors as though the investor earned the income directly.[3] The pass-through of investment income has one important disadvantage for individual investors. If you manage your own portfolio, you decide when to realize capital gains and losses on any security; therefore, you can time those realizations to efficiently manage your tax liabilities. When you invest through a mutual fund, however, the timing of the sale of securities from the portfolio is out of your control, which reduces your ability to engage in tax management.

A fund with a high portfolio turnover rate can be particularly "tax inefficient." **Turnover** is the ratio of the trading activity of a portfolio to the assets of the portfolio. It measures the fraction of the portfolio that is "replaced" each year. For example, a $100 million portfolio with $50 million in sales of some securities and purchases of other securities would have a turnover rate of 50%. High turnover means that capital gains or losses are being realized constantly, and therefore that the investor cannot time the realizations to manage his or her overall tax obligation. Turnover rates in equity funds in the last decade have typically been around 60% when weighted by assets under management. By contrast, a low-turnover fund such as an index fund may have turnover as low as 2%, which is both tax-efficient and economical with respect to trading costs.

turnover

The ratio of the trading activity of a portfolio to the assets of the portfolio.

SEC rules require funds to disclose the tax impact of portfolio turnover. Funds must include in their prospectus after-tax returns for the past 1-, 5-, and 10-year periods. Marketing literature that includes performance data also must include after-tax results. The after-tax returns are computed accounting for the impact of the taxable distributions of income and capital gains passed through to the investor, assuming the investor is in the maximum federal tax bracket.

CONCEPT check 4.3

An investor's portfolio currently is worth $1 million. During the year, the investor sells 1,000 shares of FedEx at a price of $90 per share and 5,000 shares of Cisco Systems at a price of $15 per share. The proceeds are used to buy 1,000 shares of IBM at $165 per share.

a. What was the portfolio turnover rate?

b. If the shares in FedEx originally were purchased for $80 each and those in Cisco were purchased for $12.50, and if the investor's tax rate on capital gains income is 15%, how much extra will the investor owe on this year's taxes as a result of these transactions?

4.6 EXCHANGE-TRADED FUNDS

Exchange-traded funds (ETFs) are offshoots of mutual funds first introduced in 1993 that allow investors to trade index portfolios just as they do shares of stock. The first ETF was the "Spider," a nickname for SPDR or Standard & Poor's Depository Receipt, which is a unit investment trust holding a portfolio matching the S&P 500 Index. Unlike mutual funds, which can be bought or sold only at the end of the day when NAV is calculated, investors could trade Spiders throughout the day, just like any other share of stock. Spiders gave rise to many similar products such as "Diamonds" (based on the Dow Jones Industrial Average, ticker DIA), Qubes (pronounced "cubes", based on the NASDAQ 100 Index, ticker QQQ), and WEBS (World Equity Benchmark Shares, which are shares in portfolios of foreign stock market indexes). By early 2011, about $1 trillion was invested in over 900 ETFs in five general classes: broad U.S. market indexes, narrow industry or "sector" portfolios, international indexes, commodities, and bond portfolios. Table 4.3, Panel A, presents some of the sponsors of ETFs; Panel B is a small sample of ETFs, which we include to give you a flavor of the sort of products available.

exchange-traded funds

Offshoots of mutual funds that allow investors to trade index portfolios.

[3]An interesting problem that an investor needs to be aware of derives from the fact that capital gains and dividends on mutual funds are typically paid out to shareholders once or twice a year. This means that an investor who has just purchased shares in a mutual fund can receive a capital gain distribution (and be taxed on that distribution) on transactions that occurred long before he or she purchased shares in the fund. This is particularly a concern late in the year when such distributions typically are made.

TABLE 4.3 ETF sponsors and products

A. ETF Sponsors

Sponsor	Product Name
Barclays Global Investors	i-Shares
Merrill Lynch	HOLDRS (Holding Company Depository Receipts: "Holders")
StateStreet/Merrill Lynch	Select Sector SPDRs (S&P Depository Receipts: "Spiders")
Vanguard	Vanguard ETFs

B. Sample of ETF Products

Name	Ticker	Index Tracked
Broad U.S. Indexes		
Spiders	SPY	S&P 500
Diamonds	DIA	Dow Jones Industrials
Qubes	QQQ	NASDAQ 100
iShares Russell 2000	IWM	Russell 2000
Total Stock Market (Vanguard)	VTI	Wilshire 5000
Industry Indexes		
Energy Select Spider	XLE	S&P 500 energy companies
iShares Energy Sector	IYE	Dow Jones energy companies
Oil Service HOLDRS	OIH	Portfolio of oil service firms
Financial Sector Spider	XLF	S&P 500 financial companies
iShares Financial Sector	IYF	Dow Jones financial companies
Vanguard Financials ETF	VFH	MSCI financials index
International Indexes		
WEBS United Kingdom	EWU	MCSI U.K. Index
WEBS France	EWQ	MCSI France Index
WEBS Japan	EWJ	MCSI Japan Index

Figure 4.2 shows the rapid growth in the ETF market since 1998. Until 2008, most ETFs were required to track specified indexes, and ETFs tracking broad indexes still dominate the industry. However, there are dozens of industry-sector ETFs, and as Figure 4.2 makes clear, commodity, bond, and international ETFs have grown especially dramatically in recent years. While only $1 billion was invested in commodity ETFs in 2004, by 2010 this value had grown to $101 billion. Gold and silver ETFs dominate this sector, accounting for about three-quarters of commodity-based funds. Indeed, ETFs have become the main way for investors to speculate in precious metals. Figure 4.3 shows that by 2010 ETFs had captured a significant portion of the assets under management in the investment company universe.

Barclay's Global Investors was long the market leader in the ETF market, using the product name iShares. Since Barclay's 2009 merger with Blackrock, iShares have operated under the Blackrock name. The firm sponsors ETFs for several dozen equity index funds, including many broad U.S. equity indexes, broad international and single-country funds, and U.S. and global industry sector funds. Blackrock also offers several bond ETFs and a few commodity funds such as ones for gold and silver. For more information, on these funds, go to **www.iShares.com.**

More recently, a variety of new ETF products have been devised. Among these are leveraged ETFs, with daily returns that are a targeted *multiple* of the returns on an index, and inverse ETFs, which move in the opposite direction to an index. In addition, there is now a small number of actively managed ETF funds that, like actively managed mutual funds, attempt to outperform market indexes. But these account for only about 3% of assets under management in the ETF industry.

Other even more exotic variations are so-called synthetic ETFs such as exchange-traded notes (ETNs) or exchange-traded vehicles (ETVs). These are nominally debt securities, but

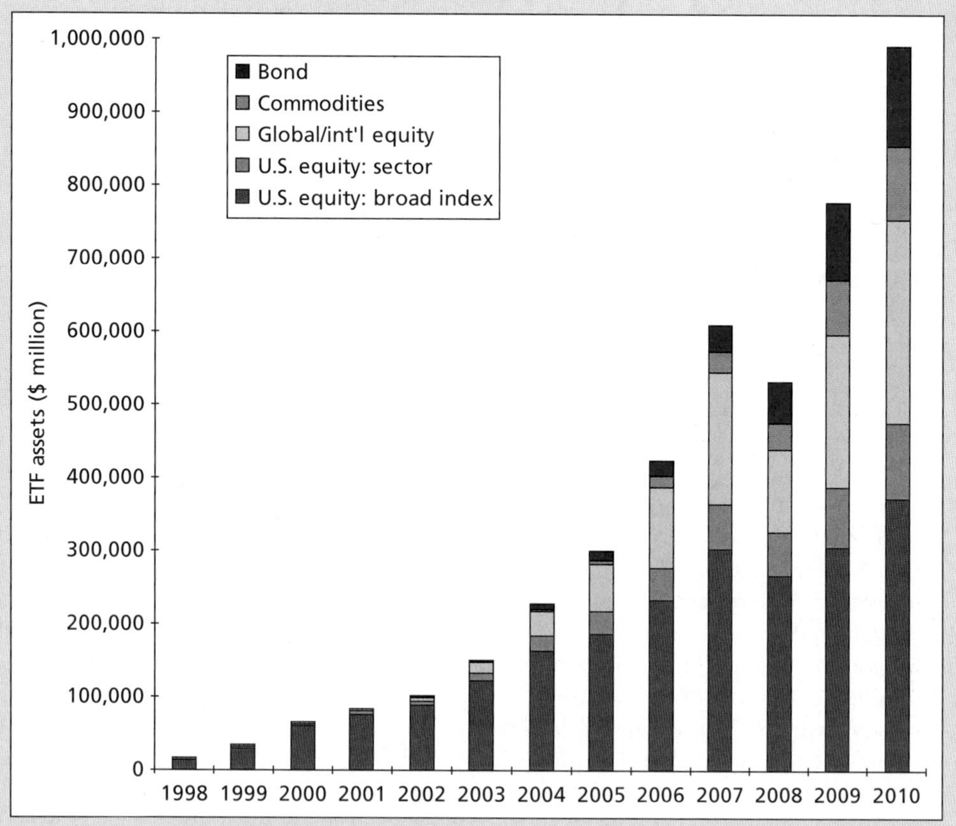

FIGURE 4.2

Assets in ETFs

Source: Investment Company Institute, *2011 Investment Company Fact Book.* Washington, DC 2011. Used with permission.

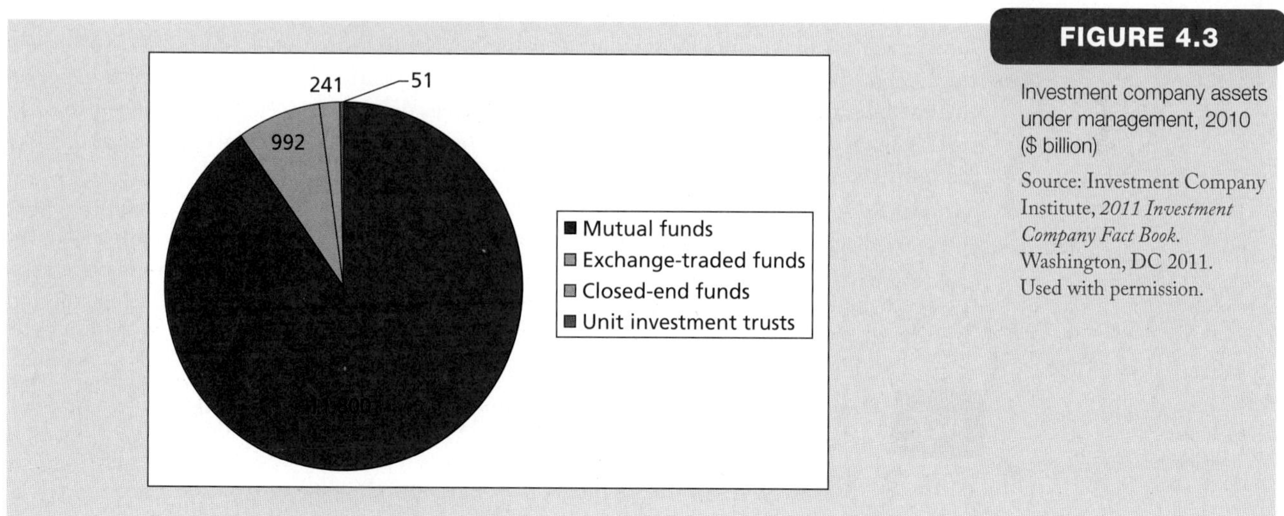

FIGURE 4.3

Investment company assets under management, 2010 ($ billion)

Source: Investment Company Institute, *2011 Investment Company Fact Book.* Washington, DC 2011. Used with permission.

with payoffs linked to the performance of an index. Often that index measures the performance of an illiquid and thinly traded asset class, so the ETF gives the investor the opportunity to add that asset class to his or her portfolio. However, rather than invest in those assets directly, the ETF achieves this exposure by entering a "total return swap" with an investment bank in which the bank agrees to pay the ETF the return on the index in exchange for a relatively fixed fee. These have become controversial, as the ETF is then exposed to risk that in a period of financial stress, the investment bank will be unable to fulfill its obligation, leaving investors without the returns they were promised.

ETFs offer several advantages over conventional mutual funds. First, as we just noted, a mutual fund's net asset value is quoted—and therefore, investors can buy or sell their shares in the fund—only once a day. In contrast, ETFs trade continuously. Moreover, like other shares, but unlike mutual funds, ETFs can be sold short or purchased on margin.

ETFs also offer a potential tax advantage over mutual funds. When large numbers of mutual fund investors redeem their shares, the fund must sell securities to meet the redemptions. The sale can trigger capital gains taxes, which are passed through to and must be paid by the remaining shareholders. In contrast, when small investors wish to redeem their position in an ETF they simply sell their shares to other traders, with no need for the fund to sell any of the underlying portfolio. Moreover, when large traders wish to redeem their position in the ETF, redemptions are satisfied with shares of stock in the underlying portfolio. Again, a redemption does not trigger a stock sale by the fund sponsor.

The ability of large investors to redeem ETFs for a portfolio of stocks constituting the index, or to exchange a portfolio of stocks for shares in the corresponding ETF, ensures that the price of an ETF cannot depart for long from the NAV of that portfolio. Any meaningful discrepancy would offer arbitrage trading opportunities for these large traders, which would quickly eliminate the disparity.

ETFs are also cheaper than mutual funds. Investors who buy ETFs do so through brokers, rather than buying directly from the fund. Therefore, the fund saves the cost of marketing itself directly to small investors. This reduction in expenses translates into lower management fees. For example, the expense ratio on Vanguard's Total Stock Market mutual fund, which tracks the Wilshire 5000 Index, is .18%, whereas the ratio on its Total Stock Market ETF is only .07%.

There are some disadvantages to ETFs, however. First, while mutual funds can be bought for NAV with no expense from no-load funds, ETFs must be purchased from brokers for a fee. Investors also incur a bid–ask spread when purchasing an ETF.

In addition, because ETFs trade as securities, their prices can depart from NAV, at least for short periods, and these price discrepancies can easily swamp the cost advantage that ETFs otherwise offer. While those discrepancies typically are quite small, they can spike unpredictably when markets are stressed. Chapter 3 briefly discussed the so-called flash crash of May 6, 2010, when the Dow Jones Industrial Average fell by 583 points in *seven minutes,* leaving it down nearly 1,000 points for the day. Remarkably, the index recovered more than 600 points in the next 10 minutes. In the wake of this incredible volatility, the stock exchanges canceled many trades that had gone off at what were viewed as distorted prices. Around one-fifth of all ETFs changed hands on that day at prices less than one-half of their closing price, and ETFs accounted for about two-thirds of all canceled trades.

At least two problems were exposed in this episode. First, when markets are not working properly, it can be hard to measure the net asset value of the ETF portfolio, especially for ETFs that track less liquid assets. And, reinforcing this problem, some ETFs may be supported by only a very small number of dealers. If they drop out of the market during a period of turmoil, prices may swing wildly.

4.7 MUTUAL FUND INVESTMENT PERFORMANCE: A FIRST LOOK

We noted earlier that one of the benefits of mutual funds for the individual investor is the ability to delegate management of the portfolio to investment professionals. The investor retains control over the broad features of the overall portfolio through the asset allocation decision: Each individual chooses the percentages of the portfolio to invest in bond funds versus equity funds versus money market funds, and so forth, but can leave the specific security selection decisions within each investment class to the managers of each fund. Shareholders hope that these portfolio managers can achieve better investment performance than they could obtain on their own.

What is the investment record of the mutual fund industry? This seemingly straightforward question is deceptively difficult to answer because we need a standard against which to evaluate performance. For example, we clearly would not want to compare the investment performance of an equity fund to the rate of return available in the money market. The vast differences in the risk of these two markets dictate that year-by-year as well as average performance will differ considerably. We would expect to find that equity funds outperform money market funds (on average) as compensation to investors for the extra risk incurred in equity markets. How can we determine whether mutual fund portfolio managers are performing up to par *given* the level of risk they incur? In other words, what is the proper benchmark against which investment performance ought to be evaluated?

Measuring portfolio risk properly and using such measures to choose an appropriate benchmark is an extremely difficult task. We devote all of Parts Two and Three of the text to issues surrounding the proper measurement of portfolio risk and the trade-off between risk and return. In this chapter, therefore, we will satisfy ourselves with a first look at the question of fund performance by using only very simple performance benchmarks and ignoring the more subtle issues of risk differences across funds. However, we will return to this topic in Chapter 8, where we take a closer look at mutual fund performance after adjusting for differences in the exposure of portfolios to various sources of risk.

Here, we will use as a benchmark for the performance of equity fund managers the rate of return on the Wilshire 5000 Index. Recall from Chapter 2 that this is a value-weighted index of more than 5,000 stocks that trade on the NYSE, NASDAQ, and Amex stock markets. It is the most inclusive index of the performance of U.S. equities. The performance of the Wilshire 5000 is a useful benchmark with which to evaluate professional managers because it corresponds to a simple passive investment strategy: Buy all the shares in the index in proportion to their outstanding market value. Moreover, this is a feasible strategy for even small investors, because the Vanguard Group offers an index fund (its Total Stock Market Index Fund) designed to replicate the performance of the Wilshire 5000 Index. Using the Wilshire 5000 Index as a benchmark, we may pose the problem of evaluating the performance of mutual fund portfolio managers this way: How does the typical performance of actively managed equity mutual funds compare to the performance of a passively managed portfolio that simply replicates the composition of a broad index of the stock market?

Casual comparisons of the performance of the Wilshire 5000 Index versus that of professionally managed mutual fund portfolios show disappointing results for most fund managers. Figure 4.4 shows that the average return on diversified equity funds was below the return on the Wilshire 5000 Index in 24 of the 40 years from 1971 to 2010. The average return on the index was 10.3%, which was .8% greater than that of the average mutual fund.[4]

This result may seem surprising. After all, it would not seem unreasonable to expect that professional money managers should be able to outperform a very simple rule such as "hold an indexed portfolio." As it turns out, however, there may be good reasons to expect such a result. We will explore them in detail in Chapter 8, where we discuss the efficient market hypothesis.

Of course, one might argue that there are good managers and bad managers, and that good managers can, in fact, consistently outperform the index. To test this notion, we examine whether managers with good performance in one year are likely to repeat that performance in a following year. Is superior performance in any particular year due to luck, and therefore random, or due to skill, and therefore consistent from year to year?

To answer this question, we can examine the performance of a large sample of equity mutual fund portfolios, divide the funds into two groups based on total investment return, and ask: "Do funds with investment returns in the top half of the sample in one period continue to perform well in the subsequent period?"

Table 4.4 presents such an analysis from a study by Malkiel (1995). The table shows the fraction of "winners" (i.e., top-half performers) in each year that turn out to be winners or losers in the following year. If performance were purely random from one period to the next, there would be entries of 50% in each cell of the table, as top- or bottom-half performers

[4]Of course, actual funds incur trading costs while indexes do not, so a fair comparison between the returns on actively managed funds versus those on a passive index would first reduce the return on the Wilshire 5000 by an estimate of such costs. Vanguard's Total Stock Market Index portfolio, which tracks the Wilshire 5000, charges an expense ratio of .18%, and, because it engages in little trading, incurs low trading costs. Therefore, it would be reasonable to reduce the returns on the index by about .30%. This reduction would not erase the difference in average performance.

FIGURE 4.4

Average returns on diversified equity funds versus Wilshire 5000 Index

Source: Data compiled from **www.wilshire.com**. Used with permission of Wilshire Associates.

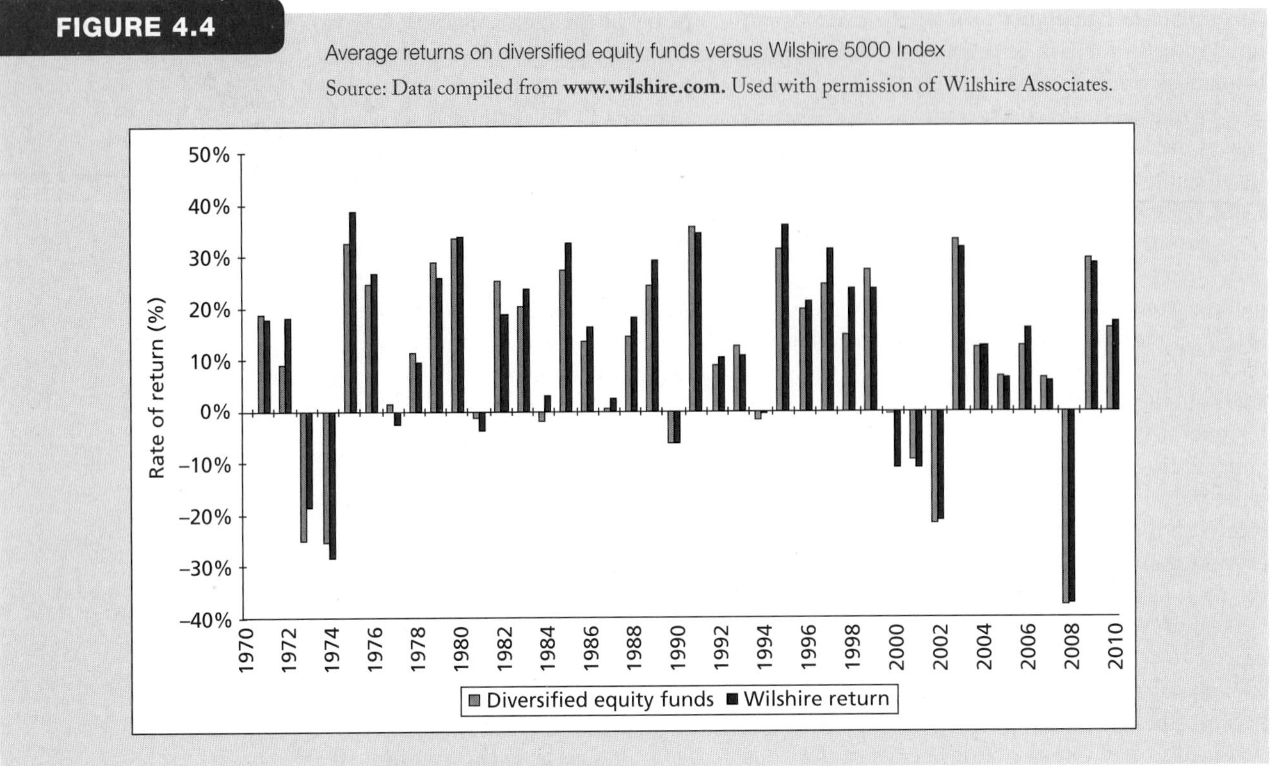

TABLE 4.4 Consistency of investment results

Initial Period Performance	Successive Period Performance: Top Half	Bottom Half
A. Malkiel study, 1970s		
Top half	65.1%	34.9%
Bottom half	35.5%	64.5%
B. Malkiel study, 1980s		
Top half	51.7%	48.3%
Bottom half	47.5%	52.5%

Source: Burton G. Malkiel, "Returns from Investing in Equity Mutual Funds 1971–1991," *Journal of Finance* 50 (June 1995), pp. 549–72. Used with permission of John Wiley and Sons, via Copyright Clearance Center.

would be equally likely to perform in either the top or bottom half of the sample in the following period. On the other hand, if performance were due entirely to skill, with no randomness, we would expect to see entries of 100% on the diagonals and entries of 0% on the off-diagonals: Top-half performers would all remain in the top half while bottom-half performers similarly would all remain in the bottom half. In fact, Panel A shows that 65.1% of initial top-half performers in the 1970s fall in the top half of the sample in the following period, while 64.5% of initial bottom-half performers fall in the bottom half in the following period. This evidence is consistent with the notion that at least part of a fund's performance is a function of skill as opposed to luck, so that relative performance tends to persist from one period to the next.[5]

[5]Another possibility is that performance consistency is due to variation in fee structure across funds. We return to this possibility in Chapter 8.

On the other hand, this relationship does not seem stable across different sample periods. While initial-year performance predicts subsequent-year performance in the 1970s (see Panel A), the pattern of persistence in performance virtually disappears in the 1980s (Panel B).

Other studies suggest that bad performance is more likely to persist than good performance. This makes some sense: It is easy to identify fund characteristics that will predictably lead to consistently poor investment performance, notably, high expense ratios and high turnover ratios with associated trading costs. It is far harder to identify the secrets of successful stock picking. (If it were easy, we would all be rich!) Thus the consistency we do observe in fund performance may be due in large part to the poor performers. This suggests that the real value of past performance data is to avoid truly poor funds, even if identifying the future top performers is still a daunting task.

CONCEPT check 4.4

Suppose you observe the investment performance of 400 portfolio managers and rank them by investment returns during the year. Twenty percent of all managers are truly skilled, and therefore always fall in the top half, but the others fall in the top half purely because of good luck. What fraction of these top-half managers would you expect to be top-half performers next year? Assume skilled managers always are top-half performers.

4.8 INFORMATION ON MUTUAL FUNDS

The first place to find information on a mutual fund is in its prospectus. The Securities and Exchange Commission requires that the prospectus describe the fund's investment objectives and policies in a concise "Statement of Investment Objectives" as well as in lengthy discussions of investment policies and risks. The fund's investment adviser and its portfolio manager also are described. The prospectus also presents the costs associated with purchasing shares in the fund in a fee table. Sales charges such as front-end and back-end loads as well as annual operating expenses such as management fees and 12b-1 fees are detailed in the fee table.

Funds provide information about themselves in two other sources. The Statement of Additional Information, or SAI, also known as Part B of the prospectus, includes a list of the securities in the portfolio at the end of the fiscal year, audited financial statements, a list of the directors and officers of the fund as well as their personal investments in the fund, and data on brokerage commissions paid by the fund. Unlike the fund prospectus, however, investors do not receive the SAI unless they specifically request it; one industry joke is that SAI stands for "something always ignored." The fund's annual report also includes portfolio composition and financial statements, as well as a discussion of the factors that influenced fund performance over the last reporting period.

With more than 8,000 mutual funds to choose from, it can be difficult to find and select the fund that is best suited for a particular need. Several publications now offer "encyclopedias" of mutual fund information to help in the search process. One prominent source is Morningstar's *Mutual Fund Sourcebook.* Morningstar's website, **www.morningstar.com,** is another excellent source of information, as is Yahoo!'s site, **finance.yahoo.com/funds.** The Investment Company Institute—the national association of mutual funds, closed-end funds, and unit investment trusts—publishes an annual *Directory of Mutual Funds* that includes information on fees as well as phone numbers to contact funds. To illustrate the range of information available about funds, we consider a sample report from Morningstar, reproduced in Figure 4.5.

Some of Morningstar's analysis is qualitative. The top box on the left-hand side of the report reproduced in the figure provides a short description of fund strategy, in particular the types of securities in which the fund manager tends to invest. The bottom box on the left ("Morningstar's Take") is a more detailed discussion of the fund's income strategy. The short statement of the fund's investment policy is in the top right-hand corner: Laudus is a "large

FIGURE 4.5

Morningstar report

Source: Morningstar Mutual Funds. © 2011 Morningstar, Inc. All rights reserved. Used with permission.

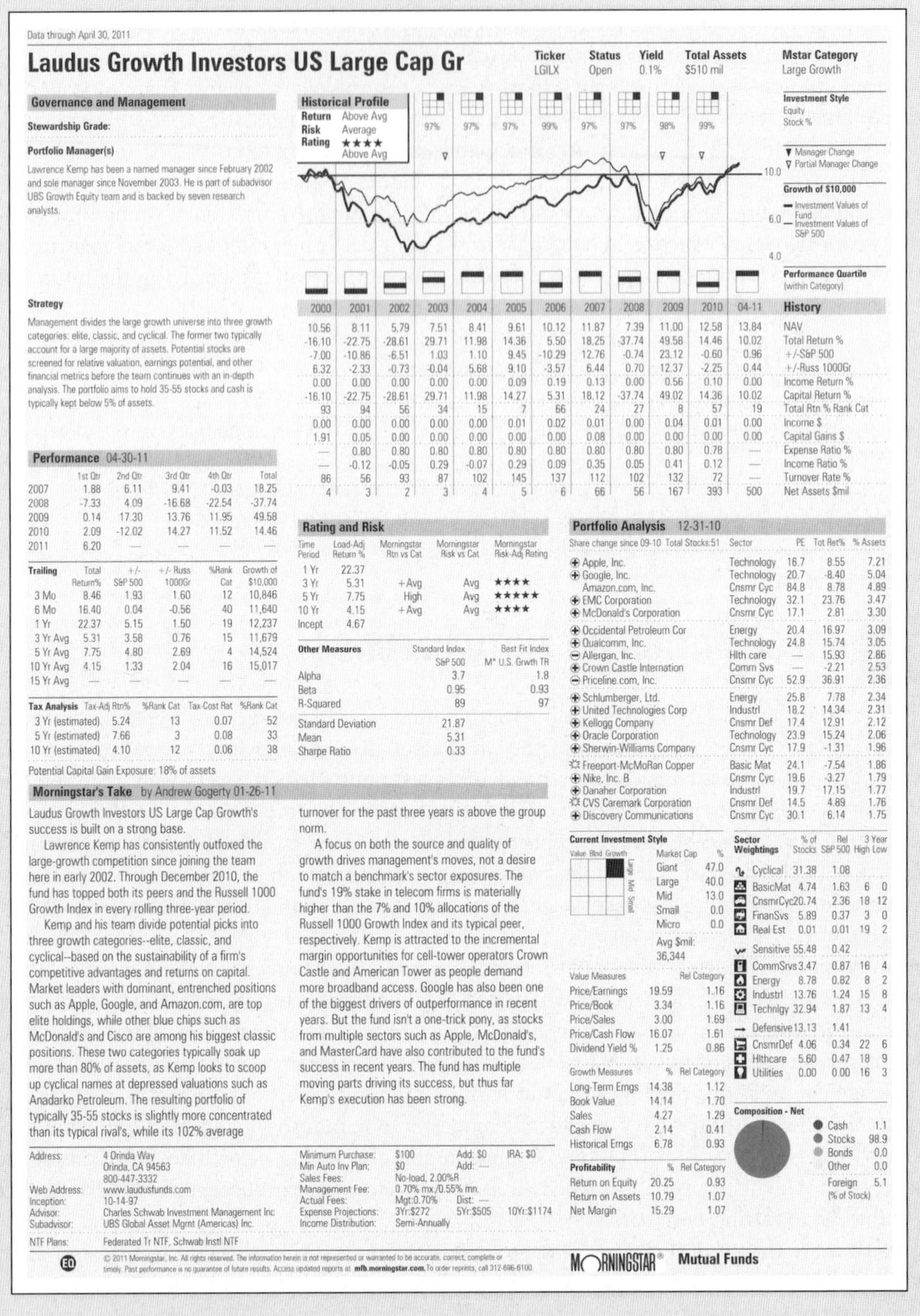

Data through April 30, 2011

Laudus Growth Investors US Large Cap Gr

Ticker	Status	Yield	Total Assets	Mstar Category
LGILX	Open	0.1%	$510 mil	Large Growth

Governance and Management

Stewardship Grade:

Portfolio Manager(s)

Lawrence Kemp has been a named manager since February 2002 and sole manager since November 2003. He is part of subadvisor UBS Growth Equity team and is backed by seven research analysts.

Strategy

Management divides the large growth universe into three growth categories: elite, classic, and cyclical. The former two typically account for a large majority of assets. Potential stocks are screened for relative valuation, earnings potential, and other financial metrics before the team continues with an in-depth analysis. The portfolio aims to hold 35-55 stocks and cash is typically kept below 5% of assets.

Historical Profile
Return: Above Avg
Risk: Average
Rating: ★★★★ Above Avg

2000	2001	2002	2003	2004	2005	2006	2007	2008	2009	2010	04-11	History
10.56	8.11	5.79	7.51	8.41	9.61	10.12	11.87	7.39	11.00	12.58	13.84	NAV
-16.10	-22.75	-28.61	29.71	11.98	14.36	5.50	18.25	-37.74	49.58	14.46	10.02	Total Return %
-7.00	-10.86	-6.51	1.03	1.10	9.45	-10.29	12.76	-0.74	23.12	-0.60	0.96	+/-S&P 500
6.32	-2.33	-0.73	-0.04	5.68	9.10	-3.57	6.44	0.70	12.37	-2.25	0.44	+/-Russ 1000Gr
0.00	0.00	0.00	0.00	0.00	0.09	0.19	0.13	0.00	0.56	0.10	0.00	Income Return %
-16.10	-22.75	-28.61	29.71	11.98	14.27	5.31	18.12	-37.74	49.02	14.36	10.02	Capital Return %
93	94	56	34	15	7	66	24	27	8	57	19	Total Rtn % Rank Cat
0.00	0.00	0.00	0.00	0.00	0.01	0.02	0.01	0.00	0.04	0.01	0.00	Income $
1.91	0.05	0.00	0.00	0.00	0.00	0.00	0.08	0.00	0.00	0.00	0.00	Capital Gains $
—	0.80	0.80	0.80	0.80	0.80	0.80	0.80	0.80	0.80	0.78	—	Expense Ratio %
—	-0.12	-0.05	0.29	-0.07	0.29	0.09	0.35	0.05	0.41	0.12	—	Income Ratio %
86	56	93	87	102	145	137	112	102	132	72	—	Turnover Rate %
4	3	2	3	4	5	6	66	56	167	393	500	Net Assets $mil

Performance 04-30-11

	1st Qtr	2nd Qtr	3rd Qtr	4th Qtr	Total
2007	1.88	6.11	9.41	-0.03	18.25
2008	-7.33	4.09	-16.68	-22.54	-37.74
2009	0.14	17.30	13.76	11.95	49.58
2010	2.09	-12.02	14.27	11.52	14.46
2011	6.20	—	—	—	—

Trailing	Total Return%	+/- S&P 500	+/- Russ 1000Gr	%Rank Cat	Growth of $10,000
3 Mo	8.46	1.93	1.60	12	10,846
6 Mo	16.40	0.04	-0.56	40	11,640
1 Yr	22.37	5.15	1.50	19	12,237
3 Yr Avg	5.31	3.58	0.76	15	11,679
5 Yr Avg	7.75	4.80	2.69	4	14,524
10 Yr Avg	4.15	1.33	2.04	16	15,017
15 Yr Avg	—	—	—	—	—

Tax Analysis	Tax-Adj Rtn%	%Rank Cat	Tax-Cost Rat	%Rank Cat
3 Yr (estimated)	5.24	13	0.07	52
5 Yr (estimated)	7.66	3	0.08	33
10 Yr (estimated)	4.10	12	0.06	38

Potential Capital Gain Exposure: 18% of assets

Rating and Risk

Time Period	Load-Adj Return %	Morningstar Rtn vs Cat	Morningstar Risk vs Cat	Morningstar Risk-Adj Rating
1 Yr	22.37			
3 Yr	5.31	+Avg	Avg	★★★★
5 Yr	7.75	High	Avg	★★★★★
10 Yr	4.15	+Avg	Avg	★★★★
Incept	4.67			

Other Measures	Standard Index S&P 500	Best Fit Index M* U.S. Grwth TR
Alpha	3.7	1.8
Beta	0.95	0.93
R-Squared	89	97
Standard Deviation	21.87	
Mean	5.31	
Sharpe Ratio	0.33	

Portfolio Analysis 12-31-10

Share change since 09-10 Total Stocks:51	Sector	PE	Tot Ret%	% Assets
⊕ Apple, Inc.	Technology	16.7	8.55	7.21
⊕ Google, Inc.	Technology	20.7	-8.40	5.04
Amazon.com, Inc.	Cnsmr Cyc	84.8	8.78	4.89
⊕ EMC Corporation	Technology	32.1	23.76	3.47
⊕ McDonald's Corporation	Cnsmr Cyc	17.1	2.81	3.30
⊕ Occidental Petroleum Cor	Energy	20.4	16.97	3.09
⊕ Qualcomm, Inc.	Technology	24.8	15.74	3.05
⊖ Allergan, Inc.	Hlth care	—	15.93	2.86
⊕ Crown Castle Internation	Comm Svs	—	-2.21	2.53
⊖ Priceline.com, Inc.	Cnsmr Cyc	52.9	36.91	2.36
⊕ Schlumberger, Ltd.	Energy	25.8	7.78	2.34
⊕ United Technologies Corp	Industrl	18.2	14.34	2.31
⊕ Kellogg Company	Cnsmr Def	17.4	12.91	2.12
⊕ Oracle Corporation	Technology	23.9	15.24	2.06
⊕ Sherwin-Williams Company	Cnsmr Cyc	17.9	-1.31	1.96
☼ Freeport-McMoRan Copper	Basic Mat	24.1	-7.54	1.86
⊕ Nike, Inc. B	Cnsmr Cyc	19.6	-3.27	1.79
⊕ Danaher Corporation	Industrl	19.7	17.15	1.77
☼ CVS Caremark Corporation	Cnsmr Def	14.5	4.89	1.76
⊕ Discovery Communications	Cnsmr Cyc	30.1	6.14	1.75

Current Investment Style

Value Blnd Growth / Large Mid Small

Market Cap	%
Giant	47.0
Large	40.0
Mid	13.0
Small	0.0
Micro	0.0
Avg $mil: 36,344	

Value Measures		Rel Category
Price/Earnings	19.59	1.16
Price/Book	3.34	1.16
Price/Sales	3.00	1.69
Price/Cash Flow	16.07	1.61
Dividend Yield %	1.25	0.86

Growth Measures	%	Rel Category
Long-Term Erngs	14.38	1.12
Book Value	14.14	1.70
Sales	4.27	1.29
Cash Flow	2.14	0.41
Historical Erngs	6.78	0.93

Profitability	%	Rel Category
Return on Equity	20.25	0.93
Return on Assets	10.79	1.07
Net Margin	15.29	1.07

Sector Weightings	% of Stocks	Rel S&P 500	3 Year High	Low
Cyclical	31.38	1.08		
BasicMat	4.74	1.63	6	0
CnsmrCyc	20.74	2.36	18	12
FinanSvs	5.89	0.37	3	0
Real Est	0.01	0.01	19	2
Sensitive	55.48	0.42		
CommSrvs	3.47	0.87	16	4
Energy	8.78	0.82	8	2
Industrl	13.76	1.24	15	8
Technlgy	32.94	1.87	13	4
Defensive	13.13	1.41		
CnsmrDef	4.06	0.34	22	6
Hlthcare	5.60	0.47	18	9
Utilities	0.00	0.00	16	3

Composition - Net

Cash	1.1
Stocks	98.9
Bonds	0.0
Other	0.0
Foreign (% of Stock)	5.1

Morningstar's Take by Andrew Gogerty 01-26-11

Laudus Growth Investors US Large Cap Growth's success is built on a strong base.

Lawrence Kemp has consistently outfoxed the large-growth competition since joining the team here in early 2002. Through December 2010, the fund has topped both its peers and the Russell 1000 Growth Index in every rolling three-year period.

Kemp and his team divide potential picks into three growth categories--elite, classic, and cyclical--based on the sustainability of a firm's competitive advantages and returns on capital. Market leaders with dominant, entrenched positions such as Apple, Google, and Amazon.com, are top elite holdings, while other blue chips such as McDonald's and Cisco are among his biggest classic positions. These two categories typically soak up more than 80% of assets, as Kemp looks to scoop up cyclical names at depressed valuations such as Anadarko Petroleum. The resulting portfolio of typically 35-55 stocks is slightly more concentrated than its typical rival's, while its 102% average turnover for the past three years is above the group norm.

A focus on both the source and quality of growth drives management's moves, not a desire to match a benchmark's sector exposures. The fund's 19% stake in telecom firms is materially higher than the 7% and 10% allocations of the Russell 1000 Growth Index and its typical peer, respectively. Kemp is attracted to the incremental margin opportunities for cell-tower operators Crown Castle and American Tower as people demand more broadband access. Google has also been one of the biggest drivers of outperformance in recent years. But the fund isn't a one-trick pony, as stocks from multiple sectors such as Apple, McDonald's, and MasterCard have also contributed to the fund's success in recent years. The fund has multiple moving parts driving its success, but thus far Kemp's execution has been strong.

Address:	4 Orinda Way, Orinda, CA 94563, 800-447-3332	Minimum Purchase:	$100	Add: $0	IRA: $0
		Min Auto Inv Plan:	$0	Add: —	
		Sales Fees:	No-load, 2.00%R		
Web Address:	www.laudusfunds.com	Management Fee:	0.70% mx./0.55% mn.		
Inception:	10-14-97	Actual Fees:	Mgt:0.70%	Dist: —	
Advisor:	Charles Schwab Investment Management Inc	Expense Projections:	3Yr:$272	5Yr:$505	10Yr:$1174
Subadvisor:	UBS Global Asset Mgmt (Americas) Inc.	Income Distribution:	Semi-Annually		
NTF Plans:	Federated Tr NTF, Schwab Instl NTF				

MORNINGSTAR® Mutual Funds

growth" fund, meaning that it tends to invest in large firms, with an emphasis on growth over value stocks.

The table on the left in the figure, labeled "Performance," reports on the fund's quarterly returns over the last few years and then over longer periods up to 15 years. Comparisons of returns to relevant indexes, in this case, the S&P 500 and the Russell 1000 indexes, are provided to serve as benchmarks in evaluating the performance of the fund. The values under these columns give the performance of the fund relative to the index. The returns reported for the fund are calculated net of expenses, 12b-1 fees, and any other fees automatically deducted from fund assets, but they do not account for any sales charges such as front-end loads or back-end charges. Next appear the percentile ranks of the fund compared to all other funds with the same investment objective (see column headed "%Rank Cat"). A rank of 1 means the fund is a top performer. A rank of 80 would mean that it was beaten by 80% of funds in the comparison group. Finally, growth of $10,000 invested in the fund over various periods ranging from the past three months to the past 15 years is given in the last column.

More data on the performance of the fund are provided in the graph near the top of the figure. The line graph compares the growth of $10,000 invested in the fund and the S&P 500 over the last 10 years. Below the graph are boxes for each year that depict the relative performance of the fund for that year. The shaded area on the box shows the quartile in which the fund's performance falls relative to other funds with the same objective. If the shaded band is at the top of the box, the firm was a top quartile performer in that period, and so on. The table below the bar charts presents historical data on characteristics of the fund such as return data and expense ratios.

The table on the right entitled "Portfolio Analysis" presents the 20 largest holdings of the portfolio, showing the price–earnings ratio and year-to-date return of each of those securities. Investors can thus get a quick look at the manager's biggest bets.

Below the portfolio analysis table is a box labeled "Current Investment Style." In this box, Morningstar evaluates style along two dimensions: One dimension is the size of the firms held in the portfolio as measured by the market value of outstanding equity; the other dimension is a value/growth measure. Morningstar defines *value stocks* as those with low ratios of market price per share to various measures of value. It puts stocks on a growth-value continuum based on the ratios of stock price to the firm's earnings, book value, sales, cash flow, and dividends. Value stocks are those with a low price relative to these measures of value. In contrast, *growth stocks* have high ratios, suggesting that investors in these firms must believe that the firm will experience rapid growth to justify the prices at which the stocks sell. The shaded box for Laudus shows that the portfolio tends to hold larger firms (top row) and growth stocks (right column). A year-by-year history of Laudus's investment style is presented in the sequence of such boxes at the top of Figure 4.5.

The center of the figure, labeled "Rating and Risk," is one of the more complicated but interesting facets of Morningstar's analysis. The column labeled "Load-Adj Return" rates a fund's return compared to other funds with the same investment policy. Returns for periods ranging from 1 to 10 years are calculated with all loads and back-end fees applicable to that investment period subtracted from total income. The return is then compared to the average return for the comparison group of funds to obtain the Morningstar Return vs. Category. Similarly, risk measures compared to category are computed and reported in the next column.

The last column presents Morningstar's risk-adjusted rating, ranging from one to five stars. The rating is based on the fund's return score minus risk score compared to other funds with similar investment styles. To allow funds to be compared to other funds with similar investment styles, Morningstar employs a large number of categories; there are now 48 separate stock and bond fund categories. Of course, we are accustomed to the disclaimer that "past performance is not a reliable measure of future results," and this is true as well of the coveted Morningstar five-star rating.

The "Tax Analysis" box shown on the left in Figure 4.5 provides some evidence on the tax efficiency of the fund. The after-tax return, given in the first column, is computed based on the dividends paid to the portfolio as well as realized capital gains, assuming the investor is in the maximum federal tax bracket at the time of the distribution. State and local taxes are ignored. The tax efficiency of the fund is measured by the "Tax-Cost Ratio," which is an estimate of the impact of taxes on the investor's after-tax return. Morningstar ranks each fund compared to its category for both tax-adjusted return and tax-cost ratio.

The bottom of the page in Figure 4.5 provides information on the expenses and loads associated with investments in the fund, as well as information on the fund's investment adviser. Thus, Morningstar provides a considerable amount of the information you would need to decide among several competing funds.

SUMMARY

- Unit investment trusts, closed-end management companies, and open-end management companies are all classified and regulated as investment companies. Unit investment trusts are essentially unmanaged in the sense that the portfolio, once established, is fixed. Managed investment companies, in contrast, may change the composition of the portfolio as deemed fit by the portfolio manager. Closed-end funds are traded like other securities; they do not redeem shares for their investors. Open-end funds will redeem shares for net asset value at the request of the investor.
- Net asset value equals the market value of assets held by a fund minus the liabilities of the fund divided by the shares outstanding.
- Mutual funds free the individual from many of the administrative burdens of owning individual securities and offer professional management of the portfolio. They also offer advantages that are available only to large-scale investors, such as lower trading costs. On the other hand, funds are assessed management fees and incur other expenses, which reduce the investor's rate of return. Funds also eliminate some of the individual's control over the timing of capital gains realizations.
- Mutual funds often are categorized by investment policy. Major policy groups include money market funds; equity funds, which are further grouped according to emphasis on income versus growth; fixed-income funds; balanced and income funds; asset allocation funds; index funds; and specialized sector funds.
- Costs of investing in mutual funds include front-end loads, which are sales charges; back-end loads, which are redemption fees or, more formally, contingent-deferred sales charges; fund operating expenses; and 12b-1 charges, which are recurring fees used to pay for the expenses of marketing the fund to the public.
- Income earned on mutual fund portfolios is not taxed at the level of the fund. Instead, as long as the fund meets certain requirements for pass-through status, the income is treated as being earned by the investors in the fund.
- The average rate of return of the average equity mutual fund in the last 40 years has been below that of a passive index fund holding a portfolio to replicate a broad-based index like the S&P 500 or Wilshire 5000. Some of the reasons for this disappointing record are the costs incurred by actively managed funds, such as the expense of conducting the research to guide stock-picking activities, and trading costs due to higher portfolio turnover. The record on the consistency of fund performance is mixed. In some sample periods, the better-performing funds continue to perform well in the following periods; in other sample periods they do not.

KEY TERMS

closed-end fund, 86
exchange-traded funds, 95
funds of funds, 90
hedge fund, 88
investment companies, 85
load, 87
net asset value (NAV), 85
open-end fund, 86
soft dollars, 94
turnover, 95
12b-1 fees, 92
unit investment trust, 86

PROBLEM SETS

Select problems are available in McGraw-Hill's *Connect Finance.* Please see the Supplements section of the book's frontmatter for more information.

Basic

1. What are the benefits to small investors of investing via mutual funds? What are the costs? *(LO 4-1)*
2. Why can closed-end funds sell at prices that differ from net value while open-end funds do not? *(LO 4-2)*
3. What is a 12b-1 fee? *(LO 4-1)*
4. What are some differences between a unit investment trust and a closed-end fund? *(LO 4-2)*

5. What are the advantages and disadvantages of exchange-traded funds versus mutual funds? *(LO 4-2)*
6. What are some differences between hedge funds and mutual funds? *(LO 4-2)*
7. Would you expect a typical open-end fixed-income mutual fund to have higher or lower operating expenses than a fixed-income unit investment trust? Why? *(LO 4-2)*
8. Balanced funds and asset allocation funds invest in both the stock and bond markets. What is the difference between these types of funds? *(LO 4-4)*
9. What are some comparative advantages of investing your assets in the following: *(LO 4-2)*
   a. Unit investment trusts.
   b. Open-end mutual funds.
   c. Individual stocks and bonds that you choose for yourself.
10. Open-end equity mutual funds find it necessary to keep a significant percentage of total investments, typically around 5% of the portfolio, in very liquid money market assets. Closed-end funds do not have to maintain such a position in "cash-equivalent" securities. What difference between open-end and closed-end funds might account for their differing policies? *(LO 4-2)*

Intermediate

11. An open-end fund has a net asset value of $10.70 per share. It is sold with a front-end load of 6%. What is the offering price? *(LO 4-3)*
12. If the offering price of an open-end fund is $12.30 per share and the fund is sold with a front-end load of 5%, what is its net asset value? *(LO 4-3)*
13. The composition of the Fingroup Fund portfolio is as follows:

Stock	Shares	Price
A	200,000	$35
B	300,000	40
C	400,000	20
D	600,000	25

   The fund has not borrowed any funds, but its accrued management fee with the portfolio manager currently totals $30,000. There are 4 million shares outstanding. What is the net asset value of the fund? *(LO 4-3)*
14. Reconsider the Fingroup Fund in the previous problem. If during the year the portfolio manager sells all of the holdings of stock D and replaces it with 200,000 shares of stock E at $50 per share and 200,000 shares of stock F at $25 per share, what is the portfolio turnover rate? *(LO 4-5)*
15. The Closed Fund is a closed-end investment company with a portfolio currently worth $200 million. It has liabilities of $3 million and 5 million shares outstanding. *(LO 4-3)*
   a. What is the NAV of the fund?
   b. If the fund sells for $36 per share, what is its premium or discount as a percent of NAV?
16. Corporate Fund started the year with a net asset value of $12.50. By year-end, its NAV equaled $12.10. The fund paid year-end distributions of income and capital gains of $1.50. What was the rate of return to an investor in the fund? *(LO 4-3)*
17. A closed-end fund starts the year with a net asset value of $12. By year-end, NAV equals $12.10. At the beginning of the year, the fund is selling at a 2% premium to NAV. By the end of the year, the fund is selling at a 7% discount to NAV. The fund paid year-end distributions of income and capital gains of $1.50. *(LO 4-3)*
   a. What is the rate of return to an investor in the fund during the year?
   b. What would have been the rate of return to an investor who held the same securities as the fund manager during the year?

www.mhhe.com/bkm

18. Loaded-Up Fund charges a 12b-1 fee of 1% and maintains an expense ratio of .75%. Economy Fund charges a front-end load of 2%, but has no 12b-1 fee and an expense ratio of .25%. Assume the rate of return on both funds' portfolios (before any fees) is 6% per year. How much will an investment in each fund grow to after: ***(LO 4-5)***
    a. 1 year?
    b. 3 years?
    c. 10 years?
19. City Street Fund has a portfolio of $450 million and liabilities of $10 million. ***(LO 4-3)***
    a. If there are 44 million shares outstanding, what is net asset value?
    b. If a large investor redeems 1 million shares, what happens to the portfolio value, to shares outstanding, and to NAV?
20. *a.* Impressive Fund had excellent investment performance last year, with portfolio returns that placed it in the top 10% of all funds with the same investment policy. Do you expect it to be a top performer next year? Why or why not?
    b. Suppose instead that the fund was among the poorest performers in its comparison group. Would you be more or less likely to believe its relative performance will persist into the following year? Why? ***(LO 4-5)***
21. Consider a mutual fund with $200 million in assets at the start of the year and with 10 million shares outstanding. The fund invests in a portfolio of stocks that provides dividend income at the end of the year of $2 million. The stocks included in the fund's portfolio increase in price by 8%, but no securities are sold, and there are no capital gains distributions. The fund charges 12b-1 fees of 1%, which are deducted from portfolio assets at year-end. What is net asset value at the start and end of the year? What is the rate of return for an investor in the fund? ***(LO 4-3)***
22. The New Fund had average daily assets of $2.2 billion in the past year. The fund sold $400 million and purchased $500 million worth of stock during the year. What was its turnover ratio? ***(LO 4-5)***
23. If New Fund's expense ratio was 1.1% and the management fee was .7%, what were the total fees paid to the fund's investment managers during the year? What were the other administrative expenses? ***(LO 4-5)***
24. You purchased 1,000 shares of the New Fund at a price of $20 per share at the beginning of the year. You paid a front-end load of 4%. The securities in which the fund invests increase in value by 12% during the year. The fund's expense ratio is 1.2%. What is your rate of return on the fund if you sell your shares at the end of the year? ***(LO 4-5)***
25. The Investments Fund sells Class A shares with a front-end load of 6% and Class B shares with 12b-1 fees of .5% annually as well as back-end load fees that start at 5% and fall by 1% for each full year the investor holds the portfolio (until the fifth year). Assume the portfolio rate of return net of operating expenses is 10% annually. If you plan to sell the fund after four years, are Class A or Class B shares the better choice for you? What if you plan to sell after 15 years? ***(LO 4-5)***
26. You are considering an investment in a mutual fund with a 4% load and an expense ratio of .5%. You can invest instead in a bank CD paying 6% interest. ***(LO 4-5)***
    a. If you plan to invest for two years, what annual rate of return must the fund portfolio earn for you to be better off in the fund than in the CD? Assume annual compounding of returns.
    b. How does your answer change if you plan to invest for six years? Why does your answer change?
    c. Now suppose that instead of a front-end load the fund assesses a 12b-1 fee of .75% per year. What annual rate of return must the fund portfolio earn for you to be better off in the fund than in the CD? Does your answer in this case depend on your time horizon?

27. Suppose that every time a fund manager trades stock, transaction costs such as commissions and bid–ask spreads amount to .4% of the value of the trade. If the portfolio turnover rate is 50%, by how much is the total return of the portfolio reduced by trading costs? ***(LO 4-5)***
28. You expect a tax-free municipal bond portfolio to provide a rate of return of 4%. Management fees of the fund are .6%. What fraction of portfolio income is given up to fees? If the management fees for an equity fund also are .6%, but you expect a portfolio return of 12%, what fraction of portfolio income is given up to fees? Why might management fees be a bigger factor in your investment decision for bond funds than for stock funds? Can your conclusion help explain why unmanaged unit investment trusts tend to focus on the fixed-income market? ***(LO 4-4)***
29. Why would it be challenging to properly compare the performance of an equity fund to a fixed-income mutual fund? ***(LO 4-4)***

Challenge

30. Suppose you observe the investment performance of 350 portfolio managers for five years and rank them by investment returns during each year. After five years, you find that 11 of the funds have investment returns that place the fund in the top half of the sample in each and every year of your sample. Such consistency of performance indicates to you that these must be the funds whose managers are in fact skilled, and you invest your money in these funds. Is your conclusion warranted? ***(LO 4-5)***

WEB *master*

Go to **www.morningstar.com.** In the Morningstar Tools section, click on the link for the *Mutual Fund Screener.* Set the criteria you desire, then click on the *Show Results* tab. If you get no funds that meet all of your criteria, choose the criterion that is least important to you and relax that constraint. Continue the process until you have several funds to compare.

1. Examine all of the views available in the drop-down box menu (*Snapshot, Performance, Portfolio,* and *Nuts and Bolts*) to answer the following questions:
   - Which fund has the best expense ratio?
   - Which funds have the lowest Morningstar Risk rating?
   - Which fund has the best 3-year return? Which has the best 10-year return?
   - Which fund has the lowest turnover ratio? Which has the highest?
   - Which fund has the longest manager tenure? Which has the shortest?
   - Do you need to eliminate any of the funds from consideration due to a minimum initial investment that is higher than you are capable of making?
2. Based on what you know about the funds, which one do you think would be the best one for your investment?
3. Select up to five funds that are of the most interest to you. Click on the button that says *Score These Results.* Customize the criteria listed by indicating their importance to you. Examine the score results. Does the fund with the highest score match the choice you made in part 2?

SOLUTIONS TO CONCEPT *checks*

4.1 NAV = ($3,352 − $270.3)/110.2 = $27.96

4.2 The net investment in the Class A shares after the 4% commission is $9,600. If the fund earns a 10% return, the investment will grow after n years to $\$9,600 \times (1.10)^n$. The Class B shares have no front-end load. However, the net return to the investor after 12b-1 fees will be only 9.5%. In addition, there is a back-end load that reduces the sales proceeds by a percentage equal to (5 − years until sale) until the fifth year, when the back-end load expires.

	Class A Shares	Class B Shares
Horizon	$9,600 × (1.10)^n	$10,000 × (1.095)^n × (1 − percentage exit fee)
1 year	$10,560.00	$10,000 × (1.095) × (1 − .04) = $10,512.00
4 years	$14,055.36	$10,000 × (1.095)^4 × (1 − .01) = $14,232.89
10 years	$24,899.93	$10,000 × (1.095)^{10} = $24,782.28

For a very short horizon such as one year, the Class A shares are the better choice. The front-end and back-end loads are equal, but the Class A shares don't have to pay the 12b-1 fees. For moderate horizons such as four years, the Class B shares dominate because the front-end load of the Class A shares is more costly than the 12b-1 fees and the now-smaller exit fee. For long horizons of 10 years or more, Class A again dominates. In this case, the one-time front-end load is less expensive than the continuing 12b-1 fees.

4.3 *a.* Turnover = $165,000 in trades per $1 million of portfolio value = 16.5%.
b. Realized capital gains are $10 × 1,000 = $10,000 on FedEx and $2.50 × 5,000 = $12,500 on Cisco. The tax owed on the capital gains is therefore .15 × $22,500 = $3,375.

4.4 Twenty percent of the managers are skilled, which accounts for .2 × 400 = 80 of those managers who appear in the top half. There are 120 slots left in the top half, and 320 other managers, so the probability of an unskilled manager "lucking into" the top half in any year is 120/320, or .375. Therefore, of the 120 lucky managers in the first year, we would expect .375 × 120 = 45 to repeat as top-half performers next year. Thus, we should expect a total of 80 + 45 = 125, or 62.5%, of the better initial performers to repeat their top-half performance.

Portfolio Theory

PART 2

The last 90 years witnessed the Great Depression, seven additional recessions of varying severity, and the deep recession that began in 2007. Yet even with these downturns, a dollar invested in a broad portfolio of stocks over this period still grew to a value about 120 times greater than a dollar invested (and reinvested) in safe assets. Why then would anyone invest in a safe asset? Because investors are risk averse, and risk is as important to them as the expected value of returns. Chapter 5, the first of five in Part Two, provides the tools needed to interpret the history of rates of return, and the lessons that history offers for how investors might go about constructing portfolios using both safe and risky assets.

Deciding the proportion an investor desires to put at risk must be augmented by a decision of how to construct an efficient portfolio of risky assets. Chapter 6 lays out modern portfolio theory (MPT), which involves the construction of the risky portfolio. It aims to accomplish efficient diversification across asset classes like bonds and stocks and across individual securities within these asset classes.

This analysis quickly leads to other questions. For example, how should one measure the risk of an individual asset held as part of a diversified portfolio? You may be surprised at the answer. Once we have an acceptable measure of risk, what precisely should be the relation between risk and return? And what is the minimally acceptable rate of return for an investment to be considered attractive? These questions also are addressed in this part of the text. Chapter 7 introduces the Capital Asset Pricing Model (CAPM) and Arbitrage Pricing Theory (APT), as well as index and multi-index models, all mainstays of applied financial economics. These models link risk with the return investors can reasonably expect on various securities.

Next, we come to one of the most controversial topics in investment management, the question of whether portfolio managers—amateur or professional—can outperform simple investment strategies such as "buy a market index fund." The evidence in Chapter 8 will at least make you pause before pursuing active strategies. You will come to appreciate how good active managers must be to outperform passive strategies. Finally, Chapter 9 on behavioral finance is concerned with lessons from psychology that have been proposed to explain irrational investor behavior that leads to observed anomalies in patterns of asset returns.

Chapters in This Part:

Chapter 5

Risk and Return: Past and Prologue

Learning Objectives:

LO5-1 Compute various measures of return on multi-year investments.

LO5-2 Use data on the past performance of stocks and bonds or scenario analysis to characterize the risk and return features of these investments.

LO5-3 Determine the expected return and risk of portfolios that are constructed by combining risky assets with risk-free investments in Treasury bills.

LO5-4 Use the Sharpe ratio to evaluate the investment performance of a portfolio and provide a guide for capital allocation.

What constitutes a satisfactory investment portfolio? Until the early 1970s, a reasonable answer would have been a federally insured bank savings account (a risk-free asset) plus a risky portfolio of U.S. stocks. Nowadays, investors have access to a vast array of assets and can easily construct portfolios that include foreign stocks and bonds, real estate, precious metals, and collectibles. Even more complex strategies may include futures, options, and other derivatives to insure portfolios against specified risks.

Clearly every individual security must be judged on its contributions to both the expected return and the risk of the entire portfolio. We begin with an examination of various conventions for measuring and reporting rates of return. Next, we turn to the historical performance of several broadly diversified investment portfolios. In doing so, we use a risk-free portfolio of Treasury bills as a benchmark to evaluate the historical performance of diversified stock and bond portfolios.

We then consider the trade-offs that arise when investors practice the simplest form of risk control, capital allocation: choosing the fraction of the portfolio invested in virtually risk-free securities versus risky securities. We show how to calculate the performance one may expect from various allocations between a risk-free asset and a risky portfolio and contemplate the mix that would best suit different investors. With this background, we can evaluate a passive strategy that will serve as a benchmark for the active strategies considered in the next chapter.

Related websites for this chapter are available at www.mhhe.com/bkm.

5.1 RATES OF RETURN

A key measure of investors' success is the rate at which their funds have grown during the investment period. The total **holding-period return (HPR)** of a share of stock depends on the increase (or decrease) in the price of the share over the investment period as well as on any dividend income the share has provided. The rate of return is defined as dollars earned over the investment period (price appreciation as well as dividends) per dollar invested:

holding-period return (HPR)

Rate of return over a given investment period.

$$\text{HPR} = \frac{\text{Ending price} - \text{Beginning price} + \text{Cash dividend}}{\text{Beginning price}} \quad \textbf{(5.1)}$$

This definition of the HPR assumes that the dividend is paid at the end of the holding period. When dividends are received earlier, the definition ignores reinvestment income between the receipt of the dividend and the end of the holding period. The percentage return from dividends, cash dividends/beginning price, is called the *dividend yield,* and so the dividend yield plus the capital gains yield equals the HPR.

This definition of holding return is easy to modify for other types of investments. For example, the HPR on a bond would be calculated using the same formula, except that the bond's interest or coupon payments would take the place of the stock's dividend payments.

EXAMPLE 5.1

Holding-Period Return

Consider investing some of your money, now all invested in a bank account, in a stock market index fund. The price of a share in the fund is currently $100, and your time horizon is one year. You expect the cash dividend during the year to be $4, so your expected dividend yield is 4%.

Your HPR will depend on the price one year from now. Suppose your best guess is that it will be $110 per share. Then your *capital gain* will be $10, so your capital gains yield is $10/$100 = .10, or 10%. The total holding-period rate of return is the sum of the dividend yield plus the capital gains yield, 4% + 10% = 14%.

$$\text{HPR} = \frac{\$110 - \$100 + \$4}{\$100} = .14, \text{ or } 14\%$$

Measuring Investment Returns over Multiple Periods

The holding-period return is a simple and unambiguous measure of investment return over a single period. But often you will be interested in average returns over longer periods of time. For example, you might want to measure how well a mutual fund has performed over the preceding five-year period. In this case, return measurement is more ambiguous.

Consider a fund that starts with $1 million under management. It receives additional funds from new and existing shareholders and also redeems shares of existing shareholders so that net cash inflow can be positive or negative. The fund's quarterly results are as given in Table 5.1, with negative numbers in parentheses.

The numbers indicate that when the firm does well (i.e., achieves a high HPR), it attracts new funds; otherwise it may suffer a net outflow. For example, the 10% return in the first quarter by itself increased assets under management by .10 × $1 million = $100,000; it also elicited new investments of $100,000, thus bringing assets under management to $1.2 million

TABLE 5.1 Quarterly cash flows and rates of return of a mutual fund

	1st Quarter	2nd Quarter	3rd Quarter	4th Quarter
Assets under management at start of quarter ($ million)	1.0	1.2	2.0	0.8
Holding-period return (%)	10.0	25.0	(20.0)	20.0
Total assets before net inflows	1.1	1.5	1.6	0.96
Net inflow ($ million)*	0.1	0.5	(0.8)	0.6
Assets under management at end of quarter ($ million)	1.2	2.0	0.8	1.56

*New investment less redemptions and distributions, all assumed to occur at the end of each quarter.

by the end of the quarter. An even better HPR in the second quarter elicited a larger net inflow, and the second quarter ended with $2 million under management. However, HPR in the third quarter was negative, and net inflows were negative.

How would we characterize fund performance over the year, given that the fund experienced both cash inflows and outflows? There are several candidate measures of performance, each with its own advantages and shortcomings. These are the *arithmetic average,* the *geometric average,* and the *dollar-weighted return.* These measures may vary considerably, so it is important to understand their differences.

arithmetic average

The sum of returns in each period divided by the number of periods.

Arithmetic average The **arithmetic average** of the quarterly returns is just the sum of the quarterly returns divided by the number of quarters; in the above example: $(10 + 25 - 20 + 20)/4 = 8.75\%$. Since this statistic ignores compounding, it does not represent an equivalent, single quarterly rate for the year. However, without information beyond the historical sample, the arithmetic average is the best forecast of performance for the next quarter.

geometric average

The single per-period return that gives the same cumulative performance as the sequence of actual returns.

Geometric average The **geometric average** of the quarterly returns is equal to the single per-period return that would give the same cumulative performance as the sequence of actual returns. We calculate the geometric average by compounding the actual period-by-period returns and then finding the per-period rate that will compound to the same final value. In our example, the geometric average quarterly return, r_G, is defined by:

$$(1 + .10) \times (1 + .25) \times (1 - .20) \times (1 + .20) = (1 + r_G)^4$$

The left-hand side of this equation is the compounded year-end value of a $1 investment earning the four quarterly returns. The right-hand side is the compounded value of a $1 investment earning r_G *each* quarter. We solve for r_G:

$$r_G = [(1 + .10) \times (1 + .25) \times (1 - .20) \times (1 + .20)]^{1/4} - 1 = .0719, \text{ or } 7.19\% \quad \textbf{(5.2)}$$

The geometric return is also called a *time-weighted average return* because it ignores the quarter-to-quarter variation in funds under management. In fact, an investor will obtain a larger cumulative return when high returns are earned in periods when larger sums have been invested and low returns are earned when less money is at risk. In Table 5.1, the higher returns (25% and 20%) were achieved in quarters 2 and 4, when the fund managed $1,200,000 and $800,000, respectively. The lower returns (−20% and 10%) occurred when the fund managed $2,000,000 and $1,000,000, respectively. In this case, better returns were earned when *less* money was under management—an unfavorable combination.

Published data on past returns earned by mutual funds actually are *required* to be time-weighted returns. The rationale for this practice is that since the fund manager does not have full control over the amount of assets under management, we should not weight returns in one period more heavily than those in other periods when assessing "typical" past performance.

Dollar-weighted return To account for varying amounts under management, we treat the fund cash flows as we would a capital budgeting problem in corporate finance and compute the portfolio manager's internal rate of return (IRR). The initial value of $1 million and the net cash inflows are treated as the cash flows associated with an investment "project." The year-end "liquidation value" of the portfolio is the final cash flow of the project. In our example, the investor's net cash flows are as follows:

	Quarter				
	0	**1**	**2**	**3**	**4**
Net cash flow ($ million)	−1.0	−.1	−.5	.8	−.6 + 1.56 = .96

The entry for time 0 reflects the starting contribution of $1 million; the negative entries for times 1 and 2 are additional net inflows in those quarters, while the positive value for quarter 3 signifies a withdrawal of funds. Finally, the entry for time 4 represents the sum of the final (negative) cash inflow plus the value of the portfolio at the end of the fourth quarter. The latter is the value for which the portfolio could have been liquidated at year-end.

The **dollar-weighted average return** is the internal rate of return of the project, which is 3.38%. The IRR is the interest rate that sets the present value of the cash flows realized on the portfolio (including the $1.56 million for which the portfolio can be liquidated at the end of the year) equal to the initial cost of establishing the portfolio. It therefore is the interest rate that satisfies the following equation:

dollar-weighted average return

The internal rate of return on an investment.

$$0 = -1.0 + \frac{-.1}{1 + \text{IRR}} + \frac{-.5}{(1 + \text{IRR})^2} + \frac{.8}{(1 + \text{IRR})^3} + \frac{.96}{(1 + \text{IRR})^4} \quad \textbf{(5.3)}$$

The dollar-weighted return in this example is less than the time-weighted return of 7.19% because, as we noted, the portfolio returns were higher when less money was under management. The difference between the dollar- and time-weighted average return in this case is quite large.

CONCEPT check 5.1

A fund begins with $10 million and reports the following three-month results (with negative figures in parentheses):

	Month		
	1	**2**	**3**
Net inflows (end of month, $ million)	3	5	0
HPR (%)	2	8	(4)

Compute the arithmetic, time-weighted, and dollar-weighted average returns.

Conventions for Annualizing Rates of Return

We've seen that there are several ways to compute average rates of return. There also is some variation in how the mutual fund in our example might annualize its quarterly returns.

Returns on assets with regular cash flows, such as mortgages (with monthly payments) and bonds (with semiannual coupons), usually are quoted as annual percentage rates, or APRs, which annualize per-period rates using a simple interest approach, ignoring compound interest:

$$\text{APR} = \text{Per-period rate} \times \text{Periods per year}$$

However, because it ignores compounding, the APR does not equal the rate at which your invested funds actually grow. This is called the *effective annual rate,* or EAR. When there are n compounding periods in the year, we first recover the rate per period as APR/n and then compound that rate for the number of periods in a year. (For example, $n = 12$ for monthly payment mortgages and $n = 2$ for bonds making payments semiannually.)

$$1 + \text{EAR} = (1 + \text{Rate per period})^n = \left(1 + \frac{\text{APR}}{n}\right)^n \quad \textbf{(5.4)}$$

Since you can earn the APR each period, after one year (when n periods have passed), your cumulative return is $(1 + \text{APR}/n)^n$. Note that one needs to know the holding period when given an APR in order to convert it to an effective rate.

Rearranging Equation 5.4, we can also find APR given EAR:

$$\text{APR} = [(1 + \text{EAR})^{1/n} - 1] \times n$$

The EAR diverges by greater amounts from the APR as n becomes larger (we compound cash flows more frequently). In the limit, we can envision continuous compounding when n becomes extremely large in Equation 5.4. With continuous compounding, the relationship between the APR and EAR becomes

$$1 + \text{EAR} = e^{\text{APR}}$$

or, equivalently,

$$\text{APR} = \ln(1 + \text{EAR})$$

More generally, the EAR of any investment can be converted to an equivalent continuously compounded rate, r_{cc}, using the relationship

$$r_{cc} = \ln(1 + \text{EAR}) \quad \textbf{(5.5)}$$

We will return to continuous compounding later in the chapter.

EXAMPLE 5.2

Annualizing Treasury-Bill Returns

Suppose you buy a $10,000 face value Treasury bill maturing in one month for $9,900. On the bill's maturity date, you collect the face value. Since there are no other interest payments, the holding-period return for this one-month investment is

$$\text{HPR} = \frac{\text{Cash income} + \text{Price change}}{\text{Initial price}} = \frac{\$100}{\$9{,}900} = .0101 = 1.01\%$$

The APR on this investment is therefore 1.01% × 12 = 12.12%. The effective annual rate is higher:

$$1 + \text{EAR} = (1.0101)^{12} = 1.1282$$

which implies that EAR = .1282 = 12.82%.

A warning: Terminology can be loose. Occasionally, *annual percentage yield* or *APY* and even *APR* are used interchangeably with effective annual rate, and this can lead to confusion. To avoid error, you must be alert to context.

The difficulties in interpreting rates of return over time do not end here. Two thorny issues remain: the uncertainty surrounding the investment in question and the effect of inflation.

5.2 RISK AND RISK PREMIUMS

Any investment involves some degree of uncertainty about future holding-period returns, and in many cases that uncertainty is considerable. Sources of investment risk range from macroeconomic fluctuations, to the changing fortunes of various industries, to asset-specific unexpected developments. Analysis of these multiple sources of risk is presented in Part Four, "Security Analysis."

Scenario Analysis and Probability Distributions

When we attempt to quantify risk, we begin with the question: What HPRs are possible, and how likely are they? A good way to approach this question is to devise a list of possible economic outcomes, or *scenarios,* and specify both the likelihood (probability) of each scenario and the HPR the asset will realize in that scenario. Therefore, this approach is called **scenario analysis.** The list of possible HPRs with associated probabilities is the **probability distribution** of HPRs. Consider an investment in a broad portfolio of stocks, say, an index fund, which we will refer to as the "stock market." A very simple scenario analysis for the stock market (assuming only four possible scenarios) is illustrated in Spreadsheet 5.1.

scenario analysis

Process of devising a list of possible economic scenarios and specifying the likelihood of each one, as well as the HPR that will be realized in each case.

The probability distribution lets us derive measurements for both the reward and the risk of the investment. The reward from the investment is its **expected return,** which you can think of as the average HPR you would earn if you were to repeat an investment in the asset many times. The expected return also is called the *mean of the distribution* of HPRs and often is referred to as the *mean return.*

probability distribution

List of possible outcomes with associated probabilities.

To compute the expected return from the data provided, we label scenarios by s and denote the HPR in each scenario as $r(s)$, with probability $p(s)$. The expected return, denoted $E(r)$, is then the weighted average of returns in all possible scenarios, $s = 1, \ldots, S$, with weights equal to the probability of that particular scenario.

expected return

The mean value of the distribution of HPR.

$$E(r) = \sum_{s=1}^{S} p(s)r(s) \tag{5.6}$$

Each entry in column D of Spreadsheet 5.1 corresponds to one of the products in the summation in Equation 5.6. The value in cell D7, which is the sum of these products, is therefore the expected return. Therefore, $E(r) = 10\%$.

Because there is risk to the investment, the actual return may be (a lot) more or less than 10%. If a "boom" materializes, the return will be better, 30%, but in a severe recession the return will be a disappointing −37%. How can we quantify this uncertainty?

The "surprise" return in any scenario is the difference between the actual return and the expected return. For example, in a boom (scenario 4) the surprise is $r(4) - E(r) = 30\% - 10\% = 20\%$. In a severe recession (scenario 1), the surprise is $r(1) - E(r) = -37\% - 10\% = -47\%$.

SPREADSHEET 5.1

Scenario analysis for the stock market

	A	B	C	D	E	F
1				Column B x	Deviation from	Column B x
2	Scenario	Probability	HPR (%)	Column C	Mean Return	Squared Deviation
3	1. Severe recession	.05	−37	−1.85	−47.00	110.45
4	2. Mild recession	.25	−11	−2.75	−21.00	110.25
5	3. Normal growth	.40	14	5.60	4.00	6.40
6	4. Boom	.30	30	9.00	20.00	120.00
7	Column sums:		Expected return =	10.00	Variance =	347.10
8			Square root of variance = Standard deviation (%) =			18.63

Please visit us at www.mhhe.com/bkm

variance

The expected value of the squared deviation from the mean.

Uncertainty surrounding the investment is a function of both the magnitudes and the probabilities of the possible surprises. To summarize risk with a single number, we define the **variance** as the expected value of the *squared* deviation from the mean (the expected squared "surprise" across scenarios).

$$\mathrm{Var}(r) \equiv \sigma^2 = \sum_{s=1}^{S} p(s)[r(s) - E(r)]^2 \qquad \textbf{(5.7)}$$

We square the deviations because negative deviations would offset positive deviations otherwise, with the result that the expected deviation from the mean return would necessarily be zero. Squared deviations are necessarily positive. Squaring (a nonlinear -transformation) exaggerates large (positive or negative) deviations and deemphasizes small deviations.

Another result of squaring deviations is that the variance has a dimension of percent squared. To give the measure of risk the same dimension as expected return (%), we use the **standard deviation,** defined as the square root of the variance:

standard deviation

The square root of the variance.

$$SD(r) \equiv \sigma = \sqrt{\mathrm{Var}(r)} \qquad \textbf{(5.8)}$$

EXAMPLE 5.3

Expected Return and Standard Deviation

Applying Equation 5.6 to the data in Spreadsheet 5.1, we find that the expected rate of return on the stock index fund is

$$E(r) = .05 \times (-37) + .25 \times (-11) + .40 \times 14 + .30 \times 30 = 10\%$$

We use Equation 5.7 to find the variance. First we take the difference between the holding-period return in each scenario and the mean return, then we square that difference, and finally we multiply by the probability of each scenario. The sum of the probability-weighted squared deviations is the variance.

$$\sigma^2 = .05(-37 - 10)^2 + .25(-11 - 10)^2 + .40(14 - 10)^2 + .30(30 - 10)^2 = 347.10$$

and so the standard deviation is

$$\sigma = \sqrt{347.10} = 18.63\%$$

Column F of Spreadsheet 5.1 replicates these calculations. Each entry in that column is the squared deviation from the mean multiplied by the probability of that scenario. The sum of the probability-weighted squared deviations that appears in cell F7 is the variance, and the square root of that value is the standard deviation (in cell F8).

The Normal Distribution

The normal distribution is central to the theory *and* practice of investments. Its familiar bell-shaped plot is symmetric, with identical values for all three standard measures of "typical" results: the mean (the expected value discussed earlier), the median (the value above and below which we expect 50% of the observations), and the mode (the most likely value).

Figure 5.1 illustrates a normal distribution with a mean of 10% and standard deviation (SD) of 20%. Notice that the probabilities are highest for outcomes near the mean and are significantly lower for outcomes far from the mean. But what do we mean by an outcome "far" from the mean? A return 15% below the mean would hardly be noteworthy if typical volatility were high, for example, if the standard deviation of returns were 20%, but that same outcome would be highly unusual if the standard deviation were only 5%. For this reason, it is often useful to think about deviations from the mean in terms of how many standard deviations they represent. If the standard deviation is 20%, that 15% negative surprise would be only three-fourths of a standard deviation, unfortunate perhaps but not uncommon. But if the standard deviation were only 5%, a 15% deviation would be a "three-sigma event," and quite rare.

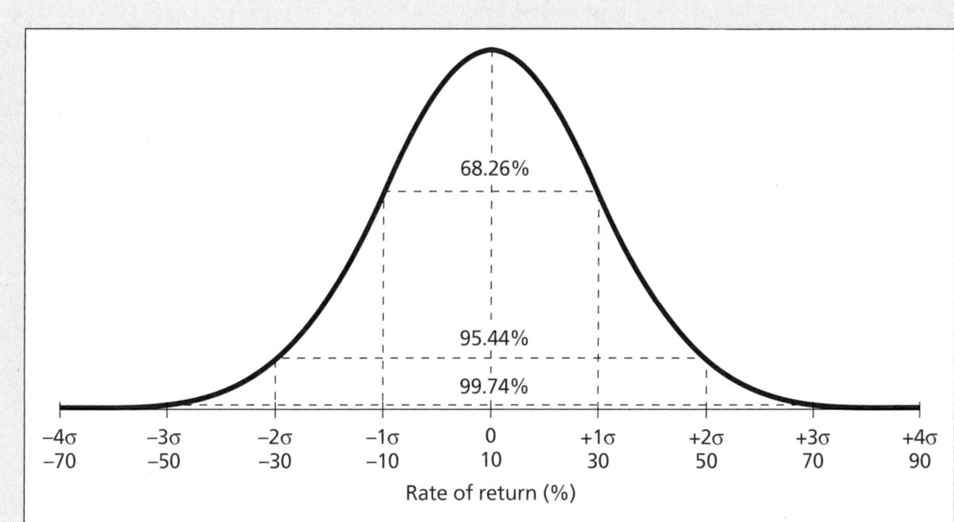

FIGURE 5.1

The normal distribution with mean return 10% and standard deviation 20%

We can transform any normally distributed return, r_i, into a "standard deviation score," by first subtracting the mean return (to obtain distance from the mean or return "surprise") and then dividing by the standard deviation (which enables us to measure distance from the mean in units of standard deviations).

$$sr_i = \frac{r_i - E(r_i)}{\sigma_i} \quad \textbf{(5.9A)}$$

This standardized return, which we have denoted sr_i, is normally distributed with a mean of zero and a standard deviation of 1. We therefore say that sr_i is a "standard normal" variable.

Conversely, we can start with a standard normal return, sr_i, and recover the original return by multiplying by the standard deviation and adding back the mean return:

$$r_i = E(r_i) + sr_i \times \sigma_i \quad \textbf{(5.9B)}$$

In fact, this is how we drew Figure 5.1. Start with a standard normal (mean = 0 and SD = 1); next, multiply the distance from the mean by the assumed standard deviation of 20%; finally, recenter the mean away from zero by adding 10%. This gives us a normal variable with mean 10% and standard deviation 20%.

Figure 5.1 shows that when returns are normally distributed, roughly two-thirds (more precisely, 68.26%) of the observations fall within one standard deviation of the mean, that is, the probability that any observation in a sample of returns would be no more than one standard deviation away from the mean is 68.26%. Deviations from the mean of more than two SDs are even rarer: 95.44% of the observations are expected to lie within this range. Finally, only 2.6 out of 1,000 observations are expected to deviate from the mean by three or more SDs.

Two special properties of the normal distribution lead to critical simplifications of investment management when returns are normally distributed:

1. The return on a portfolio comprising two or more assets whose returns are normally distributed also will be normally distributed.
2. The normal distribution is completely described by its mean and standard deviation. No other statistic is needed to learn about the behavior of normally distributed returns.

These two properties in turn imply this far-reaching conclusion:

3. The standard deviation is the appropriate measure of risk for a portfolio of assets with normally distributed returns. In this case, no other statistic can improve the risk assessment conveyed by the standard deviation of a portfolio.

value at risk (VaR)

Measure of downside risk. The worst loss that will be suffered with a given probability, often 5%.

Suppose you worry about large investment losses in worst-case scenarios for your portfolio. You might ask: "How much would I lose in a fairly extreme outcome, for example, if my return were in the fifth percentile of the distribution?" You can expect your investment experience to be worse than this value only 5% of the time and better than this value 95% of the time. In investments parlance, this cutoff is called the **value at risk** (denoted by **VaR,** to distinguish it from Var, the common notation for variance). A loss-averse investor might desire to limit portfolio VaR, that is, limit the loss corresponding to a probability of 5%.

For normally distributed returns, VaR can be derived from the mean and standard deviation of the distribution. We calculate it using Excel's standard normal function =NORMSINV(0.05). This function computes the fifth percentile of a normal distribution with a mean of zero and a variance of 1, which turns out to be −1.64485. In other words, a value that is 1.64485 standard deviations below the mean would correspond to a VaR of 5%, that is, to the fifth percentile of the distribution.

$$\text{VaR} = E(r) + (-1.64485)\sigma \quad \textbf{(5.10)}$$

We can obtain this value directly from Excel's nonstandard normal function =NORMINV (.05, $E(r)$, σ).

When faced with a sample of actual returns that may not be normally distributed, we must estimate the VaR directly. The 5% VaR is the fifth-percentile rate of return. For a sample of 100 returns this is straightforward: If the rates are ordered from high to low, count the fifth observation from the bottom.

Calculating the 5% VaR for samples where 5% of the observations don't make an integer requires interpolation. Suppose we have 72 monthly observations so that 5% of the sample is 3.6 observations. We approximate the VaR by going .6 of the distance from the third to the fourth rate from the bottom. Suppose these rates are −42% and −37%. The interpolated value for VaR is then −42 + .6 (42 − 37) = −39%.

In practice, analysts sometimes compare the historical sample VaR to the VaR implied by a normal distribution with the same mean and SD as the sample rates. The difference between these VaR values indicates the deviation of the observed rates from normality.

Please visit us at www.mhhe.com/bkm

a. The current value of a stock portfolio is $23 million. A financial analyst summarizes the uncertainty about next year's holding-period return using the scenario analysis in the following spreadsheet. What are the annual holding-period returns of the portfolio in each scenario? Calculate the expected holding-period return, the standard deviation of returns, and the 5% VaR. What is the VaR of a portfolio with normally distributed returns with the same mean and standard deviation as this stock? The spreadsheet is available at the Online Learning Center (go to **www.mhhe.com/bkm,** and link to the Chapter 5 material).

	A	B	C	D	E
1	**Business Conditions**	**Scenario, *s***	**Probability, *p***	**End-of-Year Value ($ million)**	**Annual Dividend ($ million)**
2	High growth	1	.30	35	4.40
3	Normal growth	2	.45	27	4.00
4	No growth	3	.20	15	4.00
5	Recession	4	.05	8	2.00

b. Suppose that the worst three rates of return in a sample of 36 monthly observations are 17%, −5%, and 2%. Estimate the 5% VaR.

Normality over Time

The fact that portfolios of normally distributed assets also are normally distributed greatly simplifies analysis of risk because standard deviation, a simple-to-calculate number, is the appropriate risk measure for normally distributed portfolios.

But even if returns are normal for any particular time period, will they also be normal for other holding periods? Suppose that monthly rates are normally distributed with a mean of 1%. The expected annual rate of return is then $1.01^{12} - 1$. Can this annual rate, which is a nonlinear function of the monthly return, also be normally distributed? Unfortunately, the answer is no. Similarly, why would monthly rates be normally distributed when a monthly rate is $(1 + \text{daily rate})^{30} - 1$? Indeed, they are not. So, do we really get to enjoy the simplifications offered by the normal distribution?

Despite these potential complications, when returns over very short time periods (e.g., an hour or even a day) are normally distributed, then HPRs up to holding periods as long as a month will be *nearly* normal, and we can treat them as if they are normal. Longer-term, for example, annual, HPRs will indeed deviate more substantially from normality, but even here, if we expressed those HPRs as continuously compounded rates, they will remain normally distributed. The practical implication is this: Use continuously compounded rates in all work where normality plays a crucial role, as in estimating VaR from actual returns.

To see why relatively short-term rates are still nearly normal, consider these calculations: Suppose that rates are normally distributed over an infinitesimally short period. Beyond that, compounding, strictly speaking, takes them adrift from normality. But those deviations will be very small. Suppose that on an annual basis the continuously compounded rate of return has a mean of .12 (i.e., 12%; we must work with decimals when using continuously compounded rates). Equivalently, the effective annual rate has an expected value of $E(r) = e^{.12} - 1 = 0.1275$. So the difference between the effective annual rate and continuously compounded rate is meaningful, .75%, or 75 basis points. On a monthly basis, however, the equivalent continuously compounded expected holding-period return is 1%, implying an expected monthly effective rate of $e^{.01} - 1 = .01005$. The difference between effective annual and continuously compounded rates here is trivial, only one-half of a basis point. For shorter periods the difference will be smaller still. So, when continuously compounded rates are exactly normal, rates over periods up to a month are so close to those continuously compounded values that we can treat them as if they are effectively normal.

Another important aspect of (normal) continuously compounded rates over time is this: Just as the total continuously compounded rate and the risk premium grow in direct proportion to the length of the investment period, so does the variance (*not* the standard deviation) of the total continuously compounded return and the risk premium. Hence, for an asset with annual continuously compounded SD of .20 (20%), the variance is .04, and the quarterly variance will be .01, implying a quarterly standard deviation of .10, or 10%. (Verify that the monthly standard deviation is 5.77%.) Because variance grows in direct proportion to time, the standard deviation grows in proportion to the square root of time.

Deviation from Normality and Value at Risk

The scenario analysis laid out in Spreadsheet 5.1 offers insight about the issue of normality in practice. While a four-scenario analysis is quite simplistic, even this simple example can nevertheless shed light on how practical analysis might take shape.[1]

How can the returns specified in the scenario analysis in Spreadsheet 5.1 be judged against the normal distribution? (As prescribed above, we first convert the effective rates specified

[1]You may wonder: Is the fact that the probability of the worst-case scenario is .05 in Spreadsheet 5.1 just a lucky happenstance given our interest in the 5% VaR? The answer is no. Given investor concern about VaR, it is fair (in fact, necessary) to demand of analysts that their scenario analysis explicitly take a stand on the rate of return corresponding to the probability of the VaR of interest, here .05.

FIGURE 5.2

Comparing scenario analysis (from Spreadsheet 5.1) to a normal distribution with the same mean and standard deviation

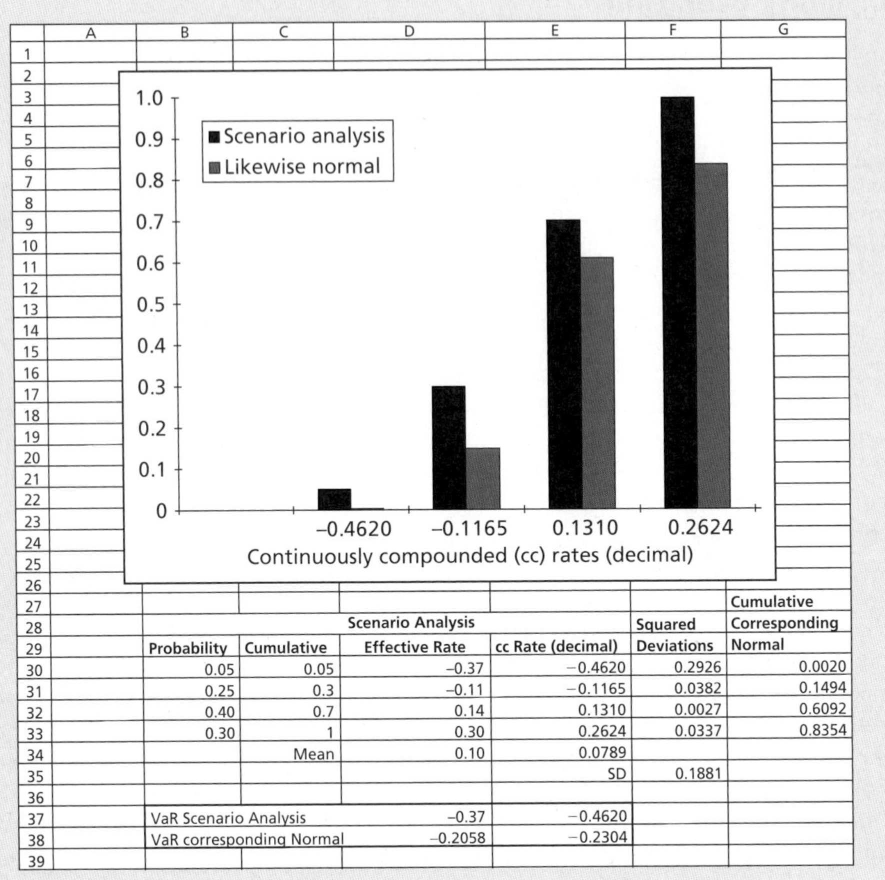

	B	C	D	E	F	G
27						Cumulative
28			Scenario Analysis		Squared	Corresponding
29	Probability	Cumulative	Effective Rate	cc Rate (decimal)	Deviations	Normal
30	0.05	0.05	−0.37	−0.4620	0.2926	0.0020
31	0.25	0.3	−0.11	−0.1165	0.0382	0.1494
32	0.40	0.7	0.14	0.1310	0.0027	0.6092
33	0.30	1	0.30	0.2624	0.0337	0.8354
34		Mean	0.10	0.0789		
35				SD	0.1881	
36						
37	VaR Scenario Analysis		−0.37	−0.4620		
38	VaR corresponding Normal		−0.2058	−0.2304		
39						

in each scenario to their equivalent continuously compounded rates using Equation 5.5.) Obviously, it is naive to believe that this simple analysis includes all possible rates. But while we cannot explicitly pin down probabilities of rates other than those given in the table, we can get a good sense of the entire spectrum of potential outcomes by examining the distribution of the assumed scenario rates, as well as their mean and standard deviation.

Figure 5.2 shows the known points from the cumulative distribution of the scenario analysis next to the corresponding points from a "likewise normal distribution" (a normal distribution with the same mean and standard deviation, SD). Below the graph, we see a table of the actual distributions. The mean in cell D34 is computed from the formula =SUMPRODUCT($B$30:$B$33, D30:D33), where the probability cells B30:B33 are fixed to allow copying to the right.[2] Similarly, the SD in cell F35 is computed from =SUMPRODUCT(B30:B33, F30:F33)^0.5. The 5% VaR of the normal distribution in cell E38 is computed from =NORMINV(0.05, E34, F35).

VaR values appear in cells D37 and D38. The VaR from the scenario analysis, −37%, is far worse than the VaR derived from the corresponding normal distribution, −20.58%. This immediately suggests that the scenario analysis entails a higher probability of extreme losses than would be consistent with a normal distribution. On the other hand, the normal distribution allows for the possibility of extremely large returns, beyond the maximum return of 30% envisioned in the scenario analysis. We conclude that the scenario analysis has a distribution that is skewed to the left compared to the normal. It has a longer left tail (larger losses) and a

[2]The Excel function SUMPRODUCT multiplies each term in the first column specified (in this case, the probabilities in column B) with the corresponding terms in the second column specified (in this case, the returns in column D), and then adds up those products. This gives us the expected rate of return across scenarios.

shorter right tail (smaller gains). It makes up for this negative attribute with a larger probability of positive, but not extremely large, gains (14% and 30%).

This example shows when and why the VaR is an important statistic. When returns are normal, knowing just the mean and standard deviation allows us to fully describe the entire distribution. In that case, we do not need to estimate VaR explicitly—we can calculate it exactly from the properties of the normal distribution. But when returns are not normal, the VaR conveys important additional information beyond mean and standard deviation. It gives us additional insight into the shape of the distribution, for example, skewness or risk of extreme negative outcomes.[3]

Because risk is largely driven by the likelihood of extreme negative returns, two additional statistics are used to indicate whether a portfolio's probability distribution differs significantly from normality with respect to potential extreme values. The first is **kurtosis,** which compares the frequency of extreme values to that of the normal distribution. The kurtosis of the normal distribution is zero, so positive values indicate higher frequency of extreme values than this benchmark. A negative value suggests that extreme values are less frequent than with the normal distribution. Kurtosis sometimes is called "fat tail risk," as plots of probability distributions with higher likelihood of extreme events will be higher than the normal distribution at both ends or "tails" of the distribution; in other words, the distributions exhibit "fat tails." Similarly, exposure to extreme events is often called *tail risk,* because these are outcomes in the far reaches or "tail" of the probability distribution.

kurtosis

Measure of the fatness of the tails of a probability distribution relative to that of a normal distribution. Indicates likelihood of extreme outcomes.

The second statistic is the **skew,** which measures the asymmetry of the distribution. Skew takes on a value of zero if, like the normal, the distribution is symmetric. Negative skew suggests that extreme negative values are more frequent than extreme positive ones. Nonzero values for kurtosis and skew indicate that special attention should be paid to the VaR, in addition to the use of standard deviation as measure of portfolio risk.

skew

Measure of the asymmetry of a probability distribution.

Using Time Series of Return

Scenario analysis postulates a probability distribution of future returns. But where do the probabilities and rates of return come from? In large part, they come from observing a sample history of returns. Suppose we observe a 10-year time series of monthly returns on a diversified portfolio of stocks. We can interpret each of the 120 observations as one potential "scenario" offered to us by history. Adding judgment to this history, we can develop a scenario analysis of future returns.

As a first step, we estimate the expected return, standard deviation, and VaR for the sample history. We assume that each of the 120 returns represents one independent draw from the historical probability distribution. Hence, each return is assigned an equal probability of 1/120 = .0083. When you use a fixed probability in Equation 5.6, you obtain the simple average of the observations, often used to estimate the mean return.

As mentioned earlier, the same principle applies to the VaR. We sort the returns from high to low. The bottom six observations comprise the lower 5% of the distribution. The sixth observation from the bottom is just at the fifth percentile, and so would be the 5% VaR for the historical sample.

Estimating variance from Equation 5.7 requires a minor correction. Remember that variance is the expected value of squared deviations from the mean return. But the true mean is not observable; we *estimate* it using the sample average. If we compute variance as the average of squared deviations from the sample average, we will slightly underestimate it because this procedure ignores the fact that the average necessarily includes some estimation error. The necessary correction turns out to be simple: With a sample of n observations, we divide the sum of the squared deviations from the sample average by $n - 1$ instead of n. Thus, the estimates of variance and standard deviation from a time series of returns, r_t, are

$$\text{Var}(r_t) = \frac{1}{n-1}\Sigma(r_t - \bar{r}_t)^2 \quad \text{SD}(r_t) = \sqrt{\text{Var}(r_t)} \quad \bar{r}_t = \frac{1}{n}\Sigma r_t \qquad \textbf{(5.11)}$$

[3]The financial crisis of 2008–2009 demonstrated that bank portfolio returns are far from normally distributed, with exposure to unlikely but catastrophic returns in extreme market meltdowns. The international Basel accord on bank regulation requires banks to monitor portfolio VaR to better control risk.

EXAMPLE 5.4

Historical Means and Standard Deviations

To illustrate how to calculate average returns and standard deviations from historical data, let's compute these statistics for the returns on the S&P 500 portfolio using five years of data from the following table. The average return over this period is 16.7%, computed by dividing the sum of column (1), below, by the number of observations. In column (2), we take the deviation of each year's return from the 16.7% average return. In column (3), we calculate the squared deviation. The variance is, from Equation 5.11, the sum of the five squared deviations divided by (5 − 1). The standard deviation is the square root of the variance. If you input the column of rates into a spreadsheet, the AVERAGE and STDEV functions will give you the statistics directly.

Year	(1) Rate of Return	(2) Deviation from Average Return	(3) Squared Deviation
1	16.9%	0.2%	0.0
2	31.3	14.6	213.2
3	−3.2	−19.9	396.0
4	30.7	14.0	196.0
5	7.7	−9.0	81.0
Total	83.4%		886.2

$$\text{Average rate of return} = 83.4/5 = 16.7$$

$$\text{Variance} = \frac{1}{5-1} \times 886.2 = 221.6$$

$$\text{Standard deviation} = \sqrt{221.6} = 14.9\%$$

Risk Premiums and Risk Aversion

How much, if anything, would you invest in the index stock fund described in Spreadsheet 5.1? First, you must ask how much of an expected reward is offered to compensate for the risk involved in stocks.

We measure the "reward" as the difference between the expected HPR on the index fund and the **risk-free rate,** the rate you can earn on Treasury bills. We call this difference the **risk premium.** If the risk-free rate in the example is 4% per year, and the expected index fund return is 10%, then the risk premium on stocks is 6% per year.

risk-free rate

The rate of return that can be earned with certainty.

risk premium

An expected return in excess of that on risk-free securities.

The rate of return on Treasury bills also varies over time. However, we know the rate of return on T-bills *at the beginning* of the holding period, while we can't know the return we will earn on risky assets until the end of the holding period. Therefore, to study the risk premium on risky assets we compile a series of **excess returns,** that is, returns in excess of the T-bill rate in each period. A reasonable forecast of an asset's risk premium is the average of its historical excess returns.

excess return

Rate of return in excess of the risk-free rate.

The degree to which investors are willing to commit funds to stocks depends on **risk aversion.** It seems obvious that investors are risk averse in the sense that, without a positive risk premium, they would not be willing to invest in stocks. In theory then, there must always be a positive risk premium on all risky assets in order to induce risk-averse investors to hold the existing supply of these assets.

risk aversion

Reluctance to accept risk.

A positive risk premium distinguishes speculation from gambling. Investors taking on risk to earn a risk premium are speculating. Speculation is undertaken *despite* the risk because of a favorable risk-return trade-off. In contrast, gambling is the assumption of risk for no purpose beyond the enjoyment of the risk itself. Gamblers take on risk even without a risk premium.[4]

[4]Sometimes a gamble might *seem* like speculation to the participants. If two investors differ in their forecasts of the future, they might take opposite positions in a security, and both may have an expectation of earning a positive risk premium. In such cases, only one party can, in fact, be correct.

To determine an investor's optimal portfolio strategy, we need to quantify his degree of risk aversion. To do so, we look at how he is willing to trade off risk against expected return. An obvious benchmark is the risk-free asset, which has neither volatility nor risk premium: It pays a certain rate of return, r_f. Risk-averse investors will not hold risky assets without the prospect of earning some premium above the risk-free rate. An individual's degree of risk aversion can be inferred by contrasting the risk premium on the investor's entire wealth (the complete portfolio, C), $E(r_C) - r_f$, against the variance of the portfolio return, σ_C^2. Notice that the risk premium and the level of risk that can be attributed to *individual* assets in the complete wealth portfolio are of no concern to the investor here. All that counts is the bottom line: *complete portfolio* risk premium versus *complete portfolio* risk.

A natural way to proceed is to measure risk aversion by the risk premium necessary to compensate an investor for investing his entire wealth in a portfolio, say Q, with a variance, σ_Q^2. This approach relies on the principle of *revealed preference:* We infer preferences from the choices individuals are willing to make. We will measure risk aversion by the risk premium offered by the complete portfolio per unit of variance. This ratio measures the compensation that an investor has apparently required (per unit of variance) to be induced to hold this portfolio. For example, if we were to observe that the entire wealth of an investor is held in a portfolio with annual risk premium of .10 (10%) and variance of .0256 (SD = 16%), we would infer this investor's degree of risk aversion as:

$$A = \frac{E(r_Q) - r_f}{\sigma_Q^2} = \frac{0.10}{0.0256} = 3.91 \quad \textbf{(5.12)}$$

We call the ratio of a portfolio's risk premium to its variance the **price of risk.**[5] Later in the section, we turn the question around and ask how an investor with a given degree of risk aversion, say, $A = 3.91$, should allocate wealth between the risky and risk-free assets.

price of risk

The ratio of portfolio risk premium to variance.

To get an idea of the level of the risk aversion exhibited by investors in U.S. capital markets, we can look at a representative portfolio held by these investors. Assume that all short-term borrowing offsets lending; that is, average borrowing/lending is zero. In that case, the average investor holds a complete portfolio represented by a stock-market index;[6] call it M. A common proxy for the market index is the S&P 500 Index. Using a long-term series of historical returns on the S&P 500 to estimate investors' expectations about mean return and variance, we can recast Equation 5.12 with these stock market data to obtain an estimate of average risk aversion:

$$\overline{A} = \frac{\text{Average}(r_M) - r_f}{\text{Sample } \sigma_M^2} \approx \frac{0.08}{0.04} = 2 \quad \textbf{(5.13)}$$

The price of risk of the market index portfolio, which reflects the risk aversion of the average investor, is sometimes called the *market price of risk.* Conventional wisdom holds that plausible estimates for the value of A lie in the range of 1.5–4. (Take a look at average excess returns and SD of the stock portfolios in Table 5.2, and compute the risk aversion implied by their histories to investors that invested in them their entire wealth.)

The Sharpe (Reward-to-Volatility) Ratio

Risk aversion implies that investors will accept a lower reward (as measured by their portfolio risk premium) in exchange for a sufficient reduction in the standard deviation. A statistic

[5]Notice that when we use variance rather than the SD, the price of risk of a portfolio does not depend on the holding period. The reason is that variance is proportional to the holding period. Since portfolio return and risk premium also are proportional to the holding period, the portfolio pays the same price of risk for any holding period.

[6]In practice, a broad market index such as the S&P 500 often is taken as representative of the entire market.

TABLE 5.2 Annual rate-of-return statistics for diversified portfolios for 1926–2010 and three subperiods (%)

	World Portfolio		U.S. Market		
	Equity Return in U.S. Dollars	Bond Return in U.S. Dollars	Small Stocks	Large Stocks	Long-Term T-Bonds
Total Return—Geometric Average					
1926–2010	9.21	5.42	11.80	9.62	5.12
1926–1955	8.31	2.54	11.32	9.66	3.46
1956–1985	10.28	5.94	13.81	9.52	4.64
1986–2010	9.00	8.34	9.99	9.71	7.74
Total Real Return—Geometric Average					
1926–2010	6.03	2.35	8.54	6.43	2.06
1926–1955	6.86	1.16	9.82	8.18	2.07
1956–1985	5.23	1.09	8.60	4.51	−0.15
1986–2010	5.99	5.36	6.96	6.68	4.77
Excess Return Statistics					
Arithmetic average					
1926–2010	7.22	2.09	13.91	8.00	1.76
1926–1955	9.30	1.75	20.02	11.67	2.43
1956–1985	5.55	0.38	12.18	5.01	−0.87
1986–2010	6.74	4.54	8.66	7.19	4.11
Standard deviation					
1926–2010	18.98	8.50	37.56	20.70	7.93
1926–1955	21.50	8.10	49.25	25.40	4.12
1956–1985	16.33	8.42	32.31	17.58	8.29
1986–2010	19.27	8.81	25.82	17.83	10.07
Minimum (lowest excess return)					
1926–2010	−41.97	−18.50	−55.34	−46.65	−13.43
1926–1955	−41.03	−13.86	−55.34	−46.65	−6.40
1956–1985	−32.49	−18.50	−45.26	−34.41	−13.09
1986–2010	−41.97	−11.15	−41.47	−38.44	−13.43
Maximum (highest excess return)					
1926–2010	70.51	28.96	152.88	54.26	26.07
1926–1955	70.51	28.96	152.88	54.26	10.94
1956–1985	35.25	26.40	99.94	42.25	24.96
1986–2010	36.64	24.40	73.73	32.11	26.07
Deviation from the Normal Distribution*					
Kurtosis					
1926–2010	1.49	1.01	0.65	1.05	0.24
1926–1955	1.88	3.05	0.03	0.97	−0.24
1956–1985	0.25	1.52	−0.08	0.04	0.99
1986–2010	1.85	−0.31	0.53	1.93	−0.45
Skew					
1926–2010	−0.83	0.44	−0.40	−0.86	0.16
1926–1955	−0.67	0.64	−0.49	−1.01	−0.20
1956 1985	−0.61	0.44	−0.31	−0.52	0.79
1986–2010	−1.36	0.26	−0.45	−1.30	−0.26
Performance Statistics					
Sharpe ratio					
1926–2010	0.38	0.25	0.37	0.39	0.22
1926–1955	0.43	0.22	0.41	0.46	0.59

(continued)

TABLE 5.2 (concluded)

	World Portfolio		U.S. Market		
	Equity Return in U.S. Dollars	**Bond Return in U.S. Dollars**	**Small Stocks**	**Large Stocks**	**Long-Term T-Bonds**
1956–1985	0.34	0.05	0.38	0.28	−0.11
1986–2010	0.35	0.51	0.34	0.40	0.41
VaR*					
1926–2010	−27.41	−10.81	−65.13	−36.86	−11.69
1926–1955	−40.04	−14.55	−78.60	−53.43	−5.48
1956–1985	−29.08	−13.53	−49.53	−30.51	−12.46
1986–2010	−46.35	−10.25	−49.16	−42.28	−13.85
Difference of actual VaR from VaR of a Normal distribution with same mean and SD					
1926–2010	−2.62	0.34	−18.22	−9.40	−0.99
1926–1955	−13.58	−3.32	−16.51	−20.34	−1.22
1956–1985	−8.19	−1.15	−10.38	−6.89	1.16
1986–2010	−18.66	−1.03	−15.33	−18.26	−1.83

*Applied to continuously compounded (cc) excess returns (= cc total return − cc T-bill rates).

Source: Inflation data: BLS; T-bills and U.S. small stocks: Fama and French, **http://mba.tuck.dart mouth.edu/pages/faculty/ken.french/data_library.html;** Large U.S. stocks: S&P500; Long-term U.S. government bonds: 1926–2003 return on 20-Year U.S. Treasury bonds, and 2004–2008 Lehman Brothers long-term Treasury index; World portfolio of large stocks: Datastream; World portfolio of Treasury bonds: 1926–2003 Dimson, Elroy, and Marsh, and 2004–2008 Datastream.

Please visit us at www.mhhe.com/bkm

commonly used to rank portfolios in terms of this risk-return trade-off is the **Sharpe (or reward-to-volatility) ratio,** defined as

Sharpe (or reward-to-volatility) ratio

Ratio of portfolio risk premium to standard deviation.

$$S = \frac{\text{Portfolio risk premium}}{\text{Standard deviation of portfolio excess return}} = \frac{E(r_P) - r_f}{\sigma_P} \quad \textbf{(5.14)}$$

A risk-free asset would have a risk premium of zero and a standard deviation of zero. Therefore, the reward-to-volatility ratio of a risky portfolio quantifies the incremental reward (the increase in risk premium) for each increase of 1% in the portfolio standard deviation. For example, the Sharpe ratio of a portfolio with an annual risk premium of 8% and standard deviation of 20% is 8/20 = 0.4. A higher Sharpe ratio indicates a better reward per unit of volatility, in other words, a more efficient portfolio. Portfolio analysis in terms of mean and standard deviation (or variance) of excess returns is called **mean-variance analysis.**

mean-variance analysis

Ranking portfolios by their Sharpe ratios.

A warning: We will see in the next chapter that while standard deviation and VaR of returns are useful risk measures for diversified portfolios, these are not useful ways to think about the risk of individual securities. Therefore, the Sharpe ratio is a valid statistic only for ranking portfolios; it is *not* valid for individual assets. For now, therefore, let's examine the historical reward-to-volatility ratios of broadly diversified portfolios that reflect the performance of some important asset classes.

CONCEPT check 5.3

a. A respected analyst forecasts that the return of the S&P 500 Index portfolio over the coming year will be 10%. The one-year T-bill rate is 5%. Examination of recent returns of the S&P 500 Index suggests that the standard deviation of returns will be 18%. What does this information suggest about the degree of risk aversion of the average investor, assuming that the average portfolio resembles the S&P 500?

b. What is the Sharpe ratio of the portfolio in (*a*)?

5.3 THE HISTORICAL RECORD

World and U.S. Risky Stock and Bond Portfolios

We begin our examination of risk with an analysis of a long sample of return history (85 years) for five risky asset classes. These include three well-diversified stock portfolios—world large stocks, U.S. large stocks, and U.S. small stocks—as well as two long-term bond portfolios—world and U.S. Treasury bonds. The 85 annual observations for each of the five time series of returns span the period 1926–2010.

Until 1969, the "World Portfolio" of stocks was constructed from a diversified sample of large capitalization stocks of 16 developed countries weighted in proportion to the relative size of gross domestic product. Since 1970 this portfolio has been diversified across 24 developed countries (almost 6,000 stocks) with weights determined by the relative capitalization of each market. "Large Stocks" is the Standard & Poor's market value–weighted portfolio of 500 U.S. common stocks selected from the largest market capitalization stocks. "Small U.S. Stocks" are the smallest 20% of all stocks trading on the NYSE, NASDAQ, and Amex (currently almost 1,000 stocks).

The World Portfolio of bonds was constructed from the same set of countries as the World Portfolio of stocks, using long-term bonds from each country. Until 1996, "Long-Term T-Bonds" were represented by U.S. government bonds with at least a 20-year maturity and approximately current-level coupon rate.[7] Since 1996, this bond series has been measured by the Barclay's (formerly the Lehman Brothers) Long-Term Treasury Bond Index.

Look first at Figure 5.3, which shows histograms of total (continuously compounded) returns of the five risky portfolios and of Treasury bills. Notice the hierarchy of risk: Small stocks are the most risky, followed by large stocks and then long-term bonds. At the same time, the higher average return offered by riskier assets is evident, consistent with investor risk aversion. T-bill returns are by far the least volatile. In fact, despite the variability in their returns, bills are actually riskless, since you know the return you will earn at the beginning of the holding period. The small dispersion in these returns reflects the variation in interest rates over time.

Figure 5.4 provides another view of the hierarchy of risk. Here we plot the year-by-year returns on U.S. large stocks, long-term Treasury bonds, and T-bills. Risk is reflected by wider swings of returns from year to year.

Table 5.2 presents statistics of the return history of the five portfolios over the full 85-year period, 1926–2010, as well as for three subperiods.[8] The first 30-year subperiod, 1926–1955, includes the Great Depression (1929–1939), World War II, the postwar boom, and a subsequent recession. The second subperiod (1956–1985) includes four recessions (1957–1958, 1960–1961, 1973–1975, and 1980–1982) and a period of "stagflation" (poor growth combined with high inflation (1974–1980). Finally, the most recent 25-year subperiod (1986–2010) included two recessions (1990–1991, 2001–2003) bracketing the so-called high-tech bubble of the 1990s, and a severe recession that started in December 2007 and is estimated to have ended in the second half of 2009. Let us compare capital asset returns in these three subperiods.

We start with the geometric averages of total returns in the top panel of the table. This is the equivalent, constant annual rate of return that an investor would have earned over the period. To appreciate these rates, you must consider the power of compounding. Think about an investor who might have chosen to invest in either large U.S. stocks or U.S. long-term T-bonds at the end of 1985. The geometric averages for 1986–2010 tell us that over the most recent 25-year period, the stock portfolio would have turned \$1 into $\$1 \times 1.0971^{25} = \$10.13$, while the same investment in the T-bond portfolio would have brought in $\$1 \times 1.0774^{25} = \$6.45$. We will see later that T-bills would have provided only \$2.74.

[7]The importance of the coupon rate when comparing returns on bonds is discussed in Part Three.

[8]Year-by-year returns are available on the Online Learning Center. Go to **www.mhhe.com/bkm,** and link to material for Chapter 5.

FIGURE 5.3

Frequency distribution of annual, continuously compounded rates of return, 1926–2010

Source: Prepared from data used in Table 5.2.

World Equity Portfolio (MSCI World)
Average return = 10.81
Standard deviation = 18.06
T-Bills
Average return = 3.56
Standard deviation = 2.95
U.S. Large Stocks (S&P 500)
Average return = 9.19
Standard deviation = 19.96
Long-Term U.S. Treasury Bonds
Average return = 4.99
Standard deviation = 7.58
U.S. Small Stocks (Lowest Capitalization Quintile)
Average return = 11.15
Standard deviation = 32.72
World Bond Portfolio (Barclay's World Treasuries)
Average return = 5.28
Standard deviation = 7.92

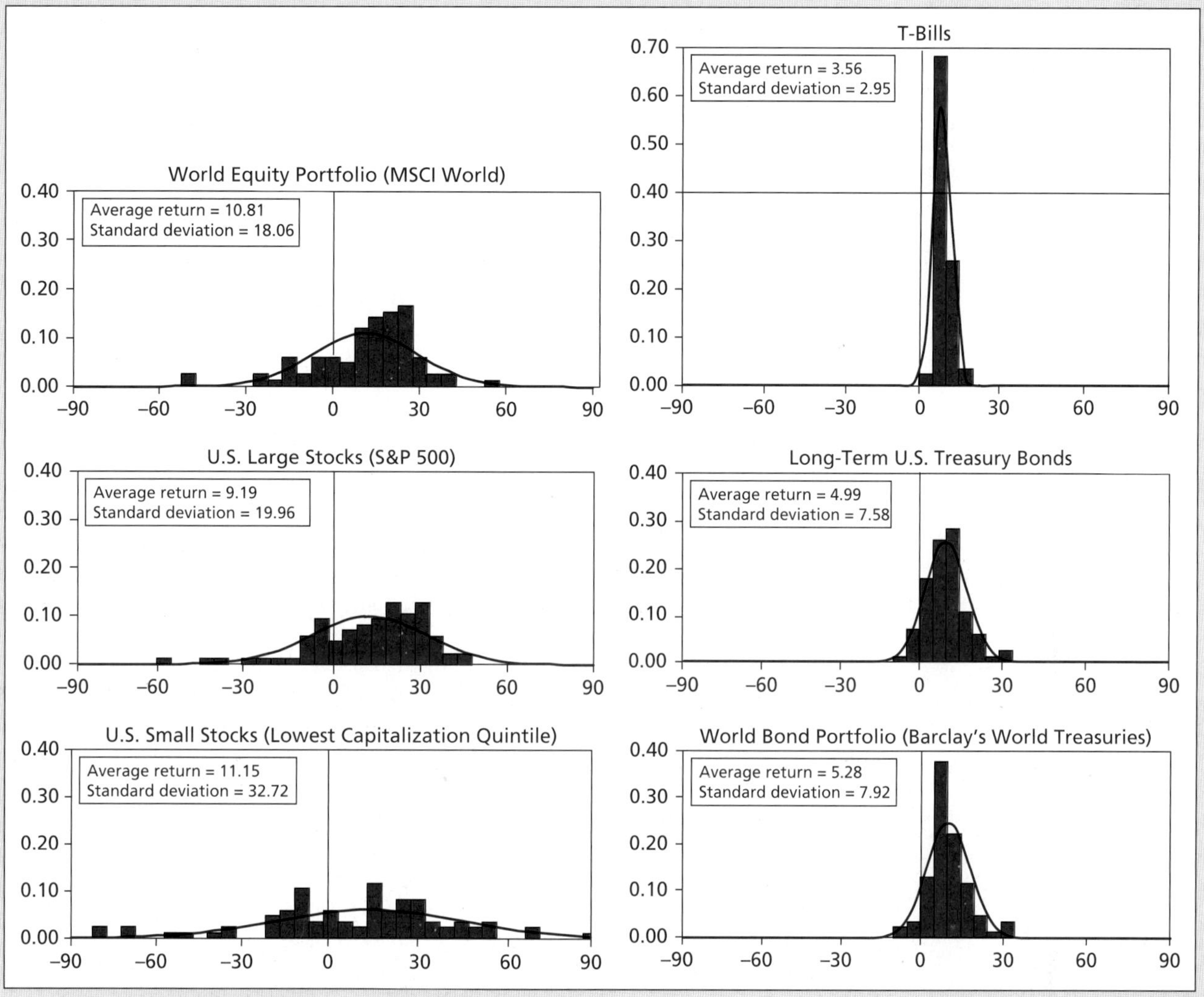

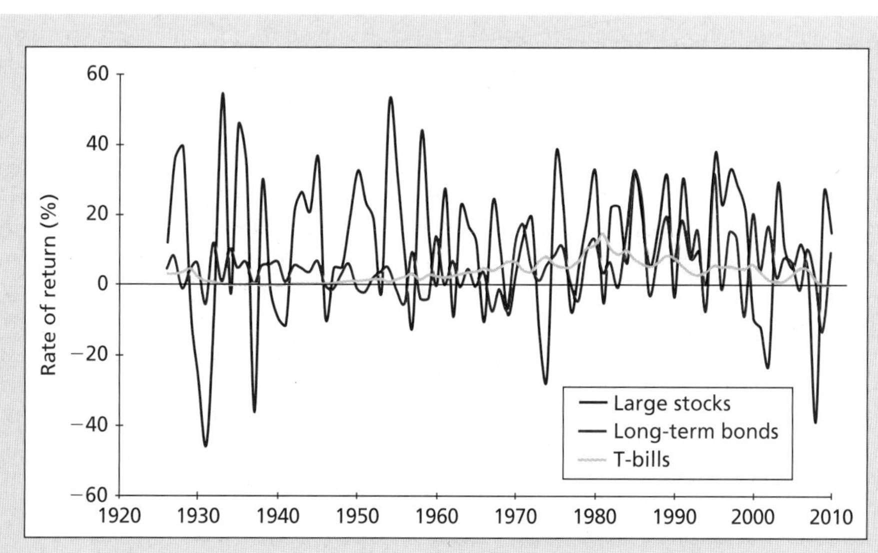

FIGURE 5.4

Rates of return on stocks, bonds, and bills, 1926–2010

Source: Prepared from data used in Table 5.2.

Rate of return (%)
Large stocks
Long-term bonds
T-bills

Thus, while the differences in average returns in Table 5.2 may seem modest at first glance, they imply great differences in long-term results. Naturally, the reason all investors don't invest everything in stocks is the higher risk that strategy would entail.

The geometric average is always less than the arithmetic average. For a normal distribution, the difference is exactly half the variance of the return (with returns measured as decimals, not percentages). Here are the arithmetic averages (from Figure 5.3) and geometric averages (from Table 5.2) for the three stock portfolios over the period (1926–2010), the differences between the two averages, as well as half the variance computed from the respective standard deviations.

	Average Portfolio Return (%)		
	World Stocks	**U.S. Small Stocks**	**U.S. Large Stocks**
Arithmetic average	10.89	17.57	11.67
Geometric average	9.21	11.80	9.62
Difference	1.68	5.78	2.04
Half historical variance	1.75	6.84	2.09

You can see that the differences between the geometric and arithmetic averages are consequential and generally close to one-half the variance of returns, suggesting that these distributions may be approximately normal, but there is a greater discrepancy for small stocks; therefore, VaR will still add important information about risk beyond standard deviation, at least for this asset class.

We have suggested that the geometric average is the correct measure for historical perspective. But investors are concerned about their *real* (inflation-adjusted) rates of return, not the paper profits indicated by the nominal (dollar) return. The real geometric averages suggest that the real cost of equity capital for large corporations has been about 6%. Notice from Table 5.2 that the average real rate on small stocks has been consistently declining, steadily approaching that of large stocks. One reason is that the average size of small, publicly traded firms has grown tremendously. Although they are still far smaller than the larger firms, their size apparently has reached the level where there is little remaining small-firm premium. The higher-than-historical-average returns recently provided by long-term bonds are due largely to capital gains earned as interest rates plunged in the recessions of the decade ending in 2010.

In the previous section we discussed the importance of risk and risk premiums. Let us now turn to the excess-return panel of Table 5.2. Notice first that excess returns do not need to be adjusted for inflation because they are returns over and above the nominal risk-free rate. Second, bond portfolios, albeit an important asset class, are not really candidates for an investor's sole-investment vehicle, because they are not sufficiently diversified. Third, the large differences in average returns across historical periods reflect the tremendous volatility of annual returns. One might wonder whether the differences across subperiods are statistically significant. Recalling that the standard deviation of the average return is the annual standard deviation divided by the square root of the number of observations, none of the differences between these subperiod averages and the 1926–2010 average exceeds one standard deviation for stocks and 1.8 standard deviations for bonds. Thus, differences in these subperiod results might well reflect no more than statistical noise.

The minimum and maximum historical returns also reflect the large variability in annual returns. Notice the large worst-case annual losses (around 50%) and even larger best-case gains (50%–150%) on the stock portfolios, as well as the more moderate extreme returns on the bond portfolios. Interestingly, the small and large U.S. stock portfolios each experienced both their maximum and minimum returns during the Great Depression; indeed, that period is also associated with the largest standard deviations of stock portfolio returns.

EXAMPLE 5.5

The Risk Premium and Growth of Wealth

The potential import of the risk premium can be illustrated with a simple example. Consider two investors with $1 million as of December 31, 2000. One invests in the small-stock portfolio, and the other in T-bills. Suppose both investors reinvest all income from their portfolios and liquidate their investments 10 years later, on December 31, 2010. We can find the annual rates of return for this period from the spreadsheet of returns at the Online Learning Center. (Go to **www.mhhe.com/bkm.** Look for the link to Chapter 5 material.) We compute a "wealth index" for each investment by compounding wealth at the end of each year by the return earned in the following year. For example, we calculate the value of the wealth index for small stocks as of 2003 by multiplying the value as of 2002 (1.1404) by 1 plus the rate of return earned in 2003 (measured in decimals), that is, by 1 + .7475, to obtain 1.9928.

	Small Stocks		T-Bills	
Year	**Return (%)**	**Wealth Index**	**Return (%)**	**Wealth Index**
2000		1		1
2001	29.25	1.2925	3.86	1.0386
2002	−11.77	1.1404	1.63	1.0555
2003	74.75	1.9928	1.02	1.0663
2004	14.36	2.2790	1.19	1.0790
2005	3.26	2.3533	2.98	1.1111
2006	17.69	2.7696	4.81	1.1646
2007	−8.26	2.5408	4.67	1.2190
2008	−39.83	1.5288	1.64	1.2390
2009	36.33	2.0842	0.05	1.2396
2010	29.71	2.7034	0.08	1.2406

The final value of each portfolio as of December 31, 2010, equals its initial value ($1 million) multiplied by the wealth index at the end of the period:

Date	Small Stocks	T-Bills
December 31, 2000	$1,000,000	$1,000,000
December 31, 2010	$2,703,420	$1,240,572

The difference in total return is dramatic. Even with its devasting 2008 return, the value of the small-stock portfolio after 10 years is 118% more than that of the T-bill portfolio.

We can also calculate the geometric average return of each portfolio over this period. For T-bills, the geometric average over the 10-year period is computed from:

$$(1 + r_G)^{10} = 1.2406$$
$$1 + r_G = 1.2406^{1/10} = 1.0218$$
$$r_G = 2.18\%$$

Similarly, the geometric average for small stocks is 10.46%. The difference in geometric average reflects the difference in cumulative wealth provided by the small-stock portfolio over this period.

Are these portfolios normally distributed? The next section of Table 5.2 shows the kurtosis and skew of the distributions. As discussed earlier, testing for normality requires us to use continuously compounded rates. Accordingly, we use Equation 5.5 to compute continuously compounded rates of return. We calculate ln(1 + annual rate) for each asset and compute excess returns by subtracting the continuously compounded rate of return on T-bills. Because these measures derive from higher exponents of deviations from the mean (the cubed deviation for skew and the fourth power of the deviation for kurtosis), these measures are highly sensitive to rare but extreme outliers; therefore, we can rely on these measures only in very large samples that allow for sufficient observations to be taken as exhibiting a "representative" number of such events. You can see that these measures also vary considerably across subperiods. The picture is quite unambiguous with respect to stock portfolios. There is excess positive kurtosis and negative skew. These indicate extreme gains and, even more so, extreme losses that are significantly more likely than would be predicted by the normal distribution. We must conclude that VaR (and similar risk measures) to augment standard deviation is in order.

The last section in Table 5.2 presents performance statistics, Sharpe ratios, and value at risk. Sharpe ratios of stock portfolios are in the range of 0.37–0.39 for the overall history and range between 0.34–0.46 across all subperiods. We can estimate that the return-risk trade-off in stocks on an annual basis is about a .4% risk premium for each increment of 1% to standard deviation. In fact, just as with the average excess return, the differences between subperiods are not significant. The same can be said about the three stock portfolios: None showed significant superior performance. Bonds can outperform stocks in periods of falling interest rates, as we see from the Sharpe ratios in the most recent subperiod. But, as noted earlier, bond portfolios are not sufficiently diversified to allow for the use of the Sharpe ratio as a performance measure. (As we will discuss in later chapters, standard deviation as a risk measure makes sense for an investor's overall portfolio but not for one relatively narrow component of it.)

The VaR panel in Table 5.2 shows unambiguously for stocks, and almost so for bonds, that potential losses are larger than suggested by likewise normal distributions. To highlight this observation, the last panel of the table shows the difference of actual 5% VaR from likewise normal distributions; the evidence is quite clear and consistent with the kurtosis and skew statistics.

Finally, investing internationally is no longer considered exotic, and Table 5.2 also provides some information on the historical results from international investments. It appears that for passive investors who focus on investments in index funds, international diversification doesn't deliver impressive improvement over investments in the U.S. alone. However, international investments do hold large potential for active investors. We elaborate on these observations in Chapter 19, which is devoted to international investing.

CONCEPT check 5.4

Compute the average excess return on large-company stocks (over the T-bill rate) and the standard deviation for the years 1926–1934. You will need to obtain data from the spreadsheet available at the Online Learning Center at **www.mhhe.com/bkm.** Look for Chapter 5 material.

5.4 INFLATION AND REAL RATES OF RETURN

A 10% annual rate of return means that your investment was worth 10% more at the end of the year than it was at the beginning of the year. This does not necessarily mean, however, that you could have bought 10% more goods and services with that money, for it is possible that in the course of the year prices of goods also increased. If prices have changed, the increase in your purchasing power will not match the increase in your dollar wealth.

At any time, the prices of some goods may rise while the prices of other goods may fall; the *general* trend in prices is measured by examining changes in the consumer price index, or CPI. The CPI measures the cost of purchasing a representative bundle of goods, the "consumption basket" of a typical urban family of four. The **inflation rate** is measured by the rate of increase of the CPI.

inflation rate

The rate at which prices are rising, measured as the rate of increase of the CPI.

Suppose the rate of inflation (the percentage change in the CPI, denoted by i) for the last year amounted to $i = 6\%$. The purchasing power of money was thus reduced by 6%. Therefore, part of your investment earnings were offset by the reduction in the purchasing power of the dollars you received at the end of the year. With a 10% interest rate, for example, after you netted out the 6% reduction in the purchasing power of money, you were left with a net increase in purchasing power of about 4%. Thus, we need to distinguish between a **nominal interest rate**—the growth rate of money—and a **real interest rate**—the growth rate of purchasing power. If we call R the nominal rate, r the real rate, and i the inflation rate, then we conclude

nominal interest rate

The interest rate in terms of nominal (not adjusted for purchasing power) dollars.

$$r \approx R - i \tag{5.15}$$

real interest rate

The excess of the interest rate over the inflation rate. The growth rate of purchasing power derived from an investment.

In words, the real rate of interest is the nominal rate reduced by the loss of purchasing power resulting from inflation.

In fact, the exact relationship between the real and nominal interest rates is given by

$$1 + r = \frac{1 + R}{1 + i} \tag{5.16}$$

In words, the growth factor of your purchasing power, $1 + r$, equals the growth factor of your money, $1 + R$, divided by the new price level that is $1 + i$ times its value in the previous period. The exact relationship can be rearranged to

$$r = \frac{R - i}{1 + i} \tag{5.17}$$

which shows that the approximate rule overstates the real rate by the factor $1 + i$.[9]

EXAMPLE 5.6

Real versus Nominal Rates

If the interest rate on a one-year CD is 8%, and you expect inflation to be 5% over the coming year, then using the approximation given in Equation 5.15, you expect the real rate to be $r = 8\% - 5\% = 3\%$. Using the exact formula given in Equation 5.17, the real rate is $r = \frac{.08 - .05}{1 + .05} = .0286$, or 2.86%. Therefore, the approximation rule overstates the expected real rate by only .14 percentage points. The approximation rule of Equation 5.16 is more accurate for small inflation rates and is perfectly exact for continuously compounded rates.

The Equilibrium Nominal Rate of Interest

We've seen that the real rate of return is approximately the nominal rate minus the inflation rate. Because investors should be concerned with real returns—the increase in their purchasing power—they will demand higher nominal rates of return on their investments. This higher rate is necessary to maintain the expected real return as inflation increases.

Irving Fisher (1930) argued that the nominal rate ought to increase one-for-one with increases in the expected inflation rate. Using $E(i)$ to denote the current expected inflation over the coming period, then the so-called Fisher equation is

$$R = r + E(i) \tag{5.18}$$

Suppose the real rate of interest is 2%, and the inflation rate is 4%, so that the nominal interest rate is about 6%. If the expected inflation rate rises to 5%, the nominal interest rate should climb to roughly 7%. The increase in the nominal rate offsets the increase in expected inflation, giving investors an unchanged growth of purchasing power at a 2% rate.

[9]Notice that for continuously compounded rates, Equation 5.16 is perfectly accurate. Because $\ln(x/y) = \ln(x) - \ln(y)$, the continuously compounded real rate of return, r_{cc}, can be derived from the annual rates as

$$r_{cc} = \ln(1 + r) = \ln\left(\frac{1 + R}{1 + i}\right) = \ln(1 + R) - \ln(1 + i) = R_{cc} - i_{cc}$$

CONCEPT check 5.5

a. Suppose the real interest rate is 3% per year, and the expected inflation rate is 8%. What is the nominal interest rate?

b. Suppose the expected inflation rate rises to 10%, but the real rate is unchanged. What happens to the nominal interest rate?

U.S. History of Interest Rates, Inflation, and Real Interest Rates

Figure 5.5 plots nominal interest rates, inflation rates, and real rates in the U.S. between 1926 and 2010. Since the mid-1950s, nominal rates have increased roughly in tandem with inflation, broadly consistent with the Fisher equation. The 1930s and 1940s, however, show us that very volatile levels of unexpected inflation can play havoc with realized *real* rates of return.

Table 5.3 quantifies what we see in Figure 5.5. One interesting pattern that emerges is the steady increase in the average real interest rate across the three subperiods reported in the table. Perhaps this reflects the shrinking national savings rate (and therefore reduced availability of funds to borrowers) over this period. Another striking observation from Table 5.3 is the dramatic reduction in the variability of the inflation rate and the real interest rate. This is reflected in the decline in standard deviations as well as in the steady attenuation of minimum and maximum values. This reduction in variability also is related to the patterns in correlation that we observe. According to the Fisher equation, an increase in expected inflation translates directly into an increase in nominal interest rates; therefore, the correlation between nominal rates and inflation rates should be positive and high. In contrast, the correlation between real rates and inflation should be zero, because expected inflation is fully factored into the nominal interest rate and does not affect the expected real rate of return. The table indicates that during the early period, 1926–1955, market rates did not accord to this logic, possibly due to the extraordinarily high and almost certainly unforeseen variability in inflation rates. Since 1955, however, the nominal T-bill rate and inflation rate have tracked each other far more closely (as is clear from Figure 5.5), and the correlations show greater consistency with Fisher's logic.

Inflation-indexed bonds called Treasury Inflation-Protected Securities (TIPS) were introduced in the U.S. in 1997. These are bonds of 5- to 30-year original maturities with coupons and principal that increase at the rate of inflation. (We discuss these bonds in more detail in Chapter 10.) The difference between nominal rates on conventional T-bonds and the rates on equal-maturity TIPS provides a measure of expected inflation (often called *break-even inflation*) over that maturity.

FIGURE 5.5

Interest rates, inflation, and real interest rates, 1926–2010

Source: T-bills: Prof. Kenneth French, **http://mba.tuck.dartmouth.edu/pages/faculty/ken.french/data_library.html;** Inflation: Bureau of Labor Statistics, **www.bls.gov;** Real rate: authors' calculations.

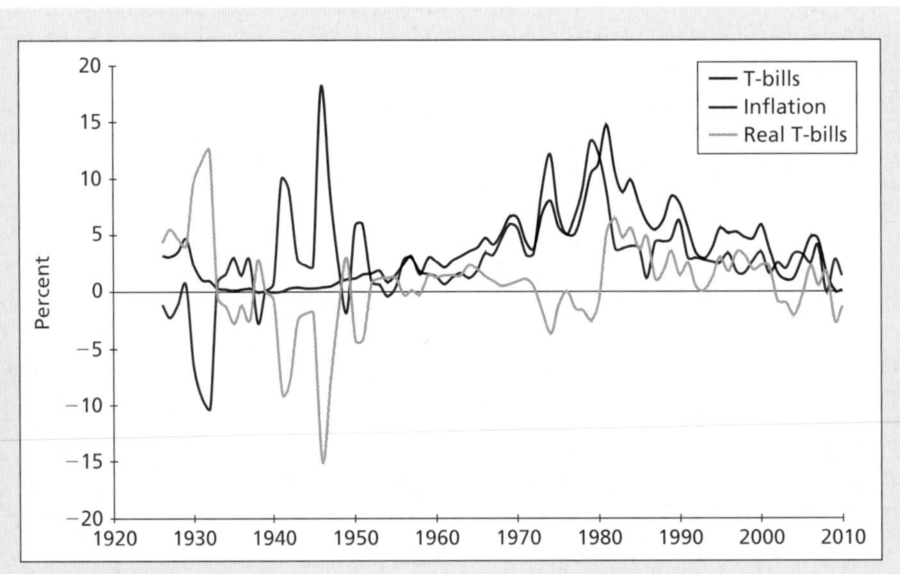

TABLE 5.3 Annual rates of return statistics for U.S. T-bills, inflation, and real interest rates, 1926–2010 and three subperiods (%)

	U.S. Market		
	T-Bills	**Inflation**	**Real T-Bills**
Arithmetic average			
1926–2010	3.66	3.08	0.68
1926–1955	1.10	1.51	−0.11
1956–1985	5.84	4.85	0.98
1986–2010	4.14	2.84	1.26
Standard deviation			
1926–2010	3.09	4.17	3.89
1926–1955	1.22	5.55	5.84
1956–1985	3.19	3.50	2.39
1986–2010	2.25	1.31	1.87
Correlations	**T-bills+inflation**	**Real bills+inflation**	
1926–2010	0.41	−0.46	
1926–1955	−0.30	−0.59	
1956–1985	0.72	−0.53	
1986–2010	0.53	0.35	
Minimum (lowest rate)			
1926–2010	−0.04	−10.27	−15.04
1926–1955	−0.04	−10.27	−15.04
1956–1985	1.53	0.67	−3.65
1986–2010	0.05	−0.04	−2.64
Maximum (highest rate)			
1926–2010	14.72	18.13	12.50
1926–1955	4.74	18.13	12.50
1956–1985	14.72	13.26	6.45
1986–2010	8.38	6.26	4.91

* Two slightly negative interest rates occurred in the 1930s, before T-bills were introduced. In those days, the Treasury instead guaranteed short-term bonds. In highly uncertain times, great demand for these bonds could result in a negative rate.

Source: T-bills: Fama and French risk-free rate; Inflation data: Bureau of Labor Statistics (inflation-cpiu-dec2dec).

5.5 ASSET ALLOCATION ACROSS RISKY AND RISK-FREE PORTFOLIOS

History shows us that long-term bonds have been riskier investments than investments in Treasury bills and that stock investments have been riskier still. On the other hand, the riskier investments have offered higher average returns. Investors, of course, do not make all-or-nothing choices from these investment classes. They can and do construct their portfolios using securities from all asset classes.

A simple strategy to control portfolio risk is to specify the fraction of the portfolio invested in broad asset classes such as stocks, bonds, and safe assets such as Treasury bills. This aspect of portfolio management is called **asset allocation** and plays an important role in the determination of portfolio performance. Consider this statement by John Bogle, made when he was the chairman of the Vanguard Group of Investment Companies:

asset allocation
Portfolio choice among broad investment classes.

> The most fundamental decision of investing is the allocation of your assets: How much should you own in stock? How much should you own in bonds? How much should you own in cash reserves? . . . That decision [has been shown to account] for an astonishing 94% of the differences

in total returns achieved by institutionally managed pension funds. . . . There is no reason to believe that the same relationship does not also hold true for individual investors.[10]

capital allocation

The choice between risky and risk-free assets.

The most basic form of asset allocation envisions the portfolio as dichotomized into risky versus risk-free assets. The fraction of the portfolio placed in risky assets is called the **capital allocation** to risky assets and speaks directly to investor risk aversion.

To focus on the capital allocation decision, we think about an investor who allocates funds between T-bills and a portfolio of risky assets. We can envision the risky portfolio, *P*, as a mutual fund or ETF (exchange-traded fund) that includes a bundle of risky assets in desired, fixed proportions. Thus, when we shift wealth into and out of *P*, we do not change the relative proportion of the various securities within the risky portfolio. We put off until the next chapter the question of how to best construct the risky portfolio. We call the overall portfolio composed of the risk-free asset and the risky portfolio, *P*, the **complete portfolio** that includes the entire investor's wealth.

complete portfolio

The entire portfolio including risky and risk-free assets.

The Risk-Free Asset

The power to tax and to control the money supply lets the government, and only the government, issue default-free (Treasury) bonds. The default-free guarantee by itself is not sufficient to make the bonds risk-free in real terms, since inflation affects the purchasing power of the proceeds from the bonds. The only risk-free asset in real terms would be a price-indexed government bond such as TIPS. Even then, a default-free, perfectly indexed bond offers a guaranteed real rate to an investor only if the maturity of the bond is identical to the investor's desired holding period. These qualifications notwithstanding, it is common to view Treasury bills as *the* risk-free asset. Any inflation uncertainty over the course of a few weeks, or even months, is negligible compared to the uncertainty of stock market returns.[11]

In practice, most investors treat a broader range of money market instruments as effectively risk-free assets. All the money market instruments are virtually immune to interest rate risk (unexpected fluctuations in the price of a bond due to changes in market interest rates) because of their short maturities, and all are fairly safe in terms of default or credit risk.

Money market mutual funds hold, for the most part, three types of securities: Treasury bills, bank certificates of deposit (CDs), and commercial paper. The instruments differ slightly in their default risk. The yields to maturity on CDs and commercial paper, for identical maturities, are always slightly higher than those of T-bills. A history of this yield spread for 90-day CDs is shown in Figure 2.2 in Chapter 2.

Money market funds have changed their relative holdings of these securities over time, but by and large, the risk of such blue-chip, short-term investments as CDs and commercial paper is minuscule compared to that of most other assets, such as long-term corporate bonds, common stocks, or real estate. Hence, we treat money market funds, as well as T-bills, as representing the most easily accessible risk-free asset for most investors.

Portfolio Expected Return and Risk

We can examine the risk-return combinations that result from various capital allocations in the complete portfolio to risky versus risk-free assets. Finding the available combinations of

[10]John C. Bogle, *Bogle on Mutual Funds* (Burr Ridge, IL: Irwin Professional Publishing, 1994), p. 235.

[11]In the wake of the euro crisis as well as the credit downgrade of the United States in the summer of 2011, one clearly needs to consider whether (or when) sovereign debt can be treated as risk-free. Governments that issue debt in their home currency can in principle always repay that debt, if need be by printing more money in that currency. This strategy, however, can lead to runaway inflation, so the real return on that debt would hardly be risk-free. Moreover, the cost of possible hyperinflation can be so great that they might justifiably conclude that default is the lesser of the two evils. Governments that issue debt in currencies they do not control (e.g., euro-denominated Greek debt) cannot fall back on the printing press, even under extreme duress, so default in that situation is certainly possible. Since the euro crisis, analysts have focused considerable attention on measures of sovereign fiscal health such as the ratio of indebtedness to GDP. As is also true of corporate debt, long- and medium-term debt issues are typically riskier, as they allow more time for credit conditions to deteriorate before the loan is paid off.

risk and return is the "technical" part of capital allocation; it deals only with the opportunities available to investors. In the next section, we address the "personal preference" part of the problem, the individual's choice of the preferred risk-return combination, given his degree of risk aversion.

Since we assume that the composition of the risky portfolio, *P*, already has been determined, the only concern here is with the proportion of the investment budget (y) to be allocated to it. The remaining proportion ($1 - y$) is to be invested in the risk-free asset, which has a rate of return denoted r_f.

We denote the *actual* risky rate of return by r_P, the *expected* rate of return on *P* by $E(r_P)$, and its standard deviation by σ_P. In the numerical example, $E(r_P) = 15\%$, $\sigma_P = 22\%$, and $r_f = 7\%$. Thus, the risk premium on the risky asset is $E(r_P) - r_f = 8\%$.

Let's start with two extreme cases. If you invest all of your funds in the risky asset, that is, if you choose $y = 1$, the expected return on your complete portfolio will be 15% and the standard deviation will be 22%. This combination of risk and return is plotted as point *P* in Figure 5.6. At the other extreme, you might put all of your funds into the risk-free asset, that is, you choose $y = 0$. In this case, you would earn a riskless return of 7%. (This choice is plotted as point *F* in Figure 5.6.)

Now consider more moderate choices. For example, if you allocate equal amounts of your *complete portfolio, C,* to the risky and risk-free assets, that is, you choose $y = .5$, the expected return on the complete portfolio will be the average of $E(r_P)$ and r_f. Therefore, $E(r_C) = .5 \times 7\% + .5 \times 15\% = 11\%$. The risk premium of the complete portfolio is therefore $11\% - 7\% = 4\%$, which is half of the risk premium of *P*. The standard deviation of the portfolio also is one-half of *P*'s, that is, 11%. When you reduce the fraction of the complete portfolio allocated to the risky asset by half, you reduce both the risk and risk premium by half.

To generalize, the risk premium of the complete portfolio, *C*, will equal the risk premium of the risky asset times the fraction of the portfolio invested in the risky asset.

$$E(r_C) - r_f = y[E(r_P) - r_f] \tag{5.19}$$

The standard deviation of the complete portfolio will equal the standard deviation of the risky asset times the fraction of the portfolio invested in the risky asset.

$$\sigma_C = y\sigma_P \tag{5.20}$$

In sum, both the risk premium and the standard deviation of the complete portfolio increase in proportion to the investment in the risky portfolio. Therefore, the points that describe the risk and return of the complete portfolio for various capital allocations of y all plot on the

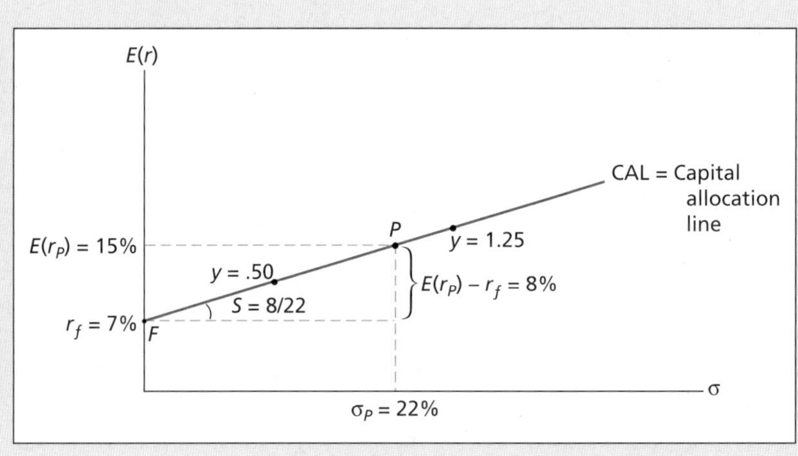

FIGURE 5.6

The investment opportunity set with a risky asset and a risk-free asset straight line connecting F and P, as shown in Figure 5.6, with an intercept of r_f and slope (rise/run) equal to the familiar Sharpe ratio of P:

$$S = \frac{E(r_P) - r_f}{\sigma_P} = \frac{15 - 7}{22} = .36 \tag{5.21}$$

CONCEPT check 5.6

What are the expected return, risk premium, standard deviation, and ratio of risk premium to standard deviation for a complete portfolio with $y = .75$?

The Capital Allocation Line

capital allocation line (CAL)

Plot of risk-return combinations available by varying portfolio allocation between a risk-free asset and a risky portfolio.

The line plotted in Figure 5.6 depicts the risk-return combinations available by varying capital allocation, that is, by choosing different values of y. For this reason it is called the **capital allocation line,** or **CAL.** The slope, S, of the CAL equals the increase in expected return that an investor can obtain per unit of additional standard deviation or extra return per extra risk. It is obvious why it is also called the *reward-to-volatility ratio,* or Sharpe ratio, after William Sharpe who first suggested its use.

Notice that the Sharpe ratio is the same for risky portfolio P and the complete portfolio that mixes P and the risk-free asset in equal proportions.

	Expected Return	Risk Premium	Standard Deviation	Reward-to-Volatility Ratio
Portfolio *P*:	15%	8%	22%	$\frac{8}{22} = 0.36$
Portfolio *C*:	11%	4%	11%	$\frac{4}{11} = 0.36$

In fact, the reward-to-volatility ratio is the same for all complete portfolios that plot on the capital allocation line. While the risk-return combinations differ according to the investor's choice of y, the *ratio* of reward to risk is constant.

What about points on the CAL to the right of portfolio P in the investment opportunity set? You can construct complete portfolios to the right of point P by borrowing, that is, by choosing $y > 1$. This means that you borrow a proportion of $y - 1$ and invest both the borrowed funds and your own wealth in the risky portfolio P. If you can borrow at the risk-free rate, $r_f = 7\%$, then your rate of return will be $r_C = -(y - 1)r_f + y\, r_P = r_f + y(r_P - r_f)$. This complete portfolio has risk premium of $y[E(r_P) - r_f]$ and SD $= y\,\sigma_P$. Verify that your Sharpe ratio equals that of any other portfolio on the same CAL.

EXAMPLE 5.7

Levered Complete Portfolios

Suppose the investment budget is \$300,000, and an investor borrows an additional \$120,000, investing the \$420,000 in the risky asset. This is a levered position in the risky asset, which is financed in part by borrowing. In that case

$$y = \frac{420{,}000}{300{,}000} = 1.4$$

and $1 - y = 1 - 1.4 = -.4$, reflecting a short position in the risk-free asset, or a borrowing position. Rather than lending at a 7% interest rate, the investor borrows at 7%. The portfolio rate of return is

$$E(r_C) = 7 + (1.4 \times 8) = 18.2$$

Another way to find this portfolio rate of return is as follows: You expect to earn \$63,000 (15% of \$420,000) and pay \$8,400 (7% of \$120,000) in interest on the loan. Simple subtraction yields an

(continued)

EXAMPLE 5.7

Levered Complete Portfolios (concluded)

expected profit of \$54,600, which is 18.2% of your investment budget of \$300,000. Therefore, $E(r_C) = 18.2\%$.

Your portfolio still exhibits the same reward-to-volatility ratio:

$$\sigma_C = 1.4 \times 22 = 30.8$$

$$S = \frac{E(r_C) - r_f}{\sigma_C} = \frac{11.2}{30.8} = .36$$

As you might have expected, the levered portfolio has both a higher expected return and a higher standard deviation than an unlevered position in the risky asset.

Risk Aversion and Capital Allocation

We have developed the CAL, the graph of all feasible risk-return combinations available from allocating the complete portfolio between a risky portfolio and a risk-free asset. The investor confronting the CAL now must choose one optimal combination from the set of feasible choices. This choice entails a trade-off between risk and return. Individual investors with different levels of risk aversion, given an identical capital allocation line, will choose different positions in the risky asset. Specifically, the more risk-averse investors will choose to hold *less* of the risky asset and *more* of the risk-free asset.

How can we find the best allocation between the risky portfolio and risk-free asset? Recall that a particular investor's degree of risk aversion (A) measures the price of risk she demands from the complete portfolio in which her entire wealth is invested. The compensation for risk demanded by the investor must be compared to the price of risk offered by the risky portfolio, P. We can find the investor's preferred capital allocation, y, by dividing the risky portfolio's price of risk by the investor's risk aversion, her *required* price of risk:

$$y = \frac{\text{Available risk premium to variance ratio}}{\text{Required risk premium to variance ratio}} = \frac{[E(r_P) - r_f]/\sigma_P^2}{A} = \frac{[E(r_P) - r_f]}{A\sigma_P^2} \quad \textbf{(5.22)}$$

Notice that when the price of risk of the available risky portfolio exactly matches the investor's degree of risk aversion, her entire wealth will be invested in it ($y = 1$).

What would the investor of Equation 5.12 (with $A = 3.91$) do when faced with the market index portfolio of Equation 5.13 (with price of risk = 2)? Equation 5.22 tells us that this investor would invest $y = 2/3.91 = 0.51$ (51%) in the market index portfolio and a proportion $1 - y = 0.49$ in the risk-free asset.

Graphically, more risk-averse investors will choose portfolios near point F on the capital allocation line plotted in Figure 5.6. More risk-tolerant investors will choose points closer to P, with higher expected return and higher risk. The most risk-tolerant investors will choose portfolios to the right of point P. These levered portfolios provide even higher expected returns, but even greater risk.

The investor's asset allocation choice also will depend on the trade-off between risk and return. When the reward-to-volatility ratio increases, investors might well decide to take on riskier positions. Suppose an investor reevaluates the probability distribution of the risky portfolio and now perceives a greater expected return without an accompanying increase in the standard deviation. This amounts to an increase in the reward-to-volatility ratio or, equivalently, an increase in the slope of the CAL. As a result, this investor will choose a higher y, that is, a greater position in the risky portfolio.

One role of a professional financial adviser is to present investment opportunity alternatives to clients, obtain an assessment of the client's risk tolerance, and help determine the appropriate complete portfolio.[12]

[12]"Risk tolerance" is simply the flip side of "risk aversion." Either term is a reasonable way to describe attitudes toward risk. We generally find it easier to talk about risk *aversion,* but practitioners often use the term risk *tolerance.*

5.6 PASSIVE STRATEGIES AND THE CAPITAL MARKET LINE

passive strategy

Investment policy that avoids security analysis.

A **passive strategy** is based on the premise that securities are fairly priced, and it avoids the costs involved in undertaking security analysis. Such a strategy might at first blush appear to be naive. However, we will see in Chapter 8 that intense competition among professional money managers might indeed force security prices to levels at which further security analysis is unlikely to turn up significant profit opportunities. Passive investment strategies may make sense for many investors.

To avoid the costs of acquiring information on any individual stock or group of stocks, we may follow a "neutral" diversification approach. Select a diversified portfolio of common stocks that mirrors the corporate sector of the broad economy. This results in a value-weighted portfolio, which, for example, invests a proportion in GE stock that equals the ratio of GE's market value to the market value of all listed stocks.

Such strategies are called *indexing*. The investor chooses a portfolio of all the stocks in a broad market index such as the S&P 500. The rate of return on the portfolio then replicates the return on the index. Indexing has become a popular strategy for passive investors. We call the capital allocation line provided by one-month T-bills and a broad index of common stocks the **capital market line** (CML). That is, a passive strategy using the broad stock market index as the risky portfolio generates an investment opportunity set that is represented by the CML.

capital market line

The capital allocation line using the market index portfolio as the risky asset.

Historical Evidence on the Capital Market Line

Table 5.4 is a small cut-and-paste from Table 5.3, which concentrates on S&P 500 data, a popular choice for a broad stock-market index. As we discussed earlier, the large standard deviation of its rate of return implies that we cannot reject the hypothesis that the entire 85-year period is characterized by the same Sharpe ratio. Using this history as a guide, investors might reasonably forecast a risk premium of around 8% coupled with a standard deviation of approximately 20%, resulting in a Sharpe ratio of .4.

We also have seen that to hold a complete portfolio with these risk-return characteristics, the "average" investor (with $y = 1$) would need to have a coefficient of risk aversion of $.08/.20^2 = 2$. But that average investor would need some courage. As the VaR figures in Table 5.4 indicate, the market index has exhibited a probability of 5% of a 36.86% or worse loss in a year; surely this is no picnic. This substantial risk, together with differences in risk aversion across individuals, might explain the large differences we observe in portfolio positions across investors.

Finally, notice the instability of the excess returns on the S&P 500 across the 30-year subperiods in Table 5.4. The great variability in excess returns raises the question of whether the 8% historical average really is a reasonable estimate of the risk premium looking into the future. It also suggests that different investors may come to different conclusions about future excess returns, another reason for capital allocations to vary.

In fact, there has been considerable recent debate among financial economists about the "true" equity risk premium, with an emerging consensus that the historical average may be an unrealistically high estimate of the future risk premium. This argument is based on several

TABLE 5.4 Excess return statistics for the S&P 500

	Excess Return (%)			
	Average	Std Dev	Sharpe Ratio	5% VaR
1926–2010	8.00	20.70	.39	−36.86
1926–1955	11.67	25.40	.46	−53.43
1956–1985	5.01	17.58	.28	−30.51
1986–2010	7.19	17.83	.40	−42.28

On the MARKET FRONT

TRIUMPH OF THE OPTIMISTS

As a whole, the last eight decades have been very kind to U.S. equity investors. Even accounting for miserable 2008 returns, stock investments have outperformed investments in safe Treasury bills by more than 7% per year. The real rate of return averaged more than 6%, implying an expected doubling of the real value of the investment portfolio about every 12 years!

Is this experience representative? A book by three professors at the London Business School, Elroy Dimson, Paul Marsh, and Mike Staunton, extends the U.S. evidence to other countries and to longer time periods. Their conclusion is given in the book's title, *Triumph of the Optimists**: In every country in their study (which included markets in North America, Europe, Asia, and Africa), the investment optimists—those who bet on the economy by investing in stocks rather than bonds or bills—were vindicated. Over the long haul, stocks beat bonds everywhere.

On the other hand, the equity risk premium is probably not as large as the post-1926 evidence from Table 5.3 would seem to indicate. First, results from the first 25 years of the last century (which included the first World War) were less favorable to stocks. Second, U.S. returns have been better than those of most other countries, and so a more representative value for the historical risk premium may be lower than the U.S. experience. Finally, the sample that is amenable to historical analysis suffers from a self-selection problem. Only those markets that have survived to be studied can be included in the analysis. This leaves out countries such as Russia or China, whose markets were shut down during communist rule, and whose results if included would surely bring down the average historical performance of equity investments. Nevertheless, there is powerful evidence of a risk premium that shows its force everywhere the authors looked.

*Elroy Dimson, Paul Marsh, Mike Staunton, *Triumph of the Optimists: 101 Years of Global Investment Returns* (Princeton, NJ: Princeton University Press, 2002).

factors: the use of longer time periods in which equity returns are examined; a broad range of countries rather than just the U.S. in which excess returns are computed (Dimson, Marsh, and Staunton, 2001); direct surveys of financial executives about their expectations for stock market returns (Graham and Harvey, 2001); and inferences from stock market data about investor expectations (Jagannathan, McGrattan, and Scherbina, 2000; Fama and French, 2002). The nearby box discusses some of this evidence.

Costs and Benefits of Passive Investing

The fact that an individual's capital allocation decision is hard does not imply that its implementation needs to be complex. A passive strategy is simple and inexpensive to implement: Choose a broad index fund or ETF and divide your savings between it and a money market fund. To justify spending your own time and effort or paying a professional to pursue an active strategy requires some evidence that those activities are likely to be profitable. As we shall see later in the text, this is much harder to come by than you might expect!

To choose an active strategy, an investor must be convinced that the benefits outweigh the cost, and the cost can be quite large. As a benchmark, annual expense ratios for index funds are around 20 and 50 basis points for U.S. and international stocks, respectively. The cost of utilizing a money market fund is smaller still, and T-bills can be purchased at no cost.

Here is a very cursory idea of the cost of active strategies: The annual expense ratio of an active stock mutual fund averages around 1% of invested assets, and mutual funds that invest in more exotic assets such as real estate or precious metals can be more expensive still. A hedge fund will cost you 1% to 2% of invested assets plus 10% or more of any returns above the risk-free rate. If you are wealthy and seek more dedicated portfolio management, costs will be even higher.

Because of the power of compounding, an extra 1% of annual costs can have large consequences for the future value of your portfolio. With a risk-free rate of 2% and a risk premium of 8%, you might expect your wealth to grow by a factor of $1.10^{30} = 17.45$ over a 30-year investment horizon. If fees are 1%, then your net return is reduced to 9%, and your wealth grows by a factor of only $1.09^{30} = 13.26$ over that same horizon. That seemingly small management fee reduces your final wealth by about one-quarter.

The potential benefits of active strategies are discussed in detail in Chapter 8. The news is generally not that good for active investors. However, the factors that keep the active management industry going are (1) the large potential of enrichment from successful investments—the same power of compounding works in your favor if you can add even a few basis points to total return, (2) the difficulty in assessing performance (discussed in Chapter 18), and (3) uninformed investors who are willing to pay for professional money management. There is no question that some money managers can outperform passive strategies. The problem is (1) how do you identify them and (2) do their fees outstrip their potential. Whatever the choice one makes, one thing is clear: The CML using the passive market index is not an obviously inferior choice.

SUMMARY

- Investors face a trade-off between risk and expected return. Historical data confirm our intuition that assets with low degrees of risk should provide lower returns on average than do those of higher risk.
- Shifting funds from the risky portfolio to the risk-free asset is the simplest way to reduce risk. Another method involves diversification of the risky portfolio. We take up diversification in later chapters.
- U.S. T-bills provide a perfectly risk-free asset in nominal terms only. Nevertheless, the standard deviation of real rates on short-term T-bills is small compared to that of assets such as long-term bonds and common stocks, so for the purpose of our analysis, we consider T-bills the risk-free asset. Besides T-bills, money market funds hold short-term, safe obligations such as commercial paper and CDs. These entail some default risk but relatively little compared to most other risky assets. For convenience, we often refer to money market funds as risk-free assets.
- A risky investment portfolio (referred to here as the risky asset) can be characterized by its reward-to-volatility ratio. This ratio is the slope of the capital allocation line (CAL), the line connecting the risk-free asset to the risky asset. All combinations of the risky and risk-free asset lie on this line. Investors would prefer a steeper-sloping CAL, because that means higher expected returns for any level of risk.
- An investor's preferred choice among the portfolios on the capital allocation line will depend on risk aversion. Risk-averse investors will weight their complete portfolios more heavily toward Treasury bills. Risk-tolerant investors will hold higher proportions of their complete portfolios in the risky asset.
- The capital market line is the capital allocation line that results from using a passive investment strategy that treats a market index portfolio, such as the Standard & Poor's 500, as the risky asset. Passive strategies are low-cost ways of obtaining well-diversified portfolios with performance that will reflect that of the broad stock market.

KEY TERMS

arithmetic average, 112
asset allocation, 133
capital allocation, 134
capital allocation line (CAL), 136
capital market line, 138
complete portfolio, 134
dollar-weighted average return, 113
excess return, 122
expected return, 115
geometric average, 112
holding-period return (HPR), 111
inflation rate, 130
kurtosis, 121
mean-variance analysis, 125
nominal interest rate, 131
passive strategy, 138
price of risk, 123
probability distribution, 115
real interest rate, 131
risk aversion, 122
risk-free rate, 122
risk premium, 122
scenario analysis, 115
Sharpe (or reward-to-volatility) ratio, 125
skew, 121
standard deviation, 116
value at risk (VaR), 118
variance, 116

KEY FORMULAS

Arithmetic average of n returns: $(r_1 + r_2 + \cdots + r_n)/n$

Geometric average of n returns: $[(1 + r_1)(1 + r_2) \cdots (1 + r_n)]^{1/n} - 1$

Continuously compounded rate of return, r_{cc}: $\ln(1 + \text{Effective annual rate})$

Expected return: Σ [prob(Scenario) $\times$ Return in scenario]

Variance: Σ [prob(Scenario) $\times$ (Deviation from mean in scenario)^2]

Standard deviation: $\sqrt{\text{Variance}}$

Sharpe ratio: $\dfrac{\text{Portfolio risk premium}}{\text{Standard deviation of excess return}} = \dfrac{E(r_P) - r_f}{\sigma_P}$

Real rate of return: $\dfrac{1 + \text{Nominal return}}{1 + \text{Inflation rate}} - 1$

Real rate of return (continuous compounding): $r_{\text{nominal}} - \text{Inflation rate}$

Optimal capital allocation to the risky asset, y: $\dfrac{E(r_P) - r_f}{A\sigma_P^2}$

Select problems are available in McGraw-Hill's *Connect Finance.* Please see the Supplements section of the book's frontmatter for more information.

PROBLEM SETS

Basic

1. Suppose you've estimated that the fifth-percentile value at risk of a portfolio is −30%. Now you wish to estimate the portfolio's first-percentile VaR (the value below which lie 1% of the returns). Will the 1% VaR be greater or less than −30%? *(LO 5-2)*
2. To estimate the Sharpe ratio of a portfolio from a history of asset returns, we use the difference between the simple (arithmetic) average rate of return and the T-bill rate. Why not use the geometric average? *(LO 5-4)*
3. When estimating a Sharpe ratio, would it make sense to use the average excess real return that accounts for inflation? *(LO 5-4)*
4. You've just decided upon your capital allocation for the next year, when you realize that you've underestimated both the expected return and the standard deviation of your risky portfolio by 4%. Will you increase, decrease, or leave unchanged your allocation to risk-free T-bills? *(LO 5-4)*

Intermediate

5. Suppose your expectations regarding the stock market are as follows:

State of the Economy	Probability	HPR
Boom	0.3	44%
Normal growth	0.4	14
Recession	0.3	−16

Use Equations 5.6–5.8 to compute the mean and standard deviation of the HPR on stocks. *(LO 5-4)*

6. The stock of Business Adventures sells for $40 a share. Its likely dividend payout and end-of-year price depend on the state of the economy by the end of the year as follows: *(LO 5-2)*

	Dividend	Stock Price
Boom	$2.00	$50
Normal economy	1.00	43
Recession	.50	34

a. Calculate the expected holding-period return and standard deviation of the holding-period return. All three scenarios are equally likely.

b. Calculate the expected return and standard deviation of a portfolio invested half in Business Adventures and half in Treasury bills. The return on bills is 4%.

7. XYZ stock price and dividend history are as follows:

Year	Beginning-of-Year Price	Dividend Paid at Year-End
2010	$100	$4
2011	$110	$4
2012	$ 90	$4
2013	$ 95	$4

An investor buys three shares of XYZ at the beginning of 2010, buys another two shares at the beginning of 2011, sells one share at the beginning of 2012, and sells all four remaining shares at the beginning of 2013. ***(LO 5-1)***

a. What are the arithmetic and geometric average time-weighted rates of return for the investor?

b. What is the dollar-weighted rate of return? (*Hint:* Carefully prepare a chart of cash flows for the *four* dates corresponding to the turns of the year for January 1, 2010, to January 1, 2013. If your calculator cannot calculate internal rate of return, you will have to use a spreadsheet or trial and error.)

8. *a.* Suppose you forecast that the standard deviation of the market return will be 20% in the coming year. If the measure of risk aversion in Equation 5.13 is $A = 4$, what would be a reasonable guess for the expected market risk premium?

b. What value of A is consistent with a risk premium of 9%?

c. What will happen to the risk premium if investors become more risk tolerant? ***(LO 5-4)***

9. Using the historical risk premiums as your guide, what is your estimate of the expected annual HPR on the S&P 500 stock portfolio if the current risk-free interest rate is 5%? ***(LO 5-3)***

10. What has been the historical average *real* rate of return on stocks, Treasury bonds, and Treasury bills? ***(LO 5-2)***

11. Consider a risky portfolio. The end-of-year cash flow derived from the portfolio will be either $50,000 or $150,000, with equal probabilities of .5. The alternative riskless investment in T-bills pays 5%. ***(LO 5-3)***

a. If you require a risk premium of 10%, how much will you be willing to pay for the portfolio?

b. Suppose the portfolio can be purchased for the amount you found in (*a*). What will the expected rate of return on the portfolio be?

c. Now suppose you require a risk premium of 15%. What is the price you will be willing to pay now?

d. Comparing your answers to (*a*) and (*c*), what do you conclude about the relationship between the required risk premium on a portfolio and the price at which the portfolio will sell?

For Problems 12–16, assume that you manage a risky portfolio with an expected rate of return of 17% and a standard deviation of 27%. The T-bill rate is 7%.

12. Your client chooses to invest 70% of a portfolio in your fund and 30% in a T-bill money market fund. ***(LO 5-3)***

a. What is the expected return and standard deviation of your client's portfolio?

b. Suppose your risky portfolio includes the following investments in the given proportions:

Stock A	27%
Stock B	33%
Stock C	40%

What are the investment proportions of your client's overall portfolio, including the position in T-bills?

c. What is the reward-to-volatility ratio (*S*) of your risky portfolio and your client's overall portfolio?

d. Draw the CAL of your portfolio on an expected return/standard deviation diagram. What is the slope of the CAL? Show the position of your client on your fund's CAL.

13. Suppose the same client in the previous problem decides to invest in your risky portfolio a proportion (*y*) of his total investment budget so that his overall portfolio will have an expected rate of return of 15%. ***(LO 5-3)***
   a. What is the proportion *y*?
   b. What are your client's investment proportions in your three stocks and the T-bill fund?
   c. What is the standard deviation of the rate of return on your client's portfolio?
14. Suppose the same client as in the previous problem prefers to invest in your portfolio a proportion (*y*) that maximizes the expected return on the overall portfolio subject to the constraint that the overall portfolio's standard deviation will not exceed 20%. ***(LO 5-3)***
   a. What is the investment proportion, *y*?
   b. What is the expected rate of return on the overall portfolio?
15. You estimate that a passive portfolio invested to mimic the S&P 500 stock index yields an expected rate of return of 13% with a standard deviation of 25%. Draw the CML and your fund's CAL on an expected return/standard deviation diagram. ***(LO 5-4)***
   a. What is the slope of the CML?
   b. Characterize in one short paragraph the advantage of your fund over the passive fund.
16. Your client (see previous problem) wonders whether to switch the 70% that is invested in your fund to the passive portfolio. ***(LO 5-4)***
   a. Explain to your client the disadvantage of the switch.
   b. Show your client the maximum fee you could charge (as a percent of the investment in your fund deducted at the end of the year) that would still leave him at least as well off investing in your fund as in the passive one. (*Hint:* The fee will lower the slope of your client's CAL by reducing the expected return net of the fee.)
17. What do you think would happen to the expected return on stocks if investors perceived an increase in the volatility of stocks? ***(LO 5-4)***
18. You manage an equity fund with an expected risk premium of 10% and a standard deviation of 14%. The rate on Treasury bills is 6%. Your client chooses to invest $60,000 of her portfolio in your equity fund and $40,000 in a T-bill money market fund. What is the expected return and standard deviation of return on your client's portfolio? ***(LO 5-3)***
19. What is the reward-to-volatility ratio for the *equity fund* in the previous problem? ***(LO 5-4)***

For Problems 20–22, download the spreadsheet containing the data for Table 5.2, "Rates of return, 1926–2010," from www.mhhe.com/bkm.

Please visit us at www.mhhe.com/bkm

20. Calculate the same subperiod means and standard deviations for small stocks as Table 5.4 of the text provides for large stocks. ***(LO 5-2)***
   a. Have small stocks provided better reward-to-volatility ratios than large stocks?
   b. Do small stocks show a similar higher standard deviation in the earliest subperiod as Table 5.4 documents for large stocks?

Please visit us at www.mhhe.com/bkm

21. Convert the nominal returns on both large and small stocks to real rates. Reproduce Table 5.4 using real rates instead of excess returns. Compare the results to those of Table 5.4. ***(LO 5-1)***

Please visit us at www.mhhe.com/bkm

22. Repeat the previous problem for small stocks and compare with the results for nominal rates. ***(LO 5-1)***

www.mhhe.com/bkm

Challenge

Please visit us at www.mhhe.com/bkm

23. Download the annual returns on the combined NYSE/NASDAQ/AMEX markets as well as the S&P 500 from the Online Learning Center at **www.mhhe.com/bkm.** For both indexes, calculate: ***(LO 5-2)***
    a. Average return.
    b. Standard deviation of return.
    c. Skew of return.
    d. Kurtosis of return.
    e. The 5% value at risk.
    f. Based on your answers to parts (*b*)–(*e*), compare the risk of the two indexes.

CFA Problems

1. A portfolio of nondividend-paying stocks earned a geometric mean return of 5% between January 1, 2005, and December 31, 2011. The arithmetic mean return for the same period was 6%. If the market value of the portfolio at the beginning of 2005 was $100,000, what was the market value of the portfolio at the end of 2011? ***(LO 5-1)***
2. Which of the following statements about the standard deviation is/are *true?* A standard deviation: ***(LO 5-2)***
    a. Is the square root of the variance.
    b. Is denominated in the same units as the original data.
    c. Can be a positive or a negative number.
3. Which of the following statements reflects the importance of the asset allocation decision to the investment process? The asset allocation decision: ***(LO 5-3)***
    a. Helps the investor decide on realistic investment goals.
    b. Identifies the specific securities to include in a portfolio.
    c. Determines most of the portfolio's returns and volatility over time.
    d. Creates a standard by which to establish an appropriate investment time horizon.

Use the following data in answering CFA Questions 4–6.

Investment	Expected Return, $E(r)$	Standard Deviation, σ
1	.12	.30
2	.15	.50
3	.21	.16
4	.24	.21

Investor "satisfaction" with portfolio increases with expected return and decreases with variance according to the "utility" formula: $U = E(r) - \frac{1}{2}A\sigma^2$ where $A = 4$.

4. Based on the formula for investor satisfaction or "utility," which investment would you select if you were risk averse with $A = 4$? ***(LO 5-4)***
5. Based on the formula above, which investment would you select if you were risk neutral? ***(LO 5-4)***
6. The variable (A) in the utility formula represents the: ***(LO 5-4)***
    a. Investor's return requirement.
    b. Investor's aversion to risk.
    c. Certainty equivalent rate of the portfolio.
    d. Preference for one unit of return per four units of risk.

Use the following scenario analysis for stocks *X* and *Y* to answer CFA Questions 7 through 9.

	Bear Market	Normal Market	Bull Market
Probability	.2	.5	.3
Stock *X*	−20%	18%	50%
Stock *Y*	−15%	20%	10%

7. What are the expected returns for stocks *X* and *Y*? ***(LO 5-2)***
8. What are the standard deviations of returns on stocks *X* and *Y*? ***(LO 5-2)***
9. Assume that of your \$10,000 portfolio, you invest \$9,000 in stock *X* and \$1,000 in stock *Y*. What is the expected return on your portfolio? ***(LO 5-3)***
10. Probabilities for three states of the economy and probabilities for the returns on a particular stock in each state are shown in the table below.

State of Economy	Probability of Economic State	Stock Performance	Probability of Stock Performance in Given Economic State
Good	.3	Good	.6
		Neutral	.3
		Poor	.1
Neutral	.5	Good	.4
		Neutral	.3
		Poor	.3
Poor	.2	Good	.2
		Neutral	.3
		Poor	.5

What is the probability that the economy will be neutral *and* the stock will experience poor performance? ***(LO 5-2)***

11. An analyst estimates that a stock has the following probabilities of return depending on the state of the economy. What is the expected return of the stock? ***(LO 5-2)***

State of Economy	Probability	Return
Good	.1	15%
Normal	.6	13
Poor	.3	7

WEB master

1. Use data from **finance.yahoo.com** to answer the following questions.
   a. Select the Company tab and enter the ticker symbol "ADBE." Click on the *Profile* tab to see an overview of the company.
   b. What is the latest price reported in the *Summary* section? What is the 12-month target price? Calculate the expected holding-period return based on these prices.
   c. Use the *Historical Prices* section to answer the question "How much would I have today if I invested \$10,000 in ADBE five years ago?" Using this information, calculate the five-year holding-period return on Adobe's stock.
2. From the *Historical Prices* tab, download Adobe's dividend-adjusted stock price for the last 24 months into an Excel spreadsheet. Calculate the monthly rate of return for each month, the average return, and the standard deviation of returns over that period.
3. Calculating the real rate of return is an important part of evaluating an investment's performance. To do this, you need to know the nominal return on your investment and

the rate of inflation during the corresponding period. To estimate the expected real rate of return before you make an investment, you can use the promised yield and the expected inflation rate.

a. Go to **www.bankrate.com** and click on the *CDs and Investments* tab. Using *Compare CDs & Investment Rates* box, find the average one-year CD rate from banks across the nation (these will be nominal rates).

b. Use the St. Louis Federal Reserve's website at **research.stlouisfed.org/fred2** as a source for data about expected inflation. Search for "MICH inflation," which will provide you with the University of Michigan Inflation Expectation data series (MICH). Click on the *View Data* link and find the latest available data point. What is the expected inflation rate for the next year?

c. On the basis of your answers to parts *(a)* and *(b),* calculate the expected real rate of return on a one-year CD investment.

d. What does the result tell you about real interest rates? Are they positive or negative, and what does this mean?

SOLUTIONS TO CONCEPT checks

5.1 *a.* The arithmetic average is $(2 + 8 - 4)/3 = 2\%$ per month.

b. The time-weighted (geometric) average is $[(1 + .02) \times (1 + .08) \times (1 - .04)]^{1/3} - 1 = .0188 = 1.88\%$ per month.

c. We compute the dollar-weighted average (IRR) from the cash flow sequence (in $ millions):

	Month		
	1	**2**	**3**
Assets under management at beginning of month	10.0	13.2	19.256
Investment profits during month (HPR × Assets)	0.2	1.056	(0.77)
Net inflows during month	3.0	5.0	0.0
Assets under management at end of month	13.2	19.256	18.486

	Time			
	0	**1**	**2**	**3**
Net cash flow*	−10	−3.0	−5.0	+18.486

*Time 0 is today. Time 1 is the end of the first month. Time 3 is the end of the third month, when net cash flow equals the ending value (potential liquidation value) of the portfolio.

The IRR of the sequence of net cash flows is 1.17% per month.

The dollar-weighted average is less than the time-weighted average because the negative return was realized when the fund had the most money under management.

5.2 *a.* Computing the HPR for each scenario, we convert the price and dividend data to rate-of-return data:

Scenario	Prob	Ending Value ($ million)	Dividend ($ million)	HPR	HPR × Prob	Deviation: HPR-mean	Prob × Dev'n Squared
1	.30	$35	$4.40	.713	.214	.406	.049
2	.45	27	4.00	.348	.157	.040	.001
3	.20	15	4.00	−.174	−.035	−.481	.046
4	.05	8	2.00	−.565	−.028	−.873	.038
Sum:					.307		.135

Expected HPR = .307 = 30.7%.

Variance = .135.

Standard deviation = $\sqrt{.135}$ = .367 = 36.7%.

5% VaR = −56.5%.

For the corresponding normal distribution, VaR would be 30.7% − 1.64485 × 36.7% = −29.67%.

b. With 36 returns, 5% of the sample would be .05 × 36 = 1.8 observations. The worst return is −17%, and the second-worst is −5%. Using interpolation, we estimate the fifth-percentile return as:

$$-17\% + .8[-5\% - (-17\%)] = -7.4\%$$

5.3 *a.* If the average investor chooses the S&P 500 portfolio, then the implied degree of risk aversion is given by Equation 5.13:

$$A = \frac{.10 - .05}{.18^2} = 1.54$$

b. $S = \dfrac{10 - 5}{18} = .28$

5.4 The mean excess return for the period 1926–1934 is 3.56% (below the historical average), and the standard deviation (using $n - 1$ degrees of freedom) is 32.55% (above the historical average). These results reflect the severe downturn of the great crash and the unusually high volatility of stock returns in this period.

5.5 *a.* Solving:

$$1 + R = (1 + r)(1 + i) = (1.03)(1.08) = 1.1124$$
$$R = 11.24\%$$

b. Solving:

$$1 + R = (1.03)(1.10) = 1.133$$
$$R = 13.3\%$$

5.6 $E(r) = 7 + .75 \times 8\% = 13\%$

$\sigma = .75 \times 22\% = 16.5\%$

Risk premium = 13 − 7 = 6%

$$\frac{\text{Risk premium}}{\text{Standard deviation}} = \frac{13 - 7}{16.5} = .36$$

Chapter 6

Efficient Diversification

Learning Objectives:

- **LO6-1** Show how covariance and correlation affect the power of diversification to reduce portfolio risk.
- **LO6-2** Calculate mean, variance, and covariance using either historical data or scenario analysis.
- **LO6-3** Construct efficient portfolios and use the Sharpe ratio to evaluate portfolio efficiency.
- **LO6-4** Calculate the composition of the optimal risky portfolio.
- **LO6-5** Use index models to analyze the risk and return characteristics of securities and portfolios.

In this chapter we describe how investors can construct the best possible risky portfolio. The key concept is efficient diversification.

The notion of diversification is age-old. The adage "Don't put all your eggs in one basket" obviously predates formal economic theory. However, a rigorous model showing how to make the most of the power of diversification was not devised until 1952, a feat for which Harry Markowitz eventually won the Nobel Prize in Economics. This chapter is largely developed from his work, as well as from later insights that built on his work.

We start with a bird's-eye view of how diversification reduces the variability of portfolio returns. We then turn to the construction of optimal risky portfolios. We follow a top-down approach, starting with asset allocation across a small set of broad asset classes, such as stocks, bonds, and money market securities. Then we show how the principles of optimal asset allocation can easily be generalized to solve the problem of security selection among many risky assets. We discuss the efficient set of risky portfolios and show how it leads us to the best attainable capital allocation. Finally, we show how index models of security returns can simplify the search for efficient portfolios and the interpretation of the risk characteristics of individual securities.

The last section examines the common fallacy that long-term investment horizons mitigate the impact of asset risk. We argue that the common belief in "time diversification" is in fact an illusion and is not real diversification.

Related websites for this chapter are available at www.mhhe.com/bkm.

6.1 DIVERSIFICATION AND PORTFOLIO RISK

Suppose you have in your risky portfolio only one stock, say, Dell Computers. What are the sources of risk affecting this "portfolio"?

We can identify two broad sources of uncertainty. The first is the risk from general economic conditions, such as business cycles, inflation, interest rates, exchange rates, and so forth. None of these macroeconomic factors can be predicted with certainty, and all affect Dell stock. Then you must add firm-specific influences, such as Dell's success in R&D, its management style and philosophy, and so on. Firm-specific factors are those that affect Dell without noticeably affecting other firms.

Now consider adding another security to the risky portfolio. If you invest half of your risky portfolio in ExxonMobil, leaving the other half in Dell, what happens to portfolio risk? Because the firm-specific influences on the two stocks differ (statistically speaking, the influences are independent), this strategy should reduce portfolio risk. For example, when oil prices fall, hurting ExxonMobil, computer prices might rise, helping Dell. The two effects are offsetting, which stabilizes portfolio return.

But why stop at only two stocks? Diversifying into many more securities continues to reduce exposure to firm-specific factors, so portfolio volatility should continue to fall. Ultimately, however, there is no way to avoid all risk. To the extent that virtually all securities are affected by common (risky) macroeconomic factors, we cannot eliminate exposure to general economic risk, no matter how many stocks we hold.

Figure 6.1 illustrates these concepts. When all risk is firm-specific, as in Figure 6.1A, diversification can reduce risk to low levels. With all risk sources independent, and with investment spread across many securities, exposure to any particular source of risk is negligible. This is an application of the law of large numbers. The reduction of risk to very low levels because of independent risk sources is called the *insurance principle.*

When a common source of risk affects all firms, however, even extensive diversification cannot eliminate all risk. In Figure 6.1B, portfolio standard deviation falls as the number of securities increases, but it is not reduced to zero. The risk that remains even after diversification is called **market risk,** risk that is attributable to marketwide risk sources. Other terms are **systematic risk** or **nondiversifiable risk.** The risk that *can* be eliminated by diversification is called **unique risk, firm-specific risk, nonsystematic risk,** or **diversifiable risk.**

market risk, systematic risk, nondiversifiable risk

Risk factors common to the whole economy.

unique risk, firm-specific risk, nonsystematic risk, diversifiable risk

Risk that can be eliminated by diversification.

This analysis is borne out by empirical studies. Figure 6.2 shows the effect of portfolio diversification, using data on NYSE stocks. The figure shows the average standard deviations of equally weighted portfolios constructed by selecting stocks at random as a function of the number of stocks in the portfolio. On average, portfolio risk does fall with diversification, but

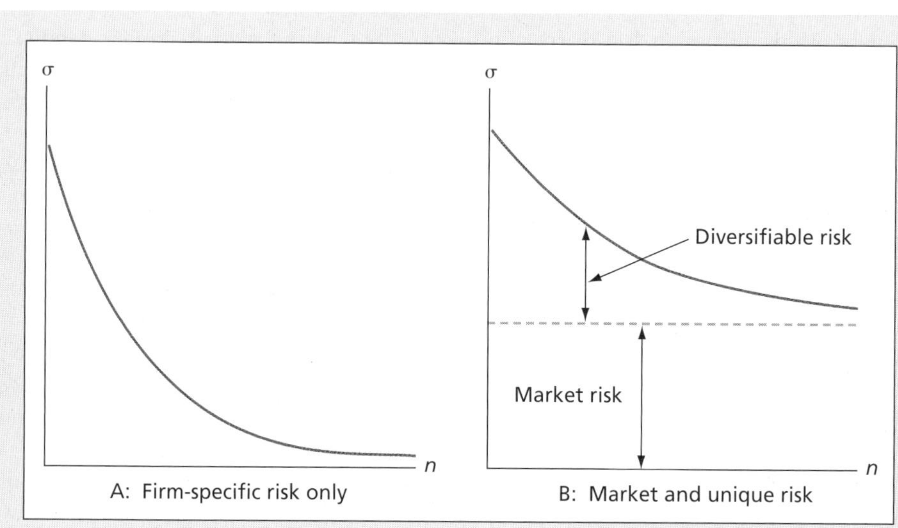

FIGURE 6.1

Portfolio risk as a function of the number of stocks in the portfolio

On the MARKET FRONT

DANGER: HIGH LEVELS OF COMPANY STOCK

Q: I'm 48 years old and have about 90% of my 401(k) invested in my company's stock and the rest in an international equity fund. I want to diversify further, but don't know where to turn. Any suggestions?

A: Diversify further? That's an understatement. You, my friend, need a total 401(k) portfolio makeover.

The glaring trouble spot, of course, is your huge concentration of company stock. Generally, I recommend that, to the extent you own your employer's stock at all in your 401(k), you limit it to 10% or so of your account's value.

The problem is that once you get beyond a small holding of company stock—or the shares of any one company for that matter—you dramatically increase the riskiness of your portfolio in two ways.

First, you expose yourself to the possibility that your company may simply implode, decimating the stock's value (and your 401(k)'s balance along with it) virtually overnight. But even if that doesn't happen, there's another risk: heightened volatility. A single stock is typically two to three times more volatile than a diversified portfolio. And when you load up your 401(k) with the stock of one company, it subjects your account value to the possibility of much wider swings.

In short, the payoff you'll likely get from investing in company stock doesn't adequately compensate you for the risk you're taking.

So, about that further diversification. Basically, you need to rebuild your portfolio from the ground up so that you not only own a broad range of stocks, but bonds as well. As for which investments you should choose from your 401(k)'s lineup, I'd recommend sticking as much as possible to low-cost funds and particularly index funds to the extent they're available.

SOURCE: Walter Updegrave, "Danger: High Levels of Company Stock," **http://money.cnn.com,** January 19, 2009.

FIGURE 6.2

Portfolio risk decreases as diversification increases

Source: Meir Statman, "How Many Stocks Make a Diversified Portfolio?" *Journal of Financial and Quantitative Analysis* 22, September 1987.

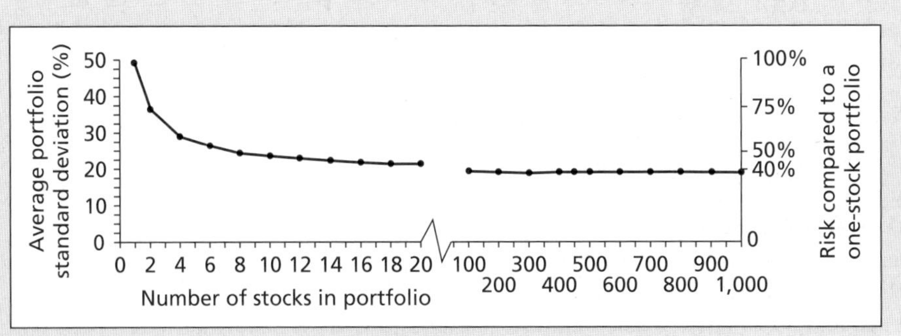

the power of diversification to reduce risk is limited by common sources of risk. The nearby box, "Danger: High Levels of Company Stock," highlights the dangers of neglecting diversification.

In light of this discussion, it is worth pointing out that general macroeconomic conditions in the U.S. do not move in lockstep with those in other countries. International diversification may further reduce portfolio risk, but here too, global economic and political factors affecting all countries to various degrees will limit the extent of risk reduction.

6.2 ASSET ALLOCATION WITH TWO RISKY ASSETS

In the last chapter we examined the capital allocation decision, how much of the portfolio to place in risk-free securities versus in a risky portfolio. Of course, investors need to choose the precise composition of the risky portfolio. In a top-down process, the first step would be an asset allocation decision. As the other nearby box, "First Take Care of Asset Allocation Needs," emphasizes, most investment professionals recognize that the asset allocation decision must take precedence over the choice of particular stocks.

We turn first to asset allocation between only two risky assets, still assumed to be a bond fund and a stock fund. Once we understand the portfolios of two risky assets, we will

On the MARKET FRONT

FIRST TAKE CARE OF ASSET ALLOCATION NEEDS

If you want to build a top-performing mutual-fund portfolio, you should start by hunting for top-performing funds, right?

Wrong.

Too many investors gamely set out to find top-notch funds without first settling on an overall portfolio strategy. Result? These investors wind up with a mishmash of funds that don't add up to a decent portfolio.

So what should you do? With thousands of stock, bond, and money-market funds to choose from, you couldn't possibly analyze all the funds available. Instead, to make sense of the bewildering array of funds available, you should start by deciding what basic mix of stock, bond, and money-market funds you want to hold. This is what experts call your "asset allocation."

This asset allocation has a major influence on your portfolio's performance. The more you have in stocks, the higher your likely long-run return.

But with the higher potential return from stocks come sharper short-term swings in a portfolio's value. As a result, you may want to include a healthy dose of bond and money-market funds, especially if you are a conservative investor or you will need to tap your portfolio for cash in the near future.

Once you have settled on your asset allocation mix, decide what sort of stock, bond, and money-market funds you want to own. This is particularly critical for the stock portion of your portfolio. One way to damp the price swings in your stock portfolio is to spread your money among large, small, and foreign stocks.

You could diversify even further by making sure that, when investing in U.S. large- and small-company stocks, you own both growth stocks with rapidly increasing sales or earnings and also beaten-down value stocks that are inexpensive compared with corporate assets or earnings.

Similarly, among foreign stocks, you could get additional diversification by investing in both developed foreign markets such as France, Germany, and Japan, and also emerging markets like Argentina, Brazil, and Malaysia.

SOURCE: Abridged from Jonathan Clements, "It Pays for You to Take Care of Asset-Allocation Needs Before Latching onto Fads," *The Wall Street Journal*, April 6, 1998. Reprinted by permission of *The Wall Street Journal*,

reintroduce the choice of the risk-free asset. This will complete the asset allocation problem across the three key asset classes: stocks, bonds, and T-bills. Constructing efficient portfolios of many risky securities is a straightforward extension of this asset allocation exercise.

Covariance and Correlation

To optimally construct a portfolio from risky assets, we need to understand how the uncertainties of asset returns interact. A key determinant of portfolio risk is the extent to which the returns on the two assets vary either in tandem or in opposition. Portfolio risk depends on the *covariance* between the returns of the assets in the portfolio. We can see why using a simple scenario analysis.

The scenario analysis in Spreadsheet 6.1 posits four possible scenarios for the economy: a severe recession, a mild recession, normal growth, and a boom. The performance of stocks follows the broad economy, returning, respectively, −37%, −11%, 14%, and 30% in the four scenarios. In contrast, bonds perform best in a mild recession, returning 15% (since falling interest rates create capital gains), and in the normal growth scenario, where their return is 8%. They suffer from defaults in severe recession, resulting in a negative return, −9%, and from

SPREADSHEET 6.1

Capital market expectations for the stock and bond funds

	A	B	C	D	E	F
1			Stock Fund		Bond Fund	
2	Scenario	Probability	Rate of Return	Col B x Col C	Rate of Return	Col B x Col E
3	Severe recession	.05	−37	−1.9	−9	−0.45
4	Mild recession	.25	−11	−2.8	15	3.8
5	Normal growth	.40	14	5.6	8	3.2
6	Boom	.30	30	9.0	−5	−1.5
7	Expected or Mean Return:		SUM:	10.0	SUM:	5.0

eXcel

Please visit us at www.mhhe.com/bkm

inflation in the boom scenario, where their return is −5%. Notice that bonds outperform stocks in both the mild and severe recession scenarios. In both normal growth and boom scenarios, stocks outperform bonds.

The expected return on each fund equals the probability-weighted average of the outcomes in the four scenarios. The last row of Spreadsheet 6.1 shows that the expected return of the stock fund is 10% and that of the bond fund is 5%. The variance is the probability-weighted average of the squared deviation of actual return from the expected return; the standard deviation is the square root of the variance. These values are computed in Spreadsheet 6.2.

What about the risk and return characteristics of a portfolio made up from the stock and bond funds? The portfolio return is the weighted average of the returns on each fund with weights equal to the proportion of the portfolio invested in each fund. Suppose we form a portfolio with 40% invested in the stock fund and 60% in the bond fund. Then the portfolio return in each scenario is the weighted average of the returns on the two funds. For example

$$\text{Portfolio return in mild recession} = .40 \times (-11\%) + .60 \times 15\% = 4.6\%$$

which appears in cell C6 of Spreadsheet 6.3.

Spreadsheet 6.3 shows the rate of return of the portfolio in each scenario. Notice that both funds suffer in a severe downturn and, therefore, the portfolio also experiences a substantial loss of 20.2%. This is a manifestation of systematic risk affecting a broad spectrum of securities. Declines of more than 25% in the S&P 500 Index have occurred five times in the past 86 years (1930, 1931, 1937, 1974, and 2008), roughly once every 17 years. Avoiding losses in these extreme outcomes would require one to devote a large allocation of the portfolio to risk-free (low return) investments or (expensive) portfolio insurance (which we will discuss in Chapter 16).

SPREADSHEET 6.2

Variance of returns

eXcel

Please visit us at www.mhhe.com/bkm

	A	B	C	D	E	F	G	H	I	J
1				Stock Fund				Bond Fund		
2				Deviation				Deviation		
3			Rate	from		Column B	Rate	from		Column B
4			of	Expected	Squared	×	of	Expected	Squared	×
5	Scenario	Prob.	Return	Return	Deviation	Column E	Return	Return	Deviation	Column I
6	Severe recession	.05	−37	−47	2209	110.45	−9	−14	196	9.80
7	Mild recession	.25	−11	−21	441	110.25	15	10	100	25.00
8	Normal growth	.40	14	4	16	6.40	8	3	9	3.60
9	Boom	.30	30	20	400	120.00	−5	−10	100	30.00
10				Variance = SUM		347.10			Variance:	68.40
11		Standard deviation = SQRT(Variance)				18.63			Std. Dev.:	8.27

SPREADSHEET 6.3

Performance of a portfolio invested in the stock and bound funds

Please visit us at www.mhhe.com/bkm

	A	B	C	D	E	F	G
1			Portfolio invested 40% in stock fund and 60% in bond fund				
2			Rate	Column B	Deviation from		Column D
3			of	×	Expected	Squared	×
4	Scenario	Probability	Return	Column C	Return	Deviation	Column F
5	Severe recession	.05	−20.2	−1.01	−27.2	739.84	36.99
6	Mild recession	.25	4.6	1.15	−2.4	5.76	1.44
7	Normal growth	.40	10.4	4.16	3.4	11.56	4.62
8	Boom	.30	9.0	2.70	2.0	4.00	1.20
9		Expected return:		7.00		Variance:	44.20
10						Standard deviation:	6.65

Extreme events such as a severe recession make for the large standard deviation of stocks, 18.63%, and even of bonds, 8.27%. Still, the overall standard deviation of the diversified portfolio, 6.65%, is considerably smaller than that of stocks and even smaller than that of bonds.

The low risk of the portfolio is due to the inverse relationship between the performances of the stock and bond funds. In a mild recession, stocks fare poorly, but this is offset by the large positive return of the bond fund. Conversely, in the boom scenario, bond prices fall, but stocks do very well. Notice that while the portfolio's expected return is just the weighted average of the expected return of the two assets, *the portfolio standard deviation is actually lower than that of either component fund.*

Portfolio risk is reduced most when the returns of the two assets most reliably offset each other. The natural question investors should ask, therefore, is how one can measure the tendency of the returns on two assets to vary either in tandem or in opposition to each other. The statistics that provide this measure are the covariance and the correlation coefficient.

The covariance is calculated in a manner similar to the variance. Instead of multiplying the difference of an asset return from its expected value by itself (i.e., squaring it), we multiply it by the deviation of the *other* asset return from *its* expectation. The sign and magnitude of this product are determined by whether deviations from the mean move together (i.e., are both positive or negative in the same scenarios) and whether they are small or large at the same time.

We start in Spreadsheet 6.4 with the deviation of the return on each fund from its expected value. For each scenario, we multiply the deviation of the stock fund return from its mean by the deviation of the bond fund. The product will be positive if both asset returns exceed their respective means or if both fall short of their respective means. The product will be negative if one asset exceeds its mean return when the other falls short. Spreadsheet 6.4 shows that the stock fund return in a mild recession falls short of its expected value by 21%, while the bond fund return exceeds its mean by 10%. Therefore, the product of the two deviations is $-21 \times 10 = -210$, as reported in column E. The product of deviations is negative if one asset performs well when the other is performing poorly. It is positive if both assets perform well or poorly in the same scenarios.

The probability-weighted average of the products is called *covariance* and measures the *average* tendency of the asset returns to vary in tandem, that is, to co-vary. The formula for the covariance of the returns on the stock and bond funds is given in Equation 6.1. Each particular scenario in this equation is labeled or "indexed" by i. In general, i ranges from scenario 1 to S (the total number of scenarios; here, $S = 4$). The probability of each scenario is denoted $p(i)$.

$$\text{Cov}(r_S, r_B) = \sum_{i=1}^{S} p(i)[r_S(i) - E(r_S)][r_B(i) - E(r_B)] \qquad \textbf{(6.1)}$$

The covariance of the stock and bond funds is computed in the next-to-last line of Spreadsheet 6.4 using Equation 6.1. The negative value for the covariance indicates that the two assets, on average, vary inversely; when one performs well, the other tends to perform poorly.

SPREADSHEET 6.4

Covariance between the returns of the stock and bond funds

	A	B	C	D	E	F
1			Deviation from Mean Return		Covariance	
2	Scenario	Probability	Stock Fund	Bond Fund	Product of Dev	Col B × Col E
3	Severe recession	.05	−47	−14	658	32.9
4	Mild recession	.25	−21	10	−210	−52.5
5	Normal growth	.40	4	3	12	4.8
6	Boom	.30	20	−10	−200	−60.0
7				Covariance =	SUM:	−74.8
8	Correlation coefficient = Covariance/(StdDev(stocks)*StdDev(bonds)) =					−0.49

Please visit us at www.mhhe.com/bkm

Like variance, the unit of covariance is percent square, which is why it is difficult to interpret its magnitude. For instance, does the covariance of −74.8 in cell F7 indicate that the inverse relationship between the returns on stock and bond funds is strong? It's hard to say. An easier statistic to interpret is the *correlation coefficient*, which is the covariance divided by the product of the standard deviations of the returns on each fund. We denote the correlation coefficient by the Greek letter rho, ρ.

$$\text{Correlation coefficient} = \rho_{SB} = \frac{\text{Cov}(r_S, r_B)}{\sigma_S \sigma_B} = \frac{-74.8}{18.63 \times 8.27} = -.49 \quad \textbf{(6.2)}$$

Correlation is a pure number and can range from values of −1 to +1. A correlation of −1 indicates that one asset's return varies perfectly inversely with the other's. If you were to do a linear regression of one asset's return on the other, the slope coefficient would be negative and the R-square of the regression would be 100%, indicating a perfect fit. The R-square is the square of the correlation coefficient and tells you the fraction of the variance of one return explained by the other return. With a correlation of −1, you could predict 100% of the variability of one asset's return if you knew the return on the other asset. Conversely, a correlation of +1 would indicate perfect positive correlation and also would imply an R-square of 100%. A correlation of zero indicates that the returns on the two assets are unrelated. The correlation coefficient of $\rho_{SB} = -.49$ in Equation 6.2 confirms the tendency of the returns on the stock and bond funds to vary inversely. In fact, a fraction of $(-.49)^2 = .24$ of the variance of stocks can be explained by the returns on bonds.

Equation 6.2 shows that whenever the covariance is called for in a calculation we can replace it with the following expression using the correlation coefficient:

$$\text{Cov}(r_S, r_B) = \rho_{SB}\sigma_S\sigma_B \quad \textbf{(6.3)}$$

We are now in a position to derive the risk and return features of portfolios of risky assets.

CONCEPT check 6.1

Suppose the rates of return of the bond portfolio in the four scenarios of Spreadsheet 6.1 are −10% in a severe recession, 10% in a mild recession, 7% in a normal period, and 2% in a boom. The stock returns in the four scenarios are −37%, −11%, 14%, and 30%. What are the covariance and correlation coefficient between the rates of return on the two portfolios?

Using Historical Data

We've seen that portfolio risk and return depend on the means and variances of the component securities, as well as on the covariance between their returns. One way to obtain these inputs is a scenario analysis as in Spreadsheets 6.1–6.4. A common alternative approach to produce these inputs is to make use of historical data. The idea is that variability and covariability change slowly over time. Thus, if we estimate these statistics from recent data, our estimates will provide useful predictions for the near future—perhaps next month or next quarter.

In this approach, we use realized returns to estimate variances and covariances. Means cannot be as precisely estimated from past returns. We discuss mean returns in great detail later. The estimate of variance is the average value of the squared deviations around the sample average; the estimate of the covariance is the average value of the cross-product of deviations. Notice that, as in scenario analysis, the focus for risk is on deviations of returns from their average value. Instead of using mean returns based on the scenario analysis, we use average returns during the sample period. We can illustrate this approach with a simple example.

EXAMPLE 6.1

Using Historical Data to Estimate Means, Standard Deviations, Covariance, and Correlation

Consider the 10 years of returns for the two mutual funds presented in the following spreadsheet. While these are far less data than most analysts would use, for the sake of illustration we will pretend that they are adequate to estimate mean returns and relevant risk statistics. In practice, analysts would use higher-frequency data (e.g., monthly or even daily data) to estimate risk coefficients and would, as well, supplement historical data with fundamental analysis to forecast future returns.

The spreadsheet starts with the raw return data in columns B and C. We use standard Excel functions to obtain average returns, standard deviation, covariance, and correlation (see rows 18–21). We also confirm (in cell F14) that covariance is the average value of the product of each asset's deviation from its mean return.

The average returns and standard deviations in this spreadsheet are similar to those of our previous scenario analysis. However, the correlation between stock and bond returns in this example is low but positive, which is more consistent with historical experience than the strongly negative correlation of −.49 implied by our scenario analysis.

	A	B	C	D	E	F
1		Rates of Return		Deviations from Average Returns		Products of
2	Year	Stock Fund	Bond Fund	Stock Fund	Bond Fund	Deviations
3	2006	30.17	5.08	20.17	0.08	1.53
4	2007	32.97	7.52	22.97	2.52	57.78
5	2008	21.04	−8.82	11.04	−13.82	−152.56
6	2009	−8.10	5.27	−18.10	0.27	−4.82
7	2010	−12.89	12.20	−22.89	7.20	−164.75
8	2011	−28.53	−7.79	−38.53	−12.79	493.00
9	2012	22.49	6.38	12.49	1.38	17.18
10	2013	12.58	12.40	2.58	7.40	19.05
11	2014	14.81	17.29	4.81	12.29	59.05
12	2015	15.50	0.51	5.50	−4.49	−24.70
13						
14	Average	10.00	5.00	Covariance = average product of deviations:		30.08
15	SD	19.00	8.00	Correlation = Covariance/(SD stocks*SD bonds):		0.20
16						
17	**Excel formulas**					
18	Average	=average(B3:B12)				
19	Std deviation	=stdevp(B3:B12)				
20	Covariance	=covar(B3:B12,C3:C12)				
21	Correlation	=correl(B3:B12,C3:C12)				
22						
23						

Two comments on Example 6.1 are in order. First, you may recall from a statistics class and from Chapter 5 that when variance is estimated from a sample of n observed returns, it is common to divide the squared deviations by $n - 1$ rather than by n. This is because we take deviations from an estimated average return rather than the true (but unknown) expected return; this procedure is said to adjust for a "lost degree of freedom." In Excel, the function STDEVP computes standard deviation dividing by n, while the function STDEV uses $n - 1$. Excel's covariance and correlation functions both use n. In Example 6.1, we ignored this fine point, and divided by n throughout. In any event, the correction for the lost degree of freedom is negligible when there are plentiful observations. For example with 60 returns (e.g., five years of monthly data), the difference between dividing by 60 or 59 will affect variance or covariance by a factor of only 1.017.

Second, we repeat the warning about the statistical reliability of historical estimates. Estimates of variance and covariance from past data are generally reliable forecasts (at least for the short term). However, averages of past returns typically provide highly noisy (i.e., imprecise) forecasts of future expected returns. In this example, we use past averages from small samples because our objective is to demonstrate the methodology. In practice, professional investors spend most of their resources on macroeconomic and security analysis to improve their estimates of mean returns.

CONCEPT check 6.2

The following tables present returns on various pairs of stocks in several periods. In part A, we show you a scatter diagram of the returns on the first pair of stocks. Draw (or prepare in Excel) similar scatter diagrams for cases B through E. Match up your diagrams (A–E) to the following list of correlation coefficients by choosing the correlation that best describes the relationship between the returns on the two stocks: $\rho = -1, 0, .2, .5, 1.0$.

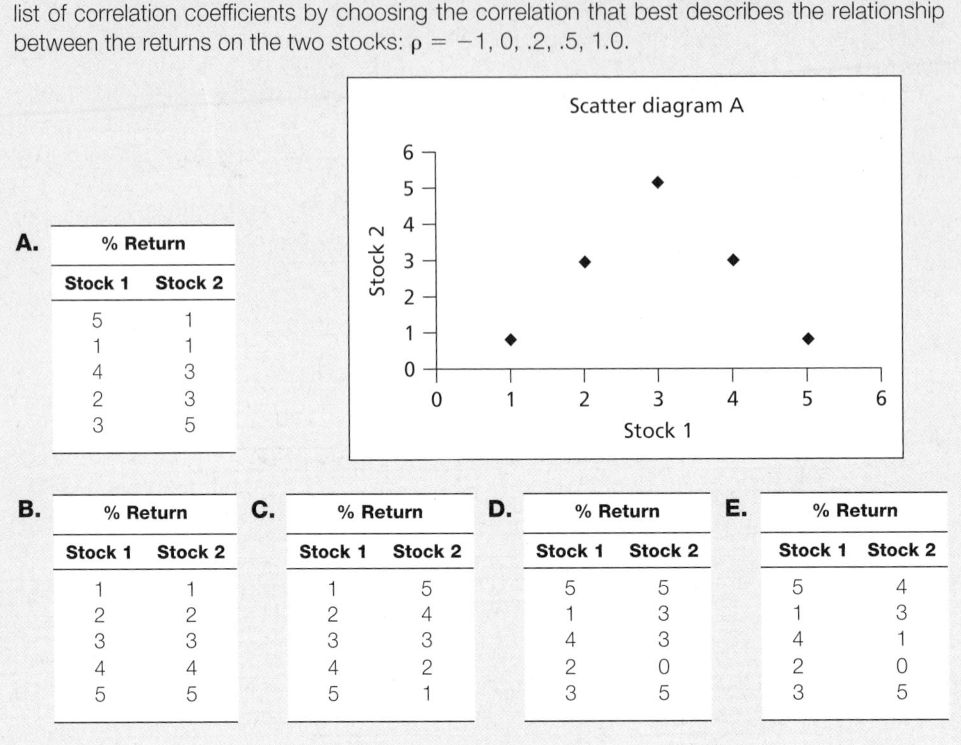

A.

% Return	
Stock 1	**Stock 2**
5	1
1	1
4	3
2	3
3	5

B.

% Return	
Stock 1	**Stock 2**
1	1
2	2
3	3
4	4
5	5

C.

% Return	
Stock 1	**Stock 2**
1	5
2	4
3	3
4	2
5	1

D.

% Return	
Stock 1	**Stock 2**
5	5
1	3
4	3
2	0
3	5

E.

% Return	
Stock 1	**Stock 2**
5	4
1	3
4	1
2	0
3	5

The Three Rules of Two-Risky-Assets Portfolios

Suppose a proportion denoted by w_B is invested in the bond fund and the remainder $1 - w_B$, denoted by w_S, is invested in the stock fund. The properties of the portfolio are determined by the following three rules governing combinations of random variables:

Rule 1: The rate of return on a portfolio is the weighted average of returns on the component securities, with the investment proportions as weights.

$$r_P = w_B r_B + w_S r_S \qquad \textbf{(6.4)}$$

Rule 2: The expected *rate of return on a portfolio is the weighted average of the* expected *returns on the component securities, with the portfolio proportions as weights.*

$$E(r_P) = w_B E(r_B) + w_S E(r_S) \qquad \textbf{(6.5)}$$

Rules 1 and 2 say that a portfolio's actual return and its mean return are linear functions of the component security returns and portfolio weights. This is not so for portfolio variance, as the third rule shows.

Rule 3: The variance of the rate of return on a two-risky-asset portfolio is

$$\sigma_P^2 = (w_B\sigma_B)^2 + (w_S\sigma_S)^2 + 2(w_B\sigma_B)(w_S\sigma_S)\rho_{BS} \qquad \textbf{(6.6)}$$

where ρ_{BS} is the correlation coefficient between the returns on the stock and bond funds. Notice that using Equation 6.3, we may replace the last term in Equation 6.6 with $2w_B w_S Cov(r_B, r_S)$.

The variance of a portfolio is the *sum* of the contributions of the component security variances *plus* a term that involves the correlation coefficient (and hence, covariance) between the returns on the component securities. We know from the last section why this last term arises. When the correlation between the component securities is small or negative, there will be a greater tendency for returns on the two assets to offset each other. This will reduce portfolio risk. Notice in Equation 6.6 that portfolio variance is lower when the correlation coefficient is lower.

The formula describing portfolio variance is more complicated than that describing portfolio return. This complication has a virtue, however: a tremendous potential for gains from diversification.

The Risk-Return Trade-Off with Two-Risky-Assets Portfolios

We can assess the benefit from diversification by using Rules 2 and 3 to compare the risk and expected return of a better-diversified portfolio to a less diversified benchmark. Suppose an investor estimates the following input data:

$$E(r_B) = 5\% \quad \sigma_B = 8\% \quad E(r_S) = 10\% \quad \sigma_S = 19\% \quad \rho_{BS} = .2$$

Currently, all funds are invested in the bond fund, but the invester ponders a portfolio invested 40% in stock and 60% in bonds. Using Rule 2, the expected return of this portfolio is

$$E(r_P) = .4 \times 10\% + .6 \times 5\% = 7\%$$

which represents a gain of 2% compared to a bond-only investment. Using Rule 3, the portfolio standard deviation is

$$\sigma = \sqrt{(.4 \times 19)^2 + (.6 \times 8)^2 + 2(.4 \times 19) \times (.6 \times 8) \times .2} = 9.76\%$$

which is less than the weighted average of the component standard deviations: $.4 \times 19 + .6 \times 8 = 12.40\%$. The difference of 2.64% reflects the benefits of diversification. This benefit is cost-free in the sense that diversification allows us to experience the full contribution of the stock's higher expected return, while keeping the portfolio standard deviation below the average of the component standard deviations.

EXAMPLE 6.2

Benefits from Diversification

Suppose we invest 85% in bonds and only 15% in stocks. We can construct a portfolio with an expected return higher than bonds $(.85 \times 5) + (.15 \times 10) = 5.75\%$ and, at the same time, a standard deviation less than bonds. Using Equation 6.6 again, we find that the portfolio variance is

$$(.85 \times 8)^2 + (.15 \times 19)^2 + 2(.85 \times 8)(.15 \times 19) \times .2 = 62.1$$

and, accordingly, the portfolio standard deviation is $\sqrt{62.1} = 7.88\%$, which is less than the standard deviation of either bonds or stocks alone. Taking on a more volatile asset (stocks) actually reduces portfolio risk! Such is the power of diversification.

We can find investment proportions that will reduce portfolio risk even further. The risk-minimizing proportions are 90.7% in bonds and 9.3% in stocks.[1] With these proportions, the portfolio standard deviation will be 7.80%, and the portfolio's expected return will be 5.47%.

Is this portfolio preferable to the one considered in Example 6.2, with 15% in the stock fund? That depends on investor preferences, because the portfolio with the lower variance also has a lower expected return.

What the analyst can and must do is show investors the entire **investment opportunity set.** This is the set of all attainable combinations of risk and return offered by portfolios formed using the available assets in differing proportions. We find the investment opportunity

investment opportunity set

Set of available portfolio risk-return combinations.

[1]The minimum-variance portfolio minimizes the variance (and hence standard deviation) of returns, regardless of the expected return. The formula for the weight in bonds is $w_B = \frac{\sigma_S^2 - \sigma_B\sigma_S\rho_{BS}}{\sigma_S^2 + \sigma_B^2 - 2\sigma_B\sigma_S\rho_{BS}}$, and the weight in stocks is $w_S = 1 - w_B$. Notice that when correlation is zero, the variance-minimizing weight simplifies to the ratio of stock variance to the sum of the variances of stocks and bonds: $w_B = \frac{\sigma_S^2}{\sigma_S^2 + \sigma_B^2}$.

SPREADSHEET 6.5

The investment opportunity set with the stock and bond funds

eXcel

Please visit us at www.mhhe.com/bkm

	A	B	C	D	E
1			Input Data		
2	$E(r_S)$	$E(r_B)$	σ_S	σ_B	ρ_{BS}
3	10	5	19	8	0.2
4	Portfolio Weights		Expected Return, $E(r_p)$		Std Dev
5	$w_S = 1 - w_B$	w_B	Col A*A3 + Col B*B3		(Equation 6.6)
6	−0.2	1.2	4.0		9.59
7	−0.1	1.1	4.5		8.62
8	0.0	1.0	5.0		8.00
9	0.0932	0.9068	5.5		7.804
10	0.1	0.9	5.5		7.81
11	0.2	0.8	6.0		8.07
12	0.3	0.7	6.5		8.75
13	0.4	0.6	7.0		9.77
14	0.5	0.5	7.5		11.02
15	0.6	0.4	8.0		12.44
16	0.7	0.3	8.5		13.98
17	0.8	0.2	9.0		15.60
18	0.9	0.1	9.5		17.28
19	1.0	0.0	10.0		19.00
20	1.1	−0.1	10.5		20.75
21	1.2	−0.2	11.0		22.53
22	Notes:				
23	1. Negative weights indicate short positions.				
24	2. The weights of the minimum-variance portfolio are computed using the formula in Footnote 1.				

set using Spreadsheet 6.5. Columns A and B set out several different proportions for investments in the stock and bond funds. The next columns present the portfolio expected return and standard deviation corresponding to each allocation. These risk-return combinations are plotted in Figure 6.3.

The Mean-Variance Criterion

Investors desire portfolios that lie to the "northwest" in Figure 6.3. These are portfolios with high expected returns (toward the "north" of the figure) and low volatility (to the "west"). These preferences mean that we can compare portfolios using a *mean-variance criterion* in the following way: Portfolio A is said to dominate portfolio B if all investors prefer A over B. This will be the case if it has higher mean return and lower variance or standard deviation:

$$E(r_A) \geq E(r_B) \quad \text{and} \quad \sigma_A \leq \sigma_B$$

FIGURE 6.3

The investment opportunity set with the stock and bond funds

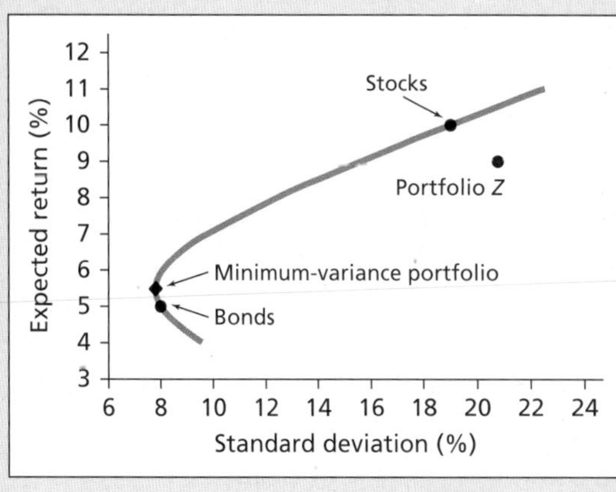

Graphically, when we plot the expected return and standard deviation of each portfolio in Figure 6.3, portfolio A will lie to the northwest of B. Given a choice between portfolios A and B, *all* investors would choose A. For example, the stock fund in Figure 6.3 dominates portfolio Z; the stock fund has higher expected return and lower volatility.

Portfolios that lie below the minimum-variance portfolio in the figure can therefore be rejected out of hand as inefficient. Any portfolio on the downward-sloping portion of the curve (including the bond fund) is "dominated" by the portfolio that lies directly above it on the upward-sloping portion of the curve since that portfolio has higher expected return and equal standard deviation. The best choice among the portfolios on the upward-sloping portion of the curve is not as obvious, because in this region higher expected return is accompanied by greater risk. We will discuss the best choice when we introduce the risk-free asset to the portfolio decision.

So far we have assumed a correlation of .2 between stock and bond returns. We know that low correlations aid diversification and that a higher correlation coefficient results in a reduced effect of diversification. What are the implications of perfect positive correlation between bonds and stocks?

A correlation coefficient of 1 simplifies Equation 6.6 for portfolio variance. Looking at it again, you will see that substitution of $\rho_{BS} = 1$ allows us to "complete the square" of the quantities $w_B\sigma_B$ and $w_S\sigma_S$ to obtain

$$\sigma_P^2 = w_B^2\sigma_B^2 + w_S^2\sigma_S^2 + 2w_B\sigma_B w_S\sigma_S = (w_B\sigma_B + w_S\sigma_S)^2$$
$$\sigma_P = w_B\sigma_B + w_S\sigma_S$$

The portfolio standard deviation is a weighted average of the component security standard deviations only in the special case of perfect positive correlation. In this circumstance, there are no gains to be had from diversification. Both the portfolio mean and the standard deviation are simple weighted averages. Figure 6.4 shows the opportunity set with perfect positive correlation—a straight line through the component securities. No portfolio can be discarded as inefficient in this case, and the choice among portfolios depends only on risk aversion. Diversification in the case of perfect positive correlation is not effective.

Perfect positive correlation is the *only* case in which there is no benefit from diversification. Whenever $\rho < 1$, the portfolio standard deviation is less than the weighted average of the standard deviations of the component securities. Therefore, *there are benefits to diversification whenever asset returns are less than perfectly positively correlated.*

Our analysis has ranged from very attractive diversification benefits ($\rho_{BS} < 0$) to no benefits at all ($\rho_{BS} = 1$). For ρ_{BS} within this range, the benefits will be somewhere in between.

A realistic correlation coefficient between stocks and bonds based on historical experience is actually around .20. The expected returns and standard deviations that we have so far assumed also reflect historical experience, which is why we include a graph for $\rho_{BS} = .2$ in Figure 6.4. Spreadsheet 6.6 enumerates some of the points on the various opportunity sets in Figure 6.4. As the figure illustrates, $\rho_{BS} = .2$ is a lot better for diversification than perfect positive correlation and a bit worse than zero correlation.

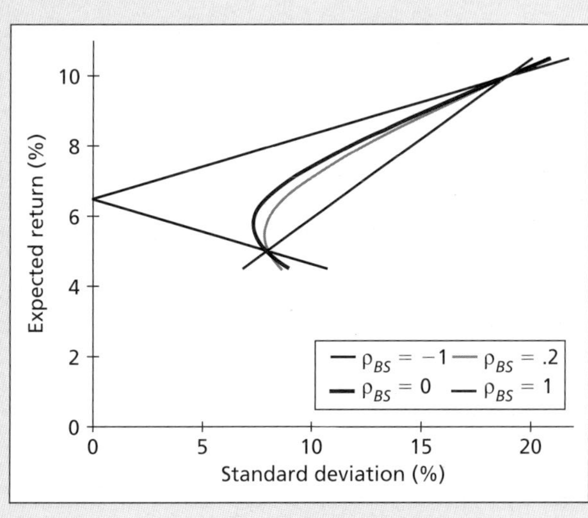

FIGURE 6.4

Investment opportunity sets for bonds and stocks with various correlation coefficients

SPREADSHEET 6.6

Investment opportunity set for stocks and bonds with various correlation coefficients

	A	B	C	D	E	F	G
1		**Input Data**					
2	$E(r_S)$	$E(r_B)$	σ_S	σ_B			
3	10	5	19	8			
4							
5	Weights in Stocks	Portfolio Expected Return	Portfolio Standard Deviation[1] for Given Correlation, ρ				
6	w_S	$E(r_P)$ = Col A*A3 + (1 − Col A)*B3	−1	0	0.2	0.5	1
7	−0.1	4.5	10.70	9.00	8.62	8.02	6.90
8	0.0	5.0	8.00	8.00	8.00	8.00	8.00
9	0.1	5.5	5.30	7.45	7.81	8.31	9.10
10	0.2	6.0	2.60	7.44	8.07	8.93	10.20
11	0.3	6.5	0.10	7.99	8.75	9.79	11.30
12	0.4	7.0	2.80	8.99	9.77	10.83	12.40
13	0.6	8.0	8.20	11.84	12.44	13.29	14.60
14	0.8	9.0	13.60	15.28	15.60	16.06	16.80
15	1.0	10.0	19.00	19.00	19.00	19.00	19.00
16	1.1	10.5	21.70	20.92	20.75	20.51	20.10
17				Minimum-Variance Portfolio[2,3,4,5]			
18	$w_S(\min) = (\sigma_B{}^\wedge 2 - \sigma_B\sigma_S\rho)/(\sigma_S{}^\wedge 2 + \sigma_B{}^\wedge 2 - 2{*}\sigma_B\sigma_S\rho) =$		0.2963	0.1506	0.0923	−0.0440	−0.7273
19		$E(r_P) = w_S(\min){*}A3 + (1 - w_S(\min)){*}B3 =$	6.48	5.75	5.46	4.78	1.36
20		$\sigma_P =$	0.00	7.37	7.80	7.97	0.00

Please visit us at www.mhhe.com/bkm

Notes:

1. σ_P = SQRT[(Col A*C3)^2 + ((1 − Col A)*D3)^2 + 2*Col A*C3*(1 − Col A)*D3*ρ]
2. The standard deviation is calculated from Equation 6.6 using the weights of the minimum-variance portfolio:

$$\sigma_P = \text{SQRT}[(w_S(\min){*}\text{C3})^\wedge 2 + ((1 - w_S(\min)){*}\text{D3})^\wedge 2 + 2{*}w_S(\min){*}\text{C3}{*}(1 - w_S(\min)){*}\text{D3}{*}\rho]$$

3. As the correlation coefficient grows, the minimum-variance portfolio requires a smaller position in stocks (even a negative position for higher correlations), and the performance of this portfolio becomes less attractive.
4. Notice that with correlation of .5 or higher, minimum variance is achieved with a short position in stocks. The standard deviation is lower than that of bonds, but the mean is lower as well.
5. With perfect positive correlation (column G), you can drive the standard deviation to zero by taking a large, short position in stocks. The mean return is then as low as 1.36%.

Negative correlation between a pair of assets is also possible. When correlation is negative, there will be even greater diversification benefits. Again, let us start with the extreme. With perfect negative correlation, we substitute $\rho_{BS} = -1$ in Equation 6.6 and simplify it by completing the square:

$$\sigma_P^2 = (w_B\sigma_B - w_S\sigma_S)^2$$

and, therefore,

$$\sigma_P = \text{ABS}[w_B\sigma_B - w_S\sigma_S] \tag{6.7}$$

The right-hand side of Equation 6.7 denotes the absolute value of $w_B\sigma_B - w_S\sigma_S$. The solution involves the absolute value because standard deviation cannot be negative.

With perfect negative correlation, the benefits from diversification stretch to the limit. Equation 6.7 yields the proportions that will reduce the portfolio standard deviation all the way to zero.[2] With our data, this will happen when $w_B = 70.37\%$. While exposing us to zero risk, investing 29.63% in stocks (rather than placing all funds in bonds) will still increase the portfolio expected return from 5% to 6.48%. Of course, we can hardly expect results this attractive in reality.

[2]The proportion in bonds that will drive the standard deviation to zero when $\rho = -1$ is

$$w_B = \frac{\sigma_S}{\sigma_B + \sigma_S}$$

Compare this formula to the formula in footnote 1 for the variance-minimizing proportions when $\rho = 0$.

CONCEPT check 6.3

Suppose that for some reason you are *required* to invest 50% of your portfolio in bonds and 50% in stocks. Use the data on mean returns and standard deviations in Spreadsheet 6.5 to answer the following questions.

a. If the standard deviation of your portfolio is 10%, what must be the correlation coefficient between stock and bond returns?
b. What is the expected rate of return on your portfolio?
c. Now suppose that the correlation between stock and bond returns is .22 instead of the value you found in part (*a*) but that you are free to choose whatever portfolio proportions you desire. Are you likely to be better or worse off than you were in part (*a*)?

6.3 THE OPTIMAL RISKY PORTFOLIO WITH A RISK-FREE ASSET

Now we can expand the asset allocation problem to include a risk-free asset. Let us continue to use the input data from Spreadsheet 6.5. Suppose then that we are still confined to the risky bond and stock funds but now can also invest in T-bills yielding 3%. When we add the risk-free asset to a stock-plus-bond risky portfolio, the resulting opportunity set is the straight line that we called the CAL (capital allocation line) in Chapter 5. We now consider various CALs constructed from risk-free bills and a variety of possible risky portfolios, each formed by combining the stock and bond funds in alternative proportions.

We start in Figure 6.5 with the opportunity set of risky assets constructed only from the bond and stock funds. The lowest-variance risky portfolio is labeled MIN (denoting the *minimum-variance portfolio*). CAL_{MIN} is drawn through it and shows the risk-return trade-off with various positions in T-bills and portfolio MIN. It is immediately evident from the figure that we could do better (i.e., obtain a higher Sharpe ratio) by using portfolio A instead of MIN as the risky portfolio. CAL_A dominates CAL_{MIN}, offering a higher expected return for any level of volatility. Spreadsheet 6.6 (see bottom panel of column E) shows that portfolio MIN's expected return is 5.46% and its standard deviation (SD) is 7.80%. Portfolio A (row 10 in Spreadsheet 6.6) offers an expected return of 6% with an SD of 8.07%.

The slope of the CAL is the Sharpe ratio of the risky portfolio, that is, the ratio of excess return to standard deviation:

$$S_P = \frac{E(r_P) - r_f}{\sigma_P} \tag{6.8}$$

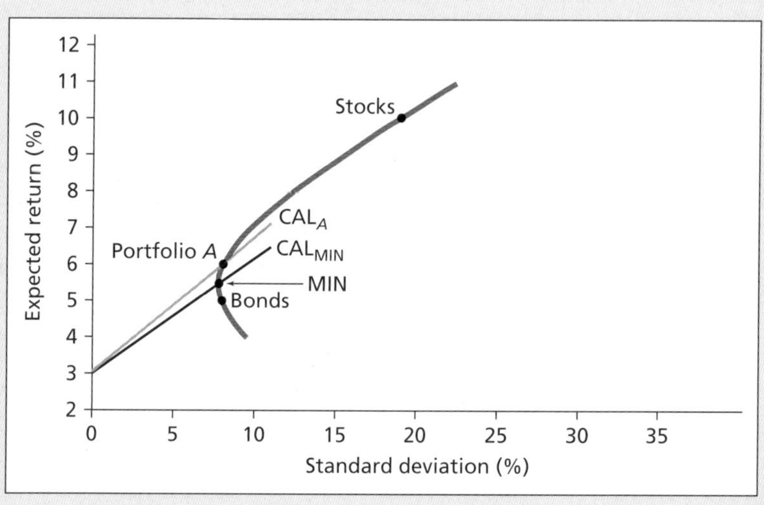

FIGURE 6.5 The opportunity set of stocks, bonds, and a risk-free asset with two capital allocation lines

FIGURE 6.6

The optimal capital allocation line with bonds, stocks, and T-bills

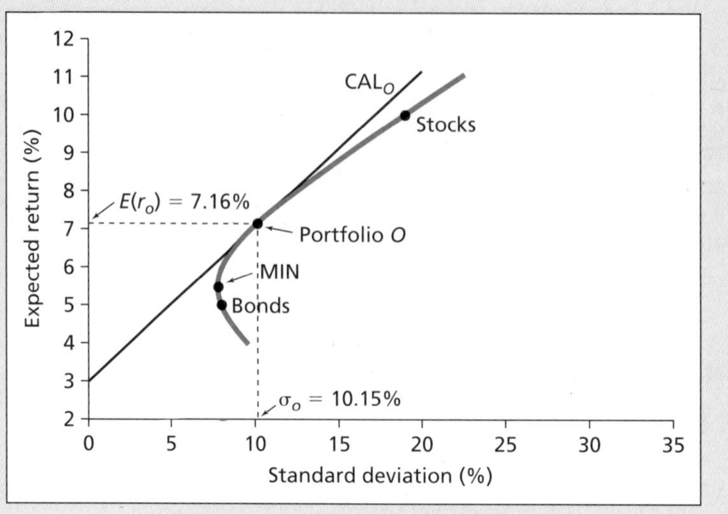

This is the rate at which the investor can increase expected return by accepting higher portfolio standard deviation. With a T-bill rate of 3% we obtain the Sharpe ratio of the two portfolios:

$$S_{\text{MIN}} = \frac{5.46 - 3}{7.80} = .32 \quad S_A = \frac{6 - 3}{8.07} = .37 \tag{6.9}$$

The higher ratio for portfolio A compared to MIN measures the improvement it offers in the risk-return trade-off.

But why stop at portfolio A? We can continue to ratchet the CAL upward until it reaches the ultimate point of tangency with the investment opportunity set. This must yield the CAL with the highest feasible reward-to-volatility (Sharpe) ratio. Therefore, the tangency portfolio (O) in Figure 6.6 is the **optimal risky portfolio** to mix with T-bills, which may be defined as the risky portfolio resulting in the highest possible CAL.

optimal risky portfolio

The best combination of risky assets to be mixed with safe assets to form the complete portfolio.

Figure 6.6 clearly shows the improvement in the risk-return trade-off obtained with CAL$_O$. For any portfolio standard deviation, CAL$_O$ offers a higher expected return than is attainable from the opportunity set constructed only from the risky bond and stock funds.

To find the composition of the optimal risky portfolio, O, we search for weights in the stock and bond funds that maximize the portfolio's Sharpe ratio. With only two risky assets, we can solve for the optimal portfolio weights using the following formula:

$$w_B = \frac{[E(r_B) - r_f]\sigma_S^2 - [E(r_S) - r_f]\sigma_B\sigma_S\rho_{BS}}{[E(r_B) - r_f]\sigma_S^2 + [E(r_S) - r_f]\sigma_B^2 - [E(r_B) - r_f + E(r_S) - r_f]\sigma_B\sigma_S\rho_{BS}}$$

$$w_S = 1 - w_B \tag{6.10}$$

Using the risk premiums (expected excess return over the risk-free rate) of the stock and bond funds, their standard deviations, and the correlation between their returns in Equation 6.10, we find that the weights of the optimal portfolio are $w_B(O) = .568$ and $w_S(O) = .432$. Using these weights, Equations 6.5, 6.6, and 6.8 imply that $E(r_O) = 7.16\%$, $\sigma_O = 10.15\%$, and therefore the Sharpe ratio of the optimal portfolio (the slope of its CAL) is

$$S_O = \frac{E(r_O) - r_f}{\sigma_O} = \frac{7.16 - 3}{10.15} = .41$$

This Sharpe ratio is significantly higher than those provided by either the bond or stock portfolios alone.

In the last chapter we saw that the preferred *complete* portfolio formed from a risky portfolio and a risk-free asset depends on the investor's risk aversion. More risk-averse investors prefer low-risk portfolios despite the lower expected return, while more risk-tolerant investors choose higher-risk, higher-return portfolios. Both investors, however, will choose portfolio O as their risky portfolio since it results in the highest return per unit of risk, that is, the steepest capital allocation line. Investors will differ only in their allocation of investment funds between portfolio O and the risk-free asset.

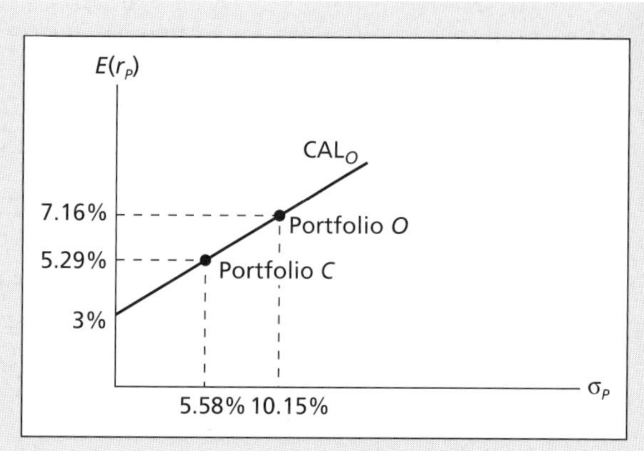

FIGURE 6.7

The complete portfolio

Figure 6.7 shows one possible choice for the preferred complete portfolio, C. The investor places 55% of wealth in portfolio O and 45% in Treasury bills. The rate of return and volatility of the portfolio are

$$E(r_C) = 3 + .55 \times (7.16 - 3) = 5.29\%$$
$$\sigma_C = .55 \times 10.15 = 5.58\%$$

We found above that the optimal risky portfolio O is formed by mixing the bond fund and stock fund with weights of 56.8% and 43.2%. Therefore, the overall asset allocation of the *complete* portfolio is as follows:

Weight in risk-free asset		45.00%
Weight in bond fund	.568 × 55% =	31.24
Weight in stock fund	.432 × 55% =	23.76
Total		100.00%

Figure 6.8 depicts the overall asset allocation. The allocation reflects considerations of both efficient diversification (the construction of the optimal risky portfolio, O) and risk aversion (the allocation of funds between the risk-free asset and the risky portfolio O to form the complete portfolio, C).

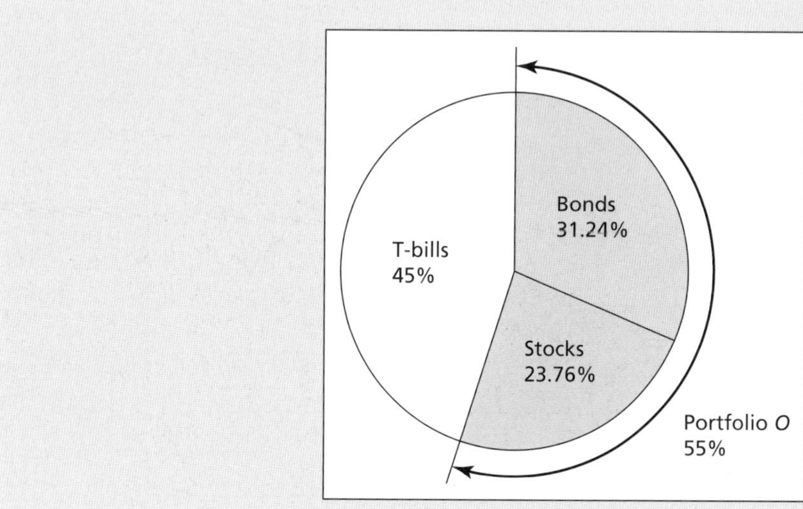

FIGURE 6.8

The composition of the complete portfolio: The solution to the asset allocation problem

CONCEPT check 6.4

A universe of securities includes a risky stock (*X*), a stock-index fund (*M*), and T-bills. The data for the universe are:

	Expected Return	Standard Deviation
X	15%	50%
M	10	20
T-bills	5	0

The correlation coefficient between *X* and *M* is −.2.

a. Draw the opportunity set of securities *X* and *M*.
b. Find the optimal risky portfolio (*O*), its expected return, standard deviation, and Sharpe ratio. Compare with the Sharpe ratio of *X* and *M*.
c. Find the slope of the CAL generated by T-bills and portfolio *O*.
d. Suppose an investor places 2/9 (i.e., 22.22%) of the complete portfolio in the risky portfolio *O* and the remainder in T-bills. Calculate the composition of the complete portfolio, its expected return, SD, and Sharpe ratio.

6.4 EFFICIENT DIVERSIFICATION WITH MANY RISKY ASSETS

We extend the two-risky-assets portfolio methodology to the case of many risky assets and a risk-free asset in three steps. First, we extend the two-risky-assets opportunity set to many assets. Next we determine the optimal risky portfolio that supports the steepest CAL, that is, maximizes its Sharpe ratio. Finally, we choose a complete portfolio on CAL_O based on the investor's risk aversion by mixing the risk-free asset with the optimal risky portfolio.

The Efficient Frontier of Risky Assets

To get a sense of how additional risky assets can improve investment opportunities, look at Figure 6.9. Points *A, B,* and *C* represent the expected returns and standard deviations of three stocks. The curve passing through *A* and *B* shows the risk-return combinations of portfolios formed from those two stocks. Similarly, the curve passing through *B* and *C* shows portfolios formed from those two stocks. Now observe point *E* on the *AB* curve and point *F* on the *BC* curve. These points represent two portfolios chosen from the set of *AB* and *BC* combinations. The curve that passes through *E* and *F* in turn represents portfolios constructed from portfolios *E* and *F.* Since *E* and *F* are themselves constructed from *A, B,* and *C,*

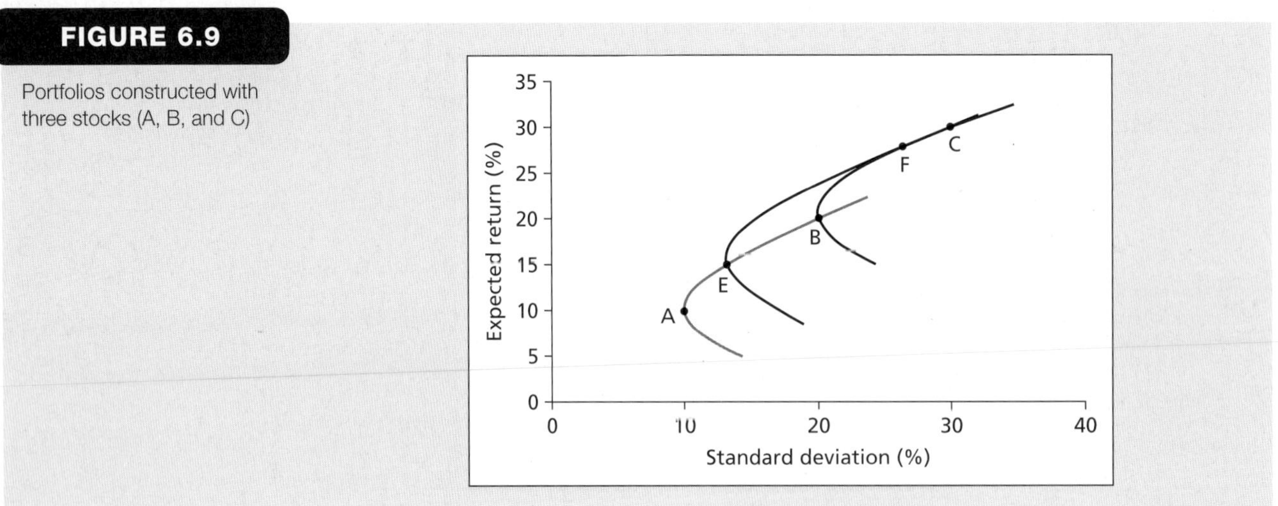

FIGURE 6.9 Portfolios constructed with three stocks (A, B, and C)

this curve shows some of the portfolios constructed from these *three* stocks. Notice that curve *EF* extends the investment opportunity set to the northwest, which is the desired direction.

Now we can continue to take other points (each representing portfolios) from these three curves and further combine them into new portfolios, thus shifting the opportunity set even farther to the northwest. You can see that this process would work even better with more stocks. Moreover, the boundary or "envelope" of all the curves thus developed, will lie quite away from the individual stocks in the northwesterly direction, as shown in Figure 6.10.

The analytical technique to derive the efficient set of risky assets was developed by Harry Markowitz in 1951 and ultimately earned him the Nobel Prize in Economics. We sketch his approach here.

First, we determine the risk-return opportunity set. The aim is to construct the northwesternmost portfolios in terms of expected return and standard deviation from the universe of securities. The inputs are the expected returns and standard deviations of each asset in the universe, along with the correlation coefficients between each pair of assets. These data come from security analysis, to be discussed in Part Four. The graph that connects all the northwesternmost portfolios is called the **efficient frontier** of risky assets. It represents the set of portfolios that offers the highest possible expected rate of return for each level of portfolio standard deviation. These portfolios may be viewed as efficiently diversified. One such frontier is shown in Figure 6.10.

efficient frontier

Graph representing a set of portfolios that maximizes expected return at each level of portfolio risk.

There are three ways to produce the efficient frontier. We will sketch each in a way that allows you to participate and gain insight into the logic and mechanics of the efficient frontier: Please take a pencil and paper and draw the graph as you follow along with our discussion. For each method, first draw the horizontal axis for portfolio standard deviation and the vertical axis for risk premium. We focus on the risk premium (expected excess returns), *R*, rather than total returns, *r*, so that the risk-free asset will lie at the origin (with zero SD and zero risk premium). We begin with the minimum-variance portfolio—mark it as point *G* (for *global* minimum variance). Imagine that *G*'s coordinates are .10 (SD = 10%) and .03 (risk premium = 3%); this is your first point on the efficient frontier. Later, we add detail about how to find these coordinates.

The three ways to draw the efficient frontier are (1) maximize the risk premium for any level of SD; (2) minimize the SD for any level of risk premium; and (3) maximize the Sharpe ratio for any level of SD (or risk premium).

For the first method, maximizing the risk premium for any level of SD, draw a few vertical lines to the right of *G* (there can be no portfolio with SD less than *G*'s). Choose the vertical line drawn at SD = 12%; we therefore search for the portfolio with the highest possible expected return consistent with an SD of 12%. So we give the computer an assignment to maximize the risk premium subject to two constraints: (i) The portfolio weights sum to 1

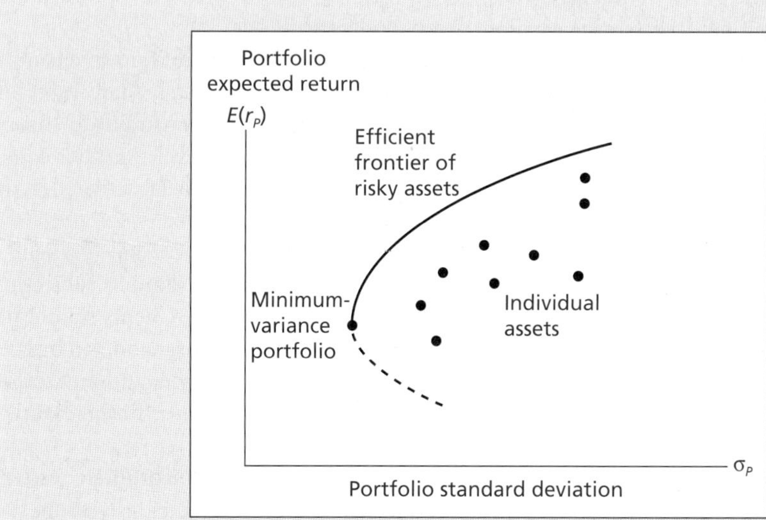

FIGURE 6.10

The efficient frontier of risky assets and individual assets (this is called the *feasibility* constraint, since any legitimate portfolio must have weights that sum to 1), and (ii) the portfolio SD must match the constraint value, $\sigma = .12$. The optimization software searches over all portfolios with $\sigma = .12$ and finds the highest feasible portfolio on the vertical line drawn at $\sigma = .12$; this is the portfolio with the highest risk premium. Assume that for this portfolio $R = .04$. You now have your second point on the efficient frontier. Do the same for other vertical lines to the right of .12, and when you "connect the dots," you will have drawn a frontier like that in Figure 6.10.

The second method is to minimize the SD for any level of risk premium. Here, you need to draw a few horizontal lines above G (portfolios lying below G are inefficient because they offer a *lower* risk premium and *higher* variance than G). Draw the first horizontal line at $R = .04$. Now the computer's assignment is to minimize the SD subject to the usual feasibility constraint. But in this method, we replace the constraint on SD by one on the portfolio's risk premium ($R = .04$). Now the computer seeks the portfolio that is farthest to the left along the horizontal line—this is the portfolio with the lowest SD consistent with a risk premium of 4%. You already know that this portfolio must be at $\sigma = .12$, since the first point on the efficient frontier that you found using method 1 was $(\sigma, R) = (.12, .04)$. Repeat this approach using other risk premiums, and you will find other points along the efficient frontier. Again, connect the dots and you will have the frontier of Figure 6.10.

The third approach to forming the efficient frontier, maximizing the Sharpe ratio for any SD or risk premium, is easiest to visualize by revisiting Figure 6.5. Observe that each portfolio on the efficient frontier provides the highest Sharpe ratio, the slope of a ray from the risk-free rate, for any choice of SD or expected return. Let's start by specifying the SD constraint, achieved by using the vertical lines to the right of G. To each line, we draw rays from the origin at ever-increasing slopes, and we assign the computer to find the *feasible* portfolio with the highest slope. This is similar to sliding up the vertical line to find the highest risk premium. We must find the same frontier as that found with either of the first two methods. Similarly, we could instead specify a risk-premium constraint and construct rays from the origin to horizontal lines. We assign the computer to find the *feasible* portfolio with the highest slope to the given horizontal line. This is similar to sliding to the left on horizontal lines in method 2.

We started the efficient frontier from the minimum-variance portfolio, G. G is found with a program that minimizes SD subject *only* to the feasibility constraint. This portfolio has the lowest SD for *any* risk premium, which is why it is called the "global" minimum-variance portfolio. By the same principle, the optimal portfolio, O, will maximize the Sharpe ratio globally, subject only to the feasibility constraint. Any *individual* asset ends up inside the efficient frontier, because single-asset portfolios are inefficient—they are not efficiently diversified.

Various constraints may preclude a particular investor from choosing portfolios on the efficient frontier, however. If an institution is prohibited by law from taking short positions in any asset, for example, the portfolio manager must add constraints to the computer-optimization program that rule out negative (short) positions.

Short-sale restrictions are only one possible constraint. Some clients may want to ensure a minimum level of expected dividend yield. In this case, input data must include a set of expected dividend yields. The optimization program is made to include a constraint to ensure that the expected *portfolio* dividend yield will equal or exceed the desired level. Another common constraint forbids investments in companies engaged in "undesirable social activity." This constraint implies that portfolio weights in these companies must equal zero.

In principle, portfolio managers can tailor an efficient frontier to meet any particular objective. Of course, satisfying constraints carries a price tag. An efficient frontier subject to additional constraints will offer a lower reward-to-volatility (Sharpe) ratio. Clients should be aware of this cost and may want to think twice about constraints that are not mandated by law.

Deriving the efficient frontier and graphing it with any number of assets and any set of constraints is quite straightforward. For a not-too-large number of assets, the efficient frontier can be computed and graphed even with a spreadsheet program.

The spreadsheet program, available at **www.mhhe.com/bkm,** can easily incorporate restrictions against short sales imposed on some portfolio managers. To impose this restriction, the program simply requires that each weight in the optimal portfolio be greater than or equal to zero. One way to see whether the short-sale constraint actually matters is to find the efficient portfolio without it. If one or more of the weights in the optimal portfolio turn out negative, we know the short-sale restrictions will result in a different efficient frontier with a less attractive risk-return trade-off.

Choosing the Optimal Risky Portfolio

The second step of the optimization plan involves the risk-free asset. Using the current risk-free rate, we search for the capital allocation line with the highest Sharpe ratio (the steepest slope), as shown in Figures 6.5 and 6.6.

The CAL formed from the optimal risky portfolio (*O*) will be tangent to the efficient frontier of risky assets discussed above. This CAL dominates all feasible CALs. Portfolio *O*, therefore, is the optimal risky portfolio. Because we know that an investor will choose a point on the CAL that mixes the *optimal* risky portfolio with T-bills, there is actually no need to either provide access to or derive the entire efficient frontier. Therefore, as a practical matter, rather than solving for the entire efficient frontier, we can proceed directly to determining the optimal portfolio. This requires maximizing the Sharpe ratio subject only to the feasibility constraint. The "global" maximum-Sharpe-ratio portfolio is the optimal portfolio *O*. The ray from the origin to *O* and beyond is the optimal CAL.

The Preferred Complete Portfolio and the Separation Property

Finally, in the third step, the investor chooses the appropriate mix between the optimal risky portfolio (*O*) and T-bills, exactly as in Figure 6.7.

A portfolio manager will offer the same risky portfolio (*O*) to all clients, no matter what their degrees of risk aversion. Risk aversion comes into play only when clients select their desired point on the CAL. More risk-averse clients will invest more in the risk-free asset and less in the optimal risky portfolio *O* than less risk-averse clients, but both will use portfolio *O* as the optimal risky investment vehicle.

This result is called a **separation property,** introduced by James Tobin (1958), the 1983 Nobel Laureate for Economics: It implies that portfolio choice can be separated into two independent tasks. The first task, to determine the optimal risky portfolio (*O*), is purely technical. Given a particular set of input data, the best risky portfolio is the same for all clients regardless of risk aversion. The second task, construction of the complete portfolio from bills and portfolio *O*, is personal and depends on risk aversion. Here the client is the decision maker.

separation property

The property that implies portfolio choice can be separated into two independent tasks: (1) determination of the optimal risky portfolio, which is a purely technical problem, and (2) the personal choice of the best mix of the risky portfolio and the risk-free asset.

Optimal risky portfolios for different clients may vary because of constraints on short sales, dividend yield, tax considerations, or other client preferences. Our analysis, though, suggests that a few portfolios may be sufficient to serve the demands of a wide range of investors. We see here the theoretical basis of the mutual fund industry. If the optimal portfolio is the same for all clients, professional management is more efficient and less costly. One management firm can serve a number of clients with relatively small incremental administrative costs.

The (computerized) optimization technique is the easiest part of portfolio construction. When different managers use different input data, they will develop different efficient frontiers and offer different "optimal" portfolios. Therefore, the real arena of the competition among portfolio managers is in the sophisticated security analysis that produces the input estimates. The rule of GIGO (garbage in–garbage out) applies fully to portfolio selection. If the quality of the security analysis is poor, a passive portfolio such as a market-index fund will yield better results than an active portfolio tilted toward *seemingly* favorable securities.

Constructing the Optimal Risky Portfolio: An Illustration

To illustrate how the optimal risky portfolio might be constructed, suppose an analyst wished to construct an efficiently diversified global portfolio using the stock market indices of six countries. The top panel of Table 6.1 shows the input list. The values for standard deviations and the correlation matrix are estimated from recent historical data, while forecasts of risk premiums are generated from fundamental analysis. Examination of the table shows the U.S. index portfolio has the highest Sharpe ratio. China and Japan have the lowest, and the correlation of

TABLE 6.1 Efficient frontiers for international diversification with and without short sales and CAL with short sales

A. Input list

	Excess Returns			
	Mean	**SD**	**Sharpe Ratio**	**INPUT LIST**
U.S.	0.0600	0.1495	0.4013	**Expected excess returns from fundamental analysis.**
U.K.	0.0530	0.1493	0.3551	**Standard deviations and correlation matrix from**
FRANCE	0.0680	0.2008	0.3386	**econometric estimates.**
GERMANY	0.0800	0.2270	0.3525	
JAPAN	0.0450	0.1878	0.2397	
CHINA	0.0730	0.3004	0.2430	

Correlation Matrix

	U.S.	**U.K.**	**France**	**Germany**	**Japan**	**China**
U.S.	1					
U.K.	0.83	1				
FRANCE	0.83	0.92	1			
GERMANY	0.85	0.88	0.96	1		
JAPAN	0.43	0.44	0.47	0.43	1	
CHINA	0.16	0.28	0.26	0.29	0.14	1

B. Efficient frontier—short sales allowed

Portfolio:	**(1)**	**(2)**	**G**	**(4)**	**(5)**	**(6)**	**(7)**	**O**	**(9)**	**(10)**	**(11)**	**(12)**	**(13)**
Risk premium	0.0325	0.0375	0.0410	0.0425	0.0450	0.0500	0.0550	0.058474	0.0600	0.0650	0.0700	0.0800	0.0850
SD	0.1147	0.1103	0.1094	0.1095	0.1106	0.1154	0.1234	0.130601	0.1341	0.1469	0.1612	0.1933	0.2104
Slope (Sharpe)	0.2832	0.3400	0.3749	0.3880	0.4070	0.4334	0.4457	0.447733	0.4474	0.4425	0.4341	0.4140	0.4040
Portfolio weights													
U.S.	0.5948	0.6268	0.6476	0.6569	0.6724	0.7033	0.7342	0.755643	0.7651	0.7960	0.8269	0.8887	0.9196
U.K.	1.0667	0.8878	0.7681	0.7155	0.6279	0.4527	0.2775	0.155808	0.1023	−0.0728	−0.2480	−0.5984	−0.7736
FRANCE	−0.1014	−0.1308	−0.1618	−0.1727	−0.1908	−0.2272	−0.2635	−0.2888	−0.2999	−0.3362	−0.3725	−0.4452	−0.4816
GERMANY	−0.8424	−0.6702	−0.5431	−0.4901	−0.4019	−0.2253	−0.0487	0.0740	0.1278	0.3044	0.4810	0.8341	1.0107
JAPAN	0.2158	0.1985	0.1866	0.1815	0.1729	0.1558	0.1386	0.126709	0.1215	0.1043	0.0872	0.0529	0.0357
CHINA	0.0664	0.0879	0.1025	0.1089	0.1195	0.1407	0.1619	0.176649	0.1831	0.2043	0.2256	0.2680	0.2892

C. Capital allocation line (CAL) with short sales

Risk premium	0.0000	0.0494	0.0490	0.0490	0.0495	0.0517	0.0553	0.0585	0.0600	0.0658	0.0722	0.0865	0.1343
SD	0.0000	0.1103	0.1094	0.1095	0.1106	0.1154	0.1234	0.1306	0.1341	0.1469	0.1612	0.1933	0.3000

D. Efficient frontier—no short sales

Portfolio	**(1)**	**(2)**	**(3)**	**(4)**	**(5)**	**Min Var**	**(7)**	**(8)**	**Optimum**	**(10)**	**(11)**	**(12)**	**(13)**
Risk premium	0.0450	0.0475	0.0490	0.0510	0.0535	0.0560	0.0573	0.0590	0.0607	0.0650	0.07	0.0750	0.0800
SD	0.1878	0.1555	0.1435	0.1372	0.1330	0.131648	0.1321	0.1337	0.1367	0.1493	0.1675332	0.1893	0.2270
Slope (Sharpe)	0.2397	0.3055	0.3414	0.3718	0.4022	0.425089	0.4339	0.4411	0.4439	0.4353	0.4178277	0.3963	0.3525
Portfolio weights													
U.S.	0.0000	0.0000	0.0000	0.0671	0.2375	0.4052	0.4964	0.6122	0.7067	0.6367	0.4223	0.1680	0.0000
U.K.	0.0000	0.3125	0.5000	0.5465	0.3967	0.2491	0.1689	0.0670	0.0000	0.0000	0.0000	0.0000	0.0000
FRANCE	0.0000	0.0000	0.0000	0.0000	0.0000	0.0000	0.0000	0.0000	0.0000	0.0000	0.0000	0.0000	0.0000
GERMANY	0.0000	0.0000	0.0000	0.0000	0.0000	0.0000	0.0000	0.0000	0.0000	0.1324	0.3558	0.5976	1.0000
JAPAN	1.0000	0.6875	0.5000	0.3642	0.3029	0.2424	0.2096	0.1679	0.1114	0.0232	0.0000	0.0000	0.0000
CHINA	0.0000	0.0000	0.0000	0.0222	0.0630	0.1032	0.1251	0.1529	0.1819	0.2077	0.2219	0.2343	0.0000

France and Germany with the U.S. is high. Given these data, one might be tempted to conclude that, *perhaps*, U.S. investors may not benefit much from international diversification during this period. But even in this sample period, we will see that diversification is beneficial.

Panel B shows the efficient frontier developed as follows: First we generate the global minimum-variance portfolio *G* by minimizing the SD with just the feasibility constraint, and then we find portfolio *O* by maximizing the Sharpe ratio subject only to the same constraint. To fill out the curve, we choose more risk premiums; for each, we maximize the Sharpe ratio subject to the feasibility constraint as well as the appropriate risk-premium constraint. In all, we have 13 points to draw the graph in Figure 6.11, one of which is the global maximum-Sharpe-ratio portfolio, *O*.

The results are quite striking. Observe that the SD of the global minimum-variance portfolio of 10.94% is far lower than that of the lowest-variance country (the U.K.), which has an SD of 14.93%. *G* is formed by taking short positions in Germany and France, as well as a large position in the relatively low-risk U.K. Moreover, the Sharpe ratio of this portfolio is higher than that of all countries but the U.S! Still, even this portfolio will be rejected in favor of the highest Sharpe-ratio portfolio.

Portfolio *O* attains a Sharpe ratio of .4477, compared to the U.S. ratio of .4013, a significant improvement that can be verified from the CAL shown in Panel C. The points shown on the CAL have the same SD as those on the efficient frontier portfolios, so the risk premium for each equals the SD times the Sharpe ratio of portfolio *O*.[3] Notice that portfolio (9) on the CAL has the same risk premium as the U.S., 6%, but an SD of 13.41%, fully 1.5% less than the 14.95% SD of the U.S. All this is achieved while still investing 76% of the portfolio in the U.S., although it does require a large short position in France (−29.99%).

Many institutional investors are prohibited from taking short positions, and individuals may be averse to large short positions because the unlimited upward potential of stock prices implies unlimited potential losses on short sales. Panel D shows the efficient frontier when an additional constraint is applied to each portfolio, namely, that all weights must be nonnegative.

Take a look at the two frontiers in Figure 6.11. The no-short-sale frontier is clearly inferior on both ends. This is because both very low-return and very high-return frontier portfolios will typically entail short positions. At the low-return/low-volatility end of the frontier,

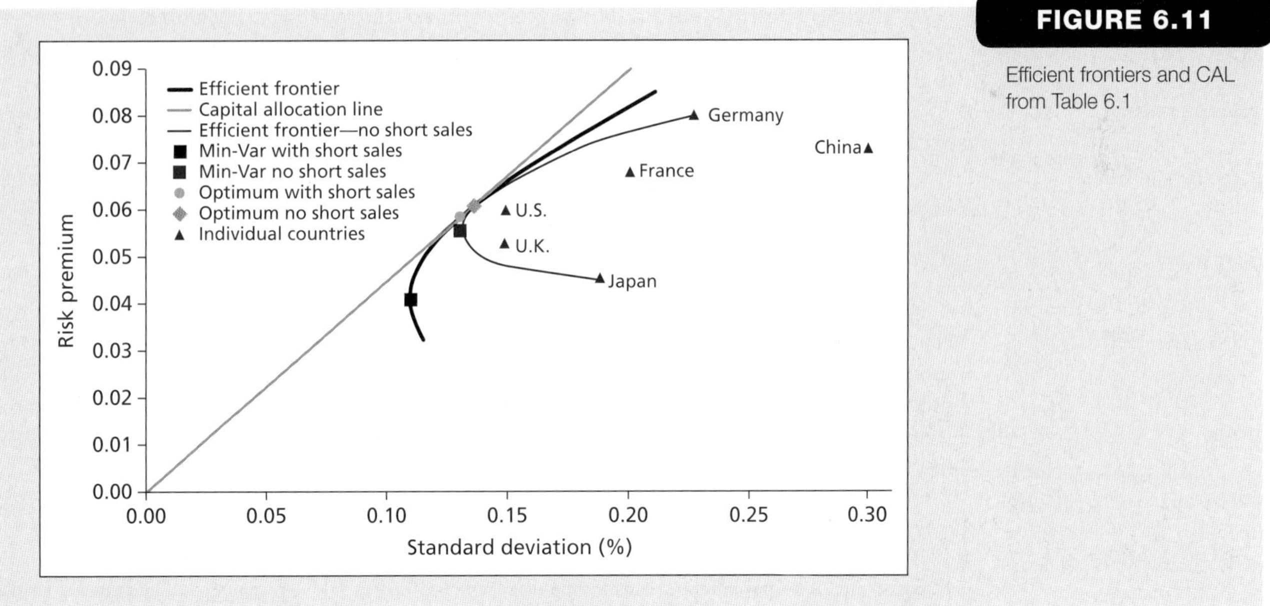

FIGURE 6.11

Efficient frontiers and CAL from Table 6.1

[3]Since the Sharpe ratio is S = risk premium/SD, we can rearrange to show that SD = risk premium/S_O. The CAL has the same slope everywhere, equal to the Sharpe ratio of portfolio *O* that supports it.

portfolios have short positions in stocks with a high correlation and low risk premium that reduce variance at low cost to expected return. At the other (high expected return) end of the frontier, we find short positions in low-risk-premium stocks in favor of larger positions in high-risk-premium stocks. At the same time, the no-short-sale frontier is restricted to begin with the lowest-risk-premium country (Japan) and end with the highest (Germany). Without short sales, we cannot achieve lower or higher risk premiums than are offered by these portfolios. Intermediate-return portfolios on each frontier, including the optimal portfolio, *O*, are not far apart. Thus, even under the no-short-sale constraint, the Sharpe ratio (.4439) is still higher than that of the U.S. portfolio. The no-short-sale CAL can match the U.S. risk premium of 6% with an SD of only 13.52%, still 1.4% less than the SD of the U.S.

CONCEPT check 6.5

Two portfolio managers work for competing investment management houses. Each employs security analysts to prepare input data for the construction of the optimal portfolio. When all is completed, the efficient frontier obtained by manager A dominates that of manager B in that A's optimal risky portfolio lies northwest of B's. Is the more attractive efficient frontier asserted by manager A evidence that she really employs better security analysts?

6.5 A SINGLE-INDEX STOCK MARKET

index model

Model that relates stock returns to returns on both a broad market index and firm-specific factors.

We started this chapter with the distinction between systematic and firm-specific risk. Systematic risk is macroeconomic, affecting all securities, while firm-specific risk factors affect only one particular firm or, at most, a cluster of firms. **Index models** are statistical models designed to estimate these two components of risk for a particular security or portfolio. The first to use an index model to explain the benefits of diversification was another Nobel Prize winner, William F. Sharpe (1963). We will introduce his major work (the capital asset pricing model) in the next chapter.

The popularity of index models is due to their practicality. To construct the efficient frontier from a universe of 100 securities, we would need to estimate 100 expected returns, 100 variances, and $100 \times 99/2 = 4{,}950$ covariances. And a universe of 100 securities is actually quite small. A universe of 1,000 securities would require estimates of $1{,}000 \times 999/2 = 499{,}500$ covariances, as well as 1,000 expected returns and variances. Assuming that one common factor is responsible for all the covariability of stock returns, with all other variability due to firm-specific factors, dramatically simplifies the analysis.

excess return

Rate of return in excess of the risk-free rate.

Let us use R_i to denote the **excess return** on a security, that is, the rate of return in excess of the risk-free rate: $R_i = r_i - r_f$. Then we can express the distinction between macroeconomic and firm-specific factors by decomposing this excess return in some holding period into three components:[4]

$$R_i = \beta_i R_M + e_i + \alpha_i \tag{6.11}$$

beta

The sensitivity of a security's returns to the market factor.

The first two terms on the right-hand side of Equation 6.11 reflect the impact of two sources of uncertainty. R_M is the excess return on a broad market index (the S&P 500 is commonly used for this purpose), so variation in this term reflects the influence of economywide or macroeconomic events that generally affect all stocks to greater or lesser degrees. The security's **beta**, β_i, is the typical response of that particular stock's excess return to changes in the market index's excess return. As such, beta measures a stock's comparative sensitivity to macroeconomic news. A value greater than 1 would indicate a stock with greater sensitivity to the

[4]Equation 6.11 is surprisingly simple and would appear to require very strong assumptions about security market equilibrium. But, in fact, if rates of return are normally distributed, then returns will be linear in one or more indexes. Statistics theory tells us that, when rates of return on a set of securities are *joint-normally* distributed, then the rate of return on each asset is linear in one identical index as in Equation 6.11. When rates of return exhibit a multivariate normal distribution, we can use a multi-index generalization of Equation 6.11. Practitioners employ index models such as 6.11 extensively because of the ease of use as we just noted, but they would not do so unless empirical evidence supported them.

economy than the average stock. These are known as *cyclical stocks.* Betas less than 1 indicate below-average sensitivity and therefore are known as *defensive stocks.* Recall that the risk attributable to the stock's exposure to uncertain market returns is called market or *systematic* risk, because it relates to the uncertainty that pervades the whole economic system.

The term e_i in Equation 6.11 represents the impact of **firm-specific** or **residual risk.** The expected value of e_i is zero, as the impact of unexpected events must average out to zero. Both residual risk and systematic risk contribute to the total volatility of returns.

firm-specific or **residual risk**

Component of return variance that is independent of the market factor.

The term α_i in Equation 6.11 is not a risk measure. Instead, α_i represents the expected return on the stock *beyond* any return induced by movements in the market index. This term is called the security **alpha.** A positive alpha is attractive to investors and suggests an underpriced security: Among securities with identical sensitivity (beta) to the market index, securities with higher alpha values will offer higher expected returns. Conversely, stocks with negative alphas are apparently overpriced; for any value of beta, they offer lower expected returns.

alpha

A stock's expected return beyond that induced by the market index; its expected excess return when the market's excess return is zero.

In sum, the index model separates the realized rate of return on a security into macro (systematic) and micro (firm-specific) components. The excess rate of return on each security is the sum of three components:

	Symbol
1. The component of return due to movements in the overall market (as represented by the index R_M); β_i is the security's responsiveness to the market.	$\beta_i R_M$
2. The component attributable to unexpected events that are relevant only to this security (firm-specific).	e_i
3. The stock's expected excess return if the market factor is neutral, that is, if the market-index excess return is zero.	α_i

Because the firm-specific component of the stock return is uncorrelated with the market return, we can write the variance of the excess return of the stock as[5]

$$\begin{aligned} \text{Variance}(R_i) &= \text{Variance}(\alpha_i + \beta_i R_M + e_i) \\ &= \text{Variance}(\beta_i R_M) + \text{Variance}(e_i) \\ &= \beta_i^2 \sigma_M^2 \qquad\quad + \sigma^2(e_i) \\ &= \text{Systematic risk} + \text{Firm-specific risk} \end{aligned} \tag{6.12}$$

Therefore, the total variance of the rate of return of each security is a sum of two components:

1. The variance attributable to the uncertainty of the entire market. This variance depends on both the variance of R_M, σ_M^2, *and* the beta of the stock on R_M.
2. The variance of the firm-specific return, e_i, which is independent of market performance.

This single-index model is convenient. It relates security returns to a market index that investors follow. Moreover, as we soon shall see, its usefulness goes beyond mere convenience.

Statistical and Graphical Representation of the Single-Index Model

Equation 6.11, $R_i = \alpha_i + \beta_i R_M + e_i$, may be interpreted as a single-variable *regression equation* of R_i on the market excess return R_M. The excess return on the security (R_i) is the dependent variable that is to be explained by the regression. On the right-hand side of the equation are the intercept α_i; the regression (slope) coefficient beta, β_i, multiplying the independent (explanatory) variable R_M; and the residual (unexplained) return, e_i. We plot this regression in Figure 6.12, which shows a scatter diagram for Dell's excess return against the excess return of the market index.

[5]Notice that because α_i is a constant, it has no bearing on the variance of R_i.

FIGURE 6.12

Scatter diagram for Dell

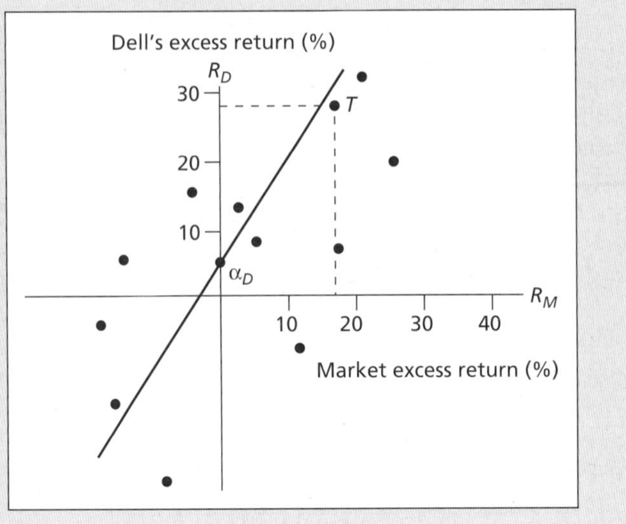

The horizontal axis of the scatter diagram measures the explanatory variable, here the market excess return, R_M. The vertical axis measures the dependent variable, here Dell's excess return, R_D. Each point on the scatter diagram represents a sample pair of returns (R_M, R_D) observed over a particular holding period. Point *T*, for instance, describes a holding period when the excess return was 17% for the market index and 27% for Dell.

Regression analysis uses a sample of historical returns to estimate the coefficients (alpha and beta) of the index model. The analysis finds the regression line, shown in Figure 6.12, that minimizes the sum of the squared deviations around it. Hence, we say the regression line "best fits" the data in the scatter diagram. The line is called the **security characteristic line,** or SCL.

security characteristic line

Plot of a security's *predicted* excess return from the excess return of the market.

The regression intercept (α_D) is measured from the origin to the intersection of the regression line with the vertical axis. Any point on the vertical axis represents zero market excess return, so the intercept gives us the *expected excess* return on Dell when market return was "neutral," that is, equal to the T-bill return. The intercept in Figure 6.12 is 4.5%.

The slope of the regression line, the ratio of the rise to the run, is called the *regression coefficient* or simply the beta. In Figure 6.12, Dell's beta is 1.4. A stock beta measures systematic risk since it predicts the response of the security to each extra 1% return on the market index.

The regression line does not represent *actual* returns; points on the scatter diagram almost never lie exactly on the regression line. Rather, the line represents average tendencies; it shows the *expectation* of R_D given the market excess return, R_M. The algebraic representation of the regression line is

$$E(R_D|R_M) = \alpha_D + \beta_D R_M \quad \textbf{(6.13)}$$

which reads: The expectation of R_D *given* a value of R_M equals the intercept plus the slope coefficient times the value of R_M.

Because the regression line represents expectations and these expectations may not be realized (as the scatter diagram shows), the *actual* returns also include a residual, e_i. This surprise (at point *T*, for example) is measured by the vertical distance between the point of the scatter diagram and the regression line. The expected return on Dell, given a market return of 17%, would have been 4.5% + 1.4 × 17% = 28.3%. The actual return was only 27%, so point *T* falls below the regression line by 1.3%.

Equation 6.12 shows that the greater the beta of a security, that is, the greater the slope of the regression, the greater the systematic risk and total variance. Because the market is composed of all securities, the typical response to a market movement must be one for one. An "aggressive" investment will have a beta higher than 1; that is, the security has above-average market risk.[6] Conversely, securities with betas lower than 1 are called defensive.

A security may have a negative beta. Its regression line will then slope downward, meaning that, for more favorable macro events (higher R_M), we would expect a *lower* return, and vice versa. The latter means that when the macro economy goes bad (negative R_M) and securities with positive beta are expected to have negative excess returns, the negative-beta security will shine. The result is that a negative-beta security provides a hedge against systematic risk.

The dispersion of the scatter of actual returns about the regression line is determined by the residual variance $\sigma^2(e_D)$. The magnitude of firm-specific risk varies across securities. One way to measure the relative importance of systematic risk is to measure the ratio of systematic variance to total variance.

$$\rho^2 = \frac{\text{Systematic (or explained) variance}}{\text{Total variance}}$$

$$= \frac{\beta_D^2\sigma_M^2}{\sigma_D^2} = \frac{\beta_D^2\sigma_M^2}{\beta_D^2\sigma_M^2 + \sigma^2(e_D)} \tag{6.14}$$

where ρ is the correlation coefficient between R_D and R_M. Its square measures the ratio of explained variance to total variance, that is, the proportion of total variance that can be attributed to market fluctuations. But if beta is negative, so is the correlation coefficient, an indication that the explanatory and dependent variables are expected to move in opposite directions.

At the extreme, when the correlation coefficient is either 1 or −1, the security return is fully explained by the market return and there are no firm-specific effects. All the points of the scatter diagram will lie exactly on the line. This is called *perfect correlation* (either positive or negative); the return on the security is perfectly predictable from the market return. A large correlation coefficient (in absolute value terms) means systematic variance dominates the total variance; that is, firm-specific variance is relatively unimportant. When the correlation coefficient is small (in absolute value terms), the market factor plays a relatively unimportant part in explaining the variance of the asset, and firm-specific factors dominate.

CONCEPT check 6.6

Interpret the eight scatter diagrams of Figure 6.13 in terms of systematic risk, diversifiable risk, and the intercept.

Example 6.3 on the following page illustrates how you can use a spreadsheet to estimate the single-index model from historical data.

Diversification in a Single-Index Security Market

Imagine a portfolio that is divided equally among securities whose returns follow the single-index model of Equation 6.11. What are the systematic and nonsystematic variances of this portfolio?

The beta of the portfolio is a simple average of the individual security betas; hence, the systematic variance equals $\beta_P^2\sigma_M^2$. This is the level of market risk in Figure 6.1B. The market variance (σ_M^2) and the beta of the portfolio determine its market risk.

[6]Note that only the *weighted* average of betas (using market values as weights) will be 1, since the stock market index is value-weighted. We know from Chapter 5 that the distribution of securities by market value is not symmetric: There are relatively few large corporations and many more smaller ones. As a result, the simple average of the betas of individual securities, when computed against a value-weighted index such as the S&P 500, will be greater than 1, pushed up by the tendency for stocks of low-capitalization companies to have betas greater than 1.

FIGURE 6.13

Various scatter diagrams

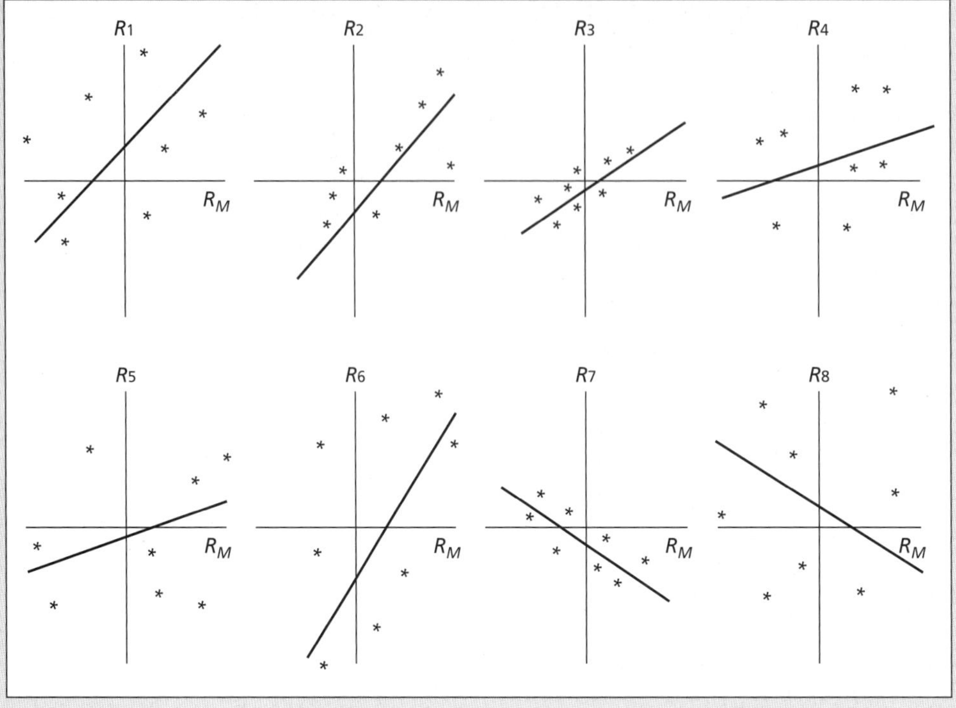

The systematic component of each security return, $\beta_i R_M$, is driven by the market factor and therefore is perfectly correlated with the systematic part of any other security's return. Hence, there are no diversification effects on systematic risk no matter how many securities are involved. As far as *market risk* goes, a single security has the same systematic risk as a diversified portfolio with the same beta. The number of securities makes no difference.

EXAMPLE 6.3

Estimating the Index Model Using Historical Data

The direct way to calculate the slope and intercept of the characteristic lines for ABC and XYZ is from the variances and covariances. Here, we use the Data Analysis menu of Excel to obtain the covariance matrix in the following spreadsheet.

The slope coefficient for ABC is given by the formula

$$\beta_{ABC} = \frac{\text{Cov}(R_{ABC}, R_{Market})}{\text{Var}(R_{Market})} = \frac{773.31}{669.01} = 1.156$$

The intercept for ABC is

$$\alpha_{ABC} = \text{Average}(R_{ABC}) - \beta_{ABC} \times \text{Average}(R_{Market})$$
$$= 15.20 - 1.156 \times 9.40 = 4.33$$

Therefore, the security characteristic line of ABC is given by

$$R_{ABC} = 4.33 + 1.156 R_{Market}$$

This result also can be obtained by using the "Regression" command from Excel's Data Analysis menu, as we show at the bottom of the spreadsheet. The minor differences between the direct regression output and our calculations above are due to rounding error.

(continued)

EXAMPLE 6.3

Estimating the Index Model Using Historical Data

(concluded)

	A	B	C	D	E	F	G	H	I
2			**Annualized Rates of Return**					**Excess Returns**	
3	Week	ABC	XYZ	Mkt. Index	Risk free		ABC	XYZ	Market
4	1	65.13	-22.55	64.40	5.23		59.90	-27.78	59.17
5	2	51.84	31.44	24.00	4.76		47.08	26.68	19.24
6	3	-30.82	-6.45	9.15	6.22		-37.04	-12.67	2.93
7	4	-15.13	-51.14	-35.57	3.78		-18.91	-54.92	-39.35
8	5	70.63	33.78	11.59	4.43		66.20	29.35	7.16
9	6	107.82	32.95	23.13	3.78		104.04	29.17	19.35
10	7	-25.16	70.19	8.54	3.87		-29.03	66.32	4.67
11	8	50.48	27.63	25.87	4.15		46.33	23.48	21.72
12	9	-36.41	-48.79	-13.15	3.99		-40.40	-52.78	-17.14
13	10	-42.20	52.63	20.21	4.01		-46.21	48.62	16.20
14	**Average:**						**15.20**	**7.55**	**9.40**
15									
16	**COVARIANCE MATRIX**								
17		ABC	XYZ	Market					
18	ABC	3020.933							
19	XYZ	442.114	1766.923						
20	Market	773.306	396.789	669.010					
21									
22	**SUMMARY OUTPUT OF EXCEL REGRESSION**								
23									
24	Regression Statistics								
25	Multiple R	0.544							
26	R-Square	0.296							
27	Adj. R-Square	0.208							
28	Standard Error	48.918							
29	Observations	10.000							
30									
31									
32		Coefficients	Std. Error	t-Stat	p-value				
33	Intercept	4.336	16.564	0.262	0.800				
34	Market return	1.156	0.630	1.834	0.104				
35									

Note: This is the output provided by the Data Analysis tool in Excel. As a technical aside, we should point out that the covariance matrix produced by Excel does not adjust for degrees of freedom. In other words, it divides total squared deviations from the sample average (for variance) or total cross product of deviations from sample averages (for covariance) by total observations, despite the fact that sample averages are estimated parameters. This procedure does not affect regression coefficients, however, because in the formula for beta, both the numerator (i.e., the covariance) and denominator (i.e., the variance) are affected equally.

It is quite different with firm-specific risk. Consider a portfolio of n securities with weights, $w_i \left(\text{where} \sum_{i=1}^{n} w_i = 1\right)$, in securities with nonsystematic risk, $\sigma_{e_i}^2$. The nonsystematic portion of the portfolio return is

$$e_P = \sum_{i=1}^{n} w_i e_i$$

Because the firm-specific terms, e_i, are uncorrelated, the portfolio nonsystematic variance is the weighted sum of the individual firm-specific variances:[7]

$$\sigma_{e_P}^2 = \sum_{i=1}^{n} w_i^2 \sigma_{e_i}^2 \tag{6.15}$$

Each individual nonsystematic variance is multiplied by the *square* of the portfolio weight. With diversified portfolios, the squared weights are very small. For example, if $w_i = .01$ (think of a portfolio with 100 securities), then $w_i^2 = .0001$. The sum in Equation 6.15 is far less than

[7]We use the result from statistics that when we multiply a random variable (in this case, e_i) by a constant (in this case, w_i), the variance is multiplied by the *square* of the constant. The variance of the sum in Equation 6.15 equals the sum of the variances because in this case all covariances are zero.

the average firm-specific variance of the stocks in the portfolio. We conclude that the impact of nonsystematic risk becomes negligible as the number of securities grows and the portfolio becomes ever-more diversified. This is why the number of securities counts more than the size of their nonsystematic variance.

In sum, when we control the systematic risk of the portfolio by manipulating the average beta of the component securities, the number of securities is of no consequence. But for *nonsystematic* risk the number of securities is more important than the firm-specific variance of the securities. Sufficient diversification can virtually eliminate firm-specific risk. Understanding this distinction is essential to understanding the role of diversification.

We have just seen that when forming highly diversified portfolios, firm-specific risk becomes *irrelevant.* Only systematic risk remains. This means that for diversified investors, the relevant risk measure for a security will be the security's beta, β, since firms with higher β have greater sensitivity to market risk. As Equation 6.12 makes clear, systematic risk will be determined by both market volatility, σ_M^2, and the firm's β.

CONCEPT check 6.7

a. What is the characteristic line of XYZ in Example 6.3?
b. Does ABC or XYZ have greater systematic risk?
c. What proportion of the variance of XYZ is firm-specific risk?

Using Security Analysis with the Index Model

Imagine that you are a portfolio manager in charge of the endowment of a small charity. Without the resources to engage in security analysis, you would choose a passive portfolio comprising one or more index funds and T-bills. Denote this portfolio as M. You estimate its standard deviation as σ_M and acquire a forecast of its risk premium as R_M. Now you find that you have sufficient resources to perform fundamental analysis on one stock, say Google. You forecast Google's risk premium as R_G and estimate its beta (β_G) and residual SD, $\sigma(e_G)$, against the benchmark portfolio M. How should you proceed?

Without access to other securities, all you can do is construct the optimal portfolio (with the highest Sharpe ratio) from M and Google using Equation 6.10. It turns out that the index model allows us to further simplify Equation 6.10.

Notice that your forecast of R_G implies that Google's alpha is $\alpha_G = R_G - \beta_G R_M$. We use two key statistics $\alpha_G/\sigma^2(e_G)$ and R_M/σ_M^2, to find the position of Google in the optimal risky portfolio in two steps. In step 1, we compute

$$w_G^0 = \frac{\alpha_G/\sigma^2(e_G)}{R_M/\sigma_M^2} \tag{6.16}$$

In step 2, we adjust the value from Equation 6.16 for the beta of Google:

$$w_G^* = \frac{w_G^0}{1 + w_G^0(1 - \beta_G)} \qquad w_M^* = 1 - w_G^* \tag{6.17}$$

The Sharpe ratio of this portfolio exceeds that of the passive portfolio M, S_M, according to

$$S_O^2 - S_M^2 = \left(\frac{\alpha_G}{\sigma(e_G)}\right)^2 \tag{6.18}$$

information ratio

Ratio of alpha to the standard deviation of the residual.

We see that the improvement over the passive benchmark is determined by the ratio $\alpha_G/\sigma(e_G)$, which is called Google's **information ratio.** This application of the index model is called the Treynor-Black model, after Fischer Black and Jack Treynor who proposed it in 1973.

The value of the Treynor-Black model becomes dramatic when you analyze more than one stock. To compute the optimal portfolio comprising the benchmark portfolio and more than two stocks, you would need to use the involved Markowitz methodology of Section 6.4. But with the Treynor-Black model, the task is straightforward. You can view Google in the previous discussion as your **active portfolio.** If instead of Google alone you analyze several stocks, a portfolio of these stocks would make up your active portfolio, which then would be mixed with the passive index. You would use the alpha, beta, and residual SD of the active portfolio in Equations 6.16–6.18 to obtain the weights of the optimal portfolio, *O,* and its Sharpe ratio. Thus, the only task left is to determine the exact composition of the active portfolio, as well as its alpha, beta, and residual standard deviation.

active portfolio

The portfolio formed by optimally combining analyzed stocks.

Suppose that in addition to analyzing Google, you analyze Dell's stock (*D*) and estimate its alpha, beta, and residual variance. You estimate the ratio for Google, $\alpha_G/\sigma^2(e_G)$, the corresponding ratio for Dell, and the sum of these ratios for all stocks in the active portfolio. Using Google and Dell,

$$\sum_i \alpha_i/\sigma^2(e_i) = \alpha_G/\sigma^2(e_G) + \alpha_D/\sigma^2(e_D) \tag{6.19}$$

Treynor and Black showed that the optimal weight of each security in the active portfolio should be

$$w_G(\text{active}) = \frac{\alpha_G/\sigma^2(e_G)}{\sum_i \alpha_i/\sigma^2(e_i)} \qquad w_D(\text{active}) = \frac{\alpha_D/\sigma^2(e_D)}{\sum_i \alpha_i/\sigma^2(e_i)} \tag{6.20}$$

Notice that the active portfolio entails two offsetting considerations. On the one hand, a stock with a higher alpha value calls for a high weight to take advantage of its attractive expected return. On the other hand, a high residual variance leads us to temper our position in the stock to avoid bearing firm-specific risk.

The alpha and beta of the active portfolio are weighted averages of each component stock's alpha and beta, and the residual variance is the weighted sum of each stock's residual variance, using the squared portfolio weights:

$$\begin{aligned} \alpha_A &= w_{GA}\alpha_{GA} + w_{DA}\alpha_{DA} \quad \beta_A = w_{GA}\beta_{GA} + w_{DA}\beta_{DA} \\ \sigma^2(e_A) &= w_{GA}^2\sigma^2(e_G) + w_{DA}^2\sigma^2(e_D) \end{aligned} \tag{6.21}$$

Given these parameters, we can now use Equations 6.16–6.18 to determine the weight of the active portfolio in the optimal portfolio and the Sharpe ratio it achieves.

EXAMPLE 6.5

The Treynor-Black Model

Suppose your benchmark portfolio is the S&P 500 Index. The input list in Panel A of Table 6.2 includes the data for the passive index as well as the two stocks, Google and Dell. Both stocks have positive alpha values, so you would expect the optimal portfolio to be tilted toward these stocks. However, the tilt will be limited to avoid excessive exposure to otherwise-diversifiable firm-specific risk. The optimal trade-off maximizes the Sharpe ratio. We use the Treynor-Black model to accomplish this task.

We begin in Panel B assuming that the *active portfolio* comprises solely Google, which has an information ratio of .115. This "portfolio" is then combined with the passive index to form the optimal risky portfolio as in Equations 6.16–6.18. The calculations in Table 6.2 show that the optimal portfolio achieves a Sharpe ratio of .20, compared with .16 for the passive benchmark. This optimal portfolio is invested 43.64% in Google and 56.36% in the benchmark.

In Panel C, we add Dell to the list of actively analyzed stocks. The optimal weights of each stock in the active portfolio are 55.53% in Google and 44.47% in Dell. This gives the active portfolio an information ratio of .14, which improves the Sharpe ratio of the optimal portfolio to .24. The optimal portfolio invests 91.73% in the active portfolio and 8.27% in the index. This large tilt is acceptable because the residual standard deviation of the active portfolio (6.28%) is far less than that of either stock. Finally, the optimal portfolio weight in Google is 50.94% and in Dell, 40.79%. Notice that the weight in Google is now *larger* than its weight without Dell! This, too, is a result of diversification within the active position that allows a larger tilt toward Google's large alpha.

TABLE 6.2 Construction of optimal portfolios using the index model

Input List

	Benchmark Portfolio (S&P 500)	Active Portfolio: Google	Active Portfolio: Dell	
A. Input data				
Risk premium	0.7	2.20	1.74	
Standard deviation	4.31	11.39	10.49	
Sharpe ratio	0.16	not applicable		
Alpha		1.04	0.75	
Beta		1.65	1.41	
Residual standard deviation		9.01	8.55	
Information ratio = alpha/residual SD		0.1154	0.0877	
Alpha/residual variance		0.0128	0.0103	
Portfolio Construction				
B. Optimal portfolio with Google only in active portfolio				
Performance data				
Sharpe ratio = SQRT (index Sharpe^2 + Google information ratio^2)	0.20			
Composition of optimal portfolio				
w^0 = (alpha/residual SD)/(index risk premium/index variance)		0.3400		
$w^* = w^0/(1 + w^0(1 - \text{beta}))$	0.5636	0.4364		
C. Optimal portfolio with Google and Dell in the active portfolio				
				Active Portfolio (sum)
Composition of the active portfolio				
w^0 of stock (Equation 6.15)		0.3400	0.2723	0.6122
w^0/Sum w^0 of analyzed stocks		0.5553	0.4447	1.0000
Performance of the active portfolio				
alpha = weight in active portfolio × stock alpha		0.58	0.33	0.91
beta = weight in active portfolio × stock beta		0.92	0.63	1.54
Residual variance = square weight × stock residual variance		25.03	14.46	39.49
Residual SD = SQRT (active portfolio residual variance)				6.28
Information ratio = active portfolio alpha/residual SD				0.14
Performance of the optimal portfolio				
Sharpe ratio	0.24			
	Index	**Active**		
Composition of optimal portfolio				
w^0		0.6122		
w^*	0.0827	0.9173		
		Google	**Dell**	
Weight of active portfolio × weight of stock in active portfolio		0.5094	0.4079	

Please visit us at www.mhhe.com/bkm

6.6 RISK OF LONG-TERM INVESTMENTS

So far we have envisioned portfolio investment for one period. We have not made any explicit assumptions about the duration of that period, so one might take it to be of any length, and thus our analysis would seem to apply as well to long-term investments. Yet investors are frequently advised that stock investments for the long run are not as risky as it might appear from the statistics presented in this chapter and the previous one. To understand this widespread misconception, we must first understand what the alternative long-term investment strategies are.

Risk and Return with Alternative Long-Term Investments

We have not yet had much to say about the investor's time horizon. From the standpoint of risk and return,[8] does it matter whether an investor's horizon is long or short? A common misconception is that long-term investors should allocate a greater proportion of wealth into stocks simply because in some sense stocks are less risky over long-term horizons. This belief that stocks become less risky over longer horizons is based on a notion of "time diversification," that spreading your risky investments over many time periods offers a similar benefit in risk reduction as spreading an investment budget over many assets in a given period (the subject we have worked on throughout this chapter). That belief, however, is incorrect.

We can gain insight into risk in the long run by comparing one-year ("short-term") and two-year ("longer-term") *risky* investments. Imagine an investment opportunity set that is identical in each of the two years. It includes a risky portfolio with a normally distributed, continuously compounded, annual risk premium of R and variance of σ^2. The one-year Sharpe ratio is therefore $S_1 = R/\sigma$, and the one-year price of risk is $P_1 = R/\sigma^2$. Investors can allocate their portfolios between that risky portfolio and a risk-free asset with zero risk premium and variance.[9] As we learned from Table 5.2, we can safely assume that the stock portfolio returns are serially uncorrelated.

Of course, you cannot properly compare a one-year to a two-year investment without specifying what the one-year investor will do in the second year. To make the comparisons meaningful, we compare the strategies of three investment companies that advertise three alternative two-year investment strategies: Company 1 calls its strategy "Two-In": Invest everything in the risky portfolio for two years. Company 2 touts its "One-In" strategy: In one year invest fully in the risk-free asset, and in the other year invest fully in the risky portfolio. Finally, Company 3 advocates a "Half-in-Two" strategy: In both years, invest half the investment budget in the risk-free asset and the other half in the risky portfolio. We must decide which strategy is best.

Recall that both the mean and variance of continuously compounded, serially uncorrelated returns (or excess returns) grow in proportion to the length of the holding period. We show the rate-of-return statistics for the three strategies in Table 6.3. The risk premium is zero for bills and R for the risky portfolio, so the first row of the table shows the accumulation of the investor's risk premium over two years using each strategy. Similarly, the second row shows the accumulation of the variance of the investor's wealth.

We see immediately that risk is *not* lower for longer-term investors. A two-year investment in stocks (the Two-In strategy) has twice the variance as the One-In strategy. This observation already should settle the debate of whether total risk in the long run is smaller—it clearly is not. Rather, it grows proportionally over time: The two-year investment in the risky portfolio has double the variance of the one-year investment.

[8]An investor may choose a specific investment horizon for a number of reasons, such as the target retirement age. Other factors that we have not considered, for example, the magnitude of one's human capital (the value of future earning power) versus current financial wealth, also may affect investment horizon and portfolio allocations.

[9]The hierarchy of portfolio choice we developed for any given holding period is this: Construct a risky portfolio with the highest Sharpe ratio. Allocate the entire investment budget between this portfolio and the risk-free asset. The optimal weight in the risky portfolio is $y = P/A$, where P is the price of risk and A is the investor's risk aversion.

TABLE 6.3 Two-year risk premium, variance, Sharpe ratio, and price of risk for three strategies

Strategy:	Two-In[1]	One-In[2]	Half-in-Two[3]
Risk premium	$R + R = 2R$	$0 + R = R$	$2^* \frac{1}{2} R = R$
Variance	$\sigma^2 + \sigma^2 = 2\sigma^2$	$0 + \sigma^2 = \sigma^2$	$2^* \frac{1}{4} \sigma^2 = \sigma^2/2$
Sharpe ratio[4]	$\dfrac{2R}{\sigma\sqrt{2}} = S_1\sqrt{2}$	$R/\sigma = S_1$	$\dfrac{R}{\sigma/\sqrt{2}} = S_1\sqrt{2}$
Price of risk[5]	$R/\sigma^2 = P_1$	$R/\sigma^2 = P_1$	$\dfrac{R}{\sigma^2/2} = 2P_1$

[1]Two-In: Invest entirely in the risky portfolio for two years.

[2]One-In: Invest entirely in the risky portfolio for one year and in the risk-free asset in the other.

[3]Half-in-Two: Invest half the budget in the risky portfolio for two years.

[4]Sharpe Ratio $= \dfrac{\text{Risk premium}}{\text{Standard deviation}}$

[5]Price of risk $= \dfrac{\text{Risk premium}}{\text{Variance}}$

While the One-In investment is less risky than the Two-In strategy, an even safer investment strategy that still offers the same risk premium as One-In is the Half-in-Two strategy, which invests half the investor's wealth in stocks in *each* of the two years. This has only one-half the variance of One-In and only one-fourth the variance of Two-In. When less risk than Two-In is desired, spreading the risk evenly over time, rather than lumping all the risk into a concentrated period (as the One-In strategy does), is the best strategy. This is evident from the Sharpe ratios of each strategy (line 3 of the table): The Sharpe ratio of Half-in-Two exceeds that of One-In by a multiple of $\sqrt{2}$. Does this mean that Half-in-Two actually does offer a meaningful benefit of time diversification? Put differently, does Half-in-Two allow investors to prudently allocate greater portfolio shares to the risky portfolio? Surprisingly, the answer is no. Even this more limited notion of time diversification is faulty.

We will compare investors' optimal capital allocations under each of these strategies. However, we can dismiss the One-In strategy out of hand, as it clearly is dominated by the Half-in-Two strategy, which has equal risk premium with only half the variance. Therefore, we need only compare Two-In with Half-in-Two. We established earlier that an investor with a degree of risk aversion A will allocate a fraction of overall wealth to the risky portfolio equal to $y = \dfrac{\text{Price of risk}}{A}$. For Two-In, that fraction is $\dfrac{R/\sigma^2}{A}$, while for Half-in-Two, it is $\dfrac{2R/\sigma^2}{A}$. So the Half-in-Two strategy gets double the allocation as All-In; but remember that Half-in-Two is only half as heavily invested in the risky portfolio. These effects precisely cancel out: The higher risk and return of Two-In are precisely offset by the investor's reduced allocation to it. So the Half-in-Two strategy that *seems* to offer the benefit of time diversification does not in fact elicit a greater overall allocation to the risky portfolio.

Would it matter if we extended the horizon from two years to some greater value? With a horizon of T years, a "time diversification strategy" (we must now change our strategy from "Half in Two" to "$1/T$ in T") puts at risk $1/T$ of the budget each year. The price of risk of the time-diversified strategy is TR/σ^2, compared to only R/σ^2 for the All-In strategy. Will this elicit greater investments in the risky portfolio as T increases? Once again, the telling point is that the time-diversified portfolio has no better Sharpe ratio than the fully invested All-In portfolio: The Sharpe ratio for both strategies is now $S_1\sqrt{T}$. Any investor will invest with the time-diversified strategy T times the fraction he would with the All-In T-year strategy; the net effect is that these alternatives are for all practical purposes equivalent. The investor choosing between these two alternatives is simply sliding up or down the CAL. Despite its higher price of risk, the overall allocation to the risky portfolio is not higher for the time-diversified portfolio.

Why the Unending Confusion?

It is no secret that the vast majority of financial advisers believe that "stocks are less risky if held for the long run," and so advise their clients. Their reasoning is this: The risk premium grows at the rate of the horizon, T. The standard deviation grows at the slower rate of only $\sqrt{T}$. The fact that risk grows more slowly than the risk premium is evident from the Sharpe ratio, $S_1\sqrt{T}$, which grows with the investment horizon.

This story sounds compelling, and in fact it contains no mathematical error. However, it is only half the story. Time diversification seems to offer a better risk-return trade-off (a higher Sharpe ratio) if you compare the All-In to the "One-In" strategy that invests all in one year and nothing later. But the relevant alternative to All-In is $1/T$ in T. The long-term $1/T$ in T investment strategy falls on the same "time CAL" as the All-In strategy, since it uses the same risky portfolio for the entire horizon. When this strategy is on the menu, complete portfolio allocations will *not* shift toward risky investments even as the investor's horizon extends.[10]

[10]You can verify that, more generally, a $1/n$ in T strategy (investing a portfolio weight of $1/n$ in the risky portfolio over T years) would give us the same results. You will find that the Sharpe ratio is $S_1\sqrt{T}$, while the price of risk is nP_1. Hence, you would invest n times more in the low-risk strategy and end with the same complete portfolio as the All-In strategy.

SUMMARY

- The expected rate of return of a portfolio is the weighted average of the component asset expected returns with the investment proportions as weights.
- The variance of a portfolio is a sum of the contributions of the component-security variances *plus* terms involving the covariance among assets.
- Even if correlations are positive, the portfolio standard deviation will be less than the weighted average of the component standard deviations, as long as the assets are not *perfectly* positively correlated. Thus, portfolio diversification is of value as long as assets are less than perfectly correlated.
- The contribution of an asset to portfolio variance depends on its correlation with the other assets in the portfolio, as well as on its own variance. An asset that is perfectly negatively correlated with a portfolio can be used to reduce the portfolio variance to zero. Thus, it can serve as a perfect hedge.
- The efficient frontier of risky assets is the graphical representation of the set of portfolios that maximizes portfolio expected return for a given level of portfolio standard deviation. Rational investors will choose a portfolio on the efficient frontier.
- A portfolio manager identifies the efficient frontier by first establishing estimates for the expected returns and standard deviations and determining the correlations among them. The input data are then fed into an optimization program that produces the investment proportions, expected returns, and standard deviations of the portfolios on the efficient frontier.
- In general, portfolio managers will identify different efficient portfolios because of differences in the methods and quality of security analysis. Managers compete on the quality of their security analysis relative to their management fees.
- If a risk-free asset is available and input data are identical, all investors will choose the same portfolio on the efficient frontier, the one that is tangent to the CAL. All investors with identical input data will hold the identical risky portfolio, differing only in how much each allocates to this optimal portfolio and to the risk-free asset. This result is characterized as the separation principle of portfolio selection.
- The single-index model expresses the excess return on a security as a function of the market excess return: $R_i = \alpha_i + \beta_i R_M + e_i$. This equation also can be interpreted as a

www.mhhe.com/bkm

regression of the security excess return on the market-index excess return. The regression line has intercept α_i and slope β_i and is called the security characteristic line.

- In a single-index model, the variance of the rate of return on a security or portfolio can be decomposed into systematic and firm-specific risk. The systematic component of variance equals β^2 times the variance of the market excess return. The firm-specific component is the variance of the residual term in the index-model equation.
- The beta of a portfolio is the weighted average of the betas of the component securities. A security with negative beta reduces the portfolio beta, thereby reducing exposure to market volatility. The unique risk of a portfolio approaches zero as the portfolio becomes more highly diversified.

KEY TERMS

KEY FORMULAS

The expected rate of return on a portfolio: $E(r_P) = w_B E(r_B) + w_S E(r_S)$

The variance of the return on a portfolio: $\sigma_P^2 = (w_B\sigma_B)^2 + (w_S\sigma_S)^2 + 2(w_B\sigma_B)(w_S\sigma_S)\rho_{BS}$

The Sharpe ratio of a portfolio: $S_P = \dfrac{E(r_P) - r_f}{\sigma_P}$

Sharpe ratio maximizing portfolio weights with two risky assets (B and S) and a risk-free asset:

$$w_B = \frac{[E(r_B) - r_f]\sigma_S^2 - [E(r_S) - r_f]\sigma_B\sigma_S\rho_{BS}}{[E(r_B) - r_f]\sigma_S^2 + [E(r_S) - r_f]\sigma_B^2 - [E(r_B) - r_f + E(r_S) - r_f]\sigma_B\sigma_S\rho_{BS}}$$

$$w_S = 1 - w_B$$

The index-model equation: $R_i = \beta_i R_M + \alpha_i + e_i$

Decomposition of variance based on the index-model equation:

$$\text{Variance}(R_i) = \beta_i^2\sigma_M^2 + \sigma^2(e_i)$$

Percent of security variance explained by the index return = the square of the correlation coefficient of the regression of the security on the market:

$$\rho^2 = \frac{\text{Systematic (or explained) variance}}{\text{Total variance}}$$

$$= \frac{\beta_D^2\sigma_M^2}{\sigma_D^2} = \frac{\beta_D^2\sigma_M^2}{\beta_D^2\sigma_M^2 + \sigma^2(e_D)}$$

Optimal position in the active portfolio, A:

$$w_A^* = \frac{w_A^0}{1 + w_A^0(1 - \beta_A)} \qquad w_M^* = 1 - w_A^*$$

$$w_A^0 = \frac{\alpha_A/\sigma^2(e_A)}{R_M/\sigma_M^2}$$

Optimal weight of a security, G, in the active portfolio: $w_G(\text{active}) = \dfrac{\alpha_G/\sigma^2(e_G)}{\sum_i \alpha_i/\sigma^2(e_i)}$

Select problems are available in McGraw-Hill's *Connect Finance.* Please see the Supplements section of the book's frontmatter for more information.

PROBLEM SETS

Basic

1. In forming a portfolio of two risky assets, what must be true of the correlation coefficient between their returns if there are to be gains from diversification? Explain. *(LO 6-1)*
2. When adding a risky asset to a portfolio of many risky assets, which property of the asset is more important, its standard deviation or its covariance with the other assets? Explain. *(LO 6-1)*
3. A portfolio's expected return is 12%, its standard deviation is 20%, and the risk-free rate is 4%. Which of the following would make for the greatest increase in the portfolio's Sharpe ratio? *(LO 6-3)*
   a. An increase of 1% in expected return.
   b. A decrease of 1% in the risk-free rate.
   c. A decrease of 1% in its standard deviation.
4. An investor ponders various allocations to the optimal risky portfolio and risk-free T-bills to construct his complete portfolio. How would the Sharpe ratio of the complete portfolio be affected by this choice? *(LO 6-3)*

Intermediate

5. The standard deviation of the market-index portfolio is 20%. Stock A has a beta of 1.5 and a residual standard deviation of 30%. *(LO 6-5)*
   a. What would make for a larger increase in the stock's variance: an increase of .15 in its beta or an increase of 3% (from 30% to 33%) in its residual standard deviation?
   b. An investor who currently holds the market-index portfolio decides to reduce the portfolio allocation to the market index to 90% and to invest 10% in stock A. Which of the changes in (*a*) will have a greater impact on the portfolio's standard deviation?
6. Suppose that the returns on the stock fund presented in Spreadsheet 6.1 were −40%, −14%, 17%, and 33% in the four scenarios. *(LO 6-2)*
   a. Would you expect the mean return and variance of the stock fund to be more than, less than, or equal to the values computed in Spreadsheet 6.2? Why?
   b. Calculate the new values of mean return and variance for the stock fund using a format similar to Spreadsheet 6.2. Confirm your intuition from part (*a*).
   c. Calculate the new value of the covariance between the stock and bond funds using a format similar to Spreadsheet 6.4. Explain intuitively the change in the covariance.
7. Use the rate-of-return data for the stock and bond funds presented in Spreadsheet 6.1, but now assume that the probability of each scenario is as follows: severe recession: .10; mild recession: .20; normal growth: .35; boom: .35. *(LO 6-2)*
   a. Would you expect the mean return and variance of the stock fund to be more than, less than, or equal to the values computed in Spreadsheet 6.2? Why?
   b. Calculate the new values of mean return and variance for the stock fund using a format similar to Spreadsheet 6.2. Confirm your intuition from part (*a*).
   c. Calculate the new value of the covariance between the stock and bond funds using a format similar to Spreadsheet 6.4. Explain intuitively why the absolute value of the covariance has changed.

The following data apply to Problems 8–12.

A pension fund manager is considering three mutual funds. The first is a stock fund, the second is a long-term government and corporate bond fund, and the third is a T-bill money market fund that yields a sure rate of 5.5%. The probability distributions of the risky funds are:

	Expected Return	Standard Deviation
Stock fund (S)	15%	32%
Bond fund (B)	9	23

The correlation between the fund returns is .15.

8. Tabulate and draw the investment opportunity set of the two risky funds. Use investment proportions for the stock fund of 0% to 100% in increments of 20%. What expected return and standard deviation does your graph show for the minimum-variance portfolio? ***(LO 6-2)***
9. Draw a tangent from the risk-free rate to the opportunity set. What does your graph show for the expected return and standard deviation of the optimal risky portfolio? ***(LO 6-3)***
10. What is the reward-to-volatility ratio of the best feasible CAL? ***(LO 6-3)***
11. Suppose now that your portfolio must yield an expected return of 12% and be efficient, that is, on the best feasible CAL. ***(LO 6-4)***
    a. What is the standard deviation of your portfolio?
    b. What is the proportion invested in the T-bill fund and each of the two risky funds?
12. If you were to use only the two risky funds and still require an expected return of 12%, what would be the investment proportions of your portfolio? Compare its standard deviation to that of the optimal portfolio in the previous problem. What do you conclude? ***(LO 6-4)***
13. Stocks offer an expected rate of return of 10% with a standard deviation of 20%, and gold offers an expected return of 5% with a standard deviation of 25%. ***(LO 6-3)***
    a. In light of the apparent inferiority of gold to stocks with respect to both mean return and volatility, would anyone hold gold? If so, demonstrate graphically why one would do so.
    b. How would you answer (*a*) if the correlation coefficient between gold and stocks were 1? Draw a graph illustrating why one would or would not hold gold. Could these expected returns, standard deviations, and correlation represent an equilibrium for the security market?
14. Suppose that many stocks are traded in the market and that it is possible to borrow at the risk-free rate, r_f. The characteristics of two of the stocks are as follows:

Stock	Expected Return	Standard Deviation
A	8%	40%
B	13	60
Correlation = −1		

Could the equilibrium r_f be greater than 10%? (*Hint:* Can a particular stock portfolio be substituted for the risk-free asset?) ***(LO 6-3)***

Please visit us at www.mhhe.com/bkm

15. You can find a spreadsheet containing the historic returns presented in Table 5.2 on the text's website at **www.mhhe.com/bkm.** (Look for the link to Chapter 5 material.) Copy the data for the last 20 years into a new spreadsheet. Analyze the risk-return trade-off that would have characterized portfolios constructed from large stocks and long-term Treasury bonds over the last 20 years. What was the average rate of return and standard deviation of each asset? What was the correlation coefficient of their annual returns? What would have been the average return and standard deviation of portfolios with differing weights in the two assets? For example, consider weights in stocks starting at zero and incrementing by .10 up to a weight of 1. What was the

average return and standard deviation of the minimum-variance combination of stocks and bonds? *(LO 6-2)*

16. Assume expected returns and standard deviations for all securities, as well as the risk-free rate for lending and borrowing, are known. Will investors arrive at the same optimal risky portfolio? Explain. *(LO 6-4)*
17. Your assistant gives you the following diagram as the efficient frontier of the group of stocks you asked him to analyze. The diagram looks a bit odd, but your assistant insists he double-checked his analysis. Would you trust him? Is it possible to get such a diagram? *(LO 6-4)*

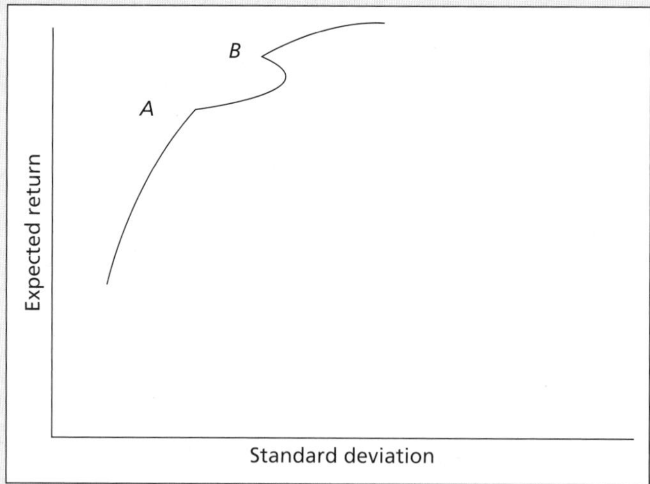

18. What is the relationship of the portfolio standard deviation to the weighted average of the standard deviations of the component assets? *(LO 6-1)*
19. A project has a .7 chance of doubling your investment in a year and a .3 chance of halving your investment in a year. What is the standard deviation of the rate of return on this investment? *(LO 6-2)*
20. Investors expect the market rate of return this year to be 10%. The expected rate of return on a stock with a beta of 1.2 is currently 12%. If the market return this year turns out to be 8%, how would you revise your expectation of the rate of return on the stock? *(LO 6-5)*
21. The following figure shows plots of monthly rates of return and the stock market for two stocks. *(LO 6-5)*
    a. Which stock is riskier to an investor currently holding her portfolio in a diversified portfolio of common stock?
    b. Which stock is riskier to an undiversified investor who puts all of his funds in only one of these stocks?

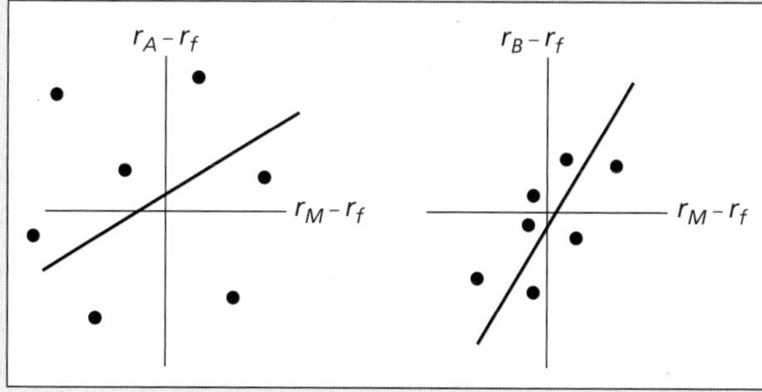

22. Go to **www.mhhe.com/bkm** and link to the material for Chapter 6, where you will find a spreadsheet containing monthly rates of return for GM, the S&P 500, and T-bills over a recent five-year period. Set up a spreadsheet just like that of Example 6.3 and find the beta of GM. *(LO 6-5)*

Please visit us at www.mhhe.com/bkm

23. Here are rates of return for six months for Generic Risk, Inc. What is Generic's beta? (*Hint:* Find the answer by plotting the scatter diagram.) ***(LO 6-5)***

Month	Market Return	Generic Return
1	0%	+2%
2	0	0
3	−1	0
4	−1	−2
5	+1	+4
6	+1	+2

Challenge

24. Go to the Online Learning Center at **www.mhhe.com/bkm,** where you will find rate-of-return data over 60 months for Google, the T-bill rate, and the S&P 500, which we will use as the market-index portfolio. ***(LO 6-4)***
    a. Use these data and Excel's regression function to compute Google's excess return each period as well as its alpha, beta, and residual standard deviation, $\sigma(e)$.
    b. What was the Sharpe ratio of the S&P 500 over this period?
    c. What was Google's information ratio over this period?
    d. If someone whose risky portfolio is currently invested in an index portfolio such as the S&P 500 wishes to take a position in Google based on the estimates from parts (*a*)–(*c*), what would be the optimal fraction of the risky portfolio to invest in Google? Use Equations 6.16 and 6.17.
    e. Based on Equation 6.18 and your answer to part (*d*), by how much would the Sharpe ratio of the optimal risky portfolio increase given the incremental position in Google?

CFA Problems

1. A three-asset portfolio has the following characteristics:

Asset	Expected Return	Standard Deviation	Weight
X	15%	22%	0.50
Y	10	8	0.40
Z	6	3	0.10

What is the expected return on this three-asset portfolio? ***(LO 6-1)***

2. George Stephenson's current portfolio of $2 million is invested as follows:

Summary of Stephenson's Current Portfolio

	Value	Percent of Total	Expected Annual Return	Annual Standard Deviation
Short-term bonds	$ 200,000	10%	4.6%	1.6%
Domestic large-cap equities	600,000	30	12.4	19.5
Domestic small-cap equities	1,200,000	60	16.0	29.9
Total portfolio	$2,000,000	100%	13.8%	23.1%

Stephenson soon expects to receive an additional $2 million and plans to invest the entire amount in an index fund that best complements the current portfolio. Stephanie Coppa, CFA, is evaluating the four index funds shown in the following table for their ability to produce a portfolio that will meet two criteria relative to the current portfolio: (1) maintain or enhance expected return and (2) maintain or reduce volatility.

www.mhhe.com/bkm

Each fund is invested in an asset class that is not substantially represented in the current portfolio.

Index Fund Characteristics			
Index Fund	**Expected Annual Return**	**Expected Annual Standard Deviation**	**Correlation of Returns with Current Portfolio**
Fund A	15%	25%	+0.80
Fund B	11	22	+0.60
Fund C	16	25	+0.90
Fund D	14	22	+0.65

State which fund Coppa should recommend to Stephenson. Justify your choice by describing how your chosen fund *best* meets both of Stephenson's criteria. No calculations are required. ***(LO 6-4)***

3. Abigail Grace has a $900,000 fully diversified portfolio. She subsequently inherits ABC Company common stock worth $100,000. Her financial adviser provided her with the following estimates: ***(LO 6-5)***

Risk and Return Characteristics		
	Expected Monthly Returns	**Standard Deviation of Monthly Returns**
Original Portfolio	0.67%	2.37%
ABC Company	1.25	2.95

The correlation coefficient of ABC stock returns with the original portfolio returns is .40.

a. The inheritance changes Grace's overall portfolio and she is deciding whether to keep the ABC stock. Assuming Grace keeps the ABC stock, calculate the:
   i. Expected return of her new portfolio which includes the ABC stock.
   ii. Covariance of ABC stock returns with the original portfolio returns.
   iii. Standard deviation of her new portfolio which includes the ABC stock.

b. If Grace sells the ABC stock, she will invest the proceeds in risk-free government securities yielding .42% monthly. Assuming Grace sells the ABC stock and replaces it with the government securities, calculate the:
   i. Expected return of her new portfolio which includes the government securities.
   ii. Covariance of the government security returns with the original portfolio returns.
   iii. Standard deviation of her new portfolio which includes the government securities.

c. Determine whether the beta of her new portfolio, which includes the government securities, will be higher or lower than the beta of her original portfolio.

d. Based on conversations with her husband, Grace is considering selling the $100,000 of ABC stock and acquiring $100,000 of XYZ Company common stock instead. XYZ stock has the same expected return and standard deviation as ABC stock. Her husband comments, "It doesn't matter whether you keep all of the ABC stock or replace it with $100,000 of XYZ stock." State whether her husband's comment is correct or incorrect. Justify your response.

e. In a recent discussion with her financial adviser, Grace commented, "If I just don't lose money in my portfolio, I will be satisfied." She went on to say, "I am more afraid of losing money than I am concerned about achieving high returns." Describe *one* weakness of using standard deviation of returns as a risk measure for Grace.

The following data apply to CFA Problems 4–6:

Hennessy & Associates manages a $30 million equity portfolio for the multimanager Wilstead Pension Fund. Jason Jones, financial vice president of Wilstead, noted that Hennessy had rather consistently achieved the best record among the Wilstead's six equity managers. Performance of the Hennessy portfolio had been clearly superior to that of the S&P 500 in four of the past five years. In the one less favorable year, the shortfall was trivial.

Hennessy is a "bottom-up" manager. The firm largely avoids any attempt to "time the market." It also focuses on selection of individual stocks, rather than the weighting of favored industries.

There is no apparent conformity of style among the six equity managers. The five managers, other than Hennessy, manage portfolios aggregating $250 million, made up of more than 150 individual issues.

Jones is convinced that Hennessy is able to apply superior skill to stock selection, but the favorable results are limited by the high degree of diversification in the portfolio. Over the years, the portfolio generally held 40–50 stocks, with about 2% to 3% of total funds committed to each issue. The reason Hennessy seemed to do well most years was that the firm was able to identify each year 10 or 12 issues that registered particularly large gains.

Based on this overview, Jones outlined the following plan to the Wilstead pension committee:

> Let's tell Hennessy to limit the portfolio to no more than 20 stocks. Hennessy will double the commitments to the stocks that it really favors and eliminate the remainder. Except for this one new restriction, Hennessy should be free to manage the portfolio exactly as before.

All the members of the pension committee generally supported Jones's proposal, because all agreed that Hennessy had seemed to demonstrate superior skill in selecting stocks. Yet the proposal was a considerable departure from previous practice, and several committee members raised questions.

4. Answer the following: ***(LO 6-1)***
   a. Will the limitation of 20 stocks likely increase or decrease the risk of the portfolio? Explain.
   b. Is there any way Hennessy could reduce the number of issues from 40 to 20 without significantly affecting risk? Explain.
5. One committee member was particularly enthusiastic concerning Jones's proposal. He suggested that Hennessy's performance might benefit further from reduction in the number of issues to 10. If the reduction to 20 could be expected to be advantageous, explain why reduction to 10 might be less likely to be advantageous. (Assume that Wilstead will evaluate the Hennessy portfolio independently of the other portfolios in the fund.) ***(LO 6-1)***
6. Another committee member suggested that, rather than evaluate each managed portfolio independently of other portfolios, it might be better to consider the effects of a change in the Hennessy portfolio on the total fund. Explain how this broader point of view could affect the committee decision to limit the holdings in the Hennessy portfolio to either 10 or 20 issues. ***(LO 6-1)***
7. Dudley Trudy, CFA, recently met with one of his clients. Trudy typically invests in a master list of 30 equities drawn from several industries. As the meeting concluded, the client made the following statement: "I trust your stock-picking ability and believe that you should invest my funds in your five best ideas. Why invest in 30 companies when you obviously have stronger opinions on a few of them?" Trudy plans to respond to his client within the context of Modern Portfolio Theory. ***(LO 6-1)***
   a. Contrast the concepts of systematic risk and firm-specific risk, and give an example of each type of risk.
   b. Critique the client's suggestion. Discuss how both systematic and firm-specific risk change as the number of securities in a portfolio is increased.

WEB *master*

1. Go to **finance.yahoo.com** and download five years of monthly closing prices for Eli Lilly (ticker = LLY), Alcoa (AA), and the S&P 500 Index (GSPC). Download the data into an Excel file and use the Adjusted-Close prices, which adjust for dividend payments, to calculate the monthly rate of return for each price series. Use an XY Scatter Plot chart with no line joining the points to plot Alcoa's returns against the S&P 500. Now select

www.mhhe.com/bkm

one of the data points, and right-click to obtain a shortcut menu allowing you to enter a trend line. This is Alcoa's characteristic line, and the slope is Alcoa's beta. Repeat this process for Lilly. What conclusions can you draw from each company's characteristic line?

2. Following the procedures in the previous question, find five years of monthly returns for Staples. Using the first two years of data, what is Staples' beta? What is the beta using the latest two years of data? How stable is the beta estimate? If you use all five years of data, how close is your estimate of beta to the estimate reported in Yahoo's *Key Statistics* section?
3. Following the procedures in the previous questions, find five years of monthly returns for the following firms: Genzyme Corporation, Sony, Cardinal Health, Inc., Black & Decker Corporation, and Kellogg Company. Copy the returns from these five firms into a single Excel workbook, with the returns for each company properly aligned. Use the full range of available data. Then do the following:
   a. Using the Excel functions for average (AVERAGE) and sample standard deviation (STDEV), calculate the average and the standard deviation of the returns for each of the firms.
   b. Using Excel's correlation function (CORREL), construct the correlation matrix for the five stocks based on their monthly returns for the entire period. What are the lowest and the highest individual pairs of correlation coefficients? (*Alternative:* You may use Excel's Data Analysis Tool to generate the correlation matrix.)
4. There are some free online tools that will calculate the optimal asset weights and draw the efficient frontier for the assets that you specify. One of the sites is **www.investorcraft.com/PortfolioTools/EfficientFrontier.aspx.**

   Go to this site and enter at least eight assets in the selection box. You can search for the companies by name or by symbol. Click on the *Next Step* button and select one of the time spans offered. Specify an appropriate risk-free rate, a minimum allowable asset weight of 0, and a maximum allowable asset weight of 100. Click on *Calculate* to get your results.
   a. What are the expected return and the standard deviation of the portfolio based on adjusted weights?
   b. How do they compare to those for the optimal portfolio and the minimum variance portfolio?
   c. Of the three portfolios shown, with which one would you feel most comfortable as an investor?

6.1 Recalculation of Spreadsheets 6.1 and 6.4 shows that the covariance is now −5.80 and the correlation coefficient is −.07.

	A	B	C	D	E	F
1			Stock Fund		Bond Fund	
2	Scenario	Probability	Rate of Return	Col B × Col C	Rate of Return	Col B × Col E
3	Severe recession	.05	−37.0	−1.9	−10	−0.5
4	Mild recession	.25	−11.0	−2.8	10	2.5
5	Normal growth	.40	14.0	5.6	7	2.8
6	Boom	.30	30.0	9.0	2	0.6
7	Expected or Mean Return:		SUM:	10.0	SUM:	5.4
8						
9			Deviation from Mean Return		Covariance	
10	Scenario	Probability	Stock Fund	Bond Fund	Product of Dev	Col B × Col E
11	Severe recession	.05	−47.0	−15.4	723.8	36.19
12	Mild recession	.25	−21.0	4.6	−96.6	−24.15
13	Normal growth	.40	4.0	1.6	6.4	2.56
14	Boom	.30	20.0	−3.4	−68.0	−20.40
15		SD =	18.63	4.65	Covariance =	−5.80
16	Correlation coefficient = Covariance/(StdDev(stocks)*StdDev(bonds)) =					−0.07

6.2 The scatter diagrams for pairs B–E are shown below. Scatter diagram A (presented with the Concept Check) shows an exact mirror image between the pattern of points 1,2,3 versus 3,4,5. Therefore, the correlation coefficient is zero. Scatter diagram B shows perfect positive correlation (1). Similarly, C shows perfect negative correlation (−1). Now compare the scatters of D and E. Both show a general positive correlation, but scatter D is tighter. Therefore, D is associated with a correlation of about .5 (use a spreadsheet to show that the exact correlation is .54), and E is associated with a correlation of about .2 (show that the exact correlation coefficient is .23).

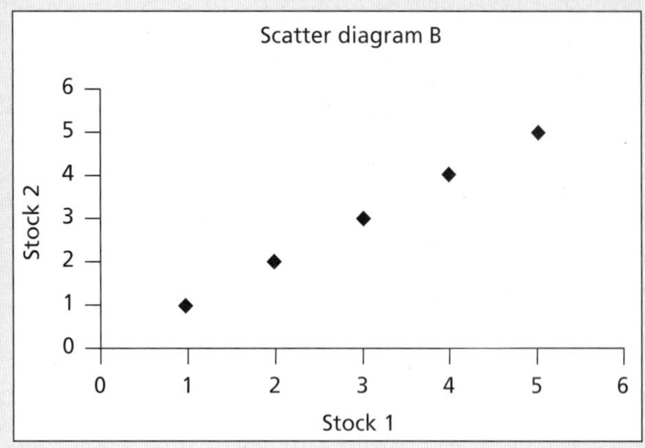

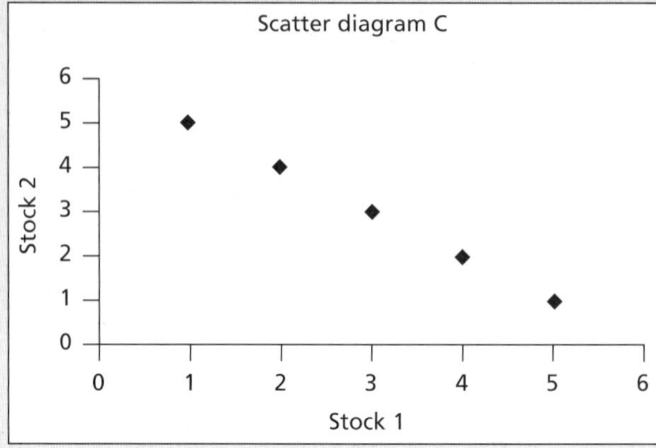

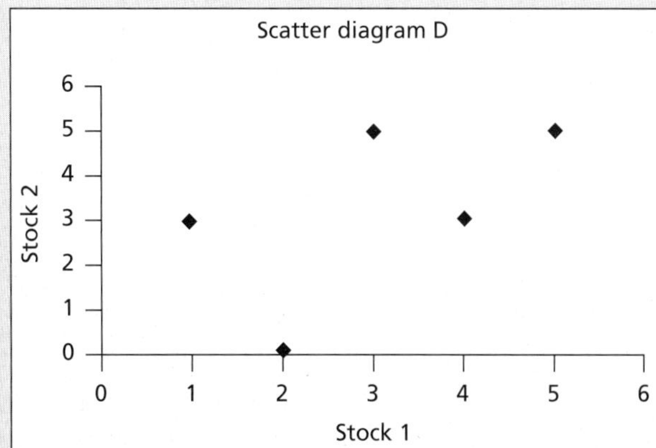

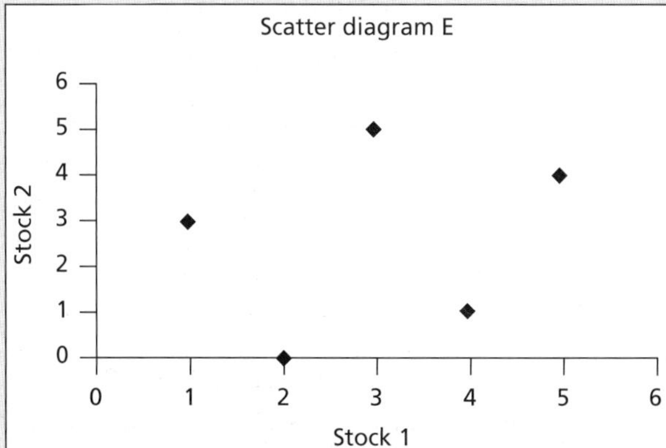

6.3 *a.* Using Equation 6.6 with the data $\sigma_B = 8$; $\sigma_S = 19$; $w_B = .5$; and $w_S = 1 - w_B = .5$, we obtain the equation

$$\sigma_P^2 = 10^2 = (w_B\sigma_B)^2 + (w_S\sigma_S)^2 + 2(w_B\sigma_B)(w_S\sigma_S)\rho_{BS}$$
$$= (.5 \times 8)^2 + (.5 \times 19)^2 + 2(.5 \times 8)(.5 \times 19)\rho_{BS}$$

which yields $\rho = -.0822$.

b. Using Equation 6.5 and the additional data $E(r_B) = 5\%$; $E(r_S) = 10\%$, we obtain

$$E(r_P) = w_B E(r_B) + w_S E(r_S) = (.5 \times 5) + (.5 \times 10) = 7.5\%$$

c. On the one hand, you should be happier with a correlation of .17 than with .22 since the lower correlation implies greater benefits from diversification and means that, for any level of expected return, there will be lower risk. On the other hand, the constraint that you must hold 50% of the portfolio in bonds represents a cost to you since it prevents you from choosing the risk-return trade-off most suited to your tastes. Unless you would choose to hold about 50% of the portfolio in bonds anyway, you are better off with the slightly higher correlation but with the ability to choose your own portfolio weights.

6.4 *a.* Implementing Equations 6.5 and 6.6, we generate data for the graph. See Spreadsheet 6.7 and Figure 6.14 on the following pages.

b. Implementing the formulas indicated in Spreadsheet 6.6, we generate the optimal risky portfolio (O) and the minimum-variance portfolio.

c. The slope of the CAL is equal to the risk premium of the optimal risky portfolio divided by its standard deviation, $(11.28 - 5)/17.59 = .357$.

d. The mean of the complete portfolio is $.2222 \times 11.28 + .7778 \times 5 = 6.395\%$, and its standard deviation is $.2222 \times 17.58 = 3.91\%$. Sharpe ratio $= (6.395 - 5)/3.91 = .357$.

SPREADSHEET 6.7

For Concept Check 4. Mean and standard deviation for various portfolio applications

	A	B	C	D	E	F	G
5		Data	X	M	T-Bills		
6		Mean (%)	15	10	5		
7		Std. Dev. (%)	50	20	0		
8		Corr. Coeff. X and S		-0.20			
9		Portfolio Opportunity set					
10		Weight in X	Weight in S	Pf Mean (%)	Pf Std Dev (%)		
11		-1.00	2.00	5.00	70.00		
12		-0.90	1.90	5.50	64.44		
13		-0.80	1.80	6.00	58.92		
14		-0.70	1.70	6.50	53.45	=B13*$C$6+C13*$D$6	
15		-0.60	1.60	7.00	48.04		
16		-0.50	1.50	7.50	42.72		
17		-0.40	1.40	8.00	37.52		
18		-0.30	1.30	8.50	32.51		
19		-0.20	1.20	9.00	27.78	=(B15^2*$C$7^2	
20		-0.10	1.10	9.50	23.52	+C15^2*$D$7^2	
21		0.00	1.00	10.00	20.00	+2*B15*C15	
22		0.10	0.90	10.50	17.69	*$C$7*$D$7*$D$8)^0.5	
23		0.20	0.80	11.00	17.09		
24		0.30	0.70	11.50	18.36		
25		0.40	0.60	12.00	21.17		
26		0.50	0.50	12.50	25.00		
27		0.60	0.40	13.00	29.46		
28		0.70	0.30	13.50	34.31		
29		0.80	0.20	14.00	39.40		
30		0.90	0.10	14.50	44.64		
31		1.00	0.00	15.00	50.00		
32		1.10	-0.10	15.50	55.43		
33		1.20	-0.20	16.00	60.93		
34		1.30	-0.30	16.50	66.46		
35		1.40	-0.40	17.00	72.03		
36		1.50	-0.50	17.50	77.62		
37		1.60	-0.60	18.00	83.23		
38		1.70	-0.70	18.50	88.87		
39		1.80	-0.80	19.00	94.51		
40		1.90	-0.90	19.50	100.16		
41		2.00	-1.00	20.00	105.83		
42	**Min. Var Pf**	0.18	0.82	10.91	17.06		
43	**Optimal Pf**	0.26	0.74	11.28	17.59		
44							
45							
46		=((C6-E6)*D7^2-(D6-E6)*C7*D7*D8)/					
47		((C6-E6)*D7^2+(D6-E6)*C7^2-(C6-E6+D6-E6)*C7*D7*D8)					
48							
49							

The composition of the complete portfolio is
$.2222 \times .26 = .06$ (i.e., 6%) in X
$.2222 \times .74 = .16$ (i.e., 16%) in M
and 78% in T-bills.

6.5 Efficient frontiers derived by portfolio managers depend on forecasts of the rates of return on various securities and estimates of risk, that is, standard deviations and correlation coefficients. The forecasts themselves do not control outcomes. Thus, to prefer a manager with a rosier forecast (northwesterly frontier) is tantamount to rewarding the bearers of good news and punishing the bearers of bad news. What the investor wants is to reward bearers of *accurate* news. Investors should monitor forecasts of portfolio managers on a regular basis to develop a track record of their forecasting accuracy. Portfolio choices of the more accurate forecasters will, in the long run, outperform the field.

6.6 *a.* Beta, the slope coefficient of the security on the factor: Securities $R_1 - R_6$ have a positive beta. These securities move, on average, in the same direction as the market (R_M). R_1, R_2, R_6 have large betas, so they are "aggressive" in that they carry more systematic risk than R_3, R_4, R_5, which are "defensive." R_7 and R_8 have a negative beta. These are hedge assets that carry negative systematic risk.

FIGURE 6.14

For Concept Check 6.4. Plot of mean return versus standard deviation using data from spreadsheet.

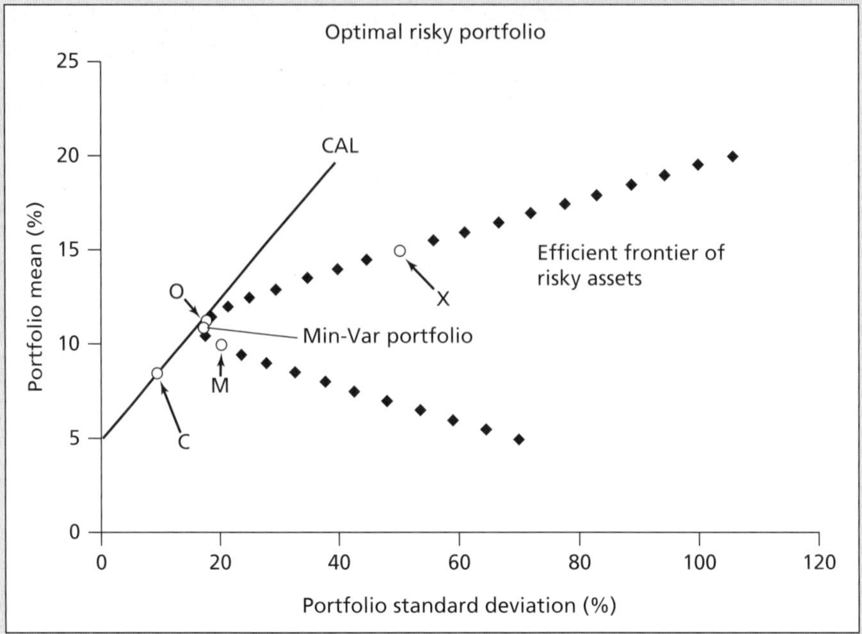

b. Intercept, the expected return when the market is neutral: The estimates show that R_1, R_4, R_8 have a positive intercept, while R_2, R_3, R_5, R_6, R_7 have negative intercepts. To the extent that one believes these intercepts will persist, a positive value is preferred.

c. Residual variance, the nonsystematic risk: R_2, R_3, R_7 have a relatively low residual variance. With sufficient diversification, residual risk eventually will be eliminated, and, hence, the difference in the residual variance is of little economic significance.

d. Total variance, the sum of systematic and nonsystematic risk: R_3 has a low beta and low residual variance, so its total variance will be low. R_1, R_6 have high betas and high residual variance, so their total variance will be high. But R_4 has a low beta and high residual variance, while R_2 has a high beta with a low residual variance. In sum, total variance often will misrepresent systematic risk, which is the part that matters.

6.7. *a.* To obtain the characteristic line of XYZ, we continue the spreadsheet of Example 6.3 and run a regression of the excess return of XYZ on the excess return of the market-index fund.

Summary Output	
Regression Statistics	
Multiple R	0.363
R-square	0.132
Adjusted R-square	0.023
Standard error	41.839
Observations	10

	Coefficients	**Standard Error**	***t*-Stat**	***p*-Value**	**Lower 95%**	**Upper 95%**
Intercept	3.930	14.98	0.262	0.800	−30.62	38.48
Market	0.582	0.528	1.103	0.302	−0.635	1.798

The regression output shows that the slope coefficient of XYZ is .582 and the intercept is 3.93%; hence the characteristic line is $R_{XYZ} = 3.93 + .582R_{\text{Market}}$.

b. The beta coefficient of ABC is 1.156, greater than XYZ's .582, implying that ABC has greater systematic risk.

c. The regression of XYZ on the market index shows an R-square of .132. Hence the proportion of unexplained variance (nonsystematic risk) is .868, or 86.8%.

Capital Asset Pricing and Arbitrage Pricing Theory

Chapter

7

Learning Objectives:

LO7-1 Use the implications of capital market theory to estimate security risk premiums.

LO7-2 Construct and use the security market line.

LO7-3 Specify and use a multifactor security market line.

LO7-4 Take advantage of an arbitrage opportunity with a portfolio that includes mispriced securities.

LO7-5 Use arbitrage pricing theory with more than one factor to identify mispriced securities.

The capital asset pricing model, almost always referred to as the CAPM, is a centerpiece of modern financial economics. It was first proposed by William F. Sharpe, who was awarded the 1990 Nobel Prize in Economics.

The CAPM provides a precise prediction of the relationship we should observe between the risk of an asset and its expected return. This relationship serves two vital functions.

First, it provides a benchmark rate of return for evaluating possible investments. For example, a security analyst might want to know whether the expected return she forecasts for a stock is more or less than its "fair" return given its risk. Second, the model helps us make an educated guess as to the expected return on assets that have not yet been traded in the marketplace. For example, how do we price an initial public offering of stock? How will a major new investment project affect the return investors require on a company's stock? Although the CAPM does not fully withstand empirical tests, it is widely used because of the insight it offers and because its accuracy suffices for many important applications.

Once you understand the intuition behind the CAPM, it becomes clear that the model may be improved by generalizing it to allow for multiple sources of risk. Therefore, we turn next to multifactor models of risk and return, and we show how these result in richer descriptions of the risk-return relationship.

Finally, we consider an alternative derivation of the risk-return relationship known as arbitrage pricing theory, or APT. Arbitrage is the exploitation of security mispricing to earn risk-free economic profits. The most basic principle of capital market theory is that prices ought to be aligned to eliminate risk-free profit opportunities. If actual prices allowed for such arbitrage, the resulting opportunities for profitable trading would lead to strong pressure on security prices that would persist until equilibrium was restored and the opportunities were eliminated. We will see that this no-arbitrage principle leads to a risk-return relationship like that of the CAPM. Like the generalized version of the CAPM, the simple APT is easily extended to accommodate multiple sources of systematic risk.

Related websites for this chapter are available at www.mhhe.com/bkm.

7.1 THE CAPITAL ASSET PRICING MODEL

Historically, the CAPM was developed prior to the index model introduced in the previous chapter (Equation 6.11). The index model was widely adopted as a natural description of the stock market immediately on the heels of the CAPM because the CAPM implications so neatly match the intuition underlying the model. So it makes sense to use the index model to help understand the lessons of the CAPM.

The index model describes an empirical relationship between the excess return on an individual stock, R_i, and that of a broad market-index portfolio, R_M: $R_i = \beta_i R_M + \alpha_i + e_i$, where alpha is the expected firm-specific return and e_i is zero-mean "noise," or firm-specific risk. Therefore, the expected excess return on a stock, given (conditional on) the market excess return, R_M, is $E(R_i | R_M) = \beta_i R_M + \alpha_i$.

What does this mean to portfolio managers? Hunt for positive-alpha stocks, don't invest in negative-alpha stocks, and, better yet, sell short negative-alpha stocks if short sales are not prohibited. Investor demand for a positive-alpha stock will increase its price. As the price of a stock rises, other things being equal, the expected return falls, reducing and ultimately eliminating the very alpha that first created the excess demand. Conversely, the drop in demand for a negative-alpha stock will reduce its price, pushing its alpha back toward zero. In the end, such buying or selling pressure will leave most securities with zero alpha values most of the time. Put another way, unless and until your own analysis of a stock tells you otherwise, you should assume alpha is zero.

When alpha is zero, there is no reward from bearing firm-specific risk; the only way to earn a higher expected return than the T-bill rate is by bearing systematic risk. Recall the Treynor-Black model, in which the position in any active portfolio is zero if the alpha is zero. In that case, the best portfolio is the one that completely eliminates nonsystematic risk, and that portfolio is an indexed portfolio that mimics the broad market. This is the conclusion of the CAPM. But science demands more than a story like this. It requires a carefully set up model with explicit assumptions in which an outcome such as the one we describe will be the only possible result. Here goes.

The Model: Assumptions and Implications

capital asset pricing model (CAPM)

A model that relates the required rate of return on a security to its systematic risk as measured by beta.

The **capital asset pricing model,** or **CAPM,** was developed by Treynor, Sharpe, Lintner, and Mossin in the early 1960s, and further refined later. The model predicts the relationship between the risk and equilibrium expected returns on risky assets. It begins by laying down the necessary, albeit unrealistic, assumptions that are necessary for the validity of the model. Thinking about an admittedly unrealistic world allows a relatively easy leap to the solution. With this accomplished, we can add realism to the environment, one step at a time, and see how the theory must be amended. This process allows us to develop a reasonably realistic model.

The conditions that lead to the CAPM ensure competitive security markets and investors who choose from identical efficient portfolios using the mean-variance criterion:

1. Markets for securities are perfectly competitive and equally profitable to all investors.
   1.A. No investor is sufficiently wealthy that his or her actions alone can affect market prices.
   1.B. All information relevant to security analysis is publicly available at no cost.
   1.C. All securities are publicly owned and traded, and investors may trade all of them. Thus, all risky assets are in the investment universe.
   1.D. There are no taxes on investment returns. Thus, all investors realize identical returns from securities.
   1.E. Investors confront no transaction costs that inhibit their trading.
   1.F. Lending and borrowing at a common risk-free rate are unlimited.
2. Investors are alike in every way except for initial wealth and risk aversion; hence, they all choose investment portfolios in the same manner.
   2.A. Investors plan for the same (single-period) horizon.
   2.B. Investors are rational, mean-variance optimizers.
   2.C. Investors are efficient users of analytical methods, and by assumption 1.B they have access to all relevant information. Hence, they use the same inputs and consider identical portfolio opportunity sets. This assumption is often called *homogeneous expectations.*

Obviously, these assumptions ignore many real-world complexities. However, they lead to powerful insights into the nature of equilibrium in security markets.

Given these assumptions, we summarize the equilibrium that will prevail in this hypothetical world of securities and investors. We elaborate on these implications in the following sections.

1. All investors will choose to hold the **market portfolio (M),** which includes all assets of the security universe. For simplicity, we shall refer to all assets as stocks. The proportion of each stock in the market portfolio equals the market value of the stock (price per share times the number of shares outstanding) divided by the total market value of all stocks.

market portfolio (M)

The portfolio for which each security is held in proportion to its total market value.

2. The market portfolio will be on the efficient frontier. Moreover, it will be the optimal risky portfolio, the tangency point of the capital allocation line (CAL) to the efficient frontier. As a result, the capital market line (CML), the line from the risk-free rate through the market portfolio, M, is also the best attainable capital allocation line. All investors hold M as their optimal risky portfolio, differing only in the amount invested in it as compared to investment in the risk-free asset.
3. The risk premium on the market portfolio will be proportional to the variance of the market portfolio and investors' typical degree of risk aversion. Mathematically,

$$E(r_M) - r_f = \overline{A}\sigma_M^2 \tag{7.1}$$

   where σ_M is the standard deviation of the return on the market portfolio and $\overline{A}$ represents the degree of risk aversion of the average investor.
4. The risk premium on individual assets will be proportional to the risk premium on the market portfolio (M) and to the *beta coefficient* of the security on the market portfolio. Beta measures the extent to which returns respond to the market portfolio. Formally, beta is the regression (slope) coefficient of the security return on the market return, representing sensitivity to fluctuations in the overall security market.

Why All Investors Would Hold the Market Portfolio

Given all our assumptions, it is easy to see why all investors hold identical risky portfolios. If all investors use mean-variance analysis (assumptions 2.A and 2.B), apply it to the same universe of securities (assumptions 1.C and 1.F) with an identical time horizon (assumption 2.A),

FIGURE 7.1

The efficient frontier and the capital market line

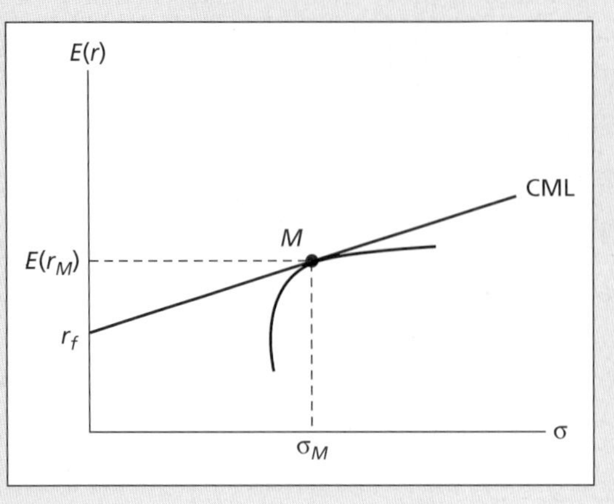

use the same security analysis (assumption 2.C), and experience identical net returns from the same securities (assumptions 1.A, 1.D, and 1.E), they all must arrive at the same determination of the optimal risky portfolio.

With everyone choosing to hold the same risky portfolio, stocks will be represented in the aggregate risky portfolio in the same proportion as they are in each investor's (common) risky portfolio. If Google represents 1% in each common risky portfolio, Google will be 1% of the aggregate risky portfolio. This in fact is the market portfolio since the market is no more than the aggregate of all individual portfolios. Because each investor uses the market portfolio for the optimal risky portfolio, the CAL in this case is called the *capital market line,* or CML, as in Figure 7.1.

Suppose the optimal portfolio of our investors does not include the stock of some company, say, Southwest Airlines. When no investor is willing to hold Southwest stock, the demand is zero, and the stock price will take a free fall. As Southwest stock gets progressively cheaper, it begins to look more attractive, while all other stocks look (relatively) less attractive. Ultimately, Southwest will reach a price at which it is desirable to include it in the optimal stock portfolio, and investors will buy.

This price adjustment process guarantees that all stocks will be included in the optimal portfolio. The only issue is the price. At a given price level, investors will be willing to buy a stock; at another price, they will not. The bottom line is this: If all investors hold an *identical* risky portfolio, this portfolio must be the *market* portfolio.

The Passive Strategy Is Efficient

The CAPM implies that a passive strategy, using the CML as the optimal CAL, is a powerful alternative to an active strategy. The market portfolio proportions are a result of profit-oriented "buy" and "sell" orders that cease only when there is no more profit to be made. And in the simple world of the CAPM, all investors use precious resources in security analysis. A passive investor who takes a free ride by simply investing in the market portfolio benefits from the efficiency of that portfolio. In fact, an active investor who chooses any other portfolio will end on a CAL that is inferior to the CML used by passive investors.

mutual fund theorem

States that all investors desire the same portfolio of risky assets and can be satisfied by a single mutual fund composed of that portfolio.

We sometimes call this result a **mutual fund theorem** because it implies that only one mutual fund of risky assets—the market index fund—is sufficient to satisfy the investment demands of all investors. The mutual fund theorem is another incarnation of the separation property discussed in Chapter 6. Assuming all investors choose to hold a market-index mutual fund, we can separate portfolio selection into two components: (1) a technical side, in which an efficient mutual fund is created by professional management; and (2) a personal side, in which an investor's risk aversion determines the allocation of the complete portfolio between the mutual fund and the risk-free asset. Here, all investors agree that the mutual fund they would like to hold is invested in the market portfolio.

While investment managers in the real world generally construct risky portfolios that differ from the market index, we attribute this to the differences in their estimates of risk and expected return (in violation of assumption 2.C). Nevertheless, a passive investor may view the market index as a reasonable first approximation to an efficient risky portfolio.

The logical inconsistency of the CAPM is this: If a passive strategy is costless *and* efficient, why would anyone follow an active strategy? But if no one does any security analysis, what brings about the efficiency of the market portfolio?

We have acknowledged from the outset that the CAPM simplifies the real world in its search for a tractable solution. Its applicability to the real world depends on whether its predictions are accurate enough. The model's use is some indication that its predictions are reasonable. We discuss this issue in Section 7.3 and in greater depth in Chapter 8.

CONCEPT check 7.1

If only some investors perform security analysis while all others hold the market portfolio (*M*), would the CML still be the efficient CAL for investors who do not engage in security analysis? Explain.

The Risk Premium of the Market Portfolio

In Chapter 5 we showed how individual investors decide how much to invest in the risky portfolio when they can include a risk-free asset in the investment budget. Returning now to the decision of how much to invest in the market portfolio *M* and how much in the risk-free asset, what can we deduce about the equilibrium risk premium of portfolio *M*?

We asserted earlier that the equilibrium risk premium of the market portfolio, $E(r_M) - r_f$, will be proportional to the degree of risk aversion of the average investor and to the risk of the market portfolio, σ_M^2. Now we can explain this result.

When investors purchase stocks, their demand drives up prices, thereby lowering expected rates of return and risk premiums. But when risk premiums fall, investors will move some of their funds from the risky market portfolio into the risk-free asset. In equilibrium, the risk premium on the market portfolio must be just high enough to induce investors to hold the available supply of stocks. If the risk premium is too high, there will be excess demand for securities, and prices will rise; if it is too low, investors will not hold enough stock to absorb the supply, and prices will fall. The *equilibrium* risk premium of the market portfolio is therefore proportional both to the risk of the market, as measured by the variance of its returns, and to the degree of risk aversion of the average investor, denoted by $\bar{A}$ in Equation 7.1.

EXAMPLE 7.1

Market Risk, the Risk Premium, and Risk Aversion

Suppose the risk-free rate is 5%, the average investor has a risk-aversion coefficient of $\bar{A} = 2$, and the standard deviation of the market portfolio is 20%. Then, from Equation 7.1, we estimate the equilibrium value of the market risk premium[1] as $2 \times .20^2 = .08$. So the expected rate of return on the market must be

$$E(r_M) = r_f + \text{Equilibrium risk premium}$$
$$= .05 + .08 = .13 = 13\%$$

If investors were more risk averse, it would take a higher risk premium to induce them to hold shares. For example, if the average degree of risk aversion were 3, the market risk premium would be $3 \times .20^2 = .12$, or 12%, and the expected return would be 17%.

CONCEPT check 7.2

Historical data for the S&P 500 Index show an average excess return over Treasury bills of about 7.5% with standard deviation of about 20%. To the extent that these averages approximate investor expectations for the sample period, what must have been the coefficient of risk aversion of the average investor? If the coefficient of risk aversion were 3.5, what risk premium would have been consistent with the market's historical standard deviation?

Expected Returns on Individual Securities

The CAPM is built on the insight that the appropriate risk premium on an asset will be determined by its contribution to the risk of investors' overall portfolios. Portfolio risk is what matters to investors, and portfolio risk is what governs the risk premiums they demand.

[1]To use Equation 7.1, we must express returns in decimal form rather than as percentages.

We know that nonsystematic risk can be reduced to an arbitrarily low level through diversification (Chapter 6); therefore, investors do not require a risk premium as compensation for bearing nonsystematic risk. They need to be compensated only for bearing systematic risk, which cannot be diversified. We know also that the contribution of a single security to the risk of a large diversified portfolio depends only on the systematic risk of the security as measured by its beta, as we saw in Section 6.5. Therefore, it should not be surprising that the risk premium of an asset is proportional to its beta; a security with double the systematic risk of another must pay twice the risk premium. Thus, the ratio of risk premium to beta should be the same for any two securities or portfolios.

If we equate the ratio of risk premium to systematic risk for the market portfolio, which has a beta of 1, to the corresponding ratio for a particular stock, for example, Dell, we find that

$$\frac{E(r_M) - r_f}{1} = \frac{E(r_D) - r_f}{\beta_D}$$

expected return (mean return)–beta relationship

Implication of the CAPM that security risk premiums (expected excess returns) will be proportional to beta.

Rearranging results in the CAPM's **expected return–beta relationship:**

$$E(r_D) = r_f + \beta_D[E(r_M) - r_f] \quad \textbf{(7.2)}$$

In words, an asset's risk premium equals the asset's systematic risk measure (its beta) times the risk premium of the (benchmark) market portfolio. This expected return (or mean return)–beta relationship is the most familiar expression of the CAPM.

The mean–beta relationship of the CAPM makes a powerful economic statement. It implies, for example, that a security with a high variance but a relatively low beta of .5 will carry one-third the risk premium of a low-variance security with a beta of 1.5. Equation 7.2 quantifies the conclusion we reached in Chapter 6: Only systematic risk matters to investors who can diversify, and systematic risk is measured by beta.

EXAMPLE 7.2

Expected Returns and Risk Premiums

Suppose the risk premium of the market portfolio is 9%, and we estimate the beta of Dell as $\beta_D = 1.3$. The risk premium predicted for the stock is therefore 1.3 times the market risk premium, or $1.3 \times 9\% = 11.7\%$. The expected rate of return on Dell is the risk-free rate plus the risk premium. For example, if the T-bill rate were 5%, the expected rate of return would be $5\% + 11.7\% = 16.7\%$ or, using Equation 7.2 directly,

$$\begin{aligned} E(r_D) &= r_f + \beta_D[\text{Market risk premium}] \\ &= 5\% + 1.3 \times 9\% = 16.7\% \end{aligned}$$

If the estimate of the beta of Dell were only 1.2, the required risk premium for Dell would fall to 10.8%. Similarly, if the market risk premium were only 8% and $\beta_D = 1.3$, Dell's risk premium would be only 10.4%.

The fact that many investors hold active portfolios that differ from the market portfolio does not necessarily invalidate the CAPM. Recall that reasonably well-diversified portfolios shed almost all firm-specific risk and are subject to only systematic risk. Even if one does not hold the precise market portfolio, a well-diversified portfolio will be so highly correlated with the market that a stock's beta relative to the market still will be a useful risk measure.

In fact, several researchers have shown that modified versions of the CAPM will hold despite differences among individuals that may cause them to hold different portfolios. A study by Brennan (1970) examines the impact of differences in investors' personal tax rates on market equilibrium. Another study by Mayers (1972) looks at the impact of nontraded assets such as human capital (earning power). Both find that while the market portfolio is no longer each investor's optimal risky portfolio, a modified version of the mean–beta relationship still holds.

If the mean–beta relationship holds for any individual asset, it must hold for any combination of assets. The beta of a portfolio is simply the weighted average of the betas of the stocks in the portfolio, using as weights the portfolio proportions. Thus, beta also predicts a portfolio's risk premium in accordance with Equation 7.2.

EXAMPLE 7.3

Portfolio Beta and Risk Premium

Consider the following portfolio:

Asset	Beta	Risk Premium	Portfolio Weight
Microsoft	1.2	9.0%	0.5
American Electric Power	0.8	6.0	0.3
Gold	0.0	0.0	0.2
Portfolio	0.84	?	1.0

If the market risk premium is 7.5%, the CAPM predicts that the risk premium on each stock is its beta times 7.5%, and the risk premium on the portfolio is .84 × 7.5% = 6.3%. This is the same result that is obtained by taking the weighted average of the risk premiums of the individual stocks. (Verify this for yourself.)

A word of caution: We often hear that a well-managed firm will provide a high rate of return. This is true when referring to the *firm's* accounting return on investments in plant and equipment. The CAPM, however, predicts returns on investments in the *securities* of the firm that trade in capital markets.

Say everyone knows a firm is well run. Its stock price will be bid up, and returns to stockholders at those high prices will not be extreme. Security *prices* reflect public information about a firm's prospects, but only the risk of the company (as measured by beta) should affect *expected returns.* In a rational market, investors receive high expected returns only if they bear systematic risk.

CONCEPT check 7.3

Suppose the risk premium on the market portfolio is estimated at 8% with a standard deviation of 22%. What is the risk premium on a portfolio invested 25% in GE with a beta of 1.15 and 75% in Dell with a beta of 1.25?

The Security Market Line

The expected return–beta relationship is a reward-risk equation. The beta of a security is the appropriate measure of its risk because beta is proportional to the variance the security contributes to the optimal risky portfolio.[2]

With approximately normal returns, we measure the risk of a portfolio by its standard deviation. Because the beta of a stock measures the stock's contribution to the standard deviation of the market portfolio, we expect the required risk premium to be a function of beta. The CAPM confirms this intuition, stating further that the security's risk premium is directly proportional to both the beta and the risk premium of the market portfolio; that is, the risk premium equals $\beta[E(r_M) - r_f]$.

The mean–beta relationship is called the **security market line (SML)** in Figure 7.2. Its slope is the risk premium of the market portfolio. At the point where $\beta = 1$ (the beta of the market portfolio), we can read off the vertical axis the expected return on the market portfolio.

security market line (SML)

Graphical representation of the expected return–beta relationship of the CAPM.

It is useful to compare the SML to the capital market line. The CML graphs the risk premiums of efficient complete portfolios (made up of the market portfolio and the risk-free asset) as a function of portfolio standard deviation. This is appropriate because standard deviation is a valid measure of risk for portfolios that are candidates for an investor's complete portfolio.

[2]The contribution of a security to portfolio variance equals the variance of the portfolio when the security is included minus the variance when the security is excluded, with the weights of all other securities increased proportionally to bring total weights to 1.

FIGURE 7.2

The security market line and a positive-alpha stock

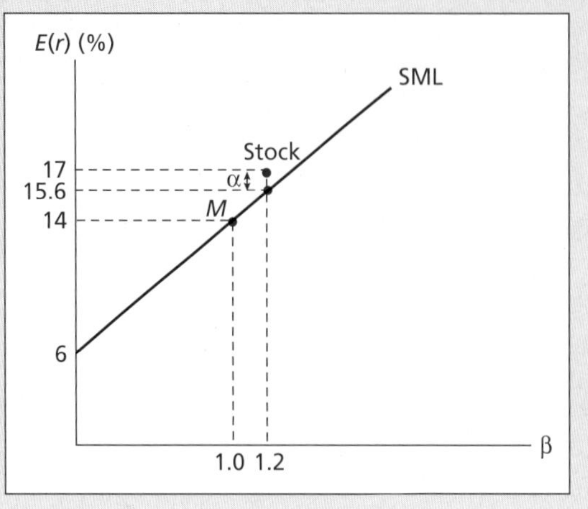

The SML, in contrast, graphs *individual-asset* risk premiums as a function of asset risk. The relevant measure of risk for an individual asset (which is held as part of a well-diversified portfolio) is not the asset standard deviation but rather the asset beta. The SML is valid both for individual assets and portfolios.

The security market line provides a benchmark for evaluation of investment performance. The SML provides the required rate of return that will compensate investors for the beta risk of that investment, as well as for the time value of money.

alpha

The abnormal rate of return on a security in excess of what would be predicted by an equilibrium model such as the CAPM.

Because the SML is the graphical representation of the mean–beta relationship, "fairly priced" assets plot exactly on the SML. The expected returns of such assets are commensurate with their risk. Whenever the CAPM holds, all securities must lie on the SML in equilibrium. Underpriced stocks plot above the SML: Given beta, their expected returns are greater than is indicated by the CAPM. Overpriced stocks plot below the SML. The difference between fair and actual expected rates of return on a stock is the **alpha,** denoted α. The expected return on a mispriced security is given by $E(r_s) = \alpha_s + r_f + \beta_s[E(r_M) - r_f]$.

EXAMPLE 7.4

The Alpha of a Security

Suppose the return on the market is expected to be 14%, a stock has a beta of 1.2, and the T-bill rate is 6%. The SML would predict an expected return on the stock of

$$E(r) = r_f + \beta[E(r_M) - r_f]$$
$$= 6 + 1.2(14 - 6) = 15.6\%$$

If one believes the stock will provide instead a return of 17%, its implied alpha would be 1.4%, as shown in Figure 7.2. If instead the expected return were only 15%, the stock alpha would be negative, −.6%.

Applications of the CAPM

One place the CAPM may be used is in the investment management industry. Suppose the SML is taken as a benchmark to assess the *fair* expected return on a risky asset. Then an analyst calculates the return she actually expects. Notice that we depart here from the simple CAPM world in that active investors apply their own analysis to derive a private "input list." If a stock is perceived to be a good buy, or underpriced, it will provide a positive alpha, that is, an expected return in excess of the fair return stipulated by the SML.

The CAPM is also useful in capital budgeting decisions. When a firm is considering a new project, the SML provides the required return demanded of the project. This is the cutoff internal rate of return (IRR) or "hurdle rate" for the project.

EXAMPLE 7.5

The CAPM and Capital Budgeting

Suppose Silverado Springs Inc. is considering a new spring-water bottling plant. The business plan forecasts an internal rate of return of 14% on the investment. Research shows the beta of similar products is 1.3. Thus, if the risk-free rate is 4%, and the market risk premium is estimated at 8%, the hurdle rate for the project should be $4 + 1.3 \times 8 = 14.4\%$. Because the IRR is less than the risk-adjusted discount or hurdle rate, the project has a negative net present value and ought to be rejected.

Yet another use of the CAPM is in utility rate-making cases. Here the issue is the rate of return a regulated utility should be allowed to earn on its investment in plant and equipment.

EXAMPLE 7.6

The CAPM and Regulation

Suppose shareholder equity invested in a utility is \$100 million, and the equity beta is .6. If the T-bill rate is 6%, and the market risk premium is 8%, then a fair annual profit will be $6 + (.6 \times 8) = 10.8\%$ of \$100 million, or \$10.8 million. Since regulators accept the CAPM, they will allow the utility to set prices at a level expected to generate these profits.

CONCEPT check 7.4

a. Stock XYZ has an expected return of 12% and $\beta = 1$. Stock ABC is expected to return 13% with a beta of 1.5. The market's expected return is 11% and $r_f = 5\%$. According to the CAPM, which stock is a better buy? What is the alpha of each stock? Plot the SML and the two stocks. Show the alphas of each on the graph.

b. The risk-free rate is 8% and the expected return on the market portfolio is 16%. A firm considers a project with an estimated beta of 1.3. What is the required rate of return on the project? If the IRR of the project is 19%, what is the project alpha?

7.2 THE CAPM AND INDEX MODELS

The CAPM has two limitations: It relies on the theoretical market portfolio, which includes *all* assets (such as real estate, foreign stocks, etc.), and it applies to *expected* as opposed to actual returns. To implement the CAPM, we cast it in the form of an *index model* and use realized, not expected, returns.

An index model replaces the theoretical all-inclusive portfolio with a market index such as the S&P 500. An important advantage of index models is that the composition and rate of return of the index is unambiguous and widely published, hence providing a clear benchmark for performance evaluation.

In contrast to an index model, the CAPM revolves around the elusive "market portfolio." However, because many assets are not traded, investors would not have full access to the market portfolio even if they could exactly identify it. Thus, the theory behind the CAPM rests on a shaky real-world foundation. But, as in all science, a theory is legitimate if it predicts real-world outcomes with sufficient accuracy. In particular, the reliance on the market portfolio shouldn't faze us if the predictions are sufficiently accurate when the index portfolio is substituted for the CAPM market portfolio.

We can start with the central prediction of the CAPM: The market portfolio is mean-variance efficient. An index model can be used to test this hypothesis by verifying that an index chosen to be representative of the full market is mean-variance efficient.

To test mean-variance efficiency of an index portfolio, we must show that the Sharpe ratio of the index is not surpassed by any other portfolio. We will examine this question in the next chapter.

The CAPM predicts relationships among *expected* returns. However, all we can observe are realized (historical) holding-period returns, which in a particular holding period seldom, if ever, match initial expectations. For example, the S&P 500 returned −39% in 2008. Could this possibly have been expected when investors could have invested in risk-free Treasury bills? In fact, this logic implies that any stock-index return less than T-bills must entail a negative departure from expectations. Since expectations must be realized on average, this means that more often than not, positive excess returns exceeded expectations.

The Index Model, Realized Returns, and the Mean-Beta Equation

To move from a model cast in expectations to a realized-return framework, we start with the single-index regression equation in realized excess returns, Equation 6.11:

$$r_{it} - r_{ft} = \alpha_i + \beta_i(r_{Mt} - r_{ft}) + e_{it} \tag{7.3}$$

On the MARKET FRONT

ALPHA BETTING

IT HAS never been easier to pay less to invest. No fewer than 136 exchange-traded funds (ETFs) were launched in the first half of 2006, more than in the whole of 2005.

For those who believe in efficient markets, this represents a triumph. ETFs are quoted securities that track a particular index, for a fee that is normally just a fraction of a percentage point. They enable investors to assemble a low-cost portfolio covering a wide range of assets from international equities, through government and corporate bonds, to commodities.

But as fast as the assets of ETFs and index-tracking mutual funds are growing, another section of the industry seems to be flourishing even faster. Watson Wyatt, a firm of actuaries, estimates that "alternative asset investment" (ranging from hedge funds through private equity to property) grew by around 20% in 2005, to $1.26 trillion. Investors who take this route pay much higher fees in the hope of better performance. One of the fastest-growing assets, funds of hedge funds, charge some of the highest fees of all.

Why are people paying up? In part, because investors have learned to distinguish between the market return, dubbed beta, and managers' outperformance, known as alpha. "Why wouldn't you buy beta and alpha separately?" asks Arno Kitts of Henderson Global Investors, a fund-management firm. "Beta is a commodity and alpha is about skill."

Clients have become convinced that no one firm can produce good performance in every asset class. That has led to a "core and satellite" model, in which part of the portfolio is invested in index trackers with the rest in the hands of specialists. But this creates its own problems. Relations with a single balanced manager are simple. It is much harder to research and monitor the performance of specialists. That has encouraged the middlemen—managers of managers (in the traditional institutional business) and funds-of-funds (in the hedge-fund world), which are usually even more expensive.

That their fees endure might suggest investors can identify outperforming fund managers in advance. However, studies suggest this is extremely hard. And even where you can spot talent, much of the extra performance may be siphoned off into higher fees. "A disproportionate amount of the benefits of alpha go to the manager, not the client," says Alan Brown at Schroders, an asset manager.

In any event, investors will probably keep pursuing alpha, even though the cheaper alternatives of ETFs and tracking funds are available. Craig Baker of Watson Wyatt says that, although above-market returns may not be available to all, clients who can identify them have a "first mover" advantage. As long as that belief exists, managers can charge high fees.

SOURCE: *The Economist,* September 14, 2006.

where r_{it} is the holding-period return (HPR) on asset i in period t and α_i and β_i are the intercept and slope of the security characteristic line that relates asset i's realized excess return to the realized excess return of the index. We denote the index return by r_M to emphasize that the index portfolio is proxying for the market. The e_{it} measures firm-specific effects during holding period t; it is the deviation in that period of security i's realized HPR from the regression line, the forecast of return based on the index's actual HPR. We set the relationship in terms of *excess* returns (over r_{ft}), consistent with the CAPM's logic of risk premiums.

To compare the index model with the CAPM predictions about expected asset returns, we take expectations in Equation 7.3. Recall that the expectation of e_{it} is zero, so in terms of expectations, Equation 7.3 becomes

$$E(r_{it}) - r_{ft} = \alpha_i + \beta_i[E(r_{Mt}) - r_{ft}] \quad \textbf{(7.4)}$$

Comparing Equation 7.4 to Equation 7.2 reveals that the CAPM predicts $\alpha_i = 0$. Thus, we have converted the CAPM prediction about unobserved expectations of security returns relative to an unobserved market portfolio into a prediction about the intercept in a regression of observed variables: realized excess returns of a security relative to those of an observed index.

Operationalizing the CAPM in the form of an index model has a drawback, however. If intercepts of regressions of returns on an index differ substantially from zero, you will not be able to tell whether it is because you chose a bad index to proxy for the market or because the theory is not useful.

In actuality, some instances of persistent, positive significant alpha values have been identified; these will be discussed in Chapter 8. Among these are (1) small versus large stocks; (2) stocks of companies that have recently announced unexpectedly good earnings; (3) stocks with high ratios of book value to market value; and (4) stocks with "momentum" that have experienced recent advances in price. In general, however, future alphas are practically impossible to predict from past values. The result is that index models are widely used to operationalize capital asset pricing theory (see the nearby box).

Estimating the Index Model

To illustrate how to estimate the index model, we will use actual data and apply the model to the stock of Google (G), in a manner similar to that followed by practitioners. Let us rewrite Equation 7.3 for Google, denoting Google's excess return as $R_G = r_G - r_f$ and denoting months using the subscript *t*.

$$R_{Gt} = \alpha_G + \beta_G R_{Mt} + e_{Gt}$$

The dependent variable in this regression equation is Google's excess return in each month, explained by the excess return on the market index in that month, R_{Mt}. The regression coefficients are intercept α_G and slope β_G.

The alpha of Google is the average of the firm-specific factors during the sample period; the zero-average surprise in each month is captured by the last term in the equation, e_{Gt}. This residual is the difference between Google's actual excess return and the excess return that would be predicted from the regression line:

$$\begin{aligned} \text{Residual} &= \text{Actual return} - \text{Predicted return for Google based on market return} \\ e_{Gt} &= R_{Gt} \qquad\qquad\quad - (\alpha_G + \beta_G R_{Mt}) \end{aligned}$$

We are interested in estimating the intercept α_G and Google's beta as measured by the slope coefficient, β_G. We estimate Google's firm-specific risk by *residual standard deviation,* which is just the standard deviation of e_{Gt}.

We conduct the analysis in three steps: Collect and process relevant data; feed the data into a statistical program (here we use Excel) to estimate the regression Equation 7.3; and use the results to answer these questions about Google's stock: (*a*) What have we learned about the behavior of Google's returns, (*b*) what required rate of return is appropriate for investments with the same risk as Google's equity, and (*c*) how might we assess the performance of a portfolio manager who invested heavily in Google stock during this period?

Collecting and processing data We start with the monthly series of Google stock prices and the S&P 500 Index, adjusted for stock splits and dividends over the period January 2006–December 2010.[3] From these series we computed monthly holding-period returns on Google and the market index.

For the same period we compiled monthly rates of return on one-month T-bills.[4] With these three series of returns we generate monthly excess return on Google's stock and the market index. Some statistics for these returns are shown in Table 7.1. Notice that the monthly variation in the T-bill return reported in Table 7.1 does not reflect risk, as investors knew the return on bills at the beginning of each month.

The period of January 2006–December 2010 includes the late stage of recovery from the mild 2001 recession, the severe recession that officially began in December 2007, as well as the first stage of the recovery that began in June 2009. Table 7.1 shows that the effect of the financial crisis was so severe that the monthly geometric average return of the market index, .107%, was less than that of T-bills, .180%. We noted in Chapter 5 that arithmetic averages exceed geometric averages, with the difference between them increasing with return volatility.[5] In

[3]Returns are available from **finance.yahoo.com.** We need to use the price series adjusted for dividends and splits in order to obtain holding-period returns (HPRs). The unadjusted price series would tell us about capital gains alone rather than total returns.

[4]We downloaded these rates from Professor Kenneth French's website: **mba.tuck.dartmouth.edu/pages/faculty/ken.french/data_library.html.**

[5]When returns are normally distributed, the relation between the arithmetic average return, r_A, and the geometric average return, r_G (expressed as decimals, not percentages), is arithmetic average = geometric average plus one-half variance of returns. This relation holds approximately when returns are not precisely normally distributed.

TABLE 7.1 Monthly return statistics: T-bills, S&P 500, and Google, January 2006–December 2010

Statistic (%)	T-bills	S&P 500	Google
Average rate of return	0.184	0.239	1.125
Average excess return	–	0.054	0.941
Standard deviation*	0.177	5.11	10.40
Geometric average	0.180	0.107	0.600
Cumulative total 5-year return	11.65	6.60	43.17
Gain Jan 2006–Oct 2007	9.04	27.45	70.42
Gain Nov 2007–May 2009	2.29	−38.87	−40.99
Gain June 2009–Dec 2010	0.10	36.83	42.36

*The rate on T-bills is known in advance, hence SD does not reflect risk.

this period, the monthly SD of the market index, 5.11%, was large enough that despite the market return's lower geometric average, its monthly arithmetic average, .239%, was greater than that of T-bills, .185%, resulting in a positive average excess return of .054% per month.

Google had a cumulative five-year return of 43.17%, a lot better than T-bills (11.65%) or the S&P 500 (6.60%). Its monthly standard deviation of 10.40%, about double that of the market, raises the question of how much of that volatility is systematic.

Google's returns over subperiods within these five years illustrate a common illusion. Observe in Table 7.1 that Google's prerecession increase between January 2006 and October 2007 was 70.42%. The subsequent financial crisis decline (November 2007–May 2009) and recovery (June 2009–December 2010) were of similar magnitudes of −40.99% and 42.36%, respectively, and you might think they should have just about canceled out. Yet the total five-year return was "only" 43.17%, around 27% less than the prerecession gain of 70.42%. Where did that 27% go? It went in the crisis: The decline and subsequent increase had a total impact on cumulative return of $(1 - .4099) \times (1 + .4236) = .8401$, resulting in a loss of about 16%. Apply that loss to the prerecession value of stock, and you obtain $.8401 \times (1 + .7042) = 1.43$, just equal to the five-year cumulative return.

Why didn't the 40.99% loss and 42.36% gain (roughly) cancel out? In general, a large gain following a large loss has a muted impact on cumulative return because it acts on a diminished investment base, while a large loss following a large gain has an amplified impact because it acts on a greater investment base. The greater the fluctuations, the greater the impact on final investment value, which is why the spread between the geometric average (which reflects cumulative return) and the arithmetic average grows with stock volatility.

Figure 7.3 Panel A shows the monthly return on the securities during the sample period. The significantly higher volatility of Google is evident, and the graph suggests that its beta is greater than 1: When the market moves, Google tends to move in the same direction, but by greater amounts.

Figure 7.3 Panel B shows the evolution of cumulative returns. It illustrates the positive index returns in the early years of the sample, the steep decline during the recession, and the significant partial recovery of losses at the end of the sample period. Whereas Google outperforms T-bills, T-bills outperform the market index over the period, highlighting the worse-than-expected realizations in the capital market.

security characteristic line (SCL)

A plot of a security's expected excess return over the risk-free rate as a function of the excess return on the market.

Estimation results We regressed Google's excess returns against those of the index using the Regression command from the Data Analysis menu of Excel.[6] The scatter diagram in Figure 7.4 shows the data points for each month as well as the regression line that best fits the data. As noted in the previous chapter, this is called the **security characteristic line (SCL),** because it describes the relevant characteristics of the stock. Figure 7.4 allows us to view the residuals, the deviation of Google's return each month from the prediction of

[6]Mac users can download a free data analysis tool kit called StatPlus from **www.AnalystSoft.com.**

FIGURE 7.3

Returns for T-bills, S&P 500 Index, and Google stock. **Panel A:** monthly returns; **Panel B:** cumulative returns.

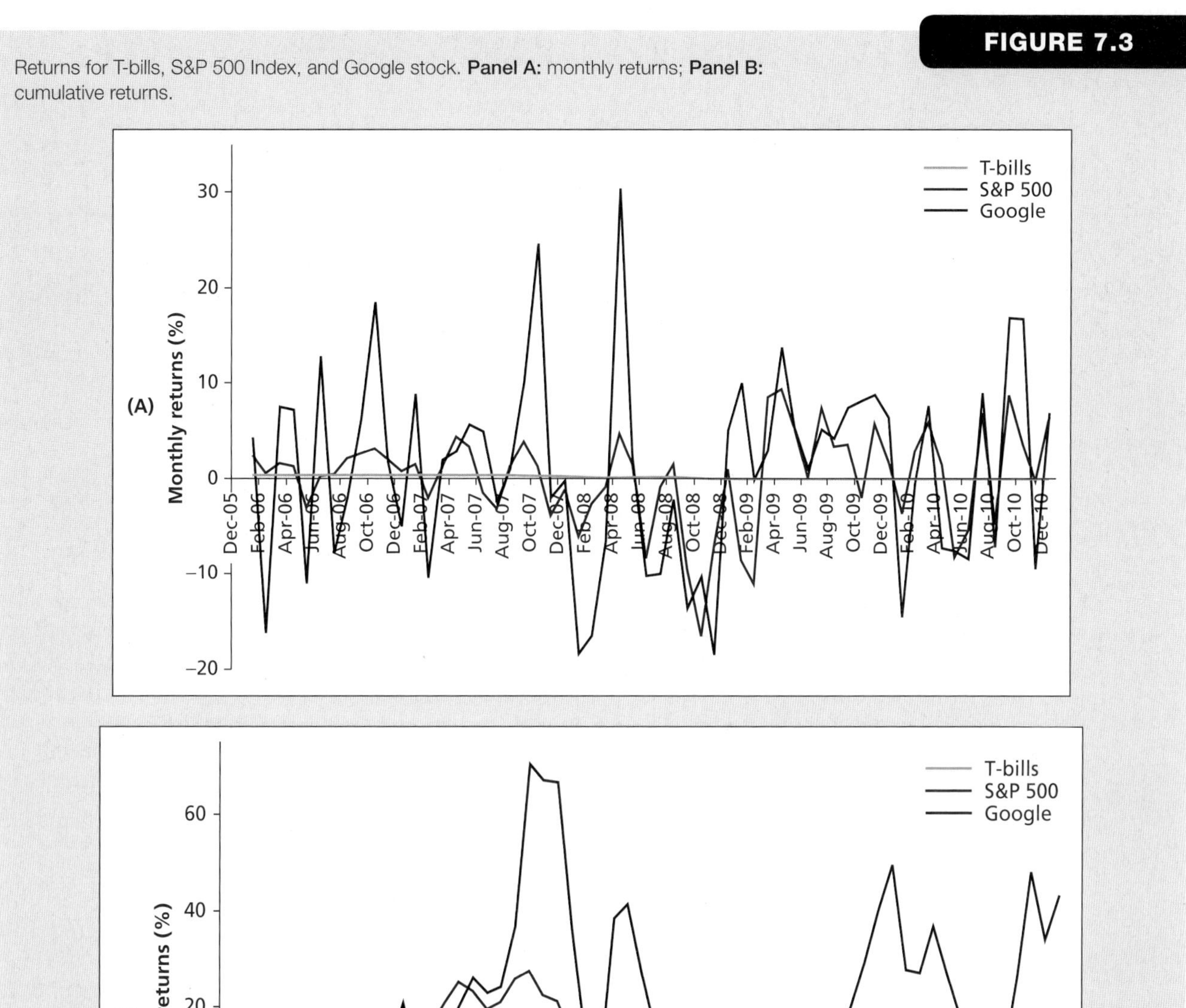

the regression equation. By construction, these residuals *average* to zero, but in any particular month, the residual may be positive or negative.

The residuals for April 2008 (23.81%) and November 2008 (−10.97%) are labeled explicitly. The April 2008 point lies above the regression line, indicating that in this month, Google's return was better than predicted from the market return. The distance between the point and the regression line is Google's firm-specific return, which is the residual for April.

The standard deviation of the residuals indicates the accuracy of predictions from the regression line. If there is a lot of firm-specific risk, there will be a wide scatter of points around the line (a high residual standard deviation), indicating that the market return will not enable a precise forecast of Google's return.

FIGURE 7.4

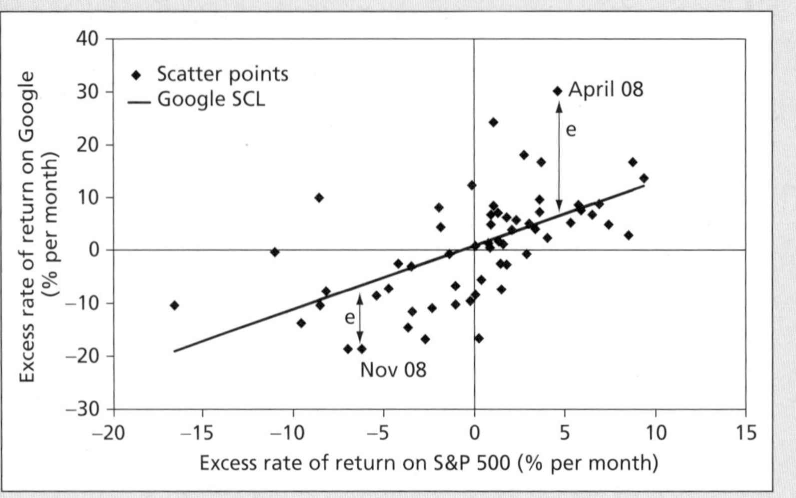

Scatter diagram and security characteristic line for Google against the S&P 500, Jan 2006–Dec 2010

Table 7.2 is the regression output from Excel. The first line shows that the correlation coefficient between the excess returns of Google and the index was .59. The more relevant statistic, however, is the *adjusted R-square* (.3497). It is the square of the correlation coefficient, adjusted downward for the number of coefficients or "degrees of freedom" used to estimate the regression line.[7] The adjusted R-square tells us that 34.97% of the variance of Google's excess returns is explained by the variation in the excess returns of the index, and hence the remainder, or 65.03%, of the variance is firm specific, or unexplained by market movements. The dominant contribution of firm-specific factors to variation in Google's returns is typical of individual stocks, reminding us why diversification can greatly reduce risk.

The standard deviation of the residuals is referred to in the output (below the adjusted R-square) as the "standard error" of the regression (8.46%). In roughly two-thirds of the months, the firm-specific component of Google's excess return was between ±8.46%. This wide spread is more evidence of Google's considerable firm-specific volatility.

The middle panel of Table 7.2, labeled "ANOVA" (for "analysis of variance"), analyzes the sources of variability in Google returns, those two sources being variation in market returns and variation due to firm-specific factors. For the most part, these statistics are not essential for our analysis. You can, however, use the total sum of squares, labeled *SS,* to find Google's variance over this period. Divide the total *SS,* or 6,381.15, by the degrees of freedom, *df,* or 59, to find that variance of excess returns was 108.16, implying a monthly standard deviation of 10.40%, as reported in Table 7.1.

Finally, the bottom panel of the table shows the estimates of the regression intercept and slope (alpha = .88% and beta = 1.20). The positive alpha means that, measured by *realized* returns, Google stock was above the security market line (SML) for this period. But the next column shows considerable imprecision in this estimate as measured by its standard error, 1.09, considerably larger than the estimate itself. The *t*-statistic (the ratio of the estimate of alpha to its standard error) is only .801, indicating low statistical significance. This is reflected in the large *p*-value in the next column, .426, which indicates the probability that an estimate of alpha this large could have resulted from pure chance even if the true alpha were zero. The last two columns give the upper and lower bounds of the 95% confidence interval around the coefficient estimate. This confidence interval tells us that, with a probability of .95, the true alpha lies in the wide interval from −1.74 to 3.49. Thus, we cannot conclude from this particular

[7]The relationship between the adjusted R-square (R_A^2) and the unadjusted (R^2) with n observations and k independent variables (plus intercept) is $1 - R_A^2 = (1 - R^2)\dfrac{n-1}{n-k-1}$, and thus a greater k will result in a larger downward adjustment to R_A^2. While R^2 cannot fall when you add an additional independent variable to a regression, R_A^2 can actually fall, indicating that the explanatory power of the added variable is not enough to compensate for the extra degree of freedom it uses. The more "parsimonious" model (without the added variable) would be considered statistically superior.

TABLE 7.2 Security characteristic line for Google (S&P 500 used as market index), January 2006–December 2010

Linear Regression

Regression Statistics	(This table produced by StatPlus patch for Mac Excel, which lacks the Data Analysis tool of Windows Excel)
R (correlation)	0.5914
R-square	0.3497
Adjusted *R*-square	0.3385
SE of regression	8.4585
Total number of observations	60

Regression equation: Google (excess return) = 0.8751 + 1.2031 * S&P 500 (excess return)

ANOVA

	df	*SS*	*MS*	*F*	*p*-level
Regression	1	2231.50	2231.50	31.19	0.0000
Residual	58	4149.65	71.55		
Total	59	6381.15			

	Coefficients	Standard Error	*t*-Statistic	*p*-value	LCL	UCL
Intercept	0.8751	1.0920	0.8013	0.4262	−1.7375	3.4877
S&P 500	1.2031	0.2154	5.5848	0.0000	0.6877	1.7185
t-Statistic (2%)	2.3924					

LCL—Lower confidence interval (95%)
UCL—Upper confidence interval (95%)

sample, with any degree of confidence, that Google's true alpha was not zero, which would be the prediction of the CAPM.

The second line in the panel gives the estimate of Google's beta, which is 1.20. The standard error of this estimate is .215, resulting in a *t*-statistic of 5.58, and a practically zero *p*-value for the hypothesis that the true beta is in fact zero. In other words, the probability of observing an estimate this large if the true beta were zero is negligible. Another important question is whether Google's beta is significantly different from the average stock beta of 1. This hypothesis can be tested by computing the *t*-statistic:

$$t = \frac{\text{Estimated value} - \text{Hypothesis value}}{\text{Standard error of estimate}} = \frac{1.2031 - 1}{.2154} = .94$$

This value is considerably below the conventional threshold for statistical significance; we cannot say with confidence that Google's beta differs from 1. The 95% confidence interval for beta ranges from .69 to 1.72.

What we learn from this regression The regression analysis reveals much about Google, but we must temper our conclusions by acknowledging that the tremendous volatility in stock market returns makes it difficult to derive strong statistical conclusions about the parameters of the index model, at least for individual stocks. With such noisy variables we must expect imprecise estimates; such is the reality of capital markets.

Despite these qualifications, we can safely say that Google is a cyclical stock, that is, its returns vary equally with or more than the overall market, as its beta is higher than the average value of 1, albeit not significantly so. Thus, we would expect Google's excess return to respond, on average, more than one-for-one with the market index. Without additional information, if we had to forecast the volatility of a portfolio that includes Google, we would use the beta estimate of 1.20 to compute the contribution of Google to portfolio variance.

Moreover, if we had to advise Google's management of the appropriate discount rate for a project that is similar in risk to its equity,[8] we would use this beta estimate in conjunction with the prevailing risk-free rate and our forecast of the expected excess return on the market index. Suppose the current T-bill rate is 2.75%, and our forecast for the market excess return is 5.5%. Then the required rate of return for an investment with the same risk as Google's equity would be

$$\begin{aligned}\text{Required rate} &= \text{Risk-free rate} + \beta \times \text{Expected excess return of index}\\ &= r_f + \beta(r_M - r_f) = 2.75 + 1.20 \times 5.5 = 9.35\%\end{aligned}$$

In light of the imprecision of both the market risk premium and Google's beta estimate, we would try to bring more information to bear on these estimates. For example, we would compute the betas of other firms in the industry, which ought to be similar to Google's, to sharpen our estimate of Google's systematic risk.

Finally, suppose we were asked to determine whether, given Google's positive alpha, a portfolio manager was correct in loading up a managed portfolio with Google stock over the period 2006–2010.

To answer this question, let's find the optimal position in Google that would have been prescribed by the Treynor-Black model of the previous chapter. Let us assume that the manager had an accurate estimate of Google's alpha and beta, as well as its residual standard deviation and correlation with the index (from Tables 7.1 and 7.2). We still need information about the manager's forecast for the index, since we know it was *not* the actual return. Suppose the manager assumed a market-index risk premium of .6%/month (near the historical average) and correctly estimated the index standard deviation of 5.11%/month. Thus, the manager's input list would have included:

Security	Risk Premium (%)	Standard Deviation (%)	Correlation
Index	0.7	5.11	
Google	0.875 + 1.203 × 0.6 = 1.60	10.40	0.59

Using Equation 6.10 we calculate for the optimized portfolio (P):

$$w_M = .3911 \quad w_G = .6089 \quad E(R_P) = 1.21\% \quad \sigma_P = 7.69\%$$

Thus, it appears the manager would have been quite right to tilt the portfolio heavily toward Google during this period. This reflects its large positive alpha over the sample period.

We can also measure the improvement in portfolio performance. Using Equation 6.8, the Sharpe ratio of the index and the optimized portfolios based on expected returns are

$$S_M = .12 \quad S_P = .16$$

So the position in Google substantially increased the Sharpe ratio.

This exercise would not be complete without the next step, where we observe the performance of the proposed "optimal" portfolio. After all, analysts commonly use available data to construct portfolios for a future period. We put *optimal* in quotes because everyone in the profession knows that past alpha values do not predict future values. Hence, a portfolio formed solely, or even primarily, by extrapolating past alpha would never qualify as optimal. However, if we treat this alpha as though it came from security analysis, we can paint a picture of what might go on in the trenches of portfolio management.

[8]A word of caution: Remember that as a general rule, equity beta is greater than asset beta, because leverage increases the exposure of equity to business risk. The required rate of return on Google's *stock* would be appropriate for an investment with the same risk as Google's *equity.* In this instance, Google has virtually no debt so this issue may be moot, but this is not generally the case.

At this writing, we have 10 additional months of returns (January 2011–October 2011) for the S&P 500, Google, and T-bills. We test the proposed portfolio for three future periods following the data collection and analysis period: the next quarter, next semiannual period, and next 10 months. For each of these periods we compare the performance of the proposed portfolio to the passive index portfolio and to T-bills. The results are as follows:

Cumulative Returns (%) of Three Alternative Strategy Portfolios

Portfolio	Proposed Google-S&P 500	Passive: S&P 500 Index	T-bills
2011 Q1	1.36	5.42	0.01
2011 First half	−7.35	5.01	0.01
January–October 2011	0.41	−0.35	0.01

We see that 2011 began as a good year for the market, with a half-year cumulative excess return of 5.01%. Up to this point, the proposed portfolio stumbled badly. Yet the next four months bring a complete reversal of fortune: The market stumbled badly, dragging its cumulative return into negative territory, while Google shined and returned the proposed "optimal" portfolio into positive territory. It is clear that evaluating performance is fraught with enormous potential estimation error. Even a nonsense portfolio can have its day when volatility is so high. This basic fact of investment life makes portfolio performance evaluation hazardous, as we discuss in Chapter 18.

Predicting Betas

A single-index model may not be fully consistent with the CAPM, which may not be a sufficiently accurate predictor of risk premiums. Still the concept of systematic versus diversifiable risk is useful. Systematic risk is approximated well by the regression equation beta and nonsystematic risk by the residual variance of the regression.

As an empirical rule, it appears that betas exhibit a statistical property called *mean reversion.* This suggests that high-β (that is, $\beta > 1$) securities tend to exhibit a lower β in the future, while low-β (that is, $\beta < 1$) securities exhibit a higher β in future periods. Researchers who desire predictions of future betas often adjust beta estimates from historical data to account for regression toward 1. For this reason, it is necessary to verify whether the estimates are already "adjusted betas."

A simple way to account for mean reversion is to forecast beta as a weighted average of the sample estimate with the value 1.

EXAMPLE 7.7

Forecast of Beta

Suppose that past data yield a beta estimate of .65. A common weighting scheme is $^2/_3$ on the sample estimate and $^1/_3$ on the value 1. Thus, the adjusted forecast of beta will be

$$\text{Adjusted beta} = {}^2/_3 \times .65 + {}^1/_3 \times 1 = .77$$

The final forecast of beta is in fact closer to 1 than the sample estimate.

A more sophisticated technique would base the weight of the sample beta on its statistical quality. A more precise estimate of beta will get a higher weight.

However, obtaining a precise statistical estimate of beta from past data on individual stocks is a formidable task, because the volatility of rates of return is so large. In particular, there is a lot of "noise" in the data due to firm-specific events. The problem is less severe with diversified portfolios because diversification reduces firm-specific variance.

One might hope that more precise estimates of beta could be obtained by using a long time series of returns. Unfortunately, this is not a solution because betas change over time[9] and old data can provide a misleading guide to current betas.

Two methods can help improve forecasts of beta. The first is an application of a technique that goes by the name of ARCH models. ARCH models better predict variance and covariance using high-frequency (daily) historical data to identify persistent changes in variance and covariance. The second method involves an additional step where beta estimates from time series regressions are augmented by other information about the firm, for example, P/E ratios.

7.3 THE CAPM AND THE REAL WORLD

In limited ways, portfolio theory and the CAPM have become accepted tools in the practitioner community. Many investment professionals think about the distinction between firm-specific and systematic risk and are comfortable with the use of beta to measure systematic risk. Still, the nuances of the CAPM are not nearly as well established in the community. For instance, compensation of portfolio managers is not based on appropriate risk-adjusted performance (see Chapter 18). What can we make of this?

New ways of thinking about the world (that is, new models or theories) displace old ones when the old models become either intolerably inconsistent with data or when the new model is demonstrably more consistent with available data. When Copernicus overthrew the age-old belief that stars orbit about the sun in circular motions, it took many years before navigators replaced old astronomical tables with superior ones based on his theory. The old tools fit the data with sufficient precision. To some extent, the slowness with which modern portfolio theory has permeated daily practice in the money management industry also has to do with its precision in fitting data and explaining variation in rates of return across assets. Let's review some of the evidence on this score.

The CAPM was first published by Sharpe in the *Journal of Finance* (the journal of the American Finance Association) in 1964 and took the world of finance by storm. Early tests by Black, Jensen, and Scholes (1972) and Fama and MacBeth (1973) were only partially supportive of the CAPM: Average returns were higher for higher-beta portfolios, but the reward for beta risk was less than predicted by the simple version of the CAPM.

While this sort of evidence against the CAPM remained largely within the ivory towers of academia, Roll's (1977) paper "A Critique of Capital Asset Pricing Tests" shook the practitioner world as well. Roll argued that since the true market portfolio can never be observed, the CAPM is *necessarily* untestable.

The publicity given the now classic "Roll's critique" resulted in popular articles such as "Is Beta Dead?" that effectively slowed the permeation of portfolio theory through the world of finance.[10] Although Roll is absolutely correct on theoretical grounds, some tests suggest that the error introduced by using a broad market index as proxy for the true, unobserved market portfolio is perhaps not the greatest problem involved in testing the CAPM.

Fama and French (1992) published a study that dealt the CAPM an even harsher blow. They claimed that in contradiction to the CAPM, certain characteristics of the firm, namely, size and the ratio of market to book value, were far more useful in predicting future returns than beta.

Fama and French and several others have published many follow-up studies of this topic. We will review some of this literature later in the chapter, and the nearby box discusses controversies about the risk-return relationship that have been reinforced in the wake of the financial crisis of 2008. It seems clear from these studies that beta does not tell the whole story of risk. There seem to be risk factors that affect security returns beyond beta's one-dimensional measurement of market sensitivity. In the next section, we introduce a theory of risk premiums that explicitly allows for multiple risk factors.

[9]*ARCH* stands for "autoregressive conditional heteroskedasticity." (The model was developed by Robert F. Engle, who received the 2003 Nobel Prize in Economics.) This is a fancy way of saying that the volatility (and covariance) of stocks changes over time in ways that can be at least partially predicted from past data.

[10]A. Wallace, "Is Beta Dead?" *Institutional Investor* 14 (July 1980), pp. 22–30.

TAKING STOCK

Since the stock market bubble of the late 1990s burst, investors have had ample time to ponder where to put the remains of their money. Economists and analysts too have been revisiting old ideas. None has been dearer to them than the capital asset pricing model (CAPM), a formula linking movements in a single share price to those of the market as a whole. The key statistic here is "beta."

Many investors and managers have given up on beta, however. Although it is useful for working out overall correlation with the market, it tells you little about share-price performance in absolute terms. In fact, the CAPM's obituary was already being written more than a decade ago when a paper by Eugene Fama and Kenneth French showed that the shares of small companies and "value stocks" (shares with low price–earnings ratios or high ratios of book value to market value) do much better over time than their betas would predict.

Another paper, by John Campbell and Tuomo Vuolteenaho of Harvard University, tries to resuscitate beta by splitting it into two.* The authors start from first principles. In essence, the value of a company depends on two things: its expected profits and the interest rate used to discount these profits. Changes in share prices therefore stem from changes in one of these factors.

From this observation, these authors propose two types of beta: one to gauge shares' responses to changes in profits; the other to pick up the effects of changes in the interest rate. Allowing for separate cash flow versus interest rate betas helps better explain the performance of small and value companies. Shares of such companies are more sensitive than the average to news about profits, in part because they are bets on future growth. Shares with high price–earnings ratios vary more with the discount rate. In all cases, above-average returns compensate investors for above-average risks.

EQUITY'S ALLURE

Beta is a tool for comparing shares with each other. Recently, however, investors have been worried about equity as an asset class. The crash left investors asking what became of the fabled equity premium, the amount by which they can expect returns on shares to exceed those from government bonds.

History says that shareholders have a lot to be optimistic about. Over the past 100 years, investors in American shares have enjoyed a premium, relative to Treasury bonds, of around seven percentage points. Similar effects have been seen in other countries. Some studies have reached less optimistic conclusions, suggesting a premium of four or five points. But even this premium seems generous.

Many answers have been put forward to explain the premium. One is that workers cannot hedge against many risks, such as losing their jobs, which tend to hit at the same time as stock market crashes; this means that buying shares would increase the volatility of their income, so that investors require a premium to be persuaded to hold them. Another is that shares, especially in small companies, are much less liquid than government debt. It is also sometimes argued that in extreme times—in depression or war, or after bubbles—equities fare much worse than bonds, so that equity investors demand higher returns to compensate them for the risk of catastrophe.

Yes, over long periods equities have done better than bonds. But the equity "premium" is unpredictable. Searching for a consistent, God-given premium is a fool's errand.

*John Campbell and Tuomo Vuolteenaho, "Bad Beta, Good Beta," *American Economic Review* 94 (December 2004), pp. 1249–1275.

Liquidity, a different kind of risk factor, was ignored for a long time. Although first analyzed by Amihud and Mendelson as early as 1986, it is yet to be accurately measured and incorporated in portfolio management. Measuring liquidity and the premium commensurate with illiquidity is part of a larger field in financial economics, namely, market structure. We now know that trading mechanisms on stock exchanges can affect the liquidity of assets traded on these exchanges and thus significantly affect their market value.

Despite all these issues, beta is not dead. Research shows that when we use a more inclusive proxy for the market portfolio than the S&P 500 (specifically, an index that includes human capital) and allow for the fact that beta changes over time, the performance of beta in explaining security returns is considerably enhanced (Jagannathan and Wang, 1996). We know that the CAPM is not a perfect model and that ultimately it will be greatly refined. Still, the logic of the model is compelling, and more sophisticated models of security pricing all rely on the key distinction between systematic and diversifiable risk. The CAPM therefore provides a useful framework for thinking rigorously about the relationship between security risk and return. This is as much as Copernicus had when he was shown the prepublication version of his book just before he passed away.

7.4 MULTIFACTOR MODELS AND THE CAPM

The index model allows us to decompose stock variance into systematic risk and firm-specific risk that can be diversified in large portfolios. In the index model, the return on the market portfolio summarized the aggregate impact of macro factors. In reality, however, systematic risk is not due to one source but instead derives from uncertainty in many economywide factors such as business-cycle risk, interest or inflation rate risk, energy price risk, and so on. It stands to reason that a more explicit representation of systematic risk, allowing stocks to exhibit different sensitivities to its various facets, would constitute a useful refinement of the single-factor model. We can expect that models that allow for several systematic factors—**multifactor models**—can provide better descriptions of security returns.

multifactor models

Models of security returns that respond to several systematic factors.

Let's illustrate with a two-factor model. Suppose the two most important macroeconomic sources of risk are the state of the business cycle reflected in returns on a broad market index such as the S&P 500 and unanticipated changes in interest rates captured by returns on a Treasury-bond portfolio. The return on any stock will respond both to sources of macro risk and to its own firm-specific influences. Therefore, we can expand the single-index model, Equation 7.3, describing the excess rate of return on stock i in some time period t as follows:

$$R_{it} = \alpha_i + \beta_{iM} R_{Mt} + \beta_{iTB} R_{TBt} + e_{it} \tag{7.5}$$

where β_{iTB} is the sensitivity of the stock's excess return to that of the T-bond portfolio and R_{TBt} is the excess return of the T-bond portfolio in month t.

How will the security market line of the CAPM generalize once we recognize the presence of multiple sources of systematic risk? Not surprisingly, a multifactor index model gives rise to a multifactor security market line in which the risk premium is determined by the exposure to *each* systematic risk factor and by a risk premium associated with each of those factors. Such a multifactor CAPM was first presented by Merton (1973).

In a two-factor economy of Equation 7.5, the expected rate of return on a security would be the sum of three terms:

1. The risk-free rate of return.
2. The sensitivity to the market index (i.e., the market beta, β_{iM}) times the risk premium of the index, $[E(r_M) - r_f]$.
3. The sensitivity to interest rate risk (i.e., the T-bond beta, β_{iTB}) times the risk premium of the T-bond portfolio, $[E(r_{TB}) - r_f]$.

This assertion is expressed mathematically as a two-factor security market line for security i:

$$E(r_i) = r_f + \beta_{iM}[E(r_M) - r_f] + \beta_{iTB}[E(r_{TB}) - r_f] \tag{7.6}$$

Equation 7.6 is an expansion of the simple security market line. Once we generalize the single-index SML to multiple risk sources, each with its own risk premium, the insights are similar.

EXAMPLE 7.8

A Two-Factor SML

Northeast Airlines has a market beta of 1.2 and a T-bond beta of .7. Suppose the risk premium of the market index is 6%, while that of the T-bond portfolio is 3%. Then the overall risk premium on Northeast stock is the sum of the risk premiums required as compensation for each source of systematic risk.

The risk premium attributable to market risk is the stock's exposure to that risk, 1.2, multiplied by the corresponding risk premium, 6%, or 1.2 × 6% = 7.2%. Similarly, the risk premium attributable to interest rate risk is .7 × 3% = 2.1%. The total risk premium is 7.2 + 2.1 = 9.3%. Therefore, if the risk-free rate is 4%, the expected return on the portfolio should be

4.0%	Risk-free rate
+ 7.2	+Risk premium for exposure to market risk
+ 2.1	+Risk premium for exposure to interest rate risk
13.3%	Total expected return

More concisely,

$$E(r) = 4\% + 1.2 \times 6\% + .7 \times 3\% = 13.3\%$$

Suppose the risk premiums in Example 7.8 were $E(r_M) - r_f = 4\%$ and $E(r_{TB}) - r_f = 2\%$. What would be the equilibrium expected rate of return on Northeast Airlines?

CONCEPT check 7.5

The multifactor model clearly gives us a richer way to think about risk exposures and compensation for those exposures than the single-index model or the CAPM. But what are the relevant additional systematic factors?

Three methodologies have been deployed to identify systematic factors in security returns, based on theory, regression analysis, or other statistical tools. The theory-based approach specifies potential extra-market risk factors on the basis of their potential impact on lifetime consumption and bequests. Broadly speaking, these variables fall into two groups: (1) prices of items that make up a substantial part of the lifetime consumption basket of many consumers, such as health care or housing, and (2) variables that affect future investment opportunities, such as interest rates or prices of inputs to major manufacturing and service industries. Investors are expected to respond to these sources of risk to their future consumption and investment opportunities by exhibiting excess demand for securities that can hedge those risks. This demand will drive up prices and drive down expected rates of return. So correlation with these sources of risk can induce its own risk premium. Variables that are important enough to affect security prices through a risk premium in such models are called *priced risk factors.* The theory therefore predicts a multi-index model in which portfolios that track each priced risk factor augment the market index in a multifactor version of the SML.

Some factors might help to explain returns but still might not carry a risk premium. For example, securities of firms in the same industry may be highly correlated. If we were to run a regression of the returns on one such security on the returns of the market index and a portfolio of the other securities in the industry, we would expect to find a significant coefficient on the industry portfolio. However, if this industry is a small part of the broad market, the industry risk can be diversified away. Thus, although an industry coefficient measures sensitivity to the industry factor, it does not necessarily represent exposure to systematic risk and will not result in a risk premium. We say that such factors are not priced, that is, they do not carry a risk premium.

The empirical content of a model of this type depends on the actual aggregate demand for these portfolios. So far, these models have not produced a clearly superior multi-index equation, suggesting that investors are not willing to pay significant premiums to hedge against these extra-market risk factors.

The regression-based approach seeks economic variables, or portfolios tracking those variables, that can significantly improve the explanatory power of the single-index equation. So far, one of these, the Fama-French factor model, has been most successful and will be discussed next.

The statistics-based approach deploys principle components and factor analysis procedures to identify systematic factors from only the return history of a security universe. This approach identifies a set of portfolios that explain returns well *within a given sample.* But in practice, the composition of these portfolios appears to change quickly over time and tends to perform poorly when applied to out-of-sample data. Consequently, this approach has largely been abandoned.

The Fama-French Three-Factor Model

Fama and French (1996) proposed a three-factor model that has become a standard tool for empirical studies of asset returns. They add to the market-index portfolios formed on the basis of firm size and book-to-market ratio to explain average returns. These additional factors are motivated by the observations that average returns on stocks of small firms and on stocks of firms with a high ratio of book value of equity to market value of equity have historically been higher than predicted by the security market line of the CAPM. This observation suggests that size or the book-to-market (B/M) ratio may be *proxies* for exposures to sources of systematic risk not captured by the CAPM beta, and thus result in return premiums. For example, Fama and French point out that firms with high ratios of book-to-market value are more likely to be in financial distress and that small stocks may be more sensitive to changes in business conditions. Thus, these variables may capture sensitivity to macroeconomic risk factors.

TABLE 7.3 Statistics for monthly rates of return (%), January 2006–December 2010

	Excess Return*		Total Return	
Security	**Average**	**Standard Deviation**	**Geometric Average**	**Cumulative Return**
T-bill	0	0	0.18	11.65
Market index†	0.26	5.44	0.30	19.51
SMB	0.34	2.46	0.31	20.70
HML	0.01	2.97	−0.03	−2.06
Google	0.94	10.40	0.60	43.17

*Total return for SMB and HML.

†Includes all NYSE, NASDAQ, and AMEX stocks.

While the high book-to-market group includes many firms in financial distress, which depresses market value relative to book value, for the most part this group includes relatively mature firms. The latter derive a larger share of their market value from assets already in place, rather than growth opportunities. This group often is called *value stocks.* In contrast, low-B/M companies are viewed as *growth firms* whose market values derive from anticipated future cash flows, rather than from assets already in place. Considerable evidence (which we will review in the following chapter) suggests that value stocks trade at lower prices than growth stocks (or, equivalently, have offered a higher average rate of return); the differential is known as the *value premium.*

While a value premium may be appropriate compensation for risk for a firm whose high B/M ratio reflects potential financial distress, it would seem paradoxical for firms whose high B/M ratio reflects maturity and thus more predictable future cash flows. It implies that, other things equal, the required rate for growth stocks is lower than that of more mature value firms. This is a puzzle; one explanation is that mature firms with large amounts of installed capital confront higher adjustment costs in adapting to shocks in the product markets in which they operate.

How can we make the Fama-French (FF) model operational? To illustrate, we will follow the same general approach that we applied for Google earlier, but now using the more general model.

Collecting and processing data To create portfolios that track the size and B/M factors, one can sort industrial firms by size (market capitalization or market "cap") and by B/M ratio. The size premium is constructed as the difference in returns between small and large firms and is denoted by SMB ("small minus big"). Similarly, the B/M premium is calculated as the difference in returns between firms with a high versus low B/M ratio and is denoted HML ("high minus low" ratio).

Taking the difference in returns between two portfolios has an economic interpretation. The SMB return, for example, equals the return from a long position in small stocks, financed with a short position in the large stocks. Note that this is a portfolio that entails no *net* investment.[11]

Summary statistics for these portfolios in our sample period are reported in Table 7.3. We use a broad market index, the value-weighted return on all stocks traded on U.S. national exchanges (NYSE, Amex, and NASDAQ) to compute the excess return on the market portfolio.

The "returns" of the SMB and HML portfolios require careful interpretation. As noted above, these portfolios do not by themselves represent investment portfolios, as they entail

[11]Interpreting the returns on the SMB and HML portfolios is a bit subtle because both portfolios are zero net investments, and therefore one cannot compute profit per dollar invested. For example, in the SMB portfolio, for every dollar held in small capitalization stocks, there is an offsetting short position in large capitalization stocks. The "return" for this portfolio is actually the profit on the overall position per dollar invested in the small-cap firms (or equivalently, per dollar shorted in the large-cap firms).

TABLE 7.4 Regression statistics for alternative specifications:
1.A Single index with S&P 500 as market proxy
1.B Single index with broad market index (NYSE + NASDAQ + Amex)
2. Fama-French three-factor model (broad market + SMB + HML)

Monthly returns January 2006–December 2010

Estimate	Single Index Specification: S&P 500	Single Index Specification: Broad Market Index	FF 3-Factor Specification with Broad Market Index
Correlation coefficient	0.59	0.61	0.70
Adjusted R-Square	0.34	0.36	0.47
Residual SD = Regression SE (%)	8.46	8.33	7.61
Alpha = Intercept (%)	0.88 (1.09)	0.64 (1.08)	0.62 (0.99)
Market beta	1.20 (0.21)	1.16 (0.20)	1.51 (0.21)
SMB (size) beta	–	–	−0.20 (0.44)
HML (book to market) beta	–	–	−1.33 (0.37)

Note: Standard errors in parenthesis.

zero net investment. Rather, they may be interpreted as side bets on whether one type of stock will beat another (e.g., large versus small ones for SMB).

To apply the FF three-factor portfolio to Google, we need to estimate Google's beta on each factor. To do so, we generalize the regression Equation 7.3 of the single-index model and fit a multivariate regression:[12]

$$r_G - r_f = \alpha_G + \beta_M (r_M - r_f) + \beta_{HML} r_{HML} + \beta_{SMB} r_{SMB} + e_G \qquad \textbf{(7.7)}$$

To the extent that returns on the size (SMB) and book-to-market (HML) portfolios proxy for risk that is not fully captured by the market index, the beta coefficients on these portfolios represent exposure to systematic risks beyond the market-index beta.[13]

Estimation results Both the single-index model (alternatively employing the S&P 500 Index and the broad market index) and the FF three-factor model are summarized in Table 7.4. The broad market index includes more than 4,000 stocks, while the S&P 500 includes only 500 of the largest U.S. stocks, in which list Google ranked fourteenth in January 2012.[14]

In this sample, the broad market index tracks Google's returns better than the S&P 500, and the three-factor model is a better specification than the one-factor model. This is reflected in three aspects of a successful specification: a higher adjusted R-square, a lower residual SD, and a smaller value of alpha. This outcome turns out to be typical, which makes a broader market index the choice of researchers and the FF model the current first-line empirical model of security returns.[15]

[12]These data are available from Kenneth French's website: **mba.tuck.dartmouth.edu/pages/faculty/ken.french/data_library.html.**

[13]When we estimate Equation 7.7, we subtract the risk-free return from the market portfolio but not from the returns on the SMB or HML portfolios. The total rate of return on the market index represents compensation for *both* the time value of money (the risk-free rate) and investment risk. Therefore, only the excess of its return above the risk-free rate represents a premium or reward for bearing risk. In contrast, as noted in footnote 11, the SMB or HML portfolios are zero-net-investment positions. As a result, there is no compensation required for time value, only for risk, and the total "return" therefore may be interpreted as a risk premium.

[14]You may ask, "Why switch to another market index?" In Table 7.2 we were concerned with typical industry practice. When using the more sophisticated FF model, it is important to use a more representative index than the S&P 500, specifically one with greater representation of smaller and younger firms.

[15]The FF model is often augmented by an additional factor, usually *momentum,* which classifies stocks according to which ones have recently increased or recently decreased in price. Liquidity is also increasingly used as yet another additional factor.

Google's market beta estimate is very different in the three-factor model (1.51 versus 1.20 or 1.16 in one-factor models). Moreover, this coefficient value implies high cyclicality and is significantly greater than 1: It exceeds 1 by 2.43 standard errors. The SMB beta is negative (−.20), as you would expect for a firm as large as Google, yet it is not significantly different from zero (standard error = .44). Google still exhibits a negative and significant book-to-market beta (coefficient = 1.33, standard error = .37), however, indicating that it is still a growth stock.

What we learn from this regression While the FF three-factor model offers a richer and more accurate description of asset returns, applying this model requires two more forecasts of future returns, namely, for the SMB and HML portfolios. We have so far in this section been using a T-bill rate of 2.75% and a market risk premium of 5.5%. If we add to these values a forecast of 2.5% for the SMB premium and 4% for HML, the required rate for an investment with the same risk as Google's equity would be

$$E(r_G) = r_f + \beta_M[E(r_M) - r_f] + \beta_{SMB}E(r_{SMB}) + \beta_{HML}E(r_{HML})$$
$$2.75 + (1.51 \times 5.5) + (-.20 \times 2.5) + (-1.33 \times 4) = 5.24\%$$

which is considerably lower than the rate derived from cyclical considerations alone (i.e., single-beta models). Notice from this example that to obtain expected rates of return, the FF model requires, in addition to a forecast of the market-index return, a forecast of the returns of the SMB and HML portfolios, making the model more difficult to apply. This can be a critical issue. If such forecasts are difficult to devise, the single-factor model may be preferred even if it is less successful in explaining *past* returns.[16]

Another reason a multi-index model is more difficult to implement is that currently it would be difficult to hold the prescribed optimal portfolio. As of yet, there are no vehicles (index funds or ETFs) to directly invest in SMB and HML.

Passive investors would have to invest in a suitable small-stock portfolio and short a large-stock portfolio to substitute for SMB. Similarly, they would have to buy value stocks and short growth stocks to substitute for HML. This is no small feat. Even for professional managers, investing in SMB and HML would be challenging. It is no wonder that while the FF model (and its variants with even additional factors) has largely superseded the single-index CAPM for the purpose of benchmarking investment performance, the single-index model still dominates the investments industry.

Multifactor Models and the Validity of the CAPM

The single-index CAPM fails empirical tests because its empirical representation, the single-index model, inadequately explains returns on too many securities. In short, too many statistically significant values of alpha (which should be zero) show up in single-index regressions. Despite this failure, it is still widely used in the industry.

Multifactor models such as the FF model may also be tested by the prevalence of significant alpha values. The three-factor model shows a material improvement over the single-index model in that regard. But the use of multi-index models comes at a price: They require forecasts of the additional factor returns. If forecasts of those additional factors are themselves subject to forecast error, these models will be less accurate than the theoretically inferior single-index model. Nevertheless, multifactor models have a definite appeal, since it is clear that real-world risk is multifaceted.

Merton (1973) first showed that the CAPM could be extended to allow for multiple sources of systematic risk. His model results in a multifactor security market line like that of Equation 7.8 but with risk factors that relate to the extra-market sources of risk that investors

[16]This is a fairly common outcome: Theoretically inferior models with fewer explanatory variables often describe out-of-sample outcomes more accurately than models employing more explanatory variables. This reflects in part the tendency of some researchers to "data mine," that is, to search too aggressively for variables that help describe a sample but have no staying power out of sample. In addition, each explanatory variable of a model must be forecast to make a prediction, and each of those forecasts adds some uncertainty to the prediction.

wish to hedge. In this light, a reasonable correct interpretation of multivariate index models such as FF is that they constitute an application of the multifactor CAPM, rather than a rejection of the underlying logic of the simple model.

7.5 ARBITRAGE PRICING THEORY

One reason for skepticism about the validity of the CAPM is the unrealistic nature of the assumptions needed to derive it. Most unappealing are assumptions 2.A-C, namely, that all investors are identical in every way but wealth and risk aversion. For this reason, as well as for its economic insights, the arbitrage pricing theory (APT) is of great interest. To understand this theory we begin with the concept of *arbitrage*.

Arbitrage is the act of exploiting mispricing of two or more securities to achieve risk-free profits. As a trivial example, consider a security that is priced differently in two markets. A long position in the cheaper market financed by a short position in the expensive market will lead to a sure profit. As investors avidly pursue this strategy, prices are forced back into alignment, so arbitrage opportunities vanish almost as quickly as they materialize.

arbitrage
Creation of riskless profits made possible by relative mispricing among securities.

The first to apply this concept to equilibrium security returns was Ross (1976), who developed the **arbitrage pricing theory (APT).** The APT depends on the observation that well-functioning capital markets preclude arbitrage opportunities. A violation of the APT's pricing relationships will cause extremely strong pressure to restore them even if only a limited number of investors become aware of the disequilibrium. Ross's accomplishment is to derive the equilibrium rates of return that would prevail in a market where prices are aligned to eliminate arbitrage opportunities. The APT thus avoids the most objectionable assumptions of the CAPM.

arbitrage pricing theory (APT)
A theory of risk-return relationships derived from no-arbitrage considerations in large capital markets.

Well-Diversified Portfolios and Arbitrage Pricing Theory

To illustrate how the APT works, we will begin with a single-index market; generalization to multi-factor markets is straightforward. The *excess* rate of return on any security, S, is then $R_S = \alpha_S + \beta_S R_M + e_S$, using an observed benchmark M.

Suppose a portfolio, P, is believed to have a positive alpha. We can use the benchmark portfolio (with a beta of 1) to hedge away or "purge" the systematic risk of P and convert it to a zero-beta portfolio. We can go even further and turn the positive-alpha, zero-beta portfolio into a zero-net-investment position by adding an appropriate position in the risk-free asset. In all, we combine the positive-alpha P with both the benchmark and T-bills to create a costless, zero-beta portfolio, A, with a positive alpha. Table 7.5 shows how.

Table 7.5 shows that portfolio A with excess return $\alpha_P + e_P$ is still risky as long as the residual variance, σ_e^2, is positive. This shows that a zero-investment, zero-beta, positive-alpha portfolio is not necessarily an arbitrage opportunity; true arbitrage implies no risk. However, if P were highly diversified, its residual risk would be small. A portfolio with practically negligible residual risk is called a **well-diversified portfolio.** The difference in the scatter diagrams of any asset versus that of a well-diversified portfolio with the same beta is shown in Figure 7.5.

well-diversified portfolio
A portfolio sufficiently diversified that nonsystematic risk is negligible.

TABLE 7.5 Steps to convert a well-diversified portfolio into an arbitrage portfolio

Portfolio Weight*	In Asset	Contribution to Excess Return
$w_P = 1$	Portfolio P	$w_P(\alpha_P + \beta_P R_M + e_P) = \alpha_P + \beta_P R_M + e_P$
$w_M = -\beta_P$	Benchmark	$w_M R_M = -\beta_P R_M$
$w_f = \beta_P - 1$	Risk-free asset	$w_f \cdot 0 = 0$
$\Sigma w = 0$	Portfolio A	$\alpha_P + e_P$

*When alpha is negative, you would reverse the signs of each portfolio weight to achieve a portfolio A with positive alpha and no net investment.

FIGURE 7.5 Security characteristic lines

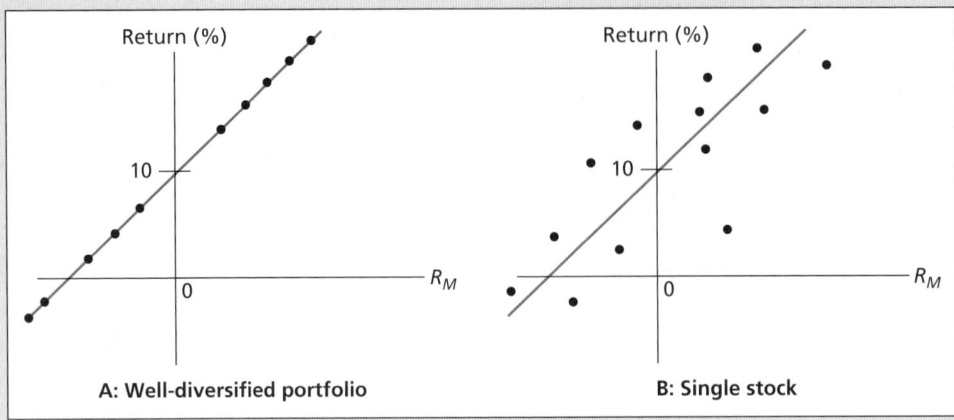

arbitrage portfolio

A zero-net-investment, risk-free portfolio with a positive return.

Portfolio A, when constructed from a *well-diversified portfolio*, is an **arbitrage portfolio.** An arbitrage portfolio is a money machine: It can generate risk-free profits with zero net investment. Therefore, investors who succeed in constructing one will scale it up as much as they can, financing with as much leverage and/or as many short positions as available.

EXAMPLE 7.9

Constructing an Arbitrage Portfolio

Suppose the benchmark, M, is the observed, broad market index that includes over 4,000 stocks (NYSE + NASDAQ + Amex). Imagine that on December 31, 2005, a portfolio manager possessed the following five-year predictions based on security and macro analyses:

1. The cumulative risk-free rate from rolling over T-bills over the next five years is estimated at 11.5%, an annual rate of 2.2%.
2. The cumulative return on the benchmark is estimated at 20%, an annual rate of 3.71%.
3. The S&P 500, which we will treat as portfolio P, is composed of large-capitalization stocks and is believed to be *overpriced.* Its expected cumulative return is forecast at 12%, an annual rate of 2.29%.
4. The S&P 500 beta against the benchmark is estimated at .95, which leads to the following calculation for its alpha: $2.29\% = 2.2\% + \alpha + .95(3.71 - 2.2)$; $\alpha = -1.34\%$ per year.

Because alpha is negative, we reverse the weights in Table 7.5 and set $w_P = -1$, $w_M = .95$, $w_f = .05$. The alpha on A is then positive: $\alpha_A = 1.34\%$.

Example 7.9 shows how to construct an arbitrage portfolio from a mispriced well-diversified portfolio. But it leaves us with an important question: While the S&P 500 is highly diversified, is even this index sufficiently diversified to make A a risk-free arbitrage portfolio? Table 7.6 shows the weight of the 10 largest stocks in the S&P 500. While these firms are only 2% of the firms in the index, they account for almost 20% of the market capitalization, and their weights in the index are far from negligible.

TABLE 7.6 Ten largest capitalization stocks in the S&P 500 portfolio and their weights (Dec. 31, 2009)

ExxonMobil	3.26	IBM	1.73
Microsoft	2.37	AT&T	1.67
Apple	1.91	JPMorgan Chase	1.65
Johnson & Johnson	1.79	GE	1.62
Procter & Gamble	1.78	Chevron	1.56
Total for 10 largest firms			19.34

TABLE 7.7 Regression statistics of the S&P 500 portfolio on the benchmark portfolio, January 2006–December 2010

Linear Regression

Regression Statistics				
R	0.9933			
R-square	0.9866			
Adjusted *R*-square	0.9864	Annualized		
Regression SE	0.5968	2.067		
Total number of observations	60			

S&P 500 = −0.1909 + 0.9337* Benchmark

	Coefficients	Standard Error	*t*-stat	*p*-level
Intercept	−0.1909	0.0771	−2.4752	0.0163
Benchmark	0.9337	0.0143	65.3434	0.0000

TABLE 7.8 Annual standard deviation of the real, inflation, and nominal rates

Period	Real Rate	Inflation Rate	Nominal Rate
1/1/2006–12/31/2010	1.46	1.46	0.61
1/1/1996–12/31/2000	0.57	0.54	0.17
1/1/1986–12/31/1990	0.86	0.83	0.37

With hindsight, we can estimate the residual risk of the S&P 500 from a regression of its monthly returns against the benchmark over the prediction period (January 1, 2006, to December 31, 2010). The essential regression output is displayed in Table 7.7. Notice that both alpha (−.19% per month or −2.27% per year) and beta (.93) are close to the 2005 prediction of 2.33% and .95. Most important is the (annualized) standard deviation of the regression residuals, called the *standard error of the regression,* which was 2.07%. Is this residual SD small enough for us to deem the S&P 500 "well-diversified"?

To answer the question, we recognize that investors who consider a zero-investment arbitrage portfolio must in any event invest their existing wealth *somewhere.* The risk of their alternative portfolio is therefore relevant to the discussion. Obviously, the lowest-risk investment would be to roll over T-bills. A measure of the risk of this strategy is the uncertainty of its real rate of return over the prediction period.[17] Table 7.8 suggests that the annual SD of the real rate from rolling over bills is in the range of .5%–1.5% per year depending on the sample period.

Our question then comes down to this: What would be the marginal increase in risk from adding an arbitrage portfolio with an SD of about 2% per year to a portfolio with an SD of .5%–1.5% per year? Since the two rates are uncorrelated, the variance of the portfolio will be the sum of the variances. The SD of this complete portfolio minus the SD of the T-bill portfolio is the *marginal* risk of the S&P 500 in its use as an arbitrage portfolio. The following table shows some examples of the marginal risk of the arbitrage portfolio, first treating T-bills as the initial portfolio to which the arbitrage portfolio is added (with three assumptions for the SD of its real return) and then treating the benchmark risky portfolio as the initial position, with an assumed SD = 20%.

[17]Obviously, five-year TIPS would carry a practically zero risk to the real rate. But we deal here with active portfolio managers who continuously rebalance their portfolios and must maintain considerable liquidity. For very short holding periods, TIPS would not be practical for these investors.

SD of Real Rate on Initial Portfolio	SD of Total Portfolio	Marginal Risk
0.5% (T-bills)	$(.005^2 + .0207^2)^{1/2} = 2.13\%$	1.63%
1.0 (T-bills)	2.30	1.30
1.5 (T-bills)	2.56	1.06
20.0 (benchmark)	20.11	0.11

There is no widely accepted threshold for the acceptable marginal risk of an arbitrage portfolio in a practical application. Nevertheless, the marginal risk in the first three lines of the table, which is just about the same as the SD of the real rate on bills, may well be above the appropriate threshold. Moreover, an alpha of 2% per year in this example is not even decisively statistically significant. We learn from this exercise that well-diversified portfolios are not easy to construct, and arbitrage opportunities are likely few and far between. On the other hand, when the arbitrage portfolio is added to the risky benchmark portfolio, the marginal increase in overall standard deviation is minimal.

We are now ready to derive the APT. Our argument follows from Example 7.9. Investors, however few, will invest large amounts in any arbitrage portfolio they can identify. This will entail large-scale purchases of positive-alpha portfolios or large-scale shorting of negative-alpha portfolios. These actions will move the prices of component securities until alpha disappears. In the end, when alphas of all well-diversified portfolios are driven to zero, their return equations become

$$r_P = r_f + \beta_P(r_M - r_f) + e_P \tag{7.8}$$

Taking the expectations in Equation 7.8 results in the familiar CAPM mean–beta equation:

$$E(r_P) = r_f + \beta_P[E(r_M) - r_f] \tag{7.9}$$

For portfolios such as the S&P 500 that shed *most* residual risk, we can still expect buying and selling pressure to drive their alpha close to zero. If alphas of portfolios with very small residual risk are near zero, then even less diversified portfolios will tend to have small alpha values. Thus, the APT implies a hierarchy of certainty about alphas of portfolios, based on the degree of diversification.

The APT and the CAPM

Why did we need so many restrictive assumptions to derive the CAPM when the APT seems to arrive at the expected return–beta relationship with seemingly fewer and less objectionable assumptions? The answer is simple: Strictly speaking, the APT applies only to well-diversified portfolios. Absence of riskless arbitrage alone cannot guarantee that, in equilibrium, the expected return–beta relationship will hold for any and all assets.

With additional effort, however, one can use the APT to show that the relationship must hold approximately even for individual assets. The essence of the proof is that if the expected return–beta relationship were violated by many individual securities, it would be virtually impossible for all well-diversified portfolios to satisfy the relationship. So the relationship must *almost* surely hold true for individual securities.

We say "almost" because, according to the APT, there is no guarantee that all individual assets will lie on the SML. If only a few securities violated the SML, their effect on well-diversified portfolios could conceivably be negligible. In this sense, it is possible that the SML relationship is violated for some securities. If many securities violate the expected return–beta relationship, however, the relationship will no longer hold for well-diversified portfolios comprising these securities, and arbitrage opportunities will be available.

The APT serves many of the same functions as the CAPM. It gives us a benchmark for fair rates of return that can be used for capital budgeting, security valuation, or performance evaluation of managed portfolios. Moreover, the APT highlights the crucial distinction between nondiversifiable risk (systematic or factor risk) that requires a reward in the form of a risk premium and diversifiable risk that does not.

The bottom line is that neither of these theories dominates the other. The APT is more general in that it gets us to the expected return–beta relationship without requiring many of the unrealistic assumptions of the CAPM, particularly the reliance on the market portfolio. The latter improves the prospects for testing the APT. But the CAPM is more general in that it applies to all assets without reservation. The good news is that both theories agree on the expected return–beta relationship.

It is worth noting that because past tests of the mean–beta relationship examined the rates of return on highly diversified portfolios, they actually came closer to testing the APT than the CAPM. Thus, it appears that econometric concerns, too, favor the APT.

Multifactor Generalization of the APT and CAPM

So far, we've examined the APT in a one-factor world. In reality, there are several sources of systematic risk such as uncertainty in the business cycle, interest rates, energy prices, and so on. Presumably, exposure to any of these factors will affect a stock's appropriate expected return. We can use a multifactor version of the APT to accommodate these multiple sources of risk.

Expanding the single-factor model of Equation 7.8 to a two-factor model:

$$R_i = \alpha_i + \beta_{i1} R_{M1} + \beta_{i2} R_{M2} + e_i \tag{7.10}$$

where R_{M1} and R_{M2} are the excess returns on portfolios that represent the two systematic factors. Factor 1 might be, for example, unanticipated changes in industrial production, while factor 2 might represent unanticipated changes in short-term interest rates. We assume again that there are many securities available with any combination of betas. This implies that we can form well-diversified **factor portfolios** with a beta of 1 on one factor and zero on all others. Thus, a factor portfolio with a beta of 1 on the first factor will have a rate of return of R_{M1}; a factor portfolio with a beta of 1 on the second factor will have a rate of return of R_{M2}; and so on. Factor portfolios can serve as the benchmark portfolios for a multifactor generalization of the security market line relationship.

factor portfolio

A well-diversified portfolio constructed to have a beta of 1 on one factor and a beta of zero on any other factor.

EXAMPLE 7.10

Multifactor SML

Suppose the two-factor portfolios, here called portfolios 1 and 2, have expected returns $E(r_1) = 10\%$ and $E(r_2) = 12\%$. Suppose further that the risk-free rate is 4%. The risk premium on the first factor portfolio is therefore 6%, while that on the second factor portfolio is 8%.

Now consider an arbitrary well-diversified portfolio (P), with beta on the first factor, $\beta_{P1} = .5$, and on the second factor, $\beta_{P2} = .75$. The multifactor APT states that the portfolio risk premium must equal the sum of the risk premiums required as compensation to investors for each source of systematic risk. The risk premium attributable to risk factor 1 is the portfolio's exposure to factor 1, β_{P1}, times the risk premium earned on the first factor portfolio, $E(r_1) - r_f$. Therefore, the portion of portfolio P's risk premium that is compensation for its exposure to the first risk factor is $\beta_{P1}[E(r_1) - r_f] = .5(10\% - 4\%) = 3\%$, while the risk premium attributable to risk factor 2 is $\beta_{P2}[E(r_2) - r_f] = .75(12\% - 4\%) = 6\%$. The total risk premium on the portfolio, therefore, should be $3 + 6 = 9\%$, and the total return on the portfolio should be 13%.

4%	Risk-free rate
+ 3%	Risk premium for exposure to factor 1
+ 6%	Risk premium for exposure to factor 2
13%	Total expected return

EXCEL APPLICATIONS

Estimating the Index Model

Please visit us at www.mhhe.com/bkm

The spreadsheet below contains monthly returns for a small sample of stocks. A related workbook (also available at **www.mhhe.com/bkm**) contains spreadsheets that show raw returns, risk premiums, and beta coefficients for the stocks in the Dow Jones Industrial Average. The security characteristic lines are estimated with five years of monthly returns.

	A	B	C	D	E	F
1				Rates of Return		
2	**Month**	**Ford**	**Honda**	**Toyota**	**S&P 500**	**T-bills**
3						
4	Dec-08	-18.34	23.02	-2.95	-8.31	0.09
5	Nov-08	-14.87	-25.44	3.71	0.97	0.02
6	Oct-08	22.83	-26.04	-17.07	-7.04	0.08
7	Sep-08	-57.88	-13.77	-11.32	-16.67	0.15
8	Aug-08	16.59	-29.61	-4.23	-9.54	0.12
9	Jul-08	-7.08	-4.92	4.11	1.40	0.15
10	Jun-08	-0.21	-11.01	-8.46	-1.07	0.17

Excel Questions

1. What were the betas of Ford, Toyota, and Honda?
2. In light of each firm's exposure to the financial crisis in 2008-2009, does the value for Ford compared to Honda and Toyota make sense to you?

Suppose portfolio P of Example 7.10 actually has an expected excess return of 11% and therefore a positive alpha of 2%. We can generalize the methodology of Table 7.5 to construct an arbitrage portfolio for this two-factor problem. Table 7.9 shows how. Because P is well diversified, e_P must be small, and the excess return on the zero-investment, zero-beta portfolio A is just $\alpha_P = 2\%$.

Here, too, extensive trade by arbitrageurs will eliminate completely alphas of well-diversified portfolios. We conclude that, in general, the APT hierarchy of possible alpha values, declining with the extent of portfolio diversification, applies to any multifactor market. In the absence of private information from security and macro analyses, investors and corporate officers must use the multifactor SML equation (with zero alpha) to determine the expected rates on securities and the required rates of return on the firm's projects.

CONCEPT check 7.6

Using the factor portfolios of Example 7.10, find the fair rate of return on a security with $\beta_1 = .2$ and $\beta_2 = 1.4$.

TABLE 7.9 Constructing an arbitrage portfolio with two systematic factors

Portfolio Weight	In Asset	Contribution to Excess Return
1	Portfolio P	$\alpha_P + \beta_{P1}R_1 + \beta_{P2}R_2 + e_P = 11\% + e_P$
$-\beta_{P1} = -0.5$	Factor portfolio 1	$\beta_{P1}R_1 = -.5 \times 6\% = -3\%$
$-\beta_{P2} = -0.75$	Factor portfolio 2	$\beta_{P2}R_2 = -.75 \times 8\% = -6\%$
$\beta_{P1} + \beta_{P1} - 1 = 0.25$	Risk-free asset	0
Total = 1	Portfolio A	$\alpha_P + e_P = 2\% + e_P$

SUMMARY

- The CAPM assumes investors are rational, single-period planners who agree on a common input list from security analysis and seek mean-variance optimal portfolios.
- The CAPM assumes ideal security markets in the sense that (*a*) markets are large and investors are price takers, (*b*) there are no taxes or transaction costs, (*c*) all risky assets are publicly traded, and (*d*) any amount can be borrowed and lent at a fixed, risk-free rate. These assumptions mean that all investors will hold identical risky portfolios. The CAPM implies that, in equilibrium, the market portfolio is the unique mean-variance efficient tangency portfolio, which indicates that a passive strategy is efficient.
- The market portfolio is a value-weighted portfolio. Each security is held in a proportion equal to its market value divided by the total market value of all securities. The risk premium on the market portfolio is proportional to its variance, σ_M^2, and to the risk aversion of the average investor.
- The CAPM implies that the risk premium on any individual asset or portfolio is the product of the risk premium of the market portfolio and the asset's beta. The security market line shows the return demanded by investors as a function of the beta of their investment. This expected return is a benchmark for evaluating investment performance.
- In a single-index security market, once an index is specified, a security beta can be estimated from a regression of the security's excess return on the index's excess return. This regression line is called the security characteristic line (SCL). The intercept of the SCL, called alpha, represents the average excess return on the security when the index excess return is zero. The CAPM implies that alphas should be zero.
- The CAPM and the security market line can be used to establish benchmarks for evaluation of investment performance or to determine appropriate discount rates for capital budgeting applications. They are also used in regulatory proceedings concerning the "fair" rate of return for regulated industries.
- The CAPM is usually implemented as a single-factor model, with all systematic risk summarized by the return on a broad market index. However, multifactor generalizations of the basic model may be specified to accommodate multiple sources of systematic risk. In such multifactor extensions of the CAPM, the risk premium of any security is determined by its sensitivity to each systematic risk factor as well as the risk premium associated with that source of risk.
- There are two general approaches to finding extra-market systematic risk factors. One is characteristics-based and looks for factors that are empirically associated with high average returns and so may be proxies for relevant measures of systematic risk. The other focuses on factors that are plausibly important sources of risk to wide segments of investors and may thus command risk premiums.
- An arbitrage opportunity arises when the disparity between two or more security prices enables investors to construct a zero net investment portfolio that will yield a sure profit. The presence of arbitrage opportunities and the resulting volume of trades will create pressure on security prices that will persist until prices reach levels that preclude arbitrage. Only a few investors need to become aware of arbitrage opportunities to trigger this process because of the large volume of trades in which they will engage.
- When securities are priced so that there are no arbitrage opportunities, the market satisfies the no-arbitrage condition. Price relationships that satisfy the no-arbitrage condition are important because we expect them to hold in real-world markets.
- Portfolios are called *well diversified* if they include a large number of securities in such proportions that the residual or diversifiable risk of the portfolio is negligible.
- In a single-factor security market, all well-diversified portfolios must satisfy the expected return–beta relationship of the SML in order to satisfy the no-arbitrage condition. If all well-diversified portfolios satisfy the expected return–beta relationship, then all but a small number of securities also must satisfy this relationship.
- The APT implies the same expected return–beta relationship as the CAPM yet does not require that all investors be mean-variance optimizers. The price of this generality is that the APT does not guarantee this relationship for all securities at all times.
- A multifactor APT generalizes the single-factor model to accommodate several sources of systematic risk.

www.mhhe.com/bkm

KEY TERMS

alpha, 200
arbitrage, 217
arbitrage portfolio, 218
arbitrage pricing theory (APT), 217
capital asset pricing model (CAPM), 194
expected return–beta relationship, 198
factor portfolio, 221
market portfolio (*M*), 195
multifactor models, 212
mutual fund theorem, 196
security characteristic line (SCL), 204
security market line (SML), 199
well-diversified portfolio, 217

KEY FORMULAS

CAPM: Market portfolio risk premium is proportional to average risk aversion and market risk:

$$E(r_M) - r_f = \bar{A}\sigma_M^2$$

SML: Expected return as a function of systematic risk:

$$E(r_i) = r_f + \beta_i[E(r_M) - r_f]$$

The index model in realized returns:

$$r_{it} - r_{ft} = \alpha_i + \beta_i(r_{Mt} - r_{ft}) + e_{it}$$

The two-index model in realized excess returns:

$$R_{it} = \alpha_i + \beta_{iM}R_{Mt} + \beta_{iTB}R_{TBt} + e_{it}$$

The two-factor SML (where TB is the second factor):

$$E(r_i) = r_f + \beta_{iM}[E(r_M) - r_f] + \beta_{iTB}[E(r_{TB}) - r_f]$$

The Fama-French three-factor model in realized returns:

$$r_i - r_f = \alpha_i + \beta_M(r_M - r_f) + \beta_{HML}r_{HML} + \beta_{SMB}r_{SMB} + e_i$$

Instructions to construct arbitrage portfolios for single- and two-factor markets are shown in Tables 7.5 and 7.9.

PROBLEM SETS

Select problems are available in McGraw-Hill's *Connect Finance.* Please see the Supplements section of the book's frontmatter for more information.

Basic

1. Suppose investors believe that the standard deviation of the market-index portfolio has increased by 50%. What does the CAPM imply about the effect of this change on the required rate of return on Google's investment projects? ***(LO 7-1)***
2. Consider the statement: "If we can identify a portfolio that beats the S&P 500 Index portfolio, then we should reject the single-index CAPM." Do you agree or disagree? Explain. ***(LO 7-1)***
3. Are the following true or false? Explain. ***(LO 7-5)***
   a. Stocks with a beta of zero offer an expected rate of return of zero.
   b. The CAPM implies that investors require a higher return to hold highly volatile securities.
   c. You can construct a portfolio with beta of .75 by investing .75 of the investment budget in T-bills and the remainder in the market portfolio.

4. Here are data on two companies. The T-bill rate is 4% and the market risk premium is 6%.

Company	$1 Discount Store	Everything $5
Forecast return	12%	11%
Standard deviation of returns	8%	10%
Beta	1.5	1.0

What would be the fair return for each company, according to the capital asset pricing model (CAPM)? **(LO 7-1)**

5. Characterize each company in the previous problem as underpriced, overpriced, or properly priced. **(LO 7-2)**

6. What is the expected rate of return for a stock that has a beta of 1 if the expected return on the market is 15%? **(LO 7-2)**
   a. 15%.
   b. More than 15%.
   c. Cannot be determined without the risk-free rate.

7. Kaskin, Inc., stock has a beta of 1.2 and Quinn, Inc., stock has a beta of .6. Which of the following statements is *most* accurate? **(LO 7-1)**
   a. The expected rate of return will be higher for the stock of Kaskin, Inc., than that of Quinn, Inc.
   b. The stock of Kaskin, Inc., has more total risk than Quinn, Inc.
   c. The stock of Quinn, Inc., has more systematic risk than that of Kaskin, Inc.
8. Which of the following statements is *true?* Explain. **(LO 7-1)**
   a. It is possible that the APT is valid and the CAPM is not.
   b. It is possible that the CAPM is valid and the APT is not.

Intermediate

9. What must be the beta of a portfolio with $E(r_P) = 20\%$, if $r_f = 5\%$ and $E(r_M) = 15\%$? **(LO 7-2)**
10. The market price of a security is $40. Its expected rate of return is 13%. The risk-free rate is 7%, and the market risk premium is 8%. What will the market price of the security be if its beta doubles (and all other variables remain unchanged)? Assume the stock is expected to pay a constant dividend in perpetuity. **(LO 7-2)**
11. You are a consultant to a large manufacturing corporation considering a project with the following net after-tax cash flows (in millions of dollars):

Years from Now	After-Tax CF
0	−20
1–9	10
10	20

The project's beta is 1.7. Assuming $r_f = 9\%$ and $E(r_M) = 19\%$, what is the net present value of the project? What is the highest possible beta estimate for the project before its NPV becomes negative? **(LO 7-2)**

12. Consider the following table, which gives a security analyst's expected return on two stocks for two particular market returns: **(LO 7-2)**

Market Return	Aggressive Stock	Defensive Stock
5%	2%	3.5%
20	32	14

   a. What are the betas of the two stocks?
   b. What is the expected rate of return on each stock if the market return is equally likely to be 5% or 20%?
   c. If the T-bill rate is 8%, and the market return is equally likely to be 5% or 20%, draw the SML for this economy.
   d. Plot the two securities on the SML graph. What are the alphas of each?
   e. What hurdle rate should be used by the management of the aggressive firm for a project with the risk characteristics of the defensive firm's stock?

If the simple CAPM is valid, which of the situations in Problems 13–19 below are possible? Explain. Consider each situation independently.

13.

Portfolio	Expected Return	Beta
A	20%	1.4
B	25	1.2

(LO 7-1)

14.

Portfolio	Expected Return	Standard Deviation
A	30%	35%
B	40	25

(LO 7-1)

15.

Portfolio	Expected Return	Standard Deviation
Risk-free	10%	0%
Market	18	24
A	16	12

(LO 7-1)

16.

Portfolio	Expected Return	Standard Deviation
Risk-free	10%	0%
Market	18	24
A	20	22

(LO 7-1)

17.

Portfolio	Expected Return	Beta
Risk-free	10%	0
Market	18	1.0
A	16	1.5

(LO 7-1)

18.

Portfolio	Expected Return	Beta
Risk-free	10%	0
Market	18	1.0
A	16	.9

(LO 7-1)

19.

Portfolio	Expected Return	Standard Deviation
Risk-free	10%	0%
Market	18	24
A	16	22

(LO 7-1)

Please visit us at www.mhhe.com/bkm

20. Go to **www.mhhe.com/bkm** and link to Chapter 7 materials, where you will find a spreadsheet with monthly returns for GM, Ford, and Toyota, the S&P 500, and Treasury bills. *(LO 7-1)*
    a. Estimate the index model for each firm over the full five-year period. Compare the betas of each firm.
    b. Now estimate the betas for each firm using only the first two years of the sample and then using only the last two years. How stable are the beta estimates obtained from these shorter subperiods?

In Problems 21–23 below, assume the risk-free rate is 8% and the expected rate of return on the market is 18%.

21. A share of stock is now selling for $100. It will pay a dividend of $9 per share at the end of the year. Its beta is 1. What do investors expect the stock to sell for at the end of the year? *(LO 7-2)*
22. I am buying a firm with an expected perpetual cash flow of $1,000 but am unsure of its risk. If I think the beta of the firm is zero, when the beta is really 1, how much *more* will I offer for the firm than it is truly worth? *(LO 7-2)*
23. A stock has an expected return of 6%. What is its beta? *(LO 7-2)*
24. Two investment advisers are comparing performance. One averaged a 19% return and the other a 16% return. However, the beta of the first adviser was 1.5, while that of the second was 1. *(LO 7-2)*
    a. Can you tell which adviser was a better selector of individual stocks (aside from the issue of general movements in the market)?
    b. If the T-bill rate were 6% and the market return during the period were 14%, which adviser would be the superior stock selector?
    c. What if the T-bill rate were 3% and the market return 15%?
25. Suppose the yield on short-term government securities (perceived to be risk-free) is about 4%. Suppose also that the expected return required by the market for a portfolio with a beta of 1 is 12%. According to the capital asset pricing model: *(LO 7-2)*
    a. What is the expected return on the market portfolio?
    b. What would be the expected return on a zero-beta stock?
    c. Suppose you consider buying a share of stock at a price of $40. The stock is expected to pay a dividend of $3 next year and to sell then for $41. The stock risk has been evaluated at $\beta = -.5$. Is the stock overpriced or underpriced?
26. Based on current dividend yields and expected capital gains, the expected rates of return on portfolios *A* and *B* are 11% and 14%, respectively. The beta of *A* is .8 while that of *B* is 1.5. The T-bill rate is currently 6%, while the expected rate of return of the S&P 500 Index is 12%. The standard deviation of portfolio *A* is 10% annually, while that of *B* is 31%, and that of the index is 20%. *(LO 7-2)*
    a. If you currently hold a market-index portfolio, would you choose to add either of these portfolios to your holdings? Explain.
    b. If instead you could invest *only* in bills and one of these portfolios, which would you choose?
27. Consider the following data for a one-factor economy. All portfolios are well diversified.

Portfolio	*E*(*r*)	Beta
A	10%	1.0
F	4	0

Suppose another portfolio *E* is well diversified with a beta of 2/3 and expected return of 9%. Would an arbitrage opportunity exist? If so, what would the arbitrage strategy be? *(LO 7-4)*

28. Assume both portfolios A and B are well diversified, that $E(r_A) = 14\%$ and $E(r_B) = 14.8\%$. If the economy has only one factor, and $\beta_A = 1$ while $\beta_B = 1.1$, what must be the risk-free rate? ***(LO 7-4)***
29. Assume a market index represents the common factor and all stocks in the economy have a beta of 1. Firm-specific returns all have a standard deviation of 30%.

    Suppose an analyst studies 20 stocks and finds that one-half have an alpha of 3%, and one-half have an alpha of −3%. The analyst then buys $1 million of an equally weighted portfolio of the positive-alpha stocks and sells short $1 million of an equally weighted portfolio of the negative-alpha stocks. ***(LO 7-4)***
    a. What is the expected profit (in dollars), and what is the standard deviation of the analyst's profit?
    b. How does your answer change if the analyst examines 50 stocks instead of 20? 100 stocks?
30. If the APT is to be a useful theory, the number of systematic factors in the economy must be small. Why? ***(LO 7-4)***
31. The APT itself does not provide information on the factors that one might expect to determine risk premiums. How should researchers decide which factors to investigate? Is industrial production a reasonable factor to test for a risk premium? Why or why not? ***(LO 7-3)***
32. Suppose two factors are identified for the U.S. economy: the growth rate of industrial production, IP, and the inflation rate, IR. IP is expected to be 4% and IR 6%. A stock with a beta of 1 on IP and .4 on IR currently is expected to provide a rate of return of 14%. If industrial production actually grows by 5%, while the inflation rate turns out to be 7%, what is your best guess for the rate of return on the stock? ***(LO 7-3)***
33. Suppose there are two independent economic factors, M_1 and M_2. The risk-free rate is 7%, and all stocks have independent firm-specific components with a standard deviation of 50%. Portfolios A and B are both well diversified.

Portfolio	Beta on M_1	Beta on M_2	Expected Return (%)
A	1.8	2.1	40
B	2.0	−0.5	10

What is the expected return–beta relationship in this economy? ***(LO 7-5)***

Challenge

34. As a finance intern at Pork Products, Jennifer Wainwright's assignment is to come up with fresh insights concerning the firm's cost of capital. She decides that this would be a good opportunity to try out the new material on the APT that she learned last semester. As such, she decides that three promising factors would be (i) the return on a broad-based index such as the S&P 500; (ii) the level of interest rates, as represented by the yield to maturity on 10-year Treasury bonds; and (iii) the price of hogs, which are particularly important to her firm. Her plan is to find the beta of Pork Products against each of these factors and to estimate the risk premium associated with exposure to each factor. Comment on Jennifer's choice of factors. Which are most promising with respect to the likely impact on her firm's cost of capital? Can you suggest improvements to her specification? ***(LO 7-3)***
35. Suppose the market can be described by the following three sources of systematic risk. Each factor in the following table has a mean value of zero (so factor values represent realized surprises relative to prior expectations), and the risk premiums associated with each source of systematic risk are given in the last column.

Systematic Factor	Risk Premium
Industrial production, IP	6%
Interest rates, INT	2
Credit risk, CRED	4

The excess return, R, on a particular stock is described by the following equation that relates realized returns to surprises in the three systematic factors:

$$R = 6\% + 1.0\text{ IP} + .5\text{ INT} + .75\text{ CRED} + e$$

Find the equilibrium expected excess return on this stock using the APT. Is the stock overpriced or underpriced? ***(LO 7-3)***

CFA Problems

1. Which of the following statements about the security market line (SML) are *true?* ***(LO 7-2)***
   a. The SML provides a benchmark for evaluating expected investment performance.
   b. The SML leads all investors to invest in the same portfolio of risky assets.
   c. The SML is a graphic representation of the relationship between expected return and beta.
   d. Properly valued assets plot exactly on the SML.
2. Karen Kay, a portfolio manager at Collins Asset Management, is using the capital asset pricing model for making recommendations to her clients. Her research department has developed the information shown in the following exhibit. ***(LO 7-2)***

Forecasted Returns, Standard Deviations, and Betas			
	Forecasted Return	**Standard Deviation**	**Beta**
Stock X	14.0%	36%	0.8
Stock Y	17.0	25	1.5
Market index	14.0	15	1.0
Risk-free rate	5.0		

   a. Calculate expected return and alpha for each stock.
   b. Identify and justify which stock would be more appropriate for an investor who wants to:
      i. Add this stock to a well-diversified equity portfolio.
      ii. Hold this stock as a single-stock portfolio.
3. Joan McKay is a portfolio manager for a bank trust department. McKay meets with two clients, Kevin Murray and Lisa York, to review their investment objectives. Each client expresses an interest in changing his or her individual investment objectives. Both clients currently hold well-diversified portfolios of risky assets. ***(LO 7-1)***
   a. Murray wants to increase the expected return of his portfolio. State what action McKay should take to achieve Murray's objective. Justify your response in the context of the capital market line.
   b. York wants to reduce the risk exposure of her portfolio but does not want to engage in borrowing or lending activities to do so. State what action McKay should take to achieve York's objective. Justify your response in the context of the security market line.

4. Jeffrey Bruner, CFA, uses the capital asset pricing model (CAPM) to help identify mispriced securities. A consultant suggests Bruner use arbitrage pricing theory (APT) instead. In comparing CAPM and APT, the consultant made the following arguments:
   a. Both the CAPM and APT require a mean-variance efficient market portfolio.
   b. The CAPM assumes that one specific factor explains security returns but APT does not.

   State whether each of the consultant's arguments is correct or incorrect. Indicate, for each incorrect argument, why the argument is incorrect. ***(LO 7-5)***
5. The security market line depicts: ***(LO 7-2)***
   a. A security's expected return as a function of its systematic risk.
   b. The market portfolio as the optimal portfolio of risky securities.
   c. The relationship between a security's return and the return on an index.
   d. The complete portfolio as a combination of the market portfolio and the risk-free asset.
6. According to CAPM, the expected rate of return of a portfolio with a beta of 1 and an alpha of 0 is: ***(LO 7-2)***
   a. Between r_M and r_f.
   b. The risk-free rate, r_f.
   c. $\beta\ (r_M - r_f)$.
   d. The expected return on the market, r_M.

The following table (for CFA Problems 7 and 8) shows risk and return measures for two portfolios.

Portfolio	Average Annual Rate of Return	Standard Deviation	Beta
R	11%	10%	0.5
S&P 500	14%	12%	1.0

7. When plotting portfolio *R* on the preceding table relative to the SML, portfolio *R* lies: ***(LO 7-2)***
   a. On the SML.
   b. Below the SML.
   c. Above the SML.
   d. Insufficient data given.
8. When plotting portfolio *R* relative to the capital market line, portfolio *R* lies: ***(LO 7-2)***
   a. On the CML.
   b. Below the CML.
   c. Above the CML.
   d. Insufficient data given.
9. Briefly explain whether investors should expect a higher return from holding portfolio *A* versus portfolio *B* under capital asset pricing theory (CAPM). Assume that both portfolios are fully diversified. ***(LO 7-2)***

	Portfolio A	Portfolio B
Systematic risk (beta)	1.0	1.0
Specific risk for each individual security	High	Low

10. Assume that both *X* and *Y* are well-diversified portfolios and the risk-free rate is 8%.

Portfolio	Expected Return	Beta
X	16%	1.00
Y	12%	0.25

In this situation you could conclude that portfolios *X* and *Y*: ***(LO 7-4)***
a. Are in equilibrium.
b. Offer an arbitrage opportunity.
c. Are both underpriced.
d. Are both fairly priced.

11. According to the theory of arbitrage: ***(LO 7-4)***
a. High-beta stocks are consistently overpriced.
b. Low-beta stocks are consistently overpriced.
c. Positive alpha investment opportunities will quickly disappear.
d. Rational investors will pursue arbitrage consistent with their risk tolerance.

12. A zero-investment well-diversified portfolio with a positive alpha could arise if: ***(LO 7-5)***
a. The expected return of the portfolio equals zero.
b. The capital market line is tangent to the opportunity set.
c. The law of one price remains unviolated.
d. A risk-free arbitrage opportunity exists.

13. An investor takes as large a position as possible when an equilibrium price relationship is violated. This is an example of: ***(LO 7-4)***
a. A dominance argument.
b. The mean-variance efficient frontier.
c. Arbitrage activity.
d. The capital asset pricing model.

14. In contrast to the capital asset pricing model, arbitrage pricing theory: ***(LO 7-4)***
a. Requires that markets be in equilibrium.
b. Uses risk premiums based on micro variables.
c. Specifies the number and identifies specific factors that determine expected returns.
d. Does not require the restrictive assumptions concerning the market portfolio.

WEB *master*

1. A firm's beta can be estimated from the slope of the characteristic line. The first step is to plot the return on the firm's stock (*y*-axis) versus the return on a broad market index (*x*-axis). Next, a regression line is estimated to find the slope.
a. Go to **finance.yahoo.com,** enter the symbol for Alcoa, and click on *Get Quotes*. On the left-side menu, click on *Historical Prices;* then enter starting and ending dates that correspond to the most recent two years. Select the *Daily* option. Save the data to a spreadsheet.
b. Repeat the process to get comparable data for the S&P 500 Index (symbol ^GSPC). Download the data and copy it into the same spreadsheet as Alcoa with dates aligned.
c. Sort the data from earliest to latest. Calculate the excess return on the stock and the return on the index for each day using the adjusted closing prices. (You can use four-week T-bill rates to calculate excess returns from the Federal Reserve website at **www.federalreserve.gov/releases/h15/data.htm.**)
d. Prepare an *xy* scatter plot with no line inserted. Be sure that the firm's excess returns represent the *y*-variable and the market's excess returns represent the *x*-variable.
e. Select one of the data points by pointing to it and clicking the left mouse button. While the point is selected, right-click to pull up a shortcut menu. Select *Add*

www.mhhe.com/bkm

Trendline, choose the linear type, then click on the *Options* tab and select *Display Equation on Chart.* When you click on OK, the trendline and the equation appear. The trendline represents the regression equation. What is Alcoa's beta?

2. In the previous question, you used 60 months of data to calculate the beta of Alcoa. Now compute the alpha of Alcoa in two consecutive periods. Estimate the index-model regression using the first 30 months of data. Now repeat the process using the second half of the sample. This will give you the alpha (intercept) and beta (slope) estimates for two consecutive time periods. How do the two alphas compare to the risk-free rate and to each other? Select 11 other firms and repeat the regressions to find the alphas for the first two-year period and the last two-year period.
3. Given your results for Question 2, investigate the extent to which beta in one period predicts beta in future periods and whether alpha in one period predicts alpha in future periods. Regress the beta of each firm in the second period (Y) against the beta in the first period (X). (If you estimated regressions for a dozen firms in Question 2, you will have 12 observations in this regression.) Do the same for the alphas of each firm. Use the coefficients you found to forecast the betas of the 12 firms for the next two-year period.
4. Our expectation is that beta in the first period predicts beta in the next period but that alpha in the first period has no power to predict alpha in the next period. (In other words, the regression coefficient on first-period beta will be statistically significant in explaining second-period beta, but the coefficient on alpha will not be.) Why does this prediction make sense? Is it borne out by the data?
5. *a.* Which of the stocks would you classify as defensive? Which would be classified as aggressive?

   b. Do the beta coefficients for the low-beta firms make sense given the industries in which these firms operate? Briefly explain.

SOLUTIONS TO CONCEPT *checks*

7.1 The CML would still represent efficient investments. We can characterize the entire population by two representative investors. One is the "uninformed" investor, who does not engage in security analysis and holds the market portfolio, while the other optimizes using the Markowitz algorithm with input from security analysis. The uninformed investor does not know what input the informed investor uses to make portfolio purchases. The uninformed investor knows, however, that if the other investor is informed, the market portfolio proportions will be optimal. Therefore, to depart from these proportions would constitute an uninformed bet, which will, on average, reduce the efficiency of diversification with no compensating improvement in expected returns.

7.2 Substituting the historical mean and standard deviation in Equation 7.1 yields a coefficient of risk aversion of

$$\overline{A} = \frac{E(r_M) - r_f}{\sigma_M^2} = \frac{.075}{.20^2} = 1.88$$

This relationship also tells us that for the historical standard deviation and a coefficient of risk aversion of 3.5, the risk premium would be

$$E(r_M) - r_f = \overline{A}\sigma_M^2 = 3.5 \times .20^2 = .14 = 14\%$$

7.3 $\beta_{\text{Dell}} = 1.25$, $\beta_{\text{GE}} = 1.15$. Therefore, given the investment proportions, the portfolio beta is

$$\beta_P = w_{\text{Dell}}\beta_{\text{Dell}} + w_{\text{GE}}\beta_{\text{GE}} = (.75 \times 1.25) + (.25 \times 1.15) = 1.225$$

and the risk premium of the portfolio will be

$$E(r_P) - r_f = \beta_P[E(r_M) - r_f] = 1.225 \times 8\% = 9.8\%$$

7.4 *a.* The alpha of a stock is its expected return in excess of that required by the CAPM.

$$\alpha = E(r) - \{r_f + \beta[E(r_M) - r_f]\}$$
$$\alpha_{XYZ} = 12 - [5 + 1.0(11 - 5)] = 1$$
$$\alpha_{ABC} = 13 - [5 + 1.5(11 - 5)] = -1\%$$

b. The project-specific required rate of return is determined by the project beta coupled with the market risk premium and the risk-free rate. The CAPM tells us that an acceptable expected rate of return for the project is

$$r_f + \beta[E(r_M) - r_f] = 8 + 1.3(16 - 8) = 18.4\%$$

which becomes the project's hurdle rate. If the IRR of the project is 19%, then it is desirable. Any project (of similar beta) with an IRR less than 18.4% should be rejected.

7.5 $E(r) = 4\% + 1.2 \times 4\% + .7 \times 2\% = 10.2\%$

7.6 Using Equation 7.11, the expected return is

$$4 + (0.2 \times 6) + (1.4 \times 8) = 16.4\%$$

Chapter 8

The Efficient Market Hypothesis

Learning Objectives:

LO8-1 Demonstrate why security price changes should be essentially unpredictable in an efficient market.

LO8-2 Cite evidence that supports and contradicts the efficient market hypothesis.

LO8-3 Provide interpretations of various stock market "anomalies."

LO8-4 Formulate investment strategies that make sense in informationally efficient markets.

One of the early applications of computers in economics in the 1950s was to analyze economic time series. Business-cycle theorists felt that tracing the evolution of several economic variables over time would clarify and predict the progress of the economy through boom and bust periods. A natural candidate for analysis was the behavior of stock market prices over time. On the assumption that stock prices reflect the prospects of the firm, recurrent patterns of peaks and troughs in economic performance ought to show up in those prices.

When Maurice Kendall (1953) examined this proposition, however, he found to his great surprise that he could identify no predictable patterns in stock prices. Prices seemed to evolve randomly. They were as likely to go up as they were to go down on any particular day, regardless of past performance. The data provided no way to predict price movements.

At first blush, Kendall's results were disturbing to some financial economists. They seemed to imply that the stock market is dominated by erratic market psychology, or "animal spirits"—that it follows no logical rules. In short, the results appeared to confirm the irrationality of the market. On further reflection, however, economists came to reverse their interpretation of Kendall's study.

It soon became apparent that random price movements indicated a well-functioning or efficient market, not an irrational one. In this chapter we explore the reasoning behind what may seem a surprising conclusion. We show how competition among analysts leads naturally to market efficiency, and we examine the implications of the efficient market hypothesis for investment policy. We also consider empirical evidence that supports and contradicts the notion of market efficiency.

Related websites for this chapter are available at www.mhhe.com/bkm.

8.1 RANDOM WALKS AND THE EFFICIENT MARKET HYPOTHESIS

Suppose Kendall had discovered that changes in stock prices can be reliably predicted. What a gold mine this would have been. If they could use Kendall's equations to predict stock prices, investors would reap unending profits simply by purchasing stocks that the computer model implied were about to increase in price and by selling those stocks about to fall in price.

A moment's reflection should be enough to convince yourself that this situation could not persist for long. For example, suppose that the model predicts with great confidence that XYZ stock price, currently at $100 per share, will rise dramatically in three days to $110. What would all investors with access to the model's prediction do today? Obviously, they would place a great wave of immediate buy orders to cash in on the forthcoming increase in stock price. No one holding XYZ, however, would be willing to sell. The net effect would be an *immediate* jump in the stock price to $110. The forecast of a future price increase will lead instead to an immediate price increase. In other words, the stock price will immediately reflect the "good news" implicit in the model's forecast.

This simple example illustrates why Kendall's attempt to find recurrent patterns in stock price movements was likely to fail. A forecast about favorable *future* performance leads instead to favorable *current* performance, as market participants all try to get in on the action before the price increase.

More generally, one might say that any information that could be used to predict stock performance should already be reflected in stock prices. As soon as there is any information indicating that a stock is underpriced and therefore offers a profit opportunity, investors flock to buy the stock and immediately bid up its price to a fair level, where only ordinary rates of return can be expected. These "ordinary rates" are simply rates of return commensurate with the risk of the stock.

However, if prices are bid immediately to fair levels, given all available information, it must be that they increase or decrease only in response to new information. New information, by definition, must be unpredictable; if it could be predicted, then the prediction would be part of today's information. Thus stock prices that change in response to new (unpredictable) information also must move unpredictably.

This is the essence of the argument that stock prices should follow a **random walk,** that is, that price changes should be random and unpredictable. Far from a proof of market irrationality, randomly evolving stock prices would be the necessary consequence of intelligent investors competing to discover relevant information on which to buy or sell stocks before the rest of the market becomes aware of that information.

random walk

The notion that stock price changes are random and unpredictable.

Don't confuse randomness in price *changes* with irrationality in the *level* of prices. If prices are determined rationally, then only new information will cause them to change. Therefore, a random walk would be the natural result of prices that always reflect all current knowledge. Indeed, if stock price movements were predictable, that would be damning evidence of stock market inefficiency, because the ability to predict prices would indicate that all available information was not already reflected in stock prices. Therefore, the notion that stocks already reflect all available information is referred to as the **efficient market hypothesis** (EMH).[1]

efficient market hypothesis

The hypothesis that prices of securities fully reflect available information about securities.

[1]Market efficiency should not be confused with the idea of efficient portfolios introduced in Chapter 6. An informationally efficient *market* is one in which information is rapidly disseminated and reflected in prices. An efficient *portfolio* is one with the highest expected return for a given level of risk.

FIGURE 8.1

Cumulative abnormal returns before takeover attempts: Target companies

Source: Arthur Keown and John Pinkerton, "Merger Announcements and Insider Trading Activity," *Journal of Finance* 36 (September 1981), pp. 855–869. Used with permission of John Wiley and Sons, via Copyright Clearance Center. Updates courtesy of Jinghua Yan.

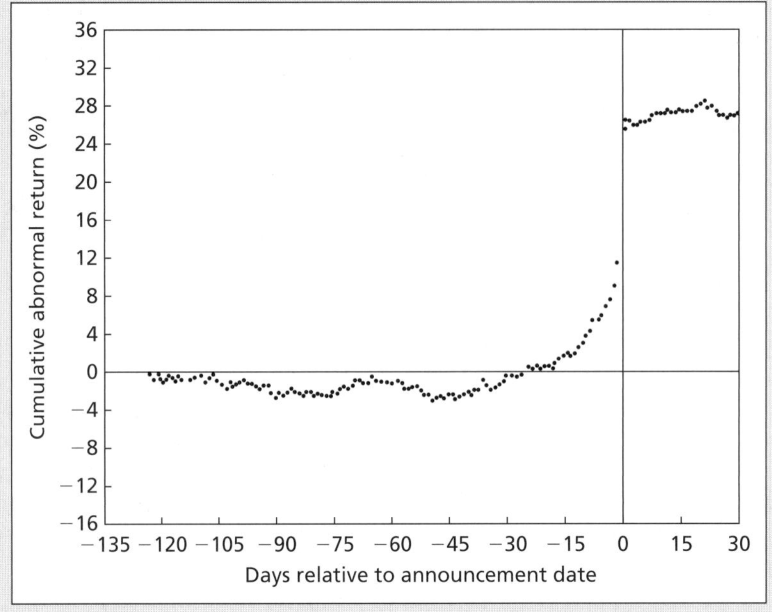

Figure 8.1 illustrates the response of stock prices to new information in an efficient market. The graph plots the price response of a sample of 194 firms that were targets of takeover attempts. In most takeovers, the acquiring firm pays a substantial premium over current market prices. Therefore, announcement of a takeover attempt should cause the stock price to jump. The figure shows that stock prices jump dramatically on the day the news becomes public. However, there is no further drift in prices *after* the announcement date, suggesting that prices reflect the new information, including the likely magnitude of the takeover premium, by the end of the trading day.

Even more dramatic evidence of rapid response to new information may be found in intraday prices. For example, Patel and Wolfson (1984) show that most of the stock price response to corporate dividend or earnings announcements occurs within 10 minutes of the announcement. A nice illustration of such rapid adjustment is provided in a study by Busse and Green (2002), who track minute-by-minute stock prices of firms that are featured on CNBC's "Morning" or "Midday Call" segments.[2] Minute 0 in Figure 8.2 is the

FIGURE 8.2

Stock price reaction to CNBC reports. The figure shows the reaction of stock prices to on-air stock reports during the "Midday Call" segment on CNBC. The chart plots cumulative returns beginning 15 minutes before the stock report.

Source: Reprinted from J. A. Busse and T. C. Green, "Market Efficiency in Real Time," *Journal of Financial Economics* 65 (2002), p. 422. Copyright 2002 with permission from Elsevier Science.

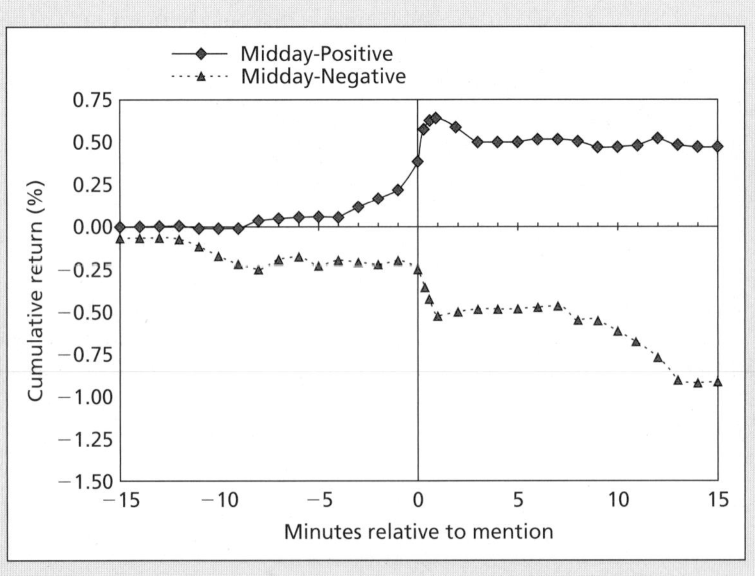

[2]You can find an intraday movie version of this figure at **www.bus.emory.edu/cgreen/docs/cnbc/cnbc.html.**

time at which the stock is mentioned on the midday show. The top line is the average price movement of stocks that receive positive reports, while the bottom line reports returns on stocks with negative reports. Notice that the top line levels off, indicating that the market has fully digested the news, within 5 minutes of the report. The bottom line levels off within about 12 minutes.

Competition as the Source of Efficiency

Why should we expect stock prices to reflect "all available information"? After all, if you are willing to spend time and money on gathering information, it might seem reasonable that you could turn up something that has been overlooked by the rest of the investment community. When information is costly to uncover and analyze, one would expect investment analysis calling for such expenditures to result in an increased expected return.

This point has been stressed by Grossman and Stiglitz (1980). They argued that investors will have an incentive to spend time and resources to analyze and uncover new information only if such activity is likely to generate higher investment returns. Thus, in market equilibrium, efficient information-gathering activity should be fruitful. Moreover, it would not be surprising to find that the degree of efficiency differs across various markets. For example, emerging markets that are less intensively analyzed than U.S. markets or in which accounting disclosure requirements are less rigorous may be less efficient than U.S. markets. Small stocks which receive relatively little coverage by Wall Street analysts may be less efficiently priced than large ones. Therefore, while we would not go so far as to say that you absolutely cannot come up with new information, it makes sense to consider and respect your competition.

EXAMPLE 8.1

Rewards for Incremental Performance

Consider an investment management fund currently managing a $5 billion portfolio. Suppose that the fund manager can devise a research program that could increase the portfolio rate of return by one-tenth of 1% per year, a seemingly modest amount. This program would increase the dollar return to the portfolio by $5 billion × .001, or $5 million. Therefore, the fund would be willing to spend up to $5 million per year on research to increase stock returns by a mere tenth of 1% per year. With such large rewards for such small increases in investment performance, it should not be surprising that professional portfolio managers are willing to spend large sums on industry analysts, computer support, and research effort, and therefore that price changes are, generally speaking, difficult to predict.

With so many well-backed analysts willing to spend considerable resources on research, easy pickings in the market will be rare. Moreover, the incremental rates of return on research activity may be so small that only managers of the largest portfolios will find them worth pursuing.

Although it may not literally be true that "all" relevant information will be uncovered, it is virtually certain that there are many investigators hot on the trail of most leads that seem likely to improve investment performance. Competition among these many well-backed, highly paid, aggressive analysts ensures that, as a general rule, stock prices ought to reflect available information regarding their proper levels.

It is often said that the most precious commodity on Wall Street is information, and the competition for it is intense. Sometimes the quest for a competitive advantage can tip over into a search for illegal inside information. In 2011, Raj Rajaratnam, the head of the Galleon Group hedge fund, which once managed $6.5 billion, was convicted on insider trading charges for soliciting tips from a network of corporate insiders and traders. Rajaratnam's case was only one of several major insider trading cases working their way through the courts in 2011. While Galleon's practices were egregious, it often can be difficult to draw a clear line separating legitimate and prohibited sources of information. For example, a large industry of *expert-network* firms has emerged in the last decade to connect (for a fee) investors to industry experts who can provide unique perspective on a company. As the nearby box discusses, this sort of arrangement can easily cross the line into insider trading.

On the MARKET FRONT

MATCHMAKERS FOR THE INFORMATION AGE

The most precious commodity on Wall Street is information, and informed players can charge handsomely for providing it. An industry of so-called *expert-network providers* has emerged to sell access to experts with unique insights about a wide variety of firms and industries to investors who need that information to make decisions. These firms have been dubbed "matchmakers for the information age." Experts can range from doctors who help predict the release of blockbuster drugs to meteorologists who forecast weather that can affect commodity prices to business executives who can provide specialized insight about companies and industries.

But it's turned out that some of those experts have peddled prohibited inside information. In 2011, Winifred Jiau, a consultant for Primary Global Research, was convicted of selling information about Nvidia and Marvell Technologies to the hedge fund SAC Capital Advisors. Several other employees of Primary Global also have been charged with insider trading.

Expert firms are supposed to provide only public information, along with the expert's insights and perspective. But the temptation to hire experts with inside information and charge handsomely for access to them is obvious. The SEC has raised concerns about the boundary between legitimate and illegal services, and several hedge funds in 2011 shut down after raids searching for evidence of such illicit activity.

In the wake of increased scrutiny, compliance efforts of both buyers and sellers of expert information have mushroomed. The largest network firm is Gerson Lehrman Group, with a stable of 300,000 experts. It now maintains down-to-the-minute records of which of its experts talks to whom and the topics they have discussed.[3] These records could be turned over to authorities in the event of an insider trading investigation. And for their part, some hedge funds have simply ceased working with expert-network firms or have promulgated clearer rules for when their employees may talk with consultants.

Even with these safeguards, however, there remains room for trouble. For example, an investor may meet an expert through a legitimate network, and then the two may establish a consulting relationship on their own. The legal matchmaking becomes the precursor to the illegal selling of insider tips. Where there is a will to cheat, there usually will be a way.

Versions of the Efficient Market Hypothesis

It is common to distinguish among three versions of the EMH: the weak, semistrong, and strong forms of the hypothesis. These versions differ by their notions of what is meant by the term "all available information."

weak-form EMH

The assertion that stock prices already reflect all information contained in the history of past trading.

The **weak-form** hypothesis asserts that stock prices already reflect all information that can be derived by examining market trading data such as the history of past prices, trading volume, or short interest. This version of the hypothesis implies that trend analysis is fruitless. Past stock price data are publicly available and virtually costless to obtain. The weak-form hypothesis holds that if such data ever conveyed reliable signals about future performance, all investors already would have learned to exploit the signals. Ultimately, the signals lose their value as they become widely known because a buy signal, for instance, would result in an immediate price increase.

semistrong-form EMH

The assertion that stock prices already reflect all publicly available information.

The **semistrong-form** hypothesis states that all publicly available information regarding the prospects of a firm already must be reflected in the stock price. Such information includes, in addition to past prices, fundamental data on the firm's product line, quality of management, balance sheet composition, patents held, earning forecasts, and accounting practices. Again, if investors have access to such information from publicly available sources, one would expect it to be reflected in stock prices.

strong-form EMH

The assertion that stock prices reflect all relevant information, including inside information.

Finally, the **strong-form** version of the efficient market hypothesis states that stock prices reflect all information relevant to the firm, even including information available only to company insiders. This version of the hypothesis is quite extreme. Few would argue with the proposition that corporate officers have access to pertinent information long enough before public release to enable them to profit from trading on that information. Indeed, much of the activity of the Securities and Exchange Commission is directed toward preventing insiders from profiting by exploiting their privileged situation. Rule 10b-5 of the Security Exchange Act of 1934 sets limits on trading by corporate officers, directors, and substantial owners, requiring them to report trades to the SEC. These insiders, their relatives, and any associates who trade on information supplied by insiders are considered in violation of the law.

[3]"Expert Networks Are the Matchmakers for the Information Age," *The Economist,* June 16, 2011.

Defining insider trading is not always easy, however. After all, stock analysts are in the business of uncovering information not already widely known to market participants. As we saw in Chapter 3 and in the nearby box, the distinction between private and inside information is sometimes murky.

Notice one thing that all versions of the EMH have in common: They all assert that prices should reflect *available* information. We do not expect traders to be superhuman or market prices to never turn out to be wrong. We will always like more information about a company's prospects than will be available. Sometimes market prices will turn out in retrospect to have been outrageously high; at other times, absurdly low. The EMH asserts only that at the given time, using current information, we cannot be sure if today's prices will ultimately prove themselves to have been too high or too low. If markets are rational, however, we can expect them to be correct on average.

CONCEPT check 8.1

a. Suppose you observed that high-level managers make superior returns on investments in their company's stock. Would this be a violation of weak-form market efficiency? Would it be a violation of strong-form market efficiency?
b. If the weak form of the efficient market hypothesis is valid, must the strong form also hold? Conversely, does strong-form efficiency imply weak-form efficiency?

8.2 IMPLICATIONS OF THE EMH

Technical Analysis

Technical analysis is essentially the search for recurrent and predictable patterns in stock prices. Although technicians recognize the value of information regarding future economic prospects of the firm, they believe that such information is not necessary for a successful trading strategy. This is because whatever the fundamental reason for a change in stock price, if the stock price responds slowly enough, the analyst will be able to identify a trend that can be exploited during the adjustment period. The key to successful technical analysis is a sluggish response of stock prices to fundamental supply-and-demand factors. This prerequisite, of course, is diametrically opposed to the notion of an efficient market.

technical analysis
Research on recurrent and predictable stock price patterns and on proxies for buy or sell pressure in the market.

Technical analysts are sometimes called *chartists* because they study records or charts of past stock prices, hoping to find patterns they can exploit to make a profit. As an example of technical analysis, consider the *relative strength* approach. The chartist compares stock performance over a recent period to performance of the market or other stocks in the same industry. A simple version of relative strength takes the ratio of the stock price to a market indicator such as the S&P 500 Index. If the ratio increases over time, the stock is said to exhibit relative strength because its price performance is better than that of the broad market. Such strength presumably may continue for a long enough period of time to offer profit opportunities.

One of the most commonly heard components of technical analysis is the notion of **resistance levels** or **support levels.** These values are said to be price levels above which it is difficult for stock prices to rise or below which it is unlikely for them to fall, and they are believed to be levels determined by market psychology.

resistance level
A price level above which it is supposedly unlikely for a stock or stock index to rise.

support level
A price level below which it is supposedly unlikely for a stock or stock index to fall.

EXAMPLE 8.2
Resistance Levels

Consider stock XYZ, which traded for several months at a price of $72 and then declined to $65. If the stock eventually begins to increase in price, $72 is considered a resistance level (according to this theory) because investors who bought originally at $72 will be eager to sell their shares as soon as they can break even on their investment. Therefore, at prices near $72 a wave of selling pressure would exist. Such activity imparts a type of "memory" to the market that allows past price history to influence current stock prospects.

The efficient market hypothesis implies that technical analysis is without merit. The past history of prices and trading volume is publicly available at minimal cost. Therefore, any information that was ever available from analyzing past prices has already been reflected in stock prices. As investors compete to exploit their common knowledge of a stock's price history, they necessarily drive stock prices to levels where expected rates of return are exactly commensurate with risk. At those levels one cannot expect abnormal returns.

As an example of how this process works, consider what would happen if the market believed that a level of $72 truly were a resistance level for stock XYZ in Example 8.2. No one would be willing to purchase the stock at a price of $71.50, because it would have almost no room to increase in price but ample room to fall. However, if no one would buy it at $71.50, then $71.50 would become a resistance level. But then, using a similar analysis, no one would buy it at $71, or $70, and so on. The notion of a resistance level is a logical conundrum. Its simple resolution is the recognition that if the stock is ever to sell at $71.50, investors *must* believe that the price can as easily increase as fall. The fact that investors are willing to purchase (or even hold) the stock at $71.50 is evidence of their belief that they can earn a fair expected rate of return at that price.

CONCEPT check 8.2

If everyone in the market believes in resistance levels, why do these beliefs not become self-fulfilling prophecies?

An interesting question is whether a technical rule that seems to work will continue to work in the future once it becomes widely recognized. A clever analyst may occasionally uncover a profitable trading rule, but the real test of efficient markets is whether the rule itself becomes reflected in stock prices once its value is discovered. Once a useful technical rule (or price pattern) is discovered, it ought to be invalidated when the mass of traders attempts to exploit it. In this sense, price patterns ought to be *self-destructing.*

Thus the market dynamic is one of a continual search for profitable trading rules, followed by destruction by overuse of those rules found to be successful, followed by more search for yet-undiscovered rules. We return to the rationale for technical analysis as well as some of its methods in the next chapter.

Fundamental Analysis

fundamental analysis

Research on determinants of stock value, such as earnings and dividend prospects, expectations for future interest rates, and risk of the firm.

Fundamental analysis uses earnings and dividend prospects of the firm, expectations of future interest rates, and risk evaluation of the firm to determine proper stock prices. Ultimately, it represents an attempt to determine the present discounted value of all the payments a stockholder will receive from each share of stock. If that value exceeds the stock price, the fundamental analyst would recommend purchasing the stock.

Fundamental analysts usually start with a study of past earnings and an examination of company financial statements. They supplement this analysis with further detailed economic analysis, ordinarily including an evaluation of the quality of the firm's management, the firm's standing within its industry, and the prospects for the industry as a whole. The hope is to attain insight into future performance of the firm that is not yet recognized by the rest of the market. Chapters 12 through 14 provide a detailed discussion of the types of analyses that underlie fundamental analysis.

Once again, the efficient market hypothesis predicts that *most* fundamental analysis also is doomed to failure. If the analyst relies on publicly available earnings and industry information, his or her evaluation of the firm's prospects is not likely to be significantly more accurate than those of rival analysts. There are many well-informed, well-financed firms conducting such market research, and in the face of such competition it will be difficult to uncover data not also available to other analysts. Only analysts with a unique insight will be rewarded.

Fundamental analysis is much more difficult than merely identifying well-run firms with good prospects. Discovery of good firms does an investor no good in and of itself if the rest of the market also knows those firms are good. If the knowledge is already public, the investor will be forced to pay a high price for those firms and will not realize a superior rate of return.

The trick is not to identify firms that are good but to find firms that are *better* than everyone else's estimate. Similarly, poorly run firms can be great bargains if they are not quite as bad as their stock prices suggest.

This is why fundamental analysis is difficult. It is not enough to do a good analysis of a firm; you can make money only if your analysis is better than that of your competitors because the market price will already reflect all commonly available information.

Active versus Passive Portfolio Management

By now it is apparent that casual efforts to pick stocks are not likely to pay off. Competition among investors ensures that any easily implemented stock evaluation technique will be used widely enough so that any insights derived will be reflected in stock prices. Only serious analysis and uncommon techniques are likely to generate the *differential* insight necessary to yield trading profits.

Moreover, these techniques are economically feasible only for managers of large portfolios. If you have only $100,000 to invest, even a 1%-per-year improvement in performance generates only $1,000 per year, hardly enough to justify herculean efforts. The billion-dollar manager, however, reaps extra income of $10 million annually from the same 1% increment.

If small investors are not in a favored position to conduct active portfolio management, what are their choices? The small investor probably is better off investing in mutual funds. By pooling resources in this way, small investors can gain from economies of scale.

More difficult decisions remain, though. Can investors be sure that even large mutual funds have the ability or resources to uncover mispriced stocks? Furthermore, will any mispricing be sufficiently large to repay the costs entailed in active portfolio management?

Proponents of the efficient market hypothesis believe that active management is largely wasted effort and unlikely to justify the expenses incurred. Therefore, they advocate a **passive investment strategy** that makes no attempt to outsmart the market. A passive strategy aims only at establishing a well-diversified portfolio of securities without attempting to find under- or overvalued stocks. Passive management is usually characterized by a buy-and-hold strategy. Because the efficient market theory indicates that stock prices are at fair levels, given all available information, it makes no sense to buy and sell securities frequently, which generates large brokerage fees without increasing expected performance.

passive investment strategy

Buying a well-diversified portfolio without attempting to search out mispriced securities.

One common strategy for passive management is to create an **index fund,** which is a fund designed to replicate the performance of a broad-based index of stocks. For example, Vanguard's 500 Index Fund holds stocks in direct proportion to their weight in the Standard & Poor's 500 stock price index. The performance of the 500 Index Fund therefore replicates the performance of the S&P 500. Investors in this fund obtain broad diversification with relatively low management fees. The fees can be kept to a minimum because Vanguard does not need to pay analysts to assess stock prospects and does not incur transaction costs from high portfolio turnover. Indeed, while the typical annual expense ratio for an actively managed equity fund is around 1% of assets, the expense ratio of the 500 Index Fund is only .17%. Today, Vanguard's 500 Index Fund is among the largest equity mutual funds with over $100 billion of assets in mid-2011. At the end of 2011, about 15% of assets in equity mutual funds were indexed.

index fund

A mutual fund holding shares in proportion to their representation in a market index such as the S&P 500.

Indexing need not be limited to the S&P 500, however. For example, some of the funds offered by the Vanguard Group track the Wilshire 5000 Index, the Barclays Capital U.S. Aggregate Bond Index, the MSCI index of small-capitalization U.S. companies, the European equity market, and the Pacific Basin equity market. Several other mutual fund complexes offer indexed portfolios, but Vanguard dominates the retail market for indexed products.

Exchange-traded funds, or ETFs, are a close (and usually lower-expense) alternative to indexed mutual funds. As noted in Chapter 4, these are shares in diversified portfolios that can be bought or sold just like shares of individual stock. ETFs matching several broad stock market indexes such as the S&P 500 or Wilshire 5000 indexes and dozens of international and industry stock indexes are available to investors who want to hold a diversified sector of a market without attempting active security selection.

CONCEPT check 8.3

What would happen to market efficiency if *all* investors attempted to follow a passive strategy?

The Role of Portfolio Management in an Efficient Market

If the market is efficient, why not throw darts at *The Wall Street Journal* instead of trying rationally to choose a stock portfolio? This is a tempting conclusion to draw from the notion that security prices are fairly set, but it is far too facile. There is a role for rational portfolio management, even in perfectly efficient markets.

You have learned that a basic principle in portfolio selection is diversification. Even if all stocks are priced fairly, each still poses firm-specific risk that can be eliminated through diversification. Therefore, rational security selection, even in an efficient market, calls for the selection of a well-diversified portfolio providing the systematic risk level that the investor wants.

Rational investment policy also requires that tax considerations be reflected in security choice. High-tax-bracket investors generally will not want the same securities that low-bracket investors find favorable. At an obvious level, high-bracket investors find it advantageous to buy tax-exempt municipal bonds despite their relatively low pretax yields, whereas those same bonds are unattractive to low-tax-bracket investors. At a more subtle level, high-bracket investors might want to tilt their portfolios in the direction of capital gains as opposed to interest income, because capital gains are taxed less heavily and because the option to defer the realization of capital gains income is more valuable the higher the current tax bracket. Hence these investors may prefer stocks that yield low dividends yet offer greater expected capital gains income. They also will be more attracted to investment opportunities for which returns are sensitive to tax benefits, such as real estate ventures.

A third argument for rational portfolio management relates to the particular risk profile of the investor. For example, a Toyota executive whose annual bonus depends on Toyota's profits generally should not invest additional amounts in auto stocks. To the extent that his or her compensation already depends on Toyota's well-being, the executive is already overinvested in Toyota and should not exacerbate the lack of diversification. This lesson was learned with considerable pain in September 2008 by Lehman Brothers employees who were famously invested in their own firm when the company failed. Roughly 30% of the shares in the firm were owned by its 24,000 employees, and their losses on those shares were around $10 billion.

Investors of varying ages also might warrant different portfolio policies with regard to risk bearing. For example, older investors who are essentially living off savings might choose to avoid long-term bonds whose market values fluctuate dramatically with changes in interest rates (discussed in Part Four). Because these investors are living off accumulated savings, they require conservation of principal. In contrast, younger investors might be more inclined toward long-term inflation-indexed bonds. The steady flow of real income over long periods of time that is locked in with these bonds can be more important than preservation of principal to those with long life expectancies.

In conclusion, there is a role for portfolio management even in an efficient market. Investors' optimal positions will vary according to factors such as age, tax bracket, risk aversion, and employment. The role of the portfolio manager in an efficient market is to tailor the portfolio to these needs, rather than to beat the market.

Resource Allocation

We've focused so far on the investments implications of the efficient market hypothesis. Deviations from efficiency may offer profit opportunities to better-informed traders at the expense of less informed traders.

However, deviations from informational efficiency would also result in a large cost that will be borne by all citizens, namely, inefficient resource allocation. Recall that in a capitalist economy, investments in *real* assets such as plant, equipment, and know-how are guided in large part by the prices of financial assets. For example, if the value of telecommunication capacity reflected in stock market prices exceeds the cost of installing such capacity, managers might justifiably conclude that telecom investments seem to have positive net present value. In this manner, capital market prices guide allocation of real resources.

If markets were inefficient and securities commonly mispriced, then resources would be systematically misallocated. Corporations with overpriced securities will be able to obtain capital too cheaply, and corporations with undervalued securities might forgo investment opportunities because the cost of raising capital will be too high. Therefore, inefficient capital markets would diminish one of the most potent benefits of a market economy. As an example of what can go wrong, consider the dot-com bubble of the late 1990s, which sent a strong but, as it turned out, wildly overoptimistic signal about prospects in Internet and telecommunication firms and ultimately led to substantial overinvestment in those industries.

Before writing off markets as a means to guide resource allocation, however, one has to be reasonable about what can be expected from market forecasts. In particular, you shouldn't confuse an efficient market, where all available information is reflected in prices, with a perfect-foresight market. Even "all available information" is still far from complete information, and generally rational market forecasts will sometimes be wrong; sometimes, in fact, they will be very wrong.

8.3 ARE MARKETS EFFICIENT?

The Issues

Not surprisingly, the efficient market hypothesis does not exactly arouse enthusiasm in the community of professional portfolio managers. It implies that a great deal of the activity of portfolio managers—the search for undervalued securities—is at best wasted effort, and quite probably harmful to clients because it costs money and leads to imperfectly diversified portfolios. Consequently, the EMH has never been widely accepted on Wall Street, and debate continues today on the degree to which security analysis can improve investment performance. Before discussing empirical tests of the hypothesis, we want to note three factors that together imply that the debate probably never will be settled: the *magnitude issue,* the *selection bias issue,* and the *lucky event issue.*

The magnitude issue We noted that an investment manager overseeing a $5 billion portfolio who can improve performance by only .1% per year will increase investment earnings by .001 × $5 billion = $5 million annually. This manager clearly would be worth her salary! Yet can we, as observers, statistically measure her contribution? Probably not: A .1% contribution would be swamped by the yearly volatility of the market. Remember, the annual standard deviation of the well-diversified S&P 500 Index has been around 20%. Against these fluctuations a small increase in performance would be hard to detect.

All might agree that stock prices are very close to fair values and that only managers of large portfolios can earn enough trading profits to make the exploitation of minor mispricing worth the effort. According to this view, the actions of intelligent investment managers are the driving force behind the constant evolution of market prices to fair levels. Rather than ask the qualitative question, "Are markets efficient?" we should instead ask a more quantitative question: "How efficient are markets?"

The selection bias issue Suppose that you discover an investment scheme that could really make money. You have two choices: either publish your technique in *The Wall Street Journal* to win fleeting fame, or keep your technique secret and use it to earn millions of dollars. Most investors would choose the latter option, which presents us with a conundrum. Only investors who find that an investment scheme cannot generate abnormal returns will be willing to report their findings to the whole world. Hence opponents of the efficient markets

On the MARKET FRONT

HOW TO GUARANTEE A SUCCESSFUL MARKET NEWSLETTER

Suppose you want to make your fortune publishing a market newsletter. You need first to convince potential subscribers that you have talent worth paying for. But what if you have no talent? The solution is simple: Start eight newsletters.

In year 1, let four of your newsletters predict an up-market and four a down-market. In year 2, let half of the originally optimistic group of newsletters continue to predict an up-market and the other half a down-market. Do the same for the originally pessimistic group. Continue in this manner to obtain the pattern of predictions in the table that follows (U = prediction of an up-market, D = prediction of a down-market).

After three years, no matter what has happened to the market, one of the newsletters would have had a perfect prediction record. This is because after three years there are $2^3 = 8$ outcomes for the market, and we have covered all eight possibilities with the eight newsletters. Now, we simply slough off the seven unsuccessful newsletters, and market the eighth newsletter based on its perfect track record. If we want to establish a newsletter with a perfect track record over a four-year period, we need $2^4 = 16$ newsletters. A five-year period requires 32 newsletters, and so on.

After the fact, the one newsletter that was always right will attract attention for your uncanny foresight and investors will rush to pay large fees for its advice. Your fortune is made, and you have never even researched the market!

WARNING: This scheme is illegal! The point, however, is that with hundreds of market newsletters, you can find one that has stumbled onto an apparently remarkable string of successful predictions without any real degree of skill. After the fact, *someone's* prediction history can seem to imply great forecasting skill. This person is the one we will read about in *The Wall Street Journal;* the others will be forgotten.

Newsletter Predictions

Year	1	2	3	4	5	6	7	8
1	U	U	U	U	D	D	D	D
2	U	U	D	D	U	U	D	D
3	U	D	U	D	U	D	U	D

view of the world always can use evidence that various techniques do not provide investment rewards as proof that the techniques that do work simply are not being reported to the public. This is a problem in *selection bias;* the outcomes we are able to observe have been preselected in favor of failed attempts. Therefore, we cannot fairly evaluate the true ability of portfolio managers to generate winning stock market strategies.

The lucky event issue In virtually any month it seems we read an article about some investor or investment company with a fantastic investment performance over the recent past. Surely the superior records of such investors disprove the efficient market hypothesis.

Yet this conclusion is far from obvious. As an analogy to the investment game, consider a contest to flip the most number of heads out of 50 trials using a fair coin. The expected outcome for any person is, of course, 50% heads and 50% tails. If 10,000 people, however, compete in this contest, it would not be surprising if at least one or two contestants flipped more than 75% heads. In fact, elementary statistics tells us that the expected number of contestants flipping 75% or more heads would be two. It would be silly, though, to crown these people the "head-flipping champions of the world." Obviously, they are simply the contestants who happened to get lucky on the day of the event. (See the nearby box.)

The analogy to efficient markets is clear. Under the hypothesis that any stock is fairly priced given all available information, any bet on a stock is simply a coin toss. There is equal likelihood of winning or losing the bet. However, if many investors using a variety of schemes make fair bets, statistically speaking, *some* of those investors will be lucky and win a great majority of the bets. For every big winner, there may be many big losers, but we never hear of these managers. The winners, though, turn up in *The Wall Street Journal* as the latest stock market gurus; then they can make a fortune publishing market newsletters.

Our point is that after the fact there will have been at least one successful investment scheme. A doubter will call the results luck; the successful investor will call it skill. The proper test would be to see whether the successful investors can repeat their performance in another period, yet this approach is rarely taken.

With these caveats in mind, we turn now to some of the empirical tests of the efficient market hypothesis.

CONCEPT check 8.4

Legg Mason's Value Trust, managed by Bill Miller, outperformed the S&P 500 in each of the 15 years ending in 2005. Is Miller's performance sufficient to dissuade you from a belief in efficient markets? If not, would *any* performance record be sufficient to dissuade you? Now consider that in the next 3 years, the fund dramatically underperformed the S&P 500; by the end of 2008, its cumulative 18-year performance was barely different from the index. Does this affect your opinion?

Weak-Form Tests: Patterns in Stock Returns

Returns over short horizons Early tests of efficient markets were tests of the weak form. Could speculators find trends in past prices that would enable them to earn abnormal profits? This is essentially a test of the efficacy of technical analysis.

One way of discerning trends in stock prices is by measuring the *serial correlation* of stock market returns. Serial correlation refers to the tendency for stock returns to be related to past returns. Positive serial correlation means that positive returns tend to follow positive returns (a momentum type of property). Negative serial correlation means that positive returns tend to be followed by negative returns (a reversal or "correction" property). Both Conrad and Kaul (1988) and Lo and MacKinlay (1988) examine weekly returns of NYSE stocks and find positive serial correlation over short horizons. However, the correlation coefficients of weekly returns tend to be fairly small, at least for large stocks for which price data are the most reliably up to date. Thus, while these studies demonstrate weak price trends over short periods,[4] the evidence does not clearly suggest the existence of trading opportunities.

While broad market indexes demonstrate only weak serial correlation, there appears to be stronger momentum in performance across market sectors exhibiting the best and worst recent returns. In an investigation of intermediate-horizon stock price behavior (using 3- to 12-month holding periods), Jegadeesh and Titman (1993) found a **momentum effect** in which good or bad recent performance of particular stocks continues over time. They conclude that while the performance of individual stocks is highly unpredictable, *portfolios* of the best-performing stocks in the recent past appear to outperform other stocks with enough reliability to offer profit opportunities. Thus, it appears that there is evidence of short- to intermediate-horizon price momentum in both the aggregate market and cross-sectionally (i.e., across particular stocks).

momentum effect

The tendency of poorly performing stocks and well-performing stocks in one period to continue that abnormal performance in following periods.

Returns over long horizons Although short- to intermediate-horizon returns suggest momentum in stock market prices, studies of long-horizon returns (i.e., returns over multiyear periods) by Fama and French (1988) and Poterba and Summers (1988) indicate pronounced *negative* long-term serial correlation in the performance of the aggregate market. The latter result has given rise to a "fads hypothesis," which asserts that the stock market might overreact to relevant news. Such overreaction leads to positive serial correlation (momentum) over short time horizons. Subsequent correction of the overreaction leads to poor performance following good performance and vice versa. The corrections mean that a run of positive returns eventually will tend to be followed by negative returns, leading to negative serial correlation over longer horizons. These episodes of apparent overshooting followed by correction give the stock market the appearance of fluctuating around its fair value.

These long-horizon results are dramatic, but the studies offer far from conclusive evidence regarding efficient markets. First, the study results need not be interpreted as evidence for stock market fads. An alternative interpretation of these results holds that they indicate only that the market risk premium varies over time. For example, when the risk premium and the required

[4]On the other hand, there is evidence that share prices of individual securities (as opposed to broad market indexes) are more prone to reversals than continuations at very short horizons. See, for example, B. Lehmann, "Fads, Martingales and Market Efficiency," *Quarterly Journal of Economics* 105 (February 1990), pp. 1–28; and N. Jegadeesh, "Evidence of Predictable Behavior of Security Returns," *Journal of Finance* 45 (September 1990), pp. 881–898. However, as Lehmann notes, this is probably best interpreted as due to liquidity problems after big movements in stock prices as market makers adjust their positions in the stock.

return on the market rises, stock prices will fall. When the market then rises (on average) at this higher rate of return, the data convey the impression of a stock price recovery. The apparent overshooting and correction is in fact no more than a rational response of market prices to changes in discount rates.

In addition to studies suggestive of overreaction in overall stock market returns over long horizons, many other studies suggest that over long horizons, extreme performance in particular securities also tends to reverse itself: The stocks that have performed best in the recent past seem to underperform the rest of the market in following periods, while the worst past performers tend to offer above-average future performance. De Bondt and Thaler (1985) and Chopra, Lakonishok, and Ritter (1992) find strong tendencies for poorly performing stocks in one period to experience sizable reversals over the subsequent period, while the best-performing stocks in a given period tend to follow with poor performance in the following period.

For example, the De Bondt and Thaler study found that if one were to rank-order the performance of stocks over a five-year period and then group stocks into portfolios based on investment performance, the base-period "loser" portfolio (defined as the 35 stocks with the worst investment performance) outperformed the "winner" portfolio (the top 35 stocks) by an average of 25% (cumulative return) in the following three-year period. This **reversal effect,** in which losers rebound and winners fade back, suggests that the stock market overreacts to relevant news. After the overreaction is recognized, extreme investment performance is reversed. This phenomenon would imply that a *contrarian* investment strategy—investing in recent losers and avoiding recent winners—should be profitable. Moreover, these returns seem pronounced enough to be exploited profitably.

reversal effect

The tendency of poorly performing stocks and well-performing stocks in one period to experience reversals in the following period.

Thus it appears that there may be short-run momentum but long-run reversal patterns in price behavior both for the market as a whole and across sectors of the market. One interpretation of this pattern is that short-run overreaction (which causes momentum in prices) may lead to long-term reversals (when the market recognizes its past error).

Predictors of Broad Market Returns

Several studies have documented the ability of easily observed variables to predict market returns. For example, Fama and French (1988) showed that the return on the aggregate stock market tends to be higher when the dividend/price ratio, the dividend yield, is high. Campbell and Shiller (1988) found that the earnings yield can predict market returns. Keim and Stambaugh (1986) showed that bond market data such as the spread between yields on high- and low-grade corporate bonds also help predict broad market returns.

Again, the interpretation of these results is difficult. On the one hand, they may imply that stock returns can be predicted, in violation of the efficient market hypothesis. More probably, however, these variables are proxying for variation in the market risk premium. For example, given a level of dividends or earnings, stock prices will be lower and dividend and earnings yields will be higher when the risk premium (and therefore the expected market return) is higher. Thus a high dividend or earnings yield will be associated with higher market returns. This does not indicate a violation of market efficiency. The predictability of market returns is due to predictability in the risk premium, not in risk-adjusted abnormal returns.

Fama and French (1989) showed that the yield spread between high- and low-grade bonds has greater predictive power for returns on low-grade bonds than for returns on high-grade bonds, and greater predictive power for stock returns than for bond returns, suggesting that the predictability in returns is in fact a risk premium rather than evidence of market inefficiency. Similarly, the fact that the dividend yield on stocks helps to predict bond market returns suggests that the yield captures a risk premium common to both markets rather than mispricing in the equity market.

Semistrong Tests: Market Anomalies

Fundamental analysis uses a much wider range of information to create portfolios than does technical analysis. Investigations of the efficacy of fundamental analysis ask whether publicly available information beyond the trading history of a security can be used to improve investment performance, and therefore they are tests of semistrong-form market efficiency. Surprisingly, several easily accessible statistics, for example a stock's price–earnings ratio or its market capitalization, seem to predict abnormal risk-adjusted returns. Findings such as these, which we will review in the following pages, are difficult to reconcile with the efficient market hypothesis and therefore are often referred to as efficient market **anomalies.**

anomalies

Patterns of returns that seem to contradict the efficient market hypothesis.

A difficulty in interpreting these tests is that we usually need to adjust for portfolio risk before evaluating the success of an investment strategy. Many tests, for example, have used the CAPM to adjust for risk. However, we know that even if beta is a relevant descriptor of stock risk, the empirically measured quantitative trade-off between risk as measured by beta and expected return differs from the predictions of the CAPM. If we use the CAPM to adjust portfolio returns for risk, inappropriate adjustments may lead to the conclusion that various portfolio strategies can generate superior returns, when in fact it simply is the risk adjustment procedure that has failed.

Another way to put this is to note that tests of risk-adjusted returns are *joint tests* of the efficient market hypothesis *and* the risk adjustment procedure. If it appears that a portfolio strategy can generate superior returns, we must then choose between rejecting the EMH and rejecting the risk adjustment technique. Usually, the risk adjustment technique is based on more-questionable assumptions than is the EMH; by opting to reject the procedure, we are left with no conclusion about market efficiency.

An example of this issue is the discovery by Basu (1977, 1983) that portfolios of low price–earnings (P/E) ratio stocks have higher returns than do high P/E portfolios. The **P/E effect** holds up even if returns are adjusted for portfolio beta. Is this a confirmation that the market systematically misprices stocks according to P/E ratio? This would be an extremely surprising and, to us, disturbing conclusion, because analysis of P/E ratios is such a simple procedure. Although it may be possible to earn superior returns by using hard work and much insight, it hardly seems plausible that such a simplistic technique is enough to generate abnormal returns.

P/E effect

Portfolios of low P/E stocks have exhibited higher average risk-adjusted returns than high P/E stocks.

Another interpretation of these results is that returns are not properly adjusted for risk. If two firms have the same expected earnings, the riskier stock will sell at a lower price and lower P/E ratio. Because of its higher risk, the low P/E stock also will have higher expected returns. Therefore, unless the CAPM beta fully adjusts for risk, P/E will act as a useful additional descriptor of risk and will be associated with abnormal returns if the CAPM is used to establish benchmark performance.

The small-firm-in-January effect The so-called size or **small-firm effect,** originally documented by Banz (1981), is illustrated in Figure 8.3. It shows the historical performance of portfolios formed by dividing the NYSE stocks into 10 portfolios each year according to firm size (i.e., the total value of outstanding equity). Average annual returns between 1926 and 2010 are consistently higher on the small-firm portfolios. The difference in average annual return between portfolio 10 (with the largest firms) and portfolio 1 (with the smallest firms) is 8.8%. Of course, the smaller-firm portfolios tend to be riskier. But even when returns are adjusted for risk using the CAPM, there is still a consistent premium for the smaller-sized portfolios.

small-firm effect

Stocks of small firms have earned abnormal returns, primarily in the month of January.

Imagine earning a premium of this size on a billion-dollar portfolio. Yet it is remarkable that following a simple (even simplistic) rule such as "invest in low-capitalization stocks" should enable an investor to earn excess returns. After all, any investor can measure firm size at little cost. One would not expect such minimal effort to yield such large rewards.

Later studies (Keim, 1983; Reinganum, 1983; and Blume and Stambaugh, 1983) showed that the small-firm effect occurs virtually entirely in January, in fact, in the first two weeks of January. The size effect is in fact a "small-firm-in-January" effect.

The neglected-firm and liquidity effects Arbel and Strebel (1983) gave another interpretation of the small-firm-in-January effect. Because they tend to be neglected by large institutional traders, information about smaller firms is less available. This information deficiency makes smaller firms riskier investments that command higher returns. "Brand-name" firms, after all, are subject to considerable monitoring from institutional investors, which promises high-quality information, and presumably investors do not purchase "generic" stocks without the prospect of greater returns.

FIGURE 8.3

Average annual return for 10 size-based portfolios, 1926–2010

Source: Authors' calculations using data obtained from Prof. Kenneth French's data library, **http://mba.tuck.dartmouth.edu/pages/faculty/ken.french/data_library.html.**

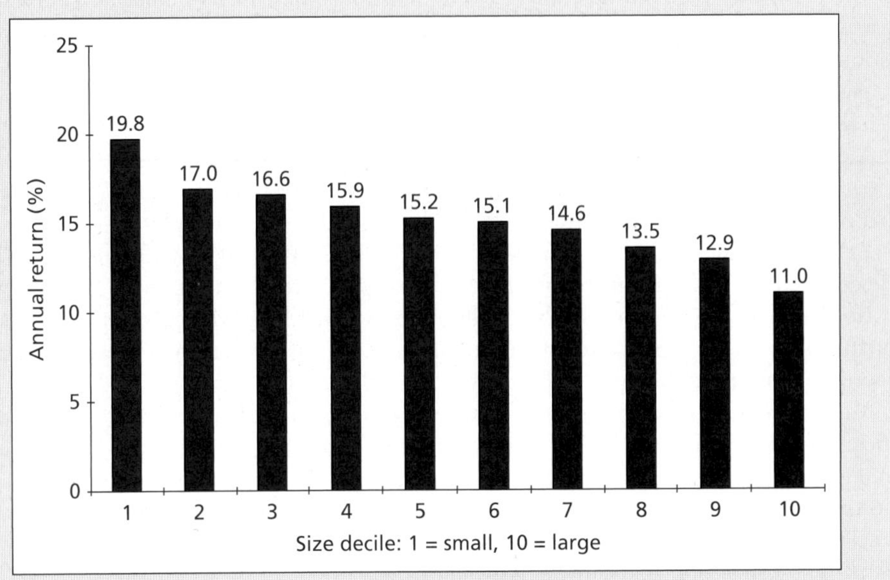

neglected-firm effect

The tendency of investments in stock of less well-known firms to generate abnormal returns.

As evidence for the **neglected-firm effect,** Arbel (1985) divided firms into highly researched, moderately researched, and neglected groups based on the number of institutions holding the stock. The January effect was in fact largest for the neglected firms. An article by Merton (1987) shows that neglected firms might be expected to earn higher equilibrium returns as compensation for the risk associated with limited information. In this sense the neglected-firm premium is not strictly a market inefficiency but is a type of risk premium.

Work by Amihud and Mendelson (1986, 1991) on the effect of liquidity on stock returns might be related to both the small-firm and neglected-firm effects. They argue that investors will demand a rate-of-return premium to invest in less liquid stocks that entail higher trading costs. In accord with their hypothesis, Amihud and Mendelson showed that these stocks show a strong tendency to exhibit abnormally high risk-adjusted rates of return. Because small and less-analyzed stocks as a rule are less liquid, the liquidity effect might be a partial explanation of their abnormal returns. However, this theory does not explain why the abnormal returns of small firms should be concentrated in January. In any case, exploiting these effects can be more difficult than it would appear. The high trading costs on small stocks can easily wipe out any apparent abnormal profit opportunity.

Book-to-market ratios Fama and French (1992) showed that a powerful predictor of returns across securities is the ratio of the book value of the firm's equity to the market value of equity. Fama and French stratified firms into 10 groups according to book-to-market ratios and examined the average rate of return of each of the 10 groups. Figure 8.4 is an updated version of their results. The decile with the highest book-to-market ratio had an average annual return of 17.3%, while the lowest-ratio decile averaged only 11%. The dramatic dependence of returns on book-to-market ratio is independent of beta, suggesting either that high book-to-market ratio firms are relatively underpriced or that the book-to-market ratio is serving as a proxy for a risk factor that affects equilibrium expected returns.

book-to-market effect

The tendency for investments in shares of firms with high ratios of book value to market value to generate abnormal returns.

In fact, Fama and French found that after controlling for the size and **book-to-market effects,** beta seemed to have no power to explain average security returns.[5] This finding is an important challenge to the notion of rational markets, since it seems to imply that a factor

[5]However, a study by S. P. Kothari, Jay Shanken, and Richard G. Sloan (1995) finds that when betas are estimated using annual rather than monthly returns, securities with high beta values do in fact have higher average returns. Moreover, the authors find a book-to-market effect that is attenuated compared to the results in Fama and French and furthermore is inconsistent across different samples of securities. They conclude that the empirical case for the importance of the book-to-market ratio may be somewhat weaker than the Fama and French study would suggest.

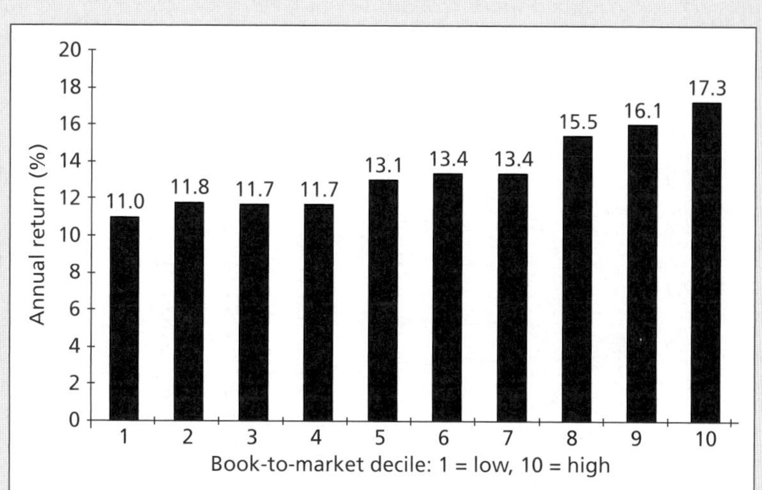

FIGURE 8.4

Average annual return as a function of the book-to-market ratio, 1926–2010

Source: Website of Prof. Kenneth French, **http://mba.tuck.dartmouth.edu/pages/faculty/ken.french/data_library.html.**

that should affect returns—systematic risk—seems not to matter, while a factor that should not matter—the book-to-market ratio—seems capable of predicting future returns. We will return to the interpretation of this anomaly.

Post-earnings-announcement price drift A fundamental principle of efficient markets is that any new information ought to be reflected in stock prices very rapidly. When good news is made public, for example, the stock price should jump immediately. A puzzling anomaly, therefore, is the apparently sluggish response of stock prices to firms' earnings announcements, as uncovered by Ball and Brown (1968). Their results were later confirmed and extended in many other papers.[6]

The "news content" of an earnings announcement can be evaluated by comparing the announcement of actual earnings to the value previously expected by market participants. The difference is the "earnings surprise." (Market expectations of earnings can be roughly measured by averaging the published earnings forecasts of Wall Street analysts or by applying trend analysis to past earnings.) Rendleman, Jones, and Latané (1982) provide an influential study of sluggish price response to earnings announcements. They calculate earnings surprises for a large sample of firms, rank the magnitude of the surprise, divide firms into 10 deciles based on the size of the surprise, and calculate abnormal returns for each decile. The abnormal return of each portfolio is the return adjusting for both the market return in that period and the portfolio beta. It measures return over and above what would be expected given market conditions in that period. Figure 8.5 plots cumulative abnormal returns by decile.

Their results are dramatic. The correlation between ranking by earnings surprise and abnormal returns across deciles is as predicted. There is a large abnormal return (a jump in cumulative abnormal return) on the earnings announcement day (time 0). The abnormal return is positive for positive-surprise firms and negative for negative-surprise firms.

The more remarkable, and interesting, result of the study concerns stock price movement *after* the announcement date. The cumulative abnormal returns of positive-surprise stocks continue to rise—in other words, exhibit momentum—even after the earnings information becomes public, while the negative-surprise firms continue to suffer negative abnormal returns. The market appears to adjust to the earnings information only gradually, resulting in a sustained period of abnormal returns.

[6]There is a voluminous literature on this phenomenon, often referred to as post-earnings-announcement price drift. For more recent papers that focus on why such drift may be observed, see V. Bernard and J. Thomas, "Evidence That Stock Prices Do Not Fully Reflect the Implications of Current Earnings for Future Earnings," *Journal of Accounting and Economics* 13 (1990), pp. 305–340, or R. H. Battalio and R. Mendenhall, "Earnings Expectation, Investor Trade Size, and Anomalous Returns around Earnings Announcements," *Journal of Financial Economics* 77 (2005), pp. 289–319.

FIGURE 8.5

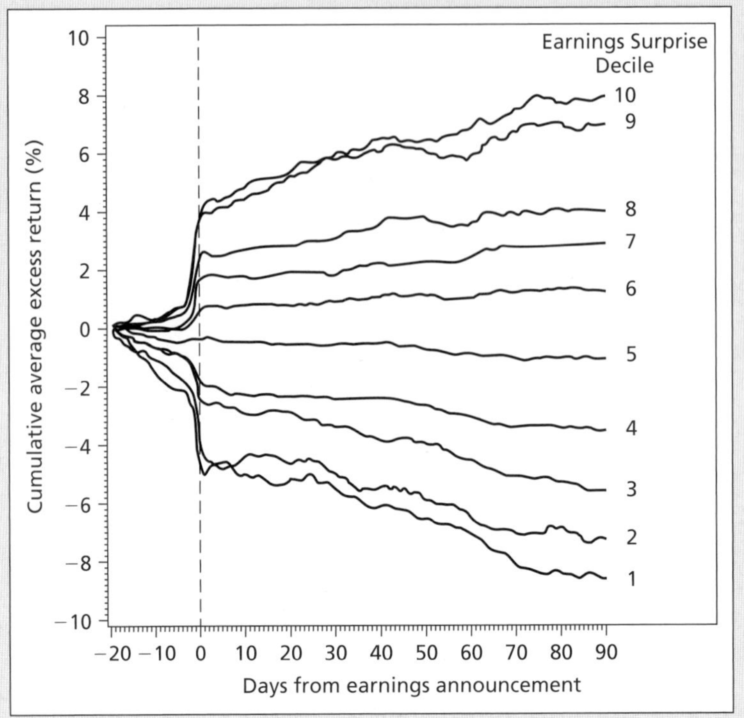

Cumulative abnormal returns in response to earnings announcements

Source: Reprinted from R. J. Rendleman Jr., C. P. Jones, and H. A. Latané, "Empirical Anomalies Based on Unexpected Earnings and the Importance of Risk Adjustments," *Journal of Financial Economics* 10 (1982), pp. 269–287. Copyright 1982 with permission from Elsevier Science.

Evidently, one could have earned abnormal profits simply by waiting for earnings announcements and purchasing a stock portfolio of positive-earnings-surprise companies. These are precisely the types of predictable continuing trends that ought to be impossible in an efficient market.

Bubbles and market efficiency Every so often, it seems (at least in retrospect) that asset prices lose their grounding in reality. For example, in the tulip mania in seventeenth-century Holland, tulip prices peaked at several times the annual income of a skilled worker. This episode has become the symbol of a speculative "bubble" in which prices appear to depart from any semblance of intrinsic value. Less than a century later, the South Sea bubble in England became almost as famous. In this episode, the share price of the South Sea Company rose from £128 in January 1720 to £550 in May and peaked at around £1,000 in August—just before the bubble burst and the share price collapsed to £150 in September, leading to widespread bankruptcies among those who had borrowed to buy shares on credit. In fact, the company was a major lender of money to investors willing to buy (and thus bid up) its shares. This sequence may sound familiar to anyone who lived through the dot-com boom and bust of 1995–2002[7] or, more recently, the financial turmoil of 2008, with origins widely attributed to a collapsing housing price bubble (see Chapter 1).

It is hard to defend the position that security prices in these instances represented rational, unbiased assessments of intrinsic value. And, in fact, some economists, most notably Hyman Minsky, have suggested that bubbles arise naturally. During periods of stability and rising prices, investors extrapolate that stability into the future and become more willing to take on risk. Risk premiums shrink, leading to further increases in asset prices, and expectations become even more optimistic in a self-fulfilling cycle. But, in the end, pricing and risk taking become excessive and the bubble bursts. Ironically, the initial period of stability fosters behavior that ultimately results in instability.

[7]The dot-com boom gave rise to the term *irrational exuberance.* In this vein consider that one company, going public in the investment boom of 1720, described itself simply as "a company for carrying out an undertaking of great advantage, but nobody to know what it is."

But beware of jumping to the conclusion that asset prices may generally be thought of as arbitrary and obvious trading opportunities abundant. First, most bubbles become "obvious" only *after* they have burst. At the time, there is often a seemingly defensible rationale for the price run-up. In the dot-com boom, for example, many contemporary observers rationalized stock price gains as justified by the prospect of a new and more profitable economy, driven by technological advances. Even the irrationality of the tulip mania may have been overblown in its later retelling.[8] In addition, security valuation is intrinsically difficult. Given the considerable imprecision of estimates of intrinsic value, large bets on perceived mispricing may entail hubris.

Moreover, even if you suspect that prices are in fact "wrong," it can be difficult to take advantage of them. We explore these issues in more detail in the following chapter. For now, we can simply point out some impediments to making aggressive bets against an asset: the costs of short-selling overpriced securities as well as potential problems obtaining the securities to sell short and the possibility that, even if you are ultimately correct, the market may disagree and prices still can move dramatically against you in the short term, thus wiping out your portfolio.

Strong-Form Tests: Inside Information

It would not be surprising if insiders were able to make superior profits trading in their firm's stock. In other words, we do not expect markets to be strong-form efficient; we regulate and limit trades based on inside information. The ability of insiders to trade profitably in their own stock has been documented in studies by Jaffe (1974), Seyhun (1986), Givoly and Palmon (1985), and others. Jaffe's was one of the earlier studies that documented the tendency for stock prices to rise after insiders intensively bought shares and to fall after intensive insider sales.

Can other investors benefit by following insiders' trades? The Securities and Exchange Commission requires all insiders to register their trading activity, and it publishes these trades in an *Official Summary of Security Transactions and Holdings.* Since 2002, insiders must report large trades to the SEC within two business days. Once the *Official Summary* is published, the trades become public information. At that point, if markets are efficient, fully and immediately processing the information released in the *Official Summary* of trading, an investor should no longer be able to profit from following the pattern of those trades. Several Internet sites contain information on insider trading.

The study by Seyhun, which carefully tracked the public release dates of the *Official Summary,* found that following insider transactions would be to no avail. Although there is some tendency for stock prices to increase even after the *Official Summary* reports insider buying, the abnormal returns are not of sufficient magnitude to overcome transaction costs.

Interpreting the Anomalies

How should we interpret the ever-growing anomalies literature? Does it imply that markets are grossly inefficient, allowing for simplistic trading rules to offer large profit opportunities? Or are there other, more-subtle interpretations?

Risk premiums or inefficiencies? The price–earnings, small-firm, market-to-book, momentum, and long-term reversal effects are currently among the most puzzling phenomena in empirical finance. There are several interpretations of these effects. First note that to some extent, some of these phenomena may be related. The feature that small firms, low-market-to-book firms, and recent "losers" seem to have in common is a stock price that has fallen considerably in recent months or years. Indeed, a firm can become a small firm or a low-market-to-book firm by suffering a sharp drop in price. These groups therefore may contain a relatively high proportion of distressed firms that have suffered recent difficulties.

[8]For interesting discussions of this possibility, see Peter Garber, *Famous First Bubbles: The Fundamentals of Early Manias* (Cambridge: MIT Press, 2000), and Anne Goldgar, *Tulipmania: Money, Honor, and Knowledge in the Dutch Golden Age* (Chicago: University of Chicago Press, 2007).

FIGURE 8.6

Return to style portfolio as a predictor of GDP growth. Average difference in the return on the style portfolio in years before good GDP growth versus in years before bad GDP growth. Positive value means the style portfolio does better in years prior to good macroeconomic performance. HML = high minus low portfolio, sorted on ratio of book-to-market value. SMB = small minus big portfolio, sorted on firm size.

Source: Reprinted from J. Liew and M. Vassalou, "Can Book-to-Market, Size, and Momentum Be Risk Factors That Predict Economic Growth?" *Journal of Financial Economics* 57 (2000), pp. 221–245. Copyright 2000 with permission from Elsevier Science.

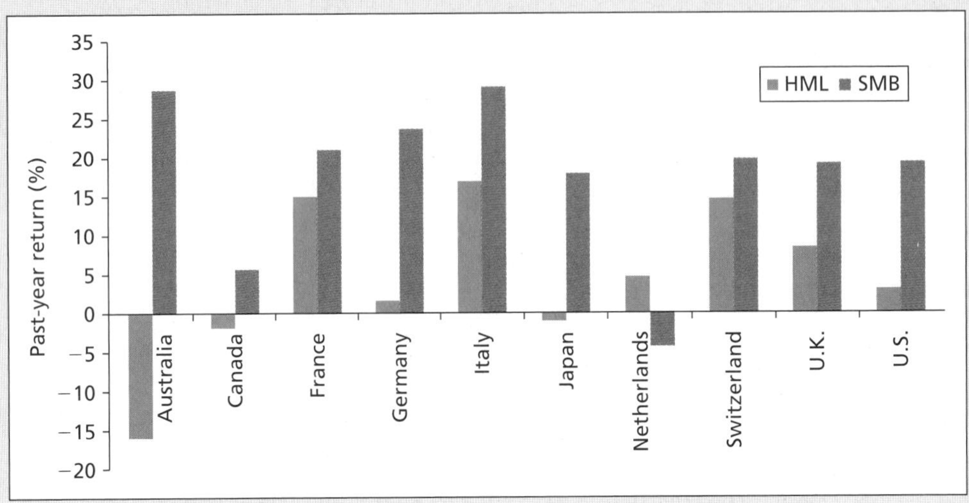

Fama and French (1993) argue that these effects can be explained as manifestations of risk premiums. Using their three-factor model, they show that stocks with higher "betas" (also known as factor loadings) on size or market-to-book factors have higher average returns; they interpret these returns as evidence of a risk premium associated with the factor. This model does a much better job than the one-factor CAPM in explaining security returns. While size or book-to-market ratios per se are obviously not risk factors, they perhaps might act as proxies for more fundamental determinants of risk. Fama and French argue that these patterns of returns may therefore be consistent with an efficient market in which expected returns are consistent with risk. In this regard, it is worth noting that returns to "style portfolios," for example, the return on portfolios constructed based on the ratio of book-to-market value (specifically, the Fama-French high minus low book-to-market portfolio) or firm size (the return on the small minus big firm portfolio) do indeed seem to predict business cycles in many countries. Figure 8.6 shows that returns on these portfolios tend to have positive returns in years prior to rapid growth in gross domestic product.

The opposite interpretation is offered by Lakonishok, Shleifer, and Vishny (1995), who argue that these phenomena are evidence of inefficient markets, more specifically, of systematic errors in the forecasts of stock analysts. They believe that analysts extrapolate past performance too far into the future and therefore overprice firms with recent good performance and underprice firms with recent poor performance. Ultimately, when market participants recognize their errors, prices reverse. This explanation is consistent with the reversal effect and also, to a degree, is consistent with the small-firm and book-to-market effects because firms with sharp price drops may tend to be small or have high book-to-market ratios.

If Lakonishok, Shleifer, and Vishney are correct, we ought to find that analysts systematically err when forecasting returns of recent "winner" versus "loser" firms. A study by La Porta (1996) is consistent with this pattern. He finds that shares of firms for which analysts predict low growth rates of earnings actually perform better than those with high expected earnings growth. Analysts seem overly pessimistic about firms with low growth prospects and overly optimistic about firms with high growth prospects. When these too-extreme expectations are "corrected," the low-expected-growth firms outperform high-expected-growth firms.

Anomalies or data mining? We have covered many of the so-called anomalies cited in the literature, but our list could go on and on. Some wonder whether these anomalies are really unexplained puzzles in financial markets or whether they instead are an artifact of data mining. After all, if one reruns the computer database of past returns over and over and examines stock returns along enough dimensions, simple chance will cause some criteria to *appear* to predict returns.

In this regard, it is noteworthy that some anomalies have not shown much staying power after being reported in the academic literature. For example, after the small-firm effect was published in the early 1980s, it promptly disappeared for much of the rest of the decade. Similarly, the book-to-market strategy, which commanded considerable attention in the early 1990s, was ineffective for the rest of that decade.

Still, even acknowledging the potential for data mining, a common thread seems to run through many of the anomalies we have considered, lending support to the notion that there is a real puzzle to explain. Value stocks—defined by low P/E ratio, high book-to-market ratio, or depressed prices relative to historic levels—seem to have provided higher average returns than "glamour" or growth stocks.

One way to address the problem of data mining is to find a data set that has not already been researched and see whether the relationship in question shows up in the new data. Such studies have revealed size, momentum, and book-to-market effects in other security markets around the world. While these phenomena may be a manifestation of a systematic risk premium, the precise nature of that risk is not fully understood.

8.4 MUTUAL FUND AND ANALYST PERFORMANCE

We have documented some of the apparent chinks in the armor of efficient market proponents. For investors, the issue of market efficiency boils down to whether skilled investors can make consistent abnormal trading profits. The best test is to look at the performance of market professionals to see if they can generate performance superior to that of a passive index fund that buys and holds the market. We will look at two facets of professional performance: that of stock market analysts who recommend investment positions and that of mutual fund managers who actually manage portfolios.

Stock Market Analysts

Stock market analysts historically have worked for brokerage firms, which presents an immediate problem in interpreting the value of their advice: Analysts have tended to be overwhelmingly positive in their assessment of the prospects of firms.[9] For example, Barber, Lehavy, McNichols, and Trueman (2001) find that on a scale of 1 (strong buy) to 5 (strong sell), the average recommendation for 5,628 covered firms in 1996 was 2.04. As a result, one cannot take positive recommendations (e.g., to buy) at face value. Instead, we must look at either the relative enthusiasm of analyst recommendations compared to those for other firms or at the change in consensus recommendations.

Womack (1996) focuses on changes in analysts' recommendations and finds that positive changes are associated with increased stock prices of about 5% and negative changes result in average price decreases of 11%. One might wonder whether these price changes reflect the market's recognition of analysts' superior information or insight about firms or, instead, simply result from new buy or sell pressure brought on by the recommendations themselves. Womack argues that price impact seems to be permanent and, therefore, consistent with the hypothesis that analysts do in fact reveal new information. Jegadeesh, Kim, Krische, and Lee (2004) also find that changes in consensus recommendations are associated with price changes, but that the *level* of consensus recommendations is an inconsistent predictor of future stock performance.

[9]This problem may be less severe in the future; as noted in Chapter 3, one recent reform intended to mitigate the conflict of interest in having brokerage firms that sell stocks also provide investment advice is to separate analyst coverage from the other activities of the firm.

Barber, Lehavy, McNichols, and Trueman (2001) focus on the level of consensus recommendations and show that firms with the most favorable recommendations outperform those with the least favorable recommendations. While their results seem impressive, the authors note that portfolio strategies based on analyst consensus recommendations would result in extremely heavy trading activity with associated costs that probably would wipe out the potential profits from the strategy.

In sum, the literature suggests some value is added by analysts but some ambiguity remains. Are superior returns following analyst upgrades due to revelation of new information or due to changes in investor demand in response to the changed outlook? Also, are these results exploitable by investors who necessarily incur trading costs?

Mutual Fund Managers

As we pointed out in Chapter 4, casual evidence does not support the claim that professionally managed portfolios can consistently beat the market. Figure 4.4 in that chapter demonstrated that between 1972 and 2010 the returns of a passive portfolio indexed to the Wilshire 5000 typically would have been better than those of the average equity fund. On the other hand, there was some (admittedly inconsistent) evidence of persistence in performance, meaning that the better managers in one period tended to be better managers in following periods. Such a pattern would suggest that the better managers can with some consistency outperform their competitors, and it would be inconsistent with the notion that market prices already reflect all relevant information.

The analyses cited in Chapter 4 were based on total returns; they did not properly adjust returns for exposure to systematic risk factors. In this section we revisit the question of mutual fund performance, paying more attention to the benchmark against which performance ought to be evaluated.

As a first pass, we can examine the risk-adjusted returns (i.e., the alpha, or return in excess of required return based on beta and the market return in each period) of a large sample of mutual funds. But the market index may not be an adequate benchmark against which to evaluate mutual fund returns. Because mutual funds tend to maintain considerable holdings in equity of small firms, whereas the S&P 500 exclusively comprises large firms, mutual funds as a whole will tend to outperform the S&P when small firms outperform large ones and underperform when small firms fare worse. Thus a better benchmark for the performance of funds would be an index that incorporates the stock market performance of smaller firms.

The importance of the benchmark can be illustrated by examining the returns on small stocks in various subperiods.[10] In the 20-year period between 1945 and 1964, for example, a small-stock index underperformed the S&P 500 by about 4% per year (i.e., the alpha of the small-stock index after adjusting for systematic risk was −4%). In the following 20-year period, between 1965 and 1984, small stocks outperformed the S&P 500 Index by 10%. Thus if one were to examine mutual fund returns in the earlier period, they would tend to look poor, not necessarily because fund managers were poor stock pickers but simply because mutual funds as a group tended to hold more small stocks than were represented in the S&P 500. In the later period, funds would look better on a risk-adjusted basis relative to the S&P 500 because small stocks performed better. The "style choice," that is, the exposure to small stocks (which is an asset allocation decision) would dominate the evaluation of performance even though it has little to do with managers' stock-picking ability.[11]

The conventional performance benchmark today is a four-factor model, which employs the three Fama-French factors (the return on the market index, and returns to portfolios based on size and book-to-market ratio) augmented by a momentum factor (a portfolio constructed based on prior-year stock return). Alphas constructed using an expanded index

[10] This illustration and the statistics cited are based on E. J. Elton, M. J. Gruber, S. Das, and M. Hlavka, "Efficiency with Costly Information: A Reinterpretation of Evidence from Managed Portfolios," *Review of Financial Studies* 6 (1993), pp. 1–22.

[11] Remember that the asset allocation decision is usually in the hands of the individual investor. Investors allocate their investment portfolios to funds in asset classes they desire to hold, and they can reasonably expect only that mutual fund portfolio managers will choose stocks advantageously *within* those asset classes.

FIGURE 8.7

Mutual fund alphas computed using a four-factor model of expected return, 1993–2007. (The best and worst 2.5% of observations are excluded from this distribution.)

Source: Professor Richard Evans, University of Virginia, Darden School of Business. Used with permission.

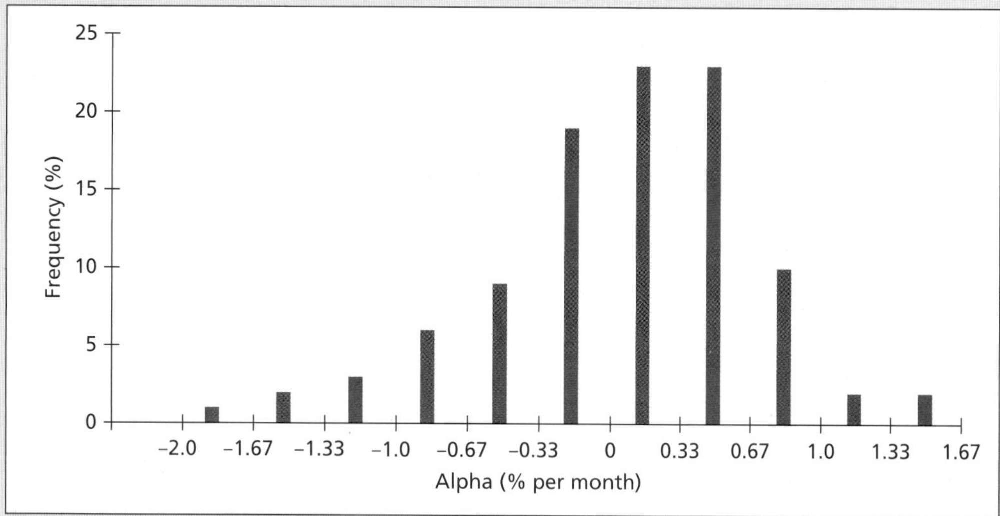

model using these four factors control for a wide range of mutual fund–style choices that may affect average returns, for example, an inclination to growth versus value or small-versus large-capitalization stocks. Figure 8.7 shows a frequency distribution of four-factor alphas for U.S. domestic equity funds.[12] The results show that the distribution of alpha is roughly bell-shaped, with a slightly negative mean. On average, it does not appear that these funds outperform their style-adjusted benchmarks.

Consistent with Figure 8.7, Fama and French (2010) use the four-factor model to assess the performance of equity mutual funds and show that while they may exhibit positive alphas *before* fees, after the fees charged to their customers, alphas were negative. Likewise, Wermers (2000), who uses both style portfolios as well as the characteristics of the stocks held by mutual funds to control for performance, also finds positive gross alphas but negative net alphas after controlling for fees and risk.

Carhart (1997) reexamines the issue of consistency in mutual fund performance to see whether better performers in one period continue to outperform in later periods. He uses the four-factor extension described above and finds that after controlling for these factors, there is only minor persistence in relative performance across managers. Moreover, much of that persistence seems due to expenses and transactions costs rather than gross investment returns.

Even allowing for expenses and turnover, some amount of performance persistence seems to be due to differences in investment strategy. Carhart finds, however, that the evidence of persistence is concentrated at the two extremes. Figure 8.8, from his study, documents performance persistence. Equity funds are ranked into 1 of 10 groups by performance in the formation year, and the performance of each group in the following years is plotted. It is clear that except for the best-performing top-decile group and the worst-performing 10th-decile group, performance in future periods is almost independent of earlier-year returns. Carhart's results suggest that there may be a small group of exceptional managers who can with some consistency outperform a passive strategy, but that for the majority of managers over- or underperformance in any period is largely a matter of chance.

Bollen and Busse (2004) find more evidence of performance persistence, at least over short horizons. They rank mutual fund performance using the four-factor model over a base

[12] We are grateful to Professor Richard Evans for this data.

FIGURE 8.8

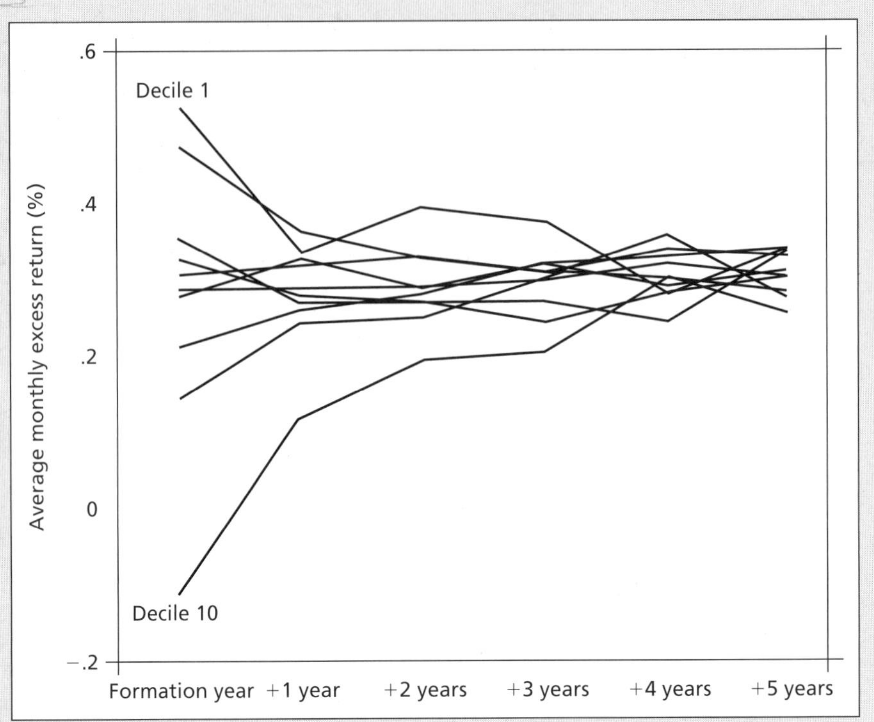

Persistence of mutual fund performance. Performance over time of mutual fund groups ranked by initial-year performance

Source: Mark M. Carhart, "On Persistence in Mutual Fund Performance," *Journal of Finance* 52 (March 1997), pp. 57–82. Used with permission of John Wiley and Sons, via Copyright Clearance Center.

quarter, assign funds into one of 10 deciles according to base-period alpha, and then look at performance in the following quarter. Figure 8.9 illustrates their results. The solid line is the average alpha of funds within each of the deciles in the base period (expressed on a quarterly basis). The steepness of that line reflects the considerable dispersion in performance in the ranking period. The dashed line is the average performance of the funds in each decile in the following quarter. The shallowness of this line indicates that most of the original performance differential disappears. Nevertheless, the plot is still clearly downward-sloping, so it appears that at least over a short horizon such as one quarter, there is some performance consistency. However, that persistence is probably too small a fraction of the original performance differential to justify performance chasing by mutual fund customers.

This pattern is actually consistent with the prediction of an influential paper by Berk and Green (2004). They argue that skilled mutual fund managers with abnormal performance will attract new funds until the additional costs and complexity of managing those extra funds

FIGURE 8.9

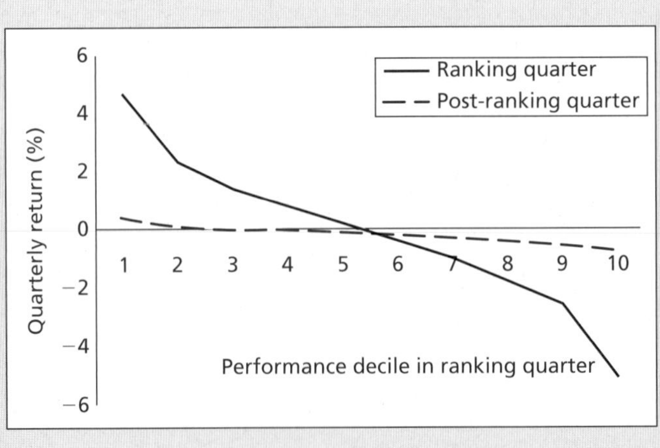

Risk-adjusted performance in ranking quarter and following quarter

Source: Nicolas P. B. Bollen and Jeffrey A. Busse, "Short-Term Persistence in Mutual Fund Performance," *Review of Financial Studies* 19 (2004), pp. 569–597, by permission of Oxford University Press.

drive alphas down to zero. Thus, skill will show up not in superior returns but rather in the amount of funds under management. Therefore, even if managers are skilled, alphas will be short-lived, as they seem to be in Figure 8.9.

In contrast to the extensive studies of equity fund managers, there have been few studies of the performance of bond fund managers. Blake, Elton, and Gruber (1993) examined the performance of fixed-income mutual funds. They found that, on average, bond funds underperform passive fixed-income indexes by an amount roughly equal to expenses and that there is no evidence that past performance can predict future performance. More recently, Chen, Ferson, and Peters (2010) find that, on average, bond mutual funds outperform passive bond indexes in terms of gross returns but underperform once the fees they charge their investors are subtracted, a result similar to those others have found for equity funds.

Thus the evidence on the risk-adjusted performance of professional managers is mixed at best. We conclude that the performance of professional managers is broadly consistent with market efficiency. The amounts by which professional managers as a group beat or are beaten by the market fall within the margin of statistical uncertainty. In any event, it is quite clear that performance superior to passive strategies is far from routine. Studies show either that most managers cannot outperform passive strategies or that if there is a margin of superiority, it is small.

On the other hand, a small number of investment superstars—Peter Lynch (formerly of Fidelity's Magellan Fund), Warren Buffett (of Berkshire Hathaway), John Templeton (of Templeton Funds), and Mario Gabelli (of GAMCO), among them—have compiled career records that show a consistency of superior performance hard to reconcile with absolutely efficient markets. In a careful statistical analysis of mutual fund "stars," Kosowski, Timmerman, Wermers, and White (2006) conclude that the stock-picking ability of a minority of managers is sufficient to cover their costs and that their superior performance tends to persist over time. However, Nobel Prize–winner Paul Samuelson (1989) points out that the records of the vast majority of professional money managers offer convincing evidence that there are no easy strategies to guarantee success in the securities markets.

So, Are Markets Efficient?

There is a telling joke about two economists walking down the street. They spot a $20 bill on the sidewalk. One starts to pick it up, but the other one says, "Don't bother; if the bill were real someone would have picked it up already."

The lesson is clear. An overly doctrinaire belief in efficient markets can paralyze the investor and make it appear that no research effort can be justified. This extreme view is probably unwarranted. There are enough anomalies in the empirical evidence to justify the search for underpriced securities that clearly goes on.

The bulk of the evidence, however, suggests that any supposedly superior investment strategy should be taken with many grains of salt. The market is competitive *enough* that only differentially superior information or insight will earn money; the easy pickings have been picked. In the end it is likely that the margin of superiority that any professional manager can add is so slight that the statistician will not easily be able to detect it.

We conclude that markets are very efficient, but that rewards to the especially diligent, intelligent, or creative may in fact be waiting.

SUMMARY

- Statistical research has shown that to a close approximation stock prices seem to follow a random walk with no discernible predictable patterns that investors can exploit. Such findings are now taken to be evidence of market efficiency, that is, evidence that market prices reflect all currently available information. Only new information will move stock prices, and this information is equally likely to be good news or bad news.
- Market participants distinguish among three forms of the efficient market hypothesis. The weak form asserts that all information to be derived from past trading data already is reflected in stock prices. The semistrong form claims that all publicly available information is already reflected. The strong form, which generally is acknowledged to be extreme, asserts that all information, including insider information, is reflected in prices.

www.mhhe.com/bkm

- Technical analysis focuses on stock price patterns and on proxies for buy or sell pressure in the market. Fundamental analysis focuses on the determinants of the underlying value of the firm, such as current profitability and growth prospects. Because both types of analysis are based on public information, neither should generate excess profits if markets are operating efficiently.
- Proponents of the efficient market hypothesis often advocate passive as opposed to active investment strategies. The policy of passive investors is to buy and hold a broad-based market index. They expend resources neither on market research nor on frequent purchase and sale of stocks. Passive strategies may be tailored to meet individual investor requirements.
- Empirical studies of technical analysis do not generally support the hypothesis that such analysis can generate superior trading profits. One notable exception to this conclusion is the apparent success of momentum-based strategies over intermediate-term horizons.
- Several anomalies regarding fundamental analysis have been uncovered. These include the P/E effect, the small-firm-in-January effect, the neglected-firm effect, post-earnings-announcement price drift, and the book-to-market effect. Whether these anomalies represent market inefficiency or poorly understood risk premiums is still a matter of debate.
- By and large, the performance record of professionally managed funds lends little credence to claims that most professionals can consistently beat the market.

KEY TERMS

anomalies, 247
book-to-market effect, 248
efficient market hypothesis, 235
fundamental analysis, 240
index fund, 241
momentum effect, 245
neglected-firm effect, 248
passive investment strategy, 241
P/E effect, 247
random walk, 235
resistance level, 239
reversal effect, 246
semistrong-form EMH, 238
small-firm effect, 247
strong-form EMH, 238
support level, 239
technical analysis, 239
weak-form EMH, 238

PROBLEM SETS

Select problems are available in McGraw-Hill's *Connect Finance.* Please see the Supplements section of the book's frontmatter for more information.

Basic

1. If markets are efficient, what should be the correlation coefficient between stock returns for two nonoverlapping time periods? ***(LO 8-1)***
2. "If all securities are fairly priced, all must offer equal expected rates of return." Comment. ***(LO 8-1)***
3. If prices are as likely to increase as decrease, why do investors earn positive returns from the market on average? ***(LO 8-1)***
4. A successful firm like Microsoft has consistently generated large profits for years. Is this a violation of the EMH? ***(LO 8-2)***
5. At a cocktail party, your co-worker tells you that he has beaten the market for each of the last three years. Suppose you believe him. Does this shake your belief in efficient markets? ***(LO 8-2)***
6. Which of the following statements are *true* if the efficient market hypothesis holds? ***(LO 8-1)***
   a. It implies that future events can be forecast with perfect accuracy.
   b. It implies that prices reflect all available information.
   c. It implies that security prices change for no discernible reason.
   d. It implies that prices do not fluctuate.
7. In an efficient market, professional portfolio management can offer all of the following benefits *except* which of the following? ***(LO 8-4)***
   a. Low-cost diversification.
   b. A targeted risk level.

c. Low-cost record keeping.

d. A superior risk-return trade-off.

8. Which version of the efficient market hypothesis (weak, semistrong, or strong-form) focuses on the most inclusive set of information? ***(LO 8-1)***
9. "Highly variable stock prices suggest that the market does not know how to price stocks." Respond. ***(LO 8-1)***
10. Which of the following sources of market inefficiency would be most easily exploited? ***(LO 8-4)***
    a. A stock price drops suddenly due to a large block sale by an institution.
    b. A stock is overpriced because traders are restricted from short sales.
    c. Stocks are overvalued because investors are exuberant over increased productivity in the economy.

Intermediate

11. Which of the following most appears to contradict the proposition that the stock market is *weakly* efficient? Explain. ***(LO 8-3)***
    a. Over 25% of mutual funds outperform the market on average.
    b. Insiders earn abnormal trading profits.
    c. Every January, the stock market earns abnormal returns.
12. Suppose that, after conducting an analysis of past stock prices, you come up with the following observations. Which would appear to *contradict* the *weak form* of the efficient market hypothesis? Explain. ***(LO 8-3)***
    a. The average rate of return is significantly greater than zero.
    b. The correlation between the return during a given week and the return during the following week is zero.
    c. One could have made superior returns by buying stock after a 10% rise in price and selling after a 10% fall.
    d. One could have made higher-than-average capital gains by holding stocks with low dividend yields.
13. Which of the following observations would provide evidence *against* the *semistrong form* of the efficient market theory? Explain. ***(LO 8-3)***
    a. Mutual fund managers do not on average make superior returns.
    b. You cannot make superior profits by buying (or selling) stocks after the announcement of an abnormal rise in dividends.
    c. Low P/E stocks tend to have positive abnormal returns.
    d. In any year approximately 50% of pension funds outperform the market.
14. Steady Growth Industries has never missed a dividend payment in its 94-year history. Does this make it more attractive to you as a possible purchase for your stock portfolio? ***(LO 8-4)***
15. Suppose you find that prices of stocks before large dividend increases show on average consistently positive abnormal returns. Is this a violation of the EMH? ***(LO 8-3)***
16. "If the business cycle is predictable, and a stock has a positive beta, the stock's returns also must be predictable." Respond. ***(LO 8-1)***
17. Which of the following phenomena would be either consistent with or a violation of the efficient market hypothesis? Explain briefly. ***(LO 8-3)***
    a. Nearly half of all professionally managed mutual funds are able to outperform the S&P 500 in a typical year.
    b. Money managers that outperform the market (on a risk-adjusted basis) in one year are likely to outperform in the following year.
    c. Stock prices tend to be predictably more volatile in January than in other months.
    d. Stock prices of companies that announce increased earnings in January tend to outperform the market in February.
    e. Stocks that perform well in one week perform poorly in the following week.

18. Why are the following "effects" considered efficient market anomalies? Are there rational explanations for these effects? ***(LO 8-2)***
    a. P/E effect
    b. Book-to-market effect
    c. Momentum effect
    d. Small-firm effect
19. Dollar-cost averaging means that you buy equal dollar amounts of a stock every period, for example, $500 per month. The strategy is based on the idea that when the stock price is low, your fixed monthly purchase will buy more shares, and when the price is high, fewer shares. Averaging over time, you will end up buying more shares when the stock is cheaper and fewer when it is relatively expensive. Therefore, by design, you will exhibit good market timing. Evaluate this strategy. ***(LO 8-4)***
20. We know that the market should respond positively to good news and that good-news events such as the coming end of a recession can be predicted with at least some accuracy. Why, then, can we not predict that the market will go up as the economy recovers? ***(LO 8-1)***
21. You know that firm XYZ is very poorly run. On a scale of 1 (worst) to 10 (best), you would give it a score of 3. The market consensus evaluation is that the management score is only 2. Should you buy or sell the stock? ***(LO 8-4)***
22. Good News, Inc., just announced an increase in its annual earnings, yet its stock price fell. Is there a rational explanation for this phenomenon? ***(LO 8-1)***
23. Shares of small firms with thinly traded stocks tend to show positive CAPM alphas. Is this a violation of the efficient market hypothesis? ***(LO 8-3)***

Challenge

24. Examine the accompanying figure, which presents cumulative abnormal returns both before and after dates on which insiders buy or sell shares in their firms. How do you interpret this figure? What are we to make of the pattern of CARs before and after the event date? ***(LO 8-3)***

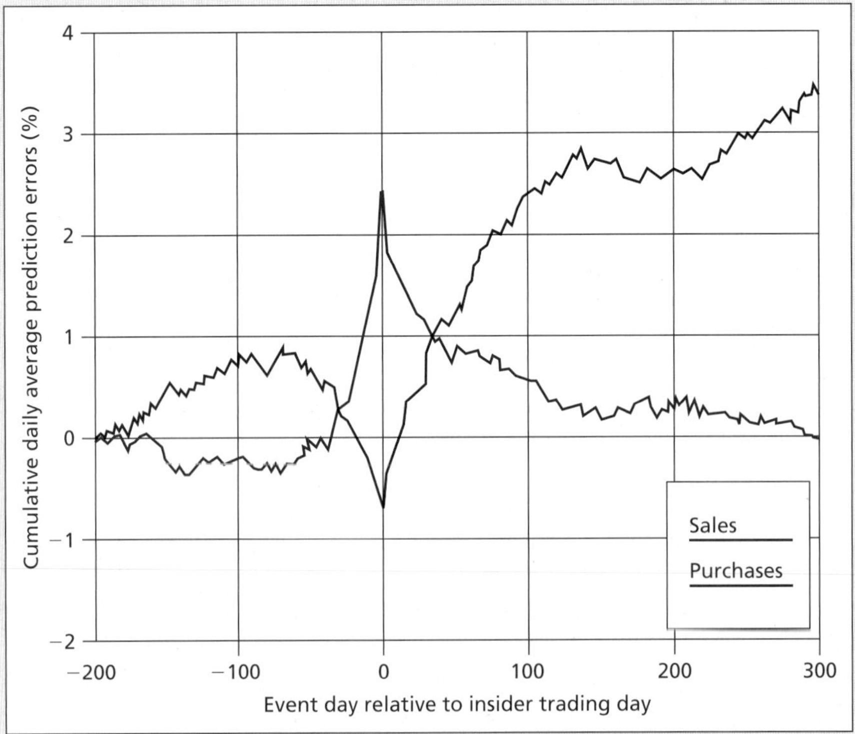

Source: Reprinted from Nejat H. Seyhun, "Insiders, Profits, Costs of Trading and Market Efficiency," *Journal of Financial Economics* 16 pp. 189–212, copyright June 1986, with permission from Elsevier.

25. Suppose that as the economy moves through a business cycle, risk premiums also change. For example, in a recession when people are concerned about their jobs, risk tolerance might be lower and risk premiums might be higher. In a booming economy, tolerance for risk might be higher and risk premiums lower. ***(LO 8-3)***
    a. Would a predictably shifting risk premium such as described here be a violation of the efficient market hypothesis?
    b. How might a cycle of increasing and decreasing risk premiums create an appearance that stock prices "overreact," first falling excessively and then seeming to recover?

CFA Problems

1. The semistrong form of the efficient market hypothesis asserts that stock prices: ***(LO 8-1)***
    a. Fully reflect all historical price information.
    b. Fully reflect all publicly available information.
    c. Fully reflect all relevant information including insider information.
    d. May be predictable.
2. Assume that a company announces an unexpectedly large cash dividend to its shareholders. In an efficient market *without* information leakage, one might expect: ***(LO 8-1)***
    a. An abnormal price change at the announcement.
    b. An abnormal price increase before the announcement.
    c. An abnormal price decrease after the announcement.
    d. No abnormal price change before or after the announcement.
3. Which one of the following would provide evidence *against* the *semistrong form* of the efficient market theory? ***(LO 8-3)***
    a. About 50% of pension funds outperform the market in any year.
    b. You cannot make abnormal profits by buying stocks after an announcement of strong earnings.
    c. Trend analysis is worthless in forecasting stock prices.
    d. Low P/E stocks tend to have positive abnormal returns over the long run.
4. According to the efficient market hypothesis: ***(LO 8-3)***
    a. High-beta stocks are consistently overpriced.
    b. Low-beta stocks are consistently overpriced.
    c. Positive alphas on stocks will quickly disappear.
    d. Negative-alpha stocks consistently yield low returns for arbitrageurs.
5. A "random walk" occurs when: ***(LO 8-1)***
    a. Stock price changes are random but predictable.
    b. Stock prices respond slowly to both new and old information.
    c. Future price changes are uncorrelated with past price changes.
    d. Past information is useful in predicting future prices.
6. A market anomaly refers to: ***(LO 8-3)***
    a. An exogenous shock to the market that is sharp but not persistent.
    b. A price or volume event that is inconsistent with historical price or volume trends.
    c. A trading or pricing structure that interferes with efficient buying and selling of securities.
    d. Price behavior that differs from the behavior predicted by the efficient market hypothesis.
7. Some scholars contend that professional managers are incapable of outperforming the market. Others come to an opposite conclusion. Compare and contrast the assumptions about the stock market that support (*a*) passive portfolio management and (*b*) active portfolio management. ***(LO 8-2)***

www.mhhe.com/bkm

8. You are a portfolio manager meeting a client. During the conversation that follows your formal review of her account, your client asks the following question: ***(LO 8-2)***

   My grandson, who is studying investments, tells me that one of the best ways to make money in the stock market is to buy the stocks of small-capitalization firms late in December and to sell the stocks one month later. What is he talking about?

   a. Identify the apparent market anomalies that would justify the proposed strategy.
   b. Explain why you believe such a strategy might or might not work in the future.
9. *a.* Briefly explain the concept of the efficient market hypothesis (EMH) and each of its three forms—weak, semistrong, and strong—and briefly discuss the degree to which existing empirical evidence supports each of the three forms of the EMH. ***(LO 8-2)***
   b. Briefly discuss the implications of the efficient market hypothesis for investment policy as it applies to: ***(LO 8-4)***
      i. Technical analysis in the form of charting.
      ii. Fundamental analysis.
   c. Briefly explain the roles or responsibilities of portfolio managers in an efficient market environment. ***(LO 8-4)***
10. Growth and value can be defined in several ways. *Growth* usually conveys the idea of a portfolio emphasizing or including only companies believed to possess above-average future rates of per-share earnings growth. Low current yield, high price-to-book ratios, and high price-to-earnings ratios are typical characteristics of such portfolios. *Value* usually conveys the idea of portfolios emphasizing or including only issues currently showing low price-to-book ratios, low price-to-earnings ratios, above-average levels of dividend yield, and market prices believed to be below the issues' intrinsic values. ***(LO 8-3)***
    a. Identify and provide reasons why, over an extended period of time, value-stock investing might outperform growth-stock investing.
    b. Explain why the outcome suggested in (*a*) should not be possible in a market widely regarded as being highly efficient.
11. Your investment client asks for information concerning the benefits of active portfolio management. She is particularly interested in the question of whether active managers can be expected to consistently exploit inefficiencies in the capital markets to produce above-average returns without assuming higher risk.

    The semistrong form of the efficient market hypothesis asserts that all publicly available information is rapidly and correctly reflected in securities prices. This implies that investors cannot expect to derive above-average profits from purchases made after information has become public because security prices already reflect the information's full effects. ***(LO 8-2)***
    a. Identify and explain two examples of empirical evidence that tend to support the EMH implication stated above.
    b. Identify and explain two examples of empirical evidence that tend to refute the EMH implication stated above.
    c. Discuss reasons why an investor might choose not to index even if the markets were, in fact, semistrong-form efficient.

WEB *master*

1. Use data from **finance.yahoo.com** to answer the following questions.
   a. Collect the following data for 25 firms of your choosing.
      i. Book-to-market ratio.
      ii. Price–earnings ratio.
      iii. Market capitalization (size).
      iv. Price–cash flow ratio (i.e, market capitalization/operating cash flow).
      v. Another criterion that interests you.

www.mhhe.com/bkm

You can find this information by choosing a company and then clicking on *Key Statistics.* Rank the firms based on each of the criteria separately, and divide the firms into five groups based on their ranking for each criterion. Calculate the average rate of return for each group of firms.

Do you confirm or reject any of the anomalies cited in this chapter? Can you uncover a new anomaly? Note: For your test to be valid, you must form your portfolios based on criteria observed at the *beginning* of the period when you form the stock groups. Why?

b. Use the price history from the *Historical Prices* tab to calculate the beta of each of the firms in part (*a*). Use this beta, the T-bill rate, and the return on the S&P 500 to calculate the risk-adjusted abnormal return of each stock group. Does any anomaly uncovered in the previous question persist after controlling for risk?

c. Now form stock groups that use two criteria simultaneously. For example, form a portfolio of stocks that are both in the lowest quintile of price–earnings ratio and in the highest quintile of book-to-market ratio. Does selecting stocks based on more than one characteristic improve your ability to devise portfolios with abnormal returns? Repeat the analysis by forming groups that meet three criteria simultaneously. Does this yield any further improvement in abnormal returns?

2. Several websites list information on earnings surprises. Much of the information supplied is from Zacks.com. Each day the largest positive and negative surprises are listed. Go to **www.zacks.com/research/earnings/today_eps.php** and identify the top positive and the top negative earnings surprises for the day. The table will list the time and date of the announcement.

a. Do you notice any difference between the times of day that positive announcements tend to be made versus negative announcements?

b. Identify the tickers for the top three positive surprises. Once you have identified the top surprises, go to **finance.yahoo.com.** Enter the ticker symbols and obtain quotes for these securities. Examine the five-day charts for each of the companies. Is the information incorporated into price quickly? Is there any evidence of prior knowledge or anticipation of the disclosure in advance of the trading?

c. Choose one of the stocks listed and click on its symbol to follow the link for more information. Click on the link for *Interactive Java Charting* that appears under the graph. In the *Graph Control* dialog box choose a period of five years and select the box that says "EPS Surprise." The resulting chart will show positive earnings surprises as green bars and negative surprises as red bars. You can move the cursor over various parts of the graph to investigate what happened to the price and trading volume of the stock around each of the surprise events. Do you notice any patterns?

8.1 *a.* A high-level manager might well have private information about the firm. Her ability to trade profitably on that information is not surprising. This ability does not violate weak-form efficiency: The abnormal profits are not derived from an analysis of past price and trading data. If they were, this would indicate that there is valuable information that can be gleaned from such analysis. But this ability does violate strong-form efficiency. Apparently, there is some private information that is not already reflected in stock prices.

b. The information sets that pertain to the weak, semistrong, and strong form of the EMH can be described by the following illustration:

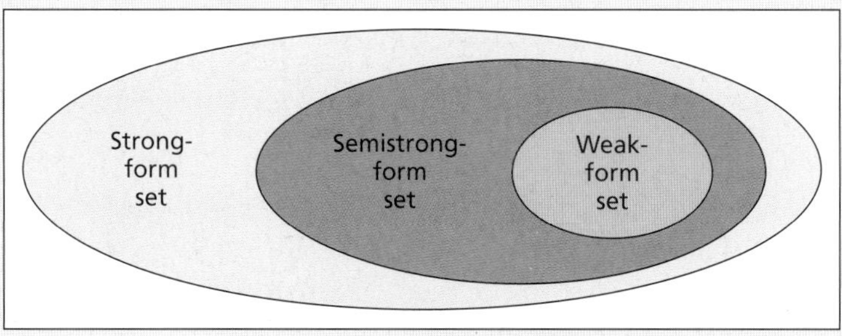

The weak-form information set includes only the history of prices and volumes. The semistrong-form set includes the weak form set *plus* all other publicly available information. In turn, the strong-form set includes the semistrong set *plus* insiders' information. It is illegal to act on this incremental information (insiders' private information). The direction of *valid* implication is

$$\text{Strong-form EMH} \Rightarrow \text{Semistrong-form EMH} \Rightarrow \text{Weak-form EMH}$$

The reverse direction implication is *not* valid. For example, stock prices may reflect all past price data (weak-form efficiency) but may not reflect relevant fundamental data (semistrong-form inefficiency).

8.2 The point we made in the preceding discussion is that the very fact that we observe stock prices near so-called resistance levels belies the assumption that the price can be a resistance level. If a stock is observed to sell *at any price,* then investors must believe that a fair rate of return can be earned if the stock is purchased at that price. It is logically impossible for a stock to have a resistance level *and* offer a fair rate of return at prices just below the resistance level. If we accept that prices are appropriate, we must reject any presumption concerning resistance levels.

8.3 If *everyone* follows a passive strategy, sooner or later prices will fail to reflect new information. At this point there are profit opportunities for active investors who uncover mispriced securities. As they buy and sell these assets, prices again will be driven to fair levels.

8.4 The answer depends on your prior beliefs about market efficiency. Miller's initial record was incredibly strong. On the other hand, with so many funds in existence, it is less surprising that *some* fund would appear to be consistently superior after the fact. Exceptional past performance of a small number of managers is possible by chance even in an efficient market. A better test is provided in "continuation studies." Are better performers in one period more likely to repeat that performance in later periods? Miller's record in the last three years fails the continuation or consistency criterion.

Behavioral Finance and Technical Analysis

Chapter

9

Learning Objectives:

LO9-1 Describe several behavioral biases, and explain how they could lead to anomalies in stock market prices and returns.

LO9-2 Explain why limits to arbitrage might allow anomalies due to behavioral biases to persist over time.

LO9-3 Identify reasons why technical analysis may be profitable.

LO9-4 Use indicators such as volume, put/call ratios, breadth, short interest, or confidence indexes to measure the "technical conditions" of the market.

The efficient market hypothesis makes two important predictions. First, it implies that security prices properly reflect whatever information is available to investors. A second implication follows immediately: Active traders will find it difficult to outperform passive strategies such as holding market indexes. To do so would require differential insight; this in a highly competitive market is very hard to come by.

Unfortunately, it is hard to devise measures of the "true" or intrinsic value of a security, and correspondingly difficult to test directly whether prices match those values. Therefore, most tests of market efficiency have focused on the performance of active trading strategies. These tests have been of two kinds. The anomalies literature has examined strategies that apparently *would* have provided superior risk-adjusted returns (e.g., investing in stocks with momentum or in value rather than glamour stocks). Other tests have looked at the results of *actual* investments by asking whether professional managers have been able to beat the market.

Neither class of tests has proven fully conclusive. The anomalies literature suggests that several strategies would have provided superior returns. But there are questions as to whether some of these apparent anomalies reflect risk premiums not captured by simple models of risk and return, or even if they merely reflect data mining. Moreover, the apparent inability of the typical money manager to turn these anomalies into superior returns on actual portfolios casts additional doubt on their "reality."

A relatively new school of thought dubbed *behavioral finance* argues that the sprawling literature on trading strategies has missed a larger and more important point by overlooking the first implication of efficient markets—the correctness of security prices. This may be the more important implication, since market economies rely on prices to allocate resources efficiently. The behavioral school argues that even if security prices are wrong, it still can be difficult to exploit them, and, therefore, that the failure to uncover obviously successful trading rules or traders cannot be taken as proof of market efficiency.

Whereas conventional theories presume that investors are rational, behavioral finance starts with the assumption that they are not. We will examine some of the information-processing and behavioral irrationalities uncovered by psychologists in other contexts and show how these tendencies applied to financial markets might result in some of the anomalies discussed in the previous chapter. We then consider the limitations of strategies designed to take advantage of behaviorally induced mispricing. If the limits to such arbitrage activity are severe, mispricing can survive even if some rational investors attempt to exploit it. We turn next to technical analysis and show how behavioral models give some support to techniques that clearly would be useless in efficient markets. We close the chapter with a brief survey of some of these technical strategies.

Related websites for this chapter are available at www.mhhe.com/bkm.

9.1 THE BEHAVIORAL CRITIQUE

behavioral finance

Models of financial markets that emphasize potential implications of psychological factors affecting investor behavior.

The premise of **behavioral finance** is that conventional financial theory ignores how real people make decisions and that people make a difference.[1] A growing number of economists have come to interpret the anomalies literature as consistent with several "irrationalities" that seem to characterize individuals making complicated decisions. These irrationalities fall into two broad categories: first, that investors do not always process information correctly and therefore infer incorrect probability distributions about future rates of return; and second, that even given a probability distribution of returns, they often make inconsistent or systematically suboptimal decisions.

Of course, the existence of irrational investors would not by itself be sufficient to render capital markets inefficient. If such irrationalities did affect prices, then sharp-eyed arbitrageurs taking advantage of profit opportunities might be expected to push prices back to their proper values. Thus, the second leg of the behavioral critique is that in practice the actions of such arbitrageurs are limited and therefore insufficient to force prices to match intrinsic value.

This leg of the argument is important. Virtually everyone agrees that if prices are right (i.e., price = intrinsic value), then there are no easy profit opportunities. But the converse is not necessarily true. If behaviorists are correct about limits to arbitrage activity, then the absence of profit opportunities does not necessarily imply that markets are efficient. We've noted that most tests of the efficient market hypothesis have focused on the existence of profit opportunities, often as reflected in the performance of money managers. But their failure to systematically outperform passive investment strategies need not imply that markets are in fact efficient.

We will start our summary of the behavioral critique with the first leg of the argument, surveying a sample of the informational processing errors uncovered by psychologists in

[1]The discussion in this section is based on an excellent survey article: Nicholas Barberis and Richard Thaler, "A Survey of Behavioral Finance," in the *Handbook of the Economics of Finance,* eds. G. M. Constantinides, M. Harris, and R. Stulz (Amsterdam: Elsevier, 2003).

other areas. We next examine a few of the behavioral irrationalities that seem to characterize decision makers. Finally, we look at limits to arbitrage activity and conclude with a tentative assessment of the import of the behavioral debate.

Information Processing

Errors in information processing can lead investors to misestimate the true probabilities of possible events or associated rates of return. Several such biases have been uncovered. Here are four of the more important ones.

Forecasting errors A series of experiments by Kahneman and Tversky (1972, 1973) indicates that people give too much weight to recent experience compared to prior beliefs when making forecasts (sometimes dubbed a *memory bias*) and tend to make forecasts that are too extreme given the uncertainty inherent in their information. De Bondt and Thaler (1990) argue that the P/E effect can be explained by earnings expectations that are too extreme. In this view, when forecasts of a firm's future earnings are high, perhaps due to favorable recent performance, they tend to be *too* high relative to the objective prospects of the firm. This results in a high initial P/E (due to the optimism built into the stock price) and poor subsequent performance when investors recognize their error. Thus, high P/E firms tend to be poor investments.

Overconfidence People tend to overestimate the precision of their beliefs or forecasts, and they tend to overestimate their abilities. In one famous survey, 90% of drivers in Sweden ranked themselves as better-than-average drivers. Such overconfidence may be responsible for the prevalence of active versus passive investment management—itself an anomaly to adherents of the efficient market hypothesis. Despite the growing popularity of indexing, only about 15% of the equity in the mutual fund industry is held in indexed accounts. The dominance of active management in the face of the typical underperformance of such strategies (consider the generally disappointing performance of actively managed mutual funds reviewed in Chapter 4 as well as in the previous chapter) is consistent with a tendency to overestimate ability.

An interesting example of overconfidence in financial markets is provided by Barber and Odean (2001), who compare trading activity and average returns in brokerage accounts of men and women. They find that men (in particular, single men) trade far more actively than women, consistent with the generally greater overconfidence among men well-documented in the psychology literature. They also find that trading activity is highly predictive of poor investment performance. The top 20% of accounts ranked by portfolio turnover had average returns seven percentage points lower than the 20% of the accounts with the lowest turnover rates. As they conclude, "Trading [and by implication, overconfidence] is hazardous to your wealth."

Overconfidence appears to be a widespread phenomenon, also showing up in many corporate finance contexts. For example, overconfident CEOs are more likely to overpay for target firms when making corporate acquisitions (Malmedier and Tate, 2008). Just as overconfidence can degrade portfolio investments, it also can lead such firms to make poor investments in real assets.

Conservatism A **conservatism bias** means that investors are too slow (too conservative) in updating their beliefs in response to new evidence. This means that they might initially underreact to news about a firm, so that prices will fully reflect new information only gradually. Such a bias would give rise to momentum in stock market returns.

conservatism bias

Investors are too slow (too conservative) in updating their beliefs in response to recent evidence.

Sample-size neglect and representativeness The notion of **representativeness bias** holds that people commonly do not take into account the size of a sample, acting as if a small sample is just as representative of a population as a large one. They may therefore infer a pattern too quickly based on a small sample and extrapolate apparent trends too far into the future. It is easy to see how such a pattern would be consistent with overreaction and correction anomalies. A short-lived run of good earnings reports or high stock returns would lead such investors to revise their assessments of likely future performance and

representativeness bias

People are too prone to believe that a small sample is representative of a broad population and infer patterns too quickly.

thus generate buying pressure that exaggerates the price run-up. Eventually, the gap between price and intrinsic value becomes glaring and the market corrects its initial error. Interestingly, stocks with the best recent performance suffer reversals precisely in the few days surrounding earnings announcements, suggesting that the correction occurs just as investors learn that their initial beliefs were too extreme (Chopra, Lakonishok, and Ritter, 1992).

CONCEPT check 9.1

We saw in the previous chapter that stocks seem to exhibit a pattern of short- to middle-term momentum, along with long-term reversals. How might this pattern arise from an interplay between the conservatism and representativeness biases?

Behavioral Biases

Even if information processing were perfect, many studies conclude that individuals would tend to make less-than-fully rational decisions using that information. These behavioral biases largely affect how investors frame questions of risk versus return, and therefore make risk-return trade-offs.

framing

Decisions are affected by how choices are posed, for example, as gains relative to a low baseline level or losses relative to a higher baseline.

Framing Decisions seem to be affected by how choices are **framed.** For example, an individual may reject a bet when it is posed in terms of the risk surrounding possible gains but may accept that same bet when described in terms of the risk surrounding potential losses. In other words, individuals may act risk averse in terms of gains but risk seeking in terms of losses. But in many cases, the choice of how to frame a risky venture—as involving gains or losses—can be arbitrary.

EXAMPLE 9.1

Framing

Consider a coin toss with a payoff of $50 for tails. Now consider a gift of $50 that is bundled with a bet that imposes a loss of $50 if that coin toss comes up heads. In both cases, you end up with zero for heads and $50 for tails. But the former description frames the coin toss as posing a risky gain while the latter frames the coin toss in terms of risky losses. The difference in framing can lead to different attitudes toward the bet.

mental accounting

A specific form of framing in which people segregate certain decisions.

Mental accounting **Mental accounting** is a specific form of framing in which people segregate certain decisions. For example, an investor may take a lot of risk with one investment account but establish a very conservative position with another account that is dedicated to her child's education. Rationally, it might be better to view both accounts as part of the investor's overall portfolio with the risk-return profiles of each integrated into a unified framework. Statman (1997) argues that mental accounting is consistent with some investors' irrational preference for stocks with high cash dividends (they feel free to spend dividend income, but would not "dip into capital" by selling a few shares of another stock with the same total rate of return) and with a tendency to ride losing stock positions for too long (since "behavioral investors" are reluctant to realize losses). In fact, investors are more likely to sell stocks with gains than those with losses, precisely contrary to a tax-minimization strategy (Shefrin and Statman, 1985; Odean, 1998).

Mental accounting effects also can help explain momentum in stock prices. The *house money effect* refers to gamblers' greater willingness to accept new bets if they currently are ahead. They think of (i.e., frame) the bet as being made with their "winnings account," that is, with the casino's and not with their own money, and thus are more willing to accept risk. Analogously, after a stock market run-up, individuals may view investments as largely funded out of a "capital gains account," become more tolerant of risk, discount future cash flows at a lower rate, and thus further push up prices.

Regret avoidance Psychologists have found that individuals who make decisions that turn out badly have more regret (blame themselves more) when that decision was more unconventional. For example, buying a blue-chip portfolio that turns down is not as painful as experiencing the same losses on an unknown start-up firm. Any losses on the blue-chip stocks can be more easily attributed to bad luck rather than bad decision making and cause less regret. De Bondt and Thaler (1987) argue that such **regret avoidance** is consistent with both the size and book-to-market effect. Higher-book-to-market firms tend to have depressed stock prices. These firms are "out of favor" and more likely to be in a financially precarious position. Similarly, smaller, less well-known firms are also less conventional investments. Such firms require more "courage" on the part of the investor, which increases the required rate of return. Mental accounting can add to this effect. If investors focus on the gains or losses of individual stocks, rather than on broad portfolios, they can become more risk averse concerning stocks with recent poor performance, discount their cash flows at a higher rate, and thereby create a value-stock risk premium.

regret avoidance

People blame themselves more for unconventional choices that turn out badly so they avoid regret by making conventional decisions.

CONCEPT check 9.2

How might the P/E effect (discussed in the previous chapter) also be explained as a consequence of regret avoidance?

Prospect theory **Prospect theory** modifies the analytic description of rational risk-averse investors found in standard financial theory.[2] Figure 9.1, Panel A, illustrates the conventional description of a risk-averse investor. Higher wealth provides higher satisfaction or "utility," but at a diminishing rate (the curve flattens as the individual becomes wealthier). This gives rise to risk aversion: A gain of $1,000 increases utility by less than a loss of $1,000 reduces it; therefore, investors will reject risky prospects that don't offer a risk premium.

prospect theory

Behavioral theory that investor utility depends on gains or losses from investors' starting position, rather than on their levels of wealth.

Figure 9.1, Panel B, shows a competing description of preferences characterized by "loss aversion." Utility depends not on the *level* of wealth, as in Panel A, but on *changes* in wealth from current levels. Moreover, to the left of zero (zero denotes no change from current wealth), the curve is convex rather than concave. This has several implications. Whereas many conventional utility functions imply that investors may become less risk averse as wealth increases, the function in Panel B always recenters on current wealth, thereby ruling out such decreases in risk aversion and possibly helping to explain high average historical equity risk premiums. Moreover, the convex curvature to the left of the origin in Panel B will induce investors to be risk seeking rather than risk averse when it comes to losses. Consistent with loss aversion, traders in the T-bond futures contract have been observed to assume significantly greater risk in afternoon sessions following morning sessions in which they have lost money (Coval and Shumway, 2005).

These are only a sample of many behavioral biases uncovered in the literature. Many have implications for investor behavior. The nearby box offers some good examples.

Limits to Arbitrage

Behavioral biases would not matter for stock pricing if rational arbitrageurs could fully exploit the mistakes of behavioral investors. Trades of profit-seeking investors would correct any misalignment of prices. However, behavioral advocates argue that in practice, several factors limit the ability to profit from mispricing.[3]

Fundamental risk Suppose that a share of IBM is underpriced. Buying it may present a profit opportunity, but it is hardly risk-free, since the presumed market underpricing can get worse. While price eventually should converge to intrinsic value, this may not happen until after the trader's investment horizon. For example, the investor may be a mutual fund manager who may lose clients (not to mention a job!) if short-term performance is poor or a trader who

[2] Prospect theory originated with a highly influential paper about decision making under uncertainty by D. Kahneman and A. Tversky, "Prospect Theory: An Analysis of Decision under Risk," *Econometrica* 47 (1979), pp. 263–291.

[3] Some of the more influential references on limits to arbitrage are J. B. DeLong, A. Schleifer, L. Summers, and R. Waldmann, "Noise Trader Risk in Financial Markets," *Journal of Political Economy* 98 (August 1990), pp. 704–738; and A. Schleifer and R. Vishny, "The Limits of Arbitrage," *Journal of Finance* 52 (March 1997), pp. 35–55.

FIGURE 9.1

Prospect theory
Panel A: A conventional utility function is defined in terms of wealth and is concave, resulting in risk aversion.
Panel B: Under loss aversion, the utility function is defined in terms of changes from current wealth. It is also convex to the left of the origin, giving rise to risk-seeking behavior in terms of losses.

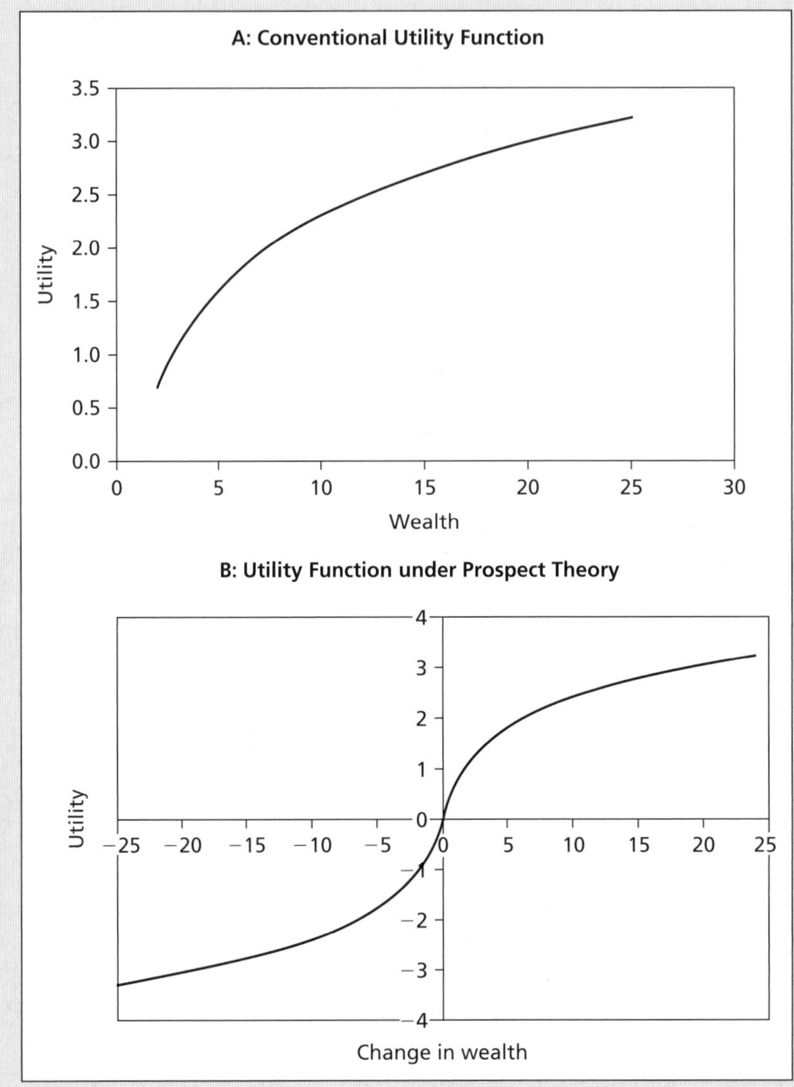

may run through her capital if the market turns against her, even temporarily. A comment often attributed to the famous economist John Maynard Keynes is that "markets can remain irrational longer than you can remain solvent." The *fundamental risk* incurred in exploiting apparent profit opportunities presumably will limit the activity of traders.

EXAMPLE 9.2

Fundamental Risk

In the first part of 2011, the NASDAQ index fluctuated at a level around 2,700. From that perspective, the value the index had reached 10 years earlier, around 5,000, seemed obviously crazy. Surely some investors living through the Internet "bubble" of the late 1990s must have identified the index as grossly overvalued, suggesting a good selling opportunity. But this hardly would have been a riskless arbitrage opportunity. Consider that NASDAQ may also have been overvalued in 1999 when it first crossed above 3,500 (30% above its value in 2011). An investor in 1999 who believed (as it turns out, quite correctly) that NASDAQ was overvalued at 3,500 and decided to sell it short would have suffered enormous losses as the index increased by another 1,500 points before finally peaking at 5,000. While the investor might have derived considerable satisfaction at eventually being proven right about the overpricing, by entering a year before the market "corrected," he might also have gone broke.

On the MARKET FRONT

WHY IT'S SO TOUGH TO FIX YOUR PORTFOLIO

If your portfolio is out of whack, you could ask an investment adviser for help. But you might have better luck with your therapist.

It's a common dilemma: You know you have the wrong mix of investments, but you cannot bring yourself to fix the mess. Why is it so difficult to change? At issue are three mental mistakes.

CHASING WINNERS

Looking to lighten up on bonds and get back into stocks? Sure, you know stocks are a long-term investment and, sure, you know they are best bought when cheap.

Yet it's a lot easier to pull the trigger and buy stocks if the market has lately been scoring gains. "People are influenced by what has happened most recently, and then they extrapolate from that," says Meir Statman, a finance professor at Santa Clara University in California. "But often, they end up being optimistic and pessimistic at just the wrong time."

Consider some results from the UBS Index of Investor Optimism, a monthly poll conducted by UBS and the Gallup Organization. Each month, the poll asks investors what gain they expect from their portfolio during the next 12 months. Result? You guessed it: The answers rise and fall with the stock market.

For instance, during the bruising bear market, investors grew increasingly pessimistic, and at the market bottom they were looking for median portfolio gains of just 5%. But true to form, last year's rally brightened investors' spirits and by January they were expecting 10% returns.

GETTING EVEN

This year's choppy stock market hasn't scared off just bond investors. It has also made it difficult for stock investors to rejigger their portfolios.

Blame it on the old "get even, then get out" syndrome. With stocks treading water, many investors are reluctant to sell, because they are a long way from recovering their bear-market losses. To be sure, investors who bought near the peak are underwater, whether they sell or not. But selling losers is still agonizing, because it means admitting you made a mistake.

"If you're rational and you have a loss, you sell, take the tax loss and move on," Prof. Statman says. "But if you're a normal person, selling at a loss tears your heart out."

MUSTERING COURAGE

Whether you need to buy stocks or buy bonds, it takes confidence to act. And right now, investors just aren't confident. "There's this status-quo bias," says John Nofsinger, a finance professor at Washington State University in Pullman, Washington. "We're afraid to do anything, because we're afraid we'll regret it."

Once again, it's driven by recent market action. When markets are flying high, folks attribute their portfolio's gains to their own brilliance. That gives them the confidence to trade more and to take greater risks. Overreacting to short-term market results is, of course, a great way to lose a truckload of money. But with any luck, if you are aware of this pitfall, maybe you will avoid it.

Or maybe [this is] too optimistic. "You can tell somebody that investors have all these behavioral biases," says Terrance Odean, a finance professor at the University of California at Berkeley. "So what happens? The investor thinks, 'Oh, that sounds like my husband. I don't think many investors say, 'Oh, that sounds like me.'"

SOURCE: Jonathan Clements, *The Wall Street Journal Online,* June 23, 2004.

Implementation costs Exploiting overpricing can be particularly difficult. Short-selling a security entails costs; short-sellers may have to return the borrowed security on little notice, rendering the horizon of the short sale uncertain; other investors such as many pension or mutual fund managers face strict limits on their discretion to short securities. This can limit the ability of arbitrage activity to force prices to fair value.

Model risk One always has to worry that an apparent profit opportunity is more apparent than real. Perhaps you are using a faulty model to value the security, and the price actually is right. Mispricing may make a position a good bet, but it is still a risky one, which limits the extent to which it will be pursued.

Limits to Arbitrage and the Law of One Price

While one can debate the implications of much of the anomalies literature, surely the Law of One Price (positing that effectively identical assets should have identical prices) should be satisfied in rational markets. Yet there are several instances where the law seems to have been violated. These instances are good case studies of the limits to arbitrage.

FIGURE 9.2

Pricing of Royal Dutch relative to Shell (*deviation from parity*)

Source: O. A. Lamont and R. H. Thaler, "Anomalies: The Law of One Price in Financial Markets," *Journal of Economic Perspectives* 17 (Fall 2003), pp. 191–202. Used with permission of American Economic Association.

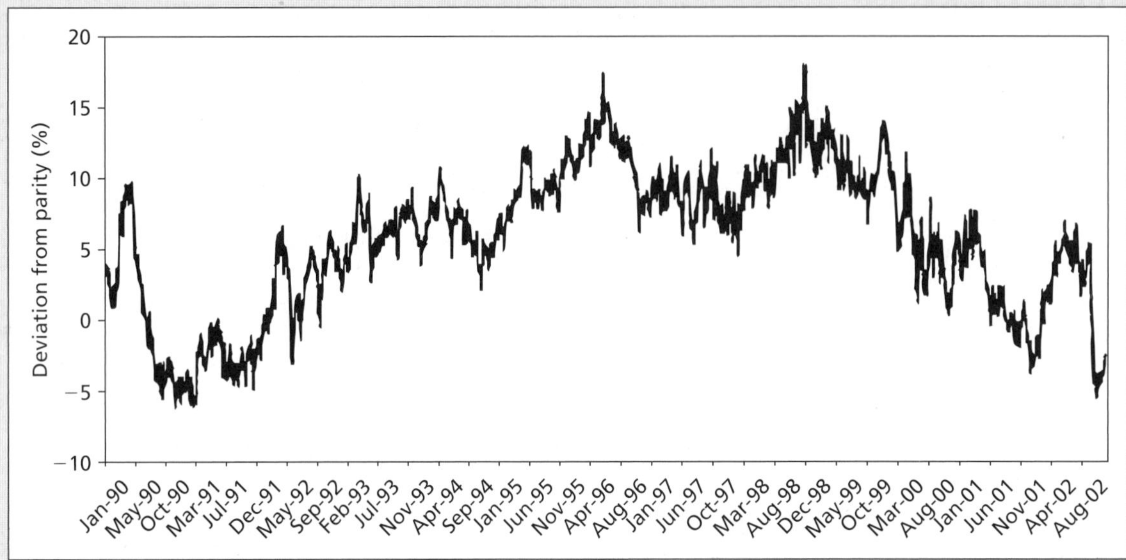

"Siamese twin" companies[4] In 1907, Royal Dutch Petroleum and Shell Transport merged their operations into one firm. The two original companies, which continued to trade separately, agreed to split all profits from the joint company on a 60/40 basis. Shareholders of Royal Dutch receive 60% of the cash flow, and those of Shell receive 40%. One would therefore expect that Royal Dutch should sell for exactly 60/40 = 1.5 times the price of Shell. But this is not the case. Figure 9.2 shows that the relative value of the two firms has departed considerably from this "parity" ratio for extended periods of time.

Doesn't this mispricing give rise to an arbitrage opportunity? If Royal Dutch sells for more than 1.5 times Shell, why not buy relatively underpriced Shell and short-sell overpriced Royal? This seems like a reasonable strategy, but if you had followed it in February 1993 when Royal sold for about 10% more than its parity value, Figure 9.2 shows that you would have lost a lot of money as the premium widened to about 17% before finally reversing after 1999. As in Example 9.2, this opportunity posed fundamental risk.

Equity carve-outs Several equity carve-outs also have violated the Law of One Price.[5] To illustrate, consider the case of 3Com, which in 1999 decided to spin off its Palm division. It first sold 5% of its stake in Palm in an IPO, announcing that it would distribute the remaining 95% of its Palm shares to 3Com shareholders six months later in a spinoff. Each 3Com shareholder would receive 1.5 shares of Palm in the spinoff.

Once Palm shares began trading, but prior to the spinoff, the share price of 3Com should have been *at least* 1.5 times that of Palm. After all, each share of 3Com entitled its owner to 1.5 shares of Palm *plus* an ownership stake in a profitable company. Instead, Palm shares at the IPO actually sold for *more* than the 3Com shares. The *stub value* of 3Com (i.e., the value of each 3Com share net of the value of the claim to Palm represented by that share) could be computed as the price of 3Com minus 1.5 times the price of Palm. This calculation, however, implies that 3Com's stub value was negative, this despite the fact that it was a profitable company with cash assets alone of about $10 per share.

[4]This discussion is based on K. A. Froot and E. M. Dabora, "How Are Stock Prices Affected by the Location of Trade?" *Journal of Financial Economics* 53 (1999), pp. 189–216.

[5]O. A. Lamont and R. H. Thaler, "Can the Market Add and Subtract? Mispricing in Tech Carve-Outs," *Journal of Political Economy* 111 (2003), pp. 227–268.

Again, an arbitrage strategy seems obvious. Why not buy 3Com and sell Palm? The limit to arbitrage in this case was the inability of investors to sell Palm short. Virtually all available shares in Palm were already borrowed and sold short, and the negative stub values persisted for more than two months.

Closed-end funds We noted in Chapter 4 that closed-end funds often sell for substantial discounts or premiums from net asset value. This is "nearly" a violation of the Law of One Price, since one would expect the value of the fund to equal the value of the shares it holds. We say nearly, because in practice, there are a few wedges between the value of the closed-end fund and its underlying assets. One is expenses. The fund incurs expenses that ultimately are paid for by investors, and these will reduce share price. On the other hand, if managers can invest fund assets to generate positive risk-adjusted returns, share price might exceed net asset value.

Lee, Shleifer, and Thaler (1991) argue that the patterns of discounts and premiums on closed-end funds are driven by changes in investor sentiment. They note that discounts on various funds move together and are correlated with the return on small stocks, suggesting that all are affected by common variation in sentiment. One might consider buying funds selling at a discount from net asset value and selling those trading at a premium, but discounts and premiums can widen, subjecting this strategy too to fundamental risk. Pontiff (1996) demonstrates that deviations of price from net asset value in closed-end funds tend to be higher in funds that are more difficult to arbitrage, for example, those with more idiosyncratic volatility.

CONCEPT check 9.3

Fundamental risk may be limited by a "deadline" that forces a convergence between price and intrinsic value. What do you think would happen to a closed-end fund's discount if the fund announced that it plans to liquidate in six months, at which time it will distribute NAV to its shareholders?

Closed-end fund discounts are a good example of apparent anomalies that also may have rational explanations. Ross (2002) demonstrates that they can be reconciled with rational investors even if expenses or fund abnormal returns are modest. He shows that if a fund has a dividend yield of δ, an alpha (risk-adjusted abnormal return) of α, and expense ratio of ε, then using the constant-growth dividend discount model (see Chapter 13), the premium of the fund over its net asset value will be

$$\frac{\text{Price} - \text{NAV}}{\text{NAV}} = \frac{\alpha - \varepsilon}{\delta + \varepsilon - \alpha}$$

If the fund manager's performance more than compensates for expenses (i.e., if $\alpha > \varepsilon$), the fund will sell at a premium to NAV; otherwise it will sell at a discount. For example, suppose $\alpha = .015$, the expense ratio is $\varepsilon = .0125$, and the dividend yield is $\delta = .02$. Then the premium will be .14, or 14%. But if the market turns sour on the manager and revises its estimate of α downward to .005, that premium quickly turns into a discount of 43%.

This analysis might explain why the public is willing to purchase closed-end funds at a premium; if investors do not expect α to exceed ε, they won't purchase shares in the fund. But the fact that most premiums eventually turn into discounts indicates how difficult it is for management to fulfill these expectations.[6]

Bubbles and Behavioral Economics

In Example 9.2, we pointed out that the stock market run-up of the late 1990s, and even more spectacularly, the run-up of the technology-heavy NASDAQ market, seems in retrospect to have been an obvious bubble. In a six-year period beginning in 1995, the NASDAQ index

[6]We might ask why this logic of discounts and premiums does not apply to open-end mutual funds since they incur similar expense ratios. Because investors in these funds can redeem shares for NAV, the shares cannot sell at a discount to NAV. Expenses in open-end funds reduce returns in each period rather than being capitalized into price and inducing a discount.

increased by a factor of more than 6. Former Fed Chairman Alan Greenspan famously characterized the dot-com boom as an example of "irrational exuberance," and his assessment turned out to be correct: By October 2002, the index fell to less than one-fourth the peak value it had reached only two and a half years earlier. This episode seems to be a case in point for advocates of the behavioral school, exemplifying a market moved by irrational investor sentiment. Moreover, in accord with behavioral patterns, as the dot-com boom developed, it seemed to feed on itself, with investors increasingly confident of their investment prowess (overconfidence bias) and apparently willing to extrapolate short-term patterns into the distant future (representativeness bias).

Only five years later, another bubble, this time in housing prices, was underway. As in the dot-com bubble, expectations of continued price increases fueled speculative demand by purchasers. Shortly thereafter, of course, housing prices stalled and then fell. The bursting bubble set off the worst financial crisis in 75 years.

On the other hand, bubbles are a lot easier to identify as such once they are over. While they are going on, it is not as clear that prices are irrationally exuberant, and, indeed, many financial commentators at the time justified the dot-com boom as consistent with glowing forecasts for the "new economy." A simple example shows how hard it can be to tie down the fair value of stock investments.[7]

EXAMPLE 9.3

A Stock Market Bubble?

In 2000, near the peak of the dot-com boom, the dividends paid by the firms included in the S&P 500 totaled $154.6 million. If the discount rate for the index was 9.2% and the expected dividend growth rate was 8%, the value of these shares according to the constant-growth dividend discount model (see Chapter 13 for more on this model) would be

$$\text{Value} = \frac{\text{Dividend}}{\text{Discount rate} - \text{Growth rate}} = \frac{\$154.6}{.092 - .08} = \$12{,}883 \text{ million}$$

This was quite close to the actual total value of those firms at the time. But the estimate is highly sensitive to the input values, and even a small reassessment of their prospects would result in a big revision of price. Suppose the expected dividend growth rate fell to 7.4%. This would reduce the value of the index to

$$\text{Value} = \frac{\text{Dividend}}{\text{Discount rate} - \text{Growth rate}} = \frac{\$154.6}{.092 - .074} = \$8{,}589 \text{ million}$$

which was about the value to which the S&P 500 firms had fallen by October 2002. In light of this example, the run-up and crash of the 1990s seems easier to reconcile with rational behavior.

Still, other evidence seems to tag the dot-com boom as at least partially irrational. Consider, for example, the results of a study by Rau, Dimitrov, and Cooper (2001) documenting that firms adding ".com" to the end of their names during this period enjoyed a meaningful stock price increase. That doesn't sound like rational valuation.

Evaluating the Behavioral Critique

As investors, we are concerned with the existence of profit opportunities. The behavioral explanations of efficient market anomalies do not give guidance as to how to exploit any irrationality. For investors, the question is still whether there is money to be made from mispricing, and the behavioral literature is largely silent on this point.

However, as we have emphasized above, one of the important implications of the efficient market hypothesis is that security prices serve as reliable guides to the allocation of real assets. If prices are distorted, then capital markets will give misleading signals (and incentives) as to where the economy may best allocate resources. In this crucial dimension, the behavioral

[7]The following example is taken from R. A. Brealey, S. C. Myers, and F. Allen, *Principles of Corporate Finance,* 9th ed. (Burr Ridge, IL: McGraw-Hill/Irwin, 2008).

critique of the efficient market hypothesis is certainly important irrespective of any implication for investment strategies.

There is considerable debate among financial economists concerning the strength of the behavioral critique. Many believe that the behavioral approach is too unstructured, in effect allowing virtually any anomaly to be explained by some combination of irrationalities chosen from a laundry list of behavioral biases. While it is easy to "reverse engineer" a behavioral explanation for any particular anomaly, these critics would like to see a consistent or unified behavioral theory that can explain a *range* of anomalies.

More fundamentally, others are not convinced that the anomalies literature as a whole is a convincing indictment of the efficient market hypothesis. Fama (1998) reviews the anomalies literature and mounts a counterchallenge to the behavioral school. He notes that the anomalies are inconsistent in terms of their support for one type of irrationality versus another. For example, some papers document long-term corrections (consistent with overreaction), while others document long-term continuations of abnormal returns (consistent with underreaction). Moreover, the statistical significance of many of these results is hard to assess. Even small errors in choosing a benchmark against which to compare returns can cumulate to large apparent abnormalities in long-term returns. Therefore, many of the results in these studies are sensitive to small benchmarking errors, and Fama argues that seemingly minor changes in methodology can have big impacts on conclusions.

The behavioral critique of full rationality in investor decision making is well taken, but the extent to which limited rationality affects asset pricing remains controversial. Whether or not investor irrationality affects asset prices, however, behavioral finance already makes important points about portfolio management. Investors who are aware of the potential pitfalls in information processing and decision making that seem to characterize their peers should be better able to avoid such errors. Ironically, the insights of behavioral finance may lead to some of the same policy conclusions embraced by efficient market advocates. For example, an easy way to avoid some behavioral minefields is to pursue passive, largely indexed portfolio strategies. It seems that only rare individuals can consistently beat passive strategies; this conclusion may hold true whether your fellow investors are behavioral or rational.

9.2 TECHNICAL ANALYSIS AND BEHAVIORAL FINANCE

Technical analysis attempts to exploit recurring and predictable patterns in stock prices to generate superior investment performance. Technicians do not deny the value of fundamental information but believe that prices only gradually close in on intrinsic value. As fundamentals shift, astute traders can exploit the adjustment to a new equilibrium.

For example, one of the best-documented behavioral tendencies is the *disposition effect,* which refers to the tendency of investors to hold on to losing investments. Behavioral investors seem reluctant to realize losses. Grinblatt and Han (2005) show that the disposition effect can lead to momentum in stock prices even if fundamental values follow a random walk. The fact that the demand of "disposition investors" for a company's shares depends on the price history of those shares means that prices close in on fundamental values only over time, consistent with the central motivation of technical analysis.

Behavioral biases may also be consistent with technical analysts' use of volume data. An important behavioral trait noted above is overconfidence, a systematic tendency to overestimate one's abilities. As traders become overconfident, they may trade more, inducing an association between trading volume and market returns (Gervais and Odean, 2001). Technical analysis thus uses volume data as well as price history to direct trading strategy.

Finally, technicians believe that market fundamentals can be perturbed by irrational or behavioral factors, sometimes labeled "sentiment variables." More or less random price fluctuations will accompany any underlying price trend, creating opportunities to exploit corrections as these fluctuations dissipate.

Trends and Corrections

Much of technical analysis seeks to uncover trends in market prices. This is in effect a search for momentum. Momentum can be absolute, in which case one searches for upward price trends, or relative, in which case the analyst looks to invest in one sector over another (or even take on a long-short position in the two sectors). Relative strength statistics (see page 280) are designed to uncover these cross-sector potential opportunities.

Momentum and moving averages While we all would like to buy shares in firms whose prices are trending upward, this begs the question of how to identify the underlying direction of prices, if in fact such trends actually exist. A primary tool for this purpose is the moving average.

The moving average of a stock price is the average price over a given interval, where that interval is updated as time passes. For example, a 50-day moving average traces the average price over the previous 50 days. The average is recomputed each day by dropping the oldest observation and adding the newest. Figure 9.3 is a moving-average chart for Intel. Notice that the moving average (the blue curve) is a "smoothed" version of the original data series (the jagged red curve).

After a period in which prices have been falling, the moving average will be above the current price (because the moving average continues to "average in" the older and higher prices until they leave the sample period). In contrast, when prices have been rising, the moving average will be below the current price.

Breaking through the moving average from below, as at point *A* in Figure 9.3, is taken as a bullish signal, because it signifies a shift from a falling trend (with prices below the moving average) to a rising trend (with prices above the moving average). Conversely, when prices drop below the moving average, as at point *B,* analysts might conclude that market momentum has become negative.

Other techniques also are used to uncover potential momentum in stock prices. Two of the more famous ones are Elliott wave theory and Kondratieff waves. Both posit the existence of long-term trends in stock market prices that may be disturbed by shorter-term trends as well as daily fluctuations of little importance. Elliott wave theory superimposes long-term and short-term wave cycles in an attempt to describe the complicated pattern of actual price movements. Once the longer-term waves are identified, investors presumably can buy when the

FIGURE 9.3

Share price and 50-day moving average for Intel

Source: Yahoo! Finance, **finance.yahoo.com,** August 11, 2011.

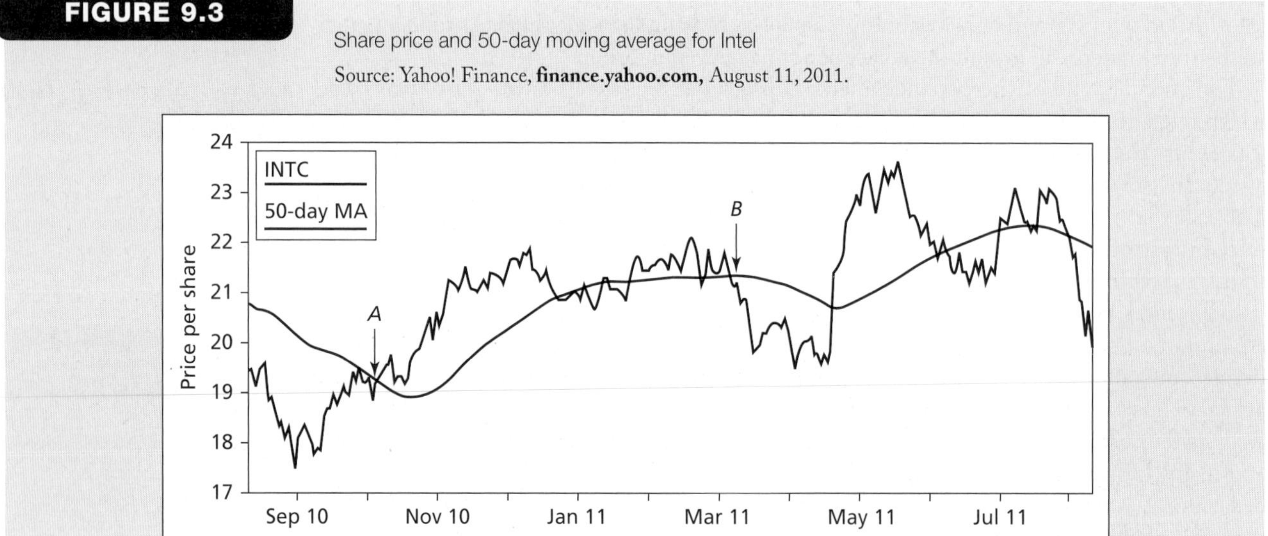

long-term direction of the market is positive. While there is considerable noise in the actual evolution of stock prices, by properly interpreting the wave cycles, one can, according to the theory, predict broad movements. Similarly, Kondratieff waves are named after a Russian economist who asserted that the macroeconomy (and therefore the stock market) moves in broad waves lasting between 48 and 60 years. Kondratieff's assertion is hard to evaluate empirically, however, because cycles that last about 50 years provide only two independent data points per century, which is hardly enough data to test the predictive power of the theory.

EXAMPLE 9.4

Moving Averages

Consider the price data in the following table. Each observation represents the closing level of the Dow Jones Industrial Average (DJIA) on the last trading day of the week. The five-week moving average for each week is the average of the DJIA over the previous five weeks. For example, the first entry, for week 5, is the average of the index value between weeks 1 and 5: 12,290, 12,380, 12,399, 12,379, and 12,450. The next entry is the average of the index values between weeks 2 and 6, and so on.

Figure 9.4 plots the level of the index and the five-week moving average. Notice that while the index itself moves up and down rather abruptly, the moving average is a relatively smooth series, since the impact of each week's price movement is averaged with that of the previous weeks. Week 16 is a bearish point according to the moving-average rule. The price series crosses from above the moving average to below it, signifying the beginning of a downward trend in stock prices.

Week	DJIA	5-Week Moving Average	Week	DJIA	5-Week Moving Average
1	12,290		11	12,590	12,555
2	12,380		12	12,652	12,586
3	12,399		13	12,625	12,598
4	12,379		14	12,657	12,624
5	12,450	12,380	15	12,699	12,645
6	12,513	12,424	16	12,647	12,656
7	12,500	12,448	17	12,610	12,648
8	12,565	12,481	18	12,595	12,642
9	12,524	12,510	19	12,499	12,610
10	12,597	12,540	20	12,466	12,563

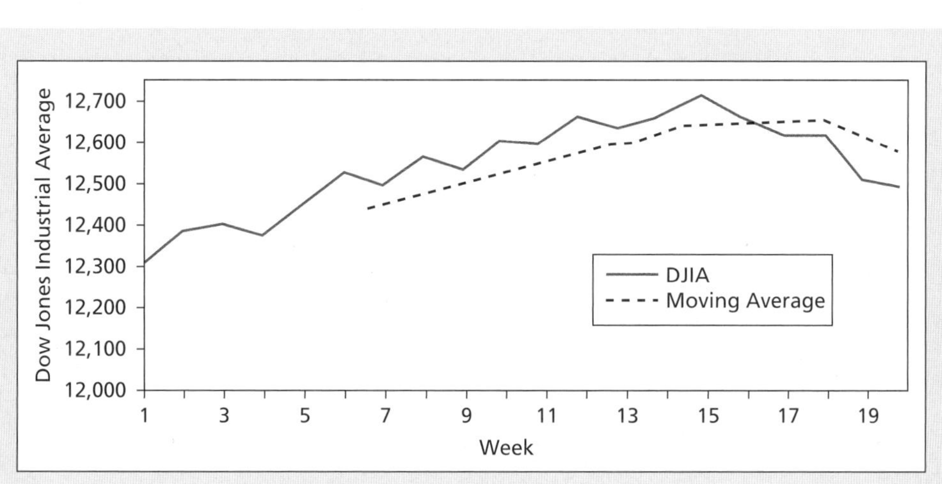

FIGURE 9.4

Moving averages

FIGURE 9.5

Point and figure chart for Table 9.1

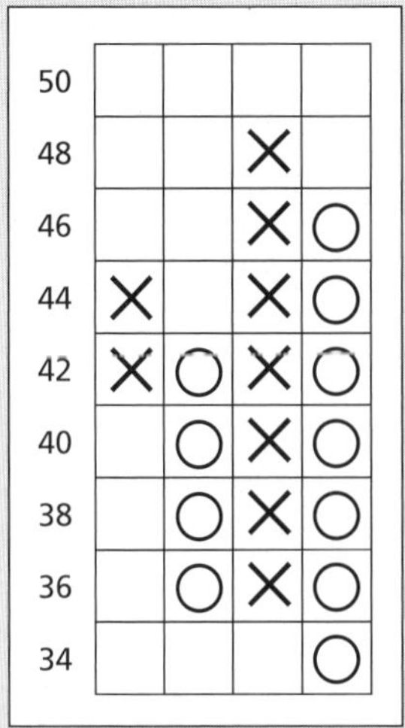

Point and figure charts A variant on pure trend analysis is the *point and figure chart* depicted in Figure 9.5. This figure has no time dimension. It simply traces significant upward or downward movements in stock prices without regard to their timing. The data for Figure 9.5 come from Table 9.1.

Suppose, as in Table 9.1, that a stock's price is currently $40. If the price rises by at least $2, you put an X in the first column at $42 in Figure 9.5. Another increase of at least $2 calls for placement of another X in the first column, this time at the $44 level. If the stock then falls by at least $2, you start a new column and put an O next to $42. Each subsequent $2 price fall results in another O in the second column. When prices reverse yet again and head upward, you begin the third column with an X denoting each consecutive $2 price increase.

The single asterisks in Table 9.1 mark an event resulting in the placement of a new X or O in the chart. The daggers denote price movements that result in the start of a new column of Xs or Os.

Sell signals are generated when the stock price *penetrates* previous lows, and buy signals occur when previous high prices are penetrated. A *congestion area* is a horizontal band of Xs and Os created by several price reversals. These regions correspond to support and resistance levels and are indicated in Figure 9.6, which is an actual chart for Atlantic Richfield.

TABLE 9.1 Stock price history

Date	Price	Date	Price
January 2	$40	February 1	$40*
January 3	40.50	February 2	41
January 4	41	February 5	40.50
January 5	42*	February 6	42*
January 8	41.50	February 7	45*
January 9	42.50	February 8	44.50
January 10	43	February 9	46*
January 11	43.75	February 12	47
January 12	44*	February 13	48*
January 15	45	February 14	47.50
January 16	44	February 15	46†
January 17	41.50†	February 16	45
January 18	41	February 19	44*
January 19	40*	February 20	42*
January 22	39	February 21	41
January 23	39.50	February 22	40*
January 24	39.75	February 23	41
January 25	38*	February 26	40.50
January 26	35*	February 27	38*
January 29	36†	February 28	39
January 30	37	March 1	36*
January 31	39*	March 2	34*

*Indicates an event that has resulted in a stock price increase or decrease of at least $2.

†Denotes a price movement that has resulted in either an upward or a downward reversal in the stock price.

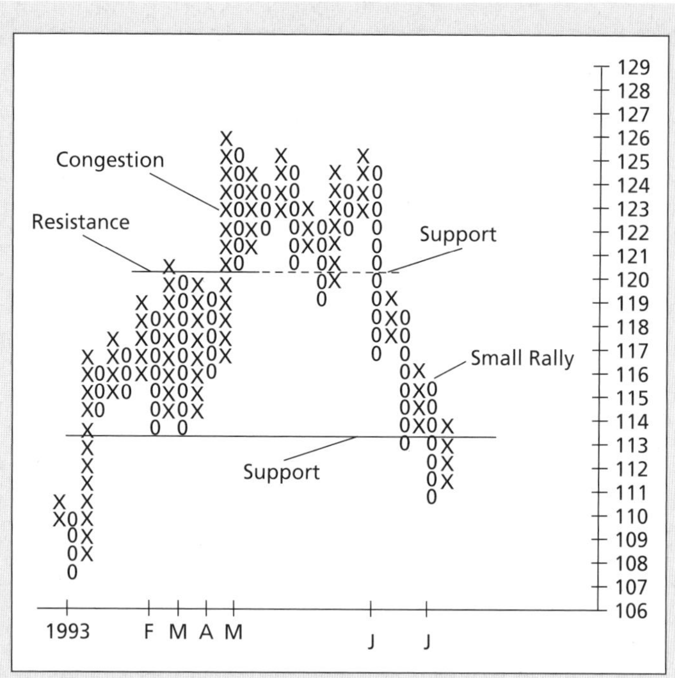

FIGURE 9.6

Point and figure chart for Atlantic Richfield

One can devise point and figure charts using price increments other than $2, but it is customary in setting up a chart to require reasonably substantial price changes before marking pluses or minuses.

CONCEPT check 9.4

Draw a point and figure chart using the history in Table 9.1 with price increments of $3.

Breadth The **breadth** of the market is a measure of the extent to which movement in a market index is reflected widely in the price movements of all the stocks in the market. The most common measure of breadth is the spread between the number of stocks that advance and decline in price. If advances outnumber declines by a wide margin, then the market is viewed as being stronger because the rally is widespread. These numbers are reported daily in *The Wall Street Journal* (see Figure 9.7).

breadth

The extent to which movements in broad market indexes are reflected widely in movements of individual stock prices.

Markets Diary

Issues	**NYSE**	**Nasdaq**	**Amex**
Advancing	2,787	2,119	308
Declining	270	441	129
Unchanged	33	64	18
Total	3,090	2,624	455
Issues at			
New 52 week high	7	6	1
New 52 week low	125	141	16
Share Volume			
Total	4,937,076,320	2,096,877,765	113,647,520
Advancing	4,681,742,414	2,010,365,013	75,275,155
Declining	231,468,687	79,349,368	36,759,430
Unchanged	23,865,219	7,163,384	1,612,935

FIGURE 9.7

Market diary

Source: *The Wall Street Journal Online,* August 11, 2011. Reprinted by permission of *The Wall Street Journal,*

TABLE 9.2 Breadth

Day	Advances	Declines	Net Advances	Cumulative Breadth
1	1,802	1,748	54	54
2	1,917	1,640	277	331
3	1,703	1,772	−69	262
4	1,512	2,122	−610	−348
5	1,633	2,004	−371	−719

Note: The sum of advances plus declines varies across days because some stock prices are unchanged.

Some analysts cumulate breadth data each day as in Table 9.2. The cumulative breadth for each day is obtained by adding that day's net advances (or declines) to the previous day's total. The direction of the cumulated series is then used to discern broad market trends. Analysts might use a moving average of cumulative breadth to gauge broad trends.

relative strength

Recent performance of a given stock or industry compared to that of a broader market index.

Relative strength **Relative strength** measures the extent to which a security has outperformed or underperformed either the market as a whole or its particular industry. Relative strength is computed by calculating the ratio of the price of the security to a price index for the industry. For example, the relative strength of Toyota versus the auto industry would be measured by movements in the ratio of the price of Toyota divided by the level of an auto industry index. A rising ratio implies Toyota has been outperforming the rest of the industry. If relative strength can be assumed to persist over time, then this would be a signal to buy Toyota.

Similarly, the relative strength of an industry relative to the whole market can be computed by tracking the ratio of the industry price index to the market price index.

Sentiment Indicators

Trin statistic Market volume is sometimes used to measure the strength of a market rise or fall. Increased investor participation in a market advance or retreat is viewed as a measure of the significance of the movement. Technicians consider market advances to be a more favorable omen of continued price increases when they are associated with increased trading volume. Similarly, market reversals are considered more bearish when associated with higher volume. The **trin statistic** is defined as

trin statistic

The ratio of average volume in declining issues to average volume in advancing issues.

$$\text{Trin} = \frac{\text{Volume declining/Number declining}}{\text{Volume advancing/Number advancing}}$$

Therefore, trin is the ratio of average trading volume in declining issues to average volume in advancing issues. Ratios above 1 are considered bearish because the falling stocks would then have higher average volume than the advancing stocks, indicating net selling pressure.

The Wall Street Journal Online provides the data necessary to compute trin in its Markets Diary section. Using the data in Figure 9.7, trin for the NYSE on this day was:

$$\text{Trin} = \frac{\$231{,}468{,}687/270}{\$4{,}681{,}742{,}414/2{,}787} = .51$$

Note, however, that for every buyer, there must be a seller of stock. Rising volume in a rising market should not necessarily indicate a larger imbalance of buyers versus sellers.

For example, a trin statistic above 1, which is considered bearish, could equally well be interpreted as indicating that there is more *buying* activity in declining issues.

Confidence index *Barron's* computes a confidence index using data from the bond market. The presumption is that actions of bond traders reveal trends that will emerge soon in the stock market.

confidence index

Ratio of the yield of top-rated corporate bonds to the yield on intermediate-grade bonds.

The **confidence index** is the ratio of the average yield on 10 top-rated corporate bonds divided by the average yield on 10 intermediate-grade corporate bonds. The ratio will always be below 100% because higher-rated bonds will offer lower promised yields to maturity. When bond traders are optimistic about the economy, however, they might require smaller default premiums on lower-rated debt. Hence, the yield spread will narrow, and the confidence index will approach 100%. Therefore, higher values of the confidence index are bullish signals.

CONCEPT check 9.5

Yields on lower-rated debt typically rise along with fears of recession. This reduces the confidence index. When these yields increase, should the stock market be expected to fall, or will it already have fallen?

Short interest **Short interest** is the total number of shares of stock currently sold short in the market. Some technicians interpret high levels of short interest as bullish, some as bearish. The bullish perspective is that, because all short sales must be covered (i.e., short-sellers eventually must purchase shares to return the ones they have borrowed), short interest represents latent future demand for the stocks. As short sales are covered, the demand created by the share purchase will force prices up.

short interest

The total number of shares currently sold short in the market.

The bearish interpretation of short interest is based on the fact that short-sellers tend to be larger, more sophisticated investors. Accordingly, increased short interest reflects bearish sentiment by those investors "in the know," which would be a negative signal of the market's prospects.

Put/call ratio Call options give investors the right to buy a stock at a fixed "exercise" price and therefore are a way of betting on stock price increases. Put options give the right to sell a stock at a fixed price and therefore are a way of betting on stock price decreases.[8] The ratio of outstanding put options to outstanding call options is called the **put/call ratio.** Because put options do well in falling markets while call options do well in rising markets, deviations of the ratio from historical norms are considered to be a signal of market sentiment and therefore predictive of market movements.

put/call ratio

Ratio of put options to call options outstanding on a stock.

Interestingly, however, a change in the ratio can be given a bullish or a bearish interpretation. Many technicians see an increase in the ratio as bearish, as it indicates growing interest in put options as a hedge against market declines. Thus, a rising ratio is taken as a sign of broad investor pessimism and a coming market decline. Contrarian investors, however, believe that a good time to buy is when the rest of the market is bearish because stock prices are then unduly depressed. Therefore, they would take an increase in the put/call ratio as a signal of a buy opportunity.

A Warning

The search for patterns in stock market prices is nearly irresistible, and the ability of the human eye to discern apparent patterns is remarkable. Unfortunately, it is possible to perceive

[8] Puts and calls were defined in Chapter 2, Section 2.5. They are discussed more fully in Chapter 15.

patterns that really don't exist. Consider Figure 9.8, which presents simulated and actual values of the Dow Jones Industrial Average during 1956 taken from a famous study by Harry Roberts (1959). In Figure 9.8B, it appears as though the market presents a classic head-and-shoulders pattern where the middle hump (the head) is flanked by two shoulders. When the price index "pierces the right shoulder"—a technical trigger point—it is believed to be heading lower, and it is time to sell your stocks. Figure 9.8A also looks like a "typical" stock market pattern.

Can you tell which of the two graphs is constructed from the real value of the Dow and which from the simulated data? Figure 9.8A is based on the real data. The graph in Panel B was generated using "returns" created by a random-number generator. These returns *by construction* were patternless, but the simulated price path that is plotted appears to follow a pattern much like that of Panel A.

Figure 9.9 shows the weekly price *changes* behind the two panels in Figure 9.8. Here the randomness in both series—the stock price as well as the simulated sequence—is obvious.

A problem related to the tendency to perceive patterns where they don't exist is data mining. After the fact, you can always find patterns and trading rules that would have generated enormous profits. If you test enough rules, some will have worked in the past. Unfortunately, picking a theory that would have worked after the fact carries no guarantee of future success.

In evaluating trading rules, you should always ask whether the rule would have seemed reasonable *before* you looked at the data. If not, you might be buying into the one arbitrary rule among many that happened to have worked in the recent past. The hard but crucial question is whether there is reason to believe that what worked in the past should continue to work in the future.

FIGURE 9.8

Actual and simulated levels for stock market prices of 52 weeks

Note: Friday closing levels, December 30, 1955–December 28, 1956, Dow Jones Industrial Average.
Source: Harry Roberts, "Stock Market 'Patterns' and Financial Analysis: Methodological Suggestions," *Journal of Finance* 14 (March 1959), pp. 1–10. Used with permission of John Wiley and Sons, via Copyright Clearance Center.

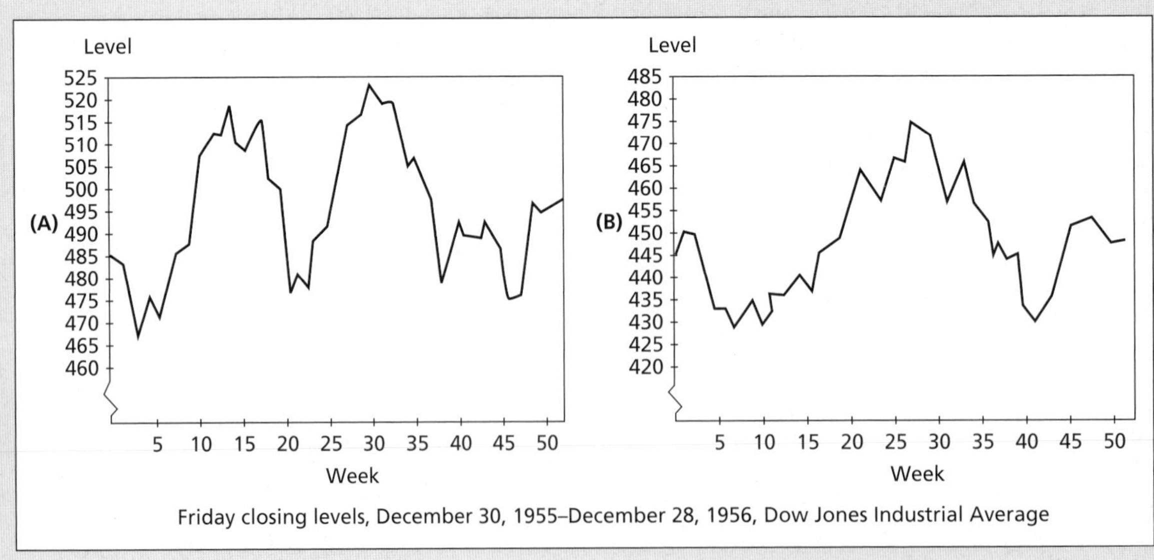

Friday closing levels, December 30, 1955–December 28, 1956, Dow Jones Industrial Average

FIGURE 9.9

Actual and simulated changes in weekly stock prices for 52 weeks

Note: Changes from Friday to Friday (closing) January 6, 1956–December 28, 1956, Dow Jones Industrial Average.

Source: Harry Roberts, "Stock Market 'Patterns' and Financial Analysis: Methodological Suggestions," *Journal of Finance* 14 (March 1959), pp. 1–10. Used with permission of John Wiley and Sons, via Copyright Clearance Center.

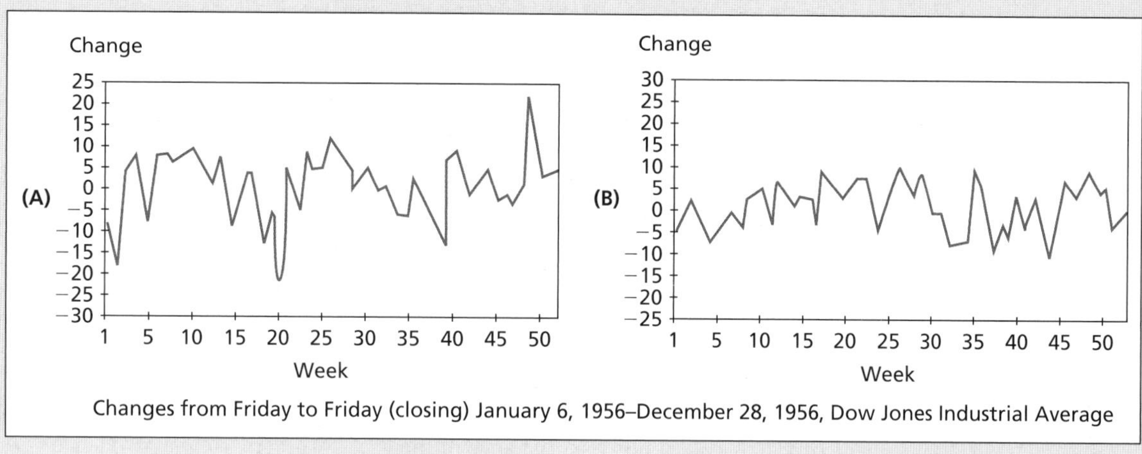

SUMMARY

- Behavioral finance focuses on systematic irrationalities that characterize investor decision making. These "behavioral shortcomings" may be consistent with several efficient market anomalies.
- Among the information processing errors uncovered in the psychology literature are memory bias, overconfidence, conservatism, and representativeness. Behavioral tendencies include framing, mental accounting, regret avoidance, and loss aversion.
- Limits to arbitrage activity impede the ability of rational investors to exploit pricing errors induced by behavioral investors. For example, fundamental risk means that even if a security is mispriced, it still can be risky to attempt to exploit the mispricing. This limits the actions of arbitrageurs who take positions in mispriced securities. Other limits to arbitrage are implementation costs, model risk, and costs to short-selling. Occasional failures of the Law of One Price suggest that limits to arbitrage are sometimes severe.
- The various limits to arbitrage mean that even if prices do not equal intrinsic value, it still may be difficult to exploit the mispricing. As a result, the failure of traders to beat the market may not be proof that markets are in fact efficient, with prices equal to intrinsic value.
- Technical analysis also uses volume data and sentiment indicators. These are broadly consistent with several behavioral models of investor activity. Technical analysis is the search for recurring and predictable patterns in stock prices. It is based on the premise that prices only gradually close in on intrinsic value. As fundamentals shift, astute traders can exploit the adjustment to a new equilibrium.
- Technical analysts try to uncover trends in stock prices and anticipate reversals of those trends. Moving averages, relative strength, and breadth are used in various trend-based strategies.
- Some sentiment indicators are the trin statistic, the confidence index, and the put/call ratio.

www.mhhe.com/bkm

KEY TERMS

behavioral finance, 266
breadth, 279
confidence index, 281
conservatism bias, 267
framing, 268
mental accounting, 268
prospect theory, 269
put/call ratio, 281
regret avoidance, 269
relative strength, 280
representativeness bias, 267
short interest, 281
trin statistic, 280

PROBLEM SETS

Select problems are available in McGraw-Hill's *Connect Finance.* Please see the Supplements section of the book's frontmatter for more information.

Basic

1. Match each example to one of the following behavioral characteristics. ***(LO 9-1)***

a. Investors are slow to update their beliefs when given new evidence.	i. Disposition effect
b. Investors are reluctant to bear losses due to their unconventional decisions.	ii. Representativeness bias
c. Investors exhibit less risk tolerance in their retirement accounts versus their other stock accounts.	iii. Regret avoidance
d. Investors are reluctant to sell stocks with "paper" losses.	iv. Conservatism bias
e. Investors disregard sample size when forming views about the future from the past.	v. Mental accounting

2. After reading about three successful investors in *The Wall Street Journal* you decide that active investing will also provide you with superior trading results. What sort of behavioral tendency are you exhibiting? ***(LO 9-1)***
3. What do we mean by fundamental risk, and why may such risk allow behavioral biases to persist for long periods of time? ***(LO 9-2)***
4. What are the strong points of the behavioral critique of the efficient market hypothesis? What are some problems with the critique? ***(LO 9-2)***
5. What are some possible investment implications of the behavioral critique? ***(LO 9-1)***

6. Jill Davis tells her broker that she does not want to sell her stocks that are below the price she paid for them. She believes that if she just holds on to them a little longer, they will recover, at which time she will sell them. What behavioral characteristic does Davis have as the basis for her decision making? ***(LO 9-1)***
   a. Loss aversion
   b. Conservatism
   c. Representativeness

7. After Polly Shrum sells a stock, she avoids following it in the media. She is afraid that it may subsequently increase in price. What behavioral characteristic does Shrum have as the basis for her decision making? ***(LO 9-1)***
   a. Fear of regret
   b. Representativeness
   c. Mental accounting

8. All of the following actions are consistent with feelings of regret *except:* ***(LO 9-1)***
   a. Selling losers quickly.
   b. Hiring a full-service broker.
   c. Holding on to losers too long.

www.mhhe.com/bkm

9. Which one of the following would be a bullish signal to a technical analyst using moving average rules? ***(LO 9-4)***
   a. A stock price crosses above its 52-week moving average.
   b. A stock price crosses below its 52-week moving average.
   c. The stock's moving average is increasing.
   d. The stock's moving average is decreasing.

Intermediate

10. What is meant by data mining, and why must technical analysts be careful not to engage in it? ***(LO 9-3)***
11. Even if prices follow a random walk, they still may not be informationally efficient. Explain why this may be true, and why it matters for the efficient allocation of capital in our economy. ***(LO 9-2)***
12. What is meant by "limits to arbitrage"? Give some examples of such limits. ***(LO 9-2)***
13. Following a shock to a firm's intrinsic value, the share price will slowly but surely approach that new intrinsic value. Is this view characteristic of a technical analyst or a believer in efficient markets? Explain. ***(LO 9-3)***
14. Use the data from *The Wall Street Journal* in Figure 9.7 to verify the trin ratio for the NYSE. Is the trin ratio bullish or bearish? ***(LO 9-4)***
15. Calculate breadth for the NYSE using the data in Figure 9.7. Is the signal bullish or bearish? ***(LO 9-4)***
16. Collect data on the DJIA for a period covering a few months. Try to identify primary trends. Can you tell whether the market currently is in an upward or downward trend? ***(LO 9-4)***
17. Suppose Baa-rated bonds currently yield 7%, while Aa-rated bonds yield 5%. Now suppose that due to an increase in the expected inflation rate, the yields on both bonds increase by 1%. What would happen to the confidence index? Would this be interpreted as bullish or bearish by a technical analyst? Does this make sense to you? ***(LO 9-4)***
18. Table 9.3 presents price data for Computers, Inc., and a computer industry index. Does Computers, Inc., show relative strength over this period? ***(LO 9-4)***
19. Use the data in Table 9.3 to compute a five-day moving average for Computers, Inc. Can you identify any buy or sell signals? ***(LO 9-4)***
20. Construct a point and figure chart for Computers, Inc., using again the data in Table 9.3. Use $2 increments for your chart. Do the buy or sell signals derived from your chart correspond to those derived from the moving-average rule (see the previous problem)? ***(LO 9-4)***
21. Yesterday, the Dow Jones industrials gained 54 points. However, 1,704 issues declined in price while 1,367 advanced. Why might a technical analyst be concerned even though the market index rose on this day? ***(LO 9-4)***
22. Table 9.4 contains data on market advances and declines. Calculate cumulative breadth and decide whether this technical signal is bullish or bearish. ***(LO 9-4)***
23. If the trading volume in advancing shares on day 1 in the previous problem was 1.1 billion shares, while the volume in declining issues was .9 billion shares, what was the trin statistic for that day? Was trin bullish or bearish? ***(LO 9-4)***
24. Given the following data on bond yields, is the confidence index rising or falling? What might explain the pattern of yield changes? ***(LO 9-4)***

	This Year	**Last Year**
Yield on top-rated corporate bonds	8%	8.5%
Yield on intermediate-grade corporate bonds	10.5	10

TABLE 9.3 Computers, Inc., stock price history

Trading Day	Computers, Inc.	Industry Index	Trading Day	Computers, Inc.	Industry Index
1	19.63	50.0	21	19.63	54.1
2	20	50.1	22	21.50	54.0
3	20.50	50.5	23	22	53.9
4	22	50.4	24	23.13	53.7
5	21.13	51.0	25	24	54.8
6	22	50.7	26	25.25	54.5
7	21.88	50.5	27	26.25	54.6
8	22.50	51.1	28	27	54.1
9	23.13	51.5	29	27.50	54.2
10	23.88	51.7	30	28	54.8
11	24.50	51.4	31	28.50	54.2
12	23.25	51.7	32	28	54.8
13	22.13	52.2	33	27.50	54.9
14	22	52.0	34	29	55.2
15	20.63	53.1	35	29.25	55.7
16	20.25	53.5	36	29.50	56.1
17	19.75	53.9	37	30	56.7
18	18.75	53.6	38	28.50	56.7
19	17.50	52.9	39	27.75	56.5
20	19	53.4	40	28	56.1

TABLE 9.4 Market advances and declines

Day	Advances	Declines	Day	Advances	Declines
1	906	704	6	970	702
2	653	986	7	1002	609
3	721	789	8	903	722
4	503	968	9	850	748
5	497	1095	10	766	766

Please visit us at www.mhhe.com/bkm

25. Go to **www.mhhe.com/bkm** and link to the material for Chapter 9, where you will find five years of weekly returns for the S&P 500. ***(LO 9-4)***
    a. Set up a spreadsheet to calculate the 26-week moving average of the index. Set the value of the index at the beginning of the sample period equal to 100. The index value in each week is then updated by multiplying the previous week's level by (1 + rate of return over previous week).
    b. Identify every instance in which the index crosses through its moving average from below. In how many of the weeks following a cross-through does the index increase? Decrease?
    c. Identify every instance in which the index crosses through its moving average from above. In how many of the weeks following a cross-through does the index increase? Decrease?
    d. How well does the moving-average rule perform in identifying buy or sell opportunities?

Please visit us at www.mhhe.com/bkm

26. Go to **www.mhhe.com/bkm** and link to the material for Chapter 9, where you will find five years of weekly returns for the S&P 500 and Fidelity's Select Banking Fund (ticker FSRBX). ***(LO 9-4)***

www.mhhe.com/bkm

a. Set up a spreadsheet to calculate the relative strength of the banking sector compared to the broad market. (*Hint:* As in the previous problem, set the initial value of the sector index and the S&P 500 Index equal to 100, and use each week's rate of return to update the level of each index.)

b. Identify every instance in which the relative strength ratio increases by at least 5% from its value five weeks earlier. In how many of the weeks immediately following a substantial increase in relative strength does the banking sector outperform the S&P 500? In how many of those weeks does the banking sector underperform the S&P 500?

c. Identify every instance in which the relative strength ratio decreases by at least 5% from its value five weeks earlier. In how many of the weeks immediately following a substantial decrease in relative strength does the banking sector underperform the S&P 500? In how many of those weeks does the banking sector outperform the S&P 500?

d. How well does the relative strength rule perform in identifying buy or sell opportunities?

Challenge

27. One apparent violation of the Law of One Price is the pervasive discrepancy between the prices and net asset values of closed-end mutual funds. Would you expect to observe greater discrepancies on diversified or less diversified funds? Why? ***(LO 9-2)***

CFA Problems

1. Don Sampson begins a meeting with his financial adviser by outlining his investment philosophy as shown below:

Statement Number	Statement
1	Investments should offer strong return potential but with very limited risk. I prefer to be conservative and to minimize losses, even if I miss out on substantial growth opportunities.
2	All nongovernmental investments should be in industry-leading and financially strong companies.
3	Income needs should be met entirely through interest income and cash dividends. All equity securities held should pay cash dividends.
4	Investment decisions should be based primarily on consensus forecasts of general economic conditions and company-specific growth.
5	If an investment falls below the purchase price, that security should be retained until it returns to its original cost. Conversely, I prefer to take quick profits on successful investments.
6	I will direct the purchase of investments, including derivative securities, periodically. These aggressive investments result from personal research and may not prove consistent with my investment policy. I have not kept records on the performance of similar past investments, but I have had some "big winners."

Select the statement from the table above that best illustrates each of the following behavioral finance concepts. Justify your selection. ***(LO 9-1)***

i. Mental accounting.
ii. Overconfidence (illusion of control).
iii. Reference dependence (framing).

www.mhhe.com/bkm

2. Monty Frost's tax-deferred retirement account is invested entirely in equity securities. Because the international portion of his portfolio has performed poorly in the past, he has reduced his international equity exposure to 2%. Frost's investment adviser has recommended an increased international equity exposure. Frost responds with the following comments:
   a. Based on past poor performance, I want to sell all my remaining international equity securities once their market prices rise to equal their original cost.
   b. Most diversified international portfolios have had disappointing results over the past five years. During that time, however, the market in country XYZ has outperformed all other markets, even our own. If I do increase my international equity exposure, I would prefer that the entire exposure consist of securities from country XYZ.
   c. International investments are inherently more risky. Therefore, I prefer to purchase any international equity securities in my "speculative" account, my best chance at becoming rich. I do not want them in my retirement account, which has to protect me from poverty in my old age.

   Frost's adviser is familiar with behavioral finance concepts but prefers a traditional or standard finance approach (modern portfolio theory) to investments.

   Indicate the behavioral finance concept that Frost most directly exhibits in each of his three comments. Explain how each of Frost's comments can be countered by using an argument from standard finance. ***(LO 9-1)***
3. Louise and Christopher Maclin live in London, United Kingdom, and currently rent an apartment in the metropolitan area. During an initial discussion of the Maclins' financial plans, Christopher Maclin makes the following statements to the Maclins' financial adviser, Grant Webb:
   a. "I have used the Internet extensively to research the outlook for the housing market over the next five years, and I believe now is the best time to buy a house."
   b. "I do not want to sell any bond in my portfolio for a lower price than I paid for the bond."
   c. "I will not sell any of my company stock because I know my company and I believe it has excellent prospects for the future."

   For each statement (*a*)–(*c*) identify the behavioral finance concept most directly exhibited. Explain how each behavioral finance concept is affecting the Maclins' investment decision making. ***(LO 9-1)***
4. During an interview with her investment adviser, a retired investor made the following two statements:
   a. "I have been very pleased with the returns I've earned on Petrie stock over the past two years, and I am certain that it will be a superior performer in the future."
   b. "I am pleased with the returns from the Petrie stock because I have specific uses for that money. For that reason, I certainly want my retirement fund to continue owning the Petrie stock."

   Identify which principle of behavioral finance is most consistent with each of the investor's two statements. ***(LO 9-1)***
5. Claire Pierce comments on her life circumstances and investment outlook:

   I must support my parents who live overseas on Pogo Island. The Pogo Island economy has grown rapidly over the past two years with minimal inflation, and consensus forecasts call for a continuation of these favorable trends for the foreseeable future. Economic growth has resulted from the export of a natural resource used in an exciting new technology application.

   I want to invest 10% of my portfolio in Pogo Island government bonds. I plan to purchase long-term bonds because my parents are likely to live more than 10 years. Experts uniformly do not foresee a resurgence of inflation on Pogo Island, so I am certain that the total returns produced by the bonds will cover my parents' spending needs for many years to come. There should be no exchange rate risk because the bonds are denominated in local currency. I want to buy the Pogo Island bonds but am not willing to distort my portfolio's long-term asset allocation to do so. The overall mix of stocks, bonds, and other investments should not change. Therefore, I am considering selling one of my U.S. bond funds to raise cash to buy the Pogo Island bonds. One possibility is my High Yield Bond Fund, which has declined 5% in value year to date. I am not excited about this fund's prospects; in fact I think it is likely to decline more, but there is a small probability that it could recover very quickly. So I have decided instead to sell my Core Bond Fund that has appreciated 5% this year. I expect this investment to continue to deliver attractive returns, but there is a small chance this year's gains might disappear quickly.

Once that shift is accomplished, my investments will be in great shape. The sole exception is my Small Company Fund, which has performed poorly. I plan to sell this investment as soon as the price increases to my original cost.

Identify three behavioral finance concepts illustrated in Pierce's comments and describe each of the three concepts. Discuss how an investor practicing standard or traditional finance would challenge each of the three concepts. ***(LO 9-1)***

WEB *master*

1. Log on to **finance.yahoo.com** to find the monthly dividend-adjusted closing prices for the most recent four years for Abercrombie & Fitch (ANF). Also collect the closing level of the S&P 500 Index over the same period.
   a. Calculate the four-month moving average of both the stock and the S&P 500 over time. For each series, use Excel to plot the moving average against the actual level of the stock price or index. Examine the instances where the moving average and price series cross. Is the stock more or less likely to increase when the price crosses through the moving average? Does it matter whether the price crosses the moving average from above or below? How reliable would an investment rule based on moving averages be? Perform your analysis for both the stock price and the S&P 500.
   b. Calculate and plot the relative strength of the stock compared to the S&P 500 over the sample period. Find all instances in which relative strength of the stock increases by more than 10 percentage points (e.g., an increase in the relative strength index from .93 to 1.03) and all those instances in which relative strength of the stock decreases by more than 10 percentage points. Is the stock more or less likely to outperform the S&P in the following two months when relative strength has increased or to underperform when relative strength has decreased? In other words, does relative strength continue? How reliable would an investment rule based on relative strength be?
2. The Yahoo! Finance charting function allows you to specify comparisons between companies by choosing the *Technical Analysis* tab. Short interest ratios are found in the *Key Statistics* table. Prepare charts of moving averages and obtain short interest ratios for GE and SWY. Prepare a one-year chart of the 50- and 200-day average price of GE, SWY, and the S&P 500 Index.
   a. Which, if either, of the companies is priced above its 50- and 200-day averages?
   b. Would you consider their charts as bullish or bearish? Why?
   c. What are the short interest ratios for the two companies?

SOLUTIONS TO CONCEPT *checks*

9.1 Conservatism implies that investors will at first respond too slowly to new information, leading to trends in prices. Representativeness can lead them to extrapolate trends too far into the future and overshoot intrinsic value. Eventually, when the pricing error is corrected, we observe a reversal.

9.2 Out-of-favor stocks will exhibit low prices relative to various proxies for intrinsic value such as earnings. Because of regret avoidance, these stocks will need to offer a more attractive rate of return to induce investors to hold them. Thus, low P/E stocks might on average offer higher rates of return.

www.mhhe.com/bkm

9.3 At liquidation, price will equal NAV. This puts a limit on fundamental risk. Investors need only carry the position for a few months to profit from the elimination of the discount. Moreover, as the liquidation date approaches, the discount should dissipate. This greatly limits the risk that the discount can move against the investor. At the announcement of impending liquidation, the discount should immediately disappear, or at least shrink considerably.

9.4

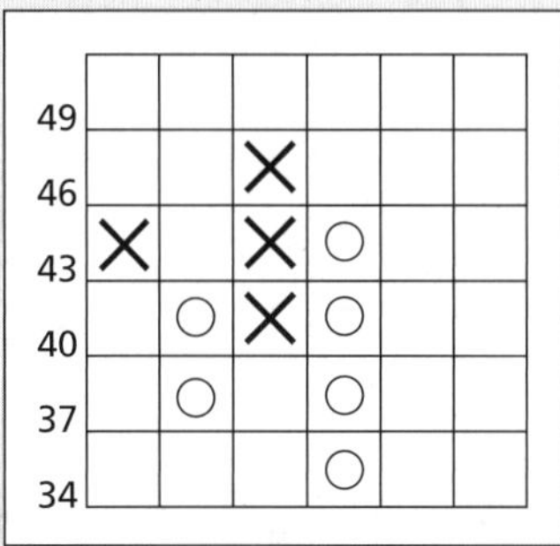

9.5 By the time the news of the recession affects bond yields, it also ought to affect stock prices. The market should fall *before* the confidence index signals that the time is ripe to sell.

Debt Securities

PART

3

Chapters in This Part:

Bond markets used to be a sedate arena for risk-averse investors who wanted worry-free investments with modest but stable returns. They are no longer so quiet. The fixed-income market was at the center of the financial crisis of 2008–2009, and the downgrade of U.S. Treasury debt by Standard & Poor's in 2011 triggered a massive one-day stock market decline of more than 6% when markets opened.

These markets are no longer free of risk. Interest rates in the last three decades have become more volatile than anyone in 1965 would have dreamed possible. Volatility means that investors have great opportunities for gain, but also for losses, and we have seen dramatic examples of both in recent years.

Long-Term Capital Management, at the time the world's most successful hedge fund, shocked Wall Street when it was felled by investment reversals in 1998, among them losses of more than $1 billion on its interest rate positions. But those losses seem almost quaint when compared to the devastation suffered in the market meltdown of 2008–2009. The beginning of that period was signaled by revelation of losses of $1 billion on mortgage bonds held by two Bear Stearns hedge funds in 2007. Over the course of the next two years, hundreds of billions were lost by investors in other mortgage-backed bonds and those who sold insurance on those securities. Of course, in many of these instances, there were traders on the other side of the transaction who did quite well. The bearish bets made by hedge fund manager John Paulson in 2007 made his funds more than $15 billion.

The chapters in Part Three provide an introduction to debt markets and securities. We will show you how to value such securities and why their values change with interest rates. We will see what features determine the sensitivity of bond prices to interest rates and how investors measure and manage interest rate risk.

Chapter 10

Bond Prices and Yields

Learning Objectives:

LO10-1 Explain the general terms of a bond contract and how bond prices are quoted in the financial press.

LO10-2 Compute a bond's price given its yield to maturity, and compute its yield to maturity given its price.

LO10-3 Calculate how bond prices will change over time for a given interest rate projection.

LO10-4 Describe call, convertibility, and sinking fund provisions, and analyze how these provisions affect a bond's price and yield to maturity.

LO10-5 Identify the determinants of bond safety and rating and how credit risk is reflected in bond yields and the prices of credit default swaps.

LO10-6 Calculate several measures of bond return, and demonstrate how these measures may be affected by taxes.

LO10-7 Analyze the factors likely to affect the shape of the yield curve at any time, and impute forward rates from the yield curve.

In the previous chapters on risk and return relationships, we have treated securities at a high level of abstraction. We have assumed implicitly that a prior, detailed analysis of each security already has been performed and that its risk and return features have been assessed.

We turn now to specific analyses of particular security markets. We examine valuation principles, determinants of risk and return, and portfolio strategies commonly used within and across the various markets.

We begin by analyzing debt securities. A debt security is a claim on a specified periodic stream of income. Debt securities are often called *fixed-income securities,* because they promise either a fixed stream of income or one determined according to a specified formula. These securities have the advantage of being relatively easy to understand because the payment formulas are specified in advance. Uncertainty about their cash flows is minimal as long as the issuer of the security is sufficiently creditworthy. That makes these securities a convenient starting point for our analysis of the universe of potential investment vehicles.

The bond is the basic debt security, and this chapter starts with an overview of bond markets, including Treasury, corporate, and international bonds. We turn next to bond pricing, showing how bond prices are set in accordance with market interest rates and why bond prices change with those rates. Given this background, we can compare the myriad measures of bond returns such as yield to maturity, yield to call, holding-period return, and realized compound rate of return. We show how bond prices evolve over time, discuss certain tax rules that apply to debt securities, and show how to calculate after-tax returns. Next, we consider the impact of default or credit risk on bond pricing and look at the determinants of credit risk and the default premium built into bond yields. Finally, we turn to the term structure of interest rates, the relationship between yield to maturity and time to maturity.

Related websites for this chapter are available at www.mhhe.com/bkm.

10.1 BOND CHARACTERISTICS

A **bond** is a security that is issued in connection with a borrowing arrangement. The borrower issues (i.e., sells) a bond to the lender for some amount of cash; the bond is in essence the "IOU" of the borrower. The arrangement obligates the issuer to make specified payments to the bondholder on specified dates. A typical coupon bond obligates the issuer to make semiannual payments of interest, called *coupon payments,* to the bondholder for the life of the bond. These are called coupon payments because, in precomputer days, most bonds had coupons that investors would clip off and present to the issuer of the bond to claim the interest payment. When the bond matures, the issuer repays the debt by paying the bond's **par value** (or equivalently, its **face value**). The **coupon rate** of the bond determines the interest payment: The annual payment equals the coupon rate times the bond's par value. The coupon rate, maturity date, and par value of the bond are part of the *bond indenture,* which is the contract between the issuer and the bondholder.

bond

A security that obligates the issuer to make specified payments to the holder over a period of time.

face value, par value

The payment to the bondholder at the maturity of the bond.

To illustrate, a bond with a par value of $1,000 and a coupon rate of 8% might be sold to a buyer for $1,000. The issuer then pays the bondholder 8% of $1,000, or $80 per year, for the stated life of the bond, say, 30 years. The $80 payment typically comes in two semiannual installments of $40 each. At the end of the 30-year life of the bond, the issuer also pays the $1,000 par value to the bondholder.

coupon rate

A bond's annual interest payment per dollar of par value.

Bonds usually are issued with coupon rates set just high enough to induce investors to pay par value to buy the bond. Sometimes, however, **zero-coupon bonds** are issued that make no coupon payments. In this case, investors receive par value at the maturity date but receive no interest payments until then: The bond has a coupon rate of zero. These bonds are issued at prices considerably below par value, and the investor's return comes solely from the difference between issue price and the payment of par value at maturity. We will return to these bonds below.

zero-coupon bond

A bond paying no coupons that sells at a discount and provides only a payment of par value at maturity.

Treasury Bonds and Notes

Figure 10.1 is an excerpt from the listing of Treasury issues from the *The Wall Street Journal Online.* Treasury notes are issued with original maturities between 1 and 10 years, while Treasury bonds are issued with maturities ranging from 10 to 30 years. Both bonds and notes may be purchased directly from the Treasury in denominations of only $100, but denominations of $1,000 are far more common. Both make semiannual coupon payments.

FIGURE 10.1

Prices and yields of U.S. Treasury bonds on August 15, 2011

Source: *The Wall Street Journal Online,* August 16, 2011. Reprinted by permission of *The Wall Street Journal.*

U.S. Treasury Quotes

Treasury note and bond data are representative over-the-counter quotations as of 3pm Eastern time.

MATURITY	Coupon	BID	ASKED	CHG	ASK YLD
Aug 15 12	1.750	101.570	101.594	–0.016	0.151
Aug 15 14	4.250	111.547	111.594	–0.094	0.358
Dec 31 15	2.125	105.789	105.820	–0.164	0.769
Aug 15 17	4.750	120.219	120.266	–0.234	1.234
Feb 15 20	8.500	152.063	152.094	–0.344	1.847
Aug 15 23	6.250	137.406	137.438	–0.688	2.598
Feb 15 27	6.625	145.547	145.594	–0.719	2.941
Feb 15 31	5.375	130.266	130.297	–0.953	3.263
Nov 15 39	4.375	111.766	111.813	–0.813	3.697
May 15 41	4.375	111.719	111.750	–0.938	3.718

The highlighted issue in Figure 10.1 matures in August 2023. Its coupon rate is 6.25%. Par value is $1,000; thus, the bond pays interest of $62.50 per year in two semiannual payments of $31.25. Payments are made in February and August of each year. Although bonds are typically sold in denominations of $1,000 par value, the bid and ask prices[1] are quoted as a percentage of par value. Therefore, the ask price is 137.438% of par, or $1,374.38.

The last column, labeled "Ask Yld," is the bond's yield to maturity based on the ask price. The yield to maturity is often interpreted as a measure of the average rate of return to an investor who purchases the bond for the ask price and holds it until its maturity date. We will have much to say about yield to maturity below.

Accrued interest and quoted bond prices The bond prices that you see quoted in the financial pages are not actually the prices that investors pay for the bond. This is because the quoted price does not include the interest that accrues between coupon payment dates.

If a bond is purchased between coupon payments, the buyer must pay the seller for accrued interest, the prorated share of the upcoming semiannual coupon. For example, if 30 days have passed since the last coupon payment, and there are 182 days in the semiannual coupon period, the seller is entitled to a payment of accrued interest of $^{30}/_{182}$ of the semiannual coupon. The sale, or *invoice price* of the bond, which is the amount the buyer actually pays, would equal the stated price plus the accrued interest.

In general, the formula for the amount of accrued interest between two dates is

$$\text{Accrued interest} = \frac{\text{Annual coupon payment}}{2} \times \frac{\text{Days since last coupon payment}}{\text{Days separating coupon payments}}$$

EXAMPLE 10.1

Accrued Interest

Suppose that the coupon rate is 8%. Then the semiannual coupon payment is $40. Because 30 days have passed since the last coupon payment, the accrued interest on the bond is $40 × ($^{30}/_{182}$) = $6.59. If the quoted price of the bond is $990, then the invoice price will be $990 + $6.59 = $996.59.

The practice of quoting bond prices net of accrued interest explains why the price of a maturing bond is listed at $1,000 rather than $1,000 plus one coupon payment. A purchaser of an 8% coupon bond one day before the bond's maturity would receive $1,040 on the following day and so should be willing to pay a total price of $1,040 for the bond. In fact,

[1]Recall that the bid price is the price at which you can sell the bond to a dealer. The ask price, which is slightly higher, is the price at which you can buy the bond from a dealer.

FIGURE 10.2

Listing of corporate bonds

Source: *The Wall Street Journal Online,* August 11, 2011. Reprinted by permission of *The Wall Street Journal.*

ISSUER NAME	SYMBOL	COUPON	MATURITY	RATING MOODY'S/S&P/ FITCH	HIGH	LOW	LAST	CHANGE	YIELD %
JPMORGAN CHASE & CO	JPM.LHD	3.125%	Dec 2011	Aaa/AA+/AAA	100.907	100.786	100.829	0.079	0.305
GOLDMAN SACHS GP	GS.AOK	5.250%	Jul 2021	–/A/–	103.899	99.790	100.490	–0.225	5.186
CITIGROUP	C.AGT	5.375%	Aug 2020	A3/A/A+	109.280	105.900	107.994	0.818	4.293
BP CAPITAL MARKETS PLC (DUPLICATE)	BP.JW	3.200%	Mar 2016	A2/A/A	106.350	105.783	105.827	–0.451	1.864
BANK OF AMERICA CORP	BAC.XQ	4.875%	Sep 2012	A2/A/A+	102.917	99.000	101.625	–0.930	3.333
AT&T	T.MA	4.450%	May 2021	A2/A–/A	111.614	108.500	110.129	1.720	3.230

$40 of that total payment constitutes the accrued interest for the preceding half-year period. The bond price is quoted net of accrued interest in the financial pages and thus appears as $1,000.[2]

Corporate Bonds

Like the government, corporations borrow money by issuing bonds. Figure 10.2 is a sample of corporate bond listings from *The Wall Street Journal Online,* which reports only the most actively traded corporate bonds. Although some bonds trade electronically on the NYSE Bonds platform, most bonds are traded over the counter in a network of bond dealers linked by a computer quotation system. In practice, the bond market can be quite "thin," in that there are few investors interested in trading a particular issue at any particular time.

The bond listings in Figure 10.2 include the coupon, maturity, price, and yield to maturity of each bond. The "Rating" column is the estimation of bond safety given by the three major bond rating agencies, Moody's, Standard & Poor's, and Fitch. Bonds with A ratings are safer than those rated B or below. Notice that as a general rule, safer bonds with the higher ratings promise lower yields to maturity. We will return to this topic toward the end of the chapter.

Call provisions on corporate bonds Some corporate bonds are issued with call provisions, allowing the issuer to repurchase the bond at a specified *call price* before the maturity date. For example, if a company issues a bond with a high coupon rate when market interest rates are high, and interest rates later fall, the firm might like to retire the high-coupon debt and issue new bonds at a lower coupon rate to reduce interest payments. The proceeds from the new bond issue are used to pay for the repurchase of the existing higher-coupon bonds at the call price. This is called *refunding.* **Callable bonds** typically come with a period of call protection, an initial time during which the bonds are not callable. Such bonds are referred to as *deferred* callable bonds.

callable bonds

Bonds that may be repurchased by the issuer at a specified call price during the call period.

The option to call the bond is valuable to the firm, allowing it to buy back the bonds and refinance at lower interest rates when market rates fall. Of course, the firm's benefit is the bondholder's burden. Holders of called bonds forfeit their bonds for the call price, thereby giving up the prospect of an attractive rate of interest on their original investment. To compensate investors for this risk, callable bonds are issued with higher coupons and promised yields to maturity than noncallable bonds.

[2]In contrast to bonds, stocks do not trade at flat prices with adjustments for "accrued dividends." Whoever owns the stock when it goes "ex-dividend" receives the entire dividend payment, and the stock price reflects the value of the upcoming dividend. The price therefore typically falls by about the amount of the dividend on the "ex day." There is no need to differentiate between reported and invoice prices for stocks.

Suppose that Verizon issues two bonds with identical coupon rates and maturity dates. One bond is callable, however, while the other is not. Which bond will sell at a higher price?

convertible bond

A bond with an option allowing the bondholder to exchange the bond for a specified number of shares of common stock in the firm.

Convertible bonds **Convertible bonds** give bondholders an option to exchange each bond for a specified number of shares of common stock of the firm. The *conversion ratio* gives the number of shares for which each bond may be exchanged. Suppose a convertible bond is issued at par value of $1,000 and is convertible into 40 shares of a firm's stock. The current stock price is $20 per share, so the option to convert is not profitable now. Should the stock price later rise to $30, however, each bond may be converted profitably into $1,200 worth of stock. The *market conversion value* is the current value of the shares for which the bonds may be exchanged. At the $20 stock price, for example, the bond's conversion value is $800. The *conversion premium* is the excess of the bond price over its conversion value. If the bond were selling currently for $950, its premium would be $150.

Convertible bondholders benefit from price appreciation of the company's stock. Not surprisingly, this benefit comes at a price; convertible bonds offer lower coupon rates and stated or promised yields to maturity than nonconvertible bonds. At the same time, the actual return on the convertible bond may exceed the stated yield to maturity if the option to convert becomes profitable.

We discuss convertible and callable bonds further in Chapter 15.

put bond

A bond that the holder may choose either to exchange for par value at some date or to extend for a given number of years.

Puttable bonds While the callable bond gives the issuer the option to extend or retire the bond at the call date, the *extendable* or **put bond** gives this option to the bondholder. If the bond's coupon rate exceeds current market yields, for instance, the bondholder will choose to extend the bond's life. If the bond's coupon rate is too low, it will be optimal not to extend; the bondholder instead reclaims principal, which can be invested at current yields.

floating-rate bonds

Bonds with coupon rates periodically reset according to a specified market rate.

Floating-rate bonds **Floating-rate bonds** make interest payments that are tied to some measure of current market rates. For example, the rate might be adjusted annually to the current T-bill rate plus 2%. If the one-year T-bill rate at the adjustment date is 4%, the bond's coupon rate over the next year would then be 6%. This arrangement means that the bond always pays approximately current market rates.

The major risk involved in floaters has to do with changing credit conditions. The yield spread is fixed over the life of the security, which may be many years. If the financial health of the firm deteriorates, then investors will demand a greater yield premium than is offered by the security. In this case, the price of the bond will fall. While the coupon rate on floaters adjusts to changes in the general level of market interest rates, it does not adjust to changes in the financial condition of the firm.

Preferred Stock

Although preferred stock strictly speaking is considered to be equity, it often is included in the fixed-income universe. This is because, like bonds, preferred stock promises to pay a specified stream of dividends. However, unlike bonds, the failure to pay the promised dividend does not result in corporate bankruptcy. Instead, the dividends owed simply cumulate, and the common stockholders may not receive any dividends until the preferred stockholders have been paid in full. In the event of bankruptcy, the claim of preferred stockholders to the firm's assets has lower priority than that of bondholders but higher priority than that of common stockholders.

Preferred stock commonly pays a fixed dividend. Therefore, it is in effect a perpetuity, providing a level cash flow indefinitely. More recently, however, adjustable or floating-rate preferred stock has become popular, in some years accounting for about half of new issues. Floating-rate preferred stock is much like floating-rate bonds. The dividend rate is linked to a measure of current market interest rates and is adjusted at regular intervals.

Unlike interest payments on bonds, dividends on preferred stock are not considered tax-deductible expenses to the firm. This reduces their attractiveness as a source of capital to issuing firms. On the other hand, there is an offsetting tax advantage to preferred stock. When one corporation buys the preferred stock of another corporation, it pays taxes on only 30% of the dividends received. For example, if the firm's tax bracket is 35%, and it receives $10,000 in preferred-dividend payments, it will pay taxes on only $3,000 of that income: Total taxes owed on the income will be .35 × $3,000 = $1,050. The firm's effective tax rate on preferred dividends is therefore only .30 × 35% = 10.5%. Given this tax rule, it is not surprising that most preferred stock is held by corporations.

Preferred stock rarely gives its holders full voting privileges in the firm. However, if the preferred dividend is skipped, the preferred stockholders will then be provided some voting power.

Other Domestic Issuers

There are, of course, several issuers of bonds in addition to the Treasury and private corporations. For example, state and local governments issue municipal bonds. The outstanding feature of these is that interest payments are tax-free. We examined municipal bonds, the value of the tax exemption, and the equivalent taxable yield of these bonds in Chapter 2.

Government agencies, such as the Federal Home Loan Bank Board, the Farm Credit agencies, and the mortgage pass-through agencies Ginnie Mae, Fannie Mae, and Freddie Mac also issue considerable amounts of bonds. These too were reviewed in Chapter 2.

International Bonds

International bonds are commonly divided into two categories: *foreign bonds* and *Eurobonds.* Foreign bonds are issued by a borrower from a country other than the one in which the bond is sold. The bond is denominated in the currency of the country in which it is marketed. For example, if a German firm sells a dollar-denominated bond in the U.S., the bond is considered a foreign bond. These bonds are given colorful names based on the countries in which they are marketed. For example, foreign bonds sold in the U.S. are called *Yankee bonds.* Like other bonds sold in the U.S., they are registered with the Securities and Exchange Commission. Yen-denominated bonds sold in Japan by non-Japanese issuers are called *Samurai bonds.* British-pound-denominated foreign bonds sold in the U.K. are called *bulldog bonds.*

In contrast to foreign bonds, Eurobonds are denominated in one currency, usually that of the issuer, but sold in other national markets. For example, the Eurodollar market refers to dollar-denominated bonds sold outside the U.S. (not just in Europe), although London is the largest market for Eurodollar bonds. Because the Eurodollar market falls outside U.S. jurisdiction, these bonds are not regulated by U.S. federal agencies. Similarly, Euroyen bonds are yen-denominated bonds selling outside Japan, Eurosterling bonds are pound-denominated Eurobonds selling outside the U.K., and so on.

Innovation in the Bond Market

Issuers constantly develop innovative bonds with unusual features; these issues illustrate that bond design can be extremely flexible. Here are examples of some novel bonds. They should give you a sense of the potential variety in security design.

Inverse floaters These are similar to the floating-rate bonds we described earlier, except that the coupon rate on these bonds *falls* when the general level of interest rates rises. Investors in these bonds suffer doubly when rates rise. Not only does the present value of each dollar of cash flow from the bond fall as the discount rate rises but the level of those cash flows falls as well. (Of course investors in these bonds benefit doubly when rates fall.)

Asset-backed bonds Walt Disney has issued bonds with coupon rates tied to the financial performance of several of its films. Similarly, "David Bowie bonds" have been issued

TABLE 10.1 Principal and interest payments for a Treasury Inflation Protected Security

Time	Inflation in Year Just Ended	Par Value	Coupon Payment	+	Principal Repayment	=	Total Payment
0		$1,000.00					
1	2%	1,020.00	$40.80		0		$ 40.80
2	3	1,050.60	42.02		0		42.02
3	1	1,061.11	42.44		$1,061.11		1,103.55

with payments tied to royalties on some of his albums. These are examples of asset-backed securities. The income from a specified group of assets is used to service the debt. More conventional asset-backed securities are mortgage-backed securities or securities backed by auto or credit card loans, as we discussed in Chapter 2.

Pay-in-kind bonds Issuers of pay-in-kind bonds may choose to pay interest either in cash or in additional bonds. If the issuer is short on cash, it will likely choose to pay with new bonds rather than scarce cash.

Catastrophe bonds Oriental Land Co., which manages Tokyo Disneyland, has issued bonds with a final payment that depends on whether there has been an earthquake near the park. The Swiss firm Winterthur once issued a bond whose payments will be cut if a severe hailstorm in Switzerland results in extensive payouts on Winterthur policies. These bonds are a way to transfer "catastrophe risk" from insurance companies to the capital markets. Investors in these bonds receive compensation in the form of higher coupon rates for taking on the risk. But in the event of a catastrophe, the bondholders will lose all or part of their investments. "Disaster" can be defined either by total insured losses or by criteria such as wind speed in a hurricane or Richter level in an earthquake. Issuance of catastrophe bonds has surged in recent years as insurers have sought ways to spread their risks across a wider spectrum of the capital market.

Indexed bonds Indexed bonds make payments that are tied to a general price index or the price of a particular commodity. For example, Mexico has issued bonds with payments that depend on the price of oil. Some bonds are indexed to the general price level. The United States Treasury started issuing such inflation-indexed bonds in January 1997. They are called Treasury Inflation Protected Securities (TIPS). By tying the par value of the bond to the general level of prices, coupon payments, as well as the final repayment of par value, on these bonds increase in direct proportion to the consumer price index. Therefore, the interest rate on these bonds is a risk-free real rate.

To illustrate how TIPS work, consider a newly issued bond with a three-year maturity, par value of $1,000, and a coupon rate of 4%. For simplicity, we will assume the bond makes annual coupon payments. Assume that inflation turns out to be 2%, 3%, and 1% in the next three years. Table 10.1 shows how the bond cash flows will be calculated. The first payment comes at the end of the first year, at $t = 1$. Because inflation over the year was 2%, the par value of the bond increases from $1,000 to $1,020; since the coupon rate is 4%, the coupon payment is 4% of this amount, or $40.80. Notice that principal value increases by the inflation rate, and because the coupon payments are 4% of principal, they too increase in proportion to the general price level. Therefore, the cash flows paid by the bond are fixed in *real* terms. When the bond matures, the investor receives a final coupon payment of $42.44 plus the (price-level-indexed) repayment of principal, $1,061.11.[3]

The *nominal* rate of return on the bond in the first year is

$$\text{Nominal return} = \frac{\text{Interest} + \text{Price appreciation}}{\text{Initial price}} = \frac{40.80 + 20}{1{,}000} = 6.08\%$$

[3]By the way, total nominal income (i.e., coupon plus that year's increase in principal) is treated as taxable income in each year.

The real rate of return is precisely the 4% real yield on the bond:

$$\text{Real return} = \frac{1 + \text{Nominal return}}{1 + \text{Inflation}} - 1 = \frac{1.0608}{1.02} = .04, \text{ or } 4\%$$

One can show in a similar manner (see Problem 19 among the end-of-chapter questions) that the rate of return in each of the three years is 4% as long as the real yield on the bond remains constant. If real yields do change, then there will be capital gains or losses on the bond. In mid-2011, the real yield on TIPS bonds with 10-year maturity was about .8%.

10.2 BOND PRICING

Because a bond's coupon and principal repayments all occur months or years in the future, the price an investor would be willing to pay for a claim to those payments depends on the value of dollars to be received in the future compared to dollars in hand today. This "present value" calculation depends in turn on market interest rates. As we saw in Chapter 5, the nominal risk-free interest rate equals the sum of (1) a real risk-free rate of return and (2) a premium above the real rate to compensate for expected inflation. In addition, because most bonds are not riskless, the discount rate will embody an additional premium that reflects bond-specific characteristics such as default risk, liquidity, tax attributes, call risk, and so on.

We simplify for now by assuming there is one interest rate that is appropriate for discounting cash flows of any maturity, but we can relax this assumption easily. In practice, there may be different discount rates for cash flows accruing in different periods. For the time being, however, we ignore this refinement.

To value a security, we discount its expected cash flows by the appropriate discount rate. The cash flows from a bond consist of coupon payments until the maturity date plus the final payment of par value. Therefore

$$\text{Bond value} = \text{Present value of coupons} + \text{Present value of par value}$$

If we call the maturity date T and call the discount rate r, the bond value can be written as

$$\text{Bond value} = \sum_{t=1}^{T} \frac{\text{Coupon}}{(1 + r)^t} + \frac{\text{Par value}}{(1 + r)^T} \qquad \textbf{(10.1)}$$

The summation sign in Equation 10.1 directs us to add the present value of each coupon payment; each coupon is discounted based on the time until it will be paid. The first term on the right-hand side of Equation 10.1 is the present value of an annuity. The second term is the present value of a single amount, the final payment of the bond's par value.

You may recall from an introductory finance class that the present value of a \$1 annuity that lasts for T periods when the interest rate equals r is $\frac{1}{r}\left[1 - \frac{1}{(1 + r)^T}\right]$. We call this expression the T-period *annuity factor* for an interest rate of r.[4] Similarly, we call $\frac{1}{(1 + r)^T}$

[4]Here is a quick derivation of the formula for the present value of an annuity. An annuity lasting T periods can be viewed as an equivalent to a perpetuity whose first payment comes at the end of the current period *less* another perpetuity whose first payment doesn't come until the end of period $T + 1$. The immediate perpetuity net of the delayed perpetuity provides exactly T payments. We know that the value of a \$1 per period perpetuity is \$1/r. Therefore, the present value of the delayed perpetuity is \$1/r discounted for T additional periods, or $\frac{1}{r} \times \frac{1}{(1 + r)^T}$. The present value of the annuity is the present value of the first perpetuity minus the present value of the delayed perpetuity, or $\frac{1}{r}\left[1 - \frac{1}{(1 + r)^T}\right]$.

the *PV factor,* that is, the present value of a single payment of $1 to be received in T periods. Therefore, we can write the price of the bond as

$$\text{Price} = \text{Coupon} \times \frac{1}{r}\left[1 - \frac{1}{(1+r)^T}\right] + \text{Par value} \times \frac{1}{(1+r)^T} \tag{10.2}$$

$$= \text{Coupon} \times \text{Annuity factor}(r, T) + \text{Par value} \times \text{PV factor}(r, T)$$

EXAMPLE 10.2

Bond Pricing

We discussed earlier an 8% coupon, 30-year maturity bond with par value of $1,000 paying 60 semiannual coupon payments of $40 each. Suppose that the interest rate is 8% annually, or $r = 4\%$ per six-month period. Then the value of the bond can be written as

$$\text{Price} = \sum_{t=1}^{60} \frac{\$40}{(1.04)^t} + \frac{\$1{,}000}{(1.04)^{60}}$$

$$= \$40 \times \text{Annuity factor}(4\%, 60) + \$1{,}000 \times \text{PV factor}(4\%, 60)$$

It is easy to confirm that the present value of the bond's 60 semiannual coupon payments of $40 each is $904.94 and that the $1,000 final payment of par value has a present value of $95.06, for a total bond value of $1,000. You can calculate the value directly from Equation 10.2, perform these calculations on any financial calculator (see Example 10.3), use a spreadsheet (see Spreadsheet 10.1 below), or a set of present value tables.

In this example, the coupon rate equals the market interest rate, and the bond price equals par value. If the interest rate were not equal to the bond's coupon rate, the bond would not sell at par value. For example, if the interest rate were to rise to 10% (5% per six months), the bond's price would fall by $189.29, to $810.71, as follows:

$$\$40 \times \text{Annuity factor }(5\%, 60) + \$1{,}000 \times \text{PV factor }(5\%, 60)$$

$$= \$757.17 + \$53.54 = \$810.71$$

At a higher interest rate, the present value of the payments to be received by the bondholder is lower. Therefore, bond prices fall as market interest rates rise. This illustrates a crucial general rule in bond valuation.[5]

Financial calculators designed with present value and future value formulas already programmed can greatly simplify calculations of the sort we just encountered in Example 10.2. The basic financial calculator uses five keys that correspond to the inputs for time-value-of-money problems such as bond pricing:

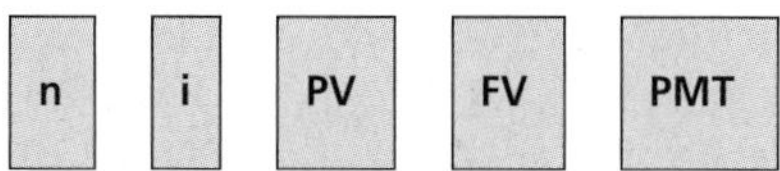

- n is the number of time periods. In the case of a bond, n equals the number of periods until the bond matures. If the bond makes semiannual payments, n is the number of half-year periods or, equivalently, the number of semiannual coupon payments. For example, if the bond has 10 years until maturity, you would enter 20 for n, since each payment period is one-half year.
- i is the interest rate per period, expressed as a percentage (not as a decimal, which is required by spreadsheet programs). For example, if the interest rate is 6%, you would enter 6, not .06.
- *PV* is the present value. Many calculators require that PV be entered as a negative number, in recognition of the fact that purchase of the bond is a cash *outflow,* while the receipt of coupon payments and face value are cash *inflows.*
- *FV* is the future value or face value of the bond. In general, FV is interpreted as a one-time future payment of a cash flow, which, for bonds, is the face (i.e., par) value.

[5]Here is a trap to avoid: You should not confuse the bond's *coupon* rate, which determines the interest paid to the bondholder, with the market interest rate. Once a bond is issued, its coupon rate is fixed. When the *market* interest rate increases, investors discount any fixed payments at a higher discount rate, which means present value, and bond prices fall.

- *PMT* is the amount of any recurring payment. For coupon bonds, PMT is the coupon payment; for zero-coupon bonds, PMT will be zero.

Given any four of these inputs, the calculator will solve for the fifth.

EXAMPLE 10.3

Bond Pricing on a Financial Calculator

We can illustrate how to use a financial calculator with the bond in Example 10.2. To find its price when the annual market interest rate is 8%, you would enter these inputs (in any order):

n	60	The bond has a maturity of 30 years, so it makes 60 semiannual payments.
i	4	The *semiannual* interest rate is 4%.
FV	1,000	The bond will provide a one-time cash flow of $1,000 when it matures.
PMT	40	Each semiannual coupon payment is $40.

On most calculators, you now punch the "compute" key (labeled "*COMP*" or "*CPT*") and then enter PV to obtain the bond price, that is, the present value today of the bond's cash flows. If you do this, you should find a value of −904.94. The negative sign signifies that while the investor receives cash flows from the bond, the price paid to *buy* the bond is a cash *out*flow, or a negative cash flow.

If you want to find the value of the bond when the interest rate is 10% (the second part of Example 10.2), just enter 5% for the semiannual interest rate (type "5" and then "*i*"), and then when you compute PV, you will find that it is −810.71.

Figure 10.3 shows the price of the 30-year, 8% coupon bond for a range of interest rates including 8%, at which the bond sells at par, and 10%, at which it sells for $810.71. The negative slope illustrates the inverse relationship between prices and yields. Note also from the figure (and from Table 10.2) that the shape of the curve implies that an increase in the interest rate results in a price decline that is smaller than the price gain resulting from a decrease of equal magnitude in the interest rate. This property of bond prices is called *convexity* because of the convex shape of the bond price curve. This curvature reflects the fact that progressive increases in the interest rate result in progressively smaller reductions in the bond price.[6] Therefore, the price curve becomes flatter at higher interest rates. We will return to convexity in the next chapter.

CONCEPT check 10.2

Calculate the price of the bond for a market interest rate of 3% per half-year. Compare the capital gains for the interest rate decline to the losses incurred when the rate increases to 5%.

Corporate bonds typically are issued at par value. This means the underwriters of the bond issue (the firms that market the bonds to the public for the issuing corporation) must choose a coupon rate that very closely approximates market yields. In a primary issue of bonds, the underwriters attempt to sell the newly issued bonds directly to their customers. If the coupon rate is inadequate, investors will not pay par value for the bonds.

TABLE 10.2 Bond prices at different interest rates (8% coupon bond, coupons paid semiannually)

Time to Maturity	Bond Price at Given Market Interest Rate				
	2%	**4%**	**6%**	**8%**	**10%**
1 year	$1,059.11	$1,038.83	$1,019.13	$1,000.00	$981.41
10 years	1,541.37	1,327.03	1,148.77	1,000.00	875.38
20 years	1,985.04	1,547.11	1,231.15	1,000.00	828.41
30 years	2,348.65	1,695.22	1,276.76	1,000.00	810.71

[6]The progressively smaller impact of interest rate increases results from the fact that at higher rates the bond is worth less. Therefore, an additional increase in rates operates on a smaller initial base, resulting in a smaller price reduction.

FIGURE 10.3

The inverse relationship between bond prices and yields: Price of an 8% coupon bond with 30-year maturity making semiannual coupon payments

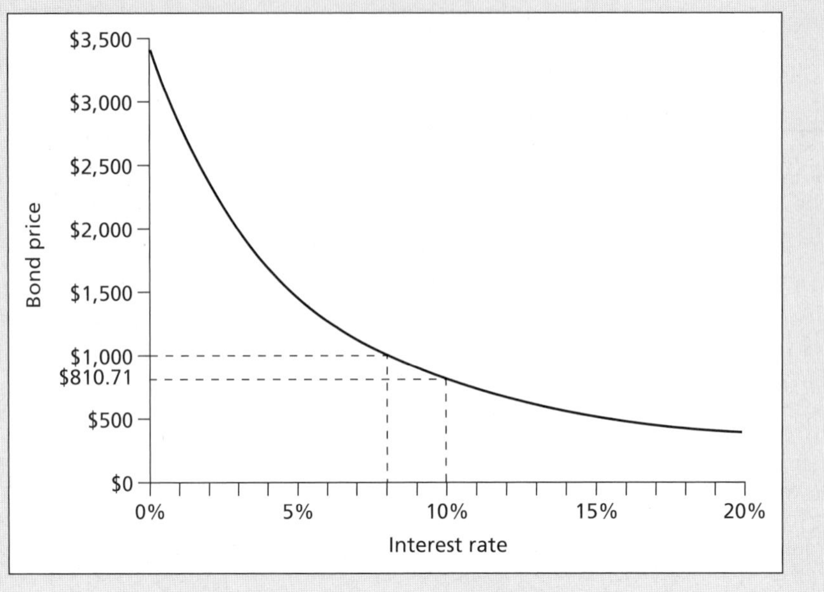

After the bonds are issued, bondholders may buy or sell bonds in secondary markets. In these markets, bond prices fluctuate inversely with the market interest rate.

The inverse relationship between price and yield is a central feature of fixed-income securities. Interest rate fluctuations represent the main source of risk in the bond market, and we devote considerable attention in the next chapter to assessing the sensitivity of bond prices to market yields. For now, however, we simply highlight one key factor that determines that sensitivity, namely, the maturity of the bond.

As a general rule, keeping all other factors the same, the longer the maturity of the bond, the greater the sensitivity of its price to fluctuations in the interest rate. For example, consider Table 10.2, which presents the price of an 8% coupon bond at different market yields and times to maturity. For any departure of the interest rate from 8% (the rate at which the bond sells at par value), the change in the bond price is greater for longer times to maturity.

This makes sense. If you buy the bond at par with an 8% coupon rate, and market rates subsequently rise, then you suffer a loss: You have tied up your money earning 8% when alternative investments offer higher returns. This is reflected in a capital loss on the bond—a fall in its market price. The longer the period for which your money is tied up, the greater the loss and, correspondingly, the greater the drop in the bond price. In Table 10.2, the row for one-year maturity bonds shows little price sensitivity—that is, with only one year's earnings at stake, changes in interest rates are not too threatening. But for 30-year maturity bonds, interest rate swings have a large impact on bond prices. The force of discounting is greatest for the longest-term bonds.

This is why short-term Treasury securities such as T-bills are considered the safest. They are free not only of default risk but also largely of price risk attributable to interest rate volatility.

Bond Pricing between Coupon Dates

Equation 10.2 for bond prices assumes that the next coupon payment is in precisely one payment period, either a year for an annual payment bond or six months for a semiannual payment bond. But you probably want to be able to price bonds all 365 days of the year, not just on the one or two dates each year that it makes a coupon payment!

In principle, the fact that the bond is between coupon dates does not affect the pricing problem. The procedure is always the same: Compute the present value of each remaining payment and sum up. But if you are between coupon dates, there will be fractional periods remaining until each payment, and this does complicate the arithmetic computations.

Fortunately, bond pricing functions are included in many financial calculators and most spreadsheet programs such as Excel. The spreadsheets allow you to enter today's date as well as the maturity date of the bond and so can provide prices for bonds at any date.

As we pointed out earlier, bond prices are typically quoted net of accrued interest. These prices, which appear in the financial press, are called *flat prices.* The actual *invoice price* that a buyer pays for the bond includes accrued interest. Thus,

$$\text{Invoice price} = \text{Flat price} + \text{Accrued interest}$$

When a bond pays its coupon, flat price equals invoice price, since at that moment accrued interest reverts to zero. However, this will be the exceptional case, not the rule.

Excel pricing functions provide the flat price of the bond. To find the invoice price, we need to add accrued interest. Excel also provides functions that count the days since the last coupon payment and thus can be used to compute accrued interest. Spreadsheet 10.1 illustrates how to use these functions. The spreadsheet provides examples using bonds that have just paid a coupon and so have zero accrued interest, as well as a bond that is between coupon dates.

Bond Pricing in Excel

Excel asks you to input both the date you buy the bond (called the *settlement date*) and the maturity date of the bond.

The Excel function for bond price is

=PRICE (settlement date, maturity date, annual coupon rate, yield to maturity, redemption value as percent of par value, number of coupon payments per year)

For the 6.25% coupon January 2012 maturity bond highlighted in Figure 10.1, we would enter the values in Spreadsheet 10.1. Alternatively, we could simply enter the following function in Excel:

=PRICE(DATE(2011,8,15), DATE(2023,8,15), .0625, .02598, 100, 2)

The DATE function in Excel, which we use for both the settlement and maturity dates, uses the format DATE(year,month,day). The first date is August 15, 2011, when the bond may be purchased, and the second is August 15, 2023, when it matures. See Spreadsheet 10.1.

Notice that the coupon rate and yield to maturity in Excel must be expressed as decimals, not percentages. In most cases, redemption value is 100 (i.e., 100% of par value), and the resulting price similarly is expressed as a percent of par value. Occasionally, however, you may encounter bonds that pay off at a premium or discount to par value. One example would be callable bonds, discussed shortly.

SPREADSHEET 10.1

Valuing bonds using a spreadsheet

	A	B	C	D	E	F	G
1		**6.25% coupon bond,**		**4.375% coupon bond,**		**8% coupon bond,**	
2		**maturing Aug 15, 2023**	**Formula in column B**	**maturing Nov 15, 2039**		**30-year maturity**	
3							
4	Settlement date	8/15/2011	=DATE(2011,8,15)	8/15/2011		1/1/2000	
5	Maturity date	8/15/2023	=DATE(2023,8,15)	11/15/2039		1/1/2030	
6	Annual coupon rate	0.0625		0.04375		0.08	
7	Yield to maturity	0.02598		0.03697		0.1	
8	Redemption value (% of face value)	100		100		100	
9	Coupon payments per year	2		2		2	
10							
11							
12	**Flat price (% of par)**	**137.444**	**=PRICE(B4,B5,B6,B7,B8,B9)**	**111.819**		**81.071**	
13	Days since last coupon	0	=COUPDAYBS(B4,B5,2,1)	92		0	
14	Days in coupon period	184	=COUPDAYS(B4,B5,2,1)	184		182	
15	Accrued interest	0	=(B13/B14)*B6*100/2	1.094		0	
16	**Invoice price**	**137.444**	**=B12+B15**	**112.913**		**81.071**	

eXcel

Please visit us at www.mhhe.com/bkm

The value of the bond returned by the pricing function is 137.444 (cell B12), which nearly matches the price reported in *The Wall Street Journal.* (The yield to maturity is reported to only three decimal places, which induces some rounding error.) This bond has just paid a coupon. In other words, the settlement date is precisely at the beginning of the coupon period, so no adjustment for accrued interest is necessary.

To illustrate the procedure for bonds between coupon payments, let's apply the spreadsheet to the 4.375% coupon November 2039 bond which also appears in Figure 10.1. Using the entries in column D of the spreadsheet, we find in cell D12 that the (flat) price of the bond is 111.819, which, except for minor rounding error, matches the price given in *The Wall Street Journal.*

What about the bond's invoice price? Rows 12 through 16 make the necessary adjustments. The function described in cell C13 counts the days since the last coupon. This day count is based on the bond's settlement date, maturity date, coupon period (1 = annual; 2 = semiannual), and day count convention (choice 1 uses actual days). The function described in cell C14 counts the total days in each coupon payment period. Therefore, the entries for accrued interest in row 15 are the semiannual coupon multiplied by the fraction of a coupon period that has elapsed since the last payment. Finally, the invoice prices in row 16 are the sum of flat price (which matches the reported price in *The Wall Street Journal*) plus accrued interest.

As a final example, suppose you wish to find the price of the bond in Example 10.2. It is a 30-year maturity bond with a coupon rate of 8% (paid semiannually). The market interest rate given in the latter part of the example is 10%. However, you are not given a specific settlement or maturity date. You can still use the PRICE function to value the bond. Simply choose an *arbitrary* settlement date (January 1, 2000, is convenient) and let the maturity date be 30 years hence. The appropriate inputs appear in column F of the spreadsheet, with the resulting price, 81.071% of face value, appearing in cell F16.

10.3 BOND YIELDS

We have noted that the current yield of a bond measures only the cash income provided by the bond as a percentage of bond price and ignores any prospective capital gains or losses. We would like a measure of rate of return that accounts for current income as well as the price increase or decrease over the bond's life. The yield to maturity is the standard measure of the total rate of return. However, it is far from perfect, and we will explore several variations of this measure.

Yield to Maturity

yield to maturity (YTM)

The discount rate that makes the present value of a bond's payments equal to its price.

In practice, an investor considering the purchase of a bond is not quoted a promised rate of return. Instead, the investor must use the bond price, maturity date, and coupon payments to infer the return offered by the bond over its life. The **yield to maturity (YTM)** is defined as the discount rate that makes the present value of a bond's payments equal to its price. This rate is often viewed as a measure of the average rate of return that will be earned on a bond if it is bought now and held until maturity. To calculate the yield to maturity, we solve the bond price equation for the interest rate given the bond's price.

For example, suppose an 8% coupon, 30-year bond is selling at $1,276.76. What average rate of return would be earned by an investor purchasing the bond at this price? We find the interest rate at which the present value of the remaining 60 semiannual payments equals the bond price. This is the rate consistent with the observed price of the bond. Therefore, we solve for r in the following equation:

$$\$1{,}276.76 = \sum_{t=1}^{60} \frac{\$40}{(1+r)^t} + \frac{\$1{,}000}{(1+r)^{60}}$$

or, equivalently,

$$1{,}276.76 = 40 \times \text{Annuity factor}(r, 60) + 1{,}000 \times \text{PV factor}(r, 60)$$

These equations have only one unknown variable, the interest rate, r. You can use a financial calculator or spreadsheet to confirm that the solution is $r = .03$, or 3% per half-year.[7] This is the bond's yield to maturity.

The financial press reports yields on an annualized basis and annualizes the bond's semiannual yield using simple interest techniques, resulting in an annual percentage rate or APR. Yields annualized using simple interest are also called *bond equivalent yields.* Therefore, the semiannual yield would be doubled and reported in the newspaper as a bond equivalent yield of 6%. The *effective* annual yield of the bond, however, accounts for compound interest. If one earns 3% interest every six months, then after one year, each dollar invested grows with interest to $\$1 \times (1.03)^2 = 1.0609$, and the effective annual interest rate on the bond is 6.09%.

The bond's yield to maturity is the internal rate of return on an investment in the bond. The yield to maturity can be interpreted as the compound rate of return over the life of the bond under the assumption that all bond coupons can be reinvested at that yield.[8] Yield to maturity therefore is widely accepted as a proxy for average return.

Yield to maturity can be difficult to calculate without a financial calculator or spreadsheet, but it is easy using either of these tools. We illustrate how in the next two examples.

EXAMPLE 10.4

Finding Yield to Maturity Using a Financial Calculator

Consider the yield to maturity problem that we just solved. On a financial calculator, we would enter the following inputs (in any order):

n	60	The bond has a maturity of 30 years, so it makes 60 semiannual payments.
PMT	40	Each semiannual coupon payment is $40.
PV	(−)1,276.76	The bond can be purchased for $1,276.76, which on some calculators must be entered as a negative number as it is a cash outflow.
FV	1,000	The bond will provide a one-time cash flow of $1,000 when it matures.

Given these inputs, you now use the calculator to find the interest rate at which $1,276.76 actually equals the present value of the 60 payments of $40 each plus the one-time payment of $1,000 at maturity. On some calculators, you first punch the "compute" key (labeled "*COMP*" or "*CPT*") and then enter i to have the interest rate computed. If you do so, you will find that $i = 3$, or 3% semiannually, as we claimed. (Notice that just as the cash flows are paid semiannually, the computed interest rate is a rate per semiannual time period.)

EXAMPLE 10.5

Finding Yield to Maturity Using Excel

Excel also provides a function for yield to maturity. It is

=YIELD(settlement date, maturity date, annual coupon rate, bond price, redemption value as percent of par value, number of coupon payments per year)

The bond price used in the function should be the reported, or "flat," price, without accrued interest. For example, to find the yield to maturity of the bond in Example 10.4, we would use column E of Spreadsheet 10.2. If the coupons were paid only annually, we would change the entry for payments per year to 1 (see cell G9), and the yield would fall slightly to 5.99%.

current yield
Annual coupon divided by bond price.

Yield to maturity differs from the **current yield** of a bond, which is the bond's annual coupon payment divided by the bond price. For example, for the 8%, 30-year bond currently selling at $1,276.76, the current yield would be $80/$1,276.76 = .0627, or 6.27% per year. In contrast, recall that the effective annual yield to maturity is 6.09%. For this bond, which is selling at a premium over par value ($1,276 rather than $1,000), the coupon rate (8%) exceeds

[7]Without a financial calculator or spreadsheet, you still could solve the equation, but you would need to use a trial-and-error approach.

[8]If the reinvestment rate does not equal the bond's yield to maturity, the compound rate of return will differ from YTM. This is demonstrated below in Examples 10.7 and 10.8.

SPREADSHEET 10.2

Finding yield to maturity using a spreadsheet (30-year maturity bond, coupon rate = 8%, price = 127.676% of par)

eXcel

Please visit us at www.mhhe.com/bkm

	A	B	C	D
1		Semiannual coupons		Annual coupons
2				
3	Settlement date	1/1/2000		1/1/2000
4	Maturity date	1/1/2030		1/1/2030
5	Annual coupon rate	0.08		0.08
6	Bond price (flat)	127.676		127.676
7	Redemption value (% of face value)	100		100
8	Coupon payments per year	2		1
9				
10	**Yield to maturity (decimal)**	0.0600		0.0599
	The formula entered here is =YIELD(B3,B4,B5,B6,B7,B8)			

the current yield (6.27%), which exceeds the yield to maturity (6.09%). The coupon rate exceeds current yield because the coupon rate divides the coupon payments by par value ($1,000) rather than by the bond price ($1,276). In turn, the current yield exceeds yield to maturity because the yield to maturity accounts for the built-in capital loss on the bond; the bond bought today for $1,276 will eventually fall in value to $1,000 at maturity.

premium bonds

Bonds selling above par value.

discount bonds

Bonds selling below par value.

This example illustrates a general rule: For **premium bonds** (bonds selling above par value), coupon rate is greater than current yield, which in turn is greater than yield to maturity. For **discount bonds** (bonds selling below par value), these relationships are reversed (see Concept Check 10.3).

It is common to hear people talking loosely about the yield on a bond. In these cases, they almost always are referring to the yield to maturity.

CONCEPT check 10.3

What will be the relationship among coupon rate, current yield, and yield to maturity for bonds selling at discounts from par? Illustrate using the 8% (semiannual payment) coupon bond assuming it is selling at a yield to maturity of 10%.

Yield to Call

Yield to maturity is calculated on the assumption that the bond will be held until maturity. What if the bond is callable, however, and may be retired prior to the maturity date? How should we measure average rate of return for bonds subject to a call provision?

Figure 10.4 illustrates the risk of call to the bondholder. The colored line is the value of a "straight" (that is, noncallable) bond with par value of $1,000, an 8% coupon rate, and a 30-year time to maturity as a function of the market interest rate. If interest rates fall, the bond price, which equals the present value of the promised payments, can rise substantially. Now consider a bond that has the same coupon rate and maturity date but is callable at 110% of par value, or $1,100. When interest rates fall, the present value of the bond's *scheduled* payments rises, but the call provision allows the issuer to repurchase the bond at the call price. If the call price is less than the present value of the scheduled payments, the issuer can call the bond at the expense of the bondholder.

The dark line in Figure 10.4 is the value of the callable bond. At high market interest rates, the risk of call is negligible because the present value of scheduled payments is substantially less than the call price; therefore, the values of the straight and callable bonds converge. At lower rates, however, the values of the bonds begin to diverge, with the difference reflecting the value of the firm's option to reclaim the callable bond at the call price. At very low market rates the present value of schedule payments significantly exceeds the call price, so the bond is called. Its value at this point is simply the call price, $1,100.

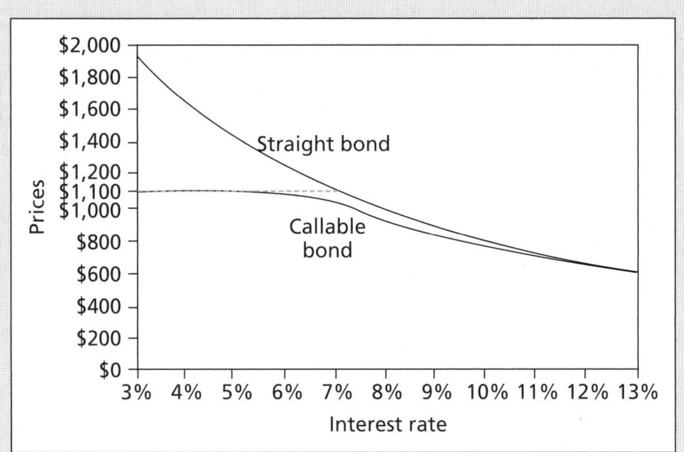

FIGURE 10.4

Bond prices: Callable and straight debt. Coupon = 8%; maturity = 30 years; semiannual payments

This analysis suggests that bond market analysts might be more interested in a bond's yield to call rather than its yield to maturity, especially if the bond is likely to be called. The yield to call is calculated just like the yield to maturity, except that the time until call replaces time until maturity and the call price replaces the par value. This computation is sometimes called "yield to first call," as it assumes the issuer will call the bond as soon as it may do so.

EXAMPLE 10.6

Yield to Call

Suppose the 8% coupon, 30-year maturity bond sells for $1,150 and is callable in 10 years at a call price of $1,100. Its yield to maturity and yield to call would be calculated using the following inputs:

	Yield to Call	Yield to Maturity
Coupon payment	$40	$40
Number of semiannual periods	20 periods	60 periods
Final payment	$1,100	$1,000
Price	$1,150	$1,150

Yield to call is then 6.64%. To confirm this on your calculator, input n = 20; PV = (−)1150; FV = 1100; PMT = 40; compute i as 3.32%, or 6.64% bond equivalent yield. In contrast, yield to maturity is 6.82%. To confirm, input n = 60; PV = (−)1150; FV = 1000; PMT = 40; compute i as 3.41%, or 6.82% bond equivalent yield. In Excel, you can calculate yield to call as =YIELD(DATE(2000,01,01), DATE(2010,01,01), .08, 115, 110, 2). Notice that redemption value is 110, that is, 110% of par value.

We have noted that most callable bonds are issued with an initial period of call protection. In addition, an implicit form of call protection operates for bonds selling at deep discounts from their call prices. Even if interest rates fall a bit, deep-discount bonds still will sell below the call price and thus will not be subject to a call.

Premium bonds that might be selling near their call prices, however, are especially apt to be called if rates fall further. If interest rates fall, a callable premium bond is likely to provide a lower return than could be earned on a discount bond whose potential price appreciation is not limited by the likelihood of a call. Investors in premium bonds therefore may be more interested in the bond's yield to call than its yield to maturity, because it may appear to them that the bond will be retired at the call date.

10.4

A 20-year maturity 9% coupon bond paying coupons semiannually is callable in five years at a call price of $1,050. The bond currently sells at a yield to maturity of 8% (bond equivalent yield). What is the yield to call?

Realized Compound Return versus Yield to Maturity

We have noted that yield to maturity will equal the rate of return realized over the life of the bond if all coupons are reinvested at an interest rate equal to the bond's yield to maturity. Consider for example, a two-year bond selling at par value paying a 10% coupon once a year. The yield to maturity is 10%. If the $100 coupon payment can be reinvested at an interest rate of 10%, the $1,000 investment in the bond will grow after two years to $1,210, as illustrated in Figure 10.5, Panel A. The coupon paid in the first year is reinvested and grows with interest to a second-year value of $110, which, together with the second coupon payment and payment of par value in the second year, results in a total value of $1,210. To summarize, the initial value of the investment is V_0 = $1,000. The final value in two years is V_2 = $1,210. The compound rate of return, therefore, is calculated as follows.

$$V_0(1 + r)^2 = V_2$$

$$\$1{,}000\,(1 + r)^2 = \$1{,}210$$

$$r = .10 = 10\%$$

realized compound return

Compound rate of return on a bond with all coupons reinvested until maturity.

With a reinvestment rate equal to the 10% yield to maturity, the **realized compound return** equals yield to maturity.

But what if the reinvestment rate is not 10%? If the coupon can be invested at more than 10%, funds will grow to more than $1,210, and the realized compound return will exceed 10%. If the reinvestment rate is less than 10%, so will be the realized compound return. Consider the following example.

EXAMPLE 10.7

Realized Compound Return

If the interest rate earned on the first coupon is less than 10%, the final value of the investment will be less than $1,210, and the realized compound yield will be less than 10%. Suppose the interest rate at which the coupon can be invested is only 8%. The following calculations are illustrated in Panel B of Figure 10.5.

Future value of first coupon payment with interest earnings	$100 × 1.08 = $ 108
Cash payment in second year (final coupon plus par value)	1,100
Total value of investment with reinvested coupons	$1,208

The realized compound return is the compound rate of growth of invested funds, assuming that all coupon payments are reinvested. The investor purchased the bond for par at $1,000, and this investment grew to $1,208.

$$\$1{,}000(1 + r)^2 = \$1{,}208$$

$$r = .0991 = 9.91\%$$

Example 10.7 highlights the problem with conventional yield to maturity when reinvestment rates can change over time. However, in an economy with future interest rate uncertainty, the rates at which interim coupons will be reinvested are not yet known. Therefore, while realized compound return can be computed *after* the investment period ends, it cannot be computed in advance without a forecast of future reinvestment rates. This reduces much of the attraction of the realized return measure.

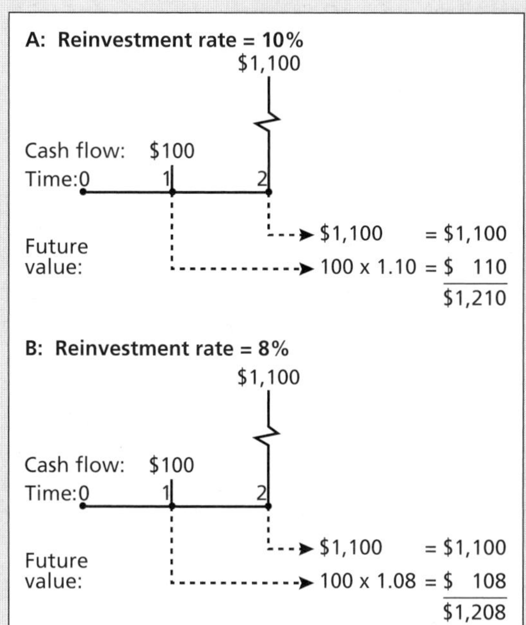

FIGURE 10.5

Growth of invested funds. In Panel A, interest payments are reinvested at 10%, the bond's yield to maturity. In Panel B, the reinvestment rate is only 8%.

We also can calculate realized compound yield over holding periods greater than one period. This is called **horizon analysis** and is similar to the procedure in Example 10.7. The forecast of total return will depend on your forecasts of *both* the yield to maturity of the bond when you sell it *and* the rate at which you are able to reinvest coupon income. With a longer investment horizon, however, reinvested coupons will be a larger component of your final proceeds.

horizon analysis

Analysis of bond returns over a multiyear horizon, based on forecasts of the bond's yield to maturity and the reinvestment rate of coupons.

EXAMPLE 10.8

Horizon Analysis

Suppose you buy a 30-year, 7.5% (annual payment) coupon bond for $980 (when its yield to maturity is 7.67%) and you plan to hold it for 20 years. Your forecast is that the bond's yield to maturity will be 8% when it is sold and that the reinvestment rate on the coupons will be 6%. At the end of your investment horizon, the bond will have 10 years remaining until expiration, so the forecast sales price (using a yield to maturity of 8%) will be $966.45. The 20 coupon payments will grow with compound interest to $2,758.92. (This is the future value of a 20-year $75 annuity with an interest rate of 6%.)

Based on these forecasts, your $980 investment will grow in 20 years to $966.45 + $2,758.92 = $3,725.37. This corresponds to an annualized compound return of 6.90%:

$$\$980\,(1+r)^{20} = \$3{,}725.37$$
$$r = .0690 = 6.90\%$$

Examples 10.7 and 10.8 demonstrate that as interest rates change, bond investors are actually subject to two sources of offsetting risk. On the one hand, when rates rise, bond prices fall, which reduces the value of the portfolio. On the other hand, reinvested coupon income will compound more rapidly at those higher rates. This **reinvestment rate risk** will offset the impact of price risk. In the next chapter, we will explore this trade-off in more detail and will discover that by carefully tailoring their bond portfolios, investors can precisely balance these two effects for any given investment horizon.

reinvestment rate risk

Uncertainty surrounding the cumulative future value of reinvested bond coupon payments.

10.4 BOND PRICES OVER TIME

As we noted earlier, a bond will sell at par value when its coupon rate equals the market interest rate. In these circumstances, the investor receives fair compensation for the time value of money in the form of the recurring coupon payments. No further capital gain is necessary to provide fair compensation.

When the coupon rate is lower than the market interest rate, the coupon payments alone will not provide investors as high a return as they could earn elsewhere in the market. To receive a competitive return on such an investment, investors also need to earn price appreciation on their bonds. The bonds, therefore, would have to sell below par value to provide a "built-in" capital gain on the investment.

EXAMPLE 10.9

Fair Holding-Period Return

To illustrate built-in capital gains or losses, suppose a bond was issued several years ago when the interest rate was 7%. The bond's annual coupon rate was thus set at 7%. (We will suppose for simplicity that the bond pays its coupon annually.) Now, with three years left in the bond's life, the interest rate is 8% per year. The bond's fair market price is the present value of the remaining annual coupons plus payment of par value. That present value is[9]

$$\$70 \times \text{Annuity factor}(8\%, 3) + \$1{,}000 \times \text{PV factor}(8\%, 3) = \$974.23$$

which is less than par value.

In another year, after the next coupon is paid and remaining maturity falls to two years, the bond would sell at

$$\$70 \times \text{Annuity factor}(8\%, 2) + \$1{,}000 \times \text{PV factor}(8\%, 2) = \$982.17$$

thereby yielding a capital gain over the year of \$7.94. If an investor had purchased the bond at \$974.23, the total return over the year would equal the coupon payment plus capital gain, or \$70 + \$7.94 = \$77.94. This represents a rate of return of \$77.94/\$974.23, or 8%, exactly the current rate of return available elsewhere in the market.

CONCEPT check 10.5

What will be the price of the bond in Example 10.9 in yet another year, when only one year remains until maturity? What is the rate of return to an investor who purchases the bond at \$982.17 and sells it one year later?

When bond prices are set according to the present value formula, any discount from par value provides an anticipated capital gain that will augment a below-market coupon rate just enough to provide a fair total rate of return. Conversely, if the coupon rate exceeds the market interest rate, the interest income by itself is greater than that available elsewhere in the market. Investors will bid up the price of these bonds above their par values. As the bonds approach maturity, they will fall in value because fewer of these above-market coupon payments remain. The resulting capital losses offset the large coupon payments so that the bondholder again receives only a competitive rate of return.

Problem 16 at the end of the chapter asks you to work through the case of the high-coupon bond. Figure 10.6 traces out the price paths of high- and low-coupon bonds (net of accrued interest) as time to maturity approaches, at least for the case in which the market interest rate is constant. The low-coupon bond enjoys capital gains, while the high-coupon bond suffers capital losses.[10]

[9]Using a calculator, enter $n = 3$, $i = 8$, PMT = 70, FV = 1000, and compute PV.

[10]If interest rates are volatile, the price path will be "jumpy," vibrating around the price path in Figure 10.6 and reflecting capital gains or losses as interest rates fluctuate. Ultimately, however, the price must reach par value at the maturity date, so, on average, the price of the premium bond will fall over time while that of the discount bond will rise.

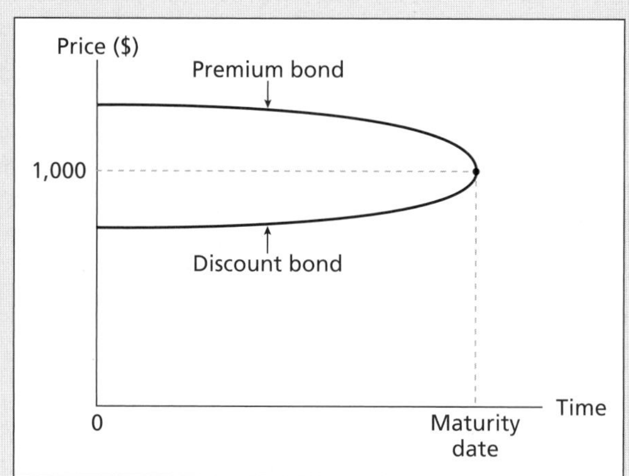

FIGURE 10.6

Price paths of coupon bonds in the case of constant market interest rates

We use these examples to show that each bond offers investors the same total rate of return. Although the capital gains versus income components differ, the price of each bond is set to provide competitive rates, as we should expect in well-functioning capital markets. Security returns all should be comparable on an after-tax risk-adjusted basis. If they are not, investors will try to sell low-return securities, thereby driving down their prices until the total return at the now-lower price is competitive with other securities. Prices should continue to adjust until all securities are fairly priced in that expected returns are comparable (given appropriate risk and tax adjustments).

Yield to Maturity versus Holding-Period Return

In Example 10.9, the holding-period return and the yield to maturity were equal. The bond yield started and ended the year at 8%, and the bond's holding-period return also equaled 8%. This turns out to be a general result. When the yield to maturity is unchanged over the period, the rate of return on the bond will equal that yield. As we noted, this should not be surprising: The bond must offer a rate of return competitive with those available on other securities.

However, when yields fluctuate, so will a bond's rate of return. Unanticipated changes in market rates will result in unanticipated changes in bond returns, and, after the fact, a bond's holding-period return can be better or worse than the yield at which it initially sells. An increase in the bond's yield to maturity acts to reduce its price, which means that the holding-period return will be less than the initial yield. Conversely, a decline in yield to maturity results in a holding-period return greater than the initial yield.

EXAMPLE 10.10

Yield to Maturity versus Holding-Period Return

Consider a 30-year bond paying an annual coupon of $80 and selling at par value of $1,000. The bond's initial yield to maturity is 8%. If the yield remains at 8% over the year, the bond price will remain at par, so the holding-period return also will be 8%. But if the yield falls below 8%, the bond price will increase. Suppose the yield falls and the price increases to $1,050. Then the holding-period return is greater than 8%:

$$\text{Holding-period return} = \frac{\$80 + (\$1,050 - \$1,000)}{\$1,000} = .13, \text{ or } 13\%$$

CONCEPT check 10.6

Show that if the yield to maturity increases, then holding-period return is *less* than that initial yield. For example, suppose in Example 10.10 that by the end of the first year, the bond's yield to maturity is 8.5%. Find the one-year holding-period return and compare it to the bond's initial 8% yield to maturity.

Here is another way to think about the difference between yield to maturity and holding-period return. Yield to maturity depends only on the bond's coupon, *current* price, and par value at maturity. All of these values are observable today, so yield to maturity can be easily calculated. Yield to maturity can be interpreted as a measure of the *average* rate of return if the investment in the bond is held until the bond matures. In contrast, holding-period return is the rate of return over a particular investment period and depends on the market price of the bond at the end of that holding period; of course this price is *not* known today. Since bond prices over the holding period will respond to unanticipated changes in interest rates, holding-period return can at most be forecast.

Zero-Coupon Bonds and Treasury STRIPS

Original-issue discount bonds are less common than coupon bonds issued at par. These are bonds that are issued intentionally with low coupon rates that cause the bond to sell at a discount from par value. An extreme example of this type of bond is the *zero-coupon bond,* which carries no coupons and provides all its return in the form of price appreciation. Zeros provide only one cash flow to their owners, on the maturity date of the bond.

U.S. Treasury bills are examples of short-term zero-coupon instruments. If the bill has face value of $10,000, the Treasury issues or sells it for some amount less than $10,000, agreeing to repay $10,000 at maturity. All of the investor's return comes in the form of price appreciation.

Longer term zero-coupon bonds are commonly created from coupon-bearing notes and bonds. A broker that purchases a Treasury coupon bond may ask the Treasury to break down the cash flows into a series of independent securities, where each security is a claim to one of the payments of the original bond. For example, a 10-year coupon bond would be "stripped" of its 20 semiannual coupons and each coupon payment would be treated as a stand-alone zero-coupon bond. The maturities of these bonds would thus range from six months to 10 years. The final payment of principal would be treated as another stand-alone zero-coupon security. Each of the payments would then be treated as an independent security and assigned its own CUSIP number, the security identifier that allows for electronic trading over the Fedwire system. The payments are still considered obligations of the U.S. Treasury. The Treasury program under which coupon stripping is performed is called STRIPS (Separate Trading of Registered Interest and Principal of Securities), and these zero-coupon securities are called *Treasury strips.*

What should happen to prices of zeros as time passes? On their maturity dates, zeros must sell for par value. Before maturity, however, they should sell at discounts from par, because of the time value of money. As time passes, price should approach par value. In fact, if the interest rate is constant, a zero's price will increase at exactly the rate of interest.

To illustrate, consider a zero with 30 years until maturity, and suppose the market interest rate is 10% per year. The price of the bond today is $\$1,000/(1.10)^{30} = \$57.31$. Next year, with only 29 years until maturity, if the yield to maturity is still 10%, the price will be $\$1,000/(1.10)^{29} = \$63.04$, a 10% increase over its previous-year value. Because the par value of the bond is now discounted for one less year, its price has increased by the one-year discount factor.

Figure 10.7 presents the price path of a 30-year zero-coupon bond for an annual market interest rate of 10%. The bond's price rises exponentially, not linearly, until its maturity.

After-Tax Returns

The tax authorities recognize that the "built-in" price appreciation on original-issue discount (OID) bonds such as zero-coupon bonds represents an implicit interest payment to the holder of the security. The Internal Revenue Service (IRS), therefore, calculates a price appreciation schedule to impute taxable interest income for the built-in appreciation during a tax year, even if the asset is not sold or does not mature until a future year. Any additional gains or losses that arise from changes in market interest rates are treated as capital gains or losses if the OID bond is sold during the tax year.

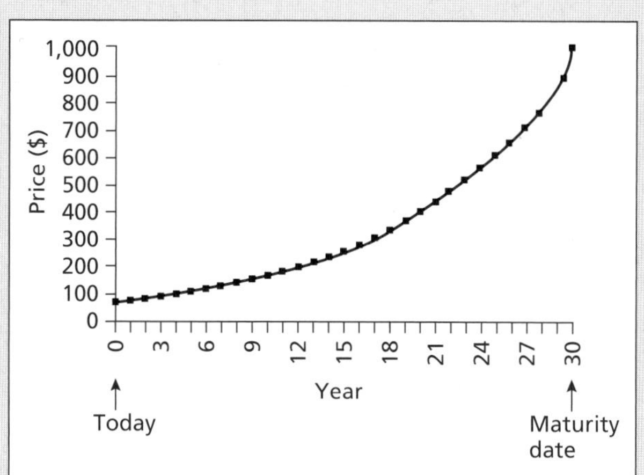

FIGURE 10.7

The price of a 30-year zero-coupon bond over time at a yield to maturity of 10%. Price equals 1,000/(1.10)^T, where T is time until maturity.

EXAMPLE 10.11

Taxation of Original-Issue Discount Bonds

If the interest rate originally is 10%, the 30-year zero would be issued at a price of $1,000/(1.10)^{30} = $57.31. The following year, the IRS calculates what the bond price would be if its yield were still 10%. This is $1,000/(1.10)^{29} = $63.04. Therefore, the IRS imputes interest income of $63.04 − $57.31 = $5.73. This amount is subject to tax. Notice that the imputed interest income is based on a "constant yield method" that ignores any changes in market interest rates.

If interest rates actually fall, let's say to 9.9%, the bond price will be $1,000/(1.099)^{29} = $64.72. If the bond is sold, then the difference between $64.72 and $63.04 will be treated as capital gains income and taxed at the capital gains tax rate. If the bond is not sold, then the price difference is an unrealized capital gain and does not result in taxes in that year. In either case, the investor must pay taxes on the $5.73 of imputed interest at the ordinary income tax rate.

The procedure illustrated in Example 10.11 applies as well to the taxation of other original-issue discount bonds, even if they are not zero-coupon bonds. Consider, as another example, a 30-year maturity bond that is issued with a coupon rate of 4% and a yield to maturity of 8%. For simplicity, we will assume that the bond pays coupons once annually. Because of the low coupon rate, the bond will be issued at a price far below par value, specifically at a price of $549.69. (Confirm this for yourself.) If the bond's yield to maturity is still 8%, then its price in one year will rise to $553.66. (Confirm this also.) This would provide a pretax holding-period return of exactly 8%:

$$\text{HPR} = \frac{\$40 + (\$553.66 - \$549.69)}{\$549.69} = .08$$

The increase in the bond price based on a constant yield, however, is treated as interest income, so the investor is required to pay taxes on imputed interest income of $553.66 − $549.69 = $3.97, as well as on the explicit coupon income of $40. If the bond's yield actually changes during the year, the difference between the bond's price and the "constant yield value" of $553.66 would be treated as capital gains income if the bond were sold at year-end.

CONCEPT check 10.7

Suppose that the yield to maturity of the 4% coupon, 30-year maturity bond falls to 7% by the end of the first year and that the investor sells the bond after the first year. If the investor's federal plus state tax rate on interest income is 38% and the combined tax rate on capital gains is 20%, what is the investor's after-tax rate of return?

10.5 DEFAULT RISK AND BOND PRICING

Although bonds generally *promise* a fixed flow of income, that income stream is not riskless unless the investor can be sure the issuer will not default on the obligation. While U.S. government bonds may be treated as free of default risk, this is not true of corporate bonds. If the company goes bankrupt, the bondholders will not receive all the payments they have been promised. Therefore, the actual payments on these bonds are uncertain, for they depend to some degree on the ultimate financial status of the firm.

Bond default risk is measured by Moody's Investor Services, Standard & Poor's Corporation, and Fitch Investors Service, all of which provide financial information on firms as well as the credit risk of large corporate and municipal bond issues. International sovereign bonds, which also entail default risk, especially in emerging markets, also are commonly rated for default risk. Each rating firm assigns letter grades to reflect its assessment of bond safety. The top rating is AAA or Aaa. Moody's modifies each rating class with a 1, 2, or 3 suffix (e.g., Aaa1, Aaa2, Aaa3) to provide a finer gradation of ratings. The other agencies use a + or − modification.

investment grade bond

A bond rated BBB and above by Standard & Poor's or Baa and above by Moody's.

speculative grade or junk bond

A bond rated BB or lower by Standard & Poor's, or Ba or lower by Moody's, or an unrated bond.

Those rated BBB or above (S&P, Fitch) or Baa and above (Moody's) are considered **investment grade bonds,** while lower-rated bonds are classified as **speculative grade** or **junk bonds.** Certain regulated institutional investors such as insurance companies have not always been allowed to invest in speculative grade bonds.

Figure 10.8 provides definitions of each bond rating classification.

Junk Bonds

Junk bonds, also known as *high-yield bonds,* are nothing more than speculative grade (low-rated or unrated) bonds. Before 1977, almost all junk bonds were "fallen angels," that is, bonds issued by firms that originally had investment grade ratings but that had since been downgraded. In 1977, however, firms began to issue "original-issue junk."

Much of the credit for this innovation is given to Drexel Burnham Lambert, and especially its trader, Michael Milken. Drexel had long enjoyed a niche as a junk bond trader and had established a network of potential investors in junk bonds. Firms not able to muster an investment grade rating were happy to have Drexel (and other investment bankers) market their bonds directly to the public, as this opened up a new source of financing. Junk issues were a lower-cost financing alternative than borrowing from banks.

High-yield bonds gained considerable notoriety in the 1980s when they were used as financing vehicles in leveraged buyouts and hostile takeover attempts. Shortly thereafter, however, the legal difficulties of Drexel and Michael Milken in connection with Wall Street's insider trading scandals of the late 1980s tainted the junk bond market.

At the height of Drexel's difficulties, the high-yield bond market nearly dried up but eventually rebounded dramatically. However, it is worth noting that the average credit quality of newly issued high-yield debt today is higher than the average quality in the boom years of the 1980s.

Of course, in periods of economic stress, junk bonds are more vulnerable than investment grade bonds. During the financial crisis of 2008–2009, prices on these bonds fell dramatically, and their yields to maturity rose equally dramatically. The spread between yields on Treasury bonds and B-rated bonds widened from around 3% in early 2007 to an astonishing 19% by the start of 2009.

Determinants of Bond Safety

Bond rating agencies base their quality ratings largely on an analysis of the level and trend of some of the issuer's financial ratios. The key ratios used to evaluate safety are:

1. *Coverage ratios.* Ratios of company earnings to fixed costs. For example, the *times-interest-earned ratio* is the ratio of earnings before interest payments and taxes to interest obligations. The *fixed-charge coverage ratio* includes lease payments and sinking fund payments

FIGURE 10.8

Definitions of each bond rating class

Sources: From Stephen A. Ross, Randolph W. Westerfield, and Jeffrey F. Jaffe, *Corporate Finance,* 9th ed. © 2010, McGraw-Hill Publishing. Data from various editions of *Standard & Poor's Bond Guide* and *Moody's Bond Guide.*

	Bond Ratings			
	Very High Quality	High Quality	Speculative	Very Poor
Standard & Poor's	AAA AA	A BBB	BB B	CCC D
Moody's	Aaa Aa	A Baa	Ba B	Caa C

At times both Moody's and Standard & Poor's use adjustments to these ratings. S&P uses plus and minus signs: A+ is the strongest A rating and A– the weakest. Moody's uses a 1, 2, or 3 designation, with 1 indicating the strongest.

Moody's	S&P	
Aaa	AAA	Debt rated Aaa and AAA has the highest rating. Capacity to pay interest and principal is extremely strong.
Aa	AA	Debt rated Aa and AA has a very strong capacity to pay interest and repay principal. Together with the highest rating, this group comprises the high-grade bond class.
A	A	Debt rated A has a strong capacity to pay interest and repay principal, although it is somewhat more susceptible to the adverse effects of changes in circumstances and economic conditions than debt in higher-rated categories.
Baa	BBB	Debt rated Baa and BBB is regarded as having an adequate capacity to pay interest and repay principal. Whereas it normally exhibits adequate protection parameters, adverse economic conditions or changing circumstances are more likely to lead to a weakened capacity to pay interest and repay principal for debt in this category than in higher-rated categories. These bonds are medium grade obligations.
Ba B Caa Ca	B CCC CC	Debt rated in these categories is regarded, on balance, as predominantly speculative with respect to capacity to pay interest and repay principal in accordance with the terms of the obligation. BB and Ba indicate the lowest degree of speculation, and CC and Ca the highest degree of speculation. Although such debt will likely have some quality and protective characteristics, these are outweighed by large uncertainties or major risk exposures to adverse conditions. Some issues may be in default.
C	C	This rating is reserved for income bonds on which no interest is being paid.
D	D	Debt rated D is in default, and payment of interest and/or repayment of principal is in arrears.

with interest obligations to arrive at the ratio of earnings to all fixed cash obligations. Low or falling coverage ratios signal possible cash flow difficulties.

2. *Leverage ratio.* Debt-to-equity ratio. A too-high leverage ratio indicates excessive indebtedness, signaling the possibility the firm will be unable to earn enough to satisfy the obligations on its bonds.
3. *Liquidity ratios.* The two common liquidity ratios are the *current ratio* (current assets/current liabilities) and the *quick ratio* (current assets excluding inventories/current liabilities). These ratios measure the firm's ability to pay bills coming due with its most liquid assets.
4. *Profitability ratios.* Measures of rates of return on assets or equity. Profitability ratios are indicators of a firm's overall performance. The *return on assets* (earnings before interest and taxes divided by total assets) or return on equity (net income/equity) are the most popular of these measures. Firms with higher return on assets or equity should be better

able to raise money in security markets because they offer prospects for better returns on the firm's investments.

5. *Cash flow-to-debt ratio.* This is the ratio of total cash flow to outstanding debt.

Standard & Poor's periodically computes median values of selected ratios for firms in several rating classes, which we present in Table 10.3. Of course, ratios must be evaluated in the context of industry standards, and analysts differ in the weights they place on particular ratios. Nevertheless, Table 10.3 demonstrates the tendency of ratios to improve along with the firm's rating class. And default rates vary dramatically with bond rating. Historically, only about 1% of industrial bonds originally rated AA or better at issuance had defaulted after 15 years. That ratio is around 7.5% for BBB-rated bonds and 40% for B-rated bonds. Credit risk clearly varies dramatically across rating classes.

Bond Indentures

indenture

The document defining the contract between the bond issuer and the bondholder.

In addition to specifying a payment schedule, the bond **indenture,** which is the contract between the issuer and the bondholder, also specifies a set of restrictions that protect the rights of the bondholders. Such restrictions include provisions relating to collateral, sinking funds, dividend policy, and further borrowing. The issuing firm agrees to these so-called protective covenants in order to market its bonds to investors concerned about the safety of the bond issue.

sinking fund

A bond indenture that calls for the issuer to periodically repurchase some proportion of the outstanding bonds prior to maturity.

Sinking funds Bonds call for the payment of par value at the end of the bond's life. This payment constitutes a large cash commitment for the issuer. To help ensure that the commitment does not create a cash flow crisis, the firm may agree to establish a **sinking fund** to spread the payment burden over several years. The fund may operate in one of two ways:

1. The firm may repurchase a fraction of the outstanding bonds in the open market each year.
2. The firm may purchase a fraction of outstanding bonds at a special call price associated with the sinking fund provision. The firm has an option to purchase the bonds at either the market price or the sinking fund price, whichever is lower. To allocate the burden of the sinking fund call fairly among bondholders, the bonds chosen for the call are selected at random based on serial number.[11]

The sinking fund call differs from a conventional call provision in two important ways. First, the firm can repurchase only a limited fraction of the bond issue at the sinking fund call price. At best, some indentures allow firms to use a *doubling option,* which allows repurchase of double the required number of bonds at the sinking fund call price. Second, while callable

TABLE 10.3 Financial ratios and default risk by rating class, long-term debt

	Three-Year (2002 to 2004) Medians						
	AAA	AA	A	BBB	BB	B	CCC
EBIT interest coverage multiple	23.8	19.5	8.0	4.7	2.5	1.2	0.4
EBITDA interest coverage multiple	25.5	24.6	10.2	6.5	3.5	1.9	0.9
Funds from operations/total debt (%)	203.3	79.9	48.0	35.9	22.4	11.5	5.0
Free operating cash flow/total debt (%)	127.6	44.5	25.0	17.3	8.3	2.8	(002.1)
Total debt/EBITDA multiple	0.4	0.9	1.6	2.2	3.5	5.3	7.9
Return on capital (%)	27.6	27.0	17.5	13.4	11.3	8.7	3.2
Total debt/total debt + equity (%)	12.4	28.3	37.5	42.5	53.7	75.9	113.5

Note: EBITDA is earnings before interest, taxes, depreciation, and amortization.

Source: *Corporate Rating Criteria,* Standard & Poor's, 2006. Reproduced by permission of Standard & Poor's, a division of The McGraw-Hill Companies, Inc.

[11]While it is uncommon, the sinking fund provision also may call for periodic payments to a trustee, with the payments invested so that the accumulated sum can be used for retirement of the entire issue at maturity.

bonds generally have call prices above par value, the sinking fund call price usually is set at the bond's par value.

Although sinking funds ostensibly protect bondholders by making principal repayment more likely, they can hurt the investor. The firm will choose to buy back discount bonds (selling below par) at their market price, while exercising its option to buy back premium bonds (selling above par) at par. Therefore, if interest rates fall and bond prices rise, a firm will benefit from the sinking fund provision that enables it to repurchase its bonds at below-market prices. In these circumstances, the firm's gain is the bondholder's loss.

One bond issue that does not require a sinking fund is a *serial bond* issue in which the firm sells bonds with staggered maturity dates. As bonds mature sequentially, the principal repayment burden for the firm is spread over time just as it is with a sinking fund. Serial bonds do not include call provisions. Unlike sinking fund bonds, serial bonds do not confront security holders with the risk that a particular bond may be called for the sinking fund. The disadvantage of serial bonds, however, is that the bonds of each maturity date are different bonds, which reduces the liquidity of the issue. Trading these bonds, therefore, is more expensive.

Subordination of further debt One of the factors determining bond safety is the total outstanding debt of the issuer. If you bought a bond today, you would be understandably distressed to see the firm tripling its outstanding debt tomorrow. Your bond would be riskier than it appeared when you bought it. To prevent firms from harming bondholders in this manner, **subordination clauses** restrict the amount of their additional borrowing. Additional debt might be required to be subordinated in priority to existing debt; that is, in the event of bankruptcy, *subordinated* or *junior* debtholders will not be paid unless and until the prior senior debt is fully paid off.

subordination clauses

Restrictions on additional borrowing that stipulate that senior bondholders will be paid first in the event of bankruptcy.

Dividend restrictions Covenants also limit the dividends firms may pay. These limitations protect the bondholders because they force the firm to retain assets rather than pay them out to stockholders. A typical restriction disallows payments of dividends if cumulative dividends paid since the firm's inception exceed cumulative retained earnings plus proceeds from sales of stock.

Collateral Some bonds are issued with specific collateral behind them. **Collateral** is a particular asset that the bondholders receive if the firm defaults. If the collateral is property, the bond is called a *mortgage bond.* If the collateral takes the form of other securities held by the firm, the bond is a *collateral trust bond.* In the case of equipment, the bond is known as an *equipment obligation bond.* This last form of collateral is used most commonly by firms such as railroads, where the equipment is fairly standard and can be easily sold to another firm should the firm default.

collateral

A specific asset pledged against possible default on a bond.

Collateralized bonds generally are considered safer than general **debenture** bonds, which are unsecured, meaning they do not provide for specific collateral; credit risk of unsecured bonds depends on the general earning power of the firm. If the firm defaults, debenture owners become general creditors of the firm. Because they are safer, collateralized bonds generally offer lower yields than general debentures.

debenture

A bond not backed by specific collateral.

Figure 10.9 shows the terms of a bond issued by Mobil as described in *Moody's Industrial Manual.* The terms of the bond are typical and illustrate many of the indenture provisions we have mentioned. The bond is registered and listed on the NYSE. It was issued in 1991, but it was not callable until 2002. Although the call price started at 105.007% of par value, it falls gradually until it reaches par after 2020.

Yield to Maturity and Default Risk

Because corporate bonds are subject to default risk, we must distinguish between the bond's promised yield to maturity and its expected yield. The promised or stated yield will be realized only if the firm meets the obligations of the bond issue. Therefore, the stated yield is the *maximum possible* yield to maturity of the bond. The expected yield to maturity must take into account the possibility of a default.

FIGURE 10.9

Callable bond issued by Mobil

Source: *Moody's Industrial Manual,* Moody's Investor Services, 1997.

& Mobil Corp. debenture 8s, due 2032:
Rating — Aa2
AUTH — $250,000,000.
OUTSTG — Dec. 31, 1993, $250,000,000.
DATED — Oct. 30, 1991.
INTEREST — F&A 12.
TRUSTEE — Chemical Bank.
DENOMINATION — Fully registered, $1,000 and integral multiples thereof. Transferable and exchangeable without service charge.
CALLABLE — As a whole or in part, at any time, on or after Aug. 12, 2002, at the option of Co. on at least 30 but not more than 60 days' notice to each Aug. 11 as follows:

2003	105.007	2004	104.756	2005	104.506
2006	104.256	2007	104.005	2008	103.755
2009	103.505	2010	103.254	2011	103.004
2012	102.754	2013	102.503	2014	102.253
2015	102.003	2016	101.752	2017	101.502
2018	101.252	2019	101.001	2020	100.751
2021	100.501	2022	100.250		

and thereafter at 100 plus accrued interest.
SECURITY — Not secured. Ranks equally with all other unsecured and unsubordinated indebtedness of Co. Co. nor any Affiliate will not incurr any indebtedness; provided that Co. will not create as security for any indebtedness for borrowed money, any mortgage, pledge, security interest or lien on any stock or indebtedness is directly owned by Co., without effectively providing that the debt securities shall be secured equally and ratably with such indebtedness, so long as such indebtedness shall be so secured.
INDENTURE MODIFICATION — Indenture may be modified, except as provided with, consent of 66⅔% of debs. outstg.
RIGHTS ON DEFAULT — Trustee, or 25% of debs. outstg., may declare principal dua nad payable (30 days' grace for payment of interest).
LISTED — On New York Stock Exchange.
PURPOSE — Proceeds used for general corporate purposes.
OFFERED — ($250,000,000) at 99.51 plus accrued interest (proceeds to Co., 99.11) on Aug. 5, 1992 thru Merrill Lynch & Co., Donaldson, Lufkin & Jenerette Securities Corp., PaineWebber Inc., Prudential Securities Inc., Smith Barney, Harris Upham & Co. Inc. and associates.

For example, at the height of the financial crisis in October 2008, as Ford Motor Company struggled, its 6.625% coupon bonds due in 2028 were rated CCC and were selling at about 33% of par value, resulting in a yield to maturity of about 20%. Investors did not really believe the expected rate of return on these bonds was 20%. They recognized the distinct possibility that bondholders would not receive all the payments promised in the bond contract and that the yield based on *expected* cash flows was far less than the yield based on *promised* cash flows. As it turned out, of course, Ford weathered the storm, and investors who purchased its bonds made a very nice profit: The bonds sell today for about 95% of par value.

EXAMPLE 10.12

Expected versus Promised Yield

Suppose a firm issued a 9% coupon bond 20 years ago. The bond now has 10 years left until its maturity date, but the firm is having financial difficulties. Investors believe that the firm will be able to make good on the remaining interest payments but that at the maturity date, the firm will be forced into bankruptcy and bondholders will receive only 70% of par value. The bond is selling at $750.

Yield to maturity (YTM) would then be calculated using the following inputs:

	Expected YTM	Stated YTM
Coupon payment	$45	$45
Number of semiannual periods	20 periods	20 periods
Final payment	$700	$1,000
Price	$750	$750

The yield to maturity based on promised payments is 13.7%. Based on the expected payment of $700 at maturity, however, the yield would be only 11.6%. The stated yield to maturity is greater than the yield to maturity investors actually expect to receive.

Example 10.12 suggests that when a bond becomes more subject to default risk, its price will fall, and therefore its promised yield to maturity will rise. Therefore, the default premium, the spread between the stated yield to maturity and that on otherwise comparable Treasury bonds, will rise. However, its expected yield to maturity, which ultimately is tied to the systematic risk of the bond, will be far less affected. Let's continue the example.

EXAMPLE 10.13

Default Risk and the Default Premium

Suppose that the condition of the firm in Example 10.12 deteriorates further, and investors now believe that the bond will pay off only 55% of face value at maturity. Investors now demand an expected yield to maturity of 12% (i.e., 6% semiannually), which is .4% higher than in Example 10.12. But the price of the bond will fall from \$750 to \$688 [n = 20; i = 6; FV = 550; PMT = \$45]. At this price, the stated yield to maturity based on promised cash flows is 15.2%. While the expected yield to maturity has increased by .4%, the drop in price has caused the promised yield to maturity (and the default premium) to rise by 1.5%.

default premium

The increment to promised yield that compensates the investor for default risk.

To compensate for the possibility of default, corporate bonds must offer a **default premium.** The default premium is the difference between the promised yield on a corporate bond and the yield of an otherwise identical government bond that is riskless in terms of default. If the firm remains solvent and actually pays the investor all of the promised cash flows, the investor will realize a higher yield to maturity than would be realized from the government bond. If, however, the firm goes bankrupt, the corporate bond is likely to provide a lower return than the government bond. The corporate bond has the potential for both better and worse performance than the default-free Treasury bond. In other words, it is riskier.

The pattern of default premiums offered on risky bonds is sometimes called the *risk structure of interest rates.* The greater the default risk, the higher the default premium. Figure 10.10 shows spreads between yields to maturity of bonds of different risk classes since 1997. You can see here clear evidence of default-risk premiums on promised yields. Note for example, the incredible run-up of credit spreads during the crisis of 2008–2009.

Credit Default Swaps

credit default swap

An insurance policy on the default risk of a corporate bond or loan.

A **credit default swap** (CDS) is in effect an insurance policy on the default risk of a corporate bond or loan. To illustrate, the annual premium in July 2011 on a five-year Citigroup CDS was about 1.3%, meaning that the CDS buyer would pay the seller an annual premium of \$1.30 for each \$100 of bond principal. The seller collects these annual payments for the term of the contract, but must compensate the buyer for loss of bond value in the event of a default.[12]

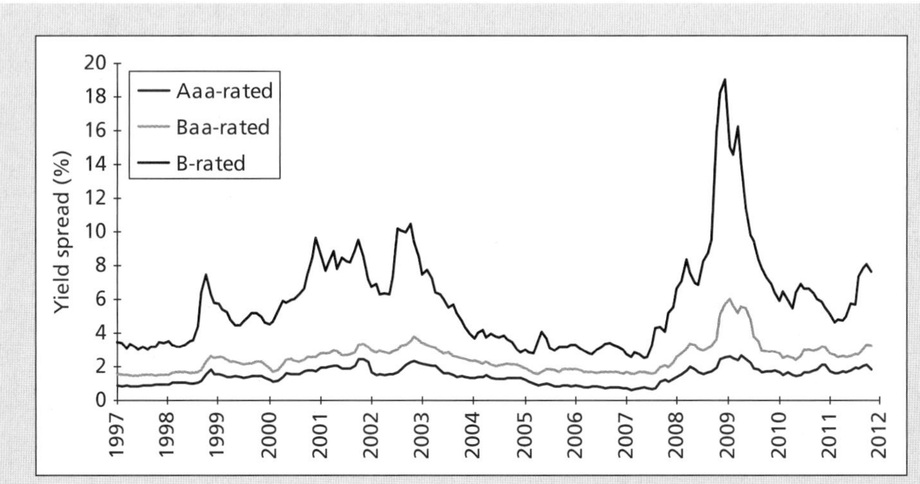

FIGURE 10.10

Yield spreads between corporate and 10-year Treasury bonds

Source: Federal Reserve Bank of St. Louis, **http://research.stlouisfed.org/fred2/categories/32348.**

[12]Actually, credit default swaps may pay off even short of an actual default. The contract specifies which particular "credit events" will trigger a payment. For example, restructuring (rewriting the terms of a firm's outstanding debt as an alternative to formal bankruptcy proceedings) may be defined as a triggering credit event.

As originally envisioned, credit default swaps were designed to allow lenders to buy protection against losses on sizable loans. The natural buyers of CDSs would then be large bondholders or banks that had made large loans and wished to enhance the creditworthiness of those loans. Even if the borrowing firm had shaky credit standing, the "insured" debt would be as safe as the issuer of the CDS. An investor holding a bond with a BB rating could, in principle, raise the effective quality of the debt to AAA by buying a CDS on the issuer.

This insight suggests how CDS contracts should be priced. If a BB-rated bond bundled with insurance via a CDS is effectively equivalent to a AAA-rated bond, then the fair price of

FIGURE 10.11

Prices of credit default swaps

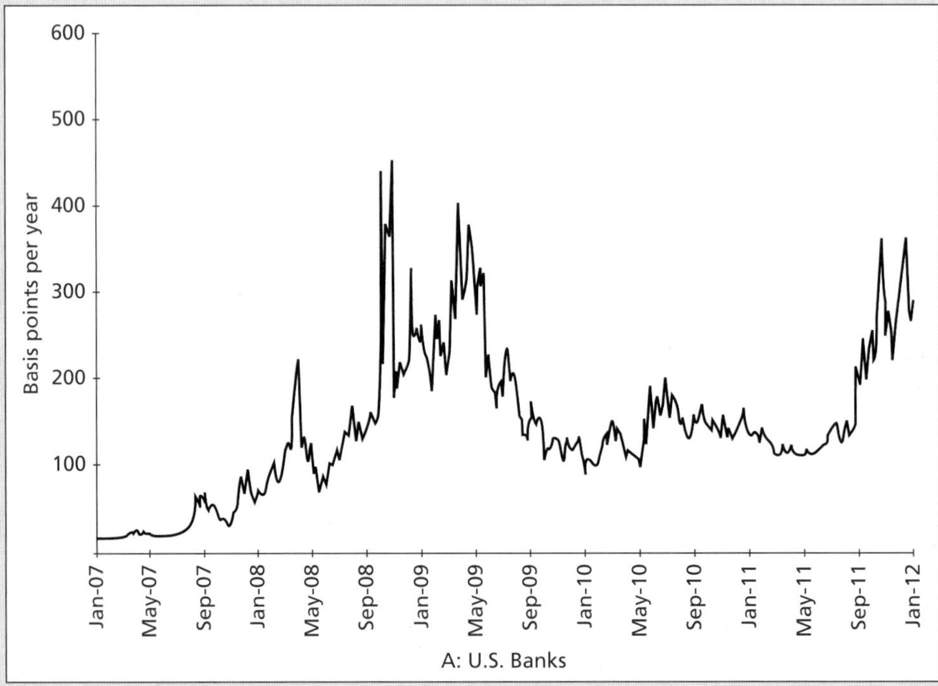

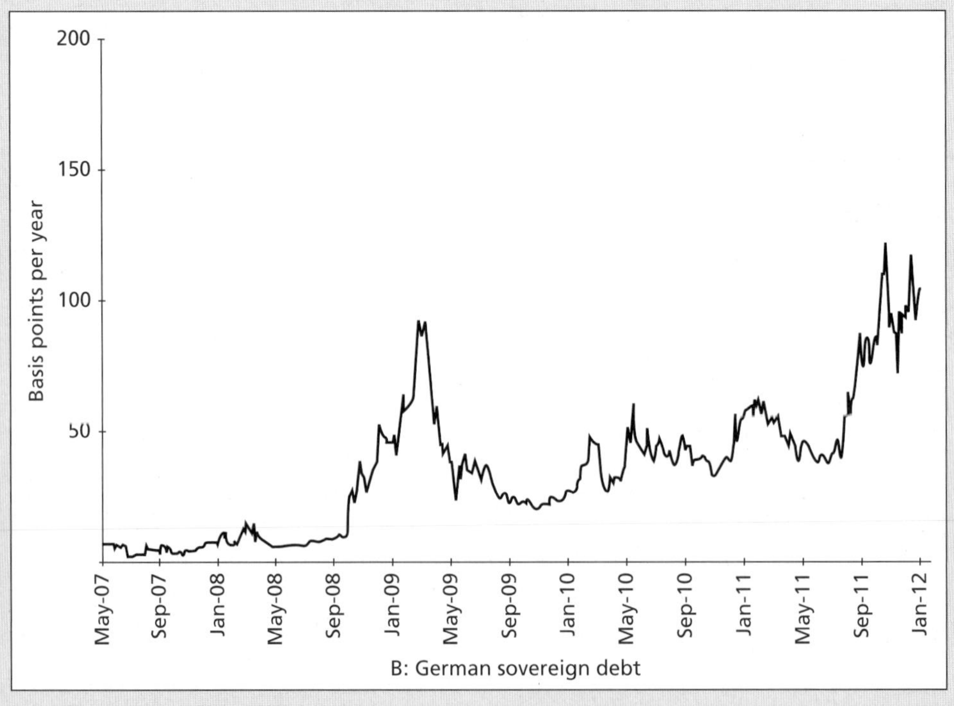

CREDIT DEFAULT SWAPS, SYSTEMIC RISK, AND THE FINANCIAL CRISIS OF 2008–2009

The credit crisis of 2008–2009, when lending among banks and other financial institutions effectively seized up, was in large measure a crisis of transparency. The biggest problem was a widespread lack of confidence in the financial standing of counterparties to a trade. If one institution could not be confident that another would remain solvent, it would understandably be reluctant to offer it a loan. When doubt about the credit exposure of customers and trading partners spiked to levels not seen since the Great Depression, the market for loans dried up.

Credit default swaps were particularly cited for fostering doubts about counterparty reliability. By August 2008, $63 trillion of such swaps were reportedly outstanding. (By comparison, U.S. gross domestic product in 2008 was about $14 trillion.) As the subprime-mortgage market collapsed and the economy entered a deep recession, the potential obligations on these contracts ballooned to levels previously considered unimaginable and the ability of CDS sellers to honor their commitments was in doubt. For example, the huge insurance firm AIG alone had sold more than $400 billion of CDS contracts on subprime mortgages and other loans and was days from insolvency. But AIG's insolvency would have triggered the insolvency of other firms that had relied on its promise of protection against loan defaults. These in turn might have triggered further defaults. In the end, the government felt compelled to rescue AIG to prevent a chain reaction of insolvencies.

Counterparty risk and lax reporting requirements made it effectively impossible to tease out firms' exposures to credit risk. One problem was that CDS positions do not have to be accounted for on balance sheets. And the possibility of one default setting off a sequence of further defaults means that lenders may be exposed to the default of an institution with which they do not even directly trade. Such knock-on effects create *systemic risk,* in which the entire financial system can freeze up. With the ripple effects of bad debt extending in ever-widening circles, it can seem imprudent to lend to anyone.

In the aftermath of the credit crisis, the Dodd-Frank Act called for new regulation and reforms. Among its proposals is the creation of a central clearinghouse for credit derivatives such as CDS contracts. Such a system would foster transparency of positions, allow netting of offsetting positions, and require daily recognition of gains or losses on positions through a margin or collateral account. If losses were to mount, positions would have to be unwound before growing to unsustainable levels. Allowing traders to accurately assess counterparty risk, and limiting such risk through margin accounts and the extra backup of the clearinghouse, would go a long way in limiting systemic risk.

the swap ought to approximate the yield spread between AAA-rated and BB-rated bonds.[13] The risk structure of interest rates and CDS prices ought to be tightly aligned.

Figure 10.11, Panel A, shows the average prices of five-year CDSs on U.S. banks between mid-2007 and 2011. Notice the sharp run-up in prices in September 2008 as Lehman Brothers entered bankruptcy and the financial crisis peaked. CDS prices fell back, but then they increased again in 2009 in the depths of the recession. As perceived credit risk increased, so did the price of insuring that debt.

CDS contracts also trade on the sovereign debt of a wide range of countries. Panel B of Figure 10.11 shows the prices of five-year CDS contracts on German debt. Even with Germany being the strongest economy in the euro zone, German CDS prices nevertheless reflect financial strain, first in the great recession of 2009 and then again in 2011 as the prospects of default (and a German-led bailout) of Greece and other euro zone countries worsened. Still, even in late 2011, German CDS prices were only about one-third of those on U.S. banks.

While CDSs were conceived as a form of bond insurance, it wasn't long before investors realized that they could be used to speculate on the financial health of particular companies. As Figure 10.11 makes clear, someone in August 2008 wishing to bet against the financial sector might have purchased CDS contracts on those firms and would have profited as CDS prices spiked in September. In fact, hedge fund manager John Paulson famously did just this. His bearish bets in 2007–2008 on commercial banks and Wall Street firms as well as on some riskier mortgage-backed securities made his funds more than $15 billion, bringing him a personal payoff of more than $3.7 billion.

[13]We say "approximately" because there are some differences between highly rated bonds and bonds synthetically enhanced with credit default swaps. For example, the term of the swap may not match the maturity of the bond. Tax treatment of coupon payments versus swap payments may differ, as may the liquidity of the bonds. Finally, some CDSs may entail one-time up-front payments as well as annual premiums.

The nearby box discusses the role of credit default swaps in the financial crisis of 2008–2009.

10.6 THE YIELD CURVE

yield curve

A graph of yield to maturity as a function of term to maturity.

term structure of interest rates

The relationship between yields to maturity and terms to maturity across bonds.

Return to Figure 10.1 again, and you will see that while yields to maturity on bonds of various maturities are reasonably similar, yields do differ. Bonds with shorter maturities generally offer lower yields to maturity than longer-term bonds. The graphical relationship between the yield to maturity and the term to maturity is called the **yield curve.** The relationship also is called the **term structure of interest rates** because it relates yields to maturity to the term (maturity) of each bond. The yield curve is published regularly and may be found in *The Wall Street Journal* or on the web at sites such as Yahoo! Finance. Four such sets of curves are reproduced in Figure 10.12. Figure 10.12 illustrates that a wide range of yield curves may be observed in practice. Panel A is an essentially flat yield curve. Panel B is an upward-sloping curve, and Panel C is a downward-sloping, or "inverted," yield curve. Finally the yield curve in Panel D is hump-shaped, first rising and then falling. Rising yield curves are most commonly observed. We will see why momentarily.

Why should bonds of differing maturity offer different yields? The two most plausible possibilities have to do with expectations of future rates and risk premiums. We will consider each of these arguments in turn.

The Expectations Theory

Suppose everyone in the market believes firmly that while the current one-year interest rate is 8%, the interest rate on one-year bonds next year will rise to 10%. What would this belief imply about the proper yield to maturity on two-year bonds issued today?

It is easy to see that an investor who buys the one-year bond and rolls the proceeds into another one-year bond in the following year will earn, on average, about 9% per year. This value is just the average of the 8% earned this year and the 10% expected for next year. More precisely, the investment will grow by a factor of 1.08 in the first year and 1.10 in the second year, for a total two-year growth factor of $1.08 \times 1.10 = 1.188$. This corresponds to an annual growth rate of 8.995% (because $1.08995^2 = 1.188$).

FIGURE 10.12

Treasury yield curves

Source: Various editions of *The Wall Street Journal.* Reprinted by permission of *The Wall Street Journal,* Copyright © 1989, 2000, 2006, 2011 Dow Jones & Company, Inc. All Rights Reserved Worldwide.

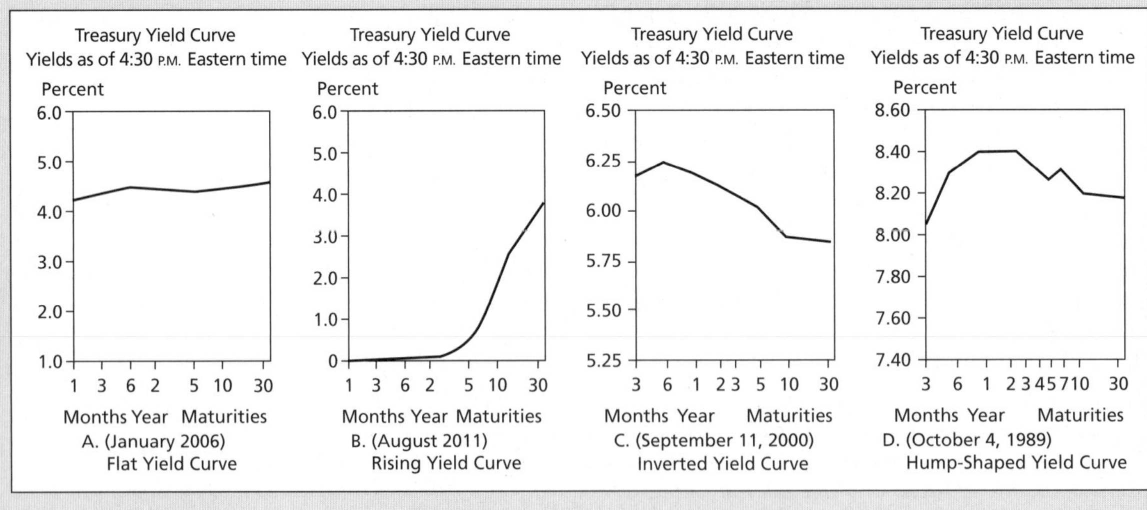

For investments in two-year bonds to be competitive with the strategy of rolling over one-year bonds, these two-year bonds also must offer an average annual return of 8.995% over the two-year holding period. This is illustrated in Figure 10.13. The current short-term rate of 8% and the expected value of next year's short-term rate are depicted above the time line. The two-year rate that provides the same expected two-year total return is below the time line. In this example, therefore, the yield curve will be upward-sloping; while one-year bonds offer an 8% yield to maturity, two-year bonds offer an 8.995% yield.

This notion is the essence of the **expectations hypothesis** of the yield curve, which asserts that the slope of the yield curve is attributable to expectations of changes in short-term rates. Relatively high yields on long-term bonds reflect expectations of future increases in rates, while relatively low yields on long-term bonds (a downward-sloping or inverted yield curve) reflect expectations of falling short-term rates.

expectations hypothesis

The theory that yields to maturity are determined solely by expectations of future short-term interest rates.

One of the implications of the expectations hypothesis is that expected holding-period returns on bonds of all maturities ought to be about equal. Even if the yield curve is upward-sloping (so that two-year bonds offer higher yields to maturity than one-year bonds), this does not necessarily mean investors expect higher rates of return on the two-year bonds. As we've seen, the higher initial yield to maturity on the two-year bond is necessary to compensate investors for the fact that interest rates the next year will be even higher. Over the two-year period, and indeed over any holding period, this theory predicts that holding-period returns will be equalized across bonds of all maturities.

EXAMPLE 10.14

Holding-Period Returns

Suppose we buy the one-year zero-coupon bond with a current yield to maturity of 8%. If its face value is $1,000, its price will be $925.93, providing an 8% rate of return over the coming year. Suppose instead that we buy the two-year zero-coupon bond at its yield of 8.995%. Its price today is $\$1,000/(1.08995)^2 = \$841.76$. After a year passes, the zero will have a remaining maturity of only one year; based on the forecast that the one-year yield next year will be 10%, it then will sell for $1,000/1.10 = $909.09. The expected rate of return over the year is thus ($909.09 − $841.76)/ $841.76 = .08, or 8%, precisely the same return provided by the one-year bond. This makes sense: If risk considerations are ignored when pricing the two bonds, they ought to provide equal expected rates of return.

In fact, advocates of the expectations hypothesis commonly invert this analysis to *infer* the market's expectation of future short-term rates. They note that we do not directly observe the expectation of next year's rate, but we *can* observe yields on bonds of different maturities. Suppose, as in this example, we see that one-year bonds offer yields of 8% and two-year bonds offer yields of 8.995%. Each dollar invested in the two-year zero would grow after two years to $\$1 \times 1.08995^2 = \$1.188$. A dollar invested in the one-year zero would grow by a factor of 1.08 in the first year and, then, if reinvested or "rolled over" into another one-year zero in the second year, would grow by an additional factor of $1 + r_2$. Final proceeds would be $\$1 \times 1.08 \times (1 + r_2)$.

The final proceeds of the rollover strategy depend on the interest rate that actually transpires in year 2. However, we can solve for the second-year interest rate that makes the

FIGURE 10.13

Returns to two two-year investment strategies

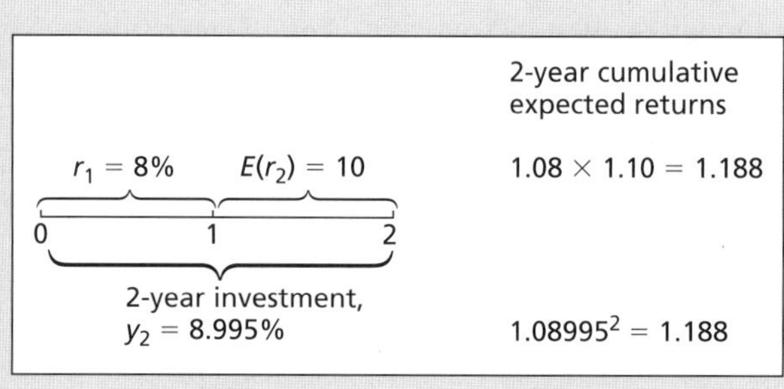

forward rate

The inferred short-term rate of interest for a future period that makes the expected total return of a long-term bond equal to that of rolling over short-term bonds.

expected payoff of these two strategies equal. This "break-even" value is called the **forward rate** for the second year, f_2, and is derived as follows:

$$1.08995^2 = 1.08 \times (1 + f_2)$$

which implies that $f_2 = .10$, or 10%. Notice that the forward rate equals the market's expectation of the year-2 short rate. Hence, we conclude that when the expected total return of a long-term bond equals that of rolling over a short-term bond, the forward rate equals the expected short-term interest rate. This is why the theory is called the expectations hypothesis.

More generally, we obtain the forward rate by equating the return on an n-period zero-coupon bond with that of an $(n - 1)$-period zero-coupon bond rolled over into a one-year bond in year n:

$$(1 + y_n)^n = (1 + y_{n-1})^{n-1}(1 + f_n) \tag{10.3}$$

The actual total returns on the two n-year strategies will be equal if the short-term interest rate in year n turns out to equal f_n.

EXAMPLE 10.15

Forward Rates

Suppose that two-year maturity bonds offer yields to maturity of 6% and three-year bonds have yields of 7%. What is the forward rate for the third year? We could compare these two strategies as follows:

1. Buy a three-year bond. Total proceeds per dollar invested will be

$$\$1 \times (1.07)^3 = \$1.2250$$

2. Buy a two-year bond. Reinvest all proceeds in a one-year bond in the third year, which will provide a return in that year of r_3. Total proceeds per dollar invested will be the result of two years' growth of invested funds at 6% plus the final year's growth at rate r_3:

$$\$1 \times (1.06)^2 \times (1 + r_3) = \$1.1236 \times (1 + r_3)$$

The forward rate is the rate in year 3 that makes the total return on these strategies equal:

$$1.2250 = 1.1236 \times (1 + f_3)$$

We conclude that the forward rate for the third year satisfies $(1 + f_3) = 1.0902$, so that f_3 is 9.02%.

While the expectations hypothesis gives us a tool to infer expectations of future market interest rates from the yield curve, it tells us nothing of what underlying considerations generated those expectations. Ultimately, interest rates reflect investors' expectations of the state of the macroeconomy. Not surprisingly, then, forward rates and the yield curve have proven themselves to be useful inputs for economic forecasts. The slope of the yield curve is one of the more important components of the index of leading economic indicators used to predict the course of economic activity. Inverted yield curves in particular, which imply falling interest rates, turn out to be among the best indicators of a coming recession.

The Liquidity Preference Theory

The expectations hypothesis starts from the assertion that bonds are priced so that "buy and hold" investments in long-term bonds provide the same returns as rolling over a series of short-term bonds. However, the risks of long- and short-term bonds are not equivalent.

We have seen that longer-term bonds are subject to greater interest rate risk than short-term bonds. As a result, investors in long-term bonds might require a risk premium to compensate them for this risk. In this case, the yield curve will be upward-sloping even in the absence of any expectations of future increases in rates. The source of the upward slope in the yield curve is investor demand for higher expected returns on assets that are perceived as riskier.

This viewpoint is called the **liquidity preference theory** of the term structure. Its name derives from the fact that shorter-term bonds have more "liquidity" than longer-term bonds, in the sense that they offer greater price certainty and trade in more active markets with lower bid–ask spreads. The preference of investors for greater liquidity makes them willing to hold these shorter-term bonds even if they do not offer expected returns as high as those of longer-term bonds.

liquidity preference theory

The theory that investors demand a risk premium on long-term bonds.

We can think of a **liquidity premium** as resulting from the extra compensation investors demand for holding longer-term bonds with greater price risk. We measure it as the spread between the forward rate of interest and the expected short rate:

liquidity premium

The extra expected return demanded by investors as compensation for the greater risk of longer-term bonds.

$$f_n = E(r_n) + \text{Liquidity premium} \quad \textbf{(10.4)}$$

In the absence of a liquidity premium, the forward rate would equal the expectation of the future short rate. But, generally, we expect the forward rate to be higher to compensate investors for the lower liquidity of longer-term bonds.

Advocates of the liquidity preference theory also note that borrowers seem to prefer to issue long-term bonds. This allows them to lock in an interest rate on their borrowing for long periods, and thus they may be willing to pay higher yields on these issues. In sum, bond buyers demand higher rates on longer-term bonds, and bond issuers are willing to pay higher rates on those bonds. As a result, the yield curve generally slopes upward.

According to the liquidity preference theory, forward rates of interest will exceed the market's expectations of future interest rates. Even if rates are expected to remain unchanged, the yield curve will slope upward because of the liquidity premium. That upward slope would be mistakenly attributed to expectations of rising rates if one were to use the pure expectations hypothesis to interpret the yield curve.

EXAMPLE 10.16

Liquidity Premiums and the Yield Curve

Suppose that the short-term rate of interest is currently 8% and that investors expect it to remain at 8% next year. In the absence of a liquidity premium, with no expectation of a change in yields, the yield to maturity on two-year bonds also would be 8%, the yield curve would be flat, and the forward rate would be 8%. But what if investors demand a risk premium to invest in two-year rather than one-year bonds? If the liquidity premium is 1%, then the forward rate would be 8% + 1% = 9%, and the yield to maturity on the two-year bond would be determined by

$$(1 + y_2)^2 = 1.08 \times 1.09 = 1.1772$$

implying that $y_2 = .085 = 8.5\%$. Here, the yield curve is upward-sloping due solely to the liquidity premium embedded in the price of the longer-term bond.

CONCEPT check 10.8

Suppose that the expected value of the interest rate for year 3 remains at 8% but that the liquidity premium for that year is also 1%. What would be the yield to maturity on three-year zeros? What would this imply about the slope of the yield curve?

A Synthesis

Of course, we do not need to make an either/or choice between expectations and risk premiums. Both influence the yield curve, and both should be considered in interpreting it.

Figure 10.14 shows two possible yield curves. In Figure 10.14A, rates are expected to rise over time. This fact, together with a liquidity premium, makes the yield curve steeply upward-sloping. In Figure 10.14B, rates are expected to fall, which by itself would make the yield curve slope downward. However, the liquidity premium lends something of an upward slope. The net effect of these two opposing factors is a "hump-shaped" curve.

FIGURE 10.14

Illustrative yield curves

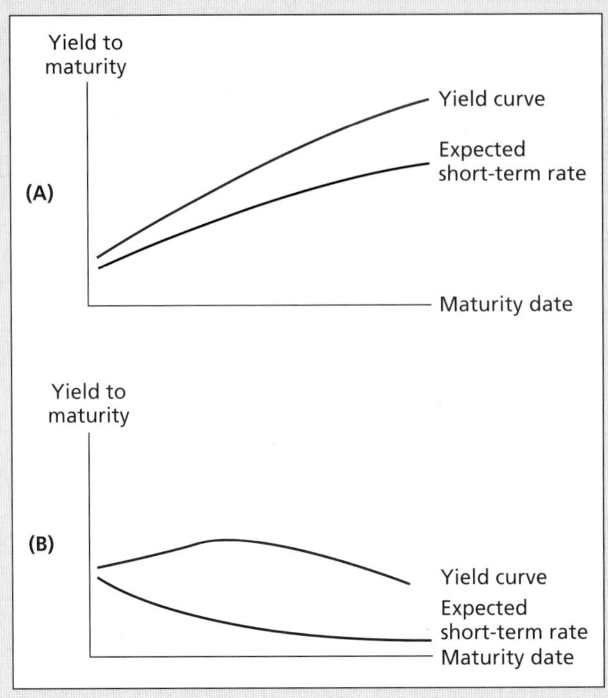

These two examples make it clear that the combination of varying expectations and liquidity premiums can result in a wide array of yield-curve profiles. For example, an upward-sloping curve does not in and of itself imply expectations of higher future interest rates, because the slope can result either from expectations or from risk premiums. A curve that is more steeply sloped than usual might signal expectations of higher rates, but even this inference is perilous.

Figure 10.15 presents yield spreads between 90-day T-bills and 10-year T-bonds since 1970. The figure shows that the yield curve is generally upward-sloping in that the longer-term bonds usually offer higher yields to maturity, despite the fact that rates could not have

FIGURE 10.15

Term spread: Yields on 10-year versus 90-day Treasury securities

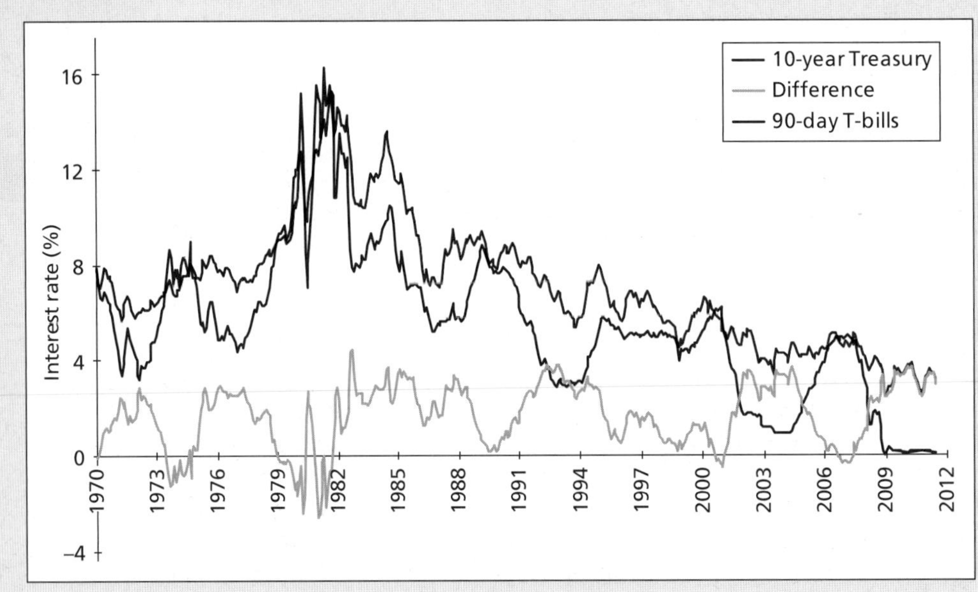

been expected to increase throughout the entire period. This tendency is the empirical basis for the liquidity premium doctrine that at least part of the upward slope in the yield curve must be due to a risk premium.

Because the yield curve normally has an upward slope due to risk premiums, a downward-sloping yield curve is taken as a strong indication that yields are more likely than not to fall. The prediction of declining interest rates is in turn often interpreted as a signal of a coming recession. Short-term rates exceeded long-term ones in each of the seven recessions since 1970. For this reason, it is not surprising that the slope of the yield curve is one of the key components of the index of leading economic indicators.

SUMMARY

- Debt securities are distinguished by their promise to pay a fixed or specified stream of income to their holders. The coupon bond is a typical debt security.
- Treasury notes and bonds have original maturities greater than one year. They are issued at or near par value, with their prices quoted net of accrued interest.
- Callable bonds should offer higher promised yields to maturity to compensate investors for the fact that they will not realize full capital gains should the interest rate fall and the bonds be called away from them at the stipulated call price. Bonds often are issued with a period of call protection. In addition, discount bonds selling significantly below their call price offer implicit call protection.
- Put bonds give the bondholder rather than the issuer the choice to terminate or extend the life of the bond.
- Convertible bonds may be exchanged, at the bondholder's discretion, for a specified number of shares of stock. Convertible bondholders "pay" for this option by accepting a lower coupon rate on the security.
- Floating-rate bonds pay a fixed premium over a referenced short-term interest rate. Risk is limited because the rate paid is tied to current market conditions.
- The yield to maturity is the single discount rate that equates the present value of a security's cash flows to its price. Bond prices and yields are inversely related. For premium bonds, the coupon rate is greater than the current yield, which is greater than the yield to maturity. These inequalities are reversed for discount bonds.
- The yield to maturity often is interpreted as an estimate of the average rate of return to an investor who purchases a bond and holds it until maturity. This interpretation is subject to error, however. Related measures are yield to call, realized compound yield, and expected (versus promised) yield to maturity.
- Treasury bills are U.S. government–issued zero-coupon bonds with original maturities of up to one year. Treasury STRIPS are longer-term default-free zero-coupon bonds. Prices of zero-coupon bonds rise exponentially over time, providing a rate of appreciation equal to the interest rate. The IRS treats this price appreciation as imputed taxable interest income to the investor.
- When bonds are subject to potential default, the stated yield to maturity is the maximum possible yield to maturity that can be realized by the bondholder. In the event of default, however, that promised yield will not be realized. To compensate bond investors for default risk, bonds must offer default premiums, that is, promised yields in excess of those offered by default-free government securities. If the firm remains healthy, its bonds will provide higher returns than government bonds. Otherwise, the returns may be lower.
- Bond safety often is measured using financial ratio analysis. Bond indentures offer safeguards to protect the claims of bondholders. Common indentures specify sinking fund requirements, collateralization, dividend restrictions, and subordination of future debt.
- Credit default swaps provide insurance against the default of a bond or loan. The swap buyer pays an annual premium to the swap seller but collects a payment equal to lost value if the loan later goes into default.
- The term structure of interest rates is the relationship between time to maturity and term to maturity. The yield curve is a graphical depiction of the term structure. The forward rate is the break-even interest rate that would equate the total return on a rollover strategy to that of a longer-term zero-coupon bond.

- The expectations hypothesis holds that forward interest rates are unbiased forecasts of future interest rates. The liquidity preference theory, however, argues that long-term bonds will carry a risk premium known as a liquidity premium. A positive liquidity premium can cause the yield curve to slope upward even if no increase in short rates is anticipated.

KEY TERMS

KEY FORMULAS

Price of a coupon bond:

$$\text{Price} = \text{Coupon} \times \frac{1}{r}\left[1 - \frac{1}{(1+r)^T}\right] + \text{Par value} \times \frac{1}{(1+r)^T}$$

$$= \text{Coupon} \times \text{Annuity factor}(r, T) + \text{Par value} \times \text{PV factor}(r, T)$$

Forward rate of interest: $1 + f_n = \dfrac{(1+y_n)^n}{(1+y_{n-1})^{n-1}}$

Liquidity premium: Forward rate − Expected short rate

PROBLEM SETS

Select problems are available in McGraw-Hill's *Connect Finance.* Please see the Supplements section of the book's frontmatter for more information.

Basic

1. Define the following types of bonds: *(LO 10-1)*
   a. Catastrophe bond.
   b. Eurobond.
   c. Zero-coupon bond.
   d. Samurai bond.
   e. Junk bond.
   f. Convertible bond.
   g. Serial bond.
   h. Equipment obligation bond.
   i. Original-issue discount bond.
   j. Indexed bond.
2. What is the option embedded in a callable bond? A puttable bond? *(LO 10-1)*
3. What would be the likely effect on the yield to maturity of a bond resulting from: *(LO 10-5)*
   a. An increase in the issuing firm's times-interest-earned ratio?
   b. An increase in the issuing firm's debt-equity ratio?
   c. An increase in the issuing firm's quick ratio?

4. A coupon bond paying semiannual interest is reported as having an ask price of 117% of its $1,000 par value. If the last interest payment was made one month ago and the coupon rate is 6%, what is the invoice price of the bond? ***(LO 10-1)***
5. A zero-coupon bond with face value $1,000 and maturity of five years sells for $746.22. What is its yield to maturity? What will happen to its yield to maturity if its price falls immediately to $730? ***(LO 10-2)***
6. Why do bond prices go down when interest rates go up? Don't investors like high interest rates? ***(LO 10-2)***
7. Two bonds have identical times to maturity and coupon rates. One is callable at 105, the other at 110. Which should have the higher yield to maturity? Why? ***(LO 10-4)***
8. Consider a bond with a 10% coupon and with yield to maturity = 8%. If the bond's YTM remains constant, then in one year will the bond price be higher, lower, or unchanged? Why? ***(LO 10-2)***
9. A bond with an annual coupon rate of 4.8% sells for $970. What is the bond's current yield? ***(LO 10-2)***
10. An investor believes that a bond may temporarily increase in credit risk. Which of the following would be the most liquid method of exploiting this? ***(LO 10-5)***
    a. The purchase of a credit default swap.
    b. The sale of a credit default swap.
    c. The short sale of the bond.

11. Which of the following *most accurately* describes the behavior of credit default swaps? ***(LO 10-5)***
    a. When credit risk increases, swap premiums increase.
    b. When credit and interest rate risk increases, swap premiums increase.
    c. When credit risk increases, swap premiums increase, but when interest rate risk increases, swap premiums decrease.

Intermediate

12. You buy an eight-year bond that has a 6% current yield and a 6% coupon (paid annually). In one year, promised yields to maturity have risen to 7%. What is your holding-period return? ***(LO 10-3)***
13. The stated yield to maturity and realized compound yield to maturity of a (default-free) zero-coupon bond will always be equal. Why? ***(LO 10-6)***
14. Which security has a higher *effective* annual interest rate? ***(LO 10-6)***
    a. A three-month T-bill with face value of $100,000 currently selling at $97,645.
    b. A coupon bond selling at par and paying a 10% coupon semiannually.
15. Treasury bonds paying an 8% coupon rate with *semiannual* payments currently sell at par value. What coupon rate would they have to pay in order to sell at par if they paid their coupons *annually*? ***(LO 10-2)***
16. Consider a bond paying a coupon rate of 10% per year semiannually when the market interest rate is only 4% per half-year. The bond has three years until maturity. ***(LO 10-6)***
    a. Find the bond's price today and six months from now after the next coupon is paid.
    b. What is the total rate of return on the bond?
17. A 20-year maturity bond with par value $1,000 makes semiannual coupon payments at a coupon rate of 8%. Find the bond equivalent and effective annual yield to maturity of the bond if the bond price is: ***(LO 10-2)***
    a. $950
    b. $1,000
    c. $1,050
18. Redo the previous problem using the same data, but now assume that the bond makes its coupon payments annually. Why are the yields you compute lower in this case? ***(LO 10-2)***

www.mhhe.com/bkm

19. Return to Table 10.1 and calculate both the real and nominal rates of return on the TIPS bond in the second and third years. *(LO 10-6)*
20. Fill in the table below for the following zero-coupon bonds, all of which have par values of $1,000. *(LO 10-2)*

Price	Maturity (years)	Yield to Maturity
$400	20	?
$500	20	?
$500	10	?
?	10	10%
?	10	8%
$400	?	8%

21. A bond has a par value of $1,000, a time to maturity of 10 years, and a coupon rate of 8% with interest paid annually. If the current market price is $800, what will be the approximate capital gain yield of this bond over the next year if its yield to maturity remains unchanged? *(LO 10-3)*
22. A bond with a coupon rate of 7% makes semiannual coupon payments on January 15 and July 15 of each year. *The Wall Street Journal* reports the ask price for the bond on January 30 at 100:02. What is the invoice price of the bond? The coupon period has 182 days. *(LO 10-1)*
23. A bond has a current yield of 9% and a yield to maturity of 10%. Is the bond selling above or below par value? Explain. *(LO 10-2)*
24. Is the coupon rate of the bond in the previous problem more or less than 9%? *(LO 10-2)*

Please visit us at www.mhhe.com/bkm

25. Consider a bond with a settlement date of February 22, 2012, and a maturity date of March 15, 2020. The coupon rate is 5.5%. If the yield to maturity of the bond is 5.34% (bond equivalent yield, semiannual compounding), what is the list price of the bond on the settlement date? What is the accrued interest on the bond? What is the invoice price of the bond? *(LO 10-1)*

Please visit us at www.mhhe.com/bkm

26. Now suppose the bond in the previous question is selling for 102. What is the bond's yield to maturity? What would the yield to maturity be at a price of 102 if the bond paid its coupons only once per year? *(LO 10-2)*
27. A 10-year bond of a firm in severe financial distress has a coupon rate of 14% and sells for $900. The firm is currently renegotiating the debt, and it appears that the lenders will allow the firm to reduce coupon payments on the bond to one-half the originally contracted amount. The firm can handle these lower payments. What are the stated and expected yields to maturity of the bonds? The bond makes its coupon payments annually. *(LO 10-5)*
28. A two-year bond with par value $1,000 making annual coupon payments of $100 is priced at $1,000. What is the yield to maturity of the bond? What will be the realized compound yield to maturity if the one-year interest rate next year turns out to be (*a*) 8%, (*b*) 10%, (*c*) 12%? *(LO 10-6)*
29. Suppose that today's date is April 15. A bond with a 10% coupon paid semiannually every January 15 and July 15 is listed in *The Wall Street Journal* as selling at an ask price of 101:04. If you buy the bond from a dealer today, what price will you pay for it? *(LO 10-1)*
30. Assume that two firms issue bonds with the following characteristics. Both bonds are issued at par.

	ABC Bonds	XYZ Bonds
Issue size	$1.2 billion	$150 million
Maturity	10 years*	20 years
Coupon	9%	10%
Collateral	First mortgage	General debenture
Callable	Not callable	In 10 years
Call price	None	110
Sinking fund	None	Starting in 5 years

*Bond is extendable at the discretion of the bondholder for an additional 10 years.

Ignoring credit quality, identify four features of these issues that might account for the lower coupon on the ABC debt. Explain. *(LO 10-4)*

31. A large corporation issued both fixed- and floating-rate notes five years ago, with terms given in the following table: *(LO 10-4)*

	9% Coupon Notes	Floating-Rate Note
Issue size	$250 million	$280 million
Maturity	20 years	15 years
Current price (% of par)	93	98
Current coupon	9%	8%
Coupon adjusts	Fixed coupon	Every year
Coupon reset rule	—	1-year T-bill rate + 2%
Callable	10 years after issue	10 years after issue
Call price	106	102
Sinking fund	None	None
Yield to maturity	9.9%	—
Price range since issued	$85–$112	$97–$102

a. Why is the price range greater for the 9% coupon bond than the floating-rate note?
b. What factors could explain why the floating-rate note is not always sold at par value?
c. Why is the call price for the floating-rate note not of great importance to investors?
d. Is the probability of call for the fixed-rate note high or low?
e. If the firm were to issue a fixed-rate note with a 15-year maturity, callable after five years at 106, what coupon rate would it need to offer to issue the bond at par value?
f. Why is an entry for yield to maturity for the floating-rate note not appropriate?

32. A 30-year maturity, 8% coupon bond paying coupons semiannually is callable in five years at a call price of $1,100. The bond currently sells at a yield to maturity of 7% (3.5% per half-year). *(LO 10-4)*
a. What is the yield to call?
b. What is the yield to call if the call price is only $1,050?
c. What is the yield to call if the call price is $1,100 but the bond can be called in two years instead of five years?

33. A newly issued 20-year maturity, zero-coupon bond is issued with a yield to maturity of 8% and face value $1,000. Find the imputed interest income in the first, second, and last year of the bond's life. *(LO 10-3)*

34. A newly issued 10-year maturity, 4% coupon bond making *annual* coupon payments is sold to the public at a price of $800. What will be an investor's taxable income from the bond over the coming year? The bond will not be sold at the end of the year. The bond is treated as an original-issue discount bond. ***(LO 10-3)***
35. Masters Corp. issues two bonds with 20-year maturities. Both bonds are callable at $1,050. The first bond is issued at a deep discount with a coupon rate of 4% and a price of $580 to yield 8.4%. The second bond is issued at par value with a coupon rate of 8.75%. ***(LO 10-2)***
    a. What is the yield to maturity of the par bond? Why is it higher than the yield of the discount bond?
    b. If you expect rates to fall substantially in the next two years, which bond would you prefer to hold?
    c. In what sense does the discount bond offer "implicit call protection"?
36. Under the expectations hypothesis, if the yield curve is upward-sloping, the market must expect an increase in short-term interest rates. True/false/uncertain? Why? ***(LO 10-7)***
37. The yield curve is upward-sloping. Can you conclude that investors expect short-term interest rates to rise? Why or why not? ***(LO 10-7)***
38. Assume you have a one-year investment horizon and are trying to choose among three bonds. All have the same degree of default risk and mature in 10 years. The first is a zero-coupon bond that pays $1,000 at maturity. The second has an 8% coupon rate and pays the $80 coupon once per year. The third has a 10% coupon rate and pays the $100 coupon once per year. ***(LO 10-3)***
    a. If all three bonds are now priced to yield 8% to maturity, what are their prices?
    b. If you expect their yields to maturity to be 8% at the beginning of next year, what will their prices be then? What is your rate of return on each bond during the one-year holding period?
39. Under the liquidity preference theory, if inflation is expected to be falling over the next few years, long-term interest rates will be higher than short-term rates. True/false/uncertain? Why? ***(LO 10-7)***
40. The current yield curve for default-free zero-coupon bonds is as follows:

Maturity (years)	YTM
1	10%
2	11
3	12

    a. What are the implied one-year forward rates? ***(LO 10-7)***
    b. Assume that the pure expectations hypothesis of the term structure is correct. If market expectations are accurate, what will the pure yield curve (that is, the yields to maturity on one- and two-year zero-coupon bonds) be next year? ***(LO 10-7)***
    c. If you purchase a two-year zero-coupon bond now, what is the expected total rate of return over the next year? What if you purchase a three-year zero-coupon bond? (*Hint:* Compute the current and expected future prices.) Ignore taxes. ***(LO 10-6)***
41. The yield to maturity on one-year zero-coupon bonds is 8%. The yield to maturity on two-year zero-coupon bonds is 9%. ***(LO 10-7)***
    a. What is the forward rate of interest for the second year?
    b. If you believe in the expectations hypothesis, what is your best guess as to the expected value of the short-term interest rate next year?
    c. If you believe in the liquidity preference theory, is your best guess as to next year's short-term interest rate higher or lower than in (*b*)?
42. The following table contains spot rates and forward rates for three years. However, the labels got mixed up. Can you identify which row of the interest rates represents spot rates and which one the forward rates? ***(LO 10-7)***

Year:	1	2	3
Spot rates or Forward rates?	10%	12%	14%
Spot rates or Forward rates?	10%	14.0364%	18.1078%

43. Consider the following $1,000 par value zero-coupon bonds:

Bond	Years until Maturity	Yield to Maturity
A	1	5%
B	2	6
C	3	6.5
D	4	7

According to the expectations hypothesis, what is the market's expectation of the one-year interest rate three years from now? ***(LO 10-7)***

44. A newly issued bond pays its coupons once a year. Its coupon rate is 5%, its maturity is 20 years, and its yield to maturity is 8%. ***(LO 10-6)***
    a. Find the holding-period return for a one-year investment period if the bond is selling at a yield to maturity of 7% by the end of the year.
    b. If you sell the bond after one year when its yield is 7%, what taxes will you owe if the tax rate on interest income is 40% and the tax rate on capital gains income is 30%? The bond is subject to original-issue discount (OID) tax treatment.
    c. What is the after-tax holding-period return on the bond?
    d. Find the realized compound yield *before taxes* for a two-year holding period, assuming that (i) you sell the bond after two years, (ii) the bond yield is 7% at the end of the second year, and (iii) the coupon can be reinvested for one year at a 3% interest rate.
    e. Use the tax rates in part (*b*) to compute the *after-tax* two-year realized compound yield. Remember to take account of OID tax rules.

CFA Problems

1. The following multiple-choice problems are based on questions that appeared in past CFA examinations.
    a. A bond with a call feature: ***(LO 10-4)***
        (1) Is attractive because the immediate receipt of principal plus premium produces a high return.
        (2) Is more apt to be called when interest rates are high because the interest saving will be greater.
        (3) Will usually have a higher yield to maturity than a similar noncallable bond.
        (4) None of the above.
    b. In which *one* of the following cases is the bond selling at a discount? ***(LO 10-2)***
        (1) Coupon rate is greater than current yield, which is greater than yield to maturity.
        (2) Coupon rate, current yield, and yield to maturity are all the same.
        (3) Coupon rate is less than current yield, which is less than yield to maturity.
        (4) Coupon rate is less than current yield, which is greater than yield to maturity.
    c. Consider a five-year bond with a 10% coupon selling at a yield to maturity of 8%. If interest rates remain constant, one year from now the price of this bond will be: ***(LO 10-3)***
        (1) Higher
        (2) Lower
        (3) The same
        (4) Par

d. Which of the following statements is *true*? *(LO 10-7)*

(1) The expectations hypothesis indicates a flat yield curve if anticipated future short-term rates exceed current short-term rates.

(2) The basic conclusion of the expectations hypothesis is that the long-term rate is equal to the anticipated short-term rate.

(3) The liquidity hypothesis indicates that, all other things being equal, longer maturities will have higher yields.

(4) The liquidity preference theory states that a rising yield curve necessarily implies that the market anticipates increases in interest rates.

2. On May 30, 2009, Janice Kerr is considering the newly issued 10-year AAA corporate bonds shown in the following exhibit: *(LO 10-3)*

Description	Coupon	Price	Callable	Call Price
Sentinal, due May 30, 2019	6.00%	100	Noncallable	NA
Colina, due May 30, 2019	6.20%	100	Currently callable	102

a. Suppose that market interest rates decline by 100 basis points (i.e., 1%). Contrast the effect of this decline on the price of each bond.

b. Should Kerr prefer the Colina over the Sentinal bond when rates are expected to rise or to fall?

c. What would be the effect, if any, of an increase in the *volatility* of interest rates on the prices of each bond?

3. A convertible bond has the following features:

Coupon	5.25%
Maturity	June 15, 2020
Market price of bond	$77.50
Market price of underlying common stock	$28.00
Annual dividend	$1.20
Conversion ratio	20.83 shares

Calculate the conversion premium for this bond. *(LO 10-4)*

4. *a.* Explain the impact on the offering yield of adding a call feature to a proposed bond issue.

b. Explain the impact on the bond's expected life of adding a call feature to a proposed bond issue.

c. Describe one advantage and one disadvantage of including callable bonds in a portfolio. *(LO 10-4)*

5. Bonds of Zello Corporation with a par value of $1,000 sell for $960, mature in five years, and have a 7% annual coupon rate paid semiannually. *(LO 10-6)*

a. Calculate the:

(1) Current yield.

(2) Yield to maturity.

(3) Horizon yield (also called realized compound return) for an investor with a three-year holding period and a reinvestment rate of 6% over the period. At the end of three years the 7% coupon bonds with two years remaining will sell to yield 7%.

b. Cite *one* major shortcoming for *each* of the following fixed-income yield measures:

(1) Current yield.

(2) Yield to maturity.

(3) Horizon yield (also called realized compound return).

WEB master

1. Go to the website of Standard & Poor's at **www.standardandpoors.com.** Look for *Rating Services (Find a Rating).* Find the ratings on bonds of at least 10 companies. Try to choose a sample with a wide range of ratings. Then go to a website such as **money.msn.com** or **finance.yahoo.com** and obtain, for each firm, as many of the financial ratios tabulated in Table 10.3 as you can find. What is the relationship between bond rating and these ratios? Can you tell from your sample which of these ratios are the more important determinants of bond rating?
2. The FINRA operates the TRACE (Trade Reporting and Compliance Engine) system, which reports over-the-counter secondary market trades of fixed-income securities. Go to the FINRA home page at **www.finra.org** and click on the link for *Industry Professionals.* Search (located at the top right) for the "TRACE Fact Book" and click the first link that appears. Find the detailed data tables and locate the table with information on issues, excluding convertible bonds (typically Table 1). For each of the last three years, calculate the following:
   a. The percentage of bonds that were publicly traded and the percentage that were privately traded.
   b. The percentage of bonds that were investment grade and the percentage that were high-yield.
   c. The percentage of bonds that had fixed coupon rates and the percentage that had floating rates.
   d. Do any patterns emerge over time?
   e. Repeat the calculations using the information for convertible bond issues (typically in Table 2).

10.1 The callable bond will sell at the *lower* price. Investors will not be willing to pay as much if they know that the firm retains a valuable option to reclaim the bond for the call price if interest rates fall.

10.2 At a semiannual interest rate of 3%, the bond is worth \$40 × Annuity factor(3%, 60) + \$1,000 × PV factor(3%, 60) = \$1,276.76, which results in a capital gain of \$276.76. This exceeds the capital loss of \$189.29 (\$1,000 − \$810.71) when the interest rate increased to 5%.

10.3 Yield to maturity exceeds current yield, which exceeds coupon rate. Take as an example the 8% coupon bond with a yield to maturity of 10% per year (5% per half year). Its price is \$810.71, and therefore its current yield is 80/810.77 = 0.0987, or 9.87%, which is higher than the coupon rate but lower than the yield to maturity.

10.4 The current price of the bond can be derived from the yield to maturity. Using your calculator, set $n = 40$ (semiannual periods); PMT = \$45 per period; FV = \$1,000; $i = 4\%$ per semiannual period. Calculate present value as \$1,098.96. Now we can calculate yield to call. The time to call is five years, or 10 semiannual periods. The price at which the bond will be called is \$1,050. To find yield to call, we set $n = 10$ (semiannual periods); PMT = \$45 per period; FV = \$1,050; PV = \$1,098.96. Calculate the semiannual yield to call as 3.72%.

10.5 Price = \$70 × Annuity factor(8%, 1) + \$1,000 × PV factor(8%, 1) = \$990.74

$$\text{Rate of return to investor} = \frac{\$70 + (\$990.74 - \$982.17)}{\$982.17} = .080 = 8\%$$

10.6 By year-end, remaining maturity is 29 years. If the yield to maturity were still 8%, the bond would still sell at par and the holding-period return would be 8%. At a higher yield, price and return will be lower. Suppose the yield to maturity is 8.5%. With annual payments of \$80 and a face value of \$1,000, the price of the bond is \$946.70

www.mhhe.com/bkm

($n = 29$; $i = 8.5\%$; PMT = \$80; FV = \$1,000). The bond initially sold at \$1,000 when issued at the start of the year. The holding-period return is

$$\text{HPR} = \frac{80 + (946.70 - 1{,}000)}{1{,}000} = .0267 = 2.67\%$$

which is less than the initial yield to maturity of 8%.

10.7 At the lower yield, the bond price will be \$631.67 [$n = 29$, $i = 7\%$, FV = \$1,000, PMT = \$40]. Therefore, total after-tax income is:

Coupon	\$40 × (1 − 0.38) =	\$24.80
Imputed interest	(\$553.66 − \$549.69) × (1 − 0.38) =	2.46
Capital gains	(\$631.67 − \$553.66) × (1 − 0.20) =	62.41
Total income after taxes:		\$89.67

Rate of return = 89.67/549.69 = .163 = 16.3%

10.8 The yield to maturity on two-year bonds is 8.5%. The forward rate for the third year is $f_3 = 8\% + 1\% = 9\%$. We obtain the yield to maturity on three-year zeros from

$$(1 + y_3)^3 = (1 + y_2)^2(1 + f_3) = 1.085^2 \times 1.09 = 1.2832$$

Therefore, $y_3 = .0867 = 8.67\%$. We note that the yield on one-year bonds is 8%, on two-year bonds is 8.5%, and on three-year bonds is 8.67%. The yield curve is upward-sloping due solely to the liquidity premium.

Managing Bond Portfolios

Chapter

11

Learning Objectives:

- LO11-1 Analyze the features of a bond that affect the sensitivity of its price to interest rates.
- LO11-2 Compute the duration of bonds, and use duration to measure interest rate sensitivity.
- LO11-3 Show how convexity affects the response of bond prices to changes in interest rates.
- LO11-4 Formulate fixed-income immunization strategies for various investment horizons.
- LO11-5 Analyze the choices to be made in an actively managed bond portfolio.

In this chapter, we turn to various strategies that bond managers can pursue, making a distinction between passive and active strategies. A *passive investment strategy* takes market prices of securities as set fairly. Rather than attempting to beat the market by exploiting superior information or insight, passive managers act to maintain an appropriate risk-return balance given market opportunities. One special case of passive management is an immunization strategy that attempts to insulate the portfolio from interest rate risk.

An *active investment strategy* attempts to achieve returns that are more than commensurate with the risk borne. In the context of bond portfolios, this style of management can take two forms. Active managers use interest rate forecasts to predict movements in the entire bond market, or they employ some form of intramarket analysis to identify particular sectors of the market (or particular securities) that are relatively mispriced.

Because interest rate risk is crucial to formulating both active and passive strategies, we begin our discussion with an analysis of the sensitivity of bond prices to interest rate fluctuations. This sensitivity is measured by the duration of the bond, and we devote considerable attention to what determines bond duration. We discuss several passive investment strategies, and show how duration-matching techniques can be used to immunize the holding-period return of a portfolio from interest rate risk. After examining the broad range of applications of the duration measure, we consider refinements in the way that interest rate sensitivity is measured, focusing on the concept of bond convexity. Duration is important in formulating active investment strategies as well, and we next explore several of these strategies. We conclude the chapter with a discussion of active fixed-income strategies. These include policies based on interest rate forecasting as well as intramarket analysis that seeks to identify relatively attractive sectors or securities within the fixed-income market.

Related websites for this chapter are available at www.mhhe.com/bkm.

11.1 INTEREST RATE RISK

You know already that there is an inverse relationship between bond prices and yields and that interest rates can fluctuate substantially. As interest rates rise and fall, bondholders experience capital losses and gains. These gains or losses make fixed-income investments risky, even if the coupon and principal payments are guaranteed, as in the case of Treasury obligations.

Why do bond prices respond to interest rate fluctuations? In a competitive market, all securities must offer investors fair expected rates of return. If a bond is issued with an 8% coupon when competitive yields are 8%, then it will sell at par value. If the market rate rises to 9%, however, who would purchase an 8% coupon bond at par value? The bond price must fall until its expected return increases to the competitive level of 9%. Conversely, if the market rate falls to 7%, the 8% coupon on the bond is attractive compared to yields on alternative investments. Investors eager for that return will respond by bidding up the bond price until the total rate of return for investors who purchase at that higher price is no better than the market rate.

Interest Rate Sensitivity

The sensitivity of bond prices to changes in market interest rates is obviously of great concern to investors. To gain some insight into the determinants of interest rate risk, turn to Figure 11.1, which presents the percentage changes in price corresponding to changes in yield to maturity for four bonds that differ according to coupon rate, initial yield to maturity, and time to maturity. All four bonds illustrate that bond prices decrease when yields rise and that the price curve is convex, meaning that decreases in yields have bigger impacts on price than increases in yields of equal magnitude. We summarize these observations in the following two propositions:

1. *Bond prices and yields are inversely related: As yields increase, bond prices fall; as yields fall, bond prices rise.*
2. *An increase in a bond's yield to maturity results in a smaller price change than a decrease in yield of equal magnitude.*

Now compare the interest rate sensitivity of bonds A and B, which are identical except for maturity. Figure 11.1 shows that bond B, which has a longer maturity than bond A, exhibits greater sensitivity to interest rate changes. This illustrates another general property:

3. *Prices of long-term bonds tend to be more sensitive to interest rate changes than prices of short-term bonds.*

This is not surprising. If rates increase, for example, the bond is less valuable as its cash flows are discounted at a now-higher rate. The impact of the higher discount rate will be greater as that rate is applied to more-distant cash flows.

FIGURE 11.1

Change in bond price as a function of change in yield to maturity

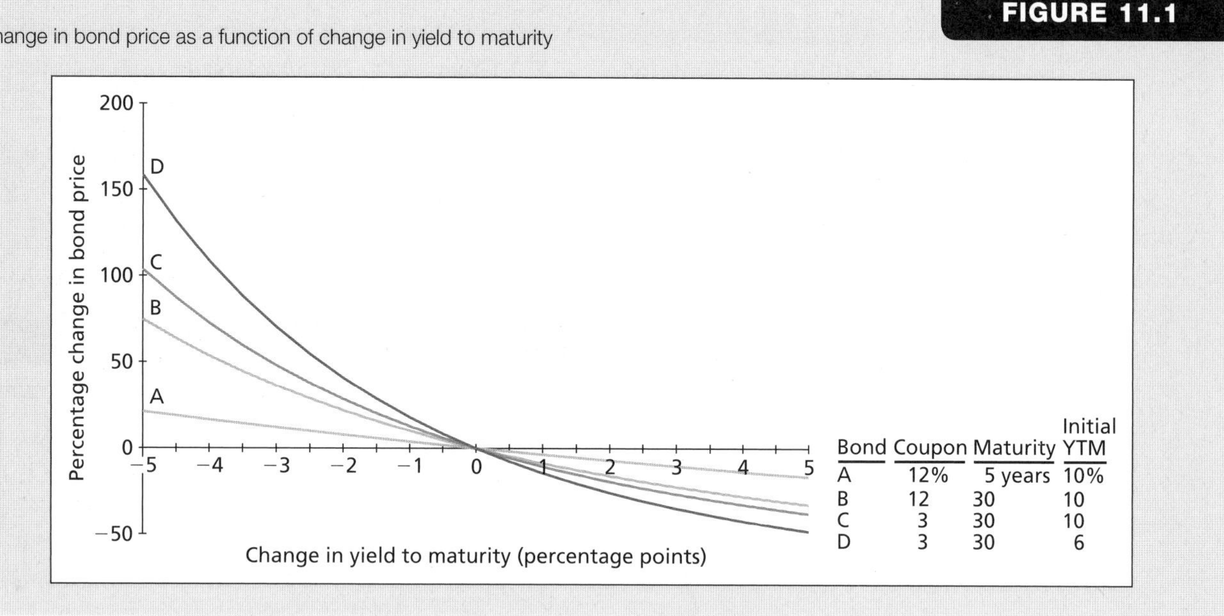

Notice that while bond B has six times the maturity of bond A, it has less than six times the interest rate sensitivity. Although interest rate sensitivity seems to increase with maturity, it does so less than proportionally as bond maturity increases. Therefore, our fourth property is that:

4. *The sensitivity of bond prices to changes in yields increases at a decreasing rate as maturity increases. In other words, interest rate risk is less than proportional to bond maturity.*

Bonds B and C, which are alike in all respects except for coupon rate, illustrate another point. The lower-coupon bond exhibits greater sensitivity to changes in interest rates. This turns out to be a general property of bond prices:

5. *Interest rate risk is inversely related to the bond's coupon rate. Prices of low-coupon bonds are more sensitive to changes in interest rates than prices of high-coupon bonds.*

Finally, bonds C and D are identical except for the yield to maturity at which the bonds currently sell. Yet bond C, with a higher yield to maturity, is less sensitive to changes in yields. This illustrates our final property:

6. *The sensitivity of a bond's price to a change in its yield is inversely related to the yield to maturity at which the bond currently is selling.*

The first five of these general properties were described by Malkiel (1962) and are sometimes known as Malkiel's bond pricing relationships. The last property was demonstrated by Homer and Liebowitz (1972).

These six propositions confirm that maturity is a major determinant of interest rate risk. However, they also show that maturity alone is not sufficient to measure interest rate sensitivity. For example, bonds B and C in Figure 11.1 have the same maturity, but the higher coupon bond has less price sensitivity to interest rate changes. Obviously, we need to know more than a bond's maturity to quantify its interest rate risk.

To see why bond characteristics such as coupon rate or yield to maturity affect interest rate sensitivity, let's start with a simple numerical example.

Table 11.1 gives bond prices for 8% annual coupon bonds at different yields to maturity and times to maturity. (For simplicity, we assume coupons are paid once a year rather than semiannually.) The shortest term bond falls in value by less than 1% when the interest rate increases from 8% to 9%. The 10-year bond falls by 6.4% and the 20-year bond by more than 9%.

TABLE 11.1 Prices of 8% annual coupon bonds

Bond's Yield to Maturity	*T* = 1 Year	*T* = 10 Years	*T* = 20 Years
8%	1,000.00	1,000.00	1,000.00
9%	990.83	935.82	908.71
Percent change in price*	−0.92%	−6.42%	−9.13%

*Equals value of bond at a 9% yield to maturity minus value of bond at (the original) 8% yield, divided by the value at 8% yield.

TABLE 11.2 Prices of zero-coupon bonds

Bond's Yield to Maturity	*T* = 1 Year	*T* = 10 Years	*T* = 20 Years
8%	925.93	463.19	214.55
9%	917.43	422.41	178.43
Percent change in price*	−0.92%	−8.80%	−16.84%

*Equals value of bond at a 9% yield to maturity minus value of bond at (the original) 8% yield, divided by the value at 8% yield.

Now look at a similar computation using a zero-coupon bond rather than the 8% coupon bond. The results are shown in Table 11.2.

For maturities beyond one year, the price of the zero-coupon bond falls by a greater proportional amount than the price of the 8% coupon bond. The observation that long-term bonds are more sensitive to interest rate movements than short-term bonds suggests that in some sense a zero-coupon bond must represent a longer-term investment than an equal-time-to-maturity coupon bond.

In fact, this insight about the effective maturity of a bond is a useful one that we can make mathematically precise. To start, note that the times to maturity of the two bonds in this example are not perfect measures of the long- or short-term nature of the bonds. The 8% bond makes many coupon payments, most of which come years before the bond's maturity date. Each payment may be considered to have its own "maturity." In this sense, it is often useful to view a coupon bond as a "portfolio" of coupon payments. The *effective* maturity of the bond would then be measured as some sort of average of the maturities of *all* the cash flows. The zero-coupon bond, by contrast, makes only one payment at maturity. Its time to maturity is well defined.

A high-coupon rate bond has a higher fraction of its value tied to coupons rather than payment of par value, and so the portfolio is more heavily weighted toward the earlier, short-maturity payments, which give it lower "effective maturity." This explains Malkiel's fifth rule, that price sensitivity falls with coupon rate.

Similar logic explains our sixth rule, that price sensitivity falls with yield to maturity. A higher yield reduces the present value of all of the bond's payments, but more so for more distant payments. Therefore, at a higher yield, a higher fraction of the bond's value is due to its earlier payments, which have lower effective maturity. The overall sensitivity of the bond price to changes in yields is thus lower.

Duration

Macaulay's duration

A measure of the effective maturity of a bond, defined as the weighted average of the times until each payment, with weights proportional to the present value of the payment.

To deal with the concept of the "maturity" of a bond that makes many payments, we need a measure of the average maturity of the bond's promised cash flows. We would also like to use such an effective maturity measure as a guide to the sensitivity of a bond to interest rate changes because price sensitivity tends to increase with time to maturity.

Frederick Macaulay (1938) called the effective maturity concept the *duration* of the bond. **Macaulay's duration** equals the weighted average of the times to each coupon or principal payment made by the bond. The weight applied to each time to payment clearly should be related to the "importance" of that payment to the value of the bond. In fact, the weight for each payment time is the proportion of the total value of the bond accounted for by that payment, the present value of the payment divided by the bond price.

We define the weight, w_t, associated with the cash flow made at time t (denoted CF_t) as

$$w_t = \frac{CF_t/(1+y)^t}{\text{Bond price}}$$

where y is the bond's yield to maturity. The numerator on the right-hand side of this equation is the present value of the cash flow occurring at time t, while the denominator is the present value of all the bond's payments. These weights sum to 1 because the sum of the cash flows discounted at the yield to maturity equals the bond price.

Using these values to calculate the weighted average of the times until the receipt of each of the bond's payments, we obtain Macaulay's formula for duration, denoted D.

$$D = \sum_{t=1}^{T} t \times w_t \tag{11.1}$$

If we write out each term in the summation sign, we can express duration as:

$$D = w_1 + 2w_2 + 3w_3 + 4w_4 + \cdots + Tw_T$$

(In $2w_2$: 2 = time until 2nd cash flow; w_2 = weight of 2nd CF. In $4w_4$: 4 = time until 4th CF; w_4 = weight of 4th CF.)

An example of how to apply Equation 11.1 appears in Spreadsheet 11.1, where we derive the durations of an 8% coupon and zero-coupon bond, each with three years to maturity. We assume that the yield to maturity on each bond is 10%. The present value of each payment is

SPREADSHEET 11.1

Calculation of the duration of two bonds using Excel spreadsheet

	A	B	C	D	E	F
1	Interest rate:	10%				
2						
3		Time until		Payment		Column (B)
4		Payment		Discounted		×
5		(Years)	Payment	at 10%	Weight*	Column (E)
6	A. 8% coupon bond	1	80	72.727	0.0765	0.0765
7		2	80	66.116	0.0696	0.1392
8		3	1080	811.420	0.8539	2.5617
9	Sum:			950.263	1.0000	2.7774
10						
11	B. Zero-coupon bond	1	0	0.000	0.0000	0.0000
12		2	0	0.000	0.0000	0.0000
13		3	1000	751.315	1.0000	3.0000
14	Sum:			751.315	1.0000	3.0000
15						
16	*Weight = Present value of each payment (column D) divided by bond price					

	A	B	C	D	E	F
1	Interest rate:	0.1				
2						
3		Time until		Payment		Column (B)
4		Payment		Discounted		×
5		(Years)	Payment	at 10%	Weight	Column (E)
6	A. 8% coupon bond	1	80	=C6/(1+$B$1)^B6	=D6/D$9	=E6*B6
7		2	80	=C7/(1+$B$1)^B7	=D7/D$9	=E7*B7
8		3	1080	=C8/(1+$B$1)^B8	=D8/D$9	=E8*B8
9	Sum:			=SUM(D6:D8)	=D9/D$9	=SUM(F6:F8)
10						
11	B. Zero-coupon	1	0	=C11/(1+$B$1)^B11	=D11/D$14	=E11*B11
12		2	0	=C12/(1+$B$1)^B12	=D12/D$14	=E12*B12
13		3	1000	=C13/(1+$B$1)^B13	=D13/D$14	=E13*B13
14	Sum:			=SUM(D11:D13)	=D14/D$14	=SUM(F11:F13)

eXcel

Please visit us at www.mhhe.com/bkm

discounted at 10% for the number of years shown in column B. The weight associated with each payment time (column E) equals the present value of the payment (column D) divided by the bond price (the sum of the present values in column D).

The numbers in column F are the products of time to payment and payment weight. Each of these products corresponds to one of the terms in Equation 11.1. According to that equation, we can calculate the duration of each bond by adding the numbers in column F.

The duration of the zero-coupon bond is exactly equal to its time to maturity, three years. This makes sense for, with only one payment, the average time until payment must be the bond's maturity. The three-year coupon bond, in contrast, has a shorter duration of 2.7774 years.

While the top panel of the spreadsheet in Spreadsheet 11.1 presents numbers for our particular example, the bottom panel presents the formulas we actually entered in each cell. The inputs in the spreadsheet—specifying the cash flows the bond will pay—are given in columns B and C. In column D we calculate the present value of each cash flow using a discount rate of 10%, in column E we calculate the weights for Equation 11.1, and in column F we compute the product of time until payment and payment weight. Each of these terms corresponds to one of the terms in Equation 11.1. The sum of these terms, reported in cells F9 and F14, is therefore the duration of each bond. Using the spreadsheet, you can easily answer several "what if" questions such as the one in Concept Check 11.1.

CONCEPT check 11.1

Suppose the interest rate decreases to 9%. What will happen to the price and duration of each bond in Spreadsheet 11.1?

Duration is a key concept in bond portfolio management for at least three reasons. First, it is a simple summary measure of the effective average maturity of the portfolio. Second, it turns out to be an essential tool in immunizing portfolios from interest rate risk. We will explore this application in the next section. Third, duration is a measure of the interest rate sensitivity of a bond portfolio, which we explore here.

We have already noted that price sensitivity to interest rate movements generally increases with maturity. Duration enables us to quantify this relationship. It turns out that when interest rates change, the percentage change in a bond's price is proportional to its duration. Specifically, the proportional change in a bond's price can be related to the change in its yield to maturity, y, according to the rule

$$\frac{\Delta P}{P} = -D \times \left[\frac{\Delta(1 + y)}{1 + y}\right] \tag{11.2}$$

The proportional price change equals the proportional change in (1 plus the bond's yield) times the bond's duration. Therefore, bond price volatility is proportional to the bond's duration, and duration becomes a natural measure of interest rate exposure.[1] This relationship is key to interest rate risk management.

modified duration

Macaulay's duration divided by 1 + yield to maturity. Measures interest rate sensitivity of bond.

Practitioners commonly use Equation 11.2 in a slightly different form. They define **modified duration** as $D^* = D/(1 + y)$ and rewrite Equation 11.2 as

$$\frac{\Delta P}{P} = -D^* \Delta y \tag{11.3}$$

The percentage change in bond price is just the product of modified duration and the change in the bond's yield to maturity. Because the percentage change in the bond price is proportional to modified duration, modified duration is a natural measure of the bond's exposure to interest rate volatility.

[1]Actually, as we will see later, Equation 11.3 is only approximately valid for large changes in the bond's yield. The approximation becomes exact as one considers smaller, or localized, changes in yields.

EXAMPLE 11.1

Duration and Interest Rate Risk

A bond with maturity of 30 years has a coupon rate of 8% (paid annually) and a yield to maturity of 9%. Its price is \$897.26, and its duration is 11.37 years. What will happen to the bond price if the bond's yield to maturity increases to 9.1%?

Equation 11.3 tells us that an increase of .1% in the bond's yield to maturity ($\Delta y = .001$ in decimal terms) will result in a price change of

$$\Delta P = -(D^* \Delta y) \times P$$

$$= -\frac{11.37}{1.09} \times .001 \times \$897.26 = -\$9.36$$

To confirm the relationship between duration and the sensitivity of bond price to interest rate changes, let's compare the price sensitivity of the three-year coupon bond in Spreadsheet 11.1, which has a duration of 2.7774 years, to the sensitivity of a zero-coupon bond with maturity and duration of 2.7774 years. Both should have equal interest rate exposure if duration is a useful measure of price sensitivity.

The three-year bond sells for \$950.263 at the initial interest rate of 10%. If the bond's yield increases by 1 basis point (1/100 of a percent) to 10.01%, its price will fall to \$950.0231, a percentage decline of .0252%. The zero-coupon bond has a maturity of 2.7774 years. At the initial interest rate of 10%, it sells at a price of $\$1{,}000/1.10^{2.7774} = \$767.425$. When the interest rate increases, its price falls to $\$1{,}000/1.1001^{2.7774} = \$767.2313$, for an identical .0252% capital loss. We conclude that equal-duration assets are equally sensitive to interest rate movements.

Incidentally, this example confirms the validity of Equation 11.2. The equation predicts that the proportional price change of the two bonds should have been $-2.7774 \times .0001/1.10 = .000252$, or .0252%, just as we found from direct computation.

CONCEPT check 11.2

a. In Concept Check 11.1, you calculated the price and duration of a three-year maturity, 8% coupon bond for an interest rate of 9%. Now suppose the interest rate increases to 9.05%. What is the new value of the bond, and what is the percentage change in the bond's price?

b. Calculate the percentage change in the bond's price predicted by the duration formula in Equation 11.2 or 11.3. Compare this value to your answer for (*a*).

The equations for the durations of coupon bonds are tedious, and spreadsheets like Spreadsheet 11.1 are cumbersome to modify for different maturities and coupon rates. Fortunately, spreadsheet programs such as Excel come with built-in functions for duration. Moreover, these functions easily accommodate bonds that are between coupon payment dates. Spreadsheet 11.2 illustrates how to use Excel to compute duration. The spreadsheets use many of the same conventions as the bond pricing spreadsheets described in Chapter 10.

SPREADSHEET 11.2

Using Excel functions to compute duration

	A	B	C
1	**Inputs**		**Formula in column B**
2	Settlement date	1/1/2000	=DATE(2000,1,1)
3	Maturity date	1/1/2003	=DATE(2003,1,1)
4	Coupon rate	0.08	0.08
5	Yield to maturity	0.10	0.10
6	Coupons per year	1	1
7			
8	**Outputs**		
9	Macaulay duration	2.7774	=DURATION(B2,B3,B4,B5,B6)
10	Modified duration	2.5249	=MDURATION(B2,B3,B4,B5,B6)

eXcel

Please visit us at www.mhhe.com/bkm

We can use the spreadsheet to reconfirm the duration of the 8% coupon bond examined in Panel A of Spreadsheet 11.1. The settlement date (i.e., today's date) and maturity date are entered in cells B2 and B3 of Spreadsheet 11.2 using Excel's date function, DATE(year, month, day). For this three-year maturity bond, we don't have a specific settlement date. We arbitrarily set the settlement date to January 1, 2000, and use a maturity date precisely three years later. The coupon rate and yield to maturity are entered as decimals in cells B4 and B5, and the payment periods per year are entered in cell B6. Macaulay and modified duration appear in cells B9 and B10. Cell B9 shows that the duration of the bond is indeed 2.7774 years. The modified duration of the bond is 2.5249, which equals 2.7774/1.10.

11.3

Consider a 9% coupon, 8-year maturity bond with annual payments, selling at a yield to maturity of 10%. Use Spreadsheet 11.2 to confirm that the bond's duration is 5.97 years. What would its duration be if the bond paid its coupon semiannually? Why intuitively does duration fall?

What Determines Duration?

Malkiel's bond price relations, which we laid out in the previous section, characterize the determinants of interest rate sensitivity. Duration allows us to quantify that sensitivity. For example, if we wish to speculate on interest rates, duration tells us how strong a bet we are making. Conversely, if we wish to remain "neutral" on rates, and simply match the interest rate sensitivity of a chosen bond market index, duration allows us to measure that sensitivity and mimic it in our own portfolio. For these reasons, it is crucial to understand the determinants of duration and convenient to have formulas to calculate the duration of some commonly encountered securities. Therefore, in this section, we present several "rules" that summarize most of its important properties. These rules are also illustrated in Figure 11.2, which contains plots of durations of bonds of various coupon rates, yields to maturity, and times to maturity.

We have already established:

Rule 1: The duration of a zero-coupon bond equals its time to maturity.

FIGURE 11.2

Duration as a function of maturity

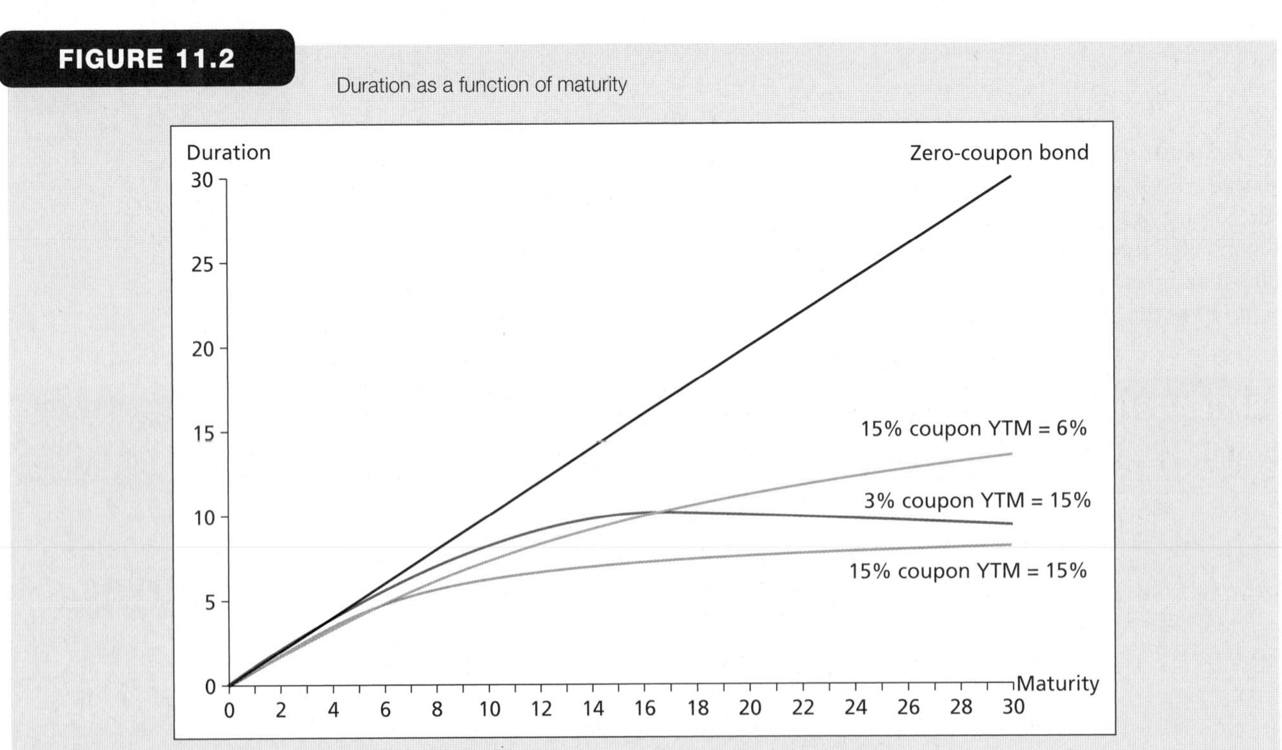

We also have seen that the three-year coupon bond has a lower duration than the three-year zero-because coupons early in the bond's life reduce the bond's weighted-average time until payments. This illustrates another general property:

Rule 2: With time to maturity and yield to maturity held constant, a bond's duration and interest rate sensitivity are higher when the coupon rate is lower.

This property corresponds to Malkiel's fifth bond pricing relationship and is attributable to the impact of early coupons on the average maturity of a bond's payments. The lower these coupons, the less weight these early payments have on the weighted-average maturity of all the bond's payments. In other words, a lower fraction of the total value of the bond is tied up in the (earlier) coupon payments whose values are relatively insensitive to yields rather than the (later and more yield-sensitive) repayment of par value. Compare the plots in Figure 11.2 of the durations of the 3% coupon and 15% coupon bonds, each with identical yields of 15%. The plot of the duration of the 15% coupon bond lies below the corresponding plot for the 3% coupon bond.

Rule 3: With the coupon rate held constant, a bond's duration and interest rate sensitivity generally increase with time to maturity. Duration always increases with maturity for bonds selling at par or at a premium to par.

This property of duration corresponds to Malkiel's third relationship and is fairly intuitive. What is surprising is that duration need not always increase with time to maturity. For some deep discount bonds, such as the 3% coupon bond selling to yield 15% in Figure 11.2, duration may eventually fall with increases in maturity. For virtually all traded bonds, however, it is safe to assume that duration increases with maturity.

Notice in Figure 11.2 that for the zero-coupon bond, maturity and duration are equal. For all the coupon bonds, however, duration increases by less than a year for each year's increase in maturity. The slope of the duration graph is less than 1, and duration is always less than maturity for positive-coupon bonds.

While long-maturity bonds generally will be high-duration bonds, duration is a better measure of the long-term nature of the bond because it also accounts for coupon payments. Maturity is an adequate measure only when the bond pays no coupons; then maturity and duration are equal.

Notice also in Figure 11.2 that the two 15% coupon bonds have different durations when they sell at different yields to maturity. The lower-yield bond has longer duration. This makes sense, because at lower yields the more distant payments have relatively greater present values and thereby account for a greater share of the bond's total value. Thus, in the weighted-average calculation of duration, the distant payments receive greater weights, which results in a higher duration measure. This establishes

Rule 4: With other factors held constant, the duration and interest rate sensitivity of a coupon bond are higher when the bond's yield to maturity is lower.

As we noted above, the intuition for this rule is that while a higher yield reduces the present value of all of the bond's payments, it reduces the value of more distant payments by a greater proportional amount. Therefore, at higher yields a higher fraction of the total value of the bond lies in its earlier payments, thereby reducing effective maturity. Rule 4, which is the sixth bond pricing relationship noted above, applies to coupon bonds. For zeros, duration equals time to maturity, regardless of the yield to maturity.

Finally, we present an algebraic rule for the duration of a perpetuity. This rule is derived from and is consistent with the formula for duration given in Equation 11.1, but it is far easier to use for infinitely lived bonds.

Rule 5: The duration of a level perpetuity is

$$\text{Duration of perpetuity} = \frac{1+y}{y} \tag{11.4}$$

TABLE 11.3 Durations of annual coupon bonds (initial bond yield = 6%)

	Coupon Rates (% per year)			
Years to Maturity	**4**	**6**	**8**	**10**
1	1.000	1.000	1.000	1.000
5	4.611	4.465	4.342	4.237
10	8.281	7.802	7.445	7.169
20	13.216	12.158	11.495	11.041
Infinite (perpetuity)	17.667	17.667	17.667	17.667

For example, at a 15% yield, the duration of a perpetuity that pays $100 once a year forever is 1.15/.15 = 7.67 years, while at a 6% yield it is 1.06/.06 = 17.67 years.

Equation 11.4 makes it obvious that maturity and duration can differ substantially. The maturity of the perpetuity is infinite, while the duration of the instrument at a 15% yield is only 7.67 years. The present value-weighted cash flows early on in the life of the perpetuity dominate the computation of duration. Notice from Figure 11.2 that as their maturities become ever longer, the durations of the two coupon bonds with yields of 15% both converge to the duration of the perpetuity with the same yield, 7.67 years.

CONCEPT check 11.4

Show that the duration of a perpetuity increases as the interest rate decreases, in accordance with Rule 4.

Durations can vary widely among traded bonds. Table 11.3 presents durations for several bonds, all paying annual coupons and yielding 6% per year. Duration decreases as coupon rates increase and increases with time to maturity. According to Table 11.3 and Equation 11.2, if the interest rate were to increase from 6% to 6.1%, the 6% coupon, 20-year bond would fall in value by about 1.15% (= $-12.158 \times .1\%/1.06$) while the 8% coupon, five-year bond would fall by only .41% (= $-4.342 \times .1\%/1.06$). Notice also from Table 11.3 that duration is independent of coupon rate only for perpetuities.

11.2 PASSIVE BOND MANAGEMENT

Passive managers take bond prices as fairly set and seek to control only the risk of their fixed-income portfolios. Generally, there are two ways of viewing this risk. Some institutions, such as banks, are concerned with protecting the portfolio's current net worth or net market value against interest rate fluctuations. Risk-based capital guidelines for commercial banks and thrift institutions require the setting aside of additional capital as a buffer against potential losses in market value, for example, due to interest rate fluctuations. The amount of capital required is directly related to the losses that may be incurred. Other investors, such as pension funds, may have an investment goal to be reached after a given number of years. These investors are more concerned with protecting the future values of their portfolios.

What is common to all investors, however, is interest rate risk. The net worth of the firm and its ability to meet future obligations fluctuate with interest rates. **Immunization** and dedication techniques refer to strategies that investors use to shield their net worth from interest rate risk.

immunization

A strategy to shield net worth from interest rate movements.

Immunization

Many banks and thrift institutions have a natural mismatch between the maturities of assets and liabilities. For example, bank liabilities are primarily the deposits owed to customers; these liabilities are short term in nature and consequently of low duration. Assets largely comprise commercial and consumer loans or mortgages. These assets are of longer duration, and their

On the MARKET FRONT

PENSION FUNDS LOSE GROUND DESPITE BROAD MARKET GAINS

The stock market had a banner year in 2003, with the S&P 500 providing a rate of return in excess of 25%. Not surprisingly, this performance showed up in the balance sheets of U.S. pension funds: Assets in these funds rose by more than $100 billion. Despite this apparent good news, pension funds actually *lost* ground in 2003, with the gap between assets and liabilities growing by about $45 billion.

How did this happen? Blame the decline in interest rates during the year that were in large part the force behind the stock market gains. As rates fell, the present value of pension obligations to retirees rose even faster than the value of the assets backing those promises. It turns out that the value of pension liabilities is more sensitive to interest rate changes than is the value of the typical assets held in those funds. So even though falling rates tend to pump up asset returns, they pump up liabilities even more so. In other words, the duration of fund investments tends to be shorter than the duration of its obligations. This duration mismatch makes funds vulnerable to interest rate declines.

Why don't funds better match asset and liability durations? One reason is that fund managers are often evaluated based on their performance relative to standard bond market indexes. Those indexes tend to have far shorter durations than pension fund liabilities. So to some extent, managers may be keeping their eyes on the wrong ball, one with the wrong interest rate sensitivity.

values are correspondingly more sensitive than deposits to interest rate fluctuations. When interest rates increase unexpectedly, banks can suffer serious decreases in net worth—their assets fall in value by more than their liabilities.

Similarly, a pension fund may have a mismatch between the interest rate sensitivity of the assets held in the fund and the present value of its liabilities—the promise to make payments to retirees. The nearby box illustrates the dangers that pension funds face when they neglect the interest rate exposure of *both* assets and liabilities. It points out that when interest rates change, the present value of the fund's liabilities change. For example, in some recent years pension funds lost ground despite the fact that they enjoyed excellent investment returns. As interest rates fell, the value of their liabilities grew even faster than the value of their assets. The conclusion: Funds should match the interest rate exposure of assets and liabilities so that the value of assets will track the value of liabilities whether rates rise or fall. In other words, the financial manager might want to *immunize* the fund against interest rate volatility.

Pension funds are not alone in this concern. Any institution with a future fixed obligation might consider immunization a reasonable risk management policy. Insurance companies, for example, also pursue immunization strategies. In fact, the notion of immunization was introduced by F. M. Redington (1952), an actuary for a life insurance company. The idea is that duration-matched assets and liabilities let the asset portfolio meet the firm's obligations despite interest rate movements.

Consider, for example, an insurance company that issues a guaranteed investment contract, or GIC, for $10,000. (GICs are essentially zero-coupon bonds issued by the insurance company to its customers. They are popular products for individuals' retirement-savings accounts.) If the GIC has a five-year maturity and a guaranteed interest rate of 8%, the insurance company promises to pay $\$10,000 \times (1.08)^5 = \$14,693.28$ in five years.

Suppose that the insurance company chooses to fund its obligation with $10,000 of 8% *annual* coupon bonds, selling at par value, with six years to maturity. As long as the market interest rate stays at 8%, the company has fully funded the obligation, as the present value of the obligation exactly equals the value of the bonds.

Table 11.4A shows that if interest rates remain at 8%, the accumulated funds from the bond will grow to exactly the $14,693.28 obligation. Over the five-year period, the year-end coupon income of $800 is reinvested at the prevailing 8% market interest rate. At the end of the period, the bonds can be sold for $10,000; they still will sell at par value because the coupon rate still equals the market interest rate. Total income after five years from reinvested coupons and the sale of the bond is precisely $14,693.28.

If interest rates change, however, two offsetting influences will affect the ability of the fund to grow to the targeted value of $14,693.28. If interest rates rise, the fund will suffer a capital loss, impairing its ability to satisfy the obligation. The bonds will be worth less in five years than if interest rates had remained at 8%. However, at a higher interest rate, reinvested

TABLE 11.4 Terminal value of a bond portfolio after five years (all proceeds reinvested)

Payment Number	Years Remaining until Obligation	Accumulated Value of Invested Payment
A. Rates remain at 8%		
1	4	$800 \times (1.08)^4 =$ 1,088.39
2	3	$800 \times (1.08)^3 =$ 1,007.77
3	2	$800 \times (1.08)^2 =$ 933.12
4	1	$800 \times (1.08)^1 =$ 864.00
5	0	$800 \times (1.08)^0 =$ 800.00
Sale of bond	0	10,800/1.08 = 10,000.00
		14,693.28
B. Rates fall to 7%		
1	4	$800 \times (1.07)^4 =$ 1,048.64
2	3	$800 \times (1.07)^3 =$ 980.03
3	2	$800 \times (1.07)^2 =$ 915.92
4	1	$800 \times (1.07)^1 =$ 856.00
5	0	$800 \times (1.07)^0 =$ 800.00
Sale of bond	0	10,800/1.07 = 10,093.46
		14,694.05
C. Rates increase to 9%		
1	4	$800 \times (1.09)^4 =$ 1,129.27
2	3	$800 \times (1.09)^3 =$ 1,036.02
3	2	$800 \times (1.09)^2 =$ 950.48
4	1	$800 \times (1.09)^1 =$ 872.00
5	0	$800 \times (1.09)^0 =$ 800.00
Sale of bond	0	10,800/1.09 = 9,908.26
		14,696.02

Note: The sale price of the bond portfolio equals the portfolio's final payment ($10,800) divided by $1 + r$, because the time to maturity of the bonds will be one year at the time of sale.

coupons will grow at a faster rate, offsetting the capital loss. In other words, fixed-income investors face two offsetting types of interest rate risk: *price risk* and *reinvestment rate risk.* Increases in interest rates cause capital losses but at the same time increase the rate at which reinvested income will grow. If the portfolio duration is chosen appropriately, these two effects will cancel out exactly. When the portfolio duration is set equal to the investor's horizon date, the accumulated value of the investment fund at the horizon date will be unaffected by interest rate fluctuations. *For a horizon equal to the portfolio's duration, price risk and reinvestment risk are precisely offsetting.* The obligation is immunized.

In our example, the duration of the six-year maturity bonds used to fund the GIC is five years. You can confirm this using either Spreadsheet 11.1 or 11.2. The duration of the (zero-coupon) GIC is also five years. Because the fully funded plan has equal duration for its assets and liabilities, the insurance company should be immunized against interest rate fluctuations. To confirm this, let's check that the bond can generate enough income to pay off the obligation in five years regardless of interest rate movements.

In Table 11.4, Panels B and C consider two possible interest rate scenarios: Rates either fall to 7% or increase to 9%. In both cases, the annual coupon payments are reinvested at the new interest rate, which is assumed to change before the first coupon payment, and the bond is sold in year 5 to help satisfy the obligation of the GIC.

Table 11.4B shows that if interest rates fall to 7%, the total funds will accumulate to $14,694.05, providing a small surplus of $.77. If rates increase to 9% as in Table 11.4C, the fund accumulates to $14,696.02, providing a small surplus of $2.74.

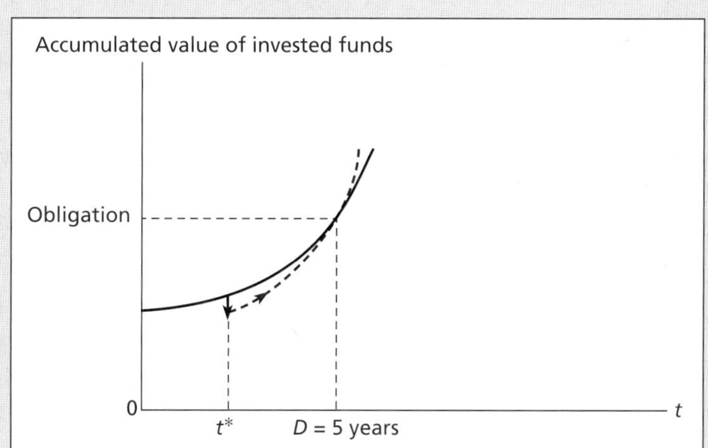

FIGURE 11.3

Growth of invested funds

Note: The solid curve represents the growth of portfolio value at the original interest rate. If interest rates increase at time t^*, the portfolio value falls but increases thereafter at the faster rate represented by the broken curve. At time D (duration) the curves cross.

Several points are worth highlighting. First, duration matching balances the difference between the accumulated value of the coupon payments (reinvestment rate risk) and the sale value of the bond (price risk). That is, when interest rates fall, the coupons grow less than in the base case, but the higher value of the bond offsets this. When interest rates rise, the value of the bond falls, but the coupons more than make up for this loss because they are reinvested at the higher rate. Figure 11.3 illustrates this case. The solid curve traces the accumulated value of the bonds if interest rates remain at 8%. The dashed curve shows that value if interest rates happen to increase. The initial impact is a capital loss, but this loss eventually is offset by the now-faster growth rate of reinvested funds. At the five-year horizon date, equal to the bond's duration, the two effects just cancel, leaving the company able to satisfy its obligation with the accumulated proceeds from the bond.

We can also analyze immunization in terms of present as opposed to future values. Table 11.5A shows the initial balance sheet for the insurance company's GIC. Both assets and the obligation have market values of $10,000, so the plan is just fully funded. Panels B and C in the table show that whether the interest rate increases or decreases, the value of the bonds funding the GIC and the present value of the company's obligation change by virtually identical amounts. Regardless of the interest rate change, the plan remains fully funded, with the surplus in Table 11.5B and C just about zero. The duration-matching strategy has ensured that both assets and liabilities react equally to interest rate fluctuations.

TABLE 11.5 Market value balance sheets

A. Interest rate = 8%			
Assets		**Liabilities**	
Bonds	$10,000	Obligation	$10,000
B. Interest rate = 7%			
Assets		**Liabilities**	
Bonds	$10,476.65	Obligation	$10,476.11
C. Interest rate = 9%			
Assets		**Liabilities**	
Bonds	$9,551.41	Obligation	$9,549.62

Notes: Value of bonds = 800 × Annuity factor(r, 6) + 10,000 × PV factor(r, 6).

Value of obligation $= \dfrac{14{,}693.28}{(1+r)^5} = 14{,}693.28 \times \text{PV factor}(r, 5)$.

Figure 11.4 is a graph of the present values of the bond and the single-payment obligation as a function of the interest rate. At the current rate of 8%, the values are equal, and the obligation is fully funded by the bond. Moreover, the two present value curves are tangent at $y = 8\%$. As interest rates change, the change in value of both the asset and the obligation are equal, so the obligation remains fully funded. For greater changes in the interest rate, however, the present value curves diverge. This reflects the fact that the fund actually shows a small surplus at market interest rates other than 8%.

Why is there *any* surplus in the fund? After all, we claimed that a duration-matched asset and liability mix would make the investor indifferent to interest rate shifts. Actually, such a claim is valid for only *small* changes in the interest rate, because as bond yields change, so too does duration. (Recall Rule 4 for duration.) In fact, while the duration of the bond in this example is equal to five years at a yield to maturity of 8%, the duration rises to 5.02 years when the bond yield falls to 7% and drops to 4.97 years at $y = 9\%$. That is, the bond and the obligation were not duration-matched *across* the interest rate shift, so the position was not fully immunized.

rebalancing

Realigning the proportions of assets in a portfolio as needed.

This example demonstrates the need for **rebalancing** immunized portfolios. As interest rates and asset durations continually change, managers must adjust the portfolio to realign its duration with the duration of the obligation. Moreover, even if interest rates do not change, asset durations *will* change solely because of the passage of time. Recall from Figure 11.2 that duration generally decreases less rapidly than maturity as time passes, so even if an obligation is immunized at the outset, the durations of the asset and liability will fall at different rates. Without portfolio rebalancing, durations will become unmatched and the goals of immunization will not be realized. Therefore, immunization is a passive strategy only in the sense that it does not involve attempts to identify undervalued securities. Immunization managers still actively update and monitor their positions.

EXAMPLE 11.2

Constructing an Immunized Portfolio

An insurance company must make a payment of $19,487 in seven years. The market interest rate is 10%, so the present value of the obligation is $10,000. The company's portfolio manager wishes to fund the obligation using three-year zero-coupon bonds and perpetuities paying annual coupons. (We focus on zeros and perpetuities to keep the algebra simple.) How can the manager immunize the obligation?

Immunization requires that the duration of the portfolio of assets equal the duration of the liability. We can proceed in four steps:

Step 1. Calculate the duration of the liability. In this case, the liability duration is simple to compute. It is a single-payment obligation with duration of seven years.

Step 2. Calculate the duration of the asset portfolio. The portfolio duration is the weighted average of duration of each component asset, with weights proportional to the funds placed in each asset. The duration of the zero-coupon bond is simply its maturity, three years. The duration of the perpetuity is 1.10/.10 = 11 years. Therefore, if the fraction of the portfolio invested in the zero is called w, and the fraction invested in the perpetuity is $(1 - w)$, the portfolio duration will be

$$\text{Asset duration} = w \times 3 \text{ years} + (1 - w) \times 11 \text{ years}$$

Step 3. Find the asset mix that sets the duration of assets equal to the seven-year duration of liabilities. This requires us to solve for w in the following equation

$$w \times 3 \text{ years} + (1 - w) \times 11 \text{ years} = 7 \text{ years}$$

This implies that $w = 1/2$. The manager should invest half the portfolio in the zero and half in the perpetuity. This will result in an asset duration of seven years.

Step 4. Fully fund the obligation. Since the obligation has a present value of $10,000, and the fund will be invested equally in the zero and the perpetuity, the manager must purchase $5,000 of the zero-coupon bond and $5,000 of the perpetuity. Note that the *face value* of the zero will be $\$5{,}000 \times (1.10)^3 = \$6{,}655$.

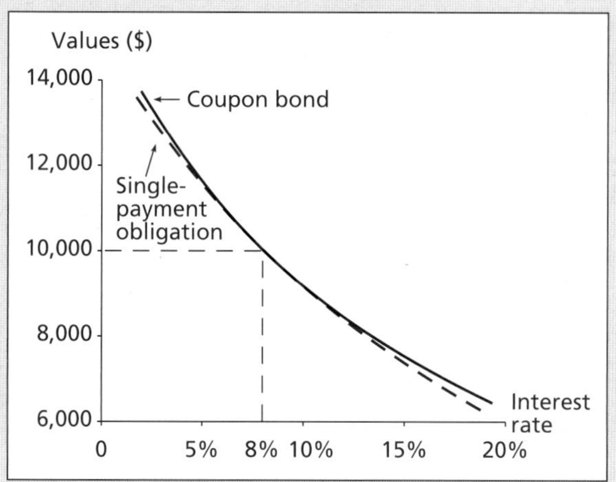

FIGURE 11.4

Immunization. The coupon bond fully funds the obligation at an interest rate of 8%. Moreover, the present value curves are tangent at 8%, so the obligation will remain fully funded even if rates change by a small amount.

Even if a position is immunized, however, the portfolio manager still cannot rest. This is because of the need for rebalancing in response to changes in interest rates. Moreover, even if rates do not change, the passage of time also will affect duration and require rebalancing. Let us continue Example 11.2 and see how the portfolio manager can maintain an immunized position.

EXAMPLE 11.3

Rebalancing

Suppose that one year has passed, and the interest rate remains at 10%. The portfolio manager of Example 11.2 needs to reexamine her position. Is the position still fully funded? Is it still immunized? If not, what actions are required?

First, examine funding. The present value of the obligation will have grown to $11,000, as it is one year closer to maturity. The manager's funds also have grown to $11,000: The zero-coupon bonds have increased in value from $5,000 to $5,500 with the passage of time, while the perpetuity has paid its annual $500 coupons and remains worth $5,000. Therefore, the obligation is still fully funded.

The portfolio weights must be changed, however. The zero-coupon bond now will have a duration of two years, while the perpetuity duration remains at 11 years. The obligation is now due in six years. The weights must now satisfy the equation

$$w \times 2 + (1 - w) \times 11 = 6$$

which implies that $w = 5/9$. To rebalance the portfolio and maintain the duration match, the manager now must invest a total of $11,000 × 5/9 = $6,111.11 in the zero-coupon bond. This requires that the entire $500 coupon payment be invested in the zero, with an additional $111.11 of the perpetuity sold and invested in the zero-coupon bond.

Of course, rebalancing the portfolio entails transaction costs as assets are bought or sold, so continuous rebalancing is not feasible. In practice, managers strike a compromise between the desire for perfect immunization, which requires continual rebalancing, and the need to control trading costs, which dictates less frequent rebalancing.

CONCEPT check 11.5

Look again at Example 11.3. What would have been the immunizing weights in the second year if the interest rate had fallen to 8%?

Cash Flow Matching and Dedication

The problems associated with immunization seem to have a simple solution. Why not simply buy a zero-coupon bond with face value equal to the projected cash outlay? This is **cash flow matching,** which automatically immunizes a portfolio from interest rate risk because the cash flow from the bond and the obligation exactly offset each other.

cash flow matching

Matching cash flows from a fixed-income portfolio with those of an obligation.

EXCEL APPLICATIONS

Immunization

Please visit us at www.mhhe.com/bkm

The Excel immunization model allows you to analyze any number of time-period or holding-period immunization examples. The model is built using the Excel-supplied formulas for bond duration, which allow the investigation of any maturity bond without building a table of cash flows.

	A	B	C	D	E	F	G	H
1			Holding Period Immunization					
2								
3	YTM	0.0800	Mar Price	1000.00				
4	Coupon R	0.0800						
5	Maturity	6			Duration	#NAME?		
6	Par Value	1000.00						
7	Holding P	5						
8	Duration	4.9927						
9								
10								
11	If Rates Increase by 200 basis points				If Rates Increase by 100 basis points			
12	Rate	0.1000			Rate	0.0900		
13	FV of CPS	488.41			FV of CPS	478.78		
14	SalesP	981.82			SalesP	990.83		
15	Total	1470.23			Total	1469.60		
16	IRR	0.0801			IRR	0.0800		
17								
18								
19								
20	If Rates Decrease by 200 basis points				If Rates Decrease by 100 basis points			
21	Rate	0.0600			Rate	0.0700		
22	FV of CPS	450.97			FV of CPS	460.06		
23	SalesP	1018.87			SalesP	1009.35		
24	Total	1469.84			Total	1469.40		
25	IRR	0.0801			IRR	0.0800		

Excel Questions

1. When rates increase by 100 basis points, what is the change in the future sales price of the bond? The value of reinvested coupons?
2. What if rates increase by 200 basis points?
3. What is the relation between price risk and reinvestment rate risk as we consider larger changes in bond yields?

dedication strategy

Refers to multiperiod cash flow matching.

Cash flow matching on a multiperiod basis is referred to as a **dedication strategy.** In this case, the manager selects either zero-coupon or coupon bonds with total cash flows that match a series of obligations. The advantage of dedication is that it is a once-and-for-all approach to eliminating interest rate risk. Once the cash flows are matched, there is no need for rebalancing. The dedicated portfolio provides the cash necessary to pay the firm's liabilities regardless of the eventual path of interest rates.

Cash flow matching is not widely pursued, however, probably because of the constraints it imposes on bond selection. Immunization/dedication strategies are appealing to firms that do not wish to bet on general movements in interest rates, yet these firms may want to immunize using bonds they believe are undervalued. Cash flow matching places enough constraints on bond selection that it can make it impossible to pursue a dedication strategy using only "underpriced" bonds. Firms looking for underpriced bonds exchange exact and easy dedication for the possibility of achieving superior returns from their bond portfolios.

Sometimes, cash flow matching is not even possible. To cash flow match for a pension fund that is obligated to pay out a perpetual flow of income to current and future retirees, the pension fund would need to purchase fixed-income securities with maturities ranging up to hundreds of years. Such securities do not exist, making exact dedication infeasible. Immunization is easy, however. If the interest rate is 8%, for example, the duration of the pension fund

fund obligation is 1.08/.08 = 13.5 years (see Rule 5 on page 345). Therefore, the fund can immunize its obligation by purchasing zero-coupon bonds with maturity of 13.5 years and a market value equal to that of the pension liabilities.

CONCEPT check 11.6

a. Suppose that this pension fund is obligated to pay out $800,000 per year in perpetuity. What should be the maturity and face value of the zero-coupon bond it purchases to immunize its obligation?

b. Now suppose the interest rate immediately increases to 8.1%. How should the fund rebalance in order to remain immunized against further interest rate shocks? Ignore transaction costs.

CONCEPT check 11.7

How would an increase in trading costs affect the attractiveness of dedication versus immunization?

11.3 CONVEXITY

Duration clearly is a key tool in bond portfolio management. Yet, the duration rule for the impact of interest rates on bond prices is only an approximation. Equation 11.3, which we repeat here, states that the percentage change in the value of a bond approximately equals the product of modified duration times the change in the bond's yield:

$$\frac{\Delta P}{P} = -D^*\Delta y$$

This equation asserts that the percentage price change is directly proportional to the change in the bond's yield. If this were *exactly* so, however, a graph of the percentage change in bond price as a function of the change in its yield would plot as a straight line, with slope equal to $-D^*$. Yet we know from Figure 11.1, and more generally from Malkiel's five bond pricing relationships (specifically Relationship 2), that the relationship between bond prices and yields is *not* linear. The duration rule is a good approximation for small changes in bond yield, but it is less accurate for larger changes.

Figure 11.5 illustrates this point. Like Figure 11.1, this figure presents the percentage change in bond price in response to a change in the bond's yield to maturity. The curved

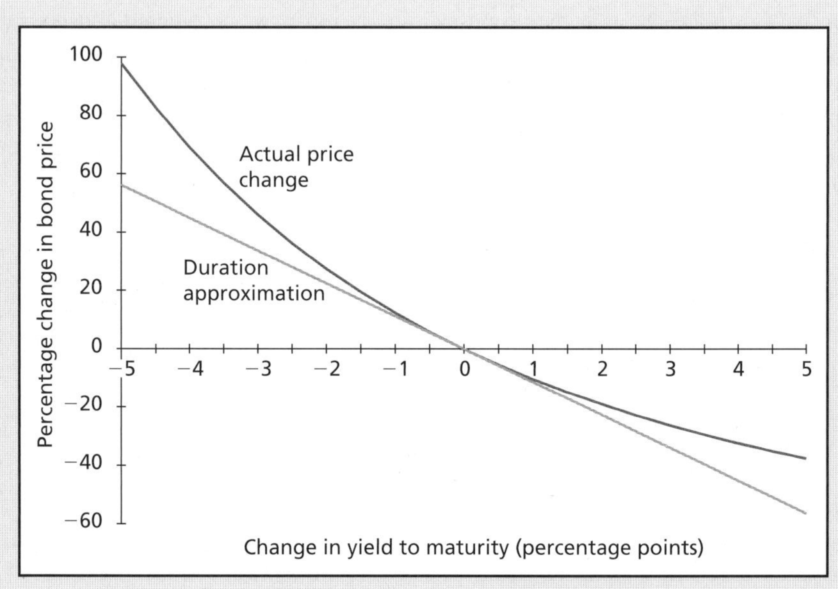

FIGURE 11.5

Bond price convexity. The percentage change in bond price is a convex function of the change in yield to maturity.

line is the percentage price change for a 30-year maturity, 8% coupon bond, selling at an initial yield to maturity of 8%. The straight line is the percentage price change predicted by the duration rule: The modified duration of the bond at its initial yield is 11.26 years, so the straight line is a plot of $-D^*\Delta y = -11.26 \times \Delta y$. Notice that the two plots are tangent at the initial yield. Thus, for small changes in the bond's yield to maturity, the duration rule is quite accurate. However, for larger changes in yield, there is progressively more "daylight" between the two plots, demonstrating that the duration rule becomes progressively less accurate.

Notice from Figure 11.5 that the duration approximation (the straight line) always understates the value of the bond; it underestimates the increase in bond price when the yield falls, and it overestimates the decline in price when the yield rises. This is due to the curvature of the true price-yield relationship. Curves with shapes such as that of the price-yield relationship are said to be convex, and the curvature of the price-yield curve is called the **convexity** of the bond.

convexity

The curvature of the price-yield relationship of a bond.

We can quantify convexity as the rate of change of the slope of the price-yield curve, expressed as a fraction of the bond price.[2] As a practical rule, you can view bonds with higher convexity as exhibiting higher curvature in the price-yield relationship. The convexity of noncallable bonds, such as that in Figure 11.5, is positive: The slope increases (i.e., becomes less negative) at higher yields.

Convexity allows us to improve the duration approximation for bond price changes. Accounting for convexity, Equation 11.3 can be modified as follows:[3]

$$\frac{\Delta P}{P} = -D^*\Delta y + \tfrac{1}{2} \times \text{Convexity} \times (\Delta y)^2 \qquad \textbf{(11.5)}$$

The first term on the right-hand side is the same as the duration rule, Equation 11.3. The second term is the modification for convexity. Notice that for a bond with positive convexity, the second term is positive, regardless of whether the yield rises or falls. This insight corresponds to the fact noted just above that the duration rule always underestimates the new value of a bond following a change in its yield. The more accurate Equation 11.5, which accounts for convexity, always predicts a higher bond price than Equation 11.3. Of course, if the change in yield is small, the convexity term, which is multiplied by $(\Delta y)^2$ in Equation 11.5, will be extremely small and will add little to the approximation. In this case, the linear approximation given by the duration rule will be sufficiently accurate. Thus, convexity is more important as a practical matter when potential interest rate changes are large.

Convexity is the reason that the immunization examples we considered above resulted in small errors. For example, if you turn back to Table 11.5 and Figure 11.4, you will see that the single-payment obligation that was funded with a coupon bond of the same duration was well immunized for small changes in yields. However, for larger yield changes, the two pricing curves diverged a bit, implying that such changes in yields would result in small surpluses. This is due to the greater convexity of the coupon bond.

[2]If you have taken a calculus class, you will recognize that Equation 11.3 for modified duration can be written as $dP/P = -D^*dy$. Thus, $-D^* = 1/P \times dP/dy$ is the slope of the price-yield curve expressed as a fraction of the bond price. Similarly, the convexity of a bond equals the second derivative (the rate of change of the slope) of the price-yield curve divided by bond price: Convexity $= 1/P \times d^2P/dy^2$. The formula for the convexity of a bond with a maturity of n years making annual coupon payments is

$$\text{Convexity} = \frac{1}{P \times (1+y)^2} \sum_{t=1}^{n} \left[\frac{CF_t}{(1+y)^t} (t^2 + t) \right]$$

where CF_t is the cash flow paid to the bondholder at date t; CF_t represents either a coupon payment before maturity or final coupon plus par value at the maturity date.

[3]To use the convexity rule, you must express interest rates as decimals rather than percentages.

EXAMPLE 11.4

Convexity

The bond in Figure 11.5 has a 30-year maturity, an 8% coupon, and sells at an initial yield to maturity of 8%. Because the coupon rate equals yield to maturity, the bond sells at par value, or $1,000. The modified duration of the bond at its initial yield is 11.26 years, and its convexity is 212.4, which can be calculated using the formula in footnote 2. (You can find a spreadsheet to calculate the convexity of a 30-year bond at the book's website, **www.mhhe.com/bkm.** See also the nearby Excel Application.) If the bond's yield increases from 8% to 10%, the bond price will fall to $811.46, a decline of 18.85%. The duration rule, Equation 11.3, would predict a price decline of

$$\frac{\Delta P}{P} = -D^*\Delta y = -11.26 \times .02 = -.2252 = -22.52\%$$

which is considerably more than the bond price actually falls. The duration-with-convexity rule, Equation 11.5, is far more accurate:

$$\frac{\Delta P}{P} = -D^*\Delta y + \tfrac{1}{2} \times \text{Convexity} \times (\Delta y)^2$$
$$= -11.26 \times .02 + \tfrac{1}{2} \times 212.4 \times (.02)^2 = -.1827 = -18.27\%$$

which is far closer to the exact change in bond price. (Notice that when we use Equation 11.5, we must express interest rates as decimals rather than percentages. The change in rates from 8% to 10% is represented as $\Delta y = .02$.)

If the change in yield were smaller, say, .1%, convexity would matter less. The price of the bond actually would fall to $988.85, a decline of 1.115%. Without accounting for convexity, we would predict a price decline of

$$\frac{\Delta P}{P} = -D^*\Delta y = -11.26 \times .001 = -.01126 = -1.126\%$$

Accounting for convexity, we get almost the precisely correct answer:

$$\frac{\Delta P}{P} = -11.26 \times .001 + \tfrac{1}{2} \times 212.4 \times (.001)^2 = -.01115 = -1.115\%$$

Nevertheless, the duration rule is quite accurate in this case, even without accounting for convexity.

Why Do Investors Like Convexity?

Convexity is generally considered a desirable trait. Bonds with greater curvature gain more in price when yields fall than they lose when yields rise. For example, in Figure 11.6 bonds A and B have the same duration at the initial yield. The plots of their proportional price changes as a function of interest rate changes are tangent, meaning that their sensitivities to changes in

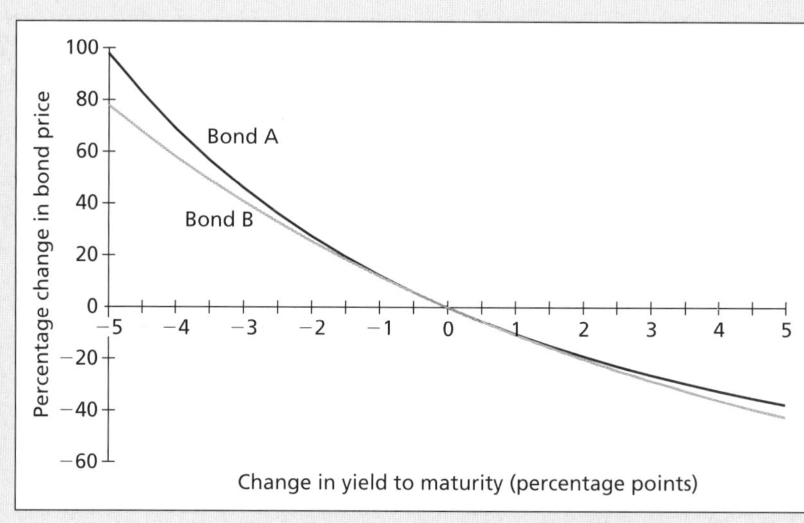

FIGURE 11.6

Convexity of two bonds. Bond A has greater convexity than bond B.

EXCEL APPLICATIONS

Convexity

Please visit us at www.mhhe.com/bkm

The Convexity spreadsheet allows you to calculate bond convexity. You can specify yield to maturity and coupon and allow for short maturities by setting later cash flows equal to zero and setting the last cash flow equal to principal plus final coupon payment.

	A	B	C	D	E	F	G	H
1					**Chapter 11**			
2					**Convexity**			
3								
4			Time (t)	Cash flow	PV(CF)	t + t^2	(t + t^2) x PV(CF)	
5								
6	Coupon	3	1	3	2.871	2	5.742	
7	YTM	0.045	2	3	2.747	6	16.483	
8	Maturity	10	3	3	2.629	12	31.547	
9	Price	$88.13	4	3	2.516	20	50.314	
10			5	3	2.407	30	72.221	
11			6	3	2.304	42	96.755	
12			7	3	2.204	56	123.451	
13			8	3	2.110	72	151.888	
14			9	3	2.019	90	181.684	
15			10	103	66.325	110	7295.701	
16								
17			Sum:		88.13092273		8025.785	
18								
19				Convexity:			83.392425	

Excel Questions

1. Calculate the convexity of a "bullet" fixed-income portfolio, that is, a portfolio with a single cash flow. Suppose a single $1,000 cash flow is paid in year 5.
2. Now calculate the convexity of a "barbell" fixed-income portfolio, that is, a portfolio with equal cash flows over time. Suppose the security makes $100 cash flows in each of years 1–9, so that its duration is close to the bullet in Question 1.
3. Do barbells or bullets have greater convexity?

yields at that point are equal. However, bond A is more convex than bond B. It enjoys greater price increases and smaller price decreases when interest rates fluctuate by larger amounts. If interest rates are volatile, this is an attractive asymmetry that increases the expected return on the bond, since bond A will benefit more from rate decreases and suffer less from rate increases. Of course, if convexity is desirable, it will not be available for free: Investors will have to pay more and accept lower yields on bonds with greater convexity.

11.4 ACTIVE BOND MANAGEMENT

Sources of Potential Profit

Broadly speaking, there are two sources of potential value in active bond management. The first is interest rate forecasting, that is, anticipating movements across the entire spectrum of the fixed-income market. If interest rate declines are forecast, managers will increase portfolio duration; if increases seem likely, they will shorten duration. The second source of potential profit is identification of relative mispricing within the fixed-income market. An analyst might believe, for example, that the default premium on one bond is unnecessarily large and the bond is underpriced.

These techniques will generate abnormal returns only if the analyst's information or insight is superior to that of the market. You can't profit from knowledge that rates are about to fall if everyone else in the market is onto this. In that case, the anticipated lower future rates will be built into bond prices in the sense that long-duration bonds already sell at higher prices, reflecting the anticipated fall in future short rates. If you do not have information before the market does, you will be too late to act—prices will have already responded to the news. You know this from our discussion of market efficiency.

For now we simply repeat that valuable information is differential information. And it is worth noting that interest rate forecasters have a notoriously poor track record.

Homer and Leibowitz (1972) have developed a popular taxonomy of active bond portfolio strategies. They characterize portfolio rebalancing activities as one of four types of *bond swaps.* In the first two swaps, the investor typically believes the yield relationship between bonds or sectors is only temporarily out of alignment. Until the aberration is eliminated, gains can be realized on the underpriced bond during a period of realignment called the *workout period.*

1. The **substitution swap** is an exchange of one bond for a nearly identical substitute. The substituted bonds should be of essentially equal coupon, maturity, quality, call features, sinking fund provisions, and so on. A substitution swap would be motivated by a belief that the market has temporarily mispriced the two bonds, with a discrepancy representing a profit opportunity.

   An example of a substitution swap would be a sale of a 20-year maturity, 8% coupon Toyota bond that is priced to provide a yield to maturity of 8.05% coupled with a purchase of an 8% coupon Honda bond with the same time to maturity that yields 8.15%. If the bonds have about the same credit risk, there is no apparent reason for the Honda bonds to provide a higher yield. Therefore, the higher yield actually available in the market makes the Honda bond seem relatively attractive. Of course, the equality of credit risk is an important condition. If the Honda bond is in fact riskier, then its higher promised yield does not represent a bargain.

substitution swap

Exchange of one bond for a bond with similar attributes but more attractively priced.

2. The **intermarket spread swap** is an exchange of two bonds from different sectors of the bond market. It is pursued when an investor believes the yield spread between two sectors of the bond market is temporarily out of line.

   For example, if the yield spread between 10-year Treasury bonds and 10-year Baa-rated corporate bonds is now 3%, and the historical spread has been only 2%, an investor might consider selling holdings of Treasury bonds and replacing them with corporates. If the yield spread eventually narrows, the Baa-rated corporate bonds will outperform the Treasury bonds.

   Of course, the investor must consider carefully whether there is a good reason that the yield spread seems out of alignment. For example, the default premium on corporate bonds might have increased because the market is expecting a severe recession. In this case, the wider spread would not represent attractive pricing of corporates relative to Treasuries but would simply be an adjustment for a perceived increase in credit risk.

intermarket spread swap

Switching from one segment of the bond market to another.

3. The **rate anticipation swap** is an exchange of bonds with different maturities. It is pegged to interest rate forecasting. Investors who believe rates will fall will swap into bonds of longer duration. For example, the investor might sell a five-year maturity Treasury bond, replacing it with a 25-year maturity Treasury bond. The new bond has the same lack of credit risk as the old one, but it has longer duration.

rate anticipation swap

A switch made in response to forecasts of interest rate changes.

4. The **pure yield pickup swap** is an exchange of a shorter-duration bond for a longer-duration bond. This swap is pursued not in response to perceived mispricing but as a means of increasing return by holding higher-yielding, longer-maturity bonds. The investor is willing to bear the interest rate risk this strategy entails.

   A yield pickup swap can be illustrated using the Treasury bond listings in Figure 10.1 in the previous chapter. You can see from that table that longer-term T-bonds offered higher yields to maturity than shorter ones. The investor who swaps the shorter-term bond for the longer one will earn a higher rate of return as long as the yield curve does not shift upward during the holding period. Of course, if it does, the longer-duration bond will suffer a greater capital loss.

pure yield pickup swap

Moving to higher yield bonds, usually with longer maturities.

We can add a fifth swap, called a **tax swap,** to this list. This refers to a swap to exploit some tax advantage. For example, an investor may swap from one bond that has decreased in price to another similar bond if realization of capital losses is advantageous for tax purposes.

tax swap

Swapping two similar bonds to receive a tax benefit.

Horizon Analysis

horizon analysis

Forecast of bond returns based largely on a prediction of the yield curve at the end of the investment horizon.

One form of interest rate forecasting, which we encountered in the last chapter, is called **horizon analysis.** The analyst selects a particular investment period and predicts bond yields at the end of that period. Given the predicted yield to maturity at the end of the investment period, the bond price can be calculated. The coupon income earned over the period is then added to the predicted capital gain or loss to obtain a forecast of the total return on the bond over the holding period.

EXAMPLE 11.5

Horizon Analysis

A 20-year maturity bond with a 10% coupon rate (paid annually) currently sells at a yield to maturity of 9%. A portfolio manager with a two-year horizon needs to forecast the total return on the bond over the coming two years. In two years, the bond will have an 18-year maturity. The analyst forecasts that two years from now 18-year bonds will sell at yields to maturity of 8% and that coupon payments can be reinvested in short-term securities over the coming two years at a rate of 7%.

To calculate the two-year return on the bond, the analyst would perform the following calculations:

1. Current price = \$100 × Annuity factor(9%, 20 years) = \$1,000 × PV factor(9%, 20 years)
   = \$1,091.29
2. Forecast price = \$100 × Annuity factor(8%, 18 years) + \$1,000 × PV factor(8%, 18 years)
   = \$1,187.44
3. The future value of reinvested coupons will be (\$100 × 1.07) + \$100 = \$207
4. The two-year return is $\frac{\$207 + (\$1,187.44 - \$1,091.29)}{\$1,091.29} = .278$, or 27.8%

The annualized rate of return over the two-year period would then be $(1.278)^{1/2} - 1 = .13$, or 13%.

CONCEPT check 11.8

What will be the rate of return in Example 11.5 if the manager forecasts that in two years the yield to maturity on 18-year maturity bonds will be 10% and that the reinvestment rate for coupons will be 8%?

An Example of a Fixed-Income Investment Strategy

To demonstrate a reasonable, active fixed-income portfolio strategy, we discuss here the policies of Sanford Bernstein & Co., as explained in a speech by its manager of fixed-income investments, Francis Trainer. The company believes big bets on general marketwide interest movements are unwise. Instead, it concentrates on exploiting numerous instances of perceived *relative* minor pricing misalignments *within* the fixed-income sector. The firm takes as a risk benchmark the Barclays Aggregate Bond Index, which includes the vast majority of publicly traded bonds with maturities greater than one year. Any deviation from this passive or neutral position must be justified by active analysis. Bernstein considers a neutral portfolio duration to be equal to that of the index.

The firm is willing to make only limited bets on interest rate movements. As Francis Trainer puts it in his speech:

> If we set duration of our portfolios at a level equal to the index and never allow them to vary, this would imply that we are perpetually neutral on the direction of interest rates. However, we believe the utilization of these forecasts will add value and, therefore, we incorporate our economic forecast into the bond management process by altering the durations of our portfolios.
>
> However, in order to prevent fixed-income performance from being dominated by the accuracy of just a single aspect of our research effort, we limit the degree to which we are willing to alter our interest rate exposure. Under the vast majority of circumstances, we will not permit the duration of our portfolios to differ from that of the [Barclays] Index by more than one year.

The company expends most of its effort in exploiting numerous but minor inefficiencies in bond prices that result from lack of attention by its competitors. Its analysts follow about

1,000 securities, attempting to "identify specific securities that are attractive or unattractive as well as identify trends in the richness or cheapness of industries and sectors." These two activities would be characterized as substitution swaps and intermarket spread swaps in the Homer–Leibowitz scheme.

Sanford Bernstein & Co. realizes that market opportunities will arise, if at all, only in sectors of the bond market that present the least competition from other analysts. For this reason, it tends to focus on relatively more complicated bond issues in the belief that extensive research efforts give the firm a comparative advantage in that sector. Finally, the company does not take unnecessary risks. If there do not appear to be enough seemingly attractive bonds, funds are placed in Treasury securities as a "neutral" parking space until new opportunities are identified.

To summarize the key features of this sort of strategy, we make the following observations:

1. A firm such as Bernstein has a respect for market prices. It believes that only minor mispricing usually can be detected. It works toward meaningful abnormal returns by combining numerous *small* profit opportunities, not by hoping for the success of one big bet.
2. To have value, information cannot already be reflected in market prices. A large research staff must focus on market niches that appear to be neglected by others.
3. Interest rate movements are extremely hard to predict, and attempts to time the market can wipe out all the profits of intramarket analysis.

SUMMARY

- Even default-free bonds such as Treasury issues are subject to interest rate risk. Longer-term bonds generally are more sensitive to interest rate shifts than short-term bonds. A measure of the average life of a bond is Macaulay's duration, defined as the weighted average of the times until each payment made by the security, with weights proportional to the present value of the payment.
- Modified duration is a direct measure of the sensitivity of a bond's price to a change in its yield. The proportional change in a bond's price approximately equals the negative of modified duration times the change in the bond's yield.
- Immunization strategies are characteristic of passive bond portfolio management. Such strategies attempt to render the individual or firm immune from movements in interest rates. This may take the form of immunizing net worth or, instead, immunizing the future accumulated value of a bond portfolio.
- Immunization of a fully funded plan is accomplished by matching the durations of assets and liabilities. To maintain an immunized position as time passes and interest rates change, the portfolio must be periodically rebalanced.
- Convexity refers to the curvature of a bond's price-yield relationship. Accounting for convexity can substantially improve on the accuracy of the duration approximation for the response of bond prices to changes in yields.
- A more direct form of immunization is dedication or cash flow matching. If a portfolio is perfectly matched in cash flow with projected liabilities, rebalancing will be unnecessary.
- Active bond management can be decomposed into interest rate forecasting techniques and intermarket spread analysis. One popular taxonomy classifies active strategies as substitution swaps, intermarket spread swaps, rate anticipation swaps, and pure yield pickup swaps.

KEY TERMS

www.mhhe.com/bkm

PROBLEM SETS

Select problems are available in McGraw-Hill's *Connect Finance.* Please see the Supplements section of the book's frontmatter for more information.

Basic

1. How can a perpetuity, which has an infinite maturity, have a duration as short as 10 or 20 years? ***(LO 11-1)***
2. You predict that interest rates are about to fall. Which bond will give you the highest capital gain? ***(LO 11-1)***
   a. Low coupon, long maturity
   b. High coupon, short maturity
   c. High coupon, long maturity
   d. Zero coupon, long maturity
3. The historical yield spread between AAA bonds and Treasury bonds widened dramatically during the credit crisis in 2008. If you believed the spread would soon return to more typical historical levels, what should you have done? This would be an example of what sort of bond swap? ***(LO 11-4)***
4. A bond currently sells for $1,050, which gives it a yield to maturity of 6%. Suppose that if the yield increases by 25 basis points, the price of the bond falls to $1,025. What is the duration of this bond? ***(LO 11-2)***
5. Macaulay's duration is less than modified duration except for: ***(LO 11-2)***
   a. Zero-coupon bonds.
   b. Premium bonds.
   c. Bonds selling at par value.
   d. None of the above.
6. Is the decrease in a bond's price corresponding to an increase in its yield to maturity more or less than the price increase resulting from a decrease in yield of equal magnitude? ***(LO 11-3)***
7. Short-term interest rates are more volatile than long-term rates. Despite this, the rates of return of long-term bonds are more volatile than returns on short-term securities. How can these two empirical observations be reconciled? ***(LO 11-1)***
8. Find the duration of a 6% coupon bond making *annual* coupon payments if it has three years until maturity and a yield to maturity of 6%. What is the duration if the yield to maturity is 10%? ***(LO 11-2)***
9. A nine-year bond has a yield of 10% and a duration of 7.194 years. If the bond's yield changes by 50 basis points, what is the percentage change in the bond's price? ***(LO 11-2)***

Intermediate

10. A pension plan is obligated to make disbursements of $1 million, $2 million, and $1 million at the end of each of the next three years, respectively. Find the duration of the plan's obligations if the interest rate is 10% annually. ***(LO 11-2)***
11. If the plan in the previous problem wants to fully fund and immunize its position, how much of its portfolio should it allocate to one-year zero-coupon bonds and perpetuities, respectively, if these are the only two assets funding the plan? ***(LO 11-4)***
12. You own a fixed-income asset with a duration of five years. If the level of interest rates, which is currently 8%, goes down by 10 basis points, how much do you expect the price of the asset to go up (in percentage terms)? ***(LO 11-2)***
13. Rank the interest rate sensitivity of the following pairs of bonds. ***(LO 11-1)***
    a. Bond A is an 8% coupon, 20-year maturity bond selling at par value.
    Bond B is an 8% coupon, 20-year maturity bond selling below par value.
    b. Bond A is a 20-year, noncallable coupon bond with a coupon rate of 8%, selling at par.
    Bond B is a 20-year, callable bond with a coupon rate of 9%, also selling at par.

14. Long-term Treasury bonds currently are selling at yields to maturity of nearly 8%. You expect interest rates to fall. The rest of the market thinks that they will remain unchanged over the coming year. In each question, choose the bond that will provide the higher capital gain if you are correct. Briefly explain your answer. ***(LO 11-2)***
    a. (1) A Baa-rated bond with coupon rate 8% and time to maturity 20 years.
    (2) An Aaa-rated bond with coupon rate 8% and time to maturity 20 years.
    b. (1) An A-rated bond with coupon rate 4% and maturity 20 years, callable at 105.
    (2) An A-rated bond with coupon rate 8% and maturity 20 years, callable at 105.
    c. (1) A 6% coupon noncallable T-bond with maturity 20 years and YTM = 8%.
    (2) A 9% coupon noncallable T-bond with maturity 20 years and YTM = 8%.
15. You will be paying $10,000 a year in tuition expenses at the end of the next two years. Bonds currently yield 8%. ***(LO 11-2)***
    a. What is the present value and duration of your obligation?
    b. What maturity zero-coupon bond would immunize your obligation?
    c. Suppose you buy a zero-coupon bond with value and duration equal to your obligation. Now suppose that rates immediately increase to 9%. What happens to your net position, that is, to the difference between the value of the bond and that of your tuition obligation? What if rates fall to 7%?
16. Pension funds pay lifetime annuities to recipients. If a firm remains in business indefinitely, the pension obligation will resemble a perpetuity. Suppose, therefore, that you are managing a pension fund with obligations to make perpetual payments of $2 million per year to beneficiaries. The yield to maturity on all bonds is 16%. ***(LO 11-4)***
    a. If the duration of 5-year maturity bonds with coupon rates of 12% (paid annually) is 4 years and the duration of 20-year maturity bonds with coupon rates of 6% (paid annually) is 11 years, how much of each of these coupon bonds (in market value) will you want to hold to both fully fund and immunize your obligation?
    b. What will be the *par value* of your holdings in the 20-year coupon bond?
17. Frank Meyers, CFA, is a fixed-income portfolio manager for a large pension fund. A member of the Investment Committee, Fred Spice, is very interested in learning about the management of fixed-income portfolios. Spice has approached Meyers with several questions. Specifically, Spice would like to know how fixed-income managers position portfolios to capitalize on their expectations of future interest rates.

    Meyers decides to illustrate fixed-income trading strategies to Spice using a fixed-rate bond and note. Both bonds have semiannual coupon periods. Unless otherwise stated all interest rate (yield curve) changes are parallel. The characteristics of these securities are shown in the following table. He also considers a nine-year floating-rate bond (floater) that pays a floating rate semiannually and is currently yielding 5%.

Characteristics of Fixed-Rate Bond and Fixed-Rate Note

	Fixed-Rate Bond	Fixed-Rate Note
Price	107.18	100.00
Yield to maturity	5.00%	5.00%
Period to maturity	18	8
Modified duration	6.9848	3.5851

Spice asks Meyers about how a fixed-income manager would position his portfolio to capitalize on expectations of increasing interest rates. Which of the following would be the most appropriate strategy? ***(LO 11-5)***
a. Shorten his portfolio duration.
b. Buy fixed-rate bonds.
c. Lengthen his portfolio duration.

18. Spice asks Meyers (see previous problem) to quantify price changes from changes in interest rates. To illustrate, Meyers computes the value change for the fixed-rate note in the table. Specifically, he assumes an increase in the level of interest rate of 100 basis points. Using the information in the table, what is the predicted change in the price of the fixed-rate note? *(LO 11-2)*
19. You are managing a portfolio of $1 million. Your target duration is 10 years, and you can choose from two bonds: a zero-coupon bond with maturity 5 years, and a perpetuity, each currently yielding 5%. *(LO 11-4)*
    a. How much of each bond will you hold in your portfolio?
    b. How will these fractions change *next year* if target duration is now nine years?

eXcel Please visit us at **www.mhhe.com/bkm**

20. Find the duration of a bond with settlement date May 27, 2012, and maturity date November 15, 2021. The coupon rate of the bond is 7%, and the bond pays coupons semi-annually. The bond is selling at a yield to maturity of 8%. You can use Spreadsheet 11.2, available at **www.mhhe.com/bkm;** link to Chapter 11 material. *(LO 11-2)*

eXcel Please visit us at **www.mhhe.com/bkm**

21. What is the duration of the bond in the previous problem if coupons are paid annually? Explain why the duration changes in the direction it does. *(LO 11-2)*
22. You manage a pension fund that will provide retired workers with lifetime annuities. You determine that the payouts of the fund are essentially going to resemble level perpetuities of $1 million per year. The interest rate is 10%. You plan to fully fund the obligation using 5-year and 20-year maturity zero-coupon bonds. *(LO 11-2)*
    a. How much *market value* of each of the zeros will be necessary to fund the plan if you desire an immunized position?
    b. What must be the *face value* of the two zeros to fund the plan?

eXcel Please visit us at **www.mhhe.com/bkm**

23. Find the convexity of a seven-year maturity, 6% coupon bond selling at a yield to maturity of 8%. The bond pays its coupons annually. (*Hint:* You can use the spreadsheet from this chapter's Excel Application on Convexity, setting cash flows after year 7 equal to zero. The spreadsheet is available at **www.mhhe.com/bkm;** link to Chapter 11 material.) *(LO 11-3)*

eXcel Please visit us at **www.mhhe.com/bkm**

24. *a.* Use a spreadsheet to calculate the durations of the two bonds in Spreadsheet 11.1 if the interest rate increases to 12%. Why does the duration of the coupon bond fall while that of the zero remains unchanged? (*Hint:* Examine what happens to the weights computed in column E.)
    b. Use the same spreadsheet to calculate the duration of the coupon bond if the coupon were 12% instead of 8%. Explain why the duration is lower. (Again, start by looking at column E.) *(LO 11-2)*

eXcel Please visit us at **www.mhhe.com/bkm**

25. *a.* Footnote 2 in the chapter presents the formula for the convexity of a bond. Build a spreadsheet to calculate the convexity of the 8% coupon bond in Spreadsheet 11.1 at the initial yield to maturity of 10%.
    b. What is the convexity of the zero-coupon bond? *(LO 11-3)*

eXcel Please visit us at **www.mhhe.com/bkm**

26. A 30-year maturity bond making annual coupon payments with a coupon rate of 12% has duration of 11.54 years and convexity of 192.4. The bond currently sells at a yield to maturity of 8%. Use a financial calculator or spreadsheet to find the price of the bond if its yield to maturity falls to 7% or rises to 9%. What prices for the bond at these new yields would be predicted by the duration rule and the duration-with-convexity rule? What is the percent error for each rule? What do you conclude about the accuracy of the two rules? *(LO 11-3)*
27. Currently, the term structure is as follows: One-year bonds yield 7%, two-year bonds yield 8%, three-year bonds and greater maturity bonds all yield 9%. You are choosing between one-, two-, and three-year maturity bonds all paying *annual* coupons of 8%, once a year. Which bond should you buy if you strongly believe that at year-end the yield curve will be flat at 9%? *(LO 11-5)*
28. A 30-year maturity bond has a 7% coupon rate, paid annually. It sells today for $867.42. A 20-year maturity bond has a 6.5% coupon rate, also paid annually. It sells today for

$879.50. A bond market analyst forecasts that in five years, 25-year maturity bonds will sell at yields to maturity of 8% and that 15-year maturity bonds will sell at yields of 7.5%. Because the yield curve is upward-sloping, the analyst believes that coupons will be invested in short-term securities at a rate of 6%. Which bond offers the higher expected rate of return over the five-year period? ***(LO 11-5)***

Challenge

29. A 12.75-year maturity zero-coupon bond selling at a yield to maturity of 8% (effective annual yield) has convexity of 150.3 and modified duration of 11.81 years. A 30-year maturity 6% coupon bond making annual coupon payments also selling at a yield to maturity of 8% has nearly identical modified duration—11.79 years—but considerably higher convexity of 231.2. ***(LO 11-3)***
    a. Suppose the yield to maturity on both bonds increases to 9%. What will be the actual percentage capital loss on each bond? What percentage capital loss would be predicted by the duration-with-convexity rule?
    b. Repeat part (*a*), but this time assume the yield to maturity decreases to 7%.
    c. Compare the performance of the two bonds in the two scenarios, one involving an increase in rates, the other a decrease. Based on their comparative investment performance, explain the attraction of convexity.
    d. In view of your answer to (*c*), do you think it would be possible for two bonds with equal duration, but different convexity, to be priced initially at the same yield to maturity if the yields on both bonds always increased or decreased by equal amounts, as in this example? Would anyone be willing to buy the bond with lower convexity under these circumstances?

CFA Problems

CFA® PROBLEMS

1. Rank the following bonds in order of descending duration. ***(LO 11-2)***

Bond	Coupon	Time to Maturity	Yield to Maturity
A	15%	20 years	10%
B	15	15	10
C	0	20	10
D	8	20	10
E	15	15	15

2. Philip Morris has issued bonds that pay annually with the following characteristics: ***(LO 11-2)***

Coupon	Yield to Maturity	Maturity	Macaulay Duration
8%	8%	15 years	10 years

    a. Calculate modified duration using the information above.
    b. Explain why modified duration is a better measure than maturity when calculating the bond's sensitivity to changes in interest rates.
    c. Identify the direction of change in modified duration if:
        i. The coupon of the bond were 4%, not 8%.
        ii. The maturity of the bond were 7 years, not 15 years.
3. As part of your analysis of debt issued by Monticello Corporation, you are asked to evaluate two specific bond issues, shown in the table below. ***(LO 11-2)***

MONTICELLO CORPORATION BOND INFORMATION

	Bond A (callable)	Bond B (noncallable)
Maturity	2019	2019
Coupon	11.50%	7.25%
Current price	125.75	100.00
Yield to maturity	7.70%	7.25%
Modified duration to maturity	6.20	6.80
Call date	2013	—
Call price	105	—
Yield to call	5.10%	—
Modified duration to call	3.10	—

a. Using the duration and yield information in the table, compare the price and yield behavior of the two bonds under each of the following two scenarios:
   i. Strong economic recovery with rising inflation expectations.
   ii. Economic recession with reduced inflation expectations.

b. Using the information in the table, calculate the projected price change for bond B if the yield-to-maturity for this bond falls by 75 basis points.

c. Describe the shortcoming of analyzing bond A strictly to call or to maturity.

4. One common goal among fixed-income portfolio managers is to earn high incremental returns on corporate bonds versus government bonds of comparable durations. The approach of some corporate-bond portfolio managers is to find and purchase those corporate bonds having the largest initial spreads over comparable-duration government bonds. John Ames, HFS's fixed-income manager, believes that a more rigorous approach is required if incremental returns are to be maximized.

   The following table presents data relating to one set of corporate/government spread relationships (in basis points, bp) present in the market at a given date: ***(LO 11-5)***

CURRENT AND EXPECTED SPREADS AND DURATIONS OF HIGH-GRADE CORPORATE BONDS (ONE-YEAR HORIZON)

Bond Rating	Initial Spread over Governments	Expected Horizon Spread	Initial Duration	Expected Duration One Year from Now
Aaa	31 bp	31 bp	4 years	3.1 years
Aa	40	50	4	3.1

a. Recommend purchase of *either* Aaa *or* Aa bonds for a one-year investment horizon given a goal of maximizing incremental returns.

b. Ames chooses not to rely solely on initial spread relationships. His analytical framework considers a full range of other key variables likely to impact realized incremental returns, including call provisions and potential changes in interest rates. Describe other variables that Ames should include in his analysis, and explain how each of these could cause realized incremental returns to differ from those indicated by initial spread relationships.

5. Noah Kramer, a fixed-income portfolio manager based in the country of Sevista, is considering the purchase of a Sevista government bond. Kramer decides to evaluate two strategies for implementing his investment in Sevista bonds. Table 11.6 gives the details of the two strategies, and Table 11.7 contains the assumptions that apply to both strategies.

TABLE 11.6 Investment strategies (amounts are market value invested)

Strategy	5-Year Maturity (Modified Duration = 4.83 Years)	15-Year Maturity (Modified Duration = 14.35 Years)	25-Year Maturity (Modified Duration = 23.81 Years)
I	$5 million	0	$5 million
II	0	$10 million	0

TABLE 11.7 Investment strategy assumptions

Market Value of Bonds	$10 Million
Bond maturities	5 and 25 years or 15 years
Bond coupon rates	0.00%
Target modified duration	15 years

Before choosing one of the two bond investment strategies, Kramer wants to analyze how the market value of the bonds will change if an instantaneous interest rate shift occurs immediately after his investment. The details of the interest rate shift are shown in Table 11.8. Calculate, for the instantaneous interest rate shift shown in Table 11.8, the percent change in the market value of the bonds that will occur under each strategy. *(LO 11-2)*

TABLE 11.8 Instantaneous interest rate shift immediately after investment

Maturity	Interest Rate Change
5 year	Down 75 basis points
15	Up 25 bp
25	Up 50 bp

6. *a.* Janet Meer is a fixed-income portfolio manager. Noting that the current shape of the yield curve is flat, she considers the purchase of a newly issued, option-free corporate bond priced at par; the bond is described in Table 11.9. Calculate the duration of the bond.

TABLE 11.9 7% option-free bond, maturity = 10 years

	Change in Yields	
	Up 10 Basis Points	Down 10 Basis Points
Price	99.29	100.71
Convexity	35.00	

b. Meer is also considering the purchase of a second newly issued, option-free corporate bond, which is described in Table 11.10. She wants to evaluate this second bond's price sensitivity to an instantaneous, downward parallel shift in the yield curve of 200 basis points. Estimate the total percentage price change for the bond if the yield curve experiences an instantaneous, downward parallel shift of 200 basis points. *(LO 11-2)*

TABLE 11.10 7.25% option-free bond, maturity = 12 years

Original issue price	Par value, to yield 7.25%
Modified duration (at original price)	7.90
Convexity measure	41.55
Convexity adjustment (yield change of 200 basis points)	1.66

7. Sandra Kapple presents Maria VanHusen with a description, given in the following exhibit, of the bond portfolio held by the Star Hospital Pension Plan. All securities in the bond portfolio are noncallable U.S. Treasury securities. ***(LO 11-2)***

STAR HOSPITAL PENSION PLAN BOND PORTFOLIO

				Price if Yields Change		
Par Value (U.S. $)	**Treasury Security**	**Market Value (U.S. $)**	**Current Price**	**Up 100 Basis Points**	**Down 100 Basis Points**	**Effective Duration**
$48,000,000	2.375% due 2010	$48,667,680	$101.391	99.245	103.595	2.15
50,000,000	4.75% due 2035	50,000,000	100.000	86.372	116.887	
98,000,000	Total bond portfolio	98,667,680	—	—	—	

a. Calculate the effective duration of each of the following:
   i. The 4.75% Treasury security due 2035
   ii. The total bond portfolio

b. VanHusen remarks to Kapple, "If you changed the maturity structure of the bond portfolio to result in a portfolio duration of 5.25, the price sensitivity of that portfolio would be identical to the price sensitivity of a single, noncallable Treasury security that has a duration of 5.25." In what circumstance would VanHusen's remark be correct?

8. The ability to *immunize* a bond portfolio is very desirable for bond portfolio managers in some instances. ***(LO 11-4)***

a. Discuss the components of interest rate risk—that is, assuming a change in interest rates over time, explain the two risks faced by the holder of a bond.

b. Define *immunization* and discuss why a bond manager would immunize his or her portfolio.

c. Explain why a duration-matching strategy is a superior technique to a maturity-matching strategy for the minimization of interest rate risk.

9. You are the manager for the bond portfolio of a pension fund. The policies of the fund allow for the use of active strategies in managing the bond portfolio.

It appears that the economic cycle is beginning to mature, inflation is expected to accelerate, and, in an effort to contain the economic expansion, central bank policy is moving toward constraint. For each of the situations below, state which one of the two bonds you would prefer. Briefly justify your answer in each case. ***(LO 11-5)***

a. Government of Canada (Canadian pay), 4% due in 2017, and priced at 101.25 to yield 3.50% to maturity;

or

Government of Canada (Canadian pay), 4% due in 2027, and priced at 95.75 to yield 4.19% to maturity.

b. Texas Power and Light Co., 5½% due in 2022, rated AAA, and priced at 85 to yield 8.1% to maturity;

or

Arizona Public Service Co., 5.45% due in 2022, rated A−, and priced at 80 to yield 9.1% to maturity.

c. Commonwealth Edison, 2¾% due in 2021, rated Baa, and priced at 81 to yield 7.2% to maturity;

or

Commonwealth Edison, 9⅜% due in 2021, rated Baa, and priced at 114 to yield 7.2% to maturity.

d. Shell Oil Co., 6¾% sinking fund debentures due in 2026, rated AAA (sinking fund begins in 2015 at par), and priced at 89 to yield 7.1% to maturity;

or

Warner-Lambert, 6⅞% sinking fund debentures due in 2026, rated AAA (sinking fund begins in 2016 at par), and priced at 95 to yield 7% to maturity.

e. Bank of Montreal (Canadian pay), 4% certificates of deposit due in 2014, rated AAA, and priced at 100 to yield 4% to maturity;

or

Bank of Montreal (Canadian pay), floating-rate notes due in 2018, rated AAA. Coupon currently set at 3.7% and priced at 100 (coupon adjusted semiannually to .5% above the three-month Government of Canada Treasury bill rate).

10. *a.* Which set of conditions will result in a bond with the greatest price volatility? ***(LO 11-1)***
    (1) A high coupon and a short maturity.
    (2) A high coupon and a long maturity.
    (3) A low coupon and a short maturity.
    (4) A low coupon and a long maturity.

    b. An investor who expects declining interest rates would be likely to purchase a bond that has a ______________ coupon and a ______________term to maturity. ***(LO 11-1)***
    (1) Low, long
    (2) High, short
    (3) High, long
    (4) Zero, long

    c. With a zero-coupon bond: ***(LO 11-1)***
    (1) Duration equals the weighted-average term to maturity.
    (2) Term to maturity equals duration.
    (3) Weighted-average term to maturity equals the term to maturity.
    (4) All of the above.

    d. As compared with bonds selling at par, deep discount bonds will have: ***(LO 11-1)***
    (1) Greater reinvestment risk.
    (2) Greater price volatility.
    (3) Less call protection.
    (4) None of the above.

11. A member of a firm's investment committee is very interested in learning about the management of fixed-income portfolios. He would like to know how fixed-income managers position portfolios to capitalize on their expectations concerning three factors which influence interest rates. Assuming that no investment policy limitations apply, formulate and describe a fixed-income portfolio management strategy for each of the following interest rate factors that could be used to exploit a portfolio manager's expectations about that factor. (*Note:* Three strategies are required, one for each of the listed factors.) ***(LO 11-5)***

    a. Changes in the level of interest rates.
    b. Changes in yield spreads across/between sectors.
    c. Changes in yield spreads as to a particular instrument.

12. The following bond swaps could have been made in recent years as investors attempted to increase the total return on their portfolio.

From the information presented below, identify possible reason(s) that investors may have made each swap. ***(LO 11-5)***

Action		Call	Price	YTM (%)
a. Sell	Baa1 Electric Pwr. 1st mtg. 6⅜% due 2017	108.24	95	7.71
Buy	Baa1 Electric Pwr. 1st mtg. 2⅜% due 2018	105.20	79	7.39
b. Sell	Aaa Phone Co. notes 5½% due 2018	101.50	90	7.02
Buy	U.S. Treasury notes 6½% due 2018	NC	97.15	6.78
c. Sell	Aa1 Apex Bank zero coupon due 2020	NC	45	7.51
Buy	Aa1 Apex Bank float rate notes due 2033	103.90	90	—
d. Sell	A1 Commonwealth Oil & Gas 1st mtg. 6% due 2023	105.75	72	8.09
Buy	U.S. Treasury bond 5½% due 2029	NC	80.60	7.40
e. Sell	A1 Z mart convertible deb. 3% due 2023	103.90	62	6.92
Buy	A2 Lucky Ducks deb. 7¾% due 2029	109.86	75	10.43

WEB *master*

1. Use data from **finance.yahoo.com** to answer the following questions. Enter the stock symbol "S" to locate information for Sprint Nextel Corp. Find the company's most recent annual balance sheet in the *Financials* section.
   a. Examine the company's assets and liabilities. What proportion of total assets are current assets? What proportion of total liabilities are current liabilities? Does it seem that there is a good match between the duration of the assets and the duration of the liabilities?
   b. Look at the *Annual Statement of Cash Flows* for Sprint Nextel, which is also found in the *Financials* section. Check the *Financing Activities* section to see if the company has issued new debt or reduced its debt outstanding. How much interest did the firm pay during the period?
   c. Repeat the exercise with several other companies of your choice. Try to pick companies in different industries. Do you notice any patterns that might be due to the industrial environments in which the firms operate?
2. Many bond calculators are offered on the web. You can retrieve information about a particular bond issue and then calculate duration and convexity with the click of a button.
   a. Select a bond from the most actively traded corporate bond list at **www.investinginbonds.com.** Go to the *Bond Markets and Prices* link; then select *Corporate Market At-a-Glance* to link to the most active list. Select a bond that has a maturity date a few years away and click on its CUSIP number to find further information.
   b. Choose the most recent trading date listed and click on the *Run Calculations* link. The bond's characteristics are entered for you.
   c. Confirm the amount of the accrued interest and the cash flow schedule listed.
   d. Confirm the bond's duration by either performing the calculations in a spreadsheet or using Excel's DURATION function.
   e. Based on the bond's current price, by what percent would the price change if the yield were to change by .5%?
   f. Repeat the calculations by entering assumed prices of 90, 100, and 110; then answer the following questions:
      i. What are the duration and the convexity for the bond at the each of the prices?
      ii. Is the bond price more or less sensitive to interest rates at higher prices relative to lower ones? How does convexity change as the price changes? Is the change in convexity symmetrical? That is, as the price decreases by $10 (from 100 to 90) and increases by $10 (from 100 to 110), are the changes in convexity equal but opposite in sign?

SOLUTIONS TO CONCEPT checks

11.1 Interest rate: 0.09

	(B) Time until Payment (years)	(C) Payment	(D) Payment Discounted at 9%	(E) Weight	Column (B) times Column (E)
A. 8% coupon bond	1	80	73.394	0.0753	0.0753
	2	80	67.334	0.0691	0.1382
	3	1,080	833.958	0.8556	2.5668
Sum:			974.687	1.0000	2.7803
B. Zero-coupon bond	1	0	0.000	0.0000	0.0000
	2	0	0.000	0.0000	0.0000
	3	1,000	772.183	1.0000	3.0000
Sum:			772.183	1.0000	3.0000

The duration of the 8% coupon bond rises to 2.7803 years. Price increases to $974.687. The duration of the zero-coupon bond is unchanged at 3 years, although its price also increases when the interest rate falls.

11.2 *a.* If the interest rate increases from 9% to 9.05%, the bond price falls from $974.687 to $973.445. The percentage change in price is −.127%.

b. The duration formula would predict a price change of

$$-\frac{2.7802}{1.09} \times .0005 = -.00127 = -.127\%$$

which is the same answer that we obtained from direct computation in part (*a*).

11.3 Use Excel to confirm that DURATION(DATE(2000,1,1), DATE(2008,1,1), .09, .10, 1) = 5.97 years. If you change the last argument of the duration function from 1 to 2 (to allow for semiannual coupons), you will find that DURATION(DATE(2000,1,1), DATE(2008,1,1), .09, .10, 2) = 5.80 years. Duration is lower when coupons are paid semiannually rather than annually because, on average, payments come earlier. Instead of waiting until year-end to receive the annual coupon, investors receive half the coupon midway through the year.

11.4 The duration of a level perpetuity is $(1 + y)/y$ or $1 + 1/y$, which clearly falls as y increases. Tabulating duration as a function of y we get:

y	*D*
.01 (i.e., 1%)	101 years
.02	51
.05	21
.10	11
.20	6
.25	5
.40	3.5

11.5 The perpetuity's duration now would be 1.08/.08 = 13.5. We need to solve the following equation for w

$$w \times 2 + (1 - w) \times 13.5 = 6$$

Therefore, $w = .6522$.

11.6 *a.* The present value of the fund's obligation is \$800,000/.08 = \$10 million. The duration is 13.5 years. Therefore, the fund should invest \$10 million in zeros with a 13.5-year maturity. The face value of the zeros will be $\$10,000,000 \times 1.08^{13.5} =$ \$28,263,159.

b. When the interest rate increases to 8.1%, the present value of the fund's obligation drops to 800,000/.081 = \$9,876,543. The value of the zero-coupon bond falls by roughly the same amount, to $\$28,263,159/1.081^{13.5} = \$9,875,835$. The duration of the perpetual obligation falls to 1.081/.081 = 13.346 years. The fund should sell the zero it currently holds and purchase \$9,876,543 in zero-coupon bonds with maturity of 13.346 years.

11.7 Dedication would be more attractive. Cash flow matching eliminates the need for rebalancing and, thus, saves transaction costs.

11.8 Current price = \$1,091.29

Forecast price = \$100 × Annuity factor (10%,18 years) + \$1,000 × PV factor(10%,18 years) = \$1,000

The future value of reinvested coupons will be (\$100 × 1.08) + \$100 = \$208

$$\text{The two-year return is } \frac{\$208 + (\$1{,}000 - \$1{,}091.29)}{\$1{,}091.29} = .107, \text{ or } 10.7\%$$

The annualized rate of return over the two-year period would then be $(1.107)^{1/2} - 1 = .052$, or 5.2%.

Security Analysis

PART

4

Tell your friends or relatives that you are studying investments and they will ask you, "What stocks should I buy?" This is the question at the heart of security analysis. How do analysts choose the stocks and other securities to hold in their portfolios?

Security analysis requires a wide mix of skills. You need to be a decent economist with a good grasp of both macroeconomics and microeconomics, the former to help you form forecasts of the general direction of the market and the latter to help you assess the relative position of particular industries or firms. You need a good sense of demographic and social trends to help identify industries with bright prospects. You need to be a quick study of the ins and outs of particular industries to choose the firms that will succeed within each industry. You need a good accounting background to analyze the financial statements that firms provide to the public. You also need to have mastered corporate finance, since security analysis at its core is the ability to value a firm. In short, a good security analyst will be a generalist, with a grasp of the widest range of financial issues. This is where there is the biggest premium on "putting it all together."

The chapters in Part Four are an introduction to security analysis. We will provide you with a "top-down" approach to the subject, starting with an overview of international, macroeconomic, and industry issues, and only then progressing to the analysis of particular firms. These topics form the core of fundamental analysis. After reading these chapters, you will have a good sense of the various techniques used to analyze stocks and the stock market.

Chapters in This Part:

Macroeconomic and Industry Analysis

Chapter

12

Learning Objectives:

LO12-1 Predict the effect of exchange rates as well as monetary, fiscal, and supply-side policies on business conditions.

LO12-2 Use leading, coincident, and lagging economic indicators to describe and predict the economy's path through the business cycle.

LO12-3 Predict which industries will be more or less sensitive to business-cycle fluctuations.

LO12-4 Analyze the effect of industry life cycles and competitive structure on earnings prospects.

fundamental analysis

The analysis of determinants of firm value, such as prospects for earnings and dividends.

To determine a proper price for a firm's stock, the security analyst must forecast the dividends and earnings that can be expected from the firm. This is the heart of **fundamental analysis,** that is, the analysis of determinants of value such as earnings prospects. Ultimately, the business success of the firm determines the dividends it can pay to shareholders and the price it will command in the stock market. Because the prospects of the firm are tied to those of the broader economy, however, valuation analyses must consider the business environment in which the firm operates. For some firms, macroeconomic and industry circumstances might have a greater influence on profits than the firm's relative performance within its industry. In other words, investors need to keep the big economic picture in mind.

Therefore, in analyzing a firm's prospects it often makes sense to start with the broad economic environment, examining the state of the aggregate economy and even the international economy. From there, one considers the implications of the outside environment on the industry in which the firm operates. Finally, the firm's position within the industry is examined.

This chapter examines the broad-based aspects of fundamental analysis—macroeconomic and industry analysis. The following two chapters cover firm-specific analysis. We begin with a discussion of international factors relevant to firm performance and move on to an overview of the significance of the key variables usually used to summarize the state of the economy. We then discuss government macroeconomic policy and the determination of interest rates. We conclude the analysis of the macroeconomic environment with a discussion of business cycles. Next, we move to industry analysis, treating issues concerning the sensitivity of the firm to the business cycle, the typical life cycle of an industry, and strategic issues that affect industry performance.

Related websites for this chapter are available at www.mhhe.com/bkm.

12.1 THE GLOBAL ECONOMY

A top-down analysis of a firm's prospects must start with the global economy. The international economy might affect a firm's export prospects, the price competition it faces from foreign competitors, or the profits it makes on investments abroad. Table 12.1 shows the importance of the global macroeconomy to firms' prospects. The effects of the euro zone debt crisis were widespread in 2011, and fears of a worldwide recession dampened stock markets in virtually all countries. Market returns across the world ranged from strikingly negative to just barely positive, reflecting the feared global slowdown.

Despite the obvious importance of global macroeconomic factors, there is also considerable variation in economic performance across countries. The Greek economy was expected to continue its painful contraction, with a forecast decline in GDP of 7.5% in 2012. At the other extreme, China's rapid growth was expected to continue, with a forecast expansion in 2012 of 8.2%. You can see from the table that the European economies were expected to be under the greatest stress in 2012 as the euro crisis continued, with expected growth rates all around zero.

TABLE 12.1 Economic performance

	Stock Market Return (%), 2011		
	In Local Currency	**In U.S. Dollars**	**Forecast Growth in GDP (%), 2012**
Brazil	−22.9	−28.9	3.5
Britain	−3.9	−4.2	0.2
Canada	−9.1	−10.9	2.0
China	−22.7	−19.1	8.2
France	−16.1	−19.2	−0.3
Germany	−11.6	−14.9	0.1
Greece	−53.2	−54.9	−7.5
India	−22.6	−34.6	7.8
Italy	−24.0	−26.9	−1.1
Japan	−16.3	−11.6	1.7
Mexico	−3.0	−12.9	3.1
Russia	−15.4	−19.0	3.7
Singapore	−15.0	−15.5	4.0
South Korea	−9.0	−10.1	3.8
Thailand	0.3	−3.9	3.1
U.S.	1.6	1.6	2.0

Source: *The Economist,* January 7, 2012. © 2012 The Economist Newspaper Limited, London. Reprinted with permission via Copyright Clearance Center.

Asia was forecast to have much healthier growth, and the so-called BRIC countries (Brazil, Russia, India, and China), often grouped together because of their rapid recent development, were by and large expected to continue that performance.

These data illustrate that the national economic environment can be a crucial determinant of industry performance. It is far harder for businesses to succeed in a contracting economy than in an expanding one. This observation highlights the role of a big-picture macroeconomic analysis as a fundamental part of the investment process.

In addition, the global environment presents political risks of considerable magnitude. The euro crisis offers a compelling illustration of the interplay between politics and economics. The prospects of a bailout for Greece, as well as support for struggling but much larger economies such as Italy or Spain, are in large part political issues, but with enormous consequences for the world economy. Government bailouts of large banks during the financial crisis of 2008–2009 were similarly the stage for pitched political battles with huge economic consequences. And, of course, the ongoing political battle over government budget deficits is of tremendous import for the economy. At this level of analysis, it is clear that politics and economics are intimately entwined.

Other political issues that are less sensational but still extremely important to economic growth and investment returns include issues of protectionism and trade policy, the free flow of capital, and the status of a nation's workforce.

exchange rate

The rate at which domestic currency can be converted into foreign currency.

One obvious factor that affects the international competitiveness of a country's industries is the exchange rate between that country's currency and other currencies. The **exchange rate** is the rate at which domestic currency can be converted into foreign currency. For example, in early 2012, it took about 77 Japanese yen to purchase one U.S. dollar. We would say that the exchange rate is ¥77 per dollar or, equivalently, $.013 per yen.

As exchange rates fluctuate, the dollar value of goods priced in foreign currency similarly fluctuates. For example, in 1980, the dollar–yen exchange rate was about $.0045 per yen. Since the exchange rate in 2012 was $.013 per yen, a U.S. citizen would have needed 2.88 times as many dollars in 2012 to buy a product selling for ¥10,000 as would have been required in 1980. If the Japanese producer were to maintain a fixed yen price for its product, the price expressed in U.S. dollars would nearly triple. This would make Japanese products more expensive to U.S. consumers, however, and result in lost sales. Obviously, appreciation of the yen creates a problem for Japanese producers such as automakers that must compete with U.S. producers.

The nearby box discusses Honda's response to the dramatic increase in the value of the yen. It is moving a good part of its manufacturing operations to North America to take advantage of the reduced cost of production (as measured in yen) in the U.S. and Mexico. Moreover, by moving some production to North America, Honda diversifies its exposure to future exchange rate fluctuations.

Figure 12.1 shows the change in the purchasing power of the U.S. dollar relative to the purchasing power of several major currencies in the last decade. The ratio of purchasing

FIGURE 12.1

Change in real exchange rate: U.S. dollar versus major currencies, 1999–2010

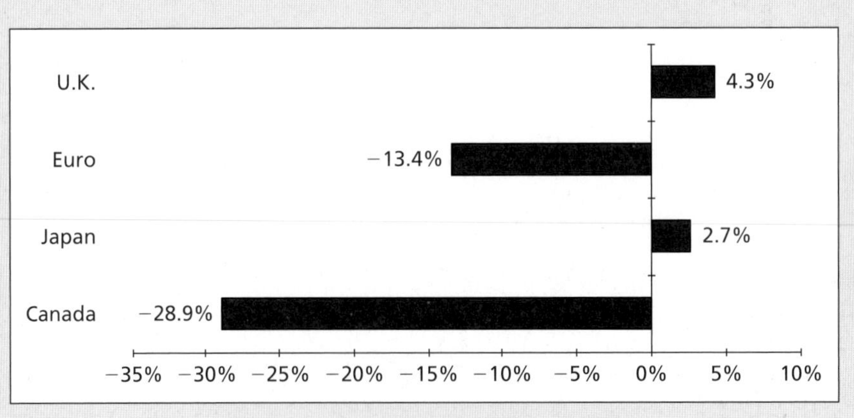

On the MARKET FRONT

HONDA REVS UP OUTSIDE JAPAN

Honda Motor Co. plans to shift a major chunk of its manufacturing to North America over the next two years, bulking up production capacity in the region by as much as 40% to combat a strengthening yen that has made Japanese cars too expensive to export around the world.

The drive to bulk up in North America is led by the yen's strength against the U.S. dollar, a change that is causing Honda and other Japanese automakers to lose money on many of the vehicles they now export from Japan. A stronger yen erodes the value of dollar-denominated profit and makes exports less price competitive.

Honda, which produced 1.29 million vehicles in North America in 2010, plans to build a new plant in Celaya, Mexico, and expand all seven of its existing assembly plants, aiming to build just short of 2 million cars and trucks a year, Tetsuo Iwamura, president of American Honda, the company's North American arm, said in an interview with *The Wall Street Journal.*

The strategic shift is "directly linked to the yen," Mr. Iwamura said. "It is virtually impossible to make money [on exporting vehicles from Japan] in the short and medium term."

Honda's shift is indicative of the broad impact the yen is having on Japanese automakers facing a currency that has strengthened by nearly 40% in the last four years. The yen was trading at 77.89 to the dollar Tuesday and as recently as 2007 was at 120 to the dollar.

The dramatic strengthening of the yen makes it particularly hard to make money on small cars because profit margins are already thin. To help reduce the number of Fits that Honda exports from Japan, the company recently began shipping Fit cars from China to Canadian dealers as a stopgap measure.

SOURCE: Excerpted from Mike Ramsey and Neal E. Boudette, "Honda Revs Up outside Japan," *The Wall Street Journal,* December 21, 2011. Reprinted by permission of *The Wall Street Journal,* Copyright © 2011 Dow Jones & Company, Inc. All Rights Reserved Worldwide.

powers is called the "real" or inflation-adjusted exchange rate. The change in the real exchange rate measures how much more or less expensive foreign goods have become to U.S. citizens, accounting for both exchange rate fluctuations and inflation differentials across countries. A positive value in Figure 12.1 means that the dollar has gained purchasing power relative to another currency; a negative number indicates a depreciating dollar. Therefore, the figure shows that goods priced in terms of euros or Canadian dollars became considerably more expensive to U.S. consumers in the last 10 years but that goods priced in British pounds or yen became slightly cheaper. Conversely, goods priced in U.S. dollars became more expensive to Japanese consumers but more affordable to Canadian consumers.

12.2 THE DOMESTIC MACROECONOMY

The macroeconomy is the environment in which all firms operate. The importance of the macroeconomy in determining investment performance is illustrated in Figure 12.2, which compares the level of the S&P 500 stock price index to estimates of earnings per share of the

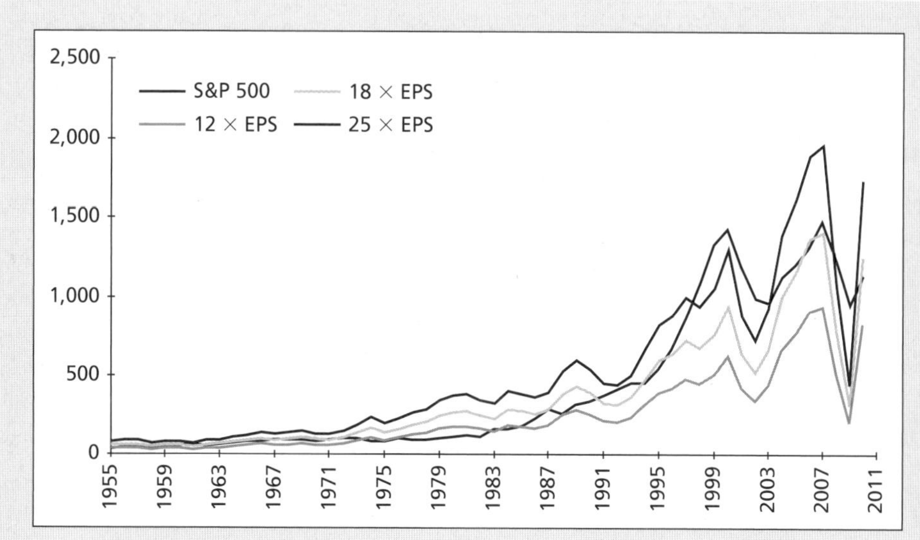

FIGURE 12.2

S&P 500 Index versus earnings per share

Source: Authors' calculations using data from *The Economic Report of the President.*

S&P 500 companies. The graph shows that stock prices tend to rise along with earnings. While the exact ratio of stock price to earnings per share varies with factors such as interest rates, risk, inflation rates, and other variables, the graph does illustrate that, as a general rule, the ratio has tended to be in the range of 12 to 25. Given "normal" price-to-earnings ratios, we would expect the S&P 500 Index to fall within these boundaries. While the earnings-multiplier rule clearly is not perfect—note the dramatic increase in the P/E multiple during the dot-com boom of the late 1990s—it also seems clear that the level of the broad market and aggregate earnings do trend together. Thus, the first step in forecasting the performance of the broad market is to assess the status of the economy as a whole.

The ability to forecast the macroeconomy can translate into spectacular investment performance. But it is not enough to forecast the macroeconomy well. One must forecast it *better* than one's competitors to earn abnormal profits. In this section, we will review some of the key economic statistics used to describe the state of the macroeconomy.

Gross Domestic Product

gross domestic product (GDP)

The market value of goods and services produced over a period of time.

Gross domestic product, or **GDP,** is the measure of the economy's total production of goods and services. Rapidly growing GDP indicates an expanding economy with ample opportunity for a firm to increase sales. Another popular measure of the economy's output is *industrial production.* This statistic provides a measure of economic activity more narrowly focused on the manufacturing side of the economy.

Employment

unemployment rate

The ratio of the number of people classified as unemployed to the total labor force.

The **unemployment rate** is the percentage of the total labor force (i.e., those who are either working or actively seeking employment) yet to find work. The unemployment rate measures the extent to which the economy is operating at full capacity. The unemployment rate is a statistic related to workers only, but further insight into the strength of the economy can be gleaned from the employment rate of other factors of production. For example, analysts also look at the factory *capacity utilization rate,* which is the ratio of actual output from factories to potential output.

Inflation

inflation

The rate at which the general level of prices for goods and services is rising.

Inflation is the rate at which the general level of prices is rising. High rates of inflation often are associated with "overheated" economies, that is, economies where the demand for goods and services is outstripping productive capacity, which leads to upward pressure on prices. Most governments walk a fine line in their economic policies. They hope to stimulate their economies enough to maintain nearly full employment but not so much as to bring on inflationary pressures. The perceived trade-off between inflation and unemployment is at the heart of many macroeconomic policy disputes. There is considerable room for disagreement as to the relative costs of these policies as well as the economy's relative vulnerability to these pressures at any particular time.

Interest Rates

High interest rates reduce the present value of future cash flows, thereby reducing the attractiveness of investment opportunities. For this reason, real interest rates are key determinants of business investment expenditures. Demand for housing and high-priced consumer durables such as automobiles, which are commonly financed, also is highly sensitive to interest rates because interest rates affect interest payments. In Section 12.3 we will examine the determinants of real interest rates.

Budget Deficit

budget deficit

The amount by which government spending exceeds government revenues.

The **budget deficit** of the federal government is the difference between government spending and revenues. Any budgetary shortfall must be offset by government borrowing. Large amounts of government borrowing can force up interest rates by increasing the total demand for credit in the economy. Economists generally believe excessive government borrowing will "crowd out" private borrowing and investing by forcing up interest rates and choking off business investment.

Sentiment

Consumers' and producers' optimism or pessimism concerning the economy are important determinants of economic performance. If consumers have confidence in their future income levels, for example, they will be more willing to spend on big-ticket items. Similarly, businesses will increase production and inventory levels if they anticipate higher demand for their products. In this way, beliefs influence how much consumption and investment will be pursued and affect the aggregate demand for goods and services.

CONCEPT check 12.1

Consider an economy where the dominant industry is automobile production for domestic consumption as well as export. Now suppose the auto market is hurt by an increase in the length of time people use their cars before replacing them. Describe the probable effects of this change on (*a*) GDP, (*b*) unemployment, (*c*) the government budget deficit, and (*d*) interest rates.

12.3 INTEREST RATES

The level of interest rates is perhaps the most important macroeconomic factor to consider in one's investment analysis. Forecasts of interest rates directly affect the forecast of returns in the fixed-income market. If your expectation is that rates will increase by more than the consensus view, you will want to shy away from longer term fixed-income securities. Similarly, increases in interest rates tend to be bad news for the stock market. Unanticipated increases in rates generally are associated with stock market declines. Thus, a superior technique to forecast rates would be of immense value to an investor attempting to determine the best asset allocation for his or her portfolio.

Unfortunately, forecasting interest rates is one of the most notoriously difficult parts of applied macroeconomics. Nonetheless, we do have a good understanding of the fundamental factors that determine the level of interest rates:

1. The supply of funds from savers, primarily households.
2. The demand for funds from businesses to be used to finance physical investments in plant, equipment, and inventories.
3. The government's net supply and/or demand for funds as modified by actions of the Federal Reserve Bank.
4. The expected rate of inflation.

Although there are many different interest rates economywide (as many as there are types of securities), these rates tend to move together, so economists frequently talk as though there were a single representative rate. We can use this abstraction to gain some insights into determining the real rate of interest if we consider the supply and demand curves for funds.

Figure 12.3 shows a downward-sloping demand curve and an upward-sloping supply curve. On the horizontal axis, we measure the quantity of funds, and on the vertical axis, we measure the real rate of interest.

The supply curve slopes up from left to right because the higher the real interest rate, the greater the supply of household savings. The assumption is that at higher real interest rates, households will choose to postpone some current consumption and set aside or invest more of their disposable income for future use.

The demand curve slopes down from left to right because the lower the real interest rate, the more businesses will want to invest in physical capital. Assuming that businesses rank projects by the expected real return on invested capital, firms will undertake more projects the lower the real interest rate on the funds needed to finance those projects.

FIGURE 12.3

Determination of the equilibrium real rate of interest

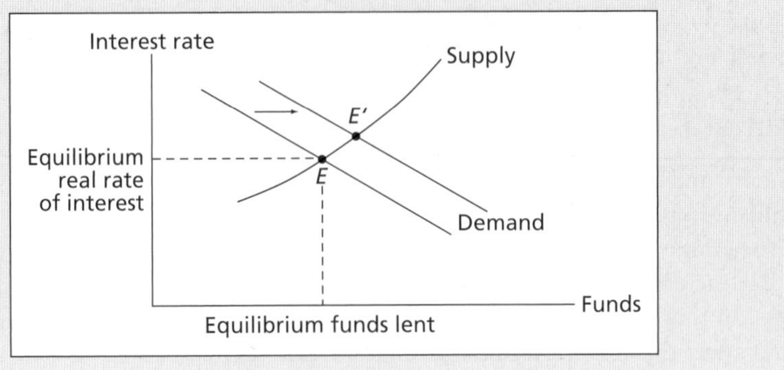

Equilibrium is at the point of intersection of the supply and demand curves, point *E* in Figure 12.3.

The government and the central bank (the Federal Reserve) can shift these supply and demand curves either to the right or to the left through fiscal and monetary policies. For example, consider an increase in the government's budget deficit. This increases the government's borrowing demand and shifts the demand curve to the right, which causes the equilibrium real interest rate to rise to point *E*′. That is, a forecast that indicates higher than previously expected government borrowing increases expectations of future interest rates. The Fed can offset such a rise through an increase in the money supply, which will increase the supply of loanable funds, and shift the supply curve to the right.

Thus, while the fundamental determinants of the real interest rate are the propensity of households to save and the expected productivity (or we could say profitability) of firms' investment in physical capital, the real rate can be affected as well by government fiscal and monetary policies.

The supply and demand framework illustrated in Figure 12.3 is a reasonable first approximation to the determination of the real interest rate. To obtain the *nominal* interest rate, one needs to add the expected inflation rate to the equilibrium real rate. As we discussed in Section 5.4, the inflation premium is necessary for investors to maintain a given real rate of return on their investments.

While monetary policy can clearly affect nominal interest rates, there is considerable controversy concerning its ability to affect real rates. There is widespread agreement that, in the long run, the ultimate impact of an increase in the money supply is an increase in prices with no permanent impact on real economic activity. A rapid rate of growth in the money supply, therefore, ultimately would result in a correspondingly high inflation rate and nominal interest rate, but it would have no sustained impact on the real interest rate. However, in the shorter run, changes in the money supply may well have an effect on the real interest rate.

12.4 DEMAND AND SUPPLY SHOCKS

demand shock

An event that affects the demand for goods and services in the economy.

supply shock

An event that influences production capacity and costs in the economy.

A useful way to organize your analysis of the factors that might influence the macroeconomy is to classify any impact as a supply or demand shock. A **demand shock** is an event that affects the demand for goods and services in the economy. Examples of positive demand shocks are reductions in tax rates, increases in the money supply, increases in government spending, or increases in foreign export demand. A **supply shock** is an event that influences production capacity and costs. Examples of supply shocks are changes in the price of imported oil; freezes, floods, or droughts that might destroy large quantities of agricultural crops; changes in the educational level of an economy's workforce; or changes in the wage rates at which the labor force is willing to work.

Demand shocks usually are characterized by aggregate output moving in the same direction as interest rates and inflation. For example, a big increase in government spending will tend to stimulate the economy and increase GDP. It also might increase interest rates by increasing the demand for borrowed funds by the government as well as by businesses that might desire to borrow to finance new ventures. Finally, it could increase the inflation rate if the demand for goods and services is raised to a level at or beyond the total productive capacity of the economy.

Supply shocks usually are characterized by aggregate output moving in the opposite direction of inflation and interest rates. For example, a big increase in the price of imported oil will be inflationary because costs of production will rise, which eventually will lead to increases in prices of finished goods. The increase in inflation rates over the near term can lead to higher nominal interest rates. Against this background, aggregate output will be falling. With raw materials more expensive, the productive capacity of the economy is reduced, as is the ability of individuals to purchase goods at now-higher prices. GDP, therefore, tends to fall.

How can we relate this framework to investment analysis? You want to identify the industries that will be most helped or hurt in any macroeconomic scenario you envision. For example, if you forecast a tightening of the money supply, you might want to avoid industries such as automobile producers that might be hurt by the likely increase in interest rates. We caution you again that these forecasts are no easy task. Macroeconomic predictions are notoriously unreliable. And again, you must be aware that in all likelihood your forecast will be made using only publicly available information. Any investment advantage you have will be a result only of better analysis—not better information.

12.5 FEDERAL GOVERNMENT POLICY

As the previous section would suggest, the government has two broad classes of macroeconomic tools—those that affect the demand for goods and services and those that affect their supply. For much of postwar history, demand-side policy has been of primary interest. The focus has been on government spending, tax levels, and monetary policy. Since the 1980s, however, increasing attention has also been focused on supply-side economics. Broadly interpreted, supply-side concerns have to do with enhancing the productive capacity of the economy, rather than increasing the demand for the goods and services the economy can produce. In practice, supply-side economists have focused on the appropriateness of the incentives to work, innovate, and take risks that result from our system of taxation. However, issues such as national policies on education, infrastructure (such as communication and transportation systems), and research and development also are properly regarded as part of supply-side macroeconomic policy.

Fiscal Policy

Fiscal policy refers to the government's spending and tax actions and is part of "demand-side management." Fiscal policy is probably the most direct way either to stimulate or to slow the economy. Decreases in government spending directly deflate the demand for goods and services. Similarly, increases in tax rates immediately siphon income from consumers and result in fairly rapid decreases in consumption.

fiscal policy

The use of government spending and taxing for the specific purpose of stabilizing the economy.

Ironically, although fiscal policy has the most immediate impact on the economy, the formulation and implementation of such policy is usually painfully slow and involved. This is because fiscal policy requires enormous amounts of compromise between the executive and legislative branches. Tax and spending policy must be initiated and voted on by Congress, which requires considerable political negotiations, and any legislation passed must be signed by the president, requiring more negotiation. Thus, while the impact of fiscal policy is relatively immediate, its formulation is so cumbersome that fiscal policy cannot in practice be used to fine-tune the economy.

Moreover, much of government spending, such as that for Medicare or Social Security, is nondiscretionary, meaning that it is determined by formula rather than policy and cannot be changed in response to economic conditions. This places even more rigidity into the formulation of fiscal policy.

A common way to summarize the net impact of government fiscal policy is to look at the government's budget deficit or surplus, which is simply the difference between revenues and expenditures. A large deficit means the government is spending considerably more than it is taking in by way of taxes. The net effect is to increase the demand for goods (via spending) by more than it reduces the demand for goods (via taxes), therefore, stimulating the economy.

Monetary Policy

monetary policy

Actions taken by the Board of Governors of the Federal Reserve System to influence the money supply or interest rates.

Monetary policy refers to the manipulation of the money supply to affect the macroeconomy and is the other main leg of demand-side policy. Monetary policy works largely through its impact on interest rates. Increases in the money supply lower short-term interest rates, ultimately encouraging investment and consumption demand. Over longer periods, however, most economists believe a higher money supply leads only to a higher price level and does not have a permanent effect on economic activity. Thus, the monetary authorities face a difficult balancing act. Expansionary monetary policy probably will lower interest rates and thereby stimulate investment and some consumption demand in the short run, but these circumstances ultimately will lead only to higher prices. The stimulation/inflation trade-off is implicit in all debate over proper monetary policy.

Fiscal policy is cumbersome to implement but has a fairly direct impact on the economy, while monetary policy is easily formulated and implemented but has a less immediate impact. Monetary policy is determined by the Board of Governors of the Federal Reserve System. Board members are appointed by the president for 14-year terms and are reasonably insulated from political pressure. The board is small enough and often sufficiently dominated by its chairperson that policy can be formulated and modulated relatively easily.

Implementation of monetary policy also is quite direct. The most widely used tool is the open market operation, in which the Fed buys or sells Treasury bonds for its own account. When the Fed buys securities, it simply writes a check, thereby increasing the money supply. (Unlike us, the Fed can pay for the securities without drawing down funds at a bank account.) Conversely, when the Fed sells a security, the money paid for it leaves the money supply. Open market operations occur daily, allowing the Fed to fine-tune its monetary policy.

Other tools at the Fed's disposal are the *discount rate,* which is the interest rate it charges banks on short-term loans, and the *reserve requirement,* which is the fraction of deposits that banks must hold as cash on hand or as deposits with the Fed. Reductions in the discount rate signal a more expansionary monetary policy. Lowering reserve requirements allows banks to make more loans with each dollar of deposits and stimulates the economy by increasing the effective money supply.

While the discount rate is under the direct control of the Fed, it is changed relatively infrequently. The *federal funds rate* is by far the better guide to Federal Reserve policy. The federal funds rate is the interest rate at which banks make short-term, usually overnight, loans to each other. These loans occur because some banks need to borrow funds to meet reserve requirements, while other banks have excess funds. Unlike the discount rate, the fed funds rate is a market rate, meaning that it is determined by supply and demand rather than being set administratively. Nevertheless, the Federal Reserve Board targets the fed funds rate, expanding or contracting the money supply through open market operations as it nudges the fed funds to its targeted value. This is the benchmark short-term U.S. interest rate, and as such it has considerable influence over other interest rates in the U.S. and the rest of the world.

Monetary policy affects the economy in a more roundabout way than fiscal policy. While fiscal policy directly stimulates or dampens the economy, monetary policy works largely through its impact on interest rates. Increases in the money supply lower interest rates, which stimulates investment demand. As the quantity of money in the economy increases, investors will find that their portfolios of assets include too much money. They will rebalance their portfolios by buying securities such as bonds, forcing bond prices up and interest rates down. In the longer run, individuals may increase their holdings of stocks as well and ultimately

On the MARKET FRONT

THE NEW OLD BIG THING IN ECONOMICS: J. M. KEYNES

The U.S. and dozens of other nations are returning to massive government spending as a recession fighter. Around the world, interest rates have been slashed and trillions of dollars have been committed to bailouts. But the global recession is deepening anyway. So policy makers are invoking the ideas of British economist John Maynard Keynes (pronounced "canes"), who argued in the 1930s that governments should fight the Great Depression with heavy spending. With consumer and business spending so weak, he argued, governments had to boost demand directly.

Keynesian policies fell out of favor in the 1970s, as government spending was blamed for helping to spur inflation around the world. But with the global economic turmoil being compared to the 1930s, government spending is once again back in vogue.

Critics argue that government deficits drive up interest rates and reduce investments in the private sector, which they say is more efficient at deploying capital. Still, with the U.S. economy facing 1930s-style threats, the Obama administration is looking back to the Great Depression for guidance. President Franklin Roosevelt's Works Progress Administration provided jobs to millions of Americans.

Keynesian fiscal stimulus remained popular globally into the 1960s, particularly in rebuilding Europe and Japan after the war. But limits of Keynes-inspired growth were reached in the following decades. Many countries mistimed their spending, pouring money into their economies and leading to economic overheating. Many nations also wasted their money: Japan became notorious for investing in little-used airports and bridges leading into sparsely populated islands. With the rise of Ronald Reagan and Britain's Margaret Thatcher, critics of stimulus policy came to the fore. The goal became to shrink government.

Monetary policy also began to play a bigger role, as central bankers drove up interest rates to bring down inflation. Recessions seemed to grow more distant and less painful. The era from the early 1980s until the recent crisis became known as "the Great Moderation," when economic activity and inflation became less volatile. But during this latest period of financial turmoil, monetary policy has been inadequate. The U.S. Federal Reserve lowered its interest-rate target to near zero last month, but the economy has continued to spiral downward.

So, nations are turning again to government stimulus spending to try knocking the economy back on track. Economists say that if governments can get money into the economy quickly, targeting projects that will have the biggest effect, and make sure the spending is temporary, they can avoid inflation and wasteful spending.

To ensure money is spent, the U.S. and other nations are focusing on infrastructure investment to create jobs. President-elect Barack Obama plans to use stimulus funds to repair schools, expand broadband Internet access, and put energy-efficient technologies in public buildings.

Inflation has quickly disappeared as a concern around the world. It's likely to reappear once growth perks up. That leaves a big test for the resurgence of fiscal stimulus: Once the economy revives, Mr. Keynes warned, the spending needs to be reversed and deficits cut. That's something nations have had a hard time doing.

SOURCE: Excerpted from Sudeep Reddy, "The New Old Big Thing in Economics: J. M. Keynes," *The Wall Street Journal,* January 8, 2009. Reprinted by permission of *The Wall Street Journal,*

buy real assets, which stimulates consumption demand directly. The ultimate effect of monetary policy on investment and consumption demand, however, is less immediate than that of fiscal policy.

The nearby box focuses on the choices facing economic policy makers who were attempting to mitigate a developing recession during the financial crisis of 2008–2009. The box touches on many of the themes of economic policy, noting for example that with short-term interest rates near zero, monetary policy had already neared its limits, forcing governments to turn to fiscal policy. The article notes the danger that huge resulting federal deficits could increase interest rates and crowd out private investment and that, as the economy recovered, such deficits would need to be trimmed quickly to avoid the risk of reigniting inflation. Indeed, as the last paragraph of the article predicts, reigning in deficits has proved to be a difficult and contentious challenge.

CONCEPT check 12.2

Suppose the government wants to stimulate the economy without increasing interest rates. What combination of fiscal and monetary policy might accomplish this goal?

Supply-Side Policies

Fiscal policy and monetary policy are demand-oriented tools that affect the economy by stimulating the total demand for goods and services. The implicit belief is that the economy will not by itself arrive at a full-employment equilibrium and that macroeconomic policy can push the economy toward this goal. In contrast, supply-side policies treat the issue of the productive capacity of the economy. The goal is to create an environment in which workers and owners of capital have the maximum incentive and ability to produce and develop goods.

Supply-side economists also pay considerable attention to tax policy. While demand-siders look at the effect of taxes on consumption demand, supply-siders focus on incentives and marginal tax rates. They argue that lowering tax rates will elicit more investment and improve incentives to work, thereby enhancing economic growth. Some go so far as to claim that reductions in tax rates can lead to increases in tax revenues because the lower tax rates will cause the economy and the revenue tax base to grow by more than the tax rate is reduced.

CONCEPT check 12.3

Large tax cuts in 2001 were followed by relatively rapid growth in GDP. How would demand-side and supply-side economists differ in their interpretations of this phenomenon?

12.6 BUSINESS CYCLES

We've looked at the tools the government uses to fine-tune the economy, attempting to maintain low unemployment and low inflation. Despite these efforts, economies repeatedly seem to pass through good and bad times. One determinant of the broad asset allocation decision of many analysts is a forecast of whether the macroeconomy is improving or deteriorating. A forecast that differs from the market consensus can have a major impact on investment strategy.

The Business Cycle

business cycles

Recurring cycles of recession and recovery.

peak

The transition from the end of an expansion to the start of a contraction.

trough

The transition point between recession and recovery.

cyclical industries

Industries with above-average sensitivity to the state of the economy.

defensive industries

Industries with below-average sensitivity to the state of the economy.

The economy recurrently experiences periods of expansion and contraction, although the length and depth of these cycles can be irregular. These recurring patterns of recession and recovery are called **business cycles.** Figure 12.4 presents graphs of several measures of production and output. The production series all show clear variation around a generally rising trend. The bottom graph of capacity utilization also evidences a clear cyclical (although irregular) pattern.

The transition points across cycles are called peaks and troughs, identified by the boundaries of the shaded areas of the graph. A **peak** is the transition from the end of an expansion to the start of a contraction. A **trough** occurs at the bottom of a recession just as the economy enters a recovery. The shaded areas in Figure 12.4 all represent periods of recession.

As the economy passes through different stages of the business cycle, the relative profitability of different industry groups might be expected to vary. For example, at a trough, just before the economy begins to recover from a recession, one would expect that **cyclical industries,** those with above-average sensitivity to the state of the economy, would tend to outperform other industries. Examples of cyclical industries are producers of durable goods, such as automobiles or washing machines. Because purchases of these goods can be deferred during a recession, sales are particularly sensitive to macroeconomic conditions. Other cyclical industries are producers of capital goods, that is, goods used by other firms to produce their own products. When demand is slack, few companies will be expanding and purchasing capital goods. Therefore, the capital goods industry bears the brunt of a slowdown but does well in an expansion.

In contrast to cyclical firms, **defensive industries** have little sensitivity to the business cycle. These are industries that produce goods for which sales and profits are least sensitive to the state of the economy. Defensive industries include food producers and processors, pharmaceutical firms, and public utilities. These industries will outperform others when the economy enters a recession.

The cyclical/defensive classification corresponds well to the notion of systematic or market risk introduced in our discussion of portfolio theory. When perceptions about the health of the economy become more optimistic, for example, the prices of most stocks will increase as forecasts of profitability rise. Because the cyclical firms are most sensitive to such developments,

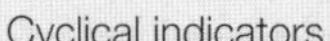

FIGURE 12.4

Cyclical indicators

Source: The Conference Board, *Business Cycle Indicators,* December 2008. Used with permission of The Conference Board, Inc.

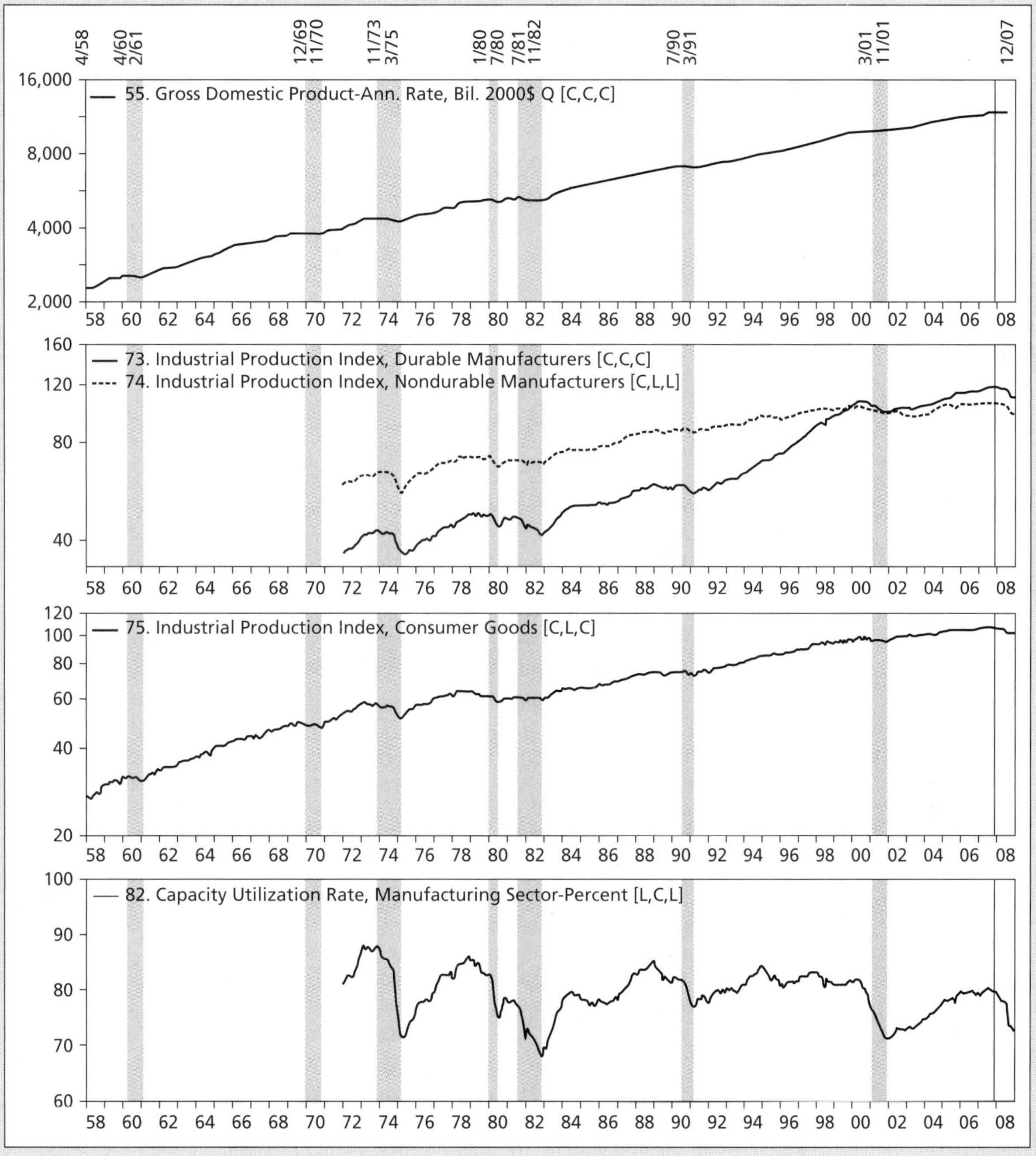

their stock prices will rise the most. Thus, firms in cyclical industries will tend to have high-beta stocks. In general, then, stocks of cyclical firms will show the best results when economic news is positive, but they will also show the worst results when that news is bad. Conversely, defensive firms will have low betas and performance that is comparatively unaffected by overall market conditions.

If your assessments of the state of the business cycle were reliably more accurate than those of other investors, choosing between cyclical and defensive industries would be easy. You would choose cyclical industries when you were relatively more optimistic about the economy, and you would choose defensive firms when you were relatively more pessimistic. As we know from our discussion of efficient markets, however, attractive investment choices will rarely be obvious. It is usually not apparent that a recession or expansion has started or ended until several months after the fact. With hindsight, the transitions from expansion to recession and back might seem obvious, but it is often quite difficult to say whether the economy is heating up or slowing down at any moment.

Economic Indicators

leading economic indicators

Economic series that tend to rise or fall in advance of the rest of the economy.

Given the cyclical nature of the business cycle, it is not surprising that to some extent the cycle can be predicted. The Conference Board publishes a set of cyclical indicators to help forecast, measure, and interpret short-term fluctuations in economic activity. **Leading economic indicators** are those economic series that tend to rise or fall in advance of the rest of the economy. Coincident and lagging indicators, as their names suggest, move in tandem with or somewhat after the broad economy.

Ten series are grouped into a widely followed composite index of leading economic indicators. Similarly, four coincident and seven lagging indicators form separate indexes. The composition of these indexes appears in Table 12.2.

Figure 12.5 graphs these three series. The dates at the top of the charts correspond to the turning points between expansions and contractions. While the index of leading indicators consistently turns before the rest of the economy, the lead time is somewhat erratic. Moreover, the lead time for peaks is consistently longer than that for troughs.

The stock market price index is a leading indicator. This is as it should be, as stock prices are forward-looking predictors of future profitability. Unfortunately, this makes the series of

TABLE 12.2 Indexes of economic indicators

A. Leading indicators

1. Average weekly hours of production workers (manufacturing)
2. Initial claims for unemployment insurance
3. Manufacturers' new orders (consumer goods and materials industries)
4. Fraction of companies reporting slower deliveries
5. New orders for nondefense capital goods
6. New private housing units authorized by local building permits
7. Yield curve: spread between 10-year T-bond yield and federal funds rate
8. Stock prices, 500 common stocks
9. Money supply (M2) growth rate
10. Index of consumer expectations

B. Coincident indicators

1. Employees on nonagricultural payrolls
2. Personal income less transfer payments
3. Industrial production
4. Manufacturing and trade sales

C. Lagging indicators

1. Average duration of unemployment
2. Ratio of trade inventories to sales
3. Change in index of labor cost per unit of output
4. Average prime rate charged by banks
5. Commercial and industrial loans outstanding
6. Ratio of consumer installment credit outstanding to personal income
7. Change in consumer price index for services

Source: The Conference Board, *Business Cycle Indicators*, November 2012.

FIGURE 12.5

Indexes of leading, coincident, and lagging indicators

Source: The Conference Board, *Business Cycle Indicators,* December 2008. Used with permission of The Conference Board, Inc.

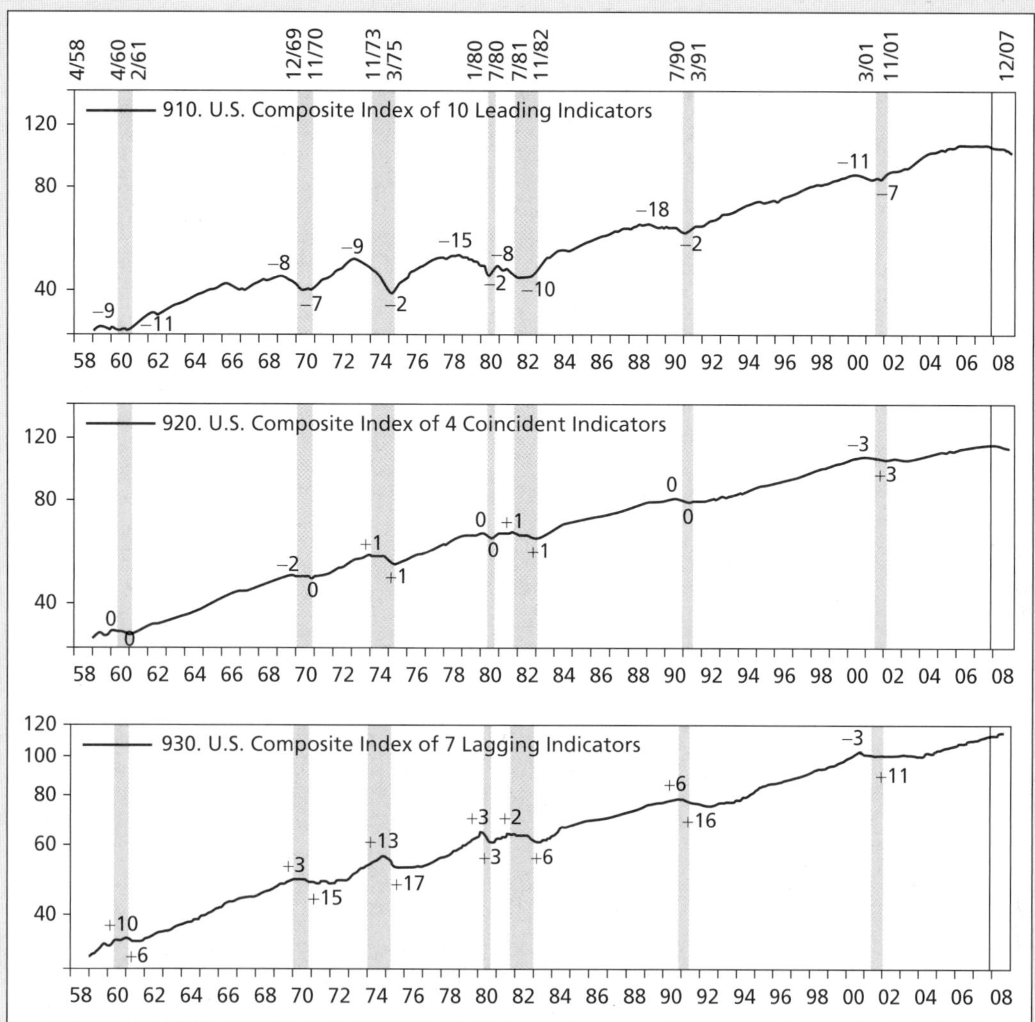

leading indicators much less useful for investment policy—by the time the series predicts an upturn, the market has already made its move. While the business cycle may be somewhat predictable, the stock market may not be. This is just one more manifestation of the efficient market hypothesis.

The money supply is another leading indicator. This makes sense in light of our earlier discussion concerning the lags surrounding the effects of monetary policy on the economy. An expansionary monetary policy can be observed fairly quickly, but it might not affect the economy for several months. Therefore, today's monetary policy might well predict future economic activity.

Other leading indicators focus directly on decisions made today that will affect production in the near future. For example, manufacturers' new orders for goods, contracts and orders for plant and equipment, and housing starts all signal a coming expansion in the economy.

A wide range of economic indicators are released to the public on a regular "economic calendar." Table 12.3 lists the public announcement dates and sources for about 20 statistics of interest. These announcements are reported in the financial press, for example, *The Wall Street Journal,* as they are released. They also are available at many sites on the web, for

TABLE 12.3 Economic calendar

Statistic	Release Date*	Source	Website (www.)
Auto and truck sales	2nd of month	Commerce Department	commerce.gov
Business inventories	15th of month	Commerce Department	commerce.gov
Construction spending	1st business day of month	Commerce Department	commerce.gov
Consumer confidence	Last Tuesday of month	Conference Board	conference-board.org
Consumer credit	5th business day of month	Federal Reserve Board	federalreserve.gov
Consumer price index (CPI)	13th of month	Bureau of Labor Statistics	bls.gov
Durable goods orders	26th of month	Commerce Department	commerce.gov
Employment cost index	End of first month of quarter	Bureau of Labor Statistics	bls.gov
Employment record (unemployment, average workweek, nonfarm payrolls)	1st Friday of month	Bureau of Labor Statistics	bls.gov
Existing home sales	25th of month	National Association of Realtors	realtor.org
Factory orders	1st business day of month	Commerce Department	commerce.gov
Gross domestic product	3rd–4th week of month	Commerce Department	commerce.gov
Housing starts	16th of month	Commerce Department	commerce.gov
Industrial production	15th of month	Federal Reserve Board	federalreserve.gov
Initial claims for jobless benefits	Thursdays	Department of Labor	dol.gov
International trade balance	20th of month	Commerce Department	commerce.gov
Index of leading economic indicators	Beginning of month	Conference Board	conference-board.org
Money supply	Thursdays	Federal Reserve Board	federalreserve.gov
New home sales	Last business day of month	Commerce Department	commerce.gov
Producer price index	11th of month	Bureau of Labor Statistics	bls.gov
Productivity and costs	2nd month in quarter (approx. 7th day of month)	Bureau of Labor Statistics	bls.gov
Retail sales	13th of month	Commerce Department	commerce.gov
Survey of purchasing managers	1st business day of month	Institute for Supply Management	ism.ws

*Many of these release dates are approximate.

example, at Yahoo!'s site. Figure 12.6 is a brief excerpt from a recent Economic Calendar page at Yahoo!. The page gives a list of the announcements released during the week of January 3, 2012. Notice that recent forecasts of each variable are provided along with the actual value of each statistic. This is useful, because in an efficient market, security prices will already reflect market expectations. The *new* information in the announcement will determine the market response.

Other Indicators

You can find lots of important information about the state of the economy from sources other than the official components of the economic calendar or the components of business-cycle indicators. Table 12.4, which is derived from some suggestions in *Inc.* magazine, contains a few.[1]

[1]Gene Sperling and illustrations by Thomas Fuchs, "The Insider's Guide to Economic Forecasting," *Inc.,* August 2003, p. 96.

FIGURE 12.6

Economic calendar at Yahoo! for the week of January 3, 2012

Source: Yahoo! Briefing Economic Calendar, **biz.yahoo.com/c/e.html**, downloaded, January 10, 2012. Yahoo! Finance, finance.yahoo.com.

Last Week Next Week

Date	Time (ET)	Statistic	For	Actual	Briefing Forecast	Market Expects	Prior	Revised From
Jan 3	10:00 A.M.	Construction Spending	Nov	1.2%	0.2%	0.5%	−0.2%	0.8%
Jan 4	7:00 A.M.	MBA Mortgage Index	12/31	−3.7%	NA	NA	−2.6%	–
Jan 4	10:00 A.M.	Factory Orders	Nov	1.8%	2.6%	2.1%	−0.2%	−0.4%
Jan 5	8:15 A.M.	ADP Employment Change	Dec	325K	200K	180K	204K	206K
Jan 5	8:30 A.M.	Initial Claims	12/31	372K	375K	375K	387K	381K
Jan 5	10:00 A.M.	ISM Services	Dec	52.6	53.0	53.0	52.0	–
Jan 6	8:30 A.M.	Nonfarm Private Payrolls	Dec	212K	200K	170K	120K	140K
Jan 6	8:30 A.M.	Unemployment Rate	Dec	8.5%	8.7%	8.7%	8.7%	8.6%
Jan 6	8:30 A.M.	Hourly Earnings	Dec	0.2%	0.1%	0.2%	0.0%	−0.1%

TABLE 12.4 Useful economic indicators

CEO polls **http://businessroundtable.org**	The business roundtable surveys CEOs about planned spending, a good measure of their optimism about the economy.
Temp jobs: Search for "Temporary Help Services" at **www.bls.gov**	A useful leading indicator. Businesses often hire temporary workers as the economy first picks up, until it is clear that an upturn is going to be sustained. This series is available at the Bureau of Labor Statistics website.
Walmart sales **www.walmartstores.com**	Walmart sales are a good indicator of the retail sector. It publishes its same-store sales weekly.
Commercial and industrial loans **www.federalreserve.gov**	These loans are used by small and medium-sized firms. Information is published weekly by the Federal Reserve.
Semiconductors **www.semi.org**	The book-to-bill ratio (i.e., new sales versus actual shipments) indicates whether demand in the technology sector is increasing (ratio > 1) or falling. This ratio is published by Semiconductor Equipment and Materials International.
Commercial structures **www.bea.gov**	Investment in structures is an indicator of businesses' forecasts of demand for their products in the near future. This is one of the series compiled by the Bureau of Economic Analysis as part of its GDP series.

12.7 INDUSTRY ANALYSIS

Industry analysis is important for the same reason that macroeconomic analysis is: Just as it is difficult for an industry to perform well when the macroeconomy is ailing, it is unusual for a firm in a troubled industry to perform well. Similarly, just as we have seen that economic performance can vary widely across countries, performance also can vary widely across industries. Figure 12.7 illustrates the dispersion of industry performance. It shows return on equity for several major industry groups in 2011. ROE ranged from 6.7% for money center banks to 36.4% for computer systems.

Given this wide variation in profitability, it is not surprising that industry groups exhibit considerable dispersion in their stock market performance. Figure 12.8 presents the 2011

FIGURE 12.7

Return on equity, 2011

Source: Yahoo! Finance, finance.yahoo.com, January 11, 2012.

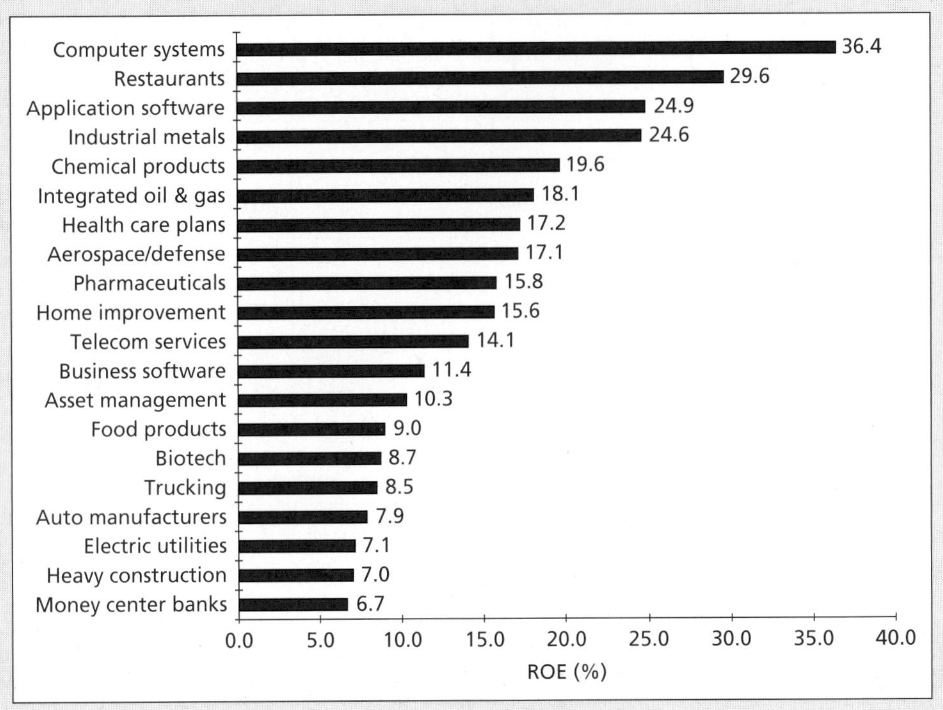

FIGURE 12.8

Industry stock price performance, 2011

Source: *The Wall Street Journal*, January 3, 2012.

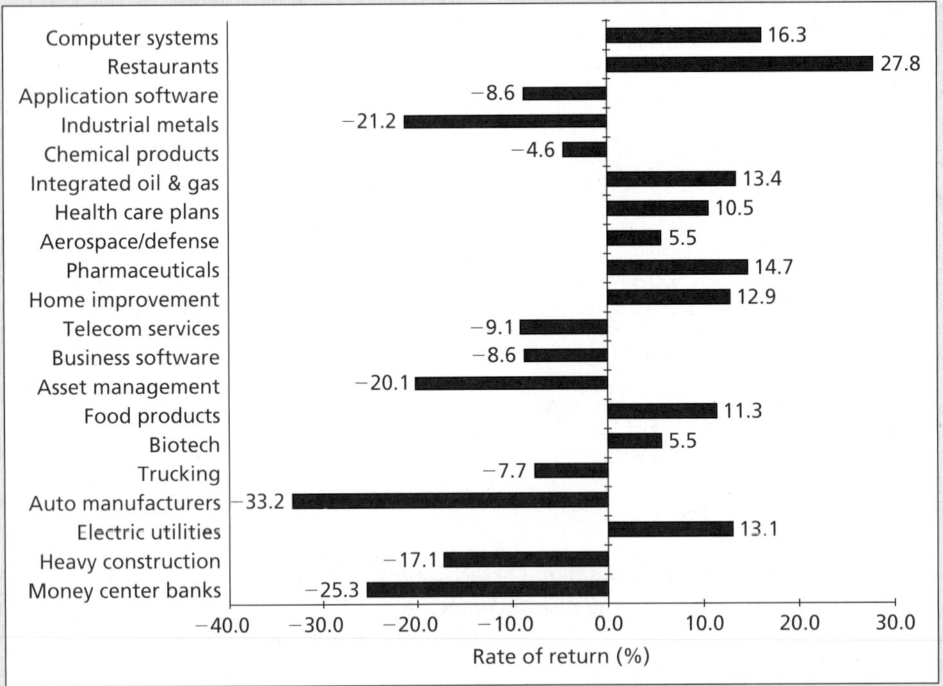

stock market performance of the same industries included in Figure 12.7. The spread in performance across industries is remarkable, ranging from a 27.8% gain in the restaurant industry to a 33.2% loss in auto manufacturing stocks. This range of performance was very much available to virtually all investors in 2011. Recall that iShares are exchange-traded funds (see Chapter 4) that trade like stocks and thus allow even small investors to take a position in each traded industry. Alternatively, one can invest in mutual funds with an industry focus. For example, Fidelity offers over 40 sector funds, each with a particular industry focus.

Defining an Industry

While we know what we mean by an industry, it can be difficult in practice to decide where to draw the line between one industry and another. Consider, for example, one of the industries depicted in Figure 12.7, application software firms. Even within this industry, there is substantial variation by focus and product line. Their differences may result in considerable dispersion in financial performance. Figure 12.9 shows 2012 ROE for a sample of the firms included in this industry, and performance did indeed wary widely: from 15.2% for Adobe to 44.2% for Microsoft.

A useful way to define industry groups in practice is given by the North American Industry Classification System, or **NAICS, codes.**[2] These are codes assigned to group firms for statistical analysis. The first two digits of the NAICS codes denote very broad industry classifications. For example, Table 12.5 shows that the codes for all construction firms start with 23. The next digits define the industry grouping more narrowly. For example, codes starting with 236 denote *building* construction, 2361 denotes *residential* construction, and 236115 denotes *single-family* construction. Firms with the same four-digit NAICS codes are commonly taken to be in the same industry.

NAICS codes

Classification of firms into industry groups using numerical codes to identify industries.

Industry classifications are never perfect. For example, both JCPenney and Neiman Marcus might be classified as department stores. Yet the former is a high-volume "value" store, while the latter is a high-margin elite retailer. Are they really in the same industry? Still, these classifications are a tremendous aid in conducting industry analysis since they provide a means of focusing on very broadly or fairly narrowly defined groups of firms.

Several other industry classifications are provided by other analysts; for example, Standard & Poor's reports on the performance of about 100 industry groups. S&P computes stock price indexes for each group, which is useful in assessing past investment performance. The *Value Line Investment Survey* reports on the conditions and prospects of about 1,700 firms, grouped into about 90 industries. Value Line's analysts prepare forecasts of the performance of industry groups as well as of each firm.

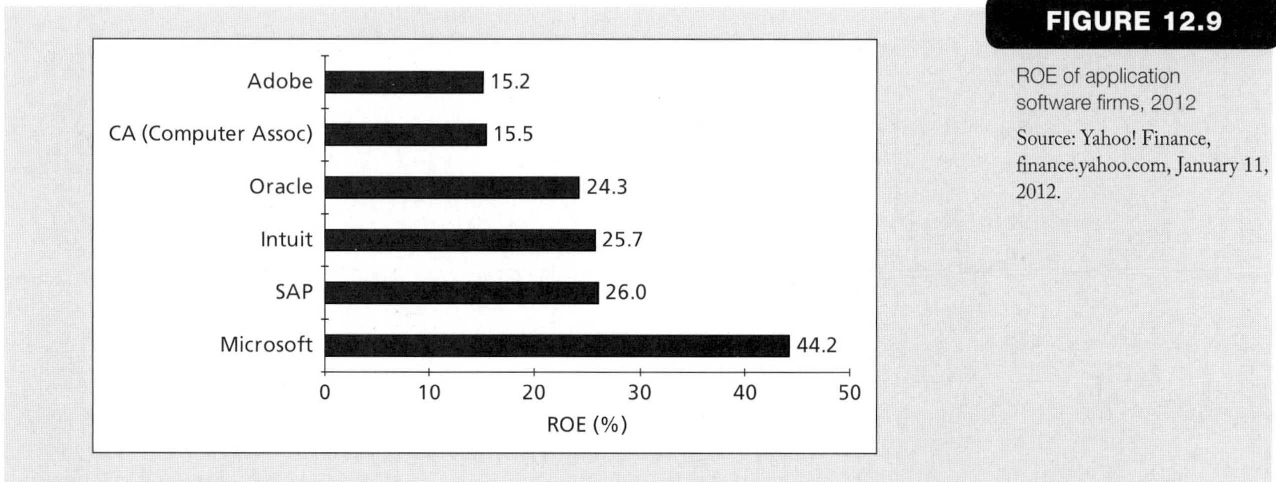

FIGURE 12.9

ROE of application software firms, 2012

Source: Yahoo! Finance, finance.yahoo.com, January 11, 2012.

[2]These codes are used for firms operating inside the NAFTA (North American Free Trade Agreement) region, which includes the U.S., Mexico, and Canada. NAICS codes replaced the Standard Industry Classification, or SIC, codes previously used in the U.S.

TABLE 12.5 Examples of NAICS industry codes

NAICS Code	NAICS Title
23	Construction
236	Construction of Buildings
2361	Residential Building Construction
23611	Residential Building Construction
236115	New Single-Family Housing Construction
236116	New Multifamily Housing Construction
236117	New Housing Operative Builders
236118	Residential Remodelers
2362	Nonresidential Building Construction
23621	Industrial Building Construction
236210	Industrial Building Construction
23622	Commercial and Institutional Building Construction
236220	Commercial and Institutional Building Construction

Sensitivity to the Business Cycle

Once the analyst forecasts the state of the macroeconomy, it is necessary to determine the implication of that forecast for specific industries. Not all industries are equally sensitive to the business cycle. For example, Figure 12.10 plots changes in retail sales (year over year) in two industries: jewelry and grocery stores. Clearly, sales of jewelry, which is a luxury good, fluctuate more widely than those of grocery stores. Jewelry sales jumped in 1999 at the height of the dot-com boom but fell steeply in the recessions of 2001 and 2008-2009. In contrast, sales growth in the grocery industry is relatively stable, with no years in which sales meaningfully decline. These patterns reflect the fact that jewelry is a discretionary good, whereas most grocery products are staples for which demand will not fall significantly even in hard times.

FIGURE 12.10

Industry cyclicality. Growth in sales, year over year, in two industries.

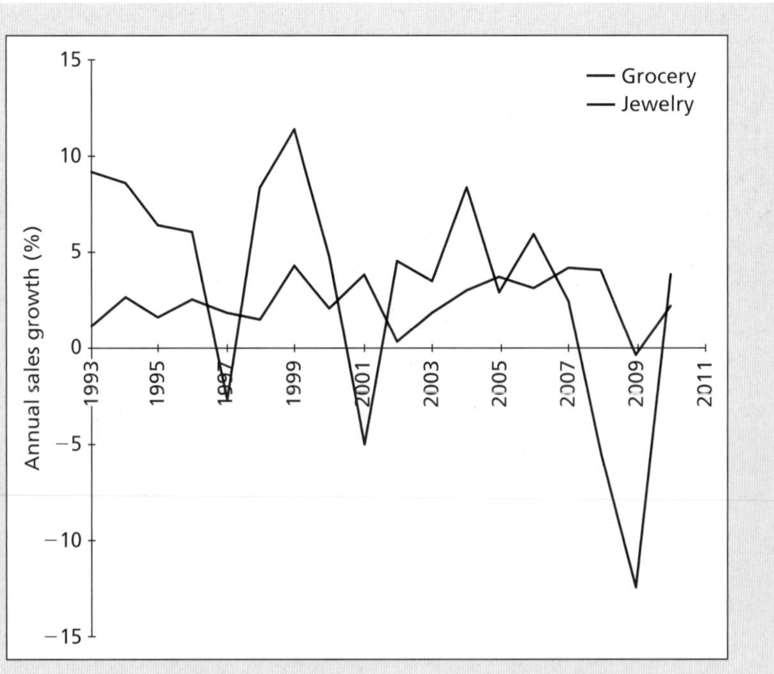

Three factors will determine the sensitivity of a firm's earnings to the business cycle. First is the sensitivity of sales. Necessities will show little sensitivity to business conditions. Examples of industries in this group are food, drugs, and medical services. Other industries with low sensitivity are those for which income is not a crucial determinant of demand. Tobacco products are examples of this type of industry. Another industry in this group is movies, because consumers tend to substitute movies for more expensive sources of entertainment when income levels are low. In contrast, firms in industries such as machine tools, steel, autos, and transportation are highly sensitive to the state of the economy.

The second factor determining business-cycle sensitivity is operating leverage, which refers to the division between fixed and variable costs. (Fixed costs are those the firm incurs regardless of its production levels. Variable costs are those that rise or fall as the firm produces more or less product.) Firms with greater amounts of variable as opposed to fixed costs will be less sensitive to business conditions. This is because, in economic downturns, these firms can reduce costs as output falls in response to falling sales. Profits for firms with high fixed costs will swing more widely with sales because costs do not move to offset revenue variability. Firms with high fixed costs are said to have high operating leverage, as small swings in business conditions can have large impacts on profitability.

The third factor influencing business-cycle sensitivity is financial leverage, which is the use of borrowing. Interest payments on debt must be paid regardless of sales. They are fixed costs that also increase the sensitivity of profits to business conditions. We will have more to say about financial leverage in Chapter 14.

Investors should not always prefer industries with lower sensitivity to the business cycle. Firms in sensitive industries will have high-beta stocks and are riskier. But while they swing lower in downturns, they also swing higher in upturns. As always, the issue you need to address is whether the expected return on the investment is fair compensation for the risks borne.

Sector Rotation

One way that many analysts think about the relationship between industry analysis and the business cycle is the notion of **sector rotation.** The idea is to shift the portfolio more heavily into industry or sector groups that are expected to outperform based on one's assessment of the state of the business cycle.

sector rotation

An investment strategy that entails shifting the portfolio into industry sectors that are expected to outperform others based on macroeconomic forecasts.

Figure 12.11 is a stylized depiction of the business cycle. Near the peak of the business cycle, the economy might be overheated with high inflation and interest rates and price pressures on basic commodities. This might be a good time to invest in firms engaged in natural resource extraction and processing such as minerals or petroleum.

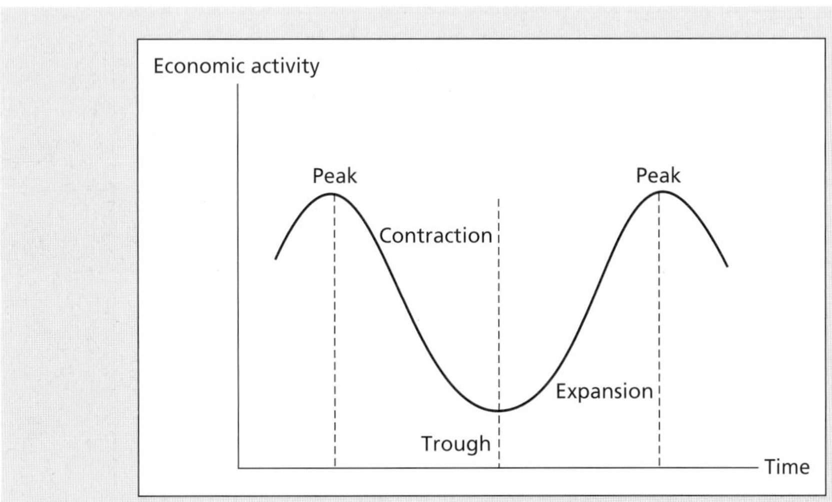

FIGURE 12.11

A stylized depiction of the business cycle

Following a peak, when the economy enters a contraction or recession, one would expect defensive industries that are less sensitive to economic conditions, for example, pharmaceuticals, food, and other necessities, to be the best performers. At the height of the contraction, financial firms will be hurt by shrinking loan volume and higher default rates. Toward the end of the recession, however, contractions induce lower inflation and interest rates, which favor financial firms.

At the trough of a recession, the economy is poised for recovery and subsequent expansion. Firms might thus be spending on purchases of new equipment to meet anticipated increases in demand. This, then, would be a good time to invest in capital goods industries, such as equipment, transportation, or construction.

Finally, in an expansion, the economy is growing rapidly. Cyclical industries such as consumer durables and luxury items will be most profitable in this stage of the cycle. Banks might also do well in expansions, since loan volume will be high and default exposure low when the economy is growing rapidly.

Figure 12.12 illustrates sector rotation. When investors are relatively pessimistic about the economy, they will shift into noncyclical industries such as consumer staples or health care. When anticipating an expansion, they will prefer more cyclical industries such as materials and technology.

Let us emphasize again that sector rotation, like any other form of market timing, will be successful only if one anticipates the next stage of the business cycle better than other investors. The business cycle depicted in Figure 12.11 is highly stylized. In real life, it is never as clear how long each phase of the cycle will last, nor how extreme it will be. These forecasts are where analysts need to earn their keep.

CONCEPT check 12.4

In which phase of the business cycle would you expect the following industries to enjoy their best performance?

(*a*) Newspapers (*b*) Machine tools (*c*) Beverages (*d*) Timber

Industry Life Cycles

Examine the biotechnology industry and you will find many firms with high rates of investment, high rates of return on investment, and very low dividends as a percentage of profits. Do the same for the electric utility industry and you will find lower rates of return, lower investment rates, and higher dividend payout rates. Why should this be?

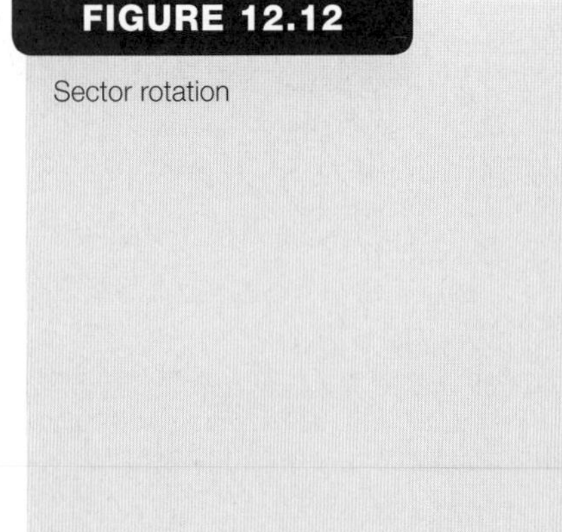

FIGURE 12.12

Sector rotation

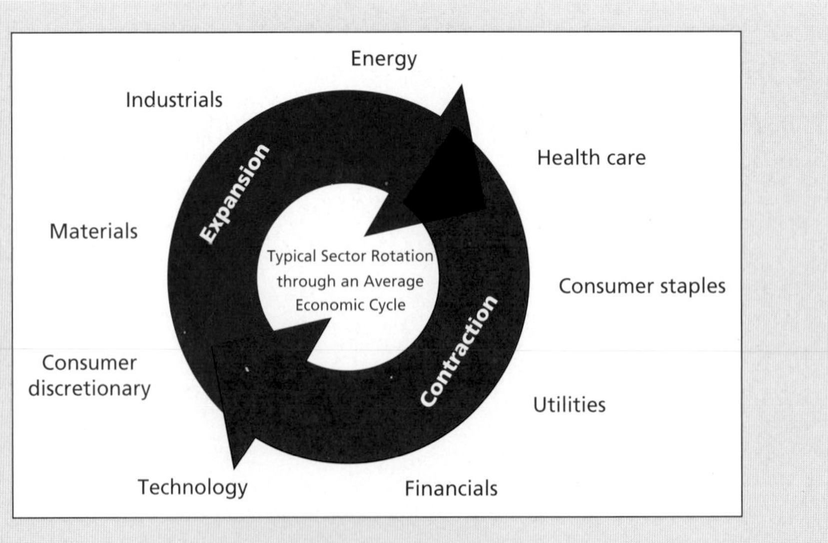

The biotech industry is still new. Recently available technologies have created opportunities for the highly profitable investment of resources. New products are protected by patents, and profit margins are high. With such lucrative investment opportunities, firms find it advantageous to put all profits back into the firm. The companies grow rapidly on average.

Eventually, however, growth must slow. The high profit rates will induce new firms to enter the industry. Increasing competition will hold down prices and profit margins. New technologies become proven and more predictable, risk levels fall, and entry becomes even easier. As internal investment opportunities become less attractive, a lower fraction of profits is reinvested in the firm. Cash dividends increase.

Ultimately, in a mature industry, we observe "cash cows," firms with stable dividends and cash flows and little risk. Their growth rates might be similar to that of the overall economy. Industries in early stages of their life cycles offer high-risk/high-potential-return investments. Mature industries offer lower-risk, lower-return combinations.

This analysis suggests that a typical **industry life cycle** might be described by four stages: a start-up stage characterized by extremely rapid growth; a consolidation stage characterized by growth that is less rapid but still faster than that of the general economy; a maturity stage characterized by growth no faster than the general economy; and a stage of relative decline, in which the industry grows less rapidly than the rest of the economy or actually shrinks. This industry life cycle is illustrated in Figure 12.13. Let us turn to an elaboration of each of these stages.

industry life cycle
Stages through which firms typically pass as they mature.

Start-up stage The early stages of an industry are often characterized by a new technology or product, such as desktop personal computers in the 1980s, cell phones in the 1990s, or the new generation of 4G smart phones being introduced today. At this stage, it is difficult to predict which firms will emerge as industry leaders. Some firms will turn out to be wildly successful, and others will fail altogether. Therefore, there is considerable risk in selecting one particular firm within the industry. For example, in the smart phone industry, there is still a battle among competing technologies, such as Google's Android phones versus Apple's iPhone, and it is still difficult to predict ultimate market shares.

At the industry level, however, it is clear that sales and earnings will grow at an extremely rapid rate since the new product has not yet saturated its market. For example, in 2000 very few households had smart phones. The potential market for the product therefore was huge. In contrast to this situation, consider the market for a mature product like refrigerators. Almost all households in the U.S. already have refrigerators, so the market for this good is primarily composed of households replacing old ones. Obviously, the growth rate in this market in the next decade will be far lower than for smart phones.

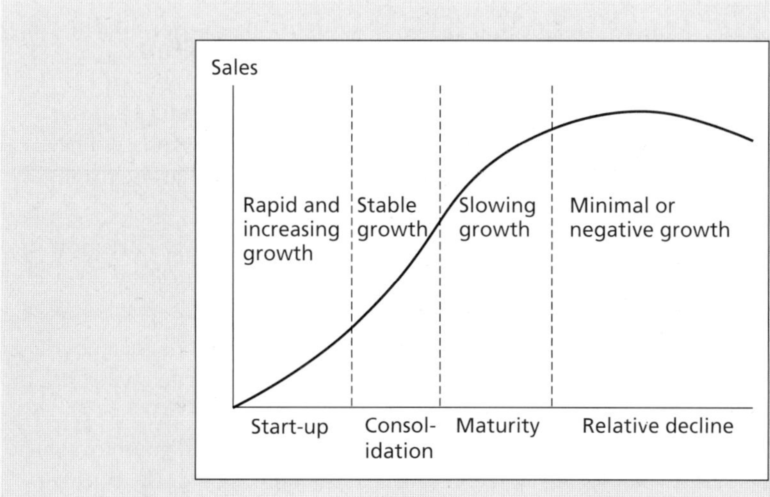

FIGURE 12.13
The industry life cycle

Consolidation stage After a product becomes established, industry leaders begin to emerge. The survivors from the start-up stage are more stable, and market share is easier to predict. Therefore, the performance of the surviving firms will more closely track the performance of the overall industry. The industry still grows faster than the rest of the economy as the product penetrates the marketplace and becomes more commonly used.

Maturity stage At this point, the product has reached its potential for use by consumers. Further growth might merely track growth in the general economy. The product has become far more standardized, and producers are forced to compete to a greater extent on the basis of price. This leads to narrower profit margins and further pressure on profits. Firms at this stage sometimes are characterized as "cash cows," firms with reasonably stable cash flow but offering little opportunity for profitable expansion. The cash flow is best "milked from" rather than reinvested in the company.

We pointed to desktop personal computers as a start-up industry in the 1980s. By the mid-1990s it was a mature industry, with high market penetration, considerable price competition, low profit margins, and slowing sales. By the 1990s, desktops were progressively giving way to laptops, which were in their own start-up stage. Within a dozen years, laptops had in turn entered a maturity stage, with standardization, considerable market penetration, and dramatic price competition. Today, tablet computers are in a start-up stage.

Relative decline In this stage, the industry might grow at less than the rate of the overall economy, or it might even shrink. This could be due to obsolescence of the product, competition from new products, or competition from new low-cost suppliers; consider, for example, the steady displacement of desktops by laptops.

At which stage in the life cycle are investments in an industry most attractive? Conventional wisdom is that investors should seek firms in high-growth industries. This recipe for success is simplistic, however. If the security prices already reflect the likelihood for high growth, then it is too late to make money from that knowledge. Moreover, high growth and fat profits encourage competition from other producers. The exploitation of profit opportunities brings about new sources of supply that eventually reduce prices, profits, investment returns, and, finally, growth. This is the dynamic behind the progression from one stage of the industry life cycle to another. The famous portfolio manager Peter Lynch makes this point in *One Up on Wall Street.* He says:

> Many people prefer to invest in a high-growth industry, where there's a lot of sound and fury. Not me. I prefer to invest in a low-growth industry. . . . In a low-growth industry, especially one that's boring and upsets people [such as funeral homes or the oil-drum retrieval business], there's no problem with competition. You don't have to protect your flanks from potential rivals . . . and this gives [the individual firm] the leeway to continue to grow. [page 131]

In fact, Lynch uses an industry classification system in a very similar spirit to the life-cycle approach we have described. He places firms in the following six groups:

1. *Slow growers.* Large and aging companies that will grow only slightly faster than the broad economy. These firms have matured from their earlier fast-growth phase. They usually have steady cash flow and pay a generous dividend, indicating that the firm is generating more cash than can be profitably reinvested in the firm.
2. *Stalwarts.* Large, well-known firms like Coca-Cola or Colgate-Palmolive. They grow faster than the slow growers but are not in the very rapid growth start-up stage. They also tend to be in noncyclical industries that are relatively unaffected by recessions.
3. *Fast growers.* Small and aggressive new firms with annual growth rates in the neighborhood of 20% to 25%. Company growth can be due to broad industry growth or to an increase in market share in a more mature industry.
4. *Cyclicals.* These are firms with sales and profits that regularly expand and contract along with the business cycle. Examples are auto companies, steel companies, or the construction industry.

5. *Turnarounds.* These are firms that are in bankruptcy or soon might be. If they can recover from what might appear to be imminent disaster, they can offer tremendous investment returns. A good example of this type of firm would be Chrysler in 1982, when it required a government guarantee on its debt to avoid bankruptcy. The stock price rose 15-fold in the next five years.
6. *Asset plays.* These are firms that have valuable assets not currently reflected in the stock price. For example, a company may own or be located on valuable real estate that is worth as much or more than the company's business enterprises. Sometimes the hidden asset can be tax-loss carryforwards. Other times the assets may be intangible. For example, a cable company might have a valuable list of cable subscribers. These assets do not immediately generate cash flow and so may be more easily overlooked by other analysts attempting to value the firm.

Industry Structure and Performance

The maturation of an industry involves regular changes in the firm's competitive environment. As a final topic, we examine the relationship between industry structure, competitive strategy, and profitability. Michael Porter (1980, 1985) has highlighted these five determinants of competition: threat of entry from new competitors, rivalry between existing competitors, price pressure from substitute products, the bargaining power of buyers, and the bargaining power of suppliers.

Threat of entry New entrants to an industry put pressure on price and profits. Even if a firm has not yet entered an industry, the potential for it to do so places pressure on prices, since high prices and profit margins will encourage entry by new competitors. Therefore, barriers to entry can be a key determinant of industry profitability. Barriers can take many forms. For example, existing firms may already have secure distribution channels for their products based on long-standing relationships with customers or suppliers that would be costly for a new entrant to duplicate. Brand loyalty also makes it difficult for new entrants to penetrate a market and gives firms more pricing discretion. Proprietary knowledge or patent protection also may give firms advantages in serving a market. Finally, an existing firm's experience in a market may give it cost advantages due to the learning that takes place over time.

Rivalry between existing competitors When there are several competitors in an industry, there will generally be more price competition and lower profit margins as competitors seek to expand their share of the market. Slow industry growth contributes to this competition since expansion must come at the expense of a rival's market share. High fixed costs also create pressure to reduce prices since fixed costs put greater pressure on firms to operate near full capacity. Industries producing relatively homogeneous goods also are subject to considerable price pressure since firms cannot compete on the basis of product differentiation.

Pressure from substitute products Substitute products mean that the industry faces competition from firms in related industries. For example, sugar producers compete with corn syrup producers. Wool producers compete with synthetic fiber producers. The availability of substitutes limits the prices that can be charged to customers.

Bargaining power of buyers If a buyer purchases a large fraction of an industry's output, it will have considerable bargaining power and can demand price concessions. For example, auto producers can put pressure on suppliers of auto parts. This reduces the profitability of the auto parts industry.

Bargaining power of suppliers If a supplier of a key input has monopolistic control over the product, it can demand higher prices for the good and squeeze profits out of the industry. One special case of this issue pertains to organized labor as a supplier of a key input to the production process. Labor unions engage in collective bargaining to increase the wages paid to workers. When the labor market is highly unionized, a significant share of the potential profits in the industry can be captured by the workforce.

The key factor determining the bargaining power of suppliers is the availability of substitute products. If substitutes are available, the supplier has little clout and cannot extract higher prices.

SUMMARY

- Macroeconomic policy aims to maintain the economy near full employment without aggravating inflationary pressures. The proper trade-off between these two goals is a source of ongoing debate.
- The traditional tools of macro policy are government spending and tax collection, which constitute fiscal policy, and manipulation of the money supply via monetary policy. Expansionary fiscal policy can stimulate the economy and increase GDP but tends to increase interest rates. Expansionary monetary policy works by lowering interest rates.
- The business cycle is the economy's recurring pattern of expansions and recessions. Leading economic indicators can be used to anticipate the evolution of the business cycle because their values tend to change before those of other key economic variables.
- Industries differ in their sensitivity to the business cycle. More sensitive industries tend to be those producing high-priced durable goods for which the consumer has considerable discretion as to the timing of purchase. Examples are automobiles or consumer durables. Other sensitive industries are those that produce capital equipment for other firms. Operating leverage and financial leverage increase sensitivity to the business cycle.

KEY TERMS

budget deficit, 376
business cycles, 382
cyclical industries, 382
defensive industries, 382
demand shock, 378
exchange rate, 374
fiscal policy, 379
fundamental analysis, 372
gross domestic product (GDP), 376
industry life cycle, 393
inflation, 376
leading economic indicators, 384
monetary policy, 380
peak, 382
sector rotation, 391
NAICS codes, 389
supply shock, 378
trough, 382
unemployment rate, 376

PROBLEM SETS

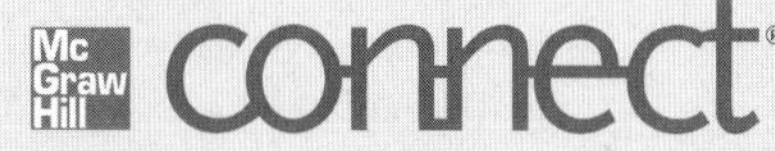

Select problems are available in McGraw-Hill's *Connect Finance.* Please see the Supplements section of the book's frontmatter for more information.

Basic

1. What are the differences between bottom-up and top-down approaches to security valuation? What are the advantages of a top-down approach? ***(LO 12-1)***
2. Why does it make intuitive sense that the slope of the yield curve is considered a leading economic indicator? ***(LO 12-2)***
3. Which one of the following firms would be described as having below-average sensitivity to the state of the economy? ***(LO 12-3)***
   a. An asset play firm
   b. A cyclical firm
   c. A defensive firm
   d. A stalwart firm
4. The price of imported oil fell dramatically in late 2008. What sort of macroeconomic shock would this be considered? ***(LO 12-1)***
5. How do each of the following affect the sensitivity of profits to the business cycle? ***(LO 12-3)***
   a. Financial leverage
   b. Operating leverage

6. The present value of a firm's projected cash flows are $15 million. The break-up value of the firm if you were to sell the major assets and divisions separately would be $20 million. This is an example of what Peter Lynch would call a(n): *(LO 12-4)*
   a. Stalwart
   b. Slow-growth firm
   c. Turnaround
   d. Asset play
7. Define each of the following in the context of a business cycle. *(LO 12-2)*
   a. Peak
   b. Contraction
   c. Trough
   d. Expansion
8. Which of the following is consistent with a steeply upwardly sloping yield curve? *(LO 12-2)*
   a. Monetary policy is expansive and fiscal policy is expansive.
   b. Monetary policy is expansive while fiscal policy is restrictive.
   c. Monetary policy is restrictive and fiscal policy is restrictive.

9. Which of the following is *not* a governmental structural policy that supply-side economists believe would promote long-term growth in an economy? *(LO 12-1)*
   a. A redistributive tax system.
   b. A promotion of competition.
   c. Minimal government interference in the economy.

10. What is typically true of corporate dividend payout rates in the early stages of an industry life cycle? Why does this make sense? *(LO 12-4)*
11. If the nominal interest rate is 5% and the inflation rate is 3%, then what is the real interest rate? *(LO 12-1)*
12. FinanceCorp has fixed costs of $7 million and profits of $4 million. What is its degree of operating leverage (DOL)? *(LO 12-3)*

Intermediate

13. Choose an industry and identify the factors that will determine its performance in the next three years. What is your forecast for performance in that time period? *(LO 12-3)*
14. What monetary and fiscal policies might be prescribed for an economy in a deep recession? *(LO 12-1)*
15. If you believe the U.S. dollar is about to depreciate more dramatically than do other investors, what will be your stance on investments in U.S. auto producers? *(LO 12-1)*
16. Unlike other investors, you believe the Fed is going to dramatically loosen monetary policy. What would be your recommendations about investments in the following industries? *(LO 12-1)*
    a. Gold mining
    b. Construction
17. Consider two firms producing smart phones. One uses a highly automated robotics process, while the other uses human workers on an assembly line and pays overtime when there is heavy production demand. *(LO 12-3)*
    a. Which firm will have higher profits in a recession? In a boom?
    b. Which firm's stock will have a higher beta?
18. According to supply-side economists, what will be the long-run impact on prices of a reduction in income tax rates? *(LO 12-1)*
19. Here are four industries and four forecasts for the macroeconomy. Choose the industry that you would expect to perform best in each scenario. *(LO 12-3)*

    Industries: housing construction, health care, gold mining, steel production.

    Economic Forecasts:

    Deep recession: falling inflation, falling interest rates, falling GDP.

    Superheated economy: rapidly rising GDP, increasing inflation and interest rates.

Healthy expansion: rising GDP, mild inflation, low unemployment.

Stagflation: falling GDP, high inflation.

20. For each pair of firms, choose the one that you think would be more sensitive to the business cycle. ***(LO 12-3)***
    a. General Autos or General Pharmaceuticals
    b. Friendly Airlines or Happy Cinemas
21. In which stage of the industry life cycle would you place the following industries? (*Warning:* There is considerable room for disagreement concerning the "correct" answers to this question.) ***(LO 12-4)***
    a. Oil well equipment
    b. Computer hardware
    c. Computer software
    d. Genetic engineering
    e. Railroads
22. Why do you think the index of consumer expectations is a useful leading indicator of the macroeconomy? (See Table 12.2.) ***(LO 12-2)***
23. Why do you think the change in the index of labor cost per unit of output is a useful lagging indicator of the macroeconomy? (See Table 12.2.) ***(LO 12-2)***
24. You have $5,000 to invest for the next year and are considering three alternatives:
    a. A money market fund with an average maturity of 30 days offering a current annualized yield of 3%.
    b. A one-year savings deposit at a bank offering an interest rate of 4.5%.
    c. A 20-year U.S. Treasury bond offering a yield to maturity of 6% per year.

    What role does your forecast of future interest rates play in your decision? ***(LO 12-1)***
25. General Weedkillers dominates the chemical weed control market with its patented product Weed-ex. The patent is about to expire, however. What are your forecasts for changes in the industry? Specifically, what will happen to industry prices, sales, the profit prospects of General Weedkillers, and the profit prospects of its competitors? What stage of the industry life cycle do you think is relevant for the analysis of this market? ***(LO 12-4)***

Use the following case in answering Problems 26–28: Institutional Advisors for All Inc., or IAAI, is a consulting firm that primarily advises all types of institutions such as foundations, endowments, pension plans, and insurance companies. IAAI also provides advice to a select group of individual investors with large portfolios. One of the claims the firm makes in its advertising is that IAAI devotes considerable resources to forecasting and determining long-term trends; then it uses commonly accepted investment models to determine how these trends should affect the performance of various investments. The members of the research department of IAAI recently reached some conclusions concerning some important macroeconomic trends. For instance, they have seen an upward trend in job creation and consumer confidence and predict that this should continue for the next few years. Other domestic leading indicators that the research department at IAAI wishes to consider are industrial production, average weekly hours in manufacturing, S&P 500 stock prices, M2 money supply, and the index of consumer expectations.

In light of the predictions for job creation and consumer confidence, the investment advisers at IAAI want to make recommendations for their clients. They use established theories that relate job creation and consumer confidence to inflation and interest rates and then incorporate the forecast movements in inflation and interest rates into established models for explaining asset prices. Their primary concern is to forecast how the trends in job creation and consumer confidence should affect bond prices and how those trends should affect stock prices.

The members of the research department at IAAI also note that stocks have been trending up in the past year, and this information is factored into the forecasts of the overall economy that they deliver. The researchers consider an upward-trending stock market a positive economic indicator in itself; however, they disagree as to the reason this should be the case.

26. The researchers at IAAI have forecast positive trends for both job creation and consumer confidence. Which, if either, of these trends should have a positive effect on stock prices? *(LO 12-1)*
27. Stock prices are useful as a leading indicator. To explain this phenomenon, which of the following is *most* accurate? Stock prices: *(LO 12-2)*
    a. Predict future interest rates and reflect the trends in other indicators.
    b. Do not predict future interest rates, nor are they correlated with other leading indicators; the usefulness of stock prices as a leading indicator is a mystery.
    c. Reflect the trends in other leading indicators only and do not have predictive power of their own.
28. Which of the domestic series that the IAAI research department listed for use as leading indicators is *least* appropriate? *(LO 12-2)*
    a. Industrial production
    b. Manufacturing average weekly hours
    c. M2 money supply

Use the following case in answering Problems 29–32: Mary Smith, a Level II CFA candidate, was recently hired for an analyst position at the Bank of Ireland. Her first assignment is to examine the competitive strategies employed by various French wineries.

Smith's report identifies four wineries that are the major players in the French wine industry. Key characteristics of each are cited in Table 12.6. In the body of Smith's report, she includes a discussion of the competitive structure of the French wine industry. She notes that over the past five years, the French wine industry has not responded to changing consumer tastes. Profit margins have declined steadily, and the number of firms representing the industry has decreased from 10 to 4. It appears that participants in the French wine industry must consolidate in order to survive.

TABLE 12.6 Characteristics of four major French wineries

	South Winery	North Winery	East Winery	West Winery
Founding date	1750	1903	1812	1947
Generic competitive strategy	?	Cost leadership	Cost leadership	Cost leadership
Major customer market (more than 80% concentration)	France	France	England	U.S.
Production site	France	France	France	France

Smith's report notes that French consumers have strong bargaining power over the industry. She supports this conclusion with five key points, which she labels "Bargaining Power of Buyers":

- Many consumers are drinking more beer than wine with meals and at social occasions.
- Increasing sales over the Internet have allowed consumers to better research the wines, read opinions from other customers, and identify which producers have the best prices.
- The French wine industry is consolidating and consists of only 4 wineries today compared to 10 wineries five years ago.
- More than 65% of the business for the French wine industry consists of purchases from restaurants. Restaurants typically make purchases in bulk, buying four to five cases of wine at a time.
- Land where the soil is fertile enough to grow grapes necessary for the wine production process is scarce in France.

After completing the first draft of her report, Smith takes it to her boss, Ron VanDriesen, to review. VanDriesen tells her that he is a wine connoisseur himself and often makes purchases from the South Winery. Smith tells VanDriesen, "In my report I have classified the South Winery as a stuck-in-the-middle firm. It tries to be a cost leader by selling its wine at a price that is slightly below the other firms, but it also tries to differentiate itself from its competitors by producing wine in bottles with curved necks, which increases its cost structure. The end result is that the South Winery's profit margin gets squeezed from both sides." VanDriesen replies, "I have met members of the management team from the South Winery at a couple of the wine conventions I have attended. I believe that the South Winery could succeed at following both a cost leadership and a differentiation strategy if its operations were separated into distinct operating units, with each unit pursuing a different competitive strategy." Smith makes a note to do more research on generic competitive strategies to verify VanDriesen's assertions before publishing the final draft of her report.

29. If the French home currency were to greatly appreciate in value compared to the English currency, what is the likely impact on the competitive position of the East Winery? ***(LO 12-1)***
    a. Make the firm less competitive in the English market.
    b. No impact, since the major market for East Winery is England, not France.
    c. Make the firm more competitive in the English market.
30. Which of Smith's points effectively support the conclusion that consumers have strong bargaining power over the industry? ***(LO 12-4)***
31. Smith notes in her report that the West Winery might differentiate its wine product on attributes that buyers perceive to be important. Which of the following attributes would be the *most likely* area of focus for the West Winery to create a differentiated product? ***(LO 12-4)***
    a. The method of delivery for the product
    b. The price of the product
    c. A focus on customers aged 30 to 45
32. Smith knows that a firm's generic strategy should be the centerpiece of a firm's strategic plan. On the basis of a compilation of research and documents, Smith makes three observations about the North Winery and its strategic planning process:
    i. North Winery's price and cost forecasts account for future changes in the structure of the French wine industry.
    ii. North Winery places each of its business units into one of three categories: build, hold, or harvest.
    iii. North Winery uses market share as the key measure of its competitive position.

    Which of these observation(s) *least* support the conclusion that the North Winery's strategic planning process is guided and informed by its generic competitive strategy? ***(LO 12-4)***

Challenge

33. OceanGate sells external hard drives for $200 each. Its total fixed costs are $30 million, and its variable costs per unit are $140. The corporate tax rate is 30%. If the economy is strong, the firm will sell 2 million drives, but if there is a recession, it will sell only half as many. What is the firm's degree of operating leverage? If the economy enters a recession, what will be the firm's after-tax profit? ***(LO 12-3)***

CFA Problems

1. As a securities analyst you have been asked to review a valuation of a closely held business, Wigwam Autoparts Heaven, Inc. (WAH), prepared by the Red Rocks Group (RRG). You are to give an opinion on the valuation and to support your opinion by analyzing each part of the valuation. WAH's sole business is automotive parts retailing. The RRG valuation includes a section called "Analysis of the Retail Auto Parts Industry," based completely on the data in Table 12.7 and the following additional information:
    - WAH and its principal competitors each operated more than 150 stores at year-end 2010.
    - The average number of stores operated per company engaged in the retail auto parts industry is 5.3.

TABLE 12.7 Selected retail auto parts industry data

	2010	2009	2008	2007	2006	2005	2004	2003	2002	2001
Population 18–29 years old (percentage change)	−1.8%	−2.0%	−2.1%	−1.4%	−0.8%	−0.9%	−1.1%	−0.9%	−0.7%	−0.3%
Number of households with income more than $40,000 (percentage change)	6.0%	4.0%	8.0%	4.5%	2.7%	3.1%	1.6%	3.6%	4.2%	2.2%
Number of households with income less than $40,000 (percentage change)	3.0%	−1.0%	4.9%	2.3%	−1.4%	2.5%	1.4%	−1.3%	0.6%	0.1%
Number of cars 5–15 years old (percentage change)	0.9%	−1.3%	−6.0%	1.9%	3.3%	2.4%	−2.3%	−2.2%	−8.0%	1.6%
Automotive aftermarket industry retail sales (percentage change)	5.7%	1.9%	3.1%	3.7%	4.3%	2.6%	1.3%	0.2%	3.7%	2.4%
Consumer expenditures on automotive parts and accessories (percentage change)	2.4%	1.8%	2.1%	6.5%	3.6%	9.2%	1.3%	6.2%	6.7%	6.5%
Sales growth of retail auto parts companies with 100 or more stores	17.0%	16.0%	16.5%	14.0%	15.5%	16.8%	12.0%	15.7%	19.0%	16.0%
Market share of retail auto parts companies with 100 or more stores	19.0%	18.5%	18.3%	18.1%	17.0%	17.2%	17.0%	16.9%	15.0%	14.0%
Average operating margin of retail auto parts companies with 100 or more stores	12.0%	11.8%	11.2%	11.5%	10.6%	10.6%	10.0%	10.4%	9.8%	9.0%
Average operating margin of all retail auto parts companies	5.5%	5.7%	5.6%	5.8%	6.0%	6.5%	7.0%	7.2%	7.1%	7.2%

- The major customer base for auto parts sold in retail stores consists of young owners of old vehicles. These owners do their own automotive maintenance out of economic necessity. ***(LO 12-1)***

  a. One of RRG's conclusions is that the retail auto parts industry as a whole is in the maturity stage of the industry life cycle. Discuss three relevant items of data from Table 12.7 that support this conclusion.

  b. Another RRG conclusion is that WAH and its principal competitors are in the consolidation stage of their life cycle. Cite three items from Table 12.7 that suggest this conclusion. How can WAH be in a consolidation stage while its industry is in a maturity stage?

2. Universal Auto is a large multinational corporation headquartered in the United States. For segment reporting purposes, the company is engaged in two businesses: production of motor vehicles and information processing services.

   The motor vehicle business is by far the larger of Universal's two segments. It consists mainly of domestic United States passenger car production, but it also includes small truck manufacturing operations in the United States and passenger car production in other countries. This segment of Universal has had weak operating results for the past several years, including a large loss in 2012. Although the company does not reveal the operating results of its domestic passenger car segments, that part of Universal's business is generally believed to be primarily responsible for the weak performance of its motor vehicle segment.

   Idata, the information processing services segment of Universal, was started by Universal about 15 years ago. This business has shown strong, steady growth that has been entirely internal: No acquisitions have been made.

An excerpt from a research report on Universal prepared by Paul Adams, a CFA candidate, states: "Based on our assumption that Universal will be able to increase prices significantly on U.S. passenger cars in 2013, we project a multibillion-dollar profit improvement . . ." ***(LO 12-4)***

a. Discuss the concept of an industrial life cycle by describing each of its four phases.

b. Identify where each of Universal's two primary businesses—passenger cars and information processing—is in such a cycle.

c. Discuss how product pricing should differ between Universal's two businesses, based on the location of each in the industrial life cycle.

3. Adams's research report (see the previous problem) continued as follows: "With a business expansion already under way, the expected profit surge should lead to a much higher price for Universal Auto stock. We strongly recommend purchase." ***(LO 12-3)***

   a. Discuss the business-cycle approach to investment timing. (Your answer should describe actions to be taken on both stocks and bonds at different points over a typical business cycle.)

   b. Assuming Adams's assertion is correct (that a business expansion is already under way), evaluate the timeliness of his recommendation to purchase Universal Auto, a cyclical stock, based on the business-cycle approach to investment timing.

4. Janet Ludlow is preparing a report on U.S.-based manufacturers in the electric toothbrush industry and has gathered the information shown in Tables 12.8 and 12.9. Ludlow's report concludes that the electric toothbrush industry is in the maturity (i.e., late) phase of its industry life cycle. ***(LO 12-4)***

   a. Select and justify three factors from Table 12.8 that support Ludlow's conclusion.

   b. Select and justify three factors from Table 12.9 that refute Ludlow's conclusion.

5. The following questions have appeared on CFA examinations. ***(LO 12-1)***

   a. Which one of the following statements *best* expresses the central idea of countercyclical fiscal policy?

   (1) Planned government deficits are appropriate during economic booms, and planned surpluses are appropriate during economic recessions.

   (2) The balanced-budget approach is the proper criterion for determining annual budget policy.

   (3) Actual deficits should equal actual surpluses during a period of deflation.

   (4) Government deficits are planned during economic recessions, and surpluses are utilized to restrain inflationary booms.

TABLE 12.8 Ratios for electric toothbrush industry index and broad stock market index

Year	2005	2006	2007	2008	2009	2010
Return on equity						
Electric toothbrush industry index	12.5%	12.0%	15.4%	19.6%	21.6%	21.6%
Market index	10.2	12.4	14.6	19.9	20.4	21.2
Average P/E						
Electric toothbrush industry index	28.5 ×	23.2 ×	19.6 ×	18.7 ×	18.5 ×	16.2 ×
Market index	10.2	12.4	14.6	19.9	18.1	19.1
Dividend payout ratio						
Electric toothbrush industry index	8.8%	8.0%	12.1%	12.1%	14.3%	17.1%
Market index	39.2	40.1	38.6	43.7	41.8	39.1
Average dividend yield						
Electric toothbrush industry index	0.3%	0.3%	0.6%	0.7%	0.8%	1.0%
Market index	3.8	3.2	2.6	2.2	2.3	2.1

TABLE 12.9 Characteristics of the electric toothbrush manufacturing industry

- **Industry sales growth**—Industry sales have grown at 15%–20% per year in recent years and are expected to grow at 10%–15% per year over the next three years.
- **Non-U.S. markets**—Some U.S. manufacturers are attempting to enter fast-growing non-U.S. markets, which remain largely unexploited.
- **Mail order sales**—Some manufacturers have created a new niche in the industry by selling electric toothbrushes directly to customers through mail order. Sales for this industry segment are growing at 40% per year.
- **U.S. market penetration**—The current penetration rate in the United States is 60% of households and will be difficult to increase.
- **Price competition**—Manufacturers compete fiercely on the basis of price, and price wars within the industry are common.
- **Niche markets**—Some manufacturers are able to develop new, unexploited niche markets in the United States based on company reputation, quality, and service.
- **Industry consolidation**—Several manufacturers have recently merged, and it is expected that consolidation in the industry will increase.
- **New entrants**—New manufacturers continue to enter the market.

b. Which *one* of the following propositions would a strong proponent of supply-side economics be *most* likely to stress?
(1) Higher marginal tax rates will lead to a reduction in the size of the budget deficit and lower interest rates because they expand government revenues.
(2) Higher marginal tax rates promote economic inefficiency and thereby retard aggregate output because they encourage investors to undertake low-productivity projects with substantial tax-shelter benefits.
(3) Income redistribution payments will exert little impact on real aggregate supply because they do not consume resources directly.
(4) A tax reduction will increase the disposable income of households. Thus, the primary impact of a tax reduction on aggregate supply will stem from the influence of the tax change on the size of the budget deficit or surplus.

WEB *master*

1. Use data from **finance.yahoo.com** to answer the following questions.
   a. Go to the *Investing* tab and click on *Industries.* Find the price/book ratios for Medical Instruments & Supplies and for Electric Utilities. Do the differences make sense in light of their different stages in the industry life cycle?
   b. Now look at each industry's price–earnings ratio and dividend yield. Again, do the differences make sense in light of their different stages in the industry life cycle?
2. This exercise will give you a chance to examine data on some of the leading economic indicators.
   a. Download the data for new privately owned housing units authorized by building permits from **www.census.gov/construction/bps.** Choose the seasonally adjusted data for the United States in an Excel format. Graph the "Total" series.
   b. Download the last five years of data for manufacturers' new orders of nondefense capital goods from the St. Louis Federal Reserve site at **research.stlouisfed.org/fred2/series/NEWORDER.** Graph the data.
   c. Locate data for the average weekly hours of production workers in manufacturing, available at **www.bls.gov/lpc/lpcover.htm#Data.** Select the historical time series link, and then choose the *Index* data. Choose *Manufacturing* as the sector and *Average Weekly Hours* as the measure. Retrieve the report for the past five years. Create a graph of the data that shows the quarterly trend over the last five years.
   d. The data series you retrieved are all leading economic indicators. Based on the tables and your graphs, what is your opinion of where the economy is heading in the near future?

www.mhhe.com/bkm

12.1 The downturn in the auto industry will reduce the demand for the product in this economy. The economy will, at least in the short term, enter a recession. This would suggest that:

a. GDP will fall.

b. The unemployment rate will rise.

c. The government deficit will increase. Income tax receipts will fall, and government expenditures on social welfare programs probably will increase.

d. Interest rates should fall. The contraction in the economy will reduce the demand for credit. Moreover, the lower inflation rate will reduce nominal interest rates.

12.2 Expansionary fiscal policy coupled with expansionary monetary policy will stimulate the economy, with the loose monetary policy keeping down interest rates.

12.3 A traditional demand-side interpretation of the tax cuts is that the resulting increase in after-tax income increased consumption demand and stimulated the economy. A supply-side interpretation is that the reduction in marginal tax rates made it more attractive for businesses to invest and for individuals to work, thereby increasing economic output.

12.4 *a.* Newspapers will do best in an expansion when advertising volume is increasing.

b. Machine tools are a good investment at the trough of a recession, just as the economy is about to enter an expansion and firms may need to increase capacity.

c. Beverages are defensive investments, with demand that is relatively insensitive to the business cycle. Therefore, they are good investments if a recession is forecast.

d. Timber is a good investment at a peak period, when natural resource prices are high and the economy is operating at full capacity.

Equity Valuation

Chapter

13

Learning Objectives:

LO13-1 Use financial statements and market comparables to estimate firm value.

LO13-2 Calculate the intrinsic value of a firm using either a constant-growth or multistage dividend discount model.

LO13-3 Assess the growth prospects of a firm, and relate growth opportunities to the P/E ratio.

LO13-4 Value a firm using free cash flow models.

You saw in our discussion of market efficiency that finding undervalued securities is hardly easy. At the same time, there are enough chinks in the armor of the efficient market hypothesis that the search for such securities should not be dismissed out of hand. Moreover, it is the ongoing search for mispriced securities that maintains a nearly efficient market. Even minor mispricing would allow a stock market analyst to earn his salary.

This chapter describes the ways stock market analysts try to uncover mispriced securities. The models presented are those used by *fundamental analysts,* those analysts who use information concerning the current and prospective profitability of a company to assess its fair market value. Fundamental analysts are different from *technical analysts,* who largely use trend analysis to uncover trading opportunities.

We start with a discussion of alternative measures of the value of a company. From there, we progress to quantitative tools called *dividend discount models* that security analysts commonly use to measure the value of a firm as an ongoing concern. Next, we turn to price–earnings, or P/E, ratios, explaining why they are of such interest to analysts but also highlighting some of their shortcomings. We explain how P/E ratios are tied to dividend valuation models and, more generally, to the growth prospects of the firm.

We close the chapter with a discussion and extended example of free cash flow models

Related websites for this chapter are available at www.mhhe.com/bkm.

used by analysts to value firms based on forecasts of the cash flows that will be generated from the firm's business endeavors. We apply the several valuation tools covered in the chapter to a real firm and find that there is some disparity in their conclusions—a conundrum that will confront any security analyst—and consider reasons for these discrepancies.

13.1 VALUATION BY COMPARABLES

The purpose of fundamental analysis is to identify stocks that are mispriced relative to some measure of "true" value that can be derived from observable financial data. Of course, true value can only be estimated. In practice, stock analysts use models to estimate the fundamental value of a corporation's stock from observable market data and from the financial statements of the firm and its competitors. These valuation models differ in the specific data they use and in the level of their theoretical sophistication. But, at their heart, most of them use the notion of valuation by comparables: They look at the relationship between price and various determinants of value for similar firms and then extrapolate that relationship to the firm in question.

The Internet makes it convenient to obtain relevant data. For U.S. companies, the Securities and Exchange Commission provides information available to the public at its EDGAR website, **www.sec.gov/edgar.shtml.** The SEC requires all public companies (except foreign companies and companies with less than $10 million in assets and 500 shareholders) to file registration statements, periodic reports, and other forms electronically through EDGAR. Many websites such as **finance.yahoo.com, money.msn.com,** and **finance.google.com** also provide analysis and data derived from the EDGAR reports.

Table 13.1 shows some financial highlights for Microsoft as well as some comparable data for other firms in the software applications industry. The price per share of Microsoft's common stock is $28.25, and the total market value or capitalization of those shares (called *market cap* for short) is $237.6 billion. Under the heading "Valuation," Table 13.1 shows the ratio of Microsoft's stock price to five benchmarks. Its share price is 10.3 times its (per-share) earnings in the most recent 12 months, 4 times its recent book value, 3.3 times its sales, and 13.9 times its cash flow. The last valuation ratio, PEG, is the P/E ratio divided by the growth rate of earnings. We would expect more rapidly growing firms to sell at higher multiples of *current* earnings (more on this below), so PEG normalizes the P/E ratio by the growth rate.

These valuation ratios are commonly used to assess the valuation of one firm compared to others in the same industry, and we will consider all of them. The column to the right gives comparable ratios for other firms in the software applications industry. For example, an analyst might note that Microsoft's price–earnings ratio and price/CF ratio are both considerably below the industry average. Similarly, Microsoft's ratio of market value to **book value,** the net worth of the company as reported on the balance sheet, is also considerably below industry norms, 4 versus 10.5. These ratios might indicate that its stock is underpriced. However, Microsoft is a more mature firm than many in the industry, and perhaps this discrepancy reflects a lower expected future growth rate of sales. In fact, its PEG ratio is comparable to others in the industry. Clearly, rigorous valuation models will be necessary to sort through these sometimes conflicting signals of value.

book value

The net worth of common equity according to a firm's balance sheet.

Limitations of Book Value

Shareholders in a firm are sometimes called "residual claimants," which means that the value of their stake is what is left over when the liabilities of the firm are subtracted from its assets. Shareholders' equity is this net worth. However, the values of both assets and liabilities recognized in financial statements are based on historical—not current—values. For example, the book value of an asset equals the *original* cost of acquisition less some adjustment for depreciation, even if the market price of that asset has changed over time. Moreover, depreciation allowances are used to allocate the original cost of the asset over several years but do not reflect loss of actual value.

TABLE 13.1 Financial highlights for Microsoft, January 2012

Price per share	$28.25	
Common shares outstanding (billion)	8.41	
Market capitalization ($ billion)	237.6	
Latest 12 Months		
Sales ($ billion)	71.12	
EBITDA ($ billion)	30.15	
Net income ($ billion)	23.48	
Earnings per share	$2.75	
Valuation	**Microsoft**	**Industry Avg**
P/E ratio	10.3	17.5
Price/Book (equivalently, Market/Book)	4.0	10.5
Price/Sales	3.3	2.7
Price/Cash flow	13.9	20.5
PEG	1.1	1.2
Profitability		
ROE (%)	44.16	24.9
ROA (%)	17.33	
Operating profit margin (%)	38.78	8.58
Net profit margin (%)	33.01	23.2

Source: Compiled from data available at **finance.yahoo.com,** January 16, 2012.

Whereas book values are based on original cost, market values measure *current* values of assets and liabilities. The market value of the shareholders' equity investment equals the difference between the current values of all assets and liabilities. We've emphasized that current values generally will not match historical ones. Equally or even more important, many assets, for example, the value of a good brand name or specialized expertise developed over many years, may not even be included on the financial statements but certainly influence market price. Market prices reflect the value of the firm as a going concern.

Can book value represent a "floor" for the stock's price, below which level the market price can never fall? Although Microsoft's book value per share is considerably less than its market price, other evidence disproves this notion. While it is not common, there are always some firms selling at a market price below book value. In early 2012, for example, such troubled firms included Sprint/Nextel, Citigroup, Mitsubishi, and AOL.

A better measure of a floor for the stock price is the firm's **liquidation value** per share. This represents the amount of money that could be realized by breaking up the firm, selling its assets, repaying its debt, and distributing the remainder to the shareholders. If the market price of equity drops below the liquidation value of the firm, the firm becomes attractive as a takeover target. A corporate raider would find it profitable to buy enough shares to gain control and then actually liquidate because the liquidation value exceeds the value of the business as a going concern.

liquidation value

Net amount that can be realized by selling the assets of a firm and paying off the debt.

Another measure of firm value is the **replacement cost** of assets less liabilities. Some analysts believe the market value of the firm cannot get too far above its replacement cost for long because, if it did, competitors would enter the market. The competitive pressure would drive down the market value of all firms until they fell to replacement cost.

replacement cost

Cost to replace a firm's assets.

This idea is popular among economists, and the ratio of market price to replacement cost is known as **Tobin's *q*,** after the Nobel Prize–winning economist James Tobin. In the long run, according to this view, the ratio of market price to replacement cost will tend toward 1, but the evidence is that this ratio can differ significantly from 1 for very long periods of time.

Tobin's *q*

Ratio of market value of the firm to replacement cost.

Although focusing on the balance sheet can give some useful information about a firm's liquidation value or its replacement cost, the analyst usually must turn to expected future cash flows for a better estimate of the firm's value as a going concern. We therefore turn to the quantitative models that analysts use to value common stock based on forecasts of future earnings and dividends.

13.2 INTRINSIC VALUE VERSUS MARKET PRICE

The most popular model for assessing the value of a firm as a going concern starts from the observation that the return on a stock investment comprises cash dividends and capital gains or losses. We begin by assuming a one-year holding period and supposing that ABC stock has an expected dividend per share, $E(D_1)$, of \$4; that the current price of a share, P_0, is \$48; and that the expected price at the end of a year, $E(P_1)$, is \$52. For now, don't worry about how you derive your forecast of next year's price. At this point we ask only whether the stock seems attractively priced *today* given your forecast of *next year's* price.

The expected holding-period return is $E(D_1)$ plus the expected price appreciation, $E(P_1) - P_0$, all divided by the current price P_0.

$$\text{Expected HPR} = E(r) = \frac{E(D_1) + [E(P_1) - P_0]}{P_0}$$

$$= \frac{4 + (52 - 48)}{48} = .167 = 16.7\%$$

Note that $E(\ )$ denotes an expected future value. Thus, $E(P_1)$ represents the expectation today of the stock price one year from now. $E(r)$ is referred to as the stock's expected holding-period return. It is the sum of the expected dividend yield, $E(D_1)/P_0$, and the expected rate of price appreciation, the capital gains yield, $[E(P_1) - P_0]/P_0$.

But what is the required rate of return for ABC stock? The capital asset pricing model (CAPM) asserts that when stock market prices are at equilibrium levels, the rate of return that investors can expect to earn on a security is $r_f + \beta[E(r_M) - r_f]$. Thus, the CAPM may be viewed as providing an estimate of the rate of return an investor can reasonably expect to earn on a security given its risk as measured by beta. This is the return that investors will require of any other investment with equivalent risk. We will denote this required rate of return as k. If a stock is priced "correctly," it will offer investors a "fair" return, that is, its *expected* return will equal its *required* return. Of course, the goal of a security analyst is to find stocks that are mis-priced. For example, an underpriced stock will provide an expected return greater than the required return.

Suppose that $r_f = 6\%$, $E(r_M) - r_f = 5\%$, and the beta of ABC is 1.2. Then the value of k is

$$k = 6\% + 1.2 \times 5\% = 12\%$$

The rate of return the investor expects exceeds the required rate based on ABC's risk by a margin of 4.7%. Naturally, the investor will want to include more of ABC stock in the portfolio than a passive strategy would dictate.

intrinsic value

The present value of a firm's expected future net cash flows discounted by the required rate of return.

Another way to see this is to compare the intrinsic value of a share of stock to its market price. The **intrinsic value,** denoted V_0, of a share of stock is defined as the present value of all cash payments to the investor in the stock, including dividends as well as the proceeds from the ultimate sale of the stock, discounted at the appropriate risk-adjusted interest rate, k. Whenever the intrinsic value, or the investor's own estimate of what the stock is really worth, exceeds the market price, the stock is considered undervalued and a good investment. For ABC, using a one-year investment horizon and a forecast that the stock can be sold at the end of the year at price $P_1 = \$52$, the intrinsic value is

$$V_0 = \frac{E(D_1) + E(P_1)}{1 + k} = \frac{\$4 + \$52}{1.12} = \$50$$

Equivalently, at a price of \$50, the investor would derive a 12% rate of return—just equal to the required rate of return—on an investment in the stock. However, at the current price of \$48, the stock is underpriced compared to intrinsic value. At this price, it provides better than a fair rate of return relative to its risk. Using the terminology of the CAPM, it is a positive-alpha stock, and investors will want to buy more of it than they would following a passive strategy.

In contrast, if the intrinsic value turns out to be lower than the current market price, investors should buy less of it than under the passive strategy. It might even pay to go short on ABC stock, as we discussed in Chapter 3.

In market equilibrium, the current market price will reflect the intrinsic value estimates of all market participants. This means the individual investor whose V_0 estimate differs from the market price, P_0, in effect must disagree with some or all of the market-consensus estimates of $E(D_1)$, $E(P_1)$, or k. A common term for the market-consensus value of the required rate of return, k, is the **market capitalization rate,** which we use often throughout this chapter.

market capitalization rate

The market-consensus estimate of the appropriate discount rate for a firm's cash flows.

You expect the price of IBX stock to be \$59.77 per share a year from now. Its current market price is \$50, and you expect it to pay a dividend one year from now of \$2.15 per share.

a. What are the stock's expected dividend yield, rate of price appreciation, and expected holding-period return?
b. If the stock has a beta of 1.15, the risk-free rate is 6% per year, and the expected rate of return on the market portfolio is 14% per year, what is the required rate of return on IBX stock?
c. What is the intrinsic value of IBX stock, and how does it compare to the current market price?

13.3 DIVIDEND DISCOUNT MODELS

Consider an investor who buys a share of Steady State Electronics stock, planning to hold it for one year. The intrinsic value of the share is the present value of the dividend to be received at the end of the first year, D_1, and the expected sales price, P_1. We will henceforth use the simpler notation P_1 instead of $E(P_1)$ to avoid clutter. Keep in mind, though, that future prices and dividends are unknown, and we are dealing with expected values, not certain values. We've already established that

$$V_0 = \frac{D_1 + P_1}{1 + k} \quad \textbf{(13.1)}$$

While this year's dividend is fairly predictable given a company's history, you might ask how we can estimate P_1, the year-end price. According to Equation 13.1, V_1 (the year-end value) will be

$$V_1 = \frac{D_2 + P_2}{1 + k}$$

If we assume the stock will be selling for its intrinsic value next year, then $V_1 = P_1$, and we can substitute this value for P_1 into Equation 13.1 to find

$$V_0 = \frac{D_1}{1 + k} + \frac{D_2 + P_2}{(1 + k)^2}$$

This equation may be interpreted as the present value of dividends plus sales price for a two-year holding period. Of course, now we need to come up with a forecast of P_2. Continuing in the same way, we can replace P_2 by $(D_3 + P_3)/(1 + k)$, which relates P_0 to the value of dividends plus the expected sales price for a three-year holding period.

More generally, for a holding period of H years, we can write the stock value as the present value of dividends over the H years plus the ultimate sales price, P_H.

$$V_0 = \frac{D_1}{1+k} + \frac{D_2}{(1+k)^2} + \cdots + \frac{D_H + P_H}{(1+k)^H} \quad \textbf{(13.2)}$$

Note the similarity between this formula and the bond valuation formula developed in Chapter 10. Each relates price to the present value of a stream of payments (coupons in the case of bonds, dividends in the case of stocks) and a final payment (the face value of the bond or the sales price of the stock). The key differences in the case of stocks are the uncertainty of dividends, the lack of a fixed maturity date, and the unknown sales price at the horizon date. Indeed, one can continue to substitute for price indefinitely to conclude

$$V_0 = \frac{D_1}{1+k} + \frac{D_2}{(1+k)^2} + \frac{D_3}{(1+k)^3} + \cdots \quad \textbf{(13.3)}$$

dividend discount model (DDM)

A formula for the intrinsic value of a firm equal to the present value of all expected future dividends.

Equation 13.3 states the stock price should equal the present value of all expected future dividends into perpetuity. This formula is called the **dividend discount model (DDM)** of stock prices.

It is tempting, but incorrect, to conclude from Equation 13.3 that the DDM focuses exclusively on dividends and ignores capital gains as a motive for investing in stock. Indeed, we assume explicitly in Equation 13.1 that capital gains (as reflected in the expected sales price, P_1) are part of the stock's value. At the same time, the price at which you can sell a stock in the future depends on dividend forecasts at that time.

The reason only dividends appear in Equation 13.3 is not that investors ignore capital gains. It is instead that those capital gains will be determined by dividend forecasts at the time the stock is sold. That is why in Equation 13.2 we can write the stock price as the present value of dividends plus sales price for *any* horizon date. P_H is the present value at time H of all dividends expected to be paid after the horizon date. That value is then discounted back to today, time 0. The DDM asserts that stock prices are determined ultimately by the cash flows accruing to stockholders, and those are dividends.

The Constant-Growth DDM

Equation 13.3 as it stands is still not very useful in valuing a stock because it requires dividend forecasts for every year into the indefinite future. To make the DDM practical, we need to introduce some simplifying assumptions. A useful and common first pass at the problem is to assume that dividends are trending upward at a stable growth rate that we will call g. For example, if $g = .05$ and the most recently paid dividend was $D_0 = 3.81$, expected future dividends are

$$D_1 = D_0(1+g) = 3.81 \times 1.05 = 4.00$$

$$D_2 = D_0(1+g)^2 = 3.81 \times (1.05)^2 = 4.20$$

$$D_3 = D_0(1+g)^3 = 3.81 \times (1.05)^3 = 4.41 \text{ etc.}$$

Using these dividend forecasts in Equation 13.3, we solve for intrinsic value as

$$V_0 = \frac{D_0(1+g)}{1+k} + \frac{D_0(1+g)^2}{(1+k)^2} + \frac{D_0(1+g)^3}{(1+k)^3} + \cdots$$

This equation can be simplified to

$$V_0 = \frac{D_0(1+g)}{k-g} = \frac{D_1}{k-g} \quad \textbf{(13.4)}$$

Note in Equation 13.4 that we divide D_1 (not D_0) by $k - g$ to calculate intrinsic value. If the market capitalization rate for Steady State is 12%, we can use Equation 13.4 to show that the intrinsic value of a share of Steady State stock is

$$\frac{\$4.00}{.12 - .05} = \$57.14$$

Equation 13.4 is called the **constant-growth DDM** or the Gordon model, after Myron J. Gordon, who popularized the model. It should remind you of the formula for the present value of a perpetuity. If dividends were expected not to grow, then the dividend stream would be a simple perpetuity, and the valuation formula for such a nongrowth stock would be $P_0 = D_1/k$.[1] Equation 13.4 is a generalization of the perpetuity formula to cover the case of a *growing* perpetuity. As g increases, the stock price also rises.

constant-growth DDM

A form of the dividend discount model that assumes dividends will grow at a constant rate.

EXAMPLE 13.1

Preferred Stock and the DDM

Preferred stock that pays a fixed dividend can be valued using the constant-growth dividend discount model. The constant growth rate of dividends is simply zero. For example, to value a preferred stock paying a fixed dividend of \$2 per share when the discount rate is 8%, we compute

$$V_0 = \frac{\$2}{.08 - 0} = \$25$$

EXAMPLE 13.2

The Constant-Growth DDM

High Flyer Industries has just paid its annual dividend of \$3 per share. The dividend is expected to grow at a constant rate of 8% indefinitely. The beta of High Flyer stock is 1, the risk-free rate is 6%, and the market risk premium is 8%. What is the intrinsic value of the stock? What would be your estimate of intrinsic value if you believed that the stock was riskier, with a beta of 1.25?

Because a \$3 dividend has just been paid and the growth rate of dividends is 8%, the forecast for the year-end dividend is \$3 × 1.08 = \$3.24. The market capitalization rate is 6% + 1.0 × 8% = 14%. Therefore, the value of the stock is

$$V_0 = \frac{D_1}{k - g} = \frac{\$3.24}{.14 - .08} = \$54$$

If the stock is perceived to be riskier, its value must be lower. At the higher beta, the market capitalization rate is 6% + 1.25 × 8% = 16%, and the stock is worth only

$$\frac{\$3.24}{.16 - .08} = \$40.50$$

The constant-growth DDM is valid only when g is less than k. If dividends were expected to grow forever at a rate faster than k, the value of the stock would be infinite. If an analyst derives an estimate of g that is greater than k, that growth rate must be unsustainable in the long run. The appropriate valuation model to use in this case is a multistage DDM such as those discussed below.

The constant-growth DDM is so widely used by stock market analysts that it is worth exploring some of its implications and limitations. The constant growth rate DDM implies that a stock's value will be greater:

1. The larger its expected dividend per share.
2. The lower the market capitalization rate, k.
3. The higher the expected growth rate of dividends.

Another implication of the constant-growth model is that the stock price is expected to grow at the same rate as dividends. To see this, suppose Steady State stock is selling at its intrinsic value of \$57.14, so that $V_0 = P_0$. Then

[1]Recall from introductory finance that the present value of a \$1-per-year perpetuity is $1/k$. For example, if k = 10%, the value of the perpetuity is \$1/.10 = \$10. Notice that if $g = 0$ in Equation 13.4, the constant-growth DDM formula is the same as the perpetuity formula.

$$P_0 = \frac{D_1}{k - g}$$

Note that price is proportional to dividends. Therefore, next year, when the dividends paid to Steady State stockholders are expected to be higher by g = 5%, price also should increase by 5%. To confirm this, note

$$D_2 = \$4(1.05) = \$4.20$$

$$P_1 = D_2/(k - g) = \$4.20/(.12 - .05) = \$60.00$$

which is 5% higher than the current price of $57.14. To generalize

$$P_1 = \frac{D_2}{k - g} = \frac{D_1(1 + g)}{k - g} = \frac{D_1}{k - g}(1 + g) = P_0(1 + g)$$

Therefore, the DDM implies that, in the case of constant expected growth of dividends, the expected rate of price appreciation in any year will equal that constant growth rate, g. For a stock whose market price equals its intrinsic value ($V_0 = P_0$) the expected holding-period return will be

$$E(r) = \text{Dividend yield} + \text{Capital gains yield}$$

$$= \frac{D_1}{P_0} + \frac{P_1 - P_0}{P_0} = \frac{D_1}{P_0} + g \qquad \textbf{(13.5)}$$

This formula offers a means to infer the market capitalization rate of a stock, for if the stock is selling at its intrinsic value, then $E(r) = k$, implying that $k = D_1/P_0 + g$. By observing the dividend yield, D_1/P_0, and estimating the growth rate of dividends, we can compute k. This equation is known also as the *discounted cash flow (DCF) formula.*

This is an approach often used in rate hearings for regulated public utilities. The regulatory agency responsible for approving utility pricing decisions is mandated to allow the firms to charge just enough to cover costs plus a "fair" profit, that is, one that allows a competitive return on the investment the firm has made in its productive capacity. In turn, that return is taken to be the expected return investors require on the stock of the firm. The $D_1/P_0 + g$ formula provides a means to infer that required return.

EXAMPLE 13.3

The Constant-Growth Model

Suppose that Steady State Electronics wins a major contract for its revolutionary computer chip. The very profitable contract will enable it to increase the growth rate of dividends from 5% to 6% without reducing the current dividend from the projected value of $4 per share. What will happen to the stock price? What will happen to future expected rates of return on the stock?

The stock price ought to increase in response to the good news about the contract, and indeed it does. The stock price jumps from its original value of $57.14 to a postannouncement price of

$$\frac{D_1}{k - g} = \frac{\$4}{.12 - .06} = \$66.67$$

Investors who are holding the stock when the good news about the contract is announced will receive a substantial windfall.

On the other hand, at the new price the expected rate of return on the stock is 12%, just as it was before the new contract was announced.

$$E(r) = \frac{D_1}{P_0} + g = \frac{\$4}{\$66.67} + .06 = .12, \text{ or } 12\%$$

This result makes sense, of course. Once the news about the contract is reflected in the stock price, the expected rate of return will be consistent with the risk of the stock. Since the risk of the stock has not changed, neither should the expected rate of return.

CONCEPT check 13.2

a. IBX's stock dividend at the end of this year is expected to be $2.15, and it is expected to grow at 11.2% per year forever. If the required rate of return on IBX stock is 15.2% per year, what is its intrinsic value?

b. If IBX's current market price is equal to this intrinsic value, what is next year's expected price?

c. If an investor were to buy IBX stock now and sell it after receiving the $2.15 dividend a year from now, what is the expected capital gain (i.e., price appreciation) in percentage terms? What is the dividend yield, and what would be the holding-period return?

Stock Prices and Investment Opportunities

Consider two companies, Cash Cow, Inc., and Growth Prospects, each with expected earnings in the coming year of $5 per share. Both companies could in principle pay out all of these earnings as dividends, maintaining a perpetual dividend flow of $5 per share. If the market capitalization rate were $k = 12.5\%$, both companies would then be valued at $D_1/k = \$5/.125 = \$40$ per share. Neither firm would grow in value, because with all earnings paid out as dividends, and no earnings reinvested in the firm, both companies' capital stock and earnings capacity would remain unchanged over time; earnings[2] and dividends would not grow.

Now suppose one of the firms, Growth Prospects, engages in projects that generate a return on investment of 15%, which is greater than the required rate of return, $k = 12.5\%$. It would be foolish for such a company to pay out all of its earnings as dividends. If Growth Prospects retains or plows back some of its earnings into its highly profitable projects, it can earn a 15% rate of return for its shareholders, whereas if it pays out all earnings as dividends, it forgoes the projects, leaving shareholders to invest the dividends in other opportunities at a fair market rate of only 12.5%. Suppose, therefore, Growth Prospects chooses a lower **dividend payout ratio** (the fraction of earnings paid out as dividends), reducing payout from 100% to 40% and maintaining a **plowback ratio** (the fraction of earnings reinvested in the firm) of 60%. The plowback ratio also is referred to as the **earnings retention ratio.**

dividend payout ratio

Percentage of earnings paid out as dividends.

The dividend of the company, therefore, will be only $2 (40% of $5 earnings) instead of $5. Will the share price fall? No, it will rise! Although dividends initially fall under the earnings reinvestment policy, subsequent growth in the assets of the firm because of reinvested profits will generate growth in future dividends, which will be reflected in today's share price.

plowback ratio or earnings retention ratio

The proportion of the firm's earnings that is reinvested in the business (and not paid out as dividends).

Figure 13.1 illustrates the dividend streams generated by Growth Prospects under two dividend policies. A low reinvestment rate plan allows the firm to pay higher initial dividends

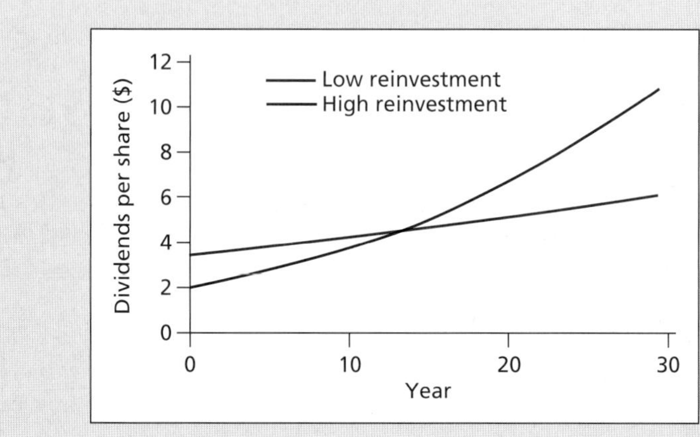

FIGURE 13.1

Dividend growth for two earnings reinvestment policies

[2]Actually, we are referring here to earnings net of the funds necessary to maintain the productivity of the firm's capital, that is, earnings net of "economic depreciation." In other words, the earnings figure should be interpreted as the maximum amount of money the firm could pay out each year in perpetuity without depleting its productive capacity. For this reason, the net earnings number may be quite different from the accounting earnings figure that the firm reports in its financial statements. We will explore this further in the next chapter.

but results in a lower dividend growth rate. Eventually, a high reinvestment rate plan will provide higher dividends. If the dividend growth generated by the reinvested earnings is high enough, the stock will be worth more under the high reinvestment strategy.

How much growth will be generated? Suppose Growth Prospects starts with plant and equipment of \$100 million and is all-equity-financed. With a return on investment or equity (ROE) of 15%, total earnings are ROE × \$100 million = .15 × \$100 million = \$15 million. There are 3 million shares of stock outstanding, so earnings per share are \$5, as posited above. If 60% of the \$15 million in this year's earnings is reinvested, then the value of the firm's capital stock will increase by .60 × \$15 million = \$9 million, or by 9%. The percentage increase in the capital stock is the rate at which income was generated (ROE) times the plowback ratio (the fraction of earnings reinvested in more capital), which we will denote as b.

Now endowed with 9% more capital, the company earns 9% more income and pays out 9% higher dividends. The growth rate of the dividends, therefore, is[3]

$$g = \text{ROE} \times b = 15\% \times .60 = 9\%$$

If the stock price equals its intrinsic value, and this growth rate can be sustained (i.e., if the ROE and payout ratios are consistent with the long-run capabilities of the firm), then the stock should sell at

$$P_0 = \frac{D_1}{k - g} = \frac{\$2}{.125 - .09} = \$57.14$$

When Growth Prospects pursued a no-growth policy and paid out all earnings as dividends, the stock price was only \$40. Therefore, you can think of \$40 as the value per share of the assets the company already has in place.

When Growth Prospects decided to reduce current dividends and reinvest some of its earnings in new investments, its stock price increased. The increase in the stock price reflects the fact that planned investments provide an expected rate of return greater than the required rate. In other words, the investment opportunities have positive net present value. The value of the firm rises by the NPV of these investment opportunities. This net present value is also called the **present value of growth opportunities,** or **PVGO.**

present value of growth opportunities (PVGO)

Net present value of a firm's future investments.

Therefore, we can think of the value of the firm as the sum of the value of assets already in place, or the no-growth value of the firm, plus the net present value of the future investments the firm will make, which is the PVGO. For Growth Prospects, PVGO = \$17.14 per share:

$$\text{Price} = \text{No-growth value per share} + \text{PVGO}$$

$$P_0 = \frac{E_1}{k} + \text{PVGO}$$

$$\$57.14 = \$40 + \$17.14 \qquad \textbf{(13.6)}$$

We know that, in reality, dividend cuts almost always are accompanied by steep drops in stock prices. Does this contradict our analysis? Not necessarily: Dividend cuts are usually taken as bad news about the future prospects of the firm, and it is the *new information* about the firm—not the reduced dividend yield per se—that is responsible for the stock price decline.

For example, when J.P. Morgan cut its quarterly dividend from 38 cents to 5 cents a share in 2009, its stock price actually increased by about 5%: The company was able to convince investors that the cut would conserve cash and prepare the firm to weather a severe recession. When

[3]We can derive this relationship more generally by noting that with a fixed ROE, earnings (which equal ROE × Book value) will grow at the same rate as the book value of the firm. Abstracting from net new capital raised by the firm, the growth rate of book value equals reinvested earnings/book value. Therefore,

$$g = \frac{\text{Reinvested earnings}}{\text{Book value}} = \frac{\text{Reinvested earnings}}{\text{Total earnings}} \times \frac{\text{Total earnings}}{\text{Book value}} = b \times \text{ROE}$$

investors were convinced that the dividend cut made sense, the stock price actually increased. Similarly, when BP announced in the wake of the massive 2010 Gulf oil spill that it would suspend dividends for the rest of the year, its stock price did not budge. The cut already had been widely anticipated, so it was not new information. These examples show that stock price declines in response to dividend cuts are really a response to the information conveyed by the cut.

It is important to recognize that growth per se is not what investors desire. Growth enhances company value only if it is achieved by investment in projects with attractive profit opportunities (i.e., with ROE > k). To see why, let's now consider Growth Prospects' unfortunate sister company, Cash Cow. Cash Cow's ROE is only 12.5%, just equal to the required rate of return, k. Therefore, the NPV of its investment opportunities is zero. We've seen that following a zero-growth strategy with $b = 0$ and $g = 0$, the value of Cash Cow will be $E_1/k = \$5/.125 = \$40$ per share. Now suppose Cash Cow chooses a plowback ratio of $b = .60$, the same as Growth Prospects' plowback. Then g would be

$$g = \text{ROE} \times b = .125 \times .60 = .075$$

but the stock price is still

$$P_0 = \frac{D_1}{k - g} = \frac{\$2}{.125 - .075} = \$40$$

no different from the no-growth strategy.

In the case of Cash Cow, the dividend reduction that frees funds for reinvestment in the firm generates only enough growth to maintain the stock price at the current level. This is as it should be: If the firm's projects yield only what investors can earn on their own, then NPV is zero, and shareholders cannot be made better off by a high reinvestment rate policy. This demonstrates that "growth" is not the same as growth opportunities. To justify reinvestment, the firm must engage in projects with better prospective returns than those shareholders can find elsewhere. Notice also that the PVGO of Cash Cow is zero: PVGO $= P_0 - E_1/k = 40 - 40 = 0$. With ROE $= k$, there is no advantage to plowing funds back into the firm; this shows up as PVGO of zero. In fact, this is why firms with considerable cash flow, but limited investment prospects, are called "cash cows." The cash these firms generate is best taken out of or "milked from" the firm.

EXAMPLE 13.4

Growth Opportunities

Takeover Target is run by entrenched management that insists on reinvesting 60% of its earnings in projects that provide an ROE of 10%, despite the fact that the firm's capitalization rate is $k = 15\%$. The firm's year-end dividend will be $2 per share, paid out of earnings of $5 per share. At what price will the stock sell? What is the present value of growth opportunities? Why would such a firm be a takeover target for another firm?

Given current management's investment policy, the dividend growth rate will be

$$g = \text{ROE} \times b = 10\% \times .6 = 6\%$$

and the stock price should be

$$P_0 = \frac{\$2}{.15 - .06} = \$22.22$$

The present value of growth opportunities is

$$\begin{aligned} \text{PVGO} &= \text{Price per share} - \text{No-growth value per share} \\ &= \$22.22 - E_1/k = \$22.22 - \$5/.15 = -\$11.11 \end{aligned}$$

PVGO is *negative.* This is because the net present value of the firm's projects is negative: The rate of return on those assets is less than the opportunity cost of capital.

Such a firm would be subject to takeover, because another firm could buy the firm for the market price of $22.22 per share and increase the value of the firm by changing its investment policy. For example, if the new management simply paid out all earnings as dividends, the value of the firm would increase to its no-growth value, $E_1/k = \$5/.15 = \$33.33$.

CONCEPT check 13.3

a. Calculate the price of a firm with a plowback ratio of .60 if its ROE is 20%. Current earnings, E_1, will be \$5 per share, and $k = 12.5\%$.
b. What if ROE is 10%, which is less than the market capitalization rate? Compare the firm's price in this instance to that of a firm with the same ROE and E_1 but a plowback ratio of $b = 0$.

Life Cycles and Multistage Growth Models

As useful as the constant-growth DDM formula is, you need to remember that it is based on a simplifying assumption, namely, that the dividend growth rate will be constant forever. In fact, firms typically pass through life cycles with very different dividend profiles in different phases. In early years, there are ample opportunities for profitable reinvestment in the company. Payout ratios are low, and growth is correspondingly rapid. In later years, the firm matures, production capacity is sufficient to meet market demand, competitors enter the market, and attractive opportunities for reinvestment may become harder to find. In this mature phase, the firm may choose to increase the dividend payout ratio, rather than retain earnings. The dividend level increases, but thereafter it grows at a slower rate because the company has fewer growth opportunities.

Table 13.2 illustrates this profile. It gives Value Line's forecasts of return on capital, dividend payout ratio, and projected three-year growth rate in earnings per share of a sample of the firms included in the computer software and services industry versus those of East Coast electric utilities. (We compare return on capital rather than return on equity because the latter is affected by leverage, which tends to be far greater in the electric utility industry than in the software industry. Return on capital measures operating income per dollar of total long-term

TABLE 13.2 Financial ratios in two industries

	Return on Capital	Payout Ratio	Growth Rate 2012–2015
Computer Software			
Adobe Systems	13.0%	0.0%	15.4%
Cognizant	19.0	0.0	21.0
Compuware	16.5	0.0	18.6
Intuit	21.0	21.0	13.3
Microsoft	31.5	30.0	10.2
Oracle	20.0	14.0	10.3
Red Hat	14.0	0.0	17.9
Parametric Tech	15.5	0.0	9.6
SAP	18.5	28.0	6.7
Median	18.5%	0.0%	13.3%
Electric Utilities			
Central Hudson G&E	6.0%	67.0%	2.6%
Central Vermont	6.0	54.0	1.9
Consolidated Edison	6.0	63.0	2.7
Duke Energy	5.5	65.0	4.4
Northeast Utilities	6.5	47.0	6.3
NStar	9.0	60.0	8.4
Pennsylvania Power (PPL Corp.)	7.0	55.0	3.6
Public Services Enter.	6.5	45.0	8.4
United Illuminating	5.0	73.0	2.2
Median	6.0%	60.0%	3.6%

Source: From *Value Line Investment Survey*, November and December 2011. Reprinted with permission of Value Line Investment Survey © 2012 Value Line, Inc. All Rights Reserved Worldwide. "Value Line" is a registered trademark of Value Line Inc.

financing, regardless of whether the source of the capital supplied is debt or equity. We will return to this issue in the next chapter.)

By and large, software firms have attractive investment opportunities. The median return on capital of these firms is forecast to be 18.5%, and the firms have responded with quite high plowback ratios. Most of these firms pay no dividends at all. The high returns on capital and high plowback ratios result in rapid growth. The median growth rate of earnings per share in this group is projected at 13.3%.

In contrast, the electric utilities are more representative of mature firms. Their median return on capital is lower, 6%; dividend payout is higher, 60%; and average growth rate is lower, 3.6%. We conclude that the higher payouts of the electric utilities reflect their more limited opportunities to reinvest earnings at attractive rates of return.

To value companies with temporarily high growth, analysts use a multistage version of the dividend discount model. Dividends in the early high-growth period are forecast and their combined present value is calculated. Then, once the firm is projected to settle down to a steady growth phase, the constant-growth DDM is applied to value the remaining stream of dividends.

We can illustrate this with a real-life example using a **two-stage DDM.** Figure 13.2 is a *Value Line Investment Survey* report on Honda Motor Co. Some of Honda's relevant information of the end of 2011 is highlighted.

two-stage DDM

Dividend discount model in which dividend growth is assumed to level off only at some future date.

Honda's beta appears at the circled A, its recent stock price at the B, the per-share dividend payments at the C, the ROE (referred to as "return on shareholder equity") at the D, and the dividend payout ratio (referred to as "all dividends to net profits") at the E.[4] The rows ending at C, D, and E are historical time series. The boldfaced italicized entries under 2012 are estimates for that year. Similarly, the entries in the far right column (labeled 14–16) are forecasts for some time between 2014 and 2016, which we will take to be 2015.

Value Line provides explicit dividend forecasts over the relative short term, with dividends rising from $.72 in 2012 to $1 in 2015. We can obtain dividend inputs for this initial period by using the explicit forecasts for 2012–2015 and linear interpolation for the years between:

2012	$ .72
2013	$ .81
2014	$ .90
2015	$1.00

Now let us assume the dividend growth rate will be steady beyond 2015. What is a reasonable guess for that steady-state growth rate? Value Line forecasts a dividend payout ratio of .25 and an ROE of 10%, implying long-term growth will be

$$g = \text{ROE} \times b = 10\% \times (1 - .25) = 7.5\%$$

Our estimate of Honda's intrinsic value using an investment horizon of 2015 is therefore obtained from Equation 13.2, which we restate here:

$$\begin{aligned} V_{2011} &= \frac{D_{2012}}{(1+k)} + \frac{D_{2013}}{(1+k)^2} + \frac{D_{2014}}{(1+k)^3} + \frac{D_{2015} + P_{2015}}{(1+k)^4} \\ &= \frac{.72}{(1+k)} + \frac{.81}{(1+k)^2} + \frac{.90}{(1+k)^3} + \frac{1.00 + P_{2015}}{(1+k)^4} \end{aligned}$$

Here, P_{2015} represents the forecast price at which we can sell our shares of Honda at the end of 2015, when dividends enter their constant-growth phase. That price, according to the constant-growth DDM, should be

[4]Because Honda is a Japanese firm, Americans would hold its shares via ADRs, or American Depository Receipts. ADRs are not shares of the firm but are *claims* to shares of the underlying foreign stock that are then traded in U.S. security markets. Value Line notes that each Honda ADR is a claim on one common share, but in other cases, each ADR may represent a claim to either multiple shares or even fractional shares.

FIGURE 13.2

Value Line Investment Survey report on Honda Motor Co.

Source: From *Value Line Investment Survey,* November 25, 2011. © 2011 Value Line, Inc. All Rights Reserved Worldwide. "Value Line" is a registered trademark of Value Line Inc.

HONDA MOTOR (ADR) NYSE-HMC | RECENT PRICE 29.54 | P/E RATIO 13.0 (Trailing: 20.2 Median: 11.0) | RELATIVE P/E RATIO 0.93 | DIV'D YLD 1.4% | VALUE LINE

(A)

TIMELINESS 3 Raised 8/26/11
SAFETY 2 Raised 3/2/07
TECHNICAL 3 Lowered 11/18/11
BETA .90 (1.00 = Market)

High:	22.7	23.1	23.8	23.6	26.1	29.7	39.9	40.8	36.4	34.5	39.7	44.6
Low:	16.1	13.6	17.0	15.5	19.3	23.8	27.1	31.3	17.3	20.3	28.3	28.0

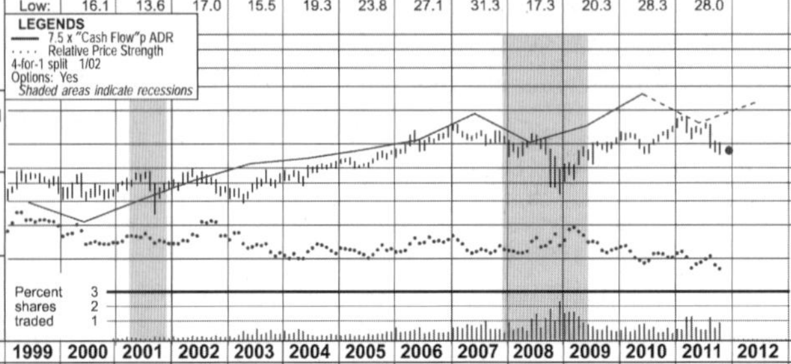

LEGENDS
— 7.5 x "Cash Flow"p ADR
.... Relative Price Strength
4-for-1 split 1/02
Options: Yes
Shaded areas indicate recessions

Target Price Range 2014 | 2015 | 2016

2014-16 PROJECTIONS

	Price	Gain	Ann'l Total Return
High	65	(+120%)	23%
Low	50	(+70%)	15%

Insider Decisions

NOT REPORTED

U.S. Institutional Decisions

	4Q2010	1Q2011	2Q2011
to Buy	87	105	114
to Sell	103	89	87
Hld's(000)	55739	54719	62595

Percent shares traded

% TOT. RETURN 10/11

	THIS STOCK	VL ARITH.* INDEX
1 yr.	-17.0	4.9
3 yr.	21.4	82.1
5 yr.	-13.3	27.6

(C)

1995	1996	1997	1998	1999	2000	2001	2002	2003	2004	2005	2006	2007	2008	2009	2010	2011	2012	© VALUE LINE PUB. LLC	14-16
107	124	133	121	106	124	133	120	106	107	118	118	100	98.23	93.04	83.19	*80.0*	*80.0*	Translation Rate (Yen/$)[A]	*80.0*
20.39	21.89	23.15	26.52	29.52	26.77	28.41	34.09	40.49	43.55	45.82	51.53	65.99	56.16	50.82	59.61	*58.45*	*65.75*	Sales per ADR [B]	*81.25*
.94	1.48	1.60	2.05	2.10	1.67	2.15	2.77	3.36	3.58	3.97	4.48	6.15	4.35	5.32	7.82	*5.50*	*7.00*	"Cash Flow" per ADR	*7.90*
.34	.90	1.01	1.30	1.27	.96	1.40	1.83	2.30	2.42	2.76	2.75	3.30	.77	1.59	3.55	*1.70*	*3.20*	Earnings per ADR [BC]	*4.00*
.07	.06	.07	.09	.10	.09	.10	.13	.15	.23	.33	.66	.76	.75	.37	.65	*.68*	*.72*	Gross Div'ds Decl'd/ADR [D]	*1.00*
.72	.90	1.19	1.01	1.08	1.18	1.17	1.36	1.43	1.88	2.13	2.78	3.60	3.56	2.32	2.12	*2.50*	*2.65*	Cap'l Spending per ADR	*3.05*
5.49	5.74	6.20	7.51	9.34	9.24	9.93	11.25	14.26	16.56	19.08	20.83	24.98	22.48	25.64	29.68	*31.05*	*33.45*	Book Value per ADR	*39.60*
1948.6	1948.7	1948.8	1948.8	1948.8	1948.8	1948.8	1948.8	1907.3	1849.7	1840.8	1824.7	1815.4	1814.6	1814.6	1802.3	*1800.0*	*1800.0*	Equiv ADRs Outst'g [E]	*1795.0*
26.5	14.3	16.5	13.6	16.0	19.3	14.3	10.8	8.8	10.0	9.8	12.7	10.1	35.8	19.8	10.0	*Bold figures are*		Avg Ann'l P/E Ratio	*14.0*
1.77	.90	.95	.71	.91	1.25	.73	.59	.50	.53	.52	.69	.54	2.15	1.32	.64	*Value Line*		Relative P/E Ratio	*.95*
.7%	.4%	.4%	.5%	.5%	.5%	.5%	.7%	.8%	1.0%	1.2%	1.9%	2.3%	2.7%	1.2%	1.8%	*estimates*		Avg Ann'l Div'd Yield	*2.3%*

CAPITAL STRUCTURE as of 9/30/11
Total Debt $49008 mill. **Due in 5 Yrs** $47876 mill.
LT Debt $23330 mill. **LT Interest** $1550 mill.
(LT int. earned and total int. coverage: over 25X) (31% of Cap'l)

Pension Assets-3/11 $13.8 bill. **Oblig.** $19.5 bill.

Pfd Stock None

Common Stock 1,802.3 mill. shares (equivalent to 1,802.3 ADRs)

MARKET CAP: $53.2 billion (Large Cap)

2001	2002	2003	2004	2005	2006	2007	2008	2009	2010	2011	2012		14-16
55357	66429	77232	80549	84345	94018	119801	101916	92210	107430	*105250*	*118380*	Sales ($mill) [B]	*145850*
11.3%	11.4%	10.0%	9.9%	10.0%	11.0%	12.3%	8.3%	11.6%	13.5%	*9.0%*	*9.0%*	Operating Margin	*12.5%*
1466.0	1840.6	2019.5	2102.2	2232.0	3150.0	5174.0	6491.0	6768.0	7665.1	*6700*	*6900*	Depreciation ($mill)	*7000*
2727.0	3555.5	4393.4	4527.4	5082.0	5023.0	5989.0	1395.0	2885.0	6420.3	*3190*	*5735*	Net Profit ($mill)	*7210*
41.9%	40.2%	39.4%	40.6%	38.9%	35.8%	43.3%	67.9%	43.7%	32.8%	*32.0%*	*35.0%*	Income Tax Rate	*35.0%*
4.9%	5.4%	5.7%	5.6%	6.0%	5.3%	5.0%	1.4%	3.1%	6.0%	*3.0%*	*4.8%*	Net Profit Margin	*4.9%*
d162.0	1416.4	3013.0	2422.7	5418.0	8182.0	5520.0	3907.0	12840	13486	*27630*	*36835*	Working Cap'l ($mill)	*48020*
5388.0	9501.5	13195	14522	15996	16160	18332	19675	24861	24562	*27500*	*30000*	Long-Term Debt ($mill)	*25000*
19353	21914	27197	30629	35122	38012	45356	40795	46525	53493	*55850*	*60200*	Shr. Equity ($mill)	*71095*
11.1%	11.4%	10.9%	10.1%	10.0%	9.8%	10.3%	2.7%	4.2%	8.2%	*4.0%*	*6.5%*	Return on Total Capital	*7.5%*
14.1%	16.2%	16.2%	14.8%	14.5%	13.2%	13.2%	3.4%	6.2%	12.0%	*5.5%*	*9.5%*	Return on Shr. Equity	*10.0%*
13.1%	15.1%	15.0%	13.3%	12.7%	10.7%	9.8%	NMF	4.8%	9.9%	*3.5%*	*7.5%*	Retained to Com Eq	*7.5%*
7%	7%	7%	10%	12%	19%	25%	102%	23%	17%	*38%*	*23%*	All Div'ds to Net Prof	*25%*

(D)

(E)

CURRENT POSITION ($MILL.)	2009	2010	9/30/11
Cash Assets	12037	15375	17161
Receivables	9496	23065	21220
Inventory (FIFO)	10056	10817	10603
Other	18000	7122	7261
Current Assets	49589	56379	56245
Accts Payable	8625	8616	8990
Debt Due	7763	24730	25678
Other	20361	9547	8970
Current Liab.	36749	42893	43638

ANNUAL RATES of change (per ADR)	Past 10 Yrs.	Past 5 Yrs.	Est'd '08-'10 to '14-'16
Sales	7.0%	5.0%	*6.5%*
"Cash Flow"	11.5%	10.0%	*5.0%*
Earnings	5.5%	-4.5%	*12.5%*
Dividends	20.5%	20.0%	*9.0%*
Book Value	11.5%	9.5%	*7.5%*

Fiscal Year Begins	QUARTERLY SALES ($ mill.) [B] Jun.30	Sep.30	Dec.31	Mar.31	Full Fiscal Year
2008	29189	28778	25789	18160	101916
2009	21520	22105	24084	24501	92210
2010	28387	27070	25369	26604	107430
2011	21431	24536	*28650*	*30633*	*105250*
2012	*28550*	*28840*	*30060*	*30930*	*118380*

Fiscal Year Begins	EARNINGS PER ADR [BC] Jun.30	Sep.30	Dec.31	Mar.31	Full Fiscal Year
2008	1.01	.69	.11	d1.04	.77
2009	.04	.33	.81	.43	1.59
2010	1.81	.90	.54	.30	3.55
2011	.22	.44	*.50*	*.54*	*1.70*
2012	*.80*	*.90*	*.75*	*.75*	*3.20*

Cal-endar	GROSS QUARTERLY DIV'DS PAID [D] Mar.31	Jun.30	Sep.30	Dec.31	Full Year
2007	.140	--	.353	.202	.70
2008	.204	--	.403	.23	.81
2009	.116	--	.168	.091	.38
2010	.103	--	.251	.13	.48
2011	.216	--	.185	.195	

BUSINESS: Honda Motor Company, Ltd. is Japan's second-largest auto maker & the world's biggest motorcycle producer. Manufactures cars in Japan, United States, Canada, United Kingdom; cycles in 32 countries. Fiscal 2009 unit sales: autos, 3.4 million; cycles, 9.6 mill.; power products, 4.7 mill. Sales by region: United States & Canada, 44%; Japan, 18%; Europe, 9%; other, 29%. Research & development, 5.4% of sales. Has about 176,815 employees. Financial institutions control 13.7% of common stock (12/09 20-F). President & CEO: Takanobu Ito. Inc.: Japan. Address: 1-1, 2-chome, Minami-Aoyama, Minato-ku. Tokyo 107, Japan. United States address: 156 West 56th St., 20th Floor, New York, NY 10019. Telephone: 212-355-9191. Internet: www.honda.com.

Honda Motor Company's results have remained under pressure. The automaker struggled in the first half of fiscal 2011 (year ends March 31, 2012) as a result of the natural disasters in Japan. Second-quarter sales fell 12% on a constant-currency basis, with a 14% drop in automobile unit sales. The reduced volume was attributable to ongoing supply shortages and production disruptions. This resulted in increased fixed costs per vehicle that, together with unfavorable currency translation, weighed on the bottom line. Indeed, earnings per ADR fell 51%, to $0.44. Yet, the bottom-line result was relatively decent, considering the significant challenges. Honda's strong diversity has helped support the bottom line, and keep the company out of the loss column. Notably, the motorcycle segment posted a 20% increase in units, while power products volume improved 9%.

The near-term outlook remains challenging. Honda had just begun to emerge from the natural disasters in Japan, with a pickup in production. However, the company now has to deal with the impact from severe flooding in Thailand. The flooding has damaged plants, equipment, and inventory, while resulting in production disruptions and stoppages. The actual impact remains unclear, and management is evaluating the extent of the damage. Full-year guidance was withheld as a result of the uncertainty.

The company's performance should improve in fiscal 2012. The recent problems in Thailand should be largely worked through by the end of this fiscal year. Meanwhile, production in other regions should continue to ramp. Top-line growth should also receive a boost from the rollout of new models, while improved capacity utilization ought to lift margins.

These neutrally ranked shares may face some additional pressure in the near term. Yet, the stock has decent 3- to 5-year appreciation potential.

Joel Schwed *November 25, 2011*

Sales (and Operating Margins*) by Business Line

	2009	2010	2011	2012
Automobiles	70452(1.9%)	81768(3.9%)	*76825(4.0%)*	*86520(5.0%)*
Motorcycles	12256(5.2%)	15485(10.8%)	*18250(10.0%)*	*20025(10.0%)*
Fin'l Svcs & Other	9502(19.3%)	10177(21.2%)	*10175(20.0%)*	*11835(20.0%)*
Company Total	92210(4.2%)	107430(6.4%)	*105250(6.0%)*	*118380(6.5%)*

*After depreciation and corporate expenses

(A) At fiscal yearend. (B) FY ends March 31 of following year. Most recent quarterly figs. based on est'd avg. exch. rate for the full year. (C) Dil. egs., based on U.S. accounting; primary through 1996. Excl. nonrecur. gains: '96, 8¢; '10 8¢. Next egs. rpt. due early February. Quarterly total may not sum due to rounding. (D) Before 15% Japanese withholding tax. Dividends historically paid in early March, July, Sept., and December. (E) In mill. of American Depositary Receipts, adj. for split. Each common share represents 1 ADR.

Company's Financial Strength	B++
Stock's Price Stability	85
Price Growth Persistence	75
Earnings Predictability	15

$$P_{2015} = \frac{D_{2016}}{k - g} = \frac{D_{2015}(1 + g)}{k - g} = \frac{1.00 \times 1.075}{k - .075}$$

The only variable remaining to be determined to calculate intrinsic value is the market capitalization rate, k.

One way to obtain k is from the CAPM. Observe from the Value Line data that Honda's beta is .90. The risk-free rate on long-term T-bonds in late 2011 was about 2.9%.[5] Suppose that the market risk premium were forecast at 8%, roughly in line with its historical average. This would imply that the forecast for the market return was

$$\text{Risk-free rate} + \text{Market risk premium} = 2.9\% + 8\% = 10.9\%$$

Therefore, we can solve for the market capitalization rate for Honda as

$$\begin{aligned} k &= r_f + \beta[E(r_M) - r_f] \\ &= 2.9\% + .90\,(10.9 - 2.9) = 10.1\% \end{aligned}$$

Our forecast for the stock price in 2015 is thus

$$P_{2015} = \frac{\$1.00 \times 1.075}{.101 - .075} = \$41.35$$

and today's estimate of intrinsic value is

$$V_{2011} = \frac{.72}{1.101} + \frac{.81}{(1.101)^2} + \frac{.90}{(1.101)^3} + \frac{1.00 + 41.35}{(1.101)^4} = \$30.81$$

We know from the Value Line report that Honda's actual price was $29.54 (at the circled B). Our intrinsic value analysis indicates Honda was underpriced by about 4.1%. Should we increase our holdings of Honda stock?

Perhaps. But before betting the farm, stop to consider how much confidence you should place in this estimate. We've had to guess at dividends in the near future, the ultimate growth rate of those dividends, and the appropriate discount rate. Moreover, we've assumed Honda will follow a relatively simple two-stage growth process. In practice, the growth of dividends can follow more complicated patterns. Even small errors in these approximations could upset a conclusion.

For example, we saw in Chapter 7 that betas are typically estimated with considerable imprecision. Suppose that Honda's beta is actually 1 rather than .9. Then its risk premium will be larger, and its market capitalization rate will be 10.9%. At this higher capitalization rate, the intrinsic value of the firm based on the two-stage model falls to $23.53, which is *less* than its recent stock price. Our conclusion regarding mispricing is reversed.

The exercise highlights the importance of assessing the sensitivity of your analysis to changes in underlying assumptions when you attempt to value stocks. Your estimates of stock values are no better than your assumptions. Sensitivity analysis will highlight the inputs that need to be most carefully examined. For example, we just found that even small changes in the estimated risk premium of the stock can result in big changes in intrinsic value. Similarly, small changes in the assumed growth rate change intrinsic value substantially. On the other hand, reasonable changes in the dividends forecast between 2012 and 2015 have a small impact on intrinsic value.

CONCEPT check 13.4

Confirm that the intrinsic value of Honda using the same data as in our example, but assuming its beta is 1, is $23.53. (*Hint:* First calculate the discount rate and stock price in 2015. Then calculate the present value of all interim dividends plus the present value of the 2015 sales price.)

[5] When valuing long-term assets such as stocks, it is common to treat the long-term Treasury bond, rather than short-term T-bills, as the risk-free asset.

SPREADSHEET 13.1

A three-stage growth model for Honda

eXcel

Please visit us at www.mhhe.com/bkm

	A	B	C	D	E	F	G	H	I
1	**Inputs**			Year	Dividend	Div growth	Term value	Investor CF	
2	beta	0.9		2012	0.72			0.72	
3	mkt_prem	0.08		2013	0.81			0.81	
4	rf	0.029		2014	0.91			0.91	
5	k_equity	0.1010		2015	1.00			1.00	
6	plowback	0.75		2016	1.12	0.1157		1.12	
7	roe	0.1		2017	1.24	0.1116		1.24	
8	term_gwth	0.075		2018	1.37	0.1076		1.37	
9				2019	1.52	0.1035		1.52	
10				2020	1.67	0.0994		1.67	
11				2021	1.83	0.0954		1.83	
12	Value Line			2022	1.99	0.0913		1.99	
13	forecasts of			2023	2.17	0.0872		2.17	
14	annual dividends			2024	2.35	0.0831		2.35	
15				2025	2.53	0.0791		2.53	
16				2026	2.72	0.0750		2.72	
17	Transitional period			2027	2.93	0.0750	120.96	123.89	
18	with slowing dividend								
19	growth							36.79	= PV of CF
20		Beginning of constant			E17*(1+F17)/(B5−F17)				
21		growth period						NPV(B5,H2:H17)	

Multistage Growth Models

The two-stage growth model that we just considered for Honda is a good start toward realism, but clearly we could do even better if our valuation model allowed for more flexible patterns of growth. Multistage growth models allow dividends per share to grow at several different rates as the firm matures. Many analysts use three-stage growth models. They may allow for year-by-year forecasts of dividends for the short term, a final period of sustainable growth, and a transition period in between, during which dividend growth rates taper off from the initial rate to the ultimate sustainable rate. These models are conceptually no harder to work with than a two-stage model, but they require many more calculations and can be tedious to do by hand. It is easy, however, to build an Excel spreadsheet for such a model.

Spreadsheet 13.1 is an example of such a model. Column B contains the inputs we have used so far for Honda. Column E contains dividend forecasts. In cells E2 through E5 we present the Value Line estimates for the next four years. Dividend growth in this period is about 11.57% annually. Rather than assume a sudden transition to constant dividend growth starting in 2015, we assume instead that the dividend growth rate in 2015 will be 11.57% and that it will decline linearly through 2026 (see column F), finally reaching the constant terminal growth rate of 7.5% in 2026. Each dividend in the transition period is the previous year's dividend times that year's growth rate. Terminal value once the firm enters a constant-growth stage (cell G17) is computed from the constant-growth DDM. Finally, investor cash flow in each period (column H) equals dividends in each year plus the terminal value in 2027. The present value of these cash flows is computed in cell H19 as $36.79, about 20% more than the value we found in the two-stage model. We obtain a greater intrinsic value in this case because we assume that dividend growth, which at the current rate of 11.57% is extremely rapid, only gradually declines to its steady state value.

13.4 PRICE–EARNINGS RATIOS

The Price–Earnings Ratio and Growth Opportunities

price–earnings multiple

The ratio of a stock's price to its earnings per share.

Much of the real-world discussion of stock market valuation concentrates on the firm's **price–earnings multiple,** the ratio of price per share to earnings per share, commonly called the P/E ratio. In fact, one common approach to valuing a firm is to use an earnings multiplier. The value of the stock is obtained by multiplying projected earnings per share by a forecast of the P/E ratio. This procedure seems simple, but its apparent simplicity is deceptive. First, forecasting earnings is challenging. As we saw in the previous chapter, earnings will depend on international, macroeconomic, and industry as well as firm-specific factors, many of which are highly unpredictable. Second, forecasting the P/E multiple is even more difficult. P/E ratios vary across industries and over time. Nevertheless, our discussion of stock valuation provides some insight into the factors that ought to determine a firm's P/E ratio.

Recall our discussion of growth opportunities, in which we compared two firms, Growth Prospects and Cash Cow, each of which had earnings per share of \$5. Growth Prospects reinvested 60% of its earnings in prospects with an ROE of 15%, while Cash Cow paid out all of its earnings as dividends. Cash Cow had a price of \$40, giving it a P/E multiple of 40/5 = 8, while Growth Prospects sold for \$57.14, giving it a multiple of 57.14/5 = 11.4. This observation suggests the P/E ratio might serve as a useful indicator of expectations of growth opportunities. We can see this explicitly by rearranging Equation 13.6 to

$$\frac{P_0}{E_1} = \frac{1}{k}\left[1 + \frac{\text{PVGO}}{E_1/k}\right] \tag{13.7}$$

When PVGO = 0, Equation 13.7 shows that $P_0 = E_1/k$. The stock is valued like a nongrowing perpetuity of EPS_1. The P/E ratio is just $1/k$. However, as PVGO becomes an increasingly dominant contributor to price, the P/E ratio can rise dramatically.

The ratio of PVGO to E/k has a simple interpretation. It is the ratio of the component of firm value reflecting growth opportunities to the component of value reflecting assets already in place (i.e., the no-growth value of the firm, E/k). When future growth opportunities dominate the estimate of total value, the firm will command a high price relative to current earnings. Thus, a high P/E multiple appears to indicate that a firm is endowed with ample growth opportunities.

EXAMPLE 13.5

P/E Ratios and Growth Opportunities

Return again to Takeover Target, the firm we first encountered in Example 13.4. Earnings are \$5 per share and the capitalization rate is 15%, implying that the no-growth value of the firm is E_1/k = \$5/.15 = \$33.33. The stock price actually is \$22.22, implying that the present value of growth opportunities equals −\$11.11. This implies that the P/E ratio should be

$$\frac{P_0}{E_1} = \frac{1}{k}\left[1 + \frac{\text{PVGO}}{E/k}\right] = \frac{1}{.15}\left[1 + \frac{-\$11.11}{\$33.3}\right] = 4.44$$

In fact, the stock price is \$22.22 and earnings are \$5 per share, so the P/E ratio is \$22.22/\$5 = 4.44.

Let's see if P/E multiples do vary with growth prospects. Between 1995 and 2011, for example, Intel's P/E ratio averaged about 24.3 while Consolidated Edison's average P/E was only 13.3. These numbers do not necessarily imply that Intel was overpriced compared to Con Ed. If investors believed Intel would grow faster than Con Ed, the higher price per dollar would be justified. That is, investors might well pay a higher price per dollar of *current earnings* if they expect that earnings stream to grow more rapidly. In fact Intel's growth rate has been consistent with its higher P/E multiple. In this period, its earnings per share grew nearly fivefold, while Con Ed's earnings grew by only 20%. Figure 13.4 (on page 427) shows the EPS history of the two companies.

Clearly, the differences in expected growth opportunities justify differentials in P/E ratios across firms. The P/E ratio is in large part a reflection of the market's optimism concerning a firm's growth prospects. In their use of a P/E ratio, analysts must decide whether they are more or less optimistic than the market. If they are more optimistic, they will recommend buying the stock.

TABLE 13.3 Effect of ROE and plowback on growth and the P/E ratio

	Plowback Ratio (b)			
	0	**.25**	**.50**	**.75**
	A. Growth rate, g			
ROE				
10%	0%	2.5%	5.0%	7.5%
12	0	3.0	6.0	9.0
14	0	3.5	7.0	10.5
	B. P/E ratio			
ROE				
10%	8.33	7.89	7.14	5.56
12	8.33	8.33	8.33	8.33
14	8.33	8.82	10.00	16.67

Note: Assumption: $k = 12\%$ per year.

There is a way to make these insights more precise. Look again at the constant-growth DDM formula, $P_0 = D_1/(k - g)$. Now recall that dividends equal the earnings that are *not* reinvested in the firm: $D_1 = E_1(1 - b)$. Recall also that $g = \text{ROE} \times b$. Hence, substituting for D_1 and g, we find that

$$P_0 = \frac{E_1(1 - b)}{k - (\text{ROE} \times b)}$$

implying that the P/E ratio for a firm growing at a long-run sustainable pace is

$$\frac{P_0}{E_1} = \frac{1 - b}{k - (\text{ROE} \times b)} \tag{13.8}$$

It is easy to verify that the P/E ratio increases with ROE. This makes sense, because high ROE projects give the firm good opportunities for growth.[6] We also can verify that the P/E ratio increases for higher plowback, b, as long as ROE exceeds k. This too makes sense. When a firm has good investment opportunities, the market will reward it with a higher P/E multiple if it exploits those opportunities more aggressively by plowing back more earnings into those opportunities.

Remember, however, that growth is not desirable for its own sake. Examine Table 13.3, where we use Equation 13.8 to compute both growth rates and P/E ratios for different combinations of ROE and b. While growth always increases with the plowback ratio (move across the rows in Panel A of Table 13.3), the P/E ratio does not (move across the rows in Panel B). In the top row of Table 13.3B, the P/E falls as the plowback rate increases. In the middle row, it is unaffected by plowback. In the third row, it increases.

This pattern has a simple interpretation. When the expected ROE is less than the required return, k, investors prefer that the firm pay out earnings as dividends rather than reinvest earnings in the firm at an inadequate rate of return. That is, for ROE lower than k, the value of the firm falls as plowback increases. Conversely, when ROE exceeds k, the firm offers superior investment opportunities, so the value of the firm is enhanced as those opportunities are more fully exploited by increasing the plowback ratio.

Finally, where ROE just equals k, the firm offers "break-even" investment opportunities with a fair rate of return. In this case, investors are indifferent between reinvestment of earnings in the firm or elsewhere at the market capitalization rate, because the rate of return in either case is 12%. Therefore, the stock price is unaffected by the plowback ratio.

[6]Note that Equation 13.8 is a simple rearrangement of the DDM formula, with $\text{ROE} \times b = g$. Because that formula requires that $g < k$, Equation 13.8 is valid only when $\text{ROE} \times b < k$.

We conclude that the higher the plowback ratio, the higher the growth rate, but a higher plowback ratio does not necessarily mean a higher P/E ratio. Higher plowback increases P/E only if investments undertaken by the firm offer an expected rate of return higher than the market capitalization rate. Otherwise, increasing plowback hurts investors because more money is sunk into prospects with inadequate rates of return.

Notwithstanding these fine points, P/E ratios commonly are taken as proxies for the expected growth in dividends or earnings. In fact, a common Wall Street rule of thumb is that the growth rate ought to be roughly equal to the P/E ratio. In other words, the ratio of P/E to g, often called the **PEG ratio,** should be about 1. Peter Lynch, the famous portfolio manager, puts it this way in his book *One Up on Wall Street:*

PEG ratio
Ratio of P/E multiple to earnings growth rate.

> The P/E ratio of any company that's fairly priced will equal its growth rate. I'm talking here about growth rate of earnings. . . . If the P/E ratio of Coca-Cola is 15, you'd expect the company to be growing at about 15% per year, etc. But if the P/E ratio is less than the growth rate, you may have found yourself a bargain.

Let's try his rule of thumb.

EXAMPLE 13.6

P/E Ratio versus Growth Rate

Assume:

$$r_f = 8\% \text{ (about the value when Peter Lynch was writing)}$$

$$r_M - r_f = 8\% \text{ (about the historical average market risk premium)}$$

$$b = .4 \text{ (a typical value for the plowback ratio in the U.S.)}$$

Therefore, $r_M = r_f +$ Market risk premium $= 8\% + 8\% = 16\%$, and $k = 16\%$ for an average ($\beta = 1$) company. If we also accept as reasonable that ROE $= 16\%$ (the same value as the expected return on the stock) we conclude that

$$g = \text{ROE} \times b = 16\% \times .4 = 6.4\%$$

and

$$\text{P/E} = \frac{1-.4}{.16-.064} = 6.26$$

Thus the P/E ratio and g are about equal using these assumptions, consistent with the rule of thumb.

However, note that this rule of thumb, like almost all others, will not work in all circumstances. For example, the yield on long-term Treasury bonds today is more like 3%, so a comparable forecast of r_M today would be

$$r_f + \text{Market risk premium} = 3\% + 8\% = 11\%$$

If we continue to focus on a firm with $\beta = 1$, and ROE still is about the same as k, then

$$g = 11\% \times .4 = 4.4\%$$

while

$$\text{P/E} = \frac{1-.4}{.11-.044} = 9.1$$

The P/E ratio and g now diverge, and the PEG ratio is now $9.1/4.4 = 2.1$. Nevertheless, lower-than-average PEG ratios are still widely seen as signaling potential underpricing.

Whatever its shortcomings, the PEG ratio is widely followed. The PEG ratio for the S&P over the last 20 years typically has fluctuated within the range between 1 and 1.5.

CONCEPT check 13.5

ABC stock has an expected ROE of 12% per year, expected earnings per share of \$2, and expected dividends of \$1.50 per share. Its market capitalization rate is 10% per year.

a. What are its expected growth rate, its price, and its P/E ratio?

b. If the plowback rate were .4, what would be the firm's expected dividend per share, growth rate, price, P/E, and PEG ratio?

On the MARKET FRONT

FACEBOOK'S $100 BILLION QUESTION

WHAT IS FACEBOOK WORTH?

As investors dug into the company's freshly released financials Wednesday, analysts and investors began circulating a range of values—from as little as $50 billion to as much as $125 billion—for the social-networking website.

It will be months before the market sets a final price, but already the valuation question has become a tug of war over two essential questions: Just how fast can the company continue to grow? And can it extract value from advertising in the way it plans?

Facebook's revenue grew 88% in 2011, and net income grew 65%. Facebook's growth has already decelerated from 154% from 2009 to 2010, to the 88% it experienced last year.

Francis Gaskins, president of IPOdesktop.com, which analyzes IPOs for investors, says he doesn't believe Facebook is worth more than $50 billion—50 times its reported profits for 2011 of $1 billion, or more than triple the market's average price-to-earnings ratio. Google Inc.'s profits are 10 times that of Facebook, but its stock-market value is $190 billion, he notes.

A $100 billion valuation "would have us believe that Facebook is worth 53% of Google, even though Google's sales and profits are 10 times that of Facebook," he said.

Martin Pyykkonen, an analyst at Denver banking boutique Wedge Partners, is more bullish, saying the value could top $100 billion. He says Facebook could trade at 15 to 18 times next year's expected earnings before interest, taxes, and certain noncash charges, a cash-flow measure known as EBITDA. By comparison, he says, mature companies trade at eight to 10 times EBITDA. Microsoft Corp. trades at seven times, and Google about 10 times.

While that math only justifies an $81 billion valuation, he says Facebook may be able to unlock faster growth in ad spending and reach $5.5 billion in EBITDA, which could justify a higher multiple of 20 times, implying a $110 billion valuation.

SOURCE: Excerpted from Randall Smith, "Facebook's $100 Billion Question," *The Wall Street Journal,* February 3, 2012. Reprinted by permission of *The Wall Street Journal.*

The importance of growth opportunities is most evident in the valuation of start-up firms, for example, in the Internet boom of the late 1990s. Many companies that had yet to turn a profit were valued by the market at billions of dollars. The value of these companies was *exclusively* growth opportunities. For example, the online auction firm eBay had 1998 profits of $2.4 million, far less than the $45 million profit earned by the traditional auctioneer Sotheby's; yet eBay's market value was more than 10 times greater: $22 billion versus $1.9 billion. As it turns out, the market was quite right to value eBay so much more aggressively than Sotheby's. Its net income in 2010 was $1.8 billion, more than 11 times that of Sotheby's.

Of course, when company valuation is determined primarily by growth opportunities, those values can be very sensitive to reassessments of such prospects. When the market became more skeptical of the business prospects of most Internet retailers at the close of the 1990s, that is, as it revised the estimates of growth opportunities downward, their stock prices plummeted.

As perceptions of future prospects wax and wane, share price can swing wildly. Growth prospects are intrinsically difficult to tie down; ultimately, however, those prospects drive the value of the most dynamic firms in the economy.

The nearby box is an example of a simple valuation analysis. As Facebook headed toward its highly anticipated IPO in 2012, there was widespread speculation about the price at which it would eventually trade in the stock market. Notice that the discussion in the article focuses on two key questions. First, what is a reasonable projection of the growth rate of Facebook's profits? Second, what multiple of earnings is appropriate to translate an earnings forecast into a price forecast? These are precisely the questions addressed by our stock valuation models.

P/E Ratios and Stock Risk

One important implication of any stock valuation model is that (holding all else equal) riskier stocks will have lower P/E multiples. We can see this in the context of the constant-growth model by examining the formula for the P/E ratio (Equation 13.8):

$$\frac{P}{E} = \frac{1 - b}{k - g}$$

Riskier firms will have higher required rates of return (i.e., higher values of k). Therefore, their P/E multiples will be lower. This is true even outside the context of the constant-growth model. For *any* expected earnings and dividend stream, the present value of those cash flows will be lower when the stream is perceived to be riskier. Hence the stock price and the ratio of price to earnings will be lower.

Of course, many small, risky, start-up companies have very high P/E multiples. This does not contradict our claim that P/E multiples should fall with risk: Instead, it is evidence of the market's expectations of high growth rates for those companies. This is why we said that high-risk firms will have lower P/E ratios *holding all else equal.* Given a growth projection, the P/E multiple will be lower when risk is perceived to be higher.

Pitfalls in P/E Analysis

No description of P/E analysis is complete without mentioning some of its pitfalls. First, consider that the denominator in the P/E ratio is accounting earnings, which are influenced by somewhat arbitrary accounting rules such as the use of historical cost in depreciation and inventory valuation. In times of high inflation, historic cost depreciation and inventory costs will tend to underrepresent true economic values because the replacement cost of both goods and capital equipment will rise with the general level of prices. As Figure 13.3 demonstrates, P/E ratios fell dramatically in the 1970s when inflation spiked. This reflected the market's assessment that earnings in these periods are of "lower quality," artificially distorted by inflation, and warranting lower P/E ratios.

Earnings management is the practice of using flexibility in accounting rules to manipulate the apparent profitability of the firm. We will have much to say on this topic in the next chapter on interpreting financial statements. A version of earnings management that became common in recent years was the reporting of "pro forma earnings" measures. These measures are sometimes called *operating earnings,* a term with no precise generally accepted definition.

earnings management
The practice of using flexibility in accounting rules to manipulate the apparent profitability of the firm.

Pro forma earnings are calculated ignoring certain expenses, for example, restructuring charges, stock-option expenses, or write-downs of assets from continuing operations. Firms

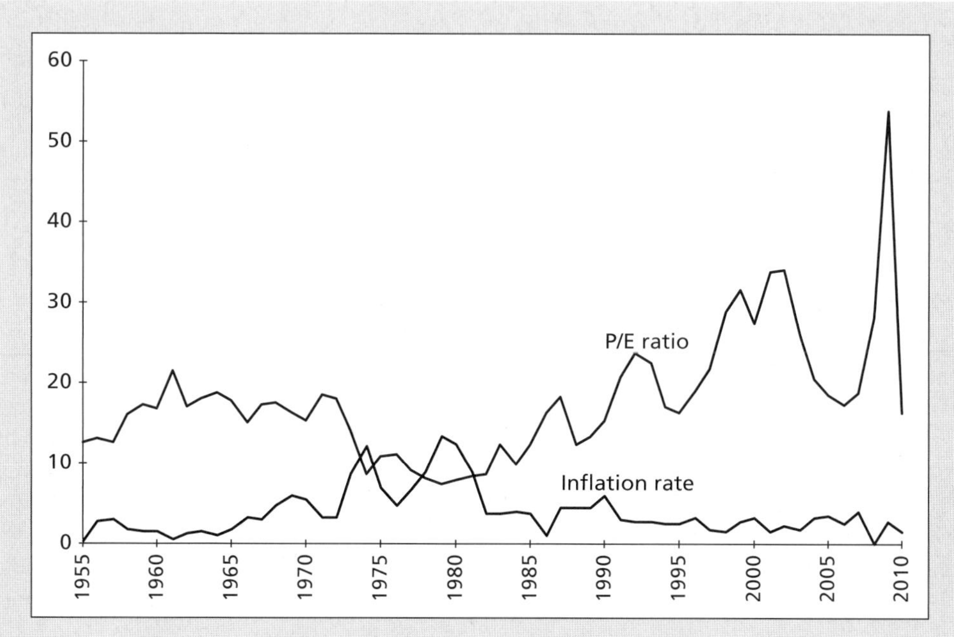

FIGURE 13.3
P/E ratio of the S&P 500 Index and inflation

argue that ignoring these expenses gives a clearer picture of the underlying profitability of the firm.

But when there is too much leeway for choosing what to exclude it becomes hard for investors or analysts to interpret the numbers or to compare them across firms. The lack of standards gives firms considerable leeway to manage earnings.

Even GAAP allows firms considerable discretion to manage earnings. For example, in the late 1990s, Kellogg took restructuring charges, which are supposed to be one-time events, nine quarters in a row. Were these really one-time events, or were they more appropriately treated as ordinary expenses? Given the available leeway in reporting earnings, the justified P/E multiple becomes difficult to gauge.

Another confounding factor in the use of P/E ratios is related to the business cycle. We were careful in deriving the DDM to define earnings as being net of *economic* depreciation, that is, the maximum flow of income that the firm could pay out without depleting its productive capacity. And reported earnings, as we note above, are computed in accordance with generally accepted accounting principles and need not correspond to economic earnings. Beyond this, however, notions of a normal or justified P/E ratio, as in Equation 13.7 or 13.8, assume implicitly that earnings rise at a constant rate, or, put another way, on a smooth trend line. In contrast, reported earnings can fluctuate dramatically around a trend line over the course of the business cycle.

Another way to make this point is to note that the "normal" P/E ratio predicted by Equation 13.8 is the ratio of today's price to the trend value of future earnings, E_1. The P/E ratio reported in the financial pages of the newspaper, by contrast, is the ratio of price to the most recent *past* accounting earnings. Current accounting earnings can differ considerably from future economic earnings. Because ownership of stock conveys the right to future as well as current earnings, the ratio of price to most recent earnings can vary substantially over the business cycle, as accounting earnings and the trend value of economic earnings diverge by greater and lesser amounts.

As an example, Figure 13.4 graphs the earnings per share of Intel and Consolidated Edison since 1995. Note that Intel's EPS fluctuates around its trend line more than Con Ed's. Because the market values the entire stream of future dividends generated by the company, when earnings are temporarily depressed, the P/E ratio should tend to be high—that is, the denominator of the ratio responds more sensitively to the business cycle than the numerator. This pattern is borne out well.

Figure 13.5 graphs the P/E ratios of the two firms. Intel has greater earnings volatility and more variability in its P/E ratio. Its clearly higher average growth rate shows up in its generally higher P/E ratio. The only period in which Con Ed's ratio exceeded Intel's was 2010–2011, a period when Intel's earnings rose at a far faster rate than its underlying trend. The market seems to have recognized that this earnings performance was not likely to be sustainable, and Intel's price did not respond dramatically to this fluctuation in earnings. Consequently, its P/E ratio declined.

This example shows why analysts must be careful in using P/E ratios. There is no way to say a P/E ratio is overly high or low without referring to the company's long-run growth prospects, as well as to current earnings per share relative to the long-run trend line.

Nevertheless, Figures 13.4 and 13.5 demonstrate a clear relationship between P/E ratios and growth. Despite short-run fluctuations, Intel's EPS clearly trended upward over the period. Its compound rate of growth in the 1995–2011 period was 10.3%. Con Edison's earnings grew far less rapidly, with a compound growth rate of 1.2%. Intel's growth prospects are reflected in its consistently higher P/E multiple.

This analysis suggests that P/E ratios should vary across industries and, in fact, they do. Figure 13.6 shows P/E ratios for a sample of industries. Notice that the industries with the two highest multiples—biotech and business software—have attractive investment opportunities, whereas the industries with the lowest multiples—defense, oil and gas, and electric utilities—are in more mature industries with limited growth prospects. The relationship between P/E and growth is not perfect, which is not surprising in light of the pitfalls discussed in this section, but as a general rule, the P/E multiple tracks growth opportunities.

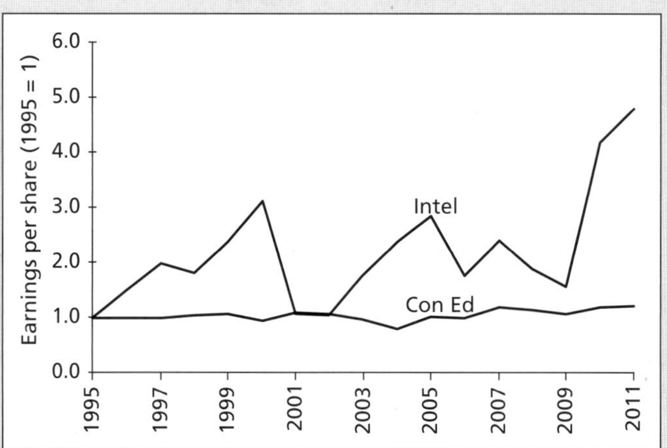

FIGURE 13.4

Earnings growth for two companies

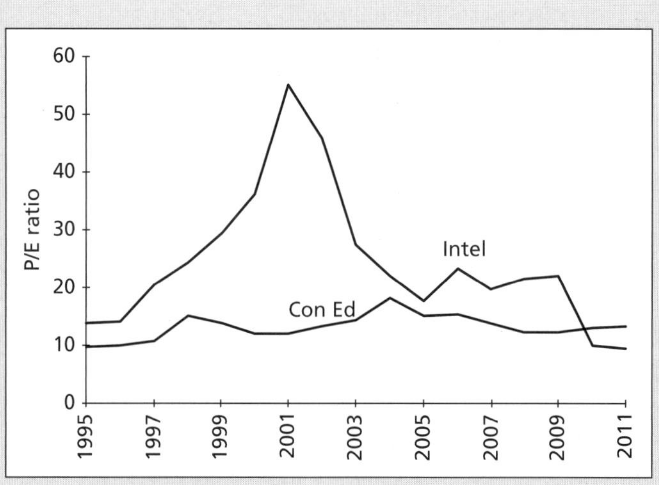

FIGURE 13.5

Price–earnings ratios

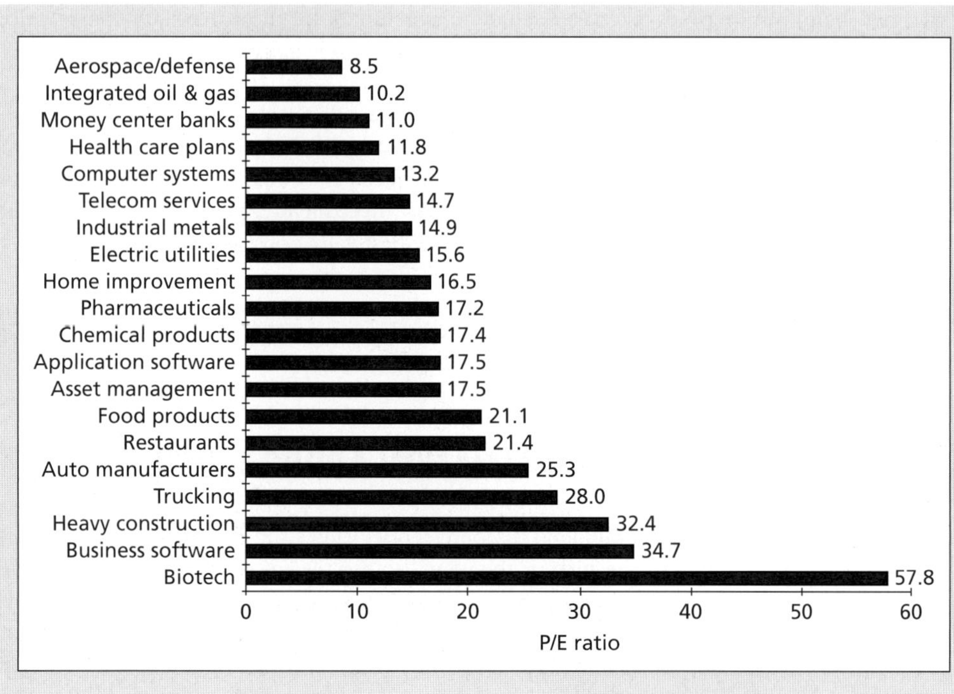

FIGURE 13.6

P/E ratios

Source: Yahoo! Finance, finance.yahoo.com, January 24, 2012.

Combining P/E Analysis and the DDM

Some analysts use P/E ratios in conjunction with earnings forecasts to estimate the price of stock at an investor's horizon date. The Honda analysis in Figure 13.2 shows that Value Line forecast a P/E ratio for 2015 of 14. EPS for 2015 was forecast at $4, implying a price in 2015 of 14 × $4 = $56. Given an estimate of $56 for the 2015 sales price, we would compute Honda's intrinsic value as

$$V_{2011} = \frac{.72}{(1.101)} + \frac{.81}{(1.101)^2} + \frac{.90}{(1.101)^3} + \frac{1.00 + \$56}{(1.101)^4} = \$40.79$$

Other Comparative Valuation Ratios

The price–earnings ratio is an example of a comparative valuation ratio. Such ratios are used to assess the valuation of one firm versus another based on a fundamental indicator such as earnings. For example, an analyst might compare the P/E ratios of two firms in the same industry to test whether the market is valuing one firm "more aggressively" than the other. Other such comparative ratios are commonly used.

Price-to-book ratio This is the ratio of price per share divided by book value per share. As we noted earlier in this chapter, some analysts view book value as a useful measure of fundamental value and therefore treat the ratio of price to book value as an indicator of how aggressively the market values the firm.

Price-to-cash-flow ratio Earnings as reported on the income statement can be affected by the company's choice of accounting practices and thus are commonly viewed as subject to some imprecision and even manipulation. In contrast, cash flow—which tracks cash actually flowing into or out of the firm—is less affected by accounting decisions. As a result, some analysts prefer to use the ratio of price to cash flow per share rather than price to earnings per share. Some analysts use operating cash flow when calculating this ratio; others prefer free cash flow, that is, operating cash flow net of new investment.

Price-to-sales ratio Many start-up firms have no earnings. As a result, the P/E ratio for these firms is meaningless. The price-to-sales ratio (the ratio of stock price to the annual sales per share) is sometimes taken as a valuation benchmark for these firms. Of course, price-to-sales ratios can vary markedly across industries, since profit margins vary widely.

Be creative Sometimes a standard valuation ratio will simply not be available, and you will have to devise your own. In the 1990s, some analysts valued retail Internet firms based on the number of hits their websites received. In retrospect, they valued these firms using too generous "price-to-hits" ratios. Nevertheless, in a new investment environment, these analysts used the information available to them to devise the best valuation tools they could.

Figure 13.7 presents the behavior of these valuation measures for the S&P 500. While the levels of these ratios differ considerably, for the most part they track each other fairly closely, with upturns and downturns at the same times.

13.5 FREE CASH FLOW VALUATION APPROACHES

An alternative approach to the dividend discount model values the firm using free cash flow, that is, cash flow available to the firm or the equityholders net of capital expenditures. This approach is particularly useful for firms that pay no dividends, for which the dividend discount model would be difficult to implement. But free cash flow models are valid for any firm, and can provide useful insights about firm value beyond the DDM.

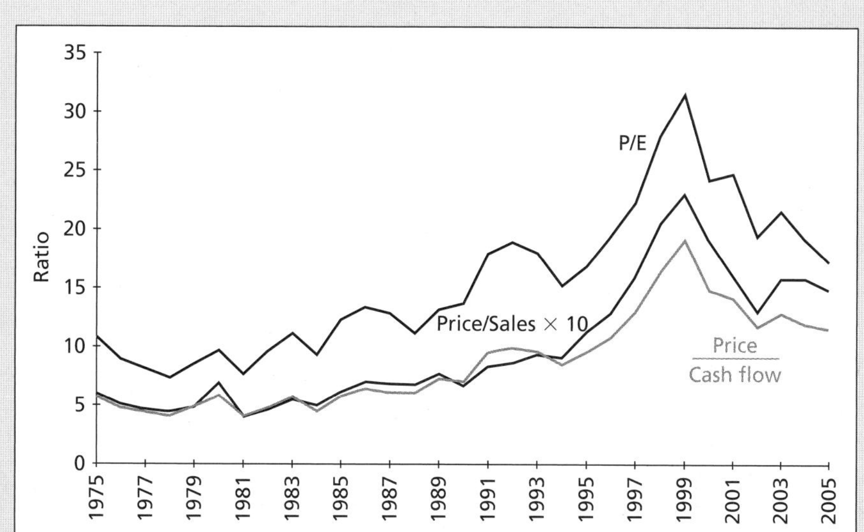

FIGURE 13.7

Valuation ratios for the S&P 500

One approach is to discount the *free cash flow* for the *firm* (FCFF) at the weighted-average cost of capital to obtain the value of the firm and then subtract the then-existing value of debt to find the value of equity. Another is to focus from the start on the free cash flow to *equityholders* (FCFE), discounting those directly at the cost of equity to obtain the market value of equity.

The free cash flow to the firm is given as follows:

$$\text{FCFF} = \text{EBIT}(1 - t_c) + \text{Depreciation} - \text{Capital expenditures} - \text{Increase in NWC} \quad \textbf{(13.9)}$$

where

EBIT = earnings before interest and taxes

t_c = the corporate tax rate

NWC = net working capital

This is the cash flow that accrues from the firm's operations, net of investments in capital and net working capital. It includes cash flows available to both debt- and equityholders.[7]

Alternatively, we can focus on cash flow available to equityholders. This will differ from free cash flow to the firm by after-tax interest expenditures, as well as by cash flow associated with net issuance or repurchase of debt (i.e., principal repayments minus proceeds from issuance of new debt).

$$\text{FCFE} = \text{FCFF} - \text{Interest expense} \times (1 - t_c) + \text{Increases in net debt} \quad \textbf{(13.10)}$$

The free cash flow to the firm approach discounts year-by-year cash flows plus some estimate of terminal value, P_T. In Equation 13.11,we use the constant-growth model to estimate terminal value. The appropriate discount rate is the weighted-average cost of capital.

$$\text{Firm value} = \sum_{t=1}^{T} \frac{1 + \text{FCFF}_t}{(1 + \text{WACC})^t} + \frac{P_T}{(1 + \text{WACC})^T} \quad \textbf{(13.11)}$$

where

$$P_T = \frac{\text{FCFF}_{T+1}}{\text{WACC} - g}$$

[7]This is firm cash flow assuming all-equity financing. Any tax advantage to debt financing is recognized by using an after-tax cost of debt in the computation of weighted-average cost of capital. This issue is discussed in any introductory corporate finance text.

To find equity value, we subtract the existing market value of debt from the derived value of the firm.

Alternatively, we can discount free cash flows to *equity* (FCFE) at the cost of *equity*, k_E,

$$\text{Market value of equity} = \sum_{t=1}^{T} \frac{\text{FCFE}_t}{(1 + k_E)^t} + \frac{P_T}{(1 + k_E)^T} \tag{13.12}$$

where

$$P_T = \frac{\text{FCFE}_{T+1}}{k_E - g}$$

As in the dividend discount model, free cash flow models use a terminal value to avoid adding the present values of an infinite sum of cash flows. That terminal value may simply be the present value of a constant-growth perpetuity (as in the formulas above), or it may be based on a multiple of EBIT, book value, earnings, or free cash flow. As a general rule, estimates of intrinsic value depend critically on terminal value.

Spreadsheet 13.2 presents a free cash flow valuation of Honda using the data supplied by Value Line in Figure 13.2. We start with the free cash flow to the firm approach given in Equation 13.9. Panel A of the spreadsheet lays out values supplied by Value Line. (Entries for middle years are interpolated from beginning and final values.) Panel B calculates free cash flow. The sum of after-tax profits in row 11 plus after-tax interest payments in row 12 [that is, interest expense × $(1 - t_c)$] equals EBIT$(1 - t_c)$. In row 13 we subtract the change in net working capital, in row 14 we add back depreciation, and in row 15 we subtract capital expenditures. The result in row 17 is the free cash flow to the firm, FCFF, for each year between 2012 and 2015.

To find the present value of these cash flows, we will discount at WACC, which is calculated in panel C. WACC is the weighted average of the after-tax cost of debt and the cost of equity in each year. When computing WACC, we must account for the change in leverage forecast by Value Line. To compute the cost of equity, we will use the CAPM as in our earlier (dividend discount model) valuation exercise but account for the fact that equity beta will decline each year as the firm reduces leverage.[8]

A reasonable approximation to Honda's cost of debt, which was rated A+ in 2012, is the yield to maturity on comparably rated long-term debt, approximately 4.2% (cell B25). Honda's debt-to-value ratio (assuming its debt is selling near par value) is computed in row 29. In 2011, the ratio was .32. Based on Value Line forecasts, it will fall to .20 by 2015. We interpolate the debt-to-value ratio for the intermediate years. WACC is computed in row 32. WACC increases slightly over time as the debt-to-value ratio steadily declines between 2012 and 2015. The present value factor for cash flows accruing in each year is the previous year's factor divided by (1 + WACC) for that year. The present value of each cash flow (row 37) is the free cash flow times the cumulative discount factor.

[8]Call β_L the firm's equity beta at the initial level of leverage as provided by Value Line. Equity betas reflect both business risk and financial risk. When a firm changes its capital structure (debt/equity mix), it changes financial risk, and therefore equity beta changes. How should we recognize the change in financial risk? As you may remember from an introductory corporate finance class, you must first unleverage beta. This leaves us a beta that reflects only business risk. We use the following formula to find unleveraged beta, β_U, (where D/E is the firm's current debt-equity ratio):

$$\beta_U = \frac{\beta_L}{1 + (D/E)(1 - t_c)}$$

Then, we re-leverage beta in any particular year using the forecast capital structure (which reintroduces the financial risk associated with that year's capital structure):

$$\beta_L = \beta_U[1 + (D/E)(1 - t_c)]$$

SPREADSHEET 13.2

Free cash flow valuation of Honda Motor

	A	B	C	D	E	F	G	H	I	J	K	L	M
1			**2011**	**2012**	**2013**	**2014**	**2015**						
2	**A. Input data**												
3	P/E		18.00	14.50	14.33	14.17	14.00						
4	Cap spending/shr		2.50	2.65	2.78	2.92	3.05						
5	LT debt		27500	30000	28333	26667	25000						
6	Shares		1800	1800	1798	1797	1795						
7	EPS		1.70	3.20	3.47	3.73	4.00						
8	Working capital		27630	36835	40563	44292	48020						
9													
10	**B. Cash flow calculations**												
11	Profits (after tax)		3190.0	5735.0	6226.7	6718.3	7210.0						
12	Interest (after tax)		750.8	819.0	773.5	728.0	682.5			=(1-tax_rate) × r_debt × LT Debt			
13	Chg working cap			9205.0	3728.3	3728.3	3728.3						
14	Depreciation			6900.0	6933	6967	7000.0						
15	Cap spending			4770.0	5004.9	5239.8	5474.8						
16								**Terminal value**					
17	FCFF			−521.0	5200.3	5444.8	5689.4	106504.6					
18	FCFE			1160.0	2760.1	3050.2	3340.3	85210.4		assumes fixed debt ratio after 2015			
19													
20	**C. Discount rate calculations**												
21	Current beta	0.9								from Value Line			
22	Unlevered beta	0.686								current beta /[1+(1-tax)*debt/equity)]			
23	Terminal growth	0.025											
24	Tax_rate	0.35								from Value Line			
25	r_debt	0.042								YTM in 2012 on A+rated LT debt			
26	Risk-free rate	0.029											
27	Market risk prem	0.08											
28	MV equity		57420				100940			Row 3 × Row 11			
29	Debt/Value		0.32	0.29	0.26	0.23	0.20			linear trend from initial to final value			
30	Levered beta		0.900	0.871	0.844	0.819	0.797			unlevered beta × [1+(1-tax)*debt/equity]			
31	k_equity		0.101	0.099	0.097	0.095	0.093	0.093		from CAPM and levered beta			
32	WACC		0.77	0.078	0.078	0.079	0.080	0.080		(1-t)*r_debt*D/V+k_equity*(1-D/V)			
33	PV factor for FCFF		1.000	0.928	0.860	0.797	0.738	0.738		Discount each year at WACC			
34	PV factor for FCFE		1.000	0.910	0.830	0.758	0.694	0.694		Discount each year at k_equity			
35													
36	**D. Present values**									**Intrinsic val**	**Equity val**	**Intrin/share**	
37	PV(FCFF)			−483	4474	4341	4201	78641		91174	63674	35.37	
38	PV(FCFE)			1056	2291	2313	2318	59136		67114	67114	37.29	

eXcel

Please visit us at www.mhhe.com/bkm

The terminal value of the firm (cell H17) is computed from the constant-growth model as $FCFF_{2015} \times (1 + g)/(WACC_{2015} - g)$, where g (cell B23) is the assumed value for the steady growth rate.[9] We assume in the spreadsheet that $g = .025$, roughly the long-run growth rate of the broad economy.[10] Terminal value is also discounted back to 2011 (cell H37), and the intrinsic value of the firm is thus found as the sum of discounted free cash flows between 2012 and 2015 plus the discounted terminal value. Finally, the value of debt in 2011 is subtracted from firm value to arrive at the intrinsic value of equity in 2011 (cell K37), and value per share is calculated in cell L37 as equity value divided by number of shares in 2011.

The free cash flow to equity approach yields a similar intrinsic value for the stock. FCFE (row 18) is obtained from FCFF by subtracting after-tax interest expense and net debt repurchases. The cash flows are then discounted at the equity rate. Like WACC, the cost of equity changes each period as leverage changes. The present value factor for equity cash flows is presented in row 34. Equity value is reported in cell J38, which is put on a per-share basis in cell L38.

Spreadsheet 13.2 is available at the Online Learning Center, **www.mhhe.com/bkm.**

[9]Over the 2011–2015 period, Value Line predicts that Honda will retire a considerable fraction of its outstanding debt. The implied debt repurchases are a use of cash and reduce the cash flow available to equity. Such repurchases cannot be sustained indefinitely, however, for debt outstanding would soon be run down to zero. Therefore, in our estimate of terminal value, we compute the final cash flow assuming that by 2015 Honda will begin *issuing* enough debt to maintain its debt-to-value ratio unchanged. This approach is consistent with the assumption of constant growth and constant discount rates after 2015.

[10]In the long run a firm can't grow forever at a rate higher than the aggregate economy. So by the time we assert that growth is in a stable stage, it seems reasonable that the growth rate should not be significantly greater than that of the overall economy (although it can be less if the firm is in a declining industry).

Comparing the Valuation Models

In principle, the free cash flow approach is fully consistent with the dividend discount model and should provide the same estimate of intrinsic value if one can extrapolate to a period in which the firm begins to pay dividends growing at a constant rate. This was demonstrated in two famous papers by Modigliani and Miller (1958, 1961). However, in practice, you will find that values from these models may differ, sometimes substantially. This is due to the fact that in practice, analysts are always forced to make simplifying assumptions. For example, how long will it take the firm to enter a constant-growth stage? How should depreciation best be treated? What is the best estimate of ROE? Answers to questions like these can have a big impact on value, and it is not always easy to maintain consistent assumptions across the models.

We have now valued Honda using several approaches, with estimates of intrinsic value as follows:

Model	Intrinsic Value
Two-stage dividend discount model	$30.81
DDM with earnings multiple terminal value	40.79
Three-stage DDM	36.79
Free cash flow to the firm	35.37
Free cash flow to equity	37.29
Market price in 2011	29.54

What should we make of these differences? The two-stage dividend discount model is the most conservative of the estimates, probably because it assumes that Honda's dividend growth rate will fall to its terminal value after only three years. In contrast, the three-stage DDM allows growth to taper off over a longer period, and the estimate of intrinsic value from this model is extremely close to those from both free cash flow models. The DDM with a terminal value provided by the earnings multiple results in a higher estimate of intrinsic value. All of these models produce intrinsic values greater than Honda's market price. Perhaps the assumed terminal growth rate used in our valuation exercise is unrealistically high, or perhaps the stock is indeed underpriced compared to intrinsic value.

This valuation exercise shows that finding bargains is not as easy as it seems. While these models are easy to apply, establishing proper inputs is more of a challenge. This should not be surprising. In even a moderately efficient market, finding profit opportunities will be more involved than analyzing Value Line data for a few hours. The models are extremely useful to analysts, however. They provide ballpark estimates of intrinsic value. More than that, they force rigorous thought about underlying assumptions and highlight the variables with the greatest impact on value and the greatest payoff to further analysis.

The Problem with DCF Models

Our estimates of Honda's intrinsic value are all based on discounted cash flow (DCF) models, in which we calculate the present value of forecast cash flows and a terminal sales price at some future date. It is clear from the calculations for Honda that most of the action in these models is in the terminal value and that this value can be highly sensitive to even small changes in some input values (see, for example, Concept Check 13.4). Therefore, you must recognize that DCF valuation estimates are almost always going to be imprecise. Growth opportunities and future growth rates are especially hard to pin down.

For this reason, many value investors employ a hierarchy of valuation. They view the most reliable components of value as the items on the balance sheet that allow for a reasonable estimate of market price. Real estate, plant, and equipment would fall in this category.

A somewhat less reliable component of value is the economic profit on assets already in place. For example, a company like Intel earns a far higher ROE on its investments in chip-making facilities than its cost of capital. The present value of these "economic profits," or economic value added,[11] is a major component of Intel's market value. This component of value is less certain than its balance sheet assets, however, because there is always a concern that new competitors will enter the market, force down prices and profit margins, and reduce the return on Intel's investments. Thus, one needs to carefully assess the barriers to entry that protect Intel's pricing and profit margins. We noted some of these barriers in the last chapter, where we discussed the role of industry analysis, market structure, and competitive position (see Section 12.7).

Finally, the least reliable components of value are growth opportunities, the purported ability of firms like Intel to invest in positive-NPV ventures that contribute to high market valuations today. Value investors don't deny that such opportunities exist, but they are skeptical that precise values can be attached to them and, therefore, tend to be less willing to make investment decisions that turn on the value of those opportunities.

13.6 THE AGGREGATE STOCK MARKET

The most popular approach to forecasting the overall stock market is the earnings multiplier approach applied at the aggregate level. The first step is to forecast corporate profits for the coming period. Then we derive an estimate of the earnings multiplier, the aggregate P/E ratio, based on a forecast of long-term interest rates. The product of the two forecasts is the estimate of the end-of-period level of the market.

The forecast of the P/E ratio of the market is sometimes derived from a graph similar to that in Figure 13.8, which plots the *earnings yield* (earnings per share divided by price per share, the reciprocal of the P/E ratio) of the S&P 500 and the yield to maturity on 10-year Treasury bonds. The two series clearly move in tandem over time and suggest that one might

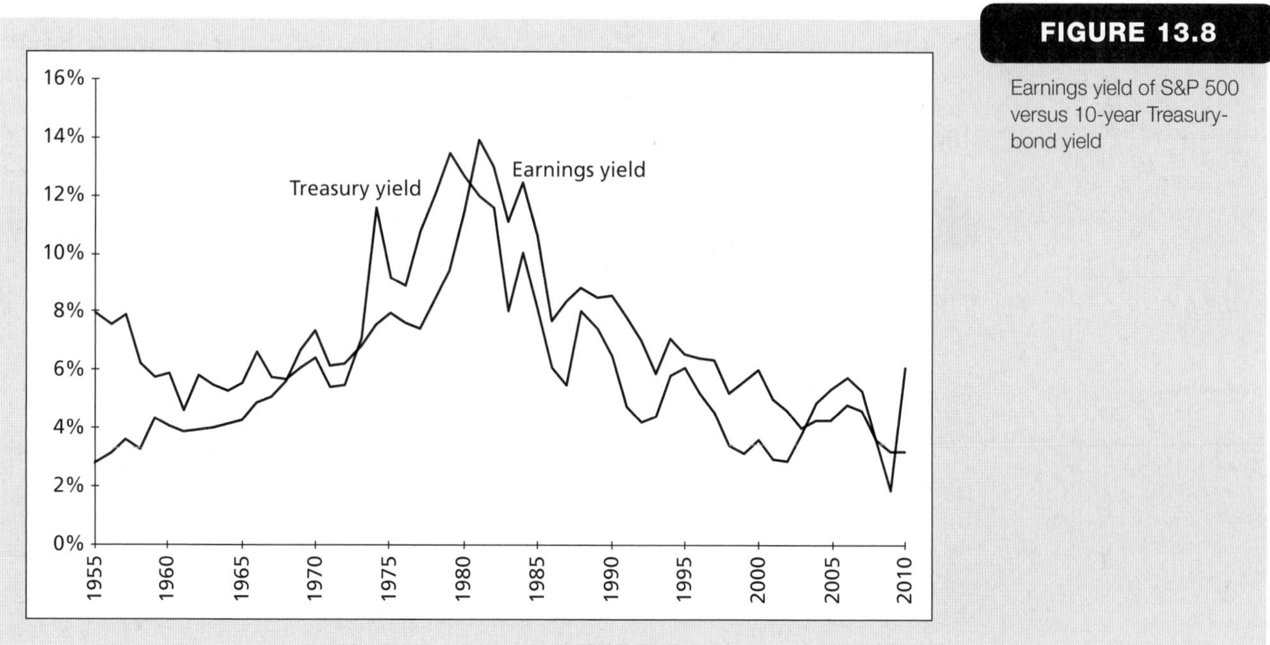

FIGURE 13.8

Earnings yield of S&P 500 versus 10-year Treasury-bond yield

[11]We discuss economic value added in greater detail in the next chapter.

use this relationship and the current yield on 10-year Treasury bonds to forecast the earnings yield on the S&P 500. Given that earnings yield, a forecast of earnings could be used to predict the level of the S&P in some future period. Let's consider a simple example of this procedure.

EXAMPLE 13.7

Forecasting the Aggregate Stock Market

In early 2012, the S&P 500 was at 1,350. The forecast for 12-month forward earnings per share for the S&P 500 portfolio was about $93. The long-term Treasury-bond yield at this time was about 3.1%. As a first approach, we might posit that the spread between the earnings yield and the Treasury yield, which was around 2.9% at the start of 2012, will remain at that level by the end of the year. Given the Treasury yield of 3.1%, this would imply an earnings yield for the S&P of 6% and a P/E ratio of 1/.06 = 16.67. Our forecast for the level of the S&P Index would then be 16.67 × 93 = 1,550. This would imply a one-year capital gain on the index of 200/1,350 = 14.8%.[12]

Of course, there is uncertainty regarding all three inputs into this analysis: the actual earnings on the S&P 500 stocks, the level of Treasury yields at year-end, and the spread between the Treasury yield and the earnings yield. One would wish to perform sensitivity or scenario analysis to examine the impact of changes in all of these variables. To illustrate, consider Table 13.4, which shows a simple scenario analysis treating possible effects of variation in the Treasury-bond yield. The scenario analysis shows that the forecast level of the stock market varies inversely and with dramatic sensitivity to interest rate changes.

Some analysts use an aggregate version of the dividend discount model rather than an earnings multiplier approach. All of these models, however, rely heavily on forecasts of such macroeconomic variables as GDP, interest rates, and the rate of inflation, which are difficult to predict accurately.

Because stock prices reflect expectations of future dividends, which are tied to the economic fortunes of firms, it is not surprising that the performance of a broad-based stock index like the S&P 500 is taken as a leading economic indicator, that is, a predictor of the performance of the aggregate economy. Stock prices are viewed as embodying consensus forecasts of economic activity and are assumed to move up or down in anticipation of movements in the economy. The government's index of leading economic indicators, which is taken to predict the progress of the business cycle, is made up in part of recent stock market performance. However, the predictive value of the market is far from perfect. A well-known joke, often attributed to Paul Samuelson, is that the market has forecast eight of the last five recessions.

TABLE 13.4 S&P 500 Index forecasts under various scenarios

	Pessimistic Scenario	Most Likely Scenario	Optimistic Scenario
Treasury-bond yield	3.6%	3.1%	2.6%
Earnings yield	6.5%	6.0%	5.5%
Resulting P/E ratio	15.4	16.7	18.2
EPS forecast	93	93	93
Forecast for S&P 500	1431	1550	1691

Note: The forecast for the earnings yield on the S&P 500 equals the Treasury-bond yield plus 2.9%. The P/E ratio is the reciprocal of the forecast earnings yield.

[12]A capital gain of this magnitude is quite high by historical standards and suggests that the forecast of either earnings or the year-end P/E multiple is too optimistic. Perhaps the current value of the index has been driven down by the euro crisis and fears that a recession in Europe could reduce the profitability of U.S. firms. In that case, we might want to build a comparable discount into predictions of the year-end P/E multiple. The bottom line: These models are a good way to organize your analysis, make your assumptions explicit, and find clues about possible investment opportunities, but they cannot be applied mechanically.

SUMMARY

- One approach to firm valuation is to focus on the firm's book value, either as it appears on the balance sheet or adjusted to reflect the current replacement cost of assets or the liquidation value. Another approach is to focus on the present value of expected future dividends.
- The dividend discount model holds that the price of a share of stock should equal the present value of all future dividends per share, discounted at an interest rate commensurate with the risk of the stock.
- The constant-growth version of the DDM asserts that if dividends are expected to grow at a constant rate forever, then the intrinsic value of the stock is determined by the formula

$$V_0 = \frac{D_1}{k - g}$$

- This version of the DDM is simplistic in its assumption of a constant value of g. There are more sophisticated multistage versions of the model for more complex environments. When the constant-growth assumption is reasonably satisfied, however, the formula can be inverted to infer the market capitalization rate for the stock:

$$k = \frac{D_1}{P_0} + g$$

- Stock market analysts devote considerable attention to a company's price–earnings ratio. The P/E ratio is a useful measure of the market's assessment of the firm's growth opportunities. Firms with no growth opportunities should have a P/E ratio that is just the reciprocal of the capitalization rate, k. As growth opportunities become a progressively more important component of the total value of the firm, the P/E ratio will increase.
- Many analysts form their estimates of a stock's value by multiplying their forecast of next year's EPS by a predicted P/E multiple. Some analysts mix the P/E approach with the dividend discount model. They use an earnings multiplier to forecast the terminal value of shares at a future date and add the present value of that terminal value with the present value of all interim dividend payments.
- The free cash flow approach is the one used most in corporate finance. The analyst first estimates the value of the firm as the present value of expected future free cash flows to the entire firm and then subtracts the value of all claims other than equity. Alternatively, the free cash flows to equity can be discounted at a discount rate appropriate to the risk of the stock.
- The models presented in this chapter can be used to explain or to forecast the behavior of the aggregate stock market. The key macroeconomic variables that determine the level of stock prices in the aggregate are interest rates and corporate profits.

KEY TERMS

book value, 406
constant-growth DDM, 411
dividend discount model (DDM), 410
dividend payout ratio, 413
earnings management, 425
earnings retention ratio, 413
intrinsic value, 408
liquidation value, 407
market capitalization rate, 409
PEG ratio, 423
plowback ratio, 413
present value of growth opportunities (PVGO), 414
price–earnings multiple, 420
replacement cost, 407
Tobin's q, 407
two-stage DDM, 417

KEY FORMULAS

Intrinsic value: $V_0 = \frac{D_1}{1+k} + \frac{D_2}{(1+k)^2} + \cdots + \frac{D_H + P_H}{(1+k)^H}$

Constant-growth DDM: $V_0 = \frac{D_1}{k - g}$

Growth opportunities: $\text{Price} = \dfrac{E_1}{k} + \text{PVGO}$

Determinant of *P/E* ratio: $\dfrac{P_0}{E_1} = \dfrac{1}{k}\left(1 + \dfrac{\text{PVGO}}{E_1/k}\right)$

Free cash flow to the firm:

$$\text{FCFF} = \text{EBIT}(1 - t_c) + \text{Depreciation} - \text{Capital expenditures} - \text{Increases in NWC}$$

Free cash flow to equity:

$$\text{FCFE} = \text{FCFF} - \text{Interest expense} \times (1 - t_c) + \text{Increase in net debt}$$

PROBLEM SETS

Select problems are available in McGraw-Hill's *Connect Finance*. Please see the Supplements section of the book's frontmatter for more information.

Basic

1. In what circumstances would you choose to use a dividend discount model rather than a free cash flow model to value a firm? ***(LO 13-4)***
2. In what circumstances is it most important to use multistage dividend discount models rather than constant-growth models? ***(LO 13-2)***
3. If a security is underpriced (i.e., intrinsic value > price), then what is the relationship between its market capitalization rate and its expected rate of return? ***(LO 13-2)***

KAPLAN SCHWESER

4. Deployment Specialists pays a current (annual) dividend of $1 and is expected to grow at 20% for two years and then at 4% thereafter. If the required return for Deployment Specialists is 8.5%, what is the intrinsic value of Deployment Specialists stock? ***(LO 13-2)***

KAPLAN SCHWESER

5. Jand, Inc., currently pays a dividend of $1.22, which is expected to grow indefinitely at 5%. If the current value of Jand's shares based on the constant-growth dividend discount model is $32.03, what is the required rate of return? ***(LO 13-2)***

KAPLAN SCHWESER

6. A firm pays a current dividend of $1, which is expected to grow at a rate of 5% indefinitely. If the current value of the firm's shares is $35, what is the required return applicable to the investment based on the constant-growth dividend discount model (DDM)? ***(LO 13-2)***

KAPLAN SCHWESER

7. Tri-coat Paints has a current market value of $41 per share with earnings of $3.64. What is the present value of its growth opportunities (PVGO) if the required return is 9%? ***(LO 13-2)***
8. A firm has current assets that could be sold for their book value of $10 million. The book value of its fixed assets is $60 million, but they could be sold for $90 million today. The firm has total debt with a book value of $40 million, but interest rate declines have caused the market value of the debt to increase to $50 million. What is this firm's market-to-book ratio? ***(LO 13-1)***
9. The market capitalization rate for Admiral Motors Company is 8%. Its expected ROE is 10% and its expected EPS is $5. If the firm's plowback ratio is 60%, what will be its P/E ratio? ***(LO 13-2)***
10. Miltmar Corporation will pay a year-end dividend of $4, and dividends thereafter are expected to grow at the constant rate of 4% per year. The risk-free rate is 4%, and the expected return on the market portfolio is 12%. The stock has a beta of .75. What is the intrinsic value of the stock? ***(LO 13-2)***
11. Sisters Corp expects to earn $6 per share next year. The firm's ROE is 15% and its plowback ratio is 60%. If the firm's market capitalization rate is 10%, what is the present value of its growth opportunities? ***(LO 13-3)***

12. Eagle Products' EBIT is $300, its tax rate is 35%, depreciation is $20, capital expenditures are $60, and the planned increase in net working capital is $30. What is the free cash flow to the firm? ***(LO 13-4)***

Intermediate

13. FinCorp's free cash flow to the firm is reported as $205 million. The firm's interest expense is $22 million. Assume the tax rate is 35% and the net debt of the firm increases by $3 million. What is the market value of equity if the FCFE is projected to grow at 3% indefinitely and the cost of equity is 12%? ***(LO 13-4)***
14. A common stock pays an annual dividend per share of $2.10. The risk-free rate is 7% and the risk premium for this stock is 4%. If the annual dividend is expected to remain at $2.10, what is the value of the stock? ***(LO 13-2)***
15. The risk-free rate of return is 5%, the required rate of return on the market is 10%, and High-Flyer stock has a beta coefficient of 1.5. If the dividend per share expected during the coming year, D_1, is $2.50 and $g = 4\%$, at what price should a share sell? ***(LO 13-2)***
16. Explain why the following statements are true/false/uncertain. ***(LO 13-3)***
    a. With all else held constant, a firm will have a higher P/E if its beta is higher.
    b. P/E will tend to be higher when ROE is higher (assuming plowback is positive).
    c. P/E will tend to be higher when the plowback rate is higher.
17. *a.* Computer stocks currently provide an expected rate of return of 16%. MBI, a large computer company, will pay a year-end dividend of $2 per share. If the stock is selling at $50 per share, what must be the market's expectation of the growth rate of MBI dividends?
    b. If dividend growth forecasts for MBI are revised downward to 5% per year, what will happen to the price of MBI stock? What (qualitatively) will happen to the company's price–earnings ratio? ***(LO 13-3)***
18. Even Better Products has come out with a new and improved product. As a result, the firm projects an ROE of 20%, and it will maintain a plowback ratio of .30. Its earnings this year will be $2 per share. Investors expect a 12% rate of return on the stock. ***(LO 13-3)***
    a. At what price and P/E ratio would you expect the firm to sell?
    b. What is the present value of growth opportunities?
    c. What would be the P/E ratio and the present value of growth opportunities if the firm planned to reinvest only 20% of its earnings?
19. *a.* MF Corp. has an ROE of 16% and a plowback ratio of 50%. If the coming year's earnings are expected to be $2 per share, at what price will the stock sell? The market capitalization rate is 12%.
    b. What price do you expect MF shares to sell for in three years? ***(LO 13-2)***
20. The market consensus is that Analog Electronic Corporation has an ROE = 9% and a beta of 1.25. It plans to maintain indefinitely its traditional plowback ratio of 2/3. This year's earnings were $3 per share. The annual dividend was just paid. The consensus estimate of the coming year's market return is 14%, and T-bills currently offer a 6% return. ***(LO 13-3)***
    a. Find the price at which Analog stock should sell.
    b. Calculate the P/E ratio.
    c. Calculate the present value of growth opportunities.
    d. Suppose your research convinces you Analog will announce momentarily that it will immediately reduce its plowback ratio to 1/3. Find the intrinsic value of the stock. The market is still unaware of this decision. Explain why V_0 no longer equals P_0 and why V_0 is greater or less than P_0.
21. The FI Corporation's dividends per share are expected to grow indefinitely by 5% per year. ***(LO 13-3)***
    a. If this year's year-end dividend is $8 and the market capitalization rate is 10% per year, what must the current stock price be according to the DDM?

b. If the expected earnings per share are $12, what is the implied value of the ROE on future investment opportunities?
c. How much is the market paying per share for growth opportunities (that is, for an ROE on future investments that exceeds the market capitalization rate)?

22. The stock of Nogro Corporation is currently selling for $10 per share. Earnings per share in the coming year are expected to be $2. The company has a policy of paying out 50% of its earnings each year in dividends. The rest is retained and invested in projects that earn a 20% rate of return per year. This situation is expected to continue indefinitely. ***(LO 13-3)***
   a. Assuming the current market price of the stock reflects its intrinsic value as computed using the constant-growth DDM, what rate of return do Nogro's investors require?
   b. By how much does its value exceed what it would be if all earnings were paid as dividends and nothing were reinvested?
   c. If Nogro were to cut its dividend payout ratio to 25%, what would happen to its stock price? What if Nogro eliminated the dividend?
23. The risk-free rate of return is 8%, the expected rate of return on the market portfolio is 15%, and the stock of Xyrong Corporation has a beta coefficient of 1.2. Xyrong pays out 40% of its earnings in dividends, and the latest earnings announced were $10 per share. Dividends were just paid and are expected to be paid annually. You expect that Xyrong will earn an ROE of 20% per year on all reinvested earnings forever. ***(LO 13-2)***
   a. What is the intrinsic value of a share of Xyrong stock?
   b. If the market price of a share is currently $100, and you expect the market price to be equal to the intrinsic value one year from now, what is your expected one-year holding-period return on Xyrong stock?
24. The MoMi Corporation's cash flow from operations before interest and taxes was $2 million in the year just ended, and it expects that this will grow by 5% per year forever. To make this happen, the firm will have to invest an amount equal to 20% of pretax cash flow each year. The tax rate is 35%. Depreciation was $200,000 in the year just ended and is expected to grow at the same rate as the operating cash flow. The appropriate market capitalization rate for the unleveraged cash flow is 12% per year, and the firm currently has debt of $4 million outstanding. Use the free cash flow approach to value the firm's equity. ***(LO 13-4)***

eXcel
Please visit us at www.mhhe.com/bkm

25. Recalculate the intrinsic value of Honda using the three-stage growth model of Spreadsheet 13.1 (available at **www.mhhe.com/bkm;** link to Chapter 13 material). Treat each of the following scenarios independently. ***(LO 13-2)***
   a. ROE in the constant-growth period will be 9%.
   b. Honda's actual beta is .95.
   c. The market risk premium is 8.5%.

eXcel
Please visit us at www.mhhe.com/bkm

26. Recalculate the intrinsic value of Honda shares using the free cash flow model of Spreadsheet 13.2 (available at **www.mhhe.com/bkm;** link to Chapter 13 material). Treat each scenario independently. ***(LO 13-4)***
   a. Honda's P/E ratio starting in 2015 will be 13.5.
   b. Honda's unlevered beta is .7.
   c. The market risk premium is 8.5%.

Challenge

27. Chiptech, Inc., is an established computer chip firm with several profitable existing products as well as some promising new products in development. The company earned $1 per share last year and just paid out a dividend of $.50 per share. Investors believe the company plans to maintain its dividend payout ratio at 50%. ROE equals 20%. Everyone in the market expects this situation to persist indefinitely. ***(LO 13-2)***
   a. What is the market price of Chiptech stock? The required return for the computer chip industry is 15%, and the company has just gone ex-dividend (i.e., the next dividend will be paid a year from now, at $t = 1$).

b. Suppose you discover that Chiptech's competitor has developed a new chip that will eliminate Chiptech's current technological advantage in this market. This new product, which will be ready to come to the market in two years, will force Chiptech to reduce the prices of its chips to remain competitive. This will decrease ROE to 15%, and, because of falling demand for its product, Chiptech will decrease the plowback ratio to .40. The plowback ratio will be decreased at the end of the second year, at $t = 2$: The annual year-end dividend for the second year (paid at $t = 2$) will be 60% of that year's earnings. What is your estimate of Chiptech's intrinsic value per share? (*Hint:* Carefully prepare a table of Chiptech's earnings and dividends for each of the next three years. Pay close attention to the change in the payout ratio in $t = 2$.)

c. No one else in the market perceives the threat to Chiptech's market. In fact, you are confident that no one else will become aware of the change in Chiptech's competitive status until the competitor firm publicly announces its discovery near the end of year 2. What will be the rate of return on Chiptech stock in the coming year (i.e., between $t = 0$ and $t = 1$)? In the second year (between $t = 1$ and $t = 2$)? The third year (between $t = 2$ and $t = 3$)? (*Hint:* Pay attention to when the *market* catches on to the new situation. A table of dividends and market prices over time might help.)

CFA Problems

1. At Litchfield Chemical Corp. (LCC), a director of the company said that the use of dividend discount models by investors is "proof" that the higher the dividend, the higher the stock price. ***(LO 13-2)***
   a. Using a constant-growth dividend discount model as a basis of reference, evaluate the director's statement.
   b. Explain how an increase in dividend payout would affect each of the following (holding all other factors constant):
      i. Sustainable growth rate.
      ii. Growth in book value.
2. Phoebe Black's investment club wants to buy the stock of either NewSoft, Inc. or Capital Corp. In this connection, Black prepared the following table. You have been asked to help her interpret the data, based on your forecast for a healthy economy and a strong stock market over the next 12 months. ***(LO 13-2)***

	NewSoft, Inc.	Capital Corp.	S&P 500 Index
Current price	$30	$32	
Industry	Computer software	Capital goods	
P/E ratio (current)	25	14	16
P/E ratio (5-year average)	27	16	16
Price/book ratio (current)	10	3	3
Price/book ratio (5-year average)	12	4	2
Beta	1.5	1.1	1.0
Dividend yield	.3%	2.7%	2.8%

   a. Newsoft's shares have higher price–earnings (P/E) and price–book value (P/B) ratios than those of Capital Corp. (The price–book ratio is the ratio of market value to book value.) Briefly discuss why the disparity in ratios may not indicate that NewSoft's shares are overvalued relative to the shares of Capital Corp. Answer the question in terms of the two ratios, and assume that there have been no extraordinary events affecting either company.
   b. Using a constant-growth dividend discount model, Black estimated the value of NewSoft to be $28 per share and the value of Capital Corp. to be $34 per share.

Briefly discuss weaknesses of this dividend discount model, and explain why this model may be less suitable for valuing NewSoft than for valuing Capital Corp.

c. Recommend and justify a more appropriate dividend discount model for valuing NewSoft's common stock.

3. Peninsular Research is initiating coverage of a mature manufacturing industry. John Jones, CFA, head of the research department, gathered the following fundamental industry and market data to help in his analysis: ***(LO 13-3)***

Forecast industry earnings retention rate	40%
Forecast industry return on equity	25%
Industry beta	1.2
Government bond yield	6%
Equity risk premium	5%

a. Compute the price-to-earnings (P_0/E_1) ratio for the industry based on this fundamental data.

b. Jones wants to analyze how fundamental P/E ratios might differ among countries. He gathered the following economic and market data:

Fundamental Factors	Country A	Country B
Forecast growth in real GDP	5%	2%
Government bond yield	10%	6%
Equity risk premium	5%	4%

Determine whether each of these fundamental factors would cause P/E ratios to be generally higher for Country A or higher for Country B.

4. Janet Ludlow's firm requires all its analysts to use a two-stage DDM and the CAPM to value stocks. Using these measures, Ludlow has valued QuickBrush Company at $63 per share. She now must value SmileWhite Corporation. ***(LO 13-2)***

a. Calculate the required rate of return for SmileWhite using the information in the following table:

	December 2010	
	QuickBrush	**SmileWhite**
Beta	1.35	1.15
Market price	$45.00	$30.00
Intrinsic value	$63.00	?

Note: Risk-free rate = 4.50%; expected market return = 14.50%.

b. Ludlow estimates the following EPS and dividend growth rates for SmileWhite:

First three years:	12% per year
Years thereafter:	9% per year

Estimate the intrinsic value of SmileWhite using the table above and the two-stage DDM. Dividends per share in 2010 were $1.72.

c. Recommend QuickBrush or SmileWhite stock for purchase by comparing each company's intrinsic value with its current market price.

d. Describe *one* strength of the two-stage DDM in comparison with the constant-growth DDM. Describe *one* weakness inherent in all DDMs.

5. Rio National Corp. is a U.S.-based company and the largest competitor in its industry. Tables 13.5–13.8 present financial statements and related information for the company. Table 13.9 presents relevant industry and market data.

   The portfolio manager of a large mutual fund comments to one of the fund's analysts, Katrina Shaar: "We have been considering the purchase of Rio National Corp. equity shares, so I would like you to analyze the value of the company. To begin, based on

TABLE 13.5 Rio National Corp. summary year-end balance sheets (U.S. $ millions)

	2012	2011
Cash	$ 13.00	$ 5.87
Accounts receivable	30.00	27.00
Inventory	209.06	189.06
Current assets	$252.06	$221.93
Gross fixed assets	474.47	409.47
Accumulated depreciation	(154.17)	(90.00)
Net fixed assets	320.30	319.47
Total assets	$572.36	$541.40
Accounts payable	$ 25.05	$ 26.05
Notes payable	0.00	0.00
Current portion of long-term debt	0.00	0.00
Current liabilities	$ 25.05	$ 26.05
Long-term debt	240.00	245.00
Total liabilities	$265.05	$271.05
Common stock	160.00	150.00
Retained earnings	147.31	120.35
Total shareholders' equity	$307.31	$270.35
Total liabilities and shareholders' equity	$572.36	$541.40

TABLE 13.6 Rio National Corp. summary income statement for the year ended December 31, 2012 (U.S. $ millions)

Revenue	$300.80
Total operating expenses	(173.74)
Operating profit	127.06
Gain on sale	4.00
Earnings before interest, taxes, depreciation & amortization (EBITDA)	131.06
Depreciation and amortization	(71.17)
Earnings before interest & taxes (EBIT)	59.89
Interest	(16.80)
Income tax expense	(12.93)
Net income	$ 30.16

TABLE 13.7 Rio National Corp. supplemental notes for 2012

Note 1: Rio National had $75 million in capital expenditures during the year.

Note 2: A piece of equipment that was originally purchased for $10 million was sold for $7 million at year-end, when it had a net book value of $3 million. Equipment sales are unusual for Rio National.

Note 3: The decrease in long-term debt represents an unscheduled principal repayment; there was no new borrowing during the year.

Note 4: On 1 January 2012, the company received cash from issuing 400,000 shares of common equity at a price of $25 per share.

Note 5: A new appraisal during the year increased the estimated market value of land held for investment by $2 million, which was not recognized in 2012 income.

TABLE 13.8 Rio National Corp. common equity data for 2012

Dividends paid (U.S. $ millions)	$3.20
Weighted-average shares outstanding during 2012	16,000,000
Dividend per share	$0.20
Earnings per share	$1.89
Beta	1.80

Note: The dividend payout ratio is expected to be constant.

TABLE 13.9 Industry and market data December 31, 2012

Risk-free rate of return	4.00%
Expected rate of return on market index	9.00%
Median industry price–earnings (P/E) ratio	19.90
Expected industry earnings growth rate	12.00%

Rio National's past performance, you can assume that the company will grow at the same rate as the industry." *(LO 13-2)*

a. Calculate the value of a share of Rio National equity on December 31, 2012, using the constant-growth model and the capital asset pricing model.

b. Calculate the sustainable growth rate of Rio National on December 31, 2012. Use 2012 beginning-of-year balance sheet values.

6. While valuing the equity of Rio National Corp. (from the previous problem), Katrina Shaar is considering the use of either free cash flow to the firm (FCFF) or free cash flow to equity (FCFE) in her valuation process. *(LO 13-4)*

   a. State two adjustments that Shaar should make to FCFF to obtain free cash flow to equity.

   b. Shaar decides to calculate Rio National's FCFE for the year 2012, starting with net income. Determine for each of the five supplemental notes given in Table 13.7 whether an adjustment should be made to net income to calculate Rio National's free cash flow to equity for the year 2012, and the dollar amount of any adjustment.

   c. Calculate Rio National's free cash flow to equity for the year 2012.

7. Shaar (from the previous problem) has revised slightly her estimated earnings growth rate for Rio National and, using normalized (underlying trend) EPS, which is adjusted for temporary impacts on earnings, now wants to compare the current value of Rio National's equity to that of the industry, on a growth-adjusted basis. Selected information about Rio National and the industry is given in Table 13.10.

TABLE 13.10 Rio National Corp. vs. industry

Rio National	
Estimated earnings growth rate	11.00%
Current share price	$25.00
Normalized (underlying trend) EPS for 2012	$ 1.71
Weighted-average shares outstanding during 2012	16,000,000
Industry	
Estimated earnings growth rate	12.00%
Median price–earnings (P/E) ratio	19.90

Compared to the industry, is Rio National's equity overvalued or undervalued on a P/E-to-growth (PEG) basis, using normalized (underlying) earnings per share? Assume that the risk of Rio National is similar to the risk of the industry. *(LO 13-3)*

8. Helen Morgan, CFA, has been asked to use the DDM to determine the value of Sundanci, Inc. Morgan anticipates that Sundanci's earnings and dividends will grow at 32% for two years and 13% thereafter.

   Calculate the current value of a share of Sundanci stock by using a two-stage dividend discount model and the data from Tables 13.11 and 13.12. *(LO 13-2)*

TABLE 13.11 Sundanci actual 2012 and forecast 2013 financial statements for fiscal years ending May 31 ($ million, except per-share data)

Income Statement	2012	2013
Revenue	$ 474	$ 598
Depreciation	20	23
Other operating costs	368	460
Income before taxes	86	115
Taxes	26	35
Net income	60	80
Dividends	18	24
Earnings per share	$0.714	$0.952
Dividend per share	$0.214	$0.286
Common shares outstanding (millions)	84.0	84.0
Balance Sheet	**2012**	**2013**
Current assets	$ 201	$ 326
Net property, plant, and equipment	474	489
Total assets	675	815
Current liabilities	57	141
Long-term debt	0	0
Total liabilities	57	141
Shareholders' equity	618	674
Total liabilities and equity	675	815
Capital expenditures	34	38

TABLE 13.12 Selected financial information

Required rate of return on equity	14%
Growth rate of industry	13%
Industry P/E ratio	26

9. To continue with Sundanci, Abbey Naylor, CFA, has been directed to determine the value of Sundanci's stock using the free cash flow to equity (FCFE) model. Naylor

believes that Sundanci's FCFE will grow at 27% for two years and 13% thereafter. Capital expenditures, depreciation, and working capital are all expected to increase proportionately with FCFE. ***(LO 13-4)***

a. Calculate the amount of FCFE per share for the year 2013, using the data from Table 13.11.

b. Calculate the current value of a share of Sundanci stock based on the two-stage FCFE model.

c. i. Describe one limitation of the two-stage DDM model that is addressed by using the two-stage FCFE model.

ii. Describe one limitation of the two-stage DDM model that is *not* addressed by using the two-stage FCFE model.

10. Christie Johnson, CFA, has been assigned to analyze Sundanci using the constant-dividend-growth price–earnings (P/E) ratio model. Johnson assumes that Sundanci's earnings and dividends will grow at a constant rate of 13%. ***(LO 13-2)***

a. Calculate the P/E ratio based on information in Tables 13.11 and 13.12 and on Johnson's assumptions for Sundanci.

b. Identify, within the context of the constant-dividend-growth model, how each of the following factors would affect the P/E ratio.

- Risk (beta) of Sundanci.
- Estimated growth rate of earnings and dividends.
- Market risk premium.

WEB *master*

1. Choose 10 firms that interest you and download their financial statements from any of these websites: **finance.yahoo.com, finance.google.com,** or **money.msn.com.**

a. For each firm, find the return on equity (ROE), the number of shares outstanding, the dividends per share, and the net income. Record them in a spreadsheet.

b. Calculate the total amount of dividends paid (dividends per share × number of shares outstanding), the dividend payout ratio (total dividends paid/net income), and the plowback ratio (1 − dividend payout ratio).

c. Compute the sustainable growth rate, $g = b \times \text{ROE}$, where b equals the plowback ratio.

d. Compare the growth rates (g) with the P/E ratios of the firms by plotting the P/Es against the growth rates in a scatter diagram. Is there a relationship between the two?

e. Find the price-to-book, price-to-sales, and price-to-cash-flow ratios for your sample of firms. Use a line chart to plot these three ratios on the same set of axes. What relationships do you see among the three series?

f. For each firm, compare the three-year growth rate of earnings per share with the growth rate you calculated above. Is the actual rate of earnings growth correlated with the sustainable growth rate you calculated?

2. Now calculate the intrinsic value of three of the firms you selected in the previous question. Make reasonable judgments about the market risk premium and the risk-free rate, or find estimates from the Internet.

a. What is the required return on each firm based on the CAPM?

b. Try using a two-stage growth model, making reasonable assumptions about how future growth rates will differ from current growth rates. Compare the intrinsic values derived from the two-stage model to the intrinsic values you find assuming a constant growth rate. Which estimate seems more reasonable for each firm?

3. Now choose one of your firms and look up the other firms in the same industry. Perform a "Valuation by Comparables" analysis by looking at the price/earnings, price/book value, price/sales, and price/cash flow ratios of the firms relative to each other and to the industry average. Which of the firms seem to be overvalued? Which seem to be undervalued? Can you think of reasons for any apparent mispricings?

4. The actually expected return on a stock based on estimates of future dividends and future price can be compared to the "required" or equilibrium return given its risk. If the expected return is greater than the required return, the stock may be an attractive investment.

a. First calculate the expected holding-period return (HPR) on Target Corporation's stock based on its current price, its expected price and its expected dividend.

i. Go to **moneycentral.msn.com/investor/home.asp** and link to the *Stock Research Wizard*. Enter "TGT" to find information about Target Corporation. Find the average estimated target price for the next fiscal year.
ii. Click on the *Company Report* link and collect information about today's price and the dividend rate. Calculate the company's expected dividend in dollars for the next fiscal year.
iii. Use these inputs to calculate Target's expected HPR for the next year.

b. Calculate the required return based on the capital asset pricing model (CAPM).
i. Use a risk-free rate from **moneycentral.msn.com/investor/market/treasuries.aspx.**
ii. Use the beta coefficient shown in Target's Company Report.
iii. Calculate the historical return on a broad-based market index of your choice. You may use any time period that you deem appropriate. Your goal is to derive an estimate of the expected return on the market index for the coming year.
iv. Use the data you've collected as inputs for the CAPM to find the required rate of return for Target Corporation.

c. Compare the expected HPR you calculated in part (*a*) to the required CAPM return you calculated in part (*b*). What is your best judgment about the stock's current status—do you think it is selling at an appropriate price?

13.1 *a.* Dividend yield = \$2.15/\$50 = 4.3%
Capital gains yield = (59.77 − 50)/50 = 19.54%
Total return = 4.3% + 19.54% = 23.84%
b. $k = 6\% + 1.15(14\% - 6\%) = 15.2\%$
c. $V_0 = (\$2.15 + \$59.77)/1.152 = \$53.75$, which exceeds the market price. This would indicate a "buy" opportunity.

13.2 *a.* $D_1/(k - g) = \$2.15/(.152 - .112) = \$53.75$
b. $P_1 = P_0(1 + g) = \$53.75(1.112) = \$59.77$
c. The expected capital gain equals \$59.77 − \$53.75 = \$6.02, for a percentage gain of 11.2%. The dividend yield is $D_1/P_0 = 2.15/53.75 = 4\%$, for a holding-period return of 4% + 11.2% = 15.2%.

13.3 *a.* $g = \text{ROE} \times b = .20 \times .60 = .12$
$P_0 = 2/(.125 - .12) = 400$
b. When the firm invests in projects with ROE less than *k*, its stock price falls.
If $b = .60$, then $g = 10\% \times .60 = 6\%$ and $P_0 = \$2/(.125 - .06) = \$30.77$. In contrast, if $b = 0$, then $P_0 = \$5/.125 = \$40$.

13.4 Because $\beta = 1$, $k = 2.9\% + 1 \times 8\% = 10.9\%$.

$$V_{2011} = \frac{.72}{1.109} + \frac{.81}{(1.109)^2} + \frac{.90}{(1.109)^3} + \frac{1.00 + P_{2015}}{(1.109)^4}$$

Now compute the sales price in 2015 using the constant-growth dividend discount model.

$$P_{2015} = \frac{1.00 \times (1 + g)}{k - g} = \frac{1.00 \times 1.075}{.109 - .075} = \$31.62$$

Therefore, $V_{2011} = \$23.53$.

13.5 *a.* ROE = 12%
$b = \$.50/\$2.00 = .25$
$g = \text{ROE} \times b = 12\% \times .25 = 3\%$
$P_0 = D_1/(k - g) = \$1.50/(.10 - .03) = \$21.43$
$P_0/E_1 = 21.43/\$2 = 10.71$
b. If $b = .4$, then $.4 \times \$2 = \$.80$ would be reinvested and the remainder of earnings, or \$1.20, would be paid as dividends.
$g = 12\% \times .4 = 4.8\%$
$P_0 = D_1/(k - g) = \$1.20/(.10 - .048) = \$23.08$
$P_0/E_1 = \$23.08/\$2.00 = 11.54$
PEG = 11.54/4.8 = 2.4

Chapter 14

Financial Statement Analysis

Learning Objectives:

LO14-1 Interpret a firm's income statement, balance sheet, and statement of cash flows, and calculate standard measures of a firm's operating efficiency, leverage, and liquidity.

LO14-2 Calculate and interpret performance measures such as economic value added and rates of return on assets, capital, and equity.

LO14-3 Use ratio decomposition analysis to show how profitability depends on efficient use of assets, profit margin, and leverage.

LO14-4 Identify possible sources of biases in conventional accounting data.

In the previous chapter, we explored equity valuation techniques. These techniques take as inputs the firm's dividends and earnings prospects. While the valuation analyst is interested in economic earnings streams, only financial accounting data are readily available. What can we learn from a company's accounting data that can help us estimate the intrinsic value of its common stock?

In this chapter, we show how investors can use financial data as inputs into stock valuation analysis. We start by reviewing the basic sources of such data: the income statement, the balance sheet, and the statement of cash flows. We note the difference between economic and accounting earnings. While economic earnings are more important for issues of valuation, they can at best be estimated, so, in practice, analysts always begin their evaluation of the firm using accounting data. We next show how analysts use financial ratios to explore the sources of a firm's profitability and evaluate the "quality" of its earnings in a systematic fashion. We also examine the impact of debt policy on various financial ratios.

Finally, we conclude with a discussion of the challenges you will encounter when using financial statement analysis as a tool in uncovering mispriced securities. Some of these issues arise from differences in firms' accounting procedures. Others are due to inflation-induced distortions in accounting numbers.

Related websites for this chapter are available at www.mhhe.com/bkm.

14.1 THE MAJOR FINANCIAL STATEMENTS

The Income Statement

The **income statement** is a summary of the profitability of the firm over a period of time, such as a year. It presents revenues generated during the operating period, the expenses incurred during that same period, and the company's net earnings or profits, which are simply the difference between revenues and expenses.

income statement

A financial statement showing a firm's revenues and expenses during a specified period.

It is useful to distinguish among four broad classes of expenses: cost of goods sold, which is the direct cost attributable to producing the product sold by the firm; general and administrative expenses, which correspond to overhead expenses, salaries, advertising, and other costs of operating the firm that are not directly attributable to production; interest expense on the firm's debt; and taxes on earnings owed to federal and local governments.

Table 14.1 presents an income statement for Home Depot (HD). At the top are the company's revenues. Next come operating expenses, the costs incurred in the course of generating these revenues, including a depreciation allowance. The difference between operating revenues and operating costs is called *operating income.* Income (or expenses) from other, primarily nonrecurring, sources is then added to obtain earnings before interest and taxes (EBIT), which is what the firm would have earned if not for obligations to its creditors and the tax authorities. EBIT is a measure of the profitability of the firm's operations abstracting from any interest burden attributable to debt financing. The income statement then goes on to subtract net interest expense from EBIT to arrive at taxable income. Finally, the income tax due the government is subtracted to arrive at net income, the "bottom line" of the income statement.

Analysts also commonly prepare a *common-size income statement,* in which all items on the income statement are expressed as a fraction of total revenue. This makes it easier to compare firms of different sizes. The right-hand column of Table 14.1 is HD's common-size income statement.

economic earnings

The real flow of cash that a firm could pay out without impairing its productive capacity.

In the previous chapter, we saw that stock valuation models require a measure of **economic earnings**—the sustainable cash flow that can be paid out to stockholders without impairing

TABLE 14.1 Home Depot income statement

	$ Million	Percent of Revenue
Operating revenues		
Net sales	$67,997	100.0%
Operating expenses		
Cost of goods sold	$42,975	63.2
Selling, general, & administrative expenses	15,849	23.3
Other	1,652	2.4
Depreciation	1,718	2.5
Earnings before interest and income taxes	$ 5,803	8.5
Interest expense	530	0.8
Taxable income	$ 5,273	7.8
Taxes	1,935	2.8
Net income	$ 3,338	4.9
Allocation of net income		
Dividends	1,569	2.3
Addition to retained earnings	1,769	2.6

Note: Sums subject to rounding error.

Source: Home Depot Annual Report, year ending January 2011.

accounting earnings

Earnings of a firm as reported on its income statement.

the productive capacity of the firm. In contrast, **accounting earnings** are affected by several conventions regarding the valuation of assets such as inventories (e.g., LIFO versus FIFO treatment) and by the way some expenditures such as capital investments are recognized over time (as depreciation expenses). We will discuss problems with some of these accounting conventions in greater detail later in the chapter. In addition to these accounting issues, as the firm makes its way through the business cycle, its earnings will rise above or fall below the trend line that might more accurately reflect sustainable economic earnings. This introduces an added complication in interpreting net income figures. One might wonder how closely accounting earnings approximate economic earnings and, correspondingly, how useful accounting data might be to investors attempting to value the firm.

In fact, the net income figure on the firm's income statement does convey considerable information concerning a firm's products. We see this in the fact that stock prices tend to increase when firms announce earnings greater than market analysts or investors had anticipated.

The Balance Sheet

balance sheet

An accounting statement of a firm's financial position at a particular time.

While the income statement provides a measure of profitability over a period of time, the **balance sheet** provides a "snapshot" of the financial condition of the firm at a particular time. The balance sheet is a list of the firm's assets and liabilities at that moment. The difference in assets and liabilities is the net worth of the firm, also called *stockholders' equity* or, equivalently, *shareholders' equity.* Like income statements, balance sheets are reasonably standardized in presentation. Table 14.2 is HD's balance sheet for 2011.

The first section of the balance sheet gives a listing of the assets of the firm. Current assets are presented first. These are cash and other items such as accounts receivable or inventories that will be converted into cash within one year. Next comes a listing of long-term or "fixed" assets. *Tangible fixed assets* are items such as buildings, equipment, or vehicles. HD also has several intangible assets such as a respected brand name and expertise. But accountants generally are reluctant to include these assets on the balance sheet, as they are so hard to value. However, when one firm purchases another for a premium over its book value, that difference is called *goodwill* and is listed on the balance sheet as an *intangible fixed asset.* HD lists goodwill at $1,187 million.[1]

The liability and shareholders' equity section is arranged similarly. Listed first are short-term or "current" liabilities, such as accounts payable, accrued taxes, and debts that are due within one year. Long-term debt and other liabilities due in more than a year follow. The difference between total assets and total liabilities is shareholders' equity. This is the net worth or book value of the firm. Shareholders' equity is divided into par value of stock, capital surplus (additional paid-in capital), and retained earnings, although this division is usually unimportant. Briefly, par value plus capital surplus represents the proceeds realized from the sale of stock to the public, while retained earnings represent the buildup of equity from profits plowed back into the firm. Even if the firm issues no new equity, book value will typically increase each year due to reinvested earnings.

The entries in the first column of the balance sheet in Table 14.2 present the dollar value of each asset. To make it easier to compare firms of different sizes, analysts often present each item on the balance sheet as a percentage of total assets. This is called a *common-size balance sheet* and is presented in the second column.

The Statement of Cash Flows

The income statement and balance sheets are based on accrual methods of accounting, which means revenues and expenses are recognized at the time of a sale even if no cash has yet been

[1]Firms are required to test their goodwill assets for "impairment" each year. If it becomes apparent that the value of the acquired firm is less than its purchase price, that amount must be charged off as an expense. AOL Time Warner set a record when it recognized an impairment of $99 billion in 2002 following the January 2001 merger of Time Warner with AOL.

TABLE 14.2 Home Depot balance sheet

Assets	$ Million	Percent of Total Assets
Current assets		
Cash and marketable securities	$ 545	1.4%
Receivables	1,085	2.7
Inventories	10,625	26.5
Other current assets	1,224	3.1
Total current assets	$13,479	33.6%
Fixed assets		
Tangible fixed assets		
Property, plant, and equipment	$25,060	62.5%
Long-term investments	139	0.3
Total tangible fixed assets	$25,199	62.8%
Intangible fixed assets		
Goodwill	$ 1,187	3.0%
Total fixed assets	$26,386	65.8
Other assets	260	0.6
Total assets	$40,125	100.0%

Liabilities and Shareholders' Equity	$ Million	Percent of Total Assets
Current liabilities		
Debt due for repayment	$ 1,042	2.6%
Accounts payable	7,903	19.7
Other current liabilities	1,177	2.9
Total current liabilities	$10,122	25.2%
Long-term debt	8,707	21.7
Other long-term liabilities	2,407	6.0
Total liabilities	$21,236	52.9%
Shareholders' equity		
Common stock and other paid-in capital	$ 3,894	9.7%
Retained earnings	14,995	37.4
Total shareholders' equity	$18,889	47.1%
Total liabilities and shareholders' equity	$40,125	100.0%

Note: Column sums subject to rounding error.

Source: Home Depot Annual Report, year ending January 2011.

exchanged. In contrast, the **statement of cash flows** recognizes only transactions in which cash changes hands. For example, if goods are sold now, with payment due in 60 days, the income statement will treat the revenue as generated when the sale occurs, and the balance sheet will be immediately augmented by accounts receivable, but the statement of cash flows will not recognize the transaction until the bill is paid and the cash is in hand.

statement of cash flows

A financial statement showing a firm's cash receipts and cash payments during a specified period.

Table 14.3 is the statement of cash flows for HD. The first entry listed under "Cash provided by operations" is net income. The following entries modify that figure for components of income that have been recognized but for which cash has not yet changed hands. For example, HD's accounts receivable increased by $102 million. This portion of its income was claimed on the income statement, but the cash had not yet been collected. Increases in accounts receivable are in effect an investment in working capital and, therefore, reduce the cash flows realized from operations. Similarly, increases in accounts payable mean expenses have been recognized, but cash has not yet left the firm. Any payment delay increases the company's net cash flows in this period.

TABLE 14.3 Home Depot statement of cash flows

	$ Million
Cash provided by operations	
Net income	$ 3,338
Adjustments to net income	
Depreciation	1,718
Changes in working capital	
Decrease (increase) in receivables	(102)
Decrease (increase) in inventories	(355)
Increase (decrease) in other current liabilities	(269)
Changes due to other operating activities	255
Total adjustments	$ 1,247
Cash provided by operations	4,585
Cash flows from investments	
Gross investment in tangible fixed assets	$(1,096)
Investments in other assets	84
Cash provided by (used for) investments	$(1,012)
Cash provided by (used for) financing activities	
Additions to (reductions in) long-term debt	$ (31)
Net issues (repurchases of) shares	(2,504)
Dividends	(1,569)
Other	(347)
Cash provided by (used for) financing activities	$(4,451)
Net increase in cash	$ (878)

Source: Home Depot Annual Report, year ending January 2011.

Another major difference between the income statement and the statement of cash flows involves depreciation, which accounts for a substantial addition in the adjustment section of the statement of cash flows in Table 14.3. The income statement attempts to "smooth" large capital expenditures over time. The depreciation expense on the income statement does this by recognizing capital expenditures over a period of many years rather than at the specific time of purchase. In contrast, the statement of cash flows recognizes the cash implication of a capital expenditure when it occurs. Therefore, it adds back the depreciation "expense" that was used to compute net income; instead, it acknowledges a capital expenditure when it is paid. It does so by reporting cash flows separately for operations, investing, and financing activities. This way, any large cash flows, such as those for big investments, can be recognized without affecting the measure of cash flow provided by operations.

The second section of the statement of cash flows is the accounting of cash flows from investing activities. For example, HD used $1,096 million of cash investing in tangible fixed assets. These entries are investments in the assets necessary for the firm to maintain or enhance its productive capacity.

Finally, the last section of the statement lists the cash flows realized from financing activities. Issuance of securities contributes positive cash flows, while redemption of outstanding securities uses cash. For example, HD expended $31 million to repurchase shares of its stock, which was a use of cash. Its dividend payments, $1,569 million, also used cash. In total, HD's financing activities absorbed $4,451 million of cash.

To summarize, HD's operations generated a cash flow of $4,585 million. The company laid out $1,012 million to pay for new investments, and financing activities used another $4,451 million. HD's cash holdings therefore changed by $4,585 − $1,012 − $4,451 = −$878 million. This is reported on the last line of Table 14.3.

The statement of cash flows provides important evidence on the well-being of a firm. If a company cannot pay its dividends and maintain the productivity of its capital stock out of cash flow from operations, for example, and it must resort to borrowing to meet these demands, this is a serious warning that the firm cannot maintain payout at its current level in the long run. The statement of cash flows will reveal this developing problem when it shows that cash flow from operations is inadequate and that borrowing is being used to maintain dividend payments at unsustainable levels.

14.2 MEASURING FIRM PERFORMANCE

In Chapter 1, we noted that a natural goal of the firm is to maximize value but that various agency problems, or conflicts of interest, may impede that goal. How can we measure how well the firm is actually performing? Financial analysts have come up with a mind-numbing list of financial ratios that measure many aspects of firm performance. Before getting lost in the trees, therefore, let's first pause to consider what sorts of ratios may be related to the ultimate objective of added value.

Two broad activities are the responsibility of a firm's financial managers: investment decisions and financing decisions. Investment, or capital budgeting, decisions pertain to the firm's *use* of capital: the business activities in which it is engaged. Here, the questions we will wish to answer pertain to the profitability of those projects. How should profitability be measured? How does the acceptable level of profitability depend on risk and the opportunity cost of the funds used to pay for the firm's many projects? In contrast, financial decisions pertain to the firm's *sources* of capital. Is there a sufficient supply of financing to meet projected needs for growth? Does the financing plan rely too heavily on borrowed funds? Is there sufficient liquidity to deal with unexpected cash needs?

These questions suggest that we organize the ratios we choose to construct along the lines given in Figure 14.1. The figure shows that when evaluating the firm's investment activities, we will ask two questions: How efficiently does the firm deploy its assets, and how profitable are its sales? In turn, aspects of both efficiency and profitability can be measured with several ratios: Efficiency is typically assessed using several turnover ratios, while the profitability of sales is commonly measured with various profit margins. Similarly, when evaluating financing decisions, we look at both leverage and liquidity, and we will see that aspects of each of these two concepts also can be measured with an array of statistics.

The next section shows how to calculate and interpret some of these key financial ratios and shows how many of them are related.

14.3 PROFITABILITY MEASURES

Big firms naturally earn greater profits than smaller ones. Therefore, most profitability measures focus on earnings per dollar employed. The most common measures are return on assets, return on capital, and return on equity.

FIGURE 14.1

Important financial questions and some ratios that help answer them

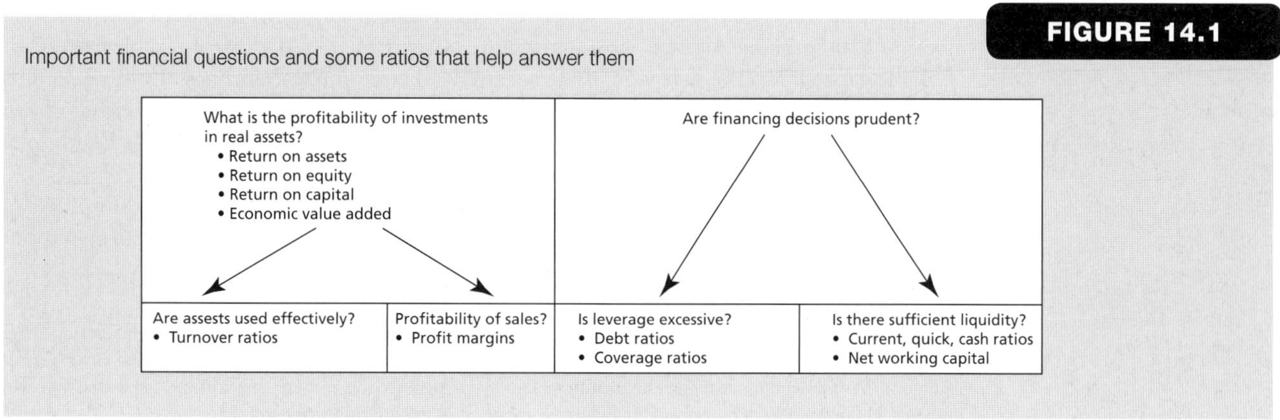

Return on Assets

return on assets (ROA)

Earnings before interest and taxes divided by total assets.

Return on assets (ROA) equals EBIT as a fraction of the firm's total assets.[2]

$$ROA = \frac{EBIT}{\text{Total assets}}$$

The numerator of this ratio may be viewed as total operating income of the firm. Therefore, ROA tells us the income earned per dollar deployed in the firm.

Return on Capital

Return on capital ROC expresses EBIT as a fraction of long-term capital, shareholders' equity plus long-term debt. It tells us the income earned per dollar of long-term capital invested in the firm.

$$ROC = \frac{EBIT}{\text{Long-term capital}}$$

Return on Equity

return on equity (ROE)

The ratio of net profits to common equity.

Whereas ROA and ROC measure profitability relative to funds raised by both debt and equity financing, **return on equity (ROE)** focuses only on the profitability of equity investments. It equals net income realized by shareholders per dollar they have invested in the firm.

$$ROE = \frac{\text{Net income}}{\text{Shareholders' equity}}$$

We noted in Chapter 13 that return on equity (ROE) is one of the two basic factors in determining a firm's growth rate of earnings. Sometimes it is reasonable to assume that future ROE will approximate its past value, but a high ROE in the past does not necessarily imply a firm's future ROE will be high. A declining ROE, on the other hand, is evidence that the firm's new investments have offered a lower ROE than its past investments. The vital point for a security analyst is not to accept historical values as indicators of future values. Data from the recent past may provide information regarding future performance, but the analyst should always keep an eye on the future. Expectations of *future* dividends and earnings determine the intrinsic value of the company's stock.

Not surprisingly, ROA and ROE are linked, but as we will see next, the relationship between them is affected by the firm's financial policies.

Financial Leverage and ROE

An analyst interpreting the past behavior of a firm's ROE or forecasting its future value must pay careful attention to the firm's debt–equity mix and to the interest rate on its debt. An example will show why. Suppose Nodett is a firm that is all-equity-financed and has total assets of $100 million. Assume it pays corporate taxes at the rate of 40% of taxable earnings.

Table 14.4 shows the behavior of sales, earnings before interest and taxes, and net profits under three scenarios representing phases of the business cycle. It also shows the behavior of two of the most commonly used profitability measures: operating ROA, which equals EBIT/total assets, and ROE, which equals net profits/equity.

Somdett is an otherwise identical firm to Nodett, but $40 million of its $100 million of assets are financed with debt bearing an interest rate of 8%. It pays annual interest expenses of $3.2 million. Table 14.5 shows how Somdett's ROE differs from Nodett's.

[2]ROA sometimes is computed using EBIT × (1 − Tax rate) in the numerator. Sometimes it is computed using after-tax operating income, that is: Net income + Interest × (1 − Tax rate). Sometimes, it even is calculated using just net income in the numerator, although this definition ignores altogether the income the firm has generated for debt investors. Unfortunately, definitions of many key financial ratios are not fully standardized.

TABLE 14.4 Nodett's profitability over the business cycle

Scenario	Sales ($ million)	EBIT ($ million)	ROA (% per year)	Net Profit ($ million)	ROE (% per year)
Bad year	$ 80	$ 5	5%	$3	3%
Normal year	$100	10	10	6	6
Good year	120	15	15	9	9

TABLE 14.5 Impact of financial leverage on ROE

		Nodett		Somdett	
Scenario	EBIT ($ million)	Net Profit ($ million)	ROE (%)	Net Profit* ($ million)	ROE† (%)
Bad year	$ 5	$3	3%	$1.08	1.8%
Normal year	10	6	6	4.08	6.8
Good year	15	9	9	7.08	11.8

*Somdett's after-tax profits equal .6(EBIT − $3.2 million).
†Somdett's equity is only $60 million.

Note that annual sales, EBIT, and therefore ROA for both firms are the same in each of the three scenarios; that is, business risk for the two companies is identical. It is their financial risk that differs. Although Nodett and Somdett have the same ROA in each scenario, Somdett's ROE exceeds that of Nodett in normal and good years and is lower in bad years.

We can summarize the exact relationship among ROE, ROA, and leverage in the following equation:[3]

$$\text{ROE} = (1 - \text{Tax rate})\left[\text{ROA} + (\text{ROA} - \text{Interest rate})\frac{\text{Debt}}{\text{Equity}}\right] \quad \textbf{(14.1)}$$

The relationship has the following implications. If there is no debt or if the firm's ROA equals the interest rate on its debt, its ROE will simply equal (1 − tax rate) times ROA. If its ROA exceeds the interest rate, then its ROE will exceed (1 − tax rate) times ROA by an amount that will be greater the higher the debt/equity ratio.

This result makes sense: If ROA exceeds the borrowing rate, the firm earns more on its money than it pays out to creditors. The surplus earnings are available to the firm's owners, the equityholders, which raises ROE. If, on the other hand, ROA is less than the interest rate paid on debt, then ROE will decline by an amount that depends on the debt/equity ratio.

[3]The derivation of Equation 14.1 is as follows:

$$\text{ROE} = \frac{\text{Net profit}}{\text{Equity}} = \frac{\text{EBIT} - \text{Interest} - \text{Taxes}}{\text{Equity}} = \frac{(1 - \text{Tax rate})(\text{EBIT} - \text{Interest})}{\text{Equity}}$$

$$= (1 - \text{Tax rate})\frac{(\text{ROA} \times \text{Assets} - \text{Interest rate} \times \text{Debt})}{\text{Equity}}$$

$$= (1 - \text{Tax rate})\left[\text{ROA} \times \frac{(\text{Equity} + \text{Debt})}{\text{Equity}} - \text{Interest rate} \times \frac{\text{Debt}}{\text{Equity}}\right]$$

$$= (1 - \text{Tax rate})\left[\text{ROA} + (\text{ROA} - \text{Interest rate})\frac{\text{Debt}}{\text{Equity}}\right]$$

EXAMPLE 14.1

Leverage and ROE

To illustrate the application of Equation 14.1, we can use the numerical example in Table 14.5. In a normal year, Nodett has an ROE of 6%, which is (1 − tax rate), or .6, times its ROA of 10%. However, Somdett, which borrows at an interest rate of 8% and maintains a debt/equity ratio of $^2/_3$, has an ROE of 6.8%. The calculation using Equation 14.1 is

$$\text{ROE} = .6[10\% + (10\% - 8\%)^2/_3]$$
$$= .6(10\% + {}^4/_3\%) = 6.8\%$$

The important point is that increased debt will make a positive contribution to a firm's ROE only if the firm's ROA exceeds the interest rate on the debt.

Notice that financial leverage increases the risk of the equityholder returns. Table 14.5 shows that ROE on Somdett is worse than that of Nodett in bad years. Conversely, in good years, Somdett outperforms Nodett because the excess of ROA over ROE provides additional funds for equityholders. The presence of debt makes Somdett's ROE more sensitive to the business cycle than Nodett's. Even though the two companies have equal business risk (reflected in their identical EBIT in all three scenarios), Somdett's stockholders carry greater financial risk than Nodett's because all of the firm's business risk is absorbed by a smaller base of equity investors.

Even if financial leverage increases the expected ROE of Somdett relative to Nodett (as it seems to in Table 14.5), this does not imply that Somdett's share price will be higher. Financial leverage increases the risk of the firm's equity as surely as it raises the expected ROE, and the higher discount rate will offset the higher expected earnings.

CONCEPT check 14.1

Mordett is a company with the same assets as Nodett and Somdett but a debt/equity ratio of 1 and an interest rate of 9%. What would its net profit and ROE be in a bad year, a normal year, and a good year?

Economic Value Added

economic value added or residual income

A measure of the dollar value of a firm's return in excess of its opportunity cost.

While it is common to use profitability measures such as ROA, ROC, or ROE to evaluate performance, profitability is really not enough. A firm should be viewed as successful only if the return on its projects is better than the rate investors could expect to earn for themselves (on a risk-adjusted basis) in the capital market. Plowing back funds into the firm increases share value only if the firm earns a higher rate of return on the reinvested funds than the opportunity cost of capital, that is, the market capitalization rate. To account for this opportunity cost, we might measure the success of the firm using the *difference* between the return on assets, ROA, and the opportunity cost of capital. **Economic value added** (EVA) is the spread between ROA and the cost of capital multiplied by the capital invested in the firm. It therefore measures the dollar value of the firm's return in excess of its opportunity cost. Another term for EVA (the term coined by Stern Stewart, a consulting firm that has promoted the concept) is **residual income.**

EXAMPLE 14.2

Economic Value Added

In 2011, Walmart had a weighted-average cost of capital of 5.5% (based on its cost of debt, its capital structure, its equity beta, and estimates derived from the CAPM for the cost of equity). Walmart's return on assets was 8.6%, fully 3.1% greater than the opportunity cost of capital on its investments in plant, equipment, and know-how. In other words, each dollar invested by Walmart earned about 3.1 cents more than the return that investors could have anticipated by investing in equivalent-risk stocks. Walmart earned this superior rate of return on a capital base of $125.8 billion. Its economic value added, that is, its return in excess of opportunity cost, was therefore (.086 − .055) × $125.8 = $3.87 billion.

TABLE 14.6 Economic value added, 2011

	EVA ($ billion)	Capital ($ billion)	ROA (%)	Cost of Capital (%)
ExxonMobil	6.90	171.31	10.8	6.8
Intel	4.29	52.87	16.1	8.0
Walmart	3.87	125.80	8.6	5.5
GlaxoSmithKline	3.02	34.75	15.3	6.6
Google	2.60	61.38	12.0	7.7
Hewlett Packard	−0.91	68.86	5.9	7.2
AT&T	−1.60	183.99	4.6	5.5
Honda	−3.63	105.20	1.7	5.1

Source: Authors' calculations using data from **finance.yahoo.com.**

Table 14.6 shows EVA for a small sample of firms.[4] The EVA leader in this sample was ExxonMobil. Notice that its EVA was greater than GlaxoSmithKline's, despite a considerably smaller margin between ROA and the cost of capital. This is because ExxonMobil applied its margin to a much larger capital base. At the other extreme, Honda earned less than its opportunity cost on a very large capital base, which resulted in a large negative EVA.

Notice that even the EVA "losers" in Table 14.6 had positive profits. For example, by conventional standards, AT&T was solidly profitable in 2011, with an ROA of 4.6%. But its cost of capital was higher, 5.5%. By this standard, AT&T did not cover its opportunity cost of capital, and its EVA in 2011 was negative. EVA treats the opportunity cost of capital as a real cost that, like other costs, should be deducted from revenues to arrive at a more meaningful "bottom line." A firm that is earning profits but is not covering its opportunity cost might be able to redeploy its capital to better uses. Therefore, a growing number of firms now calculate EVA and tie managers' compensation to it.[5]

14.4 RATIO ANALYSIS

Decomposition of ROE

To understand the factors affecting a firm's ROE, including its trend over time and its performance relative to competitors, analysts often "decompose" ROE into the product of a series of ratios. Each component ratio is in itself meaningful, and the process serves to focus the analyst's attention on the separate factors influencing performance. This kind of decomposition of ROE is often called the **DuPont system.**

DuPont system

Decomposition of profitability measures into component ratios.

One useful decomposition of ROE is

$$\text{ROE} = \frac{\text{Net profit}}{\text{Equity}} = \underset{(1)}{\frac{\text{Net profit}}{\text{Pretax profit}}} \times \underset{(2)}{\frac{\text{Pretax profit}}{\text{EBIT}}} \times \underset{(3)}{\frac{\text{EBIT}}{\text{Sales}}} \times \underset{(4)}{\frac{\text{Sales}}{\text{Assets}}} \times \underset{(5)}{\frac{\text{Assets}}{\text{Equity}}} \tag{14.2}$$

[4]Actual EVA estimates reported by Stern Stewart differ from the values in Table 14.6 because of adjustments to the accounting data involving issues such as treatment of research and development expenses, taxes, advertising expenses, and depreciation. The estimates in Table 14.6 are designed to show the logic behind EVA but must be taken as imprecise.

[5]Because it accounts for the opportunity cost of capital, EVA is a better measure of profitability than income, and this explains why firms might prefer it when evaluating their managers' performance. Nevertheless, as a measure of performance, even EVA can be distorted by factors beyond management's control. For example, a good part of Honda's poor EVA in 2011 was due to the effects of the tsunami that hit Japan in March of that year—hardly the fault of Honda's management.

TABLE 14.7 Ratio decomposition analysis for Nodett and Somdett

	ROE	(1) Net Profit / Pretax Profit	(2) Pretax Profit / EBIT	(3) EBIT / Sales (Margin)	(4) Sales / Assets (Turnover)	(5) Assets / Equity	(6) Compound Leverage Factor (2) × (5)
Bad year							
Nodett	.030	.6	1.000	.0625	0.800	1.000	1.000
Somdett	.018	.6	0.360	.0625	0.800	1.667	0.600
Normal year							
Nodett	.060	.6	1.000	.100	1.000	1.000	1.000
Somdett	.068	.6	0.680	.100	1.000	1.667	1.134
Good year							
Nodett	.090	.6	1.000	.125	1.200	1.000	1.000
Somdett	.118	.6	0.787	.125	1.200	1.667	1.311

Table 14.7 shows all these ratios for Nodett and Somdett under the three different economic scenarios. Let us first focus on factors 3 and 4. Notice that their product gives us the firm's ROA = EBIT/Assets.

profit margin or return on sales

The ratio of operating profits per dollar of sales (EBIT divided by sales).

Factor 3 is known as the firm's operating **profit margin,** or **return on sales,** which equals operating profit per dollar of sales. In an average year, Nodett's margin is .10, or 10%; in a bad year, it is .0625, or 6.25%; and in a good year, it is .125, or 12.5%.

total asset turnover (ATO)

The annual sales generated by each dollar of assets (sales/assets).

Factor 4, the ratio of sales to total assets, is known as **total asset turnover (ATO).** It indicates the efficiency of the firm's use of assets in the sense that it measures the annual sales generated by each dollar of assets. In a normal year, Nodett's ATO is 1 per year, meaning that sales of $1 per year were generated per dollar of assets. In a bad year, this ratio declines to .8 per year, and in a good year, it rises to 1.2 per year.

Comparing Nodett and Somdett, we see that factors 3 and 4 do not depend on a firm's financial leverage. The firms' ratios are equal to each other in all three scenarios.

Similarly, factor 1, the ratio of net income after taxes to pretax profit, is the same for both firms. We call this the tax-burden ratio. Its value reflects both the government's tax code and the policies pursued by the firm in trying to minimize its tax burden. In our example, it does not change over the business cycle, remaining a constant .6.

While factors 1, 3, and 4 are not affected by a firm's capital structure, factors 2 and 5 are. Factor 2 is the ratio of pretax profits to EBIT. The firm's pretax profits will be greatest when there are no interest payments to be made to debtholders. In fact, another way to express this ratio is

$$\frac{\text{Pretax profits}}{\text{EBIT}} = \frac{\text{EBIT} - \text{Interest expense}}{\text{EBIT}}$$

We will call this factor the *interest-burden (IB) ratio.* It takes on its highest possible value, 1, for Nodett, which has no financial leverage. The higher the degree of financial leverage, the lower the IB ratio. Nodett's IB ratio does not vary over the business cycle. It is fixed at 1, reflecting the total absence of interest payments. For Somdett, however, because interest expense is fixed in a dollar amount while EBIT varies, the IB ratio varies from a low of .36 in a bad year to a high of .787 in a good year.

interest coverage ratio or times interest earned

A financial leverage measure arrived at by dividing earnings before interest and taxes by interest expense.

A closely related statistic to the interest-burden ratio is the **interest coverage ratio,** or **times interest earned.** The ratio is defined as

$$\text{Interest coverage} = \frac{\text{EBIT}}{\text{Interest expense}}$$

A high coverage ratio indicates that the likelihood of bankruptcy is low because annual earnings are significantly greater than annual interest obligations. It is widely used by both lenders and borrowers in determining the firm's debt capacity and is a major determinant of the firm's bond rating.

Factor 5, the ratio of assets to equity, is a measure of the firm's degree of financial leverage. It is called the **leverage ratio** and is equal to 1 plus the debt/equity ratio.[6] In our numerical example in Table 14.7, Nodett has a leverage ratio of 1, while Somdett's is 1.667.

leverage ratio

Measure of debt to total capitalization of a firm.

From our discussion of Equation 14.1, we know that financial leverage helps boost ROE only if ROA is greater than the interest rate on the firm's debt. How is this fact reflected in the ratios of Table 14.7?

The answer is that to measure the full impact of leverage in this framework, the analyst must take the product of the IB and leverage ratios (that is, factors 2 and 5, shown in Table 14.7 as column 6). For Nodett, factor 6, which we call the compound leverage factor, remains a constant 1 under all three scenarios. But for Somdett, we see that the compound leverage factor is greater than 1 in normal years (1.134) and in good years (1.311), indicating the positive contribution of financial leverage to ROE. It is less than 1 in bad years, reflecting the fact that when ROA falls below the interest rate, ROE falls with increased use of debt.

We can summarize all of these relationships as follows:

$$\text{ROE} = \text{Tax burden} \times \text{Interest burden} \times \text{Margin} \times \text{Turnover} \times \text{Leverage}$$

Because

$$\text{ROA} = \text{Margin} \times \text{Turnover} \quad \textbf{(14.3)}$$

and

$$\text{Compound leverage factor} = \text{Interest burden} \times \text{Leverage}$$

we can decompose ROE equivalently as follows:

$$\text{ROE} = \text{Tax burden} \times \text{ROA} \times \text{Compound leverage factor}$$

Equation 14.3 shows that ROA is the *product* of margin and turnover. High values of one of these ratios are often accompanied by low values of the other. For example, Walmart has low profit margins but high turnover, while Tiffany has high margins but low turnover. Firms would love to have high values for both margin and turnover, but this generally will not be possible: Retailers with high markups will sacrifice sales volume, and, conversely, those with low turnover need high margins just to remain viable. Therefore, comparing these ratios in isolation usually is meaningful only in evaluating firms following similar strategies in the same industry. Cross-industry comparison can be misleading.

Figure 14.2 shows evidence of the turnover-profit margin trade-off. Industries with high turnover such as groceries or retail apparel tend to have low profit margins, while industries with high margins such as utilities tend to have low turnover. The two curved lines in the figure trace out turnover-margin combinations that result in an ROA of either 3% or 6%. You can see that most industries lie inside this range, so ROA across industries demonstrates far less variation than either turnover or margin taken in isolation.

EXAMPLE 14.3

Margin vs. Turnover

Consider two firms with the same ROA of 10% per year. The first is a discount supermarket chain and the second is a gas and electric utility.

As Table 14.8 shows, the supermarket chain has a "low" profit margin of 2% and achieves a 10% ROA by "turning over" its assets five times per year. The capital-intensive utility, on the other hand, has a "low" asset turnover ratio (ATO) of only .5 times per year and achieves its 10% ROA through its higher, 20%, profit margin. The point here is that a "low" margin or ATO ratio need not indicate a troubled firm. Each ratio must be interpreted in light of industry norms.

[6] $\frac{\text{Assets}}{\text{Equity}} = \frac{\text{Equity} + \text{Debt}}{\text{Equity}} = 1 + \frac{\text{Debt}}{\text{Equity}}$

FIGURE 14.2

Median ROA, profit margin, and asset turnover for 23 industries, 1990–2004

Source: "Figure D: ROAs of Sample Firms (1977-1986)" from Thomas I. Selling and Clyde P. Stickney, "The Effects of Business Environments and Strategy on a Firm's Rate of Return on Assets." Copyright 1989, CFA Institute. Reproduced and republished from *Financial Analysts Journal,* January–February 1989, pp. 43–52, with permission from the CFA Institute. All rights reserved. Updates courtesy of Professors James Wahlen, Stephen Baginski, and Mark Bradshaw.

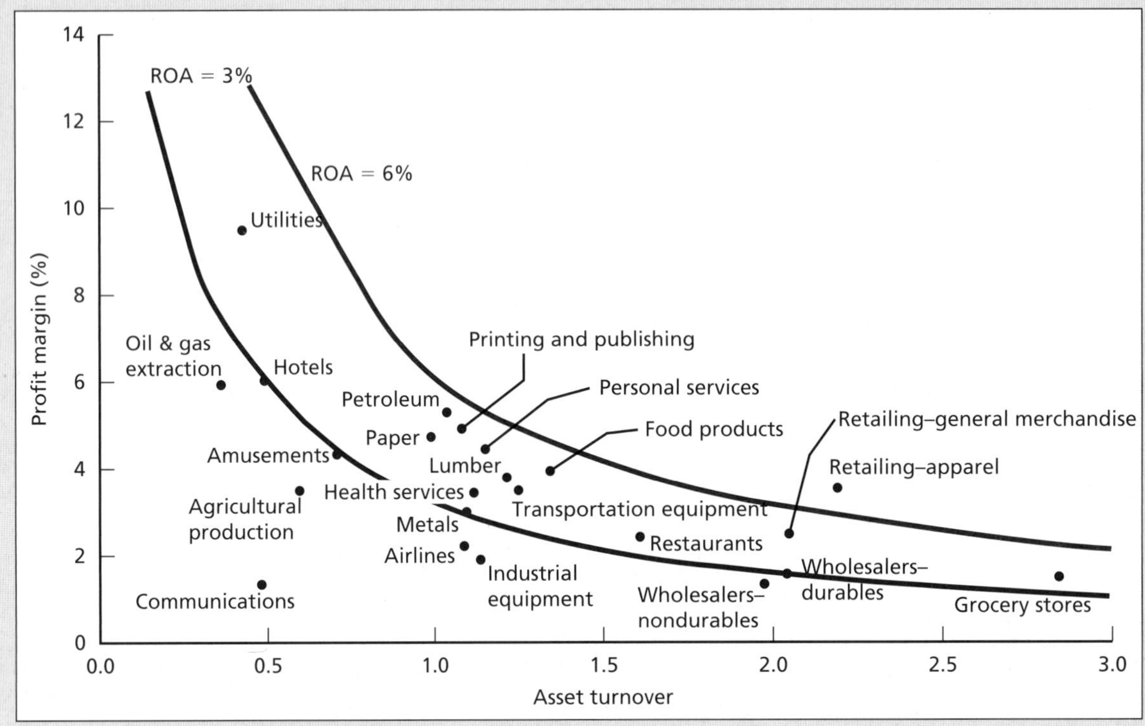

TABLE 14.8 Differences between profit margin and asset turnover across industries

	Margin	×	ATO	=	ROA
Supermarket chain	2%		5.0		10%
Utility	20%		0.5		10%

CONCEPT check 14.2

Do a ratio decomposition analysis for the Mordett corporation of Concept Check 14.1 preparing a table similar to Table 14.7.

Turnover and Asset Utilization

It is often helpful in understanding a firm's ratio of sales to assets to compute comparable efficiency-of-utilization, or turnover, ratios for subcategories of assets. For example, fixed-asset turnover would be

$$\frac{\text{Sales}}{\text{Fixed assets}}$$

This ratio measures sales per dollar of the firm's money tied up in fixed assets.

To illustrate how you can compute this and other ratios from a firm's financial statements, consider Growth Industries, Inc. (GI). GI's income statement and opening and closing balance sheets for the years 2012–2014 appear in Table 14.9.

GI's total asset turnover in 2014 was .303, which was below the industry average of .4. To understand better why GI underperformed, we compute asset utilization ratios separately for fixed assets, inventories, and accounts receivable.

GI's sales in 2014 were $144 million. Its only fixed assets were plant and equipment, which were $216 million at the beginning of the year and $259.2 million at year's end. Average fixed assets for the year were, therefore, $237.6 million [($216 million + $259.2 million)/2]. GI's fixed-asset turnover for 2014 was $144 million per year/$237.6 million = .606 per year. In other words, for every dollar of fixed assets, there was $.606 in sales during 2012.

Comparable figures for the fixed-asset turnover ratio for 2012 and 2013 and the 2014 industry average are:

2012	2013	2014	2014 Industry Average
.606	.606	.606	.700

GI's fixed-asset turnover has been stable over time and below the industry average.

Notice that when a financial ratio includes one item from the income statement, which covers a period of time, and another from the balance sheet, which is a "snapshot" at a particular time, common practice is to take the average of the beginning and end-of-year balance sheet figures. Thus, in computing the fixed-asset turnover ratio, you divide sales (from the income statement) by average fixed assets (from the balance sheet).

TABLE 14.9 Growth Industries financial statements ($ thousand)

	2011	2012	2013	2014
Income statements				
Sales revenue		$100,000	$120,000	$144,000
Cost of goods sold (including depreciation)		55,000	66,000	79,200
Depreciation		15,000	18,000	21,600
Selling and administrative expenses		15,000	18,000	21,600
Operating income		30,000	36,000	43,200
Interest expense		10,500	19,095	34,391
Taxable income		19,500	16,905	8,809
Income tax (40% rate)		7,800	6,762	3,524
Net income		11,700	10,143	5,285
Balance sheets (end of year)				
Cash and marketable securities	$ 50,000	$ 60,000	$ 72,000	$ 86,400
Accounts receivable	25,000	30,000	36,000	43,200
Inventories	75,000	90,000	108,000	129,600
Net plant and equipment	150,000	180,000	216,000	259,200
Total assets	$300,000	$360,000	$432,000	$518,400
Accounts payable	$ 30,000	$ 36,000	$ 43,200	$ 51,840
Short-term debt	45,000	87,300	141,957	214,432
Long-term debt (8% bonds maturing in 2022)	75,000	75,000	75,000	75,000
Total liabilities	$150,000	$198,300	$260,157	$341,272
Shareholders' equity (1 million shares outstanding)	$150,000	$161,700	$171,843	$177,128
Other data				
Market price per common share at year-end		$ 93.60	$ 61.00	$ 21.00

inventory turnover ratio

Cost of goods sold divided by average inventory.

Another widely followed turnover ratio is the **inventory turnover ratio,** which is the ratio of cost of goods sold per dollar of inventory. We use the cost of goods sold (instead of sales revenue) in the numerator to maintain consistency with inventory, which is valued at cost. This ratio measures the speed with which inventory is turned over.

In 2012, GI's cost of goods sold (less depreciation) was $40 million, and its average inventory was $82.5 million [($75 million + $90 million)/2]. Its inventory turnover was .485 per year ($40 million/$82.5 million). In 2013 and 2014, inventory turnover remained the same and continued below the industry average of .5 per year. In other words, GI was burdened with a higher level of inventories per dollar of sales than its competitors. This higher investment in working capital in turn resulted in a higher level of assets per dollar of sales or profits and a lower ROA than its competitors.

days sales in receivables or average collection period

Accounts receivable per dollar of daily sales.

Another aspect of efficiency surrounds management of accounts receivable, which is often measured by **days sales in receivables,** that is, the average level of accounts receivable expressed as a multiple of daily sales. It is computed as average accounts receivable/sales × 365 and may be interpreted as the number of days' worth of sales tied up in accounts receivable. You can also think of it as the average lag between the date of sale and the date payment is received, and it is therefore also called the **average collection period.**

For GI in 2014, this number was 100.4 days:

$$\frac{(\$36 \text{ million} + \$43.2 \text{ million})/2}{\$144 \text{ million}} \times 365 = 100.4 \text{ days}$$

The industry average was 60 days. This statistic tells us that GI's average receivables per dollar of sales exceeds that of its competitors. Again, this implies a higher required investment in working capital and ultimately a lower ROA.

In summary, use of these ratios lets us see that GI's poor total asset turnover relative to the industry is in part caused by lower-than-average fixed-asset turnover and inventory turnover and higher-than-average days receivables. This suggests GI may be having problems with excess plant capacity along with poor inventory and receivables management practices.

Liquidity Ratios

liquidity

The ability to convert assets into cash at short notice.

Leverage is one measure of the safety of a firm's debt. Debt ratios compare the firm's indebtedness to broad measures of its assets, and coverage ratios compare various measures of earning power against the cash flow needed to satisfy debt obligations. But leverage is not the only determinant of financial prudence. You also want to know that a firm can lay its hands on cash either to pay its scheduled obligations or to meet unforeseen obligations. **Liquidity** is the ability to convert assets into cash at short notice. Liquidity is commonly measured using the current ratio, quick ratio, and cash ratio.

current ratio

Current assets/current liabilities.

1. **Current ratio:** current assets/current liabilities. This ratio measures the ability of the firm to pay off its current liabilities by liquidating its current assets (that is, turning them into cash). It indicates the firm's ability to avoid insolvency in the short run. GI's current ratio in 2012, for example, was (60 + 30 + 90)/(36 + 87.3) = 1.46. In other years, it was:

2012	2013	2014	2014 Industry Average
1.46	1.17	0.97	2.0

This represents an unfavorable time trend and poor standing relative to the industry. This troublesome pattern is not surprising given the working capital burden resulting from GI's subpar performance with respect to receivables and inventory management.

quick ratio or acid test ratio

A measure of liquidity similar to the current ratio except for exclusion of inventories.

2. **Quick ratio:** (cash + marketable securities + receivables)/current liabilities. This ratio is also called the **acid test ratio.** It has the same denominator as the current ratio, but its numerator includes only cash, cash equivalents such as marketable securities, and receivables. The quick ratio is a better measure of liquidity than the current ratio for

firms whose inventory is not readily convertible into cash. GI's quick ratio shows the same disturbing trends as its current ratio:

2012	2013	2014	2014 Industry Average
0.73	0.58	0.49	1.0

3. **Cash ratio.** A company's receivables are less liquid than its holdings of cash and marketable securities. Therefore, in addition to the quick ratio, analysts also compute a firm's cash ratio, defined as

cash ratio

Another liquidity measure. Ratio of cash and marketable securities to current liabilities.

$$\text{Cash ratio} = \frac{\text{Cash} + \text{Marketable securities}}{\text{Current liabilities}}$$

GI's cash ratios are:

2012	2013	2014	2014 Industry Average
.487	.389	.324	.70

GI's liquidity ratios have fallen dramatically over this three-year period, and by 2014, they are far below the industry average. The decline in the liquidity ratios combined with the decline in coverage ratio (you can confirm that times interest earned also has fallen over this period) suggest that its credit rating has been declining as well and, no doubt, GI is considered a relatively poor credit risk in 2014.

Market Price Ratios

The **market-to-book-value ratio** (P/B) equals the market price of a share of the firm's common stock divided by its *book value,* that is, shareholders' equity per share. Some analysts consider the stock of a firm with a low market-to-book value to be a "safer" investment, seeing the book value as a "floor" supporting the market price. These analysts presumably view book value as the level below which market price will not fall because the firm always has the option to liquidate, or sell, its assets for their book values. However, this view is questionable. In fact, some firms do sometimes sell for less than book value. For example, in early 2012, shares in both Bank of America and Citigroup sold for less than 50% of book value per share. Nevertheless, a low market-to-book-value ratio is seen by some as providing a "margin of safety," and some analysts will screen out or reject high P/B firms in their stock selection process.

market-to-book-value ratio

Market price of a share divided by book value per share.

In fact, a better interpretation of the price-to-book ratio is as a measure of growth opportunities. Recall from the previous chapter that we may view the two components of firm value as assets in place and growth opportunities. As the next example illustrates, firms with greater growth opportunities will tend to exhibit higher multiples of market price to book value.

EXAMPLE 14.4

Price-to-Book and Growth Options

Consider two firms, both of which have book value per share of \$10, a market capitalization rate of 15%, and a plowback ratio of .60.

Bright Prospects has an ROE of 20%, which is well in excess of the market capitalization rate; this ROE implies that the firm is endowed with ample growth opportunities. With ROE = .20, Bright Prospects will earn $.20 \times 10 = \$2$ per share this year. With its plowback ratio of .60, it pays out a dividend of $D_1 = (1 - .6) \times \$2 = \$.80$, has a growth rate of $g = b \times \text{ROE} = .60 \times .20 = .12$, and a stock price of $D_1/(k - g) = \$.80/(.15 - .12) = \$26.67$. Its P/B ratio is 26.67/10 = 2.667.

In contrast, Past Glory has an ROE of only 15%, just equal to the market capitalization rate. It therefore will earn $.15 \times 10 = \$1.50$ per share this year and will pay a dividend of $D_1 = .4 \times \$1.50 = \$.60$. Its growth rate is $g = b \times \text{ROE} = .60 \times .15 = .09$, and its stock price is $D_1/(k - g) = \$.60/(.15 - .09) = \$10$. Its P/B ratio is \$10/\$10 = 1. Not surprisingly, a firm that earns just the required rate of return on its investments will sell for book value, and no more.

We conclude that the price-to-book-value ratio is determined in large part by growth prospects.

price–earnings ratio (P/E)

The ratio of a stock's price to its earnings per share. Also referred to as the P/E multiple.

Another measure used to place firms along a growth versus value spectrum is the **price–earnings ratio (P/E).** In fact, we saw in the last chapter that the ratio of the present value of growth options to the value of assets in place largely determines the P/E multiple. While low P/E stocks allow you to pay less per dollar of *current* earnings, the high P/E stock may still be a better bargain if its earnings are expected to grow quickly enough.[7]

Many analysts nevertheless believe that low P/E stocks are more attractive than high P/E stocks. And in fact, low P/E stocks have generally been positive-alpha investments using the CAPM as a return benchmark. But an efficient market adherent would discount this track record, arguing that such a simplistic rule could not really generate abnormal returns and that the CAPM may not be a good benchmark for returns in this case.

In any event, the important points to remember are that ownership of the stock conveys the right to future as well as current earnings and, therefore, that a high P/E ratio may best be interpreted as a signal that the market views the firm as enjoying attractive growth opportunities.

Before leaving the P/B and P/E ratios, it is worth pointing out an important relationship between them.

$$\text{ROE} = \frac{\text{Earnings}}{\text{Book value}} = \frac{\text{Market price}}{\text{Book value}} \div \frac{\text{Market price}}{\text{Earnings}} \tag{14.4}$$

$$= \text{P/B ratio} \div \text{P/E ratio}$$

Rearranging terms, we find that a firm's P/E ratio equals its price-to-book ratio divided by ROE:

$$\frac{P}{E} = \frac{\text{P/B}}{\text{ROE}}$$

Thus, a company with a high ROE can have a relatively low earnings yield because its P/B ratio is high.

Wall Street often distinguishes between "good firms" and "good investments." A good firm may be highly profitable, with a correspondingly high ROE. But if its stock price is bid up to a level commensurate with this ROE, its P/B ratio will also be high, and the stock price may be a relatively large multiple of earnings, thus reducing its attractiveness as an investment. The high ROE of the *firm* does not by itself imply that the *stock* is a good investment. Conversely, troubled firms with low ROEs can be good investments if their prices are low enough.

Table 14.10 summarizes the ratios reviewed in this section.

CONCEPT check 14.3

What were GI's ROE, P/E, and P/B ratios in the year 2014? How do they compare to these industry average ratios: ROE = 8.64%, P/E = 8, and P/B = .69? How does GI's earnings yield in 2014 compare to the industry average?

Choosing a Benchmark

We have discussed how to calculate the principal financial ratios. To evaluate the performance of a given firm, however, you need a benchmark to which you can compare its ratios. One obvious benchmark is the ratio for the same company in earlier years. For example, Figure 14.3 shows Home Depot's return on assets, profit margin, and asset turnover ratio for the last few years. You can see there that most of the variation in HD's return on assets has been driven by the variation in its profit margin. In contrast, its turnover ratio was almost constant between 2001 and 2005.

[7]Remember, though, P/E ratios reported in the financial pages are based on *past* earnings, while price is determined by the firm's prospects of *future* earnings. Therefore, reported P/E ratios may reflect variation in current earnings around a trend line.

TABLE 14.10 Summary of key financial ratios

Ratio	Formula
Leverage ratios:	
Interest burden	$\dfrac{\text{EBIT} - \text{Interest expense}}{\text{EBIT}}$
Interest coverage (Times interest earned)	$\dfrac{\text{EBIT}}{\text{Interest expense}}$
Leverage	$\dfrac{\text{Assets}}{\text{Equity}} = 1 + \dfrac{\text{Debt}}{\text{Equity}}$
Compound leverage factor	Interest burden × Leverage
Asset utilization:	
Total asset turnover	$\dfrac{\text{Sales}}{\text{Average total assets}}$
Fixed-asset turnover	$\dfrac{\text{Sales}}{\text{Average fixed assets}}$
Inventory turnover	$\dfrac{\text{Cost of goods sold}}{\text{Average inventories}}$
Days sales in receivables	$\dfrac{\text{Average accounts receivables}}{\text{Annual sales}} \times 365$
Liquidity:	
Current ratio	$\dfrac{\text{Current assets}}{\text{Current liabilities}}$
Quick ratio	$\dfrac{\text{Cash} + \text{Marketable securities} + \text{Receivables}}{\text{Current liabilities}}$
Cash ratio	$\dfrac{\text{Cash} + \text{Marketable securities}}{\text{Current liabilities}}$
Profitability ratios:	
Return on assets	$\dfrac{\text{EBIT}}{\text{Average total assets}}$
Return on equity	$\dfrac{\text{Net income}}{\text{Average stockholders' equity}}$
Return on sales (Profit margin)	$\dfrac{\text{EBIT}}{\text{Sales}}$
Market price ratios:	
Market-to-book	$\dfrac{\text{Price per share}}{\text{Book value per share}}$
Price–earnings ratio	$\dfrac{\text{Price per share}}{\text{Earnings per share}}$
Earnings yield	$\dfrac{\text{Earnings per share}}{\text{Price per share}}$

It is also helpful to compare financial ratios to those of other firms in the same industry. Financial ratios for industries are published by the U.S. Department of Commerce, Dun & Bradstreet, the Risk Management Association, and others, and many ratios are available on the web, for example, on the Yahoo! Finance site.

Table 14.11 presents ratios for a sample of major industry groups to give you a feel for some of the differences across industries. Some ratios such as asset turnover or total debt ratio tend to be relatively stable. For example, asset turnover in drug development and production companies will be consistently lower than in the motor vehicle or clothing industries.

FIGURE 14.3

DuPont decomposition for Home Depot

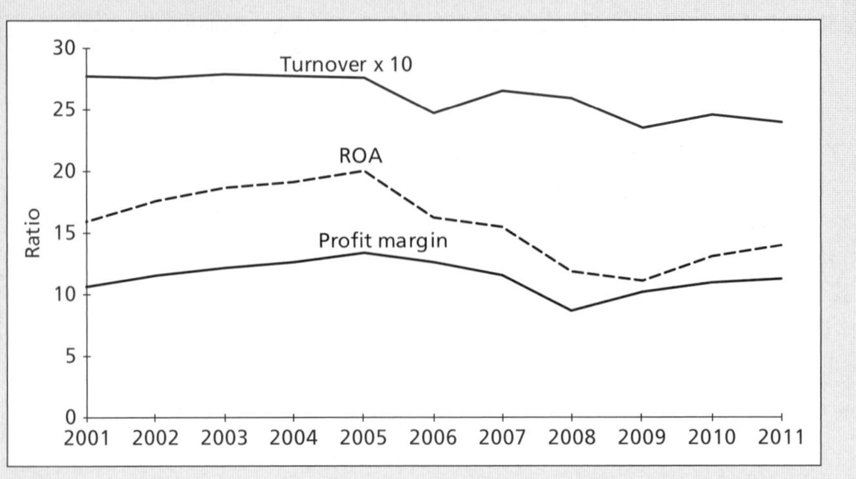

TABLE 14.11 Financial ratios for major industry groups

	LT Debt / Assets	Interest Coverage	Current Ratio	Quick Ratio	Asset Turnover	Profit Margin (%)	Return on Assets (%)	Return on Equity (%)	Payout Ratio
All manufacturing	0.21	5.01	1.42	0.98	0.84	8.03	6.78	17.12	0.27
Food products	0.29	3.83	1.28	0.76	1.15	5.95	6.87	5.59	0.87
Clothing	0.19	7.02	2.32	1.31	1.28	9.29	11.91	22.03	0.21
Printing/publishing	0.40	3.04	1.52	1.19	1.32	7.40	9.75	25.69	0.23
Chemicals	0.26	4.41	1.28	0.94	0.51	14.08	7.14	17.38	0.30
Drugs	0.25	4.47	1.28	1.00	0.35	20.44	7.08	16.26	0.28
Machinery	0.17	5.18	1.39	0.92	0.83	8.78	7.25	16.27	0.19
Electrical	0.12	4.37	1.17	0.75	0.51	7.06	3.63	11.47	0.59
Motor vehicles	0.14	4.28	1.29	0.99	1.17	4.15	4.86	22.58	0.19
Computer and electronic	0.15	5.12	1.62	1.33	0.55	7.42	4.11	15.23	0.18

Source: U.S. Department of Commerce, *Quarterly Financial Report for Manufacturing, Mining and Trade Corporations,* third quarter 2011. Available at **www2.census.gov/econ/qfr/current/qfr_pub.pdf.**

However, other ratios, for example, return on assets or equity, are more sensitive to current business conditions. A value in one year cannot be assumed to reflect fundamental differences.

14.5 AN ILLUSTRATION OF FINANCIAL STATEMENT ANALYSIS

In her 2014 annual report to the shareholders of Growth Industries, Inc., the president wrote: "2014 was another successful year for Growth Industries. As in 2013, sales, assets, and operating income all continued to grow at a rate of 20%."

Is she right?

We can evaluate her statement by conducting a full-scale ratio analysis of Growth Industries. Our purpose is to assess GI's performance in the recent past, to evaluate its future prospects, and to determine whether its market price reflects its intrinsic value.

Table 14.12 shows some key financial ratios we can compute from GI's financial statements. The president is certainly right about the growth in sales, assets, and operating income. Inspection of GI's key financial ratios, however, contradicts her first sentence: 2014 was not another successful year for GI—it appears to have been another miserable one.

TABLE 14.12 Key financial ratios of Growth Industries, Inc.

Year	ROE	(1) Net Profit / Pretax Profit	(2) Pretax Profit / EBIT	(3) EBIT / Sales (Margin)	(4) Sales / Assets (Turnover)	(5) Assets / Equity	(6) Compound Leverage Factor (2) × (5)	(7) ROA (3) × (4)	P/E	P/B
2012	7.51%	.6	.650	30%	.303	2.117	1.376	9.09%	8	.58
2013	6.08	.6	.470	30	.303	2.375	1.116	9.09	6	.35
2014	3.03	.6	.204	30	.303	2.723	0.556	9.09	4	.12
Industry average	8.64	.6	.800	30	.400	1.500	1.200	12.00	8	.69

ROE has been declining steadily from 7.51% in 2012 to 3.03% in 2014. A comparison of GI's 2014 ROE to the 2014 industry average of 8.64% makes the deteriorating time trend especially alarming. The low and falling market-to-book-value ratio and the falling price–earnings ratio indicate that investors are less and less optimistic about the firm's future profitability.

The fact that ROA has not been declining, however, tells us that the source of the declining time trend in GI's ROE must be due to financial leverage. And, in fact, as GI's leverage ratio climbed from 2.117 in 2012 to 2.723 in 2014, its interest-burden ratio worsened from .650 to .204—with the net result that the compound leverage factor fell from 1.376 to .556.

The rapid increase in short-term debt from year to year and the concurrent increase in interest expense make it clear that, to finance its 20% growth rate in sales, GI has incurred sizable amounts of short-term debt at high interest rates. The firm is paying rates of interest greater than the ROA it is earning on the investment financed with the new borrowing. As the firm has expanded, its situation has become ever more precarious.

In 2014, for example, the average interest rate on short-term debt was 20% versus an ROA of 9.09%. (You can calculate the interest rate on GI's short-term debt using the data in Table 14.9 as follows: The balance sheet shows us that the coupon rate on its long-term debt was 8% and its par value was $75 million. Therefore the interest paid on the long-term debt was .08 × $75 million = $6 million. Total interest paid in 2013 was $34,391,000, so the interest paid on the short-term debt must have been $34,391,000 − $6,000,000 = $28,391,000. This is 20% of GI's short-term debt at the start of the year.)

GI's problems become clear when we examine its statement of cash flows in Table 14.13. The statement is derived from the income statement and balance sheet data in Table 14.9. GI's cash flow from operations is falling steadily, from $12,700,000 in 2012 to $6,725,000 in 2014. The firm's investment in plant and equipment, by contrast, has increased greatly. Net plant and equipment (i.e., net of depreciation) rose from $150,000,000 in 2011 to $259,200,000 in 2014. This near doubling of capital assets makes the decrease in cash flow from operations all the more troubling.

The source of the difficulty is GI's enormous amount of short-term borrowing. In a sense, the company is being run as a pyramid scheme. It borrows more and more each year to maintain its 20% growth rate in assets and income. However, the new assets are not generating enough cash flow to support the extra interest burden of the debt, as the falling cash flow from operations indicates. Eventually, when the firm loses its ability to borrow further, its growth will be at an end.

At this point, GI stock might be an attractive investment. Its market price is only 12% of its book value, and with a P/E ratio of 4, its earnings yield is 25% per year. GI is a likely candidate for a takeover by another firm that might replace GI's management and build shareholder value through a radical change in policy.

TABLE 14.13 Growth Industries statement of cash flows ($ thousand)

	2012	2013	2014
Cash flow from operating activities			
Net income	$ 11,700	$ 10,143	$ 5,285
+ Depreciation	15,000	18,000	21,600
+ Decrease (increase) in accounts receivable	(5,000)	(6,000)	(7,200)
+ Decrease (increase) in inventories	(15,000)	(18,000)	(21,600)
+ Increase in accounts payable	6,000	7,200	8,640
Cash provided by operations	$ 12,700	$ 11,343	$ 6,725
Cash flow from investing activities			
Investment in plant and equipment*	$(45,000)	$(54,000)	$(64,800)
Cash flow from financing activities			
Dividends paid†	$ 0	$ 0	$ 0
Short-term debt issued	42,300	54,657	72,475
Change in cash and marketable securities‡	$ 10,000	$ 12,000	$ 14,400

*Gross investment equals increase in net plant and equipment plus depreciation.

†We can conclude that no dividends are paid because stockholders' equity increases each year by the full amount of net income, implying a plowback ratio of 1.

‡Equals cash flow from operations plus cash flow from investment activities plus cash flow from financing activities. Note that this equals the yearly change in cash and marketable securities on the balance sheet.

CONCEPT check 14.4

You have the following information for IBX Corporation for the years 2012 and 2015 (all figures are in $ millions):

	2015	2012
Net income	$ 253.7	$ 239.0
Pretax income	411.9	375.6
EBIT	517.6	403.1
Average assets	4,857.9	3,459.7
Sales	6,679.3	4,537.0
Shareholders' equity	2,233.3	2,347.3

What is the trend in IBX's ROE, and how can you account for it in terms of tax burden, margin, turnover, and financial leverage?

14.6 COMPARABILITY PROBLEMS

Financial statement analysis gives us a good amount of ammunition for evaluating a company's performance and future prospects. But comparing financial results of different companies is not so simple. There is more than one acceptable way to represent various items of revenue and expense according to generally accepted accounting principles (GAAP). This means two firms may have exactly the same economic income yet very different accounting incomes.

Furthermore, interpreting a single firm's performance over time is complicated when inflation distorts the dollar measuring rod. Comparability problems are especially acute in this case because the impact of inflation on reported results often depends on the particular method the firm adopts to account for inventories and depreciation. The security analyst must adjust the earnings and the financial ratio figures to a uniform standard before attempting to compare financial results across firms and over time.

Comparability problems can arise out of the flexibility of GAAP guidelines in accounting for inventories and depreciation and in adjusting for the effects of inflation. Other important potential sources of noncomparability include the capitalization of leases and other expenses, the treatment of pension costs, and allowances for reserves.

Inventory Valuation

There are two commonly used ways to value inventories: **LIFO** (last-in, first-out) and **FIFO** (first-in, first-out). We can explain the difference using a numerical example.

LIFO

The last-in first-out accounting method of valuing inventories.

FIFO

The first-in first-out accounting method of valuing inventories.

Suppose Generic Products, Inc. (GPI), has a constant inventory of 1 million units of generic goods. The inventory turns over once per year, meaning the ratio of cost of goods sold to inventory is 1.

The LIFO system calls for valuing the million units used up during the year at the current cost of production, so that the last goods produced are considered the first ones to be sold. They are valued at today's cost. The FIFO system assumes that the units used up or sold are the ones that were added to inventory first, and goods sold should be valued at original cost.

If the price of generic goods were constant, at the level of $1, say, the book value of inventory and the cost of goods sold would be the same, $1 million under both systems. But suppose the price of generic goods rises by 10 cents per unit during the year as a result of inflation.

LIFO accounting would result in a cost of goods sold of $1.1 million, while the end-of-year balance sheet value of the 1 million units in inventory remains $1 million. The balance sheet value of inventories is given as the cost of the goods still in inventory. Under LIFO, the last goods produced are assumed to be sold at the current cost of $1.10; the goods remaining are the previously produced goods, at a cost of only $1. You can see that, although LIFO accounting accurately measures the cost of goods sold today, it understates the current value of the remaining inventory in an inflationary environment.

In contrast, under FIFO accounting, the cost of goods sold would be $1 million, and the end-of-year balance sheet value of the inventory is $1.1 million. The result is that the LIFO firm has both a lower reported profit and a lower balance sheet value of inventories than the FIFO firm.

LIFO is preferred over FIFO in computing economics earnings (that is, real sustainable cash flow), because it uses up-to-date prices to evaluate the cost of goods sold. However, LIFO accounting induces balance sheet distortions when it values investment in inventories at original cost. This practice results in an upward bias in ROE because the investment base on which return is earned is undervalued.

Depreciation

Another source of problems is the measurement of depreciation, which is a key factor in computing true earnings. The accounting and economic measures of depreciation can differ markedly. According to the *economic* definition, depreciation is the amount of a firm's operating cash flow that must be reinvested in the firm to sustain its real cash flow at the current level.

The *accounting* measurement is quite different. Accounting depreciation is the amount of the original acquisition cost of an asset that is allocated to each accounting period over an arbitrarily specified life of the asset. This is the figure reported in financial statements.

Assume, for example, that a firm buys machines with a useful economic life of 20 years at $100,000 apiece. In its financial statements, however, the firm can depreciate the machines over 10 years using the straight-line method, for $10,000 per year in depreciation. Thus, after

10 years, a machine will be fully depreciated on the books, even though it remains a productive asset that will not need replacement for another 10 years.

In computing accounting earnings, this firm will overestimate depreciation in the first 10 years of the machine's economic life and underestimate it in the last 10 years. This will cause reported earnings to be understated compared with economic earnings in the first 10 years and overstated in the last 10 years.

Depreciation comparability problems add one more wrinkle. A firm can use different depreciation methods for tax purposes than for other reporting purposes. Most firms use accelerated depreciation methods for tax purposes and straight-line depreciation in published financial statements. There also are differences across firms in their estimates of the depreciable life of plant, equipment, and other depreciable assets.

Another complication arises from inflation. Because conventional depreciation is based on historical costs rather than on the current replacement cost of assets, measured depreciation in periods of inflation is understated relative to replacement cost, and *real* economic income (sustainable cash flow) is correspondingly overstated.

For example, suppose Generic Products, Inc., has a machine with a three-year useful life that originally cost \$3 million. Annual straight-line depreciation is \$1 million, regardless of what happens to the replacement cost of the machine. Suppose inflation in the first year turns out to be 10%. Then the true annual depreciation expense is \$1.1 million in current terms, while conventionally measured depreciation remains fixed at \$1 million per year. Accounting income therefore overstates *real* economic income.

Inflation and Interest Expense

While inflation can cause distortions in the measurement of a firm's inventory and depreciation costs, it has perhaps an even greater effect on the calculation of *real* interest expense. Nominal interest rates include an inflation premium that compensates the lender for inflation-induced erosion in the real value of principal. From the perspective of both lender and borrower, therefore, part of what is conventionally measured as interest expense should be treated more properly as repayment of principal.

EXAMPLE 14.5

Inflation and Real Income

Suppose Generic Products has debt outstanding with a face value of \$10 million at an interest rate of 10% per year. Interest expense as conventionally measured is \$1 million per year. However, suppose inflation during the year is 6%, so that the real interest rate is approximately 4%. Then \$.6 million of what appears as interest expense on the income statement is really an inflation premium, or compensation for the anticipated reduction in the real value of the \$10 million principal; only \$.4 million is *real* interest expense. The \$.6 million reduction in the purchasing power of the outstanding principal may be thought of as repayment of principal, rather than as an interest expense. Real income of the firm is, therefore, understated by \$.6 million.

Mismeasurement of real interest means that inflation results in an underestimate of real income. The effects of inflation on the reported values of inventories and depreciation that we have discussed work in the opposite direction.

CONCEPT check 14.5

In a period of rapid inflation, companies ABC and XYZ have the same *reported* earnings. ABC uses LIFO inventory accounting, has relatively fewer depreciable assets, and has more debt than XYZ. XYZ uses FIFO inventory accounting. Which company has the higher *real* income and why?

Fair Value Accounting

Many major assets and liabilities are not traded in financial markets and do not have easily observable values. For example, we cannot simply look up the values of employee stock options, health care benefits for retired employees, or buildings and other real estate. While the true financial status of a firm may depend critically on these values, which can swing widely over time, common practice has been to simply value them at historic cost. Proponents of **fair value accounting,** also known as **mark-to-market accounting,** argue that financial statements would give a truer picture of the firm if they better reflected the current market values of all assets and liabilities.

fair value or mark-to-market accounting

Use of current market values rather than historic cost in the firm's financial statements.

The Financial Accounting Standards Board's Statement No. 157 on fair value accounting places assets in one of three "buckets." Level 1 assets are traded in active markets and therefore should be valued at their market price. Level 2 assets are not actively traded, but their values still may be estimated using observable market data on similar assets. These assets can be "marked to a matrix" of comparable securities. Level 3 assets are hardest to value. Here, it is difficult even to identify other assets that are similar enough to serve as benchmarks for their market values; one has to resort to pricing models to estimate their intrinsic values. Rather than mark to market, these values are often called "mark to model," although they are also disparagingly known as mark-to-make-believe, as the estimates are so prone to manipulation by creative use of model inputs.

Critics of fair value accounting argue that it relies too heavily on estimates. Such estimates potentially introduce considerable noise in firms' accounts and can induce great profit volatility as fluctuations in asset valuations are recognized. Even worse, subjective valuations may offer management a tempting tool to manipulate earnings or the apparent financial condition of the firm at opportune times. As just one example, Bergstresser, Desai, and Rauh (2006) find that firms make more aggressive assumptions about returns on defined benefit pension plans (which lowers the computed present value of pension obligations) during periods in which executives are actively exercising their stock options.

A contentious debate over the application of fair value accounting to troubled financial institutions erupted in 2008 when even values of financial securities such as subprime mortgage pools and derivative contracts backed by these pools came into question as trading in these instruments dried up. Without well-functioning markets, estimating (much less observing) market values was, at best, a precarious exercise.

Some felt that mark-to-market accounting exacerbated the financial meltdown by forcing banks to excessively write down asset values; others, that a failure to mark would have been tantamount to willfully ignoring reality and abdicating the responsibility to redress problems at nearly or already insolvent banks. The nearby box discusses the debate.

Quality of Earnings and Accounting Practices

Many firms make accounting choices that present their financial statements in the best possible light. The different choices that firms can make give rise to the comparability problems we have discussed. As a result, earnings statements for different companies may be more or less rosy presentations of true "economic earnings"—sustainable cash flow that can be paid to shareholders without impairing the firm's productive capacity. Analysts commonly evaluate the **quality of earnings** reported by a firm. This concept refers to the realism and conservatism of the earnings number, in other words, the extent to which we might expect the reported level of earnings to be sustained.

quality of earnings

The realism and sustainability of reported earnings.

Examples of the accounting choices that influence quality of earnings are:

- *Allowance for bad debt.* Most firms sell goods using trade credit and must make an allowance for bad debt. An unrealistically low allowance reduces the quality of reported earnings. Look for a rising average collection period on accounts receivable as evidence of potential problems with future collections.
- *Nonrecurring items.* Some items that affect earnings should not be expected to recur regularly. These include asset sales, effects of accounting changes, effects of exchange rate movements, or unusual investment income. For example, in years with large equity returns, some firms enjoy large capital gains on securities held. These contribute to that year's earnings but should not be expected to repeat regularly. They would be considered a "low-quality" component of earnings. Similarly gains in corporate pension plans can generate large, but one-time, contributions to reported earnings.

On the **MARKET FRONT**

MARK-TO-MARKET ACCOUNTING: CURE OR DISEASE?

As banks and other institutions holding mortgage-backed securities revalued their portfolios throughout 2008, their net worth fell along with the value of those securities. The losses on these securities were painful enough but, in addition, they led to knock-on effects that only increased the banks' woes. For example, banks are required to maintain adequate levels of capital relative to assets. If capital reserves decline, a bank may be forced to shrink until its remaining capital is once again adequate compared to its asset base. But such shrinkage may require the bank to cut back on its lending, which restricts its customers' access to credit. It may also have to sell some of its assets; and if many banks attempt to shrink their portfolios at once, waves of forced sales may put further pressure on prices, resulting in additional write-downs and reductions to capital in a self-feeding cycle. Critics of mark-to-market accounting therefore conclude that it acted to exacerbate the problems of an already reeling economy.

Advocates, however, contend that the critics confuse the message with the messenger. Mark-to-market accounting makes transparent losses that have already been incurred, but it does not cause those losses. But the critics retort that when markets are faltering, market prices may be unreliable. If trading activity has largely broken down, and assets can be sold only at fire-sale prices, then those prices may no longer be indicative of fundamental value. Markets cannot be efficient if they are not even functioning. In the turmoil surrounding the defaulted mortgages weighing down bank portfolios, one of the early proposals of then–Treasury Secretary Henry Paulson was for the government to buy bad assets at "hold to maturity" prices based on estimates of intrinsic value in a normally functioning market. In the same spirit, in April 2009, FASB granted financial firms more leeway to put off write-downs on assets deemed to be only "temporarily impaired."

Waiving write-down requirements may best be viewed as thinly veiled regulatory forbearance. Regulators know that losses have been incurred and that capital has been impaired. But by allowing firms to carry assets on their books at model rather than market prices, the unpleasant implications of that fact for capital adequacy may be politely ignored for a time. Even so, if the goal is to avoid forced sales in a distressed market, transparency may nevertheless be the best policy. Better to acknowledge losses and explicitly modify capital regulations to help institutions recover their footing in a difficult economy than to deal with losses by ignoring them. After all, why bother preparing financial statements if they are allowed to obscure the true condition of the firm?

Before abandoning fair value accounting, it would be prudent to consider the alternative. Traditional historic-cost accounting, which would allow firms to carry assets on the books at their original purchase price, has even less to recommend it. It would leave investors without an accurate sense of the condition of shaky institutions and, by the same token, lessen the pressure on those firms to get their houses in order. Dealing with losses must surely first require acknowledging them.

- *Earnings smoothing.* In 2003, Freddie Mac was the subject of a major accounting scandal, with the disclosure that it had improperly reclassified mortgages held in its portfolio in an attempt to *reduce* its current earnings. Why would it take such actions? Because later, if earnings turned down, Freddie could "release" earnings by reversing these transactions and thereby create the appearance of steady earnings growth. Similarly, in 2011, 10 of the largest U.S. banks "released" $26.7 billion in reserves, which bolstered reported profits in a year when operating performance was disappointing. More than half of Citigroup's earnings in that year were due to reserve releases.[8] Such "earnings" also must be considered low quality.
- *Revenue recognition.* Under GAAP accounting, a firm is allowed to recognize a sale before it is paid. This is why firms have accounts receivable. But sometimes it can be hard to know when to recognize sales. For example, suppose a computer firm signs a contract to provide products and services over a five-year period. Should the revenue be booked immediately or spread out over five years? A more extreme version of this problem is called "channel stuffing," in which firms "sell" large quantities of goods to customers but give them the right to later either refuse delivery or return the product. The revenue from the "sale" is booked now, but the likely returns are not recognized until they occur (in a future accounting period). If you see accounts receivable increasing far faster than sales, or becoming a larger percentage of total assets, beware of these practices. Given the wide latitude firms have in how they recognize revenue, many analysts choose instead to concentrate on cash flow, which is far harder for a company to manipulate.
- *Off-balance-sheet assets and liabilities.* Suppose that one firm guarantees the outstanding debt of another firm, perhaps a firm in which it has an ownership stake. That obligation ought to be disclosed as a *contingent liability,* since it may require payments down the road. But these obligations may not be reported as part of the firm's outstanding debt. Similarly, leasing may be used to manage off-balance-sheet assets and liabilities. Airlines, for example, may show no aircraft on their balance sheets but have long-term leases that are virtually

[8]Michael Rapoport, "Banks Depleting Earnings Backstop," *The Wall Street Journal,* February 3, 2012.

equivalent to debt-financed ownership. However, if the leases are treated as operating rather than capital leases, they may appear only as footnotes to the financial statements.

International Accounting Conventions

The examples cited above illustrate some of the problems that analysts can encounter when attempting to interpret financial data. Even greater problems arise in the interpretation of the financial statements of foreign firms. This is because these firms do not follow GAAP guidelines. Accounting practices in various countries differ to greater or lesser extents from U.S. standards. Here are some of the major issues that you should be aware of when using the financial statements of foreign firms.

Reserving practices Many countries allow firms considerably more discretion in setting aside reserves for future contingencies than is typical in the United States. Because additions to reserves result in a charge against income, reported earnings are far more subject to managerial discretion than in the United States.

Depreciation In the United States, firms typically maintain separate sets of accounts for tax and reporting purposes. For example, accelerated depreciation is used for tax purposes, while straight-line depreciation is used for reporting purposes. In contrast, most other countries do not allow dual sets of accounts, and most firms in foreign countries use accelerated depreciation to minimize taxes despite the fact that it results in lower reported earnings. This makes reported earnings of foreign firms lower than they would be if the firms were allowed to follow the U.S. practice.

Intangibles Treatment of intangibles can vary widely. Are they amortized or expensed? If amortized, over what period? Such issues can have a large impact on reported profits.

The effect of different country practices can be substantial. Figure 14.4, compares average P/E ratios for several countries as reported and restated on a common basis. While P/E multiples have changed considerably since this study was published, these results illustrate how different accounting rules can have a big impact on these ratios.

Adjusted versus reported price–earnings ratios

Source: Figure J: Adjusted versus Reported Price/Earnings Ration: from Lawrence S. Speidell and Vinod Bavishi, "GAAP Arbitrage: Valuation Opportunities in International Accounting Standards," *Financial Analysts Journal,* November–December 1992, pp. 58–66. Copyright 1992, CFA Institute. Reproduced and republished from *Financial Analysts Journal* with permission from the CFA Institute. All Rights Reserved.

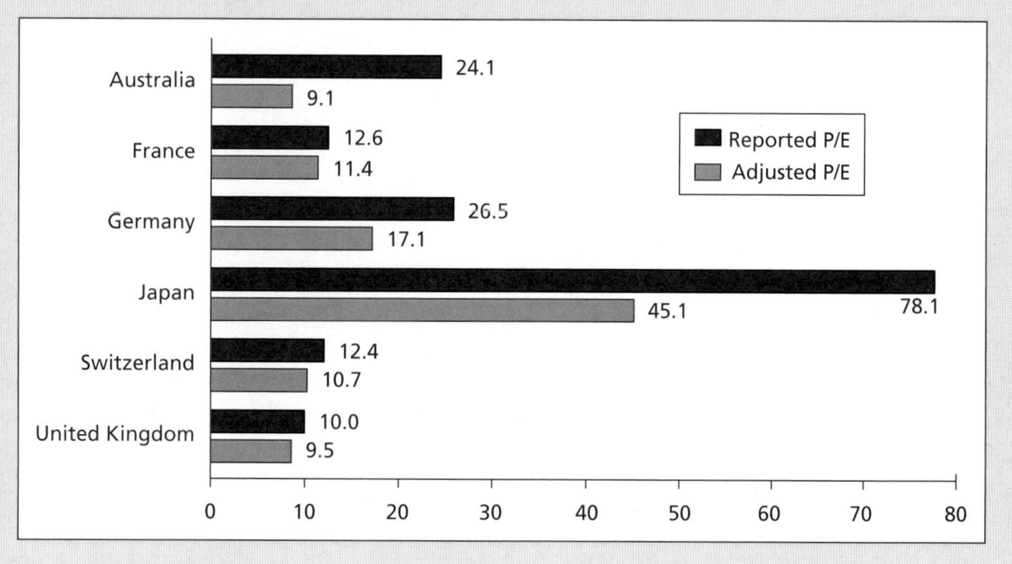

Some of the differences between U.S. and European accounting standards arise from different philosophies regarding regulating accounting practice. GAAP accounting in the U.S. is "rules-based," with detailed, explicit, and lengthy rules governing almost any circumstance that can be anticipated. In contrast, the **international financial reporting standards** (IFRS) used in the European Union are "principles-based," setting out general approaches for the preparation of financial statements. While EU rules are more flexible, firms must be prepared to demonstrate that their accounting choices are consistent with IFRS principles.

international financial reporting standards

A principles-based set of accounting rules adopted by about 100 countries around the world, including the European Union.

IFRS seem on their way to becoming global standards, even outside the European Union. By 2008, over 100 countries had adopted them, and they are making inroads even in the United States. In November 2007, the SEC began allowing foreign firms to issue securities in the U.S. if their financial statements are prepared using IFRS. In 2008, the SEC went even further when it proposed allowing large U.S. multinational firms to report earnings using IFRS rather than GAAP starting in 2010, with all U.S. firms to follow by 2014. The goal of these regulatory innovations is to make cross-border financial statements more consistent and comparable, thereby improving the quality of information available to investors.

14.7 VALUE INVESTING: THE GRAHAM TECHNIQUE

No presentation of fundamental security analysis would be complete without a discussion of the ideas of Benjamin Graham, the greatest of the investment "gurus." Until the evolution of modern portfolio theory in the latter half of the twentieth century, Graham was the single most important thinker, writer, and teacher in the field of investment analysis. His influence on investment professionals remains very strong.

Graham's magnum opus is *Security Analysis,* written with Columbia Professor David Dodd in 1934. Its message is similar to the ideas presented in this chapter. Graham believed careful analysis of a firm's financial statements could turn up bargain stocks. Over the years, he developed many different rules for determining the most important financial ratios and the critical values for judging a stock to be undervalued. Through many editions, his book has had a profound influence on investment professionals. It has been so influential and successful, in fact, that widespread adoption of Graham's techniques has led to elimination of the very bargains they are designed to identify.

In a 1976 seminar Graham said[9]

> I am no longer an advocate of elaborate techniques of security analysis in order to find superior value opportunities. This was a rewarding activity, say, forty years ago, when our textbook "Graham and Dodd" was first published; but the situation has changed a good deal since then. In the old days any well-trained security analyst could do a good professional job of selecting under-valued issues through detailed studies; but in the light of the enormous amount of research now being carried on, I doubt whether in most cases such extensive efforts will generate sufficiently superior selections to justify their cost. To that very limited extent I'm on the side of the "efficient market" school of thought now generally accepted by the professors.

Nonetheless, in that same seminar, Graham suggested a simplified approach to identifying bargain stocks:

> My first, more limited, technique confines itself to the purchase of common stocks at less than their working-capital value, or net current-asset value, giving no weight to the plant and other fixed assets, and deducting all liabilities in full from the current assets. We used this approach extensively in managing investment funds, and over a thirty-odd-year period we must have earned an average of some 20% per year from this source. For awhile, however, after the mid-1950s, this brand of buying opportunity became very scarce because of the pervasive bull market. But it has returned in quantity since the 1973–1974 decline. In January 1976 we counted over 100 such issues in the Standard & Poor's *Stock Guide*—about 10% of the total. I consider it a foolproof method of systematic investment—once again, not on the basis of individual results but in terms of the expectable group outcome.

[9]Graham's full interview is reproduced in *Financial Analysts Journal* Vol. 32, No. 5 (Sep.-Oct., 1976), pp. 20–23.

There are two convenient sources of information for those interested in trying out the Graham technique. Both Standard & Poor's *Outlook* and *The Value Line Investment Survey* carry lists of stocks selling below net working capital value.

SUMMARY

- The primary focus of the security analyst should be the firm's real economic earnings rather than its reported earnings. Accounting earnings as reported in financial statements can be a biased estimate of real economic earnings, although empirical studies confirm that reported earnings convey considerable information concerning a firm's prospects.
- A firm's ROE is a key determinant of the growth rate of its earnings. ROE is affected profoundly by the firm's degree of financial leverage. An increase in a firm's debt/equity ratio will raise its ROE and hence its growth rate only if the interest rate on the debt is less than the firm's return on assets.
- It is often helpful to the analyst to decompose a firm's ROE ratio into the product of several accounting ratios and to analyze their separate behavior over time and across companies within an industry. A useful breakdown is

$$\text{ROE} = \frac{\text{Net profits}}{\text{Pretax profits}} \times \frac{\text{Pretax profits}}{\text{EBIT}} \times \frac{\text{EBIT}}{\text{Sales}} \times \frac{\text{Sales}}{\text{Assets}} \times \frac{\text{Assets}}{\text{Equity}}$$

- Other accounting ratios that have a bearing on a firm's profitability and/or risk are fixed-asset turnover, inventory turnover, days sales in receivables, and the current, quick, and interest coverage ratios.
- Two ratios that make use of the market price of the firm's common stock in addition to its financial statements are the ratios of market-to-book value and price to earnings. Analysts sometimes take low values for these ratios as a margin of safety or a sign that the stock is a bargain.
- A major problem in the use of data obtained from a firm's financial statements is comparability. Firms have a great deal of latitude in how they choose to compute various items of revenue and expense. It is, therefore, necessary for the security analyst to adjust accounting earnings and financial ratios to a uniform standard before attempting to compare financial results across firms.
- Comparability problems can be acute in a period of inflation. Inflation can create distortions in accounting for inventories, depreciation, and interest expense.
- Fair value or mark-to-market accounting requires that most assets be valued at current market value rather than historical cost. This policy has proved to be controversial because in many instances it is difficult to ascertain true market value, and critics contend that it makes financial statements unduly volatile. Advocates argue that financial statements should reflect the best estimate of current asset values.
- International financial reporting standards have become progressively accepted throughout the world, including the United States. They differ from traditional U.S. GAAP procedures in that they are principles-based rather than rules-based.

KEY TERMS

accounting earnings, 448
acid test ratio, 460
average collection period, 460
balance sheet, 448
cash ratio, 461
current ratio, 460
days sales in receivables, 460
DuPont system, 455
economic earnings, 447
economic value added, 454
fair value accounting, 469
FIFO, 467
income statement, 447
interest coverage ratio, 456
international financial reporting standards, 472
inventory turnover ratio, 460
leverage ratio, 457
LIFO, 467
liquidity, 460
mark-to-market accounting, 469
market-to-book-value ratio, 461
price–earnings ratio (P/E), 462
profit margin, 456
quality of earnings, 469
quick ratio, 460

KEY FORMULAS

ROE and leverage: $ROE = (1 - \text{Tax rate})\left(ROA + (ROA - \text{Interest rate})\frac{\text{Debt}}{\text{Equity}}\right)$

DuPont formula: $ROE = \frac{\text{Net profit}}{\text{Pretax profit}} \times \frac{\text{Pretax profit}}{\text{EBIT}} \times \frac{\text{EBIT}}{\text{Sales}} \times \frac{\text{Sales}}{\text{Assets}} \times \frac{\text{Assets}}{\text{Equity}}$

Another DuPont formula: $ROA = \text{Margin} \times \text{Turnover}$

PROBLEM SETS

Select problems are available in McGraw-Hill's *Connect Finance.* Please see the Supplements section of the book's frontmatter for more information.

Basic

1. Use the following financial statements of Heifer Sports Inc. in Table 14.14 to find Heifer's: *(LO 14-1)*
   a. Inventory turnover ratio in 2012.
   b. Debt/equity ratio in 2012.
   c. Cash flow from operating activities in 2012.
   d. Average collection period.
   e. Asset turnover ratio.
   f. Interest coverage ratio.
   g. Operating profit margin.
   h. Return on equity.
   i. P/E ratio.
   j. Compound leverage ratio.
   k. Net cash provided by operating activities.
2. Use the following cash flow data for Rocket Transport to find Rocket's: *(LO 14-1)*
   a. Net cash provided by or used in investing activities.
   b. Net cash provided by or used in financing activities.
   c. Net increase or decrease in cash for the year.

Cash dividend	$ 80,000
Purchase of bus	$ 33,000
Interest paid on debt	$ 25,000
Sales of old equipment	$ 72,000
Repurchase of stock	$ 55,000
Cash payments to suppliers	$ 95,000
Cash collections from customers	$300,000

3. The Crusty Pie Co., which specializes in apple turnovers, has a return on sales higher than the industry average, yet its ROA is the same as the industry average. How can you explain this? *(LO 14-3)*
4. The ABC Corporation has a profit margin on sales below the industry average, yet its ROA is above the industry average. What does this imply about its asset turnover? *(LO 14-3)*
5. A company's current ratio is 2. If the company uses cash to retire notes payable due within one year, would this transaction increase or decrease the current ratio? What about the asset turnover ratio? *(LO 14-1)*

TABLE 14.14 Heifer Sports financial statements

Income Statement	**2012**	
Sales	$5,500,000	
Cost of goods sold	2,850,000	
Depreciation	280,000	
Selling & administrative expenses	1,500,000	
EBIT	870,000	
Interest expense	130,000	
Taxable income	740,000	
Taxes	330,000	
Net income	$ 410,000	
Balance Sheet, year-end	**2012**	**2011**
Assets		
Cash	$ 50,000	$ 40,000
Accounts receivable	660,000	690,000
Inventory	490,000	480,000
Total current assets	$1,200,000	$1,210,000
Fixed assets	3,100,000	2,800,000
Total assets	$4,300,000	$4,010,000
Liabilities and shareholders' equity		
Accounts payable	$ 340,000	$ 450,000
Short-term debt	480,000	550,000
Total current liabilities	$ 820,000	$1,000,000
Long-term bonds	2,520,000	2,200,000
Total liabilities	$3,340,000	$3,200,000
Common stock	$ 310,000	$ 310,000
Retained earnings	650,000	500,000
Total shareholders' equity	$ 960,000	810,000
Total liabilities and shareholders' equity	$4,300,000	$4,010,000

6. Cash flow from investing activities *excludes:* *(LO 14-1)*
   a. Cash paid for acquisitions.
   b. Cash received from the sale of fixed assets.
   c. Inventory increases due to a new (internally developed) product line.
   d. All of the above.
7. Cash flow from operating activities *includes:* *(LO 14-1)*
   a. Inventory increases resulting from acquisitions.
   b. Inventory changes due to changing exchange rates.
   c. Interest paid to bondholders.
   d. Dividends paid to stockholders.

Intermediate

8. Recently, Galaxy Corporation lowered its allowance for doubtful accounts by reducing bad debt expense from 2% of sales to 1% of sales. Ignoring taxes, what are the immediate effects on (*a*), operating income and (*b*) operating cash flow? *(LO 14-1)*

Use the following case in answering Problems 9–11: Hatfield Industries is a large manufacturing conglomerate based in the United States with annual sales in excess of $300 million. Hatfield is currently under investigation by the Securities and Exchange Commission (SEC)

for accounting irregularities and possible legal violations in the presentation of the company's financial statements. A due-diligence team from the SEC has been sent to Hatfield's corporate headquarters in Philadelphia for a complete audit in order to further assess the situation.

Several unique circumstances at Hatfield are discovered by the SEC due-diligence team during the course of the investigation:

- Management has been involved in ongoing negotiations with the local labor union, of which approximately 40% of its full-time labor force are members. Labor officials are seeking increased wages and pension benefits, which Hatfield's management states is not possible at this time due to decreased profitability and a tight cash flow situation. Labor officials have accused Hatfield's management of manipulating the company's financial statements to justify not granting any concessions during the course of negotiations.
- All new equipment obtained over the past several years has been established on Hatfield's books as operating leases, although past acquisitions of similar equipment were nearly always classified as capital leases. Financial statements of industry peers indicate that capital leases for this type of equipment are the norm. The SEC wants Hatfield's management to provide justification for this apparent deviation from "normal" accounting practices.
- Inventory on Hatfield's books has been steadily increasing for the past few years in comparison to sales growth. Management credits improved operating efficiencies in its production methods that have contributed to boosts in overall production. The SEC is seeking evidence that Hatfield somehow may have manipulated its inventory accounts.

The SEC due-diligence team is not necessarily searching for evidence of fraud but of possible manipulation of accounting standards for the purpose of misleading shareholders and other interested parties. Initial review of Hatfield's financial statements indicates that, at a minimum, certain practices have resulted in low-quality earnings.

9. Labor officials believe that the management of Hatfield is attempting lo understate its net income to avoid making any concessions in the labor negotiations. Which of the following actions by management will *most likely* result in low-quality earnings? ***(LO 14-4)***
   a. Lengthening the life of a depreciable asset in order to lower the depreciation expense.
   b. Lowering the discount rate used in the valuation of the company's pension obligations.
   c. The recognition of revenue at the time of delivery rather than when payment is received.
10. Hatfield has begun recording all new equipment leases on its books as operating leases, a change from its consistent past use of capital leases, in which the present value of lease payments is classified as a debt obligation. What is the *most likely* motivation behind Hatfield's change in accounting methodology? Hatfield is attempting to: ***(LO 14-4)***
    a. Improve its leverage ratios and reduce its perceived leverage.
    b. Reduce its cost of goods sold and increase it profitability.
    c. Increase its operating margins relative to industry peers.
11. The SEC due-diligence team is searching for the reason behind Hatfield's inventory build-up relative to its sales growth. One way to identify a deliberate manipulation of financial results by Hatfield is to search for: ***(LO 14-4)***
    a. A decline in inventory turnover.
    b. Receivables that are growing faster than sales.
    c. A delay in the recognition of expenses.
12. Use the DuPont system and the following data to find return on equity. ***(LO 14-3)***
    - Leverage ratio 2.2
    - Total asset turnover 2.0
    - Net profit margin 5.5%
    - Dividend payout ratio 31.8%
13. A firm has an ROE of 3%, a debt/equity ratio of .5, a tax rate of 35%, and pays an interest rate of 6% on its debt. What is its operating ROA? ***(LO 14-2)***
14. A firm has a tax burden ratio of .75, a leverage ratio of 1.25, an interest burden of .6, and a return on sales of 10%. The firm generates $2.40 in sales per dollar of assets. What is the firm's ROE? ***(LO 14-3)***

15. An analyst gathers the following information about Meyer, Inc.:
    - Meyer has 1,000 shares of 8% cumulative preferred stock outstanding, with a par value of $100 and liquidation value of $110.
    - Meyer has 20,000 shares of common stock outstanding, with a par value of $20.
    - Meyer had retained earnings at the beginning of the year of $5,000,000.
    - Net income for the year was $70,000.
    - This year, for the first time in its history, Meyer paid no dividends on preferred or common stock.

    What is the book value per share of Meyer's common stock? ***(LO 14-1)***
16. Here are data on two firms: ***(LO 14-2)***

	Equity ($ million)	Debt ($ million)	ROC (%)	Cost of capital (%)
Acme	100	50	17	9
Apex	450	150	15	10

a. Which firm has the higher economic value added?
b. Which has higher economic value added per dollar of invested capital?

CFA Problems

1. Jones Group has been generating stable after-tax return on equity (ROE) despite declining operating income. Explain how it might be able to maintain its stable after-tax ROE. ***(LO 14-3)***
2. Which of the following *best* explains a ratio of "net sales to average net fixed assets" that *exceeds* the industry average? ***(LO 14-3)***
   a. The firm added to its plant and equipment in the past few years.
   b. The firm makes less efficient use of its assets than other firms.
   c. The firm has a lot of old plant and equipment.
   d. The firm uses straight-line depreciation.
3. The information in the following table comes from the 2010 financial statements of QuickBrush Company and SmileWhite Corporation:

Notes to the 2010 Financial Statements		
	QuickBrush	**SmileWhite**
Goodwill	The company amortizes goodwill over 20 years.	The company amortizes goodwill over 5 years.
Property, plant, and equipment	The company uses a straight-line depreciation method over the economic lives of the assets, which range from 5 to 20 years for buildings.	The company uses an accelerated depreciation method over the economic lives of the assets, which range from 5 to 20 years for buildings.
Accounts receivable	The company uses a bad-debt allowance of 2% of accounts receivable.	The company uses a bad-debt allowance of 5% of accounts receivable.

   Determine which company has the higher quality of earnings by discussing *each* of the *three* notes. ***(LO 14-4)***
4. The financial statements for Chicago Refrigerator Inc. (see Tables 14.15 and 14.16) are to be used to compute the ratios *a* through *h* for 2013. ***(LO 14-2)***
   a. Quick ratio.
   b. Return on assets.
   c. Return on common shareholders' equity.
   d. Earnings per share of common stock.

TABLE 14.15 Chicago Refrigerator Inc. balance sheet, as of December 31 ($ thousand)

	2012	2013
Assets		
Current assets		
Cash	$ 683	$ 325
Accounts receivable	1,490	3,599
Inventories	1,415	2,423
Prepaid expenses	15	13
Total current assets	$3,603	$6,360
Property, plant, equipment, net	1,066	1,541
Other	123	157
Total assets	$4,792	$8,058
Liabilities		
Current liabilities		
Notes payable to bank	$ —	$ 875
Current portion of long-term debt	38	115
Accounts payable	485	933
Estimated income tax	588	472
Accrued expenses	576	586
Customer advance payment	34	963
Total current liabilities	$1,721	$3,945
Long-term debt	122	179
Other liabilities	81	131
Total liabilities	$1,924	$4,255
Shareholders' equity		
Common stock, $1 par value 1,000,000 shares authorized; 550,000 and 829,000 outstanding, respectively	$ 550	$ 829
Preferred stock, Series A 10%; $25.00 par value; 25,000 authorized; 20,000 and 18,000 outstanding, respectively	500	450
Additional paid-in capital	450	575
Retained earnings	1,368	1,949
Total shareholders' equity	$2,868	$3,803
Total liabilities and shareholders' equity	$4,792	$8,058

TABLE 14.16 Chicago Refrigerator Inc. income statement, years ending December 31 ($ thousand)

	2012	2013
Net sales	$7,570	$12,065
Other income, net	261	345
Total revenues	$7,831	$12,410
Cost of goods sold	$4,850	$ 8,048
General administrative and marketing expenses	1,531	2,025
Interest expense	22	78
Total costs and expenses	$6,403	$10,151
Net income before tax	$1,428	$ 2,259
Income tax	628	994
Net income	$ 800	$ 1,265

e. Profit margin.
f. Times interest earned.
g. Inventory turnover.
h. Leverage ratio.

5. Janet Ludlow is a recently hired analyst. After describing the electric toothbrush industry, her first report focuses on two companies, QuickBrush Company and SmileWhite Corporation, and concludes:

   QuickBrush is a more profitable company than SmileWhite, as indicated by the 40% sales growth and substantially higher margins it has produced over the last few years. SmileWhite's sales and earnings are growing at a 10% rate and produce much lower margins. We do not think SmileWhite is capable of growing faster than its recent growth rate of 10% whereas QuickBrush can sustain a 30% long-term growth rate. *(LO 14-3)*

   a. Criticize Ludlow's analysis and conclusion that QuickBrush is more profitable, as defined by return on equity (ROE), than SmileWhite and that it has a higher

TABLE 14.17 Quickbrush Company financial statements: Yearly data ($000 except per-share data)

Income Statement	**December 2011**	**December 2012**	**December 2013**	
Revenue	$3,480	$5,400	$7,760	
Cost of goods sold	2,700	4,270	6,050	
Selling, general, and admin. expense	500	690	1,000	
Depreciation and amortization	30	40	50	
Operating income (EBIT)	$ 250	$ 400	$ 660	
Interest expense	0	0	0	
Income before taxes	$ 250	$ 400	$ 660	
Income taxes	60	110	215	
Income after taxes	$ 190	$ 290	$ 445	
Diluted EPS	$ 0.60	$ 0.84	$ 1.18	
Average shares outstanding (000)	317	346	376	
Financial Statistics	**December 2011**	**December 2012**	**December 2013**	**3-Year Average**
COGS as % of sales	77.59%	79.07%	77.96%	78.24%
General & admin. as % of sales	14.37	12.78	12.89	13.16
Operating margin (%)	7.18	7.41	8.51	
Pretax income/EBIT (%)	100.00	100.00	100.00	
Tax rate (%)	24.00	27.50	32.58	
Balance Sheet	**December 2011**	**December 2012**	**December 2013**	
Cash and cash equivalents	$ 460	$ 50	$ 480	
Accounts receivable	540	720	950	
Inventories	300	430	590	
Net property, plant, and equipment	760	1,830	3,450	
Total assets	$2,060	$3,030	$5,470	
Current liabilities	$ 860	$1,110	$1,750	
Total liabilities	$ 860	$1,110	$1,750	
Stockholders' equity	1,200	1,920	3,720	
Total liabilities and equity	$2,060	$3,030	$5,470	
Market price per share	$21.00	$30.00	$45.00	
Book value per share	$ 3.79	$ 5.55	$ 9.89	
Annual dividend per share	$ 0.00	$ 0.00	$ 0.00	

TABLE 14.18 Smilewhite Corporation financial statements: Yearly data ($000 except per share data)

Income Statement	December 2011	December 2012	December 2013	
Revenue	$104,000	$110,400	$119,200	
Cost of goods sold	72,800	75,100	79,300	
Selling, general, and admin. expense	20,300	22,800	23,900	
Depreciation and amortization	4,200	5,600	8,300	
Operating income (EBIT)	$ 6,700	$ 6,900	$ 7,700	
Interest expense	600	350	350	
Income before taxes	$ 6,100	$ 6,550	$ 7,350	
Income taxes	2,100	2,200	2,500	
Income after taxes	$ 4,000	$ 4,350	$ 4,850	
Diluted EPS	$ 2.16	$ 2.35	$ 2.62	
Average shares outstanding (000)	1,850	1,850	1,850	
Financial Statistics	**December 2011**	**December 2012**	**December 2013**	**3-Year Average**
COGS as % of sales	70.00%	68.00%	66.53%	68.10%
General & admin. as % of sales	19.52	20.64	20.05	20.08
Operating margin (%)	6.44	6.25	6.46	
Pretax income/EBIT (%)	91.04	94.93	95.45	
Tax rate (%)	34.43	33.59	34.01	
Balance Sheet	**December 2011**	**December 2012**	**December 2013**	
Cash and cash equivalents	$ 7,900	$ 3,300	$ 1,700	
Accounts receivable	7,500	8,000	9,000	
Inventories	6,300	6,300	5,900	
Net property, plant, and equipment	12,000	14,500	17,000	
Total assets	$ 33,700	$ 32,100	$ 33,600	
Current liabilities	$ 6,200	$ 7,800	$ 6,600	
Long-term debt	9,000	4,300	4,300	
Total liabilities	$ 15,200	$ 12,100	$ 10,900	
Stockholders' equity	18,500	20,000	22,700	
Total liabilities and equity	$ 33,700	$ 32,100	$ 33,600	
Market price per share	$ 23.00	$ 26.00	$ 30.00	
Book value per share	$ 10.00	$ 10.81	$ 12.27	
Annual dividend per share	$ 1.42	$ 1.53	$ 1.72	

sustainable growth rate. Use only the information provided in Tables 14.17 and 14.18. Support your criticism by calculating and analyzing:

- The five components that determine ROE.
- The two ratios that determine sustainable growth: ROE and plowback.

b. Explain how QuickBrush has produced an average annual earnings per share (EPS) growth rate of 40% over the last two years with an ROE that has been declining. Use only the information provided in Table 14.17.

6. Scott Kelly is reviewing MasterToy's financial statements in order to estimate its sustainable growth rate. Using the information presented in Table 14.19: ***(LO 14-3)***
   a. Identify and calculate the components of the DuPont formula.
   b. Calculate the ROE for 2013 using the components of the DuPont formula.
   c. Calculate the sustainable growth rate for 2013 from the firm's ROE and plowback ratios.

TABLE 14.19 Mastertoy, Inc.: Actual 2012 and estimated 2013 financial statements for fiscal year ending December 31 ($ million, except per-share data)

	2012	2013
Income Statement		
Revenue	$4,750	$5,140
Cost of goods sold	2,400	2,540
Selling, general, and administrative	1,400	1,550
Depreciation	180	210
Goodwill amortization	10	10
Operating income	$ 760	$ 830
Interest expense	20	25
Income before taxes	$ 740	$ 805
Income taxes	265	295
Net income	$ 475	$ 510
Earnings per share	$ 1.79	$ 1.96
Average shares outstanding (millions)	265	260
Balance Sheet		
Cash	$ 400	$ 400
Accounts receivable	680	700
Inventories	570	600
Net property, plant, and equipment	800	870
Intangibles	500	530
Total assets	$2,950	$3,100
Current liabilities	$ 550	$ 600
Long-term debt	300	300
Total liabilities	$ 850	$ 900
Stockholders' equity	2,100	2,200
Total liabilities and equity	$2,950	$3,100
Book value per share	$ 7.92	$ 8.46
Annual dividend per share	0.55	0.60

7. The DuPont formula defines the net return on shareholders' equity as a function of the following components: *(LO 14-3)*
   - Operating margin
   - Asset turnover
   - Interest burden
   - Financial leverage
   - Income tax rate

Using *only* the data in Table 14.20:

a. Calculate each of the five components listed above for 2010 and 2013, and calculate the return on equity (ROE) for 2010 and 2013, using all of the five components.

b. Briefly discuss the impact of the changes in asset turnover and financial leverage on the change in ROE from 2010 to 2013.

TABLE 14.20 Income statements and balance sheets

	2010	2013
Income statement data		
Revenues	$542	$979
Operating income	38	76
Depreciation and amortization	3	9
Interest expense	3	0
Pretax income	32	67
Income taxes	13	37
Net income after tax	$ 19	$ 30
Balance sheet data		
Fixed assets	$ 41	$ 70
Total assets	245	291
Working capital	123	157
Total debt	16	0
Total shareholders' equity	$159	$220

WEB *master*

1. Go to **finance.yahoo.com** to find information about Vulcan Materials Company (VMC), Southwest Airlines (LUV), Honda Motor Company (HMC), Nordstrom, Inc. (JWN), and Abbott Laboratories (ABT). Download the most recent income statement and balance sheet for each company.
   a. Calculate the operating profit margin (operating profit/sales) and the asset turnover (sales/assets) for each firm.
   b. Calculate the return on assets directly (ROA = Operating profit/Total assets), and then confirm it by calculating ROA = Operating margin × Asset turnover.
   c. In what industries do these firms operate? Do the ratios make sense when you consider the industry types?
   d. For the firms that have relatively low ROAs, does the source of the problem seem to be the operating profit margin, the asset turnover, or both?
   e. Calculate the return on equity (ROE = Net income/Equity) for each firm. For the two firms with the lowest ROEs, perform a DuPont analysis to isolate the source(s) of the problem.
2. From the *Investing* tab, select *Industries* and then the Toys & Games industry. Pick two companies from the list and do the following for each firm:
   a. Retrieve the latest annual balance sheet for each company. Calculate the common-size percentages for the balance sheet in the new column.
   b. Compare the firms' investments in accounts receivable, inventory, and net plant, property, and equipment. Which firm has more invested in these items on a percentage basis?
   c. Compare the firms' investments in current liabilities and long-term liabilities. Does one firm have a significantly higher burden in either of these areas?
   d. Analyze the firms' capital structures by examining the debt ratios and the percentages of preferred and common equity. How much do the firms' capital structures differ from each other?
3. Select a company of interest to you and link to its annual cash flow statement under the company's *Financial* tab. Answer the following questions about the firm's cash flow activities.
   a. Did the firm have positive or negative cash flow from operations?
   b. Did the firm invest in or sell off long-term investments?
   c. What were the major sources of financing for the firm?
   d. What was the net change in cash?
   e. Did exchange rates have any effect on the firm's cash flows?

Now answer these questions:

f. How liquid is the firm?
g. How well is the firm using its assets?
h. How effectively is the firm using leverage?
i. Is the firm profitable?

14.1 A debt/equity ratio of 1 implies that Mordett will have \$50 million of debt and \$50 million of equity. Interest expense will be .09 × \$50 million, or \$4.5 million per year. Mordett's net profits and ROE over the business cycle will therefore be

		Nodett		Mordett	
Scenario	**EBIT**	**Net Profits**	**ROE**	**Net Profits***	**ROE†**
Bad year	\$ 5M	\$3M	3%	\$0.3M	0.6%
Normal year	10	6	6	3.3	6.6
Good year	15	9	9	6.3	12.6%

*Mordett's after-tax profits are given by: 0.6(EBIT − \$4.5 million).

†Mordett's equity is only \$50 million.

14.2 Ratio decomposition analysis for Mordett Corporation:

		(1)	(2)	(3)	(4)	(5)	(6)
Year	**ROE**	**Net Profit / Pretax Profit**	**Pretax Profit / EBIT**	**EBIT / Sales (Margin)**	**Sales / Assets (Turnover)**	**Assets / Equity**	**Compound Leverage Factor (2) × (5)**
a. Bad year							
Nodett	.030	.6	1.000	.0625	0.800	1.000	1.000
Somdett	.018	.6	0.360	.0625	0.800	1.667	0.600
Mordett	.006	.6	0.100	.0625	0.800	2.000	0.200
b. Normal year							
Nodett	.060	.6	1.000	.100	1.000	1.000	1.000
Somdett	.068	.6	0.680	.100	1.000	1.667	1.134
Mordett	.066	.6	0.550	.100	1.000	2.000	1.100
c. Good year							
Nodett	.090	.6	1.000	.125	1.200	1.000	1.000
Somdett	.118	.6	0.787	.125	1.200	1.667	1.311
Mordett	.126	.6	0.700	.125	1.200	2.000	1.400

14.3 GI's ROE in 2014 was 3.03%, computed as follows:

$$\text{ROE} = \frac{\$5{,}285}{.5(\$171{,}843 + \$177{,}128)} = .0303, \text{ or } 3.03\%$$

Its P/E ratio was \$21/\$5.285 = 4, and its P/B ratio was \$21/\$177 = .12. Its earnings yield was 25% compared with an industry average of 12.5%.

Note that in our calculations the P/E does not equal (P/B)/ROE because (following common practice) we have computed ROE with *average* shareholders' equity in the denominator and P/B with *end*-of-year shareholders' equity in the denominator.

www.mhhe.com/bkm

14.4 IBX ratio analysis:
ROE increased despite a decline in operating margin and a decline in the tax burden ratio because of increased leverage and turnover. Note that ROA declined from 11.65% in 2012 to 10.65% in 2015.

		(1)	(2)	(3)	(4)	(5)	(6)	(7)
Year	ROE	Net Profit / Pretax Profit	Pretax Profit / EBIT	EBIT / Sales (Margin)	Sales / Assets (Turnover)	Assets / Equity	Compound Leverage Factor (2) × (5)	ROA (3) × (4)
2015	11.4%	0.616	0.796	7.75%	1.375	2.175	1.731	10.65%
2012	10.2	0.636	0.932	8.88	1.311	1.474	1.374	11.65

14.5 LIFO accounting results in lower reported earnings than does FIFO. Fewer assets to depreciate result in lower reported earnings because there is less bias associated with the use of historic cost. More debt results in lower reported earnings because the inflation premium in the interest rate is treated as part of interest.

Derivative Markets

PART

5

Horror stories about large losses incurred by high-flying traders in derivatives markets such as those for futures and options periodically become a staple of the evening news. Indeed, there were some amazing losses to report in the last decade: several totaling hundreds of millions of dollars, and a few amounting to more than a billion dollars. Among the most notorious of these were the loss of $7.2 billion in equity futures contracts by Société Générale in January 2008 and the loss of more than $100 billion on positions in credit derivatives by American International Group that resulted in a massive government bailout in September 2008. In the wake of these debacles, some venerable institutions have gone under, notable among them Barings Bank, which once helped the U.S. finance the Louisiana Purchase and the British Empire finance the Napoleonic Wars.

These stories, while important, fascinating, and even occasionally scandalous, often miss the point. Derivatives, when misused, can indeed provide a quick path to insolvency. Used properly, however, they are potent tools for risk management and control. In fact, you will discover in these chapters that one firm was sued for *failing* to use derivatives to hedge price risk. One article in *The Wall Street Journal* on hedging applications using derivatives was entitled "Index Options Touted as Providing Peace of Mind." Hardly material for bankruptcy court or the *National Enquirer.*

Derivatives provide a means to control risk that is qualitatively different from the techniques traditionally considered in portfolio theory. In contrast to the mean-variance analysis we discussed in Parts Two and Three, derivatives allow investors to change the *shape* of the probability distribution of investment returns. An entirely new approach to risk management follows from this insight.

The following chapters will explore how derivatives can be used as parts of a well-designed portfolio strategy. We will examine some popular portfolio strategies utilizing these securities and take a look at how derivatives are valued.

Chapters in This Part:

Chapter 15

Options Markets

Learning Objectives:

LO15-1 Calculate the profit to various option positions as a function of ultimate security prices.

LO15-2 Formulate option strategies to modify portfolio risk-return attributes.

LO15-3 Identify embedded options in various securities and determine how option characteristics affect the prices of those securities.

Derivative securities, or simply *derivatives,* play a large and increasingly important role in financial markets. These are securities whose prices are determined by, or "derive from," the prices of other securities.

Options and futures contracts are both derivative securities. Their payoffs depend on the value of other securities. Swap contracts, which we will discuss in Chapter 17, also are derivatives. Because the value of derivatives depends on the value of other securities, they can be powerful tools for both hedging and speculation. We will investigate these applications in the next three chapters, beginning in this chapter with options.

Trading of standardized options on a national exchange started in 1973 when the Chicago Board Options Exchange (CBOE) began listing call options. These contracts were almost immediately a great success, crowding out the previously existing over-the-counter options market.

Options contracts now are traded on several exchanges. They are written on common stock, stock indexes, foreign exchange, agricultural commodities, precious metals, and interest rates. In addition, the over-the-counter market also has enjoyed a tremendous resurgence in recent years as its trading in custom-tailored options has exploded. Popular and potent for modifying portfolio characteristics, options have become essential tools that every portfolio manager must understand.

This chapter is an introduction to options markets. It explains how puts and calls work and examines their investment characteristics. Popular option strategies are considered next. Finally, we will examine a range of securities with embedded options such as callable or convertible bonds.

Related websites for this chapter are available at www.mhhe.com/bkm.

15.1 THE OPTION CONTRACT

A **call option** gives its holder the right to purchase an asset for a specified price, called the **exercise** or **strike price,** on or before some specified expiration date. For example, a September call option on IBM stock with exercise price $170 entitles its owner to purchase IBM stock for a price of $170 at any time up to and including the expiration date in September. The holder of the call is not required to exercise the option. She will choose to exercise only if the market value of the asset exceeds the exercise price. In this case, the option holder may "call away" the asset for the exercise price. Otherwise, the option may be left unexercised. If it is not exercised before the expiration date of the contract, a call option simply expires and becomes valueless. Therefore, if the stock price is greater than the exercise price on the expiration date, the value of the call option will equal the difference between the stock price and the exercise price; but if the stock price is less than the exercise price at expiration, the call will be worthless. The *net profit* on the call is the value of the option minus the price originally paid to purchase it.

call option

The right to buy an asset at a specified exercise price on or before a specified expiration date.

exercise or strike price

Price set for calling (buying) an asset or putting (selling) an asset.

The purchase price of the option is called the **premium.** It represents the compensation the purchaser of the call must pay for the ability to exercise the option only when exercise is profitable. Sellers of call options, who are said to *write* calls, receive premium income now as payment against the possibility they will be required at some later date to deliver the asset in return for an exercise price less than the market value of the asset. If the option is left to expire worthless, the writer of the call clears a profit equal to the premium income derived from the initial sale of the option. But if the call is exercised, the profit to the option writer is the premium income *minus* the difference between the value of the stock that must be delivered and the exercise price that is paid for those shares. If that difference is larger than the initial premium, the writer will incur a loss.

premium

Purchase price of an option.

EXAMPLE 15.1

Profits and Losses on a Call Option

Consider the September 2011 expiration call option on a share of IBM with an exercise price of $170 selling on August 25, 2011, for $3. Exchange-traded options expire on the third Friday of the expiration month, which for this option was September 16. Until the expiration date, the call holder may buy shares of IBM for $170. On August 25, IBM sells for $166.76. Because the stock price is currently less than $170 a share, it clearly would not make sense at the moment to exercise the option to buy at $170. Indeed, if IBM remains below $170 by the expiration date, the call will be left to expire worthless. On the other hand, if IBM is selling above $170 at expiration, the call holder will find it optimal to exercise. For example, if IBM sells for $172 on September 16, the option will be exercised, as it will give its holder the right to pay $170 for a stock worth $172. The value of each option on the expiration date would then be

$$\text{Value at expiration} = \text{Stock price} - \text{Exercise price} = \$172 - \$170 = \$2$$

Despite the $2 payoff at expiration, the call holder still realizes a loss of $1 on the investment because the initial purchase price was $3:

$$\text{Profit} = \text{Final value} - \text{Original investment} = \$2 - \$3 = -\$1$$

Nevertheless, exercise of the call is optimal at expiration if the stock price exceeds the exercise price because the exercise proceeds will offset at least part of the purchase price. The call buyer will clear a profit if IBM is selling above $173 at the expiration date. At that stock price, the proceeds from exercise will just cover the original cost of the call.

A **put option** gives its holder the right to *sell* an asset for a specified exercise or strike price on or before some expiration date. A September put on IBM with exercise price $170 entitles its owner to sell IBM stock to the put writer at a price of $170 at any time before expiration in September, even if the market price of IBM is less than $170. While profits on call options increase when the asset price rises, profits on put options increase when the asset price falls. A put will be exercised only if the exercise price is greater than the price of the underlying asset, that is, only if its holder can deliver for the exercise price an asset with market value less than that amount. (One doesn't need to own the shares of IBM to exercise the IBM put option.

put option

The right to sell an asset at a specified exercise price on or before a specified expiration date.

Upon exercise, the investor's broker purchases the necessary shares of IBM at the market price and immediately delivers or "puts them" to an option writer for the exercise price. The owner of the put profits by the difference between the exercise price and market price.)

EXAMPLE 15.2

Profits and Losses on a Put Option

Now consider the September 2011 expiration put option on IBM with an exercise price of $170, selling on August 25 for $6.20. It entitled its owner to sell a share of IBM for $170 at any time until September 16. If the holder of the put buys a share of IBM and immediately exercises the right to sell it at $170, net proceeds will be $170 − $166.76 = $3.24. Obviously, an investor who pays $6.20 for the put has no intention of exercising it immediately. If, on the other hand, IBM were selling for $162 at expiration, the put would turn out to be a profitable investment. Its value at expiration would be

$$\text{Value at expiration} = \text{Exercise price} - \text{Stock price} = \$170 - \$162 = \$8$$

and the investor's profit would be $8 − $6.20 = $1.80. This is a holding-period return of $1.80/$6.20 = .29, or 29%—over only 22 days! Obviously, put option sellers on August 25 (who are on the other side of the transaction) did not consider this outcome very likely.

in the money

An option where exercise would generate a positive cash flow.

out of the money

An option which, if exercised, would produce a negative cash flow. Out-of-the-money options are therefore never exercised.

at the money

An option where the exercise price equals the asset price.

An option is described as **in the money** when its exercise would produce a positive cash flow. Therefore, a call option is in the money when the asset price exceeds the exercise price, and a put option is in the money when the asset price is less than the exercise price. Conversely, a call is **out of the money** when the exercise price exceeds the asset value; no one would exercise the right to purchase for the exercise price an asset worth less than that amount. A put option is out of the money when the exercise price is less than the asset price. Options are **at the money** when the exercise price and asset price are equal.

Options Trading

Some options trade on over-the-counter (OTC) markets. The OTC market offers the advantage that the terms of the option contract—the exercise price, expiration date, and number of shares committed—can be tailored to the needs of the traders. The costs of establishing an OTC option contract, however, are relatively high. Today, most option trading occurs on organized exchanges.

Options contracts traded on exchanges are standardized by allowable expiration dates and exercise prices for each listed option. Each stock option contract provides for the right to buy or sell 100 shares of stock (except when stock splits occur after the contract is listed and the contract is adjusted for the terms of the split).

Standardization of the terms of listed option contracts means all market participants trade in a limited and uniform set of securities. This increases the depth of trading in any particular option, which lowers trading costs and results in a more competitive market. Exchanges, therefore, offer two important benefits: ease of trading, which flows from a central marketplace where buyers and sellers or their representatives congregate, and a liquid secondary market where buyers and sellers of options can transact quickly and cheaply.

Until recently, most options trading in the U.S. took place on the Chicago Board Options Exchange. However, by 2003 the International Securities Exchange, an electronic exchange based in New York, had displaced the CBOE as the largest options market. Options trading in Europe is uniformly transacted in electronic exchanges.

Figure 15.1 is a reproduction of listed stock option quotations for IBM from *The Wall Street Journal Online.* The last recorded price on the New York Stock Exchange for IBM stock was $166.76 per share.[1] Figure 15.1 includes options with exercise prices of $160 through $170, in $5 increments. These values also are called the *strike prices.*

The exercise or strike prices bracket the stock price. While exercise prices generally are set at five-point intervals for stocks, larger intervals may be set for stocks selling above $100,

[1]Occasionally, this price may not match the closing price listed for the stock on the stock market page. This is because some NYSE stocks also trade on exchanges that close after the NYSE, and the stock pages may reflect the more recent closing price. The options exchanges, however, close with the NYSE, so the closing NYSE stock price is appropriate for comparison with the closing option price.

IBM (IBM)					Underlying stock price: 166.76		
		Call			Put		
Expiration	Strike	Last	Volume	Open Interest	Last	Volume	Open Interest
Sep 2011	160.00	9.15	796	1835	2.62	1271	4298
Oct 2011	160.00	11.95	301	2369	5.35	296	7443
Jan 2012	160.00	15.00	101	7890	9.40	102	4920
Apr 2012	160.00	17.35	111	122	13.30	4	71
Sep 2011	165.00	5.80	1805	3542	4.10	1711	5085
Oct 2011	165.00	8.70	329	3866	7.00	131	2651
Jan 2012	165.00	11.70	93	4045	10.85	303	4466
Apr 2012	165.00	14.30	58	781	–	–	54
Sep 2011	170.00	3.00	3053	7959	6.20	2744	12436
Oct 2011	170.00	5.86	457	7506	9.25	148	4584
Jan 2012	170.00	8.93	73	6876	13.00	58	2929
Apr 2012	170.00	11.32	36	58	–	–	52

FIGURE 15.1

Options on IBM, August 24, 2011

Source: *The Wall Street Journal Online,* August 25, 2011. Reprinted by permission of *The Wall Street Journal,*

and intervals of $2.50 may be used for stocks selling at low prices.[2] If the stock price moves outside the range of exercise prices of the existing set of options, new options with appropriate exercise prices may be offered. Therefore, at any time, both in-the-money and out-of-the-money options will be listed, as in this example.

Figure 15.1 shows both call and put options listed for each exercise price and expiration date. The three sets of columns for each option report closing price, trading volume in contracts (each contract is for 100 shares of stock), and open interest (number of outstanding contracts).

When we compare the prices of call options with the same expiration date but different exercise prices in Figure 15.1, we see that the value of the call is lower when the exercise price is higher. This makes sense, for the right to purchase a share is not as valuable when the purchase price is higher. Thus, the September expiration IBM call option with strike price $160 sells for $9.15, while the $170 exercise price September call sells for only $3. Conversely, put options are worth *more* when the exercise price is higher: You would rather have the right to sell IBM shares for $170 than for $160, and this is reflected in the prices of the puts. The September expiration put option with strike price $170 sells for $6.20, while the $160 exercise price September put sells for only $2.62.

Not infrequently, you will find some options that go an entire day without trading. A lack of trading is denoted by a dash in the volume and price columns in Figure 15.1. Because trading is infrequent, it is not unusual to find option prices that appear out of line with other prices. You might see, for example, two calls with different exercise prices that seem to sell for the same price. This discrepancy arises because the last trades for these options may have occurred at different times during the day. At any moment, the call with the lower exercise price must be worth more, and the put less, than an otherwise-identical call or put with a higher exercise price.

Expirations of most exchange-traded options tend to be fairly short, ranging up to only several months. For larger firms and several stock indexes, however, longer-term options are traded with expirations ranging up to three years. These options are called LEAPS (for Long-term Equity AnticiPation Securities).

CONCEPT check 15.1

a. What will be the proceeds and net profits to an investor who purchases the October 2011 expiration IBM calls with exercise price $165 if the stock price at option expiration is $155? What if the stock price at expiration is $175?

b. Now answer part (*a*) for an investor who purchases the October expiration IBM put option with exercise price $165.

[2]If a stock splits, the terms of the option—such as the exercise price—are adjusted to offset the impact of the split. Therefore, stock splits will also result in exercise prices that are not multiples of $5.

American and European Options

American option

Can be exercised on or before its expiration.

European option

Can be exercised only at expiration.

An **American option** allows its holder to exercise the right to purchase (if a call) or sell (if a put) the underlying asset on or *before* the expiration date. **European options** allow for exercise of the option only on the expiration date. American-style options, because they allow more leeway than their European-style counterparts, generally will be more valuable. Most traded options in the U.S. are American-style. Foreign currency options and some stock-index options are notable exceptions to this rule, however.

The Option Clearing Corporation

The Option Clearing Corporation (OCC), the clearinghouse for options trading, is jointly owned by the exchanges on which stock options are traded. The OCC places itself between options traders, becoming the effective buyer of the option from the writer and the effective writer of the option to the buyer. All individuals, therefore, deal only with the OCC, which effectively guarantees contract performance.

When an option holder exercises an option, the OCC arranges for a member firm with clients who have written that option to make good on the option obligation. The member firm selects from among its clients who have written that option to fulfill the contract. The selected client must deliver 100 shares of stock at a price equal to the exercise price for each call option contract written or must purchase 100 shares at the exercise price for each put option contract written.

Because the OCC guarantees contract performance, it requires option writers to post margin to guarantee that they can fulfill their contract obligations. The margin required is determined in part by the amount by which the option is in the money, because that value is an indicator of the potential obligation of the option writer upon exercise of the option. When the required margin exceeds the posted margin, the writer will receive a margin call. The *holder* of the option need not post margin because the holder will exercise the option only if it is profitable to do so. After purchasing the option, no further money is at risk.

Margin requirements also depend on whether the underlying asset is held in portfolio. For example, a call option writer owning the stock against which the option is written can satisfy the margin requirement simply by allowing a broker to hold that stock in the brokerage account. The stock is then guaranteed to be available for delivery should the call option be exercised. If the underlying security is not owned, however, the margin requirement is determined by the value of the underlying security as well as by the amount by which the option is in or out of the money. Out-of-the-money options require less margin from the writer, for expected payouts are lower.

Other Listed Options

Options on assets other than stocks also are widely traded. These include options on market indexes and industry indexes, on foreign currency, and even on the futures prices of agricultural products, gold, silver, fixed-income securities, and stock indexes. We will discuss these in turn.

Index options An index option is a call or put based on a stock market index such as the S&P 500. Index options are traded on several broad-based indexes as well as on several industry-specific indexes. We discussed many of these indexes in Chapter 2.

The construction of the indexes can vary across contracts or exchanges. For example, the S&P 100 Index is a value-weighted average of the 100 stocks in the Standard & Poor's 100 stock group. The weights are proportional to the market value of outstanding equity for each stock. The Dow Jones Industrial Average, by contrast, is a price-weighted average of 30 stocks.

Options contracts on many foreign stock indexes also trade. For example, options on the Nikkei Stock Index of Japanese stocks trade on the Singapore as well as the Chicago Mercantile Exchange. Options on European indexes such as the Financial Times Share Exchange (FTSE 100) trade on the NYSE-Euronext exchange. The Chicago Board Options Exchange also lists options on industry indexes such as the oil or high-tech industries.

In contrast to stock options, index options do not require that the call writer actually "deliver the index" upon exercise or that the put writer "purchase the index." Instead, a cash settlement procedure is used. The payoff that would accrue upon exercise of the option is calculated, and the option writer simply pays that amount to the option holder. The payoff is equal to the difference between the exercise price of the option and the value of the index. For example, if the S&P index is at 1,280 when a call option on the index with exercise price 1,270 is exercised, the holder of the call receives a cash payment equal to the difference, 1,280 − 1,270, times the contract multiplier of $100, or $1,000 per contract.

Options on the major indexes, that is, the S&P 100 contract, often called the OEX after its ticker symbol, the S&P 500 Index (the SPX), and the Dow Jones Industrials (the DJX), are by far the most actively traded contracts on the CBOE. Together, these contracts dominate CBOE volume.

Futures options Futures options give their holders the right to buy or sell a specified futures contract, using as a futures price the exercise price of the option. Although the delivery process is slightly complicated, the terms of futures options contracts are designed in effect to allow the option to be written on the futures price itself. The option holder receives upon exercise net proceeds equal to the difference between the current futures price on the specified asset and the exercise price of the option. Thus, if the futures price is, say, $37, and the call has an exercise price of $35, the holder who exercises the call option on the futures gets a payoff of $2.

Foreign currency options A currency option offers the right to buy or sell a quantity of foreign currency for a specified amount of domestic currency. Currency option contracts call for purchase or sale of the currency in exchange for a specified number of U.S. dollars. Contracts are quoted in cents or fractions of a cent per unit of foreign currency.

There is an important difference between currency options and currency *futures* options. The former provide payoffs that depend on the difference between the exercise price and the exchange rate at expiration. The latter are foreign exchange futures options that provide payoffs that depend on the difference between the exercise price and the exchange rate *futures price* at expiration. Because exchange rates and exchange rate futures prices generally are not equal, the options and futures options contracts will have different values, even with identical expiration dates and exercise prices. Today, trading volume in currency futures options dominates by far trading in currency options.

Interest rate options Options also are traded on Treasury notes and bonds, Treasury bills, and government bonds of other major economies such as the U.K. or Japan. Options on several interest rates also trade. Among them are contracts on Treasury bond, Treasury note, federal funds, LIBOR, Eurodollar, and British and euro-denominated yields.

15.2 VALUES OF OPTIONS AT EXPIRATION

Call Options

Recall that a call option gives the right to purchase a security at the exercise price. If you hold a call on Fin Corp stock with an exercise price of $80, and Fin Corp is now selling at $90, you can exercise your option to purchase the stock at $80 and simultaneously sell the shares at the market price of $90, clearing $10 per share. Yet if the shares sell below $80, you can sit on the option and do nothing, realizing no further gain or loss. The value of the call option at expiration equals

$$\text{Payoff to call holder at expiration} = \begin{cases} S_T - X & \text{if } S_T > X \\ 0 & \text{if } S_T \leq X \end{cases}$$

where S_T is the value of the stock at the expiration date and X is the exercise price. This formula emphasizes the option property because the payoff cannot be negative. The option is exercised

FIGURE 15.2

Payoff and profit to call option at expiration

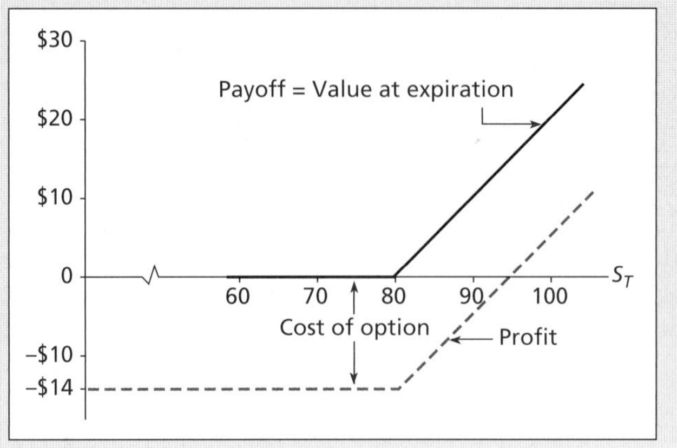

only if S_T exceeds X. If S_T is less than X, the option expires with zero value. The loss to the option holder in this case equals the price originally paid. More generally, the *profit* to the option holder is the option payoff minus the original purchase price.

The value at expiration of the call with exercise price $80 is given by the following schedule:

Stock price	$60	$70	$80	$90	$100
Option value	0	0	0	10	20

For stock prices at or below $80, the option expires worthless. Above $80, the option is worth the excess of the stock price over $80. The option's value increases by one dollar for each dollar increase in the stock price. This relationship can be depicted graphically, as in Figure 15.2.

The solid line in Figure 15.2 depicts the value of the call at expiration. The net *profit* to the holder of the call equals the gross payoff less the initial investment in the call. Suppose the call cost $14. Then the profit to the call holder would be as given in the dashed (bottom) line of Figure 15.2. At option expiration, the investor has suffered a loss of $14 if the stock price is less than or equal to $80.

Profits do not become positive until the stock price at expiration exceeds $94. The break-even point is $94, because at that price the payoff to the call, $S_T - X = \$94 - \$80 = \$14$, equals the cost paid to acquire the call. Hence, the call holder shows a profit only if the stock price is higher.

Conversely, the writer of the call incurs losses if the stock price is high. In that scenario, the writer will receive a call and will be obligated to deliver a stock worth S_T for only X dollars.

$$\text{Payoff to call writer} = \begin{cases} -(S_T - X) & \text{if } S_T > X \\ 0 & \text{if } S_T \leq X \end{cases}$$

The call writer, who is exposed to losses if the stock price increases, is willing to bear this risk in return for the option premium.

Figure 15.3 depicts the payoff and profit diagrams for the call writer. These are the mirror images of the corresponding diagrams for call holders. The break-even point for the option writer also is $94. The (negative) payoff at that point just offsets the premium originally received when the option was written.

Put Options

A put option conveys the right to sell an asset at the exercise price. In this case, the holder will not exercise unless the asset price is *less* than the exercise price. For example, if Fin Corp shares were to fall to $70, a put option with exercise price $80 could be exercised to give

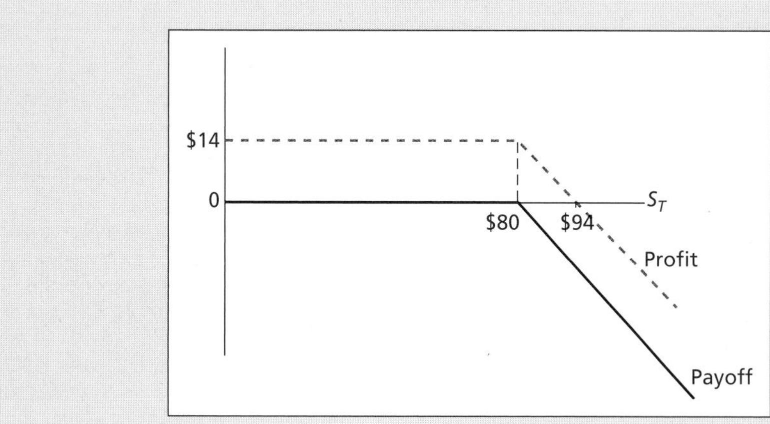

FIGURE 15.3

Payoff and profit to call writers at expiration

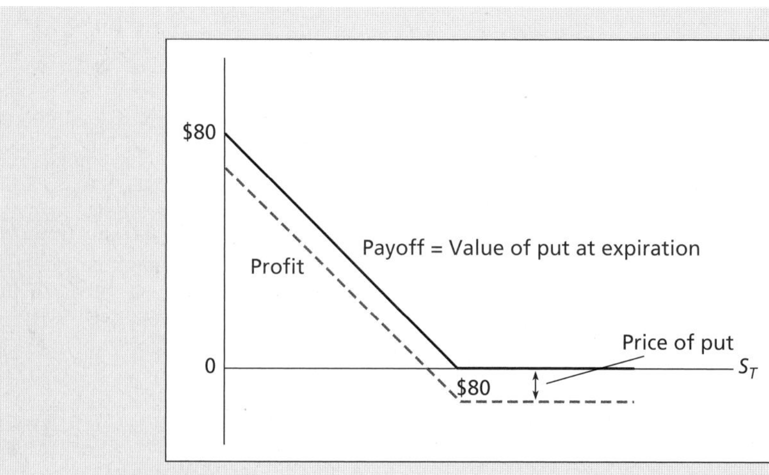

FIGURE 15.4

Payoff and profit to put option at expiration

a \$10 payoff. The holder would purchase a share for \$70 and simultaneously deliver it to the put option writer for the exercise price of \$80.

The value of a put option at expiration is

$$\text{Payoff to put holder} = \begin{cases} 0 & \text{if } S_T \geq X \\ X - S_T & \text{if } S_T < X \end{cases}$$

The solid line in Figure 15.4 illustrates the payoff at expiration to the holder of a put option on Fin Corp stock with an exercise price of \$80. If the stock price at option expiration is above \$80, the put has no value, as the right to sell the shares at \$80 would not be exercised. Below a price of \$80, the put value at expiration increases by \$1 for each dollar the stock price falls. The dashed line in Figure 15.4 is a graph of the put option owner's profit at expiration, net of the initial cost of the put.

Writing puts *naked* (i.e., writing a put without an offsetting short position in the stock for hedging purposes) exposes the writer to losses if the market falls. Writing naked, deep, out-of-the-money puts was once considered an attractive way to generate income, as it was believed that as long as the market did not fall sharply before the option expiration, the option premium could be collected without the put holder ever exercising the option against the writer. Because only sharp drops in the market could result in losses to the writer of the put, the strategy was not viewed as overly risky. However, the nearby box notes that in the wake of the market crash of October 1987, such put writers suffered huge losses. Participants now perceive much greater risk to this strategy.

On the MARKET FRONT

THE BLACK HOLE: PUTS AND THE MARKET CRASH

THEIR SALES OF "NAKED PUTS" QUICKLY COME TO GRIEF, DAMAGE SUITS ARE FILED

When Robert O'Connor got involved in stock-index options, he hoped his trading profits would help put his children through college. His broker, Mr. O'Connor explains, "said we would make about $1,000 a month, and if our losses got to $2,000 to $3,000, he would close out the account."

Instead, Mr. O'Connor got caught in one of the worst investor blowouts in history. In a few minutes on October 19, he lost everything in his account plus an *additional* $91,000—a total loss of 175% of his original investment.

SCENE OF DISASTER

For Mr. O'Connor and hundreds of other investors, a little-known corner of the Chicago Board Options Exchange was the "black hole" of Black Monday's market crash. In a strategy marketed by brokers nationwide as a sure thing, these customers had sunk hundreds of millions of dollars into "naked puts"—unhedged, highly leveraged bets that the stock market was in no danger of plunging. Most of these naked puts seem to have been options on the Standard & Poor's 100 stock index, which are traded on the CBOE. When stocks crashed, many traders with unhedged positions got margin calls for several times their original investment.

THE "PUT" STRATEGY

The losses were especially sharp in "naked, out-of-the-money puts." A seller of puts agrees to buy stock or stock-index contracts at a set price before the put expires. These contracts are usually sold "out of the money"—priced at a level below current market prices that makes it unprofitable to exercise the option so long as the market rises or stays flat. The seller pockets a small amount per contract.

But if the market plunges, as it did October 19, the option swings into the money. The seller, in effect, has to pay pre-plunge stock prices to make good on his contract—and he takes a big loss.

"You have to recognize that there is unlimited potential for disaster" in selling naked options, says Peter Thayer, executive vice president of Gateway Investment Advisors Inc. Last September [1987], Gateway bought out-of-the-money put options on the S&P 100 stock index on the CBOE at $2 to $3 a contract as "insurance" against a plunging market. By October 20, the day after the crash, the value of those contracts had soared to $130. Although Gateway profited handsomely, the parties on the other side of the trade were clobbered.

FIRM SUED

Brokers who were pushing naked options assumed that the stock market wouldn't plunge into uncharted territory. Frank VanderHoff, one of the two main brokers who put 50 to 70 H.B. Shaine clients into stock-index options, says he told clients that the strategy's risk was "moderate barring a nuclear attack or a crash like 1929." It wasn't speculative. The market could go up or down, but not *substantially* up or down. If the crash had only been as bad as '29, he adds, "we would have made it."

SOURCE: Abridged from *The Wall Street Journal,* December 2, 1987. Reprinted by permission of *The Wall Street Journal,* © 1987 Dow Jones & Company, Inc. All Rights Reserved Worldwide.

CONCEPT check 15.2

Consider these four option strategies: (i) buy a call; (ii) write a call; (iii) buy a put; (iv) write a put.

a. For each strategy, plot both the payoff and profit diagrams as a function of the final stock price.

b. Why might one characterize both buying calls and writing puts as "bullish" strategies? What is the difference between them?

c. Why might one characterize both buying puts and writing calls as "bearish" strategies? What is the difference between them?

Options versus Stock Investments

Purchasing call options is a bullish strategy; that is, the calls provide profits when stock prices increase. Purchasing puts, in contrast, is a bearish strategy. Symmetrically, writing calls is bearish, while writing puts is bullish. Because option values depend on the price of the underlying stock, the purchase of options may be viewed as a substitute for direct purchase or sale of a stock. Why might an option strategy be preferable to direct stock transactions? We can begin to answer this question by comparing the values of option versus stock positions in Fin Corp.

Suppose you believe the stock will increase in value from its current level, which we assume is $90. You know your analysis could be incorrect, however, and the share price also could fall.

Suppose a six-month maturity call option with exercise price of $90 sells for $10 and the semiannual interest rate is 2%. Consider the following three strategies for investing a sum of $9,000. Suppose the firm will not pay any dividends until after the options expire.

Strategy *A:* Invest entirely in stock. Buy 100 shares, each selling for $90.

Strategy *B:* Invest entirely in at-the-money call options. Buy 900 calls, each selling for $10. (This would require 9 contracts, each for 100 shares.)

Strategy *C:* Purchase 100 call options for $1,000. Invest the remaining $8,000 in six-month T-bills, to earn 2% interest.

Let us trace the possible values of these three portfolios when the options expire in six months as a function of the stock price at that time.

	Stock Price					
Portfolio	**$85**	**$90**	**$95**	**$100**	**$105**	**$110**
A: 100 shares stock	$8,500	$9,000	$9,500	$10,000	$10,500	$11,000
B: 900 call options	0	0	4,500	9,000	13,500	18,000
C: 100 calls plus $8,000 in T-bills	8,160	8,160	8,660	9,160	9,660	10,160

Portfolio *A* will be worth 100 times the share price. Portfolio *B* is worthless unless the shares sell for more than the exercise price of the call. Once that point is reached, the portfolio is worth 900 times the excess of the stock price over the exercise price. Finally, portfolio *C* is worth $8,160 from the investment in T-bills ($8,000 × 1.02 = $8,160) plus any profits from the 100 call options. Remember that each of these portfolios involves the same $9,000 initial investment. The rates of return on these three portfolios are as follows:

	Stock Price					
Portfolio	**$85**	**$90**	**$95**	**$100**	**$105**	**$110**
A: 100 shares stock	−5.56%	0.0%	5.56%	11.11%	16.67%	22.22%
B: 900 call options	−100.0	−100.0	−50.00	0.0	50.0	100.0
C: 100 calls plus $8,000 in T-bills	−9.33	−9.33	−3.78	1.78	7.33	12.89

These rates of return are graphed in Figure 15.5.

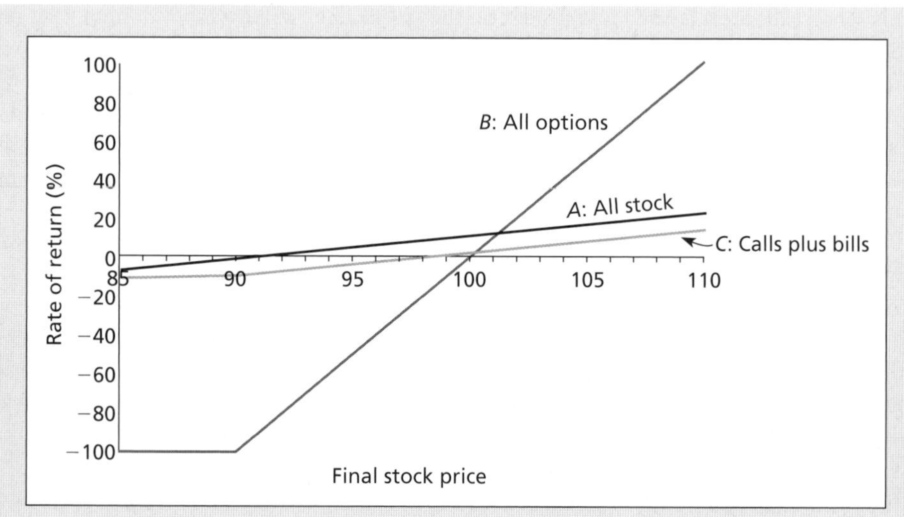

FIGURE 15.5

Rate of return to three strategies

EXCEL APPLICATIONS

Options, Stock, and Lending

Please visit us at www.mhhe.com/bkm

An Excel model based on the Fin Corp example discussed in the text is shown below. The model allows you to use any variety of options, stock, and lending or borrowing with a set investment amount and demonstrates the investment flexibility of options.

	A	B	C	D	E	F	G	H
1	Current stock price	90						
2	Exercise price	90						
3	Interest rate	0.02						
4	Investment budget	9000						
5	Call price	10						
6								
7			Dollar value of portfolio as a function of Fin Corp price					
8	**Portfolio**		**$85**	**$90**	**$95**	**$100**	**$105**	**$110**
9	Portfolio A: All stock		$8,500	$9,000	$9,500	$10,000	$10,500	$11,000
10	Portfolio B: All call options		0	0	4,500	9,000	13,500	18,000
11	Portfolio C: Call plus bills		8,160	8,160	8,660	9,160	9,660	10,160
12								
13								
14			Rate of return as a function of Fin Corp price					
15	**Portfolio**		**$85**	**$90**	**$95**	**$100**	**$105**	**$110**
16	Portfolio A: All stock		-5.6%	0.00%	5.6%	11.1%	16.7%	22.2%
17	Portfolio B: All call options		-100.0%	-100.0%	-50.0%	0.0%	50.0%	100.0%
18	Portfolio C: Call plus bills		-9.33%	-9.33%	-3.78%	1.78%	7.33%	12.89%

Excel Questions

1. Plot the rate of return to the call-plus-bills strategy using a diagram like that in Figure 15.5 but now assuming the investor uses an in-the-money call option with a strike price of $80. Assume the calls sell for $15. The higher cost for these calls compared to the at-the-money calls will result in less money being placed in T-bills, since the investment budget is still $9,000.
2. Compare the plots of rate of return for the strategies using at-the-money calls (as in Figure 15.5) and your solution to Question 1. Which strategy is riskier?

Comparing the returns of portfolios *B* and *C* to those of the simple investment in stock represented by portfolio *A*, we see that options offer two interesting features. First, an option offers leverage. Compare the returns of portfolios *B* and *A*. When the stock fares poorly, ending anywhere below $90, the value of portfolio *B* falls precipitously to zero—a rate of return of negative 100%. Conversely, modest increases in the rate of return on the stock result in disproportionate increases in the option rate of return. For example, a 4.8% increase in the stock price from $105 to $110 would increase the rate of return on the call from 50% to 100%. In this sense, calls are a levered investment on the stock. Their values respond more than proportionately to changes in the stock value.

Figure 15.5 vividly illustrates this point. For stock prices above $90, the slope of the all-option portfolio is far steeper than that of the all-stock portfolio, reflecting its greater proportional sensitivity to the value of the underlying security. The leverage factor is the reason that investors (illegally) exploiting inside information commonly choose options as their investment vehicle.

The potential insurance value of options is the second interesting feature, as portfolio *C* shows. The T-bill-plus-option portfolio cannot be worth less than $8,160 after six months, as the option can always be left to expire worthless. The worst possible rate of return on portfolio *C* is −9.33%, compared to a (theoretically) worst possible rate of return on the stock of −100% if the company were to go bankrupt. Of course, this insurance comes at a price: When the share price increases, portfolio *C* does not perform as well as portfolio *A*, the all-stock portfolio. For stock prices above $90, portfolio *C* underperforms portfolio *A* by about 9.33 percentage points.

This simple example makes an important point. While options can be used by speculators as effectively leveraged stock positions, as in portfolio *B*, they also can be used by investors who desire to tailor their risk exposures in creative ways, as in portfolio *C*. For example, the call-plus-T-bills strategy of portfolio C provides a rate of return profile quite unlike that of the stock alone. The absolute limitation on downside risk is a novel and attractive feature of this strategy. In the next section we will discuss several option strategies that provide other novel risk profiles that might be attractive to hedgers and other investors.

Option Strategies

An unlimited variety of payoff patterns can be achieved by combining puts and calls with various exercise prices. Below we explain the motivation and structure of some of the more popular ones.

Protective put Imagine you would like to invest in a stock but you are unwilling to bear potential losses beyond some given level. Investing in the stock alone seems risky to you because in principle you could lose all the money you invest. You might consider instead investing in stock and purchasing a put option on the stock.

Table 15.1 shows the total value of your portfolio at option expiration. Whatever happens to the stock price, you are guaranteed a payoff equal to the put option's exercise price because the put gives you the right to sell the share for the exercise price even if the stock price is below that value.

protective put

An asset combined with a put option that guarantees minimum proceeds equal to the put's exercise price.

Figure 15.6 illustrates the payoff and profit to this **protective put** strategy. The solid line in Figure 15.6C is the total payoff. The dashed line is displaced downward by the cost of establishing the position, $S_0 + P$. Notice that potential losses are limited.

EXAMPLE 15.3

Protective Put

Suppose the strike price is $X = \$90$ and the stock is selling for \$87 at option expiration. Then the value of your total portfolio is \$90: The stock is worth \$87 and the value of the expiring put option is

$$X - S_T = \$90 - \$87 = \$3$$

Another way to look at it is that you are holding the stock and a put contract giving you the right to sell the stock for \$90. Even if $S < \$90$, you can still sell the stock for \$90 by exercising the put. On the other hand, if the stock price is above \$90, say, \$94, then the right to sell a share at \$90 is worthless. You allow the put to expire unexercised, ending up with a share of stock worth $S_T = \$94$.

It is instructive to compare the profit on the protective put strategy with that of the stock investment. For simplicity, consider an at-the-money protective put, so that $X = S_0$. Figure 15.7 compares the profits for the two strategies. The profit on the stock is zero if the stock price remains unchanged, and $S_T = S_0$. It rises or falls by \$1 for every dollar swing in the ultimate stock price. The profit on the protective put is negative and equal to the cost of the put if S_T is below S_0. The profit on the protective put increases one for one with increases in the stock price once the stock price exceeds X.

Figure 15.7 makes it clear that the protective put offers some insurance against stock price declines in that it limits losses. As we shall see in the next chapter, protective put strategies are the conceptual basis for the portfolio insurance industry. The cost of the protection is that, in the case of stock price increases, your profit is reduced by the cost of the put, which turned out to be unneeded.

This example also shows that despite the common perception that "derivatives mean risk," derivative securities can be used effectively for **risk management.** In fact, such risk management is becoming accepted as part of the fiduciary responsibility of financial managers. Indeed, in a highly cited court case, *Brane* v. *Roth,* a company's board of directors was successfully sued for failing to use derivatives to hedge the price risk of grain held in storage. Such hedging might have been accomplished using protective puts. Some observers believe that this case will ultimately lead to a broad legal obligation for firms to use derivatives and other techniques to manage risk.

risk management

Strategies to limit the risk of a portfolio.

The claim that derivatives are best viewed as risk management tools may seem surprising in light of the credit crisis of the last few years. The crisis was immediately precipitated when

TABLE 15.1 Payoff to protective put strategy

	$S_T \le X$	$S_T > X$
Stock	S_T	S_T
Put	$X - S_T$	0
Total	X	S_T

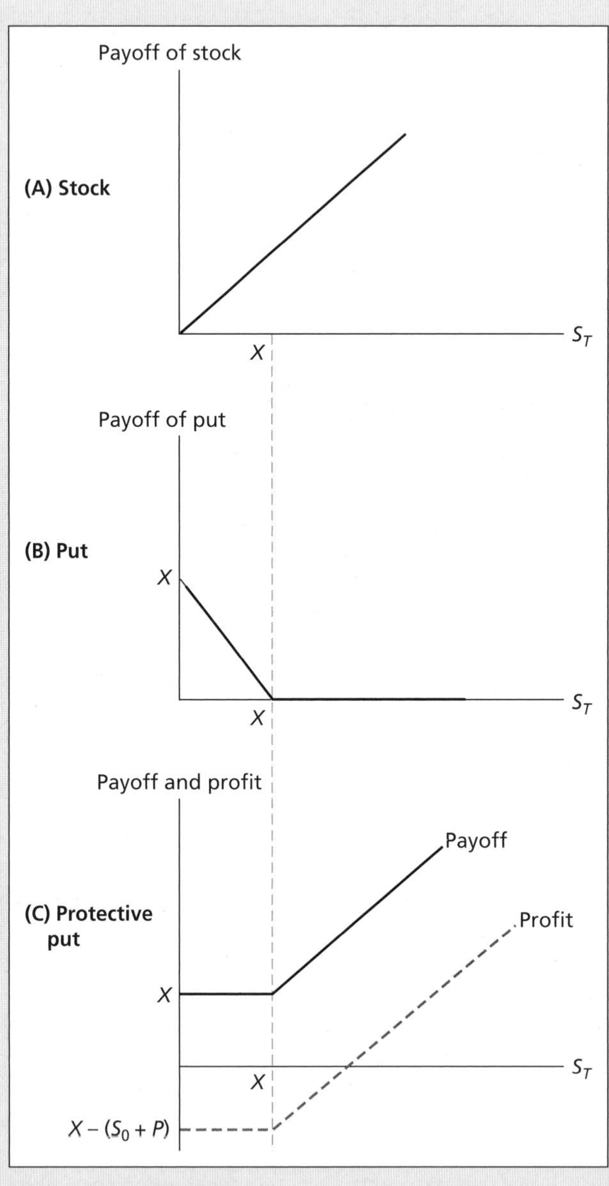

FIGURE 15.6 Value of a protective put position at expiration

the highly risky positions that many financial institutions had established in credit derivatives blew up in 2007–2008, resulting in large losses and government bailouts. Still, the same characteristics that make derivatives potent tools to increase risk also make them highly effective in managing risk, at least when used properly. Derivatives have aptly been compared to power tools: very useful in skilled hands but also very dangerous when not handled with care. The nearby box makes the case for derivatives as central to risk management.

On the MARKET FRONT

THE CASE FOR DERIVATIVES

They've been dubbed financial weapons of mass destruction, attacked for causing the financial turmoil sweeping the nation and identified as the kryptonite that brought down the global economy. Yet few Main Streeters really know what [derivatives] are—namely, financial contracts between a buyer and a seller that derive value from an underlying asset, such as a mortgage or a stock. There seems to be near consensus that derivatives were a source of undue risk.

And then there's Robert Shiller. The Yale economist believes just the opposite is true. A champion of financial innovation and an expert in management of risk, Shiller contends that derivatives, far from being a problem, are actually the solution. Derivatives, Shiller says, are merely a risk-management tool the same way insurance is. "You pay a premium and if an event happens, you get a payment." That tool can be used well or, as happened recently, used badly. Shiller warns that banishing the tool gets us nowhere.

For all the trillions in derivative trading, there were very few traders. Almost all the subprime mortgages that were bundled and turned into derivatives were sold by a handful of Wall Street institutions, working with a small number of large institutional buyers. It was a huge but illiquid and opaque market.

Meanwhile, the system was built on the myriad decisions of individual homeowners and lenders around the world. None of them, however, could hedge their bets the way large institutions can. Those buying a condo in Miami had no way to protect themselves if the market went down.

Derivatives, according to Shiller, could be used by homeowners—and, by extension, lenders—to insure themselves against falling prices. In Shiller's scenario, you would be able to go to your broker and buy a new type of financial instrument, perhaps a derivative that is inversely related to a regional home-price index. If the value of houses in your area declined, the financial instrument would increase in value, offsetting the loss. Lenders could do the same thing, which would help them hedge against foreclosures. The idea is to make the housing market more liquid. More buyers and sellers means that markets stay liquid and functional even under pressure.

Some critics dismiss Shiller's basic premise that more derivatives would make the housing market more liquid and more stable. They point out that futures contracts haven't made equity markets or commodity markets immune from massive moves up and down. They add that a ballooning world of home-based derivatives wouldn't lead to homeowners' insurance: it would lead to a new playground for speculators.

In essence, Shiller is laying the intellectual groundwork for the next financial revolution. We are now suffering through the first major crisis of the Information Age economy. Shiller's answers may be counterintuitive, but no more so than those of doctors and scientists who centuries ago recognized that the cure for infectious diseases was not flight or quarantine, but purposely infecting more people through vaccinations. "We've had a major glitch in derivatives and securitization," says Shiller. "The Titanic sank almost a century ago, but we didn't stop sailing across the Atlantic."

Of course, people did think twice about getting on a ship, at least for a while. But if we listen only to our fears, we lose the very dynamism that has propelled us this far. That is the nub of Shiller's call for more derivatives and more innovation. Shiller's appeal is a tough sell at a time when derivatives have produced so much havoc. But he reminds us that the tools that got us here are not to blame; they can be used badly and they can be used well. And trying to stem the ineffable tide of human creativity is a fool's errand.

SOURCE: Excerpted from Zachary Karabell, "The Case for Derivatives," *Newsweek,* February 2, 2009.

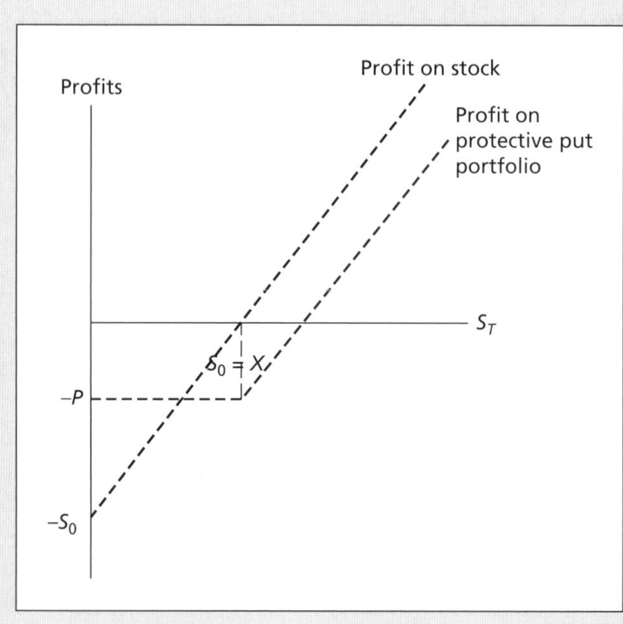

FIGURE 15.7

Protective put versus stock investment (at-the-money put option)

EXCEL APPLICATIONS
Straddles and Spreads

eXcel

Please visit us at www.mhhe.com/bkm

Using spreadsheets to analyze combinations of options is very helpful. Once the basic models are built, it is easy to extend the analysis to different bundles of options. The Excel model "Spreads and Straddles" shown below can be used to evaluate the profitability of different strategies.

	A	B	C	D	E	F	G	H	I	J	K	L
1					**Spreads and Straddles**							
2												
3	**Stock Prices**											
4	Beginning Market Price	116.5										
5	Ending Market Price	130						**X 110 Straddle**			**X 120 Straddle**	
6							**Ending**	**Profit**		**Ending**	**Profit**	
7	**Buying Options:**						**Stock Price**	-15.40		**Stock Price**	-24.00	
8	**Call Options Strike**	**Price**	**Payoff**	**Profit**	**Return %**		50	24.60		50	36.00	
9	110	22.80	20.00	-2.80	-12.28%		60	14.60		60	26.00	
10	120	16.80	10.00	-6.80	-40.48%		70	4.60		70	16.00	
11	130	13.60	0.00	-13.60	-100.00%		80	-5.40		80	6.00	
12	140	10.30	0.00	-10.30	-100.00%		90	-15.40		90	-4.00	
13							100	-25.40		100	-14.00	
14	**Put Options Strike**	**Price**	**Payoff**	**Profit**	**Return %**		110	-35.40		110	-24.00	
15	110	12.60	0.00	-12.60	-100.00%		120	-25.40		120	-34.00	
16	120	17.20	0.00	-17.20	-100.00%		130	-15.40		130	-24.00	
17	130	23.60	0.00	-23.60	-100.00%		140	-5.40		140	-14.00	
18	140	30.50	10.00	-20.50	-67.21%		150	4.60		150	-4.00	
19							160	14.60		160	6.00	
20	**Straddle**	**Price**	**Payoff**	**Profit**	**Return %**		170	24.60		170	16.00	
21	110	35.40	20.00	-15.40	-43.50%		180	34.60		180	26.00	
22	120	34.00	10.00	-24.00	-70.59%		190	44.60		190	36.00	
23	130	37.20	0.00	-37.20	-100.00%		200	54.60		200	46.00	
24	140	40.80	10.00	-30.80	-75.49%		210	64.60		210	56.00	
25												

Excel Question

1. Use the data in this spreadsheet to plot the profit on a bullish spread (see Figure 15.10) with $X_1 = 120$ and $X_2 = 130$.

covered call

Writing a call on an asset together with buying the asset.

Covered calls A **covered call** position is the purchase of a share of stock with the simultaneous sale of a call option on that stock. The written option is "covered" because the potential obligation to deliver the stock can be satisfied using the stock held in the portfolio. Writing an option without an offsetting stock position is called by contrast *naked option writing.* The payoff to a covered call, presented in Table 15.2, equals the stock value minus the payoff of the call. The call payoff is subtracted because the covered call position involves issuing a call to another investor who can choose to exercise it to profit at your expense.

The solid line in Figure 15.8C illustrates the payoff pattern. You see that the total position is worth S_T when the stock price at time T is below X and rises to a maximum of X when S_T exceeds X. In essence, the sale of the call option means the call writer has sold the claim to any stock value above X in return for the initial premium (the call price). Therefore, at expiration, the position is worth at most X. The dashed line of Figure 15.8C is the net profit to the covered call.

Writing covered call options has been a popular investment strategy among institutional investors. Consider the managers of a fund invested largely in stocks. They might find it appealing to write calls on some or all of the stock in order to boost income by the premiums collected. Although they thereby forfeit potential capital gains should the stock price rise above the exercise price, if they view X as the price at which they plan to sell the stock anyway, then the call may be viewed as enforcing a kind of "sell discipline." The written call guarantees the stock sale will occur as planned.

TABLE 15.2 Payoff to a covered call

	$S_T \le X$	$S_T > X$
Payoff of stock	S_T	S_T
−Payoff of call	−0	$-(S_T - X)$
Total	S_T	X

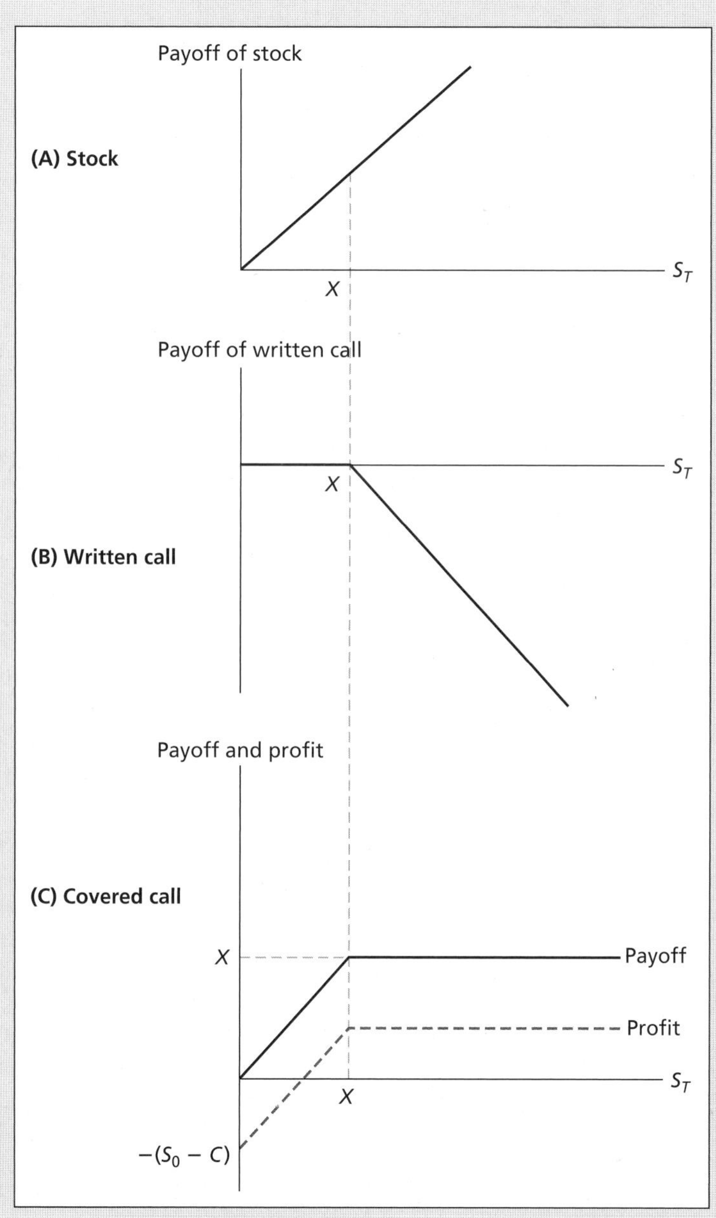

FIGURE 15.8

Value of a covered call position at expiration

EXAMPLE 15.4

Covered Call

Assume a pension fund holds 1,000 shares of GXX stock, with a current price of $130 per share. Suppose the portfolio manager intends to sell all 1,000 shares if the share price hits $140, and a call expiring in 90 days with an exercise price of $140 currently sells for $5. By writing 10 GXX call

(continued)

EXAMPLE 15.4

Covered Call (concluded)

contracts (100 shares each) the fund can pick up $5,000 in extra income. The fund would lose its share of profits from any movement of GXX stock above $140 per share, but given that it would have sold its shares at $140, it would not have realized those profits anyway.

straddle

A combination of a call and a put, each with the same exercise price and expiration date.

Straddle A long **straddle** is established by buying both a call and a put on a stock, each with the same exercise price, X, and the same expiration date, T. Straddles are useful strategies for investors who believe a stock will move a lot in price but are uncertain about the direction of the move. For example, suppose you believe an important court case that will make or break a company is about to be settled, and the market is not yet aware of the situation. The stock will either double in value if the case is settled favorably or will drop by half if the settlement goes against the company. The straddle position will do well regardless of the outcome because its value is highest when the stock price makes extreme upward or downward moves from X.

The worst-case scenario for a straddle is no movement in the stock price. If S_T equals X, both the call and the put expire worthless, and the investor's outlay for the purchase of both options is lost. Straddle positions basically are bets on volatility. An investor who establishes a straddle must view the stock as more volatile than the market does. Conversely, investors who *write* straddles—selling both a call and a put—must believe the market is less volatile. They accept the option premiums now, hoping the stock price will not change much before option expiration.

The payoff to a straddle is presented in Table 15.3. The solid line of Figure 15.9C illustrates this payoff. Notice that the portfolio payoff is always positive, except at the one point where the portfolio has zero value, $S_T = X$. You might wonder why all investors don't pursue such a no-lose strategy. To see why, remember that the straddle requires that both the put and the call be purchased. The value of the portfolio at expiration, while never negative, still must exceed the initial cash outlay for a straddle investor to clear a profit.

The dashed line of Figure 15.9C is the profit to the straddle. The profit line lies below the payoff line by the cost of purchasing the straddle, $P + C$. It is clear from the diagram that the straddle position generates a loss unless the stock price deviates substantially from X. The stock price must depart from X by the total amount expended to purchase the call *and* the put in order for the purchaser of the straddle to clear a profit.

Strips and *straps* are variations of straddles. A strip is two puts and one call on a security with the same exercise price and expiration date. A strap is two calls and one put.

CONCEPT check 15.3

Graph the profit and payoff diagrams for strips and straps.

spread

A combination of two or more call options or put options on the same asset with differing exercise prices or times to expiration.

Spreads A **spread** is a combination of two or more call options (or two or more puts) on the same stock with differing exercise prices or times to expiration. Some options are bought, while others are sold, or written. A *money spread* involves the purchase of one option and the simultaneous sale of another with a different exercise price. A *time spread* refers to the sale and purchase of options with differing expiration dates.

Consider a money spread in which one call option is bought at an exercise price X_1, while another call with identical expiration date, but higher exercise price, X_2, is written. The payoff to this position will be the difference in the value of the call held and the value of the call written, as in Table 15.4.

There are now three instead of two outcomes to distinguish: the lowest-price region, where S_T is below both exercise prices; a middle region, where S_T is between the two exercise prices; and a high-price region, where S_T exceeds both exercise prices. Figure 15.10 illustrates the payoff and profit to this strategy, which is called a *bullish spread* because the payoff either increases or is unaffected by stock price increases. Holders of bullish spreads benefit from stock price increases.

One motivation for a bullish spread might be that the investor thinks one option is overpriced relative to another. For example, an investor who believes an $X = \$50$ call is cheap

TABLE 15.3 Payoff to a straddle

	$S_T \le X$	$S_T > X$
Payoff of call	0	$S_T - X$
+Payoff of put	$+(X - S_T)$	+0
Total	$X - S_T$	$S_T - X$

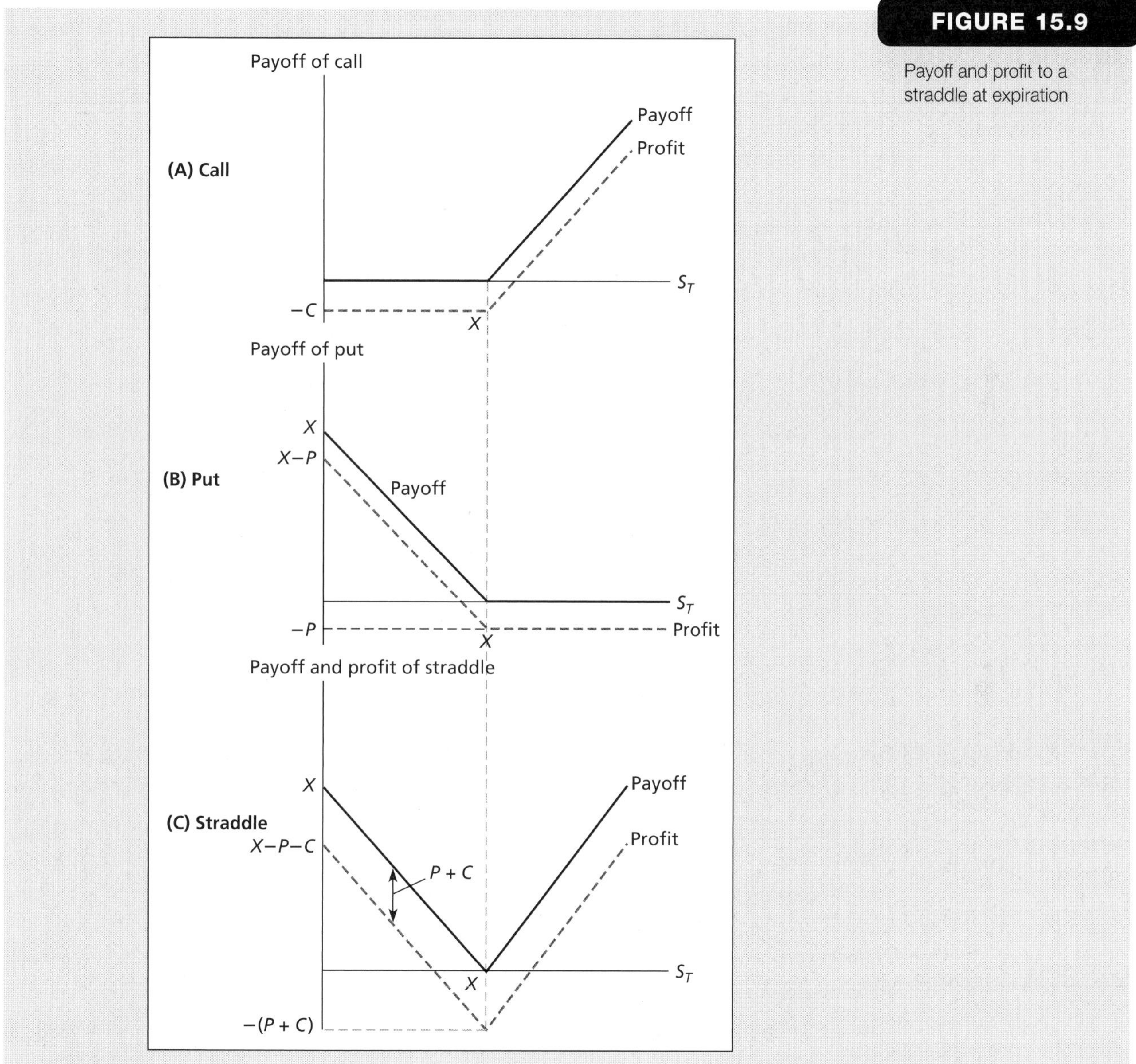

FIGURE 15.9 Payoff and profit to a straddle at expiration

compared to an $X = \$55$ call might establish the spread, even without a strong desire to take a bullish position in the stock.

collar An options strategy that brackets the value of a portfolio between two bounds.

Collars A **collar** is an options strategy that brackets the value of a portfolio between two bounds. Suppose that an investor currently is holding a large position in Eagle Corp., which is currently selling at $70 per share. A lower bound of $60 can be placed on the value of the

TABLE 15.4 Payoff to a bullish spread

	$S_T \le X_1$	$X_1 < S_T \le X_2$	$S_T > X_2$
Payoff of first call, exercise price = X_1	0	$S_T - X_1$	$S_T - X_1$
−Payoff of second call, exercise price = X_2	−0	−0	$-(S_T - X_2)$
Total	0	$S_T - X_1$	$X_2 - X_1$

FIGURE 15.10

Value of a bullish spread position at expiration

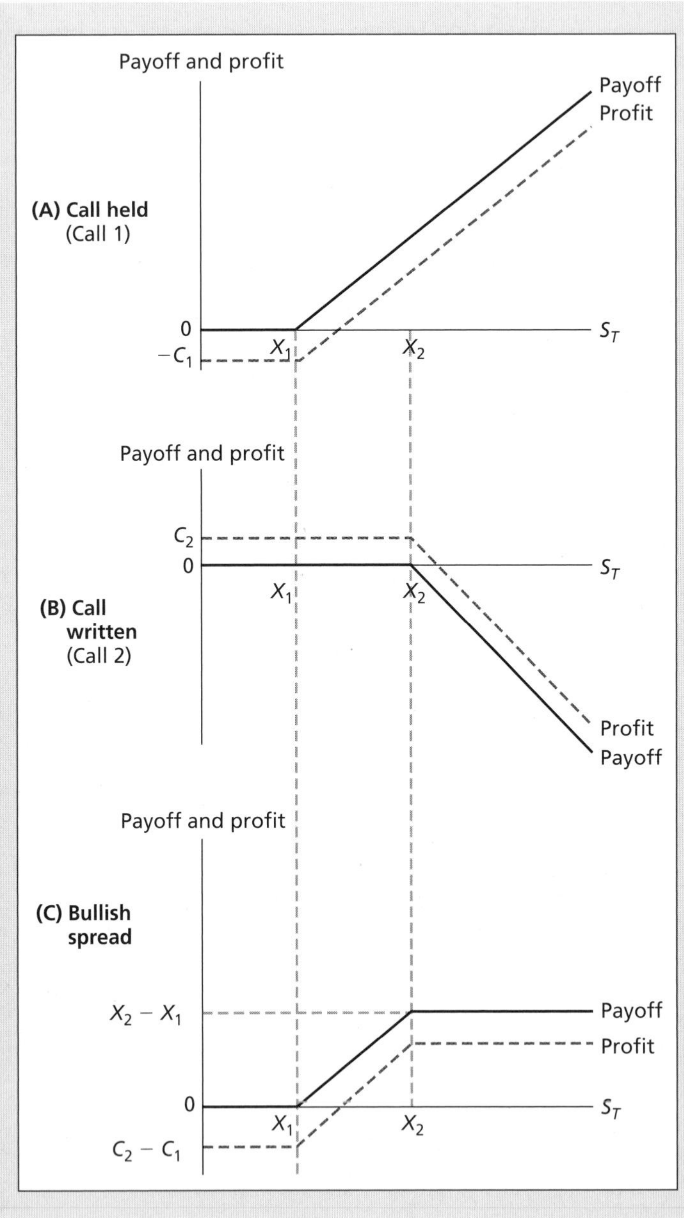

portfolio by buying a protective put with exercise price \$60. This protection, however, requires that the investor pay the put premium. To raise the money to pay for the put, the investor might write a call option, say, with exercise price \$80. The call might sell for roughly the same price as the put, meaning that the net outlay for the two options positions is approximately zero. Writing the call limits the portfolio's upside potential. Even if the stock price moves above $80, the investor will do no better than $80, because at a higher price the stock will be called away. Thus the investor obtains the downside protection represented by the exercise price of the put by selling her claim to any upside potential beyond the exercise price of the call.

EXAMPLE 15.5

Collars

A collar would be appropriate for an investor who has a target wealth goal in mind but is unwilling to risk losses beyond a certain level. Suppose you are contemplating buying a house for $160,000, for example. You might set this figure as your goal. Your current wealth may be $140,000, and you are unwilling to risk losing more than $20,000. A collar established by (1) purchasing 2,000 shares of stock currently selling at $70 per share, (2) purchasing 2,000 put options (20 option contracts) with exercise price $60, and (3) writing 2,000 calls with exercise price $80 would give you a good chance to realize the $20,000 capital gain without risking a loss of more than $20,000.

CONCEPT check 15.4

Graph the payoff diagram for the collar described in Example 15.5.

15.3 OPTIONLIKE SECURITIES

Suppose you never intend to trade an option directly. Why do you need to appreciate the properties of options in formulating an investment plan? Many financial instruments and agreements have features that convey implicit or explicit options to one or more parties. To value and use these securities correctly, you must understand their embedded option attributes.

Callable Bonds

You know from Chapter 10 that many corporate bonds are issued with call provisions entitling the issuer to buy bonds back from bondholders at some time in the future at a specified call price. A call provision conveys a call option to the issuer, where the exercise price is equal to the price at which the bond can be repurchased. A callable bond arrangement is essentially a sale of a *straight bond* (a bond with no option features such as callability or convertibility) to the investor and the concurrent sale of a call option by the investor to the bond-issuing firm.

Investors must receive some compensation for offering this implicit call option. If the callable bond were issued with the same coupon rate as a straight bond, we would expect it to sell at a discount to the straight bond equal to the value of the call. To sell callable bonds at par, firms must issue them with coupon rates higher than the coupons on straight debt. The higher coupons are the investor's compensation for the call option retained by the issuer. Coupon rates usually are selected so that the newly issued bond will sell at par value.

Figure 15.11 illustrates this optionlike property. The horizontal axis is the value of a straight bond with otherwise identical terms as the callable bond. The dashed 45-degree line represents the value of straight debt. The solid line is the value of the callable bond, and the dotted line is the value of the call option retained by the firm. A callable bond's potential for capital gains is limited by the firm's option to repurchase at the call price.

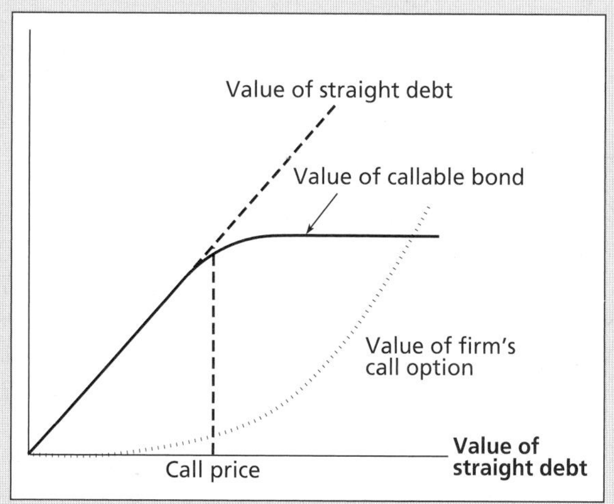

FIGURE 15.11

Values of callable bond compared with straight bond

CONCEPT check 15.5

How is a callable bond similar to a covered call strategy on a straight bond?

The option inherent in callable bonds actually is more complex than an ordinary call option because usually it may be exercised only after some initial period of call protection. The price at which the bond is callable may change over time also. Unlike exchange-listed options, these features are defined in the initial bond covenants and will depend on the needs of the issuing firm and its perception of the market's tastes.

CONCEPT check 15.6

Suppose the period of call protection is extended. How will this affect the coupon rate the company needs to offer to enable it to sell the bonds at par value?

Convertible Securities

Convertible bonds and convertible preferred stock convey options to the holder of the security rather than to the issuing firm. A convertible security typically gives its holder the right to exchange each bond or share of preferred stock for a fixed number of shares of common stock, regardless of the market prices of the securities at the time.

CONCEPT check 15.7

Should a convertible bond issued at par value have a higher or lower coupon rate than a non-convertible bond issued at par?

For example, a bond with a conversion ratio of 10 allows its holder to convert one bond of par value $1,000 into 10 shares of common stock. Alternatively, we say the conversion price in this case is $100: To receive 10 shares of stock, the investor sacrifices bonds with face value $1,000 or $100 of face value per share. If the present value of the bond's scheduled payments is less than 10 times the value of one share of stock, it may pay to convert; that is, the conversion option is in the money. A bond worth $950 with a conversion ratio of 10 could be converted profitably if the stock were selling above $95, as the value of the 10 shares received for each bond surrendered would exceed $950. Most convertible bonds are issued "deep out of the money." That is, the issuer sets the conversion ratio so that conversion will not be profitable unless there is a substantial increase in stock prices and/or decrease in bond prices from the time of issue.

A bond's conversion value equals the value it would have if you converted it into stock immediately. Clearly, a bond must sell for at least its conversion value. If it did not, you could purchase the bond, convert it immediately, and clear a riskless profit. This condition could never persist, for all investors would pursue such a strategy and quickly bid up the price of the bond.

The straight bond value or "bond floor" is the value the bond would have if it were not convertible into stock. The bond must sell for more than its straight bond value because a convertible bond has more value; it is in fact a straight bond plus a valuable call option. Therefore, the convertible bond has two lower bounds on its market price: the conversion value and the straight bond value.

Figure 15.12 illustrates the optionlike properties of the convertible bond. Figure 15.12A shows the value of the straight debt as a function of the stock price of the issuing firm. For healthy firms, the straight debt value is almost independent of the value of the stock because default risk is small. However, if the firm is close to bankruptcy (stock prices are low), default risk increases, and the straight bond value falls. Panel B shows the conversion value of the bond. Panel C compares the value of the convertible bond to these two lower bounds.

When stock prices are low, the straight bond value is the effective lower bound, and the conversion option is nearly irrelevant. The convertible will trade like straight debt. When stock prices are high, the bond's price is determined by its conversion value. With conversion all but guaranteed, the bond is essentially equity in disguise.

We can illustrate with two examples.

FIGURE 15.12

Value of a convertible bond as a function of stock price

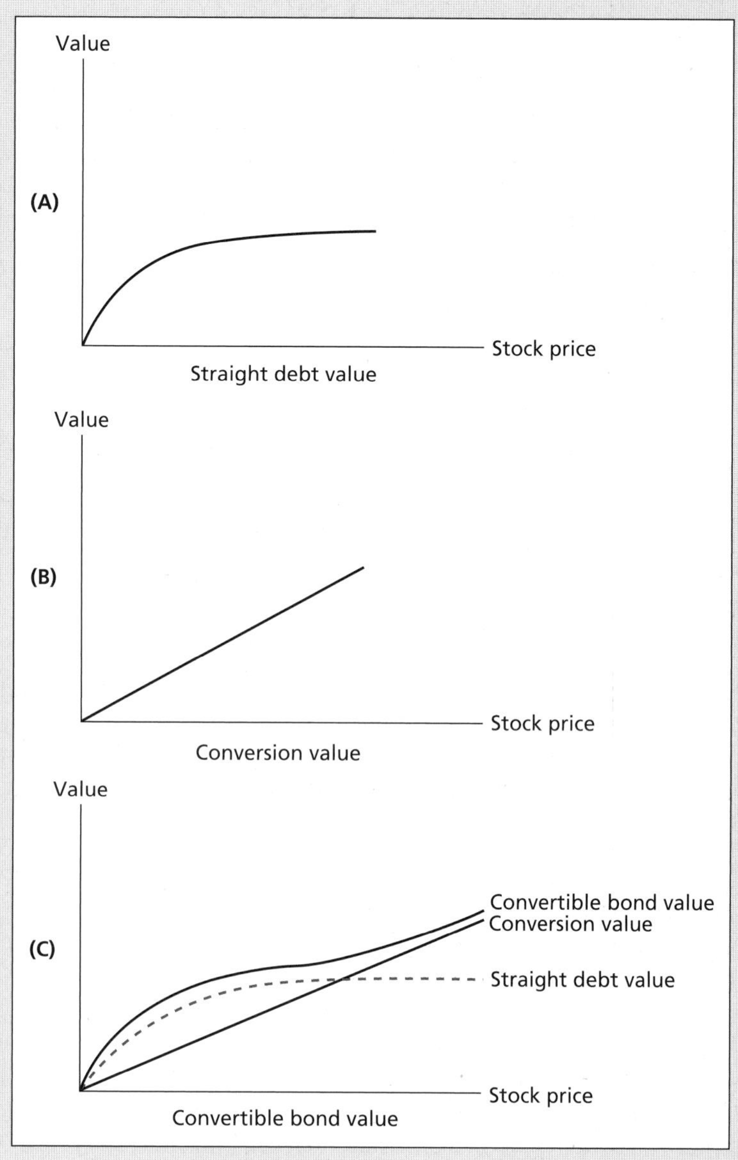

	Bond A	Bond B
Annual coupon	$80	$80
Maturity date	10 years	10 years
Quality rating	Baa	Baa
Conversion ratio	20	25
Stock price	$30	$50
Conversion value	$600	$1,250
Market yield on 10-year Baa-rated bonds	8.5%	8.5%
Value as straight debt	$967	$967
Actual bond price	$972	$1,255
Reported yield to maturity	8.42%	4.76%

Bond A has a conversion value of only $600. Its value as straight debt, in contrast, is $967. This is the present value of the coupon and principal payments at a market rate for straight debt of 8.5%. The bond's price is $972, so the premium over straight bond value is only $5, reflecting the low probability of conversion. Its reported yield to maturity based on scheduled coupon payments and the market price of $972 is 8.42%, close to that of straight debt.

The conversion option on bond B is in the money. Conversion value is $1,250, and the bond's price, $1,255, reflects its value as equity (plus $5 for the protection the bond offers against stock price declines). The bond's reported yield is 4.76%, far below the comparable yield on straight debt. The big yield sacrifice is attributable to the far greater value of the conversion option.

In theory, we could value convertible bonds by treating them as straight debt plus call options. In practice, however, this approach is often impractical for several reasons:

1. The conversion price frequently increases over time, which means the exercise price for the option changes.
2. Stocks may pay several dividends over the life of the bond, further complicating the option value analysis.
3. Most convertibles also are callable at the discretion of the firm. In essence, both the investor and the issuer hold options on each other. If the issuer exercises its call option to repurchase the bond, the bondholders typically have a month during which they still can convert. When issuers use a call option, knowing that bondholders will choose to convert, the issuer is said to have *forced a conversion.* These conditions together mean the actual maturity of the bond is indeterminate.

Warrants

warrant

An option issued by the firm to purchase shares of the firm's stock.

Warrants are essentially call options issued by a firm. One important difference between calls and warrants is that exercise of a warrant requires the firm to issue a new share of stock to satisfy its obligation—the total number of shares outstanding increases. Exercise of a call option requires only that the writer of the call deliver an already-issued share of stock to discharge the obligation. In this case, the number of shares outstanding remains fixed. Also unlike call options, warrants result in a cash flow to the firm when the warrant holder pays the exercise price. These differences mean warrant values will differ somewhat from the values of call options with identical terms.

Like convertible debt, warrant terms may be tailored to meet the needs of the firm. Also like convertible debt, warrants generally are protected against stock splits and dividends in that the exercise price and the number of warrants held are adjusted to offset the effects of the split.

Warrants often are issued in conjunction with another security. Bonds, for example, may be packaged together with a warrant "sweetener," frequently a warrant that may be sold separately. This is called a *detachable warrant.*

Issues of warrants and convertible securities create the potential for an increase in outstanding shares of stock if exercise occurs. Exercise obviously would affect financial statistics that are computed on a per-share basis, so annual reports must provide earnings per share figures under the assumption that all convertible securities and warrants are exercised. These figures are called *fully diluted earnings per share.*[3]

Collateralized Loans

Many loan arrangements require that the borrower put up collateral to guarantee the loan will be paid back. In the event of default, the lender takes possession of the collateral. A *nonrecourse loan* gives the lender no recourse beyond the right to the collateral. That is, the lender may not sue the borrower for further payment if the collateral turns out not to be valuable enough to repay the loan.[4]

[3]We should note that the exercise of a convertible bond need not reduce earnings per share (EPS). Diluted EPS will be less than undiluted EPS only if interest saved (per share) on the converted bonds is less than the prior EPS.

[4]In reality, of course, defaulting on a loan is not so simple. Losses of reputation are involved as well as considerations of ethical behavior. This is a description of a pure nonrecourse loan where both parties agree from the outset that only the collateral backs the loan and that default is not to be taken as a sign of bad faith if the collateral is insufficient to repay the loan.

This arrangement gives an implicit call option to the borrower. Assume the borrower is obligated to pay back L dollars at the maturity of the loan. The collateral will be worth S_T dollars at maturity. (Its value today is S_0.) The borrower has the option to wait until loan maturity and repay the loan only if the collateral is worth more than the L dollars necessary to satisfy the loan. If the collateral is worth less than L, the borrower can default on the loan, discharging the obligation by forfeiting the collateral, which is worth only S_T.

Another way of describing such a loan is to view the borrower as turning over collateral to the lender but retaining the right to reclaim it by paying off the loan. The transfer of the collateral with the right to reclaim it is equivalent to a payment of S_0 dollars less a simultaneous recovery of a sum that resembles a call option with exercise price L. In effect, the borrower turns over collateral but keeps an option to "repurchase" it for L dollars at the maturity of the loan if L turns out to be less than S_T. This is a call option.

A third way to look at a collaterized loan is to assume the borrower will repay the L dollars with certainty but also retain the option to sell the collateral to the lender for L dollars, even if S_T is less than L. In this case, the sale of the collateral would generate the cash necessary to satisfy the loan. The ability to "sell" the collateral for a price of L dollars represents a put option, which guarantees the borrower can raise enough money to satisfy the loan simply by turning over the collateral.

Figure 15.13 illustrates these interpretations. Figure 15.13A is the value of the payment to be received by the lender, which equals the minimum of S_T or L. Panel B shows that this amount can be expressed as S_T minus the payoff of the call implicitly written by the lender and held by the borrower. Panel C shows it also can be viewed as a receipt of L dollars minus the proceeds of a put option.

Leveraged Equity and Risky Debt

Investors holding stock in incorporated firms are protected by limited liability, which means that if the firm cannot pay its debts, the firm's creditors may attach only the firm's assets and may not sue the corporation's equityholders for further payment. In effect, any time the corporation borrows money, the maximum possible collateral for the loan is the total of the firm's assets. If the firm declares bankruptcy, we can interpret this as an admission that the assets of the firm are insufficient to satisfy the claims against it. The corporation may discharge its obligations by transferring ownership of the firm's assets to the creditors.

Just as is true for nonrecourse collateralized loans, the required payment to the creditors represents the exercise price of the implicit option, while the value of the firm is the underlying asset. The equityholders have a put option to transfer their ownership claims on the firm to the creditors in return for the face value of the firm's debt.

Alternatively, we may view the equityholders as retaining a call option. They have, in effect, already transferred their ownership claim to the firm to the creditors but have retained the right to reacquire the ownership claim by paying off the loan. Hence, the equityholders have the option to "buy back" the firm for a specified price, or they have a call option.

The significance of this observation is that analysts can value corporate bonds using option-pricing techniques. The default premium required of risky debt in principle can be estimated using option valuation models. We will consider some of these models in the next chapter.

15.4 EXOTIC OPTIONS

Investors clearly value the portfolio strategies made possible by trading options; this is reflected in the heavy trading volume in these markets and their tremendous success. Success breeds imitation, and in recent years we have witnessed tremendous innovation in the range of option instruments available to investors. Part of this innovation has occurred in the market for customized options, which now trade in active over-the-counter markets. Many of these options have terms that would have been highly unusual even a few years ago; they therefore are called *exotic options.* In this section, we will survey a few of the more interesting variants of these new instruments.

FIGURE 15.13

Collateralized loan

A: Payoff to collateralized loan

B: Lender can be viewed as collecting the collateral from the borrower but issuing an option to the borrower to call back the collateral for the face value of the loan

C: Lender can be viewed as collecting a risk-free loan from the borrower but issuing a put to the borrower to sell the collateral for the face value of the loan

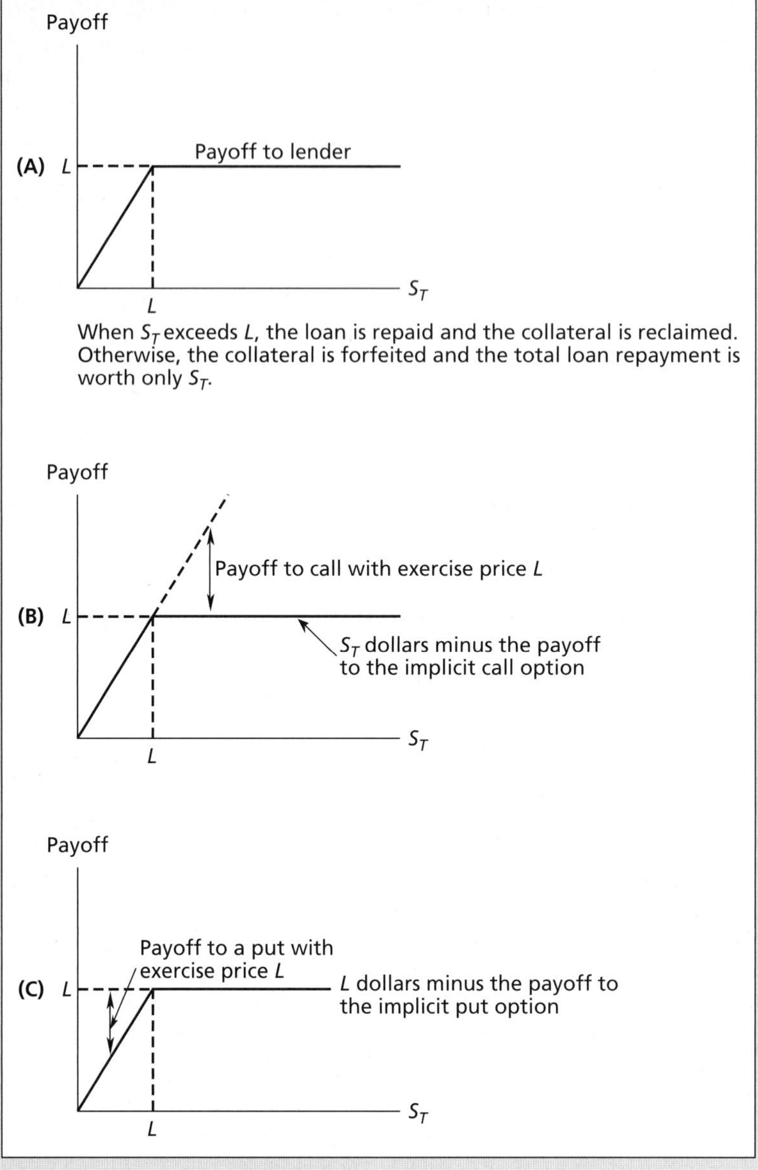

Asian Options

You already have been introduced to American and European options. *Asian options* are options with payoffs that depend on the average (rather than final) price of the underlying asset during at least some portion of the life of the option. For example, an Asian call option may have a payoff equal to the average stock price over the last three months minus the exercise price, if that value is positive or zero. These options may be of interest to firms that wish to hedge a profit stream that depends on the average price of a commodity over some period of time.

Currency-Translated Options

Currency-translated options have either asset or exercise prices denominated in a foreign currency. A good example of such an option is the *quanto,* which allows an investor to fix in advance the exchange rate at which an investment in a foreign currency can be converted back into dollars. The right to translate a fixed amount of foreign currency into dollars at a given exchange rate is a simple foreign exchange option. Quantos are more interesting, however, because the amount of currency that will be translated into dollars depends on the investment performance of the foreign security. Therefore, a quanto in effect provides a *random number* of options.

Digital Options

Digital options, also called *binary* or "bet" options, have fixed payoffs that depend on whether a condition is satisfied by the price of the underlying asset. For example, a binary call option might pay off a fixed amount of $100 if the stock price at expiration exceeds the exercise price. The Chicago Board of Options Exchange lists binary options on the S&P 500, but, to date, trading volume has been limited.

SUMMARY

- A call option is the right to buy an asset at an agreed-upon exercise price. A put option is the right to sell an asset at a given exercise price.
- American-style options allow exercise on or before the exercise date. European-style options allow exercise only on the expiration date. Most traded options are American in nature.
- Options are traded on stocks, stock indexes, foreign currencies, fixed-income securities, and several futures contracts.
- Options can be used either to lever up an investor's exposure to an asset price or to provide insurance against volatility of asset prices. Popular option strategies include covered calls, protective puts, straddles, and spreads.
- Many commonly traded securities embody option characteristics. Examples of these securities are callable bonds, convertible bonds, and warrants. Other arrangements, such as collateralized loans and limited-liability borrowing, can be analyzed as conveying implicit options to one or more parties.

KEY TERMS

American option, 490
at the money, 488
call option, 487
collar, 503
covered call, 500
European option, 490
exercise price, 487
in the money, 488
out of the money, 488
premium, 487
protective put, 497
put option, 487
risk management, 497
spread, 502
straddle, 502
strike price, 487
warrant, 508

KEY FORMULAS

$$\text{Payoff to call option} = \begin{cases} S - X & \text{if } S > X \\ 0 & \text{if } S \leq X \end{cases}$$

$$\text{Payoff to put option} = \begin{cases} 0 & \text{if } S_T > X \\ X - S_T & \text{if } S_T \leq X \end{cases}$$

PROBLEM SETS

Select problems are available in McGraw-Hill's *Connect Finance.* Please see the Supplements section of the book's frontmatter for more information.

Basic

1. We said that options can be used either to scale up or reduce overall portfolio risk. What are some examples of risk-increasing and risk-reducing options strategies? Explain each. *(LO 15-2)*

www.mhhe.com/bkm

2. Why do you think the most actively traded options tend to be the ones that are near the money? ***(LO 15-1)***
3. The following price quotations are for exchange-listed options on Primo Corporation common stock.

Company	Strike	Expiration	Call	Put
Primo 61.12	55	Feb	7.25	.48

   With transaction costs ignored, how much would a buyer have to pay for one call option contract? ***(LO 15-1)***
4. Turn back to Figure 15.1, which lists the prices of various IBM options. Use the data in the figure to calculate the payoff and the profits for investments in each of the following January 2012 expiration options, assuming that the stock price on the expiration date is $165. ***(LO 15-1)***
   a. Call option, $X = 160$
   b. Put option, $X = 160$
   c. Call option, $X = 165$
   d. Put option, $X = 165$
   e. Call option, $X = 170$
   f. Put option, $X = 170$
5. You purchase one IBM September 160 put contract for a premium of $2.62. What is your maximum possible profit? (See Figure 15.1.) ***(LO 15-1)***
6. An investor buys a call at a price of $4.50 with an exercise price of $40. At what stock price will the investor break even on the purchase of the call? ***(LO 15-1)***
7. You establish a straddle on Walmart using September call and put options with a strike price of $50. The call premium is $4.25 and the put premium is $5. ***(LO 15-2)***
   a. What is the most you can lose on this position?
   b. What will be your profit or loss if Walmart is selling for $58 in September?
   c. At what stock prices will you break even on the straddle?
8. The following diagram shows the value of a put option at expiration:

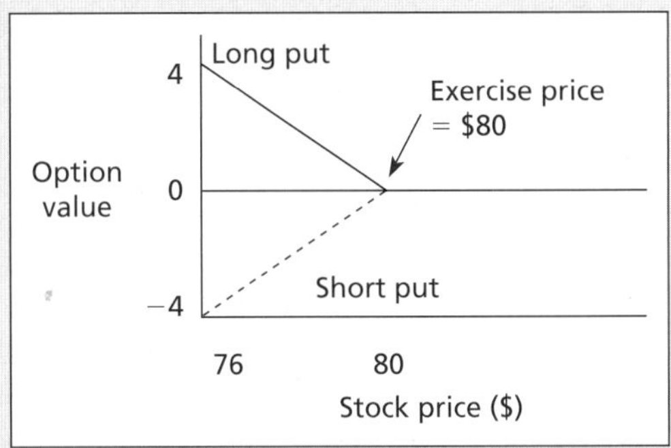

   Ignoring transaction costs, which of the following statements about the value of the put option at expiration is *true*? ***(LO 15-1)***
   a. The expiration value of the short position in the put is $4 if the stock price is $76.
   b. The expiration value of the long position in the put is −$4 if the stock price is $76.
   c. The long put has a positive expiration value when the stock price is below $80.
   d. The value of the short position in the put is zero for stock prices equaling or exceeding $76.

Intermediate

9. You are a portfolio manager who uses options positions to customize the risk profile of your clients. In each case, what strategy is best given your client's objective? ***(LO 15-2)***

a.
- Performance to date: Up 16%.
- Client objective: Earn at least 15%.
- Your scenario: Good chance of large stock price gains or large losses between now and end of year.
  - i. Long straddle
  - ii. Long bullish spread
  - iii. Short straddle

b.
- Performance to date: Up 16%.
- Client objective: Earn at least 15%.
- Your Scenario: Good chance of large stock price losses between now and end of year.
  - i. Long put options
  - ii. Short call options
  - iii. Long call options

10. An investor purchases a stock for $38 and a put for $.50 with a strike price of $35. The investor sells a call for $.50 with a strike price of $40. What is the maximum profit and loss for this position? Draw the profit and loss diagram for this strategy as a function of the stock price at expiration. ***(LO 15-1)***

11. Imagine that you are holding 5,000 shares of stock, currently selling at $40 per share. You are ready to sell the shares but would prefer to put off the sale until next year due to tax reasons. If you continue to hold the shares until January, however, you face the risk that the stock will drop in value before year-end. You decide to use a collar to limit downside risk without laying out a good deal of additional funds. January call options with a strike price of $45 are selling at $2, and January puts with a strike price of $35 are selling at $3. What will be the value of your portfolio in January (net of the proceeds from the options) if the stock price ends up at (*a*) $30? (*b*) $40? (*c*) $50? Compare these proceeds to what you would realize if you simply continued to hold the shares. ***(LO 15-2)***

12. Suppose you think FedEx stock is going to appreciate substantially in value in the next year. Say the stock's current price, S_0, is $100, and the call option expiring in one year has an exercise price, X, of $100 and is selling at a price, C, of $10. With $10,000 to invest, you are considering three alternatives:
    a. Invest all $10,000 in the stock, buying 100 shares.
    b. Invest all $10,000 in 1,000 options (10 contracts).
    c. Buy 100 options (one contract) for $1,000 and invest the remaining $9,000 in a money market fund paying 4% interest annually.

    What is your rate of return for each alternative for four stock prices one year from now? Summarize your results in the table and diagram below. ***(LO 15-1)***

Rate of return on investment

	Price of Stock 1 Year from Now			
	$80	**$100**	**$110**	**$120**
a. All stocks (100 shares)				
b. All options (1,000 shares)				
c. Bills + 100 options				

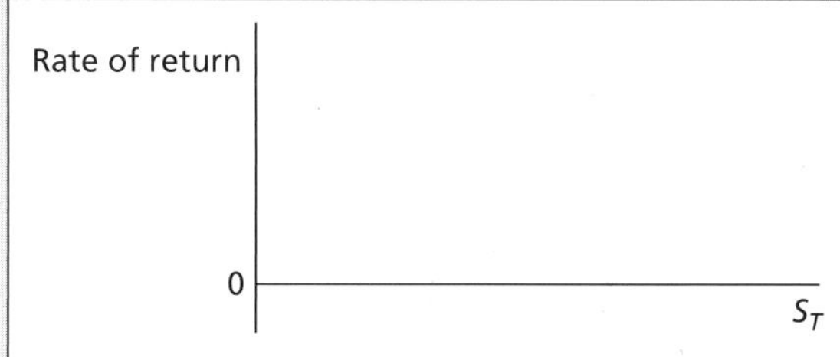

13. The common stock of the P.U.T.T. Corporation has been trading in a narrow price range for the past month, and you are convinced it is going to break far out of that range in the next three months. You do not know whether it will go up or down, however. The current price of the stock is $100 per share, the price of a three-month call option with an exercise price of $100 is $10, and a put with the same expiration date and exercise price costs $7. ***(LO 15-2)***
    a. What would be a simple options strategy to exploit your conviction about the stock price's future movements?
    b. How far would the price have to move in either direction for you to make a profit on your initial investment?
14. The common stock of the C.A.L.L. Corporation has been trading in a narrow range around $50 per share for months, and you believe it is going to stay in that range for the next three months. The price of a three-month put option with an exercise price of $50 is $4, and a call with the same expiration date and exercise price sells for $7. ***(LO 15-2)***
    a. What would be a simple options strategy using a put and a call to exploit your conviction about the stock price's future movement?
    b. What is the most money you can make on this position? How far can the stock price move in either direction before you lose money?
    c. How can you create a position involving a put, a call, and riskless lending that would have the same payoff structure as the stock at expiration? The stock will pay no dividends in the next three months. What is the net cost of establishing that position now?
15. Joseph Jones, a manager at Computer Science, Inc. (CSI), received 10,000 shares of company stock as part of his compensation package. The stock currently sells at $40 a share. Joseph would like to defer selling the stock until the next tax year. In January, however, he will need to sell all his holdings to provide for a down payment on his new house. Joseph is worried about the price risk involved in keeping his shares. At current prices, he would receive $40,000 for the stock. If the value of his stock holdings falls below $35,000, his ability to come up with the necessary down payment would be jeopardized. On the other hand, if the stock value rises to $45,000, he would be able to maintain a small cash reserve even after making the down payment. Joseph considers three investment strategies:
    a. Strategy A is to write January call options on the CSI shares with strike price $45. These calls are currently selling for $3 each.
    b. Strategy B is to buy January put options on CSI with strike price $35. These options also sell for $3 each.
    c. Strategy C is to establish a zero-cost collar by writing the January calls and buying the January puts.

    Evaluate each of these strategies with respect to Joseph's investment goals. What are the advantages and disadvantages of each? Which would you recommend? ***(LO 15-2)***
16. *a.* A butterfly spread is the purchase of one call at exercise price X_1, the sale of two calls at exercise price X_2, and the purchase of one call at exercise price X_3. X_1 is less than X_2, and X_2 is less than X_3 by equal amounts, and all calls have the same expiration date. Graph the payoff diagram to this strategy.
    b. A vertical combination is the purchase of a call with exercise price X_2 and a put with exercise price X_1, with X_2 greater than X_1. Graph the payoff to this strategy. ***(LO 15-2)***
17. A bearish spread is the purchase of a call with exercise price X_2 and the sale of a call with exercise price X_1, with X_2 greater than X_1. Graph the payoff to this strategy and compare it to Figure 15.10. ***(LO 15-2)***
18. You are attempting to formulate an investment strategy. On the one hand, you think there is great upward potential in the stock market and would like to participate in the upward move if it materializes. However, you are not able to afford substantial stock market losses and so cannot run the risk of a stock market collapse, which you

recognize is also possible. Your investment adviser suggests a protective put position: Buy shares in a market-index stock fund *and* put options on those shares with three-months until expiration and exercise price of $1,040. The stock index is currently at $1,200. However, your uncle suggests you instead buy a three-month call option on the index fund with exercise price $1,120 and buy three-month T-bills with face value $1,120. ***(LO 15-2)***

a. On the same graph, draw the *payoffs* to each of these strategies as a function of the stock fund value in three months. (*Hint*: Think of the options as being on one "share" of the stock index fund, with the current price of each share of the index equal to $1,200.)

b. Which portfolio must require a greater initial outlay to establish? (*Hint*: Does either portfolio provide a final payoff that is always at least as great as the payoff of the other portfolio?)

c. Suppose the market prices of the securities are as follows:

Stock fund	$1,200
T-bill (face value $1,120)	1,080
Call (exercise price $1,120)	160
Put (exercise price $1,040)	8

Make a table of profits realized for each portfolio for the following values of the stock price in three months: S_T = $0, $1,040, $1,120, $1,200, and $1,280. Graph the profits to each portfolio as a function of S_T on a single graph.

d. Which strategy is riskier? Which should have a higher beta?

19. Use the spreadsheet from the Excel Application boxes on spreads and straddles (available at **www.mhhe.com/bkm;** link to Chapter 15 material) to answer these questions. ***(LO 15-1)***

Please visit us at www.mhhe.com/bkm

a. Plot the payoff and profit diagrams to a straddle position with an exercise (strike) price of $130. Assume the options are priced as they are in the Excel Application.

b. Plot the payoff and profit diagrams to a spread position with exercise (strike) prices of $120 and $130. Assume the options are priced as they are in the Excel Application.

20. In what ways is owning a corporate bond similar to writing a put option? A call option? ***(LO 15-3)***

21. An executive compensation scheme might provide a manager a bonus of $1,000 for every dollar by which the company's stock price exceeds some cutoff level. In what way is this arrangement equivalent to issuing the manager call options on the firm's stock? ***(LO 15-3)***

22. Consider the following options portfolio: You write a January 2012 expiration call option on IBM with exercise price $170. You also write a January expiration IBM put option with exercise price $165. ***(LO 15-2)***

a. Graph the payoff of this portfolio at option expiration as a function of IBM's stock price at that time.

b. What will be the profit/loss on this position if IBM is selling at $167 on the option expiration date? What if IBM is selling at $175? Use *The Wall Street Journal* listing from Figure 15.1 to answer this question.

c. At what two stock prices will you just break even on your investment?

d. What kind of "bet" is this investor making; that is, what must this investor believe about IBM's stock price in order to justify this position?

23. Consider the following portfolio. You *write* a put option with exercise price $90 and *buy* a put with the same expiration date with exercise price $95. ***(LO 15-2)***

a. Plot the value of the portfolio at the expiration date of the options.

b. On the same graph, plot the profit of the portfolio. Which option must cost more?

www.mhhe.com/bkm

24. A put option with strike price \$60 trading on the Acme options exchange sells for \$2. To your amazement, a put on the firm with the same expiration selling on the Apex options exchange but with strike price \$62 also sells for \$2. If you plan to hold the options position until expiration, devise a zero-net-investment arbitrage strategy to exploit the pricing anomaly. Draw the profit diagram at expiration for your position. ***(LO 15-1)***
25. You buy a share of stock, write a one-year call option with $X = \$10$, and buy a one-year put option with $X = \$10$. Your net outlay to establish the entire portfolio is \$9.50. What must be the risk-free interest rate? The stock pays no dividends. ***(LO 15-1)***
26. Joe Finance has just purchased a stock-index fund, currently selling at \$1,200 per share. To protect against losses, Joe plans to purchase an at-the-money European put option on the fund for \$60, with exercise price \$1,200, and three-month time to expiration. Sally Calm, Joe's financial adviser, points out that Joe is spending a lot of money on the put. She notes that three-month puts with strike prices of \$1,170 cost only \$45, and suggests that Joe use the cheaper put. ***(LO 15-2)***
    a. Analyze Joe's and Sally's strategies by drawing the *profit* diagrams for the stock-plus-put positions for various values of the stock fund in three months.
    b. When does Sally's strategy do better? When does it do worse?
    c. Which strategy entails greater systematic risk?
27. You write a call option with $X = \$50$ and buy a call with $X = \$60$. The options are on the same stock and have the same expiration date. One of the calls sells for \$3; the other sells for \$9. ***(LO 15-2)***
    a. Draw the *payoff* graph for this strategy at the option expiration date.
    b. Draw the *profit* graph for this strategy.
    c. What is the break-even point for this strategy? Is the investor bullish or bearish on the stock?
28. Devise a portfolio using only call options and shares of stock with the following value (payoff) at the option expiration date. If the stock price is currently \$53, what kind of bet is the investor making? ***(LO 15-2)***

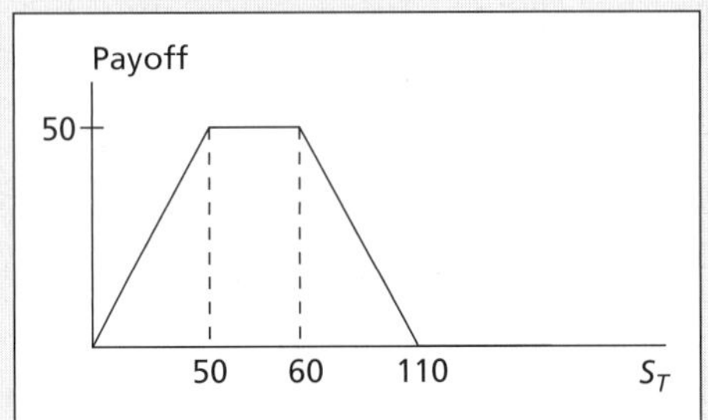

Challenge

29. The agricultural price support system guarantees farmers a minimum price for their output. Describe the program provisions as an option. What is the asset? The exercise price? ***(LO 15-3)***

CFA Problems

1. Which one of the following statements about the value of a call option at expiration is *false?* ***(LO 15-1)***
    a. A short position in a call option will result in a loss if the stock price exceeds the exercise price.
    b. The value of a long position equals zero or the stock price minus the exercise price, whichever is higher.
    c. The value of a long position equals zero or the exercise price minus the stock price, whichever is higher.
    d. A short position in a call option has a zero value for all stock prices equal to or less than the exercise price.

2. Donna Donie, CFA, has a client who believes the common stock price of TRT Materials (currently $58 per share) could move substantially in either direction in reaction to an expected court decision involving the company. The client currently owns no TRT shares, but asks Donie for advice about implementing a strangle strategy to capitalize on the possible stock price movement. A strangle is a portfolio of a put and a call with different exercise prices but the same expiration date. Donie gathers the following TRT option price data: ***(LO 15-2)***

Characteristic	Call Option	Put Option
Price	$5	$4
Strike price	$60	$55
Time to expiration	90 days from now	90 days from now

a. Recommend whether Donie should choose a long strangle strategy or a short strangle strategy to achieve the client's objective.
b. Calculate, at expiration for the appropriate strangle strategy in part (*a*), the:
i. Maximum possible loss per share.
ii. Maximum possible gain per share.
iii. Break-even stock price(s).

3. A member of an investment committee interested in learning more about fixed-income investment procedures recalls that a fixed-income manager recently stated that derivative instruments could be used to control portfolio duration, saying, "A futures-like position can be created in a portfolio by using put and call options on Treasury bonds." ***(LO 15-3)***
a. Identify the options market exposure or exposures that create a "futures-like position" similar to being long Treasury-bond futures. Explain why the position you created is similar to being long Treasury-bond futures.
b. Explain in which direction and why the exposure(s) you identified in part (*a*) would affect portfolio duration.
c. Assume that a pension plan's investment policy requires the fixed-income manager to hold portfolio duration within a narrow range. Identify and briefly explain circumstances or transactions in which the use of Treasury-bond futures would be helpful in managing a fixed-income portfolio when duration is constrained.

4. Suresh Singh, CFA, is analyzing a convertible bond. The characteristics of the bond and the underlying common stock are given in the following exhibit:

Convertible Bond Characteristics	
Par value	$1,000
Annual coupon rate (annual pay)	6.5%
Conversion ratio	22
Market price	105% of par value
Straight value	99% of par value
Underlying Stock Characteristics	
Current market price	$40 per share
Annual cash dividend	$1.20 per share

Compute the bond's: ***(LO 15-3)***
a. Conversion value.
b. Market conversion price.

www.mhhe.com/bkm

5. Rich McDonald, CFA, is evaluating his investment alternatives in Ytel Incorporated by analyzing a Ytel convertible bond and Ytel common equity. Characteristics of the two securities are given in the following exhibit: ***(LO 15-3)***

Characteristics	Convertible Bond	Common Equity
Par value	$1,000	—
Coupon (annual payment)	4%	—
Current market price	$980	$35 per share
Straight bond value	$925	—
Conversion ratio	25	—
Conversion option	At any time	—
Dividend	—	$0
Expected market price in 1 year	$1,125	$45 per share

a. Calculate, based on the exhibit, the
   i. Current market conversion price for the Ytel convertible bond.
   ii. Expected one-year rate of return for the Ytel convertible bond.
   iii. Expected one-year rate of return for the Ytel common equity.

One year has passed and Ytel's common equity price has increased to $51 per share. Also, over the year, the yield to maturity on Ytel's nonconvertible bonds of the same maturity increased, while credit spreads remained unchanged.

b. Name the two components of the convertible bond's value. Indicate whether the value of each component should decrease, stay the same, or increase in response to the:
   i. Increase in Ytel's common equity price.
   ii. Increase in bond yield.

WEB *master*

1. Use data from **finance.yahoo.com** to answer the following questions. In the *Get Quotes* box, enter stock symbol "GE" for General Electric. Go to the S&P Stock Reports section for GE.
   a. Locate the 52-week range for GE.
   b. At what price did GE last trade?
   c. Click on the link to *Options* on the left side of the Yahoo! Finance screen. Choose an expiration date three months in the future, and then choose one of the call options listed by selecting an exercise (strike) price. What is the last price (premium) shown for the call option?
   d. Is the call option in the money?
   e. Draw a graph that shows the payoff and the profit to the holder of this call option over a range of prices, including the prices you found in the 52-week range of the S&P Stock Report.
   f. Repeat the steps for a put option on GE with the same expiration date and the same strike price.
2. Go to **www.nasdaq.com** and select *IBM* in the quote section. Once you have the information quote, request the information on options. You will be able to access the prices for the calls and puts that are closest to the money. For example, if the price of IBM is $96.72, you will use the options with the $95 exercise price. Use near-term options. For example, in February, you would select April and July expirations.
   a. What are the prices for the put and call with the nearest expiration date?
   b. What would be the cost of a straddle using these options?
   c. At expiration, what would be the break-even stock prices for the straddle?
   d. What would be the percentage increase or decrease in the stock price required to break even?

e. What are the prices for the put and call with a later expiration date?
f. What would be the cost of a straddle using the later expiration date? At expiration, what would be the break-even stock prices for the straddle?
g. What would be the percentage increase or decrease in the stock price required to break even?

SOLUTIONS TO CONCEPT checks

15.1 *a.* Proceeds $= S_T - X = S_T -$ \$165 if this value is positive; otherwise, the call expires worthless. Profit = Proceeds − Price of call option = Proceeds − \$8.70.

	S_T = \$155	S_T = \$175
Proceeds	\$0	\$10
Profits	−8.70	1.30

b. Proceeds $= X - S_T =$ \$165 $- S_T$ if this value is positive; otherwise, the put expires worthless. Profit = Proceeds − Price of put option = Proceeds − \$7.

	S_T = \$155	S_T = \$175
Proceeds	\$10	\$0
Profits	3	−7

15.2 *a.*

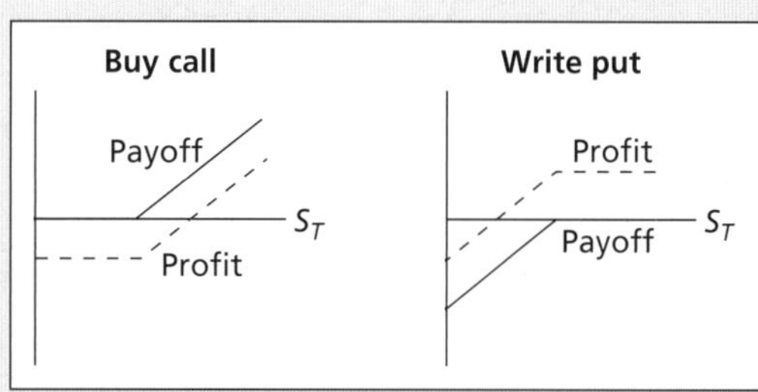

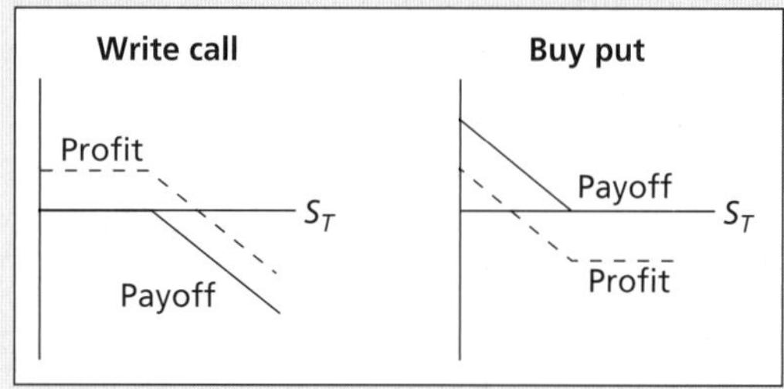

b. The payoffs and profits to both buying calls and writing puts generally are higher when the stock price is higher. In this sense, both positions are bullish. Both involve potentially taking delivery of the stock. However, the call holder will *choose* to take delivery when the stock price is high, while the put writer *is obligated* to take delivery when the stock price is low.

c. The payoffs and profits to both writing calls and buying puts generally are higher when the stock price is lower. In this sense, both positions are bearish. Both involve potentially making delivery of the stock. However, the put holder will *choose* to make delivery when the stock price is low, while the call writer *is obligated* to make delivery when the stock price is high.

15.3

Payoff to a Strip		
	$S_T \leq X$	$S_T > X$
2 Puts	$2(X - S_T)$	0
1 Call	0	$S_T - X$

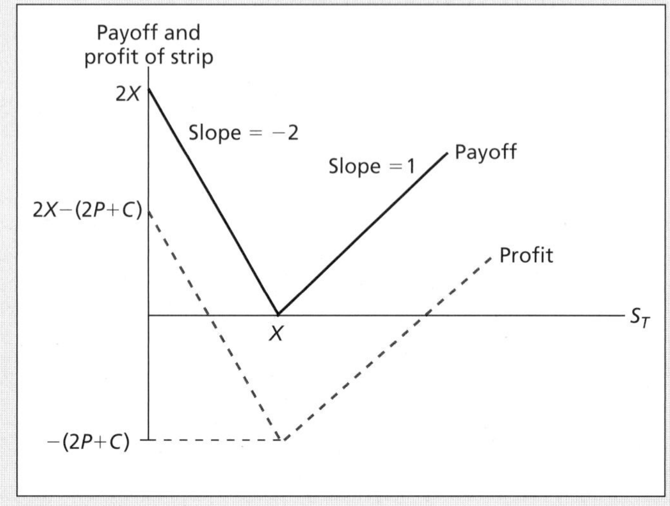

Payoff to a Strap		
	$S_T \leq X$	$S_T > X$
1 Put	$X - S_T$	0
2 Calls	0	$2(S_T - X)$

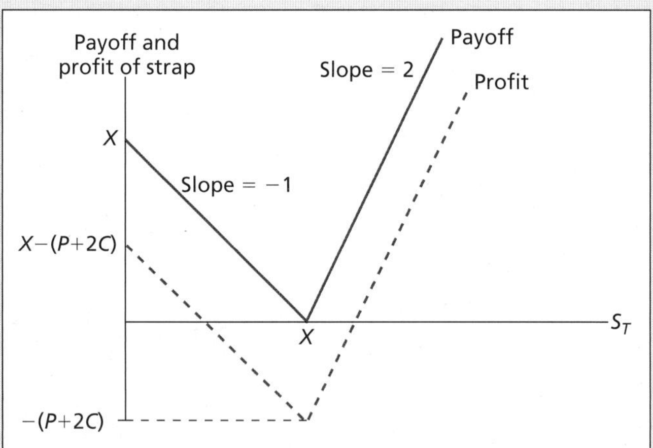

15.4 The payoff table on a per-share basis is as follows:

	$S_T < 60$	$60 < S_T < 80$	$S_T > 80$
Buy put ($X = 60$)	$60 - S_T$	0	0
Share	S_T	S_T	S_T
Write call ($X = 80$)	0	0	$-(S_T - 80)$
Total	60	S_T	80

The graph of the payoff follows. If you multiply the per-share values by 2,000, you will see that the collar provides a minimum payoff of $120,000 (representing a maximum loss of $20,000) and a maximum payoff of $160,000 (which is the cost of the house).

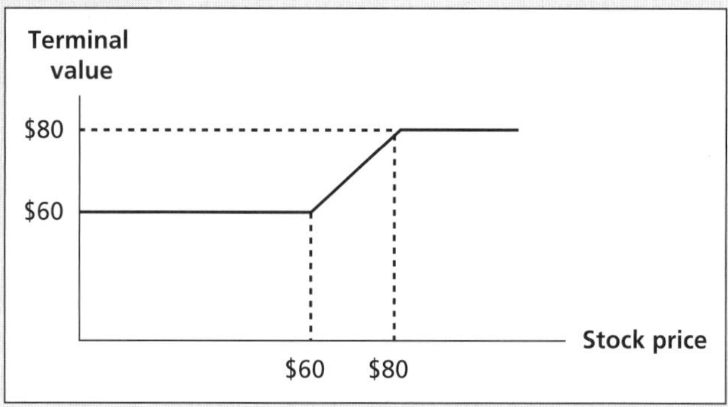

15.5 The covered call strategy would consist of a straight bond with a call written on the bond. The payoff value of the covered call position at option expiration as a function of the value of the straight bond is given in the following figure, and is virtually identical to the value of the callable bond in Figure 15.11.

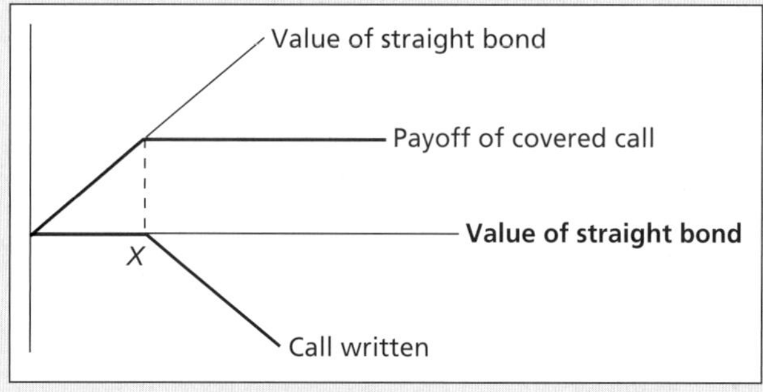

15.6 The call option is less valuable as call protection is expanded. Therefore, the coupon rate need not be as high.

15.7 Lower. Investors will accept a lower coupon rate in return for the conversion option.

Chapter 16

Option Valuation

Learning Objectives:

LO16-1 Identify the features of an option that affect its market value.

LO16-2 Compute an option value in two-scenario and binomial models of the economy.

LO16-3 Compute the Black-Scholes value and implied volatility of an option.

LO16-4 Compute the proper relationship between call and put prices.

LO16-5 Compute the hedge ratio of an option, and use that ratio to manage risk.

In the previous chapter, we examined option markets and strategies. We ended by noting that many securities contain embedded options that affect both their values and their risk-return characteristics. In this chapter, we turn our attention to option valuation issues. Understanding most of these models requires considerable mathematical and statistical background. Still, many of their ideas and insights can be demonstrated in simple examples, and we will concentrate on these.

We start with a discussion of the factors that ought to affect option prices. After this qualitative discussion, we present a simple "two-state" quantitative option valuation model and show how we can generalize it into a useful and accurate pricing tool. Next, we move on to one particular option valuation formula, the famous Black-Scholes model. Option-pricing models allow us to "back out" market estimates of stock price volatility, and we will examine these estimates of implied volatility.

Next we turn to some of the more important applications of option-pricing theory in risk management. Finally, we take a brief look at some of the empirical evidence on option pricing and the implications of that evidence concerning the limitations of the Black-Scholes model.

Related websites for this chapter are available at www.mhhe.com/bkm.

16.1 OPTION VALUATION: INTRODUCTION

Intrinsic and Time Values

Consider a call option that is out of the money at the moment, with the stock price below the exercise price. This does not mean the option is valueless. Even though immediate exercise would be unprofitable, the call retains a positive value because there is always a chance the stock price will increase sufficiently by the expiration date to allow for profitable exercise. If not, the worst that can happen is that the option will expire with zero value.

The value $S_0 - X$ is sometimes called the **intrinsic value** of an in-the-money call option because it gives the payoff that could be obtained by immediate exercise. Intrinsic value is set equal to zero for out-of-the-money or at-the-money options. The difference between the actual call price and the intrinsic value is commonly called the **time value** of the option.

intrinsic value

Stock price minus exercise price, or the cash flow that could be attained by immediate exercise of an in-the-money call option.

time value

Difference between an option's price and its intrinsic value.

Time value is an unfortunate choice of terminology because it may confuse the option's time value with the time value of money. Time value in the options context simply refers to the difference between the option's price and the value the option would have if it were expiring immediately. It is the part of the option's value that may be attributed to the fact that it still has positive time to expiration.

Most of an option's time value typically is a type of "volatility value." As long as the option holder can choose not to exercise, the payoff cannot be worse than zero. Even if a call option is out of the money now, it still will sell for a positive price because it offers the potential for a profit if the stock price increases, while imposing no risk of additional loss should the stock price fall. The volatility value lies in the right *not* to exercise the option if that action would be unprofitable. The option to exercise, as opposed to the obligation to exercise, provides insurance against poor stock price performance.

As the stock price increases substantially, it becomes more likely that the call option will be exercised by expiration. In this case, with exercise all but assured, the volatility value becomes minimal. As the stock price gets ever larger, the option value approaches the "adjusted" intrinsic value—the stock price minus the present value of the exercise price, $S_0 - \text{PV}(X)$.

Why should this be? If you *know* the option will be exercised and the stock purchased for X dollars, it is as though you own the stock already. The stock certificate might as well be sitting in your safe-deposit box now, as it will be there in only a few months. You just haven't paid for it yet. The present value of your obligation is the present value of X, so the present value of the net payoff of the call option is $S_0 - \text{PV}(X)$.[1]

Figure 16.1 illustrates the call option valuation function. The value curve shows that when the stock price is low, the option is nearly worthless because there is almost no chance that it will be exercised. When the stock price is very high, the option value approaches adjusted intrinsic value. In the midrange case, where the option is approximately at the money, the option curve diverges from the straight lines corresponding to adjusted intrinsic value. This is because, while exercise today would have a negligible (or negative) payoff, the volatility value of the option is quite high in this region.

The call option always increases in value with the stock price. The slope is greatest, however, when the option is deep in the money. In this case, exercise is all but assured, and the option increases in price one-for-one with the stock price.

Determinants of Option Values

We can identify at least six factors that should affect the value of a call option: the stock price, the exercise price, the volatility of the stock price, the time to expiration, the interest rate,

[1]This discussion presumes the stock pays no dividends until after option expiration. If the stock does pay dividends before expiration, then there *is* a reason you would care about getting the stock now rather than at expiration—getting it now entitles you to the interim dividend payments. In this case, the adjusted intrinsic value must subtract the value of the dividends the stock will pay out before the call is exercised. Adjusted intrinsic value would more generally be defined as $S_0 - \text{PV}(X) - \text{PV}(D)$, where D represents dividends to be paid before option expiration.

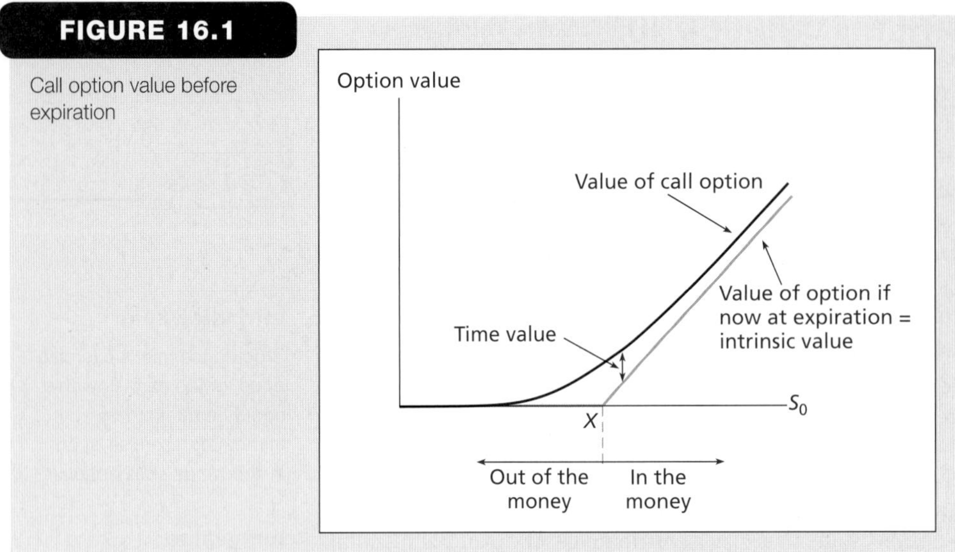

FIGURE 16.1 Call option value before expiration

and the dividend rate of the stock. The call option should increase in value with the stock price and decrease in value with the exercise price because the payoff to a call, if exercised, equals $S_T - X$. The magnitude of the expected payoff from the call increases with the difference $S_0 - X$.

Call option value also increases with the volatility of the underlying stock price. To see why, consider circumstances where possible stock prices at expiration may range from \$10 to \$50 compared to a situation where stock prices may range only from \$20 to \$40. In both cases, the expected, or average, stock price will be \$30. Suppose the exercise price on a call option is also \$30. What are the option payoffs?

High-Volatility Scenario					
Stock price	\$10	\$20	\$30	\$40	\$50
Option payoff	0	0	0	10	20
Low-Volatility Scenario					
Stock price	\$20	\$25	\$30	\$35	\$40
Option payoff	0	0	0	5	10

If each outcome is equally likely, with probability .2, the expected payoff to the option under high-volatility conditions will be \$6, but under the low-volatility conditions, the expected payoff to the call option is half as much, only \$3.

Despite the fact that the average stock price in each scenario is \$30, the average option payoff is greater in the high-volatility scenario. The source of this extra value is the limited loss an option holder can suffer, or the volatility value of the call. No matter how far below \$30 the stock price drops, the option holder will get zero. Obviously, extremely poor stock price performance is no worse for the call option holder than moderately poor performance.

In the case of good stock performance, however, the call option will expire in the money, and it will be more profitable the higher the stock price. Thus, extremely good stock outcomes can improve the option payoff without limit, but extremely poor outcomes cannot worsen the payoff below zero. This asymmetry means volatility in the underlying stock price increases the expected payoff to the option, thereby enhancing its value.[2]

CONCEPT check 16.1 Should a put option increase in value with the volatility of the stock?

[2]You should be careful interpreting the relationship between volatility and option value. Neither the focus of this analysis on total (as opposed to systematic) volatility nor the conclusion that options buyers seem to like volatility contradicts modern portfolio theory. In conventional discounted cash flow analysis, we find the discount rate appropriate for a *given* distribution of future cash flows. Greater risk implies a higher discount rate and lower present value. Here, however, the cash flow from the *option* depends on the volatility of the *stock*. The option value increases not because traders like risk but because the expected cash flow to the option holder increases along with the volatility of the underlying asset.

TABLE 16.1 Determinants of call option values

If This Variable Increases	The Value of a Call Option
Stock price, S	Increases
Exercise price, X	Decreases
Volatility, σ	Increases
Time to expiration, T	Increases
Interest rate, r_f	Increases
Dividend payouts	Decreases

Similarly, longer time to expiration increases the value of a call option. For more distant expiration dates, there is more time for unpredictable future events to affect prices, and the range of likely stock prices increases. This has an effect similar to that of increased volatility. Moreover, as time to expiration lengthens, the present value of the exercise price falls, thereby benefiting the call option holder and increasing the option value. As a corollary to this issue, call option values are higher when interest rates rise (holding the stock price constant), because higher interest rates also reduce the present value of the exercise price.

Finally, the dividend payout policy of the firm affects option values. A high dividend payout policy puts a drag on the rate of growth of the stock price. For any expected total rate of return on the stock, a higher dividend yield must imply a lower expected rate of capital gain. This drag on stock appreciation decreases the potential payoff from the call option, thereby lowering the call value. Table 16.1 summarizes these relationships.

CONCEPT check 16.2

Prepare a table like Table 16.1 for the determinants of put option values. How should put values respond to increases in S, X, T, σ, r_f, and dividend payout?

16.2 BINOMIAL OPTION PRICING

Two-State Option Pricing

A complete understanding of commonly used option valuation formulas is difficult without a substantial mathematics background. Nevertheless, we can develop valuable insight into option valuation by considering a simple special case. Assume a stock price can take only two possible values at option expiration: The stock will either increase to a given higher price or decrease to a given lower price. Although this may seem an extreme simplification, it allows us to come closer to understanding more complicated and realistic models. Moreover, we can extend this approach to describe far more reasonable specifications of stock price behavior. In fact, several major financial firms employ variants of this simple model to value options and securities with optionlike features.

Suppose the stock now sells at $100, and the price will either increase by a factor of $u = 1.2$ to $120 ($u$ stands for "up") or fall by a factor of $d = .9$ to $90 ($d$ stands for "down") by year-end. A call option on the stock might specify an exercise price of $110 and a time to expiration of one year. The interest rate is 10%. At year-end, the payoff to the holder of the call option will be either zero, if the stock falls, or $10, if the stock price goes to $120.

These possibilities are illustrated by the following "value trees":

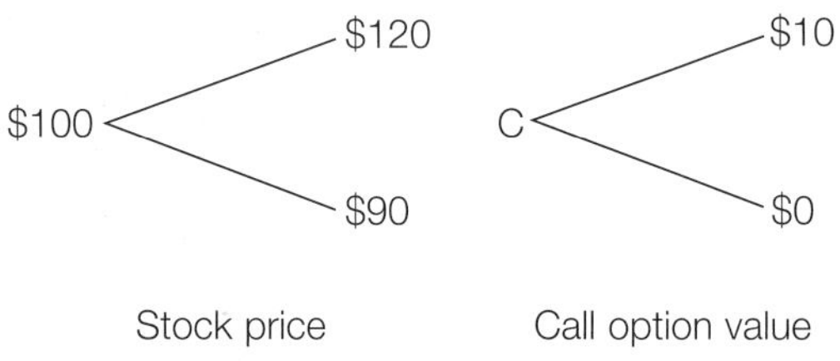

Compare this payoff to that of a portfolio consisting of one share of the stock and borrowing of \$81.82 at the interest rate of 10%. The payoff of this portfolio also depends on the stock price at year-end.

Value of stock at year-end	\$ 90	\$120
−Repayment of loan with interest	−90	−90
Total	\$ 0	\$ 30

We know the cash outlay to establish the portfolio is \$18.18: \$100 for the stock less the \$81.82 proceeds from borrowing. Therefore, the portfolio's value tree is

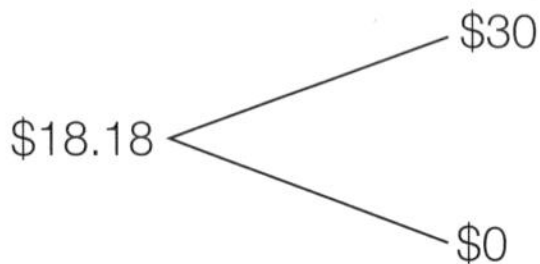

The payoff of this portfolio is exactly three times that of the call option for either value of the stock price. In other words, three call options will exactly replicate the payoff to the portfolio; it follows that three call options should have the same price as the cost of establishing the portfolio. Hence, the three calls should sell for the same price as the "replicating portfolio." Therefore,

$$3C = \$18.18$$

or each call should sell at $C = \$6.06$. Thus, given the stock price, exercise price, interest rate, and volatility of the stock price (as represented by the magnitude of the up or down movements), we can derive the fair value for the call option.

This valuation approach relies heavily on the notion of *replication.* With only two possible end-of-year values of the stock, the payoffs to the levered stock portfolio replicate the payoffs to three call options and so need to command the same market price. This notion of replication is behind most option-pricing formulas. For more complex price distributions for stocks, the replication technique is correspondingly more complex, but the principles remain the same.

One way to view the role of replication is to note that, using the numbers assumed for this example, a portfolio made up of one share of stock and three call options written is perfectly hedged. Its year-end value is independent of the ultimate stock price:

Stock value	\$90	\$120
−Obligations from 3 calls written	−0	−30
Net payoff	\$90	\$ 90

The investor has formed a riskless portfolio with a payout of \$90. Its value must be the present value of \$90, or \$90/1.10 = \$81.82. The value of the portfolio, which equals \$100 from the stock held long minus $3C$ from the three calls written, should equal \$81.82. Hence, $\$100 - 3C = \$81.82$, or $C = \$6.06$.

The ability to create a perfect hedge is the key to this argument. The hedge locks in the end-of-year payout, which therefore can be discounted using the *risk-free* interest rate. To find the value of the option in terms of the value of the stock, we do not need to know the option's or the stock's beta or expected rate of return. The perfect hedging, or replication, approach enables us to express the value of the option in terms of the current value of the stock without this information. With a hedged position, the final stock price does not affect the investor's payoff, so the stock's risk and return parameters have no bearing.

The hedge ratio of this example is one share of stock to three calls, or one-third. For every call option written, one-third share of stock must be held in the portfolio to hedge away risk.

This ratio has an easy interpretation in this context: It is the ratio of the range of the values of the option to those of the stock across the two possible outcomes. The stock, which originally sells for $S_0 = \$100$, will be worth either $d \times \$100 = \$90$ or $u \times \$100 = \$120$, for a range of \$30. If the stock price increases, the call will be worth $C_u = \$10$, whereas if the stock price decreases, the call will be worth $C_d = 0$, for a range of \$10. The ratio of ranges, \$10/\$30, is one-third, which is the hedge ratio we have established.

The hedge ratio equals the ratio of ranges because the option and stock are perfectly correlated in this two-state example. Because they are perfectly correlated, a perfect hedge requires that the option and stock be held in a fraction determined only by relative volatility.

We can generalize the hedge ratio for other two-state option problems as

$$H = \frac{C_u - C_d}{uS_0 - dS_0}$$

where C_u or C_d refers to the call option's value when the stock goes up or down, respectively, and uS_0 and dS_0 are the stock prices in the two states. The hedge ratio, H, is the ratio of the swings in the possible end-of-period values of the option and the stock. If the investor writes one option and holds H shares of stock, the value of the portfolio will be unaffected by the stock price. In this case, option pricing is easy: Simply set the value of the hedged portfolio equal to the present value of the known payoff.

Using our example, the option-pricing technique would proceed as follows:

1. Given the possible end-of-year stock prices, $uS_0 = \$120$ and $dS_0 = \$90$, and the exercise price of \$110, calculate that $C_u = \$10$ and $C_d = \$0$. The stock price range is \$30, while the option price range is \$10.
2. Find that the hedge ratio is \$10/\$30 = ⅓.
3. Find that a portfolio made up of ⅓ share with one written option would have an end-of-year value of \$30 with certainty.
4. Show that the present value of \$30 with a one-year interest rate of 10% is \$27.27.
5. Set the value of the hedged position equal to the present value of the certain payoff:

$$\tfrac{1}{3}S_0 - C_0 = \$27.27$$
$$\$33.33 - C_0 = \$27.27$$

6. Solve for the call's value, $C_0 = \$6.06$.

What if the option were overpriced, perhaps selling for \$6.50? Then you can make arbitrage profits. Here is how:

		Cash Flow in 1 Year for Each Possible Stock Price	
	Initial Cash Flow	S_1 = \$90	S_1 = \$120
1. Write 3 options	\$ 19.50	\$ 0	\$−30
2. Purchase 1 share	−100	90	120
3. Borrow \$80.50 at 10% interest; repay in 1 year	80.50	−88.55	−88.55
Total	\$ 0	\$ 1.45	\$ 1.45

Although the net initial investment is zero, the payoff in one year is positive and riskless. If the option were underpriced, one would simply reverse this arbitrage strategy: Buy the option, and sell the stock short to eliminate price risk. Note, by the way, that the present value of the profit to the above arbitrage strategy equals three times the amount by which the option is overpriced. The present value of the risk-free profit of \$1.45 at a 10% interest rate is \$1.32. With three options written in the strategy above, this translates to a profit of \$.44 per option, exactly the amount by which the option was overpriced: \$6.50 versus the "fair value" of \$6.06.

CONCEPT check 16.3

Suppose the call option had been underpriced, selling at \$5.50. Formulate the arbitrage strategy to exploit the mispricing, and show that it provides a riskless cash flow in one year of \$.6167 per option purchased. Compare the present value of this cash flow to the option mispricing.

Generalizing the Two-State Approach

Although the two-state stock price model seems simplistic, we can generalize it to incorporate more realistic assumptions. To start, suppose we were to break up the year into two six-month segments and then assert that over each half-year segment the stock price could take on two values. In this example, we will say it can increase 10% (i.e., $u = 1.10$) or decrease 5% (i.e., $d = .95$). A stock initially selling at \$100 could follow the following possible paths over the course of the year:

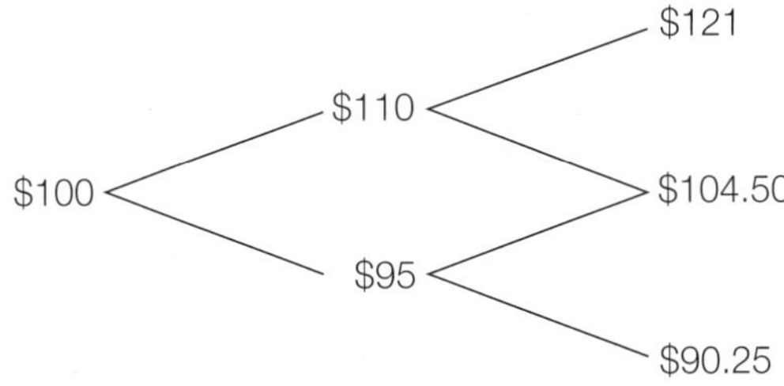

The midrange value of \$104.50 can be attained by two paths: an increase of 10% followed by a decrease of 5%, or a decrease of 5% followed by an increase of 10%.

There are now three possible end-of-year values for the stock and three for the option:

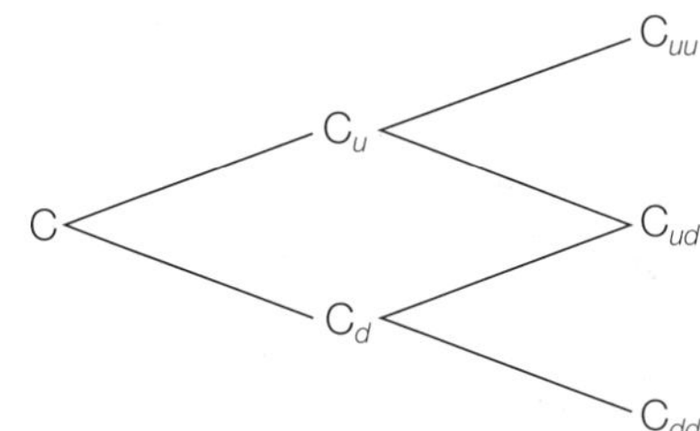

Using methods similar to those we followed above, we could value C_u from knowledge of C_{uu} and C_{ud}, then value C_d from knowledge of C_{du} and C_{dd}, and finally value C from knowledge of C_u and C_d. And there is no reason to stop at six-month intervals. We could next break the year into 4 three-month units, or 12 one-month units, or 365 one-day units, each of which would be posited to have a two-state process. Although the calculations become quite numerous and correspondingly tedious, they are easy to program into a computer, and such computer programs are used widely by participants in the options market.

EXAMPLE 16.1

Binomial Option Pricing

Suppose that the risk-free interest rate is 5% per six-month period and we wish to value a call option with exercise price \$110 on the stock described in the two-period price tree just above. We start by finding the value of C_u. From this point, the call can rise to an expiration-date value of C_{uu} = \$11 (since at this point the stock price is $u \times u \times S_0$ = \$121) or fall to a final value of $C_{ud} = 0$

(continued)

EXAMPLE 16.1

Binomial Option Pricing (concluded)

(since at this point the stock price is $u \times d \times S_0$ = \$104.50, which is less than the \$110 exercise price). Therefore, the hedge ratio at this point is

$$H = \frac{C_{uu} - C_{ud}}{uuS_0 - udS_0} = \frac{\$11 - 0}{\$121 - \$104.5} = \frac{2}{3}$$

Thus, the following portfolio will be worth \$209 at option expiration regardless of the ultimate stock price:

	udS_0 = \$104.50	uuS_0 = \$121
Buy 2 shares at price uS_0 = \$110	\$209	\$242
Write 3 calls at price C_u	0	−33
Total	\$209	\$209

The portfolio must have a current market value equal to the present value of \$209:

$$2 \times \$110 - 3C_u = \$209/1.05 = \$199.047$$

Solve to find that C_u = \$6.984.

Next we find the value of C_d. It is easy to see that this value must be zero. If we reach this point (corresponding to a stock price of \$95), the stock price at option expiration will be either \$104.50 or \$90.25; in both cases, the option will expire out of the money. (More formally, we could note that with $C_{ud} = C_{dd} = 0$, the hedge ratio is zero, and a portfolio of *zero* shares will replicate the payoff of the call!)

Finally, we solve for C by using the values of C_u and C_d. The following Concept Check leads you through the calculations that show the option value to be \$4.434.

CONCEPT check 16.4

Show that the initial value of the call option in Example 16.1 is \$4.434.

a. Confirm that the spread in option values is $C_u - C_d$ = \$6.984.
b. Confirm that the spread in stock values is $uS_0 - dS_0$ = \$15.
c. Confirm that the hedge ratio is .4656 shares purchased for each call written.
d. Demonstrate that the value in one period of a portfolio comprising .4656 shares and one call written is riskless.
e. Calculate the present value of this payoff.
f. Solve for the option value.

Making the Valuation Model Practical

As we break the year into progressively finer subintervals, the range of possible year-end stock prices expands. For example, when we increase the number of subperiods to three, the number of possible stock prices increases to four, as demonstrated in the following stock price tree:

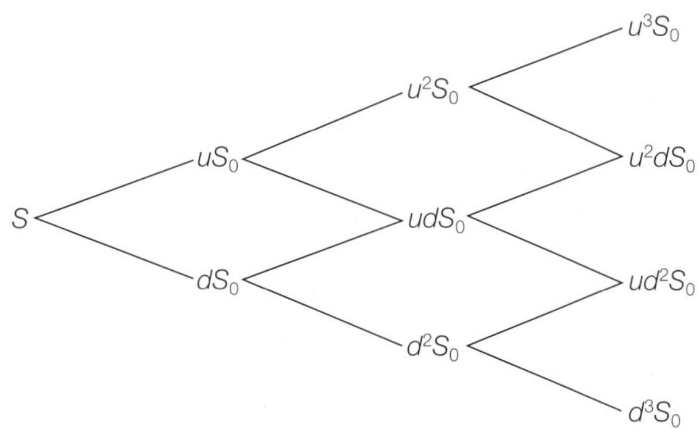

Thus, by allowing for an ever-greater number of subperiods, we can overcome one of the apparent limitations of the valuation model: that the number of possible end-of-period stock prices is small.

Notice that extreme outcomes such as u^3S_0 or d^3S_0 will be relatively rare, as they require either three consecutive increases or decreases in the three subintervals. More moderate, or midrange, results such as u^2dS_0 can be arrived at by more than one path; any combination of two price increases and one decrease will result in stock price u^2dS_0. There are three of these paths: *uud, udu, duu.* In contrast, only one path, *uuu,* results in a stock price of u^3S_0. Thus, midrange values are more likely. The probability of each outcome can be described by the binomial distribution, and this multiperiod approach to option pricing is called the **binomial model.**

binomial model

An option valuation model predicated on the assumption that stock prices can move to only two values over any short time period.

To make the model more realistic, we can break up the option maturity into more and more subperiods. As we do, the probability distribution for the final stock price will more and more resemble the familiar bell-shaped curve, with highly unlikely extreme outcomes and far more likely midrange outcomes.

But we still need to answer an important practical question. Before the model can be used to value actual options, we need a way to choose reasonable values for u and d. The spread between up and down movements in the price of the stock reflects the volatility of its rate of return, so the choice for u and d should depend on that volatility. Call σ your estimate of the standard deviation of the stock's continuously compounded annualized rate of return and Δt the length of each subperiod. To make the standard deviation of the stock in the binomial model match your estimate of σ, it turns out that you can set $u = \exp(\sigma\sqrt{\Delta t})$ and $d = \exp(-\sigma\sqrt{\Delta t})$.[3] You can see that the proportional difference between u and d increases with annualized volatility as well as the duration of the subperiod. This makes sense, as both higher σ and longer holding periods make future stock prices more uncertain. The following example illustrates how to use this calibration.

EXAMPLE 16.2

Calibrating u and d to Stock Volatility

Suppose you are using a three-period model to value a one-year option on a stock with volatility (i.e., annualized standard deviation) of $\sigma = .30$. With a time to expiration of $T = 1$ year, and three subperiods, you would calculate $\Delta t = T/n = 1/3$, $u = \exp(\sigma\sqrt{\Delta t}) = \exp(.30\sqrt{1/3}) = 1.189$ and $d = \exp(-\sigma\sqrt{\Delta t}) = \exp(-.30\sqrt{1/3}) = .841$. Given the probability of an up movement, you could then work out the probability of any final stock price. For example, suppose the probability that the stock price increases is .554 and the probability that it decreases is .446.[4] Then the probability of stock prices at the end of the year would be as follows:

Event	Possible Paths	Probability	Final Stock Price
3 down movements	*ddd*	$.446^3 = 0.089$	$59.48 = 100 \times .841^3$
2 down and 1 up	*ddu, dud, udd*	$3 \times .446^2 \times .554 = 0.330$	$84.10 = 100 \times 1.189 \times .841^2$
1 down and 2 up	*uud, udu, duu*	$3 \times .446 \times .554^2 = 0.411$	$118.89 = 100 \times 1.189^2 \times .841$
3 up movements	*uuu*	$.554^3 = 0.170$	$168.09 = 100 \times 1.189^3$

We plot this probability distribution in Figure 16.2, Panel A. Notice that the two middle end-of-period stock prices are, in fact, more likely than either extreme.

[3]Notice that $d = 1/u$. This is the most common, but not the only, way to calibrate the model to empirical volatility. For alternative methods, see Robert L. McDonald, *Derivatives Markets,* 2nd ed. (Boston: Pearson/Addison-Wesley, 2006), chap. 11, sec. 11.3.

[4]Using this probability, the continuously compounded expected rate of return on the stock is .10. In general, the formula relating the probability of an upward movement with the annual expected rate of return, r, is $p = \dfrac{\exp(r\Delta t) - d}{u - d}$.

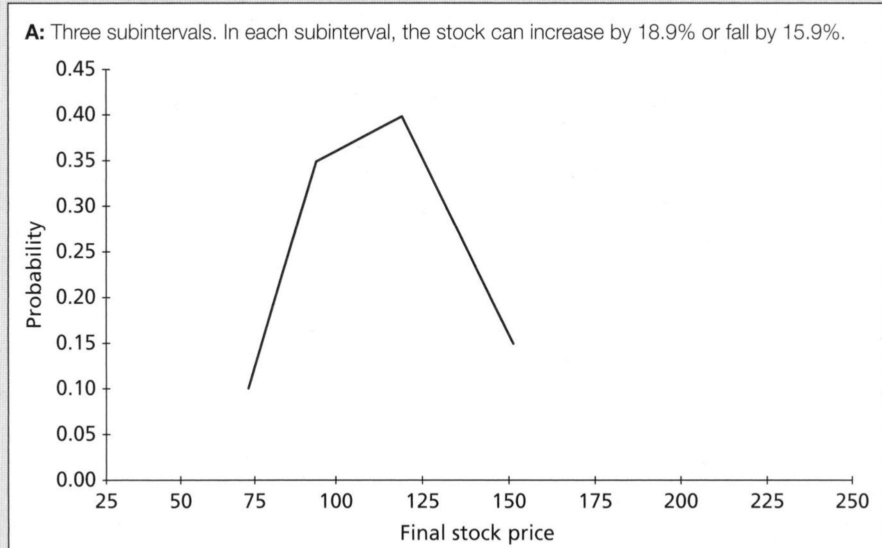

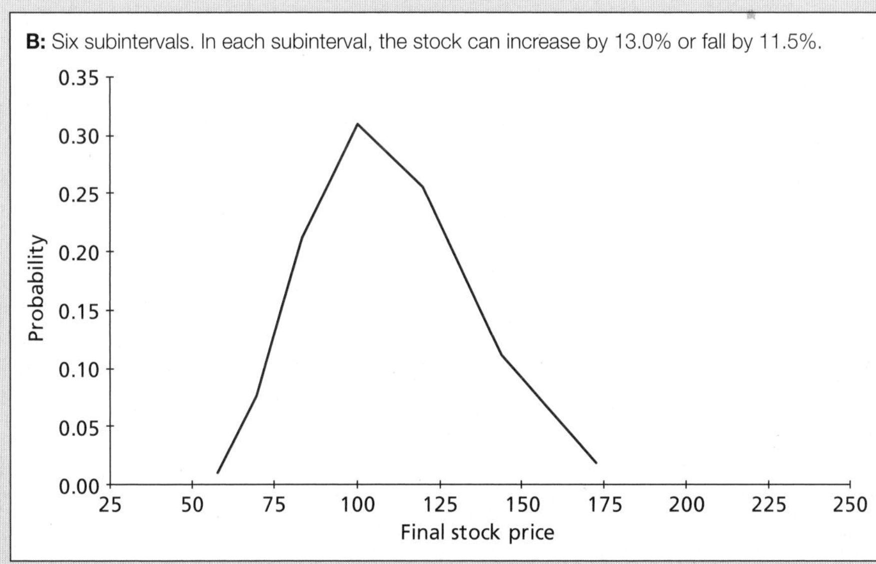

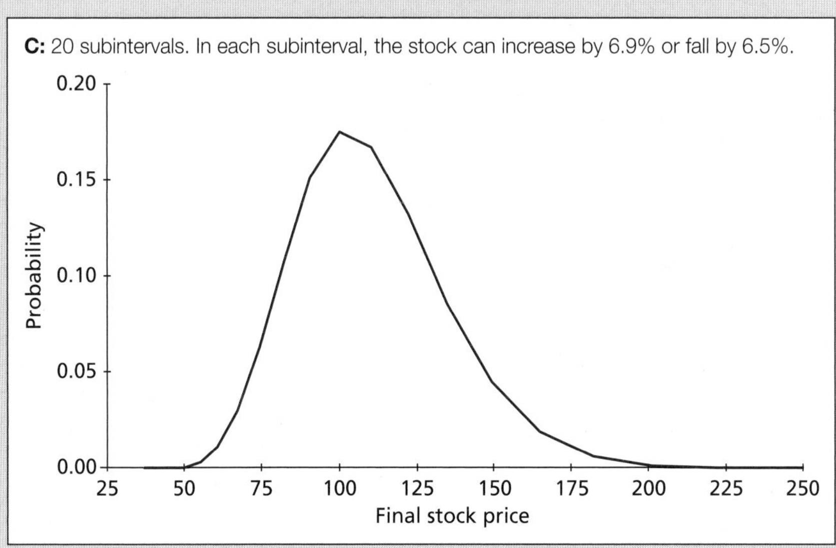

FIGURE 16.2

Probability distributions for final stock price: possible outcomes and associated probabilities. In each panel, the stock's expected annualized, continuously compounded rate of return is 10% and its standard deviation is 30%.

Now we can extend Example 16.2 by breaking up the option maturity into ever-shorter subintervals. As we do, the stock price distribution becomes increasingly plausible, as we demonstrate in Example 16.3.

EXAMPLE 16.3

Increasing the Number of Subperiods

In Example 16.2, we broke up the year into three subperiods. Let's also look at the cases of 6 and 20 subperiods.

Subperiods, n	$\Delta t = T/n$	$u = \exp(\sigma\sqrt{\Delta t})$	$d = \exp(-\sigma\sqrt{\Delta t})$
3	.333	exp(.173) = 1.189	exp(−.173) =.841
6	.167	exp(.123) = 1.130	exp(−.095) =.885
20	.015	exp(.067) = 1.069	exp(−.067) =.935

We plot the resulting probability distributions in Panels B and C of Figure 16.2.[5]

Notice that the right tail of the distribution in Panel C is noticeably longer than the left tail. In fact, as the number of intervals increases, the distribution progressively approaches the skewed lognormal (rather than the symmetric normal) distribution. Even if the stock price were to decline in *each* subinterval, it can never drop below zero. But there is no corresponding upper bound on its potential performance. This asymmetry gives rise to the skewness of the distribution.

Eventually, as we divide the option maturity into an ever-greater number of subintervals, each node of the event tree would correspond to an infinitesimally small time interval. The possible stock price movement within that time interval would be correspondingly small. As those many intervals passed, the end-of-period stock price would more and more closely resemble a lognormal distribution.[6] Thus, the apparent oversimplification of the two-state model can be overcome by progressively subdividing any period into many subperiods.

At any node, one still could set up a portfolio that would be perfectly hedged over the next time interval. Then, at the end of that interval, on reaching the next node, a new hedge ratio could be computed and the portfolio composition could be revised to remain hedged over the coming small interval. By continuously revising the hedge position, the portfolio would remain hedged and would earn a riskless rate of return over each interval. This is called *dynamic hedging,* the continued updating of the hedge ratio as time passes. As the dynamic hedge becomes ever finer, the resulting option valuation procedure becomes more precise. The nearby box offers further refinements on the use of the binomial model.

CONCEPT check 16.5

Would you expect the hedge ratio to be higher or lower when the call option is more in the money?

16.3 BLACK-SCHOLES OPTION VALUATION

While the binomial model we have described is extremely flexible, it requires a computer to be useful in actual trading. An option-pricing *formula* would be far easier to use than the tedious algorithm involved in the binomial model. It turns out that such a formula can be derived if

[5]We adjust the probabilities of up versus down movements using the formula in footnote 4 to make the distributions in Figure 16.2 comparable. In each panel, p is chosen so that the stock's expected annualized, continuously compounded rate of return is 10%.

[6]Actually, more complex considerations enter here. The limit of this process is lognormal only if we assume also that stock prices move continuously, by which we mean that over small time intervals only small price movements can occur. This rules out rare events such as sudden, extreme price moves in response to dramatic information (like a takeover attempt). For a treatment of this type of "jump process," see John C. Cox and Stephen A. Ross, "The Valuation of Options for Alternative Stochastic Processes," *Journal of Financial Economics* 3 (January–March 1976), pp. 145–166; or Robert C. Merton, "Option Pricing When Underlying Stock Returns Are Discontinuous," *Journal of Financial Economics* 3 (January–March 1976), pp. 125–144.

On the **MARKET FRONT**

A RISK-NEUTRAL SHORTCUT

We pointed out earlier in the chapter that the binomial-model valuation approach is arbitrage-based. We can value the option by replicating it with shares of stock plus borrowing. The ability to replicate the option means that its price relative to the stock and the interest rate must be based only on the technology of replication, and *not* on risk preferences. It cannot depend on risk aversion or the capital asset pricing model or any other model of equilibrium risk-return relationships.

This insight—that the pricing model must be independent of risk aversion—leads to a very useful shortcut to valuing options. Imagine a *risk-neutral economy,* that is, an economy in which all investors are risk-neutral. This hypothetical economy must value options the same as our real one, because risk aversion cannot affect the valuation formula.

In a risk-neutral economy, investors would not demand risk premiums and would therefore value all assets by discounting expected payoffs at the risk-free rate of interest. Therefore, a security such as a call option would be valued by discounting its expected cash flow at the risk-free rate: $C = \frac{"E"(CF)}{1 + r_f}$. We put the expectation operator in quotation marks to signify that this is not the true expectation but the expectation that would prevail in the hypothetical risk-neutral economy. To be consistent, we must calculate this expected cash flow using the expected rate of return the stock *would* have in the risk-neutral economy as one of our inputs, *not* using its actual expected rate of return. But if we successfully maintain consistency, the value derived for the hypothetical economy should match the one in our own.

How do we compute the expected cash flow from the option in the risk-neutral economy? Because there are no risk premiums, the stock's expected rate of return must equal the risk-free rate. Call p the probability that the stock price increases. Then p must be chosen to equate the expected rate of increase of the stock price to the risk-free rate (we ignore dividends here):

$$"E"(S_1) = p(uS) + (1 - p)\, dS = (1 + r_f)\, S$$

This implies that $p = \frac{1 + r_f - d}{u - d}$. We call p a *risk-neutral probability* to distinguish it from the true or "objective" probability. To illustrate, in our two-state example at the beginning of Section 16.2, we had $u = 1.2$, $d = .9$, and $r_f = .10$. Given these values, $p = \frac{1 + .10 - .9}{1.2 - .9} = \frac{2}{3}$.

Now let's see what happens if we use the discounted cash flow formula to value the option in the risk-neutral economy. We continue to use the two-state example from Section 16.2. We find the present value of the option payoff using the risk-neutral probability and discount at the risk-free interest rate:

$$C = \frac{"E"(CF)}{1 + r_f} = \frac{p\, C_u + (1 - p)\, C_d}{1 + r_f} = \frac{2/3 \times 10 + 1/3 \times 0}{1.10} = 6.06$$

This answer exactly matches the value we found using our no-arbitrage approach!

We repeat: This is not truly an expected discounted value.

- The *numerator* is not the true expected cash flow from the option because we use the risk-neutral probability, p, rather than the true probability.
- The *denominator* is not the proper discount rate for option cash flows because we do not account for the risk.
- In a sense these two "errors" cancel out. But this is not just luck: We are *assured* to get the correct result because the no-arbitrage approach implies that risk preferences cannot affect the option value. Therefore, the value computed for the risk-neutral economy *must* equal the value that we obtain in our economy.

When we move to the more realistic multiperiod model, the calculations are more cumbersome but the idea is the same. Footnote 4 shows how to relate p to any expected rate of return and volatility estimate. Simply set the expected rate of return on the stock equal to the risk-free rate, use the resulting probability to work out the expected payoff from the option, discount at the risk-free rate, and you will find the option value. These calculations are actually fairly easy to program in Excel.

one is willing to make just two more assumptions: that both the risk-free interest rate and stock price volatility are constant over the life of the option. In this case, as the time to expiration is divided into ever more subperiods, the distribution of the stock price at expiration progressively approaches the lognormal distribution, as suggested by Figure 16.2. When the stock price distribution is actually lognormal, we can derive an exact option-pricing formula.

The Black-Scholes Formula

Financial economists searched for years for a workable option-pricing model before Black and Scholes (1973) and Merton (1973) derived a formula for the value of a call option. Now widely used by options market participants, the **Black-Scholes pricing formula** for a European-style call option is

$$C_0 = S_0 e^{-\delta T} N(d_1) - X e^{-rT} N(d_2) \qquad \textbf{(16.1)}$$

Black-Scholes pricing formula

A formula to value an option that uses the stock price, the risk-free interest rate, the time to expiration, and the standard deviation of the stock return.

where

$$d_1 = \frac{\ln(S_0/X) + (r - \delta + \sigma^2/2)T}{\sigma\sqrt{T}}$$

$$d_2 = d_1 - \sigma\sqrt{T}$$

and where

C_0 = Current call option value.

S_0 = Current stock price.

$N(d)$ = The probability that a random draw from a standard normal distribution will be less than d. This equals the area under the normal curve up to d, as in the shaded area of Figure 16.3. In Excel, this function is called NORMSDIST( ).

X = Exercise price.

e = The base of the natural log function, approximately 2.71828. In Excel, e^x can be evaluated using the function EXP(x).

δ = Annual dividend yield of underlying stock. (We assume for simplicity that the stock pays a continuous income flow, rather than discrete periodic payments, such as quarterly dividends.)

r = Risk-free interest rate, expressed as a decimal (the annualized continuously compounded rate[7] on a safe asset with the same maturity as the expiration date of the option, which is to be distinguished from r_f, the discrete period interest rate).

T = Time remaining until expiration of option (in years).

ln = Natural logarithm function. In Excel, ln(x) can be calculated as LN(x).

σ = Standard deviation of the annualized continuously compounded rate of return of the stock, expressed as a decimal, not a percent.

Notice a surprising feature of Equation 16.1: The option value does not depend on the expected rate of return on the stock. In a sense, this information is already built into the formula with inclusion of the stock price, which itself depends on the stock's risk and return characteristics. This version of the Black-Scholes formula is predicated on the assumption that the underlying asset has a constant dividend (or income) yield.

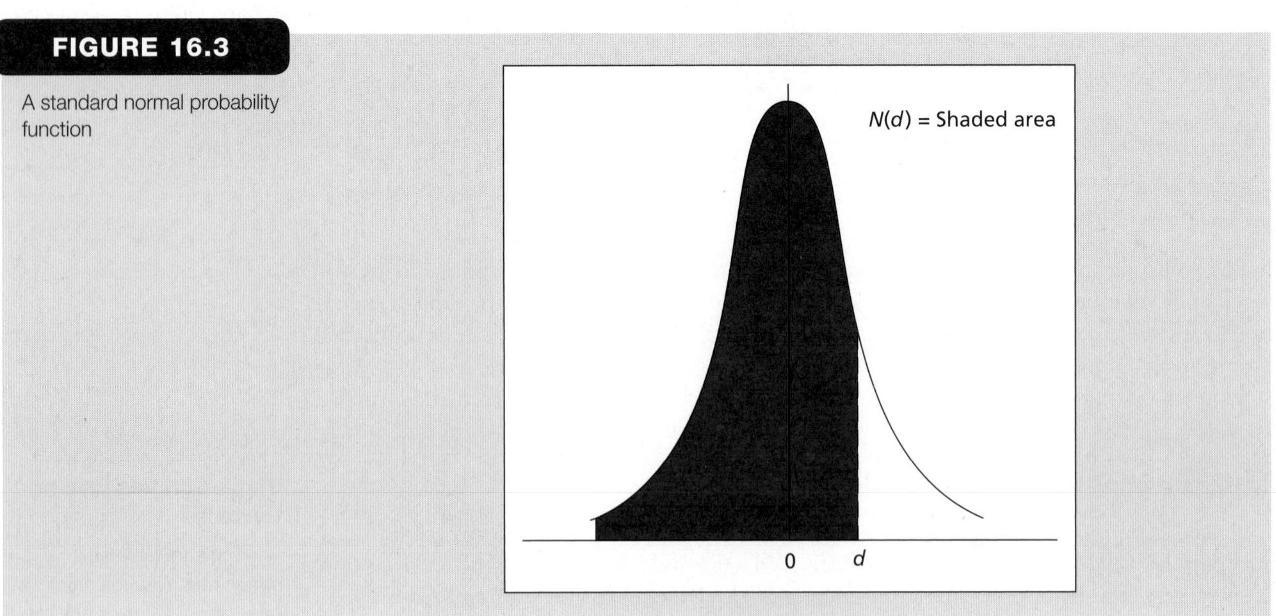

FIGURE 16.3

A standard normal probability function

[7]See Chapter 5, Section 5.1, for a review of continuous compounding.

Although you may find the Black-Scholes formula intimidating, we can explain it at a somewhat intuitive level. Consider a nondividend-paying stock, for which $\delta = 0$. Then $S_0 e^{-\delta T} = S_0$.

The trick is to view the $N(d)$ terms (loosely) as risk-adjusted probabilities that the call option will expire in the money. First, look at Equation 16.1 assuming both $N(d)$ terms are close to 1, that is, when there is a very high probability that the option will be exercised. Then the call option value is equal to $S_0 - Xe^{-rT}$, which is what we called earlier the adjusted intrinsic value, $S_0 - \text{PV}(X)$. This makes sense; if exercise is certain, we have a claim on a stock with current value S_0 and an obligation with present value PV(X), or with continuous compounding, Xe^{-rT}.

Now look at Equation 16.1 assuming the $N(d)$ terms are close to zero, meaning the option almost certainly will not be exercised. Then the equation confirms that the call is worth nothing. For middle-range values of $N(d)$ between 0 and 1, Equation 16.1 tells us that the call value can be viewed as the present value of the call's potential payoff adjusting for the probability of in-the-money expiration.

How do the $N(d)$ terms serve as risk-adjusted probabilities? This question quickly leads us into advanced statistics. Notice, however, that d_1 and d_2 both increase as the stock price increases. Therefore, $N(d_1)$ and $N(d_2)$ also increase with higher stock prices. This is the property we would desire of our "probabilities." For higher stock prices relative to exercise prices, future exercise is more likely.

EXAMPLE 16.4

Black-Scholes Call Option Valuation

You can use the Black-Scholes formula fairly easily. Suppose you want to value a call option under the following circumstances:

Stock price	$S_0 = 100$
Exercise price	$X = 95$
Interest rate	$r = .10$
Dividend yield	$\delta = 0$
Time to expiration	$T = .25$ (one-quarter year)
Standard deviation	$\sigma = .50$

First calculate

$$d_1 = \frac{\ln(100/95) + (.10 - 0 + .5^2/2).25}{.5\sqrt{0.25}} = .43$$

$$d_2 = .43 - .5\sqrt{.25} = .18$$

Next find $N(d_1)$ and $N(d_2)$. The normal distribution function is tabulated and may be found in many statistics textbooks. A table of $N(d)$ is provided as Table 16.2. The normal distribution function $N(d)$ is also provided in any spreadsheet program. In Microsoft Excel, for example, the function name is NORMSDIST. Using either Excel or Table 16.2 (using interpolation for .43), we find that

$$N(.43) = .6664$$
$$N(.18) = .5714$$

Finally, remember that with $\delta = 0$, $S_0 e^{-\delta T} = S_0$. Thus, the value of the call option is

$$C = 100 \times .6664 - 95e^{-0.10 \times 0.25} \times .5714$$
$$= 66.64 - 52.94 = \$13.70$$

CONCEPT check 16.6

Calculate the call option value if the standard deviation on the stock is .6 instead of .5. Confirm that the option is worth more using this higher volatility.

What if the option price in Example 16.4 were \$15 rather than \$13.70? Is the option mispriced? Maybe, but before betting your career on that, you may want to reconsider the

TABLE 16.2 Cumulative normal distribution

d	*N(d)*	*d*	*N(d)*	*d*	*N(d)*	*d*	*N(d)*	*d*	*N(d)*	*d*	*N(d)*
−3.00	0.0013	−1.58	0.0571	−0.76	0.2236	0.06	0.5239	0.88	0.8106	1.70	0.9554
−2.95	0.0016	−1.56	0.0594	−0.74	0.2297	0.08	0.5319	0.90	0.8159	1.72	0.9573
−2.90	0.0019	−1.54	0.0618	−0.72	0.2358	0.10	0.5398	0.92	0.8212	1.74	0.9591
−2.85	0.0022	−1.52	0.0643	−0.70	0.2420	0.12	0.5478	0.94	0.8264	1.76	0.9608
−2.80	0.0026	−1.50	0.0668	−0.68	0.2483	0.14	0.5557	0.96	0.8315	1.78	0.9625
−2.75	0.0030	−1.48	0.0694	−0.66	0.2546	0.16	0.5636	0.98	0.8365	1.80	0.9641
−2.70	0.0035	−1.46	0.0721	−0.64	0.2611	0.18	0.5714	1.00	0.8414	1.82	0.9656
−2.65	0.0040	−1.44	0.0749	−0.62	0.2676	0.20	0.5793	1.02	0.8461	1.84	0.9671
−2.60	0.0047	−1.42	0.0778	−0.60	0.2743	0.22	0.5871	1.04	0.8508	1.86	0.9686
−2.55	0.0054	−1.40	0.0808	−0.58	0.2810	0.24	0.5948	1.06	0.8554	1.88	0.9699
−2.50	0.0062	−1.38	0.0838	−0.56	0.2877	0.26	0.6026	1.08	0.8599	1.90	0.9713
−2.45	0.0071	−1.36	0.0869	−0.54	0.2946	0.28	0.6103	1.10	0.8643	1.92	0.9726
−2.40	0.0082	−1.34	0.0901	−0.52	0.3015	0.30	0.6179	1.12	0.8686	1.94	0.9738
−2.35	0.0094	−1.32	0.0934	−0.50	0.3085	0.32	0.6255	1.14	0.8729	1.96	0.9750
−2.30	0.0107	−1.30	0.0968	−0.48	0.3156	0.34	0.6331	1.16	0.8770	1.98	0.9761
−2.25	0.0122	−1.28	0.1003	−0.46	0.3228	0.36	0.6406	1.18	0.8810	2.00	0.9772
−2.20	0.0139	−1.26	0.1038	−0.44	0.3300	0.38	0.6480	1.20	0.8849	2.05	0.9798
−2.15	0.0158	−1.24	0.1075	−0.42	0.3373	0.40	0.6554	1.22	0.8888	2.10	0.9821
−2.10	0.0179	−1.22	0.1112	−0.40	0.3446	0.42	0.6628	1.24	0.8925	2.15	0.9842
−2.05	0.0202	−1.20	0.1151	−0.38	0.3520	0.44	0.6700	1.26	0.8962	2.20	0.9861
−2.00	0.0228	−1.18	0.1190	−0.36	0.3594	0.46	0.6773	1.28	0.8997	2.25	0.9878
−1.98	0.0239	−1.16	0.1230	−0.34	0.3669	0.48	0.6844	1.30	0.9032	2.30	0.9893
−1.96	0.0250	−1.14	0.1271	−0.32	0.3745	0.50	0.6915	1.32	0.9066	2.35	0.9906
−1.94	0.0262	−1.12	0.1314	−0.30	0.3821	0.52	0.6985	1.34	0.9099	2.40	0.9918
−1.92	0.0274	−1.10	0.1357	−0.28	0.3897	0.54	0.7054	1.36	0.9131	2.45	0.9929
−1.90	0.0287	−1.08	0.1401	−0.26	0.3974	0.56	0.7123	1.38	0.9162	2.50	0.9938
−1.88	0.0301	−1.06	0.1446	−0.24	0.4052	0.58	0.7191	1.40	0.9192	2.55	0.9946
−1.86	0.0314	−1.04	0.1492	−0.22	0.4129	0.60	0.7258	1.42	0.9222	2.60	0.9953
−1.84	0.0329	−1.02	0.1539	−0.20	0.4207	0.62	0.7324	1.44	0.9251	2.65	0.9960
−1.82	0.0344	−1.00	0.1587	−0.18	0.4286	0.64	0.7389	1.46	0.9279	2.70	0.9965
−1.80	0.0359	−0.98	0.1635	−0.16	0.4365	0.66	0.7454	1.48	0.9306	2.75	0.9970
−1.78	0.0375	−0.96	0.1685	−0.14	0.4443	0.68	0.7518	1.50	0.9332	2.80	0.9974
−1.76	0.0392	−0.94	0.1736	−0.12	0.4523	0.70	0.7580	1.52	0.9357	2.85	0.9978
−1.74	0.0409	−0.92	0.1788	−0.10	0.4602	0.72	0.7642	1.54	0.9382	2.90	0.9981
−1.72	0.0427	−0.90	0.1841	−0.08	0.4681	0.74	0.7704	1.56	0.9406	2.95	0.9984
−1.70	0.0446	−0.88	0.1894	−0.06	0.4761	0.76	0.7764	1.58	0.9429	3.00	0.9986
−1.68	0.0465	−0.86	0.1949	−0.04	0.4841	0.78	0.7823	1.60	0.9452	3.05	0.9989
−1.66	0.0485	−0.84	0.2005	−0.02	0.4920	0.80	0.7882	1.62	0.9474		
−1.64	0.0505	−0.82	0.2061	0.00	0.5000	0.82	0.7939	1.64	0.9495		
−1.62	0.0526	−0.80	0.2119	0.02	0.5080	0.84	0.7996	1.66	0.9515		
−1.60	0.0548	−0.78	0.2177	0.04	0.5160	0.86	0.8051	1.68	0.9535		

valuation analysis. First, like all models, the Black-Scholes formula is based on some simplifying abstractions that make the formula only approximately valid.

Some of the important assumptions underlying the formula are the following:

1. The stock will pay a constant, continuous dividend yield until the option expiration date.
2. Both the interest rate, r, and variance rate, σ^2, of the stock are constant (or in slightly more general versions of the formula, both are *known* functions of time—any changes are perfectly predictable).
3. Stock prices are continuous, meaning that sudden extreme jumps, such as those in the aftermath of an announcement of a takeover attempt, are ruled out.

Variants of the Black-Scholes formula have been developed to deal with many of these limitations.

Second, even within the context of the Black-Scholes model, you must be sure of the accuracy of the parameters used in the formula. Four of these—S_0, X, T, and r—are straightforward. The stock price, exercise price, and time to expiration are readily determined. The interest rate used is the money market rate for a maturity equal to that of the option, and the dividend yield is usually reasonably stable, at least over short horizons.

The last input, though, the standard deviation of the stock return, is not directly observable. It must be estimated from historical data, from scenario analysis, or from the prices of other options, as we will describe momentarily. Because the standard deviation must be estimated, it is always possible that discrepancies between an option price and its Black-Scholes value are simply artifacts of error in the estimation of the stock's volatility.

In fact, market participants often give the option valuation problem a different twist. Rather than calculating a Black-Scholes option value for a given stock standard deviation, they ask instead: What standard deviation would be necessary for the option price that I actually observe to be consistent with the Black-Scholes formula? This is called the **implied volatility** of the option, the volatility level for the stock that the option price implies. Investors can then judge whether they think the actual stock standard deviation exceeds the implied volatility. If it does, the option is considered a good buy; if actual volatility seems greater than the implied volatility, the option's fair price would exceed the observed price.

implied volatility

The standard deviation of stock returns that is consistent with an option's market value.

Another variation is to compare two options on the same stock with equal expiration dates but different exercise prices. The option with the higher implied volatility would be considered relatively expensive because a higher standard deviation is required to justify its price. The analyst might consider buying the option with the lower implied volatility and writing the option with the higher implied volatility.

The Black-Scholes call option valuation formula, as well as implied volatilities, is easily calculated using an Excel spreadsheet, as in Spreadsheet 16.1. The model inputs are provided in column B, and the outputs are given in column E. The formulas for d_1 and d_2 are provided in the spreadsheet, and the Excel formula NORMSDIST(d_1) is used to calculate $N(d_1)$. Cell E6 contains the Black-Scholes call option formula.

SPREADSHEET 16.1

Spreadsheet to calculate Black-Scholes call-option values

	A	B	C	D	E	F	G	H	I	J
1	INPUTS			OUTPUTS			FORMULA FOR OUTPUT IN COLUMN E			
2	Standard deviation (annual)	.2783		d1	0.0029		(LN(B5/B6)+(B4–B7+.5*B2^2)*B3)/(B2*SQRT(B3))			
3	Expiration (in years)	.5		d2	–0.1939		E2–B2*SQRT(B3)			
4	Risk-free rate (annual)	.06		N(d1)	0.5012		NORMSDIST(E2)			
5	Stock price	100		N(d2)	0.4231		NORMSDIST(E3)			
6	Exercise price	105		B/S call value	7.0000		B5*EXP(–B7*B3)*E4–B6*EXP(–B4*B3)*E5			
7	Dividend yield (annual)	0		B/S put value	8.8967		B6*EXP(–B4*B3)*(1–E5)–B5*EXP(–B7*B3)*(1–E4)			

eXcel

Please visit us at www.mhhe.com/bkm

FIGURE 16.4 Using Goal Seek to find implied volatility

	A	B	C	D	E	F	G	H	I	J	K
1	INPUTS			OUTPUTS			FORMULA FOR OUTPUT IN COLUMN E				
2	Standard deviation (annual)	.2783		d1	0.0029		(LN(B5/B6)+(B4–B7+.5*B2^2)*B3)/(B2*SQRT(B3))				
3	Expiration (in years)	.5		d2	–0.1939		E2–B2*SQRT(B3)				
4	Risk-free rate (annual)	.06		N(d1)	0.5012		NORMSDIST(E2)				
5	Stock price	100		N(d2)	0.4231		NORMSDIST(E3)				
6	Exercise price	105		B/S call value	7.0000		B5*EXP(–B7*B3)*E4–B6*EXP(–B4*B3)*E5				
7	Dividend yield (annual)	0		B/S put value	8.8968		B6*EXP(–B4*B3)*(1–E5)–B5*EXP(–B7*B3)*(1–E4)				
8											
9											
10											
11											
12											
13											
14											
15											
16											
17											

Goal Seek

Set cell: $E$6

To value: 7

By changing cell: $B$2

OK Cancel

To compute an implied volatility, we can use the Goal Seek command from the What-If Analysis menu (which may be found under the Data tab) in Excel. (See Figure 16.4 for an illustration.) Goal Seek asks us to change the value of one cell to make the value of another cell (called the *target cell*) equal to a specific value. For example, if we observe a call option selling for $7 with other inputs as given in the spreadsheet, we can use Goal Seek to change the value in cell B2 (the standard deviation of the stock) to set the option value in cell E6 equal to $7. The target cell, E6, is the call price, and the spreadsheet manipulates cell B2. When you click *OK*, the spreadsheet finds that a standard deviation equal to .2783 is consistent with a call price of $7; therefore, 27.83% would be the call's implied volatility if it were selling at $7.

CONCEPT check 16.7

Consider the call option in Example 16.4. If it sells for $15 rather than the value of $13.70 found in the example, is its implied volatility more or less than .5? Use Spreadsheet 16.1 (available at the Online Learning Center) to find its implied volatility at this price.

The Chicago Board Options Exchange regularly computes the implied volatility of major stock indexes. Figure 16.5 is a graph of the implied (30-day) volatility of the S&P 500. During periods of turmoil, implied volatility can spike quickly. Notice the peaks in January 1991 (Gulf War), in August 1998 (collapse of Long-Term Capital Management), on September 11, 2001, in 2002 (buildup to invasion of Iraq), and, most dramatically, during the credit crisis of 2008. Because implied volatility correlates with crisis, it is sometimes called an "investor fear gauge," and, as the nearby box makes clear, observers use it to infer the market's assessment of possible stock price swings in coming months. In this case, the Food and Drug Administration's imminent ruling on the viability of an important drug being developed by Dendreon Corporation created tremendous uncertainty about its future stock price and a commensurate jump in the implied volatility of its stock options.

In March 2004, a futures contract on the 30-day implied volatility of the S&P 500 began trading on the CBOE Futures Exchange. The payoff of the contract depends on market implied volatility at the expiration of the contract. The ticker symbol of the contract is VIX.

Figure 16.5 also reveals an awkward empirical fact. While the Black-Scholes formula is derived assuming that stock volatility is constant, the time series of implied volatilities

IMPLIED VOLATILITY SPIKES ON DENDREON CORP. AHEAD OF FDA'S PROVENGE RULING

Biotech issue Dendreon Corporation (DNDN) is on the verge of a major fundamental development—the U.S. Food & Drug Administration (FDA) is slated to issue its verdict on Dendreon's prostate cancer vaccine, Provenge, by May 1. As a result, implied volatility on DNDN's options is pretty much off the charts.

Check it out: DNDN's at-the-money May 40 call is pricing in implied volatility of 155%, while the May 40 put carries implied volatility of 157% (as of Tuesday's close). By contrast, the equity's one-month historical volatility stands at 28%. It seems inevitable that DNDN will make some kind of major move on the charts following the regulatory decision.

Overall, speculators are feeling antsy ahead of the FDA's Provenge decision. DNDN's 10-day International Securities Exchange (ISE) put/call volume ratio of 0.81 ranks higher than 92% of other such readings taken during the past year, suggesting that traders [seeking downside protection] have rarely purchased puts over calls at a faster pace.

SOURCE: Elizabeth Harrow, "Implied Volatility Spikes on Dendreon Corp. Ahead of FDA's Provenge Ruling," Schaeffer's Investment Research, **www.schaeffersresearch.com**, April 28, 2010. Used with permission.

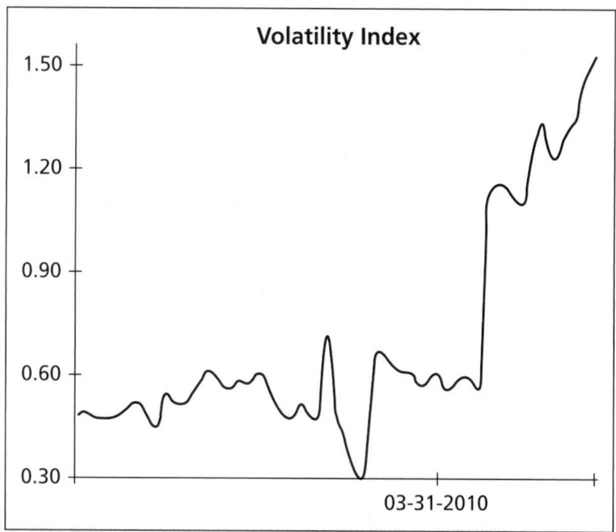

DNDN's Schaeffer's Volatility Index (SVI) is sky-high ahead of the FDA ruling

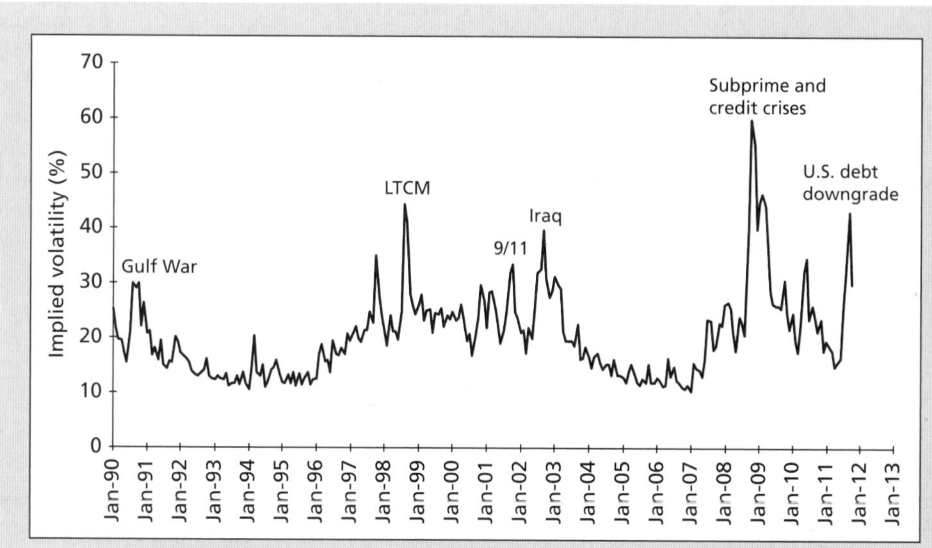

FIGURE 16.5

Implied volatility of the S&P 500 (VIX index), expressed as an annualized standard deviation

Source: Chicago Board Options Exchange. CBOE Volatility Index® (VIX®) data is provided by Chicago Board Options Exchange, Incorporated (CBOE) and CBOE makes no warranties of any kind with respect to this data. Used with permission.

consistent with that formula is in fact far from constant. This contradiction reminds us that the Black-Scholes model (like all models) is a simplification that does not capture all aspects of real markets. In this particular context, extensions of the pricing model that allow stock volatility to evolve randomly over time would be desirable, and, in fact, many extensions of the model along these lines have been suggested.[8]

[8]Influential articles on this topic are Hull and White (1987), Wiggins (1987), and Heston (1993). For a more recent review, see Ghysels, Harvey, and Renault (1996).

FIGURE 16.6

The payoff pattern of a long call–short put position

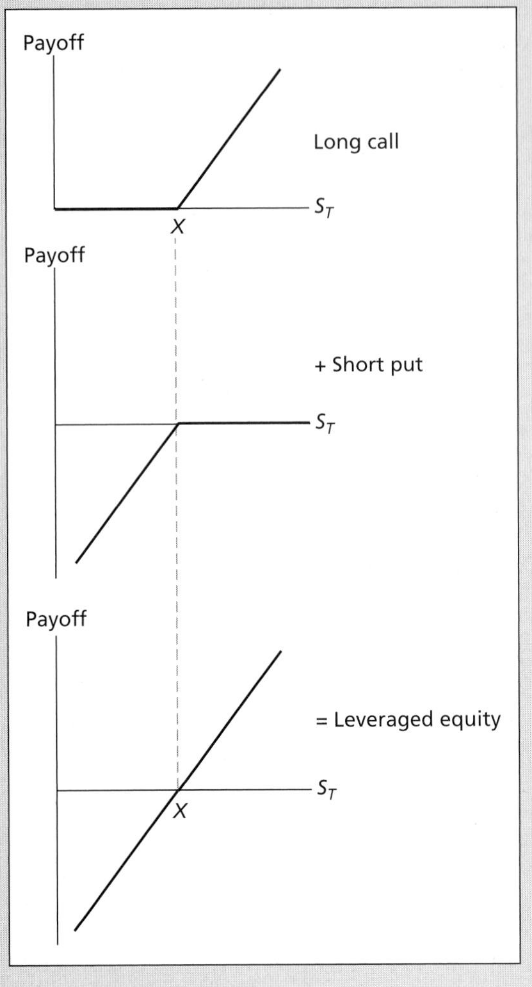

The fact that volatility changes unpredictably means that it can be difficult to choose the proper volatility input to use in any option-pricing model. A considerable amount of recent research has been devoted to techniques to predict changes in volatility. These techniques, which are known as *ARCH* and *stochastic volatility models,* posit that changes in volatility are partially predictable and that by analyzing recent levels and trends in volatility, one can improve predictions of future volatility.[9]

The Put-Call Parity Relationship

So far, we have focused on the pricing of call options. In many important cases, put prices can be derived simply from the prices of calls. This is because prices of European put and call options are linked together in an equation known as the put-call parity relationship. Therefore, once you know the value of a call, finding the value of the put is easy.

To derive the parity relationship, suppose you buy a call option and write a put option, each with the same exercise price, *X,* and the same expiration date, *T.* At expiration, the payoff on your investment will equal the payoff to the call minus the payoff that must be made on the put. The payoff for each option will depend on whether the ultimate stock price, S_T, exceeds the exercise price at contract expiration.

	$S_T \le X$	$S_T > X$
Payoff of call held	0	$S_T - X$
− Payoff of put written	$-(X - S_T)$	0
Total	$S_T - X$	$S_T - X$

Figure 16.6 illustrates this payoff pattern. Compare the payoff to that of a portfolio made up of the stock plus a borrowing position, where the money to be paid back will grow, with interest, to *X* dollars at the maturity of the loan. Such a position is a *levered* equity position in which $PV(X) = Xe^{-rT}$ dollars is borrowed today (so that *X* will be repaid at maturity), and S_0 dollars is invested in the stock. The total payoff of the levered equity position is $S_T - X$, the same as that of the option strategy. Thus, the long call–short put position replicates the levered equity position. Again, we see that option trading provides leverage.

[9]For an introduction to these models, see Alexander (2001).

Because the option portfolio has a payoff identical to that of the levered equity position, the costs of establishing them must be equal. The net cash outlay necessary to establish the option position is $C - P$: The call is purchased for C, while the written put generates income of P. Likewise, the levered equity position requires a net cash outlay of $S_0 - Xe^{-rT}$, the cost of the stock less the proceeds from borrowing. Equating these costs, we conclude

$$C - P = S_0 - Xe^{-rT} \tag{16.2}$$

put-call parity relationship
An equation representing the proper relationship between put and call prices.

Equation 16.2 is called the **put-call parity relationship** because it represents the proper relationship between put and call prices. If the parity relationship is ever violated, an arbitrage opportunity arises.

EXAMPLE 16.5

Put-Call Parity

Suppose you observe the following data for a certain stock.

Stock price	\$110
Call price (six-month maturity, X = \$105)	14
Put price (six-month maturity, X = \$105)	5
Risk-free interest rate	5% continuously compounded rate

We use these data in the put-call parity relationship to see if parity is violated.

$$C - P \stackrel{?}{=} S_0 - Xe^{-rT}$$
$$14 - 5 \stackrel{?}{=} 110 - 105e^{-.05\times 5}$$
$$9 \stackrel{?}{=} 7.59$$

This result, a violation of parity (9 does not equal 7.59) indicates mispricing and leads to an arbitrage opportunity. You can buy the relatively cheap portfolio (the stock plus borrowing position represented on the right-hand side of Equation 16.2) and sell the relatively expensive portfolio (the long call–short put position corresponding to the left-hand side, that is, write a call and buy a put).

Let's examine the payoff to this strategy. In six months, the stock will be worth S_T. You borrowed the present value of the exercise price, \$105, and must pay back the loan with interest, resulting in a cash outflow of \$105. The written call will result in a cash outflow of S_T − \$105 if S_T exceeds \$105. The purchased put pays off \$105 − S_T if the stock price is below \$105.

Table 16.3 summarizes the outcome. The immediate cash inflow is \$1.41, precisely equal to the mispricing of the option. In six months, the various positions provide exactly offsetting cash flows: The \$1.41 inflow is realized risklessly without any offsetting outflows. This is an arbitrage opportunity that investors will pursue on a large scale until buying and selling pressure restores the parity condition expressed in Equation 16.2.

TABLE 16.3 Arbitrage strategy

		Cash Flow in Six Months	
Position	**Immediate Cash Flow**	$S_T < 105$	$S_T \geq 105$
Buy stock	−110	S_T	S_T
Borrow Xe^{-rT} = \$102.41	+102.41	−105	−105
Sell call	+14	0	$-(S_T - 105)$
Buy put	−5	$105 - S_T$	0
Total	1.41	0	0

Equation 16.2 actually applies only to options on stocks that pay no dividends before the expiration date of the option. It also applies only to European options, as the cash flow streams from the two portfolios represented by the two sides of Equation 16.2 will match only if each position is held until expiration. If a call and a put may be optimally exercised at different times before their common expiration date, then the equality of payoffs cannot be assured, or even expected, and the portfolios will have different values.

The extension of the parity condition for European call options on dividend-paying stocks is, however, straightforward. Problem 32 at the end of the chapter leads you through the extension of the parity relationship. The more general formulation of the put-call parity condition is

$$P = C - S_0 + \text{PV}(X) + \text{PV}(\text{dividends}) \tag{16.3}$$

where PV(dividends) is the present value of the dividends that will be paid by the stock during the life of the option. If the stock does not pay dividends, Equation 16.3 becomes identical to Equation 16.2.

Notice that this generalization would apply as well to European options on assets other than stocks. Instead of using dividend income in Equation 16.3, we would let any income paid out by the underlying asset play the role of the stock dividends. For example, European put and call options on bonds would satisfy the same parity relationship, except that the bond's coupon income would replace the stock's dividend payments in the parity formula.

Let's see how well parity works using real data on the IBM options in Figure 15.1 from the previous chapter. The September expiration call with exercise price \$170 and time to expiration of 22 days cost \$3, while the corresponding put option cost \$6.20. IBM was selling for \$166.76, and the annualized short-term (money market) interest rate on this date was .08%. No dividends will be paid between the date of the listing and the option expiration date. According to parity, we should find that

$$P = C + \text{PV}(X) - S_0 + \text{PV}(\text{Dividends})$$

$$6.20 = 3.00 + \frac{170}{(1.0008)^{22/365}} - 166.76 + 0$$

$$6.20 = 3.00 + 169.99 - 166.76$$

$$6.20 = 6.23$$

So parity is violated by about \$.03 per share. Is this a big enough difference to exploit? Almost certainly not. You have to weigh the potential profit against the trading costs of the call, put, and stock. More important, given the fact that options may trade relatively infrequently, this deviation from parity might not be "real" but may instead be attributable to "stale" (i.e., out-of-date) price quotes at which you cannot actually trade.

Put Option Valuation

As we saw in Equation 16.3, we can use the put-call parity relationship to value put options once we know the call option value. Sometimes, however, it is easier to work with a put option valuation formula directly. The Black-Scholes formula for the value of a European put option is[10]

$$P = Xe^{-rT}[1 - N(d_2)] - S_0e^{-\delta T}[1 - N(d_1)] \tag{16.4}$$

[10]This formula is consistent with the put-call parity relationship and in fact can be derived from it. If you want to try to do so, remember to take present values using continuous compounding, and note that when a stock pays a continuous flow of income in the form of a constant dividend yield, δ, the present value of that dividend flow is $S_0(1 - e^{-\delta T})$. (Notice that $e^{-\delta T}$ approximately equals $1 - \delta T$, so the value of the dividend flow is approximately $\delta T S_0$.)

EXAMPLE 16.6

Black-Scholes Put Option Valuation

Using data from the Black-Scholes call option in Example 16.4, we find that a European put option on that stock with identical exercise price and time to expiration is worth

$$\$95e^{-.10\times.25}(1 - .5714) - \$100(1 - .6664) = \$6.35$$

Notice that this value is consistent with put-call parity:

$$P = C + PV(X) - S_0 + PV(\text{Div}) = 13.70 + 95e^{-.10\times.25} - 100 + 0 = 6.35$$

As we noted traders can do, we might then compare this formula value to the actual put price as one step in formulating a trading strategy.

Equation 16.4 is valid for European puts. Most listed put options are American-style, however, and offer the opportunity of early exercise. Because an American option allows its owner to exercise at any time before the expiration date, it must be worth at least as much as the corresponding European option. However, while Equation 16.4 describes only the lower bound on the true value of the American put, in many applications the approximation is very accurate.

16.4 USING THE BLACK-SCHOLES FORMULA

Hedge Ratios and the Black-Scholes Formula

In the last chapter, we considered two investments in FinCorp stock: 100 shares or 900 call options. We saw that the call option position was more sensitive to swings in the stock price than the all-stock position. To analyze the overall exposure to a stock price more precisely, however, it is necessary to quantify these relative sensitivities. A tool that enables us to summarize the overall exposure of portfolios of options with various exercise prices and times to expiration is the hedge ratio. An option's **hedge ratio** is the change in the price of an option for a $1 increase in the stock price. A call option, therefore, has a positive hedge ratio, and a put option has a negative hedge ratio. The hedge ratio is commonly called the option's **delta.**

hedge ratio or delta

The number of shares of stock required to hedge the price risk of holding one option.

If you were to graph the option value as a function of the stock value as we have done for a call option in Figure 16.7, the hedge ratio is simply the slope of the value function evaluated at the current stock price. For example, suppose the slope of the curve at S_0 = $120 equals .60. As the stock increases in value by $1, the option increases by approximately $.60, as the figure shows.

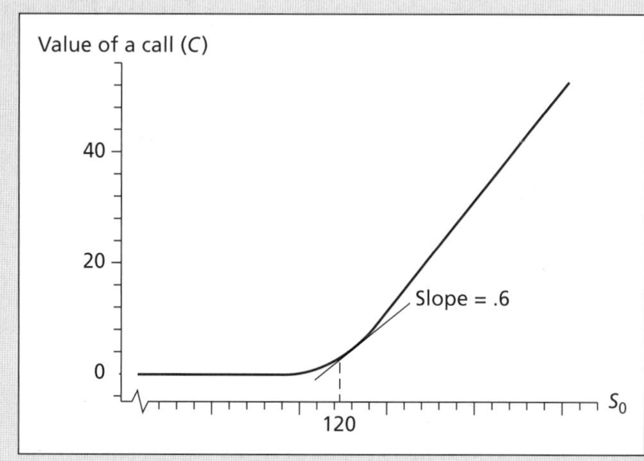

FIGURE 16.7

Call option value and hedge ratio

For every call option written, .60 shares of stock would be needed to hedge the investor's portfolio. For example, if one writes 10 options and holds six shares of stock, according to the hedge ratio of .6, a \$1 increase in stock price will result in a gain of \$6 on the stock holdings, while the loss on the 10 options written will be 10 × \$.60, an equivalent \$6. The stock price movement leaves total wealth unaltered, which is what a hedged position is intended to do. The investor holding both the stock and options in proportions dictated by their relative price movements hedges the portfolio.

Black-Scholes hedge ratios are particularly easy to compute. The hedge ratio for a call is $N(d_1)$, while the hedge ratio for a put is $N(d_1) - 1$. We defined $N(d_1)$ as part of the Black-Scholes formula in Equation 16.1. Recall that $N(d)$ stands for the area under the standard normal curve up to d. Therefore, the call option hedge ratio must be positive and less than 1.0, while the put option hedge ratio is negative and of smaller absolute value than 1.0.

Figure 16.7 verifies the insight that the slope of the call option valuation function is less than 1, approaching 1 only as the stock price becomes extremely large. This tells us that option values change less than one-for-one with changes in stock prices. Why should this be? Suppose an option is so far in the money that you are absolutely certain it will be exercised. In that case, every \$1 increase in the stock price would increase the option value by \$1. But if there is a reasonable chance the call option will expire out of the money, even after a moderate stock price gain, a \$1 increase in the stock price will not necessarily increase the ultimate payoff to the call; therefore, the call price will not respond by a full \$1.

The fact that hedge ratios are less than 1 does not contradict our earlier observation that options offer leverage and are sensitive to stock price movements. Although *dollar* movements in option prices are slighter than dollar movements in the stock price, the *rate of return* volatility of options remains greater than stock return volatility because options sell at lower prices. In our example, with the stock selling at \$120, and a hedge ratio of .6, an option with exercise price \$120 may sell for \$5. If the stock price increases to \$121, the call price would be expected to increase by only \$.60, to \$5.60. The percentage increase in the option value is \$.60/\$5 = 12%, however, while the percentage stock price increase is only \$1/\$120 = .83%. The ratio of the percent changes is 12%/.83% = 14.4. For every 1% increase in the stock price, the option price increases by 14.4%. This ratio, the percent change in option price per percent change in stock price, is called the **option elasticity.**

option elasticity

The percentage increase in an option's value given a 1% increase in the value of the underlying security.

The hedge ratio is an essential tool in portfolio management and control. An example will show why.

EXAMPLE 16.7

Portfolio Hedge Ratios

Consider two portfolios, one holding 750 FinCorp calls and 200 shares of FinCorp and the other holding 800 shares of FinCorp. Which portfolio has greater dollar exposure to FinCorp price movements? You can answer this question easily using the hedge ratio.

Each option changes in value by H dollars for each dollar change in stock price, where H stands for the hedge ratio. Thus, if H equals .6, the 750 options are equivalent to 450 shares (= .6 × 750) in terms of the response of their market value to FinCorp stock price movements. The first portfolio has less dollar sensitivity to stock price change because the 450 share-equivalents of the options plus the 200 shares actually held are less than the 800 shares held in the second portfolio.

This is not to say, however, that the first portfolio is less sensitive to the stock's rate of return. As we noted in discussing option elasticities, the first portfolio may be of lower total value than the second, so despite its lower sensitivity in terms of total market value, it might have greater rate-of-return sensitivity. Because a call option has a lower market value than the stock, its price changes more than proportionally with stock price changes, even though its hedge ratio is less than 1.

CONCEPT check 16.8

What is the elasticity of a put option currently selling for \$4 with exercise price \$120 and hedge ratio −.4 if the stock price is currently \$122?

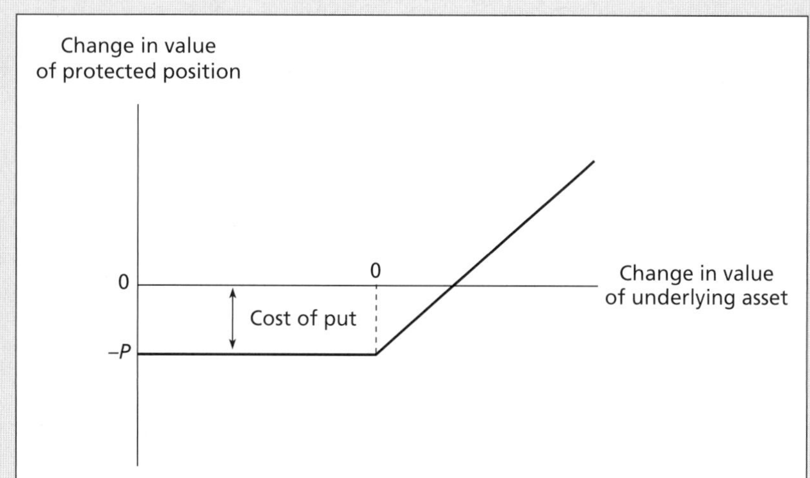

FIGURE 16.8

Profit on a protective put strategy

Portfolio Insurance

In Chapter 15, we showed that protective put strategies offer a sort of insurance policy on an asset. The protective put has proven to be extremely popular with investors. Even if the asset price falls, the put conveys the right to sell the asset for the exercise price, which is a way to lock in a minimum portfolio value. With an at-the-money put ($X = S_0$), the maximum loss that can be realized is the cost of the put. The asset can be sold for X, which equals its original price, so even if the asset price falls, the investor's net loss over the period is just the cost of the put. If the asset value increases, however, upside potential is unlimited. Figure 16.8 graphs the profit or loss on a protective put position as a function of the change in the value of the underlying asset.

While the protective put is a simple and convenient way to achieve **portfolio insurance,** that is, to limit the worst-case portfolio rate of return, there are practical difficulties in trying to insure a portfolio of stocks. First, unless the investor's portfolio corresponds to a standard market index for which puts are traded, a put option on the portfolio will not be available for purchase. And if index puts are used to protect a nonindexed portfolio, tracking error can result. For example, if the portfolio falls in value while the market index rises, the put will fail to provide the intended protection. Moreover, the maturities of traded options may not match the investor's horizon. Therefore, rather than using option strategies, investors may use trading strategies that mimic the payoff to a protective put option.

portfolio insurance

Portfolio strategies that limit investment losses while maintaining upside potential.

Here is the general idea. Even if a put option on the desired portfolio with the desired expiration date does not exist, a theoretical option-pricing model (such as the Black-Scholes model) can be used to determine how that option's price *would* respond to the portfolio's value if the option did trade. For example, if stock prices were to fall, the put option would increase in value. The option model could quantify this relationship. The net exposure of the (hypothetical) protective put portfolio to swings in stock prices is the sum of the exposures of the two components of the portfolio: the stock and the put. The net exposure of the portfolio equals the equity exposure less the (offsetting) put option exposure.

We can create "synthetic" protective put positions by holding a quantity of stocks with the same net exposure to market swings as the hypothetical protective put position. The key to this strategy is the option delta, or hedge ratio, that is, the change in the price of the protective put option per change in the value of the underlying stock portfolio.

EXAMPLE 16.8

Synthetic Protective Puts

Suppose a portfolio is currently valued at $100 million. An at-the-money put option on the portfolio might have a hedge ratio or delta of −.6, meaning the option's value swings $.60 for every dollar change in portfolio value, but in an opposite direction. Suppose the stock portfolio falls in value by

(continued)

EXAMPLE 16.8

Synthetic Protective Puts (concluded)

2%. The profit on a hypothetical protective put position (if the put existed) would be as follows (in millions of dollars):

Loss on stocks:	2% of $100 = $2.00
+Gain on put:	.6 × $2.00 = 1.20
Net loss	$0.80

We create the synthetic option position by selling a proportion of shares equal to the put option's delta (i.e., selling 60% of the shares) and placing the proceeds in risk-free T-bills. The rationale is that the hypothetical put option would have offset 60% of any change in the stock portfolio's value, so one must reduce portfolio risk directly by selling 60% of the equity and putting the proceeds into a risk-free asset. Total return on a synthetic protective put position with $60 million in risk-free investments such as T-bills and $40 million in equity is:

Loss on stocks:	2% of $40 = $.80
+Loss on bills:	0
Net loss	$.80

The synthetic and actual protective put positions have equal returns. We conclude that if you sell a proportion of shares equal to the put option's delta and place the proceeds in cash equivalents, your exposure to the stock market will equal that of the desired protective put position.

dynamic hedging

Constant updating of hedge positions as market conditions change.

The difficulty with synthetic positions is that deltas constantly change. Figure 16.9 shows that as the stock price falls, the absolute value of the appropriate hedge ratio increases. Therefore, market declines require extra hedging, that is, additional conversion of equity into cash. This constant updating of the hedge ratio is called **dynamic hedging,** as discussed in Section 16.2. Another term for such hedging is delta hedging, because the option delta is used to determine the number of shares that need to be bought or sold.

Dynamic hedging is one reason portfolio insurance has been said to contribute to market volatility. Market declines trigger additional sales of stock as portfolio insurers strive to increase their hedging. These additional sales are seen as reinforcing or exaggerating market downturns.

In practice, portfolio insurers do not actually buy or sell stocks directly when they update their hedge positions. Instead, they minimize trading costs by buying or selling stock-index futures as a substitute for sale of the stocks themselves. As you will see in the next chapter, stock prices and index future prices usually are very tightly linked by cross-market arbitrageurs

FIGURE 16.9

Hedge ratios change as the stock price fluctuates

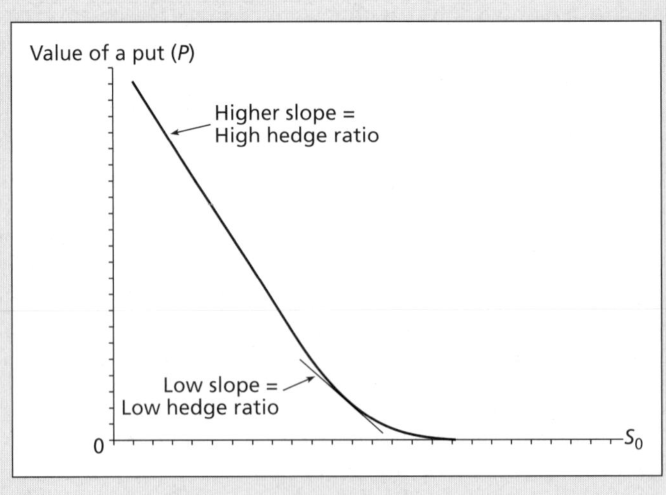

On the MARKET FRONT

J. P. MORGAN ROLLS DICE ON MICROSOFT OPTIONS

Microsoft, in a shift that could be copied throughout the technology business, said yesterday that it plans to stop issuing stock options to its employees, and instead will provide them with restricted stock.

The deal could portend a seismic shift for Microsoft's Silicon Valley rivals, and it could well have effects on Wall Street. Though details of the plan still aren't clear, J. P. Morgan effectively plans to buy the options from Microsoft employees who opt for restricted stock instead. Employee stock options are granted as a form of compensation and allow employees the right to exchange the options for shares of company stock.

The price offered to employees for the options presumably will be lower than the current value, giving J. P. Morgan a chance to make a profit on the deal. Rather than holding the options, and thus betting Microsoft's stock will rise, people familiar with the bank's strategy say J. P. Morgan probably will match each option it buys from the company's employees with a separate trade in the stock market that both hedges the bet and gives itself a margin of profit.

For Wall Street's so-called rocket scientists who do complicated financial transactions such as this one, the strategy behind J. P. Morgan's deal with Microsoft isn't particularly unique or sophisticated. They add that the bank has several ways to deal with the millions of Microsoft options that could come its way.

The bank, for instance, could hedge the options by shorting, or betting against, Microsoft stock. Microsoft has the largest market capitalization of any stock in the market, and its shares are among the most liquid, meaning it would be easy to hedge the risk of holding those options.

J. P. Morgan also could sell the options to investors, much as they would do with a syndicated loan, thereby spreading the risk. During a conference call with investors, [Microsoft Chief Executive Steve] Ballmer said employees could sell their options to "a third party or set of third parties," adding that the company was still working out the details with J. P. Morgan and the SEC.

SOURCE: Excerpt from *The Wall Street Journal,* July 9, 2003. Reprinted by permission of *The Wall Street Journal,*

so that futures transactions can be used as reliable proxies for stock transactions. Instead of selling equities based on the put option's delta, insurers will sell an equivalent number of futures contracts.[11]

Several portfolio insurers suffered great setbacks during the market "crash" of October 19, 1987, when the Dow Jones Industrial Average fell more than 20%. A description of what happened then should help you appreciate the complexities of applying a seemingly straightforward hedging concept.

1. Market volatility at the crash was much greater than ever encountered before. Put option deltas computed from historical experience were too low; insurers underhedged, held too much equity, and suffered excessive losses.
2. Prices moved so fast that insurers could not keep up with the necessary rebalancing. They were "chasing deltas" that kept getting away from them. The futures market saw a "gap" opening, where the opening price was nearly 10% below the previous day's close. Prices dropped before insurers could update their hedge ratios.
3. Execution problems were severe. First, current market prices were unavailable, with trade execution and the price quotation system hours behind, which made computation of correct hedge ratios impossible. Moreover, trading in stocks and stock futures ceased during some periods. The continuous rebalancing capability that is essential for a viable insurance program vanished during the precipitous market collapse.
4. Futures prices traded at steep discounts to their proper levels compared to reported stock prices, thereby making the sale of futures (as a proxy for equity sales) to increase hedging seem expensive. While you will see in the next chapter that stock-index futures prices normally exceed the value of the stock index, on October 19, futures sold far below the stock-index level. When some insurers gambled that the futures price would recover to its usual premium over the stock index and chose to defer sales, they remained underhedged. As the market fell farther, their portfolios experienced substantial losses.

[11]Notice, however, that the use of index futures reintroduces the problem of tracking error between the portfolio and the market index.

While most observers believe that the portfolio insurance industry will never recover from the market crash, dynamic hedges are still widely used by large firms to hedge potential losses from options positions. For example, the nearby box notes that when Microsoft ended its employee stock option program and J. P. Morgan purchased many already-issued options from Microsoft employees, it was widely expected that Morgan would protect its options position by selling shares in Microsoft in accord with a delta hedging strategy.

Option Pricing and the Crisis of 2008–2009

Merton[12] shows how option-pricing models can provide insight into the financial crisis of 2008-2009. The key to understanding his argument is to recognize that when banks lend to or buy the debt of firms with limited liability, they implicitly write a put option to the borrower. To see why, consider the payoff to the lender when the loan comes due for repayment. If the borrower has sufficient assets to pay off the loan, it will do so, and the lender will be fully repaid. But if the borrower has insufficient assets, it can declare bankruptcy and discharge its obligations by transferring ownership of the firm to its creditors. The borrower's ability to satisfy a loan by transferring ownership is equivalent to the right to "sell" itself to the creditor for the face value of the loan. This arrangement is therefore just like a put option on the firm with exercise price equal to the stipulated loan repayment.

Figure 16.10 shows the payoff to the lender at loan maturity (time T) as a function of the value of the borrowing firm, V_T, when the loan, with face value L, comes due. If $V_T \geq L$, the lender is paid off in full. But if $V_T < L$, the lender gets the firm, which is worth less than the promised payment L.

We can write the payoff in a way that emphasizes the implicit put option:

$$\text{Payoff} = \begin{cases} L \\ V_T \end{cases} = L - \begin{cases} 0 & \text{if } V_T \geq L \\ L - V_T & \text{if } V_T < L \end{cases} \qquad \textbf{(16.5)}$$

Equation 16.5 shows that the payoff on the loan equals L (when the firm has sufficient assets to pay off the debt) *minus* the payoff of a put option on the value of the firm (V_T) with an exercise price of L. Therefore, we may view risky lending as a combination of safe lending, with a guaranteed payoff of L, with a short position in a put option on the borrower.

When firms sell credit default swaps (see Chapter 10), the implicit put option is even clearer. Here, the CDS seller agrees to make up any losses due to the insolvency of a bond issuer. If the bond issuer goes bankrupt, leaving assets of only V_T for the creditors, the CDS seller is obligated to make up the difference, $L - V_T$. This is in essence a pure put option.

FIGURE 16.10

A risky loan. The payoff to the lender may be viewed as $L, the face value of the loan, minus the proceeds to a put option on the value of the firm with exercise price L.

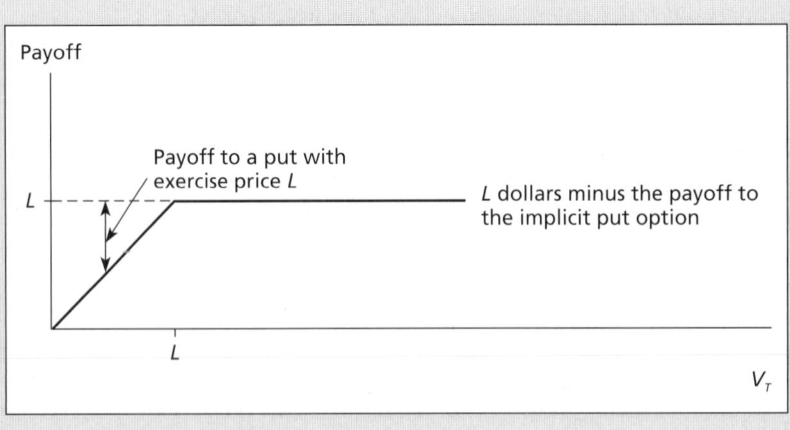

[12]This material is based on a lecture given by Robert Merton at MIT in March 2009. You can find the lecture online at **http://mitworld.mit.edu/video/659.**

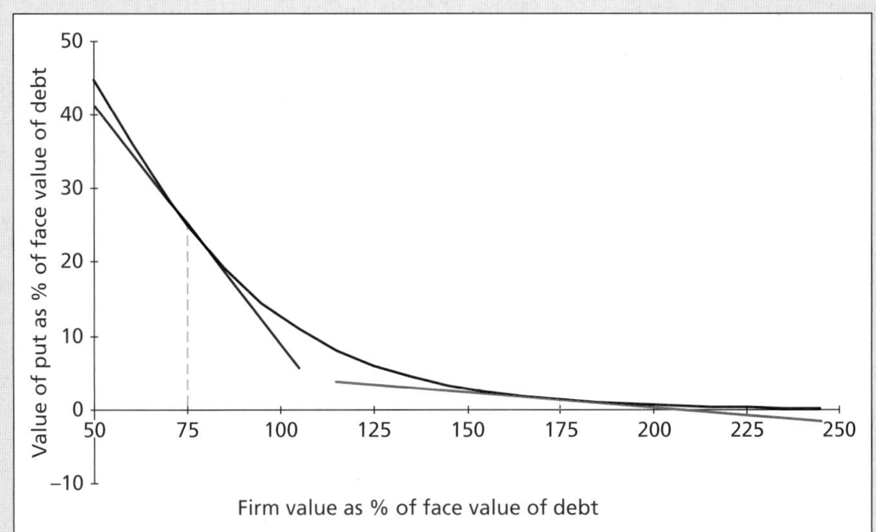

FIGURE 16.11

Value of implicit put option on a loan guarantee as a percentage of the face value of debt (debt maturity = 1 year, standard deviation of value of firm = 40%, risk free rate = 6%)

Now think about the exposure of these implicit put writers to changes in the financial health of the underlying firm. The value of a put option on V_T appears in Figure 16.11. When the firm is financially strong (i.e., V is far greater than L), the slope of the curve is nearly zero, implying that there is little exposure of the implicit put writer (either the bank or the CDS writer) to the value of the borrowing firm. For example, when firm value is 1.75 times the value of the debt, the lighter line drawn tangent to the put value curve has a slope of only −.040. But if there is a big shock to the economy, and firm value falls, not only does the value of the implicit put rise, but its slope is now steeper, implying that exposure to further shocks is now greater. When firm value is only 75% of the value of the loan, the slope of the line tangent to the put value valuation curve is far steeper, −.644. You can see how as you get closer to the edge of the cliff, it gets easier and easier to slide right off.

We often hear people say that a shock to asset values of the magnitude of the financial crisis was a 10-sigma event, by which they mean that such an event was so extreme that it would be 10 standard deviations away from an expected outcome, making it virtually inconceivable. But this analysis shows that standard deviation may be a moving target, increasing dramatically as the firm weakens. As the economy falters and put options go further into the money, their sensitivity to further shocks increases, increasing the risk that even worse losses may be around the corner. The built-in instability of risk exposures makes a scenario like the crisis more plausible and should give us pause when we discount an extreme scenario as "almost impossible."

16.5 EMPIRICAL EVIDENCE

There have been an enormous number of empirical tests of the Black-Scholes option-pricing model. For the most part, the results of the studies have been positive in that the Black-Scholes model generates option values quite close to the actual prices at which options trade. At the same time, some smaller but regular empirical failures of the model have been noted.

Whaley (1982) examines the performance of the Black-Scholes formula relative to that of more complicated option formulas that allow for early exercise. His findings indicate that formulas that allow for the possibility of early exercise do better at pricing than the Black-Scholes formula. The Black-Scholes formula seems to perform worst for options on stocks with high dividend payouts. The true American call option formula, on the other hand, seems to fare equally well in the prediction of option prices on stocks with high or low dividend payouts.

FIGURE 16.12

Implied volatility as a function of exercise price

Source: Mark Rubinstein, "Implied Binomial Trees," *Journal of Finance* 49 (July 1994), pp. 771–818, Figure 2. Used with permission of John Wiley and Sons, via Copyright Clearance Center.

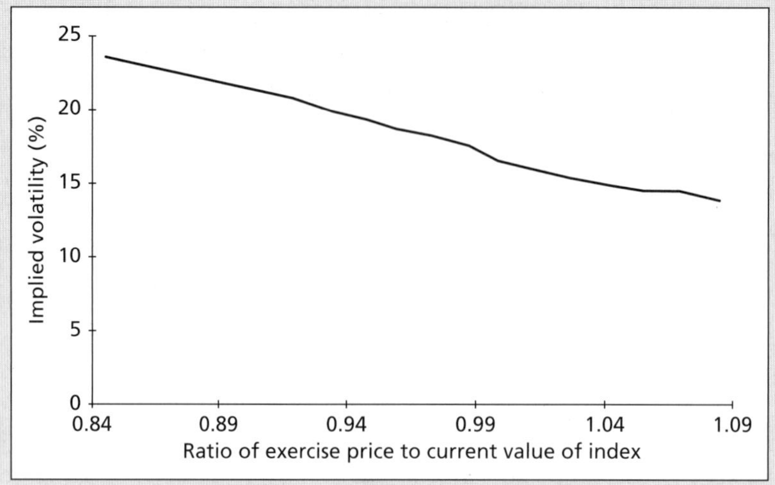

Rubinstein (1994) has emphasized a more serious problem with the Black-Scholes model. If the model were accurate, the implied volatility of all options on a particular stock with the same expiration date would be equal—after all, the underlying asset and expiration date are the same for each option, so the volatility inferred from each also ought to be the same. But, in fact, when one actually plots implied volatility as a function of exercise price, the typical results appear as in Figure 16.12, which treats S&P 500 Index options as the underlying asset. Implied volatility steadily falls as the exercise price rises. Clearly, the Black-Scholes model is missing something.

Rubinstein suggests that the problem with the model has to do with fears of a market crash like that of October 1987. The idea is that deep out-of-the-money puts would be nearly worthless if stock prices evolve smoothly, since the probability of the stock falling by a large amount (and the put option thereby moving into the money) in a short time would be very small. But a possibility of a sudden large downward jump that could move the puts into the money, as in a market crash, would impart greater value to these options. Thus, the market might price these options as though there is a bigger chance of a large drop in the stock price than would be suggested by the Black-Scholes assumptions. The result of the higher option price is a greater implied volatility derived from the Black-Scholes model.

Interestingly, Rubinstein points out that prior to the 1987 market crash, plots of implied volatility like the one in Figure 16.12 were relatively flat, consistent with the notion that the market was then less attuned to fears of a crash. However, postcrash plots have been consistently downward-sloping, exhibiting a shape often called the *option smirk.* When we use option-pricing models that allow for more general stock price distributions, including jumps and random changes in volatility, they generate downward-sloping implied volatility curves similar to the one observed in Figure 16.12.[13]

SUMMARY

- Option values may be viewed as the sum of intrinsic value plus time or "volatility" value. The volatility value is the right to choose not to exercise if the stock price moves against the holder. Thus, option holders cannot lose more than the cost of the option regardless of stock price performance.
- Call options are more valuable when the exercise price is lower, when the stock price is higher, when the interest rate is higher, when the time to expiration is greater, when the stock's volatility is greater, and when dividends are lower.

[13]For an extensive discussion of these more general models, see R. L. McDonald, *Derivatives Markets,* 2nd ed. (Boston: Pearson Education, Addison-Wesley, 2006).

- Options may be priced relative to the underlying stock price using a simple two-period, two-state pricing model. As the number of periods increases, the model can approximate more realistic stock price distributions. The Black-Scholes formula may be seen as a limiting case of the binomial option model, as the holding period is divided into progressively smaller subperiods.
- The put-call parity theorem relates the prices of put and call options. If the relationship is violated, arbitrage opportunities will result. Specifically, the relationship that must be satisfied is

$$P = C - S_0 + \text{PV}(X) + \text{PV}(\text{dividends})$$

  where X is the exercise price of both the call and the put options and PV(X) is the present value of the claim to X dollars to be paid at the expiration date of the options.
- The implied volatility of an option is the standard deviation of stock returns consistent with an option's market price. It can be backed out of an option-pricing model by finding the stock volatility that makes the option's value equal to its observed price.
- The hedge ratio is the number of shares of stock required to hedge the price risk involved in writing one option. Hedge ratios are near zero for deep out-of-the-money call options and approach 1 for deep in-the-money calls.
- Although hedge ratios are less than 1, call options have elasticities greater than 1. The rate of return on a call (as opposed to the dollar return) responds more than one-for-one with stock price movements.
- Portfolio insurance can be obtained by purchasing a protective put option on an equity position. When the appropriate put is not traded, portfolio insurance entails a dynamic hedge strategy where a fraction of the equity portfolio equal to the desired put option's delta is sold, with proceeds placed in risk-free securities.
- Empirically, implied volatilities derived from the Black-Scholes formula tend to be lower on options with higher exercise prices. This may be evidence that the option prices reflect the possibility of a sudden dramatic decline in stock prices. Such "crashes" are inconsistent with the Black-Scholes assumptions.

KEY TERMS

binomial model, 530
Black-Scholes pricing formula, 533
delta, 543
dynamic hedging, 546
hedge ratio, 543
implied volatility, 537
intrinsic value, 523
option elasticity, 544
portfolio insurance, 545
put-call parity relationship, 541
time value, 523

KEY FORMULAS

Binomial model: $u = \exp(\sigma\sqrt{\Delta t})$; $d = \exp(-\sigma\sqrt{\Delta t})$; $p = \dfrac{\exp(r\Delta t) - d}{u - d}$

Put-call parity: $P = C + \text{PV}(X) - S_0 + \text{PV}(\text{Dividends})$

Black-Scholes formula: $C_0 = S_0 e^{-\delta T} N(d_1) - Xe^{-rT} N(d_2)$

$$d_1 = \frac{\ln(S_0/X) + (r - \delta + \sigma^2/2)T}{\sigma\sqrt{T}}$$

$$d_2 = d_1 - \sigma\sqrt{T}$$

www.mhhe.com/bkm

PROBLEM SETS

Select problems are available in McGraw-Hill's *Connect Finance.* Please see the Supplements section of the book's frontmatter for more information.

Basic

1. A call option with a strike price of $50 on a stock selling at $55 costs $6.50. What are the call option's intrinsic and time values? ***(LO 16-1)***
2. A put option on a stock with a current price of $33 has an exercise price of $35. The price of the corresponding call option is $2.25. According to put-call parity, if the effective annual risk-free rate of interest is 4% and there are three months until expiration, what should be the value of the put? ***(LO 16-4)***
3. A call option on Jupiter Motors stock with an exercise price of $75 and one-year expiration is selling at $3. A put option on Jupiter stock with an exercise price of $75 and one-year expiration is selling at $2.50. If the risk-free rate is 8% and Jupiter pays no dividends, what should the stock price be? ***(LO 16-4)***
4. We showed in the text that the value of a call option increases with the volatility of the stock. Is this also true of put option values? Use the put-call parity relationship as well as a numerical example to prove your answer. ***(LO 16-4)***

Intermediate

5. In each of the following questions, you are asked to compare two options with parameters as given. The risk-free interest rate for *all* cases should be assumed to be 6%. Assume the stocks on which these options are written pay no dividends. ***(LO 16-1)***

a.

Put	*T*	*X*	σ	Price of Option
A	.5	50	.20	10
B	.5	50	.25	10

Which put option is written on the stock with the lower price?
(1) A
(2) B
(3) Not enough information

b.

Put	*T*	*X*	σ	Price of Option
A	.5	50	.2	10
B	.5	50	.2	12

Which put option must be written on the stock with the lower price?
(1) A
(2) B
(3) Not enough information

c.

Call	*S*	*X*	σ	Price of Option
A	50	50	.20	12
B	55	50	.20	10

Which call option must have the lower time to expiration?
(1) A
(2) B
(3) Not enough information

d.

Call	*T*	*X*	*S*	Price of Option
A	.5	50	55	10
B	.5	50	55	12

Which call option is written on the stock with higher volatility?
(1) A
(2) B
(3) Not enough information

e.

Call	*T*	*X*	*S*	Price of Option
A	.5	50	55	10
B	.5	55	55	7

Which call option is written on the stock with higher volatility?
(1) A
(2) B
(3) Not enough information

6. Reconsider the determination of the hedge ratio in the two-state model (Section 16.2), where we showed that one-third share of stock would hedge one option. What would be the hedge ratio for each of the following exercise prices: \$120, \$110, \$100, \$90? What do you conclude about the hedge ratio as the option becomes progressively more in the money? ***(LO 16-5)***
7. Show that Black-Scholes call option hedge ratios increase as the stock price increases. Consider a one-year option with exercise price \$50 on a stock with annual standard deviation 20%. The T-bill rate is 3% per year. Find $N(d_1)$ for stock prices \$45, \$50, and \$55. ***(LO 16-3)***
8. We will derive a two-state put option value in this problem. Data: $S_0 = 100$; $X = 110$; $1 + r = 1.10$. The two possibilities for S_T are 130 and 80. ***(LO 16-2)***
   a. Show that the range of *S* is 50 while that of *P* is 30 across the two states. What is the hedge ratio of the put?
   b. Form a portfolio of three shares of stock and five puts. What is the (nonrandom) payoff to this portfolio? What is the present value of the portfolio?
   c. Given that the stock currently is selling at 100, show that the value of the put must be 10.91.
9. Calculate the value of a *call* option on the stock in the previous problem with an exercise price of 110. Verify that the put-call parity relationship is satisfied by your answers to both Problems 8 and 9. (Do not use continuous compounding to calculate the present value of *X* in this example, because the interest rate is quoted as an effective per-period rate.) ***(LO 16-2)***

Use the following case in answering Problems 10–15: Mark Washington, CFA, is an analyst with BIC. One year ago, BIC analysts predicted that the U.S. equity market would most likely experience a slight downturn and suggested delta-hedging the BIC portfolio. As predicted, the U.S. equity markets did indeed experience a downturn of approximately 4% over a 12-month period. However, portfolio performance for BIC was disappointing, lagging its peer group by nearly 10%. Washington has been told to review the options strategy to determine why the hedged portfolio did not perform as expected.

10. Which of the following *best* explains a delta-neutral portfolio? A delta-neutral portfolio is perfectly hedged against: ***(LO 16-5)***
    a. Small price changes in the underlying asset.
    b. Small price decreases in the underlying asset.
    c. All price changes in the underlying asset.

11. After discussing the concept of a delta-neutral portfolio, Washington determines that he needs to further explain the concept of delta. Washington draws the value of an option as a function of the underlying stock price. Draw such a diagram, and indicate how delta is interpreted. Delta is the: ***(LO 16-5)***
    a. Slope in the option price diagram.
    b. Curvature of the option price graph.
    c. Level in the option price diagram.
12. Washington considers a put option that has a delta of −.65. If the price of the underlying asset decreases by $6, then what is the best estimate of the change in option price? ***(LO 16-5)***
13. BIC owns 51,750 shares of Smith & Oates. The shares are currently priced at $69. A call option on Smith & Oates with a strike price of $70 is selling at $3.50 and has a delta of .69. What is the number of call options necessary to create a delta-neutral hedge? ***(LO 16-5)***
14. Return to the previous problem. Will the number of call options written for a delta-neutral hedge increase or decrease if the stock price falls? ***(LO 16-5)***
15. Which of the following statements regarding the goal of a delta-neutral portfolio is *most* accurate? One example of a delta-neutral portfolio is to combine a: ***(LO 16-5)***
    a. Long position in a stock with a short position in call options so that the value of the portfolio does not change with changes in the value of the stock.
    b. Long position in a stock with a short position in a call option so that the value of the portfolio changes with changes in the value of the stock.
    c. Long position in a stock with a long position in call options so that the value of the portfolio does not change with changes in the value of the stock.

Please visit us at www.mhhe.com/bkm

16. Use the Black-Scholes formula to find the value of a call option on the following stock:
    Time to expiration = 6 months
    Standard deviation = 50% per year
    Exercise price = $50
    Stock price = $50
    Interest rate = 3%
    (LO 16-3)

eXcel

Please visit us at www.mhhe.com/bkm

17. Find the Black-Scholes value of a put option on the stock in the previous problem with the same exercise price and expiration as the call option. ***(LO 16-3)***

eXcel

Please visit us at www.mhhe.com/bkm

18. Recalculate the value of the option in Problem 16, successively substituting one of the changes below while keeping the other parameters as in Problem 16:
    a. Time to expiration = 3 months
    b. Standard deviation = 25% per year
    c. Exercise price = $55
    d. Stock price = $55
    e. Interest rate = 5%

    Consider each scenario independently. Confirm that the option value changes in accordance with the prediction of Table 16.1. ***(LO 16-3)***
19. What would be the Excel formula in Spreadsheet 16.1 for the Black-Scholes value of a straddle position? ***(LO 16-3)***
20. Would you expect a $1 increase in a call option's exercise price to lead to a decrease in the option's value of more or less than $1? ***(LO 16-1)***
21. All else being equal, is a put option on a high-beta stock worth more than one on a low-beta stock? The firms have identical firm-specific risk. ***(LO 16-1)***
22. All else being equal, is a call option on a stock with a lot of firm-specific risk worth more than one on a stock with little firm-specific risk? The betas of the stocks are equal. ***(LO 16-1)***

23. All else being equal, will a call option with a high exercise price have a higher or lower hedge ratio than one with a low exercise price? *(LO 16-5)*
24. Should the rate of return of a call option on a long-term Treasury bond be more or less sensitive to changes in interest rates than the rate of return of the underlying bond? *(LO 16-1)*
25. If the stock price falls and the call price rises, then what has happened to the call option's implied volatility? *(LO 16-1)*
26. If the time to expiration falls and the put price rises, then what has happened to the put option's implied volatility? *(LO 16-1)*
27. According to the Black-Scholes formula, what will be the value of the hedge ratio of a call option as the stock price becomes infinitely large? Explain briefly. *(LO 16-5)*
28. According to the Black-Scholes formula, what will be the value of the hedge ratio of a put option for a very small exercise price? *(LO 16-5)*
29. The hedge ratio of an at-the-money call option on IBM is .4. The hedge ratio of an at-the-money put option is −.6. What is the hedge ratio of an at-the-money straddle position on IBM? *(LO 16-5)*
30. Consider a six-month expiration European call option with exercise price $105. The underlying stock sells for $100 a share and pays no dividends. The risk-free rate is 5%. What is the implied volatility of the option if the option currently sells for $8? Use Spreadsheet 16.1 (available at **www.mhhe.com/bkm;** link to Chapter 16 material) to answer this question. *(LO 16-3)*

Please visit us at www.mhhe.com/bkm

    a. Go to the *Data* tab of the spreadsheet and select *Goal Seek* from the What-If menu. The dialog box will ask you for three pieces of information. In that dialog box, you should *set cell* E6 *to value* 8 *by changing cell* B2. In other words, you ask the spreadsheet to find the value of standard deviation (which appears in cell B2) that forces the value of the option (in cell E6) equal to $8. Then click *OK*, and you should find that the call is now worth $8, and the entry for standard deviation has been changed to a level consistent with this value. This is the call's implied standard deviation at a price of $8.
    b. What happens to implied volatility if the option is selling at $9? Why?
    c. What happens to implied volatility if the option price is unchanged at $8 but option expiration is lower, say, only four months? Why?
    d. What happens to implied volatility if the option price is unchanged at $8 but the exercise price is lower, say, only $100? Why?
    e. What happens to implied volatility if the option price is unchanged at $8 but the stock price is lower, say, only $98? Why?
31. These three put options all are written on the same stock. One has a delta of −.9, one a delta of −.5, and one a delta of −.1. Assign deltas to the three puts by filling in the table below. *(LO 16-5)*

Put	*X*	Delta
A	10	
B	20	
C	30	

32. In this problem, we derive the put-call parity relationship for European options on stocks that pay dividends before option expiration. For simplicity, assume that the stock makes one dividend payment of $\$D$ per share at the expiration date of the option. *(LO 16-4)*
    a. What is the value of the stock-plus-put position on the expiration date of the option?
    b. Now consider a portfolio consisting of a call option and a zero-coupon bond with the same expiration date as the option and with face value $(X + D)$. What is the value of

this portfolio on the option expiration date? You should find that its value equals that of the stock-plus-put portfolio, regardless of the stock price.

c. What is the cost of establishing the two portfolios in parts (*a*) and (*b*)? Equate the cost of these portfolios, and you will derive the put-call parity relationship, Equation 16.3.

33. A collar is established by buying a share of stock for $50, buying a six-month put option with exercise price $45, and writing a six-month call option with exercise price $55. Based on the volatility of the stock, you calculate that for an exercise price of $45 and maturity of six months, $N(d_1) = .60$, whereas for the exercise price of $55, $N(d_1) = .35$. ***(LO 16-5)***
    a. What will be the gain or loss on the collar if the stock price increases by $1?
    b. What happens to the delta of the portfolio if the stock price becomes very large? Very small?

34. You are *very* bullish (optimistic) on stock EFG, much more so than the rest of the market. In each question, choose the portfolio strategy that will give you the biggest dollar profit if your bullish forecast turns out to be correct. Explain your answer. ***(LO 16-5)***
    a. *Choice A:* $100,000 invested in calls with $X = 50$.
    Choice B: $100,000 invested in EFG stock.
    b. *Choice A:* 10 call options contracts (for 100 shares each), with $X = 50$.
    Choice B: 1,000 shares of EFG stock.

35. You are attempting to value a call option with an exercise price of $100 and one year to expiration. The underlying stock pays no dividends, its current price is $100, and you believe it has a 50% chance of increasing to $120 and a 50% chance of decreasing to $80. The risk-free rate of interest is 10%. Calculate the call option's value using the two-state stock price model. ***(LO 16-2)***

36. Consider an increase in the volatility of the stock in the previous problem. Suppose that if the stock increases in price, it will increase to $130, and that if it falls, it will fall to $70. Show that the value of the call option is higher than the value derived using the original assumptions. ***(LO 16-2)***

37. Return to Example 16.1. Use the binomial model to value a one-year European put option with exercise price $110 on the stock in that example. Does your solution for the put price satisfy put-call parity? ***(LO 16-2)***

Challenge

38. Imagine you are a provider of portfolio insurance. You are establishing a four-year program. The portfolio you manage is currently worth $100 million, and you promise to provide a minimum return of 0%. The equity portfolio has a standard deviation of 25% per year, and T-bills pay 5% per year. Assume for simplicity that the portfolio pays no dividends (or that all dividends are reinvested). ***(LO 16-5)***
    a. What fraction of the portfolio should be placed in bills? What fraction in equity?
    b. What should the manager do if the stock portfolio falls by 3% on the first day of trading?

39. You would like to be holding a protective put position on the stock of XYZ Co. to lock in a guaranteed minimum value of $100 at year-end. XYZ currently sells for $100. Over the next year, the stock price will either increase by 10% or decrease by 10%. The T-bill rate is 5%. Unfortunately, no put options are traded on XYZ Co. ***(LO 16-5)***
    a. Suppose the desired put option were traded. How much would it cost to purchase?
    b. What would have been the cost of the protective put portfolio?
    c. What portfolio position in stock and T-bills will ensure you a payoff equal to the payoff that would be provided by a protective put with $X = \$100$? Show that the payoff to this portfolio and the cost of establishing the portfolio matches that of the desired protective put.

40. Suppose you are attempting to value a one-year maturity option on a stock with volatility (i.e., annualized standard deviation) of $\sigma = .40$. What would be the appropriate values for u and d if your binomial model is set up using the following? ***(LO 16-2)***
    a. 1 period of one year
    b. 4 subperiods, each 3 months
    c. 12 subperiods, each 1 month

41. You build a binomial model with one period and assert that over the course of a year the stock price will either rise by a factor of 1.5 or fall by a factor of $\frac{2}{3}$. What is your implicit assumption about the volatility of the stock's rate of return over the next year? *(LO 16-2)*
42. Use the put-call parity relationship to demonstrate that an at-the-money call option on a nondividend-paying stock must cost more than an at-the-money put option. Show that the prices of the put and call will be equal if $S = (1 + r)^T$. *(LO 16-4)*
43. Return to Problem 35. Value the call option using the risk-neutral shortcut described in the box on page 533. Confirm that your answer matches the value you get using the two-state approach. *(LO 16-2)*
44. Return to Problem 37. What will be the payoff to the put, P_u, if the stock goes up? What will be the payoff, P_d, if the stock price falls? Value the put option using the risk-neutral shortcut described in the box on page 533. Confirm that your answer matches the value you get using the two-state approach. *(LO 16-2)*

CFA Problems

1. Ken Webster manages a $200 million equity portfolio benchmarked to the S&P 500 Index. Webster believes the market is overvalued when measured by several traditional fundamental/economic indicators. He is therefore concerned about potential losses but recognizes that the S&P 500 Index could nevertheless move above its current 883 level.

   Webster is considering the following *option collar* strategy:

   - Protection for the portfolio can be attained by purchasing an S&P 500 Index put with a strike price of 880 (just out of the money).
   - The put can be financed by selling two 900 calls (further out-of-the-money) for every put purchased.
   - Because the combined delta of the two calls (see the following table) is less than 1 (that is, 2 × .36 = .72), the options will not lose more than the underlying portfolio will gain if the market advances.

   The information in the following table describes the two options used to create the collar. *(LO 16-5)*

Characteristics	900 Call	880 Put
Option price	$8.60	$16.10
Option implied volatility	20%	22%
Option's delta	0.36	−0.44
Contracts needed for collar	602	301

Notes:

Ignore transaction costs.

S&P 500 historical 30-day volatility = 21%.

Time to option expiration 30 days.

   a. Describe the potential returns of the combined portfolio (the underlying portfolio plus the option collar) if after 30 days the S&P 500 Index has:
      i. Risen approximately 5% to 927.
      ii. Remained at 883 (no change).
      iii. Declined by approximately 5% to 841.
      (No calculations are necessary.)
   b. Discuss the effect on the hedge ratio (delta) of *each* option as the S&P 500 approaches the level for *each* of the potential outcomes listed in part (*a*).
   c. Evaluate the pricing of each of the following in relation to the volatility data provided:
      i. The put
      ii. The call

2. Michael Weber, CFA, is analyzing several aspects of option valuation, including the determinants of the value of an option, the characteristics of various models used to value options, and the potential for divergence of calculated option values from observed market prices. ***(LO 16-1)***
   a. What is the expected effect on the value of a call option on common stock if (i) the volatility of the underlying stock price decreases; (ii) the time to expiration of the option increases.
   b. Using the Black-Scholes option-pricing model, Weber calculates the price of a three-month call option and notices the option's calculated value is different from its market price. With respect to Weber's use of the Black-Scholes option-pricing model, (i) discuss why the calculated value of an out-of-the-money European option may differ from its market price; (ii) discuss why the calculated value of an American option may differ from its market price.
3. A stock index is currently trading at 50. Paul Tripp, CFA, wants to value two-year index options using the binomial model. In any year, the stock will either increase in value by 20% or fall in value by 20%. The annual risk-free interest rate is 6%. No dividends are paid on any of the underlying securities in the index. ***(LO 16-2)***
   a. Construct a two-period binomial tree for the value of the stock index.
   b. Calculate the value of a European call option on the index with an exercise price of 60.
   c. Calculate the value of a European put option on the index with an exercise price of 60.
   d. Confirm that your solutions for the values of the call and the put satisfy put-call parity.

WEB *master*

1. Use information from **finance.yahoo.com** to answer the following questions.
   a. What is Coke's current price?
   b. Now enter the ticker "KO" (for Coca-Cola) and find the *Analyst Opinion* tab. What is the mean 12-month target price for Coke? Based on this forecast, would it make more sense to buy calls or puts on Coca-Cola?
   c. What is the spread between the high and low target stock prices, expressed as a percentage of Coke's current stock price? How (qualitatively) should the spread be related to the price at which Coke options trade?
   d. Calculate the implied volatility of the call option closest to the money with time to expiration of about three months. You can use Spreadsheet 16.1 (available at the Online Learning Center, **www.mhhe.com/bkm**) to calculate implied volatility using the Goal Seek command.
   e. Now repeat the exercise for Pepsi (ticker: PEP). What would you expect to be the relationship between the high versus low target price spread and the implied volatility of the two companies? Are your expectations consistent with actual option prices?
   f. Suppose you believe that the volatility of KO is going to increase from currently anticipated levels. Would its call options be overpriced or underpriced? What about its put options?
   g. Could you take positions in both puts and calls on KO in such a manner as to speculate on your volatility beliefs without taking a stance on whether the stock price is going to increase or decrease? Would you buy or write each type of option?
   h. How would your relative positions in puts and calls be related to the delta of each option?
2. Calculating implied volatility can be difficult if you don't have a spreadsheet handy. Fortunately, many tools are available to perform the calculation; **www.numa.com** and **www.math.columbia.edu/~ smirnov/options13.html** contain options calculators that also compute implied volatility.

   Using daily price data, calculate the annualized standard deviation of the daily percentage change in a stock price. For the same stock, use **www.numa.com** or **www.math.columbia.edu/~ smirnov/options13.html** to find the implied volatility. Option price data can be retrieved from **www.cboe.com.**

Recalculate the standard deviation using three months, six months, and nine months of daily data. Which of the calculations most closely approximates implied volatility? What time frame does the market seem to use for assessing stock price volatility?

SOLUTIONS TO CONCEPT check

16.1 Yes. Consider the same scenarios as for the call.

Stock price	$10	$20	$30	$40	$50
Put payoff	20	10	0	0	0
Stock price	20	25	30	35	40
Put payoff	10	5	0	0	0

The low volatility scenario yields a lower expected payoff.

16.2

If This Variable Increases . . .	The Value of a Put Option
S	Decreases
X	Increases
σ	Increases
T	Increases/Uncertain*
r_f	Decreases
Dividend payouts	Increases

*For American puts, increase in time to expiration *must* increase value. One can always choose to exercise early if this is optimal; the longer expiration date simply expands the range of alternatives open to the option holder, thereby making the option more valuable. For a European put, where early exercise is not allowed, longer time to expiration can have an indeterminate effect. Longer maturity increases volatility value since the final stock price is more uncertain, but it reduces the present value of the exercise price that will be received if the put is exercised. The net effect on put value is ambiguous.

16.3 Because the option now is underpriced, we want to reverse our previous strategy.

		Cash Flow in 1 Year for Each Possible Stock Price	
	Initial Cash Flow	S = $90	S = $120
Buy 3 options	$−16.50	$ 0	$ 30
Short-sell 1 share; repay in 1 year	100	−90	−120
Lend $83.50 at 10% interest rate	−83.50	91.85	91.85
Total	$ 0	$ 1.85	$ 1.85

The riskless cash flow in one year per option is $1.85/3 = $.6167, and the present value is $.6167/1.10 = $.56, precisely the amount by which the option is underpriced.

16.4 *a.* $C_u - C_d = \$6.984 - 0 = \$6.984$
b. $uS_0 - dS_0 = \$110 - \$95 = \$15$
c. $6.984/15 = .4656$

d.

Action Today (time 0)	Value in Next Period as Function of Stock Price	
	$dS_0 = \$95$	$uS_0 = \$110$
Buy .4656 shares at price $S_0 = \$100$	\$44.232	\$51.216
Write 1 call at price C_0	0	−6.984
Total	\$44.232	\$44.232

The portfolio must have a market value equal to the present value of \$44.232.

e. \$44.232/1.05 = \$42.126

f. $.4656 \times \$100 - C_0 = \$42.126$

$C_0 = \$46.56 - \$42.126 = \$4.434$

16.5 Higher. For deep out-of-the-money options, an increase in the stock price still leaves the option unlikely to be exercised. Its value increases only fractionally. For deep in-the-money options, exercise is likely, and option holders benefit by a full dollar for each dollar increase in the stock, as though they already own the stock.

16.6 Because $\sigma = .6$, $\sigma^2 = .36$.

$$d_1 = \frac{\ln(100/95) + (.10 + .36/2).25}{.6\sqrt{.25}} = .4043$$

$$d_2 = d_1 - .6\sqrt{.25} = .1043$$

Using Table 16.2 and interpolation, or a spreadsheet function,

$$N(d_1) = .6570$$

$$N(d_2) = .5415$$

$$C = 100 \times .6570 - 95e^{-.10 \times .25} \times .5415 = 15.53$$

16.7 Implied volatility exceeds .5. Given a standard deviation of .5, the option value is \$13.70. A higher volatility is needed to justify the actual \$15 price. Using Spreadsheet 16.1 and Goal Seek, we find the implied volatility is .5714, or 57.14%.

16.8 A \$1 increase in stock price is a percentage increase of 1/122 = .82%. The put option will fall by (.4 × \$1) = \$.40, a percentage decrease of \$.40/\$4 = 10%. Elasticity is −10/.82 = −12.2.

Appendix A

References

Affleck-Graves, John, and Richard R. Mendenhall. "The Relation between the Value Line Enigma and Post-Earnings-Announcement Drift." *Journal of Financial Economics* 31 (February 1992), pp. 75–96.

Agarwal, Vikas; Naveen D. Daniel; and Narayan Y. Naik. "Why Is Santa So Kind to Hedge Funds? The December Return Puzzle!" March 29, 2007, **http://ssrn.com/abstract=891169.**

Alexander, C. *Market Models.* Chichester, England: Wiley, 2001.

Alexander, Sidney. "Price Movements in Speculative Markets: Trends or Random Walks, No. 2." In *The Random Character of Stock Market Prices,* ed. Paul Cootner. Cambridge, MA: MIT Press, 1964.

Amihud, Yakov, and Haim Mendelson. "Asset Pricing and the Bid-Ask Spread." *Journal of Financial Economics* 17 (December 1986), pp. 223–50.

———. "Liquidity, Asset Prices, and Financial Policy." *Financial Analysts Journal* 47 (November–December 1991), pp. 56–66.

Amin, G., and H. Kat. "Stocks, Bonds and Hedge Funds: Not a Free Lunch!" *Journal of Portfolio Management* 29 (Summer 2003), pp. 113–20.

Aragon, George O. "Share Restrictions and Asset Pricing: Evidence from the Hedge Fund Industry." *Journal of Financial Economics* 83 (2007), pp. 33–58.

Arbel, Avner. "Generic Stocks: An Old Product in a New Package." *Journal of Portfolio Management,* Summer 1985, pp. 4–13.

Arbel, Avner, and Paul J. Strebel. "Pay Attention to Neglected Firms." *Journal of Portfolio Management,* Winter 1983, pp. 37–42.

Arnott, Robert. "Orthodoxy Overwrought." *Institutional Investor,* December 18, 2006.

Asness, Cliff. "The Value of Fundamental Indexing." *Institutional Investor,* October 16, 2006, pp. 94–99.

Ball, R., and P. Brown. "An Empirical Evaluation of Accounting Income Numbers." *Journal of Accounting Research* 9 (1968), pp. 159–78.

Banz, Rolf. "The Relationship between Return and Market Value of Common Stocks." *Journal of Financial Economics* 9 (March 1981), pp. 3–18.

Barber, B.; R. Lehavy; M. McNichols; and B. Trueman. "Can Investors Profit from the Prophets? Security Analysts Recommendations and Stock Returns." *Journal of Finance* 56 (April 2001), pp. 531–63.

Barber, Brad, and Terrance Odean. "Trading Is Hazardous to Your Wealth: The Common Stock Investment Performance of Individual Investors." *Journal of Finance* 55 (2000), pp. 773–806.

———. "Boys Will Be Boys: Gender, Overconfidence, and Common Stock Investment." *Quarterly Journal of Economics* 16 (2001), pp. 262–92.

Barberis, Nicholas, and Richard Thaler. "A Survey of Behavioral Finance." In *The Handbook of the Economics of Finance,* ed. G. M. Constantinides, M. Harris, and R. Stulz. Amsterdam: Elsevier, 2003.

Basu, Sanjoy. "The Investment Performance of Common Stocks in Relation to Their Price-Earnings Ratios: A Test of the Efficient Market Hypothesis." *Journal of Finance* 32 (June 1977), pp. 663–82.

———. "The Relationship between Earnings Yield, Market Value, and Return for NYSE Common Stocks: Further Evidence." *Journal of Financial Economics* 12 (June 1983), pp. 129–56.

Battalio, R. H., and R. Mendenhall. "Earnings Expectation, Investor Trade Size, and Anomalous Returns around Earnings Announcements." *Journal of Financial Economics* 77 (2005), pp. 289–319.

Benveniste, Lawrence, and William Wilhelm. "Initial Public Offerings: Going by the Book." *Journal of Applied Corporate Finance* 10 (March 1997), pp. 98–108.

Bergstresser, D.; M. Desai; and J. Rauh. "Earnings Manipulation, Pension Assumptions, and Managerial Investment Decisions." *Quarterly Journal of Economics* 121 (2006), pp. 157–95.

Berk, J. B., and R. C. Green. "Mutual Fund Flows and Performance in Rational Markets." *Journal of Political Economy* 112 (2004), pp. 1269–95.

Bernard, Victor L., and Jacob K. Thomas. "Post-Earnings-Announcement Drift: Delayed Price Response or Risk Premium?" *Journal of Accounting Research* 27 (1989), pp. 1–36.

Bernard, V., and J. Thomas. "Evidence That Stock Prices Do Not Fully Reflect the Implications of Current Earnings for Future Earnings." *Journal of Accounting and Economics* 13 (1990), pp. 305–40.

Bernhard, Arnold. *Value Line Methods of Evaluating Common Stocks.* New York: Arnold Bernhard, 1979.

Black, Fischer. "Yes, Virginia, There Is Hope: Tests of the Value Line Ranking System." Graduate School of Business, University of Chicago, 1971.

Black, Fischer; Michael C. Jensen; and Myron Scholes. "The Capital Asset Pricing Model: Some Empirical Tests." In *Studies in the Theory of Capital Markets,* ed. Michael C. Jensen. New York: Praeger, 1972.

Black, Fischer, and Myron Scholes. "The Pricing of Options and Corporate Liabilities." *Journal of Political Economy* 81 (May–June 1973), pp. 637–59.

"From Black-Scholes to Black Holes: New Frontiers in Options." London: *Risk* Magazine, 1992.

Blake, Christopher; Edwin J. Elton; and Martin J. Gruber. "The Performance of Bond Mutual Funds." *Journal of Business* 66 (July 1993), pp. 371–404.

Blume, Marshall E., and Robert F. Stambaugh. "Biases in Computed Returns: An Application to the Size Effect." *Journal of Finance Economics,* 1983, pp. 387–404.

Bogle, John C. "Investing in the 1990s: Remembrance of Things Past, and Things Yet to Come." *Journal of Portfolio Management,* Spring 1991, pp. 5–14.

———. *Bogle on Mutual Funds.* Burr Ridge, IL: Irwin, 1994.

Bollen, Nicolas P. B., and Jeffrey A. Busse. "Short-Term Persistence in Mutual Fund Performance." *Review of Financial Studies* 19 (2004), pp. 569–97.

Brav, Alon; Christopher Geczy; and Paul A. Gompers. "Is the Abnormal Return Following Equity Issuances Anomalous?" *Journal of Financial Economics* 56 (2000), pp. 209–49.

Brennan, Michael. "Taxes, Market Valuation and Corporate Financial Policy." *National Tax Journal,* 1970.

Brinson, G.; C. R. Hood; and G. Beebower. "Determinants of Portfolio Performance." *Financial Analysts Journal,* July–August 1986.

Brinson, Gary; Brian Singer; and Gilbert Beebower. "Determinants of Portfolio Performance." *Financial Analysts Journal,* May–June 1991.

Brock, William; Josef Lakonishok; and Blake LeBaron. "Simple Technical Trading Rules and the Stochastic Properties of Stock Returns." *Journal of Finance* 47 (December 1992), pp. 1731–64.

Brown, David, and Robert H. Jennings. "On Technical Analysis." *Review of Financial Studies* 2 (1989), pp. 527–52.

Brown, Lawrence D., and Michael Rozeff. "The Superiority of Analysts' Forecasts as Measures of Expectations: Evidence from Earnings." *Journal of Finance,* March 1978.

Brown, S. J.; W. N. Goetzmann; and B. Liang. "Fees on Fees in Funds of Funds." *Journal of Investment Management* 2 (2004), pp. 39–56.

Busse, J. A., and T. C. Green. "Market Efficiency in Real Time." *Journal of Financial Economics* 65 (2002), pp. 415–37.

Campbell, John Y., and Robert Shiller. "Stock Prices, Earnings and Expected Dividends." *Journal of Finance* 43 (July 1988), pp. 661–76.

Carhart, Mark. "On Persistence in Mutual Fund Performance." *Journal of Finance* 52 (1997), pp. 57–82.

Chen, Nai-fu; Richard Roll; and Stephen Ross. "Economic Forces and the Stock Market." *Journal of Business* 59 (1986), pp. 383–403.

Chen, Y.; W. E. Ferson; and H. Peters. "Measuring the Timing Ability and Performance of Bond Mutual Funds." *Journal of Financial Economics* 98 (2010), pp. 72–89.

Chopra, Navin; Josef Lakonishok; and Jay R. Ritter. "Measuring Abnormal Performance: Do Stocks Overreact?" *Journal of Financial Economics* 31 (1992), pp. 235–68.

Clarke, Roger, and Mark P. Kritzman. *Currency Management: Concepts and Practices.* Charlottesville: Research Foundation of the Institute of Chartered Financial Analysts, 1996.

Clayman, Michelle. "In Search of Excellence: The Investor's Viewpoint." *Financial Analysts Journal,* May–June 1987.

Connolly, Robert. "An Examination of the Robustness of the Weekend Effect." *Journal of Financial and Quantitative Analysis* 24 (June 1989), pp. 133–69.

Conrad, Jennifer, and Gautam Kaul. "Time-Variation in Expected Returns." *Journal of Business* 61 (October 1988), pp. 409–25.

Copeland, Thomas E., and David Mayers. "The Value Line Enigma (1965–1978): A Case Study of Performance Evaluation Issues." *Journal of Financial Economics,* November 1982.

Coval, Joshua D., and Tyler Shumway. "Do Behavioral Biases Affect Prices?" *Journal of Finance* 60 (February 2005), pp. 1–34.

Cremers, Martijn; Antti Petajisto; and Eric Zitzewitz. "Should Benchmark Indices Have Alpha? Revisiting Performance Evaluation." 2010, available at SSRN, **http://ssrn.com/abstract=1108856.**

Davis, James L.; Eugene F. Fama; and Kenneth R. French. "Characteristics, Covariances, and Average Returns, 1929 to 1997." *Journal of Finance* 55 (2000), pp. 389–406.

De Bondt, W.F.M., and R. H. Thaler. "Does the Stock Market Overreact?" *Journal of Finance* 40 (1985), pp. 793–805.

———. "Further Evidence on Investor Overreaction and Stock Market Seasonality." *Journal of Finance* 42 (1987), pp. 557–81.

———. "Do Security Analysts Overreact?" *American Economic Review* 80 (1990), pp. 52–57.

———. "Financial Decision Making in Markets and Firms." In *Handbooks in Operations Research and Management Science, Vol. 9: Finance,* ed. R. A. Jarrow, V. Maksimovic, and W. T. Ziemba. Amsterdam: Elsevier, 1995.

DeLong, J. Bradford; Andrei Schleifer; Lawrence Summers; and Robert Waldmann. "Noise Trader Risk in Financial Markets." *Journal of Political Economy* 98 (August 1990), pp. 704–38.

DeMarzo, Peter M.; Ron Kaniel; and Ilan Kremer. "Diversification as a Public Good: Community Effects in Portfolio Choice." *Journal of Finance* 59 (August 2004), pp. 1677–1716.

de Soto, Hernando. *The Mystery of Capital: Why Capitalism Triumphs in the West and Fails Everywhere Else.* New York: Basic Books, 2000.

Dimson, E.; P. R. Marsh; and M. Staunton. *Millennium Book II: 101 Years of Investment Returns.* London: ABN-Amro and London Business School, 2001.

Douglas, George W. "Risk in Equity Markets: An Empirical Appraisal of Market Efficiency." *Yale Economic Essays* IX (Spring 1969).

Dunn, Patricia, and Rolf D. Theisen. "How Consistently Do Active Managers Win?" *Journal of Portfolio Management* 9 (Summer 1983), pp. 47–53.

Errunza, Vihang, and Etienne Losq. "International Asset Pricing under Mild Segmentation: Theory and Test." *Journal of Finance* 40 (March 1985), pp. 105–24.

Fama, Eugene. "The Behavior of Stock Market Prices." *Journal of Business* 38 (January 1965), pp. 34–105.

———. "Market Efficiencies, Long-Term Returns, and Behavioral Finance." *Journal of Financial Economics* 49 (September 1998), pp. 283–306.

Fama, Eugene, and Marshall Blume. "Filter Rules and Stock Market Trading Profits." *Journal of Business* 39 (Supplement, January 1966), pp. 226–41.

Fama, Eugene F., and Kenneth R. French. "Permanent and Temporary Components of Stock Prices." *Journal of Political Economy* 96 (1988), pp. 246–73.

———. "Dividend Yields and Expected Stock Returns." *Journal of Financial Economics* 22 (October 1988), pp. 3–25.

———. "Business Conditions and Expected Returns on Stocks and Bonds." *Journal of Financial Economics* 25 (November 1989), pp. 3–22.

———. "The Cross Section of Expected Stock Returns." *Journal of Finance* 47 (June 1992), pp. 427–65.

———. "Common Risk Factors in the Returns on Stocks and Bonds." *Journal of Financial Economics* 33 (1993), pp. 3–56.

———. "Multifactor Explanations of Asset Pricing Anomalies." *Journal of Finance* 51 (1996), pp. 55–84.

———. "The Equity Premium." *Journal of Finance* 57 (April 2002), pp. 637–60.

———. "Luck versus Skill in the Cross-Section of Mutual Fund Returns." *Journal of Finance* 65 (2010), pp. 1915–47.

Fama, Eugene, and James MacBeth. "Risk, Return and Equilibrium: Empirical Tests." *Journal of Political Economy* 81 (March 1973).

Fisher, Irving. *The Theory of Interest: As Determined by Impatience to Spend Income and Opportunity to Invest It.* New York: Augustus M. Kelley, 1965, originally published in 1930.

Flannery, Mark J., and Christopher M. James. "The Effect of Interest Rate Changes on the Common Stock Returns of Financial Institutions." *Journal of Finance* 39 (September 1984), pp. 1141–54.

Foster, George; Chris Olsen; and Terry Shevlin. "Earnings Releases, Anomalies, and the Behavior of Security Returns." *The Accounting Review* 59 (October 1984).

French, Kenneth. "Stock Returns and the Weekend Effect." *Journal of Financial Economics* 8 (March 1980), pp. 55–69.

Froot, K. A., and E. M. Dabora. "How Are Stock Prices Affected by the Location of Trade?" *Journal of Financial Economics* 53 (1999), pp. 189–216.

Fung, William, and David Hsieh. "Empirical Characteristics of Dynamic Trading Strategies: The Case of Hedge Funds." *Review of Financial Studies* 10 (1997), pp. 275–302.

———. "Performance Characteristics of Hedge Funds and CTA Funds: Natural versus Spurious Biases." *Journal of Financial and Quantitative Analysis* 35 (2000), pp. 291–307.

Gervais, S., and T. Odean. "Learning to Be Overconfident." *Review of Financial Studies* 14 (2001), pp. 1–27.

Geske, Robert, and Richard Roll. "On Valuing American Call Options with the Black-Scholes European Formula." *Journal of Finance* 39 (June 1984), pp. 443–56.

Getmansky, Mila; Andrew W. Lo; and Igor Makarov. "An Econometric Model of Serial Correlation and Illiquidity in Hedge Fund Returns." *Journal of Financial Economics* 74 (2004), pp. 529–609.

Ghysels, E.; A. Harvey; and E. Renault. "Stochastic Volatility." In *Statistical Methods in Finance,* ed. C. Rao and G. Maddala. Amsterdam: Elsevier Science, North-Holland Series in Statistics and Probability, 1996.

Gibbons, Michael, and Patrick Hess. "Day of the Week Effects and Asset Returns." *Journal of Business* 54 (October 1981), pp. 579–98.

Givoly, Dan, and Dan Palmon. "Insider Trading and Exploitation of Inside Information: Some Empirical Evidence." *Journal of Business* 58 (1985), pp. 69–87.

Goetzmann, William N., and Roger G. Ibbotson. "Do Winners Repeat?" *Journal of Portfolio Management,* Winter 1994, pp. 9–18.

Graham, J. R., and C. R. Harvey. "Grading the Performance of Market Timing Newsletters." *Financial Analysts Journal* 53 (November–December 1997), pp. 54–66.

———. "Expectations of Equity Risk Premia, Volatility and Asymmetry from a Corporate Finance Perspective." 2001, available at SSRN, **http://ssrn.com/abstract=292623.**

Grieves, Robin, and Alan J. Marcus. "Riding the Yield Curve: Reprise." *Journal of Portfolio Management,* Winter 1992.

Grinblatt, Mark, and Bing Han. "Prospect Theory, Mental Accounting, and Momentum." *Journal of Financial Economics* 78 (November 2005), pp. 311–39.

Grinblatt, Mark, and Sheridan Titman. "Mutual Fund Performance: An Analysis of Quarterly Portfolio Holdings." *Journal of Business* 62 (1989), pp. 393–416.

Grossman, Sanford J., and Joseph E. Stiglitz. "On the Impossibility of Informationally Efficient Markets." *American Economic Review* 70 (June 1980), pp. 393–408.

Hasanhodzic, Jasmina, and Andrew W. Lo. "Can Hedge Fund Returns Be Replicated? The Linear Case." *Journal of Investment Management* 5 (2007), pp. 5–45.

Haugen, Robert A. *The New Finance: The Case against Efficient Markets.* Englewood Cliffs, NJ: Prentice Hall, 1995.

Henriksson, Roy D. "Market Timing and Mutual Fund Performance: An Empirical Investigation." *Journal of Business* 57 (January 1984).

Heston, S. L. "A Closed-Form Solution for Options with Stochastic Volatility with Applications to Bonds and Currency Options." *Review of Financial Studies* 6 (1993), pp. 327–43.

Hirshleifer, David. "Investor Psychology and Asset Pricing." *Journal of Finance* 56 (August 2001), pp. 1533–97.

Homer, Sidney, and Martin L. Leibowitz. *Inside the Yield Book: New Tools for Bond Market Strategy.* Englewood Cliffs, NJ: Prentice Hall, 1972.

Hull, J. C., and A. White. "The Pricing of Options on Assets with Stochastic Volatilities." *Journal of Finance* 42 (1987), pp. 281–300.

Ibbotson, Roger G. "Price Performance of Common Stock New Issues." *Journal of Financial Economics* 2 (September 1975).

Ibbotson, Roger; Richard C. Carr; and Anthony W. Robinson. "International Equity and Bond Returns." *Financial Analysts Journal,* July–August 1982.

Ibbotson, R. G., and L. B. Siegel. "The World Market Wealth Portfolio." *Journal of Portfolio Management,* Winter 1983.

Ibbotson, R. G.; L. B. Siegel; and K. Love. "World Wealth: Market Values and Returns." *Journal of Portfolio Management,* Fall 1985.

Jacquier, Eric, and Alan Marcus. "Asset Allocation Models and Market Volatility." *Financial Analysts Journal* 57 (March–April 2001), pp. 16–30.

Jaffe, Jeffrey F. "Special Information and Insider Trading." *Journal of Business* 47 (July 1974), pp. 410–28.

———. "Gold and Gold Stocks as Investments for Institutional Portfolios." *Financial Analysts Journal* 45 (March–April 1989), pp. 53–59.

Jagannathan, R.; E. R. McGrattan; and A. Scherbina. "The Declining U.S. Equity Premium." *Federal Reserve Bank of Minneapolis Quarterly Review* 24 (Fall 2000), pp. 3–19.

Jagannathan, Ravi, and Zhenyu Wang. "The Conditional CAPM and the Cross-Section of Expected Returns." *Staff Report 208,*

Federal Reserve Bank of Minneapolis, 1996.

Jegadeesh, Narasimhan. "Evidence of Predictable Behavior of Security Returns." *Journal of Finance* 45 (September 1990), pp. 881–98.

Jegadeesh, N.; J. Kim; S. D. Krische; and C. M. Lee. "Analyzing the Analysts: When Do Recommendations Add Value?" *Journal of Finance* 59 (June 2004), pp. 1083–1124.

Jegadeesh, Narasimhan, and Sheridan Titman. "Returns to Buying Winners and Selling Losers: Implications for Stock Market Efficiency." *Journal of Finance* 48 (March 1993), pp. 65–91.

Jensen, Michael C. "The Performance of Mutual Funds in the Period 1945–1964." *Journal of Finance,* May 1968.

———. "Risk, the Pricing of Capital Assets, and the Evaluation of Investment Portfolios." *Journal of Business* 42 (April 1969), pp. 167–247.

Kahneman, D., and A. Tversky. "Subjective Probability: A Judgment of Representativeness." *Cognitive Psychology* 3 (1972), pp. 430–54.

———. "On the Psychology of Prediction." *Psychology Review* 80 (1973), pp. 237–51.

Keim, Donald B. "Size Related Anomalies and Stock Return Seasonality: Further Empirical Evidence." *Journal of Financial Economics* 12 (June 1983), pp. 13–32.

Keim, Donald B., and Robert F. Stambaugh. "Predicting Returns in the Stock and Bond Markets." *Journal of Financial Economics* 17 (1986), pp. 357–90.

Kendall, Maurice. "The Analysis of Economic Time Series, Part I: Prices." *Journal of the Royal Statistical Society* 96 (1953), pp. 11–25.

Kopcke, Richard W., and Geoffrey R. H. Woglom. "Regulation Q and Savings Bank Solvency—The Connecticut Experience." In *The Regulation of Financial Institutions,* Federal Reserve Bank of Boston Conference Series, No. 21, 1979.

Kosowski, R.; A. Timmermann; R. Wermers; and H. White. "Can Mutual Fund 'Stars' Really Pick Stocks? New Evidence from a Bootstrap Analysis." *Journal of Finance* 61 (December 2006), pp. 2551–95.

Kothari, S. P.; Jay Shanken; and Richard G. Sloan. "Another Look at the Cross-Section of Expected Stock Returns." *Journal of Finance* 50 (March 1995), pp. 185–224.

Kotlikoff, Laurence J., and Avia Spivack. "The Family as an Incomplete Annuities Market." *Journal of Political Economy* 89, no. 2 (April 1981), pp. 372–91.

Kotlikoff, Laurence J., and Lawrence H. Summers. "The Role of Intergenerational Transfers in Aggregate Capital Accumulation." *Journal of Political Economy* 89, no. 4 (August 1981), pp. 706–32.

Lakonishok, Josef; Andrei Shleifer; and Robert W. Vishny. "Contrarian Investment, Extrapolation, and Risk." *Journal of Finance* 50 (1995), pp. 1541–78.

Lamont, O. A., and R. H. Thaler. "Can the Market Add and Subtract? Mispricing in Tech Carve-Outs." *Journal of Political Economy* 111 (2003), pp. 227–68.

La Porta, Raphael. "Expectations and the Cross-Section of Stock Returns." *Journal of Finance* 51 (December 1996), pp. 1715–42.

Latane, H. A., and C. P. Jones. "Standardized Unexpected Earnings—1971–1977." *Journal of Finance,* June 1979.

Lease, R.; W. Lewellen; and G. Schlarbaum. "Market Segmentation: Evidence on the Individual Investor." *Financial Analysts Journal* 32 (1976), pp. 53–60.

Lee, C. M.; A. Shleifer; and R. H. Thaler. "Investor Sentiment and the Closed-End Fund Puzzle." *Journal of Finance* 46 (March 1991), pp. 75–109.

Lehmann, Bruce. "Fads, Martingales and Market Efficiency." *Quarterly Journal of Economics* 105 (February 1990), pp. 1–28.

Levy, Robert A. "The Predictive Significance of Five-Point Chart Patterns." *Journal of Business* 44 (July 1971), pp. 316–23.

Liebowitz, Martin L., and Alfred Weinberger. "Contingent Immunization—Part I: Risk Control Procedure." *Financial Analysts Journal* 38 (November–December 1982).

Lo, Andrew W., and Craig MacKinlay. "Stock Market Prices Do Not Follow Random Walks: Evidence from a Simple Specification Test." *Review of Financial Studies* 1 (Spring 1988), pp. 41–66.

Loeb, T. F. "Trading Cost: The Critical Link between Investment Information and Results." *Financial Analysts Journal,* May–June 1983.

Longin, F., and B. Solnik. "Is the Correlation in International Equity Returns Constant: 1960–1990?" *Journal of International Money and Finance* 14 (1995), pp. 3–26.

Lynch, Peter, with John Rothchild. *One Up on Wall Street.* New York: Penguin Books, 1989.

Macaulay, Frederick. *Some Theoretical Problems Suggested by the Movements of Interest Rates, Bond Yields, and Stock Prices in the United States since 1856.* New York: National Bureau of Economic Research, 1938.

Malkiel, Burton G. "Expectations, Bond Prices, and the Term Structure of Interest Rates." *Quarterly Journal of Economics* 76 (May 1962), pp. 197–218.

———. "Returns from Investing in Equity Mutual Funds: 1971–1991." *Journal of Finance* 50 (June 1995), pp. 549–72.

Malkiel, Burton G., and Atanu Saha. "Hedge Funds: Risk and Return." *Financial Analysts Journal* 61 (2005), pp. 80–88.

Malmendier, U., and G. Tate. "Who Makes Acquisitions? CEO Overconfidence and the Market's Reaction." *Journal of Financial Economics* 89 (July 2008) pp. 20–43.

Marcus, Alan J. "The Magellan Fund and Market Efficiency." *Journal of Portfolio Management* 17 (Fall 1990), pp. 85–88.

Mayers, David. "Nonmarketable Assets and Capital Market Equilibrium under Uncertainty." In *Studies in the Theory of Capital Markets,* ed. M. C. Jensen. New York: Praeger, 1972.

McDonald, Robert L. *Derivative Markets,* 2nd ed. Boston: Addison-Wesley, 2005.

Merton, Robert C. "Theory of Rational Option Pricing." *Bell Journal of Economics and Management Science* 4 (Spring 1973), pp. 141–83.

———. "On Market Timing and Investment Performance: An Equilibrium Theory of Value for Market Forecasts." *Journal of Business* 54 (July 1981).

———. "A Simple Model of Capital Market Equilibrium with Incomplete Information." *Journal of Finance* 42 (1987), pp. 483–510.

Miller, Merton H., and Myron Scholes. "Rate of Return in Relation to Risk: A Reexamination of Some Recent Findings." In *Studies in the Theory of Capital Markets,* ed. Michael C. Jensen. New York: Praeger, 1972.

Modigliani, Franco, and M. Miller. "The Cost of Capital, Corporation Finance, and the Theory of Investment." *American Economic Review,* June 1958.

———. "Dividend Policy, Growth, and the Valuation of Shares." *Journal of Business,* October 1961.

Modigliani, Franco, and Leah Modigliani. "Risk-Adjusted Performance." *Journal of Portfolio Management,* Winter 1997, pp. 45–54.

Morrell, John A. "Introduction to International Equity Diversification." In *International Investing for U.S. Pension Funds,* Institute for Fiduciary Education, London/Venice, May 6–13, 1989.

Niederhoffer, Victor, and Patrick Regan. "Earnings Changes, Analysts' Forecasts, and Stock Prices." *Financial Analysts Journal,* May–June 1972.

Norby, W. C. "Applications of Inflation-Adjusted Accounting Data." *Financial Analysts Journal,* March–April 1983.

Odean, T. "Are Investors Reluctant to Realize Their Losses?" *Journal of Finance* 53 (1998), pp. 1775–98.

Patel, J. M., and M. A. Wolfson. "The Intraday Speed of Adjustment of Stock Prices to Earnings and Dividend Announcements." *Journal of Financial Economics* 13 (June 1984), pp. 223–52.

Perold, André. "Fundamentally Flawed Indexing." HBS mimeo, January 2007.

Perry, Kevin, and Robert A. Taggart. "The Growing Role of Junk Bonds in Corporate Finance." *Continental Bank Journal of Applied Corporate Finance* 1 (Spring 1988).

Pontiff, Jeffrey. "Closed-End Fund Premia and Returns Implications for Financial Market Equilibrium." *Journal of Financial Economics* 37 (1995), pp. 341–70.

———. "Costly Arbitrage: Evidence from Closed-End Funds." *Quarterly Journal of Economics* 111 (November 1996), pp. 1135–51.

Porter, Michael E. *Competitive Strategy: Techniques for Analyzing Industries and Competitors.* New York: Free Press, 1980.

———. *Competitive Advantage: Creating and Sustaining Superior Performance.* New York: Free Press, 1985.

Poterba, James M., and Lawrence Summers. "Mean Reversion in Stock Market Prices: Evidence and Implications." *Journal of Financial Economics* 22 (1988), pp. 27–59.

Rau, P. R.; O. Dimitrov; and M. Cooper. "A Rose.com by Any Other Name." *Journal of Finance* 56 (2001), pp. 2371–88.

Ready, Mark J. "Profits from Technical Trading Rules." *Financial Management* 31 (Autumn 2002), pp. 43–62.

Redington, F. M. "Review of the Principle of Life-Office Valuations." *Journal of the Institute of Actuaries* 78 (1952), pp. 286–340.

Reinganum, Marc R. "The Anomalous Stock Market Behavior of Small Firms in January: Empirical Tests for Tax-Loss Effects." *Journal of Financial Economics* 12 (June 1983), pp. 89–104.

———. "The Anatomy of a Stock Market Winner." *Financial Analysts Journal,* March–April 1988, pp. 272–84.

Rendleman, Richard J., Jr.; Charles P. Jones; and Henry A. Latané. "Empirical Anomalies Based on Unexpected Earnings and the Importance of Risk Adjustments." *Journal of Financial Economics* 10 (November 1982), pp. 269–87.

Ritter, Jay R. "The Buying and Selling Behavior of Individual Investors at the Turn of the Year." *Journal of Finance* 43 (July 1988), pp. 701–17.

Roberts, Harry. "Stock Market 'Patterns' and Financial Analysis: Methodological Suggestions." *Journal of Finance* 14 (March 1959), pp. 11–25.

Roll, Richard. "A Critique of the Capital Asset Theory Tests: Part I: On Past and Potential Testability of the Theory." *Journal of Financial Economics* 4 (1977).

———. "The International Crash of October 1987." *Financial Analysts Journal,* September–October 1988.

Ross, Stephen A. "Return, Risk and Arbitrage." In *Risk and Return in Finance,* ed. I. Friend and J. Bicksler. Cambridge, MA: Ballinger, 1976.

———. "Neoclassical Finance, Alternative Finance and the Closed End Fund Puzzle." *European Financial Management* 8 (2002), pp. 129–37, **ssrn.com/abstract=313444.**

Rubinstein, Mark. "Implied Binomial Trees." *Journal of Finance* 49 (July 1994), pp. 771–818.

Sadka, Ronnie. "Liquidity Risk and the Cross-Section of Hedge-Fund Returns." *Journal of Financial Economics* 98 (October 2010), pp. 54–71.

Samuelson, Paul. "The Judgment of Economic Science on Rational Portfolio Management." *Journal of Portfolio Management* 16 (Fall 1989), pp. 4–12.

Schleifer, Andrei. *Inefficient Markets.* New York: Oxford University Press, 2000.

Schleifer, Andrei, and Robert Vishny. "Equilibrium Short Horizons of Investors and Firms." *American Economic Review* 80 (May 1990), pp. 148–53.

———. "The Limits of Arbitrage." *Journal of Finance* 52 (March 1997), pp. 35–55.

Seyhun, H. Nejat. "Insiders' Profits, Costs of Trading and Market Efficiency." *Journal of Financial Economics* 16 (1986), pp. 189–212.

Sharpe, William F. "A Simplified Model for Portfolio Analysis." *Management Science* IX (January 1963), pp. 277–93.

———. "Mutual Fund Performance." *Journal of Business* 39 (January 1966).

———. "Asset Allocation: Management Style and Performance Evaluation." *Journal of Portfolio Management,* Winter 1992, pp. 7–19.

Shefrin, Hersh. *Beyond Greed and Fear.* Boston: Harvard Business School Press, 2002.

Shefrin, Hersh, and Meir Statman. "The Disposition to Sell Winners Too Early and Ride Losers Too Long: Theory and Evidence." *Journal of Finance* 40 (July 1985), pp. 777–90.

Shiller, Robert. "Do Stock Prices Move Too Much to Be Justified by Subsequent Changes in Dividends?" *American Economic Review* 71 (June 1981).

Solnik, B. *International Investing,* 4th ed. Reading, MA: Addison-Wesley, 1999.

Solnik, Bruno, and A. De Freitas. "International Factors of Stock Price Behavior." CESA Working Paper, February 1986 (cited in Bruno Solnik, *International Investments.* Reading, MA: Addison-Wesley, 1988).

Speidell, Lawrence S., and Vinod Bavishi. "GAAP Arbitrage: Valuation Opportunities in International Accounting Standards." *Financial Analysts Journal,* November–December 1992, pp. 58–66.

Statman, Meir. "Behavioral Finance." *Contemporary Finance Digest* 1 (Winter 1997), pp. 5–22.

Stickel, Scott E. "The Effect of Value Line Investment Survey Rank Changes on Common Stock Prices." *Journal of Financial Economics* 14 (1986), pp. 121–44.

Taleb, Nassim N. *Fooled by Randomness: The Hidden Role of Chance in Life and in the Markets.* New York: TEXERE (Thomson), 2004.

———. *The Black Swan: The Impact of the Highly Improbable.* New York: Random House, 2007.

Thaler, Richard H. *The Winner's Curse.* Princeton, NJ: Princeton University Press, 1992.

———. *Advances in Behavioral Finance.* New York: Russell Sage Foundation, 1993.

Tobin, James. "Liquidity Preference as Behavior toward Risk." *Review of Economic Studies* XXVI (February 1958), pp. 65–86.

Treynor, Jack L. "How to Rate Management Investment Funds." *Harvard Business Review* 43 (January–February 1965).

Treynor, Jack, and Fischer Black. "How to Use Security Analysis to Improve Portfolio Selection." *Journal of Business* 46 (January 1973).

Treynor, Jack L., and Kay Mazuy. "Can Mutual Funds Outguess the Market?" *Harvard Business Review* 43 (July–August 1966).

Trippi, Robert R., and Duane Desieno. "Trading Equity Index Futures with Neural Networks." *Journal of Portfolio Management* 19 (Fall 1992).

Trippi, Robert R.; Duane Desieno; and Efraim Turban, eds. *Neural Networks in Finance and Investing.* Chicago: Probus, 1993.

Wallace, A. "Is Beta Dead?" *Institutional Investor* 14 (July 1980), pp. 22–30.

Wermers, R. R. "Mutual Fund Performance: An Empirical Decomposition into Stock-Picking Talent, Style, Transaction Costs, and Expenses." *Journal of Finance* 55 (2000), pp. 1655–1703.

Whaley, Robert E. "Valuation of American Call Options on Dividend-Paying Stocks: Empirical Tests." *Journal of Financial Economics* 10 (1982), pp. 29–58.

Wiggins, J. B. "Option Values under Stochastic Volatilities." *Journal of Financial Economics* 19 (1987), pp. 351–72.

Womack, K. L. "Do Brokerage Analysts' Recommendations Have Investment Value?" *Journal of Finance* 51 (March 1996), pp. 137–67.

Appendix B

References to CFA Questions

Each end-of-chapter CFA question is reprinted with permission from the CFA Institute, Charlottesville, Virginia.[1] Following is a list of the CFA questions in the end-of-chapter material and the exams/study guides from which they were taken and updated.

Chapter 2

CFA 1. 1986 Level II CFA Study Guide, © 1986.

Chapter 3

CFA 1–2. 1986 Level I CFA Study Guide, © 1986.

Chapter 5

CFA 1–3. 1998 Level I CFA Study Guide, © 1998.

CFA 4–6. 1991 Level I CFA Study Guide, © 1991.

CFA 7–11. 1993 Level I CFA Study Guide, © 1993.

Chapter 6

CFA 1. 1998 Level I CFA Study Guide, © 1998.

CFA 2. 2001 Level III CFA Study Guide, © 2001.

CFA 3. 2001 Level II CFA Study Guide, © 2001.

CFA 4–6. 1982 Level III CFA Study Guide, © 1982.

CFA 7. 2000 Level II CFA Study Guide, © 2000.

Chapter 7

CFA 1. 1998 Level I CFA Study Guide, © 1998.

CFA 2. 2000 Level II CFA Study Guide, © 2000.

CFA 3. 2002 Level II CFA Study Guide, © 2002.

CFA 4. 2001 Level II CFA Study Guide, © 2001.

CFA 5–14. Various CFA exams.

Chapter 8

CFA 1–5. 1993 Level I CFA Study Guide, © 1993.

CFA 6. 1998 Level I CFA Study Guide, © 1998.

CFA 7. 1981 Level I CFA Study Guide, © 1981.

CFA 8. 1989 Level III CFA Study Guide, © 1989.

CFA 9. 1996 Level III CFA Study Guide, © 1996.

CFA 10. 1996 Level III CFA Study Guide, © 1996.

CFA 11. 1996 Level III CFA Study Guide, © 1996.

Chapter 9

CFA 1. 2000 Level III CFA Study Guide, © 2000.

CFA 2. 2001 Level III CFA Study Guide, © 2001.

CFA 3. 2004 Level III CFA Study Guide, © 2004.

CFA 4. 2003 Level III CFA Study Guide, © 2003.

CFA 5. 2002 Level III CFA Study Guide, © 2002.

Chapter 10

CFA 1. From various CFA exams.

CFA 2. 1999 Level II CFA Study Guide, © 1999.

CFA 3. 1992 Level II CFA Study Guide, © 1992.

CFA 4. 1993 Level I CFA Study Guide, © 1993.

CFA 5. 1994 Level I CFA Study Guide, © 1994.

Chapter 11

CFA 1. 1985 Level I CFA Study Guide, © 1985.

CFA 2. 1985 Level I CFA Study Guide, © 1985.

CFA 3. 1992 Level II CFA Study Guide, © 1992.

CFA 4. 1983 Level III CFA Study Guide, © 1983.

CFA 5. 2001 Level II CFA Study Guide, © 2001.

CFA 6. 2003 Level II CFA Study Guide, © 2003.

CFA 7. 2004 Level II CFA Study Guide, © 2004.

CFA 8–9. 1983 Level III CFA Study Guide, © 1983.

CFA 10. From various CFA exams.

CFA 11–12. 1983 Level III CFA Study Guide, © 1983.

Chapter 12

CFA 1. 1995 Level II CFA Study Guide, © 1995.

CFA 2. 1993 Level II CFA Study Guide, © 1993.

CFA 3. 1993 Level II CFA Study Guide, © 1993.

CFA 4. 1998 Level II CFA Study Guide, © 1998.

CFA 5. From various CFA exams.

Chapter 13

CFA 1. 1995 Level II CFA Study Guide, © 1995.

CFA 2. 1987 Level I CFA Study Guide, © 1987.

[1] The CFA Institute does not endorse, promote, review, or warrant the accuracy of the product or services offered by The McGraw-Hill Companies.

CFA 3. 2001 Level II CFA Study Guide, © 2001.
CFA 4. 1994 Level II CFA Study Guide, © 1994.
CFA 5. 2003 Level I CFA Study Guide, © 2003.
CFA 6. 2003 Level I CFA Study Guide, © 2003.
CFA 7. 2003 Level II CFA Study Guide, © 2003.
CFA 8. 2001 Level II CFA Study Guide, © 2001.
CFA 9. 2001 Level II CFA Study Guide, © 2001.
CFA 10. 2001 Level II CFA Study Guide, © 2001.

Chapter 14

CFA 1. 2002 Level II CFA Study Guide, © 2002.
CFA 2. 1988 Level I CFA Study Guide, © 1988.
CFA 3. 1998 Level II CFA Study Guide, © 1998.
CFA 4. 1987 Level I CFA Study Guide, © 1987.
CFA 5. 1998 Level II CFA Study Guide, © 1998.
CFA 6. 1999 Level II CFA Study Guide, © 1999.
CFA 7. 1998 Level II CFA Study Guide, © 1998.

Chapter 15

CFA 1. 1984 Level III CFA Study Guide, © 1984.
CFA 2. 2000 Level II CFA Study Guide, © 2000.
CFA 3. 1984 Level III CFA Study Guide, © 1984.
CFA 4. 2001 Level II CFA Study Guide, © 2001.
CFA 5. 2002 Level II CFA Study Guide, © 2002.

Chapter 16

CFA 1. 2000 Level I CFA Study Guide, © 2000.
CFA 2. 2000 Level I CFA Study Guide, © 2000.
CFA 3. 2000 Level II CFA Study Guide, © 2000.

Chapter 17

CFA 1–3. 1998 Level I CFA Study Guide, © 1998.
CFA 4. 1982 Level III CFA Study Guide, © 1982.
CFA 5. 1986 Level III CFA Study Guide, © 1986.
CFA 6. 2000 Level II CFA Study Guide, © 2000.
CFA 7. 1993 Level I CFA Study Guide, © 1993.
CFA 8. 2000 Level III Study Guide, © 2000.
CFA 9. 2004 Level II CFA Study Guide, © 2004.

Chapter 18

CFA 1. From various CFA exams.
CFA 2. 1981 Level I Study Guide, © 1981.
CFA 3. 1981 Level I Study Guide, © 1981.
CFA 4. 2000 Level I Study Guide, © 2000.

Chapter 19

CFA 1. 1986 Level III Study Guide, © 1986.
CFA 2. 1986 Level III Study Guide, © 1986.
CFA 3. 1991 Level II Study Guide, © 1991.
CFA 4. 1998 Level II Study Guide, © 1998.

Chapter 22

CFA 1. 1988 Level I CFA Study Guide, © 1988.
CFA 2. 1988 Level I CFA Study Guide, © 1988.
CFA 3. From various CFA exams.
CFA 4. From various CFA exams.
CFA 5. 1981 Level II CFA Study Guide, © 1981.
CFA 6. 1985 Level III CFA Study Guide, © 1985.
CFA 7. 1988 Level I CFA Study Guide, © 1988.
CFA 8. 1982 Level III CFA Study Guide, © 1982.
CFA 9–10. From various CFA exams.

Index

Note: Boldface entries indicate key terms and the page numbers where they are defined. Page numbers followed by n indicate notes; f, figures; t, tables.

B

C

D

E

F

G

H

N

O

P

S

U

V

W

Y

Z